THE OXFORD
COMPANION TO
NEW ZEALAND
LITERATURE

THE OXFORD COMPANION TO NEW ZEALAND LITERATURE

EDITED BY

ROGER ROBINSON

NELSON WATTIE

Melbourne

OXFORD UNIVERSITY PRESS

Oxford   Auckland   New York

OXFORD UNIVERSITY PRESS NEW ZEALAND

Oxford New York
Athens Auckland Bangkok Bogotá Buenos Aires
Calcutta Cape Town Chennai Dar es Salaam
Delhi Florence Hong Kong Istanbul Karachi
Kuala Lumpur Madrid Melbourne Mexico City
Mumbai Nairobi Paris Port Moresby São Paolo
Singapore Taipei Tokyo Toronto Warsaw

and associated companies in
Berlin Ibadan

OXFORD is a trade mark of Oxford University Press

ISBN 0 19 558348 5

Publication is assisted by

ARTS COUNCIL OF NEW ZEALAND *TOI AOTEAROA*

Edited by Simon Cauchi
Typeset by Archetype
Printed by Australian Print Group
Published by Oxford University Press,
540 Great South Road, Greenlane, PO Box 11-149,
Auckland, New Zealand

PREFACE

The *Oxford Companion to New Zealand Literature* is designed to provide information and pleasure to anyone with an interest in New Zealand or in literature. For those with special interests in New Zealand literature and related fields, it is intended to be a reference source of a full and unprecedented kind. The contents have been shaped in part by this lack of precedent. Although the *Oxford Companion* series supplied ample guidance for general procedure, the editors were still in a situation that was doubly novel. Scholarship in New Zealand literature is far from fully established; very many of the authors and topics we chose for entries have simply never been written about before. The book has also been prepared at a time when definitions of literature worldwide have been expanding dramatically. We have sought to take account of this new inclusiveness at the same time as charting parts even of the main literary stream. Such a range of information pertaining to New Zealand literature has never before been assembled in one place.

The guiding principle has nevertheless been simple. We have sought to create a *Companion*; not a dictionary or bibliography or history or a ranking of writers, but a reference book which is friendly as well as reliable, which makes established and unfamiliar facts readily accessible, which is quick and simple to use as well as alluring to browse at leisure. Our main instructions to the contributors were to establish all facts from primary sources, to communicate their own enthusiasm for their subjects, and to write in their own voice.

Some matters of policy should be declared. First, this *Companion* follows closely on the publication of the *Oxford History of New Zealand Literature in English* (1991, 1998). Our contributors have drawn extensively and gratefully on that work, but the *Companion* has been consciously designed to complement and not replicate the *History*. The *Companion* therefore contains no surveys of literary genres, no overview essays on such topics as Māori writing, publishing or literary criticism, no formal bibliography. If such things are missed, they will usually be found in the *History*. Where the same ground is inevitably covered, as in discussions of the achievement of major writers, it is done from different viewpoints, and by different commentators. The authors of the *History*'s chapters do not (with one special-case exception) write on the same subject matter for the *Companion*. More importantly, the *Companion* goes well beyond the *History* in scope. There are separate, specially researched entries on dozens of authors and texts that are absent from the *History*, or mentioned only in passing in its genre-centred surveys. The smallness of New Zealand's literature by most international comparisons has enabled this *Companion* to give many obscure or reputedly minor figures and works their two or three hundred words of fame; and thus to give our readers a basis for making their own choices and judgments. This first *Companion* should err, we decided, in the direction of inclusiveness.

Another challenge has been to give recognition to the range of literature in a nation that has more than one official language and more than one distinct cultural tradition. There are 125 entries on Māori writers, texts and topics, and several on Pacific topics, including a reminder that New Zealand has more than two languages (see 'Tokelau'). While many of these entries are necessarily concerned with texts in English, and while the entries themselves are written in English, the significance and accomplishment of literature (primarily in oral forms) in Māori have been recognised to the best of our ability. On several occasions the different circumstances that still apply to publication by Māori writers have caused the editors to waive our standard requirement that authors should have published at least two books to be considered for inclusion.

The core of this, as of all literary *Oxford Companions*, is the author and title entries: 680 authors and 110 titles are discussed in entries that range from one hundred to over two thousand words. The space allocated indicates judgments about their relative importance in a general and approximate but not a rigid way. Some writers' lives and some texts can be more concisely summarised than others, and some contributors garnered new material that was too interesting to reject because of anxieties over relative word-count. Contributors also made different decisions about the division of material between author and title entries; we accepted their judgments, apart from ensuring that there are entries, or at least cross-references, for all titles that have acquired resonance in their own right.

Though coverage is thus extensive, it could not be comprehensive. The more inclusive you are, the more has to be left out. Writing has been such an exuberant and prolific activity in New Zealand that selection has been inevitable. There are more novelists, dramatists and poets for readers to discover, and their absence here under separate entries (for many do appear in the general articles) is normally to avoid repetitiveness in representing areas of peripheral literary interest.

Similarly, while it seemed essential to include living writers, and to make those entries as up to date as possible, full coverage and right judgments there are difficult to achieve. The entries were received and edited over a three-year period, from 1994. Every effort has been made to acknowledge newly emerged writers and to mention very recent publications, but from late 1996 to 1998 this could be only by title, without any accompanying comment.

We decided also to give recognition to many more various kinds of writing than have traditionally been placed alongside a nation's major works of drama, fiction and poetry. There will be surprises, which we will not spoil. In such areas, however, even more rigorous choices had to be made. New Zealand has produced far more film, radio and television writers, sports writers, journalists, historians and rock-music lyricists than are included, and far more visual artists and musicians whose work connects with literature than the dozen or so of each who have entries. Our intention in these areas was to acknowledge their place in the full picture of the nation's literature, and in the priorities of the public. The choices we then had to make may be debatable, but they have never been capricious or made without advice. The same applies, for instance, to the twelve entries on New Zealand's connections with other national literatures. We regret the omission of India, Russia, Spain and others, but we drew the line where it seemed best to be drawn. Entries on publishers, libraries, collectors, newspapers, regions and many others are subject to the same necessary selectiveness.

All these are part of our effort to contextualise New Zealand literature in illuminating ways. There are also entries on writers born in New Zealand (e.g. Hugh Walpole), or who lived there for a while (e.g. Fay Weldon), or who paid a memorable visit (e.g. Bernard Shaw), or whose work has some place, however indirect, in New Zealand's literary history (e.g. Shakespeare, Melville, Verne, Patrick White). We are not appropriating these names, nor affirming some new definition of a national literature; they simply seemed valuable for the kind of interesting resource a *Companion* should be. For the same reason there are entries on the meaning and literary provenance of words which recur in literature but will be strange to readers who have not lived in New Zealand: 'bush', 'mana', 'station', 'tangi'.

In some areas, however, the selections are intended to be generous. Twenty-two of Katherine Mansfield's stories are discussed in some detail, in addition to an authoritative overview essay and entries on her iconic significance and on writers whose work connects with hers (Carco, Lawrence, Murry). Every significant title by Janet Frame and Allen Curnow has a separate entry, for a *Companion* should help readers to gain access to important (and sometimes difficult) works. Other writers receive similar if less complete treatment, and the most frequently anthologised short stories have separate entries.

With children's literature (75 entries) and literary periodicals (123 entries), too, the selections and the research on which they are based almost amount to mini-*Companions* in their own right. The time will come, indeed, for such books, and for those on New Zealand theatre, film and television, art and music. This *Companion* is aware of preparing the ground as well as space, time and the availability of qualified contributors permitted. The time will also come for full books on many topics which are opened up by our entries—literature and war, literature and music, Shakespeare in New Zealand, censorship, landscape, disability, goldmining, sport and many more. Our contributors invariably found more material than there was space to use, but the role of a *Companion* is to explore such issues, not exhaust them.

One omission may be noticed by users of other *Companions* to literature: there are no entries on created literary characters. No Odysseus, Ophelia, Pickwick or Huck Finn has yet claimed a place in the national imagination. We leave readers to meditate on why the only created characters we felt impelled to list as cross-references were Barbara, Gus Tomlins, Hairy Maclary and Fred Dagg. (Other entries recognise the iconic importance of Jack Lovelock, Katherine Mansfield and Robert Muldoon, but that is a different kind of cultural process.)

A last point returns us to the user-friendliness or companionability this book aspires to. New Zealand literature has some reputation for an unremitting dourness, which New Zealand literary scholarship seems to have attempted to emulate. In preparing this volume, we have very often encountered wit, fun, absurdity, eccentricity, beauty, eloquence, passion and sheer brilliance. The surprise and admiration which we and our contributors so often felt are, we hope, captured in the entries that follow.

Roger Robinson
Nelson Wattie

ACKNOWLEDGMENTS

The principal acknowledgment for what has been an essentially collaborative work must go to the 94 individual contributors. Their time and expertise were willingly given, often under many competing demands, almost entirely for the sake of participating in a project of value to New Zealand literature. Their names are given in the list of contributors below.

We offer special thanks, however, to those who took on an exceptional number of entries, or responsibility for an area of literature, or who kindly accepted extra entries at a time when completion became urgent: Christina Barton, David Carnegie, Les Cleveland, Simon Garrett, Stephen Hamilton, Diane Hebley, Lawrence Jones, Andrew Mason, Paul Millar, Pauline Neale, Harry Orsman, Peter Simpson, Terry Sturm, John M. Thomson and Kim Worthington.

Ideas, suggestions, references and help of all sorts have come from almost all the contributors, many other friends and directly and indirectly from authorities on many areas of New Zealand literature. These are too far numerous to name in full (as are those to whom we would wish to apologise for inflicting our obsession on them); but various particular acknowledgments for aspects of the book's contents are due to Ken Arvidson, Dr R.W. Bailey, William Broughton, Ray Copland, David Dowling, Brian Easton, Ray Grover, Diane Hebley, Kevin Ireland, Carole Legge, Paul Millar, Harry Orsman, Harry Ricketts, Jack Shallcrass, Peter Simpson, Lyman Tower Sargent and Peter Whiteford.

The entries relating to Māori literature, language, culture and authors are to an even greater extent the result of collaborative effort. The name under the entry is often that of the scribe rather than the source of the information given. Consultation with the Māori community has been ongoing and extensive: more extensive than even we understand, because of widespread discussion of matters we may have raised with one individual. Those to whom we know we are most indebted are Angela Ballara, Robin Rangihuia Bargh, Jon Battista, George Bertos, Jenifer Curnow, Witi Ihimaera, Wiremu Kaa, Tīmoti S. Kāretu, Bernie Kernot, Aorewa McLeod, Jane McRae, Margaret Orbell, Charles Royal, Miria Simpson and Ngāhuia Te Awekotuku; and all at the Māori Language Commission.

Similarly, for advice and material relating to Pacific writing, we are indebted to Loimata Iupati, Don Long, Albert Wendt, Mele Wendt and Briar Wood.

Anne French and Vincent O'Sullivan contributed crucially to the concept and early development of the book, when Elizabeth Marsden was also very helpful.

At the later stages, the contribution of Simon Cauchi went much deeper than the role of copy editor usually implies. The book reflects his profound and careful scholarship in many crucial ways.

Similarly, the informed and constructive interest taken by Linda Cassells made her a valued adviser as well as a supportive publisher.

The huge labour of compiling the book's text in digital form has been lightened by vital help from Helen Heazlewood of Victoria University and Diana Patterson of Oxford University Press; similar assistance has been given by Ruth Gay and Jim Baltaxe of Victoria University, and by David Norton, who was also a supportive Head of School through most of the project.

Published sources for information are far too numerous to list, though every effort has been made to acknowledge direct indebtedness within the text. The most constant resources for the editors have been *The Oxford History of New Zealand Literature in English*, ed. Terry Sturm; *New Zealand National Bibliography to the Year 1960*, ed. A.G. Bagnall; the *Dictionary of New Zealand Biography* (ed. W.H. Oliver and Claudia Orange); E.H. McCormick, *New Zealand Literature: A Survey*; Joan Stevens, *The New Zealand Novel 1860–1965*; Patrick Evans, *The Penguin History of New Zealand Literature*; *Who's Who in New Zealand*, ed. Max Lambert; *New Zealand Who's Who Aotearoa*, ed. Alister Taylor; *The Oxford Companion to Australian Literature*, ed. William H. Wilde, Joy Hooton and Barry Andrews; and the pages of *Landfall*, *Islands*, the *NZ Listener*, the *Journal of New Zealand Literature* and *New Zealand Books*.

Almost one hundred contributors, several based overseas, will have used the resources of more libraries than the editors could even estimate. Certainly every academic collection in New Zealand and many public libraries have contributed to this work. Again, we can acknowledge by name only those which the editors themselves have most constantly used: most especially the Alexander Turnbull Library, New Zealand National Library (New Zealand Collection) and Victoria University Library; also the Hocken Library, British Library, Library of Congress (Washington, DC), New York Public Library and Chapin Library, Williams College, Mass.

We most gratefully acknowledge the crucial financial support generously given by the Lottery Grants Board, Victoria University of Wellington, and Creative New Zealand.

We also acknowledge with gratitude the hospitality and support of Victoria University of Wellington, especially its School of English, Film and Theatre; and the support and patience of our colleagues, families and friends, most especially of all Kathrine Switzer and Elfi Wattie.

RR, NW

CONTRIBUTORS

(listed in alphabetical order of their initials, as shown at the foot of each entry)

AB	Angela Ballara, Dictionary of New Zealand Biography, Wellington
AL	Alan Loney, Holloway Press, University of Auckland
ALa	Alison Laurie, Victoria University of Wellington
AM	Andrew Mason, Wellington
AMcL	Aorewa McLeod, University of Auckland
AR	Alan Riach, University of Waikato
AT	Allan Thomas, Victoria University of Wellington
BE	Brian Easton, Wellington
BS	Brent Southgate, Learning Media, Wellington
BW	Briar Wood, University of North London
CB	Christina Barton, Victoria University of Wellington
CL	Carol Legge, Victoria University of Wellington
CM	Christiane Mortelier, Wellington
CR	Charles Royal, Te Wānanga o Raukawa, Ōtaki
DB	Dale Benson, University of Otago
DC	David Carnegie, Victoria University of Wellington
DD	David Dowling, University of Northern British Columbia
DFD	D.F. Dugdale, The Law Commission
DG	David Groves, Victoria University of Wellington
DH	Diane Hebley, Taradale
DK	Diana Knowles, Auckland
DL	Don Long, Learning Media, Wellington
DM	David Mackay, Victoria University of Wellington
DMcE	Dennis McEldowney, Auckland
EB	Edmund Bohan, Christchurch
EC	Elizabeth Caffin, Auckland University Press
EM	Elizabeth Marsden, Taupo
EN	Emma Neale, University of London
FB	Fergus Barrowman, Victoria University Press

GB	Gillian Boddy, Victoria University of Wellington
HM	Heather Murray, Journal of New Zealand Literature, Dunedin
HMcQ	Harvey McQueen, Wellington
HO	Harry Orsman, Victoria University of Wellington
HR	Heather Roberts, Wellington
HRi	Harry Ricketts, Victoria University of Wellington
HRo	Hugh Roberts, University of California, Irvine
HT	Heidi Thomson, Victoria University of Wellington
IR	Ian Richards, Tottori National University, Japan
JB	Judith Binney, University of Auckland
JBa	Jon Battista, University of Auckland
JBd	James Braund, University of Auckland
JC	Jenifer Curnow, Auckland
JE	Juniper Ellis, Loyola College, Baltimore
JH	Janet Hughes, Victoria University of Wellington
JMcC	Janet McCallum, Wellington
JMcR	Jane McRae, University of Auckland
JMT	John Mansfield Thomson, Wellington
JS	Jane Stafford, Victoria University of Wellington
JT	James Traue, Wellington
JW	Janet Wilson, University of Otago
KA	Ken Arvidson, University of Waikato
KI	Kevin Ireland, Auckland
KJ	Kai Jensen, Hamilton
KO	Keith Ovenden, Warsaw, Poland
KWa	Kathryn Walls, Victoria University of Wellington
KWo	Kim Worthington, Victoria University of Wellington
LC	Les Cleveland, Wellington
LI	Loimata Iupati, Porirua
LJ	Lawrence Jones, University of Otago
LTS	Lyman Tower Sargent, University of Missouri, St Louis
MH	Mark Houlahan, University of Waikato
MPJ	MacDonald P. Jackson, University of Auckland
NN	Nina Nola, University of Auckland
NW	Nelson Wattie, Victoria University of Wellington
NWr	Niel Wright, Wellington
NWt	Noel Waite, Auckland
PB	Peter Beatson, Massey University
PE	Patrick Evans, University of Canterbury
PM	Paul Millar, Victoria University of Wellington
PMn	Phillip Mann, Victoria University of Wellington
PN	Pauline Neale, Wellington
PP	Peter Pierce, James Cook University of North Queensland
PS	Peter Simpson, University of Auckland
PW	Peter Whiteford, Victoria University of Wellington
RC	Ralph Crane, University of Waikato
RCo	Richard Corballis, Massey University
RCp	Ray Copland, Christchurch

CONTRIBUTORS

RCr	Ronda Cooper, Wellington
RG	Ray Grover, Wellington
RR	Roger Robinson, Victoria University of Wellington
RRB	Robyn Rangihuia Bargh, Huia Publishers, Wellington
SG	Simon Garrett, Learning Media, Wellington
SH	Stephen Hamilton, Alexander Turnbull Library
SS	Sarah Shieff, University of Waikato
SSa	Sarah Sandley, Sydney
SSh	Sydney Shep, Wai-te-ata Press, Victoria University of Wellington
SW	Susan Wild, Victoria University of Wellington
TD	Tony Deverson, University of Canterbury
TS	Terry Sturm, University of Auckland
VO	Vincent O'Sullivan, Victoria University of Wellington
WB	William Broughton, Massey University
WBa	Winifred Bauer, Victoria University of Wellington
WHN	William H. New, University of British Columbia
WS	Bill Sewell, Wellington

USING THIS BOOK

Entries are in alphabetical order, including personal names, titles, words and general topics. Definite and indefinite articles are disregarded in establishing the order. Headwords for authors are given in the form in which they most usually publish, and alphabetised in that form; other names are given in the text where they are of literary significance. Where there is doubt or a variant form, a cross-reference is given (e.g. **MACMILLAN BROWN, John**, see **BROWN, John Macmillan**). Names such as Du Fresne are placed under Du (preceding Duckworth); names in the Māori form such as Te Whatahoro are under Te (preceding Templeton); names beginning with Mac or Mc are all treated as if spelt Mac. Personal surnames are in bold capitals (e.g. **FRAME, Janet**); works published as separate titles are in bold italics (e.g. ***Greenstone Door, The***, and ***Ao Hou, Te***); titles not published separately, such as poems or short stories, are in bold within quotation marks (e.g. **'Doll's House, The'**; but note ***Prelude***, which was published as a separate title). Readers and playgoers will be aware of the difficulty of establishing performance or publication details for some plays. The style stated above is followed and dates given for both first performance and publication so far as possible.

The most important aspect of this book's style is the use of the asterisk before a word in the text, to designate a cross-reference, 'q.v.' or 'see'. These have been quite fully used, since this *Companion* is designed to be read in an interconnected manner as well as to be a reference source on particular items and a venue for pleasurable random browsing. Thus few entries are wholly self-contained. The entry on an author will refer the reader by asterisk to entries on individual titles by that author (where plot summary, publication details, etc., may be found), and to other pertinent topics; the entries on titles and topics, equally, refer the reader to relevant author entries, where fuller personal information is given. Words such as 'bush' or 'waiata' are habitually asterisked, since readers may be encountering them for the first time and need advice that a full exposition is provided. The same applies to key topics such as 'gold', 'landscape' or 'music'; we wish readers to know that fuller essays on such topics are provided within these pages. The asterisks are therefore intended *both* to advise that information is provided pertinent to the entry being read *and* to lead the reader on to other matters of related interest. The reader of entries on Denis Glover, Ian Milner or the Caxton Press, for instance, will thus find a fuller version of the story of *Oriflamme* under that entry; and may be led from there to relevant entries on

Phoenix, Bob Lowry, the *Press* or censorship. In each entry, an asterisk is used only on the first occasion that a particular name, title, word or topic is mentioned. Sometimes an asterisk is attached to an adjectival or other derived form; thus '*Australian' and '*Irish', for example, refer to the articles on 'Australia' and 'Ireland', and '*goldfields' to that on 'gold'.

Māori vowels which properly now take a macron have been so treated, but macrons have not been added to quotations or titles (e.g. *The Maori King*) which predate this practice.

A very few living writers asked that some personal details, such as year of birth, not be stated; the editors respected this preference. The formal cut-off date for the inclusion of material was 30 June 1997, but in many instances subsequent material has been briefly noted.

ABBREVIATIONS

In general abbreviations have been sparingly used, and the full form is used wherever it is of significance to the entry. The abbreviation NZ is generally used only where that is the form in a title or quotation, except that the *New Zealand Listener* is generally shown as *NZ Listener*. The only other frequent abbreviations are *OHNZLE*, BHS, GHS and GS.

APRA	Australasian Performing Right Association
ATL	Alexander Turnbull Library, National Library
AUP	Auckland University Press
BA	Bachelor of Arts
BBC	British Broadcasting Corporation
BHS	Boys' High School
BMus	Bachelor of Music
BSc	Bachelor of Science
c.	*circa*, about
CPA	Communist Party of Australia
Dip	Diploma (e.g. of Fine Arts)
DLit	Doctor of Literature (Waikato)
DLitt	Doctor of Literature
DNZB	*Dictionary of New Zealand Biography*
DPhil	Doctor of Philosophy (Oxford)
ed.	editor, or edited by
edn	edition
ESOL	English as a Second Language
GHS	Girls' High School
GS	Grammar School
GSO 3 (I)	General Staff Officer, Grade 3, Intelligence
JNZL	*Journal of New Zealand Literature*
LittD	Doctor of Literature
MA	Master of Arts
MBE	Member of the Order of the British Empire
MHR	Member of the House of Representatives

MP	Member of Parliament
No. *or* no.	Number *or* number
NZBC	New Zealand Broadcasting Corporation
NZE	New Zealand English
NZEF	New Zealand Expeditionary Force
NZPA	New Zealand Press Association
NZSO	New Zealand Symphony Orchestra
OBE	Officer of the Order of the British Empire
OCTU	Officer Cadets Training Unit
ODT	*Otago Daily Times*
OHNZLE	*The Oxford History of New Zealand Literature in English*
OUP	Oxford University Press
PEN	Association of Poets, Playwrights, Editors, Essayists and Novelists: see entry
PhD	Doctor of Philosophy
prod.	produced (of a play)
pub.	published
rev.	revised
Rev.	Reverend
rpt.	reprinted
RN	Royal Navy
RNZAF	Royal New Zealand Air Force
RSA	Returned Services Association
SF	science fiction
TLS	*Times Literary Supplement*
trans.	translation, or translated by
UK	United Kingdom
USA	United States of America
Vol. *or* vol.	Volume *or* volume
VUP	Victoria University Press

A

ACHESON, Frank O.V. (1887–1948), novelist and judge, was born in Southland, graduated LLM (Hons) from Victoria College, Wellington, in 1913 and, after a period in legal practice, was a judge of the Native Land Court (1919–45) and the Native Appellate Court. After retirement, he was chairman of the Southland Regional Planning Council and was elected mayor of Riverton, his birthplace, a few months before his death. He was widely respected in the Māori community, especially in the Taupo–Tongariro region, and his one novel *Plume of the Arawas* (1930) is set there in pre-European times. Very popular in its day, it was republished in 1974. Its central figure is Manaia, an ancestor of the Ngāti Tūwharetoa, who leads his people in a war against the Tūhoe. The story is spiced by a romance between Manaia and Reremoa, a girl of the Ngāti Hotu. The book contains much Māori lore, including poetic translations of *waiata and *kōrero, and fulfils most of the expectations of ripping adventure and love romance. With Wiremu Rangi of Gisborne, Acheson wrote a *haka for the 'Invincibles' (the All Blacks of 1924–25), but there is no record of other written work.   NW

Action Songs, see **Waiata-a-ringa**.

ADAMS, Arthur H. (1872–1936), was a poet, novelist, playwright and journalist. Born at Lawrence, Otago, he was educated at Otago BHS and the University of Otago (BA 1894). He went on to law studies, but abandoned them when his uncle, E.T. Gillon, editor of the *Evening Post*, offered him a start in journalism in Wellington. In 1898 he moved to Sydney, and in 1900 covered the Boxer Rebellion in China for Australian and New Zealand papers, returning to Sydney in 1901 with enteric fever. After a lecture tour in New Zealand he freelanced in England for three years, living in biting poverty. In 1905 he was back on the *Evening Post*, but a year later joined the Sydney *Bulletin, almost immediately replacing A.G. Stephens as literary editor (of the 'Red Page'). He was editor of the Sydney *Sun* from 1911 to 1917, when he returned to the *Bulletin*.

For all his work as a journalist, Adams saw himself primarily as a poet and novelist. As early as 1893 Alfred *Hill composed an opera to a libretto by Adams: *The Whipping Boy*. The collaboration continued with a concert work entitled *Time's Great Monotone*, Adams showing skill in the Australasian ballad style. In his first Wellington year he and Hill worked on a cantata on the legend of *Hinemoa; the sharp-tongued *Triad* remarked that Adams's lyrics were 'graceful, musical and in places even poetical'. Adams was celebrated for *Hinemoa* as much as the composer. It was revived for performance in Wellington in 1992. In 1902 he collaborated with Hill again, on an opera called *Tapu*. Despite scenes as surprising as the entrance of four ladies from the Emancipated Women's League on bicycles, and backgrounds as spectacular as the Pink and White Terraces, Adams's libretto was blamed for the opera's failure.

As a playwright, however, Adams enjoyed some success. Since not all his plays were published, it is not possible to record his entire output, but in 1908 the *Bulletin* reviewed 'The Tame Cat: A Somewhat Colonial Comedy in Four Acts' as 'interpreted by the Sydney "Muffs"'. With its central character torn between a London *femme fatale* and persuasions to return to *Maoriland, the play enacts the conflict between London and the colony, the most common literary topos of the time. 'The Tame Cat' was praised more for 'wit' than structure, and the published plays confirm this impression. A collection of bon mots could be assembled from them, but their overall design is conventional, the influence of Ibsen, Wilde, Shaw and Pinero being apparent. These *Three Plays for the Australian Stage* (1914) were entitled 'Mrs Pretty and the Premier', 'The Wasters' and 'Galahad Jones' (the last based on the novel mentioned below). In the introduction Adams refers to four other full-length plays and 'about a dozen one-act comedies'.

Adams's his first volume of poems, *Maoriland and Other Verses* (1899), was welcomed by the critics and achieved some degree of popularity. Its ballad-like rhythms, reminiscent of Henry *Lawson and other Australian writers, were more appreciated than the attempts at lyricism. 'The Dwellings of Our Dead' was frequently anthologised, and its melancholy tone and harsh images of the South Island tussock country make a refreshing alternative to the 'bellbird and kowhai' sentimentality of many of his contemporaries. His description of the thermal region in 'The Brave Days to Be' is no less uncompromising: 'The earth writhed / With a scrofula of quivering sores'. This use of the New Zealand scene as a source of melancholy and austerity and the recurrence of death as a topic distinguish Adams, the professional writer, from his local contemporaries. Only Blanche *Baughan can rank with him. Though the masculine eroticism of his verse can seem mawkish and clumsy, it was a sign of some courage in the puritanical context. His introduction of Māori themes, as in 'The Coming of Te Rauparaha', is one of the strongest bridges from *Domett to *Acheson in the literary imaging of Māori.

The Nazarene: A Study of a Man (1902) is an exercise in austere, yet graceful, language and in uncompromising atheistic humanism, denying the divinity of Christ while admiring his human qualities. Adams's years in London seem to have been unhappy. In some work there are traces of a relationship with a wretchedly poor washerwoman and his conscience-stricken inability to help her. Consequently, the poems in *London Streets* (1906) show none of that fascination for *'Home' that characterised many colonial jottings, presenting instead the metropolis as a 'grey cobweb', in whose sticky threads people from afar are caught. 'There, drawn by the great lure of that great name, / My alien heart, shrivelled and long sucked dry!'

Some of these poems and many previously uncollected ones, often from the *Bulletin*, were elegantly printed on expensive paper in *Collected Verses* (1913), whose 'Preface' is a farewell to poetry: the 40-year-old writer believed that poems are the art of youth. Now he was 'leaving the pleasant, twisting by-paths of poetry for the dustier, though more direct, highway of prose.'

In fact he had published his first novel in 1904: *Tussock Land*. A 'Künstlerroman', a novel of artistic development, its hero is unable to realise his ambitions in New Zealand but is discontented in Australia, despite the greater opportunities. He travels back and forth, torn between his love of art and of his New Zealand home, which is at one with his love of a Māori woman who will never consent to going to Australia. It is marked by evocative descriptions of both countries. His other major New Zealand work of fiction is *The New Chum and Other Stories* (1909). The stories are set in the *bush and contrast the practical unpolished ways of the settled workmen with a newcomer 'from a place in England called Oxford, where so many of the colonial "dead-beats" hail from.' The contrast between 'Home' and colony is again central. Though the *'new chum' earns the respect of his colonial friends, he remains an alien.

During the years of his high repute in the literary world of *Australia, Adams wrote several 'Australian' novels: *Galahad Jones* (1909) is the tale of a dry bank clerk humanised by his encounter with a dying girl; similarly *Grocer Greatheart* (1915), set on a tropical island, reveals unsuspected strengths in the soul of a middle-aged Woolloomooloo grocer who had sunk into dull routine; in *A Touch of Fantasy* (1912), a young middle-class man finds confusion rather than happiness in the arms of a working-class woman; *The Australians* (1920) tells of a lively young Englishwoman stranded in Sydney, with satiric digs at social customs and artistic pretensions. The final novel, *A Man's Life* (1929), concerned with the gradual failing of a man's creativity, has been called (by Uther Barker) 'a thinly veiled autobiography'. According to this view, Adams lost his literary skills as the demands of the practical world overwhelmed him. Indeed, the gap between romantic idealism and daily life is one common theme of his novels, the other being a similar dislocation between sexual passion and idealised love.

This last theme finds a strangely disturbing form in four novels Adams published under the pseudonym 'James James', where the titillations of partial nudity are in continual conflict with prudishness, a powerful sexual urge with the demands of *puritanism.

Now largely forgotten, Adams was once a powerful force on the Australian literary scene, though throughout his life he identified with New Zealand. In a once notorious poem, 'Written in Australia', he contrasts the dry, bleak landscape of Australia with the lush green of New Zealand. As H.M. Green, the Australian literary historian, writes, 'If Australia became his wife, New Zealand remained his first love, far off and idealized.... Although Australia was more mature than New Zealand, Adams was more mature than they were.'   NW

Adaptable Man, The, is the fifth novel by Janet *Frame (*Pegasus Press, 1965; New York, London, 1965; the typescript is held in the *Hocken Library). After the stylistic experimentation and minimal plots of Frame's earlier novels, this seems to be a concession to the conventions of realism in terms of plot and characterisation. However, by juxtaposing realist passages with fluid, intensely metaphorical passages reminiscent of the style of her earlier novels, Frame invites readers to recognise the insufficiencies of realism as a mode of representing the contemporary world. She satirically exposes the artifice of her omniscient narrator, Unity Foreman (a name loaded with implication, like so many in Frame's novels), undercutting her imposition of narrative order on a setting and cast of characters that is far from unified. The setting is the East Suffolk village of Little Burgelstatham and the focus is on several families there, the Maudes, the Baldrys and the Unwins. Unable to adapt to the reality of a twentieth-century world devoid of the moral certainties of the past, the villagers (and visitors to the village) have all retreated into fantasy, wish-fulfilment or memory. Some dream of a return to childhood (Ruby Unwin), of the recovery of lost religious faith (Rev. Aisley Maude), of an escape from domestic servitude to the excitement of London life (Dot Unwin), of migration to another country (Vic Baldry), of a lost inheritance (Rex Unwin); others steadfastly remain attached to an anachronistic past (Russell Maude), or seek vicarious fulfilment through a child, gardening or interior decoration (Greta Maude and Muriel Baldry). The novel's one 'adaptable man', Alwyn Maude, is offered as the fittest survivor of human evolution. He alone is able to adapt to his century: chillingly amoral, ruthlessly violent, he is 'a twentieth century man who would fight and kill to stay in his time'; a man who commits murder and incest with indifference. The barest details of these acts are described, and not explicated; Frame seems to suggest that we cannot ask for reasons in an amoral twentieth-century world where actions and events are arbitrary and pattern and order are imposed fictions. At the apocalyptic ending, several characters are killed by a falling chandelier, leaving Vic Baldry paralysed, condemned forever to view life in a cracked mirror from his bed. The novel concludes with the narrator's question—'don't we all live in mirrors, forever?' —suggesting the imitative and artificial nature of the human struggle to adapt and conform. The reader is left with a larger question: at what cost, adaptability? KWo

ADCOCK, Fleur (1934–), is a poet, editor and translator of medieval Latin and twentieth-century Romanian poetry. She was born in Papakura. Her family moved to England when she was five, remaining there through World War 2 until she was thirteen, when they returned to New Zealand. Her mother Irene Adcock (*NZ Poetry Society) and sister Marilyn *Duckworth are writers. Having obtained an MA in Classics at Victoria University, Adcock repeated her family's journey in 1963, and made her permanent home in Britain. Her 1952 marriage to Alistair *Campbell ended in 1957. She was married to Barry *Crump, 1962–66. A professional librarian for the British Foreign and Commonwealth Office until 1979, she has held writing fellowships at Charlotte Mason College of Education at Ambleside and at the universities of Newcastle upon Tyne, Durham, East Anglia and Adelaide, Australia.

Adcock's poetry ranges across themes from the painful negotiations of relationships to ecological, political and gender concerns. Although she is often praised for her 'anti-erotica' and her restrained, classically informed voice, underlying such defensive discursive strategies there is a genuine tenderness and sensitivity to the potential psychic scarrings of the most intimate betrayals. Tellingly, Adcock's most moving elegiac works ('The Keepsake', 1986, 'The Chiffonier', 1986) testify to the endurance of friendship or familial bonds, rather than romantic love.

Adcock's work has moved from an earlier self-concealing deployment of male narrators or characters to a more confident use of the lyrical self, and a deliberate focus on women's lives through various fictional voices. Influences include Graves, Auden, Yeats, Edna St Vincent Millay and Ursula *Bethell. The most consistent influences, however, are of various principles that may be seen as grounded in such British associations of poets as the Movement or the Group. Her accessible, declarative diction comes from a conscious wish to avoid taking advantage of the reader, and so she rejects fragmentation, academicism, disruptions of syntax or awkward, esoteric symbolism—traits that could be seen as either Neo-romantic or Modernist in succession to Ezra Pound. Adcock is also resistant to typographically or visually experimental poetry. Her ear trained to formal metrics, she delights in patterned rhymes and strict stanzaic forms. Her early work in *The Eye of the Hurricane* (1964) and *Tigers* (1967) (her British debut, based partly on the first book), shows interest in the symbolic use of fairy tale, myth and allegory. She has since moved to sharper clarity in documenting contemporary and domestic scenes. Yet she also creates vivid 'other' worlds, from the science fiction scenario in 'Gas' (*High Tide in the Garden*, 1971) to the incorporation of historical material in her libretto, *Hotspur, A Ballad for Music* (1986; composer Gillian *Whitehead).

Although Adcock's range is wide, her oeuvre like her life, she has said, is 'influenced, infected, and to some sense distorted' by questions of national identity. Many poems are written from the perspective of an ambivalent outsider; identifying with and yet withdrawing from various emotional and physical contexts. The dislocations of emigration inform several; not just poems that directly confront the experience, but also those concerned with the dream landscapes of the subconscious, or the reconstruction of a narrative of her family history. *Below Loughrigg* (1979) also deals in the literary historical pressures of place and tradition, as she explores her relationship to the Lake Poets during one of her writing fellowships. The troubling intersections of private and national identities are discussed in autobiographical pieces written for *Poetry Review* (74, 1984), 'A Lifetime of Writing' in *Beyond Expectations* (ed. Margaret Clark), *The Bloodaxe Book of Contemporary Women Poets: Eleven British Writers* (ed. Jeni Couzyn) and the *Contemporary Authors* series (Gale Research).

Ursula Bethell is the only New Zealand poetic predecessor that Adcock openly acknowledges. Yet some poems directly concern her feelings about the New Zealand side of her heritage and engage with and criticise descriptions of the ★landscape that had been standard literary fare since the 1930s. These issues crop up particularly in her main collections from the 1970s, *High Tide in the Garden* (1971), *The Scenic Route* (1974) and *The Inner Harbour* (1979). In poems such as 'Ngauranga Gorge Hill', 'Stewart Island' and 'On a Son Returned to New Zealand', Adcock expresses discomfort over the question of her own position within the language of New Zealanders. The isolation and 'peculiar pressures', which Allen ★Curnow advocated as aspects of a native New Zealand art, are present in her poems as part of a highly personal argument over origins and belonging. 'Ngauranga Gorge Hill' (1971) performs the exorcism of a painful past by depicting its physical setting as sterile, awkward and confined. Subsequent poems about England juxtapose a variety and abundance of natural forms to their perceived absences in New Zealand.

Adcock's work performs perpetual migrations. Later poems such as 'Please Identify Yourself', 'The Bullaun' (1974), 'Foreigner' and 'Immigrant' (1979) touch on the difficulties of adapting to Britain or claiming Britishness; while 'Richey', 'The Voyage Out', 'Moa Point' (1971) and 'Settlers', 'Going Back' and 'Instead of an Interview' (1979) relocate, exploring the emigrant's or backmigrant's experience within New Zealand. Fittingly, a section in *The Inner Harbour* is titled 'To and Fro'. This shuttling point of view is quintessentially Adcock; the section title emphasises the divided sense of identity she inherits from both family (or historical) emigrant experience and personal expatriation. In 'Instead of an Interview' the issue is further complicated, as Adcock

explores the loss and alienation that spring from the choice of long-term separation from family.

Adcock's translation and editorial work intensified in the 1980s, when her *Selected Poems* (1983) also appeared. The main collection of new work from this decade is *The Incident Book* (1986), in which her English childhood is mapped out through various changes in schools; the role of new girl or outsider is dramatised through small events, while an England of woods and flowers is recorded that is absent in the poems that frame this section. The rest of the volume depicts a Britain fractured by social tension, the 'Thatcherland' sequence showing how the erosions of recession, commercialisation and the creed of individualism filter down into the apparently small changes in suburban lives. Adcock's England has developed from a place which answers to New Zealand's supposed deficiencies to a more troubled depiction of social and political unease. *Meeting the Comet* (1988) shows particular skills with the topical.

Ecological and political concerns recur in *Time-Zones* (1991), which takes its title from the division of hemispheres, yet also refers to the intense presence of memory underpinning the everyday. Here Adcock's subject matter loops from the oppressive regime of Ceauşescu in Romania to the insidious workings of chemical pollution. The volume is also haunted by the death of her father. Yet, typical of Adcock's professional ability to switch registers, poems such as 'Housemartins' and 'Creosote' also confront the idealising tendencies of even the most painful nostalgia. 'Mrs Fraser's Frenzy', which explores the same events as Patrick ★White's novel *A Fringe of Leaves* (the shipwreck of the *Stirling Castle* and the ordeal of one survivor), shows Adcock's continuing fascination for the drama of migration, and the feelings of psychological division associated with the experience, as she channels these through an extreme example of deprivation and conflicting fictionalised voices.

Despite her absences and ambivalences, Adcock is well represented in New Zealand anthologies such as the most recent Oxford and Penguin, frequently reviews New Zealand books in British journals, edited the *Oxford Book of Contemporary New Zealand Poetry* (1982) and was awarded an OBE in 1996 for her contribution to New Zealand literature.   EN

ADSETT, Dell (1920–), novelist and local historian, has lived, as a sheep farmer, within the rural communities that are the subject of her two novels. *A Magpie Sings* (1963) takes a small farming community through the early years of the twentieth century. Its ★romance main plot is strengthened by her convincing portrayals of social rituals, day-to-day life at the local school, animal husbandry and the romantic and sexual impulses of young women. The impact of World War 1, as the initial excitement turns to the reality of loss, provides an unexpected ending, though softened by the obligatory romance uplift. *Leave Me in the Park* (1974) also ends well for its socially rejected, handicapped Bennie, a character associated by Lawrence *Jones with Janet *Frame's Toby Withers. Adsett's main connections are with small-community fiction such as The *Cunninghams, and with stories of growth to adulthood. She has also published local histories, *A Township Like Ours* (1974) and *Show Time 100* (1987). She has completed further adult and children's fiction.   RR

Aeronaut, one of several attempts to establish a literary periodical in the late nineteenth century, was published at the 'Evening Post Office' in Wellington from July to September 1881 (vol. 1, nos. 1–3). An 'Introductory Address to the Public' remarks optimistically that '… the want has long been felt for a publication of this description, both as an object of amusement and instruction and as a vehicle for the considerable amount of local talent which has hitherto lain dormant from the dearth of opportunity for its dissemination'. But after three issues 'the want' turned out to be insufficient for the journal's survival. Apart from an essay on 'The Rising Generation', a poem on a Wellington cemetery and two serials set in England, the contents are entirely anecdotal short fiction. All contributions were anonymous.   NW

A.H. & A.W. Reed was a leading New Zealand publisher from 1932, when it published its first major title, to 1983, when it was bought by an international company. While other local firms combined publishing with printing and/or retailing, Reeds were publishers alone throughout most of this period and at their peak in the 1960s they were, with their Australian subsidiary, publishing more titles per year than any other firm in Australasia. Between 1957 and 1967 they produced 903 new titles and 353 reprints and their turnover doubled every six years. They dominated the New Zealand publishing scene and for a time influenced the Australian one as well.

The firm was founded in Dunedin by A.H. *Reed as a Sunday school and religious supply business, but the publishing was largely the creation of his nephew A.W. *Reed after he moved to Wellington in 1932 to set up a branch there. The publishing business expanded rapidly, taking particular advantage of the wartime shortage of imported books and making the most of the Reeds' entrepreneurial flair.

After the war A.W. Reed increasingly spent his time writing books for the firm's imprint and left the publishing activities in the skilled hands of Ray Richards, publishing director, and Tom Kennedy, sales director, a team which later included Don Sinclair, Arnold *Wall and Fred Davey. In the 1950s–60s this group produced and marketed a string of best-sellers, of which Barry *Crump's books are the best known, and also established Reeds as the country's leading educational publisher.

Reed books were directed at a popular middlebrow readership and celebrated a distinctly New Zealand way of life. Mostly non-fiction, they included back-country tales, books on *sport, gardening, cooking and crafts. Māori topics were a particular strength. Well-illustrated books on natural history and books of landscape photographs and paintings appealed to both local readers and tourists.

The 1970s was however a troubled decade for the company, and changes of management were not able to halt the decline in the firm's fortunes as the market shrank and competition increased. The educational publishing and the Australian company were both sold and in 1983 the main company was purchased by British publisher ABP Methuen. Further overseas ownership changes followed, and since 1992 the firm has been owned by Reed Elsevier. The imprint retains its particularly strong list of books in and about Māori.

The firm's history is told in [A.H. and A.W. Reed], *The House of Reed: Fifty Years of New Zealand Publishing, 1907–1957* (1957), A.W. Reed, *The House of Reed, 1957–1967* (1968) and Dennis *McEldowney's chapter in the *OHNZLE (1991, 1998).   EC

ALCOCK, Peter (1922–), literary critic and poet, published poetry in a number of periodicals during the 1960s–70s, featuring in *New Zealand Poetry Yearbook* 1964. As lecturer in English at Palmerston North University College from 1960, he was a very early pioneer of courses in New Zealand literature and promoted its study overseas. Perceiving an increasing international interest in the field then known as 'Commonwealth Literature', he surveyed British libraries, established that few had significant holdings in New Zealand literature and described his findings in 'An Invisible Literature?', *Landfall 88 (1968). His representations persuaded the Department of Internal Affairs to donate collections of New Zealand literary texts and periodicals to a number of research libraries in UK and USA. In the 1970s and early 1980s he published regular surveys of New Zealand writing in the *Journal of Commonwealth Literature* and *World Literature Written in English*, and represented New Zealand on the latter's editorial board. His long-term involvement with the Association of Commonwealth Literature and Language Studies led to the honour of life membership of its

South Pacific branch. With William Broughton he compiled the reference work *Three Hundred Years of New Zealand Books: Select Chronology, literary and general, with commentary, from Tasman to 1975* (1991).   PM

Alex Quartet, The, is the name popularly given to the series of four novels for young adults by Tessa ★Duder, *Alex* (1987), *Alex in Winter* (1989), *Alessandra: Alex in Rome* (1991) and *Songs for Alex* (1992). Set principally in the Auckland of the 1950s, the quartet charts the dramatic events in 15-year-old Alex Archer's sporting, artistic and personal development. *Alex* is structured in fifteen chapters, framed by the title-character's thoughts as she swims to victory in the final of the National 100m freestyle—the race that was to have determined her selection for the 1960 Rome Olympics. It establishes her as multi-talented, having musical and artistic ability as well as a keenly critical mind. The need to make choices between her talents is a recurrent theme, as she aspires to play top-level hockey, act in school productions and gain ballet, piano and academic qualifications while in serious swimming training. A rival supported by a ruthlessly ambitious mother provides further conflict. In the far bleaker *Alex in Winter*, after the death of her boyfriend and the selectors' decision to delay announcement of the team, she turns against friends, family and the conformist, patriarchal society around her. Alex's selection is eventually confirmed and the novel ends with the New Zealand Olympic team assembling. *Alex in Rome*, more optimistic in tone, introduces a second narrator, Tom Alexander, a young New Zealand operatic student with whom Alex falls in love. Her selection is vindicated when, against the odds, she wins a bronze medal, a success which, as the youngest member of the team, exposes her to more intense media scrutiny than she is able to cope with. Resolution comes in *Songs for Alex* with a series of decisions: to retire from swimming, to remain in New Zealand to study at university and to develop a relationship with Tom. Throughout the quartet, the plot is advanced with dramatic crises. The books vividly evoke 1950s Auckland society, as well as the rigour of early-morning training in densely chlorinated pools and the extreme stress of competitive sport. Critically acclaimed, each has been recognised with awards (see author entry), which have helped to secure the quartet's place as a key work in young adult literature. Although Duder had a distinguished swimming career, winning a silver medal in the 1958 Cardiff Empire Games, she consistently downplays autobiographical interpretations. Claudia Marquis discusses the quartet in 'Telling Tales out of School: "Young Adult" Literature in New Zealand', ★*Landfall* 179 (1991), and

Duder writes on 'Is There Life After Alex?' in *Reading Forum New Zealand* 2 (1994). A film version, *Alex* (1993), directed by Megan Simpson with screenplay by Ken ★Catran, was based primarily on *Alex*.   SSa

ALEXANDER, Raewyn (1955–), is a poet and fiction writer best known for her revealing sex industry novel *Fat* (1996). She was born and grew up in Hamilton and has lived also in Auckland and Europe. She studied fine arts at Elam, and worked as a dressmaker and costume embellisher, and for a brief period as a stripper in Auckland's Pink Pussycat Club, drawing on that experience for the background of her first novel. A second novel, *Concrete*, appeared in 1998.   KI

Alexander Turnbull Library, The, in Wellington, is now a division of the National Library of New Zealand, responsible for a unique collection of materials relating to New Zealand as well as other major collections: the Pacific, voyages of discovery especially in the Pacific and Antarctica, early printed books, the history of the book and books by and relating to John Milton.

The library was founded with a bequest to the nation by Alexander Horsburgh ★Turnbull of 55 000 volumes together with prints, drawings, manuscripts, maps and photographs. The *New Zealand Times* called it 'one of the most astounding acts of public benefaction in the country's history'. The son of a successful merchant, and the manager of the firm after his father's death, Turnbull devoted his fortune to his collections: his Māori and Pacific artefacts and his coins were given to the Dominion Museum in 1913 to make room for his books. In 1916 he moved into a specially designed house in the heart of Wellington, which the government bought after his death to preserve his library. It was opened to the public in 1920 and became a part of the National Library in 1966, so that the collections are now housed in the National Library building in Molesworth Street. Turnbull's collections, including his world-famous Milton collection, have been completed and extended so that it is now the major research library for all aspects of New Zealand and many aspects of the Pacific.

The Pacific collection includes virtually all printed materials since the voyage of Magellan (1523) and many manuscripts, log books, maps, journals and the like. The Antarctic collection is also notable. The library tries to be as inclusive as possible in covering Polynesia, Melanesia and Micronesia. Australia, Asia and the Americas are generally covered in aspects that impinge on these Pacific regions. On microfilm there are thousands of documents from the Archives Nationales (Paris), the Church Missionary Society, London Missionary Society and Methodist Missionary Society. There is a collection of some quarter of a million photographs in negatives and prints, 5000 maps and 5000 pictures and prints.

The large collection of English literature includes rare editions of major poets, dramatists and novelists. The Milton collection has many rare editions, biographical and critical works and works relating to Milton's times, so that other seventeenth-century areas are also well represented. Another major area is the history of the book, with fine examples in the study of paper, binding, illustration and *typography. Naval affairs, folklore and witchcraft, Italian Renaissance statecraft and early Scottish and Irish history are also strengths.

Special attention is paid to acquiring all kinds of New Zealand materials. During the 1950s and especially 1960s the acquisition of literary manuscripts and writers' papers became a major concern, with the papers of Robin *Hyde, D'Arcy *Cresswell, Frank *Sargeson, A.R.D. *Fairburn and Denis *Glover among those acquired. Its extensive collection of manuscripts, editions, and critical, biographical and bibliographical works relating to Katherine *Mansfield makes the library a major centre for Mansfield studies and publications.   NW

ALEXANDER, W.F., see **Currie, A.E.**; *New Zealand Verse*.

'ALIEN', see **Baker, Louisa Alice.**

All Visitors Ashore (1984) won C.K. *Stead the New Zealand Book Award for Fiction. The novel presents a fictitious version of Stead's own experience in the 1950s, when he was a student at Auckland University College, and was befriended by Frank *Sargeson while Janet *Frame was living in a hut in Sargeson's garden. Stead condenses this personal history into the year 1951, the year of the *Waterfront Strike, and sets the political upheaval as background for a personal trauma: the disintegration of his protagonist's love relationship. Stead has repeatedly commented on the importance of the Waterfront Strike for his political education, and there are allusions in his poetry and other fiction to an early, traumatic affair. Curl Skidmore, central character of *All Visitors Ashore*, thus refracts Stead's own experience rather than directly representing it, and critics such as Mark *Williams and Michael *Morrissey rightly warn that the straightforward identification of Curl and Karl is a narrative trap. Indeed, the narrative tone is delightfully mischievous, particularly in its boisterous, playful syntax. Many of the sentences are a paragraph long, and rich with details of a remembered and loved 1950s Auckland. The novel's success evidently encouraged Stead to take early retirement from the University of Auckland and concentrate on his creative writing. His subsequent

novels carry on from *All Visitors Ashore* in their refraction of personal material through a variety of narrative devices, but Stead has never again ventured on so rich and extensive a syntax.   KJ

ALLAN, Rob (1945–   ), poet, was born in Birmingham, UK, and emigrated to New Zealand in 1960, where he trained as an educational psychologist and teacher of the deaf. He has for some years taught deaf children in schools around Otago. His poems, initially published in periodicals, led in 1991 to *Hazard Press publishing his first book, *Karitane Postcards*. Described by him as 'a sustained post-modern attempt to write a long poem with an epic scope', the 100 sections of *Postcards* develop the small Otago seaside settlement of Karitane into a fixed symbol about which the ebb and flow of time, history, politics and poetics deposit traces that, as they accumulate, shape the poem's language. Peter Whiteford has noted parallels between Ezra Pound's *Cantos* and Allan's deliberate raiding of local elements from diverse cultures, whose interplay then 'becomes part of the poem's meaning'. *Postcards* was named 1991's best first book of poetry by *PEN.   PM

Allen Adair is the fourth novel by Jane *Mander, published in London in 1925. As if rebutting criticism that she could only effectively portray women, Mander centres attention and sympathy on her eponymous male protagonist. A disappointment to his family, Allen has failed at whatever he turns his hand to: study at Oxford, sheep farming, clerical work. He leaves Auckland and travels north, literally and metaphorically enacting a journey towards self-discovery and fulfilment. After running a mail boat in Dargaville, he settles near Pahi. Here he runs a general store serving the local gumdiggers and sawmillers and eventually holds the lease of the gumfield. Feeling the need for a wife, Allen hastily marries Marion, an Aucklander, but the marriage is a disappointment to them both. Marion does not share Allen's love of the gum country, viewing its hardship and struggle as necessary only until they can afford to return to Auckland. As the marriage dissolves into bare mutual tolerance, the couple vie for the affection of their eldest daughter Joan. Allen is gentle and beneficent to all but his wife. Marion is given unsympathetic treatment as the embodiment of the repressive conformity that Mander believed threatened the potential of New Zealand and the sanctity and individuality of spirited pioneers like Allen. After discord and suspicion during Allen's friendship with Dick Rossiter, an apparent 'lost soul' of the gumfields, Allen, Marion and their children depart for the 'flurry' of Auckland. In contrast to the sometimes strident political voice, speech-making and long promulgatory passages that characterise Mander's earlier novels, the style is economical and the tone mellow. Gone are the contentious moral impropriety and earnest feminism of her precocious young heroines struggling for liberation. But if Mander hoped to appease her critical local audience with this very different novel, she failed to do so. It was poorly received, its virtues not fully appreciated until the first New Zealand edition in 1971. Reprinted in 1984 and published by Godwit Press in 1995, *Allen Adair* remains a compelling ode to the lost kauri forests of Northland and the men who pioneered them.   KWo

ALLEN, C.R. (Charles Richards) (1885–1962), was active in literary circles throughout the period 1920–40, when his nostalgic mannerism was eclipsed by the younger generation. His work recurs in literary journals, including a poem in the fourth issue of *Phoenix*. He published three novels set in England and then three in New Zealand, moving from a colonial to a more nationalistic set of values. Once admired, his novels are rarely read today.

His three Dunedin novels, *A Poor Scholar* (1936), *Hedge Sparrow* (1937) and *The Young Pretender* (1939) are low-key, indeed provincial; they examine the uneventful lives of suburban people, many of whom have a nostalgia for English ways of life. *A Poor Scholar* seems to be autobiographical, telling of a boy's escape from poverty into respectability by gaining academic success at Otago Boys' High School and, eventually, Otago University. His ultimate aim—England—is, however, never attained.

No doubt Allen was hindered in his ambitions by his total blindness. In a letter he once remarked: 'My method of work is to live wherever I can and to pay an amanuensis. I read Braille for relaxation, but Braille is too cumbersome for reference.' In another letter he refers to his eleven completed novels, but despairs of getting more published.

Allen edited *Tales by New Zealanders* (1938), which included stories by Eileen *Duggan and Robin *Hyde; yet even here he tended to favour stories flavoured with a nostalgic sentiment of England.   NW

ALLEY, Elizabeth, Wellington broadcaster, reviewer and editor, has influenced public perception of New Zealand literature while also creating a valuable national archive of literary resources. From 1965 she was involved in commissioning and producing radio programmes on New Zealand and other literatures and subsequently became Executive Producer and Literary Editor for the Concert Programme, later Concert FM. Literary Editor of *New Zealand Bookworld* 1974–80, she was a member of the *Literary Fund Advisory Committee 1981–83 and has frequently served as judge of literary awards.

Her notable radio productions include the outstanding series for the *Mansfield centenary in 1988, the 25-part series on 'Landmarks and Signposts in New Zealand Literature' for the 1990 sesquicentenary, and her biennial series of recordings of *Writers and Readers Week sessions. Her own broadcasts include perceptive interviews with writers such as Margaret Atwood, Alice Munro, Patrick *White, Salman Rushdie, E. Annie Proulx, Lauris *Edmond, Allen *Curnow, Margaret *Mahy, Fleur *Adcock, Albert *Wendt and two of special importance with Janet *Frame. These two were included in *In the Same Room: Conversations with New Zealand Writers* (1992), interviews remarkable for spontaneity and engagement, edited by Alley and Mark *Williams. A long-serving member of the Writers and Readers Week organising committee, for the 1994 Week Alley edited *The Inward Sun: Celebrating the Life and Work of Janet Frame* (1994).

Born in Hawkes Bay, she was educated in Wellington where she has since lived. In 1995 she was awarded the QSO, and an honorary DLit at the University of Waikato. She is now Programme Development Manager for Radio New Zealand.   GB

ALLEY, Rewi (1897–1987), poet, was born in Springfield, a farming area outside Christchurch. Of European descent, he was named after the legendary Māori chief Rewi Maniapoto, who had resisted British forces during the land wars of the 1860s. He attended Christchurch BHS, but left at the end of 1915 to enlist in the army. The war took him to France, where he received the Military Medal for bravery and was invalided home in 1919, having been shot through the hips by a machine gun round. From 1920 to 1927 he worked, in partnership, an isolated *backblocks sheep farm in Taranaki's Moeawatea Valley. The venture struggled and Alley, who had read of *China, decided to 'go and have a look at their revolution'. He travelled to Shanghai in 1927 and was soon involved in fighting the abysmal industrial conditions. When China's war with *Japan began in the late 1930s, he laboured to organise the relocation of 30 000 industrial co-operatives before the Japanese advance, to maintain China's production. He went on to found the Chinese Industrial Co-operatives Association, inventing a slogan, 'Gung Ho' (meaning 'work together'), that earned him international attention. In 1942 he helped found a school in Sandan to train peasants in simple skills to make them less vulnerable to the changing seasons and, by the 1950s, he was its headmaster. Even in retirement (with a modest state pension), Alley's energy never flagged: he laboured for the resurrection of the Industrial Co-operative movement, and the rebuilding of Sandan School to operate as an agriculture and forestry training ground for peasants. He died, and is buried, in Beijing.

At school Alley had enjoyed poems of action, bits of Shelley and Shakespeare's sonnets. He read little poetry in New Zealand's backblocks, so it was in China that he began scribbling, by 'the sides of roads or because I had nothing to read'. His first published poems, 'Lines to My Mother', marked the start of a prolific output totalling almost sixty books of poetry and prose. His writing reverberates with a strong ideological commitment to China and communism, although expressed through a direct concern with life and people, because 'without dealing with life poetry has little meaning'. Such immediacy of purpose has spared Alley the lash of critics, with Allen ★Curnow mildly locating his verse on the margins of his life's activities—'simply jottings arranged into poems'—which concurs with his own description of them as unrevised, unpolished, unworked, and scribbled 'out as they occur to me'. He characteristically employs free verse lines of varying length, generally unrhymed because in his opinion rhyme distorts and conceals meaning. He also prefers transparent imagery and crisp, condensed expressions of ideas and beliefs. Central to many poems is a sense of the immediacy of history, expressed in a unity of past and present, history and current events: 'do we start anew, with / new wine in old bottles, as we have / been taught not to do. Yet, is the wine so new?' ('Boiler in Sandan'). Indigenous writers such as Hone ★Tuwhare and Australian Aboriginals Kevin Gilbert and Oodgeroo Noonuccal (Kath Walker) are among the poets he admired.

Alley's poetry collections published in New Zealand include *Gung Ho: Poems* (1948), *Leaves from a Sandan Notebook* (1950), *This is China Today: Poems* (1951), *Fragments of Living Peking, and Other Poems* (1955), *Human China: A Diary with Poems* (1957), *Journey to Outer Mongolia: A Diary with Poems* (1957), *Beyond the Withered Oak Ten Thousand Saplings Grow* (1962), *The Mistake: Poems* (1965), *What is Sin?: Poems* (1967), *Twenty-Five Poems of Protest* (1968), *Upsurge: Asia and the Pacific: Poems* (1969), *73 Man to Be: Poems* (1970), *Poems for Aotearoa* (1972), *Winds of Change: Poems* (1972), *The Rebels* (1973), *Walkabout: 52 Poems of Australia* (1973), *Over China's Hills of Blue: Unpublished Poems and New Poems* (1974), *Today and Tomorrow: Poems* (1975), *Snow Over the Pines: Poems* (1977), and *The Freshening Breeze: Poems* (1977).

Alley learned Chinese by reading poetry and studying such classics as the three hundred poems of the Tang dynasty. Later he began translating Chinese poetry into English: *Peace Through the Ages: Translations from the Poets of China* (1954) is typical. He continued translating despite enduring ultra-leftist attacks during the cultural revolution for an activity they called 'a poisonous weed'.

In their unpretentiousness, Alley's many works of non-fiction emulate his poetry. One example, *Yo Banfa! (We Have a Way!)* (1952), is set down in typical journal form. In the process of documenting ordinary human encounters, however, its prose develops into a series of meditations on aspects of life and belief. Alley's autobiography *At 90: Memoirs of My China Years* (Beijing, 1986; rpt. as *Rewi Alley: An Autobiography*, Wellington, 1987) is supplemented by two biographies, W.T.G. Airey's *A Learner in China* (1970) and Geoff Chapple's *Rewi Alley of China* (1980). *Rewi Alley Seventy Five* (1972) includes a bibliography 'Rewi Alley: A Preliminary Checklist of Published Books and Pamphlets', by A.P.U. Millett. Alley was interviewed by David Gunby for ★*Landfall 101* (1972).   PM

'Aloe, The', an uncompleted short story by Katherine ★Mansfield, shortened, reshaped and published as ★*Prelude* (1918), was written during March 1915 and March 1916, a period marked by the accidental death of Mansfield's brother Leslie in October 1915. Referred to by Mansfield in a letter to John Middleton ★Murry as 'my first novel' (25 March 1915), it was first published posthumously, in book form, in 1930. In 1982 *The Aloe with Prelude*, edited by Vincent ★O'Sullivan, set the two stories side by side and showed all textual emendations. The MS is held at the Newberry Library, Chicago. *The Aloe* presents the Burnell family during the domestic upheaval of moving house from the city (Wellington) to the country (Karori). In four chapters, it introduces characters who are central to both 'Prelude' and ★'At the Bay': Stanley and Linda Burnell, parents of Lottie, Kezia and Isabel, Linda's unmarried sister Beryl Fairfield, and her mother Mrs Fairfield. A defining moment is Linda Burnell's encounter with the eponymous aloe, which prompts a new level of self-awareness, particularly her fear of childbirth and resentment of Stanley's pressing sexuality: 'Looking at it from below she could see the long sharp thorns that edged the Aloe leaves, and at the sight of them her heart grew hard ... for all her love and respect and admiration she hated him.' The episode is significant as Mansfield's first use of the epiphany, or 'glimpse' as the writer referred to this device, which was to become central to her fiction. The story shows Mansfield progressing towards her distinctive narrative technique in other ways: instead of a linear form it is structured episodically, through the juxtaposition of various characters' interior monologue; symbols and images illuminate temperament, as do dreams and fantasies, the latter giving rise to a fluid sense of time. Despite these mature features, it also contains passages of authorial narration and some extended 'local colour' descriptions, which (along with some incidental characters) were largely excised when the story was refined into 'Prelude'.

SSa

'Along Rideout Road That Summer', by Maurice *Duggan, has become one of the most frequently anthologised New Zealand short stories. It was published in *Landfall 65 (1963) and collected in *Summer in the Gravel Pit* (1965, 1971) and *Collected Stories*, ed. C.K. *Stead (1981). The basic story is an on-the-road summer interlude, 'the trashy clamour of boy meeting girl', 17-year-old Buster O'Leary and the 'reputedly wild' ukulele-strumming Fanny Hohepa, daughter of the Māori farmer who has given Buster summer work. The exuberant virtuosity of Duggan's writing, in which Sterne and Nabokov are discernible influences, makes it much more than just a love story. In part it is a getting of wisdom for Buster, as under the laconic but clear-sighted moral guidance of Puti Hohepa he learns to accept 'the responsibility of acting in full knowledge', and so comes to feel 'tenderly' as well as lustfully for Fanny; and learns, too, 'a passion of sympathy' for his own inept, puritanical father. In part it is an exploration of New Zealand's 'profound cultural problem', as Buster, 'a bookish lad', his head full of 'Kubla Khan' even as he drives the clattering old tractor across Hohepa's infertile ground, struggles to resolve 'a certain discrepancy between the real and the written'. Even Coleridge ('old STC ... that old hophead'), for all his word magic, is inadequate to New Zealand's unique terrain and experience.

Duggan had argued for the teaching of New Zealand literature, rather than exclusively English, in an article called 'Only Connect' in *Manuka, the magazine of Auckland Teachers' College, in 1960. The story poses the same problem, 'How connect the dulcimer with the ukulele, if you follow...'. So its narrative opens with a gauchely discrepant juxtaposition of Kiwi slang ('lugged my fibre suitcase up to the verandah') and English poetic archaisms ('apocalyptic horses browsing the marge'). It then progresses, through experiment, pastiche, parody, a pyrotechnic variety of styles and idioms, towards connection, 'the confluence ... of universal river and regional stream', a daring reconciliation of cultural elements (even the label on Puti Hohepa's gumboots—'Marathon'—brings in Ancient Athens and Lord Byron). Often very funny, as in the parodic 'crumpy' first conversation between Buster and Fanny (the allusion is to Barry *Crump), vibrantly lyrical, or wickedly high-spirited, the story is also shot through with melancholy, presented as the fragmentary memories of the older O'Leary, 'old and somewhat sour', reminiscing from the retreat of *O'Leary's Orchard.

RR

ALPERS, Antony (1919–96), was biographer, journalist, mythologist and the pre-eminent scholar of Katherine *Mansfield. He began that work with *Katherine Mansfield: A Biography* (USA 1953, UK 1954). The most significant study at that date, it derived from four years' research in London, with help from some of the first writing grants made by the New Zealand (State) *Literary Fund, supplemented by his usual profession of journalism. He returned to Mansfield during his later academic appointment in *Canada, producing the two most important books in Mansfield studies: *The Life of Katherine Mansfield* (1980) and *The Stories of Katherine Mansfield* (1984). His combination of extensive research and literary judgment makes these nearly definitive (not quite all the minor fiction is collected in *Stories*). His percipient delineation of the lasting importance of Mansfield's New Zealand origins, especially in the search for community and 'Home' in her last years, has been seminal both for his successors in New Zealand and also in readjusting the previously almost wholly English and European view of her work.

Alpers's versatility and writing strengths had been honed in journalism on the *Press, *NZ Listener (where he wrote on music among many other things) and in London. In the early 1960s he became one of the key authors during the halcyon publishing period of *Blackwood and Janet Paul. *A Book of Dolphins* (1960; 2nd edn, *Dolphins*, 1963) is an engaging and pioneering text that has remained influential. Then Blackwood Paul invited him to rewrite earlier translations and versions of Māori legends, such as those of *Grey and S. Percy *Smith. The result was *Maori Myths and Tribal Legends* (1964, 1996), its accessible and sympathetic text and the often-admired monoprint illustrations by Patrick Hanly making it 'an extremely beautiful and lively book' (Janet Paul).

Alpers was briefly editor at *Caxton Press and founding editor of *Local Government*, but left New Zealand when a Canada Council lecture tour led in 1966 to an academic post at Queen's University, Ontario. He remained there until retiring in 1982. The award of an honorary doctorate from Queen's University acknowledged the distinction of his publications during his time there, in Pacific studies and on Mansfield. An interest in the *Pacific that had begun on the *Auckland Star* in the late 1950s and developed with Paul now led to *Legends of the South Seas* (1970) and the scholarly *The World of the Polynesians: Seen Through Their Myths and Legends, Poetry and Art* (1970, 1987).

Canada, which had supported his Mansfield work, remained important to him, and his Mansfield materials are at Queen's. (But see also Patrick *White.) Retirement brought him back to Christchurch, where he was born, educated at Christ's College and had his first job, on the *Press*; and back also to editing the writings of his father, O.T.J. *Alpers, his last publication.   RR

ALPERS, O.T.J. (Oscar) (1867–1927), performed with equal brilliance as a trial lawyer, comic actor and man of letters, writing journalism, history, verse, theatre and literary criticism and history, and an autobiography, *Cheerful Yesterdays* (1928, 1951), that still gives informative and entertaining insight into early Canterbury. He wrote a regular column for the *Lyttelton Times* and contributed to other local journals, writing on topics such as the plays of Ibsen for *Monthly Review*, and to such prestigious overseas publications as the *Fortnightly Review* and *Nineteenth Century and After*. He edited the important *Jubilee Book of Canterbury Rhymes* (1900), an updating of *Canterbury Rhymes*, and *College Rhymes; An Anthology of Verse by Members of Canterbury College 1873–1923* (1923). To the latter he contributed an anecdotal and invaluable history of local drama. His talents lay in this kind of urbane disquisition, to judge from the ponderously patriotic and celebratory-historic verse he contributed to *Jubilee Rhymes*: 'Rouse ye, cubs of the lion breed … Stalwart the sons New Zealand gave'; 'The sad fens brooded, and the land / Awaited yet the Pilgrim Band—/ A bounty-wasted solitude'.

Born in Denmark, Alpers arrived in Napier with his parents at the age of 8, and quickly learned English well enough to win a bursary to Christchurch Teachers' Training College and then become a prize scholar at Canterbury University College. He taught at the university and at Christchurch BHS, but in his thirties began law studies, became an outstanding barrister and rose to appointment to the bench and then the Supreme Court in 1925. His son Antony *Alpers and Josephine Baker compiled *Confident Tomorrows: A Biographical Self-Portrait* (1993) from *Cheerful Yesterdays* and other writings by O.T.J., some unpublished.   RR

AMATO, Renato ('Michael') (1928–64), short story writer, was born in the Italian town of Potenza, south-east of Naples, in 1928. His father was a bank official. During Amato's childhood the family lived in many parts of Italy, and were in Turin in 1940 when World War 2 broke out there. In the months following the surrender of 1943, Amato became passionately involved with the ideal of fighting for the restitution of his country's honour. Aged 16, he made several attempts to go south to join the remaining Italian forces. On one such attempt he was captured by the Germans and found himself enlisted in a unit of the *Brigate Nere*, a blackshirt militia involved in the guerrilla struggle against the partisans just before the war's end. In 1945 he witnessed the execution of his former associates by a partisan firing squad in the town square of Varese. After the war, aged 17, he returned to school and thence to the University of Turin to begin a law degree.

At university he became associated with a group of aspiring young writers who called themselves 'The Rattlesnakes'. He published some short fiction and attracted the attention of the writers Cesare Pavese and Gio Rimanelli. He soon drifted from the university into a variety of jobs but about 1950 began to learn English and contemplated an escape from the humiliation of post-war Italy to some dreamed-of new, democratic and vital society.

He migrated to New Zealand in 1954, and for four years worked at various labouring and sales jobs in the North Island before settling in Wellington. Shortly after arriving in the country he took the name 'Michael' in preference to his given name. He married in 1958 and the following year enrolled at Victoria University College, where he began writing again. Drawing much of his material from his own experiences, he transformed it from autobiography into fiction with an often trenchant and ironic detachment. At first he translated his compositions from Italian into English, but soon began working directly in his adopted language. As in Turin he formed an association with other student writers, and became president of the university's Literary Society in 1960. His earliest publications in the 'little magazines' were followed in September 1961 by Charles *Brasch's acceptance for *Landfall* of the story 'Perspectives', later anthologised by C.K. *Stead in *New Zealand Short Stories*, Second Series (1966). 'One of the Titans', published in *Mate* in the same year, was included in the *Oxford Book of New Zealand Short Stories* (ed. Vincent *O'Sullivan, 1992).

In only five years Amato established a reputation as a stylistically sophisticated writer whose works showed a confidence in the handling of English and the crafting of narrative superior to many of those in whose company he published. His work raised the expectation of further achievement, and his energy as a reviewer and teacher further established his literary presence in Wellington in the early 1960s.

Amato died suddenly shortly before his thirty-sixth birthday. His life was to serve as the basis for the fictional character of Pietro Fratta in Maurice *Shadbolt's 1971 novel *An *Ear of the Dragon*. Thirteen stories, some of them fragments rather than complete works, were posthumously selected by Ian *Cross and Shadbolt, and published with an introduction by Shadbolt as *The Full Circle of the Travelling Cuckoo* (1967).   WB

America and New Zealand share the literary concerns of a new nation in precarious relationship to established cultures, both first-people's and metropolitan. James *Cowan was the earliest to point explicitly to this common history of 'white conquest' and to draw consciously on American literary models such as Fennimore Cooper. Contemporary American writers such as Louise Erdrich, N. Scott Momaday and Gerald Vizenor, and Māori authors Patricia *Grace, Keri *Hulme and Witi *Ihimaera reflect the diverse cultures that antedate writing by traders, explorers and settlers from Europe. Among those settlers came the felt need to create a literature appropriate to the settled land, and to order it through such institutions as anthologies, journals, publishing houses and the Academy. Also significantly in common is the *Pacific Ocean.

Early American travellers and cartographers of the Pacific instance New Zealand as a reference point for geographical or cultural location. Jedidiah Morse's *American Gazetteer* (1797), for instance, offers a hierarchy of Pacific cultures, ranking 'New Zealanders', 'Sandwich Islanders' and 'Friendly Islanders' in relation to one another. In their 1830s accounts, Benjamin Morrell and Abby Jane Morrell adduce Māori and missionary co-operation as examples that the rest of the 'isles of the sea' could follow. Edmund Fanning, David Porter and Charles Wilkes also invoked New Zealand to locate their observations of Pacific cultures and places. Even in the early twentieth century, *The New Zealand Pilot* (1901), a book used by Jack London on his *Snark* cruise of the South Pacific, implies that Māori people are one of the local geographical features that visitors must navigate.

US observers have tended to examine Māori people in double-edged terms: as the long-established residents and as ostensibly exotic people who disrupt linear conceptions of time and development. For Herman *Melville, Mark *Twain, Henry Adams and others, Māori culture has been the defining feature of the land they knew as travellers. Melville's portraits, such as the 'mowry' harpoonist Bembo in *Omoo*), with his emphasis on cannibalism, both employ and challenge stereotypes. Twain, with his characteristic sarcasm, and attitudes that border on evolutionary theories of culture, protests in *Following the Equator* (1897) that Māori techniques in building houses, fortresses and boats must 'modify their savagery to a semi-civilization—or at least to a quarter-civilization'. Adams and his travelling companion, painter John La Farge, suggest that Māori and other Pacific cultures are cognate with ancient Greek civilisation.

Representations of Māori appear across a range of twentieth-century US culture. Martin Johnson, who sailed with London, later toured the US and England with the animated picture series, *Wonders of the South Seas* (1913), featuring sequences of 'Happy Little Maoris at Rotorua, New Zealand, Diving for Coins, Maori War Canoes, Canoe Hurdle Race'. Frederick O'Brien, acclaimed in the early 1920s as 'the greatest writer of English today in America', lamented the rule of Pākehā in New Zealand and Samoa. Caroline Mytinger between the two world wars set out to paint the 'cannibals' of the South Pacific, funding her trip in part by portraits of white settlers. Kurt Vonnegut includes a tattooed Māori in his war novel *Slaughterhouse Five* (1970). Less familiar representations include those in the writing of the Southern Agrarian poet Merrill Moore.

Early US women travellers evince their ambivalent position as not entirely authorised visitors. Mary Davis Wallis's *Life in Feejee, or, Five Years among the Cannibals* (1851) justifies its observations, including an account of the aftermath of the land wars in the Bay of Islands, by claiming to provide 'many facts never before published in America'. Abby Jane Morrell's *Narrative of a Voyage to the Ethiopic and South Atlantic Ocean, Indian Ocean, Chinese Sea, North and South Pacific Ocean* (1833), suggests that Māori 'phrensy and fury' may inspire American women and prospective missionaries to increased efforts at conversion. Later accounts of New Zealand less focused on Māori range from Zane Grey's enthusiastic fishing narratives (see *Sport) through James Michener's portraits of New Zealand military in his best-selling World War 2 books to Kate Crane-Gartz's deprecating comments: in Auckland 'they "point with pride" to their large imposing looking Insane Asylum'.

In the other direction, New Zealand's literature of *gold-mining, with its frontier-adventures character, draws partly on American conventions, and the garrulous George Washington Pratt in Vincent *Pyke's two novels is the earliest significant appearance of what was to decline into the stereotype American. The unscrupulous 'Black Angel' in the melodrama The *Land of the Moa* (1895) is an early example of the association (still quite common) of Americans with villainy. In *Wednesday's Children* (1937), Robin *Hyde creates an American whose self-satisfied drawl and confusion between Australia and New Zealand belong to a convention that has subsequently produced the affluent opportunist GI of A *Soldier's Tale*, and the materialists and militarists of *Smith's Dream* and novels by Rachel *McAlpine, Sally Marshall, Cathie *Dunsford and others. Janet *Frame reflects anxieties of the Vietnam *War era in her New Zealand policed by American troops in *Intensive Care* (1970). Most memorable among these satiric caricatures is the white-whale-obsessed American ambassador of Vincent *O'Sullivan's *Miracle: A Romance* (1976), perhaps because it goes beyond the standard charges. War and materialism have been prominent in New Zealand's versions of America, since James Cowan drew on the American West as analogue in *The New Zealand Wars* (1922–23), and most especially at the time of the Vietnam War.

A less stereotyped image, recognising America's liberal tradition, is contained in the various narratives of Kimball Bent, an itinerant soldier from Eastport, Maine, who deserted from the British to join the Māori side in the New Zealand *Wars. Cowan's *The Adventures of Kimball Bent* (1911) is used in fictional versions by James *Sanders (*Fire in the Forest*, 1975) and Maurice *Shadbolt (*Monday's Warriors*, 1990; see *New Zealand Wars trilogy). A figure of similarly radical inclination, and tendency to get court-martialled, is Hyde's Starkie in *Passport to Hell*, 'a half-caste Red Indian' whose father is a Delaware.

At the same time the US has become the major vitalising influence on new modes of writing. Ezra Pound and C.K. *Stead, Thomas Wolfe and Bruce *Mason, the Black Mountain poets (especially Robert *Creeley) and the New Zealand 'open form' movement (Alan *Loney, Alistair *Paterson), John Ashbery and Bill *Manhire, the Beat writers and performance poetry (David *Eggleton, Jan *Kemp), Thomas Pynchon and *postmodernist fiction (Patrick *Evans, Malcolm *Fraser), American and New Zealand *detective thrillers, *science fiction and fiction of youthful urban angst (Emily *Perkins, Maria *Wilkens) are only some of the links that are now numerous and deep.

The best representations of America have, of course, tended to come from writers with extended US experience, beginning with Ian *Milner's outstanding 'American News-Letter' series in *Tomorrow*, 1937–39. Rex *Hunter wrote well of New York in poems and (as Reginald Hunter) in the novel *Porlock* (1940). Janet Frame's tenure of writing fellowships in the US and friendships there contributed to *Daughter Buffalo* (1972) and *Living in the Maniototo* (1979), a similar period produced O'Sullivan's insightful poem sequence *Brother Jonathan, Brother Kafka* (1980), Allen *Curnow made American images crucial to *Trees, Effigies, Moving Objects* (1972), Robert *Lord's New York experience gave a fresh perspective even to plays set in New Zealand and Dinah *Hawken's years there stimulated her first successful poetry. Michael *Morrissey, Barry *Southam, Michael *Harlow, Wystan *Curnow, Michele *Leggott, Witi *Ihimaera and Damien *Wilkins have also benefited in various ways from sustained time in the US, while Don *Long is American-born. Literary responses by New Zealand writers more briefly visiting America are far too numerous even to list selectively.

In an article in *Amerasia Journal*, Lisa Kahaleole Chang Hall and J. Kehaulani Kauanui point to artistic and activist connections among Māori, Pacific Islanders and Native Americans, instancing a forthcoming Firebrand Press anthology to be edited by Cathie Dunsford and Beth Brant (noted in the Mohawk community).

The response to the 'Te Māori' exhibition in Chicago, New York and San Francisco in 1986, the sustained American sales of the *bone people*, the popular success of films like The *Piano and *Once Were Warriors and the music and lyrics of Neil *Finn testify to a ready interest from the American community in a range of New Zealand culture. Equally the Fulbright-sponsored conference, 'American Popular Culture and New Zealand' at the University of Waikato in 1993 attested to the intricate ways in which US cultural influences function in Aotearoa. Film, television, theatre, popular music and tourism, as well as the full range of literature all ensure constant and intricate interactions, an exchange that continues to transform specific locations across the Pacific.   JE/RR

Among the Cinders, Maurice *Shadbolt's first novel, was published in 1965 and substantially revised in 1984. It follows Nick Flinders on his journey of maturation through New Zealand in the company of his grandfather Hubert. Through the combination of the journey and the relationship across three generations Shadbolt depicts the pioneering, male-dominated period of New Zealand's post-European history. This is familiar ground, of course, covered by a host of writers, including John *Mulgan and Frank *Sargeson. Shadbolt himself had traversed it in the story 'Ben's Land', which this first novel clearly draws on, as does the later The *Lovelock Version*. The book began as a playful parody of some New Zealand writing, including the work of C.K. *Stead, Allen *Curnow and Ian *Cross, but is best read as a straight novel, and, indeed, most of the satirical passages were omitted from the revised edition. What remains from this exercise is an early example of Shadbolt's interest in the position of the artist in society. The novel is short by Shadbolt's standards and the writing may now appear a little dated, but as Shadbolt explains in the Author's Note in the revised edition, 'it's a young man's tale'. Towards the end, Nick Flinders is described as his poet brother's 'unpolished window on reality'. Nick's voice as well as his vision is indeed unpolished and deliberately naive; to polish it would be to destroy its vitality and with it the strength of Shadbolt's narrative. A film version was made in 1983.   RC

AND was a radical literary magazine. Four issues were produced from October 1983 to October 1985, edited by Alex Calder and Leigh *Davis, who were joined by Roger Horrocks for Numbers 3 and 4. In fact, its first issue announced, 'This is a finite project with four parts only.' *AND* contained more critical essays than literary works, moving to document the state of literary–cultural play rather than simply offer more literary products. As Leigh Davis writes in his first editorial on the connection between the terms 'New Zealand' and 'literature', 'We consider some present characteristics of the discourse of New Zealand literature, and begin to present an oppositional view.' Although *AND* is often regarded as an exceptional intervention in the general trend of literary discourse, its interventions had in fact been figured in earlier magazines like *Parallax and in its contemporary *Splash. These years 1979–86 saw an intense follow-up to the promise of *Freed (1969–72). But while the other magazines staked out a territory different from the mainstream in creative terms, the purpose of *AND* was to alter the critical language to include the possibility of reading both the mainstream and the oppositional tradition in a single discourse. In this respect it was more interested in exploring different ways of writing about literature than merely coming up with a different definitive assessment of literary works. Covers were designed by the editors, except Number 3, designed by Wystan *Curnow and Roger Horrocks. Essays and articles were by Calder, Davis, Curnow, Horrocks, John Geraets, Simon During, Louis Arnoux, Kerry Buchanan, Elizabeth Eastmond, Francis Pound and others.   AL

ANDERSEN, Johannes C. (Carl) (1873–1962), was born in Klakring, Denmark, and some eighteen months later, in 1874, arrived in New Zealand, where his parents joined a Scandinavian settlement in North Canterbury before settling in Christchurch. Although Danish was spoken at home, Johannes quickly became bilingual in the urban environment. Good at school, he left at the age of 14 to join the civil service, staying in local land administration for twenty-eight years, where he was called upon to apply the radical land legislation of the Liberal government. His first publications were translations of German (Schiller, Heine) and Scandinavian poetry as well as a few original poems. In 1900 he married Catherine (Kate) McHaffie, notable for her extensive work in welfare organisations. Three years later he issued his first book, *Songs Unsung*. He composed an epic poem of several thousand lines based on Māori mythology, which was never published. Instead he put out an extensive (675-page) collection of myths and legends: *Maori Life in Ao-tea* (1907). In articles and lectures he argued that local poets should 'leave the Greek and turn to the Maori'. His short stories and articles on historical subjects appeared in newspapers, leading to the huge *Jubilee History of South Canterbury*

(1916). Andersen moved to Wellington in 1912 to take up a position in the Parliamentary Library. In 1918, on the death of Alexander *Turnbull, Andersen was appointed Librarian for the collection bequeathed as the *Alexander Turnbull Library. Close by, Elsdon *Best was working on his ethnological collections in the Dominion Museum; the two men became friends and Andersen joined four ethnographic expeditions of Best, Apirana *Ngata and Peter *Buck between 1919 and 1923. Here Andersen's main function was to collect string games and record music. He was appointed editor of the *Transactions* of the New Zealand Institute in 1920 and became a Fellow in 1923. His popularising style did not appeal to all scientists and he gradually gave up the editorship of the *Transactions* as his duties as co-editor (with Best) of the *Journal of the Polynesian Society* expanded. Throughout these years he was working on several large books, which were published in the late 1920s: *Bird-song and New Zealand Song Birds* (1926), *Place Names of Banks Peninsula* (1927), *Maori String Figures* (1927), *New Zealand Tales* (1927—a collection of short stories, fairy tales and translations from the Danish), *Laws of Verse* (1928—a study of metre) and *Myths and Legends of the Polynesians* (1928). Three other books remained in manuscript. The next ten years were largely devoted to building up the collections of the Turnbull Library until his retirement in 1937. In 1936 Andersen travelled to a *PEN conference in Buenos Aires, which he addressed on the need for form in poetry, preceded by a holiday in England, Denmark, the Netherlands and Germany, his only extensive overseas journey. In retirement Andersen continued to pursue his varied interests. After the publication of *Maori Poetry* in 1946 he moved to Auckland. *Old Christchurch* was published in 1949 as was a booklet on spiders. The last book of poems was *Tui-cymbalist* (1951). Andersen died in Auckland in his ninetieth year.   NW

ANDERSON, Barbara (1926–), became an internationally recognised fiction writer in her sixties. Born in Hastings, and educated in Hawkes Bay, she graduated BSc Otago University (1947) and BA Victoria University (1984). She has worked as a medical technologist and teacher in Hawkes Bay and Wellington. With a lifelong interest in writing and reading, she attended Bill *Manhire's creative writing course at Victoria University in 1983, having already experimented with her writing. Several stories were published in *Metro, *Landfall, *Sport and the *NZ Listener, while one of her unpublished plays won the J.C. Reid award in 1985, and several have been broadcast. Her first collection of short stories, *I Think We Should Go into the Jungle* (1989), shortlisted for the Wattie Award (1989) and the New

Zealand Book Award for Fiction (1990), demonstrated a dramatist's acute sense of dialogue and timing, together with a shrewdly observant understanding of human behaviour and a successful challenge to stylistic conventions. *Girls High* (1990) can be described structurally as a serial novel that consists of linked short stories. There is again a keen sense of the absurdity of human behaviour; the resulting comedy is, however, touched with compassion. As 1991 writing fellow at Victoria University, Anderson completed the more intricate *Portrait of the Artist's Wife* (1992). Winner of the Wattie Award (1992), and a more sustained, complex work of fiction, this spans forty years with settings in 'the Bay', Wellington, London and Europe. The humour is more muted and the story of Sarah Tandy struggling to develop her own artistic talent in spite of the inhibiting environment of 1950s New Zealand and the demands of marriage and family is told with gently wry understanding of the bewildering complexity of human relationships. The popular *All the Nice Girls* (1993) exemplifies her talent for wise and witty encapsulation of her diverse experiences, including acute observation of naval society, gained during her nomadic life as wife of a senior naval officer. Again a network of relationships is undercut by the tension between public and private lives, within the clearly established, neatly detailed context of 1960s New Zealand.

In *The House Guest* (1995) Anderson digs more deeply into the layers of human behaviour, challenging readers with the experience of love and loss, and the subsequent unexpected dilemmas. The novel differs in many ways from her earlier work, particularly in its reversal of readers' early expectations. Located in 1990s New Zealand its comedy is not as broad, the focus deliberately diffused. If in her earlier books form shaped content, in this novel, set in Wellington and Central Otago, the reverse is true. The scope is broader and the plot more ambitious in its deliberate use of uncertainty and suspense.

Proud Garments (1996) weaves a tragicomic story between Auckland and Milan. The intricate relationships are carefully woven; married love is wryly shown to be a composite of pride, passion and regret, loyalty, deceit and compromise. The differing perspectives of young and old and their equally inevitable failings are depicted with merciless clarity, and yet there is, as always in Anderson's work, a sense of empathy and understanding.

Now living in Wellington, Anderson is one of New Zealand's best-selling authors and has been well received in the UK. Her irony, compassion, awareness of the significance of small moments, neatly deflating use of anticlimax and sense of the ridiculous place her in the tradition of Jane Austen, while she responds perceptively to New Zealand society and skilfully captures its colloquialisms and speech patterns.

See also Anderson's autobiographical essay, 'Beginnings', ★*Landfall* 195 (1998). GB

ANDREWS, Isobel (1905–), was a writer of fiction and poetry, but most significant as a leading playwright of the period 1935–63, writing for the British Drama League, for radio and after World War 2 for Wellington's Unity Theatre. She also acted. Her 'Even If We Are At War' was the second short story the ★*NZ Listener* published (29 September 1939) and is reprinted in *NZ Listener Short Stories*, Vol. 2 (1978). It includes an amusing (but pointed) confusion between 'Land of Hope and Glory', 'There'll always be an England' and ★'God Defend New Zealand'. Her short stories were also included in ★*New Zealand New Writing* (Number 1 also published a poem) and collected as *Something to Tell* (1944). Her published plays were *Sudden Rain* (1935), *The Best Seller* (1937), *The Willing Horse* (1943; 1962), *When the Rangiora Blows* (1944), *A Sunny Afternoon in Spring* (London, 1957), *The Gold Fish* (1954) and *The Bride from the Hills* (1962; London 1963). She wrote over 60 plays, and won the British Drama League playwriting competition four times. Howard McNaughton in ★*OHNZLE* points out that the BDL's festival category for all-female casts encouraged women playwrights and 'plays with a strongly female perspective'. Andrews certainly develops interesting relationships among female characters and gives them convincing dialogue, most successfully around the character of the busy but potentially tragic matchmaking spinster in *The Willing Horse*. Her best novel, *Return to Marara* (London, 1969), which she wrote after receiving a Scholarship in Letters, also explores the effects of an energetic woman, this time the impact of a returned native on a small inward-looking township north of Auckland, in the midst of problems with commercial developers. The descriptive writing in her fiction tends to the florid, with the first paragraph of *Return to Marara* echoing the famous opening of *The ★End of the Golden Weather*: 'Picture Marara this year, next year, tomorrow, lulled by sub-tropical sun, lipped by sub-tropical sea....' The dialogue, by contrast, is often tight and telling. Her other novels are *Exit with Emeralds* (1971) and *Goodbye to Romance* (1989). She wrote the script for the Rudall Hayward film *To Love a Maori* (1972). Born in Scotland, she arrived in 1911, was educated at Wellington Girls' College and was active in ★PEN and on the NZ Drama Council. RR

ANDREWS, Philip, see **Dalmatians in New Zealand Literature.**

ANGAS, George French (1822–86), was born in Newcastle upon Tyne and educated in Essex. He became one of the great Victorian travel-writers and artists and was a talented naturalist. His first book, *A Ramble in Malta and Sicily in the Autumn of 1841* (1842), was written before he was 21. He was in Adelaide from January to July 1843, when he sailed to New Zealand, returning to South Australia in January 1844. These six months in the country were extremely fruitful for New Zealand art and ethnology. He travelled 1300 kilometres mainly on foot but partly by canoe, sketching and writing every day 'however much exhausted by fatigue'. In 1847, after returning to Britain, he published two impressive folio volumes, *South Australia Illustrated*, and *The New Zealanders Illustrated*, as well as a written account of his travels, *Savage Life and Scenes in Australia and New Zealand* (in two volumes). Superb facsimile editions of the first two books were produced by *A.H. & A.W. Reed in 1963, together with a large volume of previously unpublished work in the same format. Other books arising from Angas's travels illustrate the lives of South African natives, the natural life of the Barossa Range and the goldfields of Australia. From 1853 to 1860 he was secretary to the Australian Museum in Sydney, where he carried out pioneering work as a conchologist. He went to London in 1863 and stayed there till his death, publishing numerous papers in *Proceedings of the Zoological Society*. Among his writings are *Australia, a Popular Account* (1865) and *Polynesia, a Popular Description* (1866), the latter including notes on New Zealand natural and human history. His *Wreck of the 'Admella', and Other Poems* (1874) is said to have little merit. *Pomara, a Tale of Real Life* may well have been published in 1848, but no copy has survived (Angas took Hemi Pomara, the son of a Chathams Island chief, to Sydney and England in 1845). Angas wrote copiously, largely in the style of his paintings: he is a visual writer, carefully observant of small details but not concerned with inner realities. His notes on the Taupo chief Te Heuheu, for example, concentrate on his enormous size and the whiteness of his hair. Angas's drawings and paintings are admired for their portrayal of Māori 'material culture' before it was radically altered by European influence, but have also been called sentimental. This mixture of careful observation and a romantic eye for the 'sublime' is also found in his writing. NW

Angel at My Table, An, is the second volume of autobiography by Janet *Frame (Auckland, New York, London, 1984; published together with Volume One, *To the Is-Land* and Volume Three, *The *Envoy from Mirror City*, as *Janet Frame: An Autobiography*, 1989). It won the New Zealand Book Award for Non-fiction and was placed third in the Wattie Book of the Year. The volume spans the years 1943–56. Frame recounts her two years at Dunedin Teachers' Training College and the University of Otago (1943–45) while boarding in the house of an aunt. She records her excitement at the new knowledge made available by her studies, her painful sense of difference from others, and her continued writing activities (she published poems in the *NZ Listener* and the college magazine but was rejected by *Landfall*). Frame's first year as a student teacher (1945) is remembered for her delight in the teaching but her 'failure as a member of staff'. The first signs of mental breakdown are recalled, as are an attempted suicide and the death by drowning of her younger sister, Isabel, in 1947. They resulted in a series of temporary stays in psychiatric hospitals, between visits home to Oamaru and various temporary jobs as a housemaid or waitress. She was at last permanently committed to hospital in 1947, mistakenly diagnosed a schizophrenic (a diagnosis facilitated by Frame who then sought what she has called the 'distorted "privilege"' of schizophrenia 'because it allied me with the great artists more readily than my attempts to produce works of art might have done'). The years spent in hospital are sparely treated, disappointing critics hoping for clear facts about this period of Frame's life (one has referred to the 'vast *lacunae*' at the heart of the autobiography). Frame instead directs her reader to her second novel, *Faces in the Water*, in which, she writes, 'I have described in detail the surroundings and events in the several mental hospitals I experienced during the eight following years.' Nonetheless Frame stresses the fictionality of the novel: the central character is 'based on my life but given largely fictional thoughts and feelings, to create a picture of the sickness I saw around me'. Of her eventual release in 1954 Frame writes, 'it was now my writing that at last came to my rescue'. Noticing the newspaper announcement of the Hubert Church Prose Award for *The Lagoon* in 1952, Frame's doctor decided to remove her from the hospital long-stay ward, averting a planned leucotomy and initiating her 'recovery'. Frame offers a touching portrait of Frank *Sargeson, friend and mentor (who, she later wrote, 'saved my life by affirming that I could spend my time writing'), on whose property she stayed in the eighteen months after her release, while working on her first novel, *Owls Do Cry*. The volume ends with Frame's imminent departure by ship for England in 1956. KWo

Anthologies of fiction begin to appear later than *anthologies of poetry, with O.N. *Gillespie's *New Zealand Short Stories* (London, 1930) and C.R. *Allen's *Tales by New Zealanders* (1938), both largely indistinguishable from anything that might have been produced in Britain or the Empire. Frank ★Sargeson's ★*Speaking for Ourselves* (1945), intended as the first of a series, deliberately brought together writers who would give the sense that a newly localised fiction had begun in the postwar era. Anthony Stones's edition *Celebration: An Anthology of New Zealand Writing from the 'Penguin New Writing' Series* (1984), with an introduction by John Lehmann, helped to recall this period, while *Voices: New Short Stories by Modern New Zealand Writers* (1948), edited by G.L. Martin, was soon overshadowed by the seminal ★OUP World's Classics *New Zealand Short Stories* (1953), selected and introduced by Dan ★Davin, the first to attempt some kind of historical overview and to begin the process of creating a canon of central stories. A second volume in the series, edited by C.K. ★Stead, adding thirteen writers to Davin's, appeared in 1966; a third, edited by Vincent ★O'Sullivan and adding eleven more, in 1975; and a fourth, edited by Lydia Wevers, adding another fifteen writers, in 1984, now chosen to represent the 'breadth and vitality' of the preceding decade rather than a historical overview. *Landfall Country* (1966) reprinted a selection by Charles ★Brasch of fiction and other material from ★*Landfall* during 1947–61. *New Zealand Listener Short Stories*, chosen by Bill ★Manhire (1977), were followed by a second volume a year later. In 1979 ★Reed produced the curious experiment of *Tandem,* which yoked two novellas, Edith ★Campion's *The Chain* and Sargeson's *En Route.* Lauris ★Edmond's *Young Writing* appeared in 1979. John Barnett's *All the Dangerous Animals Are in Zoos* (1981) and Michael ★Morrissey's *The New Fiction* (1985) represent attempts to address the ★postmodernist element of contemporary writing. MacDonald P. Jackson and O'Sullivan's *Oxford Anthology of New Zealand Writing Since 1945* (1983), though it contains other genres, harks back to the earlier World's Classics anthologies, as does *Some Other Country: New Zealand's Best Short Stories,* chosen by Marion McLeod and Manhire (1984; new edn 1992), the first since Davin's to attempt a select overview.

Generally, however, the 1980s saw a tendency towards special-interest collections. ★Anthologies of women's writing have been especially prominent, and are recorded under that heading. Other anthologies of the period are mostly self-explanatory: *Countless Signs: The New Zealand Landscape in Literature,* ed. Trudie McNaughton (1986); *Short Stories from New Zealand,* selected by Alistair ★Paterson (1988); Louis ★Johnson (ed.), *Antipodes New Writing* (1989); Manhire's *Six By Six,* a wider sampling from six writers, especially for educational use (1989); Bernard ★Gadd (ed.), *Other Voices: New Writers and Writing in New Zealand* (1989, 1991); Susan Davis and Russell ★Haley (eds), *The Penguin Book of Contemporary New Zealand Short Stories*

(1989); *A History of New Zealand Humour,* compiled by Gordon McLauchlan (1989); *Closing the File: American Express Short Story Award Winners 1984–89* (1990); Stephanie Dowrick and Jane Parkin (eds.), *Speaking with the Sun: New Short Stories from Australian and New Zealand Writers* (1991); Sue ★McCauley and Richard McLachlan (eds), *Erotic Writing* (1992); Michael ★Gifkins (ed.), *The Good Tourist and the Laughing Cadaver: Travel Stories From Australian and New Zealand Writers* (1993); William Taylor (ed.), *Zig Zag: New Zealand Short Stories* (1993); Frances ★Cherry (ed.), *Fresh! New Stories by New Zealand Writers* (1993); Owen ★Marshall (ed.), *Burning Boats: Seventeen New Zealand Short Stories* (1994, aimed at schools); Gifkins's *Tart and Juicy: Food Stories from Australian and New Zealand Writers* (1994); Lawrence ★Jones and Heather Murray's anthology of South Island writing, *From the Mainland* (1995); and Fergus Barrowman (ed.), *The Picador Book of Contemporary New Zealand Fiction* (1996).

New Zealand stories, especially by Māori writers, are also included in anthologies of ★Pacific and 'postcolonial' literatures, such as the authoritative *Arnold Anthology of Post-Colonial Literatures,* ed. John Thieme (1996). The latest national selection, O'Sullivan's *Oxford Book of New Zealand Short Stories* (1992), emphasises by its contemporary choices and in its introduction the increased diversity of the form, whose 'extension of narrative methods … argues an ear quite as attuned to international writing as it is to closer pressures'. A sales success in the soundbite age was Graeme ★Lay's ingenious *100 New Zealand Short Short Stories* (1997), reflecting perhaps a more populist view of the story as entertainment.   PE

Anthologies of poetry begin with the regional collections, W.P. ★Reeves and J. Ward's *The Book of Canterbury Rhymes* (1866; 1883) and O.T.J. ★Alpers's *The Jubilee Book of Canterbury Rhymes* (1900). The first national collection was ★*New Zealand Verse* (1906), edited by William Alexander and Ernest ★Currie and based largely on the New Zealand poetry that had appeared in the Sydney ★*Bulletin* during the previous twenty-five years. *A Treasury of New Zealand Verse* (1926), edited by the same pair, by repeating much of their earlier volume's contents showed how little had changed. Its newer poems tended to echo the ★Georgian movement, an influence which became clearer in Quentin Pope's ★*Kowhai Gold* (1930), whose title represents its poetry's attempt to localise the earlier, idealistic phase of the English movement. Charles ★Marris's series ★*New Zealand Best Poems* (1932–43) traces the long dying echo of this late colonial Georgianism. Both editors, but particularly Pope, were criticised by the new young poets of the so-called '★*Phoenix* group', a criticism first explored at length by Allen *Curnow in the intro-duction to his A *Book of New Zealand Verse 1923–45 (1945). This anthology deliberately turned on the fore-going tradition by reducing the number of its poets to sixteen (as against over seventy in Alexander and Currie's 1926 collection) and setting out a self-consciously *nationalistic and localised poetic. It established Curnow as the dominant force in local anthologising, an author-ity reinforced in the second edition of his anthology, A *Book of New Zealand Verse 1923–50 (1951), by the exclusion of a number of newly emerged young poets. One of these, Louis *Johnson, responded by setting up the *New Zealand Poetry Yearbook (1951–64) under his own editorship, a venture which increased slightly the representation of women and gave space to a number of new writers at the expense of what was sometimes perceived as a lowering of standards. With forty-three contributors, Robert *Chapman and Jonathan Bennett's Anthology of New Zealand Verse (1956) tried to bring back the tradition of inclusiveness, but Curnow's final anthol-ogy, the Penguin Book of New Zealand Verse (1960), simply reinforced his concept of exclusive selection and his rhetorical control of the genre.

Charles *Doyle's Recent Poetry in New Zealand (1965), and the annual *Poetry New Zealand edited from 1971 by Frank *McKay and from 1984 by Elizabeth Caffin, are echoes of the conflict fomented by Curnow. Both anthologies represent a remaining opposition to his method, but the position of an established anthologiser of New Zealand poetry has continued, albeit a little less contentiously, with Vincent *O'Sullivan's An Anthology of Twentieth Century New Zealand Poetry, the first two of whose three editions (1970, 1976, 1987) recall in a lesser way the exclusiveness of Curnow. One response to these exclusions is Alistair *Paterson's 15 Contemporary New Zealand Poets (1980), an attempt to represent 'open form' poetry as the new mainstream of local writing. An earlier response is Arthur Baysting's The *Young New Zealand Poets (1973). With its single woman contributor, it is the last in the linear male tradition that dominated New Zealand poetry for forty years, and also, with its strong debt to contemporary American culture, rep-resents the end of the predominant Anglophilia of that tradition.

From this point, diversity and multiplicity of view-point mark the anthologising of poetry, as in Riemke *Ensing's Private Gardens (1977) and Lydia Wevers's Yellow Pencils (1988), both exclusively *anthologies of women's writing, and in Witi *Ihimaera and Don *Long's *Into the World of Light (1982) and the subsequent volumes of Ihimaera's Te *Ao Mārama (1992, 1993, 1993, etc.). Devoted to Māori writing, these also question the notion of genre by anthologising poetry, fiction, autobiography,

biography and drama. Barbara Petrie's The Kiwi and the Emu (1989) dissolves the notion of nationality, bringing together the poetry of New Zealand and Australian women; Fleur *Adcock's Oxford Book of Contemporary New Zealand Poetry (1982) dissolves the notion that an editor needs to live in the country whose poetry she is anthologising, while Murray *Edmond and Mary Paul's The New Poets (1987) attempts in both the gender of its editorship and in its technical presentation to dissolve the notion of authority itself. In such a context, Ian *Wedde and Harvey *McQueen's Penguin Book of New Zealand Verse (1985) is something of a contradiction in terms, an attempt to include the authoritative tradition established by Curnow while being inclusive at the same time. The result is recuperative and revisionary, an anthology whose content implies that a continuous and coherent tradition of European and Māori writing was practised, by both men and women, from the first. Wedde and McQueen's Penguin Book of Contemporary New Zealand Poetry / Nga Kupu Titohu o Aotearoa (1989) adds Miriama Evans as editor of its Māori content. Terry Locke, Peter Low and John Winslade's White Feathers: An Anthology of New Zealand and Pacific Poetry on the Theme of Peace (1990) typifies a more recent trend to special-interest antholo-gies, while collections for the schools market are also increasing, such as teacher-poet Rangi *Faith's Dangerous Landscapes (1994). Bill *Manhire's 100 New Zealand Poems (1993), which was extraordinarily successful in book-trade terms, even finding its way to best-seller lists, includes one poem from each of a hundred writers, whose names are not given above or below the poems but in a list at the back of the book. The latest major anthology, An Anthology of New Zealand Poetry in English (1997), edited by Jenny *Bornholdt, Gregory *O'Brien and Mark *Williams, includes ninety-six poets, from John *Barr (b. 1809) to Robert *Sullivan (b. 1967). PE

Anthologies of women's writing have burgeoned since 1977, making archaic such earlier volumes as Poems, ed. Alan Dunlop (New Zealand Women Writers and Artists' Society, 1953). That all have been edited by women suggests both a collective determination to over-see production of their work and heightened public self-awareness. The first anthology of women's verse, Riemke *Ensing's Private Gardens: An Anthology of New Zealand Women Poets (1977), with an afterword by Vincent *O'Sullivan, is notable for the number of poets (thirty-five), many unpublished, some previously under-estimated (Ruth *Gilbert, Gloria *Rawlinson, Helen *Shaw, Mary *Stanley). The book helped to establish then-new writers such as Christina *Beer, Lauris *Edmond and Judith *Lonie. Janet *Frame and Ruth *Dallas declined to contribute on the grounds of gender discrimination. Lydia Wevers in her *Yellow Pencils: Contemporary Poetry by New Zealand Women* (1988) notes the unevenness of *Private Gardens*, describing it as 'across a boundary, the historical boundary of feminism'. By contrast, the professionalism of Wevers's anthology, with fewer poets (twenty-eight), but a better range of theme, consistency of achievement, and more generous space, shows that the intervening decade had been crucial: poets like Edmond, Fiona *Kidman, Rachel *McAlpine and Heather *McPherson, who appeared in *Private Gardens*, are now well represented; so are Meg *Campbell and Dallas, who were not in Ensing's volume. A new generation, many now accepted as mainstream, became visible, including Michele *Leggott, Jenny *Bornholdt and Dinah *Hawken. Also represented are women now better known for their prose, notably Keri *Hulme and Fiona *Farrell. The limitation of Wevers's anthology to 1965–87 means a lack of older poets like Stanley and Frame.

Women's anthologies of fiction during this period are more numerous. The pioneer, in the same year as *Private Gardens*, was Christine Cole *Catley's *Shirley Temple Is a Wife and Mother: 34 Stories by 22 New Zealanders* (1977). This was followed by Margaret Hayward and Joy *Cowley's historical survey, *Women Writers of New Zealand 1932–82* (1982), which includes brief biographies; *Hyacinths and Biscuits*, ed. Peggy *Dunstan et al. (1985, the Diamond Jubilee Book of the *Penwomen's Club 1925–1985); *Mscellany: Women Writers' Prose and Poetry*, ed. Betty Bremner, Sonia Kellett, Julia Millen and Joy Tonks (1987); and *In Deadly Earnest: A Collection of Fiction by New Zealand Women, 1870s–1980s*, ed. Trudie McNaughton (1989), which also contains extracts from novels. The increasing range of special areas within women's writing is indicated by three 1989 collections: Suzann Olsson's *Womansight*, Anne Else and Heather Roberts's *Women's Life: Writing About Female Experience in New Zealand*, and Elizabeth Webby and Wevers's *Goodbye to Romance: Stories by New Zealand and Australian Women Writers*.

A new kind of collection focused on contemporary short fiction appears with Wevers and Marion McLeod's *Women's Work: Contemporary Short Stories by New Zealand Women* (1985), covering the previous eighteen years; this was also published as *One Whale, Singing; And Other Stories from New Zealand* (1986). The New Women's Press series confirmed the development of a new market and readership. *New Women's Fiction 1* (1986) was edited by Cathie *Dunsford; subsequent editors were Aorewa McLeod (*NWF2*, 1988), Mary *Paul and Marion Rae (*NWF3*, 1989), Wendy Harrex and Lynsey Ferrari (*NWF4*, 1991). Dunsford, who runs workshops and encourages new writers, has edited three further volumes organised around specific feminist themes: with Susan Hawthorne, *The Exploding Frangipani* (1990), lesbian writing in New Zealand and Australia; *Subversive Acts* (1991), on women's writing as subversion and survival; *Me and Marilyn Monroe* (1993), on women's bodies. Both series have published short fiction by some of the best-known women writers. Dunsford's stable of lesbian, heterosexual, established and new writers, like Shonagh *Koea, Sandi Hall, Marewa Glover, and Hulme, Edmond and Kidman, makes her probably the most enterprising and eclectic independent publisher of women's fiction. The competing Women's Press series has published fiction by Christine *Johnston, Vivienne *Plumb, Stephanie *Johnston, Anne *Kennedy and Sheridan *Keith, while Ngahuia *Te Awekotuku, Beryl *Fletcher, Sue *McCauley, Annamarie *Jagose, Sue *Reidy and poets Jan *Kemp and Elizabeth *Smither have published with both. David *Eggleton wrote of *Subversive Acts*, 'There's an unstoppable growth industry in women's writing and this collection shows some of these contemporary provocateurs rolling unchallenged and perhaps unchallengeable across the local literary landscape.'

Most anthologies include some lesbian writing, but the first devoted to this market was Miriam *Saphira's *The Power and the Glory and Other Lesbian Stories* (1987). *Spiral 7: A Collection of Lesbian Autobiography and Writing from Aotearoa/ New Zealand* (1992) was edited by Heather McPherson, Julie King, Marian Evans and Pamela Gerrish Nunn. Also recent are the anthologies of ethnic writing, such as *The Worlds of Maori Women: Toi Wāhine* (1995), illustrated by Robin *Kahukiwa, edited by Kathie Irwin and Irihapeti Ramsden, a mix of fiction and non-fiction; and Trixie Te Arama *Menzies's *He Wai: A Song: First Nations Women's Writing* (1996), published by the Waiata Koa collective, which includes photographs, poetry, prose and non-fiction by twenty-one women of different ethnicities. This growth in numbers and range suggests that anthologies of women's writing have become a significant showcase for writing by women in Aotearoa.   JW

ANTHONY, Frank (Sheldon) (1891–1927), was author of the 'Me and Gus' stories, which enjoyed wide popularity when they were adapted for radio by Francis Jackson in the 1950s. He was born at Matawhero near Gisborne and grew up in the South Taranaki *backblocks, where his father was (variously) a hotel proprietor, racehorse owner and small farmer, and his mother a teacher. At 17 he left home and spent nearly a decade at sea, working initially as a deckhand on coastal steamers, then travelling the world in the merchant service, attracted especially by the romance of the sailing ships, 'windjammers', then rapidly disappearing from service. During World War 1 he served in the Royal Navy in the Battle of Jutland, and in 1918 was invalided back to New Zealand with a permanently damaged lung.

After the war he was assisted under the government's Soldier Settlement scheme onto a small, poorly developed farm at Midhurst near Stratford, and in the evenings began to write, prolifically, stories and novels based on his seafaring and farming experiences. Between mid-1923 and mid-1924 he had considerable success publishing this fiction in the Auckland *Weekly News* and the Christchurch *Weekly ★Press*. This included two serialised novels, *Follow the Call* (a comic romance of unrequited love, set in Stratford) and *Windjammer Sailors* (an autobiographical narrative underscored with the theme of a New Zealand innocent abroad), as well as numerous of the comic-satiric stories of farming mishaps and romantic entanglements centred on the relationship of a shy bachelor-narrator, Mark Henricks, with his extroverted do-it-yourself Kiwi neighbour, Gus Tomlins.

In the wake of this success Anthony decided to give up the struggle to make his farm pay, and pursue a professional writing career in England, where he spent the last two years of his life. Here he rewrote and expanded the 'Me and Gus' stories into a novel, revised *Windjammer Sailors* and *Follow the Call* to remove much of the local vernacular that had made them such lively examples of their genre in New Zealand, and wrote other stories and novels of the sea, including a fictional account of his war experiences (entitled 'A Cog in the Wheel') of considerable historical significance. However he failed to break into the British market and, dogged by ill health and poverty, died of consumption in a boarding-house near Bournemouth.

It was through the efforts of Anthony's mother that *Follow the Call* and the 'Me and Gus' stories were eventually published in book form in 1936 and 1938 respectively. The adapted radio-broadcast and widely published versions of the stories in the 1950s emphasised comic events at the expense of Anthony's subtler stylistic effects, and it was not until the 1970s that original versions of his main works were published by ★Auckland University Press in two volumes: *Follow the Call*, with an unfinished Taranaki back-country novel, 'Dave Baird', and a biography by Terry ★Sturm, in 1975; and the original 'Me and Gus' stories, together with the novel *Gus Tomlins*, in 1977.

Anthony was one of the first New Zealand writers to exploit the possibilities of male colloquial idiom for comic purposes, perhaps drawing on earlier Australian models like Steele Rudd's 'Dad and Dave' stories. With its exaggerated images of domestically inept bachelors, comically ill-at-ease in their romantic relationships,

Anthony's fiction also offers an insight into emergent gender stereotypes in New Zealand; and beneath its highly skilled deployment of farce, it also offers an edged social comment on the conservative rural values promoted by the Massey government of the 1910s and 1920s. For all their commitment to the pioneering values of self-reliance, efficiency and hard work, Anthony's bachelor-farmers remain poverty-stricken and mortgage-ridden, victims of government bureaucracy and the economic vagaries of farming's dependence on overseas markets. Anthony was one of the first New Zealand writers (alongside Jean ★Devanny) in the 1920s to indicate the vulnerability of cherished pioneering myths.   TS

Antic started in June 1986, partly in response to the imminent demise of ★*AND*, as a journal of artwork and debate about the arts and criticism, especially from the viewpoint of feminist theory. From an interview with Ngahuia ★Te Awekotuku in Number 1 to an article by Peter ★Wells in Number 8 (1990), it was an outlet for radical arts comment, especially in relation to gender. Patrick ★Evans thought it provided 'for the first time … a language with the potential to be particular to women and to begin to articulate their world without subversion or ambiguity' (*Penguin History of New Zealand Literature*, 1990).   RR

Anvil was published in Auckland by the left-wing Anvil Club, 1945–46. Articles on social, political and educational issues dominated the literary content, which included stories by Maurice ★Duggan and Greville ★Texidor and a poem by G.R. ★Gilbert.   SH

Anzac, an acronym of 'Australian and New Zealand Army Corps', was coined in General Birdwood's Egyptian HQ originally as a codename (1915); then used as a short form of 'Anzac Cove', a landing place of the Corps on 25 April 1915, quickly extended to include the Gallipoli Peninsula and sometimes the Gallipoli campaign as a whole. By 1916 it denoted also a member of the Corps: 'The Anzacs considered the Maltese respectability too much of a good thing' (Robin ★Hyde, ★*Passport to Hell*, 1936). Since World War 1 it has been regarded as a symbol of unity, often through suffering. It forms many compounds, especially those commemorating the Gallipoli landing, as 'Anzac Day' (1916), and the names of items of food and drink, mainly from the 1920s, as 'Anzac biscuit', 'pudding', etc. It is also applied to things, projects, exercises, etc., involving both New Zealand and Australia. The terrible nature of the Gallipoli experience has left the term with strong associations of the pity of war and of national mourning or commemoration, which it carries in such titles as *After*

Anzac Day, a novel by Ian ★Cross (1961), or 'Elegy for Anzac Day', a poem by Alistair ★Campbell (1991). HO

Ao Hou, Te / The New World (1952–76) was a bilingual quarterly published by the Maori Affairs Department, and printed by ★Pegasus Press, 'to provide,' as its first issue said, 'interesting and informative reading for Maori homes ... like a ★marae on paper, where all questions of interest to the Maori can be discussed'. The earliest issues did not name the editor. From 1954 it was Erik Schwimmer, from 1960 to 1961 he was temporarily replaced by Bruce ★Mason, and from 1962 to 1966 the editor was Margaret ★Orbell, who considerably increased the literary content, including the transcription of traditional work (such as a major series by Mervyn McLean and reprints from John ★White). She was replaced by Joy Stephenson, who continued to publish much fiction and poetry.

Articles ranged from agriculture through recipes to wood carving and other crafts, as well as biographically important obituaries. There were also literary contributions, such as the bilingual presentation of legends ('How Ngarara-Huarau Was Killed' by Te Whetu, translated by T.G. Poutawera), and poems (a series of 'Nga Titotito a Te Māori', translated by Reweti Kohere).

Distinguished contributors included S.M. (Hirini) ★Mead, Pei Te Hurunui ★Jones, Reweti Kohere, Joan Metge, J.C. ★Sturm, Kingi Ihaka, Maharaia Winiata, Turoa Royal, Leo Fowler, Hone ★Tuwhare, Barry ★Mitcalfe, Rowley Habib (Rore ★Hapipi), Patricia ★Grace and Riki Erehi, while works by older poets and storytellers (Mohi ★Turei) were revived. There were also annual literary competitions in Māori and in English.

As early as September 1959, the editor commented on 'a quite recent development, the emergence of Maori writers attempting the novel, the short story and modern verse forms.... Altogether there must have been some dozens of Maoris who have recently started to write short stories, some with definite success.' In the following year, in judging a competition (won by Pita Sharples), he was even bolder: 'The Maori writer seems instinctively to understand that the English language is one of unrivalled majesty and richness, not, as many pakehas demonstrate, a convenient method of shorthand. I expect—I say this in full confidence—that the next ten years will produce a Maori novelist of outstanding talent; already the ground is being prepared for him.' Nine years later Witi ★Ihimaera published his first book.   NW

Ao Mārama, Te: Contemporary Māori Writing, is a bilingual anthology in five volumes (1992–96) edited by Witi ★Ihimaera, with the assistance of Haare ★Williams, Irihapeti Ramsden and D.S. ★Long. More than 250 writers and more than 800 individual items are included, making this—the successor to ★*Into the World of Light* (1982)—the most comprehensive collection of writing by Māori ever published. Its emphasis is on living or recently deceased writers, so that for the rich range of nineteenth-century texts it is still essential to turn to collections compiled by Margaret ★Orbell.

Many of the texts are from larger works—novels, biographies, autobiographies, essay collections, studies of Māori culture—while many more are complete in themselves and no small number are published here for the first time. The first volume, *Te Whakahuatanga o te Ao: Reflections of Reality* (1992) sets the contemporary scene with fiction, poetry, song and drama of very recent times. The high point is a generous selection from the poems of the 'old master' Hone ★Tuwhare, selected on 'Māori' principles, which make it differ radically from his selections in other anthologies. His work sits comfortably here with that of much younger men, such as Robert ★Sullivan and Apirana ★Taylor, and with that of such significant woman writers as J.C. ★Sturm, ★Renée and Ngoi ★Pēwhairangi.

Volume 2, *He Whakaatanga o to Ao: The Reality* (1993) turns to non-fiction writing, much of it associated with the politically radical movements of the 1970s–80s. As the Preface ('Kaupapa') states: 'In these years Māori confronted Government and obtained a partnership agreement ... that saw Māori move beyond the role of supplicant to become negotiators and architects of our own destiny.' The volume does not trace the history of that development in any formal way but offers highlights of passionate and thoughtful prose associated with it.

The third and central volume, entitled *Te Pūwaitanga o te Kōrero: The Flowering* (1993), concentrates on the younger generation of contemporary writers—those who began to publish in the early 1980s, some ten years after Ihimaera himself. Notably it includes items written collectively by groups of Māori exploring creative possibilities. Volume 4, *Te Ara o te Hau: The Path of the Wind* (1994) concentrates on yet another rich vein: writing for children. The growth of interest in the language is reflected in the large number of children's texts which have been published bilingually. They and others are fully represented here. The fifth volume was intended to be the final one: *Te Tōrino: The Spiral* (1996), its title being explained as the movement both forward and backward in time as traditions are explored and new discoveries made. In the introduction a sixth volume is announced, 'in the form of cassettes.... It will feature contemporary Māori oral literature.' Ranginui ★Walker described the first volume, and by implication the whole collection, as 'a treasure chest of cloaks woven by many talented authors'.   NW

Aotearoa, one of the Māori names of New Zealand, is usually translated 'Land of the Long White Cloud', and this English version was used by *Reeves for the title of his history of the country as well as by many other English-laguage writers. Eve *Langley's unpublished first novel had this title, for instance. According to some traditions, 'Aotea' was the canoe used by *Kupe, who first discovered the land, while in others he was guided on his course by a long white (or bright) cloud. The name was originally applied to the North Island by Sir George *Grey's informants for his *Polynesian Mythology* (1855), and to New Zealand as a whole certainly from the 1870s, particularly by North Island Māori and by Europeans (such as *Buller, Reeves and *Cowan). It most frequently referred to New Zealand as the homeland of the Māori. On occasion it may have been used as a literary-romantic equivalent in Māori of *'Maoriland', or of the more frequent but prosaic *'Niu Tirani'. In *The *Godwits Fly* (1938), Robin *Hyde records that 'Sometimes the school journal called New Zealand "Maoriland" or "Ao-te-aroa". There again you hardly ever saw a Maori, and if you did it was in town.' 'Aotearoa New Zealand' is a symbolic name introduced in the 1980s to emphasise the bicultural elements of New Zealand society and has become increasingly used, for instance in such titles as *New Zealand Who's Who Aotearoa* or *Aotearoa Māori Performing Arts Festival.   HO

Aotearoa Māori Performing Arts Festival, formerly the New Zealand Polynesian Festival, was inaugurated in 1972. It is the most important festival of its kind and inspires the creation of new *waiata, *haka and other forms of Māori music and poetry as well as caring for the tradition. The chairman of its committee is Tīmoti S. *Kāretu.   NW

APPLE, Billy (1935–), born Barrie Bates, is a conceptual artist who was born in Auckland. He trained at the Royal College of Art in London 1959–62 and established himself in New York in the later 1960s–70s as a performance and installation artist. He returned to New Zealand permanently in the mid-1980s. Since the mid-1970s he has been concerned to expose the systems and structures within which art is made, seen and consumed. To this end he has collaborated with Wystan *Curnow on text-based series (*Transactions,* 1981– ; *From the Collection,* 1988– ; and *The Golden Rectangle,* 1988–) and installations (for example, *From the Centre,* 1979–80, and *The Cage and the Pedestal,* 1988), in which such details as the transaction between artist and client, the work's location or destination and its physical proportions or relation to the space it occupies are made the content of the work. Thus Apple's work functions as a narrative artefact which re-presents information about its history, context and format in literal, textual form. Apple's aim is to intervene critically in the structures of the art world, exposing the architectural, ideological and cultural frames within which art is normally seen.   CB

Arachne was published in Wellington by the Victoria University College Literary Society and Crocus Publishing 1950–51. It was the immediate successor to *Hilltop* and its three issues were an important venue for the emergence of Wellington poets such as Louis *Johnson, W.H. *Oliver, Alistair *Campbell, Erik Schwimmer, Hubert *Witheford, and Pat *Wilson. SH

ARAGO, Jacques-Étienne-Victor (1790–1855), was born in France, the third of a family of brothers who in diverse ways made the name Arago famous. In addition to being a writer, novelist and dramatist, Jacques was a gifted artist and intrepid traveller. As a youth he set out to explore the world, knapsack on back and crayon in hand. He is best known for his two books about his voyage on the French naval ship, *Uranie,* commanded by Freycinet. He was the official draughtsman on board this ship, which was wrecked in the Falkland Islands near the end of a three-year voyage (1817–20). Back in France in 1821, he worked as a newspaper editor and theatre director. An illness left him without his sight for the last eighteen years of his life but he continued to write and travel. He died in Brazil.

While en route from New South Wales to Cape Horn on the *Uranie,* Arago saw Campbell Island and recorded, when they were a few leagues from the island, that they were at the precise antipodes of Paris. He could almost say, he remarked, that he was therefore dancing under the Pont-Neuf. This was the closest he came to visiting New Zealand. However, in Freycinet's volumes of the voyage, a section entitled 'Digression sur les Nouveaux Zélandais' records that during *Uranie*'s stay at Port Jackson, several New Zealand chiefs visited the ship. One of the French officers drew the faces of some of the Māori with accuracy.

The first of Arago's two books about the voyage was *Promenade autour du monde* (1821), in the form of a series of letters to a friend. Arago leaves, as he says in the preface, the scientific work and nautical details to the experts. The second book, *Souvenirs d'un aveugle, voyage autour du monde,* appeared in 1839 when, as the title suggests, the writer was blind. One chapter narrates the writer's dramatic encounter with a Māori chief during the *Uranie*'s stay in Sydney in December 1819, illustrated by Arago's fine sketch. He writes (here translated for the first time): 'This man, chief, king, whom I sketched at

Port Jackson, whom I followed and studied for twenty-four hours of his nomadic existence, the same man, about whom Mr Wollstonecraft gave me information which I pass on to you, always astonished and often frightened me. He had realised that I was following him and although he appeared very annoyed about it initially, after a few seconds my presence no longer bothered him and he behaved as if I were not there. What is more, I hasten to add that he was completely naked. His only weapons were a magnificent flint tomahawk, secured firmly to its handle, and another stone which was grey, worked to the shape of a spatula and hanging at his side. Knowing what I had to fear from his bad temper and anger, I had hidden two excellent pistols and a good dagger under my clothes. This was not excessive, I do assure you, to subdue such an impressively built fellow of five feet ten or eleven....' (Wollstonecraft was a Sydney merchant and landowner, a relative of Mary Shelley.) The style and tone of this chapter on New Zealand and its people are typical of *Souvenirs d'un aveugle*. Arago adds dialogue and suspense to incidents that are related concisely in the letters in *Promenade autour du monde*, turning them into such miniature dramas as this historically important account of his meeting with the Māori chief.   CL

Arawata Bill, a sequence of twenty related poems by Denis *Glover, was published in 1953. Unlike the *'Sings Harry' poems, which Glover worked on between 1941 and 1951, the equally significant 'Arawata Bill' sequence took only a few months to complete. Early in 1953 Glover's sometime climbing companion John *Pascoe returned from a transalpine tramping trip, reporting how his party had found cairns, marking routes, and a shovel they believed must have belonged to the legendary prospector Arawata Bill. At once Glover saw the potential of Bill's story for extended lyric treatment. The historical subject of Glover's sequence, William O'Leary (*c.*1865–1947), took his nickname from the isolated Arawata River in South Westland. Although he favoured the Arawata, the solitary Bill fossicked over most of South Westland, where he spent nearly half a century searching for *gold, doggedly returning to the mountains year after year. Near the end of his life, he commented that it was only partly the promise of gold that drew him back: 'but really it was the country. I loved the country' (*New Zealand's Heritage* 2541). O'Leary died in Dunedin in 1947, cared for by the Little Sisters of the Poor. In its mixture of fact, speculation and legend, Glover's sequence has further enhanced Arawata Bill's status as a local folk-hero.

Glover's Bill was a silent and solitary *'Man Alone' who expressed himself largely through the cairns he left to mark his traverses. He lived his life away from the company of his fellow beings: his most important relationships were with his shovel, his rusted gold-pan and his patient, wise pack-horse. Despite his relentless optimism, gold finally eluded Arawata Bill. It proved to be a kind of Grail which existed most tangibly in hope and in legend, always around the next bend. Not even sure what he would do with a fortune, Bill used the search for gold as a pretext for the isolated life he enjoyed. In a coda, Glover's narrator muses on Bill's life and alerts the reader to the moral conclusion Bill was unable to draw for himself: there was never any mother lode. All along, the gold was hiding in Bill's own heart. Denis Glover reads 'Arawata Bill' on *Arawata Bill and Other Verses* (Kiwi Records, 1971). A well-received biography of the historical O'Leary, *Arawata Bill* by Ian Dougherty, was published in 1996.   SS

Arena was the last and longest running magazine published, printed and edited by Noel Farr *Hoggard of Wellington. Entitled *Letters* for the first ten issues, it appeared quarterly 1943–75. Many young writers obtained first publication there, and established contributors included Frank *Sargeson, James K. *Baxter, Louis *Johnson, Roderick *Finlayson, G.R. *Gilbert, Helen *Shaw, Maurice *Gee, Amelia *Batistich, C.K. *Stead and Kevin *Ireland. An index to the first 70 issues was published in 1970.   SH

ARETA, Mavis, who also wrote as Mavis Winder, see **Romance fiction.**

Ariki is the leader of an *iwi.

ARMITAGE, Alan, pseudonym used by Alice *Kenny for her adventure fiction.

ARMITAGE, Ronda (author) and **David** (illustrator), won the 1978 Esther Glen Award for Children's Literature for their first book for early readers, *The Lighthouse Keeper's Lunch* (1977). It is a sprightly tale of a wife's ingenuity in saving her husband's lunch from the depredations of ruthless seagulls. The Armitages had moved in 1974 to England, which is the setting for *The Trouble with Mr Harris* (1978), in which a postmaster from the city ('Gutterville') has to win acceptance from a rural village community. Parcels posted to New Zealand show some continuing thought for the authors' place of origin, as perhaps does the suburban Australian setting of *Don't Forget, Matilda* (1978), about a koala family. Betty *Gilderdale in *A Sea Change* (1982) says 'these books demonstrate the high standard of achievement attained by authors, illustrators, publishers, and printers in books for the young during the 1970s'.   RR

ARNOLD, Thomas, the Younger (1823–1900), was the third of nine children of the great educational, religious and political reformer Thomas Arnold of Rugby School, and a brother of the poet and literary and social thinker Matthew Arnold, as well as a close friend of the poet Arthur Hugh Clough. At the age of 25, feeling repressed by an authoritarian world and disgusted by one that clung rigidly to traditions, he set out for New Zealand, hoping for a finer, more democratic way of life. His idealism was due for some knocks, and yet he remained energetic and affectionate throughout the years he spent in the colony. Later he returned to England, was converted to Catholicism and worked with Cardinal Newman. The letters from New Zealand, which were his finest literary achievement, were edited by James *Bertram in 1966. They resonate with the voice of an idealistic, self-sacrificing, generous man who was nonetheless a careful down-to-earth observer of the scene around him. His descriptions of early Wellington and Nelson are perhaps the most precise and vivid to have survived. The cadences are musical and the tone overflows with human warmth, but is never exaggerated or strident: 'The custom of the country is that when you are travelling in the bush, that is, in the wild, thinly inhabited country, you may go into any house you come to, and get food and lodging there, and it would be considered an insult if you were to offer payment on going away. Also, if you fall in with any one on your road, whether it be a poor or a rich man, you are expected to share equally with him any food you may have got. Both these are very good customs; indeed there is almost a necessity for them in a country like this.'   NW

Aroha is often translated as 'love', but is used in a wider sense than the English term usually is. Only rarely does it refer to 'man–woman love', and more frequently it is the spiritual force that creates a bond for the members of a *whānau or *hapū. It can also bind the guests (manuhiri) to the local people (*tangata whenua) on a *marae. In various situations it might be translated as respect, concern, caring, hospitality and giving. Fundamental is a concern for the welfare of others, so that 'altruism' might be yet another potential translation. Cleve Barlow, in *Tikanga Whakaaro: Key Concepts of Māori Culture* (1991), emphasises its religious quality: 'Aroha is the creative force that emanates from the gods.' For 'waiata aroha', see *Waiata.   NW

Art and New Zealand literature. Images are always woven around by words. Signatures, titles, inscriptions, iconographical sources, narrative subtexts, critical and exegetic commentary, ideological underpinnings are the textual and unspoken companions to the visual arts; while books, catalogues, journals, diaries and letters can be their physical contexts. In New Zealand this proximity has been strengthened by the prominent role writers have played as art critics, historians and biographers. Charles *Brasch, E.H. *McCormick, A.R.D. *Fairburn, Janet *Paul, John *Caselberg, James K. *Baxter, Maurice *Shadbolt, C.K. *Stead, Denys *Trussell, Ian *Wedde, Wystan *Curnow and recently Elizabeth *Knox and Gregory *O'Brien, have played a distinctive role in collaborations, and in formulating and commenting upon the history of this country's art.

On some occasions the visual and the written have especially intersected. These are in (i) the intimate relation between words and forms in Māori art; (ii) the interaction between the visual and the written in early accounts by explorers and settlers from the 1770s to the 1870s, and in later nineteenth and early twentieth century history painting; (iii) the intertwined relationship between art and literature in the construction of national identity in the 1930s to the 1950s; (iv) the role words played in the breakdown of modernist paradigms in the visual arts in the 1970s; and (v) since 1980, the redefinition of image as text undertaken by *postmodernism, which has seen an even greater merging of these once separate disciplines. (See also *Typography.)

*Kōrero, words, play a vital role in Māori culture. Narratives of creation, gods and ancestors, sacred sites and natural features, and significant events and sacred and secular rituals and lore, are recounted in chants, songs, oratory and proverbs, and are carved, painted, woven and built into precious objects and communal structures. These reinforce a sense of identity embedded in a deeply felt connection to place.

Māori art is thought of as the revered inheritance of the ancestors, passed down in forms that are valued as taonga, or treasured artefacts. Through time, the history of an artefact becomes part of its story, and new narratives add to its meaning, so that it continues to have relevance. As new technologies, materials and subjects become available, forms adapt—for example, the evolution of carved and painted meeting houses in the nineteenth century, or the creation of works of art by Māori artists in which traditional symbols and stories are reused, but in formats that conform with the different contexts of modern art—without their being severed from their original meaning and function.

Thus Māori art, whether produced in the context of the marae, or for the modern art gallery, retains a link to the past which is tangible to Māori, and therefore not mediated by the codes of representation, so that artefacts and artworks are recognised to have ihi (power), wehi (awe) and *mana (authority). It is through them that the ancestors can be directly invoked, even when the artist is Pākehā, as in the case of the recent appreciation by Māori of the portraits of their kaumātua by Charles Frederick Goldie (1870–1942).

The power and beauty of words, the authority invested in the recitation of *whakapapa and the deep cultural investment in the natural world inform Māori art, whether a carved panel in a meeting house, or a painted canvas in a gallery. Forms and symbols have also been adapted from traditional and European sources for political ends, to assert an identity alternative to the dominant power, and claim self-determination and the return of land. This has led to a particular engagement with the Treaty of Waitangi, for example in the work of Robyn *Kahukiwa and Emily Karaka (b. 1952), and to a critique of the Bible for the impact Christianity has had on traditional Māori beliefs, rituals and customs, registered in the work of Selwyn Muru (b. 1939), Para Matchitt (b. 1933), and Michael Parekowhai (b. 1968).

While Māori artists give form to narrative in their paintings, sculptures, weaving, carving and other artefacts, Pākehā artists have played a role in picturing Māori myths and histories through post-contact art and literature. These have often taken the form of illustrations to texts written by historians, ethnologists and anthologists, or in journals like Te *Ao Hou and various *School Publications from the late 1930s to the 1960s. They include Te Tohunga: The Ancient Legends and Traditions of the Maori (1907) by Wilhelm Dittmer (1868–1909); the graphic works of E. Mervyn Taylor (1906–64) for Te Ao Hou, Russell *Clark's illustrations for the 1956 reprint of George *Grey's Polynesian Mythology; Patrick Hanly's (b. 1932) illustrations to Anthony *Alpers's Maori Myths and Tribal Legends (1964); and Colin *McCahon's paintings derived from the writings of Matire Kereama in 1969–70.

The earliest representations by Europeans of New Zealand subjects were the visual corollaries to written accounts by trained and untrained artists also employed as surveyors, scientists, soldiers and settlers. These fall into three main phases. Firstly, the sketches made by professional artists, like Sydney *Parkinson, William Hodges (1744–97), John Webber (1751–93), Louis Auguste de Sainson (1800– ?) and François-Louis Lejeune (1804–after 1851), who accompanied British and French explorers, from James *Cook's three historic voyages between 1769 and 1780, and *Dumont d'Urville's last exploratory mission in 1840. Secondly, the visual and written accounts made, and later published to supply a growing demand for travel literature about the exotic destinations encountered during colonial expansion, by itinerant artists like Augustus *Earle

and George French *Angas in the pre-settlement period between the 1820s and 1840s. And, thirdly, the work of surveyors, explorers and settlers; between the 1840s and 1860s, for example Charles Heaphy (1822–81), Samuel Brees (1810–65), William Fox (1812–93) and John Alexander Gilfillan (1793–1864), who integrated visual material into their written and factual accounts chronicling first settlement, and subsequent expeditions into the hinterland.

These works were largely utilitarian; describing the land in the interests of science and cartography and its suitability for settlement, as well as recording the appearances, customs and activities of Māori and the early efforts of European inhabitants. These usually took the form of small-scale drawings and watercolour sketches illustrating journals, sketchbooks, logbooks, diaries and letters.

Engravings and lithographs were selectively made from these, to illustrate published accounts of voyages and expeditions and, after settlement, to inform and attract prospective immigrants. This task was undertaken largely under the aegis of the New Zealand Company who, for example, published the work of Heaphy, Brees and others in Illustrations to Adventure in New Zealand (1845), a lavish folio edition of lithographs describing the settlements established under the *Wakefield scheme. Thus, although the best of these works have been recontextualised as icons in the story of New Zealand art, it is as visual equivalents to scientific and factual literature that their meaning more truly lies.

After the 1870s, when an infrastructure was established to support the resident artist, the close relation between art and letters declined. Professional and amateur painters, now trained in local art schools and exhibiting their works in art society exhibitions, aspired to make work for a local market as an aesthetic end in itself. No longer couched in writing that chronicled the facts of early settlement, the growing volume of landscapes, still-lifes, and portraits were framed instead by the nascent language of art theory and criticism, penned by art world figures like William Mathew Hodgkins (1833–98) in Dunedin and Albin Martin (1813–1908) and Alfred *Sharpe in Auckland.

Only briefly, in the 1890s and 1900s, particularly in Auckland, did art itself take a narrative turn, with the activities of professional artists like Louis John Steele (1843–1917), Kennett Watkins (1847–1933) and Goldie, who painted large-scale history paintings and sentimentalised portraits of Māori subjects, designed to contribute to the construction of a distinctive New Zealand culture. These served as a visual analogue to the ethnological writings of scholars like Augustus Hamilton and Grey; as a pictorial dramatisation of myths and legends associated with a pre-historical Māori past; and as an imaginative reconstruction of the historic first encounters between the two races, which were fast becoming the foundational stories on which a New Zealand identity was being created. But rather than register the veracity of historical records, or prove an artistic equal to the qualities of their Māori sources, such paintings as *The Arrival of the Maoris in New Zealand* (1898, Auckland Art Gallery), were fictional projections, informed by the assumptions of the first native-born generation of Pākehā New Zealanders.

Nineteenth-century economic and political colonisation was followed in the twentieth century by 'imaginative colonisation'. According to Francis Pound, this occurred as a result of a crucial alliance between writers, artists, architects, designers, musicians and cultural commentators between the 1930s and the 1960s, who set out to characterise and articulate a unique cultural identity for New Zealand as an emerging nation-state. Pound argues that poets and painters were galvanised by a desire to create a New Zealand literature and art, developing a rhetoric that conceived New Zealand as an empty silent land, waiting to be 'invented' by men and women who had the clarity of vision to see its essential qualities. In painting and literature, images and metaphors were chosen to embody this unique vision (see also *Nationalism). These sprang from a reinvestment in the land both in its primal state and as the privileged site where New Zealand's pioneers had left their marks.

From 1947 to the 1960s, *Landfall* played a key role in promulgating this new art. Not only did *Landfall* reproduce the work of artists who were thought to share the vision of its editors, but their work was discussed in terms that lay the foundations for a nationalist art criticism. In this critical forum artists like Eric *Lee-Johnson, Russell Clark, Colin McCahon, Rita Angus and Toss *Woollaston were praised for their ability to communicate the essential qualities of New Zealand.

In the 1970s and early 1980s, words, texts and written formats were used by artists in ways which augur the first challenges to the hegemony of modernism, whose rigid formalism was seen as limiting the integration of artistic activities into the social realm. The desire to restore meaning and a social function to artmaking is clearly expressed by McCahon in 1972: 'As a painter, how do you get around either a Michelangelo or a Mondrian? It seems that the only way is not more "masking tape" but more involvement in the human condition' (*Colin McCahon: A Survey Exhibition*, 1972). For McCahon this meant the increasing use of words and numbers in his paintings, to create large-scale public works that refused the conventions of a mimetic tradition yet sought to communicate ideas directly. His use of found texts to

articulate metaphysical and political meanings has had a lasting impact on New Zealand art, evidenced in the practices of Ralph *Hotere, Emily Karaka, Selwyn Muru, Nigel Brown (b. 1949), and others.

Post-object artists, working in this period, in installation, performance and other site-specific and ephemeral modes, sought to resist both modernist dictums about the function and appearance of art, and its commodification in the marketplace, by shifting their focus from product to process and from object to situation. As a result, writing played a new role, now as the sole residue of the work: as instructions for or descriptions of performances or installations. This displaced the artwork from its central position as precious object into the subsidiary role of written and photographic documentation, in catalogues and archives, and as signs, wall-texts and posters, which traditionally would have surrounded the work.

Artists like Jim Allen (b. 1922), Bruce Barber (b. 1950), Billy *Apple, Andrew Drummond (b. 1951), Philip Dadson (b. 1946) and Pauline Rhodes (b. 1937) began to use writing—either their own or that of others—as an integral aspect of their work. Likewise, art writers and critics like Tony Green and especially Wystan Curnow redefined their role, seeking to deny the established guise of disinterested critic, to become exemplary witnesses of and active participants in ephemeral events, their writing now serving as a highly personal account that might become part of the artwork itself.

Another important by-product of this conceptual shift from the singular object that required only dispassionate visual attention was the creation of a new media category: the artist's book. This format required physical handling and allowed the presentation of material in linear or temporal modes, as well as proving a productive site for the reintroduction of content, by the artist's inclusion of either their own (often diaristic) writing or factual and found texts. Such works were brought together in an important exhibition: *ANZART '85 Artists' Books Show*, held in 1985 at the Auckland City Art Gallery.

Women artists, for example Joanna Margaret *Paul, Vivian Lynn (b. 1931), Juliet Batten (b. 1942) and Carole Shepheard (b. 1945), were particularly prominent in the production of artists' books. This was, in part, the outcome of a growing feminist critique of art, women artists choosing this format to explore their thoughts and feelings, bringing into the public arena the visual equivalents to women's diaries or journals, which had traditionally served as important but invisible outlets for female creativity. Women artists also helped dismantle the formal purity of modernist art by insisting on the specificity of their points of view, by making figurative art which either dealt with the particular circumstances of their lives, for example in the work of Jacqueline Fahey (b. 1929), or which addressed the situation of women in society, as in the politically engaged work of Allie Eagle (Alison Mitchell, b. 1949).

With the arrival of postmodern theory in the 1980s, the discourses within which art had been framed were further, and perhaps finally, dismantled. Crucial to this is the redefinition of the image as a 'text', which has served to break down the boundaries between the visual and the written.

Artists like Richard ★Killeen, Terence Handscomb (b. 1948), Billy Apple, Julian Dashper (b. 1960), Julia Morison (b. 1952) and Merylyn ★Tweedie, working in media that include painting, sculpture, photography, performance, installation, film, video and text-based work, now examine the visual as a language which is not transparent in its relation to reality, but a complex of material practices which mediate or even give rise to that reality.

Such theoretical concerns are shared by a variety of postmodern poets, writers and critics. This has led to the work of postmodern artists finding a context alongside that of writers like Tony Green, Wystan Curnow, Judi Stout, Michael ★Harlow, Roger Horrocks, Alex Calder, Laurence Simmons, Francis Pound, Anne Maxwell and Lita Barrie in journals like ★Parallax, ★AND, ★Splash and ★Antic. Here the visual played a role, not as illustration, nor as the object of interpretive analysis, but as 'page art', a visual intervention which often utilised words and appropriated images, or manipulated the format and the conventions of layout and typography.

Book projects and special issues have also resulted from the shared interests of artists and writers. These demonstrate a postmodern understanding of the role language plays in constructing meaning, and register the breakdown of boundaries between written and visual. Representative are Landfall 182 (June 1992), which treated the literary journal as a site-specific space for the visual play of image and text; Amending the Vulgar (1992), edited by two visual artists, Ruth Watson (b. 1962) and Mary-Louise ★Browne; and The Writing of New Zealand: Inventions and Identities (1993), an anthology selected by Alex Calder in which the visual plays a vital role.

Artists whose work combines image and text, reflects on art and writing as a system of signs or can be read through various ideological frames have been brought together in some important exhibitions. These include The Word in Art, initiated by Roger Robinson as convener of the conference of the Australasian Universities Languages and Literature Association (National Art Gallery, 1977); Sex and Sign curated by Wystan Curnow for Artspace in 1987–88; Now See Hear! Art, Language and Translation, curated by Wedde and Gregory Burke (Wellington City Art Gallery, 1990); Francis Pound's Signatures of Place at the Govett-Brewster Art Gallery in 1991; and Like They Are Now (Auckland, 1992), in which Lesley Kaiser and John Barnett invited 36 artists and writers to provide texts for display on a prominent Auckland signboard.   CB

Art in New Zealand was published in Wellington by Harry ★Tombs 1928–46. It was succeeded by The ★Yearbook of the Arts in New Zealand (1945–51). Besides promoting work in the visual and plastic arts, including the publishing of quality mounted-plate colour reproductions, its literary editor, Charles ★Marris, published a limited range of writers and poets. Marris drew his annual ★New Zealand Best Poems (1932–43) partly from the pages of Art in New Zealand, and is remembered for a conservative ★'Georgian' poetic, and as subject of Denis ★Glover's satiric Arraignment of Paris. However, while he clearly preferred the verse of Alan ★Mulgan, J.R. ★Hervey, Eileen ★Duggan or Robin ★Hyde, he also published a few poems by Allen ★Curnow and Charles ★Brasch. Following Marris's retirement in 1942 Tombs gave control to Howard Wadman, who with the assistance of Eric ★Lee-Johnson radically revamped the journal to cope with increasing costs and wartime paper shortages. A.R.D. ★Fairburn became Poetry Editor in 1945 and during the final year printed work by James K. ★Baxter, Basil ★Dowling, G.R. ★Gilbert, Glover and Kendrick ★Smithyman.   SH

Arts Council, see **Literary Fund**.

ARVIDSON, K.O. (Kenneth Owen) (1938–), born in Hamilton and educated in Catholic schools there and in Auckland, began publishing poems in ★Kiwi in the late 1950s while studying Science at the University of Auckland. He transferred to a BA after enjoying a year of German (required as a preliminary for MSc) and on the side attending English lectures by Bill ★Pearson, John ★Reid, M.K. ★Joseph, Allen ★Curnow and others. After completing his MA in English, Arvidson lectured at Flinders University of South Australia 1967–70, and in 1971 moved to the University of the South Pacific to develop a degree programme in English and Commonwealth literature. He contributed a foundation study of South Pacific writing in English to Mana (see ★Pacific). Since 1974 he has taught at the University of Waikato.

Arvidson's verse has appeared in literary magazines in New Zealand and internationally, and has been anthologised in Australia and Japan as well as the Penguin, Oxford and other New Zealand collections. The earlier verse was collected in Riding the Pendulum: Poems

1961–69 (1973). Temporal and spiritual matters balance one another in much of his poetry, in keeping with his Catholic cast of thought. His imagery often quickly acquires symbolic significance. A good example is 'Fish and Chips on the Merry-Go-Round', which takes the fish, an early symbol of Christ, and places it in a secular modern world. Although its original symbolism has largely been 'hosed out' and fish now merely 'fodder us', nothing is static: the merry-go-round of history suggests that the empty symbol may yet again be filled with significance: 'Still, / On a slow wheel, sharpening fins / Give glints.'

Arvidson's research interests include John Henry Newman, Gerard Manley Hopkins, Victorian Literature and Australian Literature. Champion of local writing, he has also made a special contribution to the criticism of Pacific nations' literatures. An autobiographical essay, 'Out of Irishtown', appears in *The Source of the Song: New Zealand Writers on Catholicism*, ed. Mark ★Williams (1995). SS

ASHTON-WARNER, Sylvia (1908–84), was a novelist, autobiographer and educational pioneer. She was born in Stratford, Taranaki, where the family income was earned by her mother Margaret Warner's teaching in various remote country schools, where she was invariably at odds with the school board and national educational authorities. Her father, who was crippled with rheumatoid arthritis, told romantic, mythic stories, some of which informed Ashton-Warner's fiction. Her childhood was marked by extreme material deprivation and interrupted schooling, as her mother moved from school to school, earning barely enough to keep the family of nine children. Without friends, Sylvia depended on her siblings and the natural world to feed her lively imagination. She was educated partly by her forceful mother and partly at various schools, where she invariably felt isolated and disliked.

Having to earn a living, Ashton-Warner became a pupil teacher in Wellington in 1926, and in 1928 she entered Auckland Teachers' College. Everything in her rebelled against becoming a teacher, because she thought that it would thwart her creativity and her potential success as a concert pianist, artist or writer—all occupations she aspired to. For her, teaching was synonymous with her mother, whose influence she spent a significant part of her adult life trying to expunge. She married in 1931, and three children were born 1935–38. Despite her resistance to teaching, Ashton-Warner stayed in the profession from 1938 to 1955, working with her husband in Māori schools in Horoera (East Cape), Pipiriki (Wanganui River) and Fernhill (Hawkes Bay).

For many years, although she was writing and paint-

ing while her husband took responsibility for most of the housekeeping and childcare, Ashton-Warner's public work was centred on her teaching, and in particular experiments with encouraging Māori children to read. Her recognition that each person has a 'key vocabulary', a set of words with a special meaning relating to their emotional life, enabled her to develop a reading scheme for children who were otherwise failing at school. Though she despaired of being recognised in New Zealand for her contribution to education, she enjoyed a warm response overseas. After her husband's death in 1969 she accepted an invitation to assist in setting up an 'alternative' school in Colorado. She also lectured at Simon Fraser University, Vancouver. She wrote a number of books about teaching, of which the best known is *Teacher* (1963).

Ashton-Warner's teaching and approach to education are closely linked to her contribution to New Zealand literature. The 'key vocabulary' not only made the teaching of reading more effective, but also provided insights into the working of children's minds and released their literary creativity. Unfortunately she was less successful in applying this method to herself, and often depended on alcohol to relieve her inner tension. Her observation that all people, but particularly children, have an inner and an outer vision is central to both her teaching and her fiction. The inner world 'behind my eyes' and the outer of 'raw reality' are often at war with each other, but the tension is also creative. This recognition is one she shares with Janet ★Frame, who similarly writes about the hidden world 'two inches behind my eyes'.

Sylvia Ashton-Warner had been writing fiction and publishing short stories for many years before ★*Spinster* burst on to the New Zealand and international literary scene in 1958. Ostensibly the story of a single teacher working in a largely Māori school, *Spinster* is also an account of Anna Vorontosov's emotional involvement with her pupils, a fellow teacher, the inspector who praises her reading scheme, and the shadowy lover Eugene. The effort to integrate Anna's emotional life (the inner world) with her teaching (the world of raw reality) makes this her most popular and successful novel. In 1960 it was made into a film starring Shirley MacLaine, Laurence Harvey and Jack Hawkins in a studio set that was a Hollywood distortion of New Zealand realities.

In presenting the clash between reality and emotion, Ashton-Warner helped to break the dominance of the realist tradition associated with Frank ★Sargeson and opened up other ways of interpreting the experience of living in this country. She lamented the poverty of creative vision in New Zealand and that the experience of many, particularly women, was negated. This also applied to Māori, children and anyone seen as 'different' from white males, whose experiences, she thought, had dominated literature since at least the turn of the century.

The test for Ashton-Warner was to create another world, in which the inner and outer could coexist in creative tension. She explored this possibility in the four novels and the collection of short stories written in the 1960s. *Spinster* had been a novel about a character with 'no top layer to (her) mind'. *Incense to Idols* (1960) is its obverse, the story of Germaine de Bauvais, who 'only live(s) the top half' of herself, burning incense to the idols of love—men, her appearance and alcohol—rather than to pure emotion itself. While *Time* magazine listed it—as it had *Spinster*—among its top ten books of the year, the New Zealand response was both muted and hostile.

In *Bell Call* (1969) Ashton-Warner achieves the integration of the two worlds in the character of Tarl Prackett, an artist, mother and educational rebel. As the novel's male narrator observes of Tarl, 'imagery ignites emotion, which in turn inspires action, and it is action which reaches others'. Ironically, Tarl is no more successful in making contact with others than Anna (in *Spinster*) or Germaine, but her vision of the world is seen as more coherent and whole than theirs. Central to this perspective on the world is Tarl's role as mother to four children, whereas Anna and Germaine were both childless. Ashton-Warner saw mothers as imbued with Madonna-like qualities: 'Without this beginning point, the love for one's children or of children in one's care, a woman seldom comes to universal love.' The mothering role grounds Tarl as well as giving her access to the world of emotion and creativity, Ashton-Warner drawing on her own experience of child rearing and teaching.

In *Three* (1970) the mother role is central, as an unnamed writer pays a prolonged and eventually acrimonious visit to her son and his wife. At first glamorising her son's marriage, the mother finally comes close to wrecking it as she implicitly passes judgement on his wife.

Greenstone (1966) and *Stories from the River* (1986) demonstrate Ashton-Warner's affinity with fantasy. The story in *Greenstone* is loosely based on her own birth family, taking the romantic and legendary—and therefore more palatable—parts and making them into a novel. To the large family, the crippled father with a long heritage, and the mother at war with her employers, Ashton-Warner adds a Māori princess and all the myth and legend she brings with her. Several of the stories in the posthumous short story collection relate to *Greenstone* in subject matter.

Ashton-Warner also produced two volumes of auto-biography. *Myself* (1966) is an account of the years she and her family spent at Pipiriki on the Wanganui River, though many people are given pseudonyms in view of the intensity of the emotional relationships. It was her full autobiography, *I Passed this Way* (1979) that gained her the kind of acclaim accorded only to *Spinster* among her fiction. It won the New Zealand Book Award for Non-fiction in 1980 and was subsequently made into a film. Though Lynley Hood's biography, *Sylvia!* (1988), refutes some of the the author's account of her life, *I Passed This Way* remains a fascinating if sometimes fantastic account of the growth of an artist. Its tense ambivalence in relationship to New Zealand seems to be resolved at the end when the ending affirms this land as the one she wants to be part of. *Sylvia*, a feature film based on her autobiographies, was made by Michael Firth in 1985.

Ashton-Warner's fear that teaching would render her incapable of making a mark elsewhere was not borne out. Her teaching enriched her fiction, and the creativity from which the fiction came underlay her innovations in education. She broke new ground in New Zealand fiction, opening the world of imagination and emotion as a legitimate subject.   HR

Association of New Zealand Literature, The, was founded (as the 'New Zealand Literature Association') in 1991 by the editorial committee of the ★*Journal of New Zealand Literature*. Membership in 1997–98 is approximately 130 individual and 30 institutional members. They receive the twice-yearly magazine *Kite* (first issue December 1991), a vehicle for informal discussion and articles of a less academic nature than those in the *Journal*, appealing to a broader community. The first and present editor is Heather Murray of the University of Otago, who is the association's secretary. The association also arranges and hosts a biennial conference, on Janet ★Frame in 1992, James K. ★Baxter in 1994, and '★Curnow, ★Caxton and the Canon' in 1996. Generally these lead to a special issue of the *Journal*.   RR

At Dead Low Water and Sonnets is a collection of poems by Allen ★Curnow published in 1949 as No. 5 of the ★Caxton Poets. Apart from the well-known title poem, all the poems are sonnets, many of which were first published in Curnow's previous collections, ★*Sailing or Drowning* (1943) and *Jack Without Magic* (1946).   PS

'At the Bay' is a short story by Katherine ★Mansfield in twelve sections, completed in 1921. It was published in the *London Mercury*, January 1922, and (with a short coda now separated as section xiii) in *The Garden Party*

and Other Stories (1922). It represents Mansfield's best mature work, a numinous example of her literary impressionism. While writing it at the Chalet des Sapins, she was coming to terms with her relationship with John Middleton *Murry, and with her own origins and identity.

The story focuses on relationships: 'That's the whole problem.' It brings together some major themes: relationships between women, and between men and women who seem to inhabit different realities; the societal expectations of gender roles; the world of children, criss-crossed by shadows from the adult world and the unknown; disillusionment and, finally, acceptance of that disillusionment and life's inevitable paradoxes.

With the same central characters as *Prelude, it is set at 'the Bay', the summer beach resort on the indented coastline across the harbour from Wellington city. She had spent holidays and weekends there at Days Bay and Muritai as a child and young woman, and had set fiction there as early as 1906. The story demonstrates her remarkable memory of these experiences and their transformation into fiction. The comic figure of Mrs Stubbs, for example, inherits the name of a bank official once a neighbour of the Beauchamps in Thorndon. Her store, with 'its two big windows for eyes, a broad verandah for a hat', is a description of the Muritai Park Store, opposite The Glen, a house the Beauchamps rented. By relocating it to the site of Martin and Jones's store further south, she was able to require Alice to walk along a long stretch of empty road and so highlight her uncertainty and nervousness. Mansfield's own family, the Beauchamps, as in Prelude, are transformed into the Burnells.

To tell the characters' individual stories Mansfield brings them together in the progress of a single summer's day from dawn to dark, each of the twelve sections centred on a moment of revelation: Stanley's sense of exclusion as he blusters off to work, the child Kezia's discovery of the universality of death, or Beryl's late-night encounter with the dangerous sexuality of Harry Kember. The societal context and the unobtrusive realisation of the physical setting disprove the claims of V.S. Pritchett and Frank O'Connor that the characters exist in a vacuum. Mansfield herself reflected, 'it is so strange to bring the dead to life again. There's my Grandmother … with her pink knitting … And one feels possessed. And then the place where it all happens … one tries to go deep—to speak to the secret self we all have.'

Apart from the distinctive location, the use of New Zealand words such as *'bush', 'paddocks' and 'toi-toi', in the first paragraph alone, would have distinguished it from English contemporaries. The dialogue ranges from the taut, brittle words of Mrs Kember to the warm gentleness of Mrs Fairfield. It also illustrates the mature development of two elements that Mansfield aspired to when only nineteen: capturing the significance of the fleeting moment, the 'glimpse'; and working through suggestion and implication rather than analysis.

Shortly before her death, Mansfield declared that she intended to write a 'third part' of the story that began with Prelude. This conclusion was never written, but 'At the Bay' remains an innovative and vividly evocative story. Rebecca West called it 'a work of genius'.   GB

ATKINSON, Tania (1943–), is a writer of junior fiction, often retelling folklore or historical stories. She was fourteen, just arrived at Christchurch GHS from her native Dublin, when her Irish fairy story 'The Piper and the Primrose' was accepted for broadcast. She continued to write for radio and, 1961–64, worked as television production assistant and scriptwriter. Her first book was Honey Mead: Some Irish Fantasies (*Caxton, 1964), a set of four fairytales marked by lively narrative and dialect. After a period back in Ireland, she graduated in English at the University of Canterbury in 1972. Mr Krenko's Wednesday Visitor (1972) is set in a South Island suburb, and satirises New Zealand conformity in its story of an apparently gauche heroine who prefers the violin to marching girls. The unconventional European immigrant Mr Krenko is contrasted with the unimaginative aspirin-chewing teacher Mr Gillespie.

Atkinson's most recent titles deal with famous New Zealand stories, Pelorus Jack: The Story of New Zealand's Famous Dolphin (1984; rev. edn, 1995) and Mackenzie and His Dog (1993), a deft retelling of the legend of the explorer-shepherd drawn from his 1855 petition to the Governor, and particularly engaging in presenting the relationship between man and dog. She now lives in Dunedin.   RR

Atom Quarterly, subtitled A Magazine Written and Illustrated by the Girls of New Zealand, was published in Auckland between about 1899 and 1903. Its editor, Dora E. Moor, solicited stories, poems and essays by members of the Atom Club and other 'unmarried girls'. It is of interest for contributions by Jessie *Mackay and Isabel Maud *Peacocke.   SH

Atua Wera (1997) is a long poem-book by Kendrick *Smithyman, published posthumously by *Auckland University Press, concerning the nineteenth-century Ngā Puhi tohunga and prophet Papahurihia, also known as Atua Wera, the fiery god. Drawing on decades of research into published and oral sources, Smithyman worked on the book for more than a dozen years, adding the last of its nearly 300 numbered poems in the final year of his life. Atua Wera is a narrative poem, a verse biography, and a work of historical scholarship, all bound into one. Smithyman presents us with everything that is known about Papahurihia (often in the precise words of his historical sources), but also with the myths, rumours, opinions, speculations and hypotheses about him as well as the documented facts. In a sense the search for Papahurihia is as much the subject of the poem as the man himself. PS

Auckland University Library, see **University of Auckland Library.**

Auckland University Press grew out of a series of scholarly 'bulletins' dating back to the 1920s. Dennis *McEldowney, editor of University Publications from 1966, became Managing Editor when the Press was formally established in 1972. Elizabeth Caffin succeeded him in 1986, becoming Director. Although the Press has published in many fields, its focus has been on New Zealand and Pacific history and literature. Its first poet was Kendrick *Smithyman, in 1968. He remained with the Press all his life. Those who followed make a distinguished list: Allen *Curnow, C.K. *Stead, Elizabeth *Smither, Bill *Manhire, Ian *Wedde and Albert *Wendt, continued by younger poets including Michele *Leggott, Murray *Edmond, Gregory *O'Brien, Anne *French, Elizabeth *Nannestad, Janet *Charman and Robert *Sullivan. Keri *Hulme's The Silences Between (1982) was her first published work. Historians, biographers and autobiographers have equally been part of the literary tradition: E.H. *McCormick, Keith *Sinclair, Judith Binney, James *Belich, Phoebe Meikle, Jessie Munro, Martin Edmond. Notable collections of letters include Mary *Taylor, Thomas *Arnold, Apirana *Ngata, Frances *Hodgkins and Peter *Buck. With the Department of Internal Affairs the Press now publishes the *Dictionary of New Zealand Biography. In the 1970s the pioneering New Zealand Fiction series, edited successively by John *Reid and Bill *Pearson, brought back into the mainstream earlier novelists almost forgotten, beginning with Robin *Hyde, George *Chamier, Jane *Mander and William *Satchell. New fiction has been less frequent, but includes interesting experimental work by Anne *Kennedy, Gregory O'Brien and others. Literary works are complemented by literary criticism: Curnow, Stead, Frank *Sargeson, Mark *Williams. Māori and Pacific studies are a growing part of the Press's activities. DMcE

AUDLEY, E.H. (Ernest Henry) (1896–1973), was born in Coromandel, and his enthusiasm for that region was to characterise all his fiction. In 1913 he joined the public service and, after war service 1917–19, became a teacher, working at primary schools throughout the Auckland region, and travelling with his wife to teach in Britain. He retired as headmaster at Manurewa in 1953, having already taken up writing as a hobby: many of his short stories appeared in the New Zealand Dairy Exporter.

His first book, Islands Float at Eleven (1952), published with the help of the New Zealand *Literary Fund, is as much reminiscence as fiction. Life in a colonial *gold-mining town (Thames) is seen through the eyes of an 11-year-old boy, who larks with others, notably flooding the mine's shower room and setting fire to the neighbour's outhouse (with the neighbour inside). The romance of ships, the smell of horses, the use of kerosene tins and their lids as baking tins, water vessels, dustpans and containers for flowery adornments, and a similar versatility in the use of sacks and flour-bags help to evoke the scene vividly and unsentimentally.

Audley's other two novels were published in Britain but are equally evocative of New Zealand realities, often with a gentle comedy. No Boots for Mr. Moehau (1963) tells of Mr. Moehau's struggle both with the company that plans to mar his home with holiday resorts and with those Māori who wish to sell land, as well as of his encounters with the Land Court. Equally, it tells of his pleasure in the company of his fellows, in the sea and its food, and in the forests and hills of Coromandel, again without sentimentality. Similarly, A New Gate for Mattie Dulivich (1965) describes the conflict between old settlers on the Coromandel and business interests planning to build a boating marina and a luxury hotel. Mattie Dulivich, a *'Dalmatian', and Amo, a Māori, combine as friends and lovers of the land to protect its uncommercialised beauty.

Audley always enjoyed the company of Māori friends and neighbours and, writing at the same time as Noel *Hilliard, shares Hilliard's ability to cross the cultural boundary without fuss or self-congratulation. His language is deft, sometimes poetic, and although his fiction is sometimes called 'light', this quality is due to maturity and sure-footedness when moving in quite difficult terrain. NW

Aussie began as a soldiers' magazine of cartoons, jokes, and humorous stories published in France in 1918. The New Zealand edition, edited by Pat *Lawlor, ran from April 1923 until January 1932 and consisted of a sixteen-page supplement to the Australian publication. Contributors included Ken Alexander, James *Cowan, Dulce *Carman, S.G. August, Alice *Kenny, A.R.D. *Fairburn, Una Currie, Margaret *Macpherson, Will *Lawson, Quentin *Pope, Alan *Mulgan, Tom Mills, Mona *Tracy and Robin *Hyde. SH

Australasia, adapted from French 'Australasie', has been used from 1838 to denote New Zealand with *Australia and their outlying islands. (Earlier Australian use, from 1793, excluded New Zealand.) Sometimes felt to be patronising, the term has had little literary currency. There was one significant anthology, *The Oxford Book of Australasian Verse* (ed. Walter Murdoch, London, 1918), which ran to four editions. But by the last, 1950, New Zealand is allocated a separate section, edited by Alan *Mulgan. From the same early twentieth century came P. Serle's *A Bibliography of Australasian Poetry and Verse* (Melbourne, 1925). The two literatures are now rarely seen as conjoint, even from a great distance, and the term is usually replaced by such locutions as 'Australia and New Zealand' or (rarely, now) *'Anzac'. HO

Australia and New Zealand were in the early colonial era closely related in their literatures. In 1827, the painter Augustus *Earle disparagingly compared the Australian Aborigines ('last link in the great chain of existence which unites man with monkeys') with the Māori, who were '"cast in beauty's perfect mould"'. Later in the century, a succession of Australian poets would also find more 'heroic' and 'noble' attributes in the Māori. The diverse productions of Charles Harpur and Henry Halloran, Bassett Dickson and Benjamin Hoare focused on the figure of Hone Heke, Māori resistance leader of the 1840s. The type of forlorn heroics, rather than re-calcitrant barbarism, Heke was a savage Christian warrior evidently more noble, and fit for verse, than any Aborigine known to history. Dickson even allowed Heke to speak on behalf of the downtrodden natives of New South Wales and Van Diemen's Land; Halloran co-opted him to the cause of Australian republicanism. While its foreground was the Waikato Wars of the 1860s, Rolf *Boldrewood's romance *War to the Knife* (1899) is imbued with memories of Heke's struggle. Samuel *Butler's *Erewhon* links New Zealand, Australia and the *Pacific in the mock proposal to ship the Erewhonians to labour on the Queensland sugar plantations, citing the actual exploitation there of Pacific Islanders.

The attraction of New Zealand material for Australian artists was strong at the turn of the century. The painters Alfred Daplyn and Arthur Fullwood visited 1898–99; Tom Roberts in the following year. Leaving a Sydney stricken by bubonic plague, Roberts delighted in the South Island, 'that land of cool air, lakes and purple mountains', as he sought to expand his range of subjects, with a view to sales. Roberts had been preceded by Henry *Lawson, whose time labouring for a telephone company in the South Island in 1893–94 produced the 'Study in the Steerage' called 'Coming Across', which described fugitives from the *Depression: 'tradesmen,

labourers, clerks and hard-up bagmen, driven out of Australia by the hard times there'. 'His Country After All' dates from this period as well. Again Australia suffers initially in a comparison, for New Zealand farming land 'would make an Australian cockatoo's mouth water'. The smell of eucalyptus is, however, sufficient to direct the disgruntled Australian homeward. Lawson was to try New Zealand a second time, as a schoolteacher at Mangamaumu in 1897–98, before returning to Sydney.

The Otago *goldfields were the nurturing ground for some writers who later wrote more of Australia than of New Zealand. They included Fergus *Hume, who baldly stated that 'I belong to New Zealand and not Australia', Benjamin *Farjeon and the playwright George Darrell. Lady *Barker, claimed by New Zealanders for the two books she set in Canterbury, in fact wrote some twenty books set in most countries of the Empire, including Australia, where her husband Frederick *Broome, author of New Zealand poems, was Governor of Western Australia.

For New Zealand writers of this period Australia was, according to Patrick *Evans in the *Penguin History of New Zealand Literature* (1990), 'the first version of Overseas and a seeming network of magazines that not only published but even paid'. Early stories by Katherine *Mansfield appeared in Australia in the *Native Companion*. By far the most popular outlet was the *Bulletin, to the extent that in the 1890s, fabled decade of Australian proto-nationalism, ten per cent of the magazine's literary content was actually contributed by New Zealanders. A number of them decided to try the Australian scene in person, beginning a pattern of expatriation that has seldom flagged and never been reversed. Notwithstanding that Eric *Beach, who arrived in Sydney in 1972, could say 'I didn't come to Australia. I just left New Zealand', his compatriots—before and since—determinedly sought more enriching careers across the Tasman.

Thus what appears to be a dearth of New Zealand writing about Australia by authors who stayed home is better understood as the process by which generations of expatriate New Zealand writers have been instrumental in contributing to the shaping of Australian literary culture. For example, Arthur *Adams, a published poet in his own country (with *Maoriland*, 1899, a name for New Zealand that the *Bulletin*, and Lawson, fondly popularised), first came to Australia as secretary to the theatrical entrepreneur J.C. Williamson. After an interlude at the Boxer Rebellion, he returned to edit the Red [literary] Page of the *Bulletin*, then the *Lone Hand* and the Sydney *Sun*. The Irish-born poet David McKee *Wright was another New Zealander to influence literary taste as editor of the Red Page, besides being a prolific contributor under such pseudonyms as 'Pat O'Maori'. In four volumes of ballads in the Australian style between 1869 and 1900 Wright wrote of New Zealand subjects in a New Zealand setting.

Will *Lawson, often treated by Australians as one of theirs, in fact spent more years in New Zealand than anywhere else in his restless, nomadic life. Many of his 'Australian' ballads were written in moments of boredom at his clerical desk in the Union Steam Ship Company in Wellington. He, too, became a major contributor to the *Bulletin*.

Another who has fallen between the two nationalities is William *Hart-Smith, the first poet to be published by Denis *Glover at the *Caxton Press but also a contributor to the Jindyworobak movement. After some years at the centre of Australian nationalism he spent another twenty in Dunedin, writing of South Island landscapes, before going back to Australia in 1962 and back again to New Zealand in 1978. When questioned about his nationality he replied, 'The poetry, that's what matters. The rest is just messing around.'

Douglas *Stewart was one of the most famous and accomplished of all writers to be in charge of the Red Page. His tenure lasted from 1940 until 1961, when he became literary editor for the publisher Angus & Robertson. Stewart's earliest volumes of verse, *Green Lions* (1936) and *The White Cry* (1939), had their settings in New Zealand. His nostalgia never abated. In 1966, *The Seven Rivers*, an account of the fishing streams of his home province of Taranaki, appeared, while his autobiography of childhood, *Springtime at Taranaki*, was published in 1983. Auckland-born writer Ruth *Park, like Stewart, turned—at 70, and after long residence in Australia—to memories of her earliest years in the autobiography *A Fence Around the Cuckoo* (1992).

A number of notable female New Zealand writers had preceded Park to Australia. By the 1920s, Dulcie *Deamer had established herself as a renowned Sydney bohemian, besides working as an actor and journalist. The long and distinguished international newspaper career of Elizabeth *Riddell began when she went to Australia in 1928 to work for *Truth*. Following assignments in Europe and the United States, she returned to Australia after World War 2 and gained a further reputation as a poet. Jean *Devanny arrived in Australia the year after Riddell. Then in her mid-thirties, she had already had four novels published. One of them, *The *Butcher Shop* (1926), was banned on both sides of the Tasman for an array of offences: socialism, feminism, sexuality and its depiction of the brutalities of rural life in New Zealand. After settling in Australia, Devanny wrote three more novels in the 1930s based in her native country, before turning to Australian subjects.

When New Zealand writers began to arrive after World War 2, often prompted by local economic problems, many knew of compatriots who had made successful careers in Australia, so could draw on a network of support. For instance, New Zealand–educated academics have made notable contributions to intellectual life in Australia, among them the etymologists, bibliographers and critics Sidney Baker, John Ferguson, Graham Johnston, Eric Partridge and George Russell. The publishing firm of Allen & Unwin was largely created by expatriate New Zealanders. Finding employment in journalism, as had some of their predecessors, numbers of writers continued to combine this with their literary output. There are few examples of such influential intellectuals moving in the other direction, H. Winston *Rhodes being the exception.

Cultural exchanges between the two countries are now probably weaker than a century ago, despite quite frequent visits by writers in both directions to appear at literary festivals like Adelaide or Wellington's *Writers and Readers Week, and some reciprocal interest in theatre and film (several David Williamson plays have been produced in New Zealand, and *The *Piano* was an Australian-produced film with a New Zealand subject). New Zealand writers have published in *Meanjin*, but not prominently. *Climate's attempt to establish a trans-Tasman literary journal soon foundered, and the efforts of *Hazard Press to do the same with a poetry series have so far had limited success in attracting Australian titles. Some writers and academics, such as Terry *Sturm, C.K. *Stead and Vincent *O'Sullivan have forged creative contacts. Like Sturm, O'Sullivan lived in Australia for several years, and Tasmania affords one of the settings for his novel, *Let the River Stand* (1993). Jane *Campion has preserved a strong New Zealand element in her artistic identity while living mainly in Australia.

More typically, writers who leave New Zealand for Australia are reconciled to making their working life in the new country, even if the home land remains a vital presence in their writing. Stephanie Dowrick, who moved to Australia in 1981, made her heroine in *Running Backwards Over Sand* (1985) a New Zealander, and edited a collection of stories by Australian and New Zealand writers, *Speaking with the Sun* (with Jane Parkin, 1991). That enterprise, at once natural and rare, illuminated the differences between the two literary cultures while showing how readily these can be bridged.

Novelist Rosie *Scott has imagined both a pre-apocalyptic Auckland in *Feral City* (1992) and the predations to which dishevelled Australian youth is subjected in *Movie Dreams* (1995). It was long after he moved to Australia that John *Sligo wrote his three novellas, *Final Things* (1989), which treat of New Zealand society from

World War 2 until 1967. Playwright Alma ★De Groen settled there in 1973, but her best-known play, *The Rivers of China* (1987–88), covers in part the last months in the life of Katherine ★Mansfield. Jennifer ★Compton retains a strong sense of New Zealand in her poetry. All these writers tend to lament the difficulty of maintaining a dual identity or of sustaining recognition in New Zealand. The awarding of literary grants and the marketing concerns of publishers determine how origins are represented.

In recent years, it has been left to historians rather than novelists or poets to insist upon the experiences in common between Australians and New Zealanders. Military historians have written of the shared experiences in war of their servicemen and women; Patrick O'Farrell, in *Vanished Kingdoms* (1990), of the lives that Irish immigrants fashioned for themselves on either side of the Tasman. Nevertheless, two countries that a century ago almost federated are now in crucial respects at greater cultural distance than at any time since European settlement, to the detriment of both. 'The Growing Strangeness', to appropriate the title of one of Douglas Stewart's early poems, is to be lamented.   PP

Authors' Week, 1936 (organised by ★PEN with John A. ★Lee as government representative), was held in the main centres during April–May to celebrate New Zealand's emerging literature. Leading writers and citizens co-opted as sponsors and helpers were Sir Harold Beauchamp (father of Katherine ★Mansfield), O.N. ★Gillespie, Jessie ★Mackay, Edith ★Lyttleton, Edith ★Howes, Johannes ★Andersen, C.A. ★Marris, Robin ★Hyde, Hilda Carr Rollett, Elsie K. ★Morton and Jane ★Mander. Gillespie, a publicist for New Zealand books, felt it was timely to acknowledge the country's excellent writers, bookshops, newspapers and magazines: New Zealand could be the new Greece, he wrote. Significantly the practising writer, Lee, was more pessimistic: our writers wrote, he said, but the populace firmly resisted reading them, so that poverty was the hallmark of New Zealand authors.

Celebrations took the form of displays of books and lectures: in Auckland, Mander, Lee, Carr Rollett, Morton, Hyde and A.R.D. ★Fairburn (stringently critical of all poetry save R.A.K. ★Mason's) and Mason gave lectures. In Dunedin book displays were held at the ★Hocken, Knox College and Dunedin Public Libraries, with radio talks by C.R. ★Allen and Muriel May. Allen's novel, *A Poor Scholar*, was launched; the Otago Women's Club Poetry Circle celebrated the poems of Blanche ★Baughan, Eileen ★Duggan, Gloria ★Rawlinson and Mackay. Considerable space was devoted in the *Evening Star* and the *Otago Daily Times*.

Evening Star editor, W.F. Alexander, who with A.E. ★Currie had compiled the first poetry anthology (★*New Zealand Verse*, 1906) noted with regret the common view that New Zealand was not a place to inspire a literature. In this he was supported by C.H. Fortune, who wrote in the *Daily Times* (24 April) that while there was some support for non-fiction books, the public largely ignored local fiction, including Mansfield. A visiting Englishman, W.J. Grant, noted (in the *Star*, 24 April) that New Zealand writing 'sings a new song', its practitioners being 'robust men and women, with a message of strength and virility; they see old things with young eyes'. In retrospect Authors' Week 1936 now seems to mark the end in fiction and poetry of a Late Colonial era in which women had dominated. Themes and forms, with a few exceptions, had been inherited from Europe, with some overlay of local colour. Many commentators were already asking why writers failed to reflect the real life of the country, and suggesting that a new path might be shown by young Auckland writers in the radical student paper ★*Phoenix* (1932–33), who were frightening their elders by their irreverence for the past, their strange forms, and sociological probing.   HM

Autumn Testament, James K. ★Baxter's last book of poetry, was published shortly after his death in 1972. Thus its title acquired a symbolic significance beyond Baxter's intention. What it might reasonably have implied—the articulation of a covenant worked out by a man at the height of his creative power—would be overshadowed by the legal connotations of a man in decay disposing of his property. Inevitably it was read as a presentiment of impending death and searched for clues that might explain his final days.

Autumn Testament comprises three poetic and two prose sequences. Two short poems bracket the titlepiece. The first of these, 'He Waiata Mo Te Kare', is Baxter's final verse letter to his wife, the second, 'Te Whiori O Te Kuri'—'the tail of the dog / That wags at the end of my book'—is a sequence of seven sonnets. The prose pieces are reminiscent of ★*Jerusalem Daybook* (1971): the first is a series of notes that follow the opening poem; the second is a letter to Baxter's friend Colin Durning that obliquely glosses the titlepiece. The forty-eight sonnets of the title poem document the life of the Jerusalem community and anticipate Baxter's own end. But his characteristic imagery of death, often a disturbing feature of his poetry, now suggests peace and acceptance. Behind the apparent simplicity of Baxter's final volume is the distilled essence of a life's writing, carrying the themes which were most significant, expressed in authenticity, shorn of imitation and derivation.   PM

AWATERE, Arapeta (Marukitepua) (1910–76), leader and scholar, wrote at length on a wide range of issues relating to Māori culture while in Mount Eden Prison, and is often quoted by other writers for the oral information on classical Māori culture they obtained from him. His tribal affiliations were Ngāti Porou, Te Whānau-a-Hinetapora, Uepohatu. He acquired great *mana as a leader of the Maori Battalion during World War 2 and devoted much of his energies to welfare issues. His poem 'Ka Huri', published in the *Penguin Book of Contemporary New Zealand Poetry* (1989) and reprinted in *Te *Ao Mārama,* is a 'genealogical tribute to the ancestors, tribes, mountains and rivers of the Māori' (Witi *Ihimaera). NW

AYLMER, Mrs J.E. (Isabella), was the author of one of the earliest New Zealand novels, *Distant Homes; or, the Graham Family in New Zealand* (1862). It was once attributed to Mrs. Isabella Aylmer (d. 1908), wife of Rev. W.J. Aylmer (1802–83), the first Anglican incumbent of Akaroa, but correspondence in the *Alexander Turnbull Library indicates that the author was another Isabella, wife of Captain J.E. Aylmer who died in the Crimean War. Consequently we must assume that the author was never in New Zealand, but based her novel on the letters of her namesake from Akaroa, and on an active fantasy.

The title, with its implications both of distance and of *home comforts, suggests major themes of early colonial fiction. The children are excited by the word 'savages', while the parents think of quiet English life. Consequently they are comforted to see that Lyttelton Harbour has 'such a busy home-look about it'. The family travels a little, giving the author opportunity to convey often erroneous geographical information. An eruption of 'Mt. Egmont' causes an earthquake that goes on for a day and a half while great water spouts shoot up in Cook Strait; a visit to the thermal region reveals that the Māori cook and swim in pools that coat everything with liquid stone; a kauri is found in a 'tropical forest' in the Southern Alps. ('The long spars of Kauri were evidently intended by nature as masts for ships.') A garbled version of Māori beliefs is provided. The smallest child is lost in the *bush, a familiar device of frontier narratives, but shows 'manliness' and 'independence' beyond his years, in contrast to the child-like Māori. On another journey Wellington is seen with its 'beautiful houses, wide streets and gay shops'. Back in Canterbury, the Māori again gratefully come to live near the Grahams and profit from being taught civilisation by the women and girls. The superiority of English manners is perceived by all, above all by the English reader for whom the book was written. NW

B

bach (or **batch**) as a noun (NZ 1924, thence to Australia 1929) derives in an indirect way from the intransitive verb 'to bach' (Australia 1882, NZ 1890), to live alone or with others of the same sex doing one's own cooking and housekeeping: 'You would live in a cheap lodging-house or batch with another girl' (Clyde, *Pagan's Love*, 1905). It is probably a familiar shortening of an obsolete, distinctively New Zealand verb, 'to bachelorise' (*Auckland Weekly News*, 20 Dec. 1879). The noun was first applied (1911) to a simple habitation rented cheap: 'And seeing a small hut in a back garden by the road, of the sort called a bach in this country … I inquired at the house if I might inhabit it' (D'Arcy *Cresswell, *Present Without Leave*, 1939). The contrast with the Otago and Southland 'crib' (a hut 1856, a weekend cottage 1909) is often quoted as one of the few obvious regional differences in New Zealand English. To go baching or live in a bach is often an affirmation of the kind of earthy pragmatic masculine pastoralism expressed in literature by Barry *Crump among others and associated with the *'Man Alone' topos. Nigel *Cox wrote on this topic in 'At the Bach' in *New Zealand Geographic*, Jan.–Mar. 1995.   HO

backblocks, usually as 'the backblocks' (or hyphenated 'back-blocks'), derives from the originally uncompounded 'back block', meaning a surveyed block of grazing land remote from a main *station or homestead, or from the coast (1852). Since 1901 it has been applied to the sparsely settled hinterland, having few urban facilities, also called 'the back-country', 'the boohai' or (humorously) 'the wopwops', similar to the American 'the boondocks' or 'boonies' in their implication of affectionate disparagement from the urban point of view.

Jean *Devanny writes of 'one of the back-blocker's pleasures, taking tea in restaurants in town' (*Bushman Burke*, 1930). The first of Mary *Scott's popular 'Barbara' books is *Barbara of the New Zealand Back-Blocks* (1935). From about 1875 'backblocks' has also been used to denote the characteristics of such remote areas, usually self-reliance, or, more pejoratively, makeshift roughness, and is thus associated with the pioneering myth (as in Scott, or Frank *Anthony) and the *'Man Alone' topos.
                                        HO

BACON, Ron or **R.L.** (1924–), is important as a children's writer who affirms the values of Māori life and the New Zealand land. He was born in Melbourne and came to New Zealand aged 8. On leaving Hastings BHS, he served in the Pacific with the RNZAF, and then went to Ardmore Teachers' College in 1948. He taught in several country schools before moving to Auckland, where he finished his teaching career as Principal of Favona School. His only novels for adults, *In the Sticks* (1963) and *Along the Road* (1964), successfully draw on humorous aspects of his early teaching experiences.

As a teacher, however, Bacon soon perceived the need for indigenous children's books. His study of Māori lore and acceptance by Māori led to an extensive output of mainly picture books, some readers, including Adult New Readers, but only one children's novel. *Again, the Bugles Blow*, illustrated by V.J. Livingston (1973), and republished in the Kotare series (1984), is notable for portraying the drama, heroics and futility of war through the experiences of a contemporary Māori boy taken by a time-slip back to the Waikato Land Wars and Battle of Orakau in 1864.

Bacon's picture books begin with *Boy and the*

Taniwha (1966) and *Rua and the Sea People* (1968), both fictionally historical, celebrating New Zealand natural life and Māori perceptions, and both outstandingly illustrated by Māori artist Para Matchitt. Later came legends such as *Hautupatu and the Bird Woman*, illustrated by Stanley Woods (1979), and *The Creation Stories* trilogy (1984). Three important books, emphasising the 'sound' of language, celebrate past life on the marae: *The House of the People* (1977); *The Fish of Our Fathers* (1984), winner of the 1985 Picture Book Award; and *The Home of the Winds* (1987), all illustrated by Robert Jahnke. Contemporary stories about Hemi, beginning with *Hemi Dances*, illustrated by Sharon O'Callaghan (1985), further demonstrate Bacon's versatility, sensitivity and interest in the natural world. Other successful picture books include *The Banjo Man* and *The Kite* (1990), both illustrated by Kelvin Hawley; and *The Clay Boy*, illustrated by Chris Gaskin (1990), which sums up his belief in the importance of art. Several non-fiction books include *Save Our Earth* (1988), and he has also published retold legends (1995) for a Junior Māori Collection.   DH

BAGNALL, Jill (1940–), is known for the children's picture book *Crayfishing with Grandmother* (illustrated by Barbara Strathdee, 1973), which is notable as a bilingual publication, with the text in Māori by Hapi Potae. Developed from friendship with Potae's family, it celebrates traditional Māori beach experiences and family relationships. Born in Wellington, Bagnall was educated at Wellington GHS and at Gilbey's Business and Wellington Teachers' Colleges.   DH

BAIGENT, Lawrence (1912–85), was an editor with *Caxton Press, novelist, reviewer and university teacher. Born in Nelson and educated at Nelson College, he arrived at Canterbury University College in 1931 when the *Depression seemed to be generating intense activity in student politics and culture. He was one of the group of students led by Denis *Glover and including Ian *Milner in launching the controversial *Oriflamme. With Charles *Spear, writing jointly as 'C.L. Spear-Baigent', he wrote a novel, *Rearguard Actions* (1936), wittily satirical and intellectual in the manner of Aldous Huxley and early Anthony Powell. Another Spear-Baigent novel exists in manuscript. Baigent also had a poem in Caxton's *New Poems*.

Baigent's teaching career at Christchurch BHS was curtailed when he was suspended for conscientious objection to military service in 1942. He joined Glover at Caxton and became editor, compositor and printer, with Leo *Bensemann also among his friends. When the teenage James K. *Baxter appeared with his mother in August 1944 with a bundle of poems, Baigent 'was com-

pletely bowled over by them'. He became, in Baxter's words, 'rather enthusiastic as a midwife', seeing *Beyond the Palisade into print. At Easter 1945 he entertained Baxter at his Christchurch flat, introducing him to such significant friends as Allen *Curnow, Basil *Dowling, Douglas *Lilburn and painter Rita Angus, though suffering from Baxter's loquacity, according to the amusing account he gave to Frank *McKay for his *Life of James K. Baxter*. Baxter's second collection, *Cold Spring*, was left with Baigent but for reasons unknown remained unpublished at that time.

Joining the Canterbury University English Department in 1946, he carried for some years a prodigious teaching load that, with his own self-effacement, restricted his writing to reviews in *Landfall and elsewhere. Though few, these were perceptive, for instance in criticising 'the mystique of violence' in the fiction of Guthrie *Wilson. He continued generously to support others, including Ngaio *Marsh and Mervyn *Thompson in their early drama work. Baxter summarised him as 'friendly, sensitive, intelligent, poetical views sound but slightly narrow for me'.   RR

BAINES, W.M. (William Mortimer) (d. 1912), of Bell Hall, Yorkshire, a Fellow of the Royal Geographical Society, wrote *The Narrative of Edward Crewe; or, Life in New Zealand* (1874). It is a probably semi-autobiographical account of Baines as master of a coastal trader, timber merchant and Auckland ship-owner, depicting an early *'Man Alone' as adventurer interested in exploiting New Zealand's natural wealth. Baines returned to Britain and published *Old Naburn* (1895) in York.   DB

BAKER, Heretaunga Pat (1920–88), wrote the first novels of Māori history presented from an inwardly Māori viewpoint. *Behind the Tattooed Face*, published 1975, two years after Witi *Ihimaera's novel of modern Māori life, *Tangi, is drawn directly from the traditional stories and legends of the Whakatōhea of the Bay of Plenty, which he had grown up hearing. It deals with one of the last great tribal conflicts fought by traditional warfare. An epilogue chapter, 'A Prophecy Fulfilled' (also published separately in *Into the World of Light, 1982), relates the arrival of *Cook's *Endeavour* within the frame of Māori cultural belief. Deeply informed in its understanding of Māori thought and of the land, the novel sustains an almost ritualistic eloquence in the writing.

The Strongest God (1990), left in manuscript at the author's death, even more ambitiously incorporates oral sonority into its narrative, with forms such as chants, songs and prayers interspersed every few pages, often in both languages. The choric effect affirms the essentially

Māori commitment. Baker called the novel 'the second in what I hope will be a series of historical novels about my people, the Whakatohea'. It deals with events of 1864, especially the British attack on Rangiaowahia and the hanging of Rev. Carl Volkner at Opotiki. The main subject of the somewhat unwieldy narrative is the complex conflict of religious belief in that turbulent period, and the often formal and elevated language reaches for the spiritual significance of events that are distressingly violent. The history is seen as essentially tragic, the outcome of misplaced certainties on all sides. The book includes forewords by the author, his editor (Christine Cole *Catley) and his daughter, Kahukore Baker, who affirms his overriding belief in *Papatua-nuku and 'the natural world in its entirety'. An appendix by Nehe Dewes deals with the exhumation of the remains of the executed leader Mokomoko and others from Mount Eden Prison.

Baker, connected through his mother with Ngāti Kahungunu, was born at Rakaia, grew up at Omaru-mutu, was educated at Te Aute College and saw action in the Merchant Navy in World War 2. He studied jour-nalism at Canterbury University College and worked variously in journalism, farming and business, serving a prison sentence from 1973 for business-related charges, which he always denied. He served as secretary of the Te Waipounamu District Māori Council, on the Māori Education Foundation, as Chairman of the Canterbury Museum of Science and Industry and in other voluntary roles. RR

BAKER, Louisa Alice (1856–1926), published her sixteen novels and one book of short stories under the pseudonym 'Alien', no doubt because of her sense of alienation both in New Zealand, where she claimed to have been 'bred' (though born in Warwickshire), and in England, where she chose to spend much of her life. Her family settled near Christchurch in 1863 and she married there at the age of 18. In 1886 she moved to Dunedin, her husband remaining in Christchurch. They were never reconciled and he died in Ashburton in 1916.

Her first work was for the *Otago Witness* where she assisted William Fenwick to edit the *children's page, 'Dot's Little Folk'. She was the first 'Dot', although the pseudonym survived her tenancy of it by many years. She gave advice to children who wrote in from near and far. As 'Alice', she also gave advice to women, but her women's column also included occasional poems and her own serials.

By 1894 she had written her first novel, *A Daughter of the King*, and had settled in London. Her connection with New Zealand was partly restored with her column

"'Alien's' Letter from England' for the *Witness* from 1903, and most of her novels are set in New Zealand, a few in Australia and England.

Today, many passages in her novels reward reading for their rhythmic prose, for their interweaving of South Island landscapes into human lives, for their observation of difficulties in human relationships and for their ambi-tious attempts at varying the narrative point of view—but none of them can be said to be rewarding in its entirety, generally because they rarely take life from their characters but are driven by feminist dogmas or plot formulae. The almost total lack of a sense of humour tends to leave the dogmas over-exposed.

An undoubted strength is her repeated use of river symbolism. Chapter 2 of *A Daughter of the King* opens with images of life: birds, flowers and the River Avon, but the 'King', a sick violinist, is dying and it is his daughter Florence who must answer the call to life. In *Another Woman's Territory* (1901) the lovers go through many difficulties but are always reconciled by their meetings beside a Canterbury river, and they discover that both share knowledge of a river in Cornwall. When Marah, in *His Neighbour's Landmark* (1907), sees one of her lovers rescued from a 'foaming' river by another, 'it was then she passed from girlhood to a woman's deep knowledge of pain', and later she marries on the Wanganui River.

Other aspects of *landscape can often bring out the artistic tendencies in characters. Bret in *The Majesty of Man* (1895) has such tendencies, and finds in Fiordland that 'No artist could place on canvas the dazzling loveli-ness of these scenes; now high banks of gold and brown mosses; now a tropical growth of ferns; now the mighty majesty of some great hill; and then a little island, which was a fairyland of greenery fringed with toi-tois and tall, graceful rushes, swiftly changing, ever varying.' Fiord-land is also a powerful presence for lovers in *Not in Fellowship* (1902). Mountains often (for example in *The Untold Half*, 1899) represent mystic aspiration (as they do in *Grossmann's *The *Heart of the Bush*).

Music can often symbolise spirituality: violinists occur in several novels and there are more subtle refer-ences such as the chapter title 'The Maid of the Mill', which has a wandering miller, in *The Devil's Half Acre* (1900). Again and again the theatre is used as a symbol of civilisation in the otherwise raw colonies. Florence in *A Daughter of the King* is thrilled by Ibsen's *A Doll's House*—and many of 'Alien's' characters bear Ibsen-like names, such as the mysterious Alma in *The Perfect Union* (1908).

The lot of a lone woman is 'Alien's' most common theme. It is inspiring for the opportunities of learning it gives but depressing for the defeat of 'natural' life it takes away. Thus Lilian, in *A Daughter of the King*, grows spiritually great, and then insane; Miss Goodyear, a blue-stocking in *Wheat in the Ear* (1898), trains her protegée Joan in 'emotionless' elocution but is defeated by Joan's spirit. Mutual love in marriage with equality of the partners is the virtually unattainable ideal.

'Alien' tackles large themes, complex interpersonal relationships, images of human dignity and enormous self-control, and broad natural and social images of impressive implication; but neither her plots nor her language are strong enough to bear all this, so that her novels, despite their inner dignity, slip into sentimentality. She shows a strong sense of symbol (especially when she uses rivers), but again her skill does not match her ambition so that such symbols remain outside the structure, imposed from without, not reaching their potential force. One is left with the impression of a considerable but sadly flawed (perhaps never adequately guided) talent. For her novel *In Golden Shackles* (1896), see *Gold.   NW

BALLANTYNE, David (1924–86), novelist and journalist, was born in Auckland and raised in Rotorua, Hicks Bay and Gisborne. After serving in the New Zealand Army 1942–43, he began a long career in journalism with the *Auckland Star*, 1943–47. He returned to the *Star* 1949–54 after a brief stay with the short-lived Wellington daily, the *Southern Cross*, 1947–48. From 1955 to 1966 he worked on Fleet Street in London, with the *Evening News*, *Evening Standard* and the periodical *Finding Out*. He returned once more to the *Auckland Star* in 1966 and remained there until his death.

In 1970 Ballantyne described himself as 'a writer who never really made it, neither kudos nor cash to show for a quarter century at the typewriter', and his career as an imaginative writer was one of unrealised hopes and unrecognised accomplishments. He began precociously with articles and short stories in little magazines in 1942, and by 1944 was at work on the first book of a planned trilogy. By 1945 that book had been accepted by an Australian publisher, who went out of business before the novel could appear. After a New Zealand publisher turned down the manuscript, the American novelist, James T. Farrell, who was in correspondence with the young Ballantyne, got his publishers to look at what by then was a completed trilogy. They accepted the first volume and a half, which appeared in New York in 1948 as The *Cunninghams*. The book was well reviewed in the United States, and in New Zealand Oliver *Duff announced in *NZ Listener*, 'It looks as if New Zealand has found a new novelist.' When Ballantyne won the Hubert Church Award for *The Cunninghams* in 1949, and in late 1948 received one of

the earliest *Literary Fund grants to write his next novel, he seemed launched. However, it was to be fourteen years before another novel appeared, with a long series of failures and mishaps in the interim. He abandoned a second, autobiographical novel in 1949 when his American publisher did not like the sample he submitted. He completed 'Freeman's Bay', a novel of Auckland working-class life, in 1950, but the American publisher reluctantly refused it as 'too New Zealand', and no New Zealand publisher would take it. From 1950 to 1955 Ballantyne worked on several novels and put together a collection of short stories, but none were accepted for publication. In England he focused more on journalism, but after several successful television plays was approached by a literary agent and for the second time his career seemed launched. In 1963 he published in England and New Zealand a second novel, *The Last Pioneer*, which had gone through five drafts between 1955 and 1962, as well as a collection of short stories, *And the Glory*, and a reprint of *The Cunninghams*. These books were followed by two more novels, *A Friend of the Family* (1966) and *Sydney Bridge Upside Down* (1968). Even after such productivity little critical attention was paid to any of the books; hence Ballantyne's comment about not having made it. A further novel was refused in 1968, and no more fiction appeared (except for a reprint of *The Cunninghams* in 1976) until *The Talkback Man* in 1978. This novel significantly dealt with an alcoholic ex-writer who had many years before published a briefly well-known novel and was haunted by its memory. It was followed by *The Penfriend* (1980) and a reprint of *Sydney Bridge Upside Down* (1981). Critical essays by C.K. *Stead in 1979 and Patrick *Evans in 1981 attempted to bring recognition to Ballantyne, but he remains relatively unknown. At his death, he left behind notes towards several other novels.

The long story of Ballantyne's failure to achieve literary fame might be only a cautionary tale if were not for the quality of his best work. *The Cunninghams* is one of the finest works of New Zealand realism, unsurpassed as a picture of working-class family life, and the unpublished sections of the trilogy and the unpublished 'Freeman's Bay' (in its revised version called 'A Corner at the Duke'), which remain in manuscript, are not markedly inferior. The best of the short stories, such as 'And the Glory', 'A Leopard's Tale' and 'Other Gardens', are among the best of the period. While neither *The Last Pioneer*, a sardonic picture of small-town New Zealand life, nor *A Friend of the Family*, a novel about the urban journalistic world, is up to the earlier fiction, *Sydney Bridge Upside Down* marks a real advance in its use of dream material and an unreliable, manipulative narrator. It ranks with Janet Frame's *Owls Do Cry* and Ian Cross's

The *God Boy among the best New Zealand novels of growing up. His last two novels are imperfect but of considerable interest for what they depict and how they are told. While the earlier novels had focused on a dour, puritanical New Zealand of the *Depression and the immediate post-war period, these focus on a very different multicultural and more affluent society no longer dominated by *puritanism. The way of telling involves sophisticated narrative games with hints of metafiction. Thus these last novels indicate a further development in Ballantyne, an abortive third start to his career. It is quite possible that his work will last longer than that of some better-known contemporaries; already The Cunninghams and Sydney Bridge Upside Down are coming to be seen as New Zealand classics.   LJ

BANKS, Joseph (1743–1829), natural historian and scientific administrator, is best known for his participation on James *Cook's first voyage around the world 1768–71. His Journal, which was not published in full until 1962, ranks with that of Cook as the first accurate written account of New Zealand and its inhabitants. Banks was the only son of a wealthy Lincolnshire landowner. Educated at Harrow, Eton and Oxford University, by 1764 his inherited wealth gave him the leisure and resources to pursue his scientific interests, and botany in particular. Unsatisfied with the conventional aristocratic destinations of the Grand Tour, in 1766 Banks journeyed to Newfoundland on HMS Niger, beginning a lifetime's work in the study and collection of natural history specimens. His broken Journal of this expedition was published in 1971 in an edition by Averil Lysaght.

Banks had been elected to the Royal Society in 1766 and the support of this body secured him a place on Cook's Endeavour, which was to journey to the Pacific to observe the transit of Venus across the disk of the sun and search for the southern continent. In 1768 he embarked with a party of eight, including two scientists and two artists, on a voyage that was to take three years. Throughout the voyage Banks took every opportunity to go ashore and collect plant, animal, ethnographic and geological specimens. His artists provided a visual record of these and they were described in the scientist's Journal, along with the accounts of the lands and peoples the ship visited. The reports of Tahiti, New Zealand and the eastern coast of Australia provided Europe with its first detailed knowledge of these regions and Banks's collections were, and remain, a rich source for scientists and ethnographers. The account of New Zealand, its people, flora and fauna provide invaluable insights into Māori language, society and material culture at the time of western contact. As a landowner Banks took particular interest in the Māori economy, especially agriculture and fishing, comparing the large kumara fields of the east coast with the most finely cultivated English farms.

Although Banks journeyed to the Western Islands of Scotland, to Iceland and to Holland after his return from the Endeavour voyage, from 1773 his collecting activities throughout the world were conducted by a large body of agents who sent shiploads of plant, rock and animal specimens to him or to Kew Gardens, over which he unofficially presided. Banks became president of the Royal Society in 1778, a position held until his death, and from this office he exercised enormous influence as a patron of science, discovery and colonisation. He advised governments on matters ranging from coinage and explosives to the exploration of America and Africa and the settlement of New South Wales. Banks played a critical role in the publication of the journals of the explorers Mungo Park, William Blight, George Vancouver and Matthew Flinders. Although he published little in his own name, he had a profound impact on the scientific world. The results of his voyage with Cook were not published in his own time, but his library and herbarium at his London house at Soho Square were visited by most of the prominent European and American scientists of his day. In 1962 The Endeavour Journal of Joseph Banks, 1768–1771 was published in an edition by J.C. *Beaglehole. Banks' Florilegium was finally printed in full between 1980 and 1990 in an edition of 100 sets, from the 738 copperplates engraved between 1771 and 1784 but not used at the time.   DM

Barbara is the *backblocks farmer's wife heroine of five popular books of stories by Mary *Scott, originally published in the New Zealand Herald.

BARKER, Lady (1831–1911), also known as Lady Broome, was born Mary Anne Stewart in Jamaica, where her father was Island Secretary. That this makes her a true daughter of the Empire is especially interesting because the persona she presents in her writing is that of an 'English' lady, and might best be understood as a fictitious narrator. She was educated in England and married Capt. George Barker, who was later knighted for services in the Indian mutiny, so that she acquired the name 'Lady Barker'. She used this even after her second marriage, until her second husband was also knighted, from which time she called herself 'Lady Broome'. She used only her title and surname in her publications.

After Barker's death she returned to England where she married another child of the Empire, Frederick Napier *Broome, who had been born in Canada in 1842 and had moved to New Zealand at the age of 15. There he became the owner of a large sheep *station in

Canterbury and it was to that remote place that he took his bride. The period which followed, and which turned Lady Barker into the author of two classic New Zealand books, lasted only three years, 1866–68. After a catastrophic snowstorm, which is vividly described in both books (and yet again in her autobiography *Colonial Memories*, 1904), the Broomes returned to England, where they worked as journalists.

There Lady Barker wrote her first book, ★*Station Life in New Zealand* (1870), which is based largely on the letters she had written to her younger sister. It was so successful that she followed it with another book of anecdotes of New Zealand life, ★*Station Amusements in New Zealand* (1873). Both remained very popular and were reprinted several times in Britain and on the continent. In more recent times (since 1950) they have been republished in New Zealand. They were in fact only two of ten books Lady Barker wrote during the eight years after her return to Britain. Another was *First Principles of Cookery* (1874), which led to her appointment as Lady Superintendent of the National School of Cooking in Kensington. In 1875 Broome was appointed Colonial Secretary to Natal. For most of his term his wife remained in England, but she spent one year in Natal (1876–77), which formed the basis of her book *A Year's Housekeeping in South Africa* (1879). When Broome moved to Mauritius she joined him there, and during the Zulu War she organised a relief fund. In 1882 Broome was appointed Governor of Western Australia (where a town was named after him), and *The Western Australian* welcomed the new governor with a notice including the words 'To the world in general he is best known as the husband of Lady Barker'. From there she wrote a series of letters to her son from her first marriage: *Letters to Guy* (1885). Broome was appointed Governor of Trinidad in 1891 and died there in 1896. After this date Lady Barker lived in London in near penury until her death in 1911.

Clearly it is an oversimplification to call her a New Zealand writer. She stayed only three years, and set various works in England, India, South Africa, Mauritius, Australia and the West Indies as well as New Zealand. On the other hand the two 'Station' books are undoubtedly the best of her twenty-two books. Some others are of New Zealand interest. In most cases she adopts a fictional mask but undermines it with references to her 'real' life, so that uncertainty about the status of the narrator is typical of her work. *A Christmas Cake in Four Quarters* tells Christmas stories for children set in England, Jamaica, India and New Zealand. The latter is a rather formless tale that begins with a boar hunt and continues with the station owners entertaining the 'hands', who tell their own tales, especially of ★gold

digging. In *Travelling About Over New and Old Ground* (1872) there is no overt fictional disguise. It consists of stories about explorers in various parts of the world, the New Zealand chapters including a summary of J.S. ★Polack's memoirs and another of Sir Charles Dilke's memoirs as well as yet another account of her own experiences in Canterbury.

Stories About — (1887) includes 'The Grave by the Rakaia': 'Going out for a ride in England is a very different affair from a New Zealand excursion. *Here* you have only to coax papa to give the order to the groom, and it is all settled; you mount quietly and set off (quietly also, I hope, but I rather doubt it). *There* the first thing necessary is to catch horses.' The use of 'here' and 'there' is symptomatic. The narrator and her husband ride out to visit a lonely man in a lonely environment. Another story in the same book, 'Aunt Anne's Stories about Horses', includes an anecdote about a reliable old New Zealand horse who rounds up a mob of wild horses with the narrator clinging to his bare back. Even in her major books, for all their vivid evocation of New Zealand life, the narrator and the implied readers never forget that they are snug in middle-class England. Lady Barker is best seen as a 'colonial' writer, rather than a New Zealand one, and her 'Station' books bear comparison with Susanna Moodie's Canadian classic *Roughing it in the Bush* (1852) and Mrs Charles Meredith's *Notes and Sketches of New South Wales* (1844). In 1996 Betty ★Gilderdale's *The Seven Lives of Lady Barker* was published.   NW

BARR, John (1809–89), of Craigilee, was 'Poet to the Caledonian Society of Otago' and inaugurated the Burns Club. Born in Paisley, Scotland, he was head of a large engineering firm before emigrating to Otago in 1852. He farmed the property he called Craigilee until retiring to Dunedin. He had a famous talent for composing songs and humorous verse for any occasion, usually in the Scots dialect. ★Hocken called him 'a general favourite'. Often strongly satiric, his verses express his Scottish identity, pride in the new colony and egalitarian criticisms of conditions back in the old country. In 1861 he published (in Edinburgh) *Poems and Songs, Descriptive and Satirical*, republished with additional pieces in Dunedin in 1874. Both editions received the unusual compliment of financial sponsorship from Otago settlers. (See also ★Scotland.)   HMcQ

BATHGATE, Alexander (1845–1930), novelist, was born in Peebles, Scotland, and came to New Zealand in 1863. His father John was manager of the Bank of Otago, managing director of the Otago Daily Times and Witness Co and even edited the *Otago Daily Times* for a few months. After working as a banker, Alexander qualified as barrister and solicitor and practised in Dunedin until 1909. With Thomas *Bracken he established the *Saturday Advertiser* in 1875. He also founded the Dunedin Art Gallery and encouraged railway development in Otago.

As a writer he is remembered for two novels. *Waitaruna* (1881) is an early example of the pastoral novel. Two lads, one cheerful and practical, the other thoughtful and book-reading, land from the same ship to make their way in the colony, accompanied at times by a comic Irishman called Mike Donovan. After impressions of the raw but lively town of Dunedin, they variously try the masculine life of a tussock country sheep *station. One sets off for the *goldfields, the other finds romantic interest with a woman who maintains an English gentility in the 'barren' surroundings: 'Do you know mamma has made a rule that no-one must talk "sheep" in the evening in the drawing room.' Jealousy intrudes, interspersed throughout with descriptions of mustering, shearing and the 'New Zealand death' of drowning while crossing a river. There is also a leitmotif of loneliness and isolation, leading to insanity and the destruction of a marriage. The pastoral hero marries happily, the gold-mining one endures a period of alcoholism before settling down as a publican. The book ends with an image of mist clearing from Port Chalmers.

Bathgate turned to the novel again thirty years later with *Sodger Sandy's Bairn* (1913). There is a kind of dialect prelude set in Scotland where two boys defy the enmity of their families. One is disinherited and goes to New Zealand, where after other scenes the action shifts many years later. The story now is of love, jealousy, gold, floods, mateship, dramatically revealed identity and wrongful arrest for murder. Another jump in time closes the narrative on scenes of marriage with children, the settled life apparently preferable to adventurous mining.

Bathgate also wrote a lively, anecdotal account of Otago, *Colonial Experiences* (1874), and an undistinguished volume of verse, *Far South Fancies* (1890). NW

BATISTICH, Amelia (1915–), fiction writer, was born in Dargaville to early *Dalmatian settlers, her father from the island of Korcula, and mother from the village Zaostrog, on the mainland coast, famed for its oral culture and monastic scholarship. The family boarding house peopled with new migrants—manual labourers and proxy brides from the former Yugoslavia on their way to the harsh life on the gumfields—provided fertile ground for her most memorable stories. Irish Catholic nuns of her convent years and local Māori also feature. Bilingual as a child, she lost contact with her Dalmatian identity when the family moved to Auckland. As a

teenager she was thrust back into the language and culture of her beginnings, among the Dalmatian stonemasons at her father's Mount Wellington quarry. She married a Dalmatian, and started to write of the vibrant community. Her first publication was in *Best Bets* in 1947, a poem about a horse in a tribute to the Dalmatian love of gambling. She contributed stories to the *NZ Listener*, *Mate and *Arena while working as a copywriter and for ten years as librarian. Asked to write about ethnic minorities for *School Journal*, she introduced children to the culture of the 'Bohemians of Puhoi', 'Vikings in the Bush', the Chinese in 'New Gold Hills' and many others. Immersing herself in the different cultures, she explained the non-British immigrant people of New Zealand as from an insider's perspective, in what she considers to be her most important work. Her stories on Māori were written from a sense of identification of 'otherness', coupled with respect for *tangata whenua.

Her journals, 'The Olive and The Vine' and 'They Came to The Gumfields', were developed into her most acclaimed publication *An Olive Tree in Dalmatia* (1963), rpt. for the Dalmatian Centenary Celebration (1980). Presenting Dalmatians as ideal migrants, the collection, packaged with sociological introduction and glossary, moves succinctly from a primarily 'Dally' sensibility to a 'Kiwi' view of the world. It tells of Dalmatian families 'finding their way from one world to another', identifying first with their Dalmatian heritage and then with their adopted land, in the end struggling to remember their past. A variation on the New Zealand preoccupation with national identity and belonging, the collection includes 'A Dalmatian Woman' and 'An Olive Tree in Dalmatia', both anthologised internationally. These stories struck a chord with New Zealanders anxious to claim a sense of place, and are Batistich's high points.

Less well received were the novels *Another Mountain Another Song* (1981) and *Sing Vila in the Mountain* (1987), first published in Serbo-Croatian translation as *Pjevaj Vilo u Planini* in the former Yugoslavia (1981) as the prize winner in an international competition for migrant writers. Fleshing out the themes, characters and predicaments introduced in the short stories, both novels are based loosely on Batistich's childhood, the first set in Auckland during the *Depression and war and the second in 1920s Dalmatian Dargaville. Childhood and small-town New Zealand are underscored by difference in a society tolerant only of homogeneity. The novels present an alternative New Zealand, a redefinition of nationalism, but they were seen as naive and sentimental. *Holy Terrors and Other Stories* (1991), a celebration of Batistich's Dalmatian writing, contains many of the original stories, and an irreverent look at convent education in the novella 'Holy Terrors'. The reception of this final publication highlights the problem of being classified as a chronicler of minority experience. Neither critics nor publishers have allowed that Batistich is an important voice on New Zealand society in general, though writers such as Patricia *Grace acknowledge her importance as a model for variant voices. Her grass roots popularity includes many appearances in the Writers in Schools programme, festivals and workshops, and she is acknowledged as the spokesperson of Dalmatian New Zealanders.   NN

BATTYE, Susan (1950–), is a playwright in the grow-ing field of theatre for young adults, and was founding president in 1985 of the New Zealand Association for Drama in Education. After education at Christchurch GHS, University of Canterbury (BA 1974) and Christ-church Teachers' College, a major influence was Dorothy Heathcote under whom she studied drama in education at Newcastle upon Tyne in 1979. Her experience includes student productions in the era of Mervyn *Thompson at Canterbury, work in opera and theatre at Greymouth while on the staff of Greymouth HS, 1974–83, and school productions there and at Epsom GGS, where she has taught since 1983 and is Head of Drama.

Battye's best-known play is probably *The Shadow of the Valley* (with Thelma Eakin; produced 1977, publ. 1980). A reconstruction of the Brunner Mine disaster of 1896, it had a major impact on its first production in Greymouth, the documentary-drama techniques making the tragedy immediate for local audiences. West Coast writer Peter *Hooper reviewed it as 'our own history transmitted into an art form'. There have been sub-sequent productions in Auckland and elsewhere. Her other published plays are *Living In* (1983), *Easy as Pie* (1985), *The Singing Lesson* (1992), based on the Katherine *Mansfield story, *Not for School but for Life* (1993) and *Radio Waves* (1996). She has also worked for television and published articles about drama in education.   RR

BAUCKE, William (1847–1931), contributed a series of articles on the Māori to the *New Zealand Herald* and the *Auckland Weekly News*, fifty-seven of which were collected and published as *Where the White Man Treads* (1905). The son of Lutheran Missionary parents, he was born and grew up on the Chatham Islands. A self-taught linguist, he became fluent in seven languages, including Māori and Moriori, which he learned during childhood. In later life he made an important linguistic contribution to the ethnology of the Moriori, when, in collaboration with H.D. Skinner, he published *The Morioris* (1928) at the invitation of the Bishop Museum, Hawaii. For most of his adult life he lived in the King Country, working as

an interpreter. T.M. *Hocken praises *Where the White Man Treads*' for its 'contribution to the history of the Maori by one who has dwelt amongst them throughout his life, and who deplores the white man's tread across their pathway'. But more recent critics have interrogated Baucke's claims to 'construct Maori history from oral narrative' and suggest that instead of his articles being factual they exhibit tropes of colonial short fiction that distance him from his Māori subjects. This assessment disregards numerous pieces that are in no way fictitious. 'The Treaty of Waitangi', for example—an impassioned appeal for justice for Māori—proposes an 'annulment of every law we have enacted that is in contravention of the Treaty'; criticises land confiscations—'if rapacity needs justifying, political dishonesty stops at no subterfuge to gratify it'; and scorns the notion that Māori willingly gave up their land: 'Given? The miles of confiscated acres and the graves of many battlefields attest the donor and the gift!' That such criticisms are familiar a century later suggests that, on certain subjects at least, Baucke not only handled facts accurately but was well ahead of his time. *Where the White Man Treads* was reprinted with some revisions in 1928.   PM

BAUGHAN, B.E. (Blanche Edith) (1870–1958), was a poet and *landscape writer, especially known for her much-anthologised poem 'A Bush Section'. She was born in Wandsworth, Surrey, suffering tragedy at the age of 10 when her father was killed in a fit of homicidal madness by her mother. The five daughters were re-sponsible for their mother's care after she was adjudged criminally insane, especially Blanche, for whom the responsibility continued through her twenties. Believing the condition to be congenital, she remained single, despite falling in love with a fellow passenger while on a world tour in 1893, during which she visited New Zealand. There are fictionalised versions of these trau-matic episodes in 'Two New Zealand Roses', an unpub-lished novel written in her seventies and held in the *Alexander Turnbull Library.

She was educated in Brighton, as a scholar at Royal Holloway College and at London University, graduating with Honours in Classics in 1892, one of the earliest female graduates in England. She was a suffragette. She worked as a private tutor and as a social worker in East London slums, still caring for her mother. She published her first book, *Verses*, in 1898. Left a small income by her father (whose memory she revered), she was able to move to New Zealand after her mother died in 1902. *Reuben and Other Poems* (1903) included three poems dramatising aspects of colonial life written after her arrival in New Zealand. She always published under the name B.E. Baughan in order not to disclose her gender.

She first worked in Ormandville in Hawkes Bay, but soon moved to a remote farm at Long Look-out near Chorlton on Banks Peninsula. Around 1910 she shifted to Clifton, near Sumner, and in 1930 retired to Akaroa on Banks Peninsula where she became a town councillor and a prominent citizen.

Her first fully New Zealand book was *Shingle-Short and Other Verses* (1908), which contains her best poetry, including 'A Bush Section', 'Maui's Fish' (an intermittently vivid version of Māori mythology), 'The Paddock' (an ambitious and curious poetic 'oratorio'), and the title poem (a long dramatic monologue in the tradition of Wordsworth and Browning). Her rhapsodic poetics also reveal a familiarity with the philosophy and versification of Walt Whitman; she was the first New Zealand poet to adopt his belief in the need for a new poetic for the New World. A fourth volume, *Poems from the Port Hills* (1923), appeared after she had largely abandoned poetry.

In her early years in New Zealand Baughan travelled widely and wrote several essays, many published as 'Souvenir Booklets' by *Whitcombe & Tombs (who published most of her work) describing her visits to notable tourist spots. First came *The Finest Walk in the World* (about the Milford Track), which went through four editions 1909–26. In 1910 *Snow Kings of the Southern Alps* was published, followed by *Uncanny Country—Rotorua and Environs* in 1911 (there were two later editions, more than 10,000 copies altogether), and *The Summit Road* (1912, 1914); *A River of Pictures and Peace* (the Wanganui) and *Forest and Ice* followed in 1913. These six booklets were collected (together with 'Stars Under the Earth', about the Waitomo Caves) as *Studies in New Zealand Scenery* (1916). *Akaroa* (1919) was added to a second edition published as *Glimpses of New Zealand Scenery* in 1922. Booklets on *Arthur's Pass and the Otira Gorge* (1925) and *Mount Egmont* (1929) completed the sequence of essays in which she expressed her passion for natural beauty and the landscape of her adopted country in vivid and subtle prose that owed much to the example of John Ruskin.

Baughan was also an occasional contributor of articles, stories and book reviews to journals, including the *New Zealand Illustrated Magazine*, the *Weekly *Press*, *Lyttelton Times*, the *Citizen* and the *Otago Witness*; most were about the mountains or country people. Her talents were less well adapted to fiction. *Brown Bread from a Colonial Oven* (1912), subtitled 'Sketches of up-country life in New Zealand', is her only published fiction. The partly autobiographical 'Two New Zealand Roses', which recounts the contrasting but linked lives of two women born on Banks Peninsula, was written 1940–46.

Baptised an Anglican, Baughan lost her Christian faith in childhood, presumably as a consequence of her father's violent death, but the religious impulse stayed with her. In 1905 she had a well-documented mystical experience at Long Look-out, and this lies behind the ecstatic tone and transcendental rhetoric of some of her poems. Visiting California in 1914 she was converted to Hinduism by a swami in San Francisco and became a devout supporter of the Vedanta philosophy. She corresponded with swamis in India and California, much preoccupied with the question of whether love of beauty and art is consistent with the quest for religious truth.

Gradually her writing was replaced by an ideal of social service, which she regarded 'as an art'. The renunciation of poetry is consistent with a lifetime pattern of such renunciations, including marriage and England. She found her resting place in Vedanta and (from about 1918) in the cause of prison reform. She formed a New Zealand branch of the Howard League for Prison Reform in 1924 and worked tirelessly as lecturer, editor, prison worker and visitor, and opened her home to released prisoners. Many of her ideas have been adopted—wider use of probation and preliminary reports, proper classification of prisoners, trained prison staff, abolition of capital punishment and training for release. She has been called the Elizabeth Fry of New Zealand. Her last book was *People in Prison*, largely a series of case studies written in collaboration with F. de la Mare, published under the pseudonym 'T.I.S.' by the Unicorn Press in 1936.   PS

BAUME, Eric (Frederick Ehrenfried) (1900–67), was an internationally renowned journalist but is remembered in New Zealand for the melodramatic romance novel *Half-Caste* (1933, 1950). His father (also Frederick Ehrenfried), a colourful Auckland lawyer and politician, founded the magazine *New Zealand Illustrated* in 1899. Eric succeeded in journalism early: at 22 he edited the *Timaru Herald*, then New Zealand's largest provincial newspaper. In 1923 he left to advance his career, going first to Australia and then on to London (1939–49). His greatest coup as a journalist was scooping the international press by being the first to predict the German invasion of Russia. After the war he returned to Australia to work in broadcasting and in 1966 received the OBE for services to Australian journalism. A prolific writer, he published, in addition to *Half-Caste*, a variety of fictional, autobiographical and documentary works including *Tragedy Track* (1932), *Burnt Sugar* (1934, 1938), *… I Lived These Years* (1941), *I've Lived Another Year: A Journalist's Diary of the Year 1941* (1942), *Sydney Duck* (1944), *Five Graves at Nijmegen* (1945), *Yankee Women* (1945), *… I'll Always Be with You* (1946), *Ponty Galler* (1947), *Devil Lord's Daughter* (1948), *Unrehearsed Incident and Other Stories* (1948), and *The Mortal Sin of Father Grossard* (1953). Most of his work has been criticised for impatience and lack of care, and only *Five Graves at Nijmegen* is considered to have 'some literary claims'. In addition to *Half-Caste*—which deals with the perceived dangers of interracial marriages between Māori and Pākehā—titles with New Zealand elements include *Devil Lord's Daughter*, about a girl brought up as a boy who comes to New Zealand on ★Cook's *Resolution*, and ... *I Lived These Years*, which recounts Baume's journalistic experiences in Australia and New Zealand. A.E. Manning has written a biography of Baume titled *Larger than Life* (1967). JMcC/PM

BAXTER, Archibald (1881–1970), was in his own way as well known as a writer as his mercurial son, James K. ★Baxter. A quiet, self-educated man who worked for most of his life on the land, he arrived at the decision that 'war—all war—was wrong, futile, and destructive alike to victor and vanquished'. He refused conscription to fight in World War 1, becoming instead one of New Zealand's most notorious pacifists. For his stand he was shipped as a prisoner to the battlefields of Europe where he endured extreme ill-treatment and was at one stage near death. He survived to recount his experiences in *We Will Not Cease* (1939, 1960, 1980). Written in a dispassionate prose curiously at odds with the descriptions of the brutality inflicted on New Zealand objectors, *We Will Not Cease* is a powerful testament to the courage of one man's convictions.

In 1921 Archie Baxter married Millicent Brown, daughter of the well-known academic Professor John Macmillan ★Brown. James K. Baxter, while crediting both parents for the fact that at the age of 7 he 'broke out in words', makes it clear that his father was the strongest influence on his desire to write. Describing Archie as 'a poet whom the time betrayed / To action', James was infected in childhood by the love of verse evidenced in his father's recitations of 'Burns and Shelley and Byron and Blake and Tom Hood and Henry ★Lawson when the mood took him'. Archie features in poems written throughout his son's life, although in James K.'s earliest published poems (for example 'Rain-Ploughs' and 'The Unicorn' from ★*Beyond the Palisade*) he is disguised as an archer, symbolising the risks and rewards of personal values that prompt a stand outside society. James K.'s ostentatious rejection of New Zealand's Calvinist ethos in his 'Jerusalem period' surely has its origins in his father's refusal to conform to values he perceived as dehumanising. PM

BAXTER, James K. (1926–72), poet, dramatist, literary critic, social commentator, was born in Dunedin into an Otago farming family. Family fable has it that Archibald ★Baxter prayed that he 'might have a poet for a son'. James, the second son, indeed became one of New Zealand's finest poets and most controversial figures, often at odds with a society unable to stomach its disturbing reflection in his work.

James Baxter (known by friends as 'Jim' or, later, 'Hemi') once described each of his poems as 'part of a large subconscious corpus of personal myth, like an island above the sea, but joined underwater to other islands', and elsewhere commented that what 'happens is either meaningless to me, or else it is mythology'. This tendency to mythologise his life in verse makes biography important in any response to his poetry.

Baxter's middle name—after the Scottish socialist, Keir Hardie—signified his parents' left-leaning politics. Their beliefs profoundly influenced him, as did their contrasting backgrounds. Whereas the quiet Archie's ancestors had been small-farmers in the Scottish highlands, Millicent was the strong-minded eldest daughter of the distinguished Professor John Macmillan ★Brown, who regarded the marriage as a mismatch, mistakenly.

Baxter's aversion to systematic schooling was symbolised by an incident on his first day at Brighton Primary School, on Otago's coast, when he burnt his hand. As the family moved, he later attended Quaker schools in Wanganui and the English Cotswolds, and, in World War 2, King's HS in Dunedin.

This was not a good period for pacifists. The family was suspected of spying, James was bullied, and his brother Terence sent into detention as a military defaulter. Adolescence was therefore a solitary time, but Baxter felt that his experiences 'created a gap in which the poems were able to grow'. Indeed, between 1942 and 1946 he drafted some 600 poems.

An able although unmotivated student, Baxter matriculated a year early, with unspectacular results, applying himself meanwhile to reading and imitating almost the entire English poetic canon. The moderns, particularly Auden, Spender, MacNeice and Day Lewis, inspired him with the voice they were giving to the social battles of the time. By his late teens, a discernible voice was developing out of adolescent imitation.

In 1944, Baxter began a 'long, unsuccessful love affair with the Higher Learning' when he enrolled at Otago University. 'Incipient alcoholism' soon became a problem, but in 1944 he won the Macmillan Brown literary prize (for 'Convoys') and ★Caxton Press published his first collection, ★*Beyond the Palisade,* to critical acclaim. Six poems from *Beyond the Palisade* were selected for Allen ★Curnow's *A* ★*Book of New Zealand Verse 1923–45.* A second book, ★*Cold Spring,* remained unpublished at that time.

Abandoning university study, from 1945 to 1947 Baxter worked in factories and on farms. Part of this period is fictionalised in his novel *Horse* (1985). His struggle with alcoholism was both cause and consequence of the failure of his first significant love affair, with a young medical student. Her enduring effect, however, is evident in three poem sequences: 'Songs of the Desert' (*c.*1946–47), 'Cressida' (1951) and 'Words to Lay a Strong Ghost' (1966). An even more important relationship began in 1947 when he met Jacqueline *Sturm.

In late 1947 Baxter moved to Christchurch, ostensibly to renew his university studies, but actually to visit a Jungian psychologist. He began incorporating Jungian symbolism into his poetic theory and practice. His behaviour, thanks to the 'irrigating river of alcohol', could be erratic as he sporadically attended lectures and took jobs as a sanatorium porter, copy editor for the Christchurch *Press* and freezing worker. He began associating with the poets Curnow and *Glover, and his reading remained copious.

Blow, Wind of Fruitfulness (1948) confirmed Baxter as the pre-eminent poet of his generation. His interest in religion culminated in baptism as an Anglican, and, despite considerable parental concern, he and Jacquie were married in St John's Cathedral, Napier.

Moving to Wellington, they enrolled at Victoria University College and associated with the generation of writers that included W.H. *Oliver, Alistair *Campbell and Louis *Johnson, and became known as the Wellington Group.

In 1951, now attending Wellington Teachers' College, Baxter enthralled the *New Zealand Writers' Conference with his lecture *Recent Trends in New Zealand Poetry*, subsequently published by Caxton. One reviewer described him as 'the profoundest critic we have'. A selection of poems in a collaborative volume, *Poems Unpleasant*, was published in 1952.

Having completed his Teachers' College course, Baxter studied full-time at Victoria University in 1953, also publishing The *Fallen House*. In 1954 he was assistant master at Lower Hutt's Epuni School. An able teacher, but no disciplinarian, his major contribution was a series of children's poems published posthumously as *The Tree House* (1974). Also in 1954, he gave three Macmillan Brown lectures on poetry at Victoria University, published, to mixed reviews from critics concerned by his simplification of issues and reliance upon anecdote, as *The Fire and the Anvil* (1955).

In late 1954, Baxter joined Alcoholics Anonymous, espousing its principle of helping others in a course of counselling and prison visitation that continued for the rest of his life. Some stability was achieved partly through a substantial legacy with which the family purchased a house in the Wellington suburb of Ngaio. He received

his BA in 1955 and published a long poem in pamphlet form, *Traveller's Litany*. He left Epuni School in 1956 to work for *School Publications, a period which provided material for numerous attacks on bureaucracy.

Baxter discovered the pitfalls of parody when his skilful imitations of seventeen New Zealand poets, *The Iron Breadboard: Studies in New Zealand Writing* (1957), was received with acrimony by some of his peers. Fourteen more serious poems appeared in a collaboration, *The Nightshift: Poems on Aspects of Love* (1957), a collection that, to quote Howard McNaughton, 'established a position of alienation that would recur in his work for two decades'. The following year Baxter received international recognition when *Oxford University Press published **In Fires of No Return*. Critics, however, thought the book loose and poorly selected.

Baxter's greatest success in 1958 was the radio play, broadcast in September, *Jack Winter's Dream*. The script was published in *Two Plays: The Wide Open Cage and Jack Winter's Dream* (1959), adapted for the stage in 1960, and filmed in 1979. Domestically, things were less successful. Jacquie was astonished by Baxter's unheralded decision to convert to Roman Catholicism and in October 1957 they separated. He was received into the Church in 1958.

A UNESCO Fellowship to study educational publishing in Japan and India gave Baxter and Jacquie a chance to reconcile. He left for Japan in September 1958 and the family joined him later in India. Baxter was overwhelmed by the poverty and the situation of ethnic minorities. The Indian poor would haunt his imagination and his poetry. His sense of displacement and disorientation is evident in the 'Asian' poems of his next collection, *Howrah Bridge* (1961). Baxter's later compulsion to leave his family and attempt an alternative lifestyle at Jerusalem must be considered in this context.

Returning to New Zealand wasted by dysentery, he showed increasing disillusionment with New Zealand society. Drama became a vehicle for such criticism. *The Wide Open Cage*, which was staged in 1959 by Richard Campion, explored themes such as guilt and alienation in relationships. Its success inspired Baxter to write *Three Women and the Sea* (1961) and *The Spots of the Leopard* (1962). In 1960 Baxter became embroiled in a controversy over Curnow's *Penguin Book of New Zealand Verse. His argument that Curnow misrepresented the state of New Zealand poetry by under-representing younger poets did little to lessen an antipathy his erstwhile champion had developed towards him.

Becoming a postman in 1963, he wrote *The Ballad of the Soap Powder Lock-Out* as a light-hearted contribution to the postal workers' industrial action against delivering heavy soap powder samples. More significant were a number of polemical poems protesting against the *Vietnam War. Themes inherited from his pacifist parents, and explored in his unpublished adolescent verse, were reworked to satiric effect in such poems as 'A Bucket of Blood for a Dollar' and 'The Gunner's Lament'. *Poetry Magazine* had published *A Selection of Poetry* in 1964, but Baxter's next major collection was the widely praised *Pig Island Letters* (1966).

In 1966–67, Baxter was *Burns Fellow at the University of Otago. It was a triumphant homecoming for the man who had left twenty years earlier under a cloud of failure. Baxter took an active part in university life, protesting against Vietnam and satirising the university prohibition against student cohabitation in his pamphlet *A Small Ode on Mixed Flatting, Elicited by the Decision of the Otago University Authorities to Forbid this Practice Among Students*. Through all this his creative output was staggering: he wrote numerous poems, and published a selection, *The Lion Skin: Poems* (1967), through the university's Bibliography Room.

Revisiting the site of his painful but formative adolescence also impelled Baxter to revisit, in his poetry, the themes and locales of the verse of that period. Family memories and Otago landscapes again feature, but always with the presence of death, at times subtly, at other times looming, within the poetic frame. A marked change in style accompanied these variations on earlier themes. Whereas the youthful poetry might, with ponderous metre and latinate diction, move towards a final grand, sonorous phrase, now unrhymed run-on couplets (increasingly the unit of choice in Baxter's later work) create a tone both direct and personal. Baxter's later poetry becomes stripped of artifice and abstraction, until all that remains is a personal voice 'almost ostentatiously matter of fact' (Vincent *O'Sullivan).

In 1967, Baxter also published two volumes of criticism—*Aspects of Poetry in New Zealand* and *The Man on the Horse*—and saw a number of his plays and mimes staged by Dunedin director Patric Carey, among them *The Band Rotunda, The Sore-Footed Man, The Bureaucrat* and *The Devil and Mr Mulcahy* (see also *Theatre). In 1971 Heinemann Educational published two volumes of his plays—*The Devil and Mr Mulcahy [and] The Band Rotunda* and *The Sore-Footed Man [and] The Temptations of Oedipus* (the latter performed in 1970). Just as Baxter's verse supplied several of the characters for these dramas, so his experiences as an alcoholic and working with alcoholics supplied a usefully emblematic 'tribal' context within which human frailties were examined through a mythical, or archetypal, lens. The majority of Baxter's drama is in Howard McNaughton's edition of his *Collected Plays* (1982).

In 1968 Dunedin's Catholic Education Office employed Baxter to prepare catechetical material and teach at Catholic schools, and his articles for the Catholic periodical *The Tablet* were collected and published in *The Flowering Cross* (1969). Yet the Fellowship appeared to have drained him of energy and refilled him with doubt. He struggled in his marriage, fearing the trap of domesticity; found difficulty relating to his children; and was dogged by the feeling that words had become impotent and should be replaced by actions.

Around April 1968 'a minor revelation' led him to think of Jerusalem (in Māori 'Hiruharama')—'the mission station on the Wanganui river'. He thought he might go to this small Māori settlement, bordered by a Catholic church and a convent, and 'form the nucleus of a community where the people, both Maori and pakeha, would try to live without money or books, worship God and work on the land'. Following the family's return to Wellington in December, Baxter left home to put his beliefs into practice.

Auckland was his initial stop. There he failed to hold down a job Hone *Tuwhare found for him at the Chelsea sugar refinery. All that came out of the experience was the trenchantly satirical poem *Ballad of the Stonegut Sugar Works*. He discovered his Auckland niche in a cluster of run-down squats in the suburb of Grafton. Number 7 Boyle Crescent, where he settled in Easter 1969, became a drop-in centre for drug addicts. Baxter, adopting the Māori transliteration of his first name, 'Hemi', set about counselling and attempting to establish a Narcotics Anonymous organisation similar to AA. His appearance—barefoot, bearded and shabbily dressed—attracted the attention of both media and police, who suspected his motives and morality. He put the drug users' side of the story in 'Ballad of the Junkies and the Fuzz', and also published a selection of twenty years' verse in *The *Rock Woman* (1969), but poetry was not his main focus. By August 1969, the Boyle Crescent period had ended and Baxter was heading for Jerusalem, to begin his commune.

He sought there to form a community structured around key 'spiritual aspects of Maori communal life', to recover values New Zealand's Pākehā urban society had lost. He recorded aspects of his philosophy of communality in *Jerusalem Sonnets* (1970) and *Jerusalem Daybook* (1971), but in practice the commune lacked order. Baxter could not regulate numbers or behaviour; the media sensationalised his activities; and the locals became increasingly uneasy. Problems compounded because he was often away—in Dunedin visiting his dying father; on speaking tours; and on 8 February 1971 protesting with young Māori radicals at Waitangi.

The commune's first phase ended in September 1971

and Baxter returned to Wellington, but in February 1972 the Jerusalem land-owners permitted him to return with a smaller, more cohesive, group. His last collection, *Autumn Testament* (1972), dates from this period.

By August 1972 Baxter was drained, physically and emotionally. He sought refuge on a small commune in Auckland. On 22 October he died of a coronary thrombosis.

A memorable literary and spiritual commemoration ensued. His body was escorted back by his family to Jerusalem where, in a rare honour for a Pākehā, he received a full Māori *tangi and was buried on tribal land, attended by hundreds of people from the many walks of life with which Baxter's intersected. A boulder inscribed 'HEMI / JAMES KEIR BAXTER / I WHANAU 1926 / I MATE 1972' marks the grave.

Other monuments included a number of posthumous publications: Futuna Press printed two small selections of religious writing, *The Six Faces of Love* (1972) and *Thoughts About the Holy Spirit* (1973); a selection of his last poems appeared in *Stonegut Sugar Works, Junkies and the Fuzz, Ode to Auckland, and Other Poems* (1972); and the Australian Max Harris paid tribute to Baxter's bawdy side by publishing *Two Obscene Poems* (1973). Of more importance were four posthumous collections edited by J.E. *Weir: *The Labyrinth: Some Uncollected Poems 1944–72* (1974), *The Bone Chanter: Unpublished Poems 1945–72* (1976); *The Holy Life and Death of Concrete Grady: Various Uncollected and Unpublished Poems* (1976); and, most significantly, *Collected Poems* (1980). Weir has also written *The Poetry of James K. Baxter* (1970), and edited, with Barbara Lyon, *A Preliminary Bibliography of Works by and Works about James K. Baxter* (1979).

Frank *McKay's *James K. Baxter as Critic* (1978) is an edition of selected critical writings, and his *Life of James K. Baxter* (1990) is the essential biography, although W.H. *Oliver's *James K. Baxter: A Portrait* (1983) offers an interesting perspective and a lavish selection of illustrations. Baxter's writing has generated a large amount of critical material, including a complete issue of the *Journal of New Zealand Literature* (vol. 13, 1995), but little has been written to rival O'Sullivan's critical monograph *James K. Baxter* (1976), although Charles *Doyle's *James K. Baxter* (1976) is more extensive.

O'Sullivan suggests that the real achievement of Baxter's verse is as 'the most complete delineation yet of a New Zealand mind. The poetic record of its shaping [being] as original an act as anything we have.' If, at times, Baxter appears to evaluate New Zealand society harshly, his judgements are always from the perspective of one intimately involved in the social process. His criticisms of national life and his ultimate decision to step out of the mainstream seemed to develop naturally from the preoccupations of a lifetime of verse. Yet these preoccupations were, as a rule, neither negative nor despairing. Rather, the deliberately mythological cast of mind that underpinned his poetry sought to place the individual (and the nation) within a wider frame by directing attention towards universal elements of human experience. The Baxter who, writing shortly before his death, found the Medusa's head of present-day urban civilisation—with its 'depersonalisation, centralisation, [and] desacralisation'—intolerable, could still find reason for hope 'in the hearts of people'.   PM

BAYNTON, Martin (1953–), children's writer, was born in London, attended art school and studied at Great Ormond St and St Bartholemew's Hospitals, before emigrating in 1987 to settle in Whangamata. He began his career in children's books in 1983 with illustrations for other writers, notably Russell Hoban. In 1991, he illustrated *Daniel's Dinosaurs* by Mary Carmine (1990), featuring a New Zealand landscape acceptable to the overseas market. Now writing and illustrating his own texts, he has made an impact particularly with *Jane and the Dragon* (1988), featuring a feisty Jane who reverses the usual male-against-dragon role of folk tale; *Why Do You Love Me?* (1989), a conversation between father and son, gently exploring fundamentals of love and behaviour; and *Baby Floats* (1991), exploring gravitational laws. He has also created the *Fifty* series about a lively tractor. Baynton has also written stories and plays for radio, and takes an active part in *Metaphor.   DH

BAYSTING, Arthur, see *Young New Zealand Poets, The.*

BEACH, Eric (1947–), born in Hastings, emigrated to Australia in 1972 where he became active as a performance poet, playwright and short story writer. He has been widely published in New Zealand and Australian periodicals. His first book of poems, *Lyrics and Blues* (1971), acknowledges, in 'Pilgrim', the influence of James K. *Baxter: 'I'm going to Jerusalem … To where the old poet / Writes a song with an axe.' Since emigrating he has published *Henry Lawson Petfoods* (1974), *Saint Kilda Meets Hugo Ball* (1974), *In Occupied Territory* (1977), *A Photo of Some People in a Football Stadium* (1978) and *Weeping for Lost Babylon* (1996). He has edited two collections of poetry, *Fair Deal Express: Writing from Kids at the Parks* (1984) and *Hey, Hey, Brass Buttons* (1990), and performs his work on the video recording *Louder than Words* (*c.*1986). In 1993 he talked to Adrienne Rewi of the Christchurch *Press (6 May) about how his self-imposed exile had allowed him to 'bloom' as a poet. Occasionally he returns to New Zealand to perform his poems, and an audio recording of him at Wellington's 'Lizard Lounge' (1987) is in the Victoria University of Wellington Library sound archives. His books cross the Tasman less readily and are difficult to obtain in New Zealand.   PM

BEAGLEHOLE, J.C. (1901–71), achieved high distinction as a historian partly because he wrote so well. M.H. *Holcroft ranked *The Life of Captain James Cook* (1974) as one of the three best New Zealand books; in *The Exploration of the Pacific* (1934, 1966), *New Zealand: A Short History* (1936) and *The Discovery of New Zealand* (1939, 1961) Beaglehole, like *Macaulay and others before him, made historical narrative a literary form, weaving complex threads into a robust and lucid prose, and sustaining a meditation on each subject's wider significance that never becomes self-displaying or opinionated. He had the true scholar's generosity, enlarging his subjects, showing James *Cook, for instance, to be not only the resourcefully pragmatic navigator the English class system had permitted, but a formidable and original mind and (most extraordinarily after two centuries of *Hawkesworth) an outstanding writer. Even such a commonly inward-looking project as a university history became, in Beaglehole's *The University of New Zealand* (1937) and *Victoria University College: An Essay Towards a History* (1949), a disquisition on the idea of a university which is still challenging and pertinent (with its emphasis on the essentially human resource and on a liberal definition of institutional culture). He won the Hubert Church Award for Prose in 1949.

The quality of his prose was honed partly by the practice of poetry. Though he has now disappeared from notice as a poet, Beaglehole was an active and representative mid-century figure. Robin *Hyde called him 'one of the finest verse-writers in New Zealand', and he was included in every anthology for three decades: Alexander and *Currie's *Treasury* (1926), Pope's *Kowhai Gold* (1930), Marris's *Best Poems* (1930s), *Curnow's *Book of New Zealand Verse* (1945) through to *Chapman and Bennett's *Anthology* (1956). He published mainly in *Spike: Victoria College Review*, which for a while he edited, and had work in the College anthology *The Old Clay Patch* (3rd edn, 1949), Auckland University's *Phoenix* and the journal *New Nation*. *Kowhai Gold* is dedicated to 'JCB', yet he survived even that to be one of Curnow's chosen in 1945. He published one collection, *Words for Music* (*Caxton, 1938).

His poems are characteristically metaphysical, meditations on often commonplace experiences like riding a bicycle, lighting a pipe, listening to music or visiting a cathedral or museum, which turn the poet's mind to the universal, the meaning and processes of life. This produces some good poems in the intellectual-contemplative mould later done rather better by M.K. *Joseph, such as 'Molecular Theory' or 'Lighting My Pipe', a 'musing' about the primeval forces of evolution. It produces some laboured ones, too, as when 'The Climber' plods upwards under a pack apparently laden with philosophy, conscious of the obligation 'Ever to strive with the fateful implacable will / Of the Invisible'. Beaglehole the poet is at his best in the few poems where he is surprised by personal feeling, as when 'In the Cotswolds' he is suddenly overwhelmed by what Curnow called (with reference to Robin Hyde) 'reversal of the colonist's nostalgia for "home"': 'A wind strikes—and my opened eyes are blind / With gazing on an unseen distant place; / My deaf ears hear Orongo-rongo's stones—/ Bloom bursts on wind-swept hills within my mind.' But even there, great lecturer that he was, he explains what he means once too often.

Beaglehole contributed to *Tomorrow* in the late 1930s and was on the *Literary Fund Advisory Committee 1959–61. He also served literature with one other of his considerable gifts, as typographic designer. Deeply informed in the new *typography of the 1930s, he was typographical editor for the *Centennial in 1940, and designer or adviser to *Whitcombe & Tombs, the New Zealand University Press, the Council for Educational Research and the Department of Internal Affairs, where he instructed the young Janet Wilkinson, later of *Blackwood and Janet Paul and Dame Janet Paul.

As one of only two New Zealanders appointed to the elite two dozen members of the Royal Order of Merit (the other is Rutherford), Beaglehole's major accomplishments and career are well known. Eric *McCormick's 'Biographical Sketch' in *Landfall* 100 (1971) is a good starting point. Born in Wellington, educated at Wellington College and Victoria University College (MA 1924) and London University (PhD 1929), he was a WEA tutor 1930–31, then lecturer at University of Auckland, until his dismissal in 1933, nominally on account of the *Depression, caused the country's greatest outcry about academic freedom (see F.A. de la Mare, *Academic Freedom in New Zealand 1932–34*, 1935). Appointment at Victoria in 1936 led eventually to promotion to professor in 1963. He was already CMG, but then came the honours—honorary doctorates at Oxford, Victoria, Otago and Sydney, FRSNZ, the OM in 1970; and many more. He was long-serving president of the New Zealand Council for Civil Liberties and the New Zealand Institute for International Affairs. His knowledge of art laid the foundations of Victoria University's important collection of New Zealand paintings.

He remained always a man of letters and of learning. His masterpiece was the editorial restoration that became *The Journals of Captain James Cook* (1955, 1961, 1967) and *The Endeavour Journal of Joseph Banks* (1962). Beaglehole's place in literature in the final summary is as an able poet, an excellent writer of prose narrative and a brilliant scholarly editor.   RR

BEALE, Fleur (1945–), author of teenage fiction, was born in Inglewood and educated there and at Victoria University and Christchurch Teachers' College. She now lives in Hamilton. She has taught at Melville HS, at first intermittently, since 1985. She began her writing career with a small reader and picture book. (Her mother, Estelle Corney, wrote *Pa's Top Hat*, 1980.) In quick succession, Beale then produced novels with strong teenage appeal: *Against the Tide* (1993), *Slide the Corner* (1993), *Driving a Bargain* (1994), *Over the Edge* (1994), *The Fortune Teller* (1995) and *Fifteen and Screaming* (1995). With an emphasis on various outdoor activities, such as rally driving and camping, and with characters intensely aware of their difficulties, social troubles and shortcomings, Beale shows her understanding of teenagers, male and female, and ability to motivate even reluctant readers.   DH

BEAMES, Margaret (1935–), children's writer, was born in Oxford, England, taught in England and Nairobi, and came to New Zealand in 1974. Part-time teaching gave her time to write children's plays and stories for radio, magazines and *School Journal*; picture books, including *The Plant that Grew and Grew*, illustrated by Donna Hoyle (1984); readers in New Zealand and Australian publications; and most notably novels, including *The Greenstone Summer* (1977); *Hidden Valley*, illustrated by Michael Dee (1983); *The Parkhurst Boys*, illustrated by Susan Opie (1986), in which Beames, like Eve *Sutton, brings a fictional boy on the only 'convict' ship to New Zealand; *Clown Magic*, illustrated by Susan Opie (1989); *The Glass Tower* (1991), a futuristic novel; *The Girl in Blue*, illustrated by Brent Putze (1993), a modern ghost story; and *Snap Happy*, with co-author and illustrator, John Tarlton (1995). Beames received the 1986 Enid Conley Memorial Award in Australia, and also wrote *Karen: Her Fight Against Leukemia* with Karen Scotson (1988).   DH

BEARDSLEY, Eric (1925–), a prolific journalist, published his significant first novel, *Blackball 08*, in 1984. It presents with sympathetic insight the causes, characters and events of the famous 1908 coalminers' strike, an important victory for the Labour movement. Lawrence *Jones in the *OHNZLE describes it as 'an

ambitious attempt to evoke the mining community of Blackball' and acknowledges the effective use of framing comments by 'an ageing Bob Semple, looking back … from the disillusioning perspective of the society of fretful sleepers of the 1950s'. Beardsley spent his early childhood on the West Coast, then from 1931 lived in Christchurch, as reporter, sub-editor and leader-writer for the *Press, 1944–64, and as the University of Canterbury's Information Officer and editor if its *Chronicle*, 1965–88. A frequent book reviewer, principally for the *Press*, he is also co-author of *A History of the University of Canterbury 1873–1973* (1972) and *Design for a Century* (1987).   RR

BEER, Christina (1942–), poet, is best known as the painter Christina Conrad, who has had numerous exhibitions. She was born at Te Marua, near Upper Hutt, and lived in rural areas of the North Island before moving to Sydney. She has published some poetry as Conrad, such as 'Song for 1988 and you' in *Kiwi & Emu* (1989), but her main literary accomplishment is the small but powerful collection *This Tree Has Thorns: Poems & Clay Paintings* (1974). These sensual, immediate poems offer a combination of early feminism, hippydom, sexual liberation and stylistic experimentation. Often about a woman's intimacy with the landscape she lives in, they have a symbolic intensity that she has also moved on to in her paintings. One of the most powerful, about the loss of a child, was revised into more acceptable form as 'waiheke 1972—rocky bay' in the *Penguin Book of New Zealand Verse* (1985). Beer is represented in *anthologies of women's writing such as *Private Gardens* (1977) and *Yellow Pencils* (1988).   AMcL

BELICH, James (1956–), historian, is recognised as a writer of merit as well as for significantly reinterpreting nineteenth-century New Zealand history, especially Māori/Pākehā relations. His *The New Zealand Wars and the Victorian Interpretation of Racial Conflict* (1980) won the international Trevor Reed Memorial Prize for historical scholarship, has sold over 20 000 copies and is the basis of a television documentary screened in 1998. (See also *War literature: New Zealand Wars.) *I Shall Not Die: Titokowaru's War, New Zealand, 1868–9* (1989) won the Adam Award for outstanding contribution to New Zealand literature 1989–90. *Making Peoples: A History of the New Zealanders: From Polynesian Settlement to the End of the Nineteenth Century* (1996) is the first of a projected two-volume history. Belich's writing is confident in its broad sweep and vigorous in its detail, whether he writes about Māori techniques of trench warfare or the courting rituals of the society elite of Tauranga in the late nineteenth century. He was born in Wellington and educated at Onslow College, Victoria University (MA 1978), and, as a Rhodes Scholar, Oxford University (DPhil 1981). He has been deputy editor of the *Dictionary of New Zealand Biography*, lecturer at Victoria University and is now professor of history at the University of Auckland.   RR

BELL, Col. George William (1832–1907), served for seven years as US Consul at Sydney, Australia, before visiting New Zealand in 1903. Anticipating a colony 'submerged with socialism' he found in Seddon's New Zealand 'the most sturdy democracy civilization has ever produced'. Unsurprisingly, fantasy was the vehicle Bell chose to reveal this. His novel *Mr. Oseba's Last Discovery* (1904) tells of Amoora Oseba, a native of the earth's hollow centre—'Symmes Hole'—who journeys for five years among the surface dwellers (the 'Outeroos') searching for a society as enlightened as his own. His last discovery is 'Zelania fair' ('New Zealand on the map'), an idyllic land in which there is such social perfection. Up to this point the novel is bad pastiche of Jules *Verne, sprinkled with Shakespearean platitudes. Shifting rhetorical gear, Bell sets about eulogising New Zealand's politics, society and culture. The *Encyclopedia of Science Fiction* comments that the novel 'promotes New Zealand real estate by comparing that country to the edenic interior.' Numerous photographs of political figures and scenic locales (mostly unrelated to the text) enforce the impression that New Zealand's Tourist and Publicity Department played a role in the book's production. While Bell's rabid anglophilia, his easy racism and his models of eugenically directed social engineering are disturbing, his poetry is truly alarming: a reverie on 'Zelania' in 105 rhymed couplets ('At eve or dawn, we gaze upon / The busy, "blowy" Wellington') looks good alongside 'The Maori Maid of Rotorua': 'Did you ever see Maggie of Rotoru'? / You would never imagine what she can do / For the mouths of hell, / With a magic spell, / This little brown maid—/ As I have said—/ Will lead you over, and under and through.' Like some of Hollywood's 'B' movies, a reprint of *Mr Oseba's Last Discovery* could see it become a cult classic.   PM

BELL, John, published his single novel, *In the Shadow of the Bush*, in 1899. The setting for this bland historical romance is Bloomsbury, a fictitious frontier town situated on the rugged margins of the Wellington province. Generously described by T.M. *Hocken as being 'full of mild incident', *In the Shadow of the Bush* depicts land-hungry settlers' attempts to roll back the bush and the Māori. The intention is metaphorically to associate successful subjugation of native flora with nation building. The melodramatic implications of colonial economics

seem to have given his imagination its greatest stimulus, however. The character Ponsonby, for example, exposes the harsh reality of courtship in late-colonial New Zealand when he discovers that only when he is a large landed proprietor does his suit excite response in his beloved's breast.   PM

BELLAMY, Edward, see **Utopian literature.**

BENNETT, Maria, is the putative author, or perhaps only the narrator of the pamphlet *A Narrative of the Sufferings of Maria Bennett* (Dublin 1846), which Bagnall classifies, with considerable probability, as fiction. Her tale bears some resemblance to that of Eliza Fraser among the Australian aborigines. Transported for pilfering, Maria finds herself shipwrecked in New Zealand. She is captured by Māori and married to one of them, to whom she bears a child. After three years in New Zealand she is taken aboard an English ship. Back in England, the Captain gives her up 'to the authorities of the law'. Here there is a sudden and unexplained switch to a third-person narrative: 'She was found guilty of being a returned convict, and received the sentence of transportation for life. The prisoner then asked permission to address the court upon her sufferings, which drew tears from all present.' Maria is pardoned. The pamphlet's concluding sentence suddenly returns to the first person—'I hope this will be a warning to all and to the rising generation'—and the curious document is then signed 'Maria Bennett, March 25th, 1846'. The image of New Zealand is of a country more terrifying than the penal colonies themselves. Memories of the *Boyd* massacre of 1809 may well have inspired or coloured the narrative.   NW

BENSEMANN, Leo (1912–86), an artist and editor closely associated with *Caxton Press, was descended from German immigrants who settled in Nelson province in the nineteenth century. Born in Takaka, he went to Nelson with his family in 1920 and attended Nelson College (1925–30). In 1931 he moved to Christchurch, working initially as a commercial artist while taking night classes at the Canterbury School of Art, though he was largely self-taught. First known for his 'weird' bookplates, he began contributing to Caxton Club publications, from *Oriflamme* (1933) onwards. While assisting with the printing of his *Fantastica: Thirteen Drawings* (Caxton Press, 1937)—a book of illustrations to a highly diverse range of literary texts, from Marlowe's *Doctor Faustus* to the Brothers Grimm—he showed an aptitude for printing that led Denis *Glover to offer him a partnership in the Caxton Press, a position he held until his retirement in 1978. *A

Second Book of Leo Bensemann's Work—a miscellany of drawings, engravings on wood, calligraphy and typography—was published in 1952, and he contributed to many other Caxton publications as designer, typographer, illustrator and printer. In 1938 he began exhibiting with the Christchurch Group, the studios he shared with his close friends Lawrence *Baigent and Rita Angus becoming for a time the unofficial headquarters of The Group, for whom he also designed and printed annual catalogues. After The Group disbanded in 1977, he held several successful solo shows in Christchurch (1979, 1981) and Wellington (1983). He was highly idiosyncratic in both graphic work and painting, and is seen at his best in his 1940s portraits and late landscapes of Takaka and Canterbury. He was involved from the outset with the production of *Landfall* and briefly became editor 1972–75. He also founded and co-edited *Ascent*, a journal of the visual arts (Caxton, 1967–69). While primarily a visual artist, Bensemann was widely read and through Caxton made significant contributions to literature as typographer, printer, illustrator, editor and publisher, and as a productive member of a literary and artistic group.   PS

BERTRAM, James (1910–93), author, foreign correspondent and academic, was the son of a Presbyterian minister. He was born at Devonport, but when he was 4 his family moved to Australia. In 1924 he returned to New Zealand and attended Waitaki BHS, where he developed enduring friendships with Charles *Brasch and Ian *Milner. At the University of Auckland he excelled academically, earning one of two 1932 Rhodes Scholarships to Oxford University, the second going to Geoffrey *Cox. Active in Auckland University's Literary Club, Bertram edited the first two issues of *Phoenix*. One incident at Auckland became the catalyst for his developing left-wing sympathies: in April 1932, the heart of the Depression, he was among students deputised to control rioting relief workers. Like John *Mulgan, who fictionalised the riots in *Man Alone*, his sympathies turned to the workers and he renounced his policing role.

At Oxford's New College, Bertram took a First in English, joined the University Labour Club and founded the Oxford branch of the Independent Labour Party. In 1935, intending to become a foreign correspondent, he joined the London *Times*, but left in 1936 to take up a Rhodes Trust offer to spend the year in *China. There he scored a major journalistic coup by witnessing the Xian incident: where officers kidnapped Chiang Kai-shek to compel him to respond to Japanese aggression. He recorded this experience in *Crisis in China: The Story of the Sian Mutiny* (1937; rpt. as *First Act in China*, New

York, 1938). Around the same time he helped smuggle Zhou Enlai's wife out of Beijing ahead of Japanese troops. In 1937, shortly after the Red Army's Long March, he became the first official 'British' visitor to interview Mao Zedong and Zhou Enlai, the Mao interviews later being included in the Chinese leader's *Selected Works*. Soon after he began working with Madame Sun Zhongshan, publicising the China Defence League (CDL) to mobilise foreign aid to help counter the Japanese invasion. In 1939 he published *Unconquered: Journal of a Year's Adventures Among the Fighting Peasants of North China* (rpt. 1975); and *North China Front*. Still working for the CDL in 1940, he was in Hong Kong when the Japanese invaded. He fought until the island surrendered. As a prisoner of war in Tokyo, labouring on near starvation diet at a railyard, he witnessed the city's incendiary bombing (see *Japan).

Returning to New Zealand in 1945, Bertram continued fund-raising for China, primarily to assist Rewi *Alley's Sandan school. He also helped found *Landfall* in 1947. The same year he accepted a lectureship in English at Victoria University of Wellington, retiring as professor in 1975. His academic publications include *Towards a New Zealand Literature* (1971); *Charles Brasch* (1976), which received the 1977 Wattie Book of the Year Award; an anthology, *New Zealand Love Poems* (1977); an edition, the *Letters of Thomas Arnold the Younger, 1850–1900* (1980); a biography of *Dan Davin* (1983); and *Flight of the Phoenix: Critical Notes on New Zealand Writers* (1985). He published one collection of poetry, *Occasional Verses* (1971). The importance of Asia is evident in his remaining publications: *The Shadow of a War: A New Zealander in the Far East, 1939–1946* (1947, rpt. as *Beneath the Shadow*, New York, 1947); *Return to China* (1957); *The Young Traveller in China Today* (1961) and his fascinating autobiography, *Capes of China Slide Away: A Memoir of Peace and War, 1910–1980* (1993).   PM

BEST, Elsdon (1856–1931), ethnologist, published extensively on traditional Māori lore, life and customs. His first contact with the Māori was inauspicious, however. In 1881, as a member of the Armed Constabulary, he participated in the destructive raid on the Māori pacifist community of Parihaka at which Te Whiti-o-Rongomai and Tohu Kakahi were arrested, with hundreds of their followers, for resisting government surveys. Yet it was also at this time that Best's interest in the Māori was stimulated by Pākehā scholars. He helped found the Polynesian Society in 1891, and began interviewing Māori tribal elders. In 1893 his mediation in a dispute over the government's attempt to survey a road through the Urewera district, without the consent of the

Tūhoe people, set him on the path to becoming New Zealand's first professional ethnographer. Living among the Tūhoe 1895–1910, as a Māori health inspector for the Department of Public Health from 1904, he wrote his major work, *Tuhoe: The Children of the Mist* (1925, 2 vols.), and published numerous articles and poems in various periodicals. He was appointed ethnologist at the Dominion Museum in 1910, publishing a further ten substantial monographs and a major work of ethnography, *The Maori* (1924, 2 vols.). Characteristic of his style, this is detailed and exact, its sources assiduously documented, and its rhetorical fabric typically woven with dry wit, terse observation and personal anecdote.

Although Best's work was acclaimed during his lifetime by Māori leaders, recent assessments have questioned his western ethnographic method and its inherent assumption that because Māori were a 'dying race' he should focus on the historical, rather than contemporary, people. Other critics express concern with Best's paternalistic portrayal of the 'primitives'; his tendency to ignore the crucial role of tribal groupings in Māori society by depicting them as a homogenous people; and his reconstructions of Māori migration and pre-European Māori society that are contradicted by archaeological findings. Ranginui ★Walker's comment that the 'expropriation of knowledge and its transformation from the spoken to the written word is ... one of many facets of colonisation' is just, but the impetus Best's work has given to recent Māori revaluation of their culture also deserves recognition. E.W.G. Craig has written a biography, *Man of the Mist* (1964).   PM

BETHELL, (Mary) Ursula (1874–1945), poet, was born in Surrey, England, on St Faith's Day, October 6—a day whose religious significance was later recalled in the name she gave to a 'House of Sacred Learning' in Christchurch. Her parents, who had both spent some years in New Zealand before their marriage in London, returned eighteen months after her birth. They settled in Christchurch, and then Rangiora, near Richard Bethell's large sheep ★station, Pahau Pastures. Rangiora, with the Ashley River in the foreground and Mount Grey in the background, quickly became a significant element in Ursula Bethell's imagination, her affection evident in the long, unfinished sequence 'By the River Ashley', published in full for the first time in her *Collected Poems* (ed. Vincent ★O'Sullivan, 1985; new edn 1997).

On her father's death in 1885, the family moved back to Christchurch, where at Christchurch GHS she came into contact with the principal, Helen Connon, maternal grandmother of James K. ★Baxter. The next phase of her education was in England at Oxford High School for Girls, then a finishing school near Nyon in Switzerland. At Oxford she met the Mayhew family, with whom she remained very close friends—in particular, Ruth, to whom many of the 'Garden' poems were addressed, and Arthur, who was influential in their publication. Though she then returned briefly to New Zealand, Bethell spent twenty of the next twenty-five years out of the country, before finally settling in Christchurch, at Rise Cottage in the Cashmere Hills.

On one European trip she studied painting in Geneva, but her talents in that direction were only modest, and when she returned to England she engaged in social work and joined an Anglican community popularly known as the Grey Ladies. Although she did not remain, and in fact expressed some strongly negative opinions about the community, she did maintain strong connections with formal institutions within the Church of England, and continued to perform social work within a broadly religious context. In New Zealand, too, during her several trips back, she displayed the same enthusiasm for social work and educational work within religious contexts. Throughout these years, another side to her religious character emerged, which, while not genuinely contemplative, did reveal that she had an attraction towards some form of withdrawal from secular society. Her intellectual growth was also coupled with an interest in philosophy and theology which she developed throughout her life.

Most of Bethell's verse—all that she published in her lifetime—was written during her ten years at Rise Cottage with her close companion, Effie Pollen. She seldom spoke of their relationship, but a letter to Monte ★Holcroft describes Pollen's death as 'a complete shattering of my life ... from her I have had love, tenderness, and understanding ... and close and happy companionship.' Later, she described the relationship as 'prevailingly maternal', a bond of mutual protection and support, and revealed, to Holcroft and others, the difficulty she had writing poetry after her friend's death.

The first of Bethell's collections, ★*From a Garden in the Antipodes*, is her best-known work, and contains some of the most frequently anthologised pieces, but it is not the volume she most valued. *Time and Place* (★Caxton, 1936) was deliberately a memorial to Effie Pollen, although it owes something of its selection and arrangement to D'Arcy ★Cresswell, who wrote to Bethell with a fine certainty about his own judgment of her verse. Denis ★Glover objected to the title, but it accurately suggests the subject matter, with its attention to seasonal cycles and focus on mutability; and it is accurate, too, in its less concrete overtones, for the poetry of *Time and Place* is quite deliberately writ larger, and attempts more by way of generalisation. *Day and Night* (Caxton, 1939) included several pieces for which there had not been a place in the earlier work, but in many ways it demonstrates similar interests and formal properties, and like the earlier volumes it preserved the anonymity she valued. Like the earlier volumes, too, it includes some poetry that celebrates the beauty of the natural world, though such celebration is not her characteristic note, nor is it her most significant, for she is not a Romantic poet. She is, as O'Sullivan suggests, 'the most firmly, traditionally Christian' of New Zealand poets. Her preoccupation with time and the natural world owes more to religious considerations than Romantic ones. Her first volume had displayed a constant awareness of her separation from 'loved and lost London', but the sense of exile is not confined to that volume of verse letters; rather, the sense of exile takes on a traditionally religious dimension, and informs much of her writing.

After Pollen's death, Bethell sold Rise Cottage and moved to a flat in the house she had gifted to the Church of England, known as St Faith's House of Sacred Learning, which was intended as a centre for training Anglican deaconesses. Despite indifferent health, she maintained an extensive correspondence and a wide circle of friends. Persuaded by some (including Lawrence ★Baigent, Charles ★Brasch and Allen ★Curnow), she agreed to the preparation of a new selection of her poetry, to be published under her own name. Interrupted by her final cancer, her *Collected Poems* was published in 1950. It brought together all the poems from the three published volumes, together with a number of others, including the intensely private sequence of six 'Memorial Poems' which record, year by year, the anniversary of the death of Effie Pollen.   PW

'Between Earth and Sky', by Patricia ★Grace, published in *The Dream Sleepers and Other Stories* (1980), has quickly become one of the most admired and anthologised of all New Zealand short stories. Told in the voice of a mother addressing her newborn baby (though this is not immediately apparent), it is structured as a triptych: her awakening and heavy walk across the paddocks to where her farmer husband is sawing trees; the arrival at hospital, greeted by high-spirited nurses familiar from her seven previous deliveries; and her first moment of intimate communication with the new baby. The movement from solitude through the noisy activity of children, nurses and the 'work' of birth, and then back to quietness alone with the child, with a brief reprise of the opening, has a musical shapeliness. Only three pages long, the story's writing is spare and elliptical but finely textured in sound and significance. The title brings in the myth of ★Rangi and Papatuanuku with its complex resonance of the universality of procreation and the tension in nature

between creation and competition. This birth frees the woman from self-preoccupation to love her husband again, brings 'freedom from the envy I'd felt … Unable to match his step … But I could love him again this morning', while the growing children move elementally between earth and sky, 'leaping and shouting through the long grass with the swamp mud drying and caking on their legs and arms'. The mix of Māori and Pākehā names for the children and nurses ('Rawhiti and Jones') strengthens the sense of a contemporary retelling of the story of Rangi and Papa. Childbirth and parenthood are treated equally directly and without sentimentality; pregnancy is a 'great hump and swelling', the baby is 'wet and grey', 'flailing and screaming', the children are boisterous or 'reluctant'. The emotional movement from resentment to love and the mythic dimension are enhanced and made credible by this honesty and directness in the story's physical world.   RR

BEYER, Tony (1948–   ), born in Auckland, was a prominent avant-garde poet of the 1970s–80s, with *Jesus Hobo* (1971) and *the meat and other poems* (1974), followed later by *Dancing Bear* (1981), *Brute Music* (1984) and *The Singing Ground* (★Caxton, 1986). He is represented in the Penguin (1985) and Oxford (1996) anthologies, as well as collections of contemporary verse, and has published frequently in ★*Landfall* and elsewhere. The earlier poems are intensely personal, often cryptic, often religious in connotation, usually bleak in tone, with recurrent images of pain and death suggestive of intense frustration or suppressed anger ('They're selling corpses / from the night train'). Poems like 'The Kill' (set in a freezing works) insist on the physical at its most repugnant: 'the necessary vile / dead breath that went / home with us all on / hair and clothes and skin'. Some later poems are more anecdotal (as in 'Coming Home', about his father coming to terms with family life after the war), even ironically humorous, though the prevailing attitude is still what Iain Sharp in *Landfall* 154 (1985) called 'fierce loathing'. Beyer's language, always resourceful, at its best can have the bite of strangeness: 'who knew without the aid / of quadrat wires and trowels and formalin / the shape of a habitat / where nothing innocent lasts long / and clean fangs weave and glint' ('Island Waters').   RR

Beyond the Palisade (1944), James K. ★Baxter's remarkable debut volume, is a selection of thirty-four poems, from some 500 written by him between the ages of 15 and 18.

The unusual events surrounding the publication of this first book mesh nicely with Baxter's mythologising of his life. In August 1944 Baxter visited the ★Caxton Press's Christchurch office with his mother. While she presented Caxton's editor, Lawrence *Baigent, with a bundle of her son's poems, the poet himself just stood there 'gazing rather vacantly around him'. Baigent's understandable misgivings about the quality of this callow youth's poetry turned to amazement upon reading it, and he promptly offered to publish a book.

Also amazed by Baxter's poetry was Allen *Curnow, whose groundbreaking A *Book of New Zealand Verse 1923–45 was in preparation for publication by Caxton the following year. Curnow selected six poems from Beyond the Palisade and added a section to his seminal introduction in which he classed Baxter's poems as 'a new occurrence in New Zealand: strong in impulse and confident in invention, with qualities of youth in verse which we have lacked'. His endorsement established Baxter's reputation before most New Zealanders had read his work. Despite this, Baxter privately acknowledged a certain unevenness in the volume and described it to Baigent as 'a sort of poet's progress'.

Delays at the binder's meant that the book did not go on sale until 1945, in time for Denis *Glover, who had just returned from the war, to design the cover. Critics commented on Baxter's style and tone, with its mix of imitation and assimilation of numerous major poets of the English canon—Yeats, Auden, MacNeice, Keats, Blake, Shelley and others. No one, however, disagreed with Curnow's observation that Baxter had also written 'some poems which could only be his and only a New Zealander's'.   PM

Bibliography. The essential bibliography for New Zealand literature is John Thomson's chapter 'Bibliography' in *OHNZLE (1991, 1998), which is a revision of his New Zealand Literature to 1977 (1980). It includes sections on reference works, history and criticism, anthologies, periodicals and bibliographical notes on selected individual writers. Māori-language material is covered by Jane McRae's chapter 'Māori Literature: A Survey', also in OHNZLE. A comprehensive annual survey from 1964 is provided by the 'Annual Bibliography of Commonwealth Literature: New Zealand' in the Journal of Commonwealth Literature. Recent criticism is listed and annotated in Mark *Williams, Post-Colonial Literatures in English: Southeast Asia, New Zealand and the Pacific, 1970–1992 (Boston, 1996). Survey articles on recent poetry, novels, short stories, theatre and criticism are published irregularly in the *Journal of New Zealand Literature.

For poetry the major bibliographies are P. Serle, A Bibliography of Australasian Poetry and Verse (Melbourne University Press, 1925) and the typescript limited edition of New Zealand Poetry: A Select Bibliography 1920–1972, compiled by J.E. *Weir and Barbara Lyon

(University of Canterbury Library, 1977). Selected living poets are listed in Contemporary Poets (St James Press, 1991, 1996).

For fiction 'A Bibliography of New Zealand Prose Fiction 1778–1948', the second part of Joan C. Gries's 1951 Auckland University College doctoral thesis 'An Outline of Prose Fiction in New Zealand', is still very useful. The standard bibliography for novels is J.A.S. Burns, New Zealand Novels and Novelists 1861–1979: An Annotated Bibliography (Auckland, 1981). Selected living novelists are listed in Contemporary Novelists (St James Press, 1992).

Drama is listed in Howard McNaughton, New Zealand Drama: A Bibliographical Guide (University of Canterbury Library, 1974). Updates are available from the author on disk, and in the Playmarket Directory of New Zealand Plays and Playwrights (Wellington, 1992). Selected living playwrights are listed in Contemporary Dramatists (St James Press, 1994).

Individual writers are listed, selectively, in Thomson and for Māori and Polynesian writers a very broad coverage is provided by Norman Simms, Writers from the South Pacific: A Bio-Bibliographic Critical Encyclopedia (Washington, DC, 1991) and Supplement (1992). Katherine *Mansfield is covered by B.J. Kirkpatrick, A Bibliography of Katherine Mansfield (Oxford, 1989), Katherine Mansfield: Manuscripts in the Alexander Turnbull Library (1988) and Nelson Wattie, A Bibliography of Katherine Mansfield References 1970–1984 (Journal of New Zealand Literature, No. 3, 1985). Other bibliographies in monographic form are A Preliminary Bibliography of Works by and Works About James K. *Baxter, compiled by J.E. Weir and Barbara Lyon (University of Canterbury, 1979) and Ngaio *Marsh: A Bibliography of English Language Publications, compiled by Rowan Gibbs and Richard Williams (Scunthorpe, 1990). Bibliographies for other writers have appeared irregularly in the periodicals Australian and New Zealand Studies in Canada and the Journal of New Zealand Literature. Selected bibliographies can be found in critical or biographical studies of individual writers.

Literary periodicals are listed in Iris Park, New Zealand Periodicals of Literary Interest (National Library Service, 1962), and in an appendix to Stephen Hamilton's 1996 University of Auckland doctoral thesis, New Zealand English Language Periodicals of Literary Interest Active 1920s–1960s: 'Appendix I: An Annotated Bibliography of New Zealand English Language Periodicals of Literary Interest Active 1920s–1960s'. Hamilton has also produced An Annotated Bibliography and Select Author Index for 'The Mirror': July 1922–March 1963 (Department of English, University of Auckland, 1993), and Annotated Bibliography and Select Author Index for 'The Triad: A Monthly Journal of Music, Science and Art' 1893–1927 as a computer file. Published indexes were produced for *Landfall, *Arena, *Mate, *Islands and *Sport, and in J.J. Herd's *Index to *'Tomorrow' 1934–40* (University of Otago, 1962), and the *Index to the *'New Zealand Listener' 1939–1987* (National Library, 1995, microfiche).

Theses are listed in 'A Checklist of Theses and Dissertations on Topics of New Zealand Literature Completed and Currently in Progress at New Zealand Universities at 1 July 1991, and Some Held in Other New Zealand Locations' in the *Journal of New Zealand Literature* No. 8, 1990, and 'Supplement', in No. 12, 1994.

Two bibliographies of publishers are worthy of note, Ian F. McLaren, *The *Caxton Press of Christchurch New Zealand: Annotated Bibliography 1933–1978*, 2nd rev. edn (Melbourne, 1995), and *The *Wai-te-ata Press, 1962–1992* (Victoria University of Wellington Library, 1992).

Literary bibliographies in progress and recently published are listed annually in *Bibliographical Work in New Zealand* (University of Waikato Library, 1980–).   JT

Big Season, The (1962), is Maurice *Gee's first novel. See also *Sport.

BIGGS, Bruce (1921–), is a major linguist and lexicographer of Māori. His *The Structure of New Zealand Maori* (USA 1961, New Zealand 1969) was a pioneering scholarly study, and his *English–Maori Dictionary* (1966) the first of the twentieth century. It was followed by his *Complete English–Maori Dictionary* (1981), *English–Maori and Māori–English Dictionary* (1990) and *Cook Islands Maori Dictionary* (1995). He also wrote *Maori Marriage: An Essay in Reconstruction* (1960) and edited and translated *Nga Iwi o Tainui: The Traditional History of the Tainui People* (1995) from the manuscript of Pei Te Hurinui *Jones. Born in Auckland, Biggs became professor of anthropology and since 1984 emeritus professor at Auckland University, and was awarded OBE (1986) and CBE (1996) for services to linguistics, education and the Māori people.   RR

BILBROUGH, Norman (1941–), has published short stories widely for twenty years, winning the *Sunday Star Times* competition in 1995. A popular and frequent contributor to the *NZ Listener* and *School Journal*, especially, and to radio, he writes with a concise narrative and tersely authentic dialogue that give credibility to the often painful subject matter. Michael *Gifkins described the stories as 'litanies of unrelieved angst', while paying tribute to their honesty and imaginative grip 'beyond the confines of the page'. At times this comes from a near-surrealist fusion of setting and metaphor: 'At meals she

would feel as wooden as the table. And the talk had the substance of wood' ('Loss'). A droll sense of humour is also distinctive. Owen *Marshall admires the stories as 'perceptive, understated, mined with wit and sub-text'. Bilbrough has published two collections of stories, *Man with Two Arms* (1991) and *The Birdman Hunts Alone* (1994). Born in Feilding, he was educated in Wellington, where he still lives, having worked as a teacher, literary assessor and writer.   RR

BILLING, Graham (1936–), novelist and journalist, was born in Dunedin and educated at Otago BHS and the University of Otago, where his father was professor of economics. After four years working on ships—an experience later turned to account in his fourth and arguably his finest novel, *The Slipway* (1973)—he became a journalist, working 1958–77 for various New Zealand newspapers and in radio. As information officer for the New Zealand Antarctic Research Programme (1962–64) he spent several months at Scott Base. He exploited this Antarctic experience in his first novel, *Forbush and the Penguins* (1965), which was adapted as a feature film and remains his best-known work (see *Existentialism). Its intense exploration of the character's inner world sets the pattern for the early novels, though *The Alpha Trip* (1969) is more a carefully plotted thriller. Set largely in Wellington (where Billing was then an investigative journalist), it is about a communist plot to overthrow an American communications base in Blenheim. Billing's early experience of hunting, shooting, fishing and sailing around Dunedin ('Port Paradise' in the books) informs the setting and, to a lesser extent, the action of his next three novels: *Statues* (1971), *The Slipway* and *The Primal Therapy of Tom Purslane* (1980). A more important autobiographical element in *The Slipway* is Billing's long battle with alcoholism, giving the book a compelling authenticity.

In *The Chambered Nautilus* (1993), Billing partly breaks the solipsistic mould; the plot spans two centuries and involves a handful of major characters. While some scenes, particularly those relating to the sea and to Antarctica, are superbly realised, the plot outlines are often obscured by the highly charged subjective style (full of symbolism and digression) carried over from his earlier work. Billing's other writing includes a cycle of poems, *Changing Countries* (1980), inspired by a two-year teaching stint in Australia (1974–75); three radio plays, 'Mervyn Gridfern versus the Baboons' (1966) plus adaptations of *Forbush and the Penguins* (1966) and *The Slipway* (1977); and the text for three works of non-fiction: *South: Man and Nature in Antarctica* (1964), *New Zealand: The Sunlit Land* (1966) and *The New Zealanders* (1975, revised 1979).   RCo

BINNEY, Don (1940–), is a painter, novelist and art writer. Born in Auckland, he studied at Elam School of Fine Arts 1958–61 and has taught painting there since 1974. Binney became widely known in the 1960s–70s for his paintings of the New Zealand landscape, to which he added iconic reminders of the specifics of his locale. These included native birds, colonial architecture, familiar landforms, especially of the west coast north of Auckland, and signs of human impact on the New Zealand environment. In 1985 he published his first novel, *Long Lives the King*. Binney's essays on the work of other artists are often published in *Art New Zealand*. Increasingly he has recognised the interdependence of his writing and his art: 'There may be few formal parallels between what I write and what I draw/paint, but there are resonances in the production process. Exogenous elements within my art-pieces, for example, are analogous to quotes, or extra-textual reference in writing' (Michael Dunn, *Contemporary Painting in New Zealand*, 1997).   CB

Biografi: An Albanian Quest (1993), a semi-fictional travel book by Lloyd *Jones, after a positive initial reception in UK and Germany achieved some notoriety when British reviewer Margaret Driscoll in the *Sunday Times* attacked it for mixing documentary and invented material. Written in a style of understated documentary reportage, the book narrates the rigorous and sometimes dangerous journey of a New Zealand journalist through post-Communist Albania, in search of Petar Shapallo, the rumoured double of the deposed dictator, Enver Hoxha. The double's appearance may have been changed by surgery, 'so I was left with the name which few people remembered, and a face fewer still had seen'. The narrator's memories of a Wairarapa short-wave radio enthusiast, Cliff Dalziel, whose global contacts had sparked his boyhood interest in Albania, link the narrative, and its implications, to New Zealand.

The book was presented and at first received as factual: 'In the last months of 1991, Lloyd Jones went looking for Petar Shapallo, the dentist who had spent half his life standing in for the Albanian dictator …' says the dust jacket, calling it 'a gripping true adventure story'. It was entered and shortlisted in the non-fiction section of the New Zealand Book Awards. 'Jones's adventures are so fantastic that one is repeatedly tempted to assure oneself that this book is not a piece of fiction. But no, this is the true story of a traveller,' said one German review of the translation. It benefited from interest at that time in the often shocking revelations about Eastern Europe's Communist regimes. When the considerable element of imaginative, almost allegorical, material became known, Jones acknowledged that major figures,

including Shapallo and Dalziel, were 'imaginative devices', and compared his procedure to that of other travel writers such as Bruce Chatwin, who had also used the quest convention, in necessarily combining the invented and the real. In this confusion of definition, the significance of the title became apparent, with its reference to the often invented 'biografis', records on citizens kept by the Albanian secret police.

Discussion in New Zealand included an interview with Jones and an article of self-defence by him in *Quote Unquote* (September, December 1993), positive reviews by James *McNeish (whose *Lovelock* had in 1986 similarly mixed documentary and fictional material) and by Mark *Williams in *Landfall 187 (1994) ('The effect is to carry us into the utter corruption of Albanian political life more radically than either a strictly realistic or a flagrantly fantastic kind of writing might have managed'), and a riposte to this by Chris *Else in *Landfall 189 (1995), drawing on his own experience of Albania to argue that 'By inventing Shapallo … Jones is to some small degree rewriting history in exactly the same way that Hoxha himself rewrote the history of his purged opponents', and comparing the result unfavourably with the 'responsibility to other people's reality' in Jung Chang's *Wild Swans*. In March 1994 Jones and Chang pursued the subject in a panel discussion on the topic 'Writing a Life' in Wellington's *Writers and Readers Week, a discussion which has several times been rebroadcast and is perhaps most memorable for the vigorous attack by Patrick *White's biographer David Marr on any confusion between invention and biography.
                                                            RR

BIRKINSHAW, Frank, see **JEPSON, Margaret.**

BISHOP, Gavin (1946–), children's writer and illustrator, was born in Invercargill and studied painting with Russell *Clark and Rudi Gopas at Canterbury University's School of Fine Arts. Currently Head of Art at Christ's College, Christchurch, he also conducts the writing–illustrating course in the National Diploma of Children's Literature for Christchurch College of Education. He has visited Japan several times, and went to Russia in 1990 on a cultural exchange. Bishop enjoys illustrating traditional folk tales set in a recognisable New Zealand landscape. These include *Mr Fox* (1982), the 1993 Grand Prix winner, International Noma Concours, Japan, and *The Three Little Pigs* (1990). He illustrated Katherine *O'Brien's *The Year of the Yelvertons* (1981) and Jeffrey Leask's *Little Red Rocking Hood* (1992). He also wrote and designed two children's ballets for the Royal New Zealand Ballet: *Terrible Tom* and *Te Maia and the Sea Devil*. His own illustrated texts include *Mrs McGinty and* *the Bizarre Plant* (1981), Russell Clark Award winner in 1982; *Bidibidi* (1982), prizewinner in the 1984 Noma Concours; and *The Horror of Hickory Bay* (1984), a powerful, surrealistic fantasy. *Bidibidi* and *Bidibidi to the Rescue* became a thirteen-part television series 1990–91.

Bishop draws on his Waikato / Ngāti Pūkeko (Ngāti Wai) affiliations for his great-aunt's journey in *Katarina* (1990), and on legend for his tale of land desecration and retribution in *Hinepau* (1993), Picture Book of the Year in 1994. His commission to illustrate Philip Bradley's *The Wedding of Mistress Fox* (New York, 1994) confirms his growing international reputation.   DH

Black Light Press (1987–91) was a private press owned and operated by Alan ★Loney at 47 Durham Street, Wellington. As in his last years with ★Hawk Press, Loney aimed to produce limited edition books, designed, printed and bound by himself, using damped handmade papers and a handpress; and to measure his products by the highest international standards of fine printing and bookmaking. *Swell* (1987) consists of poems and prints written, designed and executed by Loney; the letterpress prints made use of wood and metal types and printer's blocks in several colours. *Poems of a War* by John ★Male (1989), with poems written during the African and Italian campaigns of World War 2, accompanied by drawings by Russell ★Clark, was printed on a Vandercook SP15 proof press. Three small books were published in 1990: *Back in the U.S.A.*, poems by Wystan ★Curnow, an essay by Loney called *& the Ampersand*, and *Art of the Book*, the catalogue of an exhibition held in Wellington. *A Cargo of Flax* by Tony Simpson (1991), an essay about notorious events in Akaroa Harbour in 1830 involving Captain Stewart of the brig *Elizabeth*, printed on an Albion handpress on paper handmade from flax, was the last Black Light Press book. The excellence of Loney's handmade books is recognised in Roderick Cave's authoritative *The Private Press* (2nd edn, 1983): 'There is also an upper level … work of the same excellence, and using the best materials as those of Kelmscott, Doves or Ashendene…. It is to this small group that Alan Loney now belongs.' See also Gregory ★O'Brien, 'On and Around Creation: The Hand Made Books of Alan Loney', *Art New Zealand* 57 (1992).   PS

Blackwood and Janet Paul was the imprint adopted in 1964 by the remarkable publishing partnership that began life as Paul's Book Arcade in 1945. Blackwood Paul (1908–65), who had abandoned a law career to make a vocation of bookselling, took over his father's bookshop in 1933. He was an exacting employer who insisted on well-informed staff and a genuine service to the community. He also made his legal services available to the book trade. Janet Paul (née Wilkinson 1919) had learnt the rudiments of typography and book design with J.C. ★Beaglehole in the Historical Branch of Internal Affairs, and met Blackwood while they were serving on the committee of the ★Progressive Publishing Society. After its collapse in 1945, Blackwood Paul took over some of its titles as the basis for his own publishing list. The first publication in March 1945 was Gordon Miram's critique of the film industry, *Speaking Candidly*. Subsequent publications were similarly motivated by the desire to engender a broader understanding of New Zealand history and culture. To this end, Paul's concentrated on the essential humus of biographical memoirs, such as Helen Wilson's *My First Eighty Years* (1950), as well as astutely commissioning a number of histories. An array of significant books on Māori history and culture also distinguished their publication list: Antony ★Alpers's *Maori Myths and Tribal Legends* (1964), Maharaia Winiata's *The Changing Role of the Leader in Maori Society* (1967), Margaret ★Orbell's *Maori Folktales* and Erik Schwimmer's *Symposium* (both 1968). A number of children's books also broke new ground by treating Māori themes accompanied by a sympathetic selection of artwork and photography. These, along with Elsie ★Locke's classic *The Runaway Settler* (1965) and Maurice ★Duggan's *Falter Tom* (1958), published in association with Faber and Faber, helped to define the genre of children's literature with which New Zealand publishers were to have so much success. Although often considered ★Caxton's rival in terms of literary publications, Blackwood and Janet Paul viewed their role as more complementary than competitive, and this was borne out by the fact that Caxton printed much of their poetry. The poetry included works by Barry ★Mitcalfe, Kendrick ★Smithyman, Gloria ★Rawlinson, C.K. ★Stead, Denis ★Glover and A.E. ★Batistich, as well as the paperback *Penguin Book of New Zealand Verse* (1966). Aside from Hone ★Tuwhare's particularly successful *No Ordinary Sun* (1964), most of the poetry was subsidised by the profit from the prolific Mary ★Scott's popular novels, which appeared annually between 1956 and 1967. Bill ★Pearson's *★Coal Flat* (1963), Frank ★Sargeson's *Collected Stories* (1964) and novels by M.K. ★Joseph and Ruth ★France offered less secure returns, but evidence a worthwhile commitment to New Zealand literature. This was strengthened by critical works such as *Distance Looks Our Way* (1961). The commissioning of artists such as Colin ★McCahon, Juliet Peters, Pat Hanley, E. Mervyn Taylor and Eric ★Lee-Johnson, as well as separate works on Johnson and M.T. ★Woollaston, clearly owed much to Janet Paul's own artistic activities. Commissioned books were chosen with equal discrimination, and along with innovative moves towards joint publication and a considered reprint programme that included the likes of Sargeson, John *Mulgan and Dan *Davin, Blackwood and Janet Paul achieved a successful combination of the commercial and the quixotic. They had opened a second shop in Auckland in 1955, and well over half their list of almost 200 publications appeared in the last eight years of the firm's existence, but the death of Blackwood Paul in 1965 and a somewhat over-ambitious publishing programme led to a merger with Longmans in 1968. An exhibition of Paul's books and other materials toured in 1995–96, with an informative catalogue by Janet Paul and J.M. *Thomson.

NWt

BLAKE, Christopher (1949–), composer and arts administrator, was born in Christchurch. His major setting of a New Zealand text, *Till Human Voices Wake Us* (1986), is a widely acclaimed work for tenor and orchestra. The title (from T.S. Eliot's 'Love Song of J. Alfred Prufrock') is that of Ian Hamilton's book of 1953, a record of his sufferings as a conscientious objector in World War 2. The work was first inspired by Archibald *Baxter's *We Will Not Cease* (1939). Blake's work for chamber orchestra *Lamentations of Motuarohia* (1983) recreates the violent scene in 1840 at the Bay of Islands when the young Māori Maketu, goaded beyond endurance by a Pākehā persecutor, murdered a European family. After a sensational trial he was later hanged. Blake's next work of literary relevance was the two-act opera *Bitter Calm* (1990) for soloists, chorus and orchestra, with a libretto by Stuart *Hoar, and first performed in the Wellington International Festival of the Arts in March 1992, but handicapped by a somewhat bizarre production. A more sympathetic television screening took place later. His symphony *The Islands* (1991), first performed in 1996, is a response to the three poems by Charles *Brasch with the same title.   JMT

BLANCO WHITE, Amber, see **REEVES, Amber**.

BLAND, Peter (1934–), poet and actor, was in the 1950s–60s associated with James K. *Baxter and Louis *Johnson as 'the Wellington Group', together editing *Numbers*. Reacting against fashionable *nationalistic aspirations, Bland and Johnson insisted that poetry engage with the commonplace suburban reality of most New Zealand lives. Bland's early work—*Habitual Fevers*, in *3 Poets*, by Peter Bland, John Boyd and Victor O'Leary (1958), *My Side of the Story: Poems 1960–1964* (1964), *Domestic Interiors* (1964) and *The Man With the Carpet-Bag* (1972)—established a reductive local social realism of 'tin butterflies and plaster gnomes, / The home-made garages, the weekend roasts, / The cat's paws delicate in new-laid concrete', inverting Utopian-picturesque plati-

tudes of *landscape with 'monotonous' hills, 'The lower slopes a useful place for tips', 'A man-made beach', 'abandoned hoardings' and 'vast insurance blocks'. Indignation as well as irony gave vigour to the intonations of these poems, a sympathy perhaps sprung from his working-class northern English origins for the 'excess / Of spirit burning in too cramped a wilderness'.

Bland's acute actor's ear for timing, inflection and the accents of everyday life brought into his verse the rhythms and diction of the country's elusive vernacular, in counterpoint with the robust resonance of his native Yorkshire ('For the rest of your life / there'll be two sets of voices …'). He works often in short dramatic monologue, as in the satiric Polynesian persona of 'Mr. Maui', which he adopted on his first return to England, or the returned-migrant sequence 'The Crusoe Factor': 'A trip to the dales / gives the soul a glimpse / of lost horizons —but that north-east wind / cuts me to the bone. Friends / once envied for being "back home" / seem suddenly enclosed.'

Collections from this period are *Mr. Maui* (1976), *Primitives* (1979), *Stone Tents* (1981) and *The Crusoe Factor* (1985). It is a special irony that Bland, at first the poet of the commuter suburb of Lower Hutt, has evolved into the bard of global commuters. His later work focuses on migration and displacement, major twentieth-century themes which he explores with the insight that comes from his own life of frequent remigrations. Many poems are distant views or conjunctions of disparate images, some of the best being letters to New Zealand friends, such as 'A Last Note from Menton', the elegy for Louis Johnson, which won an Arvon Award in England and is the pivot of *Paper Boats* (1991). It rejects '"digging in" / … that old Kiwi regressive thing / disguised as growing roots', in favour of 'turn[ing] away from that well-worn path' to write 'poems adrift / like paper boats or messages in bottles, / careless of landfall, happy to be themselves'. The same tensions are evident in Bland's imagined monologues by early settlers ('Letters Home— New Zealand 1885'), his poems where migratory movements intersect with time and ageing ('Let's Meet') and his recent vignettes of cross-cultural encounter, set in Europe ('A Postcard from Barcelona', 'At Dawn the Thames is the Ganges in Flood'), or in New Zealand ('Gauguin in Auckland 1891').

Bland's clarity of meaning and realism of reference have always been subverted by his quirky obliqueness of viewpoint, his aphoristic, self-mocking wit and his taste for the surreal, as in several successful poems about children ('House with Cat or Sun', 'Happy Army'). His voice has become increasingly flexible and lyrical, as in *Paper Boats* or the uncollected 'A Potential Poem for More than Passing Strangers'.

Bland was born in Scarborough, Yorkshire, went to grammar school at Stone, Staffordshire, and after army service moved in 1954 to New Zealand. There he studied English at Victoria University (1955–59), winning the Macmillan Brown prize for his poetry, and worked in broadcasting, editing the 'Poetry' programme, and in theatre. He has a distinguished place in theatre history as co-founder of Downstage and its artistic director 1964–68. Two of his own plays were produced, 'Father's Day' (Wellington, 1967) and 'George the Mad Ad Man' (Wellington, 1967, and Coventry, England, 1969). Returning then to England, he continued to work primarily as a stage and TV actor, achieving notoriety as a Spanish butler in TV commercials and some fame in New Zealand for his inspired comic performance in the film of *Came a Hot Friday. He wrote frequently for London Magazine, which published three of his collections. His New Zealand publishers have been *Mate, *Wai-te-ata, *Caxton and *McIndoe, which published his Selected Poems in 1987. A subsequent Selected Poems was published in the UK in 1998. In 1985 Bland moved permanently back to New Zealand for four years, and now lives at Putney, near London.   RR

BLANK, Arapera (Hineira) (1932–), poet and short story writer, was born in Rangitukia, on the East Coast. Her tribal affiliations are Ngāti Porou, Ngāti Kahungunu, Rongowhakaata, Te Aitanga-a-Māhaki. She was educated at Queen Victoria School in Auckland and the University of Auckland, where she studied anthropology. With her husband, she taught in Punaruku, a small community in the Bay of Islands. In awarding her a prize in the Katherine *Mansfield Memorial Competition in 1959, the judges said, 'her work has developed through the opportunities given to Māori writers through Te *Ao Hou. It is arresting and creative.' In 1986 she published the collection Nga Kokako Huataratara: The Notched Plumes of the Kokako. It contains verse in both Māori and English, and in an earlier essay she spoke of the two languages as two legs, without either of which it would impossible for her to walk: indeed, she said, the essential aid to walking was her 'third leg', a blending of the other two. A selection of her poems and three stories are included in the first volume of Te *Ao Mārama.   NW

'Bliss', a short story by Katherine *Mansfield, was written in 1918 and published that year by the English Review, the first notable literary journal to accept her work. It was subsequently published in Mansfield's second collection Bliss and Other Stories (1920). The MS is in the Newberry Library, Chicago. It presents the perceptions of the affluent Bertha Young preparing for and then hosting a dinner party of 'modern, thrilling friends'

at which she discovers that her husband, whom she sexually desires for almost the first time, has betrayed her with a female guest, Pearl Fulton. The story is notable for the extent to which people and objects act as a cypher for Bertha's sexual self-discovery, as when she shows Pearl a flowering pear tree: 'it seemed, like the flame of a candle, to stretch up, to point, to quiver in the bright air, to grow taller and taller as they gazed—almost to touch the rim of the round, silver moon.' Beryl's ecstasy leads to a moment of inner transformation 'feeling that this self of hers was taking leave of them forever', crushed when she discovers her husband's infidelity. Although Mansfield allowed a collection to be named after the story, which she considered one of her best, and although the story has enduring popularity, 'Bliss' has always divided critics. Virginia Woolf disliked the story's conception, and in the Life *Alpers concurs with T.S. Eliot's view that 'the moral implication is negligible'. In A Literature of Their Own, Elaine Showalter describes 'Bliss' as 'cautionary and punitive; women are lured out onto the limbs of consciousness, which are then lopped off by the author.' Other critics however interpret Bertha as more artist than 'artist manqué' (a description used by Mansfield in a 1918 letter to John Middleton *Murry). The psychological unmasking in the dénouement connects the story to the later piece *'Miss Brill' (1920); the exposé of bohemian pretensions links the story to *'Je ne parle pas français' (1918) and 'Marriage à la Mode' (1921).   SSa

Blow, Wind of Fruitfulness, James K. *Baxter's second published book of poetry, was produced by the *Caxton Press in 1948, four years after his successful first collection, *Beyond the Palisade. The long interval between books was not due to a lack of content. During this period Baxter had been writing prolifically. Rather Caxton had elected not to publish a second collection, *Cold Spring, which had been offered to them early in 1945.

The interval allowed Baxter time to develop his writing. Where Beyond the Palisade is occasionally uneven and too obviously imitative, and Cold Spring dense with personal symbolism, the poems of Blow, Wind of Fruitfulness have more control and assurance. Allen *Curnow, whose interest had aided the success of Baxter's first book, described him, in a review of the second, as 'the most original of New Zealand poets now living'. Curnow argued that if 'these poems are full of echoes, they are not the echoes of mimicry but the true, if altered, accents of other voices, inherited by right of a natural eloquence.'

The New Zealand *landscape plays an important role in the poems of Blow, Wind of Fruitfulness, as it did in *Beyond the Palisade*. Its spaces are again sparsely peopled and consequently a tone of solitude and alienation recurs. What is new is what Curnow called a 'welcome gain in irony and detachment'. The pompous and laboured 'University Song', for example, is delightfully subverted in an 'Envoi' whose final lines encapsulate Baxter's reservations about 'the higher learning': '*Lost, one original heart and mind / Between the pub and the lecture room*.' PM

'Blues for Miss Laverty', a story by Maurice *Duggan, is included in the collection *Summer in the Gravel Pit*.

Boer War, see **War literature**.

BOLDREWOOD, Rolf (pseudonym of Thomas A. Browne, 1826–1915), the justly famous *Australian author of *Robbery Under Arms* (1888), set a later novel *War to the Knife or Tangata Maori* (1899) in New Zealand. Rightly considered his worst novel, it was written at a time when New Zealand might still have federated with the other Australian states (it is 'one of the Australian colonies' at one point) and when trans-Tasman literary relations were in any case close. The novel however is a botch in the post-Scott heroic romance tradition. Sir Roland Massinger loves Hypatia Tollemache, who prefers Doing Good to marrying him. He migrates to New Zealand to forget and to buy some land, and falls in love with high-born half-caste Erena Mannering. Hypatia follows him, still Doing Good, observes his love for Erena, and witnesses her death by a Māori bullet meant for Roland. Hypatia and Roland marry after all. The period is 1859–64, from the Waitara troubles through the Taranaki and *Waikato wars. Having visited Taupo and Whakarewarewa and the Pink and White Terraces in tourist-brochure prose, Roland joins Von Tempsky's Forest Rangers. In fairness it has to be said that Boldrewood had researched the New Zealand *Wars fairly well, even if Kororareka's Waka Nene is unaccountably all over the place and the novel's geography owes more to an 1890s road map than 1860s reality. But the unreadable stylistic abominations of 'wild-wooded glades' and the 'heavenly forms' of women make its main interest the now almost unbelievable attitudes adopted towards women and the Māori race a century ago. KA

BOLITHO, Hector (1898–1974), was one of the most prolific and certainly the most financially successful of New Zealand authors of his generation. He grew up on coastal farming country at Opotiki, and a good deal of his own Methodist background is present in his first novel, *Solemn Bay* (1927), with the family insistence that 'originality, individuality and personality are things to be avoided'. Of more biographical interest, perhaps, is the novel's unconvincing heterosexual romance as homosexuality almost wins the day.

After attending Seddon Memorial College in Auckland, the young Bolitho worked as a journalist on both the *New Zealand Herald* and *Auckland Star* until he accompanied the Prince of Wales on his tour of the country in 1920. The subsequent *With the Prince in New Zealand* established his flair for bland regal celebration. Soon after, Bolitho was invited to Sydney by Allan Wilkie, the English actor and theatrical manager, to found and edit *The Shakespeare Quarterly*, the first journal dedicated solely to the study of the dramatist.

In the mid-twenties, when he arrived in England, Bolitho was advised by D.H. *Lawrence to avoid the metropolis and to live on three pounds a week. Instead, he accepted the invitation of the Dean of Windsor to help edit the correspondence of Lady Augusta Stanley. And so began his ten-year residence in the Cloisters, Windsor Castle, and his calling as royal biographer and apologist. He wrote many volumes on royal personalities, including studies of Queen Victoria, *Albert the Good* (1933), and *King Edward VIII: His Life and Reign* (1938), which sold over 100 000 copies.

Bolitho's gift for converting blue blood to both purple prose and hard cash was interspersed with travel writing, collections of essays and further fiction. His second novel set in New Zealand, *Judith Silver* (1929), explores the consequences of repressive *puritanism. His volume of short stories, *The House in Half-Moon Street* (1930), included in 'Taureke's Eyes' what may justly be ranked as this country's most bizarrely tasteless story. A brilliant young Māori doctor in Edinburgh dies by swallowing glass eyes, in an irrepressible act of 'atavism'.

Among Bolitho's more than sixty books were the insistently Anglocentric *The New Zealanders* (1930), *The Emigrants: Early Travellers in the Antipodes* (1939), written with John *Mulgan, and his own superficial reminiscences of the high, the mighty, and those who contributed to his energetically pursued social diary. Perhaps most interesting to the contemporary reader are the casual autobiographical volumes, *War in the Strand* (1942) and *My Restless Years* (1962).

Bolitho was well known for his generosity to younger readers, and his admirable work for the handicapped. He was also not without a certain wryness, as when his autobiography considers his life at Windsor Castle 'dangerous, because the colonial vigour was dripping out of my heart, and instead of being a rebel, which is my nature, I was becoming smug and genteel.' VO

bone people, the (1983), is the award-winning novel by Keri *Hulme. It was published by the Spiral Collective, after other publishers had required changes and cuts. It then won the New Zealand Book Award for Fiction (1984) and the Mobil Corporation's 'Pegasus Prize', a fiction award which moves each year to a different country; it was allocated to fiction by Māori writers in conjunction with Mobil's sponsorship of the Te Māori Exhibition in New York, San Francisco and Chicago; the award carries automatic American publication by Louisiana State University Press (1985). Also in 1985 Spiral republished the novel with Hodder and Stoughton. While Hulme was still in America after the 'Pegasus' promotion, the announcement came from the UK that the novel had won the prestigious Booker Prize.

The Prologue, 'The End at the Beginning', is a dream-like incantation which foreshadows an end to the suffering of three unnamed identities who 'were nothing more than people by themselves', but together are 'the heart and muscles and mind of something perilous and new', 'the instruments of change'. This sets the tone for the rest of the book, the plot of which has been called 'implausible, even melodramatic'. Kerewin Holmes (mind), a part-Māori woman, has, after winning the lottery, retired to a well-stocked tower overlooking the sea. She lives alone, estranged from her family (we are never told why) and alienated from her community, passing her nights in alcoholic stupor and her days foraging on the beach. An artist, her capacity to paint has withered. One day she finds that a mute, blond child, Simon (heart), has taken refuge in her tower. She recoils from the intruder but reluctantly agrees to let him stay until his stepfather, Joe Gillayley (muscles) can collect him the following day. Joe, a Māori man with some Pākehā ancestry, lost his wife and infant son to influenza, leaving the bitter and angry man to care for their adopted son, Simon, found on the beach after a shipwreck. (Simon's ancestry remains a mystery, despite considerable detective work on the part of Holmes, although she does discover an *Irish connection.) In the course of the first three parts of the narrative this unlikely trio make tentative gestures towards connection but these are continually thwarted by narcissism, violence and lack of communication.

Kerewin, a master of Aikido, becomes Simon's unwilling protector after learning that Joe periodically beats him violently, despite his love for the child. After physically beating Joe, Kerewin makes him promise never to give Simon 'the hits' again without her permission. But when Simon smashes her beloved guitar, she verbally lashes the child and passes him on to Joe for physical punishment. In this harrowing scene, portrayed in graphic and economic realist prose, Joe beats the child

so severely that he is left in a coma. Potential unity is thus violently fractured and the narrative spirals downwards into despair and darkness. But the trio are saved by the intervention of the supernatural in the final (fourth) part of the book. Joe's guardianship is revoked and he is jailed for child abuse. Simon eventually recovers with only some loss of hearing; he is sent, unwillingly, to live with a foster family. Kerewin burns her tower to the ground, and leaves on an indefinite journey around the South Island. She discovers she has stomach cancer and retires to a mountain hut to die. On the point of death she is miraculously cured by a healing potion offered by a little figure of indeterminate sex. Released from prison, Joe attempts suicide by jumping off a cliff, but survives with only a broken arm. He has chosen to end his life in a sacred place, the landing site of one of the original Great Canoes (see *Waka). He is rescued by an old man, a kaumātua nearing death, who has been waiting all his life for a 'broken man' to come and take over the care of the relics of a canoe, a sacred stone and a little god he guards, which is nothing less than the spirit of the land. Joe accepts the charge and is thus reunited with his empowering Māoriness. Recovered, Kerewin rebuilds the Māori meeting house at Moerangi, her ancestral home, and is consequently reunited with her family and the Māori community. Simon escapes foster care and is adopted by Kerewin. After an earthquake buries the canoe, Joe takes the sacred stone back to Kerewin's new home, built on the foundations of her tower, where it sinks deep into the earth. Reunited (although conventional expectations of a romantic happy ending are subverted), Joe, Kerewin and Simon are now 'the bone people'—a new multicultural group, founded on Māori spirituality and traditional ritual, who offer transformative hope to a country stunted by the violence of its divided colonial legacy. The epilogue gestures towards Hulme's vision of 'commensualism', portraying Kerewin's new spiral-shaped home filled with family (including Joe and Simon) and members of the Māori community.

Negotiation through the novel requires active reader-involvement in order to reconcile the many, seemingly conflicting aspects of the text: poetry continually jostles the prose, New Zealand vernacular English and Māori phrases are intermixed, realism and supernatural elements are juxtaposed. There is rapid movement between objective reportage and stream of consciousness, the tone shifts from the self-conscious to the sacramental, from banality to lyricism. For some, the text is flawed by the 'dive from reality into wishful daydream', its 'romantic nationalism' and 'astonishing political innocence'. For others, such criticism misses Hulme's point—the supernatural elements are the very heart of her regenerative vision. Arguably, Hulme urges the need for new myths to replace the redundant inherited master narratives of Western civilisation: those of empire, race, heterosexual love, individualism, materialism, Christianity. This, it has been suggested, is the imperative behind Hulme's multicultural borrowings, extensive literary allusions, pervasive linguistic experimentation and syncretic style: social regeneration is in part to be achieved by the regeneration of the myths and language by means of which we read, write, and understand our world and others. However one responds to the novel, it must be acknowledged as one of contemporary New Zealand literature's most powerful rewritings of the ideology of *nationalism and a prophetic vision of New Zealand's multicultural future.   KWo

BOOCK, Paula (1964–), is a novelist for young adults. Born in Dunedin and educated at Queen's HS and the University of Otago, she combines writing with editorial work for publishers. She moved from *John McIndoe to Longacre Press in 1995. Stimulated by a Queen Elizabeth II Arts Council grant 1991–92, and by a year as the 1994 writing fellow at Dunedin College of Education, she writes strong fiction which shows her sympathy for modern teenagers and understanding of the social pressures they encounter in a 'corrupt' world on a 'decaying' planet. Her feisty female protagonists explore friendships and challenge traditional roles and social expectations as they cope with dysfunctional families, school and life after school, male aggression, and disasters including death. Boock won the 1992 Best First Book Award for *Out Walked Mel* (1991) and the 1994 Esther Glen Award for *Sasscat to Win* (1993). A representative cricketer for Otago, Boock's interest in *sport is reflected in *Home Run* (1995), with its focus on softball. Her interest in the theatre is reflected in her one-act play, *Song of the Shirt*, published in a 1993 collection with the same name, along with plays by *Renée and by Fiona *Farrell.   DH

Book was a literary miscellany and typographical sampler published irregularly by the *Caxton Press 1941–47. Edited by Denis *Glover, Ian *Milner and others it featured poetry, fiction, articles and criticism by contributors such as Charles *Brasch, Allen *Curnow, Basil *Dowling, A.R.D. *Fairburn, Denis *Glover, M.H. *Holcroft, R.A.K. *Mason, Frank *Sargeson, Maurice *Duggan, John Reece *Cole, G.R. *Gilbert, Helen *Shaw, Louis *Johnson and J.R. *Hervey. Illustrations were a major feature of most issues, including numerous contributions by Leo *Bensemann, portraits of Curnow and Glover by Rita Cook, and several fine engravings by Mervyn Taylor.   SH

Book Council, see **New Zealand Book Council**.

Book of Canterbury Rhymes, The, see *Canterbury Rhymes*.

Book of New Zealand Verse 1923–45, A (1945; enlarged edn, *1923–51*, 1951), chosen by Allen *Curnow and published by the *Caxton Press, canonised sixteen poets, whose work distinguished them from a horde of 'trivial if sincere' versifiers. Those making the grade were Arnold *Wall, Ursula *Bethell, J.R. *Hervey, Walter D'Arcy *Cresswell, J.C. *Beaglehole, A.R.D. *Fairburn, R.A.K. *Mason, Robin *Hyde, Charles *Brasch, Basil *Dowling, Curnow himself, Denis *Glover, Douglas *Stewart, Anton *Vogt, Hubert *Witheford and James K. *Baxter. Curnow's introduction proved more enduring than a number of his selections, however, and its forty-two pages established his eminence among critics of New Zealand poetry for decades after.

Curnow's selections, which favoured real expressions 'of what the New Zealander is', were based on the recurrence of such themes and preoccupations as the land and the people, the sea and voyaging, settler alienation amid 'a natural time, a natural order, to which [their] presence in these islands is accidental', and (in contrast to earlier traditions) uncharacteristically dystopian depictions of a society affected by the *Depression, isolation and war. He credited the poets whose work exhibited such themes with a heightened consciousness. Not mere passive reflectors, they were active creators of New Zealand as an idea.

The qualities that distinguish Curnow's poets also differentiate them from the preceding generation of versifiers. Although *Georgian was not a term he used, his criticism of *Kowhai Gold*—the anthology that best represents the period—makes characteristic criticisms of verse that lacks 'any vital relation to experience'. The Georgian phase was regarded as a sentimental twilight dividing the poets of Curnow's anthology from their appropriate ancestors, the more vigorous colonial poets of the 1890s. A major casualty of his attack on *Kowhai Gold* was Eileen *Duggan, whose work he roundly criticised. Despite conceding, in a footnote, that Duggan would have made the anthology had she not withheld her poems, his criticism has coloured most subsequent approaches to her poetry.

One notable, late, inclusion was the 18-year-old Baxter, whose first volume was in the Caxton Press around the same time. Curnow added a section to his introduction in which he pronounced that 'since Mason in 1923, no New Zealand poet has proved so early his power to say and his right to speak'. Ironically, Baxter would become the foremost critic of Curnow's later anthology, the *Penguin Book of New Zealand Verse* (1960), citing (in 'Aspects of Poetry in New Zealand', 1967) his 'tribal piety' towards the poets of his first anthology as the factor preventing him from recognising 'that much good writing, and new modes of writing, had come to light in our poetry since 1945'. Despite this—and despite other criticism that Curnow's approach is simplistic and his *nationalism restrictive—few would deny that his first anthology, however prescriptive, set standards for the production and criticism of poetry that would dominate the genre for decades.   PM

Book of Secrets, The (1985), is a historical novel by Fiona *Kidman recounting the life of Norman McLeod, who led a party of highlanders into exile after the clearances in Scotland. The events are based on oral and sparse written evidence and the author maintains that none of those directly involving McLeod are purely fictional, even though many of the other characters are. It is the tale of a man whose charisma and intelligence motivate the loyalty of a group who settle first in Nova Scotia, where they build their own ships and travel on to Australia, eventually settling in Waipu in Northland. At the same time McLeod is a tyrant over others, especially the women. Three generations of women suffer banishment from the community for defying him. The first, Isabella, lives in a cave in Nova Scotia, easing her isolation by keeping a diary, which is 'The Book of Secrets'. This is found by her granddaughter Maria, who also lives in solitude after being found guilty of 'fornication'. For more than fifty years she never leaves her small house. She is visited by a young relative escaping conscription during World War 1, with whom she has a sexual relationship. Maria's life is dominated by the hostility of the community, who nonetheless maintain standards of 'Christian socialism', assisting each other in the difficulties of pioneer and farming life. The dark portrait of an ineluctably puritanical community, merciless but, by their own lights, just towards someone who transgresses against the laws propagated by 'the Man', is relieved by the ambivalence involved in their sense of mutual support in times of need.   NW

Book of Wiremu, The (1944), by Stella Morice was the first winner of the Esther Glen Award for Children's Literature, and an influential work in its realistic yet sympathetic representation of Māori life and culture. Because of his many brothers and sisters, Wiri is brought up by his uncle Hori ('That is the Māori way'), his happy childhood centered on their modest whare and the Waitukituki River, 'always Hori's and Wiri's best and most generous friend, next of course, to the Waterfords'. Apart from this deference to Pākehā patronage, the book is for its time unusually free of condescension, its detailed

and often poetic observation affirming respect for Māori conventions and values. From his grandmother ('Her eyes were still and deep as the river') Wiri learns the stories of his ancestral heritage, while he is able to instruct a townbred Pākehā visitor in eeling and pig-hunting, winning admiration from a boy whose first response was to complain about the lack of a refrigerator. Betty *Gilderdale calls *Wiremu* 'a considerable advance' in its 'sincerely told' treatment of Māori life (*A Sea Change*, 1982). *The Book of Wiremu* was published by the *Progressive Publishing Society and reprinted five times by Paul's Book Arcade and *Blackwood and Janet Paul 1946–66, the flagship of their list of children's books on Māori themes.   RR

Bookie was a magazine of satire written, edited and published under a bewildering range of pseudonyms by R.S. *Gormack of the Nag's Head Press of Christchurch 1948–51. While its main title and format satirises the *Caxton Press miscellany *Book*, its three issues differ widely in their content. The first was a humorous celebration of the culture of horse racing; the second presented 'Three Tales of Jack Entwistle'; and the third and final, subtitled 'Swagger Jack: A Station Tale', consisted of 118 stanzas ironically reminiscent of David McKee *Wright's *Station Ballads*.   SH

BOOTH, Pat (1929–), has won awards both as novelist and journalist, most notably for investigative journalism in the Arthur Allan Thomas case and Mr Asia drug investigation. Born in Levin and educated at Hawera HS and Sacred Heart College, Auckland, he was a versatile reporter with various papers and overseas correspondent for NZPA, with one period as a pioneering aviation writer. He became deputy editor of the *Auckland Star* (1971–80) and assistant editor of *North and South* (1986–94). His first novel, *Long Night Among the Stars* (1961), prophetically explored the personal life of a man about to be put into space. It won the *Otago Daily Times* centennial award and was called a 'tour de force' by J.C. *Reid. *Footsteps in the Sea* (1964) is a return of the native story of a young man whose disillusioned view of his home town (Te Kore, Māori for 'Nowhere') is modified by a crisis of cultural encounter between commercial Japanese fishermen and the local community. *Sprint from the Bell* (1966) focuses on the personal and domestic pressures on a man similarly engaged in epoch-making action, in this case a world-class Hutt Valley middle-distance runner who breaks 3 min 50 sec for the mile. Booth's plain, functional prose brings its own strength to heroic, colourful, even sensational material, a mix that applies to the novels, to his boys' sports writings such as the immensely popular life of All Black Don Clarke, *The

Boot (1966), and to the influential investigative narratives *Trial by Ambush* (1975) and *The Mr Asia File* (1980). More experimental is the novel *Sons of the Sword* (1992), which draws on Booth's expert knowledge of Japanese weaponry and its mystiques in a collage narrative of the Pacific War. Other titles include biographies of Norman Kirk (*The Hunter and the Hill*, 1978), Edmund Hillary and Graeme Dingle. Booth received the OBE in 1981. He still writes freelance reviews and other work. His autobiography, *Deadline: My Story*, was published in 1997. RR

BOREHAM, Rev. Frank (1871–1959), the most prolific Baptist writer of his generation, travelled from England to commence ministry at the Mosgiel Baptist Church in 1895. Editor for the *New Zealand Baptist* from 1899 and a regular writer for the *Otago Daily Times*, his first book, *The Whisper of God*, was published in 1902. According to a family anecdote, an old gipsy women prophesied that with a 'pen in his hand … he'll never want for a living,' and indeed by the end of his life he had written forty-six books. He departed for Hobart in 1906 but continued to refer to New Zealand in many of his works, in particular *Loose Leaves from the Journal of My Voyage Round the World* (c.1905), *George Augustus Selwyn, D.D., Pioneer Bishop of New Zealand* (1911), *Mushrooms on the Moor* (1915), *The Other Side of the Hill and Home Again* (1917), *A Reel of Rainbow* (1920), *Shadows on the Wall* (1922), *The Crystal Pointers* (1925), *Wisps of Wildfire* (1925), *The Song of the Stars: A Maori Romance* (1927), which tells the story of Samuel ★Marsden's arrival in New Zealand, *The Fiery Crags* (1928), *My Manse in Maoriland* (1929), *When the Swans Fly High* (1931), *The Bachelors of Mosgiel* (1933), *The Merry Man of Mosgiel* (1936), *A Vagabond of the Bush: A Christmas Story* (1937), *My Pilgrimage: An Autobiography* (1940) and *A Late Lark Singing* (1949). T.H. Crago has written a biography, *The Story of F.W. Boreham* (1961). PM

BORNHOLDT, Jenny (1960–), is a poet and anthologist. Born in Wellington, she holds a BA in English Literature and a Diploma in Journalism. She began writing seriously after attending Bill ★Manhire's original composition course at Victoria University of Wellington in 1984, and has since published *This Big Face* (1988), *Moving House* (1989), *Waiting Shelter* (1991), *How We Met* (1995) and *Miss New Zealand: Selected Poems* (1997). Almost without exception, critics have praised her poetry's freshness and the concealed depths in its lucid explorations of the simple and the familiar: 'many poems … ring like the reassuring chime of crystal glass or with the resonance of a perfectly fired bell…. They reveal the hidden' (Bill Direen, ★*NZ Listener*, 17 June 1995). Characteristic of her idiosyncratic take on the world is

the way language and relationships serve similar functions in her verse. She clearly delights in language, demonstrating a sophisticated understanding of how it can fashion and refashion existence, and an acute awareness of the mutability of meaning: 'O deceptive mouth / covering up / for the heart like that' ('My mouth was singing'). She enjoys wordplay: be it a deliberate, self-conscious reiteration of themes and vocabulary to bind sequences of shorter, lyric poems; or the employment of 'found language' to surprising effect, as happened with the sign on a shelter in the Wellington Botanic Gardens that supplies the title for *Waiting Shelter*. Manhire's teaching techniques are evident behind the eighteen pieces of the first section of *How We Met*, for which Bornholdt drew inspiration from a recording of north-eastern Estonian song cycles—a variation on a creative writing course's stock exercise involving the use of something (anything) as a catalyst to set in motion the creative process. Like words, relationships regularly elude definition in Bornholdt's poetry. She makes full use of autobiographical detail, but usually as a starting point for an imaginative act that, while inventive and unexpected, invariably finds its way back to the individual or the personal relationship—'The long arms of the family rest / along the shoulders of the world' ('We Will We Do'). Bornholdt is married to poet Gregory ★O'Brien, and critics have noted the sense of ongoing conversation occurring between their respective collections; as well, he makes occasional cameo appearances in her poems. With O'Brien she co-edited *My Heart Goes Swimming: New Zealand Love Poems* (1996), and with O'Brien and Mark ★Williams *An Anthology of New Zealand Poetry in English* (1997), which won the 1997 Montana Book Award for Poetry. PM

BOWEN, Charles C. (Christopher) (1830–1917), was public servant, politician and poet, knighted for his service as a cabinet minister, especially in introducing the 1877 Act which set up national education on a free and compulsory basis. Irish-born (Milford, County Mayo), educated at Rugby and Cambridge, he arrived as one of the first Canterbury Pilgrims in 1850, aboard the *Charlotte Jane*, which also carried the printing equipment for the *Lyttelton Times*. He served in various public positions for the Canterbury provincial government and contributed leaders to the *Lyttelton Times*, of which he became part-owner in 1856. After a period of travel, he became a resident magistrate 1864–74 and MP for Kaiapoi 1874–81. He published *Poems* in Christchurch in 1861. He was included in ★*Canterbury Rhymes* and the *Jubilee Book of Canterbury Rhymes* (1900), and is recently anthologised in Harvey ★McQueen's *The New Place* (1993). The poems, while patriotically British, confidently assert the identity of the new country, especially 'Change Not the Name', a polemic against any anglicised replacement for the name ★New Zealand, partly out of respect for Abel ★Tasman: ''Twere grievous wrong to that bold voyager.' Others show the usual Victorian conventions and technical accomplishment. 'The Battle of the Free' is a rousing call for New Zealand to support Britain in the Crimea: 'Her rifles from the mountain and her horsemen from the plain, / When the foeman's ranks are reeling o'er the slain.' 'Moonlight in New Zealand' is all descriptive melancholy, with an elegiac vision of how 'the pale ghosts of Maori warriors flit / Between the moon and me'. And 'Song, from the Argonauts' advocates Tennysonian progressivism, even using the metre of 'Locksley Hall': 'To toil onward still, and onward / To the goal that must be won.' With his achievement in education, Sir Charles fulfilled this meliorist aspiration better than most.   RR

BOWMAN, Hildebrand, is the fictitious name of the narrator of an anonymous novel published in London in 1778 and entitled *The Travels of Hildebrand Bowman, Esquire, Into Carnovirria, Taupiniera, Olfactaria, and Auditante, in New-Zealand; in the Island of Bonhommica and in the powerful Kingdom of Luxo-volupto, on the Great Southern Continent. Written by himself; Who went on shore in the Adventure's large Cutter, at Queen Charlotte's Sound New-Zealand, the fatal 17th of December 1773; and escaped being cut off, and devoured, with the rest of the Boat's crew, by happening to be a-shooting in the woods; where he was afterwards unfortunately left behind by the Adventure.* On the day in question, as the diaries of ★Cook and ★Banks inform us, the *Adventure* did indeed lose the crew of a cutter, who were presumably cannibalised. Bowman claims to have escaped but only returned to the ship's anchorage after it had departed. He finds himself among the Carnovirrians, who, as their name implies, are eaters of men, but escapes across Cook Strait to the land of the Taupinierans. These consumers of shellfish are tiny people with pig-like faces and rudimentary tails (a reference to the theory of Lord Monboddo that the most primitive humans must have tails). They have no language and no form of government. Across a chain of mountains Bowman enters the land of Olfactaria, a race of hunters with a more-than-human sense of smell, whom he is able to lead to success in battle against the Carnovirrians, thus avenging the dead men from the *Adventure*. Auditante, the fourth land in New Zealand, is inhabited by nomads with flocks, herds and trains of wives and slaves. A stage higher in civilisation than the Olfactarians, they have an acute sense of hearing and devote their leisure to music, poetry recitals and carnivorous feasts—a lifestyle too self-indulgent to please the puritanical Bowman. With some travelling merchants he travels on to the island of Bonhommica, a land which meets with his approval and is very like some ideal Britain. He has travelled not only through various lands but through various levels of civilisation and now moves to yet another, a kingdom on the Great Southern Continent. Here in Luxo-volupto he finds a people very like unidealised Britons, living in wonderful surroundings but given to vice and 'profligacy'.

We sense that the narrator's true purpose is not to examine remote lands but to criticise his fellow citizens and offer an ideal for them to strive for. In this the book resembles other imaginary voyages of the eighteenth century such as Swift's *Gulliver's Travels* and Johnson's *Rasselas*. Chronologically it comes interestingly between the great satires of *Gulliver's Travels* (1727) and ★*Erewhon* (1872) but it lacks their bite and philosophical depth, and its acceptance of British 'virtues' distinguishes it from them. It is rather a fictional popularisation of pre-Darwinian theories of evolution—but its entertainment value has not entirely dated.   NW

BOYD, Brian (1952–), was born in Belfast, Ulster, and came to New Zealand when he was five; his parents were booksellers in Palmerston North. He studied at the universities of Canterbury (MA 1974) and Toronto (PhD 1979). A version of his thesis, a comprehensive two-volume study of Nabokov's last enigmatic novel, was published as *Nabokov's 'Ada': The Place of Consciousness* (1985). This was prelude to his magisterial two-volume biography: *Vladimir Nabokov: The Russian Years* (1990) and *Vladimir Nabokov: The American Years* (1991), published to international acclaim. Nabokov's widow Véra granted Boyd unprecedented access to the novelist's personal archives and facilitated Boyd's access to Nabokov's international gallery of friends. His vivid celebration of the daily texture of Nabokov's lives in Russia, Europe and America seems likely to outlast his more extreme claims for Nabokov's genius.   MH

BRACKEN, Thomas (1843–98), is remembered principally as author of ★'God Defend New Zealand', now the national anthem. In the later nineteenth century he was one of the colony's most popular poets. Born into a Protestant family in County Meath, he left Ireland aged about 12 to work in Victoria on farms and the gold-diggings. He began writing and published at least one book of poems there. He is thought to have arrived early in 1869 in Dunedin, where he soon established himself in journalism, being associated with several Otago newspaper ventures in the next twenty years. Under his editorship the *Otago Guardian* was very hospitable to local writers. He also quickly became known as a popular poet whose rhythmic compositions, whether jaunty, melodramatic or sentimental, found favour for public recitation. For some of his lighter verse he used the pseudonym 'Paddy Murphy'.

Bracken became involved in politics in the late 1870s, and entered parliament in 1881 as member for Dunedin Central. He was defeated in 1884 but re-elected in a by-election in 1886 for a term that lasted less than two months. A supporter of George *Grey and Robert Stout, his speeches in the House reveal a man whose politics were liberal and humanitarian, reflecting the values that permeate his verse. After leaving politics his fortunes declined and he spent his last years plagued by ill health and financial hardship. He was converted to Roman Catholicism in 1896.

Bracken published five collections of verse in almost thirty years in New Zealand. The first were *Behind the Tomb* (1871) and *Flowers of the Free Lands* (1877). More ambitious volumes followed: *Lays of the Land of the Maori and Moa*, introduced by Rev. Rutherford Waddell (1884) and **Musings in Maoriland* (1890). This ornate and expensive production, which was printed in Leipzig and stretched Bracken's financial resources, contained a long 'historical sketch' by Stout and a brief preface by Grey. Bracken sold more than 1000 copies by carrying them from door to door in New Zealand and Australia. Bracken's last book, *Lays and Lyrics: God's Own Country and Other Poems* (1893), was a retrospective selection from his earlier volumes. He also wrote two books of literary sketches and reminiscences, two issues of a literary annual and numerous pamphlets and compilations.

Bracken resembled Charles *Dickens in his appearance, his love of long walks and his bonhomie, so that his contemporaries saw him as a 'character'. His ability to tap into the vein of popular emotion seems to have been the secret of his appeal as a writer, though it also explains his reputation's demise, for his verse seldom goes beyond the predictable and the sentimental cliché. Performance pieces such as 'Dunedin from the Bay', 'Pax Vobiscum' and 'The Tramp of the Fire Brigade' are hard to accept now with the seriousness that their author expected. *'Not Understood' was the only poem apart from 'God Defend New Zealand' which was to remain popular even into the mid-twentieth century. The posthumous collection, *Not Understood, and Other Poems* (1905), went through many editions up to 1956. It is an indication of changes in taste that he was the only New Zealand poet apart from Alfred *Domett to receive mention in the 1916 *Cambridge History of English Literature*. An excellent discussion of Bracken's verse by MacDonald P. Jackson is in **OHNZLE*. It deals with the 'vague aura of suggestiveness', with the imagery ('a psychoanalyst's delight'), with the inflated verbal techniques of personification and

periphrasis, and with the 'Irish blarney' that enabled Bracken to write nostalgically about Scotland or resonantly about Māori without knowledge of either. Yet the continuing success of 'God Defend New Zealand' (strongly endorsed as national anthem in a 1996 survey) suggests that Bracken's populist skills and almost ritualistic emotiveness are not wholly irrelevant even to the contemporary nation.   WB

BRADLEY, Tom (1946–), is an established Auckland broadcaster whose energetic, humorous and popular children's books began with *Johnny Whistler and the Spiders*, illustrated by Trevor Pye (1992). A collection of Bradley's short stories then appeared, entitled *Baker's Dozen* (1994). His novels, fast-paced and often improbable, include *Supertall Sam* (1993), which humorously treats embarrassment; *The Screaming Tree* (1994), a horror story; *Fair Weather* (1995); and, for teenagers, *The Hunt for Samantha* (1995), in which Scott discovers he is adopted and a twin. In Bradley's 1995 series, subtitled *The Brightside Bunch*, and illustrated by Stephen Axelsen, a reconstituted family presents many humorous crises in relationships in *Crowded House, Double Dilemma, Nine Lives* and *Father Daze*.   DH

BRASCH, Charles (1909–73), was a gifted poet, the distinguished founding editor of **Landfall*, and a generous and far-sighted patron of the arts. He was born in Dunedin, the only son of parents of Jewish descent. His father was a lawyer, and his mother, who died before Charles was 5, was connected to the Hallenstein business dynasty (initially established on the Central Otago goldfields).

Brasch was a boarder at Waitaki BHS 1922–27, when the rector was the well-known Frank Milner. He established lifelong friendships with Ian *Milner, son of the rector, and James *Bertram, and published his first poems in the school magazine. At 17 he was sent by his father to St John's College, Oxford. He did not distinguish himself academically at Oxford (1927–31) but published some poems in university magazines and travelled extensively on the continent. He returned to New Zealand in 1931, and was expected by his father to enter the family business. He became involved with the group—some of them ex-Waitaki friends—who were planning **Phoenix*, to be published at Auckland University College. Brasch contributed to three of the four issues 1932–33, including some translations from Rilke's *Letters to a Young Poet*. Temperamentally unsuited to the commercial world, he was determined, despite family disapproval, to become a poet. After what has been described by Bertram as a 'bitter showdown' with his father, he went back to England where he remained until the end of World War 2 in 1945, apart from brief visits to New Zealand.

Brasch was based for most of this time in London. Between 1933 and 1935 he spent three seasons on field sites in Egypt as a cadet archaeologist. He also visited Russia with friends in 1934. In 1936 his sister, Lesley, became ill and Brasch accompanied her to Little Missenden in the Chilterns, also teaching there at an experimental school. In 1938 he went to New Zealand for several months, meeting many of those involved in the literary and artistic movement centred on the *Caxton Press in Christchurch, including Denis *Glover, Leo *Bensemann, Ursula *Bethell, Douglas *Lilburn, M.T. *Woollaston and Rodney Kennedy. He contributed to *Tomorrow—the Christchurch-based journal—and in 1939 had his first collection of poems, *The Land and the People*, published by Caxton. Among some slight and immature work the title sequence stood out as a portent of things to come.

On his way back to Europe Brasch crossed America with Milner and Bertram. In England his sister died after a long illness, and while he was travelling to New Zealand with his father after her funeral in 1939, war broke out and he decided to go back to England. Rejected for active war service, he became a fire-watcher during the London blitz and later worked as a civil servant doing intelligence work for the Foreign Office. Stimulated by the war, Brasch began writing newly mature poems which looked back to his country of origin: 'It was New Zealand I discovered, not England, because New Zealand lived in me as no other country could live, part of myself as I was part of it, the world I breathed and wore from birth, my seeing and my language' (*Indirections*). These poems include phrases still familiar for their encapsulation of New Zealand experience: 'Always, in these islands, meeting and parting / Shake us …'; 'distance looks our way' ('The Islands'). They were printed in John Lehmann's *New Writing*, along with work by other New Zealanders, including Frank *Sargeson and Allen *Curnow. Brasch's poems of the war years were published in his second volume, *Disputed Ground: Poems 1939–45* (Caxton, 1948).

During the war Brasch was visited in London by Glover, of the Caxton Press, on leave from the Royal Navy. The two writers made plans for a new literary magazine in New Zealand after the war. In these discussions *Landfall* was conceived, which Brasch was to edit for its first twenty years (1947–66). He returned to New Zealand in late 1945, this time permanently.

Being of independent means, Brasch was able to devote himself to editing *Landfall* virtually full-time and with the utmost diligence and seriousness. The journal's character owed much to his predilections. It was at his insistence that, as well as publishing poetry, stories and reviews, *Landfall* addressed itself to all the arts and to other aspects of public affairs. He included in each issue commentaries on topical activities in theatre, music, the visual arts, architecture and other cultural fields. He deliberately placed imaginative literature within a social and political context by including lengthy exploratory essays such as T.H. Scott's 'From Emigrant to Native', Bill *Pearson's *'Fretful Sleepers' and Robert *Chapman's 'Fiction and the Social Pattern'. Also noteworthy was the series of essays entitled 'New Zealand Since the War'. Brasch did much to establish a perspective that was (in his phrase) 'distinctly of New Zealand without being parochial'. He encouraged what might be called an enlightened provincialism, recognising that New Zealand was provincial in relation to Europe but nonetheless a centre in its own right, connected with other countries of British origin such as *Canada, *Australia, South Africa and India. Brasch was an exacting and even fussy editor, often insisting on detailed revision from his contributors, not all of whom appreciated his meticulous solicitude. He nevertheless maintained high standards and there was little of genuine literary value written in New Zealand in the two decades of his editorship that he did not recognise and support. He put together *Landfall Country: Work from Landfall 1947–61* (Caxton, 1962), a substantial anthology of the better contributions in poetry, short stories and essays. It also included twenty-nine pages of selections from the high-toned editorial Notes, which he contributed to every number.

Meanwhile Brasch continued to write poetry, publishing with Caxton *The Estate and Other Poems* (1957) and *Ambulando* (1964). *The Estate* was dominated by the long, uneven, personal and philosophical title-poem in thiry-four sections dedicated to the memory of his close friend T.H. Scott who was killed in a climbing accident. The shorter poems have proved more lasting. *Ambulando* represented something of a shift in style as the final poem, 'Cry Mercy', made explicit: 'Getting older, I grow more personal, / Like more, dislike more / And more intensely than ever—/ People, customs, the state, / The ghastly status quo, / And myself, black-hearted crow / In the canting off-white feathers'.

After his retirement from *Landfall* Brasch had more time to devote to his own writing, publishing his fifth, largest, and most various collection, *Not Far Off* (Caxton, 1969). He also engaged in verse translation, publishing versions of poems from the Russian, *German and Punjabi. A sixth collection, *Home Ground*, edited by Alan Roddick, was published posthumously by Caxton in 1974. It included the sinewy and impressive title-sequence and some exquisitely limpid lyrics written during his last illness. Brasch's evolution as poet from a preoccupation with issues of national identity towards broader and more personal concerns was something of a paradigm for the poets of his generation.

One less publicised aspect of Brasch's activities was his anonymous support of New Zealand artists. Sargeson, Colin *McCahon and James K. *Baxter were among those who benefited from his patronage. He bequeathed his notable collection of New Zealand books and paintings to the *Hocken Library. He also contributed substantially to the first residencies for writers, composers and painters, at the University of Otago. The *Burns Fellowship, established from his patronage, provided crucial support for writers including Baxter, Janet *Frame and Ian *Cross.

Since Brasch's death much of his writing has appeared in collected editions. An uncompleted autobiography was published as *Indirections: A Memoir 1909–47* (ed. James Bertram, 1980). This deals in great (if reticent) detail with Brasch's life from childhood up to the time he began editing *Landfall. The Universal Dance: A Selection from the Critical Prose Writings of Charles Brasch* (ed. J.L. Watson, 1981) contains a selection of his *Landfall* Notes, and texts of various essays, reviews and lectures, including *Present Company: Reflections on the Arts*, a kind of artistic manifesto, originally published in 1966. *Collected Poems* (ed. Alan Roddick, 1984) includes the contents of all six of his collections plus a selection of unpublished and uncollected pieces ranging from poems written at school to some left unfinished at his death.   PS

BRATHWAITE, Errol (1924–   ), airman, farmer, soldier, journalist and novelist, was born in Clive, Hawkes Bay, as the son of a dairy farmer. Later the family moved to the small town of Waipukurau, where Errol attended school. Somewhat to his surprise he was suddenly sent to Timaru BHS as a boarder. He was not a highly successful scholar, but did win prizes for speech-making and debating. He was saved from an unhappy life as a railways clerk in Napier when he was conscripted in 1942. He claimed to love the military life. He was trained as an air gunner in Ohakea and served in Guadalcanal, where he had some contact with Japanese forces. He returned a flight sergeant in 1945 and was discharged.

After some years as a journalist Brathwaite produced his first novel, *Fear in the Night*, in 1959. A straightforward adventure story, involving a forced landing in *Japanese territory, it created a strong visual and tactile sense of the jungle and demonstrated competence in plotting, though nothing unconventional.

These skills were developed in *An Affair of Men* (1961), Brathwaite's most successful novel, which won the *Otago Daily Times* centennial novel competition, was translated into half a dozen languages and went into

several international editions. It tells of the conflict on the island of Bougainville between the Japanese officer Itoh, seeking some allied airmen, and the village headman Sedu who is sheltering them. The convincing presentation of Itoh's thoughts and Sedu's diplomatic skills are fascinating. In the battle of wills Sedu adopts a Christian passive-resistance stance that is utterly confusing to Itoh, whose cultural background is completely different. No glib judgments are passed on either of these opponents and the reader's sympathy is never completely alienated from Itoh, despite the acts of violence he gets his men to commit.

This remarkable novel was followed by *Long Way Home* (1964), the story of two survivors from an air crash in the Southern Alps, one blind, the other unable to walk unaided, who pool their resources. The interest, as in *An Affair of Men*, lies in the behaviour of 'tough' men under stress.

Brathwaite's skill in presenting this theme in a kind of indirect free style stands him in good stead in his remarkable trilogy of the *New Zealand wars, which begins with *The Flying Fish* (1964) and with the Taranaki campaigns of the early 1860s. The primary point of view is that of a settler, William Phipps, who is seen struggling with his land and with social ostracism because of his friendship with local Māori and especially with his handyman Matiu, before he is forced like others to abandon his farm and move to New Plymouth because of the increasing danger of war. Together with other fit but socially unacceptable men he joins Captain Williams and his Dragoons, a kind of private army based on the historical Forest Rangers and their charismatic leader von Tempsky. Williams is the central figure of the trilogy, but in this first volume he is observed by the reluctant outsider Phipps, which enables the reader to see the action through the eyes of someone who is almost equally foreign to it. Characters and events, especially the battles, are from detailed historical research, but the point of view through the fictitious Phipps and Williams gives rich opportunities for the kind of identification processes and emotional responses that fiction can provide. Because of his sensitivity to Māori attitudes, Phipps is an especially good mediator—a little like Cedric Tregarthen in The *Greenstone Door. To reinforce this, the narrative sometimes takes the point of view of Matiu, now fighting with the Māori, and Brathwaite makes Matiu's very different thought patterns and attitudes as convincing as those of Itoh in *An Affair of Men*.

At the end of *The Flying Fish*, Phipps and Matiu are dead, so that a new narrative beginning is made with *The Needle's Eye* (1965). Williams and his Dragoons join General Cameron on his march into the *Waikato in 1863–64. Williams is now more mature and more cautious, his fiery aggression tempered with greater awareness of danger and a growing sympathy for the Māori cause. The advance along the Waikato River and the brilliant defensive strategies of the Māori are described in detail, but the centrepiece of the book begins when the Dragoons are sent as an advance post and find a small European settlement at Hairini, near the end-point of the advance at Rangiaowhia. Here Williams meets the irascible and intolerant Dr Harris, who refuses to treat an injured Māori, and the Anglican and Catholic missionaries, who take up opposite positions in the ensuing debate. Williams decides that as the superior officer in a war zone it is his responsibility to bring Harris to trial. Instead of pursuing the campaign he enters into a debate with his officers, the missionaries and Harris, but above all an inner debate with himself, that leads into serious and complex moral conflicts. The war zone becomes a philosophical and ethical minefield, where Williams treads with caution. This unexpected development can irritate readers who were hoping for a story of action, but it is skilfully integrated with action as tensions grow unbearably during the delay in hostilities, and no glib answers are offered.

The trilogy is completed with *The Evil Day* (1967). Major Williams has retired and married and is living the life of a peaceful citizen when he is called to assist in the fight against Titokowaru in Taranaki. His mature awareness of the conflict between civilian and military values adds yet another dimension to the philosophical range of the trilogy. Again Brathwaite tempers the issues by moving between the point of view of the two opponents, Williams and Titokowaru, and offers convincing streams of the thought of each, using his indirect free style, which never completely yields the narrator's point of view to that of the characters. Williams's maturity does not make him milder in battle but even more ruthless, determined to finish the necessary work and return to his farm and family. His strategic intelligence is high, but is matched by that of Titokowaru, a tragic figure who loses *mana by taking the wife of another man, so that the war ends inconclusively with the fading of Māori resistance. The settlers cannot be said to have won, but they take over by default. Brathwaite never presents a black-and-white picture of war but one with many degrees of sympathy for different points of view. This makes his trilogy a major achievement in New Zealand fiction, underestimated perhaps because of its one-sided masculinity. For all his narrative versatility, the feminine point of view is almost missing from his books, though it might also be said to be of little relevance to his themes. When it is of relevance, as a broader frame for the action, it can be found in the lovers and wives of Phipps and Williams and in the powerful women who dominate non-military settler society.

Brathwaite produced a novel for children, *The Flame Box* (1978), which shares a Maurice *Gee motif by having the children climb the hills (near Christchurch) and be carried into a different world, where peoples are in conflict.

However, like other New Zealand writers of fiction, Brathwaite found it hard to cope with indifference and financial restraints. After writing six novels 1959–67, he reluctantly returned to journalism. His books include a two-volume place-by-place description of New Zealand for travellers and *New Zealand and Its People* (1974), a commission from the Government Printing Office which he called 'a middle-of-the-road view of New Zealand aimed at the overseas reader'. The *Dominion* reported 'the reason why a man known as a novelist has not written a novel in seven years: "Until I can consolidate my position financially, I've got to continue taking these commission jobs." Translated that means, "I gotta eat"'.   NW

Brave Company, Guthrie *Wilson's first and best-known novel, was published in the US in 1950 and in England and New Zealand in 1951. Reviewed as one of the more successful novels to emerge from World War 2 (with frequent comparisons to Dan *Davin's *For the Rest of Our Lives*), it focuses on the daily life and ultimate destruction of a platoon of the New Zealand Division in the *Italian campaign of 1944–45. It culminates in a battle based on that at the Senio River, for which Wilson received the Military Cross. Narrated in the first person by 'Lawyer' Considine, an honest, thoughtful member of the platoon, the novel succeeds most in the detail and the sensuous feel of battle and the everyday life of the soldier. It celebrates the men's courage, capability and mateship as tested by war experience: 'Two things are of greatest moment to men—women and war. And the greater, because of its demands upon fortitude, because of its nightmare quality, is war.'   LJ

BREAM, Freda (pseudonym for Patricia Freda Whale, 1918–96), wrote popular murder mysteries set in New Zealand but published in the UK. She began her writing career in middle age, with *Chalk Dust and Chewing Gum* (1970) and *Whistles for the Postie* (1972), based on personal experience as teacher and postwoman. She then wrote twelve murder novels, all set in New Zealand or Norfolk Island (where she served in World War 2) but none published in New Zealand until a 1996 reprint of her first, *Island of Fear* (1982), set on Waiheke Island. Many are held in New Zealand libraries, however, and her short stories have been published in the *NZ Listener* and *New Zealand Women's Weekly*, and read on radio. She also wrote articles and radio plays as 'Pat Whale'. Several stories have been published in German and Norwegian translation. Strong on character and light on violence, often witty and engagingly written, her novels have a droll quality indicated by titles such as *The Vicar Dunnit* (1983), *A Case of Art Failure* (1984) or *The Corpse on the Cruise* (1985). *The Problem at Piha* (1986) is the only one to announce its New Zealand setting, though her last will be published posthumously as 'Murder at the Herald'. She was born and educated in Christchurch and from Canterbury University College won a scholarship to Oxford which the war prevented her taking up. Marrying after the war, she lived and taught in Christchurch, Te Kuiti and Morrinsville, retiring quietly to Auckland, virtually unnoticed as a writer.   RR

Breed of Women, A (1979), a novel by Fiona *Kidman, was one of the most successful works to emerge from the women's movement of the 1970s. The non-conforming Harriet Wallace is born and has her undistinguished school career in 'Ohaka', Northland. Moving to 'Weyville', a south Waikato township, to stay with her father's cousin Alice, she makes friends with Leonie, who arranges a library job and introduces her to the rugby set. There she begins an affair with Denny Rei, a Māori. Racial prejudice brings disgrace when the couple are discovered by Alice, and Harriet leaves, marries Denny and has a baby who dies. The marriage fails and Harriet returns to Weyville. A visit to Wellington leads to remarriage, to Max Taylor, with whom she has three children in their Weyville home. Harriet's continuing restlessness is expressed in poetry, in unconventional behaviour and by an affair. When this is discovered, Harriet and Max move to Wellington, where she becomes a successful television presenter and is reunited with Leonie, now unhappily married. Narrated in flashbacks, the novel ends with a nostalgic visit to Ohaka, where Harriet reflects on the ability of her generation of women to survive the pressures of social conformity.
JS

Breeze, subtitled 'Maoriland's Summer Annual: A Miscellany for Lovers of Nature and Art,' was published in Wellington in 1921. Its single issue was intended to raise capital for a monthly, *The New World*. Contributors included Arthur H. *Adams, Johannes C. *Andersen, O.N. *Gillespie, Maurice Hurst (the probable editor) and Will *Lawson.   SH

BRENSTRUM, Erick (1951–), has published one small volume of poems, *Thalassa: The Words of the Dream* (1982), of a poetic intelligence, originality and lyric intensity that constitute a distinctive voice. The book's title is misleading, as most of the poems are fresh responses to the New Zealand natural environment. Brenstrum can write about the sea, autumn, first love or farewells without cliché ('Come farewell me / the sadness of the traveller / is the losing of new friends'). His reading is international—Neruda is recognised in one poem and the poet acknowledges modern European and American poetry as influences. He writes with the same taut control, ear for cadence and intensity of tone about South American military power or the American Civil War. Or about foreign travel: 'I went to the dictionary / like a child to the beach / came away pockets full of shells / I exercised my new tongue / my ears caught some words / like stray sparrows' ('Summer Notes South Chile'). He writes well about small things, especially birds, yet connects them to big ones, as when 'Horizons' takes a European migratory bird ('body as big / as your cupped hands / drinking cold water') and in the last surprising lines makes it a metaphor for the courage and risk of the great Polynesian migrations across the Pacific.

Born in New Plymouth, Brenstrum has been a meteorologist in Wellington since 1974. Poems like 'The Wind' or 'Ruamahanga' record the weather with expert observation and a more than professional 'delight to the heart'. Though several poems have been published since *Thalassa*, he now writes mostly popular articles on meteorology, in *New Zealand Geographic* and elsewhere, and has a book on the weather in preparation.   RR

BRIDGER, Bub (1924–), poet and short story writer, was born in Napier of Irish and Ngāti Kahungunu descent, and lived in Wellington for many years before moving to Westport. A voracious reader as a child and adolescent, Robin *Hyde was, she has claimed, a particular favourite: '*The Godwits Fly* and *Wednesday's Children* shone in my heart like beacons.' Leaving school at 14, Bridger worked in a number of factory and office jobs and did not begin writing until 1974 when she attended a writer's workshop run by Michael *King. Best known as a poet, though some of her short stories have also been anthologised, her work is characterised by its erotic exuberance, comic fantasy and underlying melancholy. A notable 'live' performer, delivering her poems in a hypnotic half-chant, she has published one collection of poems, *Up Here on the Hill* (1989).   HRi

Bright was a monthly published from Masterton 1941–45, consisting for the most part of locally written stories, poems and articles. A prize of one guinea for the best story in each issue ensured a steady stream of contributions. The poetry is patriotic and clichéd and editorial taste tended towards the conservative. It is notable for five early stories by David *Ballantyne and items by C.R. *Allen and Noel *Hoggard.   SH

BRIGHT, Laurey, see **CLAIR, Daphne**.

BRITTENDEN, R.T. (Dick) (1919–), cricket writer, was born in Rakaia and worked as a journalist on the *Press* 1938–84, becoming its first sports editor in 1955. During the 1950s, 60s and 70s he acted as the NZPA correspondent on cricket tours to Australia, South Africa, India, Pakistan and England. Several of his books, such as *Silver Fern on the Veld* (1954), *Red Leather, Silver Fern* (1965), *Scoreboard '69* (1970) and *Test Series '82* (1982), commemorate these tours or a home Test series; others, notably *Great Days in New Zealand Cricket* (1958), *New Zealand Cricketers* (1961) and *The Finest Years: Twenty Years of New Zealand Cricket* (1977), celebrate key matches and offer portraits of major local figures. The doyen of New Zealand cricket writers, Brittenden's work combines a wide, enthusiastic knowledge of the game with an eye for the character-revealing detail, his style at times displaying a belletristic streak reminiscent of the great chronicler of English cricket, Neville Cardus. HRi

Broadsheet (1) was published by the Victoria University College Literary Society 1947–48. Edited and largely written by W.H. *Oliver, Pat *Wilson, Alistair *Campbell and Erik Schwimmer, its third issue constituted a literary hoax reminiscent of the Australian Ern Malley affair of 1943. After five numbers *Broadsheet* was succeeded by *Hilltop* in 1949. SH

Broadsheet (2) was also the title of an irregular cyclostyled periodical produced 1957–60 by Wellington journalist Brian Bell. Content varies from criticism and satire by Bell, influenced by H.L. Mencken, to reprints of pamphlets issued by the British Campaign for Nuclear Disarmament. James K. *Baxter contributed a poem to the second issue. SH

Broadsheet (3) was a monthly feminist magazine which began in 1972 when 'four women from Auckland Women's Liberation … felt ready to initiate some project which would further the ideals of the women's movement' (Sandra Coney and Sharyn Cederman, No. 31, July 1975). It ceased publication in 1997. Its literary content has included poetry, fiction, reviews and interviews. Especially in its first decade it provided early publication opportunities for new women writers, who included Keri *Hulme (whose 'One Whale, Rising' was first published there, No. 39, May 1976), Helen *Jacobs, Jan *Kemp, Rachel *McAlpine, Rosie *Scott and Elizabeth *Smither. Other work published includes poetry by Cathie *Dunsford and Miriam *Saphira, fiction by Yvonne *du Fresne and Heather *McPherson, and journalism, essays or review articles by Sandra Coney,

Riemke *Ensing and Sandi Hall. Cathy *Downes, Fiona *Kidman, Patricia *Grace and *Renée (Taylor) are among writers interviewed. RR

BROOME, Sir Frederick Napier (1842–96), published two volumes of poetry that drew in part on scenes observed during his years as a Canterbury sheep farmer, *Poems from New Zealand* (1868) and *The Stranger of Seriphos* (1869). Born in Canada, he was the second husband of Lady *Barker, whom he married in England in 1865, during a visit back from Canterbury, where he had worked since emigrating at the age of 15. Their life in Canterbury after marriage is described in her *Station Life in New Zealand*, in which he is affectionately featured as F—. Snowstorm and flood in 1867 caused him to sell up and the couple moved back to England, though his neighbour J.B.A. Acland attributed the farm's failure to Broome's fondness for pig-hunting and poetry-writing. The poetry shows few signs of the pigs and is mostly conventional Victorian descriptive iambics, as of Lake Coleridge: 'Thy native hills crowd countless in the sky; / How rugged are the shores thy smooth waves wet.' After a period as a journalist in London, Broome went on to a series of colonial appointments, as Governor of Western Australia (1883–89) and of Trinidad from 1891 until his death. EM/RR

BROUGHTON, John (1947–), is a Māori playwright with affiliations to Ngāti Kuhungunu and Ngāi Tahu. He grew up and had his schooling in Hastings before studying science at Massey University, where he graduated BSc, and at University of Otago, where he graduated in dentistry in 1977. After a year as dental house surgeon in the School of Dentistry he went into private practice, retiring in 1989 to become a lecturer in Māori health in the Otago Medical School. Broughton has always taken an active interest in military affairs and has been a commissioned officer in the territorials since 1977 and a member of 2 Field Ambulance (NZ) since 1980.

This interest has deeply coloured his plays, which he has been writing since 1988, when he attended a playwriting course held by Roger *Hall. In that year *Te Hara* (The Sin) was performed at Writers' Week in Dunedin. It is concerned with the effect of a belief in *tapu on Māori lives. *Te Hokinga Mai* (The Return) was performed at Writers' Week in the following year and published by Aoraki Productions in 1990. It explores a theme Broughton takes up in greater depth later—a soldier returning from Vietnam and remembering his Māori comrade—and is perhaps best understood as a didactic piece (a 'Lehrstück' in the Brecht tradition), where white audiences are introduced to Māori customs and thoughts. At the International Festival of the Arts in

Wellington in 1990, *Te Hara* was performed together with a new play: *Nga Puke* (The Hills), a love story set in World War 2. World War 1 is the background to *The Private Life of Corporal Cooper*, a one-act play about the relationship between a nun and a Kiwi soldier.

In 1991 *Michael James Minaia* was premièred at Downstage, Wellington, and selected to travel to the Edinburgh Festival. This major work deals with a part-Māori part-Pākehā youth growing up in Hastings in almost idyllic surroundings but burdened with his father's memories of European war. Later he experiences war in *Vietnam and brings his own traumas and the results of Agent Orange back to his life in New Zealand. The action's blend of Māori and Pākehā themes is even more efffective in the language and imagery. The coarse language of a semi-inarticulate but passionate New Zealander is raised to the level of poetry by means of rhythm, imagery and an unobtrusive underlying structure.

Mana and *Frankie and Hone* were written in 1991 for a schools' tour and have been seen by tens of thousands of children. They are concerned with Māori self-determination (tino rangatiratanga) but are non-didactic and entertaining in style, the stories being interwoven with *waiata and references to myths and legends. *A Day at the Races* uses similar techniques to put across an AIDS message for Māori. *1981*, premièred in Dunedin in 1995, explores the tensions surrounding the Springbok rugby tour.

Broughton sees his innovations in the dental and overall health care of Māori as his main goal and views his work as a playwright as another means of contributing to the physical, spiritual and moral health of his people.   NW

BROUGHTON, Rangiahuta Alan Herewini Ruka (Ruka or Alan) (1940–86), of Ngā Rauru Kītahi, was a significant leader in Māori oral culture and expert in *whakapapa, having been taught in the traditional ways by his elders, primarily his uncle Rakei Taituha Kingi, last of the Ngā Rauru Whanganui *tohunga. Born in Patea, Broughton grew up in the Maxwell district, was educated at Te Aute College and Wanganui Technical College, ordained an Anglican minister in 1966 and later trained at Wellington Teachers' College as a Māori language secondary school teacher. He was lecturer in Maori Studies at Victoria University of Wellington from 1980. Broughton was one of the tohunga at the opening of the Te Māori exhibition in New York in 1984, when Māori ceremonial oratory made such an impact at the event and on American television. He was a prize-winning composer of *waiata and created controversy with his book *The Origins of Ngaa Rauru Kiitahi* (1979) in which he asserted that his people,

the Ngā Rauru of Waverly, Waitotara, did not come with the Aotea canoe but were the *tangata whenua, already in the area before the canoe arrived. In 1984 he published a transcription of the letters written by Te Kāhui Kararehe of Te Āti Awa to S. Percy *Smith. He had finished the first draft of his doctoral thesis on the military leader *Tītokuwaru when he became ill.   EM

BROWN, Bernard (1934–), has been called 'an acrobat of the absurd' as a poet. Born near Ipswich, England, he arrived as a lecturer in law at Auckland University in 1962, after a career in the RAF and law lecturing at Singapore University. He spent 1966–69 with the Australian National University as foundation fellow in Papua New Guinea law, gaining the distinction of an arrow wound in New Guinea. His professional writing is chiefly in the area of legal regulation (five titles 1969–93) but early acquaintance with English poets John Heath-Stubbs and D.J. Enright encouraged him to a steady output of poetry, described as 'wise, wicked, witty'. His volumes are *Up to Nowadays* (1972), *Victims and Traders* (1980) and *Surprising the Slug* (1996).   KI

BROWN, J. Edward (1929–), has experience as a marine radio operator and of living in several of the *Pacific islands, and uses both in his fiction. *Chathams Spy Ship* (1974) and *The Glass Arm* (1982) are sea novels, the latter focused on personal and racial tensions aboard a deep-sea tramp. *The Luck of the Islands* (1963) recounts a Rarotongan family's extended visit to Auckland in affectionately amusing terms, though the comedy has an undertone of cultural sympathy that emerges more strongly in several stories in *New Neighbours* (1981). Mostly written for radio, these neatly turned sketches deal with cultural encounter and deracination among the various residents of the Pacific. Brown's stories have appeared in *School Journal*, Te *Ao Hou* and on radio internationally, and his play *Who Killed the Resident Commissioner?* was professionally produced.   RR

BROWN, John Macmillan (1846–1935), wrote, as 'Godfrey Sweven', three works of *Utopian literature, as well as three of Pacific anthropology and a volume of memoirs, after a career as 'the outstanding university teacher in New Zealand before 1900' (*History of the University of Canterbury*). Born into a seafaring Calvinist family in Ayrshire, his outstanding abilities as a student at Glasgow (MA 1869) and Oxford (1869–74) admitted him to Benjamin Jowett's famed literary and scholarly salon at Balliol College. When ill health denied him his Oxford degree, he accepted the foundation chair of classics and English at Canterbury College, arriving in 1874. A teacher of prodigious energy, his scrupulous dedication to his students won an international reputation. His preacher's zeal inspired packed audiences (who paid fees directly to the professor) at lectures that could last over three hours, and all day on Saturdays. He was particularly famed for his philosophical commentaries on English literature, which students left 'as from a sacrament'. This capacity for what Frank ★McKay called 'sustained eloquence' passed into his writings, as well as to his grandson, James K. ★Baxter.

After retirement from teaching in 1895 (though he continued active, serving long terms as vice-chancellor and chancellor of the University of New Zealand), he turned to the genre of the imaginary voyage. *Riallaro: The Archipelago of Exiles* (1901) is, however, only laboriously imaginative and only sedately satiric. Starting from New Zealand, 'with her sombre fiords and the argent glory of her mountains', the narrative travels to mist-shrouded 'dreamy archipelagoes' of the Pacific, with better prospects than 'the labyrinth of disease and wrong and crime … in old Europe'. Echoes of Arnold recur. The social philosophy is too elitist and totalitarian for modern tastes, but there are surprises, as when a chapter on 'the organization of repute' turns out to anticipate late twentieth-century methods of public relations and image-marketing, even to newspapers in the hands of publicists and sensationalists. A purist view of language, that words need to be cleansed of 'ambiguities and shifting senses', perhaps explains the lucid formality of Brown's own style. At its lightest moments it is Miltonic.

Limanora, The Island of Progress (1903) is even more perfunctory as fiction and a more consistent Utopia, though ★*Erewhon*'s 'cynical utopia' (as Brown called it) is an influence. It expounds a meliorist version of evolution, incorporating eugenics, idealised scientific progress, and the then-fashionable fantasy of human flight. But its bloodless ideal of a race free from vanity or lust is not made attractive even by its unexpectedly feminist views on work for women. Macmillan Brown's wife, Helen Connon, the British Empire's first woman honours graduate, had been principal of Christchurch GHS. Her death early in 1903 may explain the poignant note of romantic loss that tinges the book's ending. A third Utopia, 'Beyond', exists in manuscript. While their spacious eloquence now has little appeal, they have a place in the New Zealand traditions of Utopian speculation and social polemic, and they look innovatively towards a Pacific rather than European future.

A large bequest to Canterbury University College included his library of 15 000 volumes; and nationally he endowed the Macmillan Brown Prizes (the Poetry Prize at Otago was the first award won by James K. Baxter) and Memorial Lectures, a distinguished series which have often contributed to understanding of New Zealand literature, most notably when delivered by Baxter at Victoria University College in 1954. Baxter also 'struggled to edit' his grandfather's papers. *The Memoirs of John Macmillan Brown* (1974) were eventually edited by R.A. ★Copland, including a brief introduction in which Baxter confessed 'I am haunted by this ancestral voice which insists that the intellectual and moral betterment of mankind is achievable.'

RR

Brown Man's Burden (1938), a book of short stories by Roderick ★Finlayson, was printed in an edition of 250 copies by Ronald Holloway at his ★Griffin Press, after being started by Robert ★Lowry at the Unicorn Press. It contained twelve brief stories of Māori life between World War 1 and the ★Depression, strongly influenced by the Sicilian peasant stories of Giovanni Verga as translated by D.H. ★Lawrence. In his foreword, Finlayson states that the stories 'deal chiefly with the annihilation of [Māori] culture by our scientific barbarism, and the something, pathetic or humorous, that yet remains'. He saw Māori culture as having suffered a 'gradual invasion … by modern materialism', but thought that 'the Maori still retains much of the poetic life of his forefathers … a life dependent upon the forces and powers of nature.' The 'invasion' includes the Pākehā money culture, popular films and music, the legal system, tourism, technology, disease and religion. While the Māori occasionally win a skirmish, as in 'The Totara Tree' (frequently anthologised), when the attempt of the electricity department to cut down a sacred tree is thwarted, the ultimate result threatens to be the destruction of Māori culture. At the same time, in some of the stories Finlayson shows that a 'poetic life … dependent upon the forces of nature' has its own dangers when one of those forces is sexuality. Jealousy and passion lead to violence and sudden death in 'The Wedding Gift', 'New Year', 'The Tangi', 'The Storm', 'By the Calm Waters' and 'Tiki-Tiki'.

In 1973, an expanded edition, edited by Bill ★Pearson, appeared, containing all but one of the original stories, plus stories of later Māori life from Finlayson's other collections and from his uncollected works. The additional stories carry further the process of culture loss, showing landless Māori working as labourers on Chinese market gardens in the 1930s and becoming rootless and urbanised in the post-war period.   LJ

BROWN, Riwia (1957–), playwright and screenwriter, was born in Wellington, her iwi affiliations with Ngāti Porou, Te Whānau-a-Apanui and Taranaki. Her first play was 'Roimata' (The Depot, 1988), followed by its sequel, 'Te Hokinga' (Taki Rua Depot, 1990). These two plays tell the story of Roimata, who, after the death of her mother on the East Coast, comes to Wellington to meet Girlie, her half-sister, for the first time. Girlie introduces Roimata to the intricacies of city life and to her friends Mouse, Blue Boy and, in particular, Eddy. She also meets Kevin, an old friend from home, who has joined the Salvation Army. These plays were followed by 'Ngā Wahine' (Taki Rua Depot, 1992), a contemporary story about Moana and Dana, two pregnant women who meet in a maternity ward. Although their meeting is brief, they form an intimate bond. Next came 'The Debate' (Bats, 1994), a one-act play about two teams of student debaters who are contesting the final of a national debating competition on the topic 'That the Māori language should be the national language'. 'Irirangi Bay' (Taki Rua, 1996) followed, in which a seemingly perfectly married 1950s couple are the victims of a web of secrets. The play follows the consequences of a makutu (curse) laid during the Land Wars. 'Roimata' was adapted for television in a production written and directed by the author. Brown also wrote the screenplay for *Once Were Warriors, the internationally successful adaptation of Alan *Duff's novel, and adapted Debra Savage's novel, *The Flight of the Albatross*, to film.   SG

BROWNE, Mary-Louise (1957–), artist, was born in Auckland and attended Elam School of Fine Arts (MFA 1982). She has worked in performance, installation and sculpture and has made a number of limited edition artist's books, including *Off White Papers* (1979), *Black and /or White* (1982) and *Vicious Circles* (1986). She is best known for her sculptural series she calls 'Transmutations', where one word becomes another, by a sequence of single letter shifts, for example from 'deaf' to 'mute' (*Untitled (Deaf/Mute)*, 1990). Functioning as three-dimensional objects where words are visually arranged, such works have both a physical and a literal meaning. Browne is typical of a number of artists who, in the 1980s–90s, explore the interplay between word and image, forms and languages. She has said 'I am committed to exploring the possibilities of literary intermedia in regard to my interest in socio-political issues'.   CB

BRUNO, Frank (pseudonym of Albert Francis St Bruno, 1910–67), was born in Sydney and moved to New Zealand as a child. He later travelled round Australia during the *Depression years, freelancing for newspapers. Other occupations in Australia and New Zealand included hobo, lightning-caricaturist and professional boxer (Frank Bruno the 1995 world heavyweight champion is no relation). In World War 2 he was a machine gunner with the '39ers' (First Echelon) of the New Zealand Division. In middle age he produced a series of entertaining novels, mainly lurid action

adventures set in nineteenth-century New Zealand. The best-known are *The Hellbuster* (1959), located in the Bay of Islands in 1843, *Black Noon at Ngutu* (1960), a sensationalised treatment of the New Zealand *Wars in Taranaki in the 1860s, and *Fury at Finnegan's Folly* (1962), an equally colourful portrayal of life on the West Coast *goldfields. In 1965 he founded and edited an ex-Service paper called *ACTION*. He also wrote short stories, features (primarily for the *Auckland Star)* and small illustrated books, and drew cartoons. He continued to coach boxing (including at least one notable current writer among his protégés) and achieved brief fame for cornering an escaped lion in his back garden.

EM/RR

BRUNTON, Alan (1946–), is a poet, scriptwriter and performer. Born in Christchurch, he was educated at Hamilton BHS, University of Auckland (BA, 1967) and Victoria University (MA in English, 1968). He began contributing poems to student magazines from 1968, revealing connections and affinities with various strands of British, American and (later) continental modernism, and in 1969 was founding editor of *Freed, for which he wrote manifestos declaring 'the word is freed' from provincial disabilities and reactionary poetics. From 1970 Brunton spent three years in Europe and Asia, publishing his first small book, *Messengers in Blackface* (1973), in London. Back in New Zealand 1974–78 he founded (with his partner Sally Rodwell) the important experimental theatre group *Red Mole, for whom he wrote and performed around forty-five scripts 1975–95. He also co-edited (with Ian *Wedde) the tabloid-format arts magazine *Spleen, eight issues of which appeared in 1976–77. Meanwhile he wrote *Black & White Anthology* (*Hawk Press, 1976), a 33-part sequence with an Asian setting, and *Oh Ravachol* (Red Mole, 1978), highly allusive and apocalyptic poems printed in tabloid format, many of them written with performance in mind. He spent the next decade 1978–88 abroad, mostly in New York, New Mexico, London and Amsterdam, scripting and performing in Red Mole shows. Two limited editions of poetry were published in New York: *And She Said* (Red Mole, 1984) and *New Order* (Red Mole, 1986). Selections from these books together with other poems from the 'lost decade' were included in *Slow Passes 1978–88*, with an introduction by Peter Simpson (1991). Since 1988 Brunton has lived in Wellington. A selection of his performance scripts was published in 1989 as *A Red Mole Sketchbook*, and in the same year *Day for a Daughter*, with drawings by Sally Rodwell (*Untold Books). *Ephphatha* (1994), a word-and-image text, resulted from collaboration with the visual artist and publisher Richard *Killeen. An endlessly fertile, eclectic and prolific poet and scriptwriter, Brunton has also worked as an editor, director, performance tutor, literary critic and community arts worker.   PS

BUCHANAN, Dorothy (1945–   ), composer and teacher, was born in Christchurch. Many of her works are settings of New Zealand writers, such as Janet *Frame, Stevan *Eldred-Grigg, Margaret *Mahy, Witi *Ihimaera, the poets Fleur *Adcock, Lauris *Edmond, Ruth *Gilbert and Ian *Wedde and the satirist A.K. *Grant. Her *Five Vignettes of Women* (1987) for flute and female chorus gives portraits of Virginia Woolf, Olivia Spencer-Bower, Robin *Hyde, Fanny Buss and Katherine *Mansfield. Elizabeth Kerr described the work as 'unashamedly romantic … an intense and committed statement from a composer who feels no need to suppress her femaleness to achieve as a creative artist'. She has been closely associated with the New Zealand Film Archive in Wellington and has written music for classic silent films such as *Queen of Rivers* (1925) and an original score for the comedy-romance *The Adventures of Algy* (1925). She has worked closely with painters and poets, enjoys collaborating with young people, and has also played a leading role as a lecturer, writer, adjudicator and musical director. The New Zealand *landscape has been a major influence on her work. A chamber opera based on Katherine Mansfield's 'The *Woman at the Store', libretto by Jeremy Commons, had its première in 1998.   JMT

BUCK, Peter (Te Rangi Hiroa) (1877?–1951), one of the most distinguished of all Māori and New Zealand leaders, wrote three significant books on the history and life of Polynesian peoples. His anthropological learning was combined with remarkable personal gifts and accomplishments, wide experience and outstanding communication and literary skills, which place his writing outside merely academic literature.

Born at Urenui of an Anglo-Irish father and Ngāti Mutunga mother, he said he was 'binomial, bilingual, and inherit a mixture of two bloods that I would not change for a total of either.… My mother's blood enables me to appreciate a culture to which I belong, and my father's speech enables me to interpret it, inadequate though the rendering be at times.' Such personal reflections, engaging but never indulgent, are typical of the accessible writing of his major books, in which it is not far-fetched to see a mixture of Māori eloquence with Irish raconteurship; two traditions untouched by puritan earnestness through which he communicated the findings of European scholarly research.

Buck's life story is known from every book of famous New Zealanders, and has been most recently recounted in the *Dictionary of New Zealand Biography,*

Vol. 3 (1996). Educated at Te Aute College and Otago University, he graduated as a surgeon (ChB 1904, MD 1910), was also a brilliant all-round athlete, winning the New Zealand long jump championship 1900 and 1904, went on to a public career in Māori health, entered politics and rose to cabinet minister 1912–14. In World War 1 he won the DSO for gallantry and rose to second-in-command of the NZ Pioneer Batallion 1916–17. After the war he turned his considerable intellect increasingly to anthropology and in 1926 resigned as Director of Maori Hygiene to accept an invitation as research fellow at the Bishop Museum, Honolulu. Recognised by a visiting professorship at Yale 1932–34, he was appointed director of the Bishop Museum in 1936, and the position was extended virtually to his death at the age of 71. Numerous academic awards in USA testified to his standing as, in a colleague's words, 'the Great Chief of Polynesia', and in New Zealand his knighthood in 1946, many other distinctions, the symbolic canoe prow memorial over his ashes at Okoki in Taranaki, and the continued high readership of his books, all support M.P.K. Sorrensen's summary in *DNZB* that 'his standing as an anthropologist … remains untouched, as does his mana in Maoridom'.

Buck's publications comprise eleven substantial monographs, about sixty articles and the three major books. *The Coming of the Maori* began as a popular lecture and was originally published by the Cawthorne Institute, Nelson, as a paper in 1925, then expanded into book form in 1949; and has been very often reprinted. *Vikings of the Sunrise* (1938), a lucid and entertaining outline of Polynesian history and culture, was aimed at American readers, and was very successful there and locally after its New Zealand publication in 1954. *Anthropology and Religion* (1939) is a similarly readable account of Polynesian belief systems.

Together the three books, especially the first two, stand as one of New Zealand's key narratives of origin and identity. They built on and in part superseded the work of Johannes *Andersen and Elsdon *Best, with both of whom Buck undertook field trips early in his career. Scholarly, judicious, massively informative, they are also enriched like a fine novel by a sincere, wise, witty, anecdotal, personal voice, of great warmth and charisma, profoundly engaged with the subject yet never dogmatic. His own modest justification (in the Prologue to *Vikings*) was that 'personal incidents … give the story a more human atmosphere'. More than that, the voice enables the reader to participate, not merely be instructed, sharing the reflections of a mind for which one feels respect and affection. The writing is skilfully bicultural, too. The natural inclusion of sayings, songs, chants and poems within the narrative affirms the richness of the culture being described (and anticipates their use by novelists such as Heretaunga Pat *Baker and Witi *Ihimaera); while jokes like describing Whiro (who opposed Tane's plan to separate *Rangi and Papa) as leading 'the first conservative party in the South Seas' help non-Polynesian readers to a comfortable and good-humoured response.

Allen *Curnow's verse play *The Axe* (1948) derives from an incident described by Buck; Ihimaera's use of 'The New Net Goes Fishing' as a book title (1977), while the saying is of ancient provenance, must still remind most readers of Buck's famous use of it in the moving tribute and implied challenge to his people that close *Vikings of the Sunrise*. The full dissemination into literature of Buck's narratives, ideas and information is now incalculable.   RR

BUDD, Lillian, is a pseudonym. She is a text-based artist working with collage, assemblage, installation, film and video and is particularly concerned to explore language for the ways it mediates experience. The texts she uses are from a multitude of sources, including French feminists like Hélène Cixous and Julia Kristeva; film, literary and psychoanalytical theorists; manuals, self-help guides, encyclopedias and tourist brochures; colloquial speech; and recently philosophers such as Pascal and Descartes. She treats them as her material, copying, cutting, collaging and erasing, so that their meaning and narrative structure are denied. Despite this, her text-pieces allude to the physical formats of her literary sources, as books, scrolls, sheets and 'pages', and to fictional and non-fictional literary forms, like the diary, biography, novel or treatise. Her published texts include *The Woman* (1986), films like *A Narrative That Provides the Measure of Desire* (1987) and installations like *The Story of* (1991).   CB

Bulibasha (1994), a novel by Witi *Ihimaera.

BULLER, Sir Walter Lawry (1838–1906), was born in the Bay of Islands as the son of the missionary James Buller (1812–84; author of *Forty Years in New Zealand*, 1878, and *New Zealand: Past and Present*, 1880). Bilingual from childhood, he worked as a court interpreter in Wellington and later edited the didactic newspaper *Te Karere o Poneke*. He was also editor of the *Maori Messenger* and its successor *Te Manuhiri Tuarangi: The Maori Intelligencer*. However, he is best known for his ornithological masterpieces: *A History of the Birds of New Zealand* (1873) and *A Manual of the Birds of New Zealand* (1882), both beautifully illustrated with hand-coloured lithographs by J.G. Keuleman. These classificatory works are still of value to naturalists.   NW

Bulletin, *Australia's most famous weekly magazine, founded in Sydney in 1880 by J.F. Archibald and John Haynes, was a notable venue for New Zealand writing during its first eighty years, especially after the establishment of its 'Red Page' in 1896 by the influential literary editor, A.G. Stephens. Nearly 300 New Zealand authors contributed over 4000 items of verse and 700 short stories, and there were numerous reviews and commentaries on New Zealand literature by both New Zealanders and Australians. New Zealanders were also influential literary editors of the *Bulletin*. Between 1906 (when Stephens departed) and 1926 the Red Page was edited firstly by A.H. *Adams (until 1909) and, after 1912, by David McKee *Wright. In the later 1930s Douglas *Stewart joined the magazine, and was its literary editor 1940–60, when it was sold to the Australian Consolidated Press and became primarily a news magazine.

Because the *Bulletin* was a popular magazine, much of its verse and fiction was light and occasional, written under pseudonyms whose identities are now lost. However, the magazine also assisted many New Zealand writers into professional careers, especially between the 1890s and 1930s when few similar outlets existed in New Zealand. Regular contributors, among those whose careers began under the benign dictatorship of Stephens, included the poets A.H. Adams, Hubert *Church, Dora *Wilcox, Will *Lawson and Frank *Morton, and the short story writers C.A. *Jeffries and Constance Clyde. In the 1910s and 1920s, McKee Wright, then Boyce Bowden and Dulcie *Deamer, joined the still-prolific Jeffries, Adams, Lawson and Morton; and in the 1930s–40s, under Stewart, a new group emerged, including Arnold *Wall, Elizabeth *Riddell, William *Hart-Smith and Stewart himself. The longest-serving contributor, from 1900 to 1955, was the balladist Will Lawson, in later years an author of romances of pioneering days. The most prolific was McKee Wright, who contributed 1600 items 1906–28, mainly satirical verse (much of it written under the pseudonyms of 'Pat O'Maori', 'Curse O'Moses', 'Mary McCommonwealth' and 'George Street') but also short stories, playlets and a stream of often provocative Red Page editorials defending traditional versecraft and Irish culture. This is probably the most unabashed example of editorial self-promotion in Australasian literary history.

The *Bulletin* was also important for other New Zealand writers at different stages of their careers. Edith *Lyttleton ('G.B. Lancaster'), who described the *Bulletin* as her 'literary father', published forty stories there before travelling overseas in 1909. A.A. *Grace's second volume of short stories, *Tales of a Dying Race* (1901), initially appeared there. Later, numerous of the *Kowhai Gold* poets are found in its pages, and in the 1920s and 1930s there were regular contributions from the literary editors Quentin *Pope and O.N. *Gillespie (as there had been from Ernest *Currie earlier in the century), and from the poets Eileen *Duggan, Robin *Hyde and Eve *Langley. Stewart continued to champion these poets in the 1940s, as well as Wall, J.R. *Hervey and later Hart-Smith and Gloria *Rawlinson. He also published stories by A.P. *Gaskell, Roderick *Finlayson (most of whose *Tidal Creek* stories first appeared in the *Bulletin*), J.H. Melville (whose work, like that of Jeffries earlier in the century, remained unpublished), and Olaf Ruhen.

Although the *Bulletin* did not sponsor any significant 'bush ballad' tradition in New Zealand, it provided space for a new generation of largely New Zealand–born writers at the turn of the century who were reacting in different ways against the more genteel Anglophile writing represented by the mid-Victorian tradition of *Domett, *Bracken and others. Church belonged to that older tradition, but most of the others did not. Lawson's balladry of the railways and the sea, Lancaster's stories of rough back-country workers, Clyde's witty and idiosyncratic feminism, Morton's francophile fin-de-siècle bohemianism, Jeffries's satiric portrayals of New Zealand's burgeoning railway bureaucracy and the Canterbury squattocracy, Adams's poetic questionings of colonial identity and tentative gropings towards a modern style (and his later fictional efforts to render urban and suburban life as romance), and Wright's unusual mix of topical satire, Celtic romanticism and tra-ditionalist poetics—none of this work can be readily fitted into any *Bulletin* 'Australian school', nor into the older genteel pattern of New Zealand colonial writing.

Although their achievement is often uneven, such writers saw themselves as striving to represent new aspects of contemporary New Zealand life and con-sciousness, and the *Bulletin* gave them the opportunity to speak directly to a large local readership in New Zealand and Australia. A feature of the authors themselves in this period is their constant movement back and forth across the Tasman Sea. Notwithstanding New Zealand's criti-cal emphasis on the powerful Anglo-European instance of Katherine *Mansfield, the problems of location, iden-tity and allegiance typically associated with expatriation have occurred most frequently, for New Zealand writers, in relation to Australia.

As an arbiter of critical taste about New Zealand writing, the *Bulletin* was also influential. Stephens's reviews and articles were often highly critical (even of the authors he gave generous space to on the Red Page), but his judgments and insights were widely respected in New Zealand and remarkably prescient of later evaluations. Adams was also an acute, often acerbic and opinionated

critic, especially of fiction. However, by far the most sig-nificant body of critical writing about New Zealand liter-ature was contained in Stewart's long editorial reviews in the 1940s and early 1950s, including C.A. *Marris's annual *New Zealand Best Poems*, the *Caxton Press poets, the magazine *New Zealand New Writing*, fiction by Frank *Sargeson, Finlayson and Langley, and critical writings by E.H. *McCormick, M.H. *Holcroft, A.R.D. *Fairburn, Allen *Curnow and others. He used the *Bulletin's* edi-torial pages to shape an expansive critique of New Zealand literature, emphasising the comic spirit of the best writing, the value of American models for local nationalism, and the importance of the romantic lyric tradition for landscape poetry. Sceptical of the environ-mental and social determinisms he detected in McCor-mick and Holcroft, many of his assessments—of women writers like Duggan, Hyde, Langley and Rawlinson, for example—pre-dated the revisionist New Zealand literary history of the 1980s. Stewart also had first-rate editorial judgment. Although by the 1930s the *Bulletin* had ceased to be a mainstream outlet for New Zealand writers (few of the Caxton authors ever contributed to its pages), the 700 New Zealand poems and short stories, including his own, which he published in the magazine 1940–60, alongside 400 reviews and comments by himself and others, were matched in quality and quantity, in New Zealand itself, only by the *NZ Listener*.   TS

BULLOCK, Margaret (1845–1903), journalist, fem-inist and novelist, was born (as Margaret Carson) in Auckland. When her husband George Bullock, a ware-houseman, died in a shipwreck in 1877 she took her young family to Wanganui, where her brother was editor of the *Wanganui Chronicle*.

Some ten years later she began publishing short stories for English and New Zealand papers, sometimes under the name 'Madge', and acquired an eager reader-ship. Her only novel, *Utu: A Story of Love, Hate and Revenge* (1894), was published under the pseudonym 'Tua-o-Rangi'. It was based on the New Zealand visit of the French explorer Marion du Fresne in 1772. In the preface she wrote: 'Whatever may be thought of my tale, as a whole, it may justly claim to be "founded on fact", for, though the characters are imaginary, the incidents are worked up from reliable materials, and the more shocking events are but detailed reflexes of historical facts.' Her publisher had encouraged her to make the story as sensational as possible.

She also exhibited and sold portraits of Māori under the name 'Maggie Bullock'. Activity in women's rights and welfare movements brought her into association with Kate Shepherd and she campaigned for *women's suffrage in Wanganui. Her life has been researched by Bronwyn

Labrum. (See *Dictionary of New Zealand Biography*, vol. 2., and *The Book of New Zealand Women*, 1991).

In *The Maorilander* (1964) Philip *Wilson speculates that *Utu* was written by William *Satchell, but Bullock's authorship was confirmed by A.G. Bagnall from letters by her to Sir George *Grey in the Grey Collection.　NW

bullock-driver (1846) and its familiar short form *bullocky* (1854) denote a man employed to handle a bullock-team who was stereotypically notorious in early colonial life and literature for swearing ('bullock language'). Samuel *Butler's accounts in *A First Year in Canterbury Settlement* of bullocks' frustrating conduct may explain the habit. Lumbering animals with lumbering souls (he claims), they contrive tricks with the yoke that 'would make a conjurer's fortune', while their nocturnal vagrancies left 'the word "bullock" eating itself in indelible characters into his heart'. *Bullocky's joy* (1933) is treacle: 'For when dad was a boy, / Bullocky's joy, / The only jam they knew, / Was treacle black / As an old coal sack / And thick as rubber glue.' (J. Charles, *Black Billy Tea*, 1981).　HO

BUNN, Alan (1944–　), writes vigorous novels of outdoor experience for young adults. Born in Kent, he emigrated in 1954 and was educated at Southland BHS, Riccarton HS and Canterbury University. He now lives in Sumner. His years of teaching teenagers have provided him with material for convincing and appealing novels featuring tramping, surfing, canoeing and hunting, as well as the social stresses of city environments—school, peer pressures and macho cults of beer and drugs. His novels include *Water in the Blood* (1990), Best First Book Award in 1991; its independent sequel, *Driving Force* (1991), which portrays a young man's fight with cancer against the background of the Coast-to-Coast endurance race; and *Road Warriors* (1993), a sophisticated, humorous mixing of Sam's and his father's efforts in triathlon competitions and romantic attachments.　DH

BURDON, R.M. (Randal Mathews) (1896–1965), was a cavalry officer, Canterbury sheep farmer, biographer of notable New Zealanders, novelist, book reviewer and historian, who is remembered chiefly for his non-fiction. *High Country: The Evolution of a New Zealand Sheep Station* (1938) is imbued with Burdon's own experience as a practical sheep farmer, offering convincing details about the work and problems of runholders not usually found in early chronicles. Burdon's biographical approach in his three series of *New Zealand Notables* (*Caxton Press, 1941, 1945, 1950) sympathetically details his subjects' merits and deficiencies, using them to exemplify his conclusions about the implications of human behaviour.

This tendency to explicit comment is also evident in his only novel, *Outlaw's Progress* (1943), based on the Stanley Graham manhunt in Westland. Burdon's careful diagnosis of its protagonist as a victimised *'Man Alone' separates his prose from narratives by his contemporaries, Frank *Sargeson and John *Mulgan, with their modern avoidance of the authorial voice. Although Owen Marley attains an *existential appreciation of the *bush, he is not a free agent like Villiers from Erik de Mauny's treatment of the Graham manhunt, *The Huntsman in His Career* (1949), because he never accepts responsibility for his destiny. Later biographies, *The Life and Times of Sir Julius Vogel* (1948), *King Dick: A Biography of Richard John Seddon* (1955) and *Scholar Errant: A Biography of Professor A.W. Bickerton* (1956) blend accessible accounts of these notables with analyses of their social and political environments. Burdon also wrote *24 Battalion* (1953), a volume in the *Official History of New Zealand in the Second World War* series. His last publication, *The New Dominion: A Social and Political History of New Zealand, 1918–39* (1965), was praised for its biographical treatment of famous political figures but criticised for its failure to go beyond traditional interpretations of events or position them within a wider historical perspective.　DB

BURN, D.W.M. (1862–1951), poet, was born in Geelong, Victoria, but lived for most of his life in Otago, where he worked as a schoolmaster. Under the pseudonym 'Marsyas' he published screeds of verse in the *Otago Daily Times*, and occasional pamphlets. His poetry was collected in five substantial volumes, the first, *Cantilenae Nugae*, appearing in 1891. The remaining four volumes, published after Burn's retirement, were *Eggs and Olives* (1930), *Soundings* (1931), *Pedlar's Pack* (1932) and *Flax and Fernseed* (1933). Although Burn's later verse offers glimpses of New Zealand life and landscape, the bulk of it could have been penned anywhere in England. His poems are predominantly Romantic imitation; intensely personal and pastoral, and excessively burdened with religious allusion. The original Marsyas, a satyr, was flayed alive for challenging Apollo to a contest on the flute. Burn's poetry seems more likely to have induced torpor in the god than rivalry.　PM

Burning Boy, The (1990), a novel by Maurice *Gee, traces the social complexities relating to the children in a school, their parents and the headmistress, Norma, in Saxton, a small town noticeably similar to Nelson. Duncan, the eponymous boy, is disfigured in a terrible accident but develops an extraordinary intellectual ability which intimidates his elders, although Norma encourages him. The other children are more interested in matters of the body, apparently growing up to follow their parents' stultifying material values and thwarted sexuality. In rebellion against this, Les Clearwater leaves his school-teaching job and lives alone with goats, coming to resemble them until, ironically, he becomes even more a creature of the body than the people he has turned from. The vision is dark, but lightened by the humanity of Norma, who finds ways to balance the needs of the children and adults and achieves a surprisingly rich awareness of all their characters, making the provincial world look less stifling and restricted than its surface. Since *The Big Season* Gee's image of provincial New Zealand has grown more complex, but he has lost none of his sharp awareness of the limitations imposed by its *puritanism.   NW

BURNS, Carolyn, playwright, was born in Dunedin, and has lived in Auckland and Adelaide. She has worked as an actor, journalist and writer for television. Involvement with an Auckland children's theatre group prompted her to write for the stage, and her one published play, *Objection Overruled* (1985), reflects her interest in and concern for children. It explores the intergenerational consequences of emotional repression and in particular sexual abuse of children.

The play is technically adventurous, invoking the conventions of the courtroom only to subvert, disrupt and overrule them comprehensively, along with those of the theatre. The result is a challenging mixture of bold social realism, surrealism, satire, tragedy and boisterous comedy, given an unpredictable edge by the introduction of audience participation. *Objection Overruled* succeeded in its initial Christchurch production; but unsympathetic interpretation and modification of the play by a subsequent director discouraged Burns from writing further for the theatre.   JH

Burns Fellowship, The, at the University of Otago, New Zealand's first writer-in-residence position, was endowed in 1958 by a group of Dunedin citizens and academics, notably Charles *Brasch and Alan *Horsman, to mark the bicentenary of Robert Burns (1759–96) and in appreciation of service to Otago's development by the Burns family. Scotland's national poet was already the only author (so far) to be memorialised in New Zealand by a statue, the centrepiece of Dunedin's Octagon. Burns's songs and ballads in Scottish vernacular also inspired a whole school of homesick Otago settler poets, such as John *Barr. 'Auld Lang Syne', partly of Burns's composition, remains, in New Zealand as elsewhere, one of the best-known, if not best-comprehended, texts in any variety of English.

The Burns Fellowship has fulfilled its aim 'to encourage and promote the writing of imaginative New Zealand literature', contributing to the development of writers as important as Janet *Frame and Maurice *Gee. The tenure of James K. *Baxter produced a number of local and occasional verses, most notoriously 'An Ode to Mixed Flatting', and that of Roger *Hall led directly to Otago University's development of courses in creative writing. The Burns Fellows have been: 1959 Ian *Cross, 1960 Maurice *Duggan, 1961 John *Caselberg, 1962 R.A.K. *Mason, 1963 Maurice *Shadbolt, 1964 Maurice Gee, 1965 Janet Frame, 1966–67 James K. Baxter, 1968 Ruth *Dallas, 1969 Warren *Dibble and Hone *Tuwhare, 1970 O.E. *Middleton, 1971 Noel *Hilliard, 1972 Ian *Wedde, 1973 Graham *Billing, 1974 Hone *Tuwhare, 1975 Sam *Hunt and Witi *Ihimaera, 1977 Roger *Hall and Keri *Hulme, 1978 Roger Hall and Peter *Olds, 1979 Michael Noonan, 1980 Philip *Temple, 1981–82 Bill *Sewell, 1983 Rawiri *Paratene, 1984 Brian *Turner, 1985–86 Cilla *McQueen, 1987 Robert *Lord, 1988 John Dickson, 1989 *Renée, 1990 David *Eggleton, 1991 Lynley Hood, 1992 Owen *Marshall, 1993 Stuart *Hoar, 1994 Christine *Johnston, 1995 Elspeth *Sandys, 1996 Bernadette *Hall, 1997 Paddy Richardson, 1998 Michael *King.   RR

bush, 'recent, and probably a direct adoption of the Dutch 'bosch'= woodland' (OED); US 1779, South Africa 1780, Australia 1790, NZ 1810. Until the early–middle nineteenth century writers apparently preferred, in New Zealand reference, 'woods' and its derivatives, but by the mid-nineteenth century Samuel *Butler, for instance, habitually and comfortably uses 'bush'. On the first occasion he distinguishes it from European terms: 'Here, for the first time, I saw the bush; it was very beautiful; numerous creepers, and a luxuriant undergrowth among the trees, gave the forest a wholly un-European aspect, and realised, in some degree, one's idea of tropical vegetation.... The trees here are all evergreens, and are not considered very good for timber' (*A First Year in Canterbury Settlement*, 1863). The term also had a wider meaning virtually synonymous with *'backblocks', not necessarily wooded land, as in Dugald *Ferguson's *Vicissitudes of Bush Life* (1891) or when Thomas *Arnold defines it as 'the wild, thinly inhabited country'.

The mixed implications of 'clearing the bush' for farming concerned some early writers. Blanche *Baughan probably best caught both the pride at taming the wild ('That bit o' Bush paddock I fall'd myself, an' watched, each year, come clean / Don't it look fresh in the tawny ? A scrap of Old-Country green', 'The Old Place'), and the conflicting sense of loss and devastation ('Ay, the Fire went through and the Bush has departed, / The green Bush departed, green Clearing is not yet come', 'A Bush Section'). Katherine *Mansfield unembarrassedly uses 'bush' as one of the indicators (to English readers) of the New Zealand setting of the opening of *At the Bay,* along with 'paddock', 'toi–toi' and others. Barry *Crump similarly sets the scene in A *Good Keen Man with 'the dark bush', and frequented uses 'bushed' in its literal and figurative senses (cut off or lost in bush, thus metaphorically baffled, exhausted).

In the variety of its combining forms, compounds and senses, 'bush' is the most extensive and complex item in the New Zealand English lexis. Twentieth-century usage seems to confine 'forest' and its derivatives mainly to 'exotic plantation' and 'bush' to 'native forest', often with a strong conservation message in the term 'native bush'. HO/RR

Butcher Papers, The (1982), is a collection of poems by Vincent *O'Sullivan. 'Butcher', a fictional character and dramatic mouthpiece for reflections on life, had appeared in the earlier *Butcher & Co.* (1977). He interacts with his girlfriend Sheila, an intellectual cousin, Baldy, a smooth-talking rival in love, Mac, and the odd customer, and so functions in more complex ways than Denis *Glover's Harry, a ventriloquist's dummy for Glover's own bluff lyricism. Butcher's trade ensures his familiarity with flesh and blood and guts. Coarse and macho, he is 'physical man', with a touch of the Kiwi folk hero. But, along with the meat, he retails his homespun philosophy, and is not without soul. 'There's a high sweet figure / inside every butcher.' He has his instinctive wisdom. In an individual rhetoric pungent with the vernacular, he offers variations on the *carpe diem* theme, knowing well enough that 'we're all in for an end'. He is haunted by death-figure 'Rider', and retains a vivid memory of a day when, with 'the grunt before Sheila sharp beside him' on 'the top of a spur', he watched a hawk circling high over its prey. Though the poet distances himself from the dramatised and reported voices, they are subsumed within his own. MPJ

Butcher Shop, The, the first novel of Jean *Devanny, was published in 1926 by Duckworth, London. Margaret Errol, a young girl working as a housemaid on a King Country station, is courted by her employer, Barry Messenger. Despite differences in class and age, they marry, have children, and establish a life for themselves, assisted by Barry's friend, Jimmy Tutaki. However, when a new manager, Glengarry, arrives, Margaret falls in love with him, and the two have a brief, guilt-ridden affair. Barry's cousin, Miette Longstair and her invalid husband, Ian, come to stay, and the tensions of the household are brought into the open. Miette falls in love with Jimmy, who rejects her. In revenge, realising the attachment between Margaret and Glengarry, Miette lets Margaret believe that she and Glengarry are having an affair. The ensuing drama results in Barry's death by drowning and the retaliatory murder of Glengarry by Margaret.

This melodramatic plot is interspersed with discussions of feminism, sexuality and 'scientific socialism', while the rural setting is unremittingly bleak and violent. The book was viewed as 'sordid, unwholesome and unclean' by the *Censorship Appeal Board, and banned on publication. Australia followed suit in 1929, as did Boston and Nazi Germany, although the British edition sold 15 000 copies. A new edition (*Auckland University Press, 1981) has an introduction by Heather Roberts and an afterword by Bill *Pearson specifically dealing with the work's banning. JS

BUTLER, Dorothy (1925–), has, since the late 1940s, been dedicated to introducing children to reading and books in their earliest years. Her experiences as an educator, parent, founder and operator of both a children's bookshop and a centre for children with reading problems, and a number of years as a freelance children's book editor, have fully equipped her to write in the field. She has authored some thirty books for children of various ages since 1980, all of which have 'an irresistible humour and a down-to-earth quality in which young children will delight'. Butler, tongue-in-cheek, describes her picture book texts as 'a form of elderly self-indulgence', but her comment does make the point that in the wider field of children's literature her books for adults are arguably of greater importance. *Reading Begins at Home* (with Marie Clay, 1979), *Babies Need Books* (1980), and *Five to Eight* (1985) have made a major impact both nationally and internationally. *Babies Need Books*, in particular, has become the leading text in the field, and has remained in print continuously (with revisions in 1988 and 1995). In addition, *Cushla and Her Books* (1979), based on Butler's 1972 thesis for a Diploma in Education, is widely used in America and Japan and was cited by the American Library Association in 1981 as one of best books on a disabled person for twenty-five years. Butler has received numerous awards, including the Eleanor Farjeon Award (England) for distinguished services to children's literature (1980), May Hill Arbuthnot Lectureship (America) for significant contribution to children's literature (1982), Children's Literature Association of New Zealand Honour (1991), Margaret *Mahy Lecture Award (1992) and OBE (1993). PM

BUTLER, Samuel (1835–1902), lived in Canterbury from 27 January 1860 to 15 June 1864, a time which in crucial ways laid the foundations of his career as a major English ironist, novelist and controversialist. Emigrant sheep farming primarily freed him from the dominance of his father Thomas Butler and the family profession of Anglican clergyman. Born at his father's rectory at Langar, Nottinghamshire, he was educated at Shrewsbury School, where his grandfather had been a famous headmaster and his father an outstanding scholar, and followed further in their footsteps through St John's College, Cambridge, first class honours in classics, and pre-ordination parish work in London. Then he balked. Responding to the radical climate of the 1850s and his own intellectual irreverence, he began an anguished correspondence with his father about faith and career, which eventually led to the respectable compromise of emigration to the Church of England province of Canterbury.

Seeking unclaimed sheep country, the *'new chum' became an energetic explorer, penetrated to the mountain headwaters of four Canterbury rivers, narrowly missed being the first settler to find Arthur's Pass, and then discovered what was later named the Whitcombe Pass, above the Rakaia River. His distinction in exploration history is commemorated in names in that area such as Mount Butler, the Butler Range and Butler's Saddle (from which he first looked across the Rakaia to see the Pass, as described in *Erewhon, 1872). For himself he found land above Forest Creek, west of the upper Rangitata, though the 1860 winter there convinced him to move a few kilometres up river to a less exposed foothills run. After a famous race to Christchurch against a rival *squatter he managed to register this claim, named the *station Mesopotamia ('between two rivers'), and by hard work and resourcefulness that compensated for his inexperience quickly made it financially successful. After four years he had 55 000 acres, employed seven men and could live in London off the capital.

His literary writings in and about New Zealand have regrettably remained for the most part 'fugitive', as he described them later ('Autobiographical Notes', c.1883, in Butleriana, ed. A.T. Bartholomew, 1932). His first published articles were student pieces in the St John's College journal the Eagle in 1858–59. Then shortly after arriving in Christchurch he sent back an account of his voyage, published as 'Our Emigrant. Part 1' in the Eagle, vol. 2, 1860. In June 1860 he wrote a 'discursive narration' about finding and establishing himself at Forest Creek, which the Eagle published in a severely edited version as 'Our Emigrant. Part 2' (1860). The manuscript of this 'Forest Creek' journal was acquired by the Canterbury Museum in 1954 and published by Peter Bromley Maling as Samuel Butler at Mesopotamia (1960). It is a valuable, detailed and perceptive account of early settler experience.

Extracts from the Eagle articles and versions of Butler's long and entertaining letters home to his family were then compiled by his father as A First Year in Canterbury Settlement (London, 1863). This remains probably the best record of early immigrant life and impressions. It is vividly observed, nimbly mixing local and European reference, its vigorous style evincing the resolute settler spirit, yet full of self-deprecating humour. Butler had corrected the proofs but took strong exception to the preface his father added, especially the condescending apology for the author's 'young mind' and 'many faults of style'. His anonymous review in the *Press (28 Oct. 1863) comically purports to savage the book, though on careful reading its mockery is directed almost wholly against the preface, the editing and the folly of publishing material which 'though interesting enough to the family circle … ought never to be allowed to exceed that….' Butler always refused to acknowledge the book and persisted in calling it 'priggish'. A new edition of A First Year, with other early essays, was published in 1914, ed. R.A. Streatfeild, and a New Zealand edition (*Blackwood and Janet Paul) by A.C. Brassington and P.B. Maling in 1964.

That half-jesting, provocative review was typical of the occasional pieces he had begun to contribute to the Press. Their high spirits and chameleon perplexities indicate how far he now felt liberated to find his own voice. The same is true of their intellectual seriousness and adventurousness. Between building his cob hut, erecting fences and buying sheep he was still grappling with the intellectual crises of the age, reading and beginning to write on two issues which remained pivotal to his work—the dubious credibility of the Bible and the complex significance of Charles Darwin. His challenging thoughts on the first gave him a dark reputation in conformist Christchurch society: 'See 'im ? 'E don't believe in Gawd!' protested a blacksmith in an anecdote passed on by Oliver *Duff. But they led to his first publication on return to England, the pamphlet The Evidence for the Resurrection … Critically Examined (1865), and to the Swiftian exposure of pious self-delusion, The Fair Haven (1863; the fair copy MS is in Canterbury Public Library).

His unremitting scrutiny of Darwin's work and its implications lasted most of his life. Butler's continuing importance as a thinker is due to a great extent to his articulating an imaginative response to Darwin: to his challenging analyses of evolutionary science in Erewhon and his later controversial attacks; to his eschewing of the easy reassurance of such late-Victorian ideas as meliorism or 'creative evolution', so that a century later thinkers like Stephen Jay Gould look back beyond *Shaw to Butler; to the expression in his books on evolution, for all their perverse iconoclasm, of the anxieties of the age; and to the incorporation of evolutionary ideas as an organic shaping principle into *The Way of All Flesh* (1903). This work began in his cramped home-made cob hut on the upper Rangitata after lambing in late 1862; and in the Christchurch Club, where he had become acquainted, among others, with James *Fitzgerald, editor of the newly established *Press*. Butler's 'Darwin on the Origin of Species, A Dialogue' was published anonymously in the *Press*, 20 Dec. 1862. Drawing examples from *backblocks ecology, such as the devastation of bird life by introduced cats, it provides rival arguments, in a simple form of Butler's favourite later 'counterpoint' technique, about the implications for Christianity of Darwin's 1859 bombshell.

It provoked a ponderously orthodox rejoinder which Butler suspected to be by the Bishop of Wellington ('Barrel-Organs', *Press*, 17 Jan. 1863), to which Butler responded in the guise of a third correspondent, 'A.M.', with 'Darwin on Species' (21 Feb. 1863). A full controversy ensued, through which it is not easy to track Butler's mischievously elusive traces. He may be his own sarcastic antagonist, 'The Savoyard'. He is almost certainly 'Lunaticus' who submitted 'From Our Mad Correspondent' (15 Sept. 1863). This solemnly hilarious account of the evolutionary significance of communication technology ('to cork coooo-ey up in an envelope … and send the said coooo-ey to England') is a more absurdist version of the most important of all his *Press* contributions. 'Darwin Among the Machines' (13 June 1863) by 'Cellarius' (Latin for butler) is a satirical attack on the adverse effects of technology on humanity, which the twentieth century has made increasingly pertinent. Somewhat expanded, it became 'The Book of the Machines', chapters 21–23 of *Erewhon*. These also incorporate material from 'Lucubratio Ebria', a corollary argument that machines are not evolutionary competitors to humanity but our evolving supplementary limbs, which Butler sent to the *Press* after returning to England (29 July 1865).

His other 'fugitive' New Zealand pieces include 'A Note on "The Tempest"' in *Literary Foundlings*, 1864, a comment on the calculating worldliness of romantic young women which probably reflects the rebuff he had suffered when Mary Brittan chose William Rolleston; and a report on the first Canterbury vs. All England cricket match in comic mock-Shakespearean blank verse (15 Feb. 1864; see *Sport).

In his thirty-seven years as a literary London bachelor Butler did not forget New Zealand. *Erewhon* and *Erewhon Revisited* (1901) are major texts of New Zealand as well as English literature. In his four books of evolutionary controversy and in travel books like *Alps and Sanctuaries* (1882) he draws readily on New Zealand examples and comparisons, such as his recollection in *Life and Habit* (1878) of the bullock's ability to 'take an eye lash out of its eye with its hind foot'. The full notebooks, still only selectively published, contain over eighty references to New Zealand memories (the MSS are in the Chapin Library, Williams College, USA). Some recapture the vigorous, no-nonsense, laconically droll discourse he heard around him; some are notes on natural history, for instance of the kea; some are anecdotes which show how congenial he found the irrepressibility and humour of the Māori; some record echoes in the mind, as when in Italy in 1890 he notes: 'The boulders booming under the Dora as under the Rangitata.' *Erewhon Revisited*, written in his final illness, tells of recurrent dreams of the Southern Alps, and a late note headed 'Ghosts' confesses 'a good many dead people as W.S. Moorhouse … haunt me every day of my life'.

After his death Butler became a cult figure in England and a profound influence as early twentieth-century writers like Bernard *Shaw, Lytton Strachey, James Joyce and E.M. Forster took advantage of the emancipation he had achieved from Victorian values. Butler had no doubt where that emancipation began. Although the autobiographical *The Way of All Flesh* omits New Zealand, it shows Ernest Pontifex finding independence of mind and choice of lifestyle by rejecting his parents and living among the poor of London; and Butler carefully dates the dramatic beginning of that emancipation as 'the 30th of September' (1859)—the day he had sailed for New Zealand. It was not a simple crossing. Since Forster wrote that Butler 'only saved his soul by escaping to New Zealand' his Canterbury experience has been superficially seen as a sort of liberating mid-Victorian Outward Bound. The full story includes pain, loss, perplexity of belief, an acute observation of the land and people he encountered, roguish literary experimentations and profoundly intelligent scrutiny of the major issues of the age. Canterbury thus provided for Butler the significant beginnings to a literary achievement of high distinction.   RR

C

CALDER, Jason (pseudonym of John *Dunmore), author of *The Man Who Shot Rob Muldoon* (1976), see **MULDOON, Robert**.

CALLINGHAM, Judy (1944–), is the leading writer and editor of New Zealand television scripts. She has contributed substantially to almost all popular home-produced series, including *Close to Home*, *Country G.P.*, *Gloss*, *Shortland Street* and *Cover Story*, and to the *Billy T. James Show* and others. She is also a playwright for stage ('Pawn to Queen Two'), television ('Casualties of Peace') and radio ('A Nest in the Grass'). She was president of the New Zealand Writers' Guild 1991–94. Born in Christchurch and educated at Hastings GHS and Trinity College of Music, London (Fellow 1968), she worked in broadcasting and for the *NZ Listener*, and now directs Antrim Productions and lives in Auckland.   RR

Came a Hot Friday (Sydney, 1964; Auckland, 1976), Ronald Hugh *Morrieson's second novel, is set in and around the tiny imaginary south Taranaki township of Tainuia Junction. Three young men, Wes Pennington, Cyril Kiddman and Don Jackson, defraud a local bookmaker and then attempt to increase their illegal earnings at a crown-and-anchor game run by Sel Bishop, a local criminal, in his woolshed casino. Filled with its author's *puritan sensibility, the novel begins and ends with fires involving Bishop, the first an arson he has ordered, which kills an innocent old man, and the second the burning-down of his own woolshed, in which he himself dies. In between, the Pākehā world of the wool-shed casino is contrasted with the idealised world of a pā across the river, while the innocent Don contrasts with the cynical and would-be worldly Wes, the latter contrasting with the far more dangerous Bishop, who contrasts in turn with the ridiculous, comical figure of the 'cowboy' Te Whakinga Kid; while the bookmaker Cray contrasts with Don's decent, crippled returned-service-man father. In the apparently unconsciously produced religious pattern of the novel Mr Jackson is a sacrificial figure, one to whom his prodigal son eventually returns, having lost his virginity and gained a more general appreciation of the fallen nature of the world. In keeping with the puritan morality of the novel, there are earthly as well as spiritual rewards: Don, forgiven by his father, can keep his gambling earnings—although the Kid, at the novel's end, drops the bag of money he has taken from Bishop and flees, having mistaken the blazing casino wall for a *taniwha as it is swept down the novel's dark, snake-like Apuna River.

The film version directed by Ian Mune (1985) was notable for inspired performances by Peter *Bland as Wes and Billy T. James as the Te Whakinga Kid.   PE

CAMPBELL, Alistair Te Ariki (1926–), poet, playwright and novelist, was born on the Cook Islands and spent his first seven years there. His mother, a Cook Islander, married his father, a third-generation New Zealander from Dunedin, when he withdrew from post-war society, after experiencing the World War 1 trenches, to become an island storekeeper. The Polynesian and the European strains in Campbell's personality and work are inseparable. Although his early poetry makes little mention of Polynesia, in its romantic and musical tone and its intense attachment to landscape it is hard not to detect something of those origins, while his later work, more directly Polynesian, nonetheless has the form and tone provided by an education in English and classical poetry.

Although the poet lost his parents at an early age, their personalities and romantic attachment pervade his writing. His father was said to have a good command of various Island dialects and to have been consulted on them by Sir Peter *Buck. As a successful trader he achieved considerable social status in Rarotonga.

Campbell's mother, Teu, revealed in photographs as a shy beauty, was remembered for her kindness and Christian piety. Her father, the Bosini mentioned in his grandson's poems, was said to know the Bible by heart. The term 'Te Ariki' which the poet now uses in his name points to the chiefly origins of Bosini's family. Campbell later admitted that he knew his mother too little, and much of the melancholy in his personality and poetry is due to that. His father had seemed even more remote, leaving the women, family and servants to raise the children. Campbell's recorded memories of these first seven years are of South Sea warmth and a certain inner darkness, poetically personified as 'The Dark Lord of Savaiki'. As Peter Smart wrote: 'His memories included nightmares as well as dreams.'

Teu died of tuberculosis in 1932, aged 28, and Jock Campbell rapidly became addicted to alcohol. He died within a year. In interviews, Campbell confessed that the next years were a blank in his memory, a grief he had repressed. Much of his later work can be interpreted as an effort to fill that gap, although there are many less personal echoes as well.

In the *New Zealand Railways Magazine of 1 July 1933 there is a photograph of two small boys in big hats and coats, with luggage labels attached to their lapels. The taller is Alistair Campbell and the smaller his brother Bill, sent virtually as human packages from the Cook Islands to join a brother and sister in New Zealand. The next years were spent in Dunedin, the South Seas idyll replaced with an orphanage in a provincial town close to Antarctic seas.

Socially too, the boy's status had changed, from a loved member of a respected family to a child in an orphanage in the years of the Great *Depression. The sense of abandonment must have been increased by the fact that he spoke little English, Penrhyn Māori being his native language. Rather than breaking him, this situation made him determined to succeed in this new competitive world. Within a few years he was top of his class and successful at sports (he represented Otago in soccer). Nonetheless he remained a 'loner' at school, and found a warm refuge only in the home of friends in the Cromwell Gorge, Central Otago. His first important poems reflect that landscape: 'This is the kiln / That fired my shaping mind.' In 1943 he moved on to Otago

University, but the strain of competitive living told, and after a minor breakdown he suddenly moved to Wellington.

After initial difficulties he obtained a room at Weir House and was accepted as a student at Wellington Teachers' College. Considering his later major contributions to educational publishing, it is ironic that he failed to complete his College studies. He was distracted, he has said, by 'personal doubts and fears', but also by women and poetry. He helped to edit *Spike and found *Hilltop and *Arachne, publishing verse in all of them. Writing became his way of life, rather than an 'interest'. With his young friend, Roy Dickson, he travelled to familiar places in Otago and explored new ones such as the Hollyford Valley. In 1947, on another expedition, Dickson was killed, and this tragedy gave rise to the greatest of Campbell's early poems, 'Elegy', published in *Mine Eyes Dazzle (1950). It reflected the darkness that was to characterise much of his poetry, and, typically, projected it onto the landscape. At the same time Campbell was developing another theme that was to accompany him throughout his life: the beauty of inaccessible women. Many of the later attempts to order his poems into a coherent whole were to be introduced by 'Green', just such a poem written at this time.

In these early poems Campbell largely ignored his Polynesian background and wrote and argued as an inheritor of the European tradition: he was studying Latin and the history and culture of Greece, while the poet he most admired was W.B. Yeats. Together with James K. *Baxter, Louis *Johnson, Peter *Bland and others, Campbell was a member of the (informal) Wellington Group, who felt that the Auckland poets around Allen *Curnow were trying to stifle originality by focusing on 'the New Zealand thing'. This was not a question of subject matter—all of the Wellington poets wrote of local subjects—but of literary orientation. Awareness of international developments seemed essential to the Wellington Group.

After various casual jobs Campbell found employment as a gardener in the grounds of a Red Cross hospital, an ideal combination of outdoor work and opportunity to write and read when the weather turned sour. Many of his finest early poems were written in the gardener's hut. He continued to haunt Central Otago whenever possible and on one occasion was followed there by a Wellington student named Fleur *Adcock. They courted and wed. Campbell returned to the Teachers' College and was more successful this time, partly because of the support of friends among students and staff, some of whom were also poets: Anton *Vogt, Barry *Mitcalfe, Baxter and Johnson. Douglas *Lilburn, John M. *Thomson and Erik Schwimmer were also among the friends of that time. Literary conversations were intense, but Campbell was not especially productive in the 1950s. It seems that he was preparing for a later phase, and periods of silence have been typical of his career. Nonetheless the hard monosyllables of 'Aunt Lucrezia' (1954), the vision of a walking skeleton—the past recovering life—in 'Bones' (1956) and the mystery of death in 'Bitter Harvest' (1957) suggest, at least with hindsight, that the new themes of (Polynesian) childhood and death and a new harshness in style were being prepared. There is also sufficient evidence that he read widely and with passion in local and international poetry.

Having acquired his degree, Campbell worked as an editor for *School Publications and wrote a novel for children, *The Happy Summer* (1961). He also edited the first *Poetry* programme on radio (1958). In his personal life great changes were occurring. Fleur bore two sons but his attention turned to Meg Anderson (see Meg *Campbell), a beautiful young actor. Campbell divorced and remarried in 1958. Nonetheless, beneath the surface, there were tensions, and in Meg post-natal depression merged into a deep and prolonged nervous breakdown. Campbell suffered stress of his own and in 1960 he, too, suffered some kind of breakdown. For many years he had been subject to nightmares and depression—found partly in his poetry but more explicitly in his plays and later fiction—and in exorcising his devils he turned to memories of childhood. All of this is now more than a personal matter, since it has coloured his writing thematically and emotionally ever since. The poet even found something of value in his attendance at a mental hospital. In an interview with Sam *Hunt in 1969 he said: 'It was almost as if the springs of creativity had become iced over … my nervous breakdown cracked the ice and allowed the spring to flow once more.'

Perhaps the most important component of his therapy and of his poetic development was his acceptance of his Polynesian background. For years, in covering the wounds of childhood, he behaved like a 'European' poet; but now he thought and wrote of the Polynesian strain. In the first major instance, *Sanctuary of Spirits* (1963), he chose to write of the Māori history which surrounded his home at Pukerua Bay, near Wellington. A year later this sequence opened *Wild Honey* (1964), a collection published in Britain. The protagonist of the radio play *The Homecoming* (1964) is a Māori writer who resents his outsider status. The awakening of the Polynesian strain in his work was not all therapeutic joy: in 1965 he said, 'I am of mixed race. The years of solitude get you down. You are different. You are without a tribe.' He identified with the Ngāti Toa tribe of the area of his current home, but later he was to return to his original home, the Cook Islands, and find a new sense of identity there.

The Homecoming was the first of six plays for radio, a form peculiarly suited to a poet whose words resonate so musically. The best-known of the plays is *When the Bough Breaks* (1970), of which a stage version was produced and published in Howard McNaughton's *Contemporary New Zealand Plays* (1974). It is an expressionistic exploration of a stressed mind. Similarly *The Suicide* (1966) presents schizophrenia by letting an actor play each part of the personality. *Sanctuary of Spirits* was also first conceived as a radio play.

The struggle to define the best version of the poetic vision originally conceived much earlier continued into the 1970s. In 1971 these poems were collected with new ones as *Kapiti. This book sold remarkably well and constituted a statement of where Campbell had come from and where he had arrived. The early love and nature lyrics, again revised, were accompanied by poems of social awareness. *Dreams, Yellow Lions* (1975) was a more mixed collection, suggesting that the poet was experimenting with themes and forms. Personally, too, Campbell moved out to face the social world, taking part in TV documentaries on Kapiti Island and on his own life and poetry. In 1979 he took part in the 'Four Poets' tour of New Zealand with Hunt, Hone *Tuwhare and Jan *Kemp. He tutored creative writing nationally and internationally and was president of *PEN for a year.

Of special significance was his return to Rarotonga in 1976, a return to the experiences of his own childhood. Together with his brother Bill, who had also been in the photo with the railways baggage labels, he travelled to Tongareva (Penrhyn), his earliest home.

The collection *The *Dark Lord of Savaiki* (1980) showed that the poetic experiments and new life experiences had had a profound effect. These were poems of a different kind, with a different voice and a different subject matter: poems of celebration and of love for the Polynesian ancestors. They called for another reassessment, which took place in *Collected Poems* (1981), where the earlier verse was printed in definitive versions and *The Dark Lord of Savaiki*, together with some similar poems, was added. The new strain was developed into something even more relaxed in manner in *Soul Traps* (1985), published at the author's Te Kotare Press.

Work in various genres deepened this 'Polynesian strain'. The autobiographical *Island to Island* (1984), a narrative search for origin, was followed by a mythic-comic trilogy of novels: *The *Frigate Bird* (1989), which was regional finalist for the Commonwealth Writers Prize, *Sidewinder* (1991) and *Tia* (1993). At the same time, *Stone Rain: The Polynesian Strain* (1992) consolidated and highlighted these elements and concerns in the poetry.

In 1996 the ★Wai-te-ata Press published a finely printed and exquisitely bound version of a new poem, 'Death and the *Tagua*', filled with intimations of mortality, a dream of a ship carrying persons familiar to readers of Campbell's poems towards some realm of death. It makes a sombre-ironic conclusion to *Pocket Collected Poems*, also published in 1996, the most recent attempt to present the complete poetic persona, introduced with a major essay by Roger Robinson. It seems designed as a farewell, but it is accompanied by several new poems, and others that have been difficult of access, and the work of shaping a now large oeuvre into a coherent whole seems to be ongoing. Despite the hint of death, Campbell's readers are hoping that the work will be extended even further and that this dream-filled craftsman will continue to delight them.   NW

CAMPBELL, Sir John Logan (1817–1912), author of *Poenamo*, is sometimes called the 'father of Auckland', having been present at its formal foundation in 1840 and its leading businessman for half a century afterwards. He was also—reluctantly—involved in local politics. For decades at a time, however, Campbell put managers in charge and lived a '*dolce fa* [*sic*] *niente* existence' in Italy, Switzerland, France and Britain. In the depression of the 1880s, however, he claimed to be 'positively bled to death'. His numerous business ventures are analysed in R.C.J. Stone's historical biography in two parts, *Young Logan Campbell* (1986) and *The Father and His Gift* (1987).

Campbell's reminiscences of early Auckland, *Poenamo* (1881), were immediately acclaimed a classic. Unlike many such books, this is an immensely well written one and gives truthful insights into the interaction of Pākehā and Māori at a critical historical period. Campbell, an Edinburgh man (a medical graduate of the university there), struck up a friendship with a Dundee man named Brown ('we ither twa'), with whom he purchased land in the Auckland region and began a farm. They were pleasantly surprised to find Governor Hobson setting up the new capital among the huts and tents nearby. At the centre of the city-to-be 'the firm' bought building sites. Campbell's relationship with the Māori was friendly and knowledgable, backed by his friendship with his Hokianga 'neighbour' F.E. ★Maning. *Poenamo* can be well enjoyed in the company of Maning's *Old New Zealand*.

On Campbell's death, the *Auckland Star* recorded the 'Passing of a Patriarch', and he was buried at One Tree Hill, part of a large estate he had gifted to the nation; but *Poenamo* tells the story of two adventurous young men in an environment scarcely touched by European ways.

In 1903 the *Herald* published an entertaining anonymous 'novelette' called 'My Visit to Waiwera-Baden and things that I have seen and read and thought and heard in passing through the world'. Its author has been identified as John Logan Campbell. It is a have-it-both-ways sentimental love story that makes fun of sentimental love stories, and suggests that its author had both a sharp mind and a warm heart.   NW

CAMPBELL, Meg (1937–), began to write in 1969 and emerged as a notable poet in the 1980s, with *The Way Back* (1981), *A Durable Fire* (1982) and *Orpheus and Other Poems* (1990). Born in Palmerston North and brought up there with periods in Auckland, she has lived since 1951 mainly in the Wellington area, working in bookshops and libraries. Her poems are mainly short and dramatic rather than lyric, and distinctive in their strong voice with its almost muscular energy and the sense that even stronger feeling is being only with effort constrained. Elizabeth ★Smither described Campbell's voice as 'possessed of great charm, unadorned, flexible', but the poems' considerable range of tone and experience also requires to be acknowledged, compensating for the relatively slight output. They can form unexpected links, between the mythic and the domestic, for instance, as in 'Maui', or the universal and psychological, as in 'Things Random' or 'Evolution'.

Meg Campbell is now regularly anthologised, for instance in the *Penguin Book of New Zealand Verse* (1985) and *An Anthology of New Zealand Poetry in English* (1996). She is one of the four poets in *How Things Are* (1996). She lives at Pukerua Bay, married since 1958 to Alistair ★Campbell, the subject of some of his finest poems and the dedicatee of his 1996 *Collected Poems*.   RR

CAMPBELL, Thomas (1777–1844), wrote the first poem relating to New Zealand by a major British poet. 'Song of the Colonists Departing for New Zealand' (1842) is a routine patriotic exhortation, with dauntless hearts full of Britannia's pride and ★Utopian optimism: 'We go to found a realm, one day, / Like England's self to shine.' Campbell, a Scot, had achieved fame for 'The Pleasures of Hope' (1799), with lines like ''Tis distance lends enchantment to the view', and for stirring war poems like 'Lochiel's Warning'. But in 'Song of the Colonists Departing' the fading 64-year-old poet could not even match his earlier 'Lines on the Departure of Emigrants for New South Wales', which catches the poignancy of shedding 'Tears for the home that could not yield them bread'. It is revealing, too, that such a fervent critic of slavery, who could write of the stripes on the American flag that 'They mean your negroes' scars', seems to assume that New Zealand is uninhabited:

'There, tracts uncheer'd by human words, / Seclusion's wildest holds, / Shall hear the lowing of our herds, / The tinkling of our folds.' But his vision of 'vineyards girt with corn' shows some prescience. RR

CAMPION, Edith (1923–), a prominent actor, was active as a writer of fiction and poetry especially in the late 1970s. Born in Wellington and mainly educated there, after war work on the land she attended the Old Vic Theatre School in London in 1948 and returned to be co-founder of the New Zealand Players. Placing stories and poems in *Landfall, as radio readings, and elsewhere, she published A Place to Pass Through and Other Stories (1977) and a novella, 'The Chain', which was paired with Frank *Sargeson's 'En Route' in an unusual co-publication, Tandem (1979). Her stories and sketches mostly treat the lives of women, and with their strong dialogue and descriptive colour would perform well. 'The Chain' is an ambitious stream-of-consciousness, as a man chained and left to die in the bush impressionistically reviews his unfulfilled life. The treatment is again essentially dramatic, with snatches of song and poetry, reprised old dialogues and descriptive writing that is consciously, sometimes floridly, lyrical. The idea was taken from a macabre news story from Florida, with similarities to British black psychological fictions of the 1960s such as Fowles's The Collector and Golding's Pincher Martin. Edith Campion appeared as actor in her daughter Jane *Campion's film *Angel at My Table (1989), and The *Piano is dedicated to her. RR

CAMPION, Jane (1954–), won world acclaim as a film writer and director with Angel at My Table (1990) and The *Piano (1992). She has published short fiction in *Sport and Soho Square. Born in Wellington and educated at Queen Margaret's College and Victoria University (BA in Anthropology 1975), she attended art college in London and Sydney (BA in Painting 1979) and won distinction at the Australian School of Film and Television. Five short films 1982–86 all won awards, including the Palme d'Or at Cannes 1986 for Peel (1982). She co-wrote and directed Sweetie (1989) and Angel at My Table, the film dramatisation of Janet *Frame's three-volume autobiography, which won seven prizes, including the Venice Film Festival Silver Lion in 1990. Her father Richard Campion is notable as theatre director, her mother Edith *Campion as actor and fiction writer, and her sister Anna also as film director. The combination of visual, verbal and dramatic skills that she perhaps inherited distinguishes her work, in which the remarkable adaptation of Frame's complex and inward narratives into visual form and the published version of The Piano's screenplay are significant literary accomplishments. Campion lives in Sydney and has adapted and directed a film of Henry James's The Portrait of a Lady (1996). RR

CAMPION, Sarah (later Sarah Campion Alpers; also 'Mary Alpers'; 1906–), had published her English and Australian novels before settling in New Zealand in 1952. Born in Eastbourne, England, brought up in Cambridge, and always cause-oriented, she produced in the 1930s five novels concerned with pre-war European issues, particularly the treatment of the German Jews. In 1939 she visited Australia for eight months, a formative experience that inspired Turn Away No More (1940) and her 'Queensland trilogy', Mo Burdekin (1941), Bonanza (1942) and The Pommy Cow (1944), vigorous historical fictions based on the 1890s gold rush, their polemic now supporting suffragism and opposing the Boer War. There were two further novels, the popular, sensational Dr Golightly (1946) and Come Again (1951); a controversially subversive biography of her scholar-father, Father: A Portrait of G. G. Coulton at Home, etc. (1948); and an autobiographical promotion of the British welfare health scheme, National Baby (1949).

After her marriage to Antony *Alpers (later dissolved), she settled in Auckland in 1952 and focused on family and activism, especially opposing nuclear arms and racism. In 1964 she and civil liberties leader Walter Scott represented the New Zealand–China Friendship Society on a visit to the Mao regime there. She has published journalism but no further fiction. Interest in her work, especially the more feminist fictions, is rising. Mo Burdekin was reissued in 1990, edited by Elizabeth Lawson. RR

Canada's various interconnections with New Zealand literature derive in part from the common experience (though divergent in particulars) of a colonial history, and in part from other social parallels. These include paradigms of settler–native relations, of educational experience and political practice, and of literary expression. The short story, for example, has long been a pre-eminent literary form in both New Zealand and Canada, as has a literary fascination with youth and a preoccupation with the natural environment. Both societies, historically, have also expressed a belief in their own liberalism, a long-standing faith in the power of received linguistic norms, and a general desire to balance individualism against a deference to community authority.

New Zealand and Canadian political and social structures reveal the common influence of British Imperial governance, especially before World War 2. Canada's endorsement of the Statute of Westminster, giving preference to the idea of 'Commonwealth' over that of 'Empire', came earlier than New Zealand's, however, as did a widespread questioning of 'English' standards of speech and aesthetic judgment. Canada's differing trade patterns, New Zealand's island location, and Canada's continental proximity to the USA all contributed to the shaping of this difference. Canada's greater degree of multicultural and multiracial mix might also have affected current social practice and policy. By the 1990s, however, race relations and social norms in both societies had undergone significant change, taking more overtly into account the complexities of cultural practice; these changes have directly affected the subjects and the language of literature.

Specific points of contact between Canada and New Zealand began historically with the fact that the same persons—Captain James *Cook, for one—were involved in the European mapping of both coasts. Other figures, such as Edmund Burke and Edward Gibbon *Wakefield, helped shape the colonial policies that the British applied to these newly claimed territories. Further, Burke's eighteenth-century aesthetic theories of the sublime and the picturesque organised a system of perception. Because this system had the effect of establishing conventional limits of expectation as well, it long influenced received patterns of visual and verbal representation of new worlds—including the strategies that Wakefield devised in the 1830s, for the sale of colonial 'waste' lands. Wakefield's plan conceived of capitalism as a Utopian design balancing land costs, labour and private ownership; his conception of 'Responsible Government' also directly influenced both the 1839 Durham Report in Canada and the 1852 modifications to the New Zealand constitution.

Still other figures helped establish a print culture in both Canada and New Zealand. Samuel Revans, for instance, set up the early newspaper the New Zealand Gazette in 1840; but with H.S. Chapman he had previously published the Montreal Daily Advertiser—until he found it necessary to flee Lower Canada because of his 'Patriote' sympathies during the 1837 Rebellion. Despite these oppositional origins, colonial newspaper commentary tended more often to support the idea of Imperial connectedness than to challenge it, as when the *New Zealand Illustrated Magazine produced notes on 'Outposts of Empire' (including British Columbia, whose nineteenth-century origins and subsequent social history perhaps of all Canadian regions parallel New Zealand's most closely) or when *Triad praised the Yukon balladeer Robert Service and the masculine idea, as distinct from the ecological reality, of wilderness.

Actual friendships and family connections, colony to colony, reaffirmed this principle of Imperial unity,

with London as the 'centre'. Katherine *Mansfield, for instance, dedicated a 1904 poem, 'Dear friend, when back to Canada you go', to her Canadian friend Marion Creelman, whom she met at Queen's College, London. The development of the mail service, and of Pacific liner travel, reinforced the principle in practice. Yet Canadian world travellers in the late nineteenth and early twentieth centuries (Sara Jeannette Duncan, for one) often bypassed New Zealand on their way to colonies they considered more exotic. And New Zealand travellers to Canada—witness Samuel *Butler's mordant refrain 'O God O Montreal!' in 'A Psalm of Montreal'—tended to be less than enthusiastic about what they saw. European travellers to the two colonies, by contrast, usually found the sublime and picturesque in both, reconfirming European expectations of the romance, rather than the rigour, of the strange and the wild. Indeed, illustrations in nineteenth-century British children's books even treated South Pacific and North American landscapes as though (both being 'savage') they, and the narratives they accompanied, were interchangeable.

Canadian enthusiasm for New Zealand political experiment has waxed and waned throughout the twentieth century, though both left- and right-wing economic movements (Labour/Social Credit/ 'Rogernomics') found evidence in the other society to support their cause. In tandem, New Zealand writers in the *NZ Listener often used Australian and Canadian comparisons to justify New Zealand superiority, as when Hector *Bolitho in 1928 finds the New Zealand farmer to be the best of all, for his love of earth; or when D'Arcy *Cresswell in 1954 praises New Zealand by dismissing the 'speechless Canadian awe at mere space and size'.

That said, several writers in each society subsequently found their subject, their education, or their career in the other. The poet Charles *Doyle, for example, emigrated to Canada; as did the New Zealand–born Desmond Pacey and Robin Fisher, the one to become Canada's most influential literary historian prior to 1960, the other to write some of the most incisive late twentieth-century histories of Captain Cook and of race relations in British Columbia. The New Zealand literary critic Mark *Williams and the language poet Michele *Leggott were both educated at the University of British Columbia, and the Canadian critic William New, in Dreams of Speech and Violence, wrote an extended comparative study of the nature and role of the short story as it has developed in New Zealand and Canada, and has a study of Katherine Mansfield in press.

Other cross-cultural references include the observations of such writers as Bill *Manhire, Earle Birney and George Woodcock. Such texts tend to be critical rather than laudatory; Birney's attempts at dialect satire, for example, dismiss the New Zealand bourgeoisie; and passages in Woodcock's autobiographical writings critique the gap between New Zealand's modern social practices and its one-time libertarian aspirations. Manhire's observations find foible everywhere. And Russell *Haley, in references to the Canadian writer Malcolm Lowry, and in a story called 'Here Comes Your Canadian Father', reflects more generally and more abstractly on *postmodernism and the pressure of foreign influences, including the means of communication, as theorised by the Canadian Marshall McLuhan, on contemporary speech and values.

Whether these stances, collectively, are more self-defensive than critical remains unclear. The emergence of nationalism in both Canada and New Zealand can be seen as a response to, and rejection of, the ostensible universalism of Empire. The psychology of being a 'small' nation next to a 'large' one (Australia, USA) has, nevertheless, permeated much subsequent commentary and literary expression. This sensitivity does not negate a commitment to political independence, but by the 1990s, while some old colonial assumptions about cultural uniformity have obviously broken down, so have some naive assumptions about national distinctiveness begun to be questioned. The increasing speed of long-distance transport and the instantaneousness of electronic communication mean that cultural isolation is unlikely in the late twentieth century, and that intercultural influence is a fact of life. Canadian writers have been invited to New Zealand literary festivals; New Zealand writers have read at Toronto's Harbourfront and other Canadian venues; an extensive series of interviews with Canadian writers was broadcast in New Zealand by Elizabeth *Alley. Moreover, Canadian multicultural policy has diffusely affected social practice in New Zealand and, more consequentially, Māori cultural spokespersons have had a direct impact on First Nations leaders in Canada, and on their ideas about cultural vitality and political reform in the 1990s. More detailed examination of these and other historical and cultural parallels remains to be done. As both societies have perhaps more profoundly been influenced by the economic policies, the critical theoriesand the aesthetic norms and practices of Europe and the United States than by each other, however—and as both are increasingly affected by the expectations of East and Southeast Asia—the case for a simple bilateral relation between Canada and New Zealand is more tantalising than grounded in convincing argument. But the results of comparative study may yet illuminate how 'settler societies' become established under related but differing conditions, and how their subsequent cultural practices draw on related but competing systems of value.   WHN

'Canary, The', a short story by Katherine *Mansfield, written July 1922 as a gift for her artist friend Dorothy Brett, was the last story completed by Mansfield before her death in January 1923. The MS is held at the Newberry Library, Chicago. Published posthumously in *Nation and Athenaeum* (April 1923) and subsequently in the collection *The Dove's Nest and Other Stories* (June 1923), it is a monologue in which the 'I' narrator anthropomorphises her dead canary: 'But isn't it extraordinary that under his sweet, joyful little singing it was just this—sadness?—Ah, what is it?—that I heard', much as Miss *Brill anthropomorphises her fur toque. The metaphor of the cage, and the physical and emotional restriction that this implies, link the story with the earlier pieces, 'A *Married Man's Story' and 'The *Escape'. Shortly before she died, Mansfield wrote to her cousin 'Elizabeth' Countess Russell: 'I haven't written a word since October and I don't mean to until the spring. I want much more material; I am tired of my little stories like birds bred in cages.' The story is overtly sentimental and is not one of Mansfield's most popular.   SSa

Canterbury Lambs was the irregular publication of the Canterbury University College Literary Society, published 1946–49 and printed by the *Caxton Press. Contributors included W.H. *Oliver, Pat *Wilson, Alistair *Campbell and James K. *Baxter, who also edited the third and final issue.   SH

Canterbury Rhymes, or in full *The Book of Canterbury Rhymes* (1866), is a collection of verses 'chiefly of a humorous character, which have been written and first published in Canterbury' (Preface). It includes the province's earliest published poems, such as J.E. *FitzGerald's 'The Night Watch of the "Charlotte Jane"', and a selection, the Preface says, 'out of the very large number of newspaper verses which later years have produced', taken from early-1860s issues of *Canterbury Punch*, *Canterbury Times*, *Lyttelton Times* and the *Press*. Edited by William Pember *Reeves and J. Ward, and 'Printed by the "Lyttelton Times" Company', the book testifies to the prodigious literary energy of early Canterbury and to the key role of the newspapers as vehicles for its expression. A second edition, edited by Reeves, with an appendix of new verses, was published in 1883, and a selection of nine of the original poems became the basis of *The Jubilee Book of Canterbury Rhymes* edited by O.T.J. *Alpers (1900).

In the first and second editions authorship is given only by initials, on account, the Preface says, of the 'disparaging language used so generally of the country, its climate and its people, their rulers, their manners, and their pursuits'. The prevailing tone is of witty irreverence towards the province's ★Utopian aspirations: 'We left our houses, with hearts elate, / Utopian visions dreaming … Alas! alack! the space how far / 'Twixt things that seem and things that are.' E.J.W. (Edward Jerningham ★Wakefield) sardonically observes in his canine satire 'The Lay of the Last Registered Dog', 'No two dogs in the country could bark in one mind', and C.W. (Crosbie ★Ward) lambasts the slow progress of road works ('The Struggle of Papanui') and flood prevention ('The Town and the Torrent'). Wittiest of all is 'Ode to New Zealand: A Growl in a Sou'wester' by J.T.R. (Dr J. Rouse of Lyttelton), a Jeremiad which deserves to be a classic of local satire. It again sets up the Utopian ideal of emigration propaganda, 'Where the wide extended plain / Waves with fields of golden grain', only to cut it down to the dismal reality: 'Land where men with brains of fog / Built a city in a bog! … Land where all is dear and bad, / Comfort scarcely to be had; / Wooden house, with shingle roof, / Neither wind nor waterproof….' More earnestly poetic voices are the exception, such as S.R. (Sarah Raven) in 'The Avon': 'A little while / Shall see thy wastes grow lovely….'

The new poems added in 1883 are again predominantly satiric, most now depending on parody of well-known English or American models—'The Last Fly of Summer', 'The Immigrant's Carol for Christmas', 'The Ballad of the Ancient Member', or a train traveller's adaptation of Longfellow's 'Excelsior!' into 'Railroadior!' The best is the mocking application by W.M.M. of Tennyson's 'Charge of the Light Brigade' to the heavy-handed repression of the supposedly rebellious Māori at Parihaka: 'Children to the right of them, / Children to the left of them, / Women in front of them, / Saw them and wondered…. Back with their captives three / Taken so gallantly, / Rode the Twelve Hundred'.

By 1900 Canterbury poetry was taking itself more seriously. Whereas the first edition demurred modestly, 'This little book … has no pretension to the title of a Book Of Poetry. It is merely a collection of rhymes', Alpers's introduction to the *Jubilee Book* rejoices that 'enough good work has been produced in New Zealand or by New Zealanders to constitute at least no unworthy beginning'. Alpers rates Alfred ★Domett's 'Ranolf and Amohia' as 'one of the great poems of a century prolific in great poems' and finds 'a glow of pride to hear how early in our young literature the Imperialist note was sounded, and to realize how true it rings'. So here are C.C. ★Bowen, Jessie ★Mackay, Mary ★Colborne-Veal, Thomas ★Bracken, Arthur ★Adams and Johannes C. ★Andersen, here are romantic-nostalgic rondeaux and imperialist chants of triumph (such as William F. ★Alexander's 'The Battle of Omdurman'). Tennyson is now not parodied but imitated ('Across the

Bar' by 'Bohemian') and Browning is subjected to a 'Sonnet to Robert Browning' ('To crown triumphantly the prophet-bard, / The welder great of thoughts that seethe and glow') by Dolce A. Cabot. A poem like 'The Britain of the South' (by W.J. Steward, 1868) can now be offered straight, not as a mock-heroic subversion: 'And far away—upon this distant shore—/ Shall we our own, our native land ignore? / "No, no!" the answer rings from hill to hill / "We'll boast her name and love her fondly still!"'

The difference over thirty-four years between these three editions of *Canterbury Rhymes* is a reminder that terms such as 'Victorian' or 'Colonial', even applied to the literature of a small province, are neither adequate nor static. RR

Canterbury University College Review, published 1897–1945, was initially issued monthly during the university session. Editors included J.H.E. ★Schroder (1915–18, 1920), Ian ★Milner (1932), Denis ★Glover (1933–34) and J.G.A. Pocock (1945). Alexander ★Currie, Arnold ★Wall, T.M. Curnow and Schroder were notable contributors to early issues dominated by humorous verse, university news and graduate lists. With the shift to annual issues in 1930, the literary quality of the *Review* began to lift. 1931 saw the first appearance of Eric Cook and Ian ★Milner, and the following year Denis ★Glover began to contribute. Other contributors included Allen ★Curnow, Winston ★Rhodes, Charles ★Marris, Peter ★Alcock, Antony ★Alpers and John ★Weir. Many involved with the *Review* during the early 1930s were also involved in the Caxton Club and its publications ★*Oriflamme* and ★*Sirocco*. The ★Caxton Press was responsible for designing and printing all issues published after 1940. The *Review* was succeeded by ★*Canterbury Lambs*. SH

CAPE, Peter (1926–), writer, critic and photographer, has published predominantly in the area of New Zealand arts and crafts. His eclectic range of interests has also seen him producing recordings of settler and pioneer music; writing folk ballads and occasional poems; publishing photographic books for children (*Bear and Cindy*, *The Mine in the Hills*, and *Inga in the Mountains*); and, in the early 1970s, writing a regular column for the ★*NZ Listener*. PM

CARCO, Francis (1886–1958), is the nom de plume of François Marie Alexandre Carcopino-Tusoli, a French poet, novelist and memorialist who features in New Zealand literature as the 'little corporal' of Katherine ★Mansfield's 'An ★Indiscreet Journey' and as the detestable Raoul Duquette, narrator of ★'Je ne parle pas français'. A contributor to John Middleton *Murry's *Rhythm*, Carco met Murry and Mansfield in Paris, guiding their discovery of its seamy bohemian life. A brief affair with Mansfield in February 1915 at Gray, in the War Zone, appears variously in her letters and journals and is fictionalised in 'An Indiscreet Journey'. Carco used Mansfield as the model for Winnie Campbell, an amoral and voracious writer, in his novel *Les Innocents* (1916), and later wrote reminiscences of her in *Les Annales* (1933) and elsewhere. Antony *Alpers suggests that their attraction derived in part from their shared Pacific origins, as Carco was born in Nouméa. Though limited, he was a significant enough writer, especially in his Verlaine-inspired poetry and prose evocations of Montmartre's bohemian life, to deserve recognition apart from the cynical and grubby-minded Duquette.   CM

CARMAN, Dulce (1883–1970), a popular romance writer, was born in Norwich, England, and emigrated to Feilding in 1892. After marriage in 1911 she lived in Dannevirke, and from 1932 in Hastings. Carman published many short stories and serials in early twentieth-century local newspapers, and her first novel, *The Broad Stairway*, appeared in 1924, but it was not until 1948, with *Neath the Maori Moon*, that she began her prolific career as a novelist. From 1949 to 1967 she published twenty-six novels, specialising in what her English publishers called 'Maoriland romance', with titles such as *The Tapu Tree*, *The Moon Witch* and *The Miracle of Tane*. In 1962 she was elected an honorary founder member of the British Romantic Novelists' Association.

Although almost all of her novels are set in New Zealand, and although she described them as arising out of real experience, and as 'family stories, suitable for all ages', they are remarkable for their dependence on the sensational conventions of Victorian melodrama: complicated inheritance tangles, property feuds, disguises, deceptions and mistaken identities, and multiple villainies. Into little more than 200 pages she packed numerous subplots and large casts of characters reminiscent of nineteenth-century three-deckers six times as long. Though Carman's novels were praised for their 'spirit of toleration' in race relations, and for their authentic representation of Māori life and legends, they were premised on the official assimilationist attitudes of the time. Her Māori characters tend to fall into two broad categories: romanticised older figures descended from noble chiefs and princesses, and a young rootless generation whom the author never hesitates to attack as lazy, shiftless and spoilt by the Welfare State. Her novels also enact assimilation in the ways they make Māori characters dependent on the actions of Pākehā heroes and heroines, and in their blatant appropriation of Māori

mythic and legendary materials to reinforce the destinies of the Pākehā characters.   TS

Carpathians, The, the eleventh and most recent novel by Janet *Frame (Auckland, New York, London, 1988), won the New Zealand Book Award for Fiction and the Commonwealth Writers Prize for Best Book (1989); no MS is known. In Frame's early novels the artist was portrayed as alienated, forced to contemplate death or silence rather than capitulate to social conformity; here, as in *Living in the Maniototo*, Frame's vision of the artist is affirmative: one who triumphs over death through the creative utilisation of (personal and collective) memory. A note at the beginning of the novel, signed by 'J.H.B.', claims that he was inspired to write the book by his recently dead mother's visit to New Zealand and his father's 'long marriage with words'. The first section of four is a conventionally realist account by an omniscient narrator of wealthy New Yorker Mattina Brecon's journey to Puahamara (based mainly on Levin) in New Zealand, the site of the legendary Memory Flower, which has been cheapened into a tourist attraction by the inhabitants of the town. Mattina hopes to collect information to 'feed' to her husband, Jake, author of a best-selling novel, who has been stymied by a writer's block for thirty years; and also to feed her own 'passion' to know the truth about other people and places. She rents a house on Kowhai Street and settles into observing the neighbours, detailing her 'research' in notebooks. The second section is playfully metafictional. Mattina's neighbour, Dinny Wheatstone, announcing herself as an 'impostor novelist' free of the limitations of a singular and coherent self and able to adopt any point of view, offers Mattina the manuscript of her latest novel to read. Mattina discovers herself to be a character in this fiction, 'in parentheses'.

Confusingly, at several points in Dinny's embedded novel events occur before they are recounted in J.H.B.'s narrative; at times, Dinny's narrative furthers the action of the novel. In the third section Frame utilises magic realism to depict the occurrence of the 'possible impossible' on Kowhai Street. One night the street comes under the effect of the Gravity Star, which is able to collapse the distinctions between near and far, yesterday and tomorrow, near and far, 'the overturning of the old ways when distance is near and the eastern mountains of Puahamara could be the Carpathians'. The street is suffused by a rain of punctuation marks and letters of all the languages that had ever existed. The result is a 'disaster of unbeing' for all the residents who are suddenly devoid of language or the concepts that language engenders. Mattina escapes harm by imaginatively removing herself from the scene through memory—she recalls her husband and son in New York. The next day her neighbours' bodies are carried away by a small army of whitecoated people; officials deny rumours that anything strange has happened on the street; relatives receive no answers about the disappearance of their families. The fourth section returns to the mode of realism. Mattina returns to New York, determined to remember the lost people of Kowhai Street, and learns that she has inoperable cancer. Before she dies, she passes on her memories and notebooks to her husband and son. She urges Jake to travel to Puahamara, but although he complies he is unable to write the novel Mattina hoped he would. Instead her son, John Henry (J.H.B), does so, as suggested by the introductory note. But the final paragraph of the novel overturns the certainty that it comprises J.H.B's homage to his recently dead mother. He writes that his parents in fact died when he was seven and he never knew them, and 'perhaps the town of Puahamara, which I in my turn visited, never existed?'. The 'reality' of the fiction and the character, Mattina, is revealed as the product of his creative imagination.   KWo

CARR, Edwin (1926–), composer, was born in Auckland. Carr's strongly expressive melodic sense and flair for effective gesture, combined with his feeling for orchestral colour, have resulted in many instrumental works for a variety of genres. His Symphony no. 2, 'The Exile' (1983), commemorates the centenary of the birth of Karl *Wolfskehl, the notable German Jewish poet who spent the last years of his life in New Zealand. His vocal settings include the early and charming *A Blake Cantata* (1952) for two-part children's choir and small orchestra, *An Edith Sitwell Song Cycle* (1966) for oboe, soprano and piano, well-reviewed on its first performance at the Wigmore Hall, London, and *Five Wolfskehl Songs* (1977), commissioned by the New Zealand Embassy at Bonn. From 1969 to 1972 Carr worked on his three-act opera *Nastasya*. Based on Dostoyevsky's novel *The Idiot* and set to a libretto by Edward Hill, it was given a broadcast performance but still awaits a stage presentation. His ambitious *Song of Solomon* (1987) has had one performance by the NZSO.   JMT

CASELBERG, John (1927–), poet, dramatist, story writer, art critic, was born in Wakefield near Nelson and was educated at Nelson College and Otago University. After a period travelling in Europe 1949–50 he lived in Christchurch and later Auckland, becoming friendly with the painter Colin *McCahon. In Christchurch, they worked together on dramatic projects, and briefly collaborated on the journal *Issue* (1952–53). In Auckland, McCahon made several art works based on Caselberg's poems, including *The Wake* (1958);

Caselberg also provided the text (taken from the Old Testament) for McCahon's major painting *Gate II* (1961–62). Caselberg's first book was a collection of poems, *The Sound of Morning* (1954), the seventh and last in Pegasus Press's New Zealand Poets series. He also contributed several unusual stories to *Landfall, one of which, 'Eli Eli Lama Sabachthani', was awarded the *Landfall* prose award (jointly with Maurice *Shadbolt) in 1957. He was *Burns Fellow in 1961. His other publications, mostly with Nag's Head Press, are: *The Voice of the Maori, A Culture Conflict Anthology* (1969); *Six Songs and The Wake*, poems (1965); *Chart to My Country: Selected Prose, 1947–71* (1973); *Maori is My Name* (ed.), historical Māori writing in translation (1975); *Lines: Scenes and Passages from Verse Dramas with a Valedictory Sequence for Colin McCahon* (1989); and *Matins & Other Verse* (1992). He has also written a sequence of verse dramas about events in early New Zealand, consisting of *Duaterra, King* (on Samuel *Marsden's mission), read at New Independent Theatre, 1962; *Kendaro* (the introduction of muskets), 1964; *The Hour of the Right Hand* (the Treaty of Waitangi), broadcast 1975; and *John Heke Pokai*, a three-part play concerning Hone Heke, Henry *Williams and the spread of Christianity.   PS

Cash, Sam, is the rogue-hero of *Hang on a Minute Mate* and other novels by Barry *Crump.

CATLEY, Christine Cole (1922–), journalist, broadcaster, publisher and anthologist, has been an innovative promoter of literature, and especially of works by unrecognised writers and by women. The acknowledgments of her editorial work on Mary *Findlay's *Tooth and Nail* and Heretaunga Pat *Baker's *Behind the Tattooed Face* are typical. Born in Wellington, brought up in rural Rangitikei and educated at New Plymouth GHS and Canterbury University College (MA 1944), she spent one period in the Birkinshaw household, together with Fay *Weldon. Her first marriage was to fiction writer John Reece *Cole. She worked in journalism and broadcasting, and was a frequent reviewer of children's books for the *NZ Listener. She then lectured in journalism at Wellington Polytechnic and served as a member of the Broadcasting Council of New Zealand, until moving to Queen Charlotte Sound and in 1973 founding the publishing house of Cape Catley. She also founded and edited *The Picton Paper*, 1977–83, and was the founder-chairperson of the Frank *Sargeson Trust. Her anthology of short stories mainly by women, *Shirley Temple Is a Wife and Mother* (1977), was the pioneer in that field. She then edited *Celebrating Women: New Zealand Women and Their Stories* (1984), a collection of fifty biographical interviews. She has also written

Springboard for Women: New Plymouth Girls High School 1885–1985 (1985) and *The Xenophobes' Guide to Kiwis* (1996). RR

CATRAN, Ken (1944–), has written an unequalled body of teenage *science fiction and writes for film and television. Born in Auckland, he was educated at Rongotai College, and worked in the Post Office, a bank, as a radio journalist, and in a bookshop. After free-lancing for television he became a full-time scriptwriter in 1975, and now has over 100 writing credits in New Zealand film and television drama, including a dramati-sation of his own contemporary city-set novel, *Steel Riders* (1987). He won Best Script Award for Marie Stuttard's *Children of the Dog Star* (1983), and for the Hanlon series, published as *Hanlon: A Casebook* (1986). He wrote the screenplay of *Alex*, the film version of Tessa *Duder's novel. His teenage science fiction is unri-valled in New Zealand. His *Deepwater* trilogy, beginning with *Deepwater Black* (1992), uses time-slips to involve today's teenagers with power struggles in futuristic outer space travel. The *Solar Colonies* trilogy, beginning with *Doomfire on Venus* (1993), explores familiar power politics and racial struggles fifty years hence. *Space Wolf* (1994) brings satellite probes and international politics into con-temporary New Zealand, and *Focus and the Death's Head* (1994) dramatically involves hi-tech, virtual reality in a World War 2 time-warp. With increased intensity in 1995, *Dream Bite* presents a near-future, nightmarish, technological world, while *Neo's War* vividly takes a modern boy back to the Siege of Troy. DH

Cave, established in 1972 by Trevor Reeves and Norman Simms, was one of several literary journals of that time seeking to reflect overseas and especially *American developments—Simms, like Don *Long of *Edge and Michael *Harlow of *Frontiers, being American by birth. In 1976 Simms, an inveterate beget-ter of journals with his private 'Outrigger Publishers' at his Waikato University base, reinstituted it as *New Quarterly Cave* and from 1978 to 1986 as *Pacific Quarterly Moana* (sometimes shown as *Pacific Moana Quarterly*), reflecting his early interest in *Pacific writing. He also published and edited *Rimu*, 'a magazine of New Zealand history, art and culture', from 1982, merging that in 1986 with *PQM* as *Crosscurrent*. None succeeded in attracting much significant New Zealand work or public subsidy. RR

Caxton Press, The, has acquired almost mythic status for its key role in inventing and promulgating the idea (and to some extent the fact) of 'New Zealand literature'. This was achieved first by a well-focused

publishing programme of (especially) poetry, criticism and short fiction, second by establishing and sustaining *Landfall*, and third by a commitment to excellence in *typography, design and production.

The Caxton Press had its beginnings in the writing and printing activities of a group of students at Canterbury University College who established the Caxton Club in October 1932, mainly at the instigation of Denis *Glover. As a schoolboy at Auckland GS (1926–28) Glover had his interest in printing sparked by a classmate, Robert *Lowry, who a few years later estab-lished the Auckland University Students Association Press, which printed the literary magazine *Phoenix* (1932–33) and other projects. Glover, by then a student at Canterbury (1931–34), was stimulated to emulation. The Bodley Head in England was probably another model. A Kelsey hand-platen printing press was acquired and set up in a basement at the College, the Caxton Club was formed, and its members wrote and Glover printed the 'spasmodical' *Oriflamme* (April 1933), whose controversial radicalism resulted in its suppression by the college authorities. Both Glover in *Hot Water Sailor* and Ian *Milner (another club member) in his posthumous memoir *Intersecting Lines* have written accounts of this legendary episode. Forbidden to use the name *Oriflamme*, the Caxton Club (or what remained of it) produced a second magazine, *Sirocco*. The third and last publication of the Caxton Club while still connected to the university was an anthology, *New Poems* (July 1934), edited by Glover and Milner, which included verse by ten poets, several of whom were to become stalwarts of the Caxton Press list: Charles *Brasch, Allen *Curnow, A.R.D. *Fairburn, *Glover and R.A.K. *Mason. The Foreword by Glover and Milner caught the historical moment: 'The poet is the focal point of awareness in his time, and since we are living in a revo-lutionary age some interpretation of its influence is only to be expected.'

The repercussions of the *Oriflamme* affair having blocked his hopes of a career in journalism, Glover bor-rowed money and, with the idiosyncratic John Drew as partner, set up the Caxton Club Press as a commercial printer and publisher in a disused stables at 152 Peter-borough Street, Christchurch. Acquiring a larger machine-driven platen press, they began production in mid-1935. By the end of the year they had published *Another Argo* with an illustration by Leo *Bensemann and a poem each by Curnow, Fairburn and Glover, and small pamphlets of work by Curnow (*Three Poems, Poetry and Language*) and Glover (*Thistledown, A Short Reflection …*). From the start the firm also took on jobbing work (let-terheads, programmes and the like) and printed books for other publishers and institutions. Ian McLaren in *The*

Caxton Press of Christchurch, New Zealand: Annotated Bibliography 1933–1978 (2nd ed., Melbourne 1995) lists more than 1000 such commercial items as compared to some 400 publications with the Caxton imprint. In 1936 the name was shortened to 'The Caxton Press' and nine small books were published including titles by Mason, Ursula *Bethell and D'Arcy *Cresswell, new books by Glover and Curnow, and *Verse Alive*, a collection of satirical verses from the magazine *Tomorrow.

Curnow's *Enemies*, published in June 1937, was the last book printed before new premises were acquired at 129 Victoria Street, and a new press was installed (a cylinder Wharfedale). The adoption of Leo Bensemann as a new partner, and the employment (later) of D.L. Donovan (who eventually became managing director) completed the new arrangements. Bensemann's *Fantastica: Thirteen Drawings* (1937) was the most expensive, elaborate and technically complex work the press had yet produced. *A Catalogue of Publications from the Caxton Press Christchurch up to February 1941* (dating from August 1935 when a power-platen was acquired), included 25 poetry titles (Glover 5, Curnow 4, Mason 3, Bethell 2, and one each by Anton *Vogt, Fairburn, Brasch, J.C. *Beaglehole, Donald Hall and J.R. *Hervey, plus five miscellanies); 6 prose titles (by Frank *Sargeson, M.H. *Holcroft, Cresswell, Dr G.M. Smith, Curnow and Glover); and 8 under the heading 'Art & Typography': a total of 39. Some noteworthy titles were, in poetry, *Time and Place* (1936) and *Day and Night* (1939) by Ursula Bethell, *Dominion* by Fairburn (1938), *The Land and the People* by Brasch (1939), *Not in Narrow Seas* (1939) and *Island & Time* (1941) by Curnow, *This Dark Will Lighten: Selected Poems* by Mason (1941), and the landmark *Recent Poems* (by Curnow, Fairburn, Glover and Mason); and, in prose, *A Man and his Wife* by Sargeson (1940), *The Deepening Stream* by Holcroft (1940), and two pieces of fine printing, *Nastagio & the Obdurate Lady* by Boccaccio (1940) and *Areopagitica* by John Milton (1941). The longer prose works by Sargeson and Holcroft reflected the acquisition of Caxton's first fully automatic press in 1939 and the recent availability of Linotype Baskerville.

Insight into the technical aspects of Caxton's printing is afforded by *A Specimen Book of Printing Types* (1940), with revealing quotes from Caxton's chief mentors in typography, Stanley Morison and Eric Gill, which express a preference for modernity and functional plainness in typography: 'The typography of industrialism … will be plain; and in spite of the wealth of its resources it will be entirely free from exuberance and fancy' (Gill). Among the typefaces displayed in lively and miscellaneous excerpts are Caslon Old Face, Garamond, Baskerville, Perpetua, Gill Sans Serif, Goudy Modern,

and Ultra-Bodoni. A second book of printing types was produced in 1948 and expanded in 1956.

The Foreword to the 1941 catalogue articulated Caxton's philosophy: 'First to make available, as widely and therefore as reasonably as possible, what prose and poetry the directors of the press have considered of interest and value; second, to see that the work of the printing is as well carried out, typographically and technically, as has lain within our powers.' The Foreword went on to speak of the policy 'to make known any promising literature written by New Zealanders, and to provide a rallying point'. (The 'Oriflamme' or 'golden flame banner' aspiration persisted.) The Foreword ended with a restatement of the importance of 'ordered plainness' in typography.

Before Glover departed for naval service, publication began of the literary journal *Book. During the war among the few titles published were short stories by G.R. *Gilbert, essays by Frederick *Sinclaire and poems by Hervey, 'Whim-Wham' (Curnow), and Basil *Dowling. In 1944 *Beyond the Palisade, the first book by the 18-year-old prodigy James K. *Baxter, was published.

Glover marked his return with *The Wind and the Sand: Poems 1934–44* (1945), the first substantial collection of his own verse, and with two seminal anthologies (both 1945), *A *Book of New Zealand Verse 1923–45*, edited by Curnow, and *Speaking for Ourselves*, a collection of short stories edited by Sargeson and printed for Caxton by Lowry in Auckland. Curnow's anthology was especially noteworthy; thirteen of the sixteen poets were Caxton authors (only Eileen *Duggan among significant poets remained outside the fold), while the lengthy introduction made explicit the regional or national aesthetic that underlay most Caxton publications, 'the particular theme of this land and this people'. Glover later named this book (along with Holcroft's trilogy of essays in cultural nationalism, *Discovered Isles*, 1950), 'as the twin peaks of a somewhat rugged publishing career' (*Hot Water Sailor*). Just as significant was the foundation of *Landfall*, which began quarterly publication in March 1947, and celebrated its fiftieth jubilee in 1997, though no longer a quarterly under the Caxton imprint.

The Caxton tradition of fine printing was continued in the post-war period with occasional publications such as *Captain Marion* by Alexander Dumas (1949), Coleridge's *The Rime of the Ancient Mariner* (1952) and Oscar Wilde's *The Ballad of Reading Gaol* (1958). Among miscellaneous publications (many reflecting Leo Bensemann's versatile talents in calligraphy, illustration, typography and printing) were Douglas *Lilburn's *Four Preludes for Piano* (1945), books of engravings by Mervyn Taylor and Rona Dyer, and *A Second Book of Leo Bensemann's Work* (1952). Caxton gave increasing attention to fiction and other prose with collections of stories by A.P. *Gaskell, John Reece *Cole and Janet *Frame, plus longer works of fiction by Sargeson and Greville *Texidor, and several volumes of non-fictional prose by R.M. Burdon and M.H. Holcroft. In 1948 the Caxton Poets series began with collections by William *Hart-Smith, Baxter and Brasch, later joined by Hervey, Curnow, Dowling and Charles *Spear. Other poets published in this period were Rewi *Alley, Kendrick *Smithyman and Fairburn. Two landmark poetry volumes were *Collected Poems* by Ursula Bethell (1950) and *Houses by the Sea*, the posthumously published later poems of Robin *Hyde (1952). A second edition of Curnow's anthology, updated to include some younger writers, was published in 1951, its mixed reception pointing to winds of change within the literary microcosm.

A new phase came in 1951 with the move to a new building at 119 Victoria Street, the acquisition of a second fully automatic press, and the departure of Denis Glover. Fellow printer and publisher R.S. *Gormack wrote that an event which 'rather rocked the wider printing fraternity … was [Glover's] dismissal from The Caxton Press for drink-driven mismanagement. Harsh words, but somewhere near the truth of the matter' (*The Nag's Head Press*, 1992). Drew confirmed this version, describing Glover and himself as 'a pair of scalliwags'. Glover's farewell gesture to the firm he had started two decades earlier was the publication of *Sings Harry and Other Poems* (1951), perhaps his finest single collection.

After 1952 literary publishing was considerably less frequent than in the years of Glover's overreaching. There were expensive presses to keep working and the proportion of commercial publishing to material printed with the Caxton imprint greatly increased. Occasional volumes of poetry were published, titles by Baxter, Hervey, Keith *Sinclair, Paul Henderson (Ruth *France), Cresswell and W.H. *Oliver appearing in the 1950s. All six of Ruth *Dallas's poetry collections were published, from *Country Road* (1953) to *Steps of the Sun* (1979). Several further collections by Brasch were published, including the posthumous *Home Ground* (1974). Several more Sargeson titles (plays and short novels) appeared. A major undertaking was *Landfall Country: Work from Landfall 1947–1961* (1962), Brasch's selection from the first sixty numbers of the quarterly which remained central to Caxton's identity as a publisher. At 459 pages it was the largest book Caxton ever published.

Caxton briefly published *Ascent*, a quarterly of the visual arts, edited by Leo Bensemann and Barbara Brooke, but it lasted only five issues (1967–69). On Brasch's resignation, the editorship of *Landfall* and his position was taken by Robin *Dudding, who also

(1967–72) became the editor of Caxton Press publications. Initiatives during this period included a series called New Zealand Short Stories, which included volumes by Maurice *Duggan (*O'Leary's Orchard*), Sargeson (*Man of England Now*, three novellas) and James *Courage (*Such Separate Creatures*, a posthumous selection edited by Brasch). Caxton continued occasionally to introduce new poets, including (in the 1960s and 1970s) Gordon *Challis, Raymond *Ward, Kevin *Ireland, Peter *Bland, Owen *Leeming, Rob *Jackaman and Harvey *McQueen, but it was no longer the sole or dominant publisher of poetry. In some ways Caxton became more like a conventional general publisher, with titles on gardening, travel, local history, biography, politics, children's books and photography appearing as often as more specifically literary work.

Eventually in 1978 the Caxton Press was sold to Bascands, another Christchurch printer, and Bensemann and Donovan retired. The new owners kept *Landfall* going under a succession of editors and editorial boards for another fifteen years until 1992, when the rights were sold to *Oxford University Press. During the 1980s the main venture of literary interest apart from *Landfall* was the Caxton Press New Poets Series, edited by Michael *Harlow; eight titles appeared between 1985 and 1990, including volumes by Hugh *Lauder, Tony *Beyer, Murray *Edmond, Michele *Leggott, Bernadette *Hall, Gregory *O'Brien and Rob Jackaman. In 1987 Mark *Williams edited *The Caxton Press Anthology: New Zealand Poetry 1972–1986*, designed to mark the fiftieth anniversary of the founding of the Press. Of the more than ninety titles mentioned in the 'Select Bibliography' of this book, only two had been published by Caxton; this might be compared with the bibliography in the second edition of Curnow's anthology (1951) where at least half of some seventy titles listed in the bibliography were Caxton publications.   PS

Censorship in the sense of state interference in the dissemination of literature can be imposed by categorising dealings with particular classes of writings as crimes. The criminal law the European settlers brought to New Zealand, a distillation of centuries of decisions by English judges, proscribed distribution of material that was blasphemous, obscene or seditious, and these proscriptions were carried forward into the Act that in 1893 codified the judge-made law and is the ancestor of the line of statutes currently represented by the Crimes Act 1961.

In addition there has been a series of measures making the offering for sale of indecent books an offence to be dealt with summarily, that is by a magistrate rather than by jury trial. Initially these provisions were to be found in statutes (the earliest was the New Munster Ordinance to Increase the Efficiency of the Constabulary Force of 1849) concerned with the maintenance of public order generally. They were supplemented by a series of Offensive Publications Acts (each enacted in response to public pressure and designed to strengthen the legislation) passed in 1892, 1894, 1905 and 1906. Those four statutes and the earlier provisions were merged in the Police Offences Act 1908 and the Police Offences Act sections were replaced by the Indecent Publications Act 1910 (discussed with its successors below).

The imposition of criminal sanctions is not the only available censorship mechanism. From 1893 until its replacement by New Zealand Post Limited in 1988 the Post Office had a power to intercept and destroy postal articles ultimately extending to printed or written matter other than letters 'of a libellous, seditious, offensive or blasphemous nature'. More important, given New Zealand's reliance on books from abroad, has been the role of the Customs Department with its powers as guardian of the frontier to search, seize and destroy. Since 1858 the department has had power (able to be challenged only by expensive recourse to the courts) to seize indecent or obscene books and other articles. In the early 1920s the decision was made, following wartime success in blocking the inflow of material thought to be seditious, to regard customs seizure as the preferred method of censorship. This was in order to avoid both publicity and the uncertainties resulting from differing magisterial views as to what was subversive or indecent. To meet the criticism that customs clerks were ill equipped to act as censors there was established an informal censorship committee named first the Censorship Appeal Board and from 1930 the Advisory Committee on Literature. This committee, operating in secret, established an index of banned books. It was by this process that Jean Devanny's The *Butcher Shop, published in London in 1926 by Duckworth, was denied entry to New Zealand.

On the introduction of import licensing in 1938, importers of printed matter were required to undertake that 'No subversive publication or publications which give prominence to sex, obscenity, horror, terror, cruelty, or crime, will be admitted under this licence'. It was in reliance on a breach of this undertaking that in 1946 the import to New Zealand of Kathleen Winsor's *Forever Amber*, a novel memorable only for the attention it attracted from censors in various jurisdictions, was prohibited.

Involvement in such activities as publishing, subsidising literary activities and providing libraries by central (and in the case of libraries, local) government has provided further opportunities for interference. So in 1964 the *Literary Fund Advisory Committee imposed on a grant to Louis *Johnson's *New Zealand Poetry Yearbook* the condition that six poems be removed (by James K. *Baxter, Richard *Packer and Martyn Sanderson, including Baxter's 'The Girl in Yellow Jeans' and the poem later called 'Henley Pub'). Baxter referred to the incident in 'A Little Letter to Auckland Starlets'.

As to the grounds for interference, there is still in the current Crimes Act an offence of blasphemous libel. The only known prosecution (in 1922) on this charge, following the publication in the *Maoriland Worker* of a Sassoon war poem, resulted in an acquittal, though with the jury rider 'that similar publications of such literature be discouraged'. There have been periods (notably during and for some years after World War 1 and during and following the 1951 *Waterfront Strike) when governments were zealous to ban on the grounds of insufficient patriotism. Devanny believed, probably correctly, that it was because of the political unacceptability of its picture of New Zealand that action was taken against *The Butcher Shop*. It is not known whether the existence since 1971 of legislation prohibiting publications likely to incite racial disharmony has deprived New Zealand of any writing that can fairly be described as literature, but the offence is defined sufficiently broadly to embrace any local equivalent of (for example) Hilaire Belloc's anti-Semitism.

But the principal ground for interference in the dissemination of literature has always been (ignoring any nice distinction between the two terms) its obscenity or indecency, meaning its treatment of sexuality and its employment of sexual and scatological terms (usually in practice as intensifiers used in reported demotic speech). Discernible in the choice of literary targets for police attention is an insular distrust of what is not British. In 1890 five Christchurch booksellers pleaded guilty to charges based on their stocking novels by Zola. The Indecent Publications Act 1910 required magistrates in determining the issue indecent or not to consider literary, scientific and artistic merit and whether 'the act of the defendant was of an immoral or mischievous tendency', but these provisions proved not enough to ensure sophistication.

In 1917 a bookseller was convicted for offering for sale de Maupassant's *A Spa Love Affair*. 'If such books are sold indiscriminately and scattered broadcast,' said the magistrate, '... Literary hogs would be able to wallow knee-deep in sexual filth. This would tend to generate libidinous desires, ... that broad highway that leads to the mental hospital, the gaol, and the premature grave.' In 1935 another bookseller was convicted for displaying Balzac's *Droll Stories,* which the magistrate believed indecent because 'The tendency of the tales told is to glorify immorality and licentiousness and to hold purity and virtue up to ridicule.' The London Book Club was convicted by a magistrate for having Boccaccio's *Decameron* on its shelves, but in 1939 the conviction was quashed on appeal on the basis that the book was not offered for hire in a manner that drew attention to its indecency.

An amendment to the 1910 Act was hastily enacted in 1954 in the wake of a report by a committee chaired by Dr O.C. Mazengarb concerned with juvenile sexual immorality. It muddled the definition of indecency by introducing a reference to a tendency to deprave or corrupt, in this respect reversing the *Decameron* decision, and also compelled distributors of printed matter to register with the Secretary of Justice, a requirement repealed in 1958. From this time on there were two departments, Customs and Justice, making pronouncements on censorship issues which were in conflict on at least one occasion. To avoid such embarrassments, in 1960 an interdepartmental committee was established.

Until about the late 1950s censorship decisions on indecency seem to have been reasonably in step with the prevailing New Zealand social ethic. In 1934 Jane *Mander observed, 'Our writers still proceed on the theory that we are some special sort of race that never has an indecent thought; and our insides might be made of plaster of paris for all the notice that is taken of them', and there seems no reason to attribute this reticence to fear of censorship. Change followed with the shift in Western countries towards a less inhibited approach to human sexuality, a shift (in the context of censorship) symbolised in England by the 1960 acquittal by a jury of Penguin Books Limited on a charge based on its publication of D.H. *Lawrence's *Lady Chatterley's Lover*, and in New Zealand by a jury's rejection in 1972 of charges against those responsible for a production of the musical *Hair*.

There were criticisms (most loudly expressed by booksellers and librarians) of the ramshackle nature of the censorship machinery. Discontent increased when in 1960 a Supreme Court challenge by the Council for Civil Liberties to the Customs condemnation of Nabokov's novel *Lolita* failed, and when in the following year a majority of the Court of Appeal rejected an appeal against the Supreme Court decision.

The solution adopted by the Indecent Publications Act 1963, which repealed the 1910 statute, was to confer the responsibility for classifying publications on a tribunal, two of whose members were required to have special qualifications in literature or education. Mana was conferred on the tribunal by the appointment as its first chairman of Sir Kenneth Gresson, a retired President of the Court of Appeal who had dissented in the *Lolita* case. The matters the tribunal was required to take into account included the dominant effect of the book as a whole, its literary merit, its likely readers, its price, the likelihood of persons being either corrupted or benefited from reading the book, and the book's honesty of purpose. The tribunal scrupulously applied these eminently sensible criteria from its first decision, when it refused to restrict access to James Baldwin's *Another Country*, until its abolition in 1994. In consequence, interference with the availability of written material eligible to be classed as literature in any strict sense was minimal during the tribunal's thirty-one years of existence.

This position was not permitted to continue. The Films, Videos, and Publications Classification Act 1993 repealed the 1963 statute and established an Office of Film and Literature Classification comprising a politically appointed chief censor and deputy chief censor, together with classification officers. This office, assisted by inspectors of publications, is responsible for censoring and enforcing the censorship of books, films and sound and video recordings. The Act has been criticised as repressive, as shaped by the obsessions of puritans and feminists, for the width and subjectivity of its definition of what is objectionable and for processes said to breach elementary requirements of procedural justice. It is too soon to judge whether these criticisms are deserved. A verdict must likewise be postponed on whether a provision in the New Zealand Bill of Rights Act 1990—'Everyone has the right to freedom of expression, including the freedom to seek, receive, and impart information and opinions of any kind in any form'—will have any practical effect on the rules imposing censorship or whether, as seems more probable, it will prove to be mere well-intentioned exhortation.

See also *The Butcher Shop*, *Children of the Poor*, James *Courage, Sarah *Courage, John *Dunmore, Ellen *Ellis, *For the Rest of Our Lives*, *'Je ne parle pas français' and *Oriflamme*.   DFD

Centennial, The, of European settlement in New Zealand was officially marked in 1940 by the publication of the Centennial Surveys and by the Centennial Literary Competitions. The surveys were important from a literary point of view because they included E.H. *McCormick's *Letters and Art in New Zealand*, the first comprehensive New Zealand literary history and a very distinguished piece of work which was ultimately absorbed into his *New Zealand Literature: A Survey* (1959). The literary competitions brought forth, or at least rewarded, significant work in some genres, but the results in others were disappointing. The most important new work was M.H. *Holcroft's *The Deepening Stream*, which won the essay competition. A literary and cultural analysis raising serious questions about New Zealand's failure to create an organic culture at home in its environment, the essay was later incorporated into *Discovered Isles* (1950). At least as significant was Frank *Sargeson's previously published 'The Making of a New Zealander', with its dark implicit judgment on what it meant to be a New Zealander, which was first equal in the short story competition, while Roderick *Finlayson's sardonic (and also previously published) 'The Totara Tree' took third place. The other first equal story, however, was the trite 'The River' by E.A. Midgley, perhaps more typical of the other prize winners. Of the three selections in the novel competition, only one of the third-prize recipients, Beryl McCarthy's *Castles in the Soil*, seems to have achieved publication. The judges awarded no first prize in the drama competition, while J.R. *Hervey won the longer poem competition and was also first equal with Helena Henderson in the short poem competition with two rather traditional works, 'Salute to Youth' and 'The War Refugee'. None of these reflected the poetic ferment of the times.

With the exception of the works by McCormick, Holcroft, Sargeson and Finlayson, most of the writings officially associated with the centennial expressed with more or less subtlety the cultural myths of progress and *'God's Own Country'. Probably the best of these celebratory works, however, was not an official entry or publication—Eileen *Duggan's *New Zealand Poems* of 1940, which had on its cover 'In Honour of the Centennial of the Dominion of New Zealand'. 'Centenary Ode' and 'Ode' in that volume are probably the closest of all Centennial texts to such efforts as Thomas *Bracken's 'Jubilee Ode' for the 1890 celebration. Duggan celebrates the heroic Māori and Pākehā past, sees New Zealand as a society based on 'The just, the gracious way', and calls for the nation to carry out its special mission in the difficult times of World War 2. Other poems in her volume celebrate the *landscape ('New Zealand'), exploration ('The Charting'), missionary work ('Ballad to Father Petitjean') and the struggles of the pioneers ('Ballad of the Bushman').

Most of the more memorable unofficial literary responses to the centennial, however, deconstructed rather than celebrated the cultural myths. Allen *Curnow's *Island & Time* (1941), his 'attempt to assign to the New Zealander and the New Zealand scene some place in the larger current of history and Time', contains the classic anti-myth texts. 'The Unhistoric Story', notably, debunks the received views of New Zealand history and presented contemporary society as one in which the dream had died: 'The pilgrim dream pricked by a cold dawn died / Among the chemical farmers, the fresh towns; among / Miners, not husbandmen, who piercing the side / Let the land's life…'. 'House and Land', in the same volume, also presents 'a land of settlers / With never a soul at home.' In the same critical vein, Charles *Brasch's 'The Silent Land' (also 1941) shows a country where 'the cities cry for meaning' and the settlers are not at home in their environment; and Finlayson in *Our Life in This Land* (1940) mourns the loss of integrity in one hundred years of European occupation, interpreting the history in terms of the Fall instead of as progress. Summarising these critical views of the centennial five years later, Denis *Glover in 'Centennial' (1945) complained that amidst the celebrations in 'the year of centennial splendours … no one remembered our failures'.

LJ

CHALLIS, Gordon (1932–), poet, was born in a Welsh family in Birmingham, England, and raised there and in Sydney. After living for a time in Spain, he arrived in New Zealand in 1953 and worked as a postman in Wellington and studied psychology and social work at Victoria University. After working as a psychiatric social worker in Porirua Hospital 1961–62, he joined the new Hastings psychiatric unit as a psychologist. He returned to psychiatric social work in 1973, at Canberra, and retired from it in 1988, at Porirua. He lives in Nelson.

Challis began writing poetry at Victoria University. His work was widely published in literary periodicals, especially *Landfall*, and in 1960 Charles *Brasch nominated him as one of the four leading contenders for poetic fame in New Zealand in the coming decade. A poetic sequence, *The Oracle*, was published in *Landfall* 60 (1961), the first poem of which subsequently appeared in Challis's collection, *Building* (*Caxton, 1963). The intense pressures of mental health work led Challis to abandon writing poetry and, apart from translations from Spanish for *Landfall*, no further poetry appeared until several new poems in the *NZ Listener* in the late 1980s. A second collection is in preparation.

Challis's work has been linked with the other 'immigrant' poets writing in Wellington from the mid-1950s, Peter *Bland and Charles *Doyle. All three were regarded as being in the 'School of [Louis] Johnson'— that is, dealing with personal experience in a contemporary urban, often domestic, setting, and using modernist techniques. Challis's most enduring work is more distinctive. Such poems as 'The Iceman', 'The Shadowless Man', 'The Thermostatic Man', 'The Asbestos-Suited Man in Hell' and its sequel 'The Inflammable Man' explore psychological states and the development of personal identity. Others such as 'The Black One', 'The Sirens' and 'The Oracle' are an often ironic reworking of myths or archetypes into contemporary situations. Linguistically inventive yet always carefully crafted, Challis's poetry is characterised by an apparent distance, almost a clinical detachment, which subverts the immediate or expected emotional response. Beneath that, however, there is a deeper identification with psychological conditions that are unique to the individual yet common to humankind. The poems listed above have all been anthologised, some several times.   AM

CHAMIER, George (1842–1915), wrote the two most substantial nineteenth-century novels set in New Zealand, ★*Philosopher Dick: Adventures and Contemplations of a New Zealand Shepherd* (1891) and *A ★South-Sea Siren: A Novel Descriptive of New Zealand Life in the Early Days* (1895). Both were written in Australia and published in London. Born into a distinguished Huguenot family in Cheltenham, England, he lived in New Zealand only from 1860 to 1869. He had trained as a scientist in Dresden, and traces of this German background and an interest in the philosophy of science are found in his novels, together with informed interests in music and literature. In New Zealand he is recorded as a road engineer and surveyor in Canterbury, including 1866–68 in the Chief Surveyor's Department in Christchurch, and probably resided at Saltwater Creek. This Ashley River district is presumably the setting of *A South-Sea Siren*.

He left for Tasmania in 1869 and from 1873 worked on engineering projects in Victoria and South Australia, largely as a private consulting engineer. His non-fictional work includes *The Utilisation of Water in South Australia* (1886) and a book of essays entitled *War and Pessimism, and Other Studies* (1911). This 'pessimism', a rejection of religion in favour of a resigned willingness to carry out what life might demand, is a more extreme version of the irony to be found in Richard Raleigh, the novels' main figure.

With the same central figure, other recurrent characters and linked thematic developments, the novels seem almost to be one narrative, despite different settings. The thematic bond is a concern for questions relating to the individual and the community. In *Philosopher Dick* a ★'Man Alone' is able to explore his own inner nature; in *A South-Sea Siren* the same man must come to terms with social realities and, especially, encounters with women. *Philosopher Dick* concludes with first impressions of the town of Sunnydowns and the two women who feature in the sequel. The conclusion of *A South-Sea Siren*, where the main characters are planning to go to Wellington, suggests that there was to be a third novel set in the city to match those set in the remote country and a small town.

If that conjectural project had been completed we would have a remarkable trilogy of novels on early colonial life. As it is, the two novels are major milestones in the history of antipodean literature. They are highly unconventional in their characterisation and in the strong element of analysis and contemplation applied to colonial society, as well as technically skilful in incorporating these elements into an unusual narrative structure. Perhaps the very shortness of Chamier's stay enabled him to observe the pressures brought by New Zealand life on individuals with a degree of ironic detachment, yet with a wealth of significant detail. Written thirty years after the events they describe, they also have historical perspective. Because of a certain wordiness and perhaps the demanding complexities of the multi-perspectivism, Chamier's books have never won more than ambiguous praise. They are rewarding for all that.   NW

Chapbook, subtitled 'A Private Magazine of Poetry, Music and Art', appeared irregularly in Wellington 1945–50. Published by the Chapbook Society and edited by Ronald Castle it featured poetry, criticism, reviews, music and artwork. Louis ★Johnson contributed poems regularly 1946–49.   SH

CHAPMAN, Robert (1922–), historian, became professor of political studies at the University of Auckland, and was an influential critic of fiction and poetry in the 1950s. He is best known for the essay 'Fiction and the Social Pattern: Some Implications of Recent New Zealand Writing' (★*Landfall* 25, 1953), and as co-editor of *An Anthology of New Zealand Verse* (★Oxford University Press, 1956). Chapman adhered to the interpretation of F.R. Leavis's criticism that fiction writers should ultimately affirm life, showing up the destructive results when the proper human course was rejected. A type of humanitarian liberalism was the proper course for New Zealand, he argued; that is, faith in a state where 'truly human ease and depth of living' may exist. At present ★puritanism had constricted and distorted society, inducing spiritual poverty, materialism, violence, sexual repression and destruction of the family (the foundation of society). Through art, writers must show realistic pictures of life in order that society would recognise itself and act to ameliorate the distortions. Chapman's essay validated critical realism as the norm of fiction, overlooking the facts that its greatest local practitioner, Frank ★Sargeson, had exhausted the genre, that women writers often preferred more personal to societal themes, and that ★existentialism with its pessimistic view of human life was winning exponents. The essay's misogyny went largely unchallenged, so must accurately represent its age.

The Oxford *Anthology* sought to redress the under-representation of younger writers apparent at the 1951 *Writers' Conference and in Allen *Curnow's anthologies. Chapman preferred modern poets who 'feel so at ease with their environment that they can simply assume it', writing poetry in which 'New Zealand patterns of life and thought are fused without effort'. HM

Chapman's New Zealand Monthly Magazine: *Literary, Scientific, and Miscellaneous* was a journal of 1850, its title reflecting the name of its publisher, Geo. T. Chapman, an Auckland bookseller. Its aim as stated in its first issue was 'to develop a taste for writing among the colonists' and it tried to appeal to a wide range of tastes. Despite this it found too few subscribers and disappeared after a short life. Its most important contributions came from Charles Heaphy, who wrote on 'the Past Generation of Maories', using an early kind of oral history technique by reporting the memories of an old Māori 'chief' and retelling 'Puke Hina; a Legend of Mt. Eden' as recorded from a Māori informant with the help of John White. Heaphy also contributed a short descriptive series on South Island *landscapes entitled 'A Visit to the Greenstone Country'. There were a few anonymous short stories, set in England, and an anonymous recollection of a meeting with Sir Walter Scott. Otherwise, apart from a scattering of weak poems, the contents were non-literary, covering such subjects as vegetable gardening, sheep farming, a project for founding a university in Auckland, and some accounts of geology by the Rev. Richard Taylor. Some items were borrowed from abroad, including G.J. Macdonald on the Australian aborigines and an excerpt from *Macaulay's *History of England*, describing Darien's view of the Pacific. Twelve years later *The *New Zealand Magazine* was a conscious successor to *Chapman's*. NW

CHARMAN, Janet (1954–), Auckland poet, published in *AND* and *Wominspace Journal* in the 1980s. Her first collection, with Marina Bachmann and Sue Fitchett, was the Spiral publication *Drawing Together* (1985). She has subsequently published *2 deaths in 1 night* (1987), *red letter* (1992) and *end of the dry* (1995), and her work has appeared in more specialised anthologies such as *The New Poets* (ed. Murray *Edmond and Mary Paul, 1987) and *Yellow Pencils: Contemporary Poetry by New Zealand Women* (ed. Lydia Wevers, 1988). Charman shows stylistic affinities with Auckland poets like Murray Edmond and Michele *Leggott, and ideological ones with feminist poets like Heather *McPherson, Roma *Potiki and Joanna *Paul. Democratic features of her style reveal her agenda: limited capitalisation, lower-case pronominal 'I', and minimal punctuation. She focuses on women's concerns: caring for others, victimisation, literary heroines, female sexuality including lesbianism, heterosexuality, childbirth and motherhood, vocations such as midwifery and nursing. Often dense, elliptical or complex in expression, her writing displays considerable emotional range extending from sexual innuendo, to the erotic, to tenderness, or a playful wit: 'we have to pull our poems on one leg at a time'. Charman projects a distinctive voice, a living presence engaged with others, seldom at rest; her poems are unadorned, conversational, political, yet there's music in her subtle twists of perception: 'elbow heel bow / line angle jaw bone / slim scar red car loading / the baskets getting the provisos ...' She trained as a nurse, has worked as a receptionist, and now teaches English at Auckland University. JW

Check to Your King (1936) was Robin *Hyde's first novel, the first version being completed in 1935 and submitted for an American literary prize. Based on the life of Baron Charles de Thierry, it gives a vivid account of one of the most colourful characters and periods in New Zealand's colonial history. Woven into this is Hyde's perception of the subjugation of the Māori, once the 'tallest and bravest race of fighters'. She had already denounced their dispossession in trenchant newspaper articles and in the novel she looks ahead as few others had done: 'Those whose spirits have plunged from Te Reinga, the cliffs of ghosts ... have crept to earth's surface once again, back through the hollow stems of flax and *toi-toi*. The spirit tribes are abroad in the land and seek for their inheritance.' De Thierry's romantic involvement in the French Revolution, his extraordinary eccentricity and vision appealed to Hyde's poetic imagination. Drawing on his papers, she created a colourful series of tableaux as de Thierry attempted to realise his dream of setting up a sovereign state on 40 000 acres in the Hokianga, with 'unlimited brotherhood between white and brown.' Although we may now reject his imperialist aggrandisement, Hyde succeeds in winning our sympathy for him in his failure.

The novel is a blend of past and present—history, legend and speculation. As in her other novels, she employs a range of voices, moving, for example, from a description of Māori oratory to admonish the reader, 'there are excellent books on the subject, few of them read'. GB

CHEESEMAN, Clara (1852–1943), the daughter of the Rev. Thomas Cheeseman and younger sister of the distinguished scientist Thomas F. *Cheeseman, was born in Doncaster and arrived in Auckland with her family in 1854. Like many Victorian families, the Cheeseman children wrote their own newspapers and magazines, one or two of which have survived. They were still at it when grown up, using their childhood nicknames (Clara was 'Chameleon') and illustrating their Christmas annual in 1902 with photographs of themselves as children. Various relatives and family friends also contributed. Clara and her two sisters accompanied their brother on his expeditions to collect botanical specimens. She appears to have lived in Auckland for almost all her life (certainly from 1902), dying there at the age of 91.

Cheeseman's three-volume, 900-page novel *A Rolling Stone* (1886) is a remarkable but forgotten achievement. The narrator, who tends to behave coquettishly with the reader, has plenty of leisure to philosophise on the landscape and the transitions in Māori life and make excursions into botany, literary reference and the like. The rich detail gives a fascinating picture of colonial households, and there is an interesting account of the life of a professional musician in Otago, going from household to household to play the pianos. The repetitive disquisitions on weather patterns are less rewarding.

Cheeseman's essay 'Colonials in Fiction' (*New Zealand Illustrated Magazine*, Jan. 1903) is an entertaining account of the gap between truth and fiction in Australian and New Zealand novels. She mourns the amount of swearing in Marriott *Watson and William *Satchell and the alcohol consumed in Australian novels. She is harsh on Louisa *Baker too, saying that 'Her chief characters are almost always inconsistent, for while we are told in so many words that they are noble-minded, unselfish and truthful, they do not prove it by their behaviour.' Despite a 'temperance' trend, she has acute and amusing things to say of her colleagues and demonstrates a considerable range of reading.

Like so many of her contemporaries, notably Satchell, she fell silent after her industrious beginnings. Perhaps the pressures of being 'literary' in the colony were too hard to bear.   NW/PN

CHEESEMAN, Thomas Frederick (1846–1923), was primarily a botanist and, to remarkable degree, also a zoologist and ethnologist. However, his skilful prose, sense of humour and narrative interpolations which throw vivid light on remote places can only be accepted gratefully by anyone who enjoys good writing. His colleague, Sir Leonard Cockayne, praised his writings as 'distinguished by ... sound judgement, clarity of expression, and accuracy. Above all, he had the supreme gift of infinite patience; all views expressed were the result of much cautious deliberation.... And in this spirit he approached his classic work, *The Manual of the New Zealand Flora*, with the result that it ... contains the well-considered conclusions of a master mind' (cited from *An Encyclopedia of New Zealand*, 1966).

In addition to the 1200 pages of the great *Manual* (1906), he and W.B. Hemsley edited *Illustrations of the New Zealand Flora* (1914) and Cheeseman's classification of certain New Zealand molluscs—which might have been the life work of a lesser man—is still recognised as definitive. In 1923 he was awarded one of science's greatest honours, the Gold Linnean Medal of the Linnean Society. He became president of the New Zealand Institute in 1911 and an original fellow of the institute in 1918. He also made significant contributions to the substance and the classification of the ethnological and other collections of the Auckland Museum (now the Auckland War Memorial Museum).   NW

CHER, Ming (1947–), was born in Singapore and grew up there as a street-kid. He was a builder in Vietnam during the war there and then travelled widely during seven years as a merchant seaman. He settled in New Zealand in 1977, to run a business importing Indonesian goods. He speaks seven languages fluently, but was almost illiterate until he wrote his first novel, in English, using a dictionary to learn to read and write. For his second draft he taught himself to type and for the third to use a word processor. The result is *Spider Boys* (1995), published to acclaim in New Zealand, Australia and the USA, an intense novel written in a dialect which adds to its exoticism and raw colloquial force. The orphans Kwang and Kim have grown up together and now, as teenagers, discover sex and commercial success and failure. Kwang acquires riches as the owner of the most successful fighting spider. Huge sums are bet on the male spiders, which are wrought into a frenzy by the presence of females and then set on each other. The long fight descriptions are as tense as any boxing match. Kwang loses his fortune as quickly as he has won it and comes under the power of the wealthy wheeler-dealer, Yeow. He also loses Kim to Yeow. In a tense climax he tries to kill his rival, but each feels that he has been revenged and they end as friends. For other characters, such as Big Mole, who finds a doctor to remove her disfigurement, the ending is also happy, so that the overall impression is of young people successfully finding their way in a hostile and dangerous world.   NW

CHERRY, Frances (1937–), short story writer, novelist and teacher of creative writing, was born Frances Birchfield. Both parents were members of the Communist Party but were expelled in 1957 after criticising the Soviet invasion of Hungary. She lives at Paekakariki, near Wellington. Her first published story, 'Down to Earth', was in the *NZ Listener* (1977), and 'The Daughter-in-Law' in *Landfall* 127 (1978). Her stories have been extensively anthologised, published in

School Journal and broadcast on radio. Her first collection was *The Daughter-in-Law and Other Stories* (1986). Her first novel was *Dancing with Strings* (1989), a partly autobiographical story which recalls Cherry's childhood and Communist parents, and in which the main character leaves a difficult marriage and comes out as a lesbian. *The Widowhood of Jackie Bates* (1991), written on a Writer's Bursary in the house of Janet *Frame in Shannon, also deals with adjustment to a woman's solo life after marriage. *Washing Up in Parrot Bay* is forthcoming. The story 'Waiting for Jim' was filmed by Chrissie Parker as *One Man's Meat*.   ALa

Children of the Poor (1934), John A. *Lee's first published novel, is a product of the 1930s *Depression. According to Lee it was written in 1931, 'inspired by a heart-breaking parade of unemployed men', though Eric Olssen says Lee began writing it the day after the Auckland riots in April 1932. It is at any rate the first New Zealand novel of social protest, a 'Tale of the Gutter' attacking the indifference and hypocrisy of the well-off and vindicating the poor. Autobiographical in its main features, it is the story of Albany Porcello's childhood and adolescence in poorest Dunedin (Lee had attended the Albany Street School). Driven by poverty he slides into prolonged petty thieving of coal and scrap metal until he is sentenced to Burnham Industrial School. Lee is aware of the risks of determinism in social realist fiction and avoids them by celebrating the vitality of Albany's will to act and endure. This celebratory quality and the defiant *existentialism of Lee's treatment of sensitive moral issues, such as Albany's mother's extramarital pregnancy and his sister Rose's prostitution, gave the book a scandalous reputation and it was widely banned. The view that the novel misrepresented Lee's mother and sister must be revised in the light of his mother Mary Lee's own autobiography *The Not So Poor* (1992). The novel's social message earned it good literary credentials, with early recommendations from Upton Sinclair and Bernard *Shaw, though formally it is flawed through Lee's pervasive pamphleteering and moralising intrusions. It is a paradox that its more disciplined sequel, *The Hunted* (1936), lacks its range and powerful anger. Before Lee, only *Satchell and *Mander had written New Zealand novels likely to endure. Rough diamond that it is, *Children of the Poor* is a foundation work in New Zealand fiction. A stage adaptation by Mervyn *Thompson was first performed in 1989 and published in 1990.   KA

Children's Literature Association (CLA), see **New Zealand Children's Literature Association (NZCLA).**

Children's Pages of newspapers were, Robin *Hyde said, 'one of the most creditable features of journalism in this country'. When books for the young were not widely available, early exposure to writing encouraged children to feel part of a lively writing community, in which Hyde, Ruth *Dallas, Janet *Frame, Ruth *Park, Elsie *Locke and others first achieved publication. Possibly the first 'children's page' was a corner of verse, short stories, and riddles begun in the *Otago Witness* on 11 November 1876. The most famous and widely read children's feature began in the same weekly paper on 16 July 1886. Under editor William Fenwick, 'Dot's Little Folk' were given their own pages, devoted entirely to their letters, all published under a pseudonym, and each one commented on by 'Dot' herself, who wrote, 'Dot will never find any matter that interests the children too trivial to attend to, and hopes before too long to be regarded as their friend.' By the column's fiftieth jubilee in 1936, some 10 000 children's letters had been received, and members were spread throughout New Zealand. Women who assisted 'Dot' were the novelist, Louise Alice *Baker, and later the Service sisters, Eileen (*Soper) and Marna. It was not until 1906 that a poignant letter to his brother, dictated by Fenwick on the morning he died, revealed that he, a married, childless man, had himself been 'Dot'. When 'Dot's Little Folk' reappeared in the *Otago Daily Times* in 1932, the young Janet Frame became an avid reader and contributor. Given the singularly appropriate pseudonym 'Amber Butterfly' by Dot, she sent in many poems, and Dot's encouragement of her 'poetic insight and imagination' influenced her decision to become a poet. In *To the Island* Frame writes of 'the surge of performing children' at that time (1936): 'the children of the town and the province and the country began not only to perform … but also to write their own poems and stories, encouraged locally by the children's pages in the newspapers…'.

The *Southland Daily News* pages for 'Little Pakehas' edited by 'Godmother Tauira' (the editor's wife, Mrs Hutton-Potts), and later by 'Cousin Wendy', provided Ruth Dallas with inspiration and many prizes. The newspaper offices were something of a gathering place for young subscribers, with debates, plays and bazaars held there. In Christchurch the *Sun*, under the editorship of C.A. *Marris, provided pages for 'Sunbeams', clubs, plays and outings for members. Children's novelist Esther *Glen compiled the children's pages from 1925 under the name 'Lady Gay'; some 20 000 children were 'Sunbeams'. In 1935 Glen and her chief illustrator, Joan Mayo, moved to the *Press*, and were responsible for the feature 'Gay Gazette', which appeared on Saturdays to complement the 'Press Junior', a supplement edited by Jean Stevenson (Bertram), which appeared on

Thursdays. Many Christchurch writers provided material for children: Hyde, *Glover, *Curnow, *Holcroft, Somerset, *Tracy, *Mackay and *Howes. In Wellington Alison *Grant appeared as 'Fariel' in the *Evening Post*, Hyde was 'Aunt Mary' in the *Farmer's Advocate*. The weekly *Truth* also carried children's pages, and Eileen *Duggan compiled 'Pippa's Page' in the *New Zealand Tablet*. The *Sun* pages were now edited by Winifred Tennant as 'Red Feather'.

Park describes in *A Fence Around the Cuckoo* (1992) the not wholly positive impact of publishing in the *New Zealand Herald*. While she revered the *Herald*'s Elsie K. *Morton 'as if she were George Eliot', the gibes she endured from other children taught her to work 'only from imagination' and avoid 'anything that mattered to me'.

Park later worked on the children's pages of the *Star*, which offered four pages of entertainment and educational material designed to supplement the school syllabus. Historian James *Cowan wrote a weekly feature. Staff of the *Star* also created two pages for children in the *Farmers' Weekly*.

Paper shortages during World War 2 curtailed or ended many children's features and radio gave children another option for entertainment. Radio drama for children became an alternative outlet for writers, but even today Independent Newspapers' 'Newspapers in Education' feature often serves New Zealand literature well.   HM

China has occupied a significant niche in New Zealand literature since the first Chinese immigrants—men from Canton—answered an 1865 invitation to rework Central Otago's goldfields. Historian James Ng's description, in *Windows on a Chinese Past* (1993), of the miners as sojourners intent on making their fortune and returning to China, partly explains discrimination towards them out of all proportion to any threat they posed. With few assets and little English they were necessarily cooperative, and hence economically competitive. In their endurance of severe privation, dedication to work and saving, ingenuity (one designed a pioneering gold dredge), and different appearance, they provided Europeans with ample grounds for intolerance.

Consequently, the period's sporadic literary references to Chinese are almost universally negative, although David McKee *Wright, in *Station Ballads and Other Verses* (1897), while catering to his audience's prejudices, does accord them grudging respect even as he uses one of their many offensive nicknames: 'For the country as far as I've seen it's as chock full of holes as a sieve. / With the Chinkies a-mullocking through it and yet those coves manage to live.'

More recently, Chinese goldminers have captured a number of creative imaginations. These include Leon Narbey, who recreated the period in his film *Illustrious Energy* (1988); Eve *Sutton, whose children's novel *Valley of Heavenly Gold* (1987) uses the historical setting to deal with racial prejudice; and Jye Kang, whose *Guests of the New Gold Hill* (1985) fictionalises the 'Oon' family's evolution from prospectors in 1866 to Wellington fruiterers in 1947. James Ng, criticising Kang for sensationalising gambling and opium smoking, called for 'a piercing of the old caricatures which depicted [Chinese] as subhuman ... to find the real New Zealand –Chinese' (*NZ Listener*, 21 Sep. 1985).

Such caricatures were stock when Katherine *Mansfield began writing. Occasionally she introduces Chinese for local colour, as when Stanley Burnell, in *Prelude*, purchases cherries from a Chinese fruiterer. But 'Ole Underwood' provides a far grittier representation of Wellington's Chinese community to mirror Ole's madness and alienation. Initially the card-playing Chinamen, 'their long pigtails bound round their heads and their faces yellow as lemons', are a group that even he can feel superior to. But as the wind of his entry to their shop scatters their cards and their welcome turns to anger, in Underwood's demented mind the 'Chinks' become his pursuers. For Robin *Hyde in *The *Godwits Fly* (1938), the 'Chinese Dens' of Wellington's Haining Street—'a melting-pot of Asiatic shops ... in which old Chinese smoked opium and cut greasy cards'—are similarly symbolic, in this case of the conflict of aspirations in Augusta and John Hannay's marriage. Lloyd *Jones's *Splinter* (1988) contains a vicious attack on a Chinese cook in late nineteenth-century Hutt Valley. In a climate of opposition to the 'Asiatic plague', roughing up 'an unpatriotic Celestial' is, in the minds of police, no grounds for prosecution.

Manying Ip's *Dragons of the Long White Cloud: The Making of Chinese New Zealanders* (1996) offers an insider's perspective on enclaves like Haining Street. Ip's book also documents instances of Māori discrimination towards Chinese, but comments that traditionally, 'Chinese and Maori were naturally friendly: both were despised by white settlers, and both worked as soil-tillers'. So it is in Roderick *Finlayson's story 'They All Go Home to Die', from *Brown Man's Burden* (expanded 1973 edition). When a young Māori woman, Lena, tends terminally ill Ah Koo, he returns kindness of the sort she has rarely experienced. Only when he returns to China to die does she submit to an unattractive arranged marriage.

It was in the 1930s that the New Zealand–Chinese connection became of major literary significance. Rewi *Alley, who moved there in 1927, stands apart because, to quote Edgar Snow, he 'achieved greatness in a country where few foreigners ever managed to create an authentic ripple'. Alley's continuing place in the imaginations of both countries is shown in the opera 'Alley' (1998), a collaboration between composer Jack Body, librettist Geoff Chapple and Chinese-born director Chen Shi-Zheng. Among others who wrote of their Chinese experiences, James *Bertram and Hyde are key figures. Hone *Tuwhare, who visited China in the 1970s and 1980s, evokes, in poems like 'Kwantung Guest House: Canton', a country of vast spaces—'with the colours changing, banded / geometrical and moving off'—and teeming cities—'alive, / and set firmly into a dynamic base built painfully by / their heroic predecessors'.

Joy *Cowley's story 'The *Silk' reflects the ambivalence of many New Zealanders to China and Chinese. Mr Blackie's reverence for a fabric that comes 'All the way from China' is as emblematic of the attraction of difference and distance, as his contempt for the Chinese merchant—'You got to argue with these devils'—is a reflection of suspicions formed over generations. The former attitude explains why biographies like Stanley *Roche's Foreigner: The Story of Grace Morton as told to Stanley Roche (1979), which is partly set in China, are popular. And it might partially explain why Dorothy *Eden sets her novel The Time of the Dragon (1975) in Peking during the Boxer uprisings; and Claude *Evans, who lived in 1930s Canton, sets his play Far Journey (1949) in Canton during the 1938 Sino-Japanese conflict.

There have been a few exchanges across the language wall. These include *Edge, the ambitious literary journal of the 1970s, which underscored its international status by including work in Mandarin; and Murray *Edmond's signalling of his interest in Chinese poetry by incorporating Chinese brush-characters as tokens in certain poems. Of the many translations of New Zealand literature into Chinese languages, the most significant involve Mansfield's stories. Shifen Gong's doctoral thesis Katherine Mansfield in China (Auckland, 1993) studies these to discover how they construct the writer, and identifies a preference for stories that provide evidence of breakdown in bourgeois society. Gong has also published 'Katherine Mansfield in Chinese Translations' in the Journal of Commonwealth Literature (Vol. 31, No. 2, 1996) and translated Xu Zhimo's memories of meeting Mansfield in 1922, for the Turnbull Library Record (Vol. 22, No. 2, Oct. 1989).

Where poets like Alley and Tuwhare espoused communism, younger poets advance China's democratic cause. Both Edmond and Riemke *Ensing feature in the international anthology Earth Against Heaven: A Tiananmen Square Anthology (1990). James *Norcliffe presents a more personal view of cultural difference in work based on time spent teaching in China. Phil

*Mann, who wrote his first science fiction novel, The Eye of the Queen, there, draws less on place than on situation. Although not autobiographical, the character of Thorndyke, Mann has said, 'is in an analogous situation of deciphering a culture and getting it wrong'.

Tiananmen Square has had other consequences. Exiled Chinese writers have encountered similar difficulties attempting to decipher a new culture, most gravely in the case of the poet and novelist Gu Cheng (1958–93). The leading writer of the young dissidents known as the 'Misty' poets (for their supposed obscurity), and 'an icon of intellectual freedom … against the madness of the cultural revolution' (Independent on Sunday), Gu Cheng moved to Auckland in the early 1980s, settling on Waiheke Island with his wife and 'concubine' after his Auckland University post fell through. There and in Berlin in early 1993 he and his wife (writing as Lei Mi) wrote the novel Ying'er: The Kingdom of Daughters (1993; English translation 1995), about the tragic complexities of their love triangle 'on a Pacific island'. He committed suicide after gruesomely murdering his wife on Waiheke Island in October 1993. Another Chinese writer, Or Yang Lian, who moved to Auckland at the same time, writes of his apartment in Grafton, 'When was it that you stopped using the word home—When you talk about this ramshackle old house, you always say there' ('Ghost Talk', 1994). The problems of a related immigrant population are the subject of the Singaporean novelist Ming *Cher's Spider Boys (1995). Crackdowns on democracy in mainland China and the handing over of Hong Kong have generated new waves of Chinese immigration, scapegoated by some politicians riding xenophobic sentiments. In Paradise to Come (1998), Michael *Morrissey exposes the fallacy of such homogenising strategies as his character Siew Yen considers her straitened circumstances while listening to a politician rail against the influx of 'wealthy Asians'.

This new immigration has major implications for the established New Zealand–Chinese community, who, having eased into this culture over generations, are again identified as an immigrant group. But modern Chinese–New Zealanders assert themselves more readily than preceding generations. Comedian Raybon Kan, whose satirical journalism is collected in 5 Days in Las Vegas (1992), employs the 'Chinese-joke element' to make 'fun of the stereotype of Chinese people'. More significantly, the audacious work of poet, dramatist, film maker and performer Lynda Chanwai-*Earle, whose sense of self embraces distinctions—'I was meant / to be different, a / British-born Chinese Kiwi…. An Asiapean if you like'—is a new voice, speaking out about aspects of the Chinese experience in New Zealand which traditionally have remained in silence.   PM

CHURCH, Hubert (1857–1932), was a popular poet of the early twentieth century. Born at Hobart, Tasmania, he spent most of his childhood in England, where at the age of 12 a blow on the head from a cricket ball seriously damaged his hearing. Thus thrown largely on himself, he became an voracious reader. He arrived in New Zealand in 1873 and from 1879 worked in Treasury in Wellington. His first volume of verse was *The West Wind* (1902), followed by *Poems* (1904) and *Egmont* (1908). He retired in 1911 and the following year moved to Melbourne. There he published the best poems from earlier volumes, with additional pieces, as *Poems* (1912). In 1913 he went to England and was engaged in voluntary war work, publishing a novel, *Tonks: A New Zealand Yarn* in 1916. Eventually he settled in Melbourne, where he died.

Church's poems were well received and anthologised on both sides of the Tasman. Indeed, some were painted on the inside doors of Wellington trams. This recognition has declined to the point where Patrick *Evans could describe him (in his *Penguin History of New Zealand Literature*, 1990) as 'the worst poet of the period, although the title was keenly contested.' Certainly Church's conventionalised gestures and formal, archaic language are easily mocked, though there is a metrical control, an ear for cadence and a use of richly associative language which are not wholly lacking in craft. The many poems with local settings or references, too, have earned disapproval, dismissed by Ian *Wedde as 'earnest castings at the indigenous' which never 'hook into any subject'. Perhaps so, unless the real subject is the very incongruity of the English tradition among such new scenes; or the poet's own sense of isolation and religious doubt, which suffuse the verse in melancholic gloom and cause his clinging to reliable old ways of verse. There are two unpublished novels among his papers in the *Alexander Turnbull Library, 'Lucky Maidment', the life of a gambler, and 'Old Wairua', a rustic tale of early Marlborough. The 'Hubert Church Award' is presented annually by *PEN for the 'best first book of poems'.

HMcQ/RR

Citizen was successor to *Current Thought* and was published fortnightly in Wellington during 1909, edited by A.N. Field. Less concerned with literary matters than *Current Thought*, it did however publish some fiction, including work by Blanche *Baughan. SH

CLAIR, Daphne (1939–), is the publishing name of the *Mills & Boon/Harlequin romantic novelist, Daphne Clair de Jong, who also publishes Silhouette romances (often bestsellers) for the US market under the name 'Laurey Bright'. She was born in Dargaville,

trained and worked as a librarian, had five children, and lives at Maungatapere, Northland. Clair began publishing romances with Mills & Boon in the late 1970s, and by the mid-1990s had reached her fiftieth. Several have been nominated for international romance awards. She is also an author of serious fiction. She won the Katherine *Mansfield Memorial Short Story Award in 1981, and published short stories in a collection *Venus, Vagabonds & Miscellanea* (1984, with Ann Macrae and Anna Granger), and in the *Women's Work* and *New Women's Fiction* anthologies.

Clair's distinctiveness among her Mills & Boon contemporaries in New Zealand lies in the feminist edge she brings to the genre. Her essay in *Dangerous Men and Adventurous Women: Romance Writers on the Appeal of the Romance* (University of Pennsylvania Press, 1992) emphasises the historical development of the romance novel as a means of articulating women's social concerns, and argues provocatively that the novels' fundamental dynamic is an empowerment of their women readers: 'They are, and always have been, the subversive literature of sexual politics.' She has also described her own novels as 'tough love stories', their fantasies 'rooted in reality', and belonging to an 'unsentimental' strand within the romance genre. Less sexually explicit and more earnest than other contemporary romance writers, and slightly more open-ended than most, her mainly urban-based Auckland novels foreground the social problems experienced by women, and in their denouements pay particular attention to the process by which her heroines reform macho New Zealand males by enabling them to articulate their repressed emotional selves. TS

CLARK, Russell (1905–66), was a painter, sculptor and commercial artist. As principal illustrator of the *NZ Listener* he left a distinctive mark. Clark studied at Canterbury School of Art in the 1920s, then worked with John *McIndoe 1929–38. Besides his design and illustration work, he also conducted evening drawing classes, which proved popular with young artists, including Colin *McCahon. Moving to Wellington, he worked for the *Listener* and as illustrator for various *School Journals, before becoming an official war artist in the Pacific. Clark settled in Christchurch in 1947, teaching at Canterbury School of Art until his death. He contributed to a distinctive New Zealand art in his landscapes, townscapes and figure studies, which draw on a range of sources, including regionalist artists in America (Grant Wood, for example) and Australia (in particular Russell Drysdale), as well as British modernists like Henry Moore. His work as an illustrator has earned acknowledgment for its 'warmth, wit and fine skill' in its humorous anatomising of New Zealand subjects. The Russell Clark Medal (see Appendix) is awarded to children's book illustrators by the New Zealand Library and Information Association. Clark's work was used to illustrate John *Male's *Poems from a War* (1989).   CB

CLARKE, John ('Fred Dagg') (1948–), parodist, performer, scriptwriter, radio, film and television editor, was born and brought up in Palmerston North, moving at the age of 11 to Wellington, where he attended Scots College. A devotee of British radio comedy, his own comic talents emerged at Victoria University, where he flickered between law, commerce and arts, and started to make a name for himself in student sketches and 'Extravs'.

One in Five (1970), a satirical revue written and performed by Clarke, Cathy *Downes, Roger *Hall, Dave Smith and Helene Wong saw the appearance of the (as yet unnamed) Fred Dagg, the figure with whom Clarke has continued to be identified in New Zealand. After a year in London during which he had a minor role in Barry Humphries' *The Adventures of Barry McKenzie* (1972), he returned to New Zealand and developed the character of 'Fred Dagg' 1973–77. Radio and cabaret work, TV commercials, a TV pilot, *The Wonderful World of Fred Dagg* (1975), regular appearances on *Gallery*, *Country Calendar* and *Nationwide*, a short film, *Dagg Dog Afternoon* (1977), and a national tour, turned Fred into a household name and Kiwi icon. With his trademark black singlet, torn shorts, cotton hat, long hair and gumboots, he was an immediately recognisable local figure, an engaging mixture of wise fool and blunt Taihape cow-cocky. A range of Fred's songs and comic routines were collected on *Fred Dagg's Greatest Hits* (1975) and *Fred Dagg Live* (1976), and his personal anthem, the 'Gumboot Song', stayed in the singles' charts for four months, selling well over 100 000 copies. His first book, *Fred Dagg's Year*, appeared in 1975. A selection of radio monologues, *The Thoughts of Chairman Fred*, came out the following year, their unique blend of laconic humour and wacky whimsicality typified by pronouncements such as Fred on the topic of daylight saving: 'You can't play about with nature like this and expect to get away with it. Last year we had an awful lot of trouble trying to adjust, we had to tie torches onto the dogs' heads and put tail-lights onto cows' backsides. In fact, one of the Trevs got a bit mixed up about the whole thing and went out in the middle of the night and artificially inseminated the tractor. The result of that hasn't come through yet but it should be quite interesting.' Fred Dagg, Clarke has observed, 'was a collaboration I was very fortunate to have with the New Zealand public. He's not only mine, he belongs to the audience as well.'

This 'collaborative' aspect, together with Clarke's wit and originality, has ensured Fred's enduring appeal.

In 1977 Clarke moved permanently to Melbourne and has achieved acclaim in Australia, especially as a hard-hitting political satirist and performer. Australian television credits include: *Anzacs*, *The Fast Lane*, *The Gillies Report*, *A Current Affair* and *The Trouble with Men*. Film credits include: *Lonely Hearts* (1981), *Footrot Flats* (1985), *A Matter of Convenience* (1987), *Blood Oath* (1989), *Death in Brunswick* (1990), *Spotswood* (1992) and *Lust and Revenge* (1997). Other books include: *The Fred Dagg Scripts* (1981), *Daggshead Revisited* (1982), *A Complete Dagg* (1989), *Great Interviews of the Twentieth Century* (1990) and *A Dagg at My Table: Writings 1977–1996* (1996). He has also produced two excellent volumes of literary parody, *The Complete Book of Australian Verse* (1989) and *The Even More Complete Book of Australian Verse* (1994), which present the work of such well-known 'Australian' poets as 'Arnold Wordsworth', 'Emmy-Lou Dickinson', 'Pinko Brooke', 'Sir Don Betjeman' and 'Sylvia Blath'. Clarke is the son of short story writer, local historian and autobiographer Neva Clarke McKenna.   HRi

Cliffs of Fall (1945) is Dan *Davin's first novel, an *existential tale of an alienated student, Mark Burke, who, determined to free himself from the constraints of convention and commitment, murders his pregnant girlfriend Marta. After joining in the hunt for her killer, he discovers his murderous self, and falls to his death in the sea. Experimental in style, bohemian in content, it enjoyed a *succès de scandale* in New Zealand where the characters were widely recognised as drawn from life. Davin, who had finished the novel in 1939 (when it first had the title 'The Mills of God'), and whose views had been greatly altered by the experience of war, virtually disowned the book when it was published. Its critical reception was quite good, however, and it was generally described a 'brilliant failure' in London, where it was published by Nicholson & Watson, a view echoed in New Zealand by Eric *McCormick, who wrote in the *NZ Listener* (28 Sept. 1945) that its failure was 'worth a dozen timid successes'.   KO

Climate, see **Mate**.

Coal Flat, a novel by Bill *Pearson, was published in 1963, with reprints in 1970, 1976 and 1985. The novel had a long gestation, for Pearson first got the idea in 1946, and published a chapter in *Landfall as early as 1951 (as by 'Chris Bell'). It underwent extensive revisions between 1951 and 1958 as the central character, Paul Rogers, with his personal problems, was moved back and the community brought forward, and as the originally more hopeful ending was modified in line with Pearson's own changing perceptions, influenced especially by the decline of faith in Marxism after the Russian invasion of Hungary in 1956. The novel was completed in 1958 but not published until five years later, by *Blackwood Paul, after several unsuccessful submissions within New Zealand and overseas and a rejection for subsidy by the State *Literary Fund. When it finally did appear, it was accepted by many as the major realistic novel of New Zealand life that they had been awaiting, and was given enthusiastic recognition by Allen *Curnow, H. Winston *Rhodes, Charles *Brasch and, a bit later, Frank *Sargeson.

Set in a West Coast mining town (based on Blackball) in 1947, the novel provides a critical but sympathetic view of a cross-section of New Zealand society, examining such aspects of New Zealand life as schools, labour unions, political parties, churches, pubs, popular culture, Māori–Pākehā relations and, centrally, mother-dominated and dysfunctional families. The emphasis is on the strong communal pressures to conform and the difficulty of sustaining any different, non-conformist social position, acted out most dramatically by Rogers when he attempts to help a family-damaged child in one of his classes. The view of New Zealand society is consonant with Pearson's analysis in his 1952 essay, *'Fretful Sleepers'. Pearson's only novel, Coal Flat is rivalled only by David Ballantyne's The *Cunninghams (1948) as a realistic portrait of the New Zealand society of the time.

LJ

COCHRANE, Geoff (1951–), is a poet and fiction writer. He was born in Wellington, where he has lived almost all his life. One of a large Catholic family, he was educated at St Patrick's College.

His poetry first appeared in small collections from private presses: Images of Midnight City (1976), Solstice (1979, with Victoria Broome and Lindsay Rabbitt), The Sea the Landsman Knows (1980), Taming the Smoke (1983) and Kandinsky's Mirror (1989). Aztec Noon (1992) is a collection of twenty-seven new poems plus a selection from previous volumes, published by *Victoria University Press. His poems have also appeared in *Sport and *Printout, and in several anthologies. Cochrane's poetry could be described as 'pain distilled'; spare in form and precise in language, it fixes an often melancholy mood in complex shifts of thought and imagery, usually mediated through a physical setting.

Cochrane has recently published fiction. A novella, 'Quest Clinic' (Sport 9, 1992), and his first novel, Tin Nimbus (1995), both describe, in precise and polished language, an alcoholic's quest for sobriety and eventual escape from institutions that may provide it. Blood (1997)

retrospectively recaptures Wellington in the mid-1970s. The fiction's intensity and evocativeness reflect Cochrane's experience as a poet.

AM

CODY, J.F. (Joseph Frederick) (1895–1967), served during World War 1 with 1st Canterbury Battalion and received the Military Medal. In addition to writing the biography Man of Two Worlds: Sir Maui Pomare (1953), Cody drew on his war experience for two war histories: 21 Battalion (1953) and 28 (Maori) Battalion (1956). His interest in the Māori also inspired a melodramatic romance novel The Red Kaka (1955). Set in the 1830s, it tells the story of Timothy O'Hara, a young dragoon unjustly transported to the Australian penal colonies. From initial similarities to Marcus Clarke's brutal novel For the Term of His Natural Life, The Red Kaka develops into a rollicking adventure in the tradition of Rider Haggard. O'Hara survives a 500-stroke flogging, escapes to New Zealand, and joins forces with Ruru, a Māori slave of noble birth intent on restoring his *mana by defeating the rapacious chief Te Wheto. The comrades set about proving themselves: Ruru, a brave warrior, is sponsored by a *tohunga who names him 'Te Patua, the slayer of enemies'; O'Hara's own merits—military schooling, wrestling prowess, startling red hair, and uniquely tattooed back (courtesy of Sydney Cove's punishment tripod)—earn him the honorific 'Kaka Kura'—the Red Kaka. Welding enthusiastic but undisciplined warriors into a formidable force, the friends win numerous battles as a prelude to victory over Te Wheto. Cameos of Samuel *Marsden and Te Rauparaha sustain the narrative, as does the tense romantic subplot in which O'Hara is torn between two loves: Aileen—a convict maid he left in Sydney, herself a victim of British injustice—and 'Smiling Morn', the tohunga's daughter, to whom he becomes betrothed. The narrative solves O'Hara's dilemma (and negotiates the perilous waters of miscegenation) by allowing Smiling Morn to sacrifice herself saving his life. O'Hara, careless of his own safety, copes with his grief by performing prodigious feats in battle. Happily he survives and, through Marsden's good offices, is finally united with Aileen.

PM

COLBORNE-VEEL, Mary (1863?–1923), was a poet of some dramatic and narrative power. Born in Christchurch and educated at home, she began writing verse and essays for the *Press in 1887, and was an early contributor to *Zealandia. Subsequently she frequently had work published in Australian and English periodicals. The Fairest of the Angels, and Other Verse (1894) and In Memoriam Emily Sophia Foster (1898) were her only volumes, until Jessie *Mackay published the commemorative A Little Anthology of Mary Colborne-Veel (1924).

Although her poems are mostly about nature and the familiar Victorian virtues of duty and honour, she is more subtle and accomplished than this surface suggests. 'Jael' sustains its dramatic narrative with unusual power, and some skilled use of long lines (hexameters in the manner of Clough), as when the heroine recounts her slaying of the evil Sisera: 'Mine is the hand. Yet a woman's: a hand that has tended an infant, / Succoured the needy full oft, and divided the food to the hungry.' 'Saturday Night' sets the timelessness of love against the care-stricken tumult of the modern city, 'as the hundreds slow moving go' in 'the glare of the gaslight ray', in, for that date, a quite contemporary way, making the conventional refrain of 'Strephon and Chloe together move, / Walking in Arcady, land of love' sound ironic. And there is a hint of the dark side of evolutionary science, and its application to the natural world and to racial matters, in her 'Strayed Albatross': 'This alien of a race / Unskilled to live or die / Apart from sea and sky.'

HMcQ/RR

Cold Spring would have been James K. *Baxter's second published collection, had the *Caxton Press decided to proceed with it. Early in 1945, before his first book had even left the binders, the 18-year-old Baxter had his second collection ready in manuscript form. He thought it 'rather better' than *Beyond the Palisade* (1944) and spent months attempting to persuade Lawrence *Baigent—Caxton's editor at the time—to publish it. Why it was never published remains unclear, although Baxter's correspondence with Baigent suggests that breaches of publishing etiquette may have played a part. Another reason may have been that Baxter's use of dense classical allusions to express a private symbolism was at odds with the model of New Zealand poetry recently institutionalised by Allen *Curnow in A *Book of New Zealand Verse 1923–45. Curnow's praise of Baxter's first volume for poetry that could only be 'a New Zealander's' is also at odds with Cold Spring's foreword, in which Baxter defends his English influences and remains silent concerning his fellow New Zealand poets. Cold Spring was rediscovered by Paul Millar while researching Baxter's wartime correspondence with Noel *Ginn. Millar's 1996 edition fills a gap in the Baxter corpus and adds valuable detail to what is known about this period of Baxter's life.

PM/RR

COLE, John Reece (1916–84), short story writer, was born in Palmerston North. His father died when he was 2 and his mother then worked as live-in housekeeper in large country houses, where the child experienced the pain of class discrimination. He had to leave school in 1930 to work, and until 1941 clerked while also writing some freelance journalism. He opposed the war but in 1941 joined the Royal Air Force and served in England as a pilot until 1944, when he was invalided home. From 1944 to 1948 he gained education at Auckland University College and then the New Zealand Library School. In 1944 he established friendships with Frank *Sargeson and other Auckland writers, including Greville *Texidor, Maurice *Duggan and David *Ballantyne. Between 1943 and 1948 he wrote the short stories that were collected in It Was So Late and Other Stories, published by Denis *Glover at the *Caxton Press in 1949 (rpt. 1978). He had a distinguished career as a librarian 1948–65, spending 1948–52 with the National Library Service, and most of the rest of his career as deputy and then as head librarian of the *Alexander Turnbull Library, with overseas periods as UNESCO library adviser in Indonesia 1956–58 and as director of the National Library in Singapore in 1962. He took early retirement in 1965 for reasons of ill health. During these years as librarian he attempted to continue writing fiction but did not succeed, and his only further published work was a pamphlet on Pompallier House. Like his contemporaries, A.P. *Gaskell and G.R. *Gilbert, he did not develop from his promising beginning as a writer in the 'Sargeson school'. However, he continued as a member of the literary community, with close friendships with Sargeson and Duggan, and with work for *PEN and as a cultural adviser for the Department of Internal Affairs in support of aid for writers.

Cole's stories are clearly in the realist tradition, showing some relationship to Sargeson's but often more like those of John O'Hara in their use of vernacular dialogue and external observation by a first-person observer or an effaced third-person narrator to reveal character and situation. Most of them are brief, leading up to a moment of revelation, but some of the later ones, such as 'Up at the Mammoth' are longer, dealing with more complex situations over a longer time-span, and perhaps point towards the novel that was never written. Almost all of them deal with World War 2 and its aftermath. His most frequent theme is the destructive effect of war on the participants, and a number of the stories such as 'One of the Few' and 'Up at the Mammoth' show combatants and veterans suffering from post-traumatic stress disorders. An important secondary theme is the hurtful effect of class distinctions, shown in the military in 'Blues in the Night' and, most memorably, in the New Zealand country house world in 'It Was So Late'.

LJ

College Spectator was the annual magazine of the Wellington District secondary schools published 1953–54. The first issue featured poems by Marilyn Adcock (later Marilyn *Duckworth).

SH

colonial experience was formerly used to describe the training in practical agricultural work and living close to the land by which a *'new chum' was converted into an 'old hand': 'Sowing at once, with a double stitch, / Colonial experience and groans' (1853, in *Canterbury Rhymes*, 1866). Cf. *overseas experience.   HO

Colophon was an irregular miscellany produced by students of the New Zealand Library School in Wellington 1946–69. Early issues were edited and contributed to by W.J. McEldowney and Basil *Dowling. Denis *Glover contributed an article to the issue for 1957.   SH

Comment appeared in two distinct series, 1959–70 and 1977–82. W.H. *Oliver edited the first four volumes of series one and most of series two, and Vincent *O'Sullivan edited volumes five to eight of series one with the assistance of an editorial committee. As a quarterly social and political review it was liberal and Roman Catholic in its perspective. While it eschewed short fiction, it did feature poetry by James K. *Baxter, Louis *Johnson, Charles *Brasch and others, and became an important venue for the discussion of New Zealand literature.   SH

COMPTON, Jennifer (1949–   ), is a poet, playwright, radio dramatist and short story writer who made a major impact with her first full-length play, *No Man's Land*, later retitled *Crossfire* (1973). Joint winner of the Newcastle, New South Wales, playwriting award, it was first performed by Sydney's Nimrod Theatre and published by Currency Press, prior to many productions internationally, including Wellington and in the prize-winning season of the New Zealand 'Heartache and Sorrow' company at the 1978 Edinburgh Festival.

Born in Wellington, Compton lived there and in Auckland until 1971, when she began to move between Australia and New Zealand until settling in the southern highlands of New South Wales from 1981. Her poetry has been published in *Climate*, *Islands*, *Landfall* and other New Zealand journals, but she can now be read mainly in Australian publications such as *Aspect*, *Poetry Australia*, *Southerly* or *The Australian*, and her plays are written initially for Australian stage or radio production. She is thus most often seen in the Australian literary context, and has received awards such as the NSW writing fellowship, Robert Harris Poetry Prize (both 1995) and Tahale Poetry Prize (1996).

However, Alistair *Paterson's 1996 edition of *Poetry New Zealand* featured recent work and affirmed her continuing New Zealand identity. The poems themselves evince ongoing tensions between past and present,

domestic and artistic commitments, New Zealand and Australia, most strikingly in 'poetry new zealand volume one', a 'backward glance' which juxtaposes conflicting Australian 'ikons' and Māori images ('She Who Is Darkness Hine-nui-te-Po spoke / a foreign language this ancient art / knocked all my turrets down') with 'found' text from the title page and biographical notes of that 1971 edition and an inscription by its editor, Frank *McKay. She has regretted the literary separation between the two countries: 'any step forward in one is of no account in the other.' (See *Australia.)

Compton's poetry collections are *From the Other Woman* (1993) and *Blue Leaves* (1997). Her poems have been featured on radio and will be included in the *New Oxford Book of Australian Verse*, edited by Les Murray. Her short fiction has been anthologised in New Zealand and Australia, including Michael *Morrissey's *The New Fiction* (1985) and Michael Wilding's *The Art of the Story* (1989). As a playwright she has had seventeen plays produced on stage or radio or both. Particularly successful since *Crossfire* have been *Julia's Story* (1991), which was reviewed by the *Sydney Morning Herald* as 'rich ... with subtle naturalism'; *Barefoot* (1994), published by Currency and produced on both stage and TV; and *All the Time in the World*, which was showcased at the Australian National Playwrights' Centre in 1994. She is known for 'quirky dialogue' and 'seriously funny' attention to women's issues. Her latest production is 'The Big Picture' (Griffin Theatre, Sydney, October 1997).   RR

Conferences, see **Authors' Week, 1936**; **Mansfield Centenary Conference 1988**; **New Zealand Writers' Conference 1951**; **New Zealand Writers Week (Dunedin)**; **PEN/Victoria University Conference 1979**; **Writers and Readers Week**.

Conquest was a monthly magazine for young people published in Wellington 1945–47. It featured stories by Alice *Kenny.   SH

Conspectus was published in four issues by the Auckland University Literary Society 1949–64 and featured student essays, mostly on literary topics.   SH

Continuum (1988) is a collection of poems by Allen *Curnow, subtitled 'New and Later Poems 1972–1988', published by *Auckland University Press. It brings together the contents of five collections by Curnow published 1972–86, namely *Trees, Effigies, Moving Objects* (1972), *An Abominable Temper & Other Poems* (1973), *An Incorrigible Music* (1979), *You Will Know When You Get There* (1982) and *The Loop in Lone Kauri Road* (1986), plus half a dozen new poems. Several of these recreate remembered events from the poet's Canterbury childhood ('Survivors', 'A Time of Day'). The poems are printed in reverse chronological order. The book was awarded the Commonwealth Poetry Prize in 1989. PS

Conversation with My Uncle and Other Sketches (1936) was Frank *Sargeson's first volume of stories, a 29-page book published by the Unicorn Press, Auckland. It contained ten sketches and stories, eight of which had been published in the periodical *Tomorrow* over the previous fifteen months. Though Sargeson had published a few sketches and stories from 1933, the title piece, first printed on 24 July 1935, has come to be identified with the beginnings of the techniques of characterisation he was to develop in the next ten years. The sketches are brief, and easily accommodated in the few hundred words available on the single page of the periodical. They are principally concerned with the economical delineation of character, through techniques appropriate to the pictorial metaphor of the word 'sketch', suggesting an outline rather than a full portrayal. The sketches also show minimal concern with plot or sequential narration, appropriate to the term's other use, meaning a brief theatrical depiction of a single event. They are predominantly static tableaux, typified by 'A Piece of Yellow Soap', 'The Last War' and 'In the Midst of Life,' where the narrator recalls a single character or episode to illustrate a wry recognition about human attitudes or behaviour.

A few, however, anticipate the more extended narratives that Sargeson was to develop, when the sketch became expanded into the short story, whose narrator would fashion a reminiscence or conversational 'yarn' from the sequence of events. Thus the embryonic narrative of 'White Man's Burden' is developed to cover a 24-hour sojourn at a North Auckland pub, where the burden of the conversations between the narrator, the Māori ploughman and the woman tending the bar become preliminaries to the narrator's wry insight into New Zealand's bi-racial future, reflected in both *Kipling's imperialist invocation used as the story's title, and the closing reference to the current invasion of Abyssinia by Mussolini.

The clearest precursors of Sargeson's next volumes are the last two pieces, 'Sketch from Life', later retitled 'A Good Boy', and 'I've Lost My Pal'. The first has an adolescent narrator, tormented by the moral confusion of his *puritanical upbringing and incapable of coping with his own developing sexuality. The second is the recollection of someone who describes a shearing gang in which the young man sees the killing of a dog as the mirror-image of one or perhaps two murders carried out by another character, apparently a homosexual for whom the narrator acknowledges an unnerving complicit sympathy. In each piece Sargeson develops the central characters and linear plot more fully, and the yarn in more complex ways, while each introduces the images of Gothic sexual repression and violence that were to figure frequently in his later stories. WB

COOK, Captain James (1728–79), explorer and navigator, though not the first European commander to visit New Zealand (that distinction belongs to Abel *Tasman), was the first to map its coastline and to record details about its landforms, inhabitants and flora and fauna. It is these contributions that have given Cook such iconic significance in New Zealand literature and history. Cook's nautical life began in the North Sea coal trade but in 1755 he volunteered into the Royal Navy as an able seaman and through his industry and ability rose quickly to the rank of master. During the Seven Years War against France he revealed his genius as a surveyor, becoming involved in the charting of the St Lawrence River and later the coasts of Newfoundland. His success in this later enterprise secured his appointment to the command of *HMS Endeavour* for a voyage to Tahiti, to observe the transit of Venus across the disk of the sun and search for the southern continent or Great South Land.

In August 1768 Cook left Plymouth on what was to be the first of three voyages into the Pacific. On the first he charted the coasts of New Zealand (October 1769 to March 1770) and eastern Australia. During the second he finally destroyed the notion of a habitable southern continent, but also charted some of the most significant island groups in the Pacific. On his final and fatal voyage he discovered the Hawaiian Islands and charted the north-west coast of America, virtually destroying the notion of a navigable north-west passage to China. Cook spent a total of 328 days in New Zealand waters, using Queen Charlotte Sound and Dusky Sound as bases. His Journals, along with those of the botanist Joseph *Banks, who travelled as a supernumerary on the first voyage, gave Europe its first detailed knowledge of the country. The account of the first voyage was published in a version edited, or rather rewritten, by Dr John *Hawkesworth. Because of the editor's extravagant literary licence, the account was rightly criticised. As a consequence the great navigator vowed that subsequent accounts would be published under his own control with minimal editorial assistance. His death on the third voyage, however, meant that the published account for that was finished by one of his officers, James King. Between 1955 and 1967 modern and definitive versions of Cook's Journals were published under the editorship of J.C. *Beaglehole, also the author of *Cook the Writer* (1970) and *The Life of Captain Cook* (1974).

James Cook has left an impression on the New Zealand imagination out of all proportion to the periods of time he spent in the country. His likeness, usually represented as a variation of the portrait by Nathaniel Dance, is instantly recognisable. He left an indelible impression on the country's daily language in the naming of coastal landmarks, and his own name and those of his crew and ships have been given to landforms, streets, suburbs, hotels, schools and other institutions. Literary texts as recent and as different as the travel journal of Denis *McLean or poems by Chris *Orsman can allude to Cook's visits confident of continuing iconic recognition. However, it is Cook's own published Journals, with their rich and perspicacious ethnographic and cultural observations, which have had the most significant impact on New Zealand literature and culture.   DM

Co-operative Book News was the monthly publication of the Christchurch Co-Operative Book Society 1941–43. Initially cyclostyled but later printed by the *Caxton Press it carried news of the society's activities, book lists, and articles and reviews by, among others, Allen *Curnow and Winston *Rhodes.   SH

COPLAND, R.A. (Raymond Augustus) (1918–), wrote droll satiric fictions under the pen-name 'Augustus' while pursuing a career at the University of Canterbury as an exceptionally well-regarded teacher of literature. Born in Feilding, educated at Napier and Christchurch BHS and Canterbury University College, he served as navigator with the RNZAF in World War 2 before returning in 1949 to lecture at Canterbury, where he gained his PhD in 1960 and was appointed professor in 1970. Retiring in 1976, he served as chairman and then member of the *Literary Fund Advisory Committee 1980–86. A judicious and witty reviewer of New Zealand and contemporary English fiction, for *Landfall, *Islands, *NZ Listener and the *Press, he was the first, in his essay 'This Goodly Roof', to identify the consequences self-inflicted by Frank *Sargeson's choice of limited narrative vision in his earlier work: 'Hitherto Frank Sargeson's eloquence has lain in his reticence,' as he memorably put it in a review in *Landfall* 77 (1966). His *Frank Sargeson* and edition of *A.P. *Gaskell: Stories* were published in 1976. He anonymously edited *The Memoirs of John Macmillan *Brown* (1974).

As 'Augustus' he sustained a series of perceptive and funny sketches of the idiosyncrasies of New Zealand life, published irregularly in the *NZ Listener* in the 1950s. They have been anthologised in J.C. *Reid's *The Kiwi Laughs* (1961) and *Listener Short Stories 1* and *2. Augustus on the journey of the service-car ('monotonously hair-raising'), on the interchangeable ménages of weekend

suburbia or on *Coal Flat* are comic classics that deserve republication. A privately published collection, *Augustus* (undated), was produced about 1978. Copland has written at least one unpublished novel of the same sardonically comic observation of local life.   RR

CORRIN, Ruth (1939–), writer for children and young adults, was born in Invercargill, educated at Southland GHS and Dunedin Teachers' College, and began writing after teaching and working as a radio programme producer. *Grampa's Place*, illustrated by Sandra Cammell (1985), grew out of her radio programme for preschoolers, winner of seven international awards. Her media experiences also led to a children's abuse prevention programme, *Feeling Safe*, for the Child Alert Trust in 1990. After winning the 1990 Choysa Bursary, Corrin became the 1992 inaugural children's writer-in-residence, Dunedin College of Education, and artist-in-residence, Taieri Community Arts Council 1993.

Her picture books include *It Always Rains for Jackie*, illustrated by Trevor Pye (1989); *Mr Cat*, illustrated by John Hurford (1991); *And Karen Did Too*, illustrated by Mandy Nelson (1991); *The Right-Hand Man*, illustrated by Brent Putze (1992); and *Not Without Randolph*, illustrated by Fifi Colston (1993). Her novels, which draw on her love of painting and singing, explore complex family dynamics, including incest in *Secrets* (1990), and separation through adoption of twins in *Two Voices Sing* (1992). She lives at Plimmerton.   DH

COTTLE, Thomas (1845?–1923), was a journalist who wrote notable articles on tourism and historical themes for *Zealandia and The *Monthly Review and one entertaining novel of colonial times. According to his death certificate he was 78 when he died in Havelock North and had lived in New Zealand for 60 years, having been born in Watford, Northamptonshire, as the son of a clergyman. *Frank Melton's Luck; or, Off to New Zealand* was published in Auckland (by 'H. Brett, Printer and Publisher') probably in 1891, but the two *'new chums' who are at its centre disembark in 1866 into an Auckland whose streets are a mass of mud. There is probably some autobiography blended with the romance. Frank Melton learns the art of horse-breaking and other *station skills, while his friend Harry copes with city con-men. Both endure initiation in arms in the *Waikato and Taranaki wars, fighting with von Tempsky, and cope with love, jealousy and an unscrupulous rival who pretends to be of noble birth. The lads are able to expose him to Frank's uncle ('I'm sorry I didn't listen to you Frank. The new-chum nephew has put the old hand to shame.') and it is the sturdy, maturing working men who finally win the fair ladies. The well-worn theme of a change from innocence to experience and the topos of the 'making of a New Zealander' are both recognisable. The climax comes with a fortune won at the races and a double wedding. Cottle's style has some Victorian elegance but takes the use of colonial colloquialisms for granted. The result is a very readable masculine tale.   NW

COURAGE, James (1905–63), was an expatriate fiction writer of the period after World War 2, writing especially of pre-war Canterbury. Born in Christchurch, he grew up on Seadown, a sheep *station near Amberley in North Canterbury. He was sent as a boarder to a preparatory school in Sumner and then to Christ's College in Christchurch. A visit to England in 1922 led to his decision to attend Oxford, where he completed a degree in English at St John's College in 1927. He lived in London, supported by a modest grant from his family, and remained there the rest of his life, except for conva- lescence in New Zealand from tuberculosis in 1933–35. At Oxford he had some poems, short stories, criticism and a play published by 1926. He continued writing in London, with only moderate success, publishing a slight, E.M. Forster-ish novel of English country house life, *One House*, in 1933, and having an unpublished play, *Private History*, produced by a private theatre club in 1938. During World War 2 he worked in a bookshop, which he then managed from 1946 until his health broke down in 1952. From 1951 he was frequently under psychiatric care for depression.

Courage began to find himself as a writer in the 1940s when he turned to the Canterbury of his child- hood and adolescence for material. His first significant short story, 'Uncle Adam Shot a Stag', was published in *English Story* in 1945. The central character, the young Walter Blakiston, was featured in at least five other stories 1947–57, four of them in *Landfall. During these years Courage published his five New Zealand novels: *The Fifth Child* (1948), *Desire Without Content* (1950), *Fires in the Distance* (1952), *The *Young Have Secrets* (1954; rpt. 1985), and *The Call Home* (1956). All deal with the period between 1913 and 1936, and all are set in North Canterbury, Christchurch, and the area around Mt Somers Station, where Courage's beloved grand- mother had lived. All deal with the social setting he described to Phillip *Wilson in 1952 as 'the unique rural society which was an end-product of the first hundred years of Canterbury settlement, and which is already dying out, the last phase of an English liberal middle- class way of life which was transported more particularly to Canterbury than to other parts of New Zealand'. All focus on family conflict, with strong sexual implications, and show intense feeling breaking out in an externally quiet, genteel atmosphere. All are modelled on the well- made novels of Forster and L.P. Hartley, bearing little resemblance to most New Zealand fiction of the time, with their clearly marked symbolism and situations that are worked through a series of dramatic confrontations to a neat resolution. In each the central characters are forced to accept that the demands of their own needs and natures, strongly conditioned by forces of sexuality and heredity, necessarily compete with the demands of others, so that each must learn to live with civilised compromise. Unlike writers of his generation such as Frank *Sargeson, with whom he corresponded, and Roderick *Finlayson, Courage did not criticise New Zealand society (although he revealed its *puritanism and provinciality), but rather accepted the social world as a given and showed his characters struggling to make satisfactory adaptations within it. His primary concern was with the individual in relation to the family, and the tensions formed between generations and between male and female values within the family, rather than the individual in relation to larger social structures.

Courage's best works are the semi-autobiographical ones dealing with the growing-up of Walter Blakiston, such stories as 'A Smile on Sunday' (1947) and 'After the Earthquake' (1948), and the Blakiston novel, *The Young Have Secrets*. In these he looked back as an adult in England on a childhood and a New Zealand that no longer existed, drawing on the expatriate's diminishing capital of memory. By the late 1950s he seems to have used up that material, with the short stories dealing with growing up at Seadown, *The Young Have Secrets* with prep school days, *The Fifth Child, Desire Without Content* and *Fires in the Distance* with the 1920s, and *The Call Home* with a mid-1930s visit to New Zealand. The last of the Blakiston stories, 'Flowers on a Table' (1957), deals with an adult Walter in England coming to realise that his present emotional problems originate in his rela- tionship with his father during his New Zealand child- hood. Amidst his New Zealand stories and novels, Courage wrote some stories about his experiences in England, such as 'Nothing to Make Us Mad' (1954), a moving account of relationships in a mental hospital. After 1956 all of his published work was set in England in the present. His last two novels, *A Way of Love* (1959) and *The Visit to Penmorten* (1961), deal explicitly with the theme of homosexuality that had been an undercurrent in the earlier fiction. Although Courage described *A Way of Love* to Sargeson as an attempt to write 'a serious novel about homosexuality, neither jeering nor safely satirical in tone, but concerned in some degree with the heart and its deeper emotions', the novel was withdrawn from sale and from libraries in New Zealand in 1962 on the grounds of its alleged indecency.

Courage's career raises some of the problems of expatriation. Given his sexual orientation and his aesthetic interests, it is unlikely that he would have found a place in the New Zealand society of his time. Expatriation may have been a necessity; he also said that he 'found it much easier to understand things which happened in the past when he was living a good distance away from them'. On the other hand, he faced the problem of being cut off from his roots and having to rely on memory. He wrote to Sargeson in 1954 that Sargeson had 'a native authenticity' and a 'natural writing voice' that he could not reach, and he confided after the writing of *The Call Home* that he was finding it 'too difficult' to write New Zealand fiction 'at this remove'. The last novels were an attempt to get beyond that impasse and beyond the difficulty for the homosexual writer of finding a way 'to divert one's passion into acceptable channels', as he wrote to Sargeson. Thus he ended by trying to deal simultaneously with two kinds of alienation. A selection of his short stories, both English and New Zealand, *Such Separate Creatures*, was published posthumously in 1973, edited by his friend, Charles *Brasch.   LJ

COURAGE, Sarah Amelia (1845?–1901), born in Kent, sailed to New Zealand with her husband and daughter in 1864. They settled on a *station in North Canterbury. Her narrative 'Lights and Shadows' of *Colonial Life* (c.1896) is subtitled *Twenty-Six Years in Canterbury, New Zealand*. Derived from a 'diary', it provides a lively and lucid account of station life, detailing household events, difficulties with staff, problems of gardening in extremes of wind and rain, and the variety of fates suffered by children, stock and pets. Despite protestations of 'dreary' scenery, a 'pall of depression' and feelings of being 'transported for life', Courage writes with an interest that is unforced and unpretentious, and deals well with more cataclysmic events like floods, bushfires and storms as well as childbirth, sickness and domestic violence. Gatherings at church, picnics or homes are also pertinently described despite the apparent paucity of conversation, and observations are made on neighbours that are often less than flattering. This habit caused the book's curious fate of being almost destroyed as soon as it was published. Only eighteen copies were printed for private circulation, but this was too wide for some of those mentioned, and many of even those few copies were destroyed. There was a reprint in 1976. Blessed with wit as well as veracity, Courage was not an enthusiast for colonial life, but now reads as a refreshingly honest chronicler. She returned to England in 1890.
EM

Cousins (1992) is the third novel by Patricia *Grace. It weaves the separately told narratives of three female cousins into an affirmation of the continuity of the extended family to which they belong. Though many passages are set in Wellington, the focus is always on the family land and community six hours north. Separated by circumstance and family dispute, the three are eventually brought together at the *tangi of the most favoured of them: 'There we were the three of us' are almost the novel's last words. The narration begins and ends in the voice and consciousness of Mata, the shy and undistinguished orphan of a mother rejected by the family matriarch. Brought up in a 1940s Wellington institution and by an exploitative guardian, Mata endures a miserable childhood, ill-paid manual work, an unhappy marriage and a life of solitude. This story is told in fragments of memory as she sets out on an apparently aimless walk, which in fact brings her into a place in the last weeks of her more favoured cousin Makareta and thus for the first time into a role in the wider family. Makareta, chosen by her grandmother as puhi, cherished daughter, after her father is killed at El Alamein, ends her childhood of privilege and educational success by refusing the marriage arranged to secure the land. In a courageous and dramatic act her place is taken by the third cousin, Missy or Maleme, who puts family repute and interest ahead of her own romantic dreams.

The novel innovatively affirms and embodies Māori values and systems. It is more concerned with continuities than with events, more with the process of generational succession than with individual success or happiness. So births, childhoods, illnesses and deaths recur almost cyclically, and events outside the family are presented exclusively for their impact on the family and on Māori, such as World War 2, the Land March or the rise of activism over the Treaty of Waitangi. Missy's first section is narrated by her unborn twin brother, who speaks for the continued existence of the non-living members of the family, who also appear as ghostly presences accompanying the dead Makareta. While love is shown as a constant driving force, it is closely related to the need for communal belonging. Individual passion, fulfilment or tragedy are subsumed—as in the closing tangihanga for Makareta—into the proprieties of ritual and the continuities of family and land. While the narrative is sometimes too subordinate to a tendentious polemic, as in the section which tells rather than shows Makareta's supposedly distinguished role as an activist leader, Grace's descriptive and impressionistic skills, her insight into the consciousness of women and children, and the sustained inwardness of the Māori perspective, make *Cousins* a significant and uniquely Māori version of the genre of family saga.   RR

COWAN, James (1870–1943), was a prolific journalist and internationally known historian with a special affinity for Māori culture. He was born at Pakuranga, but his earliest memories were of his father's farm, which included Orakau, the field of one of the most dramatic battles of the New Zealand *Wars only six years before James's birth. During his childhood, tensions were still high and one of his earliest memories was of a farmer killed by Māori when ploughing disputed land. Within sight of the farm was the King Country, where no European could buy or even survey land. As he later said, in this frontier environment 'war memories were still raw'. Nonetheless, most of his childhood friends were Māori and he grew up completely bilingual. At the age of 16 he turned down an offer to join the Native Department and became a journalist, at first on the *Auckland Star*. He was sent to Samoa and collected stories there which became the basis of two books. The habit of collecting true stories and folk tales never left him and books such as *Tales of the Maori Coast* (1930), *Tales of the Maori Bush* (1934), *Fairy Folk Tales of the Maori* (1925) and *Legends of the Maori* (2 volumes written with Sir Maui Pomare, 1930 and 1934) arose from such collections. He moved to Wellington in 1909 and there established a reputation as a historian. This was partly built on major articles written for the *Journal of the Polynesian Society* but most of all on his two-volume study of *The New Zealand Wars* (1922–23), the result of extremely extensive research. He studied all the available documents, interviewed practically all living survivors of battles from both sides and travelled to remote places on horseback to view battlefields. Until the publication of James *Belich's book of the same name in 1986, Cowan's was the standard account, and much detail is still to be found only in his book. Another of great fascination is *The Adventures of Kimble Bent* (1911), a study of a part Native *American who deserted from the British army and became a weapons expert for the Ngāti Ruanui. Maurice *Shadbolt based part of his *New Zealand Wars trilogy on this account. Cowan's *Settlers and Pioneers*, written for the *Centennial in 1940, proved controversial, a chapter on the wars being too 'outspoken' for the young editors of the series. Altogether he wrote more than thirty books and several hundreds of popular feature articles for newspapers and magazines. Alan *Mulgan wrote of him: 'No European writer knew the Maori better at first hand; few knew him so well. And with this knowledge he combined a rare literary gift. He could interpret the Maori and his contact with the European in clear, picturesque English, which was a delight to read.'   NW

COWLEY, Joy (1936–), fiction writer for children and adults, was born in Levin and educated at Palmerston North GHS and Pharmacy College. She has been published so widely and to such acclaim that she received a Commemoration Medal in 1990, the OBE in 1992 for her services to children's literature, the Margaret Mahy Award Lecture in 1993 and an honorary doctorate from Massey University in 1993. The publisher's notice for *Heart Attack and Other Stories* (1985) states that 'during her adult life she has had many occupations: artist, freelance photographer, builder's labourer, farm worker, pharmaceutical apprentice, newspaper children's page editor, housewife, mother and writer'. Elsewhere she has noted her 'interests' as 'spinning, weaving, woodwork, sailing, fishing and an isolated farm on Marlborough Sounds'. Married to Ted Cowley in 1956, she first tried to develop as a painter but then decided to begin writing seriously in 1960 when pregnant with her fourth child, sending two or three short stories to the *NZ Listener each month. Although she sent in twenty-nine stories before one was accepted, she has always acknowledged that the editor, M.H. *Holcroft, was her main mentor and early supporter.

When a short story from *Landfall* was republished in the USA, Doubleday, a major US publisher, wrote asking for a novel. She had none to send, but wrote *Nest in a Falling Tree* in six months. It was published by Doubleday in 1967 to enthusiastic reviews and was made into a film, scripted by Roald Dahl, with his wife, Patricia Neal, in the leading role. It is a story of passion, a love affair between a 17-year-old boy, Red, and Maura, an older woman. Maura's mother, whom she is nursing, rejects Red, but dies of an overdose of medicine. Public opinion gradually turns against Maura, and when Red does too she finds herself alone.

To follow up this initial success Cowley wrote four more novels in the next decade before devoting herself entirely to writing for young people. *Man of Straw* (1972) tells of a summer in the life of a small-town family, seen mainly through the eyes of two daughters, Rosalind, aged 13, and Miranda, aged 22. Rosalind is puzzled by the passions that develop when her father is accused of seducing Miranda's friend Julie-Ann and a sense of mystery is resolved when it is revealed that he has also had an affair with Julie-Ann's mother. The people of the town throw stones at the house and kill the family dog. Rosalind runs away from home and collapses, wilfully or by accident, into the sea.

Passions are more restrained in *Of Men and Angels* (1972), which contrasts one woman, who pursues a career and has casual affairs, with another, who is unhappily married and looks for satisfaction in Catholicism and good causes. Their emotions focus on to a pregnant teenager, but it remains undecided which way of life is more satisfactory. It was followed by *The Mandrake Root* (1975), a study of a person who has recovered from mental illness, but lives on the verge between illness and health. *The Growing Season* (1979) contrasts family reactions to the coming death of James. Some are resigned, others upset, but he accepts his situation as a part of the natural order.

Heart Attack and Other Stories (1985) collects stories from various periods, the first twelve forming a loose sequence showing the journey from youth to middle age. Included is Cowley's best-known story, the often anthologised 'The *Silk'. *The Complete Short Stories* was published in 1997.

Cowley began writing for children to help her son Edward who, like her, was slow to learn reading skills. Her first picture book, which uses humour to carry a serious anti-war statement, was *The Duck and the Gun*, illustrated by Edward Sorel and published in New York in 1969, the same year as the beginning of Margaret *Mahy's remarkable publishing career. It was republished in 1985 with new illustrations by Robyn Belton, which won the Russell Clark Award in 1985. Other notable picture books include *The Terrible Taniwha of Timberditch*, illustrated by Rodney McRae (1982), which explores different cultural versions of dragons; *Salmagundi*, illustrated by Philip Webb (1985), which carries another, more anti-war message; and *The Screaming Mean Machine*, illustrated by David Cox (1993), which looks at the difficulty of overcoming fear. Cowley's short stories have featured on radio and in *Two of a Kind* (1984) in collaboration with Mona *Williams and in *Beyond the River* (1994); she has also had a play produced, 'The Haunting of Frogwash Farm' (1988). Like Mahy, Cowley has also become a prolific creator of entertaining and predominantly humorous readers, with a total of more than 400 books for the 'Storybox' series and for Wendy Pye Publishing. She now spends about three months in every year overseas, working with teachers on early reading and children's difficulties, and running writing workshops. But it is mainly for her children's novels that Cowley has won awards. *The Silent One*, illustrated by Sherryl Jordan (1981), won the 1982 inaugural Children's Book of the Year Award for its sensitive, poetic and mythic qualities. It became a feature film, released in 1985 with notable music by Jenny *McLeod. It tells the story of a deaf boy on a *Pacific island who befriends a white turtle and struggles to survive his isolated tribe's superstition and fears when the village is afflicted by a drought and a hurricane, brought on, so the tribe believes, because the turtle is an evil spirit from the depths of the sea. In 1992 *Bow Down Shadrach*, illustrated by Robyn Belton (1991), won the AIM Book of the

Year for its portrayal of twists and difficulties in family love concerning, in particular, an old horse at the end of its life. The sequel, *Gladly, Here I Come*, appeared in 1994.

Cowley now lives in the Marlborough Sounds, providing the hospitality of 'Te Aroha' to people suffering social difficulty. She contributed a statement of her view of life to *What I Believe*, edited by Allan Thomson (1993). DH/NW

COWLEY, Wanda (1924–), began writing for children while training as a playcentre supervisor. Born in Auckland, she graduated BA and DipEd from Auckland University and spent two years on Voluntary Service Overseas in Tonga. She now lives on Waiheke Island. Her stories mainly reflect her sensitive response to her Hauraki Gulf island landscape. *Biddy Alone* (1988), illustrated by Susan Opie, explores with reality and mysticism a child's responsibility for smuggling her cat into an island bird sanctuary. *Trespassers* (1991) explores an adult's damaging response to death from drunk-driving and the part two teenage protagonists must play in the healing process. Cowley has had numerous stories and poems published in periodicals and anthologies, including the *School Journal. DH

COX, Geoffrey (1910–), journalist, was one of the significant generation of New Zealand Rhodes Scholars to leave for Oxford University in the 1930s. He grew up in Southland and Otago, studied at Otago University, where he edited the student newspaper, *Critic, and entered Oriel College, Oxford, in 1932. Journalism, not academia, was his objective. In 1934 he launched his career spectacularly when he disguised himself as a member of Hanover's Hitler Youth Labour Service to investigate the rise of Nazism. The resulting articles were published in London and New York, and, at the end of his scholarship, in 1935, he began working on Fleet Street as a foreign correspondent. His reports for the *News Chronicle* and, 1937–40, the *Daily Express*, recorded conflicts from trouble spots around Europe pushing the world towards war. With John *Mulgan, he also wrote the 'Behind the Cables' column for the *New Zealand Herald*, evaluating the implications of those events. Cox's gritty prose and nose for the newsworthy combined to offer his readers immediacy and insider knowledge. This period also inspired three books: *The Defence of Madrid* (1937); *The Red Army Moves* (1941); and *Countdown to War: A Personal Memoir of Europe 1938–40* (1988). After 1940 he served with the 2nd New Zealand Division in Greece, Crete, Libya and Italy as Chief Intelligence Officer on General Bernard Freyberg's staff. *The Road to Trieste* (1946) and *The Race to Trieste* (1977) cover the last days of World War 2 in Northern Italy, while in *A Tale of Two Battles* (1987) Cox turns his attention to the war's earlier years and the New Zealand Division's role in the Mediterranean conflict. Following the war, Cox returned to journalism in England as political correspondent and then Assistant Editor for the *News Chronicle* before becoming, in 1956, Editor and Chief Executive of Independent Television News. He played a pioneering role in developing television journalism and received numerous personal and professional honours, including a knighthood in 1966. *See It Happen* (1983) and *Pioneering Television News* (1995) record the post-war activities of New Zealand's most renowned expatriate journalist.   PM

COX, Nigel (1951–), novelist, was born in Pahiatua and grew up in the Wairarapa and Lower Hutt. His two novels, *Waiting for Einstein* (1984) and *Dirty Work* (1987), were written during the period in which he worked as a bookseller in Auckland and Wellington (1977–93). Both Cox's novels are set in and around Wellington. *Waiting for Einstein* chronicles the attempts of Ralph, who lives in the Wellington fringe community of Pukerua Bay, to succeed as a painter and writer. Ralph the writer takes an active part in Cox's narrative by contributing a story which is serialised through the novel. Ralph's intention may be to 'pull off this solitary artist thing', but, as Lawrence ★Jones notes, Cox surrounds his protagonist with a small group of 'clearly delineated characters' whose intense interactions are like 'a kind of dance of relationship, as in a D.H. Lawrence novel' (★*Journal of New Zealand Literature* 3, 1985, p. 26). *Dirty Work* also focuses on a small group of characters, the inmates ('management' and 'guests') of a Wellington doss house called the Happy World Hotel. Gina, an aspiring trapeze artist and assistant to the manager, gets drawn into the lives of the Happy World's long-stay residents: those broken-winged citizens who conduct life in the hotel's cheerless rooms and dark hallways. Inevitably, as Gina's allegiance swings towards the guests, she comes into conflict with Hendy, the Happy World's controlling, intolerant owner. Jan Chilwell notes that Cox brings to both his novels 'a strong moral sense' and a 'conviction that the individual has a responsibility to work towards a better world' (★*NZ Listener*, 28 Nov. 1987).

Cox was awarded the Buckland Literary Award in 1988 and the 1991 Katherine ★Mansfield Memorial Fellowship. In 1993 he left bookselling to become a free-lance writer and, two years later, took up a position as senior writer for the Museum of New Zealand Te Papa Tongarewa.   PM

CRANNA, John (1954–), won both the New Zealand Book Award for Fiction and the Commonwealth Writers Prize for Best First Book with his debut short story volume, *Visitors* (1989). Born in Te Aroha, he grew up in the ★Waikato, lived for some years in London and then Auckland, and was 1997 writing fellow at Waikato University. His short stories have been published in the UK as well as New Zealand, and are already included in such key anthologies as *Some Other Country* (1992), the *Oxford Book of New Zealand Short Stories* (1994) and the international *Best Short Stories 1987*. Those in *Visitors* powerfully occupy the edges of normal experience. The best are built on incongruities of tone—naivety and horror in the dystopic 'Visitors' or the post-cataclysmic 'Archaeology', absurdist black fantasy in 'Huia and the Angry Earth', or dislocative cultural encounter in the tourist dramas of 'Leti' or 'History for Berliners'. Two centred on cultural conflict through work on the New Zealand land could become classics of that locale, 'Accidents', which treats men at work with unblinking realism, and 'Soft Targets', a savvy and satiric 1980s version of the ★'Along Rideout Road' situation of a young townie's temporary encounter with ★backblocks life.

Cranna's novel, *Arena* (1992), is a dystopic fable focused on the 'arena' itself, a potent and original symbol in the New Zealand context. Images of physical suffering and entrapment recur compulsively, and hallucinatory visions of the arena's roaring crowds and bizarre and protracted ceremonies read like a nightmare version of Auckland's 1990 Commonwealth Games, suffered perhaps by someone who couldn't afford a ticket. Reviewers had reservations about what Elizabeth Caffin called the 'over-emphasis on "significance"' but agreed that the force and discipline of Cranna's writing confirmed him as a serious rising talent, to be compared to J.M. Coetzee or Ian McEwan.   RR

Creative New Zealand, see **New Zealand Literary Fund**.

CREELEY, Robert (1926–), the Massachusetts-born poet who was one of the key figures in the 'Black Mountain School' of 'open form' poetry, made an influential first visit to New Zealand in March 1976. Alistair ★Paterson has described how a sense of the increasing irrelevance of the British tradition led him to 'attempt bringing a leading contemporary American poet to New Zealand … to act as a catalyst for increasing the momentum of change in New Zealand writing and the ways in which New Zealand critics were thinking.' Paterson raised financial support, and organised readings and university lectures in Auckland, Hamilton, Palmerston North, Wellington, Christchurch and Dunedin. The tour indeed provided a focus for increased awareness of recent American developments, especially in 'open form' amd *postmodernism, which Paterson, Alan *Loney, the *Freed group and others had been advocating since about 1970. Support from Robin *Dudding gave the visit exposure in *Islands 15 (1976) with a cover photo of Creeley by Russell *Haley, a long interview with Bill *Manhire and a reprint of a fairly recent (1972) Creeley poem, 'For My Mother'. Following the visit Loney's *Hawk Press published Hello: Poems by Creeley; Paterson and Michael *Morrissey visited America as Fulbright Fellows; postmodern work appeared increasingly in *Mate and Climate (then edited by Paterson) and elsewhere; changed critical ideas began to be expressed by establishment figures like C.K. *Stead in his 'Wystan to Carlos' paper at the 1979 *PEN/Victoria University Conference; and Paterson compiled his 15 Contemporary New Zealand Poets (1980) anthology, with its advocacy of open form. Paterson also published an interview with Creeley in the American journal Buff (1983).

The impact of Creeley's first visit was not all in one direction. Penelope Highet, a New Zealander among the audience at his Dunedin reading, became his third wife a year later, in 1977. They live at Buffalo, New York. Creeley has subsequently revisited New Zealand, especially as Fulbright Fellow at University of Auckland in 1995, when he wrote a long poem, 'The Dogs of Auckland', to be printed with illustrations by Max Gimblett at the *Holloway Press.   RR

CRESSWELL, D'Arcy (1896–1960), saw his life's profession as poetry. He was born into a prosperous Canterbury family, was educated at Christ's College and studied architecture in London until the outbreak of World War 1, when he enlisted with an English regiment. By 1925 he was declaring himself 'a New Zealand poet' as he peddled copies of his verses door to door on a walking tour of England. The declarations themselves, as much as the verses, were to lead Allen *Curnow some twenty years later to see Cresswell's assertions as one event (along with R.A.K. *Mason's composition of 'In the Manner of Men') that marked the beginnings of 'taking poetry seriously' in New Zealand. In the next few years Cresswell became acquainted with many of London's literary elite and began a long correspondence with Lady Ottoline Morrell. He published two small volumes of verse in 1928 and 1932, but it was his autobiography, A Poet's Progress (1930), which finally identified him as a figure of interest in the London literary milieu after its commendation by Arnold Bennett.

About this time he accepted a commission to compile an anthology for the Bodley Head entitled 'Since Byron'. The work, which the publishers finally rejected, was to become an expression of Cresswell's own increasingly obsessive belief that modern poetry was for the most part decadent and heretical, and that modern poets, seduced by post-Copernican rationalism, had almost entirely abandoned the demands of beauty and lyric form, and had turned away from the proper celebration of Nature, leaving only a handful of poets, Cresswell himself among them, to continue in the proper role of the artist.

Returning to New Zealand in 1932 he began writing the Swiftian satirical essays describing his 'discovery' of the country, which were first published in the Christchurch *Press and later formed the opening sections of his second volume of autobiography, Present Without Leave (1939). During these years he wrote the sonnet sequence Lyttelton Harbour (1936) and began to write The Forest, a didactic verse play eventually published in 1952, which proclaimed his beliefs about the role of the poet in society, the fallen nature of the modern world and the primacy of homosexual love. Cresswell returned to England in 1938. After the war he eked out a frugal existence with menial jobs while writing the poems and pamphlets that he hoped would vindicate his belief in himself as a major poet. He returned only once to New Zealand for a brief visit in 1950 and died in London.

Cresswell was an inheritor of the Romantic tradition, which emphasised the inspirational nature of poetry and stressed the moral and instructional duties of the poet. His beliefs on these subjects were transparently self-vindicating, and his beliefs about the perfection of Hellenic Greece and the order of the pre-Renaissance world, like his rejection of what he saw as the mechanistic deceptions of modern science, have a strong sense of oversimplification and unreality. Even at the time of its composition, his verse was frequently seen as mannered and archaic, and though Curnow and *Chapman and Bennet gave him generous representations in their anthologies no editor later than 1960 has to date included his work in a selection of twentieth-century poetry. It is not as a practising poet but as a forceful and romantic advocate for New Zealand verse at a time when such an idea seemed risible that Cresswell is important. His professions in the 1920s and 1930s served as starting points for the arguments of M.H. *Holcroft as essayist and Allen Curnow as anthologist. Charles *Brasch fairly summarised Cresswell's importance in the elegiac observation that 'New Zealand literature in the thirties began in a real sense under his banner'.   WB

CRESSWELL, Lyell (1944–), composer, was born in Wellington and lives in Edinburgh. A strong Salvation Army background gave him a liking for music 'of bright colours and deep feeling—music which can move people'. Although his international reputation is chiefly based on his major orchestral works such as *Salm* (1977) and his cello concerto (1984), many of these have a vocal basis. *O!* for orchestra (1982), to mark the centenary of the Salvation Army Band in New Zealand, presents 'cries of joy and sorrow, of anguish and hope, and of supplication and glorification'; *A Modern Ecstasy* (1986) is an acclaimed parable for mezzo, baritone and orchestra to a libretto by the Scottish writer Patrick Maguire; and he has also set poems by the Greek neo-imagist Yannis Ritsos. Other important vocal settings of literary texts include *Voices of Ocean Winds* (1989), for chorus and orchestra from Charles *Brasch, and *Words for Music* (1989) to a text by C.K. *Stead.   JMT

Crime Story (1994) is a novel by Maurice *Gee whose almost every character commits a crime of some sort. Indeed the society they live in commits the broadest and least accountable crimes of all. In the opening scene a petty criminal, Brent Rosser, moves through Victoria University and the Wellington suburb of Kelburn to a wealthy home, which he burgles. He finds nothing worth taking: 'You got that sort of place but it shouldn't happen in Kelburn.' What should and should not happen in various suburbs is contrasted throughout with what does and does not. In fact Rosser goes on immediately to do something he 'didn't mean to do': the result is permanent disablement for Ulla Peet, wife of Athol Peet of Athcol Properties. However, Athol and his associates are by no means the innocent victims of crime. Gwen, his mother, thinks 'All her men were greedy.' The elderly Howard is an Auckland wheeler and dealer, too cunning to be caught out committing his crimes. Her younger son, Gordon, cannot explain two million dollars not his own and is sent to prison. Meanwhile Athol and Ulla learn to cope with her suffering, while his business partners are left to be punished for actions started by him. At the other social extreme, in Wellington's Newtown, Rosser and his sister are under brutal threat; domestic violence and blackmail are only some of the crimes they encounter. Among the wealthy or the poor, it seems that crime is the only reliable survival strategy. And yet the novel is not grim—the very urge to survive is presented as a virtue and there is much entertainment in the lively style.   NW

CROSS, Ian (1925–), is known as author of *The *God Boy* and other novels and as a distinguished journalist, editor and executive manager. Born in Masterton, educated at Wanganui Tech., he became a reporter, first with the *Dominion* 1943–47 and returning as its chief reporter 1951–56. He was awarded an associate fellowship in journalism at Harvard University 1954–55. An avid reader, in his spare time he was writing fiction, winning the *Atlantic Monthly* Short Story Prize in 1956. His first novel, *The God Boy* (1957), incorporated such strengths of good reportage as immediacy, detailed observation and the sense of an authentic personal voice, as well as skilled pacing and shaping of the narrative. Its success led Cross's career in a more literary direction for a while, and he was the first holder of the *Burns Fellowship at Otago University in 1959. Two further novels followed, *The Backward Sex* in 1959 and *After Anzac Day* in 1961. Neither achieved the narratorial subtlety or tragic impact of *The God Boy*, though *After Anzac Day* sustains its position as a significant rendering of the 1951 *Waterfront Crisis. It was described as 'important in that it attempts to bring a historical dimension into the New Zealand novel' and as 'assured, efficient and beautifully shaped', by Thomas Crawford in *Landfall* 61 (1962).

With a family of four, Cross returned to more remunerative employment as public relations manager of Feltex, 1961–72, a time when he was also a successful radio and television broadcaster, especially as media analyst in 'Column Comment' 1964–72. In 1973 he was unexpectedly appointed successor to M.H. *Holcroft as editor of the *NZ Listener*, then a central position of influence and policy-shaping in the nation's cultural and intellectual life. He fulfilled its diverse demands well, fostering such new talents as Tom *Scott and cartoonist Burton Silver, just as he had earlier recognised and supported Barry *Crump. He was promoted to chairman of the then New Zealand Broadcasting Corporation in 1977, a position he held through various changes, including the exploding influence of television, until retiring as chief executive in 1986. He promptly wrote his vigorous and sometimes provocative memoir of these years of control over the electronic media, *The Unlikely Bureaucrat* (1988). This provides an important commentary on the *Muldoon years and on such issues as media censorship and the 1981 Springbok tour. He also returned to an on-camera critic's role with 'Fourth Estate' in 1988.

His career in fiction restarted with *The Family Man* (1993), a retrospect on New Zealand, especially Wellington, from the 1960s to 1990s, through a point of view whose limitations, as in *The God Boy*, produce intensity and pathos. The old vigour in narrative and clarity in description make this a better novel than its rather cool reception might suggest.

Cross also put his managerial skills and liberal judgment to the service of literature in various voluntary positions, including the presidency of *PEN 1968–72, and membership of the Queen Elizabeth II Arts Council 1967–72, the *Indecent Publications Tribunal

1964–67 and the board of Downstage Theatre 1984–87. His many public commentaries on New Zealand life, literature and media have been distinguished by integrity, liberal values and a well-informed authority, whether on camera in 'Column Comment' or 'Compass', in his *Listener* editorials, or in statements such as his opening address at the Victoria University Seminar on the New Zealand Short Story in 1978. While this authoritativeness is no doubt enhanced by his imposing physique and great height, it is also complemented by a continuing journalist's gift for the telling summative phrase.

The absence of further fiction as powerful as *The God Boy* is an indication not so much of loss of literary will as of the pressures in such a small society for a man of Cross's managerial abilities to give his energies to public life, supporting rather than producing creative work. Cross's literary consolation must be that his period in control of the *Listener*, when it was the one truly popular outlet for fiction, poetry and good feature prose, was one when New Zealand writing in all those genres was vibrantly developing self-confidence; just as his time as media overlord is now looked back to with nostalgia as the last flowering of quality state-sponsored radio and television in the era before their final capitulation to commercialism. An interview with Cross is in Neville Glasgow, *Directions* (1995). RR

Crossing the Bar (1972) was C.K. ★Stead's second collection of poetry, and included a selection from his first volume, *Whether the Will is Free* (1964). Mike ★Doyle commented that *Crossing the Bar* 'displayed as its chief technical characteristic a kind of free verse, often epigrammatic in quality'. The first line of the opening poem is 'Hard. Bright. Clean. Particular' ('You Have a Lot to Lose'), and this succinctness might stand as a manifesto. Rob ★Jackaman complained of Stead's 'stagey nostalgia or melancholy' in his earlier poems, despite their 'high degree of technical competence', and commended the advance represented by *Crossing the Bar*: 'in general the poetry is fuller and more satisfying now'. One aspect of that fullness was Stead's increasingly overt use of personal, even intimate material (not necessarily relating to his own life, however). The poems of the book's first section include treatment of the scars and losses suffered ('Old now, lacking courage') after the ending of a 'historian's' love-affair ('Long Ago'); an account of the birth of a child related to the bombing of children in ★Vietnam ('A Small Registry of Births and Deaths'); the poet's boyhood memory of impertinently hacking his name into a desk ('With a Pen-Knife'); a journal-style poem ('April Notebook'); and a sequence, strongly sexual at moments, about a love affair ('Herakles'). The second section is slighter and more

occasional, comprising poems on literary and scholarly events, and an extended myth of a park-keeper and a female sunbather. 'April Notebook' was the book's most remarkable new achievement, while 'Pictures in a Gallery Undersea' and 'The Fijian Police Band Performs in Albert Park, Auckland' stood out in the third section among work reprinted from *Whether the Will is Free*. These early sequences presaged the more relaxed form and content of Stead's poetry in the 1970s. KJ/RR

Crowded House, see **FINN, Neil**.

CRUMP, Barry (1935–96), was author of more than twenty books of comic Kiwi yarns, the first of which, *A ★Good Keen Man* (1960), was one of the most popular books ever published in New Zealand. He was born in Papatoetoe, South Auckland, grew up on dairy farms, and was educated at numerous South Auckland schools before attending Otahuhu College, which he left at the age of 15. Throughout the 1950s he was an itinerant farmhand and bushworker, and from 1952 spent several seasons as a deer-culler in the Urewera country and the Kaimanawa Ranges, employed by the Wildlife Branch of the Department of Internal Affairs. In 1959 he began writing the humorous sketches of his life as deer-culler and pighunter that were published as the book *A Good Keen Man* in 1960.

Its success was immediate, and Crump promptly produced a follow-up ('my first venture into proper fiction'), *Hang on a Minute Mate* (1961). This introduced his best-known character, Sam Cash, a shrewd, worldly-wise, hard-bitten drifter and yarn-spinner, on the run from domestic ties and suburban conformity, who educates his young mate in self-reliance and the simple life. Crump kept Sam Cash as the central character in *One of Us* (1962) and *There and Back* (1963), after which he spent two years in northern Australia, crocodile-hunting in the Gulf of Carpentaria and sailing off the north Queensland coast. The book that resulted (*Gulf*, 1964, later titled *Crocodile Country*) sold 100 000 copies in a Russian translation, according to the author. Over the next seven years Crump produced another seven books, including an attempt at a female equivalent of his 'good keen man', *A Good Keen Girl* (1970). With *Bastards I Have Met* (1971) he left ★A.H. & A.W. Reed (which in the 1950s had also promoted Frank ★Anthony's 'Me and Gus' stories, predecessors in Crump's genre of the humorous masculine yarn) and set up his own publishing company. In the late 1960s he also became well-known as a television presenter, doing skits and interviews on the local programme 'Town and Around'. Despite the success of *Bastards I Have Met*, the now well-established Crump formula appeared to be producing diminishing returns for the author, who described himself as 'bored by success' and 'restless'. His next book, *Shorty*, did not appear until 1980. In the interim he travelled for two years in England, Europe, then through Turkey and Afghanistan to India, where he developed a close friendship with a Kashmiri family and became interested in Eastern spirituality. After his return to New Zealand he joined the Baha'i faith.

From the late 1970s until his death, Crump exhibited the same mix of itinerant restlessness punctuated by brief periods of settled residence that had characterised his life in the 1960s. In the early 1980s he ran a highly successful Auckland radio talkback programme entitled 'The Bush Telegraph', and featured in award-winning Toyota television commercials. These activities confirmed his status as an icon of the rugged Kiwi *'Man Alone'. He also again began to publish books regularly, often reflecting places he briefly lived in: *Shorty* (1980), written in the Cook Islands; *Puha Road* (1982), written in the far North; *Bullock Creek* (1989), set in back-country Otago. In the mid-1980s he bought a small property and shack near Opotiki, his sole venture into private land-owning, but sold it again in 1991.

Increasingly, in his later books, Crump returned nostalgically to the material of his earlier ones, and found a new generation of interested readers. By 1992 his New Zealand sales were estimated at more than a million copies (including more than 400 000 copies of *A Good Keen Man* and *Hang on a Minute Mate*), and his overseas sales at 285 000 copies. In that year the first volume of an autobiographical trilogy appeared: *The Life and Times of a Good Keen Man*. The second, *Forty Yarns and a Song*, dedicated to 'life in New Zealand in the Fifties and Sixties. Those great days!', appeared in 1994, and the last, *Crumpy's Campfire Companion*, in 1996. In 1994 he was awarded the MBE for services to literature. He was married five times, including (briefly) to the poet Fleur *Adcock, and (for a number of years) to the novelist Jean *Watson, and had nine children, all sons. A commemorative *Tribute to Barry Crump* was published in 1997 with contributions from Kevin *Ireland and others and a selection of Crump's poems and prose.

Crump became a highly skilled practitioner in the genre of the literary yarn, a mode of male writing with a long history from colonial times. Written in a simple, intimate style which captured the feel of the idiom of the 'ordinary bloke', and with a lively sense of humour and narrative timing, his stories of abandoning the urban rat race and 'going *bush', learning to live independently and to develop practical skills of survival, appealed strongly to post-war generations of primarily city- and suburban-dwelling New Zealanders. He also became increasingly aware of the ambivalent values—freedom from domestic and other social responsibilities—which his books seemed to endorse. As early as *Hang on a Minute Mate*, Sam Cash is presented as abandoning his young mate at the end, describing his own drifting life as a 'disease'. In his later writing Crump came increasingly to share this ambivalence playfully with his readers, as if recognising the make-believe character of his fictional world and inviting them into it simply for the pleasures of nostalgia, fantasy and sheer comic story-telling skill it offered. TS

Cunninghams, The, a novel by David *Ballantyne, was first published in 1948 and reprinted in 1963, 1976 and 1986. Ballantyne began it in 1944 as a trilogy, tentatively entitled 'Dominion Testament', to be made up of 'The Pension' (successively retitled 'A Summer Storm' and 'Forty-first Summer'), 'The Cold Chain' and 'The Only Paradise'. The first was originally accepted for publication in Australia, but the publishing house failed. That novel and the first half of the second were eventually accepted by Vanguard Publishers in the United States, at the instigation of the American novelist, James T. Farrell, and appeared in 1948 as *The Cunninghams*. The realistic method, much influenced by Farrell's work, is almost documentary, the effaced third-person narrator being present only as an observer, reporting what the characters say, do, think and feel, passing no overt judgment on them, and limiting his language to their register. Farrell commented that Ballantyne told the story in 'both an objective and a human way', presenting the characters 'with an evenness of sympathy'. This relative even-handedness sets the novel apart from other New Zealand family novels, which tend to favour the sensitive child or adolescent against the parents and other siblings. Ballantyne presents Helen, the frustrated, pleasure-seeking mother, Gil, the dying father, Gilbert, the awkward and sensitive son, and Joy, the daughter, without overtly favouring any of them. In the everyday activities of the summer of 1936, their pitiful aspirations, their unfocused discontents and their failure to understand their situation and each other are dispassionately presented, as is their provincial society, with its shallow religion, furtive sexuality, small-minded social judgment, rigid gender roles, superficial and secondhand popular culture, political apathy and lack of any vision of alternatives. Perhaps the most moving section is chapter 12 of Book Two, 'Husband and Wife', in which the unspoken thoughts of Helen and Gil, when she visits him in the hospital, are interwoven, neither able to communicate to the other what he or she is feeling, and neither able to understand the other, each revealing the unquestioned and limiting values of their society. Unlike many of his contemporaries, whose critical judgment of their society could be heavy-handed, Ballantyne seemed to be saying, as he put it in an interview, 'This, for better or worse, is reality.' His reconstruction of it in the novel is an impressive accomplishment.   LJ

CURNOW, Allen (1911–) was born in Timaru, where his father—a fourth-generation New Zealander—was an Anglican clergyman; his mother was English-born. During his childhood Curnow lived in a succession of Anglican vicarages in Canterbury, at Belfast, Malvern, Lyttelton and New Brighton. He was educated at Christchurch BHS and the universities of Canterbury and Auckland. He worked for the Christchurch *Sun in 1929–30, before moving to Auckland to prepare for the Anglican ministry at St John's Theological College, 1931–33. His earliest poems appeared in the university periodicals *Kiwi in 1931 and *Phoenix (he was a member of the editorial committee) in 1932–33. Several *Phoenix* contributors, including the founding editor James *Bertram, R.A.K. *Mason, A.R.D. *Fairburn and J.C. *Beaglehole became friends (he later edited Mason's *Collected Poems*, 1962). His first collection of poems *Valley of Decision (1933)—printed, like *Kiwi* and *Phoenix*, by R.W. *Lowry—reflected a crisis of religious vocation pointing towards his decision not to be ordained, taken the following year. Biblical imagery and language remained an important element in all his writing.

In 1934 Curnow returned to the South Island. During a brief period on a South Canterbury farm he corresponded with Iris Wilkinson (Robin *Hyde) and Alan *Mulgan at the Auckland *Star*. He then found a job on the Christchurch *Press. In Christchurch he quickly established a lifelong friendship and collaboration with Denis *Glover and began contributing to *Caxton Press publications, such as *New Poems* (1934) and *Another Argo* (1935). *Three Poems* and a brief prose manifesto, *Poetry and Language*, were published by Caxton in 1935. He also contributed verse and prose to the radical periodical *Tomorrow (1934–40), often under the pseudonyms 'Amen' and 'Julian'. A shift in his poetic manner is observable in *Enemies: Poems 1934–36* (Caxton, 1937), which reveals an awareness of contemporary English poetry (including Yeats, Pound, Eliot, Auden, Day Lewis, Spender, MacNeice, Dylan Thomas and William Empson—some of these influences came in a bit later) and a sharper consciousness of the New Zealand scene, both social and physical. These tendencies continued in his next three books, *Not in Narrow Seas (Caxton, 1939), *Island & Time (Caxton, 1941) and *Sailing or Drowning (*Progressive Publishing Society, 1943), which demonstrate growing technical mastery and a progressive

widening of thematic scope. These books display a tight focus on details of New Zealand's *landscape and history and on its situation as a small island nation in the wider world—a consciousness further accentuated by the outbreak of war in Europe in 1939, and the widening of the conflict to the Pacific from late 1941. From the mid-1930s Curnow contributed frequent reviews and articles to the literary pages of the *Press*, and, after 1941, to the Caxton miscellany *Book*. *A Present for Hitler*, the first of several volumes of topical satirical verses—most of them originally printed in the *Press* (and from 1952 also the *New Zealand Herald*) under the pseudonym *'Whim-Wham'—appeared in 1940.

During the war years, Curnow—who by this time had a young family—spent his nights sub-editing foreign news at the *Press* and his days working on *The Axe*, a verse play with a *Pacific setting (performed on stage 1948, 1953, published Caxton, 1949) and an anthology, eventually published as *A *Book of New Zealand Verse 1923–45* (Caxton, 1945). This seminal anthology included the work of sixteen poets, most of whom (Ursula *Bethell, J.R. *Hervey, D'Arcy *Cresswell, Beaglehole, Fairburn, Mason, Glover, Hyde, Charles *Brasch, Basil *Dowling, Anton *Vogt, James K. *Baxter and Curnow himself) had been published by Caxton during the previous decade. The selection, together with Curnow's forty-page introduction, provided the first coherent and substantial representation and analysis of New Zealand poetry and has remained a landmark publication. The introduction was most noteworthy for his identification of recurring elements among the themes and images of the poets, in which he saw evidence of 'some common problem of the imagination' particular to the New Zealander's situation. The notion that there are circumstances reflected in the poetry which are 'peculiarly New Zealand's' ('Attitudes for a New Zealand Poet' iii) was perhaps the most influential and controversial of his critical ideas in that it engages with the complex and much debated question of 'nationalism', a keyword of the Curnow era though one he seldom used himself. An expanded edition of the anthology, including several poets who had emerged in the post-war period up to 1950 (such as Ruth *Dallas, Keith *Sinclair, Kendrick *Smithyman and Charles *Spear), was published in 1951.

During and after the war Curnow's own poetry gradually became less preoccupied with issues of history and national identity and moved towards more personal and universal themes (for example, 'At Dead Low Water', 1945). As he wrote in the Author's Note to *Collected Poems 1933–73* (1974): 'I had to get past the severities, not to say rigidities, of our New Zealand anti-myth: away from questions which present themselves as public and answerable, towards the questions which are always private and unanswerable. The geographical anxieties didn't disappear; but I began to find a personal and poetic use for them, rather than let them use me up' (p. xiii). Reflective of this tendency were the collections *Jack Without Magic* (Caxton, 1946) and *At Dead Low Water and Sonnets* (Caxton, 1949).

In 1949 Curnow was awarded a grant from the newly established *Literary Fund to travel abroad for the first time. He spent much of that year in the UK, supplementing the grant by employment on the *News Chronicle*, and with occasional work for the BBC. He spent a week with Dylan and Caitlin Thomas (then living at Laugharne village), having met the Welsh poet through the BBC; they were to see more of each other the following year in New York City, Cambridge (Massachusetts) and San Francisco. After a brief return to Christchurch and the *Press* in 1950, he and his family moved to Auckland; he took up a position in the English department at the University of Auckland where he worked from 1951 to 1976, retiring as associate professor. He received the university's LittD degree, and an honorary doctorate from the University of Canterbury.

Throughout the 1950s, Curnow—by this time recognised as one of the country's leading writers—continued to write verse (*Poems 1949–57*, 1957), including a second verse play 'Moon Section' which was professionally toured through the North Island, but he was disappointed in it, and gave up thoughts of revising it for the stage, or for print. His *Four Plays* (1972) were all produced on radio, commissioned by the New Zealand Broadcasting Corporation: *The Axe*, revised with sound images by Douglas *Lilburn (1961); *The Overseas Expert* (1962); *The Duke's Miracle* (1967); and *Resident of Nowhere* (1969). In Joseph Hirsal's translation *The Duke's Miracle* was broadcast by Prague Radio several times in the 1968–69 Czechoslovak Radio Festival of Foreign Plays; later productions were from BBC World Service and Australian Broadcasting Commission; in Italo Verri's Italian, it was published as *Il Miracolo del Duca* (Ferrara 1993).

In the 1950s and 1960s Curnow got caught up in intergenerational and interregional conflicts with the younger Wellington-based writers Louis *Johnson and Baxter, especially in connection with his reviews in *Here & Now* of the early issues of Johnson's *New Zealand Poetry Yearbook* (1951–52) and then the contents of his own second anthology, *The Penguin Book of New Zealand Verse* (1960), the publication of which was delayed by disputes about his selections and introduction.

Curnow has written about this episode: 'My critical positions, as understood from my reviews and anthologies, inevitably came under some fire: whether from an older generation who thought me unjust to respected poets of their time, or from writers younger than myself who believed themselves underrated, and who interpreted any emphasis on a New Zealand particularity or "common problem" as a restrictive desideratum—so to speak, a charge for admission to my anthologies which they were not prepared to pay. Such challenges came to a head in 1957–58, when a second anthology *The Penguin Book of New Zealand Verse* (1960) was on the point of publication in the United Kingdom. A set of galley-proofs ... fell into the hands of young Wellington poets employed in the School Publications Branch of the Education Department.... Letters were rushed off to England ... threatening a concerted withdrawal by several poets ... the threatened walk-out didn't eventuate.... But publication was delayed two years.... Invited to undertake a sequel to the 1960 Penguin, I refused.'

Debate about the contents of the anthology and its fifty-page introduction (a key document in New Zealand criticism) figured prominently in literary discussion in the 1960s. One passage in particular—'Reality must be local and special at the point where we pick up the traces: as manifold as the signs we follow and the routes we take. Whatever is true vision belongs, here, uniquely to the islands of New Zealand. The best of our verse is marked or moulded everywhere by peculiar pressures—pressures arising from the isolation of the country, its physical character, and its history'—became celebrated, seen by some as an important truth memorably expressed, while others—usually younger—took it as prescriptively nationalistic. There were clarifications and elaborations of Curnow's views in the lectures 'New Zealand Literature: The Case for a Working Definition' (1963) and 'Distraction and Definition: Centripetal Directions in New Zealand Poetry' (1968). These lectures, the anthology introductions and other miscellaneous pieces were eventually collected in *Look Back Harder: Critical Writings 1935–1984*, edited by Peter *Simpson (Auckland University Press, 1987).

After *A *Small Room with Large Windows* (Oxford University Press, 1962)—a selected poems published in the UK which contained only two previously uncollected poems—Curnow published no further verse collection until *Trees, Effigies, Moving Objects* appeared in 1972. From the perspective of the end of the 1990s it is apparent that this brilliant sequence of eighteen poems initiated a new phase of his poetic career. The increasingly elaborate and highly wrought texture of poems of the 1950s, such as 'Spectacular Blossom' and 'A Small Room with Large Windows', gave way to a more openly textured verse, often vividly colloquial, imagistic, and idiomatic in expression while still precisely calculated in its effects. Also with this book a new landscape made a forceful entry into the poetry—that of the bush-clad hills and wild beaches of Auckland's west coast, in particular Lone Kauri Road and Karekare Beach; as Curnow explained in a note in *Selected Poems 1940–1989* (1990): 'I have spent most of my summers and weekends there since 1961.'

If this beach-and-bush locale represents a kind of 'fixed foot' in the universe of Curnow's later poetry, the other 'foot' has continued to roam widely through time and space, drawing in experiences from overseas travel in Europe (including a spell as Katherine *Mansfield Fellow in Menton) and the United States, and also exploring personal and family history to a much greater extent than before. American settings are especially important in *Trees, Effigies, Moving Objects*, in which Washington DC serves with Lone Kauri Road as coordinates by which the sequence is mapped, so to speak. Family history figures especially prominently in the title poem of *An Abominable Temper & Other Poems* (1973), a ten-part sequence in which the poet adopts the persona of his great-grandfather, H.A.H. Monro, to create a portrait of *his* father, Peter Monro—the man with 'an abominable temper', the poet's great-great-grandfather —who settled in the Hokianga in the early nineteenth century. In *An *Incorrigible Music* (1979), another book-length sequence, Karekare again provides the 'home' coordinate (as in, e.g., 'Canst Thou Draw Out Leviathan with an Hook?'—the title is from the Book of Job) while Italian settings both historical and contemporary provide the 'away' coordinate, notably in two powerful multi-part poems, 'In the Duomo' (the account of a murder in Renaissance Florence) and 'Moro Assassinato' (which takes its subject from the assassination by terrorists of a contemporary Italian statesman, Aldo Moro). *You Will Know When You Get There: Poems 1979–81* (1982) is a more various sequence containing a number of out-standing short lyrics, some of which appear to focus on the imminence of death, as, for instance, in the title piece and 'The Parakeets at Karekare', while the suburban Auckland of the poet's city residence figures in such poems as 'The Weather in Tohunga Crescent'. In 'A Fellow Being', a further ten-part sequence, the poet explored his coincidental connection to an Aucklander of an earlier time, the entrepreneurial American dentist and feller of kauri forests, Dr F.J. Rayner.

Increasingly through the 1980s and 1990s, Curnow began making poems out of incidents from his Canterbury childhood. While there were isolated earlier poems of childhood reminiscence, e.g. 'Country School' from 1941, such poems became much more prominent in *The *Loop in Lone Kauri Road: Poems 1983–1985* (1986), and in the previously uncollected poems in *Continuum: New and Later Poems 1972–1988* (1988)—

which brought together five books from the 1970s and 1980s—and *Early Days Yet: New and Collected Poems 1941–1997* (1997). Between poems with Karekare settings and the poems with childhood Canterbury settings an elaborate pattern of contrasts and oppositions is implicitly established: youth and age, south and north, Canterbury and Auckland, east and west, Pacific and Tasman, plain and bush. An example of such patterning is the implied connection between two late 'car' poems, 'Early Days Yet'—in part a recollection of travelling the long dusty roads of rural Canterbury with his clergyman father in a model-T Ford—and 'The Game of Tag', a poetic fiction (in the Wallace Stevens sense of imaginative construct) in which an old Falcon is driven 'like a bat / out of Hell' around the twisting corners of Lone Kauri Road by the poet's 'spray- / gun-toting rival' whose death note is the spray-painted roadside graffito 'THANKS FOR THE TAG'.

In *Selected Poems 1940–1989* Curnow replaced the chronological arrangement of earlier collections with a broadly thematic sequence, so as to make a single poem, as it were, out of the poems of a lifetime, as if in demonstration of the statement in the Author's Note to *Collected Poems 1933–1973* (1974): 'the poetry is all one book'. *Early Days Yet* also eschews conventional practice by organising the poems in reverse chronological sequence (also adopted in *Continuum*), an arrangement in part explained by the volume's epigraph from Samuel *Butler's *Erewhon* (a fertile source text for Curnow), which begins: 'The Erewhonians say that we are drawn through life backwards; or again that we go onwards into the future as into a dark corridor.' No poet has so consistently defied expectations as to what his future will reveal as Allen Curnow; but as his career has unfolded it has revealed a logic as inevitable as it has been unpredictable. His most recent poem at the time of writing is 'Ten Steps to the Sea' (*London Review of Books*, 1 Jan. 1998).

Curnow's long and distinguished career has been marked by many awards and other forms of recognition. He received the New Zealand Book Award for Poetry on six occasions, the Commonwealth Poetry Prize in 1988, a Cholmondley Award in 1992, and in 1989 was awarded the Queen's Gold Medal for Poetry. He was made a CBE in 1986 and received the Order of New Zealand in 1990. PS

CURNOW, Wystan (1939–), critic, curator and poet, has been a positive contributor to New Zealand culture over the past three decades. Born in Christchurch, son of Allen *Curnow, and educated at Takapuna GS and the University of Auckland, he returned to the Auckland English Department in 1970 after graduate study in the United States, and is currently associate professor. He has a particular interest in contemporary *American poetry, cultural poetics, and relations between image and text.

In 1973 Curnow edited *Essays on New Zealand Literature*, the first book-length collection of criticism about New Zealand writing. He contributed essays on *postmodernism to *Parallax* in the 1970s, and produced texts in which the distinctions between writer, artist and critic are blurred in *AND*, *Splash* and *Antic* in the 1980s. Understatement and wit characterise his two collections of poems. The short pieces which make up *The Cancer Daybook* (1989) display alertness and wry humour despite the bleak circumstances in which they were written; in *Back in the USA: Poems 1980–82* (1989) Curnow revels in the incongruities and ambiguities of language. A prolific and provocative critic, he has promoted theoretical changes in New Zealand literary culture and been a prominent advocate for the avantgarde. He has collaborated with New York–based conceptual artist Billy *Apple and has written on experimental film maker Len *Lye and artists Colin *McCahon, Max Gimblett, Julia Morison and Imants Tillers, among others. In 1984 he curated *I Will Need Words: Colin McCahon's Word and Number Paintings* for the Sydney Biennale. Other curatorial projects include *Sex and Sign* (1987) and *Putting the Land on the Map: Art and Cartography in New Zealand Since 1840* (1989). An interview with Curnow appears in *Landfall* 177 (1991). SS

Current Thought, subtitled 'Literature, Science, Art, Sociology, Home Economy', was a monthly published in Christchurch by *Whitcombe & Tombs 1908–09, when it was superseded by the *Citizen*. It was typical of the period in attempting to cover a wide range of subjects, as suggested by the subtitle, which recalls that of the *Triad*. Without any explicit policy of promoting New Zealand literature it nevertheless published work by writers such as Jessie *Mackay, Blanche *Baughan, Alan *Mulgan and Edith *Lyttleton ('G.B. Lancaster').

SH

CURRIE, A.E. (Archibald Ernest) (1884–1967), was the co-editor, with his lifelong friend W.F. Alexander (1882?–1957), of the first major anthology of *New Zealand Verse* (1906). Their correspondence in more than a hundred folders in the *Alexander Turnbull Library contains many details of literary interest during the first half of the century. Currie was born in Christchurch, graduated MA, LLB from Canterbury University College and practised law in Napier, Wairoa and Wellington. He was Crown Solicitor 1925–49 and published articles on various aspects of the law. He also compiled the *Centennial Treasury of Otago* and, as a member of the lodge, *The Masonic Annals of Wellington* (1961). Although he maintained a lively interest in poetry, he published nothing except his translations, *Versions from Verlaine* (*Caxton, 1961). NW

D

DAGG, Fred, see **CLARKE, John ('Fred Dagg')**.

DALEY, Debra (1954–), was born and educated in Auckland (MA in English Literature, University of Auckland). She has worked as journalist, editor and copywriter, and has travelled extensively, living in London 1977–85. She works in Auckland as a screen-writer. As well as scripts for television series, she has also written plays for that medium. They are typically acutely observed and witty, with a satirical edge tem-pered by a compassionate perspective. She won the Lilian Ida Smith Award in 1992 and a Todd New Writer's Bursary in 1994. Her first novel, *The Strange Letter Z* (New Zealand 1995, UK 1996), achieved con-siderable success. It explores the New Zealand compul-sion to travel, focused in urban, cosmopolitan settings. A story of brilliance and emotional pathology, obsession and love, it is notable for its erudition and its deliberate manipulation of style.   JH

DALLAS, Ruth (1919–), poet and children's author, was born in Invercargill. Her working-class settler heritage and the closeness of her family relationships inform much of her writing. For example, her maternal grandmother (a midwife in the 1890s who provided for her family single-handedly) features both in poetry —'Her strength seemed large and cool, as the rock in the sea / Seemed large and cool in the green and restless waves' ('Grandmother and Child')—and as the model for the mother in Dallas's popular *Bush* series of chil-dren's novels.

As the daughter of the entrepreneurial proprietor of an Invercargill petrol-station, Dallas's background presented neither high educational opportunities nor encouragement to write. She remarks in her autobio-graphy *Curved Horizon* (1991), 'I am at a loss to account for the fact that I wrote poetry in an environment where I knew no one who was interested in poetry.' Yet she developed a love of words that, from the age of 9, mani-fested itself in poems and stories, a number of which were published in the *Southland Daily News*'s 'Little Pakehas' Page' (see ★Children's Pages). Although she left Southland Technical College in 1935 with just three years' secondary education, she never stopped reading, be it Shakespeare, ancient Greeks and Icelandic sagas, or critics like Eliot, Quiller-Couch, De Selincourt and Yeats.

Dallas chose her maternal grandmother's name in 1926 as pen-name for her earliest published poems, 'Morning Mountains', which M.H. ★Holcroft printed in the *Southland Times*. Her much anthologised 'Milking Before Dawn'—'In the drifting rain the cows in the yard are as black / And wet and shiny as rocks in an ebbing tide'—appeared in the ★*NZ Listener* the following year, and in 1948 Charles ★Brasch included her poems in ★*Landfall* 8, an issue anthologising six new poets whose work he considered important.

Dallas's first collection was published in 1953 by the ★Caxton Press, who also produced her five subsequent volumes. The following year she left Invercargill to live in Dunedin. She continued writing poetry, and stories for adults and children, and authored bulletins for ★School Publications. From 1962 to 1966 she worked with Brasch in *Landfall*'s editorial office, and in 1968 was ★Burns Fellow at the University of Otago.

Dallas's first poetry collection, *Country Road and Other Poems, 1947–52* (1953) was followed by *The Turning Wheel: Poems* (1961)—joint winner of the New

Zealand *Literary Fund Achievement Award, 1963. These two volumes exhibit a striking stylistic and thematic consistency that endures through her later work. The concentration on place—specifically the lower South Island—is intense; reflecting her permanent fascination with the 'primeval forests and cleared fields, and the history of … settlement'. This landscape, absorbed in childhood, is her 'World's Centre': 'The circle … of mountain, hill / And curving sea that once enclosed the world.' Her poems are a record of her love for 'the bright rain-washed countryside … the forests and inland mountains, [and] the long shell-strewn beaches.'

Yet Dallas's land- and city-scapes are often empty. In 'Deserted Beach' (1953) there is not 'One gull to circle through the wild salt wind / Or cry above the breaking of the waves,' nor 'One footprint or one feather on the sand'. If a poem is populated, its figures are reflections of the settler past, or poems about family that often are about loss: 'Of all the tools in my tool-cupboard, / I like best those that my father used.… Bereaved daughters have to learn / To come to their own rescue, / Or be entirely overgrown' ('Encounter', 1976).

From *The Turning Wheel* on, Dallas's natural introspection, detachment and solitude—'I don't like excitement. I like calm.'—combined with her growing interest in Asian philosophies to push her already crisp and concise verse toward even greater 'brevity and density', along the lines of *Chinese poetry and *Japanese haiku. Her collection *Day Book: Poems of a Year* (1966), was followed by *Shadow Show: Poems* (1968) and, in 1976, *Song for a Guitar and Other Songs*: a selection made by Brasch which won the 1977 Buckland Literary Award. *Walking on the Snow: Poems* (1976), joint winner of the New Zealand Book Award for Poetry, was followed by *Steps of the Sun: Poems* (1979) and, finally, *Collected Poems* (1987).

Fiona *Farrell comments that when Dallas observes some natural phenomenon, she 'writes about it with images so fresh that the lens is cleared and we see her subject for the first time' (*NZ Listener*, 11 July 1987). Elizabeth Caffin, however, finds her enduring romanticism, for all its intensity and lyricism, 'increasingly isolated from the whole field of human engagement … and in particular from any contemporary discourse about poetry' (*OHNZLE).

Dallas's children's books take her familiar southern landscapes as their settings. *The Children in the Bush* (1969), *The Wild Boy in the Bush* (1971), *The Big Flood in the Bush* (1972) and *Holiday Time in the Bush* (1983) form a series set in the 1890s featuring a mother raising her children alone. Inspired by Dallas's own mother's childhood, the series depicts settler life in some detail, leavened by a fair smattering of adventure. A limited

edition, *Ragamuffin Scarecrow* (1969), was followed by *A Dog Called Wig* (1970)—about a young boy coming to terms with his dog's preference for his father. In *The House on the Cliffs* (1975) a young woman also comes to new self-knowledge, by coming to understand an eccentric, reclusive, old lady's loneliness and her fear of removal to a retirement home. *Shining Rivers* (1979), set during Central Otago's *gold rush, tells of the relationship between a disaffected young immigrant boy and a generous old goldminer who teaches him the value of friendship.

Dallas received an honorary doctorate of the University of Otago in 1978, and a CBE in 1989. PM

Dalmatians in New Zealand literature.

Immigrants from the 'South Slav' political alliance of six ethnic groups which comprised the former Yugoslavia arrived in a series of chain migrations, primarily from the central Dalmatian coast of the Croatian constituent republic. Dalmatian migrants had been settling in New Zealand since 1857 in search of freedom from oppression by the Austro-Hungarian Empire, and a livelihood on the *goldfields of Thames, the gumfields of Northland and then through farming, fishing and horticulture.

It was not until almost a century later, when Amelia *Batistich published her first Dalmatian story 'Roots' (1948), that the voice of the migrants was heard speaking for itself in English. Batistich shared a literary heritage with gumfield poet Ante Kosovic whose collection *Dalmtinac iz Tudjine* ('From the Dalmatian in Exile', 1908) was published in Serbo-Croatian in Dalmatia. It aimed, unsuccessfully, to discourage young village men from the harsh life in inhospitable Northland. The transformation of these barren gumlands into rich farming country, and the determined settlers into prosperous, respected citizens, is traced throughout Batistich's two collections of short stories, two novels and many stories published in magazines, including *School Journal. The assimilation of Dalmatians into New Zealand society runs not so smooth a course. *An Olive Tree in Dalmatia* (1963) is a testament to the Dalmatian community's commitment to their adopted country, and in the title story the psychic dislocation suffered by representative migrant Stipan is seen as the price paid for a new life. Through the motif of bootprints on both Dalmatian and New Zealand soil, Batistich plays out the migrants' attempt to inscribe themselves on shifting terrain: fulfilling a sudden and overwhelming desire to return to the Dalmatian village he left fifty three years earlier, Stipan becomes a displaced person in the country of his birth.

Anna Roberts in *Luka* (1987) also writes from an insider's view, the hero of her historical fiction the ideal self-sufficient migrant in the early 1900s, whose lament ('our only crime in their eyes is being the wrong nationality') sums up the hatred directed by New Zealanders, particularly during World War 1, at the 'Austrians', whose passports bore an enemy stamp. The most enduring image of a Dalmatian in mainstream New Zealand literature is that of Nick the Dalmatian labourer in Frank *Sargeson's 'The Making of a New Zealander' (1940). Calling into question cultural identity, the story pivots on the narrator's observation that Nick wasn't a New Zealander, nor a Dalmatian any more: 'He knew he wasn't anything any more.' In a similar masculinist narrative vein John Yelash's collection of stories *Forty Thousand Beers Ago* (1957) depicts a narrator who has the misfortune of being the spitting image of 'Frank the Dally' whose epithet is intentionally derogatory. Vignettes of gambling, boozing and womanising are framed by the unusually poor lot of the migrants in the down-and-out world of bars and boarding houses. 'Fighting Your Own Battles' hints at racial prejudices, telling of Dalmatian boys being cleverer than the others but ending up, like Frank, struggling to survive in adulthood. Pat Radonovich, the failed gumdigger in Maurice *Shadbolt's *Among the Cinders* (1965), who arrives in New Zealand too late to cash in on gum and gold prosperity, ironically observes, in typical broken English, 'every man seem rich ... every man eat well, spend money'. He does not find the riches promised him, but he does find peace in rural isolation with his 'Dally plonk'. Pat *Booth has Dalmatian fishermen acknowledge that 'you're a Dally when they're up against you' in *Footsteps in the Sea* (1964), and Margery Godfrey's young adult fiction, *South for Gold* (1964; see *Gold), includes Ivan Ivanovich the good-natured trader, about whom there is a suspicion of unscrupulous scale fixing.

The commonest stereotype of the Dalmatian is that he—and he is invariably male—'works as if God were in him', as Robyn *Hyde claimed of Martinovitch [sic], the lumberjack in The *Godwits Fly* (1938). Industry, thrift and determination result in material wealth, as parodied in Philip Andrews's *Terese* (1967): the half-Dalmatian heroine's father owns property, racehorses and a two-storey suburban brick-and-tile display of wealth. Naive, aloof Terese is confused by her family's Catholicism and feels her difference but cannot articulate it. Emma searches throughout Joan Rosier-Jones's *Cast Two Shadows* (1985) for a sense of identity, finding it at the end by claiming the Māori side of her ancestry at the expense of both Dalmatian and Chinese inheritance. Neither Terese nor Emma are able to reconcile themselves to their Dalmatian blood, which contributes colour to both their skin and their temperaments but sees them still figured as Pākehā. Along with the Māori and Chinese, ethnicities aligned with Dalmatians include the Scots in Fiona *Kidman's The *Book of Secrets* (1987). Third-generation migrant Maria McLeod becomes infatuated with 'twinkling rough gypsy' Branco the road mender, who slides 'in and out of the landscape as if he were one of the wild creatures that inhabited it'. Using her connection with Branco to make a declaration of her independence from her puritan community, Maria finally becomes indifferent towards him; his outsider status, and the distrust the other settlers felt for the wily Dalmatians, who were seen to make a success out of any venture, makes her rejection easier.

Maurice *Gee's West Auckland includes a tapestry of Dalmatian vineyards and an appreciation of 'real' wine, as *In My Father's Den* (1972) demonstrates. E.H. *Audley's Mattie in *A New Gate for Mattie Dulivich* (1965) is unsurpassed as the Dalmatian stereotype, which bears little resemblance to the range of characters developed by Batistich, Roberts and Yelash from within the community. Stolid, square-jawed Mattie and his wife Vinka occupy a respectable position in small-town New Zealand; Audley sums up all that is positive about 'a people so powerful, so strong, they can never be broken or their identity dissolved' in the neat phrase 'decency doesn't easily die'. This indissoluble identity is in question after the conflicts of the mid-1990s as, with the Dalmatian region renamed Southern Croatia, New Zealand descendants of the community debate who they now are. There is yet to emerge a contemporary voice of the Dalmatians, known by many today as Croatians, to rival the achievement of Batistich.   NN

DANSEY, Harry (1920–79), journalist, race relations conciliator and playwright, was a member of the Ngāti Tūwharetoa and Te Arawa tribes of Taupo and Rotorua respectively. Dansey began his career working for provincial newspapers, becoming popular for his cartoons, which were collected as *Cartoons on International Affairs* (1958). However, his enduring interest was writing for Māori. He contributed regularly to Te *Ao Hou and wrote three books—*How the Maoris Came to Aotearoa* (1947, rev. 1976), *The Maori People* (1958) and *Maori Custom Today* (1971, rev. 1978). Michael *King, commenting on the difficulty of translating the 'idioms of one culture to those of another', praised Dansey's ability, as both writer and speaker, 'to convey the emotional dimensions of Maoriness in English, without mawkishness or sententiousness' (*NZ Listener, 8 Dec. 1979). Apart from an occasional poem or short story published in periodicals, Dansey's major literary work is a narrative play in two acts. *Te Raukura: The Feathers of the Albatross* (1974) mixes past and present to recount the stories of the prophet Te Ua and the pacifist Te Whiti as each man, in his own way, faces the intrusion of the

Pākehā into their lives. But for Dansey, the play's central character is Tamatane, his young narrator who 'questions the so-called lessons of history and tries to relate the agony of the past to the complexities of the present'. Harry Dansey was awarded an MBE in 1974.   PM

Dark Lord of Savaiki, The (1980), was a collection of poems in which Alistair ★Campbell demonstrated a new style and new subject matter. The voice is less troubled, yet no less urgent than before, but the urgency is of love received as well as given. The ten poems speak of the poet's Polynesian ancestors, suggesting that they had warmly welcomed him back to Tongareva (Penrhyn) and that he was welcoming them as well, after feeling uncomfortable with his origins for many years. The book was printed by Te Kotare Press, which Campbell created for the purpose but which has since been used to publish poems by Meg ★Campbell and a series of anthologies of new verse.   NW

Dark Rosaleen was the annual of the Wellington Irish Society, published in 1923 and 1924. An outlet for expressions of Irish nationalism, it featured poems and articles by Eileen ★Duggan and Jessie ★Mackay. See ★Ireland.   SH

Daughter Buffalo, the ninth novel by Janet ★Frame (New York, Toronto, 1972; Wellington, London, 1973), took second place in the Wattie Book of the Year and won the Hubert Church Prose Award; no MS is known. It is the first of Frame's novels with an American setting (New York). If in Frame's earlier novels death was frequently offered as the only, but negative, option for outcasts unable to communicate or conform, in this novel death is explored to show its proximity to love and its necessary interdependence with life. Life, Frame implies, cannot be fully lived until one fully embraces the fact of death, an act likened to love in its integration of opposites and its engendering of a necessary and fortunate fall into knowledge (imagery pertaining to the Garden of Eden myth is prolific throughout). Turnlung, a poet, an old man nearing death, travels from New Zealand to New York, 'the country of death', to complete his 'death education'. Here he meets Talbolt Edelman, a young Jewish doctor who has turned from embryology to become an assistant in the Department of Death Studies, work that affords him daily contact with the dying. But without his emotional investment in these deaths, his studies remain incomplete. The two men are offered as 'a mirror image of each other, a perfect exchange of shadow and substance'. Turnlung has experienced various deaths in his lifetime—those of the family cat, his grandfather and his lover Selwyn. Edelman, on the other hand, has been protected from the experience of death, it has been sanitised, hidden 'safely within the delusional dream of the dollar-people'; for people with money (like the Edelman family) deaths are 'marvels of cleanliness, concealment, and dispatch'. The two men become friends, and finally lovers, a consummation that figures Edelman's emotional engagement with death. In a parody of the ideal nuclear family Turnlung and Edelman adopt a young buffalo from New York Central Zoo as their 'daughter'; Turnlung dreams of setting her free on the prairie. At the end of the novel, Edelman rejects Turnlung and the old man dies soon after. After his death Edelman can find no trace that Turnlung in fact existed. In the epilogue, Turnlung has returned to New Zealand where he awaits death in the noon sun in a shadowless beach setting that replicates that of a painting, titled 'Noon', with which Edelman had been obsessed. In an act of narrative erasure typical of Frame Edelman and the New York of the novel are revealed in the epilogue to be nothing but imaginary constructs of the mad old poet who has never left New Zealand. The narrative organisation is complex, with Turnlung and Edelman alternating between the role of first-person narrator throughout: Turnlung narrates the prologue (poetry) and epilogue (prose); Edelman Part One, Turnlung Part Two (although the final chapter is narrated by a friend); the two men share the narration of Parts Three and Four, with Turnlung increasingly using poetry.   KWo

'Daughters of the Late Colonel, The', a short story by Katherine ★Mansfield, originally entitled 'Non-Compounders', was written 1920, first published in the *London Mercury* (1921) and subsequently in the collection *The Garden Party and Other Stories* (1922). The MS is held by the Newberry Library, Chicago. The story, structured in twelve sections, recounts the reflections of two middle-aged London spinsters, Josephine (Jug) and Constantia (Con) Pinner, a week after the death of their belligerent father, Colonel Pinner. The picture that emerges from a tapestry of daydream, fantasy, conjecture and recall reveals their lives to them for almost the first time. Characteristically, just as they begin to understand that they have been shaped by their circumstances, and that there may be future alternatives, they retreat into familiar ways of thinking and behaving. The denouement in section XII is one of the best-known in Mansfield's fiction, with the sun used metaphorically to illuminate familiar objects in the drawing-room before being obscured by a cloud. The story ends: 'Josephine was silent for a moment. She stared at a big cloud where the sun had been. Then she replied shortly, "I've forgotten too."'

This complex, finely crafted story is one of Mansfield's best, demonstrating many of the features of her mature technique. The form, moulded from the characters' interior monologue, *becomes* the story, with the congruence between the sisters' separate realisation that each may change their lives contributing to the pathos of the denouement. Characteristically there is no discernible narrator, and the free flow of the sisters' conjecture, fantasy, memory and deduction creates a fluid sense of time. The 'femme seule' theme and the theme of the effect of death upon the living connect the story with 'Six Years After', 'Psychology', 'The *Stranger', *'Miss Brill', 'The Lady's Maid' and 'The *Life of Ma Parker'. The story attracted little attention when first published, though from 1936 critics have concurred with David Daiches' assessment of it as a 'landmark in the history of the English short story', and it is very often included in British short story anthologies. SSa

DAVIDSON, William (1864–1916), published *Stories of New Zealand Life* in 1889. Described by himself as 'short stories of early gold-digging times', the ten tales are in fact more generalised and set in a range of locations around the South Island. Stories like 'The Beer Barrel Frolic', 'The Oyster Supper' and 'The New Chum's First Flight' recount the exploits of young Otago men making their way in colonial New Zealand. The collection's tone of hearty adventure undercuts Davidson's elevated desire to 'draw attention to a land which nature has endowed so lavishly with fair gifts, and which must come to be, in the not far distant future, a land of enlightenment and culture'. Similarly, the book's green paper covers, lavishly illustrated with advertisements, do little to enhance its stature as literature. Thus the hope Davidson expresses in his introduction, that this 'tiny craft' might return 'to port with hull undamaged' and thus 'encourage her owner to further tempt the main in search of unknown treasure', appears to have been dashed, perhaps on this prefatory reef of extended metaphor. PM

DAVIN, D.M. (Daniel Marcus) (1913–90), was born in Invercargill, fourth of six children of working-class Catholics of Irish (Galway) extraction. His father worked as a labourer, and subsequently guard, on the railways. Dan spent his early childhood in Gore, where he witnessed the flooding of the Mataura River, discovered solitude—in which he taught himself to read—and had his first formative experiences of Catholic school and Sunday church. The family returned to Invercargill, where he attended the Marist Brothers' School until 1929, then won a scholarship to Sacred Heart College in Auckland. He found himself in a class of clever boys that

included Michael *Joseph, who became a lifelong friend. Davin excelled and escaped through work from boarding school restrictions that were painful after his free life in Southland. After one year of sixth form he won a national scholarship to Otago University, where he studied history, English, French and Latin.

Soon he met Winnie Gonley (later Winifred *Davin), four years his senior, already in her MA year in English literature. Under her influence, and with his own strong work habits, Davin immersed himself in literary and linguistic study, reading widely. He adopted a bohemian style, read the 1890s poets of decadence, taught himself German, and devoured the radical fiction of the age: Dostoevsky, George Moore, Proust, D.H. *Lawrence, Aldous Huxley, *Mansfield and Joyce. His first published work appeared in the student newspaper *The Critic* and the *Otago University Review*. He took a first class MA in English (1934), and another in Latin (1935). At his second attempt (his bohemian life having caught him up in scandal the first time) he won a Rhodes Scholarship to Balliol College, Oxford, from 1936, where he read Greats (classics and philosophy).

Here he established a close friendship with Gordon Craig, later a renowned scholar of German history, and crystallised his intention to be a writer. He began a novel, provisionally titled 'The Mills of God', and wrote short stories, never published. He travelled to Galway, where he was appalled by the poverty, and to Venice. With Winnie, who joined him in 1937, he visited Ireland, Italy, Germany and France. Paris became their preferred city, the bohemian ambience of Montparnasse appealing to Davin's self-image of the literary outsider. He graduated with first class honours at Oxford in June 1939, and a month later he and Winnie were married.

At the outbreak of war he joined the British infantry, being assigned to the Royal Warwickshire Regiment, but after OCTU transferred in July 1940 to the New Zealand Division, at Mytchett, Surrey. He was writing as much as military service allowed, and began to keep a diary. His novel, retitled *Cliffs of Fall*, was finished and he began another about Parisian bohemian life. He went with the division to Greece in the spring of 1941, saw action on Mount Olympus, and took part in the withdrawal (when he lost his unfinished manuscript) and evacuation to Crete. Here he was appointed 23 Battalion Intelligence Officer. On the first day of the German airborne invasion, he was wounded in the thigh, groin and hand, and after several days of pain and delay, evacuated by sea to Egypt.

After recuperation he was appointed to Military Intelligence, 8th Army HQ, Cairo, where he made friends who were to remain important: Edgar (later Sir Edgar) Williams, later editor of the British *Dictionary of*

National Biography; Geoffrey (later Sir Geoffrey) ★Cox, eminent New Zealand journalist; Paddy Costello, another brilliant New Zealand linguist of Irish extraction, later a controversial diplomat; and John Willett, after the war a literary journalist with the *Times Literary Supplement*. Outside the community of intelligence work, Davin enjoyed the cosmopolitan side of wartime Cairo, became friends with poets Bernard Spencer and Terence Tiller, and knew writers as diverse as Lawrence Durrell, Olivia Manning and Richard Hughes. He fell in love with a Dane of German origin, Elizabeth Tylecote, by whom he later had a daughter.

In what spare time he had from work and social life he wrote short stories, mainly about his childhood in New Zealand, his student days in Dunedin and Oxford, and the war in the Middle East. Some were published in John Lehmann's *Penguin New Writing* (No. 13) and *Life and Letters Today* (Vol. 38, No. 72), and became the core of his first collection, *The ★Gorse Blooms Pale* (1947). In October 1943 he returned to the desert front and took part in the battle of Alamein and the pursuit of Rommel's Afrika Corps, in a forward intelligence unit. He later rejoined the 'Div.' in Italy as GSO 3 (I) to Lt.-Gen. Freyberg, VC, from February to July 1944, a period that included the battle for Cassino, the advance up the Liri Valley, and the fall of Arezzo. Promoted major, he served the last year of the war in the German Control Commission in London, making friends with bohemian writers such as Julian Maclaren-Ross and Dylan Thomas. ★*Cliffs of Fall* (1945) was at last published, and he began work on a war novel.

When the war ended he was invited by Kenneth Sisam (the distinguished New Zealand scholar of medieval literature) to take a job at the ★Oxford University Press. He spent the rest of his working life (1945–78) there, rising from lowly editor to Academic Publisher. He continued writing, expanding his range to include criticism with *An Introduction to English Literature* (1947, with John ★Mulgan) and reviews for the BBC, the fledgling journal ★*Landfall*, the *Review of English Studies* and *TLS*. His war novel ★*For the Rest of Our Lives* (1947), and a novel in which he drew profoundly on his experiences as a boy and young man in Southland, ★*Roads from Home* (1949), drew critical attention, and fostered high expectations. His subsequent novels were a disappointment, however, to himself and to critics. *The Sullen Bell* (1956), *No Remittance* (1959), *Not Here, Not Now* (1970) and *Brides of Price* (1972) nonetheless found an audience in New Zealand. A second volume of short stories, *Breathing Spaces* (1975), collected pieces from the 1950s–60s, many first published in *Landfall*.

Most of his disappointment as a writer of fiction may be attributed to three distracting talents: as historian, as publisher, and as friend. As historian, he contributed the volume *Crete* (1953) to the *Official History of New Zealand in the Second World War* series, a task that absorbed almost all of his energies outside OUP from 1948 to 1953. It remains a model of the genre. Its success drew him into the world of war histories, where his advice was sought for the rest of his life.

As publisher, Davin's work at OUP was recognised throughout the academic world as peerless, helping hundreds of young and established scholars to meet the demands of scholarly publication. As the Press expanded in the 1960s–70s, his role grew, absorbing the time and energy previously devoted to fiction, while what remained went to his family and friends. His home in Oxford with Winnie and their three daughters, and the thatched cottage that he renovated at Dorchester-on-Thame, were places of hospitality for writers and intellectuals from throughout the world, in particular New Zealand. For thirty years from the early 1950s Davin was recognised in Britain as the informal ambassador of New Zealand letters, and his friendships, connections and in particular reviews in the *TLS* did much to bring generations of New Zealand writers to a larger public.

In private he was generous to his many friends, particularly with guidance to younger writers, and his habitual tables at the Victoria Arms, and subsequently the Gardeners' Arms in Oxford, were places of warm companionship and witty conversation. The talent for friendship was illustrated in his volume of memoirs, *Closing Times* (1975), with portraits of Julian Maclaren-Ross, W.R. Rodgers, Louis MacNeice, Enid Starkie, Joyce Cary, Dylan Thomas and Itzik Manger, as well as a revealing introduction. It is widely considered his best book.

In retirement in the 1980s Davin struggled with poor health, in particular depressive illness. He visited New Zealand in 1978, taking part in the Victoria University Seminar on the New Zealand Short Story, in 'conversation' with James ★Bertram. He was often in pain in these last years, but his *Selected Stories* (1981); *Night Attack* (ed., 1982); and *The Salamander and the Fire: Collected War Stories* (1986) show him still thinking about the short story form in interesting ways. His other editions were *New Zealand Short Stories* (1953, in collaboration with Eric ★McCormick and Frank ★Sargeson); *Katherine Mansfield: Selected Stories* (1953); and *English Short Stories of Today* (1958), 2nd edn as *The Killing Bottle* (1988). Bertram's *Dan Davin* (1983) contains some biographical material and a critical appreciation. D.H. Akenson, *Half the World from Home* (1990), argues the case for Davin as historian. The biography is by Keith ★Ovenden, *A Fighting Withdrawal: The Life of Dan Davin, Writer, Soldier, Publisher* (1996).

KO

DAVIN, Winifred (1909–95), was born Winifred Gonley in Otautau, Southland, of Irish Catholic extraction, and attended the University of Otago 1927–31, where she met Dan *Davin. Her first ambition was to be a writer, and she published poems of promise and one short story in the *Otago University Review*, 1932–35. After working as a relieving teacher during the *Depression she travelled to Europe in 1937, living first in Paris and then London, still trying to be a writer. The outbreak of war prevented her taking up an appointment to teach in Prague. She married Davin in Oxford in July 1939, was a social worker in Bristol during the war, and returned to Oxford with her husband when he joined OUP in 1945. A close friend and subsequently literary executor of the British novelist Joyce Cary, she developed many other friendships with writers as diverse as Dylan Thomas, Christopher Hill, Julian Maclaren-Ross and Itzik Manger, who valued her advice and support. For fifty years she was indefatigable as host and confidante of New Zealand writers visiting Oxford, where her home with Dan became synonymous with New Zealand literary and intellectual hospitality. She was tireless in encouraging and promoting New Zealand writers, in particular her husband, whose talent she first nurtured, and who relied on her judgment just as he depended on her loyalty. Her wartime experiences are recorded in her essay 'A Soldier's Wife' in Lauris *Edmond, ed., *Women in Wartime* (1986).   KO

DAVIS, Leigh (1955–), co-edited *AND* magazine with academics Alex Calder and Roger Horrocks 1983–85, thereby announcing the arrival of poststructuralist literary theory and *postmodern literary practice on the New Zealand scene. Davis's book-length sonnet sequence *Willy's Gazette* (1983) was a similar announcement, and shared the informal format of *AND*: A4, typed and photocopied. On the strength of this book Davis received a large entry in the anthology *The New Poets* (ed. Murray *Edmond and Mary Paul, 1987). *Willy's Gazette* contains ninety-five sonnets divided into four parts of unequal length. The sequence bewildered some readers with its postmodern techniques of disjuncture, quotation, rapid-fire allusion and self-reflexivity. For example, a draft version of one sonnet is printed, complete with crossings-out and insertions, and the finished version appears on the next page. Another page offers a photocopied newspaper weather-map, under the title 'Diary of a Country Priest'. In retrospect, however, it is apparent that *Willy's Gazette* applied the new techniques exuberantly but unevenly, as gestures rather than as integrated practice. The sequence remains a personal narrative, well short of postmodern experimental extremes. Willy and related figures (Willis, the hawk, the picaro, the govern-ment man) are clearly based on Davis and his life as a Wellington Treasury official. The occasions of many of the poems remain embedded as substantial narratives—in particular, weekend scenes of boating and fishing. After *AND* Davis withdrew from literary activity into merchant banking: he is presently a director of Fay Richwhite. Success in such a career is probably unique for a New Zealand poet, and might be contrasted with R.A.K. *Mason's famous sacrifice of poetry to his work as a union activist.   KJ

DAVIS, Michael (1931–), wrote two popular 1960s novels. *Mutton on the Menu* (1962), a best-seller, is a *Crump-era story of the hazards of sheep farming, authentic and droll in its scenes of shearing, thistle-cutting, lambing, dog trials, hunting and the incursions of irrepressible Māori neighbours. *The Watersiders* (1964) is unusual in New Zealand, a novel set wholly in the industrial workplace and concerned with working rather than private or rural lives. The narrator is a young advertising executive working on the Napier ('Buchanan') wharves, as Davis himself did for two years. The account of wharfies' various tasks in that pre-container period challenges the widely held prejudice that they were merely indolent pilferers, and does so with humanity, wit and realistic insight into the different discomforts associated with cargoes of cement (dust), steel (rust and dangerous weight), apples (gas), meat (cold), sulphur (eye-damage and fire), and others, all involving hard labour in the moving confines of a ship's hold. The complexities of male group dynamics are conveyed with equal realism, and refreshingly undogmatically. It is especially good on 'that baffling enigma, the New Zealand labourer's relationship with his employer', with its subtly coded mix of egalitarianism and antagonism. The book's strength is less in action or ideas, however, than its lively conversational narration and convincing vernacular dialogue, skills which show Davis's experience in radio. Born in Ceylon of British parents and educated in England and Scotland, he joined the merchant navy and then worked variously and itinerantly until becoming a radio copywriter and advertising manager in New Zealand and settling in Napier. He broadcast short stories, and wrote lyrics and ballads for New Zealand music groups, several being recorded. One recorded by 'The Corvettes' acts as epigraph to *The Watersiders*.   RR

DAWSON, Lindsey (1945–), is a novelist, editor and journalist. Born Lindsey Buddle in Auckland, she began her career as a screen-printer, moved to radio in 1979 as a founding staff member of Radio Pacific, and in 1980 turned to full-time freelance journalism. She became founding editor of *More* magazine and editor-in-chief of *Home & Building* and *Your Home*. Her novel *Angel Baby* (1995) was written to amuse and entertain a world she perceived to be losing its capacity for awe, wonder and delight, and was described by Fay *Weldon as 'a bright new book for a bright New Age'. Her non-fiction title is *The 'Next' Book of Home Decorating for New Zealand* (1995), and early autobiographical material appears in her essay in *My Father and Me* (ed. Penelope Hansen, 1992).   KI

DE GOLDI, Kate, see **FLANNERY, Kate**.

DE GROEN, Alma (1941–), is a New Zealand–born playwright who has lived and worked since 1964 mainly in *Australia. Her award-winning *The Rivers of China* (1987, published 1988) dramatises the last months of Katherine *Mansfield at Gurdjieff's Institute, interweaving this theme of the dying woman artist with a 1980s dystopia of women dominating by 'the Medusa Look', a mental power that overcomes male physical superiority. Images of the diseased or dismembered body and the search for true identity run through both strands, which are eventually linked by Mansfield's works and phrases. Tightly written and often disturbing, the play was produced at Wellington's Downstage during the *Mansfield Centenary in 1988. De Groen's plays, most of which are published by Currency Press, Sydney, habitually challenge the assumptions of gender and focus on women. She has also written successfully for film, television and radio.   RR

DE HAMEL, Joan (1924–), a pioneering writer of children's fiction, was born in London, educated there and in Switzerland and Oxford, and taught French in London before arriving in New Zealand in 1955. From 1950, she wrote for magazines, radio and TV in England and New Zealand. A mother of five, she began writing longer work for children, treating traumatic personal experiences with unusual power. *X Marks the Spot* (1973), set in the Southern Alps, shows Peter, Lou and Ross confronting their survival, self-perceptions and danger from fanatics hunting kākapo for illicit export. *Take the Long Path* (1978), winner of the Esther Glen Award 1979, is among the first novels to explore dilemmas such as David's when he discovers he has a Māori heritage. His anguish is reflected in the plight of yellow-eyed penguins on the Otago Peninsula. Resolution comes from the fulfilment of a family oha at the behest of his previously unknown Māori grandfather's spirit. *The Third Eye* (1989) reintroduces Peter, Lou and Ross, confronting the old dilemma of whether the ends justify the means, here the destruction of a tuatara colony in

return for scientific knowledge that might save mankind from nuclear fallout. The preservation of the tuatara also parallels the preservation of Māori culture from commercialised tourism. *Hideaway* (1992) returns successfully to the adventure genre, and a picture book, *Hemi's Pet* (1989), portrays a warm relationship between a boy and his little sister, which rests, however, upon her being entered as his 'pet' among other children's animals in a school Pet Parade. De Hamel previously taught French at Dunedin Teachers' College, won the A.H. Reed Memorial Prize in 1985, and now combines writing with outdoor interests, including breeding goats and donkeys.   DH

DE JONG, Daphne, see **CLAIR, Daphne**.

DE MAUNY, Erik, *The Huntsman in His Career* (novel, 1949), see **Existentialism**.

DE MONTALK, Geoffrey (Wladislas Vaile Potocki) (1903–97), a colourful figure on the fringe of pre-war literature, is the only New Zealand writer to date to have laid claim to a European throne. Born in Auckland, the descendant of a Franco-Polish immigrant who was an important teacher of languages in schools and the fledgling university colleges, de Montalk himself showed great intellectual promise but never completed his degree. In the mid-1920s, as a passionately committed poet with a high view of his merits, he became acquainted with A.R.D. *Fairburn and R.A.K. *Mason, encouraging Fairburn's early verse, which had much in common with his own. Their correspondence, 1926–30, now in the *Alexander Turnbull Library, is a valuable record of the literary aspirations of that period, especially the establishnment of a poetic 'New Zealand movement'. The flamboyant de Montalk then formed higher aspirations, travelling to England in 1927 and claiming the throne of Poland (as 'Wladislaw V') and a string of related titles. He also sought recognition as a major poet. Neither claim was fulfilled, despite his extravagant brilliance and promotional skills. He did win support from major writers in 1932, when Eliot, Yeats, Forster, Virginia and Leonard Woolf and others joined protests against his imprisonment for publishing an obscene libel, a bawdy *jeu d'esprit* on the occasion of Fairburn's wedding.

Another period of internment followed during World War 2 on account of his Fascist views, to which his literary energies had increasingly been devoted during the 1930s, especially as editor of the *Right Review*. After the war his residence shifted between England, France and Switzerland, while he unremittingly wrote small books of verse, translations and contentious pamphlets. He deserves acknowledgment at least as one of the first to challenge the orthodoxy about the massacre of the Polish officer corps at Katyn and to lay the blame on Stalin's Soviet Russia instead of Nazi Germany. He also gained some recognition, ironically in the small world of the small presses, for the high quality of his *typography. He made his first return to New Zealand for over fifty years in 1983–84 and from then on alternated his domicile between the two hemispheres. WB

DE ROO, Anne (1931–), writes contemporary and historical children's fiction. Born in Gore, she was educated in Christchurch, New Plymouth and at the University of Canterbury, training as a librarian before going to England, where she worked mainly as a governess and gardener. She also began the first of numerous novels, which often portray sensitive, lonely child protagonists searching for self-identity and self-respect through association with animals. *The Gold Dog* and *Moa Valley* (both 1969) are adventure stories set in Central Otago and the Southern Alps. With a setting in the far north, *Boy and the Sea Beast* (1971) features a Māori boy and a clash of cultural values, relieved by humorous incidents concerning, mainly, his grandmothers. *Cinnamon and Nutmeg* (1972) presents the farming world of Taranaki, as does its sequel, *Mick's Country Cousins* (1974), which, after Mona *Tracy, is the first junior novel to explore dilemmas facing a protagonist of mixed blood. *Scrub Fire* (1977) traces the grim survival of three children lost in mountain country after adults ignorantly cause a bush fire.

De Roo then turned to historical novels. *Traveller* (1979) lovingly explores the just-possible fate of an immigrant boy and Mackenzie's famous dog in South Canterbury in the 1850s. *Because of Rosie* (1980), also featuring children's survival, develops cultural understandings in the Manawatu. After winning the 1983 Choysa Bursary, de Roo produced *Jacky Nobody* (1983), again about a boy of mixed ethnic heritage. Admirable for its exploration and understanding of Māori–Pākehā dilemmas in the 1840 New Zealand *Wars in the Bay of Islands (including the Treaty of Waitangi and Hone Heke), it won the 1984 Children's Book of the Year Award. *The Bats' Nest* (1986) is a fitting concluding sequel, though minor characters also reappear in *Sergeant Sal* (1991), which features a feisty heroine. *Friend Troll, Friend Taniwha* (1985), illustrated by Robert Jahnke, lightheartedly develops intercultural friendship during the wanderings of two fabled creatures. Anne de Roo lives in Palmerston North where she writes mainly short stories for her Church Mouse Press. DH

DEAMER, Dulcie (1890–1972), was born in Christchurch, where she was on the stage at the age of 9. In 1902 her family moved to Featherston, where her father was the local doctor. She attended ballet and elocution lessons in Wellington, at the time when Katherine *Mansfield was living there, which stood her in good stead in her professional acting career. In 1906 she won a short story competition in the Australian *Lone Hand*, the journal most open, after the Sydney *Bulletin*, to aspiring New Zealand writers. The story was one of several she set in the Stone Age, with a Strong Man carrying off a Red-Haired Woman after knocking her senseless. However, he cannot subdue her spirit and when she saves his life from a wild beast he comes to learn her worth. Clearly there is a touch of feminism about this 16-year-old authoress. There was also something of a sensualist about her, to her family's distress, and this aspect was taken up by Norman Lindsay, when he illustrated her stories in 1929, his pictures adding to her already considerable reputation as a defier of convention. In 1907, at the age of 17, she married a 32-year-old Australian actor, Arthur Goldberg, who adopted the name 'Goldie', and they spent some years touring the Far East before settling in Sydney. Dulcie bore six children and travelled extensively. In 1922 she left her husband and her children and lived in King's Cross as a freelance writer, often using pseudonyms.

Under her own name she published a book of short stories (*In the Beginning*, 1909, partly reprinted in 1929 as *It Was in the Beginning*) and four novels: *The Suttee of Safa: a Hindoo Romance* (1913), *Revelation* (1921), *The Street of the Gazelle* (1922) and *The Devil's Saint* (1924). During the 1930s she also wrote plays for the Sydney theatre, and there is an unpublished autobiography in the Mitchell Library, Sydney. The short stories are set in a geographically unlocated Stone Age or in Babylon and the 1909 volume also includes a short novel ('commenced at the age of 13 and finished at 16') called 'A Daughter of the Incas', which takes part of its theme from Prescott and the idea of burial alive from Poe. *The Suttee of Safa* is set at Akbar's Muslim court, which renders the topos of 'suttee' culturally inappropriate, but provides lots of opportunities for intrigues and sensuality in the harem. *Revelation* is the story of a Roman slave-girl poisoned by a rival but brought back to life by Jesus and suggests at its end the persecution of early Christians. *The Street of the Gazelle*, in which John the Baptist is heard preaching of the coming Messiah, tells of love among slaves, frustrated at every turn by the indifferent masters and by a rebellion against Roman rule, but concludes with a trip to the Elysian fields and Hades, where the lovers hear the sufferers calling, 'The Deliverer has come and his name is Love.' *The Devil's*

Saint is set in some unidentified Middle Age place where Sidonia, the lovely heroine, is pursued as a witch. Her ragged clothes have a tendency to fall from her and she is saved from embarrassment and worse by Gervais, a noble young man recently back from the Crusades. His father, the Count, is revealed as the Master of satanist worship.

Perhaps it is her failure to write of local themes that has led to Deamer being ignored by New Zealand readers, but the established Australian claim on her seems no stronger, even though she was a striking figure in the artistic life of Sydney. In 1925 she was crowned 'Queen of Bohemia' in Theo's Club, a King's Cross pub, and was notorious for acting out her Stone Age theme by wearing a leopard skin in public.   NW

Death of the Body, The (1986), is perhaps C.K. *Stead's most extreme example of metafiction, that branch of the novelistic tradition in which the narrative process is drawn to the reader's attention. The novel followed the successful *All Visitors Ashore* (1984), in which a playful, sophisticated narrative voice told a story that seemed to be based on Stead's own life in the 1950s. Where *All Visitors Ashore* set up a tantalising relationship between personal material and fiction, *The Death of the Body* offers a more blatant, structural self-consciousness. The novel moves back and forth between scenes in the story of Harry Butler, professor of philosophy at the University of Auckland, and the narrator character, struggling to write Harry's story during a prolonged stay in Europe. Harry endures marital difficulties and enjoys a risky love affair with one of his students, while becoming embroiled in a police drug squad surveillance of his next-door neighbours. An old friend of Harry's, working for the drug dealers, is murdered, thus providing the body of the title. Meanwhile the narrator figure moves from England to Italy to Denmark, seeking the conditions that will allow him to compose the story of Harry in its blue folder. The presence of Uta, the wife of a Scandinavian consul, with her willowy figure and 'pneumatic sweaters', becomes essential to this process of composition. As if this were not narrative complexity enough, the narrator frequently imagines Harry's story as a movie being filmed (Stead's next novel, *Sister Hollywood* (1989) extended this exploration of filmic fiction). Stead seems to have erected this elaborate narrative apparatus in order to handle the novel's politically sensitive material from a distance. Harry's persecution for his sexual misdemeanours by the booted, corpulent lesbians of the Philosophy Department Women's Collective evidently reflects Stead's outrage at the attack on Mervyn *Thompson, the dramatist and lecturer, who was tied to a tree by masked women in February 1984.   KJ

Depression, The, or the Great Depression, of the 1930s affected New Zealand writers and writing in various ways. The orthodox view, stated by Robin *Hyde, Eric *McCormick, Allen *Curnow and Robert *Chapman, among others, has been, as McCormick put it in *Letters and Art in New Zealand* in 1940, that the Depression 'effected a re-orientation of outlook of major importance to New Zealand's literature', or, as Hyde put it in 'Singers of Loneliness' in 1937, it 'had a stimulating effect on the thought and culture of rebellious young minds, in a silent country which at last learned to be articulate.' These writers saw a causal relation between the Depression and the outburst of imaginative literature that started with *Phoenix* in 1932 and gained force through the next decade. Revisionist historians have questioned that view, and some of their arguments must be granted: that the literary outburst had its roots in the 1920s, before the Depression, and reached its peak after it had ended, in the early 1940s; that there was little overtly political in the response to the Depression in New Zealand writing compared to what appeared in British, Australian and American literature; and that the imaginative writing of the 1930s came primarily from disaffected members of the middle class, appealed to only a small and predominantly middle-class audience, and had little effect on the popular sense of the Depression. Nonetheless, the Great Depression did have a significant effect: it influenced writers' attitudes towards their society, it gave them subject matter, and it affected their lifestyles and positions in society as writers.

M.H. *Holcroft recounted in 'Return to New Zealand' (1942) that the Depression forced him to ask 'what had gone wrong in *"God's own country"?' Other writers felt similarly. If they had viewed their society critically before the Depression, events now encouraged that tendency. As John *Mulgan said in *Report on Experience* (1945), New Zealanders 'had lived as a community in a fair state of material happiness and unconcern, and the insubstantial nature of this living came home to us'. Writers were mostly not radicalised into Marxist views, but they were made more sharply aware of the gap between the society's dream of being a 'Just City' and its imperfect social actuality.

Faced with the strains and sufferings of the Depression, writers of the 1930s felt compelled to depict them immediately, and writers of the next generations to do so retrospectively. Many dealt with the dramatic riots of 1932, which became a vivid symbol that something was wrong in 'God's Own Country'. The most famous contemporary accounts were by Hyde in *Nor the Years Condemn* (1938) and Mulgan in *Man Alone* (1939), while Jim Edwards's *Break Down These Bars* (1951) is a retrospective account by one of the leading participants, told to David *Ballantyne. Retrospective child's-eye accounts were provided by Bruce *Mason in *The *End of the Golden Weather* (1962), Amelia *Batistich in *Another Mountain, Another Song* (1981) and Heather *Marshall in *Second-Hand Children* (1984). Historical views were provided by writers of the next generation, too young to have been eyewitnesses: Maurice *Shadbolt in *Strangers and Journeys* (1972), Jack McClenaghan in *Travelling Man* (1976), Maurice *Gee in *Games of Choice* (1976) and Mervyn *Thompson in *Songs to Uncle Scrim* (1983). Writers also dealt with the less dramatic everyday effects of the Depression: in poems such as Curnow's 'On Relief' (1937), Denis *Glover's 'These Are the Men' (1934) and 'The *Magpies' (1941), and A.R.D. *Fairburn's *Dominion* (1938); in stories such as Frank *Sargeson's 'A Man and His Wife' (1940) and *'That Summer' (1943–44), G.R. *Gilbert's 'A Girl with Ambition' (1942) and Phillip *Wilson's 'A Change of Heart' (1951); in novels such as Nelle *Scanlan's *Kelly Pencarrow* (1939), Ballantyne's *The *Cunninghams* (1948), Dan *Davin's *Roads from Home* (1949), Noel *Hilliard's *Power of Joy* (1961) and, more historically, Gee's *Plumb* (1978) and *Meg* (1981). There are also many personal accounts: incidentally, in such wide-ranging autobiographies as Helen Wilson's *My First Eighty Years* (1950), Sargeson's three volumes (1973–76), Janet *Frame's *To the Is-Land* (1982), Holcroft's *Way of a Writer* (1984) and Ruth *Park's *A Fence Around the Cuckoo* (1992); more centrally in such Depression narratives as Mary *Findlay's *Tooth and Nail: The Story of a Daughter of the Depression* (1974), Elsie *Locke's *A Student at the Gates* (1981) and the collection of accounts in Tony Simpson's *The Sugarbag Years* (1974).

The widespread unemployment, as Holcroft commented in 1942, gave writers 'time to look about them at a world they had taken too much for granted', while Sargeson told Ian Reid in 1968 that it provided him 'with an excellent excuse for being out of regular work' and getting on with his writing: 'Insofar as I show myself a tolerable literary artist, it was the Slump that made it possible.' Similarly, Roderick *Finlayson told Reid that the Depression was his 'salvation' in that it freed him from uncongenial work and also showed him that the Māori way of life was 'more enduring' than the Pākehā way, which crumbled under Depression stresses. While the Depression was not the sole cause of the literary revolution of the 1930s, it had profound effects on writers and writing, and still retains the status almost of a mythic era.   LJ

Detective fiction and thrillers have been produced by numerous New Zealand writers since the late nineteenth century, though boundaries between crime or detection fiction, mysteries and thrillers are not clearcut. As with *romance, an even more successful category of popular fiction in New Zealand, the key to professional success lies in an international readership and acceptance by the international publishing industry. Fergus *Hume (1859–1932), a barrister who lived in New Zealand 1863–85, provides the earliest illustration of such market forces. After the appearance of his first, influential detective novel, *The Mystery of a Hansom Cab*, set in Melbourne and published there in 1886, he moved to London, where he produced no fewer than 140 novels.

While Australia's vigorous crime literature derived from convict origins and bushranging, New Zealand had no such significant distinctive tradition. Instead there were forays into 'melodramatic romance' by such authors as B.L. *Farjeon, Vincent *Pyke, Lady Campbell and J.H. Kirby, books replete with murder and mayhem, closely imitative of the Victorian sensation novel. However, some writers produced a distinctive variant of the popular colonial genre of the ghost story by drawing on the apparently mysterious 'otherness' of Māori culture in such concepts as *tapu (see R.H. *Horne for an early example). As late as the 1950s–60s Dulce *Carman, in what her British publishers advertised as 'romances of Maoriland', regularly exploited stereotypes associated with this 'otherness' of character, belief and custom.

In the 1930s–40s emerged New Zealand's first internationally renowned writers of detective fiction and the romantic mystery: Ngaio *Marsh and Dorothy *Eden. Both came from the heartland of New Zealand's high culture, Canterbury, but had to make accommodations to the international market. Marsh divided her life between New Zealand and England, Eden expatriated herself permanently to London in the 1950s. Their work also reflected the specialisation that from the 1930s was increasingly a requirement of the popular fiction market. Marsh's whodunnit murder mysteries derived from the classic British tradition of Conan Doyle's Sherlock Holmes stories, but were never simply imitative, subtly differing from contemporaries such as Agatha Christie, Margery Allingham and Dorothy Sayers in their realistic character development, integration of setting and plot, the comparative normality of her detective-protagonist, Roderick Alleyn, and the social hypocrisies of the upper middle-class worlds in which her novels are largely set. These qualities are especially apparent in her New Zealand detective novels and short stories, which incorporate themes of New Zealand character, identity and race relations. Eden's romantic mysteries, with their often exotic settings (including New Zealand), are purer products of their genre. They skilfully manipulate suspense, paranoia and Gothic conventions (haunted house, plausible villains with a mysterious past, eerie events) to destabilise her heroines' (and her readers') sense of normality, and plunge them into a world of menace, violence and victimisation, often sexual in nature, from which escape always seems fortuitous.

Marsh's example was influential, though none of her New Zealand successors achieved the same international breakthrough. Elizabeth Messenger, in nine novels published 1957–65, was the first to adapt the detective thriller wholly to New Zealand settings, locating her books initially in Marlborough and Nelson, then moving to tourist settings (Taupo, the Bay of Islands, Queenstown) in an effort to internationalise her readership. Mary *Scott, mainly known for light *backblocks romances, collaborated with Joyce *West in New Zealand–based whodunnits in the 1960s, using plausible plots, settings, motivations and solutions in an approach closely related to Marsh's. In the later 1950s George *Joseph was the first to succeed in the American market, publishing in the 'Bloodhound' series; and Simon Jay (Colin Alexander) wrote two lively novels in the 1960s featuring a pathologist-detective.

However, the pattern of promising beginnings which peter out in frustration is still apparent. Terence Journet was one such author, in the 1960s–70s, and in the 1980s Wellington-based Laurie Mantell published half a dozen thrillers with Marsh's British publisher, Collins, which convincingly depict the social contexts of crime in New Zealand (especially, violence against women) and feature the first Māori detective-hero, Steven Arrow. In the 1990s Picton-based Carol Dawber wrote three whodunnits in the Marsh tradition, and Marsh herself was parodied in Stevan *Eldred-Grigg's satirical Blue Blood (1997). The liveliest satirist of the whodunnit formulas, however, was Gaelyn *Gordon, in three richly comic, sophisticated parodies in the 1990s, featuring a laid-back Māori detective, Rangi Roberts, with effective satire of small town New Zealand and literary academia.

The literary provenance of Marsh and her New Zealand successors was largely British. The masculinist, post-Chandler American thriller tradition—with its hardbitten detectives, private eyes and journalists, emphasis on violent action, and extension into the international arena of espionage, corporate crime, drug-dealing and shady arms deals—began in New Zealand in the 1970s, with Journet for instance, though Frank *Bruno in the 1960s had drawn on elements in historical New Zealand novels notable for their sensationalised violence and brutality. New Zealand's most successful exponent of the American-style thriller is Colin *Peel. An admirer of Hemingway and Steinbeck, by 1997 Peel had published twenty novels on themes including the 1970s oil crisis, espionage, drug dealing, the arms and space races, terrorism and French nuclear testing in the *Pacific.

In the mid-1990s three sophisticated Auckland-based thrillers came from Paul *Thomas in the American mode of fast, complexly plotted, inventively gruesome comic action, and featuring yet another Māori detective, Tito Ihaka. Thomas's Auckland of high-flying tycoons, drug and sleaze merchants, media rednecks and bimbos, all driven by wealth, power and ego, appeals to a male fantasy of urban sophistication, a hard-edged version of the upmarket world promoted in contemporary *Mills & Boon romance.

These authors sought a popular readership with novels conceived primarily as entertainments. As with romance, the conventions have also been exploited by serious New Zealand writers. Maurice *Gee's *In My Father's Den and *Crime Story draw consciously on American detective fiction to explore the nature of violence in New Zealand society. A drugs-related murder provides an underplot to C.K. *Stead's philosophical concerns in *Death of the Body. The criminal as heroic anti-social outcast provides a motif in many *'Man Alone' fictions. Marilyn *Duckworth draws on the Gothic and suspense conventions associated with mystery thrillers to evoke paranoid and claustrophic states of mind in novels like Rest for the Wicked and Married Alive, as does Russell *Haley, for political purposes, in The Settlement. In these and numerous others, the conventions are consciously formal devices which explicitly signal, and thereby question and destabilise, the social assumptions and expectations underlying their function as entertainment in popular culture.   TS

DEVANNY, Jean (1894–1962), was born Jane Crook in Ferntown, a mining community near Collingwood, in Golden Bay. Her writing is loosely related to that of D.H. *Lawrence, and her parents, like Lawrence's, were a miner and a woman of middle-class origins (in Devanny's case the daughter of an Indian Army colonel). This class blend can be seen in the way Devanny's assertive Communism is unusually combined with 'a woman's accomplishments' such as piano-playing. Similarly, she was both a 'women's liberationist' and a devoted mother. At 17, in 1911, she married Hal Devanny, a radical union organiser. They had three children, one of whom died in infancy. In Ferntown, the couple were a part of the Marxist-Socialist movement, which was strong in study groups among West Coast miners. They met such founding members of the Socialist and Social-Democrat Parties as Paddy Webb, Pat Hickey, Harry *Holland and Bob Semple.

In 1920–22 Jean and Hal lived in Fairfield, a mining community near Dunedin, and in 1922 they moved to Wellington, where Hal joined Semple's tunnelling project through the Orongorongos. From his excellent pay they were able to buy a boarding house.

During this period Devanny wrote short stories which appeared in British and New Zealand magazines, and *Lenore Divine* (1926) is a novel with fascinating images of the twenties in Wellington. Lenore leaves her alcoholic husband for a Māori, Kowhatu Ngatoro, making this one of the first New Zealand novels of interracial marriages in which a Pākehā woman loves a Māori man rather than the reverse.

In the same year *The *Butcher Shop* was published in London. It gained instant notoriety, being banned in New Zealand, Australia, Boston and *Germany (see *Censorship). The German translation was entitled *Die Herrin*, emphasising the dominance of the woman, and Devanny herself pointed out that 'with Hitler's policy of women belonging to kitchen, church and child, to Doll's Houses etc., there was no question of a woman owning her own body either within or outside marriage'. (In fact *Die Herrin* was published in 1928, five years before the Nazis seized power.) This not only points to what Devanny thought to be a major theme of the book, but leads one to speculate on the coincidence of German and New Zealand opinion. According to the Christchurch *Sun*, the official New Zealand reason for banning it was that 'its frank portrayal of farm conditions was considered detrimental to the Dominion's immigration policy'. Since the book continued to be sold abroad—not surprisingly it sold very well—the means can hardly have been appropriate to the end.

Devanny published two more books (and seems to have written even more) before she left New Zealand. One was *Old Savage and Other Stories* (1927), a collection of passionate stories of love and of interracial relationships; the other was *Dawn Beloved* (1928). Dawn has talents that carry her far beyond the world of her mother ('… the typical New Zealand backblocks woman. Strong, inured to toil, innately religious without ever speaking of it, and attentive to the physical needs of her children without ever thinking that they might have other than physical needs'), but when she marries a miner she finds herself on the path to poverty: 'She had no clear idea of poverty. She had thought of it as a thing unknown in New Zealand.' She studies Socialism, becomes a public speaker, has an affair with a Socialist leader who is ruined by alcoholism, and finally remarries, looking forward to a more promising future.

In 1929 Devanny and her husband moved to Sydney, and in the same year *Riven* was published—the story of a woman whose love of a painter finally carries her to England. Two more novels, with New Zealand settings, followed in 1930. *Bushman Burke* (whose Australian title is *Taipo*), like many of Devanny's books, expresses a powerful attraction to New Zealand *landscapes, while despairing of its society. Burke, or Taipo, 'loved Wellington for its rugged and rough-hewn picturesqueness; perhaps the clean, solid strain in him, the strain that kept him to the practice of athletics, reacted to the cleanliness of the wind's rough play … and so the sublimity and haunting beauty of the city nestling on the finest harbour in the world claimed his allegiance.' He is impressed by Flo with her Wadestown sophistication, and marries her, but returns to the West Coast when the marriage becomes unhappy. Flo follows him to the *bush and comes to love it there, so that Taipo falls in love with her again. *Devil Made Saint* tells of a woman who dominates her sensitive husband, hating his music, but comes to love music when he is dead. Her daughter Adelaide (also the name of Beethoven's beloved) falls in love with Carl, who resembles Beethoven and whose mother is from Vienna. In a curious sequence of events, Carl turns to Adelaide's mother and composes the Song of Solomon; the older woman dies in his embrace.

During the 1930s, Devanny and her husband and children devoted their lives to the Communist Party of Australia (CPA). The *Depression made their material situation precarious. Jean worked as a domestic, in a birth-control clinic, as a journalist for *Workers' Weekly* (Hal was editor) and spent a period as a cook on a station in north-west Queensland. In 1931 she travelled to Russia and Berlin, as secretary of the Workers' International Relief Organisation, meeting Communist activists. She was an effective public speaker, described as 'having a tongue like an axe in a wood-chopping contest', and was briefly imprisoned for her political activities.

In 1932 she published the last of her novels set in New Zealand: *Poor Swine*. Its setting and themes are familiar: a West Coast mining town, alcoholism, musical talent, violent sexual relationships, small-town *'puritanism'. Like others, it also has an optimistic ending, in seeming contradiction to the bleak view of social life that predominates. The phase of bourgeois capitalism will give place to a Communist future, where people of all races and both genders will live in equality, and nature and society will be in harmony.

In 1940 Devanny was expelled from the CPA. The reasons are unclear—in her autobiography she speaks of accusations of sexual immorality—but the effect was to make her concentrate more fully on her writing. In the 1930s–40s she wrote several novels with an Australian setting, of which *Sugar Heaven* (1936) is the most notable. It tells of a cane-cutters' strike in Queensland. She also wrote her autobiography which, together with many other manuscripts, remained unpublished at her death. It was edited by Carole Ferrier and published as *Point of Departure* (1986). The account of her childhood in Golden Bay has particular merit, and belongs with New Zealand's strong tradition of narratives of childhood.

In 1944 she rejoined the party, resigned from it in 1950 and rejoined in 1957 after the death of Stalin. She confessed that her greatest intellectual effort was reserved for politics rather than literature: 'I myself might have been a good writer if I had put writing first'.   JS/NW

DICKENS, Charles (1812–70), wrote to his friend John Forster on a winter day, 8 January 1847: 'very mouldy and dull. Hardly able to write.... Disposed to go to New Zealand and start a magazine.' He had just read a review in the *Times* savaging his latest Christmas Book as 'feeble, false, artificial, worthless', thus proving that the impulse to fly overseas at such moments is not confined to New Zealand writers. Unfortunately for New Zealand literature he remained in England and in 1850 started his popular weekly magazine, *Household Words*, succeeded in 1859 by *All the Year Round*. Under his close editorship both included topical articles relating to New Zealand, which are collected in *Charles Dickens and New Zealand: A Colonial Image*, ed. J.S. Ryan, with notes by A.H. *Reed (1965). Negotiations for Dickens to make a lecture tour to Australia (and presumably New Zealand) in 1862 were not concluded, though he had proposed to write 'The Uncommercial Traveller Upside Down'. The most interesting of the New Zealand articles are R.H. *Horne's 'The New Zealand Zauberflote' (1850), 'A *Gold Digger's Notes' (1864) and 'From the Black Rocks, on Friday' (1862). The latter, supposedly the 'truthful record' of 'an English clergyman', is a short memoir, or more probably fiction, that openly draws on Defoe's *Robinson Crusoe*, shipwrecking its narrator in solitude on an island off the New Zealand coast. It is worth reading for its colourful local flora and fauna, its presentation of the narrator's friendships with Māori, and its strong views on the animosity between 'settlers' and 'missionaries'. Reed and Ryan succumb to the idea that Dickens as editor 'was partly responsible for it'; but the plainness and occasional triteness of the writing ('I can hardly describe the cold thrill of horror that tingled through my veins') make it unlikely that Dickens did more than 'hack and hew' it into shape, as he once described his editorial labours.   RR

Dictionaries of English all contain at least a few New Zealand words, though the information provided rarely gives a complete picture of their usage in New Zealand. Thus the first edition of the *Oxford English Dictionary* gives only the primary meaning of 'kiwi', the flightless bird. *Chambers* also notes its use for a New Zealander, and *Webster* adds the (non-NZ) use for 'kiwifruit'. But it is necessary to turn to a dictionary that specifically covers New Zealand usage for all the uses to which New Zealanders put the word.

Not all such words are as easily identified as 'kiwi' or other names of flora and fauna borrowed from Māori. There are also local meanings for words such as 'section', some of which New Zealand shares with Australia. There are also cases where New Zealand usage differs from usage elsewhere, as with 'kiwifruit', formerly called 'Chinese gooseberry', which in Europe and North America is just 'kiwi'. See also *New Zealand English.

Four types of dictionaries are considered: those containing only words and phrases specific to New Zealand; general English dictionaries edited specifically to cover New Zealand words; dictionaries of slang; and dictionaries of Māori.

The first dictionary to attend explicitly to New Zealand words was E.E. Morris's *Austral English* (1898), which also covers Australian English. Nearly a century passed before the next significant publications in this genre, as the scholarship of lexicographer Harry *Orsman began to reach fruition. His *Heinemann New Zealand Dictionary* (1979, revised 1989) and *Macquarie Dictionary* (1981) are general dictionaries including New Zealand (and, in the case of the *Macquarie*, Australian) content. The first significant dictionary devoted to New Zealand words was the *New Zealand Dictionary* (ed. Elizabeth and Harry Orsman, 1994), and the first New Zealand dictionary on full historical principles the *Dictionary of New Zealand English* (ed. H.W. Orsman, *Oxford University Press, 1997). The *magnum opus* of New Zealand lexicography, this provides a unique compendium of literary references, as well as a major resource for writers in all genres.

A number of general English dictionaries with New Zealand content, and sometimes Australian, were produced for schools in the early twentieth century, in some cases in a supplement. Most were derived from Morris, but the supplement to *Reed's School Dictionary* (1947) appears not to be. Two other dictionaries edited with some New Zealand material are the *New Collins Concise English Dictionary, New Zealand Edition* (ed. I.A. *Gordon, 1982) and the *New Zealand Pocket Oxford Dictionary* (ed. R. Burchfield, 1986). A new edition of the *New Zealand Pocket Oxford* is in preparation (ed. Tony Deverson). The *Oxford English Dictionary* (2nd edn, 1989) also contains many New Zealand items, as is appropriate to a volume edited by Burchfield (one of several distinguished expatriate New Zealand lexicographers) and with access to Orsman's work.

The earliest dictionary specialising in slang and colloquial New Zealand English was Sidney J. Baker's *New Zealand Slang: A Dictionary of Colloquialisms* (1941), which is chatty and not alphabetic, while there are many New Zealand items in the *Dictionary of Slang and Unconventional English* (1937), edited by Eric Partridge, another expatriate scholar (8th edn, ed. P. Beale, 1984). Recent works in this genre are *A Personal Kiwi–Yankee Dictionary* by Louis S. Leland (1980, 1990), a *Dictionary of Kiwi Slang* by David McGill (1988) and a miniature Reed *New Zealand Slang Dictionary*. *Historic Place Names of New Zealand* by L.S. Rickard (1968) is an informative introduction to that area of daily usage.

The most important dictionary of the Māori language undoubtedly remains the *Dictionary of the Maori Language* (ed. W., W.L. and H.W. *Williams), published in 1852, and now, with significant revisions, in its 7th edition (1971). It provides translations of traditional Māori words with (untranslated) illustrative quotations from early literature. It also contains a supplement of the commonest borrowings from English. A two-way dictionary, the *Concise Maori Dictionary* (ed. A.W. *Reed) was published in 1948; a revised edition is still available (Reed, 1984, ed. T.S. *Kāretu). Bruce *Biggs's *English–Maori Dictionary* (1966) provides a more substantial word-list from English to Māori. P.M. Ryan's *Dictionary of Modern Māori* (first published 1974, 4th edn 1994, Heinemann) is a two-way dictionary covering both traditional Māori words and new vocabulary. Biggs's *Complete English–Maori Dictionary* (1981) is a reverse word-list based on the Williams dictionary. P.M. Ryan has also edited a more substantial dictionary, *Reed Dictionary of Modern Māori* (1995, 1997). From this, two pocket editions have been produced, one in each direction (*Reed Pocket Dictionary of Modern Māori: English/Māori, Māori/English*). The *Māori Language Commission has published a two-way dictionary of the modern terms it has coined, *Te Matatiki* (1992; 2nd edn, Oxford, 1996). These are all finder lists with little contextual indication given for usage. Rather different from these is the *English–Maori Dictionary* (1993, ed. H.M. Ngata), which provides Māori example sentences for the use of Māori words, all with English translations, and far greater contextualisation of usage. Not least in terms of interest to the general public is *A Dictionary of Maori Place Names* (1961, 2nd edn 1982, 3rd edn as the *Reed Dictionary of Māori Place Names* 1996, ed. A.W. Reed).

WBa

Dictionary of New Zealand Biography, The, as yet uncompleted, is funded by the New Zealand government within the Department of Internal Affairs. The proposal was approved in 1982 and Volume One:

1769–1869 was published in the sesquicentennial year of 1990. The General Editor was W.H. *Oliver, who was succeeded for Volume Two by Claudia Orange.

The *DNZB*'s main precursor is G.H. *Scholefield's *A Dictionary of New Zealand Biography* (1940), which in turn acknowledges antecedents among various *Cyclopedia* and *Who's Who* volumes. By comparison, *DNZB* is far fuller, more authoritative and amply resourced, employing a team of researchers and editors. It is thus able to fulfil an intention 'to provide a broad and various image of New Zealand society' and to recognise 'the condition (and the significance) of the powerless as well as the powerful, the victims as well as the victors'.

Immensely valuable to all areas of knowledge, many of its entries are relevant to New Zealand literature. For instance, it reports the full careers of part-time authors such as C.C. *Bowen or Alfred *Domett. Its scope makes possible the inclusion of many categories of writers, such as historians, journalists and translators. It also includes writers whose texts were private or oral rather than for publication, such as letter-writers, diarists and composers of *waiata.

Further volumes are: Volume Two: *1870–1900* (1993); and Volume Three: *1901–1920* (1996); Volume Four is scheduled for 1998. There is also a separately published series of the Māori biographies from each volume, and an illustrated selection of biographies from Volume One was published as *A People's History*, selected by W.H. Oliver (1992).

RR

DIEFFENBACH, Ernst or **Ernest** (1811–55), wrote *Travels in New Zealand* (London, 1843), probably the most reliable early book on many aspects of the natural environment and particularly of Māori shortly after the Treaty of Waitangi. Born in Giessen, Hesse, his excellent scientific education was combined with humanistic concerns. Of great value in his study of New Zealand, these brought him into political disrepute in the repressive German Empire and he was driven into Swiss exile, and from there migrated to London in 1837. Though barely able to make a living, he acquired an honourable reputation among scientists and was a friend of Charles Darwin.

He joined the New Zealand Company as a naturalist and sailed to Port Nicholson (Wellington) on the *Tory* in 1839, with Edward Jerningham *Wakefield and the painter Charles Heaphy. Dieffenbach travelled in regions of interest to the Company, particularly the Marlborough Sounds, the Wellington region, Taranaki and, most significantly, the volcanic region in central North Island. His ascent of Taranaki is the first recorded. He also visited the Chatham Islands, making a separate report to the Company. Within eighteen months he had assembled large botanical, zoological and geological collections, had learned Māori, investigated Māori ways of life with intelligent sympathy and made extensive notes on large areas of the country. His application to visit other regions, especially in the South Island, was turned down, and in October 1841 he left the country.

Dieffenbach, now skilled in English, wrote and published *Travels in New Zealand* in England. His book's clear, uncluttered style reflects his quietly humane attitude to his remarkably broad subject matter. In the first volume he writes of the climate, the geological structure, the flora and fauna, which he had investigated sufficiently to have his name given to some species of fish and plants and, in keeping with his brief from the Company, of the economic, especially agricultural prospects. This work is meticulous and still of interest, yet his greatest contribution was in the second volume, where he wrote of the native inhabitants. This was pioneering work not only in the study of Māori but in the scientific study of mankind (Dieffenbach was to found the Ethnological Society in London in 1843). It was based on the thought of the philosopher Herder, who had attacked eurocentric views and noted the primacy of language in human cultures. Dieffenbach finds cannibalism and other customs distasteful, but suggests that 'If one were to reckon up the crimes and gratuitous cruelties … which civilized men have committed against the savage, the balance of humanity, and of other virtues too, would probably be found on the side of the latter.' He criticises the greed for land and culturally destructive activities of the missionaries, and was perhaps the first to note the socio-philosophical conflict between the English emphasis on individual achievement and the Māori emphasis on communal living and community values. Māori spiritual attachment to land as expressed in language and myth appealed to him.

However, for all this empathy, he suffered from the prolonged exile from his own country. He returned to Giessen after the revolutions of 1848, taking up a poorly paid academic position, translating Darwin's account of the voyage of the *Beagle* and other scientific works and continuing his own researches.   NW

Disability. The manner in which physical and mental impairment has been represented in New Zealand literature has received scant attention, but is illuminating of both social and artistic attitudes. The best-known novels, short stories and plays, without even considering films and TV soaps, provide enough disabled characters to constitute a creditable AGM for the Assembly of People with Disabilities. Types of impairment range

from amputation (as in Keri *Hulme's story 'Hooks and Feelers') through epilepsy (Janet *Frame's *Owls Do Cry*) and blindness (Bruce *Mason's *Awatea*) to post-traumatic stress disorder (Jack *Lasenby's *Dead Man's Head*) and senile dementia (Margaret *Mahy's *Memory*).

Such characters merit attention not just because they are indubitably in the foreground of much local fiction and drama, but also because of the manner in which they are habitually represented. These depictions tell us little about how people with disabilities actually live, but a great deal about the characteristic mindset of many of our authors. Disabled characters tend to be treated in terms of a restricted number of recurrent archetypes. These owe more to the cultural lenses through which people with disabilities are perceived than the realities of their lived experience.

These archetypal representations come in three broad families: Monsters, Victims and the Afflicted Elect. That is, disabled people are seen as objects of fear and loathing (or at least irritation and contempt), of pity and charity, or of admiration, even veneration. In all cases, they are objects of the able-bodied gaze, not subjects in their own right. They are the eternal Other, never 'one of us'.

Disabled monsters or villains (such as Quasimodo, Frankenstein's creature, Captains Ahab and Hook, Long John Silver and the Phantom of the Opera) abound in world literature, but play only a minor role in its New Zealand branch. A mentally deranged Māori guard in William *Satchell's The *Greenstone Door* provides a conventional melodramatic frisson, the deafness of Maurice *Gee's Plumb evokes the minor moral monstrosity of a philanthropist who behaves inhumanely to his own long-suffering wife and sexually atypical son, and AIDS in the fiction of Peter *Wells, Mike *Johnson and Witi *Ihimaera is a surreal, stalking enemy, whose victims become in their own turn agents of a monstrous pollution. The standard embitterment of mind by the body's affliction is a frequent device in television's *Shortland Street*, but only a minor element in the total oeuvre of disability.

More common in New Zealand is the Victim archetype, where the physically or mentally impaired are offered as objects of pity and charity. The most acerbic of such representations appears in Peter Sinclair's *The Frontman*, where a flock of bewildered crippled children is herded into a Telethon studio as the public whips itself up into a self-congratulatory frenzy on behalf of the disabled. The crippled David in Elizabeth *Knox's *Pomare* is physically and emotionally abused by the neighbourhood kids, Joy *Cowley's Silent One is despised and ostracised by his village, and a child with a disfiguring birthmark is the prey of kite attack at

Hulme's Doctor's Point. Disability associated with old age is also common, notably in Gee's gallery of geriatrics, such as the exuberantly senile Pitt Rimmer rebelling on the rim of the pit of death in 'A Glorious Morning, Comrade'.

Such characters are sometimes further victimised by their author's propensity to offer them up as human sacrifices. Cowley drowns her deaf protagonist, as Gaelyn *Gordon drowns the holy simpleton Pippa in *Last Summer*. Patricia *Grace despatches little, crippled Toko in *Potiki* with a blast of high explosives. Gee clearly intends 'death with dignity' for the quadriplegic Ulla in *Crime Story*. John *Broughton rips the head off a grossly deformed baby in his play *Michael James Manaia*. Albert *Wendt hangs his dwarfed Flying Fox Tagata, while Vincent *O'Sullivan in *Let the River Stand* not only hangs a hearing-impaired character but allows pigs to gnaw his dangling feet. O'Sullivan's range of the disabled also includes the dwarf narrator of 'The Snow in Spain' and the dismembered Stumpy Smith in *Miracle*.

Such victimisation of the afflicted outsider conventionally serves two related literary functions. On the one hand, if a community's ethical tonality can be judged by the way it treats its weakest members, what better means to reveal the moral bankruptcy of society than to expose its oppression of the disabled? On the other hand, respect or affection for 'approved' able-bodied characters (and also for the ethical rectitude of the author) can be generated by revealing their compassion for the afflicted. For example, the young Bruce Mason alone establishes a sympathetic rapport with the mentally handicapped Firpo, the butt of the Takapuna beach in *The *End of the Golden Weather*.

In the case of *Potiki*, the propensity for compassion extends to an entire community: Toko is the vessel into whom is poured the collective virtues of *aroha and manakitanga with which literary Māori Arcadias are frequently endowed. Thus, representing the disabled as victims allows authors simultaneously to excoriate the heartlessness of society while celebrating the virtue of an elect few able to identify with the infirm of mind or body.

However, as though in compensation, disabled characters are frequently accorded special gifts, even a transcendental aura, in a convention that goes back at least to the inspired fools of Shakespeare. Gee's disfigured *Burning Boy possesses an almost superhuman genius for figures. The mystery surrounding the sea births of Toko and of the mute Simon in *the *bone people*, like the bond between the Silent One and his mystical white turtle, confer a whiff of the supernatural upon these characters, as does the communion between Gordon's Pippa and the great Earth Mother. Sometimes grace is accorded in aesthetic terms: Tim's lameness in Maurice *Shadbolt's *Strangers and Journeys* and Ada's muteness in Jane *Campion's The *Piano* are associated with artistic ability, an association that has its apotheosis in Frame's novels, as well as Campion's treatment of mental disorder in An *Angel at My Table*.

The third archetype is perhaps a mere stereotype. Although slightly sub-human, disabled characters are also typically represented as slightly supra-human. Despite (or because of) their afflictions, they transcend the prosaic limitations of the mundane herd. Their very Otherness renders them touchstones of authenticity in an unauthentic world. The Holy Outsider is a romantic cliché. Ribald members of the real disability community prefer the less respectful term 'Supercrip'.

New Zealand writers seem to feel an especial affinity for this version of the disabled condition, perhaps because in it they find a mirror for their own self-image. Whether consciously or not, many New Zealand authors are steeped in the myth of the archer Philoctetes, whose suppurating wound made him odious to his fellow Greeks but whose unique gift rendered him indispensable to them. It is this myth which they often project onto their disabled characters.

One striking point is that the AGM of People with Disabilities proposed above would never be held. Unlike the real disabled community, disabled people in New Zealand literature never associate with one another. Nor do they rub shoulders on equal terms with the able-bodied. They do not hold down regular jobs, raise families, watch television or engage in community activities like other citizens, nor play wheelchair rugby or join self-advocacy groups in association with each other.

The 20 per cent of New Zealanders revealed by the 1996 census to have a long-term disability are not all mystical mavericks. For all the compassion and the compensatory gifts, the one thing writers will not accord their disabled characters is the right to be just ordinary. A rare exception is Lisa *Vasil's novel based on her experience of cerebral palsy, *Just an Ordinary Kid* (1987). For writers to place their disabled people in a humdrum world where disability itself is pretty ordinary would be to lose useful soulmates in the construction of their own preferred persona, that of the spiritually elite outsider.   PB

Distant Homes; *or, The Graham Family in New Zealand* (1862) is a novel by Mrs J.E. (Isabella) *Aylmer.

DODD, Lynley (1941–), is a children's writer known internationally as the creator of Hairy Maclary, canine rogue-hero. Born in Rotorua, educated at the Kaingaroa Forest School, Tauranga GHS, Elam School of Art (Dip

FA) and Auckland Teachers' College, she taught art at Queen Margaret College. She began her career in children's books in collaboration with Eve *Sutton, for whom she illustrated *My Cat Likes to Hide in Boxes* (1973). Several delightful books with her own text and illustrations then appeared: *The Nickle Nackle Tree* (1976), *Titimus Trim* (1979), *The Smallest Turtle* (1982) and *The Apple Tree* (1983). She won the 1978 Choysa Bursary, and the 1981 New Zealand Book Award for her illustrations in Clarice England's *Druscilla* (1980).

Then, in 1983, came the first of six books that would bring Dodd renown: *Hairy Maclary from Donaldson's Dairy*. With their astute evocation of animal behaviour, energetic alliterative verse and lively, cohesively designed illustrations, Dodd's characters and their memorable attendant rhymes have become internationally known: Hairy Maclary, Bitzer Maloney all skinny and bony, Schnitzel von Krumm with a very low tum, Bottomley Potts covered in spots, Muffin McLay like a bundle of hay, Hercules Morse as big as a horse, and, every suburb's fiend, SCARFACE CLAW the toughest Tom in town ('EEEEEOWWWFFTZ!'). The sequels—*Hairy Maclary's Bone* (1984), *Hairy Maclary Scattercat* (1985), *Hairy Maclary's Caterwaul Caper* (1987), *Hairy Maclary's Rumpus at the Vet* (1989) and *Hairy Maclary's Showbusiness* (1991)—were all shortlisted for the Children's Picture Book of the Year Award, which Dodd won outright in 1984, 1986, 1988 and 1992.

Many other titles have also been shortlisted: *Wake Up, Bear* (1986), *A Dragon in a Wagon* (1988), *Slinky Malinki* (1990), *Find Me a Tiger* (1992), *The Minister's Cat ABC* (1992), *Slinky Malinki Open the Door* (1993), *Schnitzel von Krumm's Basketwork* (1994) and *Sniff-Snuff-Snap!* (1995), about a bossy warthog. Now living in Tauranga, Dodd holds a special place in children's literature for her vivid wit in both word and illustration. Hairy Maclary and Slinky Malinky have each featured in stage musical versions by Paul Jarden and Jan Bolton.   DH

'Doll's House, The', a short story by Katherine *Mansfield, was written in October 1921, first published in the *Nation and Athenaeum* (1922) and subsequently in the posthumous collection *The Doves' Nest and Other Stories* (1923). Mansfield used 'At Karori' and 'The Washerwoman's Children' as working titles for the rough draft and the corrected version, which—along with a final typescript—are held at the Newberry Library, Chicago. The story, set in New Zealand, involves some of the Burnell family characters who appear in *Prelude and *'At the Bay', and incorporates others said to be drawn from recognisable people, including the Kelveys. It is structured around various characters' reactions to a doll's house, sent to the Burnell children as a gift. The

central consciousness of the story, against which other characters' speech and thoughts are drawn, is that of Kezia. Her independence contrasts with her siblings, aunt Beryl and friends, presented as spiteful gatekeepers of middle-class privilege. She responds with wonder to a miniature lamp in the house, and ultimately defies family mores by allowing the impoverished, socially outcast Kelvey children (Lil and 'our Else') to look at the toy. The poignant final lines are among the best known in Mansfield's work. They contain the only words our Else speaks and through them the lamp comes to symbolise the potential for transcendence of imposed social values: '"I seen the little lamp," she said, softly. Then both were silent once more.' Rich in implied meaning about human nature and society, the story is characteristic of Mansfield's mature work and its popularity has endured.

SSa

DOMETT, Alfred (1811–87), poet, politician and public servant, was born in London and educated at St John's College, Cambridge, and the Middle Temple. He published a number of poems in *Blackwoods Magazine* before his first collection, *Poems* (1833). Modelled on Shelley, Byron and Wordsworth, the collection is an early statement of a poetic manifesto hardly modified throughout his literary career: 'This brave bright Earth with Mind o'erflows—/ With secret soul o'erfraught; / In every form a Feeling glows, / In every tone a Thought.'

Friends attributed his subsequent travels—to the United States, Canada and Jamaica—to the lack of critical attention this work received. A diary he kept during this period, *The Canadian Journal of Alfred Domett* (edited by E.A. *Horsman) was published in 1955. Time spent in Europe resulted in *Venice* (1839), a kind of elegy on the decline of the city.

From around 1840 he became friends with Robert Browning and Domett is portrayed as the hero of Browning's poem 'Waring', published in *Dramatic Lyrics* (1842), 'a fancy portrait of a dear friend', though in the poem he travels to Moscow rather than New Zealand. Browning also refers to his friendship with Domett in the poems 'Time's Revenges' (1845) and 'The Guardian Angel' (1848). In a letter of 1843 Browning writes to Domett, ''Tis worth while running away to be so wished for again.' The friendship endured throughout Domett's life.

In 1842 Domett emigrated to New Zealand. At first he found settler society wearisome and wrote of 'the lounging, shooting-jacket existence, Mrs Wray's … aesthetic tea, Miss Essex's piano, the brandy and whist-cum-cigar evenings'. But the incident at Wairau in 1843, when twenty-one European settlers were killed by local Māori as a result of survey activities on disputed land, brought him into prominence. He travelled to Auckland to represent the views of the settlers and wrote a lengthy account in the *Nelson Examiner*, which he edited for a brief period.

Throughout the rest of his time in New Zealand he was prominent in national politics and public affairs, rising to Premier from 1862 to 1863. He founded the General Assembly Library—still an important research institution. In 1871 he returned to England.

Ranolf and Amohia: A South-Sea day-dream (1872, revised in 1883 with a different subtitle: *A dream of two lives*) is the work of Domett's retirement. Rather than use his direct experience of New Zealand, he chooses to set the poem in the early European period and, in consequence, is reliant on earlier sources, Augustus ★Earle's *A Narrative of a Nine Months' Residence in New Zealand in 1827* (1832), J.S. ★Polack's *Manners and Customs of the New Zealanders* (1840) and Sir George ★Grey's ★*Polynesian Mythology*. Romanticism rather than anthropology is the work's central influence. Its story—that of an Englishman, Ranolf, and his love for a Māori maiden, Amohia, whom he has rescued from two men tormenting her—is almost entirely obscured by a vast body of philosophical and metaphysical arguments. MacD. P. Jackson has found references to 'Locke, Berkeley, Hume, Brahma, Kapila, Spinoza, Sakya Muni, Kásyapa, Kant, Fichte, Reid, Brown, Schelling, and Hegel', pointing out that, at twenty-five cantos, *Ranolf and Amohia* is longer than *Paradise Lost*.

Domett's vast poem was well received in England and became both admired and feared in New Zealand—perhaps this was the way one had to cope with 'local colour', but its amorphous profundity was intimidating. The London *Spectator* spoke of 'its masterly grasp of the modern problem as between theism and Positivism' and also of its 'power, buoyancy and intellectual subtlety'. Tennyson's wife, Emily, told Browning, 'Alfred says your friend only wants limitation to be a very considerable poet'. Browning himself enthused of *Ranolf and Amohia*: 'I am sure it is a great and astonishing performance, of very varied beauty and power. I rank it under nothing—taken altogether—nothing that has appeared in my day and generation for subtle and clear writing about subjects of all others the most urgent for expression, and the least easy in treatment.' Longfellow also praised it.

In the introduction to ★*New Zealand Verse* (1906) Alexander and ★Currie write the fullest early appreciation of Domett—appreciation tinted with various doubts. 'Domett has taken root in the literature textbooks as one of the secondary poets of the nineteenth century; but his work is too diffuse and not distinctive enough to become the ensample of a modern school of writers.... As far as mere word-painting goes, nothing

has ever been done in Maoriland that surpasses Domett: some of his pictures of the Bush come as near to being great poetry as pure landscape can be.... The whole poem resembles a luxuriant forest, crowded with exuberant growths, vocal with the sound of bird and waterfall, and the main story meanders through it as carelessly and almost aimlessly as the two lovers thereof wander on their enchanted honeymoon.'

Allen ★Curnow, anxious to prove his own generation the 'first' in poetry, was inevitably challenged by such a figure and called *Ranolf and Amohia* a 'huge ramshackle composition'. With less at stake, more recent readers have been more tolerant, though all sigh at the poem's length. J.C. ★Reid did so in *Creative Writing in New Zealand* (1946), but added: 'At the same time there *are* good things in it and Domett has a pleasant humour that salts the whole.' In his eccentric but perceptive *Penguin History of New Zealand Literature* (1990), Patrick ★Evans remarks, 'Like a stranded whale, the poem lies rotting on the beach of New Zealand literature, an embarrassment that no-one knows what to do with', but goes on to find 'brief unexpected moments when something that has been fully imagined flows through'.

The fullest modern account of the poem is by MacD. P. Jackson in ★*OHNZLE* (1991, rev. 1998). Ironically he calls the poem 'a series of digressions', damning in varying degrees Domett's Māori-legend 'embellishments', the way ideas, feelings, things and events never 'mesh', the lack of story-telling gifts, two-dimensional characterisation and, worst, Domett's reliance on hackneyed language. Yet he too finds 'vivid passages'. Few readers seem to have the patience to search these out.

Domett published one further collection, *Flotsam and Jetsam: Rhymes Old and New* (1877), which combines poems written before going to New Zealand with poems written later in England. *The Diaries of Alfred Domett* (1953), edited by E.A. Horsman, cover Domett's retirement and are an important source for biographers of Browning's later years. Domett remained in England until his death.   JS/NW

Dominion, a long poem by A.R.D. ★Fairburn, was published by the ★Caxton Press in 1938 and later collected in *Three Poems* (1952) and the *Collected Poems* (1966). Fairburn first conceived of it in May 1935 as 'a sort of resumé of the situation of lil' ol' Enzed', and wrote the first full version 'during the heat and excitement' of the election campaign of 1935. A long negotiation with Denis ★Glover ensued, in which Fairburn agreed to reverse the order of the last two sections and to make other revisions, and the revised version was finally published in March 1938. The poem consists of five loosely related sections unified by their critical analysis of New Zealand society and history. The first, 'Utopia', is a bitter account of the country during the Great *Depression, with attacks on the government, the church, the press, business and the popular culture. The second and strongest section, 'Album Leaves', includes a critical debunking of colonial history and some effective vignettes of contemporary society. The third section, 'Elements', is a romantic hymn to the New Zealand *landscape as a source for the 'stones of a new temple' in the rebuilding of society. The fourth section, 'Dialogue', is a debate between an activist calling for 'the pure insensate / energy of destruction' and a romantic, speaking for Fairburn himself, who is given the last word in his faith that in them 'the Word endures, a seed in rock' that will eventually germinate and split the rock. That theme is resumed in the last section, 'Struggle in a Mirror', in which a vision of apocalyptic war ends in a hope of rebirth: 'the seed shall spring in blackened earth / and the Word be made flesh.'

The poem thus moves from an often specific and very critical picture of New Zealand society and history, mostly seen from the perspective of Social Credit, to a very unspecific romantic hope for social rebirth through being in tune with nature. Fairburn admitted to Glover that 'the thing doesn't hang together too well as a whole', and it is flawed both in its inconsistent intellectual structure and in the unevenness within the sections. However, such sub-sections as 'Imperial', 'Back Street', 'The Possessor', and 'Conversation in the Bush' in the 'Album Leaves' section are among his finest poems, and there are eloquent passages in the other sections. In its larger ambitions, even if not fully realised, and in its local successes, the poem is the most important New Zealand poetic work of the 1930s.   LJ

DONALD, Robyn (pseudonym of Robyn Kingston), is a prolific *Mills & Boon/Harlequin *romance novelist. Her first novel, *Bride at Whangatapu*, appeared in 1977, and her fiftieth in 1996. She grew up in Warkworth, where her father owned a stud dairy farm, trained and worked as a teacher, and is now a full-time writer at Kerikeri.

Donald's novels reflect key shifts in New Zealand Mills & Boon romance in the late 1970s–80s, from the reticent, mainly South Island–oriented Anglophile romances of Essie *Summers and her generation, to up-market, mainly Auckland, urban romances premised on the sophisticated lifestyles of the new elites: corporate executives, property investors, lawyers. The heroines in this world are feisty, independent, career-oriented, and the novels focus explicitly and intensely on sexuality and sexual fantasy. Donald's novels, whose Alpha-male

boardroom heroes often begin by seeming callous, domineering and violent, regularly relate this contemporary world to archetypal characters and narratives from myth, fairy tale and legend. In 'Mean, Moody, and Magnificent: The Hero in Romance Literature' (*Dangerous Men and Adventurous Women: Romance Writers on the Appeal of Romance*, University of Pennsylvania Press, 1992), she insists that readers are always aware of romance as fantasy, and speculates that its seductive appeal lies in the primitive idea that strong and successful men offer the greatest prospect for the survival of children. The narrative pattern suitably matches such a hero's strength against the heroine's power, resulting in 'equal commitment' at the end.   TS

DOWLING, Basil (1910–   ), was a mid-century *Caxton and Canterbury poet, now expatriate and unfashionable. Born in Southbridge, Canterbury, he gained an MA from Canterbury University College in 1932, taught in UK schools 1952–75 and now lives in Rye, Sussex. This geographical dislocation is the subject of much of his poetry, becoming a metaphor for alienation both from the English pastoral literary tradition and from a bucolic New Zealand childhood. Dowling calls himself 'The Unreturning Native' (1973), his memories 'constant as [his] pain', and wonders in the last poem of his most recent collection, *Windfalls & Other Poems* (1983), whether he has come 'full circle' back to the island of his ancestors. Although associated with other Christchurch poets like Charles *Brasch and Ruth *Dallas, his strongest influences are Edward Thomas, Andrew Young, Robert Frost and Thomas Hardy, while it is Wilfred Owen who gives him modern cynicism and anger, to counter Edwardian nature worship and to question a strongly conventional religious urge. Dowling trained for the Presbyterian ministry but lost his faith during World War 2, when he was jailed for his pacifist views. In 'Heredity' (the title alluding to Hardy), he confesses: 'My nature's an uneasy blend / of delicacy and hardihood.' That tension is traced in his many poems about his Christchurch youth, which are particularly prominent in the first three of his eight collections, *A Day's Journey* (1941), *Signs and Wonders* (1944) and *Canterbury and Other Poems* (1949; all published by Caxton). The *landscape of the Canterbury plains has nowhere been better captured than in *Canterbury and Other Poems*, where he tries to 'give what's fine some fixity'. In *Hatherley: Recollective Lyrics* (1968) he recalls the people, places and sounds of the homestead of his boyhood on the outskirts of Christchurch. His self-appointed task is to record the simple truth because 'Houses and scenes and people go.' 'The Stream: A Reverie of Boyhood' (1979) focuses on the Wairarapa

Stream flowing through his family property, while *A Little Gallery of Characters* (★Nag's Head, 1971) peoples that same landscape.

Dowling often speaks from this earlier time, with allusions to Matthew Arnold and Edward Elgar, a traditional rhyming prosody and an uncritical use of words like 'witches' and 'harlots'. He happily confesses to not understanding Māori names, preferring to make connections with his own childhood holidays: 'The pines were surf upon New Brighton beaches.' But amid such disingenuousness his philosophical and spiritual insights often have great impact, as when he complains that 'experience … is never fully now' and deftly opens up the space of resonance between past and present. In *Windfalls & Other Poems* a refreshing irony often surprises in the midst of traditional verse, as when he describes walking in the Lake District 'trying to recall what Wordsworth said'. Dowling rejects the Christian God ('a monster of depravity') in favour of a Hardyesque 'all-eluding … Inscrutable'. He celebrates the found beauty of nature (for example, the poppy) in contrast to the perversions of 'civilization' engaged in two world wars; the poppy worn like 'a bloodstain on the lapel of your soul', or the bomber pilot with his 'gentlemanly killing'. At his best, his lyrics have the concealed punch of Blake's *Songs of Innocence*, while *Bedlam: A Mid-Century Satire* (1972), written in 1958, is a powerful Blakean indictment of modern society. A child of World War 1, cut off from his childhood Eden by World War 2, Dowling finds fragile moments of peace—knowing they are 'tricks to keep the mind from thinking'.　　　　DD

DOWNES, Cathy (1950–　), has won particular acclaim for her award-winning dramatic monologue, *The Case of Katherine Mansfield* (published 1995). Compiled from ★Mansfield's *Journal*, letters and stories, it was performed first at Theater De Kikker in Utrecht, Holland, in 1978 and subsequently in Edinburgh, the USA, Australia, many times in New Zealand and in 1997 in the Southwark New Zealand Arts Festival, London. Her *Farewell Speech*, adapted from Rachel ★McAlpine's novel, won the Chapman Tripp Theatre Award for Best New New Zealand Play in 1993. Educated at Victoria University (BA 1972) and the New Zealand Drama School, she has acted and directed in many of New Zealand's major theatres, and has worked in theatre and film in Europe and Australia.　　　　GB

DOYLE, Charles (1928–　), came to prominence in the 1960s as a critic, anthologist and prolific poet. Born in Ireland, he grew up in London, and served in the Royal Navy before coming to New Zealand in 1951. He lectured in English at the University of

Auckland 1961–67, when he took up a position at a ★Canadian university.

Doyle has written critical studies of James K. ★Baxter and R.A.K. ★Mason, and a biography of Richard Aldington, and has edited collections of essays on William Carlos Williams and Wallace Stevens. His poetry collections include *A Splinter of Glass* (1956), *Distances* (1963), *A Sense of Place* and *Messages for Herod* (1965), *Earth Meditations* (1968), *Stonedancer* (1976) and *A Steady Hand* (1983).

The poetry is extremely varied, exploring the expressive range of modernist idiom, and reflecting diverse influences and trends. Doyle calls his early mode 'self-involved subjectivism'; the poems are formally strict, with a high emotional and rhetorical charge, and are often obscure. Subsequent work is more outward-looking. There follows a period marked by Jungian symbolism, ironic social comment and radically fragmented, elliptical form. The later volumes revert to more conventional syntax and versification, combined with a new concreteness, with accessible and engaging results. Through all the experimentation Doyle has always returned frequently to the fable and what one critic called the 'spare, tender lyric', modes which seem to have particularly suited his abilities.

His *Recent Poetry in New Zealand* (1965) was part of a trend away from historical or canonical anthologies. It displays an apparent bias in favour of Auckland poets and the academic temper; the inclusion of essays by the contributing poets makes it nevertheless an interesting document of the poetic climate of the time.　　　　JH

Dragon Rampant (1939), an account of Robin ★Hyde's extraordinary experiences in ★China during 1938, was written subsequently in London. Like the poems in *★Houses by the Sea*, her newspaper articles written in China and *★Passport to Hell*, it reflects her ardent desire for peace, and her horror at the savagery and tragedy of war which she witnessed in her journey to Canton, Shanghai and Hsuchow. It also describes her meetings with many of those involved in supporting China's struggle against ★Japan, some of whom, like Rewi ★Alley, were 'thinly camouflaged' to ensure their protection. It is characteristic of Hyde the journalist-novelist-poet in that it crosses genres, blending factual documentation with imaginative description and personal reflection. As in *Passport to Hell* the style is carefully controlled: 'I've deliberately kept a great deal of it light, because … if I let go with emotion throughout, a very large section of the public would yelp "Emotional woman!"' Nevertheless the trauma of war, and the urgent need for some kind of collective global action, are powerfully conveyed. Despite Hyde's own concern about the title and her publisher's desire that it should not be anti-Japanese, it won the praise of her friend James *Bertram, himself the author of several books on China, received lengthy reviews and went quickly into a second edition. GB

Drum was a single-issue magazine of poetry and social comment published in Wellington in March 1961.

DRUMMOND, John (1944–), composer, musicologist and university professor, was born in Lancaster, England. A predominant interest in opera and theatre has led him to pursue a successful career at the University of Otago music department involving production, singing, teaching, writing and composing. His compositions include several of literary significance: *The Dawning of the Year* (1976), a song cycle to poems by Charles *Brasch, and music for the Roger *Hall pantomime *Cinderella* (1978) and his revue-play comedy *The Hansard Show* (1986), with Nigel Eastgate. Drummond's three-act opera *Plague upon Eyam* (1983), to a libretto by Patrick Little, is based on events in a Peak District English village during the plague of 1665. He has also edited and translated a number of operas. JMT

DU FRESNE, Yvonne (1929–), fiction writer, was born in Takaka into a dairy-farming family dominated by Danish–French Huguenot ancestry, which provides the cultural background for her writing. After training as a teacher in Christchurch she qualified in classroom music and voice teaching, and specialised in teaching music. Forty years of full-time education employment supported her writing, including a decade at the Correspondence School, for which she was also a drama scriptwriter. First published in 1950, her early stories were an attempt at 'English' fiction. Not until encouraged by Robin *Dudding, editor of *Landfall*, did she find her own voice in a melding of her childhood experience with stories recounted by her grandparents. These provided the basis of her first collection, *Farvel* (1980), which was read on radio under the title 'Astrid of the Limberlost'. These popular stories are an affectionate testament to small-town childhood through the inquisitive eyes of an acutely observant girl 'intent on finding New Zealand'. Combining the Danish Huguenot community with Norse legends, du Fresne created in Astrid Westergaard a character whose experiences describe and scrutinise cultural difference in the homogeneous New Zealand of the 1930s, and through whom she celebrates the inheritance of the close-knit Danish community and her own affinity with the land of the Manawatu.

The Growing of Astrid Westergaard (1985), also broadcast, continues the journey of discovery, the growth suggested in the title marking a junction in Astrid's sense of cultural allegiance as she confidently claims the 'new homeland' as her own. Both collections attempt to establish an affinity between the non-British European migrants and Māori. The Women's Press (UK) published a selection of the stories, *The Bear from the North* (1989), with the subtitle 'Tales of a New Zealand Childhood'. Ester, the 50-something Danish–French Huguenot in *The Book of Ester* (1982), might be seen as a grown-up Astrid negotiating a new set of problems centring on her sense of identity. After the death of her Danish husband she tries to rationalise a life in rural New Zealand, which holds for her insufficient historical and mythical ties. Only by tracing and accepting the course of exile of her forebears ('France, Pfalz, Brandenburg, Gramzow, Russia, Denmark, New Zealand') and by finding consolation in the arms of a fellow Dane, can Ester reconcile herself to her romantic loss and cultural uncertainty. As in *Ester*, *Frédérique* (1987) retraces migrant steps but is more evocative of the strange mythical world of Danish folk lore. In this romance, richly textured with European and New Zealand settler history, nineteenth-century Denmark is intertwined with immigrant struggles and Māori uprisings in the Manawatu. The narrative uses myth and memory to conjure real and imagined dangers for Frédérique d'Albret and her persecuted Huguenot extended family. Weaving her Danish cultural heritage with its intuitive, spiritual base and deep attachment to the land and sea with the origins of New Zealand colonial society, du Fresne aligns earthy Frédérique with Māori in contrast to the English. Critics operating from realist premises have struggled both with the blurred borderline between reality and fantasy, and the claim of Danish spiritual affinity with Māori in the two novels. While they consistently celebrate du Fresne's sharp and exciting language, humorously employed to look ironically at herself and her community, they are frequently uncomfortable with her construction of an indomitable immigrant community identity and its mythical connection to another place, a superior homeland that is not England. This depiction of difference is a deliberate negotiation of New Zealandness in a distinctive style of voice du Fresne calls her 'Danish clonk'. Recognition has included nationally a *PEN award and the Scholarship in Letters, and Danish travel and writing residency awards. The autobiographical novel, *Motherland* (1996), uses this experience in Denmark to examine the cultural differences between Scandinavia and New Zealand. NN

DUCKWORTH, Marilyn (1935–), is most significant for her idiosyncratic novels of contemporary mores. Born in Otahuhu, she spent a wartime childhood in England (with her sister, Fleur *Adcock), and now lives in Wellington. She has published twelve novels since 1959, a novella, *Fooling* (1994), a collection of short stories, *Explosions on the Sun* (1989), a collection of poetry, *Other Lovers' Children* (1975), and most recently edited *Cherries on a Plate: New Zealand Writers Talk About their Sisters* (1996), to which both she and Adcock contribute chapters. Duckworth's novels investigate the way people become trapped in relationships. Although she dwells on the plight of the young to middle-aged woman in love who faces the competing claims of marriage, children, lovers and husbands, masculine narrators also perceive the vagaries of her sex, in *Pulling Faces* (1987) and *Leather Wings* (1995). Her first two novels are set in England: *A Gap in the Spectrum* (1959) reveals the prototype Duckworth heroine at her earliest stage, a virgin striving for independence from her parents whose feyness and idiosyncracy soon emerge as she becomes steadily disenchanted with her boyfriend. *The Matchbox House* (1960) demonstrates her other side: a non-coping heroine with an unfaithful husband, who shirks her responsibilities to a friend's children and sinks into fantasy. Duckworth's third novel, *A Barbarous Tongue* (1963), which won the Award for Achievement, is about a young woman pregnant to a wimpish, unreliable lover mystifyingly attached to his sister, and who finally, in the hands of a sympathetic older man, learns independence. In *Over the Fence is Out* (1969), set in England and Wellington, a passive English heroine incapacitated by her sadistic, egocentric husband is counterbalanced by his mistress, a strong and self-empowering New Zealander. This pivotal novel signalled the end of Duckworth's first phase; a fifteen years' silence ensued during which she published only the poetry collection, *Other Lovers' Children* (1975).

She resurfaced in grand style, winning the New Zealand Book Award for Fiction with *Disorderly Conduct* (1984). This is vintage Duckworth, set in 1981 during the Springbok tour, its heroine, Sophie, afflicted by a mysterious ailment, trying vainly to juggle various lovers against the competing demands of her several children by different fathers. *Married Alive* (1985), by contrast, has a futuristic theme; New Zealand is hit by a dangerous epidemic whose violent effects are symbolically reflected in the sinister, malevolent behaviour of the heroine's lover. *Rest for the Wicked* (1986) uses an English setting: Jane escapes from her family by volunteering as a guinea-pig in a Sleep Research Centre; strangers whom she encounters there catapult her into new life experiences which eventually force her to reconcile the temptations offered by a new lover with her family's demands. But Duckworth's most readable novels have a New Zealand, specifically Wellington, suburban setting, and often foreground the personal saga against contemporary public

events or themes: *Pulling Faces* (1987) interweaves its love story with the mysteries of hypnotism and a brain-reading machine; in *Message from Harpo* (1989), three generations of women confront the social upheavals which Halley's Comet apparently introduced in 1986, including homosexuality and the passage of the Homosexual Law Reform Bill, Alzheimer's disease and the Women's Movement. *Unlawful Entry* (1992) also covers three generations, an elderly woman, Joan, a teenage renegade, and Joan's daughter's friend Roey; *Seeing Red* (1993), a study of women's violence, sets on a collision course two family *mésalliances* which throw her heterosexual heroine into the worlds of incest and lesbianism; *Fooling* (1994) could be read as a cynical tale of abuse, but her heroine is deluded by love; her acquiesence makes her oblivious to masculine sexual ambiguity and the real predator, the media personality. *Leather Wings* (1995) investigates the themes of child kidnapping and paedophilia, revealing as fatally obssessed with a child's innocence that New Zealand icon of the middle class, the Rawleigh's Man. *Studmuffin* was published in 1997.

A Duckworth novel is instantly accessible almost as a generic type; her composite heroine, always vulnerable to love, lives in a welter of domestic demands and confusions, which is compounded by the doubly damning powers of her compulsive sexuality and its equally unpredictable target, the male hero. Orgasms abound, hot chocolate is an instant palliative; but inevitably her denouements restore the reader to the everyday with a sharpened sense of its oddness. Duckworth's writing has been much praised for her sharp ear for dialogue (the 'crispest and crackliest … of any of our novelists' according to Kevin *Ireland), her brilliant powers of observation, and her skilful enquiries into *les affairs du coeur*. She has also written for radio, *Home to Mother* (1976) and *Feet First* (1981), adaptations of *A Gap in the Spectrum* (1972) and *A Barbarous Tongue* (1973), and television scripts, *The Smiler and the Knife* (1971) and instalments of *Close to Home* (1975–76). She has won many fellowships and grants, including the Scholarship in Letters (1961, 1972), the Katherine *Mansfield Memorial Fellowship (1980) and the Victoria and Auckland University writing fellowships (1990, 1996). She was awarded the OBE in 1987.   JW

DUDDING, Robin (1935–), editor, publisher and journalist, was born in Hastings and, after leaving Hastings BHS, worked as a journalist on the *Hawke's Bay Herald Tribune* 1952–55, and the *Auckland Star* 1955–59. He gained a Diploma of Teaching from Auckland Teachers' College and taught in Auckland primary schools 1960–66. Dudding's career as a literary editor began with the Auckland journal *Mate, which he published and edited from 1957 to 1966, before moving to the *Caxton Press in Christchurch, where he became general editor and Charles *Brasch's chosen successor as editor of *Landfall, 1966–72 (Numbers 80–101). After being dismissed from Caxton in 1972, reputedly for late delivery of an issue of Landfall, Dudding founded, published and edited *Islands: A New Zealand Quarterly of Arts and Letters, which soon became the pre-eminent literary periodical of the 1970s, many leading writers retaining loyalty to Dudding rather than to Landfall. Initially Islands was edited from his home in Christchurch, but in 1974 he moved back to Auckland with his family and his Torbay home became the editorial base. He remained the central figure of Islands until publication ceased in 1987.

Dudding also edited *Beginnings: New Zealand Writers Tell How They Began Writing (1980), a collection of autobiographical essays which had appeared in Landfall. While editing Islands, Dudding worked as a relieving primary schoool teacher, a freelance book editor, and sometime 'Bookmarks' columnist for the *NZ Listener, where he worked as a subeditor, 1988–96. He was the first Literary Fellow at the University of Auckland in 1979. Dudding was the most distinguished periodical editor of his generation and a key figure behind the scenes in New Zealand writing for thirty years, 1957–87, engendering strong loyalty among many of the writers whose careers he nourished.   PS

DUDER, Tessa (1940–), writer for children and young adults, was educated at Diocesan GHS and Auckland University. As Tessa Stavely, she was a silver medallist in swimming at the 1958 Cardiff Empire Games (later the Commonwealth Games), national butterfly and medley record holder (1958–59) and the first New Zealand Swimmer of the Year (1959). In 1959 she was appointed a general reporter at the Auckland Star, and later deputy editor of the Women's Page. In 1964 she married and moved to London, working for two years as a feature writer for the Daily Express; she moved to Pakistan 1966–70, and returned to New Zealand in 1971, apart from spending 1981 in Malaysia. She lives in Auckland. Her first novel for children, Night Race to Kawau (1982), depicts a family's triumph over adversity when the father, an experienced sailor, is knocked unconscious at the beginning of the race, leaving the mother and three children, all experienced but untested sailors, to crew the boat. The novel bears many of the hallmarks of Duder's later work, with strong central female characters, an identifiably New Zealand setting, convincing New Zealand English dialogue and a strongly dramatic plot. Her next novel, Jellybean (1985), explores the changing relationship between Geraldine (the

Jellybean of the title) and her single-parent mother, a cellist, as the mother engages in a relationship with a fellow musician and Jellybean decides she wants to become a conductor. Duder was awarded the 1985 Choysa Bursary for Children's Writers.

The quartet of *Alex novels were all critically acclaimed. Alex won the 1988 Children's Book of the Year Award and the 1989 Esther Glen Medal; Alex in Winter the 1990 Aim Children's Book of the Year Award and the Esther Glen Medal; Alessandra—Alex in Rome was placed third in the Senior Fiction section of the 1992 Aim Award and won the Esther Glen Medal; Songs for Alex won the 1993 Aim Award. The quartet has been published in the USA, Britain and Australia, and translated into several languages. Duder has subsequently diversified into script and play writing, short stories, non-fiction and acting. She has edited several anthologies, including Falling in Love (1995), and contributed regular columns and reviews locally and overseas. Duder is also notable for her role in the establishment and promotion of the *New Zealand Children's Book Foundation. She was awarded the OBE (1994) and the Margaret Mahy Medal (the Children's Book Foundation's recognition of distinction) in 1996.   SSa

DUFF, Alan (1950–), is a novelist, newspaper columnist, polemicist and cultural phenomenon. Son of scientist Gowan Duff and Kuia Hinau (of Ngāti Rangitihi and Tūwharetoa), and grandson of Oliver *Duff, he was born and raised in a state housing area in Rotorua. After his parents separated when he was 10, Duff lived with a Māori uncle and aunt at Whakarewarewa. He was expelled from Rotorua BHS and became a runaway, ending up as a state ward at Hamilton Boys' Home. He then lived for a time with his uncle, anthropologist Roger Duff, and went to Christchurch BHS. At the age of 15 he was sentenced to a term in Waikeria borstal for assault and breaking and entering. After a period working as an installer of sheet-metal insulation and singing in a band, and with numerous convictions for petty offences, Duff went to London, where, he has said, he 'messed up but grew up'.

Back in New Zealand, Duff ran various businesses of his own, before beginning to write full-time in 1985. His first novel, a thriller, was rejected; after burning the manuscript, he began a second, *Once Were Warriors, which was taken on by literary agents Chris *Else and Barbara *Else and published by Tandem Press in 1990. It had an immediate and huge impact.

Another novel, One Night Out Stealing, appeared in 1991. After the many opposed voices of Once Were Warriors, this has just two: those of Jube, a Pākehā small-time criminal with big ambitions, and his more sensitive

Māori 'partner', Sonny. The novel traces the increasingly desperate circumstances that lead the pair to their 'one night out stealing' in Wellington, and the divergence between them that results. Where Jube sees the Harland house as a trove to plunder, and squanders his share on buying friendship, for Sonny it opens up a sophisticated alternative world of art and music, love and belonging, into which he retreats in growing fantasy. *One Night Out Stealing* is strongest in depicting the mean world of the Tavi pub and petty crime in Auckland, and in making real Jube's confused thoughts and hopeless dreams. It has been constantly in print in New Zealand, and has been published in Australia.

State Ward began as a series of episodes on National Radio in 1993, and was published as a novella in 1994. The story of 13-year-old Charlie Wilson's experiences in and escape from Riverton Boys' Home, it is a mixture of childlike simplicity and harsh realism.

Duff's toughest, most sophisticated, complex and controlled work to date is *What Becomes of the Broken Hearted?* (1996), the sequel to *Once Were Warriors*. The central focus here is Jake Heke, and his slow, sometimes bewildered and always painful growth into self-knowledge. Juxtaposed with that are the stories of his second son, Abe, joining the rival Black Hawks gang to get revenge for the death of Nig; and of his second daughter, Polly, coming to understand the suicide of her older sister, Grace. Beth, the character at the heart of *Once Were Warriors*, is now partner of Māori welfare manager Charlie Bennett and far away from Pine Block. There is an implicit contrast between her and a new character, Gloria Jones, still stuck in Pine Block, whose resentful dreams of material wealth emotionally destroy Mulla Rota, gang member and jailbird, though inwardly another lost Māori warrior looking for meaning. Again, the white and (apparently) wealthy Trambert family serve as a symbolic opposite, but their lives are shown here also from the inside as being as complicated and troubled as anyone else's. It is not your troubles that matter, the novel suggests, but how you deal with them.

What Becomes of the Broken Hearted? is less angry than *Once Were Warriors*, more mature, with a wider emotional range; acknowledging complexity and difficulty, it recognises the lack of easy solutions but the need to keep trying. The novel uses the same technique of juxtaposed interior monologues; their interweaving is controlled and subtle, leading to an understated yet forceful conclusion.

Once Were Warriors catapulted Duff to national attention, and his views on Māori issues and problems are widely sought. In 1991 he began writing a weekly (later fortnightly) column for the *Evening Post*, syndicated to eight other newspapers. In this, and in his 1993 analysis,

Maori: The Crisis and the Challenge, he has developed his ideas on the failures of Māoridom, castigating both the traditional leadership and the radical movement for dwelling on the injustices of the past and expecting others to resolve them, instead of encouraging Māori to get on and help themselves. The blame for Māori underperformance he puts squarely back on Māori, for not making the most of the opportunities given them. This somewhat simplistic message has proved highly controversial. Apparently relishing rather then resiling from the fight, Duff has gone on to prove his point with the Books in Homes scheme launched in 1995. With commercial sponsorship and government support, this scheme aims to break the cycle of illiteracy, poverty, anger and violence among underprivileged children by making books available to them to own at minimal cost, thus encouraging them to read and to enjoy and value reading. This self-help approach, which in its first year put 180 000 new books in the hands of 38 000 children, reflects the path of Duff's own remarkable career.   AM

DUFF, Oliver (1883–1967), was a notable journalist and editor. Born on the Otago ★goldfields, he was raised on a farm in Central Otago, and remained a farmer in spirit all his life. After attending Otago BHS, he served in the South African War (1901–2) and then went to Otago University to prepare for the Presbyterian ministry (BA 1905). Developing doubts, however, he went rabbiting, shearing and swagging, and spent ten years as a schoolteacher. He entered journalism in 1916 with the Christchurch ★*Sun*, and in 1920 became editor of the *Timaru Herald*. In 1922 he joined the Christchurch ★*Press* as associate editor, becoming editor in 1929. He maintained his predecessors' strong literary tradition and independent political outlook, with editorials written with robust common sense. A conflict with the *Press's* board over the Christchurch tramways strike in May 1932 saw him resign rather than compromise his editorial stance. He then established and ran the *North Canterbury Gazette* at Rangiora, but financial difficulties forced him to give it up. In 1938 Duff became editor of National Centennial Publications, establishing the range of ★Centennial surveys before being appointed editor of the National Broadcasting Service's new weekly journal, the ★*NZ Listener*, early in 1939. There, despite a restrictive brief and the chronic paper and other shortages of war, Duff's wise, firm editorial control set a new standard for New Zealand journalism, creating a successful government-sponsored magazine which not only provided broadcasting and programme information but dealt seriously and responsibly with the wider political, social and cultural issues of the day.

Duff's first published book was the well-received

centennial survey *New Zealand Now* (1940), an impressionistic sketch of the (southern, white, male) New Zealander; so shrewd was this portrait that it could be reissued in 1956 needing only a new preface and postscript. The theme was also developed in his popular *Listener* 'Sundowner' series (1946–49) exploring rural New Zealand. After retiring in 1949 to a smallholding near Christchurch, Duff wrote for the *Listener* for sixteen years a regular diary recording the unsentimental facts of farming life and his reflections on the world, his reading and the New Zealand character; the earlier columns were collected as *A Shepherd's Calendar* (1961). His only other book is the monograph *Ourselves Today* (1958), based on a winter lecture series he delivered at Otago University in 1957. AM

DUGGAN, Eileen (1894–1972), poet, was born in Tuamarina, Marlborough, where her parents (both emigrants from Co. Kerry) had settled in the 1880s. She attended Marlborough College and Victoria University College (MA 1918 with first class honours in history), also attending Wellington Teachers' Training College. She taught briefly at a secondary school and later at university, but ill health forced her to abandon teaching. For almost fifty years, she earned her living solely by full-time writing—poetry, literary and historical essays, criticism and reviews, and journalism, including a regular weekly page ('Pippa's Page', which she wrote for over forty years) for the Catholic newspaper, the *New Zealand Tablet*.

Duggan began writing poetry soon after her arrival in Wellington, and published her first volume, *Poems*, in 1921. Notable for its Irish content and religious interests, the volume skilfully evokes a range of emotions with an assured lyricism, already displaying her rare sense of words. It was well received in New Zealand and overseas, with a particularly favourable notice by George Russell ('AE'). *New Zealand Bird Songs* in 1929 included a prefatory note describing the poems as 'simply rhymes on their birds for the children of our country'. Some reviewers chose to ignore that, and the volume was greeted with an embarrassing level of *nationalistic fervour which left her alarmed that there would be nothing left to say about the subsequent 'real book'. Rhymes for children is an appropriate description of *Bird Songs*, though their skilled metrical experimentation is still of interest. The collection was very popular, and several poems proved favourite pieces for public recital or musical settings.

The first of her 'real' books was *Poems* in 1937 (American edition 1938), with an enlarged second edition in 1939, followed by *New Zealand Poems* in 1940, which also ran to second editions in Great Britain and America. Where her first volume had looked to the *Ireland of her parents, seen at times in a romantic, Celtic light, these two focus much more attentively on the New Zealand *landscape and people, and the place of the artist in a developing society. Some poems are overtly nationalistic (the cover of *New Zealand Poems* reads 'In Honour of the *Centennial of the Dominion of New Zealand'), and too often these are spoiled by a forced and uncomfortable rhetoric, or indulgence in fanciful imagery employed for its own sake. Other pieces are more successful, such as the simple ballads which she called her 'peasant poems', and the personal lyrics which are firmly tied to a vividly realised landscape, whether remembered from childhood, or known as part of her adult life. The situation of the poet in New Zealand and the nature of poetic inspiration are important themes. Her sense of the isolation of the poet (heightened perhaps by her rather secluded lifestyle) and her insistence on the primacy of an intuitive inspiration show the influence of the Romantic tradition, but the way she links poetic creativity with religious experience derives more from seventeenth-century religious poetry. Both these volumes were given a highly favourable reception by local and overseas reviewers (particularly in the United States), and for a number of years Eileen Duggan was the best-known and most widely admired of New Zealand poets. Her preference for traditional forms and for simple lyric, making often original use of the *Georgian tradition, made her a genuinely popular writer, and she received national and international honours.

The publication of *More Poems* in 1951 signalled a significant change, both in subject and in style. Like many of her contemporaries, Duggan was deeply affected by World War 2, and by the even more oppressive threat of atomic warfare. The poems of this volume mingle shock and pity as they attempt to understand the condition of that world, but still include a spirit of hope which affirms the value of fallen humanity. The writing is spare and austere, combining passion with intelligence in a way that is reminiscent of metaphysical poetry. There is some straining to handle the prophetic role that she has adopted, and there is still at times a slightly indulgent imagery, but *More Poems* is Eileen Duggan's most mature and accomplished writing.

Since *New Zealand Poems*, however, her reputation had seriously declined, victim to changing fashions in poetry and to the conscious reshaping of the canon of New Zealand poetry. She was absent from the Allen *Curnow's influential *Caxton Press anthologies of 1945 and 1951, and from the Penguin anthology of 1960, refusing permission to be represented by a selection of which she did not approve. Her refusal seems hardly surprising given Curnow's opinion expressed in the 1945 book that in her verse 'the whole effect is that of an emotional cliché'.

Duggan had been prominently associated with *Kowhai Gold (1930), an anthology that later came to stand for the worst excesses of Georgianism, romantic prettiness, and false play with Māori words as if they were 'new toys'. Duggan's reputation suffered from the attacks on Kowhai Gold and C.A. *Marris's New Zealand Best Poems (1932–43), though later critics have often exempted her from their censures of New Zealand Georgianism.

Ironically, she had written about the dangers of striving too hard to be 'indigenous', and had been aware of the risks since at least the mid-1920s. Her rejection of a modernist poetic came not from ignorance but from a deliberate criticism of its obscurity and formlessness. Undoubtedly, she is guilty of some of the Georgian weaknesses, but she writes with the strengths of that tradition and is never confined by it. Although her poetry prefers the generalising sentiment to the directly personal, it does spring from personal experiences which she treats in a subtly allusive manner, belying the conventional decorous exterior of the lyric form.

By the end of her career, Duggan had moved to a more sombre focus on the moral dimensions of human actions—what she wrote of as 'the discipline of consequences'. And correspondingly her verse lost some of its fanciful imagery and indulgent language and became itself more disciplined in style, and more conscious in its subject matter of the sadness of the post-war age. Her religious faith always formed a vital part of her poetic vision. Its beliefs and values, its legends and symbols inform much of her writing, and they, as much as any personal experience, give her poetry its concreteness and intimacy, characterising her as a lyricist whose immediate forerunners may be Georgian, but who writes at the same time within a much longer and more comprehensive tradition of religious poetry.   PW

DUGGAN, Maurice (1922–74), ranks with Katherine *Mansfield and Frank *Sargeson among New Zealand's greatest exponents of short fiction, despite his small output. He was born in Auckland and grew up on the North Shore, his father an Irish immigrant who had become manager of an Auckland department store, his mother New Zealand–born but also of Irish extraction. She died suddenly in 1930, and in 1935 Duggan's father moved with his family to Paeroa to open his own business. Duggan returned to Auckland a year later to attend Sacred Heart College, but after only nine months he returned to Paeroa to various odd jobs. He continued this lifestyle after settling in Auckland once more in

1938. Duggan displayed no interest in literature or academic pursuits as a child, and it was the loss of his left leg in 1940 through acute osteomyelitis that seems to have generated his desire to write. The amputation ended an all-absorbing interest in sports and prevented Duggan from following his friends into the army during World War 2. Early in 1944 he made contact with Frank Sargeson at Sargeson's Takapuna *bach, and the older man quickly became his mentor. Through Sargeson he also became friendly with Greville *Texidor and other writers and artists living on the North Shore. He married in 1946 and lived on and off for the remainder of his life at Forrest Hill, on the North Shore.

Unlike most of the talented younger writers encouraged by Sargeson, Duggan never adopted his mentor's famously 'New Zealand colloquial' style. Even Duggan's early stories, such as 'Sunbrown' and 'Notes on an Abstract Arachnid', display a Joycean wordiness and impatience with conventional form which remained features of his work. These first attempts were weakened by what Duggan himself later described as 'a habit of rhetoric'. This developed, however, into a stylishness and sophistication at times closer to poetry than prose, and out of step with the social realist direction of New Zealand fiction. 'Six Place Names and a Girl' (Sargeson contributed the title) proved a breakthrough with its almost minimal plot and its brief, evocative descriptions of areas on the Hauraki Plains. Its one-word sentences and composite words then seemed technically very daring. It was published in *Landfall in 1949, as was most of Duggan's later fiction.

From 1950 Duggan and his wife spent two years in London, where he attempted to write a full-length novel. It was the first of several failed novels that would provide material for successfully managed short fiction. Parts of this uncompleted work were eventually refashioned into short stories built around the lives of the Lenihans, an Irish immigrant family living in Auckland. 'Guardian' and 'In Youth is Pleasure' depict and condemn the harsh treatment meted out to boys in a Catholic boarding school. 'Race Day' describes some children watching a horse-race in the distance from the porch of their house, and their parents' unconcern at a fatal riding accident. 'A Small Story' chronicles the same children's rejection of their new stepmother after the death of Mrs Lenihan. This story's rigorous, spare prose style, and effective image of children swinging on a gate to show the futility of all action, are typical of the works of this period. Many of the events in the Lenihan stories to some extent reflect Duggan's early life. Despite the obvious influence of Joyce's Dubliners (see *Ireland), the stories form one of the finest series written by a New Zealander. They have been compared favourably to

Mansfield's Karori works on the Burnell family, written under similar circumstances (see *Prelude, 'The *Doll's House'). The Lenihan stories have remained among the most popular of Duggan's works.

During the same period of overseas travel Duggan was also working on a diary entitled 'Voyage', which in three parts describes his journey by ship to England, a holiday through *Italy and adventure in Spain. It was widely admired in New Zealand for its lyric power and evocativeness. Duggan contracted tuberculosis while in Spain in late 1952 and had to return hurriedly to New Zealand. Most of the Lenihan stories and the 'Voyage' sequence were published in his first collection, *Immanuel's Land* (1956). This book established Duggan's reputation as a literary figure of great talent. During the 1950s he worked on a second autobiographical novel, entitled 'Along the Poisoned River', which became a source of further Lenihan stories. He also wrote a children's book, *Falter Tom and the Water Boy* (1957), published by *Paul's Book Arcade jointly with Faber and Faber in England and Criterion Books in the United States. It was one of the first internationally successful New Zealand children's books.

By the end of the decade Duggan had tired of personal experience as a basis for his adult fiction. 'The Wits of Willie Graves', the story of a debt collector's journey into the outer reaches of the New Zealand countryside, marked a new departure. At the same time, in 1960, Duggan was the second recipient of the *Burns Fellowship, spending the year on yet another novel, 'The Burning Miss Bratby', and writing some of his most famous short stories. Two of these works are long monologues, the success of which pushed the New Zealand short story out of its social realist rut. 'Riley's Handbook', a novella, consists of the ravings of an artist named Fowler who has escaped his wife and family to become a barman and caretaker in a sprawling rural hotel. The work is devoid of any conventional plot and is heavily influenced by Samuel Beckett's novels. Its atmosphere of utter despair is occasionally hard to take, in contrast to the comic bravura of *'Along Rideout Road that Summer', which Duggan completed in 1961. Duggan's most reprinted work, and arguably one of the finest in New Zealand literature, this triumphantly parodies and celebrates some dominant themes of conventional New Zealand fiction. Its dense and playful style signposts a distinctly new direction for the New Zealand short story. It appeared with Duggan's work to date, except for 'Riley's Handbook', in *Summer in the Gravel Pit* (1965), which sold successfully in New Zealand (*Blackwood and Janet Paul) and England (Victor Gollancz).

From 1961 Duggan slowly moved away from writing fiction to become more involved in the Auckland advertising world. Beginning as a copywriter, his skill with language saw him rise at length to the board of directors of the prestigious firm, J. Inglis Wright. He completed only three further stories, two of which were written while he held the Scholarship in Letters in 1966 and had a year free from advertising work. These long works, 'O'Leary's Orchard' and 'An Appetite for Flowers', were published together with 'Riley's Handbook' in *O'Leary's Orchard* (1970). The book was respectfully reviewed, but by now it could be said that the enormous complexity and difficulty of Duggan's work was beyond the range of much of the reading public. A crisis with alcoholism precipitated his resignation from advertising in late 1972, and after a painful recovery he learned in late 1973 that he had contracted cancer. In his last year he completed one more story, 'The Magsman Miscellany', published posthumously in 1975. It caused a small sensation with its skilful use of metafictional form. A series of views of the relationship of Ben McGoldrick, an amateur wordsmith and traveller in pharmaceuticals, with his wife and his creative impulses, the story also contrives to be Duggan's sly self-portrait. The interest it aroused is testament to Duggan's ability to develop continually the possibilities of style, and never to be happy with less than the perfect phrase. His *Collected Stories* (1981), edited by C.K. *Stead, was another publishing event. Ian Richards's biography, *To Bed at Noon: The Life and Art of Maurice Duggan*, was published in 1997.   IR

DUMONT D'URVILLE, Jules (1790–1842), French navigator and writer, wrote one of the earliest published narratives of New Zealand. Born in Normandy, he is remembered by his countrymen for voyaging round the world, finding the remains of La Pérouse's expedition at Vanikoro, visiting Antarctica, discovering Terre Adélie and perishing in a railway accident between Versailles and Paris. New Zealanders remember him for his connection with Durville Island, French Pass and Olive Wright's book, *New Zealand 1826–1827 from the French of Dumont d'Urville* (1950). This is an English translation of his account of the voyage of the *Astrolabe* in New Zealand waters, December 1826 to March 1827.

In fact, Dumont d'Urville circumnavigated the globe three times. On each occasion he spent some time on the New Zealand coast and recorded his experiences. The first time he came, he was second in command on the *Coquille* (1822–25), the second time (1826–29) and third (1837–40) he was commander of the same ship renamed *Astrolabe*. The commander wrote copiously and his official accounts, *Voyage de la corvette l'Astrolabe* and *Voyage au Pole Sud and dans l'Océanie* were published soon after his return from each of the two later voyages.

His work from the first was not published in his lifetime. It is unique in many ways and does not fit neatly into any literary category. It is a combination of fiction and non-fiction, first published in 1992 in New Zealand in a translation by Carol Legge, with the English title *The New Zealanders: A Story of Austral Lands*. This work is Dumont d'Urville's ethnographic novel *Les Zélandais: histoire australienne*, which he was inspired to write by the Māori he met in the Bay of Islands in 1824. All the principal characters are Māori and the writer attempts to see their world through their eyes. With uncommon perception he identifies the issues arising out of the Māori contact with Europeans and, through the characters in the story, explores the cultural disruption in the transitional period before the foreign culture became dominant. The historical sequence of events is the fabric through which the writer weaves a thread of fiction. This narrative is accompanied by ethnohistorical notes compiled by the writer from diverse sources and his own observations and experiences.

Dumont d'Urville's belief that his reputation as a man of science could be compromised if his name became associated with fiction may have been one of his reasons for not getting the novel published. However, the factual information he had compiled appeared in his later publications including his very popular work, *Voyage pittoresque autour du monde*, which was published in 1834–35 and translated into other European languages (but not English). In this, Dumont d'Urville attempted to reach as many readers as possible with information about the people of Oceania in particular and to this end he used the combination of fact and fiction pioneered in his novel. However, the element of fiction in the later work is insignificant. Unlike the novel, which focuses in an imaginative way on the Māori, their culture and their regional relationships, *Voyage pittoresque autour du monde* encompasses the globe and is a factual compilation of the voyages and discoveries of many European explorers.

These publications reflect Dumont d'Urville's wide-ranging interests which included linguistics, ethnography and botany. He had an abiding concern for the peoples of the South Pacific and the Māori in particular, and was a very important observer of them.   CL

DUNCUM, Ken (1959–), poet and dramatic writer for theatre, television and radio, was born in Napier and educated at Rotorua BHS and University of Waikato (BSocSc, 1981). He then studied at Victoria University in theatre, film and creative writing during the 1980s, and had poetry published in the *★NZ Listener*, *★Islands*, *★Sport* and *Scripsi* (Australia). He became a full-time writer, and contributed sketches for satirical television comedy shows such as 'Public Eye', 'Away Laughing' and 'Skitz'. His recent television work has included writing for series such as 'Cover Story', 'Duggan' and 'Mirror, Mirror'. Duncum's first short plays 'Polythene Pam', 'Truelove' and 'Flybaby' were co-written with and starred Rebecca Rodden, and performed at Wellington's fringe Bats Theatre in 1986 and 1987. Their deliberately arbitrary structure, anarchic humour, and Rodden's punk nihilism attained a minor cult status among streetwise young audiences, reinforced by Duncum's full-length 'Jism' the following year and 'Panic' in 1993.

He then reached a much wider audience with two substantial stage plays, which each place real people from the recent past in an imagined event and explore the implicit drama. 'Blue Sky Boys' (1990, subsequently toured nationally several times) had the Everly Brothers performing rock-and-roll numbers which had middle-aged audiences stamping in the aisles, yet also locked in destructive conflict about the value of music, symbolised by their despair over an invitation to meet the Beatles (who really were in Wellington in 1964). In 'Horseplay' (1994) Duncum irreverently sets up a hypothetical meeting between the novelist Ronald Hugh ★Morrieson and the poet James K. ★Baxter in Hawera in 1972 as death approaches for them both. In the grand tradition of drunken poets, they eventually get stupefyingly sozzled together on beer, whisky, sweet sherry, down-and-out characters, Kiwi storytelling, practical jokes and a unifying hatred of critics. Morrieson is egged on by Baxter to 'give poetry a burl', while Baxter himself complains that the pioneering editors and critics of the 1950s failed to understand him. They just 'pulled their foreskins up over their heads and cried, "I see a new national literature"'. Any possibility of literary pomposity is further deflated by their sharing the stage with the rear end of a horse—which flatulates as they expire. DC

DUNLOP, Beverley (1935–), writer of children's stories, was born in Takaka, and lived there and in rural Waikato with her Russian father and part-Irish mother. She taught music and worked as a legal secretary, beginning to write for magazines in 1975. *★Landfall* and the *★School Journal* have published her stories, many of which have been anthologised. *Queen Cat and Other Stories* (1988), illustrated by Deirdre Gardiner, consists of seven of her eighty published children's stories. After receiving the 1982 Choysa Award, Dunlop completed the first of her novels. *The Dolphin Boy* (1982), illustrated by Sandra Morris, combines mysticism and exuberance as two dissimilar boys battle to save dolphins with special powers. *The Poetry Girl* (1983) poignantly portrays Natalia's difficulties at home and school. Lonely, awkwardly tall, often bronchitic, she survives rebuffs by silently reciting poetry. *Earthquake Town* (1984), illustrated by Garry

Meeson, though set in 1984, is based on the 1931 Hawkes Bay earthquake. *Spirits of the Lake* (1988) interweaves contemporary, historical and legendary threads in a dramatic tale of vengeance. Dunlop has lived in Napier since marriage in 1960. With Kay Mooney she wrote *Hawke's Bay: Profile of a Province* (1986).   DH

DUNMORE, John (1923–), has been extraordinarily active as scholar, biographer, playwright, publisher and thriller writer. In his special field, *French Explorers of the Pacific* (Vol. 1 1965; Vol. 2 1969) is still the standard work, and *The Fateful Voyage of the St Jean Baptiste* won the Wattie Book Award for 1969. These, his other scholarly publications and his many contributions to French studies earned the awards of Chevalier de la Légion d'Honneur (1976) and Officier des Palmes Académiques (1986). He began writing plays for stage and radio in 1958, with the culmination of that activity probably his sequence of 'Four New Zealand Tragedies' broadcast in 1977. He wrote often on theatre, from 'A Plea for the Playwright' (*Landfall* 11, 1957) to *A Playwright's Workbook* (1993).

If his biography *Norman Kirk: A Portrait* (1972), his introduction to *The Ballads of Thomas *Bracken* (1975) and his guidebooks to the North and South Islands (1987) were not evidence enough of Dunmore's versatility, in 1976 he began a series of thrillers under the pseudonym of 'Jason Calder'. Inspired mostly by Forsyth's *The Day of the Jackal*, these pioneered the political thriller in New Zealand. The first, *The Man Who Shot Rob Muldoon* (1976), aroused fierce controversy and some threats from supporters of the then Prime Minister (see *Muldoon), and revealed the capacity of some sections of the book retail trade to impose their own form of *censorship. The unrepentant 'Jason Calder' followed with *A Wreath for the Springboks* (1977), disturbing for its portrait of a French mercenary and for its anticipation of the unrest that actually occurred four years later. Then came *The O'Rourke Affair* (1978) and *Target Margaret Thatcher*, also set in New Zealand (1981), which sold particularly well in Britain. The Calder titles were all published by Dunmore's own innovative Dunmore Press, which later abandoned fiction and as a medium-sized non-fiction house outlasted such eminent publishers as *A.H. & A.W. Reed.

Born in France and educated there and at University of London (PhD 1962), Dunmore worked in banking in London and teaching in New Zealand before joining Massey University on its inception in 1961. He became professor of French and dean of Humanities, and served on the Queen Elizabeth II Arts Council and other arts and educational bodies. He lives in active retirement at Waikanae.   RR

DUNSFORD, Cathie (1953–), is a fiction writer, poet, anthologist and publishing consultant, with a commitment to women's, especially lesbian, issues and to postcolonialism. Born in Devonport, she was educated at Westlake GHS and University of Auckland, MA (Hons) and PhD (1983), for research on the Gothic novel. As a Fulbright Scholar at University of California, Berkeley 1983–86, she taught New Zealand and lesbian literature and women's studies. After two years as an editor in USA she returned in 1989 to posts in arts administration in Northland, and since 1990 has directed a publishing consultancy in Warkworth and taught creative writing and publishing.

She edited the first collection of new writing by New Zealand women, *New Women's Fiction* (1986) and the first Australian/New Zealand lesbian collection, *The Exploding Frangipani* (1990). Further collections are *Subversive Acts* (1991), *Me and Marilyn Monroe* (1993) and *Car Maintenance, Explosives and Love, and Other Lesbian Writing* (1997). All promote feminist, lesbian and female Māori authors, with vigorously feminist introductions.

Her volume of poems, *Survivors: Überlebende* (1990), was published in German and English by the University of Osnabrück. A short fiction, 'Cave of Tongues', was anthologised in *Erotic Writing*, ed. Sue *McCauley, 1992. Dunsford's successful novel, *Cowrie* (1994), published in Australia and New Zealand, is the story of a large-bodied, orphan New Zealand woman who searches for her ancestral roots in Hawai'i, forming a bond with a married woman there in a journey allegorical of self-discovery and the interconnectedness of indigenous Pacific cultures. In writing that is 'lyrical to the edge of lushness, but buoyant with belief and commitment' (David *Hill), the novel incorporates oral, mythic and magic realist elements. Its cultural context, including the illustrations, is almost wholly indigenous, though the narrative of discovering the cultural sources of individual creativity draws from the European 'Künstlerroman'; and attacks on US military villainy work within Western conventions of protest fiction. A sequel, *The Journey Home*, appeared in 1997, and Dunsford has received an arts grant for a further continuation.   RR

DUNSTAN, Peggy (1920–), is a poet and anthologist for children and adults. *Patterns on Glass* (1968) and *A Particular Deep* (1974) are collections of free verse poems of strong personal content, images of loss and entrapment recurring ('Two Fathoms Under', 'Ship in a Bottle'). Some deal with urban or suburban subjects ('Supermarket Special', 'City Construction') in ways that relate her to Peter *Bland, Louis *Johnson and the 'Wellington Group'. She also anticipated by nearly twenty years the main group of feminist poets of the late

1970s in poems on the tension between domestic constraints and her aspirations as a writer ('With Intent'), as well as the sexual explicitness of poems like 'Wet Summer Sunday'. She edited *A Difference in Degree: An Anthology of Verse* (1981) and was co-editor of *Hyacinths and Biscuits* (1985), the diamond jubilee prose and verse anthology of the *Penwomen's Club. Her verse for children includes *Sunflowers and Sandcastles* (1977), *In and Out the Windows* (1979) and *Behind the Stars* (1986). She also published two engaging memoirs of childhood, *A Fistful of Summer* (1981) and *The Other Side of Summer* (1983). Born in Christchurch, she was educated at Wellington East GC and served on several literary committees in Wellington. She lives in Auckland.   RR

E

EARLE, Augustus (1793–1838), known as the 'wandering artist', spent eight months in New Zealand, in the Hokianga and Bay of Islands, in 1827, from which experience he published his *Narrative of a Nine Months' Residence in New Zealand* in 1832, the first account by a professional artist prior to planned settlement. Earle's account, and his watercolour sketches which were published as lithographic prints with descriptive passages in 1838, are important examples of the literary mode of travel writing which was a popular outcome of exploration in the late eighteenth and early nineteenth centuries. His account reveals the nature of his 'European vision', as an educated and professionally trained artist, which colours his response to the 'peculiar and picturesque' land he encountered. It also provides a unique written and visual record of the lives and customs of Māori with whom he lived and of the *landscapes through which he passed. His oil painting, *The Meeting of the Artist with the Wounded Chief Hongi, Bay of Islands, November 1827* (Wellington: *Alexander Turnbull Library), is a visual corollary to the written account of that meeting recorded in his *Narrative*. It is a work whose import was recognised by Ian *Wedde, who placed the image at the centre of his exhibition: *Now See Hear! Art, Language and Translation* (1990, Wellington: City Gallery) to illustrate how questions of language and translation are at stake in historical and contemporary visual representation.   CB

EARLE, Lynda (1965–   ), also known as Lynda Chanwai-Earle, poet, playwright and film maker, was born in Britain of a Chinese mother and a New Zealand father. After some childhood years in Papua New Guinea she moved to New Zealand with her family. She attended school in Hastings, where she took part in gang life with young Māori—a strong influence on some of her poems. In 1990 she graduated from the Elam School of Fine Arts in Auckland, and has worked as designer, actor, script consultant, film maker and teacher of creative writing in a women's prison. In 1994 she published her first book of poetry, *honeypants*. It includes some dramatic monologues in colloquial verse set in irregular patterns, such as 'To Hastings with Love' and 'Dementia Praecox (or The Cowgirl Experience)', which tell mainly of erotic experience in hurried tones. They are written as much for the voice as the page and Earle is a successful performer. Other poems, such as 'HE TOOK HER', are written entirely in capital letters and long formless sentences piling sensuous image on image. In 1996 her first play, *Ka shue—Letters Home*, was performed at the Wellington International Festival of the Arts. It draws on the stories of several generations of *Chinese New Zealand women in a montage technique. She is also co-author of a documentary film, *Chinese Whispers*, about the Asian experience in New Zealand.   NW

Early Days Yet (1997) is a late collection by Allen *Curnow at the age of 86, subtitled 'New and Collected Poems 1941–1997'. Unlike Curnow's earlier *Collected Poems 1933–1973* (1974), this volume excludes the poems of the 1930s and contains nothing earlier than poems published in *Island & Time* (1941). The volume begins with a group of previously uncollected poems written in the 1990s, including two which were printed in limited editions, *Looking West, Late Afternoon, Low Water* (*Holloway Press, 1994) and *The Scrap-Book* (*Wai-te-ata Press, 1996), followed by poems printed in reverse chronological order, ending in 1941.   PS

EASON, Amanda (1959–), has had a sporadic presence as a New Zealand poet, since most of her work has been published in the UK, where she has lived since 1985. Her Master's degree in English at the University of Auckland included the creative writing course taught by C.K. *Stead. She had poems published in *Landfall*, the *NZ Listener* and *Rambling Jack* around the time of her departure for London. There she has supported herself mainly by working as a teacher at an international school. Eason's poetry has appeared in many of the leading British literary magazines, and her collection *Reasons for Loving* (1992) was published by Turret Books as part of a series of new women poets. This book was co-published in New Zealand by Brick Row, and Eason was subsequently the featured poet in *Poetry New Zealand* 8. Her poems are lyrical personal narratives; in interviews she has emphasised her keeping of journals as the basis for poetry. Eason's characteristic topics are her New Zealand childhood, an expatriate nostalgia for her homeland, vignettes of travel and, above all, bitter-sweet, transitory love-relationships.   KJ

EDEN, Dorothy (1912–82), became an internationally renowned writer in the genre of the romantic mystery novel. She was born in Canterbury near Ashburton and grew up on a farm, leaving school at 16 to become a legal secretary in Ashburton, then in Christchurch. In the 1930s she began contributing stories to journals like the New Zealand *Mirror (in which forty of her stories appeared between 1933 and 1960), and published her first novel, *Singing Shadows*, in London in 1940. In 1954, after publishing a further ten novels, she moved to London, where she continued to write prolifically, publishing a further thirty novels and many magazine stories until the year of her death. Approximately a quarter of Eden's novels are set in New Zealand, but after she left New Zealand she drew increasingly on international settings—England, Ireland, Europe and Scandinavia (which had special associations for her through family connections and because of her interest in Gothic fiction and the fairy tales of Hans Christian Andersen). She also based a number of her novels on historical events: the siege of Mafeking, the Chinese Boxer Rebellion, the love affair of Parnell and Kitty O'Shea, the colonisation of Australia.

Gothically tinged mystery and suspense, expertly contrived and resolved, were Eden's trademark. *Bride by Candlelight* (1954), the last of the novels she wrote before leaving New Zealand, in which a young woman is terrorised in a remote Canterbury mansion, reveals how knowledgeable Eden had become in the Gothic repertory of tricks of the trade, and in later novels she increasingly drew on the Gothic potential of fairy tales, myths and legends. In *Sleep in the Woods* (1960) and her last novel, *An Important Family* (1982), she applied the same techniques to New Zealand's colonial history. Eden's novels, like all Gothic fictions, invoke a world of polarised gender relations, suffused with male violence or the threat of violence. Written almost always from a female point of view, they are premised on the difficulty of 'reading' men's behaviour and speech, and plunge her heroines into nightmare, paranoid worlds in which they are unable to distinguish friends from enemies.   TS

Edge, with seven issues published 1971–76, was New Zealand's most ambitiously international literary journal. Edited by Patrick *Evans, William L. Fox, Gary *Langford, D.S. *Long, Bruce McAllister, K.K. Ruthven, Robert Stowell, David Walker and John *Weir, the journal published two generations of New Zealand writers, including James K. *Baxter, Denis *Glover, Sam *Hunt, Bill *Manhire, Kendrick *Smithyman, Brian *Turner and Ian *Wedde, alongside overseas writers like Margaret Atwood, Robert Bly, Jorge Luis Borges, Antonio Cisneros, Richard Ford, Ursula Le Guin, Stanislaw Lem, W.S. Merwin and Gary Snyder. One coup was that Richard Ford published for the first time in the pages of *Edge*. An eighth, planned joint issue with *Modern Poetry in Translation* became *Into the World of Light: An Anthology of Maori Writing*, eventually published in 1982. Contributions to *Edge* included work in Mandarin and Sinhalese, as well as English translations of contemporary French, German, Swedish, Greek, Italian, Rumanian, Serbian and Spanish writing. Edge Press also produced occasional publications such as *Gar(r)otte* (1974), a compilation by Long of poetry and stories by students of Christchurch Teachers' College.   DL

Edge of the Alphabet, The, the third novel by Janet *Frame (Christchurch, *Pegasus; New York, London, 1962; two draft MSS are held in the *Hocken Library) is the first in which she employs a device that features frequently later: an unstable, multi-selved, self-reflexive and intrusive narrator. The novel proper is prefixed by a note stating that it 'was found among the papers of Thora Pattern after her death'. Throughout the novel Thora periodically interrupts the narrative with meta-fictional passages of poetry and prose in which she reminisces, comments on her surroundings and discusses the problems of writing. The novel is her 'journey of discovery through the lives of three people—Toby, Zoe, Pat', to whom she has 'bequeathed' disowned aspects of herself. Each of these characters is on 'the edge of the alphabet', 'on the outskirts of communication', struggling to find a means to express an alternative vision without recourse to corrupt social language. All fail; each succumbs to a kind of death. Toby is a figure familiar to readers of Frame's earlier novel ★*Owls Do Cry*: the alienated epileptic son of Amy and Bob Withers. Following the death of his mother, Toby leaves home for England where he hopes to write a book on 'the Lost Tribe', the subject of a school essay once praised by his teacher. His father mocks this aspiration; indeed, Toby is barely literate. On the ship to England he meets Zoe Bryce, a spinster schoolteacher from the Midlands, who has just completed a working holiday in New Zealand. One night while recovering from sea-sickness in the ship's infirmary, Zoe experiences her first kiss, from a drunken sailor, which she interprets as a transcendental 'act beyond reason'. As a result, she gives up teaching, driven by the need to create and thus to attain the 'light' that is 'beyond [the] alphabets and lines' of reason. Also on board is Pat Keenon, returning from a failed quest to find a New Zealand wife, an insecure Irishman who works as a bus driver in London. Prejudiced, prudish and afraid to look inward, his imaginative repression is, Frame implies, tantamount to a kind of living death (attested to by his later occupation as a 'stationary' salesman). In London Zoe lives in the same boarding house as Pat, and works as a cinema usherette. Toby takes low-grade basement lodgings and is employed as a cinema commissionaire before a mysterious sore on his arm forces him to stop work. Empty and alone, his path rarely crosses that of his fellow travellers and he is unable to even begin his book. One day on the banks of the Serpentine, in the company of a sailor, a prostitute and some artists, Zoe has an intense moment of creativity, making a model forest from silver cigarette paper. Soon after she commits suicide, believing that there is only one way 'to survive. That is, to die'. Toby returns to New Zealand and another kind of death—a life of stifling conformity lived with his ailing Aunt Cora.   KWo

EDMOND, Lauris (1924–), came to prominence as a poet unusually late, her first volume being published when she was 51. Twenty-three years later she is established as one of the most significant, assured and accessible of contemporary poetic voices, and as a widely read autobiographer and commentator.

She was born in Dannevirke in southern Hawkes Bay, the province whose presence colours so much of her first volume of autobiography, *Hot October* (1989). That volume, dramatically opening with the Napier earthquake of 1931, the election of the Labour government in 1935, and the ★Depression years, recreates a strong picture of the 1930s, and demonstrates the variety and importance of extensive family links, as well as the air of difference surrounding her own parents, committed to Social Credit and opposing orthodox medicine.

In 1942, she enrolled at Wellington Teachers' Training College, and *Hot October* reproduces many of her letters to her mother. While she retained affection for Hawkes Bay, and spent time in Christchurch training as a speech therapist, it is clear from the autobiography and the poetry that Wellington came to be of central importance to her. *Hot October* concludes with the end of a war and the beginning of a marriage, and with another departure, this time to Dunedin, with her young husband Trevor Edmond. In spite of misgivings sounded in this volume, and emerging even more strongly in the second, *Bonfires in the Rain* (1991), the story told is in many ways a conventional one, following an unchallenged pattern, in which the needs of children (eventually, five daughters and a son) and the career moves of a husband determine family life. The university study she began while at training college was not finished until 1967, and included part-time or extramural enrolment at four different universities. Similarly, her training as a teacher and speech therapist was only occasionally put to use in paid employment during these years.

The importance of literature is clearly signalled from time to time in each of these volumes; as a child she experiments with writing her own poems and responds to the magic of reading, responses which continue through to training college, and are communicated in the impassioned letters home. Similarly, *Bonfires in the Rain* recalls from the early marriage a shared addiction to poets of the 1930s, recalls, too, the delight in discovering ★*Landfall*, and records the 'completely private act' of writing, an activity which could only be attempted during hastily snatched 'small islands of time'. For the most part, this 'completely private act' involved the keeping of a diary, in which were included 'bits of poems and stories' and '*very* secret thoughts—like that there was plenty of time to become a real New Zealand poet'.

But the transition implicit in the change from 'a shared addiction' to 'a completely private act' affected more than responses to literature, and *Bonfires in the Rain* also records the growing tensions within the Edmonds' marriage, tensions further described in the third volume, *The Quick World* (1992). Like the first volume, *Bonfires in the Rain* ends with momentous events and with a journey. The momentous events include the death of their fourth child, Rachel, and the publication of Lauris Edmond's first volume of poetry, *In Middle Air* (1975), and it is this which marks the author's realisation that writing is to be her 'new work', her 'next journey'.

This 'next journey' is one that led her, within ten years, to extraordinary success and acclaim as a poet, with six volumes published as well as a novel, the award of the Katherine ★Mansfield Memorial Fellowship at Menton in 1981, the Commonwealth Poetry Prize in 1985 for her *Selected Poems* (1984), the OBE in 1986 and an Honorary DLitt of Massey University in 1988. She was writer-in-residence at Deakin University, Melbourne, in 1985 and at Victoria University of Wellington in 1987. Invitations to perform at international arts festivals or on reading tours have taken her to Australia, West Germany, the United States and Great Britain as well as throughout New Zealand; and invitations to participate in creative writing courses and writers-in-schools schemes, to give talks and interviews and to contribute to university courses have been equally numerous, and have been responded to with equal generosity. In addition to the eleven volumes of poetry and three of autobiography, she has published a novel, *High Country Weather* (1984), written radio and stage drama, and edited *Letters of A.R.D. Fairburn* (1981) and *Young Writing* for ★PEN (1979).

This literary rags-to-riches story has been seen as a 'clear-cut, not to say dramatic example' of the difficulties faced by women in New Zealand in the 1950s–60s, postponing their own careers or ambitions in supporting those of their husbands. In some respects, the celebration of Edmond's emergence as a writer after years of marriage and motherhood has overshadowed a proper critical response to the writing itself, as Edmond herself has sometimes complained. (Few New Zealand poets, however, have yet received sustained critical attention.)

An unusual feature of the autobiography's narrative is the inclusion of her own poems at strategic points, which confirms for us that many poems may legitimately be read in close conjunction with the life, and that the first-person pronoun functions as more than an assumed voice. The poetry is deeply, often movingly, and at times painfully personal, from the early elegiac sequence *Wellington Letter* (1980) to the most recent *A Matter of Timing* (1996). Edmond's work is always rooted in experience—a preference that has occasionally been expressed as something of an anti-intellectual attitude. A poem, she said in one interview, is 'a confrontation with experience. It's not an idea.' That 'confrontation' is principally a way of ordering experience, 'composing feelings and experiences and ideas and events that would otherwise become chaotic … and at the end of writing about something I have the measure of it for a while'.

The 'for a while' is important. The process of ordering is primarily heuristic: 'every poem is the end of a discovery'. An early review of *In Middle Air* spoke of the 'series of delicate epiphanies', and that feature has remained distinctive, achieving a status that a reviewer twenty years later could describe as a 'stylistic signature' (and drawing some criticism elsewhere of an apparent sameness of technique). She acknowledged this primacy of the moment of vision in naming one collection *Catching It* (1983), and affirming in its title poem that

'In all of the ticking of time / it can never have happened before, / not like this, not exactly…'. Typically, her poems make use of familiar scenes and images (in that poem, 'three small brown foxy Frenchmen' on a sea wall), everyday experiences and relationships, finding in them sudden moments of significance. Poetry is 'partly idea, partly emotion, and partly a sense of surprise— seeing familiar things in different ways'. To capture that difference in familiarity, she relies for the most part on an urbane simplicity of diction and syntax, allowing herself full use of the rich resources of language that she possesses (what has been described as 'civilized middle-class discourse'), avoiding arcane word games, private spheres of reference or experimental forms.

Edmond's poetry deals, as Fleur ★Adcock has neatly expressed it, 'with topics people care about', which partly explains why she has found a wider audience than is usual for poetry. In her handling of such essential subjects as love, friendship and death, ageing, family relationships, children and grandchildren, the transience of natural beauty and of human happiness, she returns again and again to what ★Baxter called 'the big states'. But where Baxter employed myth and rhetoric to address such themes, Edmond prefers a more natural, relaxed, if always articulate and controlled speaking voice, one that generates conversational intimacy, warmth, humour and humanity. Poems quite often open with an invitation to conversation: 'Let me tell you of my country, how it / suffers the equivocal glories …' ('Wellington Letter XVI'); 'Think of her coming in from the garden …' ('Eden Cultivated'); 'I want to tell you about time, how strangely / it behaves when you haven't got much of it left …' ('In position').

She also writes often and well about response to place, most often Wellington, as in her celebratory *Scenes from a Small City* (1994): 'This is my city, the hills and harbour water / I call home, the grey sky racing over headlands, / awkward narrow streets that stirred me long ago …' ('Round Oriental Bay'). Travel poems recur, responses to scenes or encounters from Dunedin to Delphi, from Bywell with its 'squat Saxon tower' to 'the seething footlights of Fifth Avenue' ('Green').

Of all of the big subjects that her carefully measured words explore, it is perhaps death and the awareness of death which most command attention, whether seen as part of the natural process, witness to our common mortality, or confronted in the harsher circumstances of untimely illness or suicide. But there is no morbidity or dull fatalism in this. The best of the poetry (even in its grieving) is strongly life-affirming. The shift in 'The Quiet Populations' from grief to the early budding of spring is characteristic. Her poetry is vigorously intelligent, sane and clear-eyed. The essential human mortality recognised as our inheritance forms a backdrop against which the positive forces celebrated—love, compassion, friendship, sympathy, the beauty of the natural world (albeit fragmentary), family—all stand out in sharp relief and are welcomed as part of that same inheritance.

Other collections of poems not mentioned above are *The Pear Tree* (1977), *Seven* (1980), *Salt from the North* (1980), *Seasons and Creatures* (1986), *Summer Near the Arctic Circle* (1988), *New and Selected Poems* (1991) and *Selected Poems 1975–1994* (1994). Edmond frequently publishes articles and reviews, most often now in *New Zealand Books, of which she was one of the founders; she contributed guest editorials to *NZ Listener 1976–77, and was guest editor of *Landfall* 125 (March 1978). Interviews include David Dowling in *Landfall* 144 (1982) and Harry *Ricketts in his *Talking About Ourselves* (1986). Her graduation address, *Imagining Ourselves*, was published by Massey University (1988).   PW

EDMOND, Murray (1949–), poet, playwright, editor and critic, was born in Hamilton and attended Hamilton BHS and the University of Auckland, where he completed his MA and PhD in English. He also edited the third and fourth issues of *Freed 1970–71 and participated in alternative theatre groups, including Living Theatre and Beggars Bag Theatre. His first collection of poems, *Entering the Eye* (1973), incorporated 'The Grafton Notebook', a self-contained sequence which included his most anthologised poem, 'Von Tempsky's Dance'. In 1974–76 he was in Europe, mostly in London, where he worked in theatre. Back in New Zealand he resumed involvement with alternative theatre in Wellington as writer, performer and producer for groups such as Theatre Action and the Town and Country Players. *Patchwork: Poems* (1978) was a sequence focusing on domestic milestones, including the birth of his first child. *End Wall: Poems* (1983) collected poems written 1973–81, and encompassed the period abroad. Edmond wrote: 'I have aimed for a tight coherent grouping where dominant concerns are clear'; among these concerns are history, locality, language and the dynamics of personal and family relationships. In 1983 he was writer-in-residence at the University of Canterbury, where he wrote many of the poems in *Letters and Paragraphs* (1987), several of which took the form of verse letters or poems addressed to specific persons; an increasing self-referentiality and consciousness of language as the medium for poetry are also evident. After moving to Auckland in 1984 Edmond worked for Mercury Theatre and then from 1985 began teaching the University's postgraduate diploma in drama. He was also active as a director and dramaturg at several theatre workshops. His full-length musical 'A New

South Pacific' was performed in 1987. *From the Word Go* (1992) showed an increasing focus on linguistic procedures and dramatic manipulation of voice and persona, as in the sequence 'The Thirty-Six Dramatic Situations', while *The Switch* (1994), a sequence of forty-nine short poems, was described as 'a game, a show, an entertainment, a meditation about love and the passage of time'. *Names Manes* (1996), subtitled 'twenty one stories', is a collection of brief gnomic poems involving much sophisticated wordplay. Edmond edited (with Mary Paul) *The New Poets: Initiatives in New Zealand Poetry* (1987), an anthology of poets who began publishing in the 1980s. In 1996 he completed his doctoral thesis on the history of alternative theatre in New Zealand between the 1960s and 1980s, entitled 'Old Comrades of the Future'.   PS

EDWARDS, Mihipeka-Rukuhia (1918–), Te Arawa, Waikato, Ngāti Raukawa, Ngāti Maniapoto, is said to have been 'brought into the world' by her father who was carting flax in the area; the writer's exact birthplace is relayed variously as 'at the old Te Puke race course' or at Maketu. Her mother died three weeks after she was born, a victim to the flu epidemic. Mihi's life story, which is told in the first of her two books *Mihipeka: Early Years* (1990) relates her upbringing from the age of 5 by her kuia at Manakau, just north of Wellington, the period of deprivation following the deaths of her grandparents at the age of 16, an account of the succession of family homes and work experiences as people everywhere struggled to survive the years of the *Depression, and the start of her 'new false life' under an assumed non-Māori name in 1934. Self-described as 'very much a Pakeha' at this period of her life, her retelling of the indignities she suffered as a Māori child is as much the account of a socialisation of a people, even as it gives invaluable insight into her own culture. *Mihipeka: Years of Turmoil* (1992), the sequel, takes up the story from her move to Wellington in 1937, encompassing the turbulent war years, a brief childless wartime marriage, and subsequent marriage intended to give her and her three children 'the status of the Pakeha'. A social worker on a voluntary basis over a thirty-year period within main church structures, her organisational and fund-raising skills for the underprivileged were phenomenal. A healing process, which began in the late 1960s with her support of the Maori Battalion Welfare Fund, saw a return to her Māori heritage and social work focused over a twenty-five year period on Māori concerns and needs. Serving on the Advisory Board of the Salvation Army, Catholic Māori Mission and the Anglican Māori Pastorate, she campaigned tirelessly against alcohol abuse. In 1975 she took part in the Māori Land March, walking from Kaiparapara to Wellington, later inaugurated the teaching of Māori language and custom at many venues including the Health Department, and taught at a primary school, Rongotai College, Wellington HS and Victoria University. By the 1980s a prominent kuia, she accompanied many hui at Te Herenga Waka Marae, Victoria University, and among Te Arawa, her own people, as reo karanga and matriarch. She did not begin writing about her life until 1988, at the age of 70. A third volume, written 'with passion', was apparently rejected as 'too radical'. A woman of great humility, she says it is not for her to promote herself, in keeping with *mana, but in the things that matter to her, her people and the environment she says 'far too much' and believes that 'you should write on what you believe, what you see, what you have experienced…. My hand just keeps on going'.   JBa

EGGLESTON, Kim (1960–), has published *From the Face to the Bin: Poems 1978–1984* (1984); *25 Poems: The Mist Will Rise and the World Will Drip with Gold* (1985); and *The Whole Crack* (1987). Her work has also appeared in *Untold, in *Landfall, in the *Penguin Book of Contemporary New Zealand Poetry* (1989) and in *anthologies of women's writing. Her raw and raunchy style, vigorous rhythms and laid-back syntax belong to live performance, but the hard-biting, often bleak subject matter is more for private consumption. Born in Picton, Eggleston is in part a South Island regional poet, her focus on people: the coal-mining community of Greymouth, or the Otago Peninsula, Dunedin. Relationships are of the essence; settings are domestic and small-town, and the natural world, showing the same indifferent cruelty that characterises her social world, a backdrop to the real business of life. In 'Broad Bay': 'I … / … watch the sea bite the land … the sea is flat / floundering in the mud'. Eggleston's is a tough-girl persona who smokes, drinks, binges and parties in denims and leather jackets, whose playground is the pub, hamburger joint or bar with jukebox, who witnesses death and finds violence in her life, too. Her language matches this image— idiomatic, macho, free-wheeling: 'A small port town / in a flagon / of jailed hill above the sea / where the gulls whip and peeling / follow you into the pub / ushering shipgirls and disease' ('Shake'). Her poems speak of a world with little room for compromise, but as one comment on the cover of *From the Face to the Bin* reads: 'I like the way they come back at ya'.   JW

EGGLESTON, David (1952–), came to prominence in the 1980s as a performance poet in New Zealand and overseas. While his mesmeric incantations and entranced eclecticism of language are certainly at their best in performance, and while his references often draw on the alternative cultures of his audiences, he has increasingly been recognised as a distinctive voice in the development of a localised New Zealand poetic language. Ian *Wedde, Elizabeth Caffin, Damien *Wilkins and others have concurred in praising his energetic crossing of popular culture with the more formal, to produce what Wedde (in the *Penguin Book of New Zealand Verse*) called 'a confident if erratic blend of vernacular, lyric and high demotic'. Eggleton's skills and insights as one of the country's best literary reviewers also suggest that the sometimes frenetic fertility of his own verbal surfaces is, in fact, more knowingly directed than may appear. He works by accumulating allusion, demanding quick recognition of the resonance of the disparate phrases that flicker in the discontinuities familiar in music videos. By mixing local observation with the violent cacophonies of the modern, he can also bring newness to abiding images of New Zealand: 'Above, rare whales in the deep marine, brilliant silver curls of surf fold over / and pile into drifts of blubber weed bright as molten tungsten gone solar'.

Though often scoring points by mockery, especially at the expense of politicians, plutocrats and militarists, the poems celebrate their own energy as 'running commentaries' rather than pausing to condemn or propose change. 'The poet's mission is to hold the attention of the audience,' Eggleton has said. But as well as promoting poetry as popular entertainment, he has embodied the conflicts and combustions within a vibrant young culture. Part Polynesian, he was born in Auckland, grew up partly in Fiji and dropped out of high school to self-publish poetic broadsheets and begin his performance career. He is now based in Dunedin, reviewing widely. His published volumes are *South Pacific Sunrise* (1986), *After Tokyo* (short fiction, 1987), *People of the Land* (1988) and *Empty Orchestra* (1995). He has been included in most anthologies since 1984, both mainstream and avant-garde collections like Michael *Morrissey's *The New Fiction* (1984) and Murray *Edmond and Mary Paul's *The New Poets* (1987). He has published three recordings and texts for collaborations with both modern dance and sculpture. Awards include PEN Best First Book of Poetry 1987, *Burns Fellowship 1990, New Zealand Book Reviewer of the Year 1991 and, uniquely among New Zealand poets, the London *Time Out*'s Street Entertainer of the Year (Poetry) 1985.   RR

Egress was published and for the most part written by Hubert *Witheford and Patrick Hayman. Its single cyclostyled issue appeared in Wellington in March 1946.   SH

ELDRED-GRIGG, Stevan (1952–), is a social historian, fiction writer and autobiographer. His father came from a wealthy Canterbury sheep-farming family; his mother from a poor working-class family in south Christchurch. He was born in the Grey Valley but raised in prosperous suburban Christchurch. He attended Shirley BHS, Canterbury University (MA in history, 1975) and the Australian National University (PhD in history, 1978). Since then he has been a full-time writer based in Christchurch.

Eldred-Grigg is above all a historian of class and of a province: the social mores of Canterbury are an abiding preoccupation. He first became known as a historian with *A Southern Gentry: New Zealanders Who Inherited the Earth* (1980; reissued 1989), tracing the rise and fall of a powerful landed elite in the South Island, accumulating wealth through gold and wool, and the consequent rise of the class on whose work they had depended. *A New History of Canterbury* (1982) continued this rather revisionist approach by focusing not on the politics of the province but on its changing social structure and shifts in social attitudes. This last aspect was developed further in a comprehensive general study, *Pleasures of the Flesh: Sex and Drugs in Colonial New Zealand 1840–1915* (1984). Two further works on the history of class culture, coming boldly up to the 1990s, are *New Zealand Working People 1890–1990*, published by Dunmore in 1990 as part of the Trade Union History Project, and the contrasting *The Rich: A New Zealand History* (1996). As a historian, Eldred-Grigg has refined a consistent approach: categorisation first by period and then by topic, within which patterns or trends are established with the support of statistics and lavish anecdotal examples. It is popular history, impressionistic and emphasising human foible.

Eldred-Grigg's fiction has similar concerns. The family trilogy that began with *Oracles and Miracles* (1987; often reprinted) traces the lives of sisters Fag and Ginnie, born and raised in south Christchurch in the 1930s and '40s, and their efforts to escape their impoverished background. Fag marries the ineffectual son of a wealthy Canterbury sheep farmer, and the second book, *The Shining City* (1991), tells the story of their son Roddie and his close cousin Christopher, growing up in affluent suburban Christchurch and then at Canterbury University in the swinging '60s and '70s. The third, *Mum* (1995), portrays Ginnie through the eyes of two of her children, the self-deceiving Jimmy and the appalled Viv. The same technique of dual alternating first-person narratives is used in each book, and the language of each character is remarkably appropriate to his or her personality, time and place. The trilogy is strongly rooted in Eldred-Grigg's own family and personal experience.

Oracles and Miracles, the most powerful and admired book, has been treated as oral history, and adapted for radio and stage, though this highly wrought documentary quality, while increasing the authenticity, makes for a lack of emotional perspective which comes for some readers to vitiate the trilogy as fiction. The same quality is found in the early novella, *Of Ivory Accents* (New York, 1977), and the occasional short stories from the same period.

Eldred-Grigg's three other novels can also be regarded as shaped local/social history. *The Siren Celia* (1989) takes its characters, themes and historical and other detail from George ★Chamier's novel *A ★South-Sea Siren* (1895) and Sarah ★Courage's memoir *Lights and Shadows of Colonial Life* (c.1896), to portray double standards among the high society of colonial South Canterbury. *Gardens of Fire* (1993) freeze-frames the social structure of Christchurch in November 1947 by showing the complex caste system of Ballantyne's department store on the day of its great fire. *Blue Blood* (1997) takes one of Canterbury's most famous daughters, Ngaio ★Marsh, in 1929, at the outset of her career and places her in a sordid pastiche detective story that exaggeratedly resembles her own later fictions.

The tension between history, oral history, autobiography and fiction in Eldred-Grigg's work is most explicit in his memoir, *My History, I Think* (1994). Here, in an intricate game that clearly fascinates the writer, he sets out to give shape and purpose to his own life, his work as a historian and his writing of fiction by counterpointing more or less revealing glimpses of each.   AM

'Elegy' (1950), a poem sequence by Alistair ★Campbell, see *Mine Eyes Dazzle*.

ELLIS, Ellen E. (1829–95), was a novelist and women's rights activist. Born Ellen Colebrook in Guildford, England, she emigrated in 1859 with her husband and children to Auckland, where she became influenced by Rev. Samuel Edger, advocate of women's education. She read widely, became involved in temperance work and joined The Good Templars. Her only novel, *Everything is Possible to Will* (London, 1882), is autobiographical. The fictional heroine Zee marries Wrax, who like Ellis's husband is an alcoholic, and emigrates to New Zealand where he is rescued by The Good Templars. The book contains long passages strongly promoting women's rights and temperance: 'Public opinion can … strike the chains of slavery from woman's intellect and heart, and make woman's emancipation the grandest trophy of Victoria's reign'; 'Man must be taught that he can and must control his animal passions, and women must refuse to be sacrificed to his lust'; 'The Drunkard's wife and little ones are the slaves legally of the vilest slave holder that ever owned human cattle....' It may have been published with the assistance of women suffragists and temperance advocates. Her son William (who married Manawa Maniapoto, niece of chief Rewi Maniapoto) was distressed by the fictional portrayal of his father as an alcoholic, and bought up and burnt every copy of the book he could. Ellis wrote perceptive commentaries as letters home to England, one of which was published in the *Auckland Waikato Historical Journal* in 1991. The centenary of ★women's suffrage in 1993 created renewed interest in Ellis's writings. The biography, *Ellen* (Dublin, 1980), by relative Vera Colebrook, discusses connections between Ellis's life and her novel and makes Ellis better known than other nineteenth-century temperance novelists.   ALa

ELMSLY, John (1952–), composer, was born in Auckland and trained in composition at Victoria University of Wellington, the Brussels Conservatorium and the Conservatoire Royale in Liège. Among an extensive repertoire of styles and techniques, he has set poems by Charles ★Brasch, in *On Home Ground* (1985), and by other New Zealand poets.   JMT

ELSE, Barbara (1947–), playwright and fiction writer, who has also published as Barbara Neale, was born in Invercargill and educated at Otago University (MA 1969). She has lived in Wellington since 1980, working since 1988 with her husband Chris ★Else as a literary agent, editor and fiction consultant. She has published short stories in ★*Landfall*, ★*Metro*, ★*NZ Listener*, in anthologies such as *Me and Marilyn Monroe* (ed. Cathie ★Dunsford, 1993) and elsewhere, and several on radio, as well as another ten for children.

Her published plays include *Night for Clowns* (1987) and *A Very Short History of the World* (1985); four full-length plays have been performed, as have a variety of one-act plays, children's plays and radio dramas. She has won several awards and grants, including the Aoraki Festival Playwriting Award and support from the New Zealand ★Literary Fund.

The Warrior Queen (1995), Else's first novel, was received with enthusiastic acclaim. Kate Wildburn takes subtle, and sometimes unsubtle, revenge on her husband Richard for his affair with another woman. He is a surgeon and the characters are all of the trendy set in Auckland, married to their possessions as much as each other. Persuaded by a counsellor that her husband's affair can be no fault of hers, Kate sets out to embarrass him and trip him up at every turn. A series of comic events follows, rich in variety rather than insight, and both parties seem bound to a superficial level of feeling: lust on one side and hurt pride on the other. Their pursuits

are interwoven with the promiscuous affairs of Kate's sister. It is hard to sympathise with any character but easy to sense cathartic satisfaction in the practical jokes the wife succeeds in playing on her man. The book is notable for its cracking pace and sharp wit. *Gingerbread Husbands* (1997) is a suburban comedy whose protagonist fends off almost anything from importunate men to furry animals in the laundry.   NW

ELSE, Chris (1942–), has usually been discussed in the context of ★postmodernism, though his fiction has developed idiosyncratically beyond his beginnings as a writer for ★*Mate* and contributor to Michael ★Morrissey's *The New Fiction* (1985). The ten stories in *Dreams of Pythagoras* (1981) are wittily unpredictable rather than abstruse or surreal, often funny though sometimes ghoulishly so, setting up tensions between the world of the mind, especially numerological and lexical play, and dingy domesticity, and with some arresting opening sentences: 'Fourteen storeys above the street, Poultice sits in his kitchen sink scratching himself with a safety pin.' The book is tinged with an apocalyptic darkness that may derive from Else's British boyhood under the shadow of the bomb but also lifts the fiction beyond the merely local. The novel *Why Things Fall* (1991, Australia 1992) is located in New Zealand, the story of an Aucklander journeying to his father's last home in remote Northland and thus into his own past and identity; but is embedded in a polychronic narrative that includes encounters with Isaac Newton (his ancestor) in seventeenth-century Lincolnshire and Cambridge, and with Lord Rutherford in 1919. The search for scientific knowledge provides an image and context for the search for self-knowledge; hence the Newtonian title for a novel that also includes one death by falling and at least one major moral lapse. Another volume of short fiction, *Endangered Species*, was published in 1996.

Born in Hull, England, Else arrived in 1956, living in Auckland until 1977. He has worked in teaching, bookselling and data-processing. Currently he is a literary agent, technical writing consultant and partner with his wife, Barbara ★Else, in a Wellington editorial agency, which among other contributions is credited by Alan ★Duff for 'visionary advice' in the acknowledgments to ★*Once Were Warriors*.   RR

End of the Golden Weather, The (1962; revised 1970), a solo drama, is Bruce ★Mason's most popular work, and probably still the best-known dramatic piece in New Zealand literature. Mason has documented the one-man saga of presenting the show in several places, including the introduction to the 1970 edition, in *Bruce Mason Solo* (1981), in his *Beginnings* article (1980) and in *Every Kind of Weather* (1986). Of his national tour in 1960, Mason said, 'I have met 10,000 of my countrymen face to face, offering them material thrown up from our corporate life.... I regard it as the richest artistic experience—so to dignify it—of my life.'

The title of the work is from Thomas Wolfe's *The Web and the Rock* but the ideas of the play also reflect Wolfe's more famous work, *You Can't Go Home Again*. It cleverly celebrates home and simultaneously recognises home as a sentimental, mythologised construct. As Mason puts it in his monologue 'Not Christmas, but Guy Fawkes' (1976; published in *Bruce Mason Solo*), in *Golden Weather* he identified in himself 'three separate elements: the prodigious or over-reaching, the compassionate and the comic. When I can make an arch of them, deploy them in a beneficent tension, my work seems to be at its best.'

The 'territory of the heart' which Mason mines begins with the pure nostalgia of 'Sunday at Te Parenga' with its loving friends and neighbours, 'the immaculate present, endlessly pouring its essence on us'. 'The Night of the Riots' marks the end of the golden weather but the start of a more mature compassion for all members of all classes of society, including workers and policemen. 'Christmas at Te Parenga' therefore comes as a renewed blessing, the comedy turning against the narrator in his overreaching performance. The final moment of his reconciliation with his brother reprises the appearance of the social wounds in the previous section, and only an act of imaginative sympathy, as the narrator appreciates 'the complexity of human motive and behaviour', heals those cracks. The second half of the play, 'The Made Man', spans the time periods of the first half, and uses the disturbed character of Firpo to implicate the narrator in the adult world of violence and discrimination. Firpo is the overreacher, the narrator chooses compassion, and the comedy is in the eyes of the beach community. The piece's power comes from the boy's mistake in encouraging Firpo's self-deception, and its pathos from the brutal confrontation both naïfs have with reality on the beach. The satire works both ways, against the community and against the dreamer. Ian Mune's film version (1992) brought Mason's story to a new generation of New Zealanders. Predictably, it focuses on the highly dramatic and visual story of Firpo the made man, the would-be Olympic athlete. Where the play taught theatrically inexperienced audiences that they could make a man just by thinking about him, the film's emphasis is on unmaking someone by putting him or her into a levelling society where the team counts for more than the private dream.

Mason's much-loved solo drama has been hugely influential in New Zealand's theatrical tradition. For many it was their first or only encounter with live theatre. Roger *Hall has praised Mason as a *'Man Alone' of letters, embodying with resourceful independence all the indigenous theatre there was, certainly in the small towns, for at least a decade. Mervyn *Thompson's use of song-theatre and solo drama also owes much to Mason's theatre of minimal means, as do the many one-person shows popular in the 1990s, such as Cathy *Downes's *The Case of Katherine Mansfield* or John *Broughton's *Michael James Manaia*. A tribute to Mason and *Golden Weather* form part of Thompson's last play, *Passing Through*. DD

English, see *New Zealand English.

ENSING, Riemke (1939–   ), is a poet who has distinctively synthesised European and New Zealand influences. Born in Groningen, *Netherlands, she arrived in 1951 and came to attention as editor of the first New Zealand *anthology of women poets, *Private Gardens* (1977). Her own work developed slowly and deliberately as she reflected on her European heritage and absorbed local literary trends. Her first volume, *Letters* (1982), emphasised in its title a self-consciousness about the literary process that has continued to characterise her writing. Her reputation as poet and scholar has grown, especially with three books published in 1995: *Dear Mr Sargeson*, written in homage after visiting Frank *Sargeson's cottage; *Like I have seen the dark green ladder climbing*, a response to paintings by Eion Stevens; and *Gloria-in-Excelsis*, an edition of the poetry of Gloria *Rawlinson. Ensing's interest in art, evident in her reviews and her catalogue of Stanley Palmer's paintings (1992), overflows into her poetry in an arresting and original way. Her practice is similar to collage, drawing attention to the density of her texts by making their allusiveness visually apparent on the page itself. Her European background is manifest in the subject matter of many earlier poems, from *Topographies* (1984) to *Spells from Chagall* (1987). She began to absorb New Zealand voices with *The KM File and Other Poems with Katherine Mansfield* (1993), mostly written for the *Mansfield Centenary Conference in 1988. They integrate echoes of Mansfield's voice through quotations, autograph signatures, photographs and illustrations. Such experiments in layout and *typography are key to Ensing's fusion of her own cultures, re-establishing fragments from New Zealand literary icons and placing their past words in a present context. Thus many of the poems are prefaced by dedications. She teaches New Zealand literature at Auckland University. JW

Envoy from Mirror City, The, is the third and (currently) final volume of autobiography by Janet *Frame (Auckland, New York, London, 1985; published together with Volume One, *To the Is-Land and Volume Two, An *Angel at My Table, as Janet Frame: An Autobiography, 1989). It won the Wattie Book of the Year Award and the New Zealand Book Award for Non-fiction. The volume treats the years in which Frame first travelled abroad, concluding with her return to New Zealand following the death of her father (1956–65). In the first section, Frame recalls the unsettling months after her arrival in London before she journeyed to the Balearic Islands, via Paris, where she had a brief love affair with a young American history professor in Ibeza, resulting in a 'shortlived pregnancy'; and her absorption into local family life in Andorra and her unofficial engagement to an 'Italian gentleman' before her return to London. The second section details her years in London while living in a series of temporary lodgings and taking on various jobs (cinema usherette, housemaid), before being granted National Assistance which enabled her to concentrate wholly on her writing. Frame recounts her elation, and fear, when a panel of psychiatrists at the Maudsley Institute authoritatively dismissed an earlier diagnosis of schizophrenia, suggesting that any problems she now experienced were the result of her years in hospital: 'No longer, I hoped, dependent on my "schizophrenia" for comfort and attention and help, but with myself as myself, I again began my writing career.' Frame's prolific output during this period stands testimony to her new sense of professional commitment: she wrote and published three novels (*Faces in the Water, 1961; The *Edge of the Alphabet, 1962; *Scented Gardens for the Blind, 1963) and two collections of stories (The *Reservoir: Stories and Sketches, 1963, and Snowman, Snowman: Fables and Fantasies, 1963). More than a factual chronicle of her travels abroad, the autobiography recounts Frame's apprenticeship and maturation as a writer. The reader is offered the dual perspective of external factual details and inner perceptions tempered throughout by the ironic vantage point of the remembering, shaping writer. Frame not only records but exemplifies her understanding of the co-dependency, not strict separation, of the worlds of literature and life. Again and again she returns to her titular images to suggest the role of the creative self, 'The Envoy', in shaping lived experiences and memories into the 'Mirror City' of words and artistic representation. Of her return to New Zealand she writes, 'I had learned to be a citizen of the Mirror City', where the only graveyard 'is the graveyard of memories that are resurrected, reclothed with reflection and change, their essence untouched. (A truthful autobiography tries to record the essence. The renewal and change are part of the

material of fiction.)' Frame has indefinitely deferred further volumes of autobiography, claiming she is still too close to the 'recent past', the facts of which have 'not yet been transformed' by the Envoy into the 'found fiction' of autobiography.   KWo

Erewhon or Over the Range (1872), a satire by Samuel *Butler, is generally regarded as ranking with More's Utopia and Swift's Gulliver's Travels as an ironic fiction of lasting importance. Written in London six years after Butler returned from Canterbury Settlement, its title inverts 'Nowhere' and thus echoes the true meaning of *'Utopia', following More and Swift in using a journey to an imaginary country to highlight and ridicule contemporary customs and deeper human shortcomings. Its topical targets include the self-interest and mercenariness underlying Anglican Christianity (mocked in Erewhon's 'Musical Banks'), prudish Victorian censoriousness (the 'Ydgrunites') and the seductive fatuity of university education of the time (the 'Colleges of Unreason'). There are also challenges to ethical and philosophical belief, quirkily irreverent at the time, which have become profoundly pertinent in the course of the twentieth century, notably the neo-Darwinian warning about the tendency of technology to reorder human affairs, not necessarily for the better (the 'Book of the Machines'), and the exposure of the social and psychological causes of crime and obtuseness of the justice system (in the Erewhonian inversion of attitudes to crime and illness).

Its significance as a major text of New Zealand literature has received little attention, apart from documentary interest in the opening section of sheep farming and exploration. This clearly and specifically derives from Butler's Rangitata experiences of 1860–61, despite the narrator's coy avoidance of identifying New Zealand. The narrative in these five chapters is of more than biographical interest, as the taut laconic lyricism of its descriptive passages, its counterpointing of local vernacular with European cultural allusion and its subverting of the rhapsodic by the pragmatic all established an imaginative literary relationship to the New Zealand *landscape that has remained current. Some passages dealing with solitude in such surroundings ('One begins doubting one's own identity') may also mark the inception of the *'Man Alone' and *Existentialist traditions. The downbeat humour has also become a national characteristic: 'Exploring is delightful to look forward to and back upon, but it is not comfortable at the time.' After some months as a *'new chum', the narrator (named as Higgs only in the 1901 sequel, *Erewhon Revisited) bribes 'an old native, whom they had nicknamed Chowbok—though, I believe, his real name was

Kahabuka' to guide him into the ranges, in hopes of finding gold or sheep-country. Chowbok deserts when Higgs insists on approaching *tapu ground, where he encounters some forbidding giant statues, possibly derived in part from observation of carved *marae gate-posts, and in part from some upright rock-formations near Butler's first run on Forest Creek. Over the range, New Zealand scenery is replaced by that of Butler's beloved northern Italy, and after a slyly described affair between Higgs and his gaoler's daughter (in which it is tempting to find some autobiographical hints), the satiric interest takes priority over the narrative.

Here, the 'Book of the Machines' chapters are an expanded version of the essay 'Darwin among the Machines' which Butler published in the Christchurch *Press, 13 June 1863, shortly after reading Darwin's *Origins of Species* in his Rangitata sod hut. In *Erewhon Revisited* he also acknowledged that Māori practice influenced his idea of the treatment of illness and misfortune as an offence. But the main New Zealand element is the basic metaphor of inversion, the Erewhonian equivalent of Swift's manipulations of scale. This provides not only a disturbingly unpredictable ironic device, but an imaginative version of antipodean colonial experience, at various times absurdist, black comic and near-tragic. The uneasy alliance between reversed English names and romanticised Māori ones, as with Higgs's eventual wife, Arowhena Nosnibor, is only the most obvious of several signs of disjunction. The ending of *Erewhon* is the one place where this elusive and provocative satire takes on a Swiftian indignation. After escaping by balloon with Arowhena, in a well-written vignette of adventure narrative, Higgs, shifting character like Gulliver to suit the ironic purpose of the moment, plans to capitalise on the claim to have discovered the Lost Tribe of Israel, and to return to Erewhon supported by missionaries and a gunboat to convert the Erewhonians compulsorily to Christianity and ship them as slave labour to the Queensland sugar plantations. An article in the *Times* (28 Dec. 1871) about indentured Polynesians in Queensland seems to have sparked this savage satire on missionary imperialism. While it is a final shot at Victorian values rather than a considered critique of colonialism, it is consistent with the opposition by the *Press* to land theft in the name of the church, with the respect Butler expressed on several occasions for Māori, and with the not unsympathetic treatment of Chowbok/Kahubuka's spiritual trance and concern for sacred land. Only as the zealous Christian Rev. Habakkuk on the last page does he receive the lash of the irony.

Published anonymously, *Erewhon* had initial success. There were editions in March and July 1872, several further issues and a revised 'ninth edition' in conjunction with *Erewhon Revisited* in 1901. Butler's name first appeared on the 'fifth edition', 1873. The book has never been out of print and is included in all series of popular literary classics. It was issued in 'Golden Press New Zealand Classics' in 1973, a facsimile of the edition by Cape, London, 1960; a New Zealand 'illustrated' edition is forthcoming. The only scholarly edition is that edited by Hans-Peter Breuer and Daniel F. Howard (Newark, Delaware, 1981). The manuscript is in the British Library.   RR

Erewhon Revisited (1901) was the last work of Samuel *Butler. A sequel to *Erewhon*, written in poor health, its imaginative energy is in the recreation of his memories of Canterbury and the Southern Alps forty years earlier, and in the autobiographical wish-fulfilment of finding a son, rather than in the relatively uninspired satiric material. The story is supposedly told by the *Erewhon* narrator's son, John Higgs, who reconstructs his ailing father's fragmentary diaries of his return to Erewhon after the death of his wife Arowhena. These recount the discovery of an unknown son, George, from his earlier affair with Yram the gaoler's daughter, now happily married to the town's mayor. Higgs's safety is threatened by the malevolent Professors Hanky and Panky, defenders of the state religion of Sunchildism which has grown out of the supposed miracle of Higgs's ascent by balloon at the end of *Erewhon*. The manly, somewhat idealised George helps him to escape and he returns to England to die. The several partings, between the former lovers, father and son, and a year later the two brothers, are mawkishly treated, but the journeys through the mountains are strongly and vividly reconstructed, with Butler now paying open tribute to his old horse, Doctor, a hospitable high-country shepherd, and other memories such as the habits of quail and tui. Several specific 'comparisons' with New Zealand leave little doubt as to the intended setting.

The inversion metaphor is extended from *Erewhon* into the comical appearance of Professor Panky in European dress worn back to front, but is not sustained. The main satiric target is the Church for the fervour of its belief in the absurd, the rigidity of its rituals and concern with holding on to its power. The tone, however, is nostalgic and valedictory and the true subject is Butler's memories of New Zealand and sense of loss that he can never revisit them.

Fairly successful on first publication, the book went through eight impressions by 1920, and a further seven by 1964, but is rarely reprinted now. There is no New Zealand edition.   RR

'Escape, The', a short story by Katherine *Mansfield, was published in the *Athenaeum* (July 1920) and subsequently included in the collection *Bliss and Other Stories* (Dec. 1920). The date of composition is unknown. No MS is known. Presenting the reactions of an English couple to having missed their train, it is characteristic of Mansfield's mature technique in that the intermingling of and contrasts between the two characters' interior monologue and direct speech form the story. The first part of the narrative, channelled through the consciousness of the wife, establishes a tone of disgust and frustration which gives way, in the second part of the narrative, channelled through the consciousness of the husband, to acceptance. While characters attempt physical, emotional and psychological escape, they also try to accept the status quo. This makes for a thematic connection with 'The Black Cap', *'Bliss' and *'Miss Brill'. The man's experience, beginning 'As he looked at the tree he felt his breathing die away and he became part of the silence', is the nearest expression in Mansfield's fiction to a conventional Joycean epiphany. The story has not received a great deal of critical attention but W.H. New's 'Reading "The Escape"' in *Katherine Mansfield: In From the Margin*, ed. Roger Robinson (1994), argues convincingly for a more central position. SSa

ESCOTT, Margaret (1908–77), a novelist of the 1930s, who also wrote as 'C.M. Allen', was born in England and arrived in New Zealand at the age of 17. The family stayed temporarily on a Waikato farm, where she gained knowledge evident in her major novel, *Show Down*. They settled in Auckland, where she taught for a year at a technical college and wrote articles for the *New Zealand Herald* which reveal her concern for questions of social injustice. Still a teenager, she decided to pursue a career as a writer in England, where work as a lift attendant in the Times Book Club aroused the anger at the inequity of wealth and poverty that is felt in her novels. She later joined the library staff of the Club and spent her nights writing.

Much of what she wrote did not satisfy her own standards, but three novels emerged—her complete novelistic output, completed before her 26th birthday. *Insolence of Office* (1934) is the story of a talented musician with some resemblance to the author. The tension between her love for a violinist and distaste for the luxurious life he leads makes her leave him. *Awake at Noon* (1935) is also concerned with the gap between rich and poor. Its heroine, a female doctor, fights for the rights of exploited nurses and for a labour leader victimised because of his work for the unemployed.

These two novels, both set in England, were published under the pseudonym 'C.M. Allen'. When her agent asked for unpublished work, she sent him the manuscript of *Show Down*, which she had been reluctant to release, partly because of its New Zealand setting. He at once sent it to Chatto and Windus, who published it in 1936 under the name 'M. Escott', which, together with its narrative point of view, led reviewers to assume it was written by a man. It was also published in New York by W.W. Norton as *I Told My Love*. Reviewers found it 'direct' and 'very modern' and spoke of the author's 'great talent'. Its first-person narrator is a New Zealand farmer, who falls in love with a newly arrived Englishwoman. Their relationship is described with unusual sexual frankness and maturity for the work of a young woman writing in the 1930s. The narrative continues beyond marriage, presenting both partners engaged in stressful affairs and their eventual separation.

Show Down was commercially successful and admired for its bold clear style, unsentimental presentation of passionate love and balanced structure. With the royalties Escott returned to New Zealand, where she worked on her brother's farm before moving to Auckland. There she was a drama teacher, librarian, tutor, adjudicator at drama festivals and broadcaster. Dissatisfied with her novels, she turned to the theatre. She is said to have destroyed a large pile of manuscripts. In 1971 she wrote and produced *Saved*, a play to commemorate the centenary of Auckland's status as a municipality. *Show Down* was reissued by *Auckland University Press in their series 'New Zealand Fiction' in 1973. NW

Est I Rom was a little magazine of poetry and fiction published in Wellington in 1955. Its single issue was edited by Don Harris and printed by Donald St John with the cover of each copy hand-illustrated by Ivan Johnson. SH

EVANS, Charlotte (1842–82), wrote two novels, published in the same year (1874), and with the same subtitle, *A Story of New Zealand*, set in Canterbury but redolent of genteel Englishness. *A Strange Friendship* tells of two sisters, living very circumscribed lives—quite unlike contemporary tales of Māori conflicts or floods on the goldfields. 'We had only one sitting-room, but that was a good-sized room, the very pride of our hearts.... Why, it actually had a piano ... books ... a pretty work table ... pictures by Landseer and Smart.' The heart of the story is the mystery of the neighbouring Ainsleighs: are they brother and sister as they claim? In fact they are two brothers, one in disguise, and this rascal elopes with the narrator's sister. *Over the Hills, and Far Away* is presented in its preface as a sort of historical account of 'some years ago.... The land which lay waste and desolate is now fenced and under cultivation, and society has become more formal and conforms more strictly to the rules in vogue in Europe.' The dream of making the desert English is being fulfilled. There are pianos, croquet and the drinking of claret.   NW

EVANS, Claude (1903–86), wrote a series of well-made and well-received plays, late 1940s–50s, for Christchurch amateur theatre, especially the Canterbury Repertory Theatre. At least eight full-length scripts were published, extraordinary for any date, though none was performed outside Christchurch. The early ones, especially, such as *The Clock Strikes the Hour* (1946) or *Underwood* (1947), belong to that city and era—social comedies, often set nostalgically in pre–World War 2 England. *Far Journey* (1949) breaks this pattern, being about the 1938 war in *China. Later Evans used New Zealand settings, though his dramatic edge always tended to come from class issues expressed in class accents, from the corrupt lawyer of *That Man Harlington* (1952) to the cantankerous old cabinet-maker of *Overtime* (1954; publ. 1955). *So Laughs the Wind* (1959) is set at Akaroa. Ted's farewell speech at the end of *Overtime*, a lament for passing values, has more dramatic force than is usually now attributed to Evans, and might even be called a foreshadowing of the similar nostalgic incantation that was to end *Foreskin's Lament* (1980), in a very different theatrical era. Evans also deserves credit for generating local theatre in the period before Bruce *Mason and Roger *Hall.

He was as much part-time and amateur as the actors of that time. Born in Christchurch, he practised there as an accountant, specialising in accounting law and taxation and serving as chairman of several companies. RR

EVANS, Patrick (1944–), fiction writer, playwright, and literary critic and historian, is one of the funniest and most darkly satiric of contemporary writers. Born in India, he has lived in Christchurch since 1949. Educated at Linwood HS and the University of Canterbury (MA 1968, PhD 1974), he was briefly a schoolteacher, joined the university's English department in 1970 and is now associate professor. One of the first local critics to write substantially on Janet *Frame, in *An Inward Sun* (1971) and *Janet Frame* (1977), author of several essays on New Zealand fiction, and a perceptive and provocative reviewer, he is best known for his *Penguin History of New Zealand Literature* (1990). This characterful commentary manages to be both insightful and irreverent, both authoritative and downright wicked, full of roguish squibs yet also a consistently useful survey.

Evans began publishing short fiction in *Islands* and *Landfall* in the mid-1970s, and has two novels to his credit, probably best (though over-simply) described as black comedies. *Being Eaten Alive* (1980) starts as a satire on schoolteaching and modern educational pretensions, as wittily cynical as early Kingsley Amis or recent Craig *Harrison, then turns into a weirdly surrealist horror story with echoes of Thomas Pynchon, in which a television game show of pursuit and death is played out around sewage recycling ponds, a murderous clan of schoolboys mount a machine gun on the school tractor, and the hapless central character ends the story trapped inside a carnivorous television set, cooking and eating his own dismembered arm.

Making It (1989) is less unspeakable, but psychologically even darker, almost to the point of nihilism, though a perverse vestige of male romanticism lingers beneath its pungent surface. The realist narrative of the love life of a disaster-prone Christchurch real estate salesman carries something of the Jewish 'schlemiel' tradition in its self-mocking complaint and final resilience on the very brink of despair. Unlike some other imitations of American fiction, it has enough imaginative strength and local habitation to sustain its *postmodern subversion by fragmentation and fantasy, particularly effective in the dislocations and overlayerings of personal memory in the chapter 'Making It'. For all his international awareness, Evans's manic Weltschmerz remains located in territory also occupied by *Morrieson and *O'Sullivan.

He has written three award-winning short plays. All have been revived and performed outside Christchurch, though none has yet been published. 'The Meeting' won the *Christchurch Star* best new play award for 1985; 'Stuff: A Play on Words', first performed 1993, won the Theatre Foundation Award for best new playscript 1995; and 'Cold Turkey', a comedy on the tribulations of giving up smoking, won the Aoraki Festival playwriting award, 1993. First performed in 1995, it also had a season at Wellington's Circa Theatre in 1996.   RR

Existentialism in its nascent form is evident in several early New Zealand settler narratives. Articulate precursors of the *'Man Alone' like Richard Raleigh in George *Chamier's *Philosopher Dick* (1891) and *A *South-Sea Siren* (1895), Hugh Clifford in William *Satchell's *The *Land of the Lost* (1902) or Cedric Tregarthen and his adoptive father, Purcell, in *The *Greenstone Door* (1914) are deracinated, isolated and alienated, symptoms commonly associated with the existentialist mood and challenging the age's dominant myth of progress towards a Britain of the South Seas.

During the 1930s John *Mulgan and Frank *Sargeson (among others) debunked that myth with 'Men Alone' who struggled constantly against a recalcitrant Nature and yet could not prosper. Probably created independent of existentialist influences but sharing a common source in Hemingway, they are transitional figures. There are obvious similarities between Johnson in Mulgan's *Man Alone* (1939), Bill in Sargeson's *'That Summer'* and Camus' Meursault in *L'Étranger* (1942): all are drifters, their narratives emphasising present-tense sensations which they are unable to evaluate. For Mulgan and Sargeson these existentialist characteristics are a focus for criticism of New Zealand during the *Depression, rather than endorsement of Camus' suggestion of the meaninglessness of a world without transcendent values.

Dan *Davin and Guthrie *Wilson, producing novels from the mid-1940s to the 1950s, show awareness of existentialist concepts, though disapproving of them. In *Cliffs of Fall* (1945) Davin demonstrates, through the Raskolnikov-like Mark Burke, that extreme atheistic existentialism leads to murder and suicide. Davin then settled into fictions governed by assumptions of a godless, determined world, as in the Mick Connolly short stories in *The *Gorse Blooms Pale* (1947). Later, he would be less concerned with the determined fate of individuals than with how successfully they directed their own lives, as he matured into accommodation to the imperatives of modern existence.

Wilson also seemed to disapprove of existentialism, but did not moderate his reservations about its nihilistic consequences. The protagonists of *The Feared and the Fearless* (1954) and *Strip Jack Naked* (1957) recite popular existentialist dogma as they personify supermen. While living beyond the confines of morality, however, Wilson's supermen are hapless victims or criminals whose existential 'freedom' leads them inevitably to murder and self-destruction.

Other writers were more positively influenced by existentialism. A comparison between two treatments of the Stanley Graham murders, by R.M. *Burdon in *Outlaw's Progress* (1943) and Erik de Mauny in *The Huntsman in His Career* (1949), shows that as awareness of fashionable post-war existentialism grew among New Zealand writers, it changed the focus of their narratives from exposing the causes of violence to allowing characters to accept responsibility for their own destiny. Like Johnson, the protagonist of Burdon's novel is a victim of the Depression. Unable to see himself as a criminal after shooting the man he thought was threatening his farm, Marley seeks shelter in the bush, which he perceives in existential detail, until he too is hunted and killed. De Mauny's treatment of the story evinces the ideas of Sartre, whose *Portrait of the Anti-Semite* he had translated in 1948. Two main characters are victims, Cleaves of his underprivileged upbringing and Milsom of the Depression. In Villiers, however, who hunts and kills

Milsom, de Mauny has created a 'Man Alone' conscious of his existential freedom to choose his own destiny at the same time as he is aware that he must live within society. Villiers is the first existentialist in New Zealand literature who is neither mentally unbalanced nor so alienated that he is a threat to society.

Greville *Texidor also creates existentialist symbols of hopeless struggle to climb insurmountable barriers in *These Dark Glasses* (1949), while other stories seem to be pessimistic restatements of Camus' definition of the absurd. Unlike Camus, Texidor could find no cause for happiness in a meaningless world. Not one of her stories celebrates Camus' paradox of human dignity in the face of certain defeat as do Satchell or Mulgan.

By 1959 existentialism was 'in the air', as Marilyn *Duckworth has said, though she had not read any existentialist literature before writing the Sartre-like *A Gap in the Spectrum* (1959). In a situation reminiscent of Sartre's *Nausea*, the insecure, amnesiac protagonist learns to take responsibility for her destiny away from the protective confines of New Zealand, reversing the journey of the early 'Men Alone'.

Redmond *Wallis's *Point of Origin* (1962) includes explicit references to Sartre. The protagonist declares his existential freedom at the end: 'The city is a graph, the Square origin, and I a point. This time and this place is my point of origin. I begin to plot my curve.' The protagonist in Graham *Billing's *Forbush and the Penguins* (1965) similarly learns to value his existential struggle, realising that the Antarctic environment is utterly indifferent to the existence of the determined creatures that live there, falling into suicidal depression, yet surviving by understanding that his freedom to hasten his own death means that he is not completely determined.

Albert *Wendt makes explicit references to Camus' essays in *Sons for the Return Home* (1973) and *Leaves of the Banyan Tree* (1980), and ends *Sons* by connecting the legend of Maui to Camus' myth of Sisyphus.

References to French existentialism have faded gradually from New Zealand's literature. In a predominantly secular society which has come to terms with its environment, the struggle to survive in a godless, indifferent universe has been absorbed into writers' continuing preoccupation with the necessity of fellowship. DB

Experiment was the magazine of the Literary Society of Victoria University of Wellington 1956–69. After several established poets added weight to early issues it rapidly developed into an important periodical for younger writers. After a slight loss of impetus in the mid-1960s, the last few numbers were revived by contributions from the group of poets associated with *Freed. *Experiment* was a major outlet in the brief career of the

Italian immigrant writer Renato *Amato and also featured early work by Albert *Wendt.   SH

EYRE, Annette or **Anne**, is one of the publishing names of Anne Worboys, a prolific novelist of the 1960s–1970s, who also published as Vicky Maxwell and as Anne Worboys. Biographical details are uncertain. Anne Eyre's dust-jacket biographies describe her colourfully as born in Auckland, descended from a couple who arrived on the *Aurora* ('the first passenger ship to New Zealand, in 1839'), great-niece of Edward Eyre who 'discovered' Lake Eyre in Australia, brought up on her father's sheep *station, beginning to write at age 5 for *children's pages, and serving in the RNZAF in World War 2. Though a couple called Eyre did arrive on the *Aurora* (in 1840, and not the first passenger ship), no descendant corresponding to the novelist has been traced and the other details have proved unverifiable. She wrote as Anne Eyre up to 1972, as Vicky Maxwell in 1973 and as Maxwell or Anne Worboys from 1974. She probably married in Australia in 1946 and lived in Kent, England, from 1951; as Mrs Anne Worboys she was reported by the *Gisborne Herald* as visiting that area in 1962. The recurrence in her fiction of stories of young women searching for lost mothers (having been abandoned or adopted) raises the possibility that she herself may have been in that situation (e.g. *The Chosen Child*, 1973; *The Other Side of Summer*, 1977; both as Maxwell).

Her early Annette Eyre novels are usually sheep station romances. *Three Strings to a Fortune* (1962) is set on a station in the Waikato, *The Valley of Yesterday* (1965) on a farm near the Whangaparaoa Peninsula, and *Dolphin Bay* (1970) at an East Coast beach. Later, as Maxwell or Worboys, she sets romance or crime stories in exotic locations which appear to reflect extensive travel: Venice in *Venetian Inheritance* (1973), Greece in *The Lion of Delos* (1974) and Spain in *The Other Side of Summer*.   EM/PN

Faces in the Water is the second novel by Janet *Frame (Christchurch: *Pegasus; New York, London, 1961); an early draft, entitled 'Cliffhaven', is held in the *Hocken Library. In this vivid critique of the normative rationality of conformist society, Frame superbly captures the terror and the horror of those punished for their difference, and their degrading and inhumane treatment at the hands of those with the authority to enforce conformity. The novel is narrated in the first person by its protagonist, Istina Mavet, and details the nine years she spent in New Zealand psychiatric institutions. Like Daphne in *Owls Do Cry before her lobotomy, Istina is 'not yet civilised' (the novel is sometimes read as a sequel to Owls Do Cry with Istina as the metamorphosis of Daphne). The first section of the novel provides an account of her time at Cliffhaven Mental Hospital where she undergoes electric shock therapy, 'the new and fashionable means of quieting people'. After an abortive release, Istina is again hospitalised, this time at Treecroft, which forms the setting for the second, and bleakest, section of the novel. Here her behaviour deteriorates and she moves downwards through a series of wards in which patients are classified according to the degree of their insanity. She finally reaches the lowest point in her journey, 'Lawn Lodge', where the most hopelessly deranged patients are held, those who 'to all intents and purposes are dead'. After another failed attempt at social reintegration, Istina is returned to Cliffhaven, the setting of the third and final section, which records her gradual ascent from the hell of madness and culminates in her release (although the reader is left wondering about the permanence of her 'recovery'). The conclusion is typically ironical. Told by a nurse to forget everything she has undergone in the years in hospital, Istina writes

—'And by what I have written in this document you will see, won't you, that I have obeyed her?'

Structured around a pattern of descent and ascent, the novel is very carefully organised and controlled. Much of the narrative is written in a straightforward, almost 'documentary' manner, although occasionally the narrator's objective detachment gives way to fluid, impressionistic prose, usually when she is recalling her disturbed or agitated state of mind at various moments in the retrospective story. Given the fact that Frame herself spent a similar period of time in hospital many critics have insisted on reading the novel as thinly veiled autobiography. Frame has consistently rejected such an interpretation: 'Faces in the Water was autobiographical in the sense that everything happened, but the central character was invented.' Frame acknowledges having 'borrowed' from her own experiences and observations when hospitalised but suggests that conditions were actually much worse and that in the novel she left out much that actually did happen in order to create a 'subdued rather than a sensational record'. KWo

FAIRBURN, A.R.D. (Arthur Rex Dugard) (1904–57), was a a major poet of the 1920s–50s. He was a fourth-generation New Zealander, his great-grandfather having arrived as a missionary in 1819 and settled permanently in 1823. His grandfather, Edwin *Fairburn, the eleventh Pākehā child born in New Zealand (in 1827), became a surveyor and an eccentric *Utopian thinker, critic of society and novelist. The poet's father became a conservative businessman. The poet, eldest of three sons, was born in Auckland and attended Auckland GS 1918–20, leaving without academic qualifications. There he began his close friendship with the poet R.A.K. *Mason, a year younger but much more precocious as a writer. After leaving school, he worked as a clerk for New Zealand Insurance for six frustrating years, resigning in 1926 to take a trip to Norfolk Island. He was formally unemployed from his return in late 1926 until 1930, but did some freelance writing, publishing poems and articles in two of the Auckland papers, the *Star* and the *Sun*, 1927–29, and winning the poetry prize in the *Sun* Christmas Supplement in 1929. Several of these early poems were collected in Quentin Pope's *Kowhai Gold in 1930. In August of that year he went to England to join the expatriate New Zealand poet Geoffrey *de Montalk, and with de Montalk's help published at his own expense his first volume of poetry, *He Shall Not Rise*, in late 1930. He married in England in 1931. Fairburn wrote poems and articles during this time both for the Auckland papers and for English periodicals. It was a time of intellectual searching, as he formulated the rather disparate set of beliefs that remained his personal philosophy. In political and economic matters, he rejected the Marxism of his friends Mason and Clifton Firth and adopted a belief in Douglas Social Credit; at the same time he defined more explicitly a philosophy of vitalism related to that of D.H. *Lawrence and reached a belief in back-to-nature organic farming.

In October 1932 Fairburn returned to New Zealand with his wife and child. From late 1932 to 1934 he was unable to find paid employment, and experienced at first hand the relief gang work that he depicts in *Dominion*. He published poems in the 1933 issues of *Phoenix*, edited by Mason, and in the one issue of the *Caxton Club magazine *Sirocco*, edited by Denis *Glover, and began to establish himself with the new generation of writers coming together around the printers Robert *Lowry in Auckland and Glover in Christchurch. Important at this time also was a friendship with Frank *Sargeson, a relationship that later turned to enmity over the issues of state patronage of writers and the privileges and influence of homosexual writers. From its beginnings in 1934 he was one of the primary contributors to the radical Christchurch magazine *Tomorrow*, writing poetry, essays, reviews and opinions, and he contributed poetry to the *Caxton Press collections of the 1930s: *New Poems* (1934), *Another Argo* (1935), *Verse Alive* (1936, drawn from *Tomorrow*), *A Caxton Miscellany* (1937) and *Verse Alive Number Two* (1937). In 1938 Caxton published his major long poem of the Great *Depression, *Dominion*, and in 1941 he contributed to the Caxton anthology *Recent Poems* with Mason, Glover and Allen *Curnow. In 1943 Caxton brought out his collected *Poems 1929–1941* and in 1946 the slighter *The Rakehelly Man*. His anonymous pamphlet attacking the Auckland *Herald*, *Who Said Red Ruin?*, was published by

Ronald Holloway at the *Griffin Press in 1938, and his brilliant Joycean satirical pamphlet parodying the speaking style of Michael Joseph Savage, the Prime Minister, *The Sky is a Limpet: A Pollytickle Parroty*, was published by Lowry in 1939. *We New Zealanders: An Informal Essay* was brought out by the *Progressive Publishing Society in 1944.

During these years of intense literary activity Fairburn was also working at jobs related to his political and social interests. From 1934 to 1942 he held various administrative posts with the Farmers' Union, a Social Credit organisation, and helped to edit its journal, *Farming First*. He served in the army 1942–43, and then was manpowered into work with radio station 1ZB as a scriptwriter. He remained there until 1947, when he resigned to set up a business as a fabric designer and printer. At the same time he served as the editor of *Compost Magazine* 1944–49. In 1948 he became a tutor in the Department of English at Auckland University College, and in 1950 lecturer in the history and theory of fine arts at the university's Elam School of Art. He was also active as an editor in these years, doing much writing and editing for the Auckland monthly *Here and Now* 1949–52 and serving as poetry editor for the *Yearbook of the Arts* 1945–51.

Fairburn's writing of poetry continued until 1952, when his work was collected in several volumes: his two long poems from 1948 and 1949, 'The Voyage' and 'To a Friend in the Wilderness', were collected along with 'Dominion' as *Three Poems*; and his shorter poems were collected in *Strange Rendezvous: Poems 1929–1941 with Additions*, published by Caxton. In the years following, he added only light verse. This diverse career was suddenly cut short by his death from cancer in 1957. Posthumous publications included two volumes of light verse in 1958, *The Disadvantages of Being Dead* and *Poetry Harbinger* (with Glover); the *Collected Poems*, edited by Glover (1966); a selection of his prose, *The Woman Problem & Other Prose*, selected by Glover and Geoffrey Fairburn (1967); and *The Letters of A.R.D. Fairburn*, selected and edited by Lauris *Edmond (1981).

As his varied career shows, Fairburn was a remarkably diverse man. His literary activity included poetry, essays, reviews and criticism, and editing; he painted, designed and printed fabrics, wrote art criticism and lectured on art; he was a political activist at times and an organiser, with strongly held beliefs and prejudices concerning the economic system, state patronage of the arts (which he vigorously opposed for individual writers and artists), sexuality and homosexuality, the role of women (he rivalled D.H. Lawrence in the extremity of his views) and organic farming. A large, handsome man, he was physically active, a keen swimmer, sailor, long-distance walker and golfer; extremely convivial, he formed a remarkably diverse web of friendships. Perhaps inevitably with such a vigorous and varied person, the man tended to loom larger than the writings until some years after his death. Thus Curnow said in 1947 that 'More than any other New Zealand poet, Mr Fairburn has value for what he is, as much as for what he writes', and Sargeson after his death called him 'one of the most extraordinary men born in the southern hemisphere'.

However, though the presence has faded, the writings remain to be assessed independently of it. Much of this diverse body of material will come to be of historical interest only, but there is much of lasting value. The journalism and reviewing are the most ephemeral. The essays and reviews over twenty-five years in journals as varied as *Tomorrow*, *★NZ Listener*, *New English Review*, *Compost Magazine*, *Year Book of the Arts*, *★Parsons Packet* and *★Landfall* form an idiosyncratic mosaic of the intellectual life of the country and touch on most of the major issues of those years. Yet only one essay, 'Aspects of New Zealand Art and Letters' (in *Art in New Zealand* 1934), has become a landmark, one of the works that helped to set the agenda for a generation of writers. His prose *jeux d'esprit* and parodies have often dated, but his *How to Ride a Bicycle in Seventeen Lovely Colours* from 1947 (with Lowry's inspired typographical play) remains an offbeat classic, and the exuberantly punning wordplay of *The Sky is a Limpet* retains its appeal. His letters, too, are likely to hold a place in that genre, especially his playful, witty letters to Glover. Though the poetic satires and parodies were often ephemeral, the best hold up well: the playful humour of 'Poem on the Advantages of Living at the Remuera End of the North Shore', the self-parody of 'Kowhai Poem', the sharp parody of Sargeson in 'Glum Summer', the complex ambivalence of his love–hate relationship with New Zealand in 'I'm Older Than You, Please Listen', or the bitter edge of 'La Belle Dame Sans Merci', a devastating attack on the supporters of capital punishment. A few ballads such as 'Walking on My Feet' and 'Down on My Luck' are entirely successful, with the anonymous speakers taking on a role like that of Harry in Glover's *★'Sings Harry'* poems. Probably his central accomplishment is in his short lyrics on traditional themes of time, death and sexual love. There are memorable ones from every phase of his career: 'Let Us Make an End' (1927), 'Winter Night' (1931), 'A Farewell' (1942), 'Tapu' and 'The Cave' (1943) and 'Song at Summer's End' (1947). In these lyrics, his easy command of rhythm and prosodic effects, his image-making ability, and his control of a middle range of diction, neither vernacular nor consciously poetic, result in poems that are lucid, direct and deceptively simple, with great emotional resonance. His closest

approximation to major poetic works, the longer poems collected in *Three Poems*, are more ambitious but less perfect. 'Dominion' is the most significant New Zealand work to emerge from the Depression and contains many aspects of Fairburn—satirical, didactic, realistic, lyrical and discursive; yet they fail to cohere in a satisfying whole, and the influence of T.S. Eliot (in reaction against his earlier ★Georgian mode) is not fully assimilated. The lyrical quality and the lucidity of the best parts of 'The Voyage' and 'To a Friend in the Wilderness' make both poems attractive, but they lack the intellectual weight of great discursive poetry and are unlikely to be remembered as long as the best of the shorter works.

There is, in fact, no single, undeniably major work where Fairburn's many gifts come together. Rather, his lyric, satiric and discursive modes tend to operate separately, either in separate poems or as distinct parts of long poems that are not entirely integrated. However, there is a unifying thread through the work, a romantic attitude towards Nature and the 'natural'. It is most directly stated in the discursive sections of the longer poems, as in his prediction in 'Dominion' that we shall come to the 'fair earth … for the stones of a new temple', or in his statement of faith in 'The Voyage' in 'the complete, the illimitable pattern' which we cannot fully know but can serve, or in 'To a Friend in the Wilderness', his more Lawrentian celebration of the Life force expressed in 'the phallic will' and 'the logic of generation' and his faith in the knowledge gained in intense moments: 'We know in the instant of joy that our warrant is sure, / our faith not vain, our being not belied by death.' Such 'visionary' moments, when 'love's bright eye' may 'ransom life / from the entanglements of time and fear' ('Disquisition on Death') are celebrated in the lyrics, especially the love poems dealing with 'the brief eternity of the flesh' ('The Cave'), and their loss is mourned. The natural values they affirm underlie the satires, for Fairburn's targets are those individuals and institutions that block the natural and encourage the worship of false idols—capitalist greed, puritanical repression, social status and power, hypocrisy and the cult of the respectable.

While Fairburn is unlikely ever again to have quite the critical reputation he had in the decade following his death, the range of his best work in many genres, the underlying integrity of his vision and his considerable stylistic gifts secure him a place as one of the most important writers of his generation.   LJ

FAIRBURN, Edwin (1827–1911), the grandfather of A.R.D. ★Fairburn, tried his hand at writing a novel: *The Ships of Tarshish: A Sequel to Sue's 'Wandering Jew'* (1867), probably the first published novel to be written by a native New Zealander. It propagates a racial theory, according to which Germans and Russians must, by their nature, try to suppress other nations. Consequently it is necessary for England to protect herself from them. The hero, John Mandevil, has designed a ship to counter the German 'ironclads'. He is a descendent of the Wandering Jew and has inherited a huge fortune. He builds a massive but secret shipyard on the Thames and when the Germans send an 'indestructible' ship up that symbolic waterway, the iron gates of Mandevil's shipyards open and reveal the 'Vindicator' and the 'Defence'. In a battle the German ship is defeated. Mandevil gets the girl of his wishes. In a non-fictional follow-up, *The Ships of the Future*, Fairburn confesses that his novel was not a great success—of the 400 copies printed thirty were sold and 300 given away. Nonetheless he insists that his ship designs, based on tracing the shadow of an egg onto paper, are valid. In fact he was an engineer who planned the Great North Road for Auckland's North Shore and pursued his literary interests after retirement in 1892, publishing articles on the Siberian mammoth and an astronomical explanation of the Flood. Edwin and his father William are minor characters in C.K. *Stead's novel *The *Singing Whakapapa* (1994).   NW

FAITH, Rangi (1949–), is a poet, anthologist and reviewer. First published in *Te *Ao Hou*, he was substantially represented in *Into the World of Light* (1982). His collection *Unfinished Crossword* (1990) was praised for its observant and unsentimental treatment of 'the unsettled scores of a colonial history' (Tom Weston). Māori–European history and issues are taken beyond the political by the controlled and contemplative tone, by the context of a sensitive, economically evoked landscape ('Massacre Hill'), and by a deft switching between the two languages ('Whaikorero' or 'Unfinished Crossword'). Several poems draw strength from an unfamiliar point of view, the poet himself modestly reticent and undogmatic. A poetry reviewer for the *Press*, Faith edited *Dangerous Landscapes: An Anthology of New Zealand Poetry* (1994), the best recent contemporary collection for young adults, the work of a skilled teacher as well as informed reader. The issues identified—the land, history, identity, the effort of craft—are also evident in his own poems. He has lived at Woodend and Lake Brunner, and since 1988 at Rangiora.   RR

Fallen House, The, (1953), James K. *Baxter's third major published collection, exhibits greater confidence and maturity through the evenness of its tone and the less emphatic echoes of his many adolescent influences. Accents of Yeats are still evident in a poem like 'Temple Basin', as are Hardy's methods in 'The Fallen House', but

other influences are more mechanical and most obvious when Baxter chooses to demonstrate his tremendous technical virtuosity. A few poems exhibit an uncharacteristic simplicity more common in later collections. But usually, when Baxter writes about natural features or everyday events, he develops his themes to communicate a hidden meaning, or connect images of the *landscape to the wider landscapes of human experience. A number of poems from this collection—particularly 'Wild Bees', 'Poem in the Matukituki Valley', 'The Morgue', 'Rocket Show' and 'Virginia Lake'—have been frequently anthologised.   PM

FARJEON, Benjamin (1838–1903), novelist, journalist and playwright, was born in London but emigrated to Australia in 1854, aged 16, having left his family after arguments about their Jewish faith. Even on shipboard he put out a handwritten newsletter: *Ocean Record*. He sought to recover from poverty on the Victorian goldfields, occasionally making unsuccessful attempts at journalism, some of them fiction ('Salmagundi on the Goldfields'). In 1861 he followed the *gold rush to Otago but settled in Dunedin as a journalist on the *Otago Daily Times*, becoming manager and sub-editor at various times. By 1864 he was co-editor with the paper's founder, Julius *Vogel. For the *Otago Witness* he wrote an unfinished serialised novel: *Life and Adventures of Christopher Congleton* (1862–63). In 1865 he published his first book, and his only New Zealand one, *Shadows on the Snow: A Christmas Story*. This 'humble production of a colonial author' is dedicated to Charles *Dickens, who apparently encouraged Farjeon enough to make him try his luck as a writer in England. In 1866 he published *Grif: A Story of Colonial Life* (in later editions … *of Australian Life*), a tale of Dickensian sentimentality set in Victoria but written and published in Dunedin, where Farjeon also produced a dramatisation of it. Indeed, he had something of a reputation for his burlesque plays in the gold-diggers' city (his farces included 'Once Bitten Twice Shy', 1883, 'Dynamite or the Crown Jewels', 1883, and 'The Bigamist', 1886). In Britain, *Grif* was a huge success, when republished in 1870, and some fifty further novels were published under Farjeon's name, of which six reflect his Australian goldfields experiences, and perhaps implicitly similar experiences in New Zealand. Eleanor Farjeon, Benjamin's daughter, was a respected writer of children's books and wrote an account of life with her father.   NW

FARQUHAR, David (1928–), composer, university professor and pianist, born in Cambridge, New Zealand, has excelled in various musical genres, from the operatic to vocal and instrumental, including many settings of poems. Influenced by Britten's setting of Rimbaud's cycle *Les Illuminations*, performed by the Boyd Neel Orchestra on their famed 1947 New Zealand tour, he began setting William Blake songs. During the 1950s he wrote theatre music and songs including *A Unicorn for Christmas* (1962), music for a stage adaptation of Ngaio *Marsh's story *The Wyvern and the Unicorn*, presented by the New Zealand Players as a Christmas entertainment, and described by Roger Savage as having a 'fluent and intelligent score … Apt and unpretentious words' and 'pungent and inventive carol settings'. The subsequent complete destruction by fire of costumes and sets ended hopes of later productions. Farquhar's only other opera, *Shadows* (1970), not performed until 1988, is derived from the Hans Andersen story to a libretto by the composer. He continued writing for the voice, in, for instance, *Three Scots Ballads* (1964), *The Score* (1969), a collection of twenty school songs, and the notable choral symphony *Bells in their Seasons* (1974). These works include poems by Allen *Curnow, A.R.D. *Fairburn, Denis *Glover and others. In setting verse the composer seeks a poem 'that sings, or wants to sing … the problem of translating speech into song is that of sustaining a long lyrical line'.   JMT

FARRELL, Fiona (1947–), a versatile dramatist and fiction writer, was born and raised in Oamaru. She graduated from Otago University in 1968 and lived in Oxford, England 1969–71 and then Toronto, as a postgraduate student of drama and English and American literature. In 1976 she returned to New Zealand with her then husband. (She originally published as Fiona Farrell Poole.) She was lecturer in drama at Palmerston North Teachers' College 1977–82 and subsequently, as her writing career flourished, taught part-time in secondary schools. She has been a full-time writer since 1990, and was Katherine *Mansfield Memorial Fellow in Menton in 1995 and writer-in-residence at Canterbury University in 1992. Since 1993 she has lived at Otanerito, Akaroa.

A feature of Farrell's work is its variety of forms. Drama has been an abiding interest; in 1983 she won the first Bruce Mason Playwrights' Award. Plays performed on stage include 'In Confidence: Dialogues with Amy Bock' (Palmerston North, Wellington and Dunedin, 1986), 'Bonds' (Palmerston North, Wellington, 1986), 'Thatcher, Vitelli and Small' (Palmerston North, 1990), 'Passengers' (Palmerston North, 1984 and 1989, also Dunedin, Hawkes Bay and Auckland), and 'Chook Chook' (Dunedin, 1994). Radio plays include 'Images of Women' (1983), 'The Perils of Pauline Smith' (Mobil Award for Best Radio Drama, 1990), 'Looking Forward' (with Angio Farrow, 1993), and 'Chook Chook' (1994).

'Airwaves' (Palmerston North, Tauranga, Christchurch) was published in *Song of the Shirt* (1993). *Passengers* has also been published (1985), and four of its twenty 'Songs' appeared as the central sequence in Farrell's collection of poetry, *Cutting Out* (1987). Some of the shorter poems in this volume were previously published in the *NZ Listener* and have subsequently been anthologised.

It is as a writer of fiction, and especially short stories, that Farrell has made her greatest mark. Her stories began appearing in the *NZ Listener* from 1985, and later in other magazines, and have been broadcast by Radio New Zealand. A collection of twelve stories, *The Rock Garden*, was published in 1989. Her stories have won every major New Zealand short story award, including the BNZ Katherine *Mansfield Memorial Award (1984), the American Express Award (1987) and the Mobil–*Dominion Sunday Times* Award (1988). Several of her stories, notably 'Footnote', 'Rag Bag' and 'A Story about Skinny Louie', have appeared in New Zealand and Australasian anthologies; she has twice appeared in the annual international *Best Stories* collection (1990 and 1995). 'A Story about Skinny Louie' formed the starting point for Farrell's first novel, *The Skinny Louie Book* (1992), which won the 1993 New Zealand Book Award for Fiction. A second novel, *Six Clever Girls Who Became Famous Women*, appeared in 1996.

Farrell's approach to her work is equally varied. In all forms it is energetic and original, delighting in unexpected juxtapositions and sudden shifts of scene or mood. This unpredictability is matched by linguistic flair and variety. Her work is always, however, rooted in a sharply observed actual physical world and shows a compassion for human need. Two central linked themes unify Farrell's writing. One is a concern with separateness, with how society at various times judges and deals with difference in belief or appearance or behaviour. The other is the obverse: the possibility of personal emancipation through the apparently miraculous transformation of the mundane. These themes are often worked out in a historical context, as in the *Passengers* sequence, in such plays as 'In Confidence' about the transvestite confidence trickster Amy Bock, and such stories as 'Footnote', contrasting the adulteries of an early missionary wife and a late-twentieth-century woman academic. They receive their most elaborate treatment in the novels. The dazzling *Skinny Louie Book* traces the shifts in New Zealand society since World War 2 by juxtaposing the mundane and magical stories of two sisters. *Six Clever Girls* widens the perspective by spotlighting six women, first as teenage schoolgirls together on 22 September 1960, and then separately in middle age exactly thirty-five years later, tracing their often unexpected paths to maturity. This novel has a sombre tinge, being less exuberant and more complex, with a harder satirical edge. AM

Fat Man, The, (1995) by Maurice *Gee won the AIM Children's Book of the Year Award, the AIM Junior Fiction Award and the Esther Glen Award and was acclaimed in New Zealand and other countries as a major contribution to children's literature. It was also the subject of controversy. Dorothy *Butler protested in *Quote Unquote that it was too violent, too threatening, for children to read. A major debate on the nature of children's reading eventuated.

A stranger, Herbert Muskie, comes to a peaceful little town that resembles the Henderson of Gee's childhood. The boy, Colin, discovers him washing in a stream and is subjected to terror and intimidation by Muskie, who wants no one to know he is there. When Colin agrees to keep silent he becomes entangled in a series of defences and, ultimately, lies. The reader is led to see the threatening world from Colin's point of view with a mass of details that reflect his thoughts.

Judith Holloway in *New Zealand Books wrote: 'The pace never flags, the characters are all colourful and believable, the sense of time and place (small-town New Zealand, 1930s) is acutely real.... No teacher should shield children from this. It is what true literature is about.' Gee himself remarked: 'I don't believe that this book is going to upset children—because none of the central relationships are actually damaged, none of the characters in the book that children are going to identify with are damaged. They are put under terrible threat, but they're not damaged.... I meant to use pity and terror—which are a large part of fiction. But the story moves on through those things to some sort of satisfying resolution. They're not used in a way I would use them in adult fiction.' NW

FAVILLE, Barry (1939–), writes realistic and fantasy junior fiction. Born in Hamilton, educated at Waihi College and Auckland University, he has taught secondary school English since 1961 mainly in Taupo, apart from some periods overseas and work as a radio producer and scriptwriter. His fiction often draws power from the volcanic nature of the Taupo area, where he still lives. In *The Keeper* (1986), winner of the Children's Book of the Year Award in 1987, a teenage boy seeks a better way of life in a post-cataclysmic society ruled by superstition, ignorance and fear. In *Stanley's Aquarium* (1989), a teenage girl seeks to understand herself and her involvement with a vindictive man warped by bullying and social scorn. *The Return* (1987) is challenging *science-fiction set on the East Coast. Through

contact with aliens, the isolated community members confront human values and responsibilities raised by social engineering. DH

FEATON, John (1840?–1913), was the author of a book on the New Zealand *Wars, which was the standard version until James Cowan published his, forty-five years later; and also of a short work of fiction related to the wars. His non-fictional *The Waikato War, 1863–4* (1879) covers some of the major campaigns, partly from a personal point of view, so that it is realistic to assume that he was on the battlefield, perhaps as a journalist. Although it is no longer useful as a standard interpretation of the war, being heavily biased towards the Pākehā view, it is still valuable as source material on points not covered elsewhere. Featon had already published a pseudonymous work whose character is best suggested by its full title: *The Last of the Waikatos: A Sensational Tale of the Province of Auckland,* 'dedicated to the volunteers of New Zealand, by Comus' (1873). Curiously, this was treated as non-fiction in *Hocken's bibliography, which is suggestive of the narrow borderline between the fictional and the non-fictional in works of this period. In fact, it opens with an old man proposing to tell his grandson of the war 'nearly fifty years ago', which clearly places the date of narration in the future, although the events described are partly contemporary and partly of a more immediate future, if seen from 1873. The narrator is scornful of what he sees as the over-generous policy of the colonial government to the Māori, referring to it as the 'sugar and flour policy', a phrase Featon also uses in *The Waikato War*. He moves into fiction, however, when he describes a much more vigorous colonial policy, under which all Māori are driven out of the *Waikato. The imperial forces are here compared unfavourably with the Colonial ones. Nonetheless the mistake is made of not driving a railway through the district, which leads to 'devastation'. 'Shortly after' the election of Sir James Fergusson (which took place at about the time the book was published) the Kingites attack, the narration moving almost imperceptibly from the historical into the fictional. In a digression the narrator describes the town of Cambridge, fifty years after the war (and publication of the book) as 'a large town, with its woollen manufactories, its railway terminus, handsome streets lighted with gas, and a population numbering some thousands'. After a disastrous start, due to reducing capacity after the actual wars, the military forces drive deep into the King Country. Featon shows a faith in technology with his references to the construction of railways and telegraphs, and the Māori are ultimately defeated by the use of electric light, which makes them visible to the colonials and dazzles them in night fighting. After this defeat the

Waikato region gradually comes to flourish. 'Each succeeding year brought forth its good fruit.' Ultimately Arcadia, with a British flavour, is planted in the Waikato: 'The hills that had formerly been solitary wastes were converted into smiling pastures, and fields of wheat bowed their golden heads to the summer breeze in place of the useless fern and ti-tree.' NW

FERGUSON, Dugald (1833?–1920), published six books of poetry, three novels and a book of 'sketches', all extremely popular in the late nineteenth and early twentieth centuries, especially in Otago. He began with *Poems* (1878) and *Castle Gay and Other Poems* (1883), but achieved his immense popularity with *Vicissitudes of Bush Life in Australia and New Zealand* (1891), which was reprinted under variations on that title in 1893, 1898 and 1908. By that fourth edition, published in Edinburgh, it was being promoted as 'a factual account of the author's experiences of life in the bush and on farms'. No doubt in part it was, but it is also a melodramatic and romantic adventure story in which the hero pursues his love across both countries until settling down with her and his hard-earned wealth at the happy ending. On the way he shears sheep, encounters bush-rangers, meets *gold diggers and endures all the vicissitudes promised by the title.

Mates (1912) is similarly relentlessly episodic, and again carried along by Ferguson's engaging exuberance. It also includes some vivid scenes of frontier violence, with at least one hotel-bar brawl that could be said to anticipate Alan *Duff. Both novels use stereotype characters such as the *new chum and *remittance man who remain undeveloped yet are still revealing about pioneer conditions. The narrative and dialogue range from colonial slang to what Eric *McCormick called 'melodramatic bombast in the emotional scenes'.

Sketches of Gossiptown (1893), published under the pseudonym 'Daniel Frobisher', is a loose series of anecdotes, while *The King's Friend: A Tale of the Scottish Wars of Independence* (1905) is a long historical novel about William Wallace, derivative from Jane Porter's *The Scottish Chiefs* (1810) and Sir Walter Scott. It was popular among the southern Scots, whose interests are often reflected in Ferguson's work. Much of his poetry is Scots-nostalgic, quite entertaining when it is most humorous, balladic or declamatory, but at other times straining towards a lyricism he cannot master. He also wrote religious verse, usually uplifting. After *Castle Gay* his later collections are *The Book of Job* (1891), *Poems of the Heart* (1897, including poems from earlier volumes), *Job and Other Sacred Poems* (1898), *Poems and Sketches, Grave and Humorous* (1905, published as 'by A New Zealander') and another collected poems published as *Castle Gay and Other Poems* (1912).

Born in *Scotland (in 1838 according to his burial record, though 1833 elsewhere), Ferguson emigrated first to Australia and then arrived in Otago about 1870, moving on after the gold rushes to Waipu in Northland. His fictional heroes are clearly autobiographical, the DF of *Mates* (Donald Fraser) a closet poet while on the road in Australia and revealing at the end that he has written a 'bush novel' and is at work on a historical romance. This literary inclination led Ferguson himself, at the end of his career, to become a bookseller at Tapanui. NW/PN

FERGUSSON, Bernard (1911–80), biographer, autobiographer and writer of junior fiction, is the only New Zealand author to date to receive royal appointment as Governor-General (cf. Alfred *Domett) and elevation to the House of Lords. Sir Bernard at the time of his Governor-Generalship, 1962–67, he was created Lord Ballantrae of Auchairne, a life peerage, in 1972. He was already GCMG, GCVO, DSO and OBE in recognition of his military and public services. Born in Scotland, he spent part of his adolescence in New Zealand as son of Governor-General Sir Charles Fergusson. He spent several weeks travelling with Captain John Bollons (d. 1929), master of the government steamer *Tutanekai*, later describing him as 'by far the greatest hero of my boyhood'. When he returned in 1962 he was already author of several memoirs of his military career, and was stimulated to a fictional recreation for young adults of his old hero's career, *Captain John Niven* (1972). It tells of a 16-year-old Pākehā sailor who is wrecked near Bluff in 1881, and forms a close bond with the Māori hapū with whom he then lives, regarding himself as part-Māori. Friendship between individuals and reconciliation between Māori and Pākehā are the book's main themes. Though somewhat disconnectedly episodic, and struggling with its huge cast of characters, the book has admirably drawn individual characters, authentic dialogue and a grippingly readable and informative adventure story. Among Fergusson's other works are the autobiography *Travel Warrant* (1979), which again refers to New Zealand and Bollons, the novel *The Rare Adventure* and the well-known biography *Wavell*. PN

Fernfire was a left-wing magazine of fiction, poetry and social and political comment published in Auckland by Unity Writers 1957–66, edited by Murray Gittos. Prominent contributors included Noel *Hilliard, Hone *Tuwhare and James K. *Baxter. SH

Film adaptations of New Zealand literature as major features have been quite a common aspect since the New Zealand film industry's most sustained period of creativity was ushered in with *Sleeping Dogs*, Roger Donaldson's

1977 adaptation of C.K. *Stead's novel *Smith's Dream. In 1979 John Reid directed *Middle Age Spread, based on the popular play by Roger *Hall. The same year saw Albert *Wendt's much-praised *Sons for the Return Home in a version directed by Paul Maunder. In 1982 The *Scarecrow, directed by Sam Pillsbury, was the first of three films based on novels by Ronald Hugh *Morrieson, followed by Ian Mune's *Came a Hot Friday in 1985 and Lynton Butler's Pallet on the Floor in 1986. A 1983 feature co-production with German television of Maurice *Shadbolt's *Among the Cinders has had no general release. In 1984 Yvonne Mackay directed a version of Joy *Cowley's book for children, The Silent One, and 1985 saw the release of Michael Firth's Sylvia, based on the life and writings of Sylvia *Ashton-Warner, and John Laing's Other Halves, taken from the novel by Sue *McCauley, who also contributed to the screenplay. Geoff Murphy's The Quiet Earth, drawn from the *science fiction novel by Craig *Harrison, came out in 1986. An adaptation of M.K. *Joseph's novel A *Soldier's Tale was directed by Larry Parr in 1988, although not released in New Zealand until 1991. In 1989 Wendt's short story Flying Fox in a Freedom Tree was filmed by Martyn Sanderson. In 1990, Janet *Frame's autobiographical trilogy (*To the Is-Land, An *Angel at My Table, The *Envoy from Mirror City) was filmed as a three-part television drama by Jane *Campion. This was later given a theatrical release as a single film under the title Angel at My Table. In 1992, after years of work spent on developing the project, Mune brought out a film adaptation of Bruce *Mason's The *End of the Golden Weather. Both Mune and Mason had developed the multiple-character screenplay from Mason's original one-man play. Dale Bradley directed Chunuk Bair, based on Maurice *Shadbolt's play *Once on Chunuk Bair (1992). The most financially successful of all such adaptations has been 1994's *Once Were Warriors, directed by Lee Tamahori and adapted from Alan *Duff's novel by Riwia *Brown, herself a playwright.

Of all these films, perhaps only The End of the Golden Weather can be described as an act of homage to a well-known and well-loved original. In general, New Zealand directors have filmed stories they thought would work well as film, although using New Zealand literature was certainly part of the nascent film industry's desire to provide a specifically New Zealand cinema. It is possible that such stories are easier to bring to the screen with the proven success of the novel behind them, than if they had originally been written as screenplays. It is perhaps surprising that so few local plays have been turned into feature films: the two that have been are not the most obviously cinematic or the only commercially successful New Zealand plays. Conversely, a New Zealand film

(Peter Jackson's 1992 splatter-horror film Braindead) has been converted into a theatrical musical: Braindead: The Musical (1995).

It is interesting to note the number of filmed novels and stories with Māori or Pacific themes: Sons for the Return Home, The Silent One, Other Halves, Flying Fox in a Freedom Tree, Once Were Warriors. This continues an emphasis on Māori themes from the earliest days of the New Zealand cinema, in the work of Rudall Hayward and others. Most remarkable, however, is the filmmakers' concentration on recent literature. Morrieson's novels and Mason's play of the 1960s have been the oldest writings to attract the attention of our film industry, apart from the John Reid version of the relationship of Katherine *Mansfield with John Middleton *Murry, Leave All Fair (1985). In the late 1970s and early 1980s, however, the recurring thematic concerns of that industry had more in common with the literature of the 1930s–50s, or even the work of those stalwart pioneers of New Zealand cinema, Hayward and John O'Shea. Preoccupations with the *'Man Alone' in a hostile land, the search for a New Zealand identity and the attempt to invent a truly indigenous cinema were out of step with the concerns of the fledgling New Zealand film industry's literary contemporaries. The contrast between the philosophical and political speculations of Smith's Dream and the straightforward thriller action of Sleeping Dogs epitomises this discrepancy. It is not surprising that Morrieson's darkly comic small-town New Zealand Gothic proved popular for those keen to adapt New Zealand literature to the screen. By simultaneously evoking and subverting a nostalgia for a bygone New Zealand, these films managed to sidestep the questions of contemporary New Zealand identity which seemed pressing in other films of the period. Ironically, Campion's Angel at My Table, with its exploration of the artist as misfit and outsider, and its attempt to chart Frame's growing confidence as a 'New Zealand writer', while being perhaps the first literary adaptation to address these issues successfully, also made it clear that in 1990 they were firmly part of New Zealand's past.

With the exception of Riwia *Brown's adaptation of Once Were Warriors, it has been scripts written directly for the screen that have contributed most significantly to the successes of New Zealand film-making in the 1990s. What has been noticeable in the cinema of the late 1980s–90s, in addition to a striking literary allusiveness, is the ability to approach New Zealand themes with a confident and cool irony which has allowed non–New Zealand audiences in unprecedented numbers to find their own meanings and interest in the films. The open-ended symbolism of Campion's The *Piano (1993), the deliberate historical indeterminism of Peter *Wells and

Stewart Mains's *Desperate Remedies* (1993), the violent collision of fantasy and fact in Peter Jackson's and Fran Walsh's *Heavenly Creatures* (1994) all testify to this rich complexity of vision in contemporary New Zealand film.

Bill Lennox has written a book on film adaptations of New Zealand literature: *Film and Fiction: Studies of New Zealand Fiction and Film Adaptations* (Auckland, 1985). Versions of literary texts primarily for television, or shorter than feature length, are quite numerous, and include most notably Vincent Ward's *State of Siege, David Sims's *Jack Winter's Dream* (*Baxter) and Murray Reece's The *God Boy.   HRo

FINDLAY, Mary (1912–74), wrote *Tooth and Nail: The Story of a Daughter of the Depression* (1974), a memoir of her youthful struggles for survival in a society preoccupied with authoritarian hierarchies and ruthlessly dismissive of the poor. Remarkable for its unembroidered directness and close-up narration, her story provides insights into the conditions and treatment she endures as schoolgirl, domestic servant, shop assistant, billposter, public service clerk, probationer-nurse and kitchen-maid, and is a forceful chronicle of an underprivileged woman's experience of the *Depression. Its tone varies between dispassion and recalcitrance, sometimes almost automaton-like as she describes her mistreatment and decline into crime, at others truculent, resentful and scathing. Despite the absence of any sentimental appeal, the narrative is always disturbing and often moving in the immediacy of its presentation of the situation of a young woman trapped between a violent father and a series of sexually predatory employers, academically able yet denied any opportunity, desperate for affection yet subjected only to bullying and disparagement by almost every woman she encounters. Findlay was educated at Wellington East Girls' College (presented not wholly unsympathetically in the book) and worked in Wellington and itinerantly until her marriage to a Māori trainee teacher. The memoir ends with their courtship, but she went on to raise four children while helping him to graduate and progress to a headship. Though not Māori herself, the marriage enabled her to join the Maori Women's Welfare League, in which she became a national office holder, as well as being active in the English Speaking Union and Play Centre movement.
RR

FINLAYSON, Roderick (1904–92), was a prose writer known especially for his sympathetic fictional treatment of Māori society and culture. Born in Devonport, he grew up in the Auckland area but spent his summers working on farms in the Bay of Plenty until about 1930, and developed a close relationship with a Māori 'adoptive' family there. He studied architecture at Auckland Technical Institute and worked as an apprentice and then assistant to an Auckland architect until 1931. After that time he supported himself and later his family, living at Weymouth, by seasonal work and freelance writing. Wishing to capture in words the Māori society he had come to know, he began writing stories in 1933. A friendship with D'Arcy *Cresswell and, through him, with Frank *Sargeson brought encouragement to continue writing, and from Cresswell especially he gained confirmation of his critical attitude towards technological, acquisitive Pākehā society. His early stories about Māori life were collected in *Brown Man's Burden in 1938, the beginning of a long association with Ronald Holloway and the *Griffin Press. In 1940 Griffin Press published his essay, *Our Life in This Land*, his unofficial contribution to the *Centennial celebrations and a brief statement of his critical attitude towards his society. (There was a facsimile reprint in 1985.) In 1942 Holloway published Finlayson's second collection of short stories, *Sweet Beulah Land*, which had a section of stories about Māori life but also dealt with Pākehā society in the Great *Depression and in World War 2. A series of stories and sketches about 'Uncle Ted', a small farmer in Northland, were published in the Sydney *Bulletin 1944–46 and then brought together and expanded to form his first novel, *Tidal Creek*, published in Australia in 1948 (2nd edn 1979). *The Schooner Came to Atia,* a short novel exploring the culture conflict brought about by a New Zealand missionary in Western Samoa, was published by Griffin in 1952 (reissued 1974). Six Primary School Bulletins, stories illustrating the history of Māori society since European settlement, were published 1955–60 and collected as a novel, *The Springing Fern*, in 1965. *The Maoris of New Zealand*, a non-fiction descriptive booklet for children, appeared in 1958. A monograph for the Twayne World Authors Series, *D'Arcy Cresswell*, setting out in detail Cresswell's philosophy, which had greatly influenced Finlayson, appeared in 1972, followed in 1973 by the expanded collection of stories of Māori life, *Brown Man's Burden and Later Stories* (edited by Bill *Pearson). Three later novellas were collected as *Other Lovers* in 1976, and in 1988 his last book appeared, *In Georgina's Shady Garden and Other Stories*, a retrospective collection from the Griffin Press that brought together previously uncollected stories from the 1940s–80s.

Over a writing career even longer than Sargeson's, and contemporaneous with it, Finlayson struggled to support a large family (he had six children) while living as a writer. Though never as well known as Sargeson, he was a significant writer, going his own way with integrity, stating his position uncompromisingly. His primary concern was what he called 'the killing off in all of us of the naive and innocent life by which alone we can continue to live, and the ugly triumph of the sophisticated and the greedy'. Often this concern focused on the theme of the fate of Māori culture in contact with 'our ruthlessly technological and acquisitive society', a theme central to *Brown Man's Burden*, the Māori stories of *Sweet Beulah Land*, *The Springing Fern* and some of the later stories. 'The Totara Tree' has been his best-known treatment of this concern since its inclusion in Dan ⋆Davin's *New Zealand Short Stories* in 1953, and is still frequently anthologised. At other times his concern focused on the theme of the increasing corruption of Pākehā society, the fall from the 'natural piety and wonder' of the frontier society, 'Death feeding on Life'. *Our Life in This Land* discusses the negative result of the first 100 years of European settlement, while *Tidal Creek* celebrates the eccentric living on of the pioneer virtues in Uncle Ted, a humorous character but one analogous in his representative function to the maternal uncle Sargeson describes in his autobiography.

A third focus of Finlayson's primary concern is on the theme of sexual passion in both Māori and Pākehā society. In Finlayson's almost archetypal view of male and female nature, there is the 'natural' potentiality for violence and unhappiness as well as for fulfilment in the interplay of male sexual rivalry and aggression with female nest-building and nurturing instincts. Many of the Māori stories such as 'The Wedding Gift' show this potentiality for violence in a sexual situation being realised in Māori society as a primitive tragedy, shocking but natural. Other stories show the greater potentiality for unhappiness and often violence when the 'natural' gender factors are further complicated by racism and culture-clash, as in 'Jim & Miri' in *Other Lovers*, or by the restrictions of a ⋆puritanical culture, as in 'Frankie & Lena' in *Other Lovers* or in many of the stories in *Georgina's Shady Garden and Other Stories*; or by a combination of these factors, as in *The Schooner Came to Atia*. Although known primarily as a writer of Māori life, Finlayson over his lengthy career did explore this larger range of themes gathered around his central concern of the fate of the natural and the innnocent, and he played the themes in a variety of keys, from the tragedy of 'Frankie & Lena' or 'The Wedding Gift' to the humour of 'Johnny Wairua's Wonderland' or some of the episodes of *Tidal Creek*. As was appropriate to his central concern, the mode of his fiction has been an almost naive realism, with a relatively bare and primarily external presentation of events in a studiedly simple style.   LJ

FINN, Neil (1958–), lyricist and musician, was born in Te Awamutu, and began the globally successful music group Split Enz with his brother Tim Finn. The high sales of his songs make him arguably the most internationally recognised and influential of all New Zealand writers. Finn's love of the discrete phrase makes some of his lyrics look like symbolist poems; his aim is to provide 'a couple of lines that just go bang into the back of the cranium'. But there are several strong motifs, too.

The lyrics of Finn's Split Enz years range from the slightly manic rejection of the past ('That was My Mistake') and the resolve to make a new start ('History Never Repeats') to the fear of emotional entanglement ('I don't know why sometimes I get frightened' ['I Got You'], 'you slow me down, what can I do?' ['One Step Ahead']) and anger at a woman's betrayal ('I See Red' or the soaring lament, 'I Hope I Never [have to see you again]'). Even 'Message to my Girl' (from Split Enz's final album *Conflicting Emotions* [1983]) cannot give away the 'empty self-possession' of the non-risker: 'I don't want to say I love you, that would give away too much.'

In 1985 Tim Finn embarked on a solo career. Neil dissolved the band and with drummer Paul Hester formed the trio Crowded House, with bassist Nick Seymour. One of the most internationally successful groups of its generation, Crowded House broke up in 1996, though Finn has indicated that further songs will be released.

From the Crowded House decade of 1985–96, 'Don't Dream It's Over', a rare, uncomplicated profession of love from their 1986 debut album, was the first of many hits. More often, the message is wary: 'Love You 'Til the Day I Die' sings of 'teaching you how to distort the facts / Sometimes I can't be straight….' So often, the desire to make meaning out of life runs foul of women being 'Mean to me'. A song about Finn's aunt's suicide, 'Hole in the River' ('her fear inside us all') broods over the album. Salvation or damnation is always in the hands of the woman.

Despite the quiet self-assurance of 'Better be Home Soon', Finn's helplessness in the power of women continues in *Temple of Low Men* (1988). They show him 'how to give / into temptation …'; or in another striking simile, she is 'fresh like a daisy chained up in a lion's den' ('When You Come').

Finn's social conscience is clearly revealed in the Reaganite executive 'Sister Madly' stepping on people's heads in her battle to reach the top, and his revulsion at North American consumer capitalism is apparent in the hit song from *Woodface* (1991), 'Chocolate Cake'.

Finn's many allusions to religion are, he confesses, 'an ex-Catholic thing'. He remains a 'Black and White Boy' compelled to see the world in terms of paradise or damnation, seduced into love, endlessly disappointed. As he says in 'Nails in my Feet', 'My life is a house … enter the place of endless persuasion … who is that calling, you my companion, run to the water on a burning beach and it brings me release … cast me off one day, to lose my inhibitions, sit like a lapdog on a matron's knee, with nails in my feet…'.

Finn's sense that human relationships are never quite enough is seen in his increasingly urgent desire for a sea-change; after this night, 'can we look the milkman in the eye?' ('Walking on the Spot'). 'Distant Sun' deftly straddles both the cosmic ('seven worlds collide') and the domestic ('drawn to a flame') in its love imagery, but it rises an octave to desperation, and for a moment moves via Split Enz freneticism to flirt with the apocalyptic, finally leaving Finn 'fearing vengeance from above'. 'Fingers of Love' suggests the seductive ease of a life in New Zealand 'playing in the shallow water, laughing while the mad dog sleeps'. But this is the territory of Bruce *Mason's garden and the *end of the golden weather. While 'I will run for shelter, endless summer, lift the curse, it feels like nothing matters in our private universe'—the agitated underlying drumbeat belies the smooth swell of the sea wave.

'Catherine Wheels' is the essential Finn song: it modulates from a descending, ominous sequence about torture and punishment into something like rollerskates, a spinning firework, and the pleasure of love, expressed in the major key and lullaby rhythms. Its third movement describes lovers quarrelling, holding power over each other, escaping, or bruising each other in the dark. Love becomes a deadly game, and the beat becomes threateningly staccato.

In this album Finn tries to root his tangle of eros and agape in the familiar landscape of Karekare Beach, where the album was recorded. In 'Kare Kare' he finds a normality ('we gathered up our clothes, got the washing done') and a sly sense of home ('this is the only place I'll run from'). The hearty male patriotism of Split Enz's famous 'Six Months in a Leaky Boat' was the first time many New Zealand young people had heard Māori in a pop song ('Aotearoa, rugged individual'). Finn's roots show in songs like 'Weather With You' and 'Four Seasons in One Day'. The eponymous anthem 'Together Alone' from Crowded House (performed with the Te Waka Huia Cultural Group) is an elegy for a broken friendship, but it is also solemn affirmation of spiritual identity, extending from brotherhood to sexual love to a bicultural society. Here the Split Enz frenzy is finally transformed into the purposeful, communal vigour of Polynesian drumming.

While conscious that his current writing reflects 'a mixture of my own introspective, monkish work habits and a little bit of other people's influences—most of them local New Zealand characters', Finn has always resisted having his work or his bands labelled as New Zealand or Australian. At a media conference in conjunction with the farewell concert of Crowded House on the steps of Sydney Opera House in November 1996, Finn indicated that his future solo career will include 'collaboration with Polynesian, Maori and Europeans' on a forthcoming album. He now lives with his family in Auckland.   DD

Fire-Raiser, The, (1986) is a novel for children by Maurice *Gee, set in a small town (with resemblances to Nelson) during World War 1. Four children pursue a villainous arsonist, while the adults are concerned with the course of the war. A patriotic lady organises a pageant with the children playing the Kaiser, Poor Little Belgium, various other countries and New Zealand —played by the biggest boy with the cleanest teeth. The performance rouses the men in the audience to patriotic fervour, until in hysteria they march on the home of a harmless German piano teacher, and destroy her piano with an axe. The arsonist, Marwick, burns its remnants. With the aid of the children, the police hound the arsonist, but the schoolteacher marries Frau Stauffel.

Gee remarked 'I asked how would these children go through their lives? … So I … re-told the story of *The Fire-Raiser* in the first few chapters of *Prowlers* because I wanted to see … whether you could transfer the children across to an adult book. I found, of course, that you can't … the children in *Prowlers* are quite different … which is why, in the end, I changed their names, signalling that they are different beings.'   NW

First Year in Canterbury Settlement, A (1863), the first book of Samuel *Butler.

FISHER, Helen (1942–), composer, was born in Nelson, taught English, French and music and graduated BMus (Hons) in composition from Victoria University of Wellington in 1991. Appointed Composer-in-Schools for 1990–91 in the Wellington region, she teaches composition in schools. In her own music she collaborates widely with both choreographers and Māori performing artists, drawing her texts largely from Māori sources. Her own compositions include *Nga Tapuwae o Kupe* (The Footprints of Kupe) (1992).   JMT

FITZGERALD, James Edward (1818–96), poet, editor and essayist, born in Bath as the fifth son of a wealthy Irish landowner, was an Irish aristocrat in the truest sense, with a powerful sense of duty and a strong vein of quixotic idealism. A brilliant mathematics student at Christ's College, Cambridge, and a handsome young man of wit and charm, he aspired to be politician, philosopher, artist, writer and man of action. He was a good watercolourist and woodcarver, sang well, played the guitar and talked incessantly and brilliantly. Walter Savage Landor, one of the foremost men of letters of the age, guided and encouraged this precocious talent; unfortunately not even Landor could transform FitzGerald's verse into poetry, but from him FitzGerald adapted a superb prose style—fluent, clear, vigorous and often powerfully persuasive.

Between 1844 and 1850 FitzGerald was an administrator at the British Museum and a busy propagandist for emigration schemes to alleviate Irish poverty. He wrote for London's newspapers and political journals, debated at the intellectually fashionable clubs and was prominent among the influential young politicians surrounding Gladstone and John Robert Godley. Although Edward Gibbon *Wakefield appointed him secretary of the Colonial Reform Society in 1849, he was determined to be a leader of Godley's Canterbury settlement and sailed on the *Charlotte Jane* with his 18-year-old bride Fanny Erskine Draper, as multi-talented and witty as himself. During that voyage FitzGerald wrote 'The Night-Watch Song of the "Charlotte Jane"'—New Zealand's first notable settler poem and for many years its best-known. It is not good poetry but it evoked for an entire generation the immigrant's mixed emotions—nostalgia for home and the anticipation of life in an unknown land. In James Townsend's musical setting it achieved an additional popularity.

FitzGerald always aspired to be first and had some success: first Canterbury Pilgrim ashore in December 1850, first editor of Canterbury's first newspaper the *Lyttelton Times* a few weeks later, first Superintendent of Canterbury (1853), first Prime Minister of New Zealand (1854), founder of the *Press*, Christchurch (1861), and first Comptroller of Finance and Auditor-General (1867). Additionally, his wit and a flamboyance bordering on eccentricity marked him as Canterbury's first notable public figure. In New Zealand's only great age of parliamentary orators he was rated the finest, and as newspaper editor and polemical essayist he was unsurpassed. Above all he shone as the intellectual beacon for New Zealand's next generation of intellectuals, that of W.P. *Reeves and Robert Stout. W.H. *Oliver has said of him: 'In a utilitarian century he was among the few who insisted that ideas, art and literature should count, even in a colony'.   EB

FLANNERY, Kate, pseudonym of Kathleen De Goldi (1959–), has won both the American Express and Katherine *Mansfield Memorial awards for short stories, as well as writing young adult fiction and journalism as

'Kate De Goldi'. Her impressive first collection, *Like You, Really* (1994), comprises eleven linked but non-sequential narratives of a Catholic Christchurch family, especially its women, between the 1950s and the present, with glimpses further back. Each story fluctuates in time through the seemingly random movements of memory, so that characters become known almost simultaneously at different ages from childhood on, and events (like a family picnic) and people (like an eccentric teacher-nun) are retold and revisited, with some surprisingly dramatic moments of revelation and understanding, given the apparently domestic scale. Family history is satisfyingly compiled from these fragments against a background of local events and changes—fashions in clothes, children's games, cars, films and conversational idiom, developments in road surfaces and suburbs, topical news stories and changing retrospects on the past, especially the war. *Landfall reviewer Anna Smith noticed, too, that beneath this surface detail, the collection 'insists on another kind of language … sadness, anxiety, a longing for love and happiness'. The sense of identity through kinship implied in the title is the unifying concern.

Flannery's stories have been published in *Sport, the *NZ Listener, More and Tessa *Duder's collection *Falling in Love* (1995); an autobiographical sketch was in Lloyd *Jones's sports writing collection, *Into the Field of Play* (1992). As Kate De Goldi she has published *Sanctuary* (1996), a young adult story of teenage perplexities and crises, described by Ronda Cooper as 'an authentic modern fable … somewhere between a cautionary tale and a "how to" guide for pouty girls.' It won the overall Children's Book Award in 1997. A second novel on adolescence, *Love, Charlie Mike*, was published 1997. Born in Christchurch and resident there until her move to Wellington in 1997, Flannery is now a full-time writer.   RR

FLETCHER, Beryl (1938–), made a late start and quickly established herself as a feminist novelist with the 'Raglan Trilogy', centred on an intellectually vigorous engagement with changing patterns in women's identity and gender roles. *The Word Burners* (1991) follows the progress of three related but very different women to new self-definitions, a contemporary form of spiritual biography. Direct in language and immediate to the point of urgency in narration, much in journal form, it includes sections of defiantly revisionist polemic reminiscent of the earlier phases of American feminism. It won the regional Best First Book Award of the Commonwealth Writers Prize 1992. *The Iron Mouth* (1993) has the same excitement at encounter with new ideas, again in a fast-moving fragmented narrative that incorporates draft script material from a film version of *The Iliad* being written by the central character. Angry attempts to match male violence (demands to castrate rapists, etc.) and rewrite Homer's 'heroic joy of killing' are eventually replaced by the more positive statement that women need not to appropriate but to create, tell their own stories to find 'the meaning of your journey', with the novel itself offered self-referentially as example. The third novel, *The Silicon Tongue* (1996), deals with the relationship between women and technology, including assisted reproductive techniques.

Born into a socialist working-class family in Onehunga, Fletcher has lived in Auckland, Sydney and England, worked as dental nurse, horticulturalist and mother, and graduated MA (Hons) in Sociology at Waikato University in her thirties. She then, with intermittent work as university teacher, began to fulfil her youthful 'burning ambition to write novels'. Her short stories have been anthologised in women's collections by Cathie *Dunsford and others. RR

Flight was the annual of the Journalism Section of the *League of New Zealand Penwomen published 1932–34. Co-edited by Jean Boswell, it featured work by both Boswell and Ruth *Park. SH

'Fly, The', a short story by Katherine *Mansfield, was first published in the *Nation and Athenaeum* (1922), then included in the posthumously published collection *The Dove's Nest and Other Stories* (1923). It was written in Paris in 1922, over an unusually long three-week period. The MS is held at the Newberry Library, Chicago. 'The Fly' is Mansfield's artistic response to the degradation and suffering caused by war. She wrote to John Middleton *Murry: 'There *must* have been a change of heart.... I feel in the *profoundest* sense that nothing can ever be the same that as artists we are traitors if we dont feel otherwise: we have to take it in to account and find new expressions new moulds for our new thoughts & feelings' (10 Nov. 1919). It presents a symbolic episode in the inner life of 'the Boss', a successful businessman who has lost his only son in World War 1 and who, on being unexpectedly reminded of this by a visitor 'Macey', rescues, tortures and ultimately kills a fly which has fallen into his ink well. The implication is that though he empathises with the fly's fight for survival, he is compelled to destroy it, just as to survive himself he has been compelled to forget his son and destroy his grief. As a late piece in Mansfield's oeuvre, the story has a high incidence of expressive authorial narration, with which the Boss's immediate thoughts are meaningfully juxtaposed, making this one of her most discursive stories. The story has attracted much critical analysis and

debate, with F.W. Bateson and B. Shahevitch in *Essays in Criticism* (1962) challenging S. Berkman's assessment of the story as a failure in *Katherine Mansfield: A Critical Study* (1952). Parallels have been drawn with Chekhov's 'Small Fry', though it should be noted that Mansfield consistently used the image of the fly in private writings and habitually reshaped ink blots as flies. 'The Fly' has enduring popularity and is one of Mansfield's most anthologised stories. SSa

For the Rest of Our Lives (1947) is a war novel by Dan *Davin that traces the careers of three friends in the 2nd New Zealand Division, the 'Div.', through the campaigns in Greece, Crete and (mainly) North Africa from 1941 to 1943. For the time, it was experimental in style, its seventy-six short chapters or 'scenes' marrying novel to film treatment; its visual 'effects' and action passsages, particularly the love and battle scenes, are the most successful. Critics thought the characterisation thin and the reflective passages too dense and sombre, but the novel found a wide audience among returned servicemen, who recognised themselves, their language and their experience in the work. The Customs Department put the book on their monthly list, which meant that although it was not prohibited from entry into New Zealand, any bookseller who offered it for sale might become the subject of prosecution for obscenity. A second edition, with a few minor amendments (and free from such clumsy attempts at censorship), was published in 1965. KO

Forerunner was a quarterly published in Hawkes Bay 1909–14 by the Havelock Work, an esoteric religious and cultural group inspired by the writings of Annie Besant, Rudolf Steiner and William Morris. Each issue carried one or two poems, often devotional in tone, as well as articles on nature, religion, science, art and domestic life. Elsdon *Best contributed articles on Māori culture and W.H. *Guthrie-Smith a series of studies recently republished as *Birds of Tutira* (1990). Poems by Blanche *Baughan, Mona *Tracy ('Mona Tanane') and Dick *Harris were also published. SH

Foreskin's Lament (first performed 1980, published 1981) is Greg *McGee's most important play. Despite much rugby humour and vigorous comedy, it is deeply serious in its implications, using rugby as a metaphor for New Zealand society. The witty, articulate 'Foreskin' loves rugby, but after time away from his provincial home town at university, he is starting to question rugby's traditional values. Suggestively, his real name is Seymour. The brutal forward Clean has returned from *Vietnam with a cynical version of American individualism, very different from the World War 2 romanticism of the ageing coach, Tupper. And Foreskin's liberal girlfriend, Moira, is back from Europe, critical of rugby (and New Zealand) for its violence, its contempt for sensitivity and its oppressive marginalising of outsiders: women, homosexuals and intellectuals like Foreskin. In a major plot development at the after-match party, Foreskin reveals that he saw Clean kick and fatally injure their own captain during the game in order to obtain the captaincy for himself. Foreskin finally challenges his team-mates, and the audience, with a rhetorical lament for lost innocence. He ends with a repeated 'Whaddarya?' What kind of people are you? What sort of society have we become? For Foreskin, as for postcolonial New Zealand, coming of age is painful. The heroic legends of rugby are an illusion. The vaunted altruistic consensus society of ★God's Own Country is a façade for smug hypocrisy. Yet ★sport's values, New Zealand values, have created Foreskin; he cannot, and would not, cut himself from his roots. This is his impossible, tragic dilemma, the anguish to which audiences respond. The force of the first productions in 1980 and 1981, just as the civil disruption of the Springbok tour was boiling over into the streets, lay in the extraordinary correspondence between the play's analysis of New Zealand society and the experience of the audience. Seldom has a play in New Zealand so clearly articulated a defining moment in the society.   DC

FORSTER, Georg (1754–94), as the first son of J.R. ★Forster, demonstrated precocious intellectual talents. He accompanied his father on scientific expeditions in Russia 1765–66, and then to London, where the 13-year-old Georg impressed the Antiquarian Society with a lecture on a historical book he had translated from Russian into English.

In 1772 Georg joined his father on ★Cook's second voyage. After 122 days on open sea—the Forsters noting everything from cloud formations to the temperature of the sea and discovering tiny sea creatures—the voyagers landed at Dusky Bay in late March 1773. Georg took part in some land expeditions and encountered Māori. In June they sailed to Tahiti. They called in to New Zealand again on the voyage to Antarctica. After another visit to Tahiti and further explorations, the voyage arrived in New Zealand for the third time in October 1774. Both Forsters kept detailed journals of all these visits.

Returning to Britain, Georg wrote up these journals into an account of the voyage. Since he intended a wide-ranging philosophical and moral discussion of the voyage's implications, this book was in direct competition with the official accounts, authorised by the

Admiralty. It was published in English as *A Voyage round the world, in his Britannic Majesty's Sloop* Resolution *commanded by Capt. James Cook, during the Years 1772, 3, 4 and 5* (two volumes, 1777), and Forster's own translation into German was published in 1778. It was not enough to save the Forster family from bankruptcy.

This disgrace and his father's fury embarrassed him. He yearned for ★Germany. He began to write only in German and expressed sympathy with the North American rebels against Britain. When he returned to Germany in 1778 he was welcomed there as an 'ocean miracle' (*Seewunder*) by the universities but was abused by his father for abandoning the family. Forster's reports of the South Seas had an influence on German intellectual and literary life that has never been fully assessed. He was famous. He travelled extensively, celebrated by scholars, writers and the social leaders. In Weimar he dined with Goethe, Herder and Wieland. The influence of his tales from New Zealand on these and other writers is an unresearched topic.

In the confusion of revolution and war that followed the French occupation of large parts of Germany, Forster saw an opportunity to end the feudal system in the German princedoms. He joined the democratic revolutionaries, was vice-president of the national convention that declared the Rhineland free and travelled to Paris (with a fellow revolutionary named Potocki—ancestor of another New Zealand writer, ★de Montalk) to have the free Rhineland included in the French Republic, fierily condemning the 'twenty petty tyrants, who were all thirsty for human blood, all growing fat on the sweat of the poor'. The aristocrats never forgave this cosmopolitan critic of nationalism. Among his many essays is a 'Defence of the New Zealand Cannibals', arguing eloquently for the relative value of various cultures. His reputation in Germany remains ambivalent, admired as a scientist and scholar and feared as a voice of political radicalism.   NW

FORSTER, Johann Reinhold (1729–98), travelled as principal naturalist for James ★Cook's second expedition, keeping a remarkable journal that remained unpublished until it was edited by Michael E. Hoare for the Hakluyt Society in 1982. Considering that, as Hoare claims, this journal is the basis of a large part of his son Georg ★Forster's classic account of the voyage and 'is, too, the key to the science and anthropology of this voyage', the fact that it was so long unpublished has distorted scholarship relating to Cook's second voyage.

Forster was parish priest in a small Polish community, a brilliant polyglot, mathematician and scientist who in the Seven Years War was involved with diplomacy for the Prussians, because of his encyclopedic knowledge of Russian language and culture. Bored with his parish work, he spent twelve or more hours a day on scientific, especially botanical, studies in the region.

Migrating to the Lower Volga in 1765, Forster received a commission from the Russian Academy of Sciences to study the natural and agricultural features of the region. He also reported on social conditions and collected coins and other items. His botanical reports made his international reputation as a scientist, but the Russian authorities paid him nothing and he lost his parish in Poland. His voyage to London in 1766 was a desperate escape.

In London he acquired a reputation for his scientific lectures and wrote a significant study of the Volga region. He and Georg translated and annotated books from many languages and he also published a remarkable series of scientific manuals.

When *Banks suddenly withdrew from Cook's second voyage, Forster was appointed naturalist. He was more aware than the others of the limitations imposed by their lack of knowledge of the Māori language, but wrote admiringly of carving, *waka construction, flax weaving and other crafts. His zoological and botanical notes and drawings were impeccable.

Back in Britain, however, he discovered that the report he expected to bring him substantial financial gains was not wanted by the Admiralty. Since Georg was not bound by the contractual agreements, the Forsters decided that the son would publish the kind of book that the father had in mind. Consequently Georg Forster's classic *A Voyage round the world* (1777) must really have been a collaboration between father and son. Johann Reinhold's own *Observations made during a Voyage around the world, on physical geography, natural history, and ethic philosophy* (1778) confined itself perforce to what was acceptable to the Admiralty.

Believing that he had been treated dishonourably by the Admiralty, Forster reacted with a fury that won him nothing but enemies. His finances fell into a disastrous state. Georg also suffered from his blistering tongue. Politically they were at odds in later years, Forster feeling sympathy for the poor, but distrusting radical solutions. In a letter he remarked, 'Liberty is a rare thing, but democratical licentiousness is a devilish one.'

Intrigue, politics and his irascible personality obscured the his and his son's remarkable achievements. An attempt to rehabilitate him was made by Michael Hoare in his edition of the journal and in the scholarly biography, *The Tactless Philosopher: Johann Reinhold Forster 1729–1798* (1975), which includes an invaluable bibliography.   NW

FRAME, Janet (1924–), is New Zealand's most - distinguished writer (CBE; Member, Order of New Zealand; Nominee for the *Nobel Prize in Literature; Honorary Foreign Member of the American Academy and Institute of Arts and Letters; Hon DLitt, University of Otago; President of Honour, *PEN (New Zealand); Honorary Vice-President of the *New Zealand Women Writers' Society). Frame's short but suggestive autobiographical sketch, 'Beginnings' (*Landfall*, 1965), was complemented by the publication of three award-winning volumes of autobiography: *To the Is-Land* (1982), An *Angel at My Table* (1984) and The *Envoy from Mirror City* (1985). The trilogy was subsequently made into a film, *Angel at My Table*, directed by Jane *Campion.

Frame was born in Dunedin, the third of five children. George Frame was a railway worker, a job that resulted in the frequent movement of the family in the early years of Frame's life before they finally settled, in 1930, in Oamaru (the Waimaru of her first novel *Owls Do Cry*). Before her marriage Frame's mother Lottie, a Christadelphian, had worked for a time for the family of Katherine *Mansfield, the Beauchamps, and throughout her life sustained literary aspirations and wrote poetry. Critics have noted in Frame's work the deep-rooted influence of the Christadelphian faith—the investment of everyday objects with numinous significance, the recurrent themes of literalism, apocalypse and resurrection—despite overt challenges to the validity of contemporary Christian belief in many of her novels. The autobiography details a childhood in which Frame's mother's sustained faith is remarkable in the midst of poverty, debt, illness and tragedy: the severe epilepsy of Frame's only brother, George; the drowning of her eldest sister, Myrtle, in the town swimming baths when Frame was 13 and about to enter high school (1937); and the drowning of her younger sister, Isabel, at Picton almost exactly ten years later. These traumatic events and other life experiences find displaced fictional treatment in her writing, resulting in a rich store of personal metaphors and motifs that create organic links between her greatly varied novels, stories and poems. However, Frame has time and again warned against the 'blurring of the fine distinction between the writer's work and the writer's life', the naive treatment of her fictional creations as autobiography.

Despite financial hardship, the Frame family was rich in the love of language and literature: 'words were revered as instruments of magic'; 'writing poems became a family habit'. Alongside details of years of exuberant literary discovery and an intense preoccupation with language, the autobiography recalls the agonies of growing up, painfully shy, burdened by the stigma of poverty and an unusual appearance. Frame writes of a felt 'adolescent homelessness of self' and of the refuge she took in a private mental 'space', the imaginary world of 'Ardenue', prefiguring her later decision to leave 'this' external, prosaic world for 'that' world of imagination and literature. Loss of innocence and imagination in the transition from childhood to adult life in a society 'determined to drive in the rivets of conformity' is a thematic concern that haunts Frame's writing; children and social outcasts are often portrayed as the loci of imaginative truth.

After matriculating from Waitaki GHS (1942), Frame studied as a teacher at Dunedin Teachers' Training College and Otago University (1943–44). A brief spell of teaching followed, but ended abruptly in 1945 when Frame walked out of the classroom on the appearance of a visiting school inspector, never to return. During a short period of work at a boarding house she continued her childhood occupation of creative writing; her first short story, 'University Entrance', was published in the *NZ Listener on 22 March 1946. After a period of illness Frame entered Seacliff Mental Hospital as a voluntary patient in 1947. Mistakenly diagnosed as schizophrenic, she remained in mental hospitals (Seacliff and Avondale) for the next eight years and was subjected to over 200 electric shock treatments. Frame drew most extensively on her experiences of these years in her second novel, *Faces in the Water. While in hospital Frame continued to write short stories; twenty-four of these were collected by her friend John Money, given the title of the main story, 'The Lagoon' and published by the *Caxton Press in 1951 as The Lagoon: Stories. Stylistically, the stories are reminiscent of Mansfield's 'slices of (childhood) life' but they foreshadow many of the unique preoccupations and imagery of the novels that followed: a dichotomy between inner and outer worlds points towards the almost obsessive treatment of dualities in the early novels—treasure/rubbish, light/dark, insane/sane, true/false, vision/sight, innocence/experience. Most of the stories are told from the point of view of children, or of various outcasts (the insane, the simple) who are in their capacity to enter into imaginative worlds barred to, or dismissed by, socially conformist adults.

Following her release from hospital in 1954, Frame was invited by Frank *Sargeson to live in an old army hut in the garden of his Takapuna property. This provided a much needed period of isolation in which to write during the difficult period of reintegration into an unfamiliar post-war society: 'I knew only of Prospero, Caliban, King Lear, and Rilke, these for me, being occasions of the past decade.' During her time on Sargeson's property (1954–55) Frame worked on Owls Do Cry (1957). In 1956 she travelled abroad, on a State *Literary Fund grant, visiting Ibiza and Andorra before journeying to London where, at the Maudsley Clinic,

the diagnosis of schizophrenia was formally rejected by a panel of psychiatrists. During the next seven years, living in and near London, Frame was extremely prolific. In close succession she published Faces in the Water (1961) and The *Edge of the Alphabet (1962) which, together with Owls Do Cry, are thought by some to form a loose trilogy. *Scented Gardens for the Blind followed in 1963. In that same year two collections of stories were published: The *Reservoir: Stories and Sketches was followed by the less successful Snowman, Snowman: Fables and Fantasies in which, as the subtitle suggests, Frame consciously turned from the previously favoured realistic vignette towards allegorical fable.

The novels from this first decade of Frame's writing continue to develop the dualistic concerns of the early stories. In what Vincent *O'Sullivan has called 'the economy of the gifted victim', alienation figures in the novels as an index of authenticity. Frame's Romantic visionaries—eccentrics, mad people, epileptics, oddities —are pitted against the repressive forces of a sterile conformist society stultified by philistinism, materialism and the corrupt use of language. Her characters are precariously balanced on the borders between (linguistic and social) conformity and wholesale abandonment to the dissolutions of meaning and selfhood: silence, insanity, death (often suicide). Given the preponderance of death, suicide and madness in the novels, it is not surprising that some of Frame's readers have criticised the negativity of a vision that risks idealising insanity and difference as privileged sites of (incommunicable) knowledge. Frame's characters on 'the edge of the alphabet' lack an effective medium to communicate the 'treasure' to which they have privileged access: how can one express the visionary dream of wholeness in the divisive medium of social language? The ambivalent attitude towards language expressed in the novels is typically Modernist; language is understood as dual: a duel and potential jewel (to utilise one of her frequent homophonic puns). Cutting against the possibility of the healing potential of language, properly used, is an intuition of the 'deceit' of words, and the ultimate failure of language to breach the 'eternity' that lies beyond the 'hieroglyphic commonplace'. This Romantic-Modernist problematic remains central in Frame's fiction, resulting in an overt thematic concern with language and the role of the writer and persistent stylistic experimentation in novels that move increasingly away from mimetic realism, favouring destabilising narrative manœuvres, and incorporating elements of magic realism and surrealism.

Frame's father died in 1963 and she returned to New Zealand at the end of that year. She was awarded the Scholarship in Letters in 1964, and in that year completed The *Adaptable Man (1965), begun in England the previous year. Frame was awarded the *Burns Fellowship at Otago University in 1965, where she wrote *The *Rainbirds* (1968; published in the USA in 1969 as *Yellow Flowers in the Antipodean Room*). A *State of Siege*, also written in Dunedin, was published in 1966, as was *The Reservoir and Other Stories* (Buckland Literary Award in 1967), a collection including most of the stories from *The Reservoir* and *Snowman, Snowman*. The novels produced during this period in Dunedin differ in subtle but significant ways from the previous four. Frame continues to utilise and modify her personal metaphors but the focus shifts from the idealisation of the inner world of the victimised artist towards an exploration of social conditions. *The Adaptable Man*, set in England, satirises conformity (of novelistic style and human behaviour) but offers no compensatory individual consciousness as the repository of value; the parable-like *A State of Siege* exposes as mistaken the rejection by its protagonist of social interaction (despite its recognised dangers) for the solipsistic pursuit of essential truth/vision; *The Rainbirds* focuses less on the inner world of its alienated protagonist than on the Dunedin society in which he exists.

In the course of the next few years Frame travelled to the USA for several extended periods and briefly to England, returning periodically to Dunedin. She took up several fellowships at the Yaddo Foundation, a writers' colony in Saratoga Springs, New York (1967, 1969, 1971); and the McDowell Colony, Peterborough, New Hampshire (1969). *The Pocket Mirror*, Frame's only published collection of poems, was published in 1967 (Literary Fund Award for Achievement, 1969). In interview, Frame has spoken of poetry as 'the highest form of literature because you can have no dead wood in a poem'. The attraction of the genre is abundantly evident in the novels in which her already 'poetic' prose—intensely lyrical, heavily metaphorical—is at times completely pared down to poetry. Frame's only children's book, *Mona Minim and the Smell of the Sun*, was published in 1969. It was followed by *Intensive Care* (1970) and *Daughter Buffalo* (1972). The two novels written in this period of travel between New Zealand and *America continue to evidence Frame's development away from the late provincialism of the early novels; they are lighter in tone, the settings and characters are more cosmopolitan, the concerns increasingly universal. The starkly opposed dualities of the earlier work, already challenged in her previous three novels, begin to give way to a recognition of the fluidity and interpenetration of the socially/linguistically constructed boundaries between, say, inner and outer or truth and falsehood. Increasingly metafictional and ironic they utilise a barrage of narrative tricks to force a consideration of the activity of writing itself. The ambiguous

response to language still dominates, but Frame seems more willing to explore and affirm the subversive possibilities of linguistic play. Frame's habitually dense prose (described by critics as her 'baroque literary style' and 'metaphoric overdetermination') is even more thickly patterned, its hybrid of styles and registers incorporating poetry, word lists, classical myths, clichés, literary citations and advertising jargon.

In 1972 Frame moved to the Whangaparaoa Peninsula (north of Auckland), changing her surname to Clutha in the following year, although she continued to publish as Janet Frame. Awarded the Winn-Manson Menton Fellowship in 1974 (later called the Katherine *Mansfield Memorial Fellowship), she worked at Menton in France before returning to Glenfield, in Auckland, in 1975. After a silence of seven years, *Living in the Maniototo* was published (1979), followed by the three volumes of autobiography and another collection of stories, *You Are Now Entering the Human Heart* (1983). Frame was awarded the inaugural Turnovsky Prize for Outstanding Achievement in the Arts in 1984 and the Sargeson Fellowship at the University of Auckland in 1987. She lived for various periods in several North Island towns, including Wanganui, Shannon and Levin. Levin is thought to provide a model for the New Zealand setting of *The *Carpathians* (1989). She returned to Dunedin in 1997.

The term *postmodernist is often used to describe the late novels, and certainly examples of postmodernist narrative play abound within them. Feminist critics have drawn attention to Frame's persistent critique of predominantly patriarchal society throughout her oeuvre; postcolonial critics have noted in her work a challenge to an economy of imperial centre and colonised margin. While amenable to such interpretations, Frame's work eludes appropriation by any one critical approach. Her 'postmodern' style and 'feminist' or 'postcolonial' concerns are, as many critics have noted, utilised in the service of a consistently Modernist vision: the artist, and language properly used, are seen as potentially redemptive in a contemporary world marching blindly towards self-destruction (often envisaged as apocalypse). In the late novels the writer is no longer portrayed as an alienated isolate unable to communicate, but rather as one with the capacity to 'impersonate' a variety of subject positions and able to access the 'manifold' of cultural and personal memory. In a world of replicas, Frame seems to suggest, the imitations of art may prove to be the closest we come to what is real and true.

Four full-length studies of Frame have been published: Patrick *Evans's *Janet Frame* (1977); Margaret Dalziel's *Janet Frame* (1980); Judith Dell Panny's *I Have What I Gave* (1992); and Gina Mercer's *Janet Frame:*

Subversive Fictions (1994). The Janet Frame Reader, ed. Carole Ferrier, was published in 1995. Collections of essays include The Ring of Fire, ed. Jeanne Delbaere (1992), which contains an enumerative bibliography to 1990; The Inward Sun, ed. Elizabeth *Alley (1994); and Volume 11 of the *Journal of New Zealand Literature (1993), which is dedicated to discussion of Frame's writing.   KWo

France and New Zealand began their literary contact with the narratives of voyages which the Age of Enlightenment derived from the explorations of Abel *Tasman and others. The earliest was Melchisédech Thévenot's Recueil des Voyages (1681), the most eminent the Abbé Prévost's Histoire générale des voyages (1753), and the most popular Charles de Brosses's Histoire des navigations aux terres australes (1756). Imaginary voyages and *Utopias, too, in the late-eighteenth-century vogue for these genres were located in various fantasy versions of the Pacific. One of the most interesting now is Restif de la Bretonne's La Découverte australe: Le Dédale français (1781), which pursued its satiric and Utopian aims through the motifs of flight and inversion, both later closely associated with New Zealand (e.g. in *Erewhon). These early documentary and imaginary accounts are discussed in John *Dunmore's New Zealand and the French: Two Centuries of Contact (1990), Utopias and Imaginary Journeys to Australasia (1988) and The French and the Maori (1992). Voltaire was the most distinguished literary figure to draw on New Zealand contact, in a story called 'Les Oreilles du comte de Chesterfield et le chapelain Goudman' (1775; see Christiane Mortelier's essay in The French and the Maori).

France's own actual voyages of exploration, beginning with Surville's in 1769 and du Fresne's in 1772, were popularised in Abbé Rochon's Nouveau voyage à la mer du sud (1783), and in later versions which took account of James *Cook. Among the literary results listed by Dunmore was a classical-style drama, Zoraï, ou les Insulaires de la Nouvelle-Zélande by Jean-Etienne de Marignie, briefly performed in 1782, which featured a romanticised Māori warrior returning home from his tour of duty as a noble savage in France and trying to convince his home *iwi to adopt the French political system.

The most important early imaginative response, and arguably the first New Zealand novel, is *Dumont d'Urville's Les Zélandais: Histoire australienne, based on his 1824 visit. Others of interest include whaling narratives, which are the subject of an essay by Christiane Mortelier in Dunmore's New Zealand and the French, notably Félix Maynard's Les Baleiniers (1858). Its title page attributed this to Alexandre Dumas père, though Mortelier shows that he was more mentor than author. The English trans-

lation The Whalers (1937) by F.W. Reed (1874–1953), brother of A.H. *Reed and a Dumas enthusiast whose collection formed over a lifetime is now in the Auckland Public Library, remains the only one available. Accounts of the settlement at Akaroa compiled from journals written there, and thus arguably New Zealand literature in French, include Louis Thiercelin's Le Journal d'un baleinier (1866), which describes impressions from two separate visits, in 1839–40 and 1864; and the 1852–53 journal of Dr Charles Frouin. Thiercelin, Mortelier has shown, was the source for the poem 'Le Dernier des Maourys' ('The Last of the Māori') by Leconte de Lisle, published in his posthumous Derniers Poèmes (1889), a romanticised valediction in forty-one quatrains of plangent alexandrines: 'Fantôme du passé, silencieuse image / D'un peuple mort, fauché par le faim et le fer / Il s'enforça dans l'ombre …' ('A ghost from the past, a silent image of a dead race mown down by hunger and the power of arms, he moved away into the shadows …'; translation by Christiane Mortelier. See also Revue d'histoire littéraire de la France, 1990, No. 2, and Mortelier's edition of the poem, *Wai-te-ata, 1998). In late-nineteenth-century fiction the major figure is Jules *Verne, who made vivid use of New Zealand and of whaling for various exotic adventures. Voltaire received an early translation, by Goodwin Cox, whose A Selection of Voltaire's Dramas was published in Timaru in 1891.

Literary responses in the other direction naturally begin later. The dominant figure initially was Katherine *Mansfield. She knew French literature well, and drew on the symboliste poets, Proust, and others; she worked with John Middleton *Murry on the consciously international Rhythm, which published material in French by Valéry and others; she travelled often to France, lived there for extended periods, met Francis *Carco in Paris and had her brief affair with him in Gray. She wrote many of her major stories in France, especially Menton ('The *Aloe', *'Bliss', *'Daughters of the Late Colonel', 'The *Stranger') and set several there ('Honeymoon', 'An *Indiscreet Journey', *'Je ne parle pas français', 'Poison'). From France she wrote some of private literature's greatest letters. She died at Fontainebleau, southeast of Paris, and is buried in the cemetery of Avon.

France, Gillian Boddy has suggested, has created its own legend of Katherine Mansfield, a romanticised image of the innocent artist lost young, encouraged by her lyricism and insight into French sensibility (though she could be scathing in private about French furniture or flatulency). The scale of interest is certainly remarkable. A recent bibliography compiled by Saliha Azzouz, Katherine Mansfield: The French Reception 1924–1995 (1997) lists more than 300 published items, books, articles, a novel, an ode and several theses. A conference for *Mansfield's centenary was held at the University of Nice and there were commemorations at Menton and Fontainebleau. A new documentary, filmed partly in New Zealand, was shown on 'France 3' TV in March 1997, and also in 1997 Mansfield's stories became a set text in prestigious French qualifications for entering teaching or university ('Agrégation' and 'CAPES').

If this is appropriation, it is not all one way. Bandol, Menton, Fontainebleau and Avon are places of pilgrimage, on the map of New Zealand's imagined identity perhaps as clearly as Stratford-upon-Avon or Westminster Abbey. Menton becomes more familiar each year with the annual residence there of each Katherine *Mansfield Memorial Fellow, many of whom have naturally written about France, Mansfield and Menton. Michael *Gifkins collects some of these responses in *From a Room of Their Own: A Celebration of the Katherine Mansfield Fellowship* (1993). One who has drawn fruitfully on the experience is Lauris *Edmond, 1981 Fellow, especially in the poems in *Catching It* (1983) and the Menton journal which forms part of *The Quick World* (1992). Edmond has also identified one recurrent response of New Zealanders to the perfected cultivation of France: 'I am a child of exiles who dreamt / of the lost garden' ('Jardin des Colombières').

Other responses to France in New Zealand literature are numerous but could be said to be dominated by three things: war, French nuclear policies and tourism. *World War 1 made 'the wound of France ... an endless hurt' (O.N. *Gillespie) the prevailing image, with Archibald *Baxter's *We Will Not Cease* (1939), John A. *Lee's *Civilian into Soldier* (1937, 63) and Basil *Dowling's 'Twenty Years After' characteristic texts of that period. A different perspective is given by Esther *Glen in her story 'Grand-père', about a French veteran of the Franco-Prussian War agonisedly following World War 1 from Akaroa. The classic of France in *World War 2, and probably the best New Zealand writing about France since Mansfield, is M.K. *Joseph's novel *A *Soldier's Tale* (1976).

For the considerable literature of protest against France's nuclear testing, see *Pacific, with Keith *Ovenden the writer most inward with French thought and policy.

Writing by New Zealanders as tourists or short-term visitors is too plentiful to catalogue. A select list could include Greville *Texidor's sharp-edged recapturing of the South of France during the Spanish Civil War in the short fiction 'These Dark Glasses' (1949); Owen *Leeming's poem, popular in the 1960s, 'The Priests of Serabonne'; Ian *Wedde's *Homage to Matisse* (1971); James K. *Baxter's 'At Serrières' (1974, reworked from *'Letter to Noel Ginn', 1944); Charles *Brasch on Paris in *Indirections* (1980); C.K. *Stead's 'Paris: A Poem' (1984); some Allen *Curnow poems such as 'Gare SCNF Garavan'; and Michael Gifkins's stories like 'Summer is the Côte d'Azur' or 'Carnival', if Monaco may be included.

For the realities of French life recorded with more than a visitor's observation one looks outside consciously literary work to a piece like John Saker's excellent autobiographical essay about playing professional basketball in France, 'French Bread', in *Into the Field of Play*, ed. Lloyd *Jones (1992). Or one returns to M.K. *Joseph. He spent his early childhood in Belgium and France, learned English and French simultaneously, went to school in Rouen, and wrote exquisitely about these memories in the poem 'Fragment of an Autobiography' (in *The Living Countries*, 1959) and an unpublished prose memoir, 'A Private Movie'. Poems like 'Matisse' and 'Rouault' show the same empathy with the French consciousness, as do even his several fictional scenes of French history in times of conflict, such as medieval Paris in *Kaspar's Journey* (1988) or the 1871 Commune in The *Time of Achamoth* (1977).

Awareness of New Zealand literature is sustained in France by a small group of scholars, notably Jacqueline Bardolph and Jean-Paul Durix, while numerous New Zealand fiction writers have been translated into French. In the other direction, implicit influences are probably stronger than explicit literary treatments. A very few scattered texts (apart from those of history, literary history or protest) acknowledge the presence of French in New Zealand and the Pacific, such as Claude *Evans's play about Akaroa, *So Laughs the Wind* (1959) or Henrietta Mason's use of her New Hebrides experience in *White Orchid* (1953) and elsewhere. But French painting, music and cinema are all profoundly evident in New Zealand writing, currently especially through cinéma noir. *Existentialism, Foucault, Derrida, Tintin and Astérix have all made their mark. The two nations have never been formally hostile; rugby, wine and Katherine Mansfield provide much cultural common ground. If any ambivalence remains, its source will lie near Mururoa Atoll.   RR

FRANCE, Ruth (1913–68), who also wrote as 'Paul Henderson', was born Ruth Henderson in North Canterbury, one of six children in an Irish Catholic family. Her mother Helena Henderson was a prolific *Georgian poet. France began to write at Christchurch GHS, with encouragement from the *Sun children's editor, Esther *Glen. Marrying during the *Depression, she moved to Australia to find work and escape an apparently domineering father, later returning to live at Redcliffs, Christchurch. Her writing life was fitted around domestic obligations as a mother (of two sons born in the 1940s) and as wife to a successful engineer. Though her husband encouraged her, she was slow to publish, but by 1955 had enough poems in magazines for collection, *Unwilling Pilgrim* (*Caxton). It was published under the pseudonym 'Paul Henderson', as was *The Halting Place* (1961). She continued to publish verse under both names. A controversy in the *NZ Listener* over her 1949 prize-winning Royal Ode, 'The Stream and the Discovery', may have precipitated the disguise, perhaps with a feeling that male poets received better treatment. She was published frequently in the *Listener* and *Landfall*, where her Canterbury *landscape poems fitted the preference for elegiac, somewhat morbid verse, often rather floridly depicting a harsh, uncaring environment which humankind struggled to understand. Other poems failed to find a market because they were outside this genre, metaphysical debates full of anger, regret and cynicism. Though these lacked the refinement and emotional distancing favoured by Charles *Brasch, they are strong poems, where France was developing a form of Modernism ahead of most of her local contemporaries. It seems regrettable if she was not encouraged to develop this style, where her greatest strengths as poet almost certainly lay.

Her first novel, *The Race* (1958), was well received. Based on an actual incident, a disastrous yacht race sailed by her husband, it contained fashionable elements of male action, with strong passages describing tempests and danger. Outside this mode, however, were alternate chapters showing the emotional stress suffered by wives and families waiting onshore. Seen by some as interruptions to a rattling good yarn, these sections show remarkable qualities as interior monologue, and help place *The Race* among New Zealand's best *sports novels. The female heart of France's fiction was inescapable in her second novel, *Ice Cold River* (1961), which with the exception of a description of the Waimakariri River in flood lacked external action and showed women at home, preoccupied by family, inward-looking and uneasy. Through a largely stream-of-consciousness technique and some rather desultory dialogue, it depicts the insecurities of women in a male-dominated society. France's themes are bleak: an *existential isolation confounds the human spirit, unrelieved by faith in God, or hope of accommodation with the environment. She died disillusioned as a writer, sadly before perceptions of women's writing changed in the 1970s.   HM

FRASER, Malcolm (1942–), was one of the 'new fiction' generation of the 1970s–80s. The primary concern of his short fictions (not yet collected) is with New Zealand history and myth, often satirically treating the pretensions of myth fabrication. Characteristically they purport to be documentary or first-person accounts, employing a machinery of multi-layered commentary and supposedly scholarly annotations. Fraser's authorship is often suppressed, as when 'An Auckland Festival' was published as by 'Ralph E. Bodle' (*Islands 18, 1977), or 'The Legend of the Lost Mythology' as co-written with 'F.P. Wilkins' (*Islands* 7, 1974). His 'The Original Community of James Fox' (*Mate 20) was widely received as authentic research into the invented polygamous nineteenth-century commune. Other devices include the 'Questions for Discussion' and 'Suggested Further Reading' attached to 'Every Story Tells One' (*Landfall* 152, 1984), published the same year Julian Barnes employed such techniques in *Flaubert's Parrot*. Michael *Morrissey introducing *The New Fiction* (1985) compares Fraser's work to Nabokov's *Pale Fire*, while the Australian Frank Moorhouse also employed this kind of ludic authenticity in the 1970s (see *PEN/Victoria University Writers' Conference).

Fraser was born in Christchurch and has lived mainly in Auckland, working in a great variety of occupations. He has written several workshopped plays. His penchant for testing and teasing the reader is also evident in his *Diversions: Exercises for Mental Athletes* (1982), a book of puzzles contributed to the *NZ Listener* under the name 'Wilkins'.   RR

Freed, a magazine, was issued from July 1969 to July 1972. It was, in fact, variously titled—No. 1, *The Word is Freed*; Nos 2, 3 and 4, *Freed*; and No. 5, *Freed at Last*. As with the titles, editors also changed—No. 1, Alan *Brunton and Jim Stevenson; No. 2, Brunton and Chris *Else; Nos 3 and 4, Murray *Edmond; and No. 5, Russell *Haley. Only Nos 4 and 5 shared the same page size and format. Since it was intended by initiating editor Brunton that there would be four issues only, the fifth was 'unauthorised', even though it contained much material by Brunton. Except for No. 5, all were published by the Auckland University Students Association for the Auckland University Literary Society. *Freed* was the first major indication that contemporary literary theory, mainly from Europe, and *American poetry, especially from the Black Mountain and the Objectivist poets, were being registered in New Zealand literary thinking. Determinedly iconoclastic in both form and content, it began an alternative and oppositional tradition in the local scene, which has not only survived, but increased its readership and membership over the years. This can still arouse opposition, showing that the argument set up by *Freed* almost thirty years ago, with its overt manifestos and international allegiances, is by no means resolved. In addition, the literary works in this magazine were integrated, rather than illustrated, with graphics that came from a wide variety of sources—a *postmodernity of iconoclasm and integration, of seriousness and irreverence, of careful attention and play. In layouts by David Kisler, artists included Pat Hanly, Barry Linton, Hal Chapman, and authors included Brunton, David *Mitchell, Haley, Ian *Wedde, Edmond, Arthur Bates, Bob *Orr, Jan *Kemp, Roger Horrocks and Rhys Pasley. Several of these were at the heart of an important new generation, so that Freed has now a somewhat legendary status. Its daring integration of theory and practice, of *typography and graphics, of local and international sources, remains a potent image of change in the poetry of its time.   AL/SH

FREED, Dorothy (1919–), composer and librarian, born in Dunedin, was part of the early group of Frederick Page's and Douglas *Lilburn's students at Victoria University of Wellington. In 1958 she won the NZBC/APRA Award for a New Zealand song, in 1959 the Philip Neill Memorial Prize in composition and in 1980 the APRA Award for outstanding services to music. She has set poems by Ruth *Dallas, Basil *Dowling, A.R.D. *Fairburn, Katherine *Mansfield, Keith *Sinclair, Anton *Vogt and James K. *Baxter. Her career as professional librarian has enabled her to disseminate invaluable bibliographical information about New Zealand music through her numerous publications.
                                                                    JMT

FRENCH, Anne (1956–), is a poet, critic and editor. Born and raised in Wellington, she was educated at Wellington GC and Victoria University (MA 1979). After joining *Oxford University Press in Wellington as an editor in 1979, she became OUP's New Zealand managing editor in 1982. In 1993 she became the inaugural writing fellow at Massey University and since 1995 has been managing editor at the Museum of New Zealand Te Papa Tongarewa. She is also a regular reviewer, usually of New Zealand writing.

French gained early success as a poet, winning the *PEN Young Writer's Incentive Award in 1973 and 1974. Her poetry began to appear in *Landfall and other periodicals from the mid-1970s, but her first collection, All Cretans Are Liars, was not published until 1987. It attracted considerable attention, winning both the New Zealand Book Award for Poetry and the PEN Best First Book of Poetry Award in 1988. Three other collections have since been published: The Male as Evader (1988), Cabin Fever (1990) and Seven Days on Mykonos (1993).

Central to French's poetry are questions of identity and definition. A major concern is how a poet writing at the end of the twentieth century defines herself in relation to the Western poetic tradition in general and the New Zealand poetic canon in particular. Always acutely aware of itself and of the reader, her poetry plays with both traditional and open forms and contains deliberate echoes of earlier poets. Identity established through language and place is another preoccupation: what it means to live here, with a bicultural heritage (expressed for example in the evocative identification of Hauraki Gulf placenames in Cabin Fever), rather than somewhere else (the home/abroad contrasts of Seven Days on Mykonos). The definition of oneself through others is a constant theme, made most explicit in the elegant and ironic cataloguing of love and lust, need and betrayal from a feminist perspective in The Male as Evader, but recurring throughout French's poetry. The positions thus arrived at are never fixed, however; her work to date can be read as a kind of ongoing debate, both for the poet, forever redefining herself, and with her readers.   AM

'Fretful Sleepers' (1952) is a much-quoted essay by Bill *Pearson on the conformist torpidity of New Zealand society, with the subtitle 'A Sketch of New Zealand Behaviour and its Implications for the Artist'. It was written in London in 1951, published in *Landfall 23, September 1952, and reprinted in Charles *Brasch's selection Landfall Country (1962). The essay's eleven sections present New Zealanders as docile, conformist, lacking moral and artistic integrity, cynical, mindlessly deluded by a false ideal of egalitarianism, conservative, anti-intellectual, sneeringly hedonistic, exploitative of the land, and provincial. These censures are delivered with a memorable acidity: 'I doubt if a New Zealander has any other moral referee than public opinion'; 'I hate talking anything but gossip in a bus or train … otherwise you sense the rest of the bus listening united in one unspoken sneer at half-cock'. The Heinemann Dictionary of New Zealand Quotations (1988) lists eighteen such taunts, its highest citation from any single work; and the essay was still current enough to be the subject of a public lecture series at Auckland University in 1996. Its title served for some decades almost as a codeword for national inertia, and self-exiled New Zealanders overseas were known to thrust copies on anyone contemplating migration from Europe, like a deterrent emetic.

Pearson's observation of a basic national pragmatism is almost certainly valid and goes back at least to Samuel *Butler: 'A mountain here is only beautiful if it has good grass on it'; recurring in such key literary locations as *Mansfield's Stanley Burnell ('At the Bay' 2) and John *Mulgan's Report on Experience. Pearson's omissions are now striking: he makes no allowance for the two wars, which had left much of the world exhausted and paranoid in 1951; he disdains popular culture in such forms as *sport; he disregards the national literature, which was emergent by that date. But he deftly pulled together many strands of feeling about New Zealand's lost *Utopian potential, and articulated the artistic community's inveterate sense of neglect. His mainly anecdotal procedure is weak as argument but gains from its overtly personal tone, from the opening childhood reminiscence of dangerously neglected mineshafts to the nightmare Miltonic-Orwellian prophecy of the ending: '… impounding of one's writing equipment, closing of printing presses….' As summative assessment or as the voice of self-loathing, the essay still has impact.   RR

Frigate Bird, The (1989), is the first novel in a trilogy by Alistair *Campbell. It is set partly in the Cook Islands and partly in a New Zealand psychiatric hospital. The narrator, who lives on the edge of insanity and blends fantasy with reality, paranoia with love, returns to his childhood home in search of the identity he has lost. There he undergoes a severe psychiatric crisis and is brought into a hospital, where the people he and the readers encounter could be fellow patients or mythical Polynesian figures. Since their own fantasies are as lively as the narrator's, the reader is faced with an insoluble problem of sorting out imagined reality from real imagination. One is well advised to leave that unsolved and enjoy the wealth of poetic images and exquisite language. In the trilogy's middle volume, *Sidewinder* (1991), the demon of that name, who has already tormented the narrator in the previous novel, now seems to be driving him apart from Tia, the Cook Islands woman he has married and loves. Sidewinder is supported by two imps, Belial and Beelzebub, who are intimidating yet offer much in the way of comic relief—they resemble Laurel and Hardy. The images of strongly scented flowering tropical trees and of a gentle warmth in the air provide a different, more 'romantic' kind of relief and a curious setting for the crises the narrator suffers. Western and Polynesian imagery are blended in surprising ways—at a peculiarly Polynesian moment, when a woman gives birth in 'the warm maternal waters of a lagoon … as countless generations of women had done before her' the narrator's 'fiend' murmurs, 'What a masterpiece Raphael would have made of it!' The ending is 'happy' as the narrator and Tia found the family they have always wanted. The trilogy is completed with *Tia* (1993). When the narrator is again tormented by Sidewinder, he tries to contact his New Zealand doctor but is unable to. Furthermore he finds himself accused of murder. Interrogated by an inspector and in a different way by the increasingly bungling Sidewinder, he must struggle constantly to keep his mental bearings. Throughout it all he is repeatedly trying to get a flight to New Zealand. The trilogy moves to an unexpected conclusion when Tia makes a compact with the narrator's fiend. The mixture of comedy, tragedy, sanity, insanity, self-parody, surrealism, South-Sea romanticism, realistic Polynesian life, weariness and exuberance keeps the reader in a constant state of suspense and uncertainty.   NW

From a Garden in the Antipodes (1929) is the best-known poetry collection of Ursula *Bethell. For many readers, Bethell is inextricably linked to the garden she tended at Rise Cottage, its careful cultivation lovingly recorded in this first volume. It includes her most frequently anthologised work, although she herself preferred *Time and Place*, the carefully chosen memorial to Effie Pollen. *From a Garden in the Antipodes* was published in London by Sidgwick and Jackson, having been submitted to them by Arthur Mayhew, brother of Lady Ruth Head—the correspondent who is named in the first poem in the volume. Sidgwick's initial response was guarded, revealing the customary difficulty of publishing 'stuff of colonial or provincial interest', but within a fortnight he responded more positively that 'we cannot afford to give the go-by to anything as good as this'. Bethell's correspondence with Sidgwick reveals her hesitancy about submitting the poems, her readiness to defer to his judgment about matters of selection, ordering and titles, and her surprise at their acceptance 'en bloc', describing them as 'the slight inventions of an unknown dépaysée.'

About some aspects of the publication, though, she was quite clear. The book was published pseudonymously, as by 'Evelyn Hayes'. The 'positive passion' with which she clung to anonymity is quoted by Vincent *O'Sullivan; her draft letter also speaks of 'desperation', 'nervous persistence' and 'positive claustrophobia', and she asserts that 'in provincial New Zealand … publicity is a really painful affair'. She is equally firm that the word 'from' is to be part of the title, stating that it 'helps to describe the nature of the work's content which … began as metrical messages to Ruth Mayhew…. Nine of the pieces are directly addressed to her and … many have an absent acquaintance in mind.'

The collection received generally favourable reviews, both in England and in New Zealand, although some of the remarks about charm and grace have a faintly patronising air about them. The most substantial and perceptive was by J.H.E. *Schroder in the Christchurch *Press*, who remarks on 'the vividness of phrase … exhilarating quickness of mind … and corresponding range and suppleness of feeling', and who is particularly attentive to Bethell's subtle use of rhythms. Ostensibly, as the 'garden' of the title suggests, the poems deal with a small domestic world, but throughout the volume the activity of gardening is carried on against a wider backdrop of mountains and oceans, constant reminders of the permanent forces of nature and the brevity of human effort. Close observation of the seasonal cycles and a consequent focus on time and mortality are important elements in the verse, which faces this awareness of death with irony and quiet humour. Equally important, though, are the celebratory responses to new life and growth which vividly convey her delight in the natural world.

Conversational in tone and rhythm, the poems nevertheless reveal a fondness for unusual and technical words, and a delight in 'the accompaniment of words' which offsets the solitariness of the gardener. Indeed, words and language are as much a presence in these poems as the garden which is their setting and subject, from the 'plain words' of the opening 'Foreword', through the 'lovely sounding names' of 'Catalogue' and the 'silence vibrant with words' in 'Name', to the concluding 'Dirge' which closes by proposing to 'say no word more'. Although many of the poems of the following two volumes were written at the same time, they are quite different in style and subject, and Bethell's instinct for keeping them separate was a sound one. *From a Garden in the Antipodes* has a greater coherence and integrity than her cautious letters to Sidgwick would lead us to expect. PW

Frontiers was one of the literary magazines that gave voice to the diversified international awareness of the late 1960s. Edited in Christchurch by David Prescott, it had poets John *Weir and Michael *Harlow as poetry editors, the latter securing contributions from major overseas writers like Bernard Brodsky, Christopher Middleton and the South African Peter Horn, especially in the earlier issues of the six published (1968–70). A genuinely open local selection policy gave early opportunity to new writers such as Alan *Brunton, Riemke *Ensing, Gary *Langford, Bill *Manhire, Brian *Turner and Ian *Wedde (and several others whose names are not now familiar), as well as contributions from the

established, including James K. *Baxter, Ruth *Dallas and Louis *Johnson. RR

FROUDE, James Anthony (1818–94), Oxford scholar and the friend and biographer of Carlyle, was best-known for his twelve-volume *A History of England from the Fall of Wolsey to the Defeat of the Spanish Armada* (1856–70). He was meticulous in observation and research, liberal in his views and notable for a superb prose style, which manages to suggest both magisterial authority and intimacy with the reader. These virtues make his *Oceana, or England and her Colonies* (1886, 1888), an account of his travels to the southern hemisphere, still very readable. A visit to his friend Sir George *Grey on the island retreat of Kawau, for example, leads to a model pen portrait of a fascinating personality, while his description of the legendary pink and white terraces at Tarawera is highly entertaining. Like many other visitors he compared the thermal region to Hades, reporting the exclamation of 'a Scotchman' at the sight: 'By God, I will never swear again.' Froude disliked Auckland, believing that colonies should represent an escape from cities into a kind of rural bliss: his only hope for the debt-ridden country, after *Vogel's borrowings, was that when the economy collapsed people would abandon 'industry' (including the destruction of forests, which distressed him) for 'agriculture'. He compared the Māori with the Irish, finding their houses almost identical but the Māori variant 'neater, cleaner and better kept'. In both societies 'it was the wrong sex that was doing the hardest work.... We saw more than one young mother, with a child slung in a pouched shawl at her back as if she were an inverted marsupial, hoeing maize and turning up potatoes, while the husband sat smoking his pipe composedly as if he had been bred in Connemara.' He was impressed and moved by Māori poetry, which he probably encountered through Grey. His general comments on colonisation can be sharp: 'We have killed a great many thousand people to teach them to love us.' But on the whole he enjoyed what he saw in New Zealand: 'so varied, so remarkable, the future home, as I believe it to be, of the greatest nation in the Pacific.' NW

G

GADD, Bernard (1935–), is a prolific writer and editor, notable as a pioneer in work with a multicultural emphasis for high school students. Born in Hamilton and educated at Ardmore and Auckland Teachers' Colleges, he has taught mainly at Hillary College. His commitment to social justice and to providing texts reflecting his students' Polynesian lives have led to works such as *Five Stories* (1982) for Hillary College, *I Have Seen the Future* (1986) for Longman Paul and *It Started with a Scream* (1990) and *That Secret Smile* (1992) for his publishing co-operative Te Ropu Kahurangi. Plays for classroom use include *Bone City: A Fantasy of New Zealand's Future* (1995). His three novels explore the past. *Laya* (1985) tells of a 13-year-old girl in a pre-historical migration across the Pacific, *Dare Not Fail* (1987) of the search for spiritual self-worth among the Moriori of the Chatham Islands, and *Blood of Tainui* (1991) portrays tragic racial conflict during the Waikato Land ★Wars.

Adult work has been published in many journals, including ★*Landfall* and ★*NZ Listener*, his poetry being represented in *Oracle Bones* (1992); always accomplished, serious in intent, occasionally simplistically didactic, often dependent on models, sometimes explicitly pastiche (as in the 'Harry in the Rest Home' extension of Glover's ★*Sings Harry* or in 'Jackie's Rap'). Gadd also wrote a history of Papatoetoe, but deserves most recognition for validating ★Pacific peoples and texts in his own work and by editing anthologies such as the very early *Pacific Voices* (1977). DH/RR

Games of Choice (1976), the fourth novel of Maurice ★Gee, is set in a provincial town called Hardinge, clearly identifiable as Napier. It begins as the marriage of Kingsley and Alison Pratt (the name suggests the unheroic character of the protagonist) is on the point of falling apart. The adolescent miseries of the children, Miranda and Malcolm, have been exacerbated by unspoken tensions in their parents' unsuccessful marriage. Now the children take revenge, Miranda by flaunting her sexuality and Malcolm by choosing the profession his father most hates: the army. A contrast seems to be offered by the idyllic family of German silversmith Gunter Spohn and his wife Jenny, a potter, in their picturesque home, minimal clothing, many naked children and the authenticity of their art. But Gunter shows himself capable of gross violence when challenged and both he and Jenny are promiscuous without tenderness. In a brilliantly comic scene Kingsley plays golf with Alison's lover, triumphing at first, but ending in the rough. Ultimately he and his senile father are left alone: Alison, Malcolm and Miranda have all gone their unhappy ways. Though summary sounds melodramatic, Gee's tight control over language and action draws the reader constantly deeper into complex psychological territory. NW

Garden in the Antipodes (Bethell), see **From a Garden in the Antipodes**.

'Garden Party, The', a short story by Katherine ★Mansfield, was written in October 1921. A drastically cut version was first published in the *Weekly Westminster Gazette* in February 1922; later that month *The Garden Party and Other Stories* was published, containing the story in full. The MS is in the Newberry Library, Chicago. The story, based on actual events that occurred in 1907 at 75 Tinakori Road, Wellington, concerns a garden party held by the Sheridan family. The central consciousness is that of Laura whose ecstatic excitement in the first part of the story ('… there were two tiny spots of sun…. Darling little spots…. She could have kissed it') gives way to shock when news of the accidental death of a carter who lived nearby reaches her. In what Sheridan family members call an 'absurd' and 'extravagant' reaction, Laura pleads for the party to be cancelled. It goes ahead but afterwards her mother suggests she take a basket of leftover food to the bereaved family ('it will be the greatest treat for the children'). Her sighting of the corpse results in a transforming, epiphanic experience ('What did garden parties and lace frocks matter to him? He was far from all those things. He was wonderful, beautiful') which completes the emergence of Laura's individual voice and consciousness from that of the Sheridan family. Aside from its treatment of the effect of death on the living, the story is a subtle commentary on class consciousness, a quality it shares with 'The *Doll's House'. In a 1922 letter Mansfield wrote that she wanted to convey 'The diversity of life and how we try to fit in everything, Death included … it seems to me there is beauty in that inevitability.' Although the story changed the title of her collection (originally to be named *At the Bay*), she judged it in a note on the manuscript as only 'moderately successful'. Critics disagree, making this one of her most popular and admired stories.   SSa

GARRARD, Phillis, was the pseudonym under which Phillis Garrard Rowley published her pioneering 'Hilda' school stories with rural New Zealand settings. Born in England, she also lived in Canada and Bermuda. She used her home in Taihape to give attractive colour to stories of a country day school in the central North Island, at a time when it was virtually obligatory for school stories to be set in English private boarding schools. *Hilda at School: A New Zealand Story*, published in London in 1929, declared its regional interest and dealt with home life, the antics of a horse called Roger the Red and activities in various extremes of weather, as well as school events and characters. It was followed by *The Doings of Hilda* (1932), *Hilda's Adventures* (1938) and *Hilda Fifteen* (1944), which take the lively heroine from primary through secondary classes, always with the same male teacher. All were published by Blackie in London, who reissued the first three as *New Zealand Schoolgirl* in 1958, with a further 1980s edition.

Betty *Gilderdale comments that 'The books are certainly not museum pieces…. They are infused with the vitality of Hilda, a high-spirited character whose strong will is tempered by a disarming honesty' and that they vividly present a school system 'which aims at making its pupils hardy and self-reliant as well as educated'.   EM

GASKELL, A.P. (pseudonym of Alec Gaskell Pickard, 1913–), short story writer, was born in Kurow, North Otago, educated at Otago University and Dunedin Teachers' College, and worked as a schoolteacher until his retirement in 1974. After several false starts as a writer, in 1940 his discovery of the stories of Frank *Sargeson provided him with a model, and he published several stories in periodicals. Sargeson immediately recognised the affinity and initiated a correspondence, encouraging Gaskell's writing, giving him suggestions for reading and helping him to find publication. Gaskell published stories in New Zealand and Australian periodicals 1942–47, and also appeared in Sargeson's anthology *Speaking for Ourselves* (1945). A collection was published by *Caxton Press as *The Big Game and Other Stories* (1947). Gaskell added several other stories in the next few years, including his best-known, 'All Part of the Game', but published little after that, with only two further stories appearing, in 1961–62. His published fiction was collected in 1978 as *All Part of the Game: The Stories of A.P. Gaskell*, edited by R.A. *Copland.

Gaskell became one of the leading members of the 'Sargeson school' of vernacular realism, and his work clearly reveals the influence of Sargeson himself ('You Can't Go Three Days'), Sargeson's major model, Sherwood Anderson ('The Cave'), and other related writers, notably Ernest Hemingway ('Tidings of Joy') and James Joyce ('The Fire of Life'). These influences are evident in his method: a restricted point of view, usually first person, with the narrator or central consciousness not fully understanding the implications of the story; a vernacular style; and a structure built on irony or implicit revelation. The Sargesonian tradition is likewise evident in the underlying 'humanism, though of a rather special colonial variety' (as Sargeson described it). Like Sargeson, but without his sophistication and complexity, Gaskell reveals and implicitly judges the deficiencies of *puritan provincial New Zealand society: its censoriousness ('Purity Squad'); its racism ('School Picnic'); its puritan self-righteousness ('Fight the Good Fight'); its sour egalitarian resentments ('No Sound of Battle'); its limited marital patterns ('Who Steals My Purse'); its possessive parents ('He Was Lost' and 'Poor Young Man'); its authoritarian child-rearing practices ('Tell Me the Old Old Story'); its quietly destructive family relationships ('Holiday' and 'All Part of the Game'). However, Gaskell's stories give the sense of an author much more a part of the society he depicts than do Sargeson's, with a greater appreciation for ordinary social life, as on a rugby team ('The Big Game'), in an army camp ('As You Were'), or in a small community attempting to deal with an emergency ('The Cave'). Sargeson held high hopes for Gaskell, reviewing *The Big Game* very positively in the first issue of *Landfall*, and stating later that for Gaskell's best stories he had 'an admiration beyond anything [he had] felt for the work of almost any New Zealand prose writer'. He encouraged Gaskell to attempt a novel, and was disappointed that his career did not develop. However, Gaskell did leave a legacy of some of the most revealing pictures of New Zealand life in the 1930s–40s. LJ

Gaudeamus appeared in five irregular monthly issues in Christchurch in 1951. Largely published to counter the suppression of information surrounding the nationwide *waterfront strike, it featured poetry by James K. *Baxter, Louis *Johnson, Charles *Spear and Pat *Wilson. SH

GEARY, David (1963–), is a playwright and fiction writer. Born in Feilding and educated at Palmerston North BHS and Victoria University, he began a law degree before turning to Arts. After completing the creative writing paper at Victoria, and while enrolled at the Te Kura Toi Whakaari/The New Zealand Drama School, he submitted 'Kandy Cigarettes' to the 1988 New Zealand Playwrights' Workshop, under the pseudonym of Kurt Davidson. Parts of this script then became a series of revue sketches entitled 'Gothic But Staunch' and 'Dry, White and Friendly'. His first full-length play was 'Pack of Girls' (Downstage, 1991), a comedy in which a rugby widow forms a women's rugby team. This was followed by *Lovelock's Dream Run*, first seen at the Australia and New Zealand Playwrights' Conference in Canberra in 1990, opening at The Watershed (Auckland Theatre Company) in 1993 and published by *Victoria University Press in 1993. Drawing on his experience of boarding school, Geary gives a highly imaginative and empathetic account of what life might have been like for *Lovelock (the future runner) as a boarding student in Timaru, and then later in Berlin at Hitler's Olympics. His next full-length play was 'The Learner's Stand' (Circa, 1995), about the experiences of a student who joins a rather atypical shearing gang for the summer. 'The King of Stains', a short play about a drycleaner with a fish fetish, followed (Bats, 1996). With Mick Rose and Tim Spite, he co-authored 'Backstage with the Quigleys' (Bats, 1992) and 'The Rabbiter's Daughter' (Bats, 1994), two one-act plays which satirise, respectively, the theatrical and the literary worlds. He also collaborated with Theatre at Large to create 'Manawa Taua/Savage Hearts' (Watershed, 1994) and with a group of actors to create 'Ruapehu', one half of a double bill with Fiona Samuel's 'Untitled'; these two plays appeared under the title 'One Flesh' at Downstage, 1996. Geary's plays are characterised by their

physicality, their mordant humour and their critique of entrenched Kiwi mythologies. He has written for film (*The Smell of Money*, a documentary) and for television. He was awarded the Dominion Sunday Times Bruce Mason Playwrights' Award in 1991 and in 1994 won the Adam Foundation Playwrights' Award for 'The Learner's Stand'. SG

GEE, Maurice (1931–), one of New Zealand's most distinguished novelists, born in Whakatane, passed much of his childhood in the country town of Henderson (now contained by Auckland's urban sprawl), and this background plays a major role in his fiction. Again and again his plots are set in Henderson, usually under another name, or other small towns. Even in the most recent, where Wellington and Auckland play a major part, it is their subdivisions—Wadestown, Karori or present-day Henderson—which dominate.

Of special significance is Henderson Creek, where, Gee said, 'I seem to have spent half my boyhood'. A place of 'marvellous and terrible things', it became a source of his ambivalent imagery. There 'I got my first sight of death.... I'd run home from the creek to the safety and security of the kitchen ... one the place of safety and affection, the other the place of adventure, danger, excitement. And death' (*New Zealand Books*, Aug. 1995). Echoes of Henderson Creek, in various transformations, pervade his fiction.

Gee's father was a carpenter, whose sons made the most of their access to tools and materials for making boats for paddling down the creek to Waitemata Harbour. In the fiction, both children and adults have such adventures. Later, Gee lived a while in Napier and then moved to Nelson with his wife and family, to find a rural town near the sea, both resembling and differing from the Henderson of his childhood.

His mother's tales of family history were equally important to Gee's developing sense of storytelling, providing a sense of social history and its implications for families, couples and individuals. His description of his grandfather is immediately recognisable to readers of *Plumb*: 'He had an ear trumpet that now and then we were allowed to shout into.... He spent his time in the study where there were shelves of books that went up to the ceiling.... The years of his ministry were years of dispute and rebellion' ('Beginnings', *Islands* 17, 1977, an important essay for the grounding of Gee's fiction in his own and his family's life). His memories of primary school in Henderson are obviously intense and detailed. Furthermore, he seems able to transfer their atmosphere to other schools. There can be few accounts of a primary school as vivid as Gee's *Nelson Central School: A History* (1978), a major contribution to the history of education based on extensive oral research and Gee's sensitivity to social issues.

Gee then attended Avondale College and University of Auckland (MA in English 1954). He played rugby skilfully, basing the games in *The Big Season* (1962) on first-hand experience. For two years he was a school-teacher in Paeroa, but found little to enjoy in the profession. After three years' casual work in various parts of New Zealand, he spent 1961 teaching and writing in England, partly supported by a grant from the New Zealand *Literary Fund.

This acknowledged his growing literary status. Ever since university he had been writing. Short stories were published in *Landfall* in 1955 ('The Widow'), 1957 ('A Sleeping Face') and 1960 ('The Losers'), and in *Mate* in 1960 ('Schooldays'). 'The Losers' and 'Eleventh Holiday' in the British collection *New Authors Short Story I* (1961) created a wider audience for this new voice.

A year later *The Big Season*, Gee's first published novel, was greeted enthusiastically. In the *Hawkes Bay Herald Tribune*, Louis *Johnson wrote that it refuted the criticism that the New Zealand novel shows our way of life as dull. The conservative *New Zealand Herald* found it 'not always pleasant, but certainly forceful and sincere' and the *Press* commented on the 'almost cruel accuracy' of its version of a New Zealand township. The *Southland Times* went further: 'Gee must have decided he would outmodernize the modernists in vulgarity.'

This dislike of Gee's 'sordidness' and 'violence', combined with inability to fault his technique, has accompanied newspaper reviews ever since, up to the controversy surrounding the children's novel *The *Fat Man* (1995). The best answer to such pettifogging is the popularity of his work with readers of all ages, including those in other countries. Like many New Zealand writers, Gee confronts the mental constriction of local *puritanism, and the backlash shows that it is not just a fictitious construct.

The Big Season celebrates exhilarated joy in the game of rugby, while throwing severe doubt on the social ethos that surrounds it (see also *Sport). The central character, Rob Andrews, is diverted from success on the field by fascination for what makes a burglar tick. He is diverted again by the burglar's girl. He seems to have betrayed both the 'élite' of the rugby world and his lower-class friend, but he has not betrayed himself: for all his confusion he is discovering his own potential. It might be too glib to say that the author is doing so too, but patterns and themes that will shape later books are here in embryo: tension between family members, the failure of community leaders to grow up, violence as a normal element of social life, social constraint and inner freedom and the moral courage of individuals who oppose powerful taboos.

Family tensions dominate *A Special Flower* (1964), written while Gee was *Burns Fellow. Donald Pinnock, a fussy bachelor at 46, is engaged and then married to Coralie Marsh, twenty years younger and of a different social background. The encounter of Donald's refined mother with Coralie's railway-worker father is the most powerful of many tragicomic scenes. As in *The Big Season*, the protagonist's family view his attachment to someone of another class as a betrayal—one might also be reminded of the ambitious mother and blunt working father in D.H. *Lawrence's life and fiction. The energetic Coralie leaves to live with (another) rugby hero. Donald, now pathetic, dies in an accident, and gradually his mother, sister and widow come to understand each other better, the three women being sensitively drawn. Raw energy and lifeless gentility reach out for each other, and reconciliation is, as elsewhere, Gee's antidote to his more vivid theme of intolerance.

Gee's third novel was *In My Father's Den* (1972), a kind of mystery story (see *Detective fiction) set in Wadesville, another version of Henderson. Despite a rather melodramatic ending, Gee's voice seems confidently in control for the first time.

It was followed by the collection *A *Glorious Morning, Comrade* (1975), though many of these eleven short stories had been written before the novels and could be viewed as apprentice work. Nonetheless, they are carefully crafted. When Gee came to publish his *Collected Stories* (1986), he had added just two more; his mature work has tended to be longer fiction. (There are some half-dozen uncollected stories.) Dysfunctional families and acts of extreme violence, often a group attacking an individual, recur, as do creeks and drownings, while many characters and situations remind the reader of later novels.

In *Games of Choice* (1976) there is increased subtlety, complexity and tautness of writing. The violence is as much potential, in the attitudes of people towards each other, as actual. (There is a potentially dangerous dog called *Muldoon.) These strengths reach their fruition in the masterpiece *Plumb* (1978), one of the finest novels written in New Zealand. The trilogy of *Plumb*, *Meg* (1981) and *Sole Survivor* (1983) provides a broadly conceived image of life in New Zealand over three generations. Local critical response has been enthusiastic and ongoing and all three books have been successfully published abroad.

Clearly at the height of his powers, and pleased to be writing full-time, Gee combined work on the trilogy with his first children's fiction. *Under the Mountain* (1979) is an Auckland tale stimulated by the volcanoes that dot the cityscape. Strange creatures like massive slugs are planning to turn the world into their own muddy element by force of eruption and only Rachel and Theo, possessors of magic stones and with access to the mind of the slugs' pure enemy, can save the world. Similarly, in *The World Around the Corner* (1980) Caroline opposes evil beings who wish to turn a perfect world into a desolate one. In this case both worlds are outside Caroline's—on the other side of a gate on a hill 'at the centre of New Zealand', near Nelson. Illustrations are by Gary Hebley, who provided cover illustrations for others of Gee's children's books.

The battle between good and evil, a beautiful natural and social world and a dreary one, is the common theme of these books. It leads into fantasy and ultimately *science fiction in the trilogy *The *Halfmen of O* (1982), *The Priests of Ferris* (1984) and *Motherstone* (1985). Gee's children's novels also include *The *Fire-Raiser* (1986) and *The Champion* (1989), the story, originally a television series, of a black American in a small New Zealand town in 1943, who brings thrills and hero-worship to the children and arouses racism among the adults.

Going West (1992) is significant for its exploration of the nature of literary creation, and for much encoded autobiography. Rex Petley's poetry has a creek as a repeating image, and the novel's 'Loomis' is almost indistinguishable from Gee's Henderson. Gee has said that he will never write an autobiography, because he cannot betray the people who would appear in it, but as Skeat says of Petley, 'Rex wrote no autobiographical pieces … but the images of small town, country school, kitchen, workshop, creek … make a kind of autobiography. He points them out, makes sure that we understand that this is no imaginary country, then lets the poems speak for themselves.' Grounded in reality, but reaching out into a greater meaning than bare reality can provide, such images and changes shape the richness of Gee's fictional world.

In *Prowlers* (1987) and *The *Burning Boy* (1990), Gee confirms skills he has developed to high art: the historical novel grounded firmly in the present, and the complex novel of social life and unexpected yet seemingly inevitable modern behaviour, looking forward to *Crime Story*.

Each of Gee's novels bountifully gives us a rich vision of some region and aspect of New Zealand life, and of human life in general. Each is peopled with a variety of intensely living and unique personalities together with lush images of the natural and social worlds. Taken together his books can overwhelm us with their wealth, density and complexity of life. Yet there is always an awareness of living at the edge of an abyss: one false move and we shall leave this abundance for nothingness. Trevor James has pointed out the frequency of such words as *void, abyss, hole, missing,* and extends their sig-nificance beyond Gee to 'the tendency toward authoritarian conformity which characterises New Zealand society', inseparable from the *'puritanism' that obsesses many New Zealand writers (*London Magazine*, 24, 11, 1985). Plumb is many things, including a puritan in the religious, secular, local and international senses of the word, and it is not the least of Gee's achievements to have taken the traditional struggle with puritanism, a major element in the pattern of New Zealand literature, and enriched it by taking the opponent seriously, showing us the integrity, virtue and vitality of puritanism as well as its destructiveness, authoritarian repression and stultifying conformity.   NW

Geographies (1982), though presented as a relatively homogeneous volume in four related sections, is actually a miscellany, and indeed encapsulates the fragmented nature of C.K. *Stead's poetic production. The collection offers the high point of Stead's experimentation with postmodern styles, yet also many examples of the more conventional personal narrative to which he has returned throughout his career. Part I, 'Scoria: A Reconstruction', is a long poem that gives an impression of rapid composition, setting the poet's Auckland childhood in a geological framework, with some dabbling in Māori myth. 'Yes T.S.' is a more fruitful experiment in postmodern journal-style composition: a series of vignettes, puns, translations, quotations, jokes, reveries and language lessons, written during a sabbatical journey to Europe. The sequence is frenetic with excitement over the possibilities of the new form, but the novelty has not been digested, and Stead did not submit himself to the discipline of further, sustained exploration. The third part of *Geographies*, 'The Clodian Songbook', comprises fifteen adaptations of the poems of Catullus to contemporary and personal situations. This marriage of classical learning and personal narrative suited Stead better: insistence on the European literary tradition is a staple of his creative and critical writing; and the role of disgruntled lover meshed with his other confessional writing. Stead had already written isolated imitations of Catullus in earlier collections, and would extend the 'Clodian Songbook' in *Between* (1988). The fourth part of *Geographies* is a series of well-wrought but conventional meditations on the poet's life in Auckland.   KJ

'Georgian' as a literary term began with the five *Georgian Poetry* collections, published in England between 1912 and 1922, edited by Edward Marsh. George V had been King only since 1910, so the name affirmed a belief in innovation, the first volume (*1911–1912*) claiming that 'English poetry is now … putting on a new strength'. But although unconventional poets such as D.H. *Lawrence and Robert Graves were included, there was a reaction, as Modernism took hold after World War 1, against the description 'Georgian'; and ironically a term chosen to suggest innovative vitality soon meant only an exhausted post-Victorian traditionalism.

In this pejorative sense it passed to New Zealand, Charles *Brasch defining the recent history of New Zealand poetry in *Phoenix in 1933 as 'that Drinkwaterish simpering which is the curse of most colonial poetry when it has passed its first, wild-west stage'. (John Drinkwater was a *Georgian Poetry* regular.) While Allen *Curnow did not directly use the word in introducing his anthologies, he castigated the 'lamentable anthology' *Kowhai Gold (1930) for its 'imported insipidities', and the distinction between Georgian and progressive is given local application in his rejection of the 'escapist' lyricism, 'emotional cliché' and 'puerilities' of New Zealand's 'sickly second-growth of verse'. His attack on the first *New Zealand Poetry Yearbook was also on grounds of the 'stray local infection' of its 'renovated Georgian' spirit' (*Here & Now, Dec. 1951). James K. *Baxter in 'Recent Trends in New Zealand Poetry' (1951) described his study at school of Walter de la Mare (another regular) and made a similar argument of New Zealand verse that 'excepting Eileen *Duggan, the poets writing in the Georgian tradition do not seem to … meet their country on its own terms'. In 'The Fire and the Anvil' (1954) he extended this to a *'Fretful Sleepers'–like social critique: 'The Georgian dilemma had its roots in the structure of New Zealand society: in the great pressure towards conformity which prevented poets … from exercising a free and critical insight.… Many Georgians seemed afflicted by a genuine paralysis of the will.'

The word is now disparagingly applied to the whole *Kowhai Gold* period of the 1920s. Ian *Wedde, in the *Penguin Book of New Zealand Verse* (1985), writes of 'a saccharine variety of literary Georgianism' and again singles out Duggan for the extent to which she 'subverts [the] Georgian decorum'. MacD.P. Jackson in the *OHNZLE makes the link between *Kowhai Gold* and the English *Georgian Poetry*, and dismisses the 'bulk of the verse in Pope's collection' as 'fanciful, cosy, decorative and precious'.

Such enjoyable denigration still keeps the term in wide use, as a badge of shame to attach to poetic opponents. It often now loosely implies any 'conventional' notions of form, rather than derivation from the English pre–World War 1 tradition. In the 'open form' disputes of the 1970s it was liberally applied to all those who did not conform to that new orthodoxy, and it still sometimes appears in reviews to disparage those who write in ways regarded for the moment or from the perspective of the reviewer as old-fashioned.   RR

Germany and New Zealand are bound by more substantial literary ties than one might expect. Apart from the influence of particular German writers, some New Zealand writers have preserved impressions of Germany, its people and culture in various literary forms. Similarly, a small number of German writers have secured a modest place for New Zealand in German consciousness. New Zealand authors who have written about their experience of German-speaking Europe include Katherine *Mansfield, Charles *Brasch, James *Bertram (who occasionally translated Goethe, Mörike and Rilke), James *McNeish and Cilla *McQueen.

Sometimes their impressions have taken creative form, as in Mansfield's first published collection of short stories *In A German Pension (1911). Partly inspired by her stay in the Bavarian resort town of Bad Wörishofen between June and December 1909, these take a satirical view of German manners, pretensions, and sensibilities, while not sparing the naive English narrator. In turn Mansfield has long had a prominent place in German schools and universities, through several German publications of her work in English, a long series of translations and German academic studies of her work, which frequently cite her in discussions of modernist fiction. Book-length studies include Peter Halter's *Katherine Mansfield und die Kurzgeschichte: Zur Entwicklung und Struktur einer Erzählform* (1972) and Nelson Wattie's *Nation und Literatur: Zur Bestimmung der nationalen Merkmale literarischer Werke am Beispiel von Katherine Mansfields Kurzgeschichten* (1979).

Among memoirs, Brasch's posthumous *Indirections* (1980) and Bertram's *Capes of China Slide Away* (1993) both provide recollections of Germany between the late-1920s and mid-1930s, a culturally and intellectually rich nation sliding into the darkness of totalitarian rule. McNeish's biographical novel *Lovelock* (1986), set substantially in Berlin around the 1936 Olympic Games, offers a further perspective on this period, as does his later prose piece *The Man from Nowhere* (1991). This journal of his 1983 research on the athlete Jack *Lovelock also provides fascinating glimpses of everyday Berlin life in the early 1980s, and could be regarded as a companion piece to Cilla McQueen's *Berlin Diary* (1990), a poetic record of her stay there in the summer of 1988. Both works, but particularly McQueen's, capture the frenetic yet claustrophobic metropolis which showed World War 2 scars as well as cold war tensions. The poet Hugh *Lauder relates the personal and political in poems on revisiting Germany, where he was born during the occupation, and Roger Robinson wrote about the reunification in a memoir in *Into the Field of Play*, ed. Lloyd *Jones (1992).

For German influences on New Zealand writers, Mansfield and Brasch merit attention. Mansfield's German connections, particularly during her literary apprenticeship, are not always appreciated. An enthusiastic student of German at Queen's College in London (1903–06), she read Heine, Dehmel, Mörike and Nietzsche and had a 'crush' on her German teacher Walter Rippmann; her older cousin, Mary Beauchamp, married a German nobleman and as Elizabeth von Arnim found fame through best-selling books set in Germany; and friends with a strong knowledge of German literature included D.H. *Lawrence and his wife Frieda von Richthofen, the intimate of many German writers and intellectuals. Antony *Alpers believed that the magazine *Jugend* (which gave its name to *Jugendstil*, the German *art nouveau*) influenced Mansfield's modernistic style, and A.R. Orage once wrote accusing her of German sensationalism and both her and *Murry of 'sousing us with Continental wash'.

Brasch's ties were manifested more in his deep reading of authors such as Goethe, Hölderlin and Rilke and such recent poets as Günter Eich, Peter Huchel and Johannes Bobrowski. Brasch published translations of Huchel (in *Islands)*, Rilke (in *Phoenix* and *Rostrum)* and the collection *Gedichte aus Neuseeland* (private press, n.d.) by Hilde Zissermann, a refugee friend in Dunedin. Janet *Frame's early novels and autobiographical writings attest to her reading of Grimms' tales and Rilke's poetry.

German literary ties to New Zealand are dominated by Georg *Forster and Karl *Wolfskehl. The former, with his father Johann Reinhold *Forster, served as naturalists on *Cook's second voyage, visiting New Zealand three times 1773–74. Forster's literary fame rests primarily on his *A Voyage round the world*, (1777), published in German 1778–80 as *Reise um die Welt*. Forster devotes more space to New Zealand than any other country visited (approximately one-sixth of the total work), describing the virtually untouched *landscape and the Māori in vivid detail and surprising objectivity. As a work of natural history, Forster's account was the first in a line of important descriptive and scientific works by nineteenth-century German visitors, among them Ernest *Dieffenbach's *Travels in New Zealand* (1843) and Ferdinand von *Hochstetter's *Neu-Seeland* (1863). In a more artistic context, Forster's description of the exotic flora, fauna and human inhabitants of the South Seas met with enormous acclaim in continental Europe, firing the imagination of artists and thinkers receptive to the Storm-and-Stress emphasis on 'Feeling' and 'Nature', and eager to learn of lands untainted by European values. Gottfried August Bürger's poem

'Neuseeländisches Schlachtlied' (1782), for instance, was almost certainly inspired by Forster's description of a *haka; even Goethe seems to have been an attentive reader of Forster's account.

Karl Wolfskehl arrived in Auckland in 1938, one of the most important German-Jewish refugees from Nazi Germany to settle in New Zealand. He stayed for his remaining ten years, two as a naturalised citizen. For all his efforts to acquaint himself with his new homeland and its inhabitants, whom he found friendly though uncomprehending of his concerns as a European poet, the almost totally blind Wolfskehl remained largely unnoticed. However, he was befriended and admired by such literary figures as R.A.K. *Mason, A.R.D. *Fairburn, Denis *Glover and, for a time, Frank *Sargeson. Wolfskehl regarded his literary output in New Zealand as among his best, a judgment echoed by critics. Some New Zealand motifs and settings occur in his later poems (e.g. Auckland's St Heliers Bay in 'Glocke vom Strand'), but the lot of the exile and a metaphysical sense of universal destruction and transformation remain his dominant themes.

Other refugees from Nazi Germany helped New Zealand's growing international awareness and the decline in provincial remoteness, while the post-war period has also seen a number of German writers attending writers' conferences or arts festivals or touring the universities. Such visitors have included Siegfried Lenz (1968), Gerhard Köpf (1988), Jurek Becker (1990) and Hans Magnus Enzensberger (1996). Three of these had translations of their work published in *Landfall*, and Köpf published a large Modernist novel set in New Zealand.

Since about 1980 there has been an immense leap in German awareness of New Zealand, partly because of a belief that this is a European society without Europe's environmental hazards, and partly because of applause for New Zealand's stand on nuclear issues. This awareness has had effect on literature. In 1985 the Austrian writer Erwin Einzinger published *Kopfschmück für Mansfield*, a novel which tells the life of Katherine Mansfield through the life of the narrator, Sandbach, who becomes obsessed by her role-playing, her kaleidoscope of personalities which overlap each other and Sandbach's experiences and personality changes. In Christa Moog's novel *Aus tausend grünen Spiegeln* (1988) a search for Mansfield's life is similarly combined with a search for the narrator's own identity. As Mansfield comes nearer, her own past in East Germany seems to recede, and her similarity to the author adds to her insecurity of identity. In *Das Kind, oder die Vernichtung von Neuseeland (The Child, or the Destruction of New Zealand)*, a play by Bodo Kirchhoff (1981), the 'New Zealand' that is destroyed is an image in the mind of 'The Child', handicapped with an absence of intellect but blessed with a rich imagination. He digs a huge hole in his parents' garden hoping to reach New Zealand, but is hindered by adults who conspire to destroy his imagination, leaving him a human vegetable. Though indirectly, this has much to do with the place of New Zealand in the contemporary German construct of the world.

The continuing place of each country in the consciousness of the other owes much to the availability of Rilke, Mann, Kafka, Hesse, Grass and others in English translation, and the translation of Mary *Scott, Frame, Keri *Hulme, Witi *Ihimaera, Alan *Duff and Hone *Tuwhare into German, some with massive sales, supported in the cases of Frame and Duff by film successes. The story of Mary Scott in Germany is phenomenal, especially considering that the other writers named have only recently become known there. Since 1957 her *Frühstück um Sechs: Ich und Paul und 1000 Schafe* (*Breakfast at Six*) has enjoyed some twenty reprints, and was followed by more than thirty other titles. Her paperbacks still fill German shelves, sometimes in the form of 'omnibus' editions of three novels. Especially during the 1960s–70s, in the tensions of a Germany socially torn by the economic miracle and divided by the East–West conflict, Scott's novels provided an escapist alternative, where the greatest tension derived from whether Freddie would marry Jane and from financial problems focused, exotically, on the price of wool. In those decades her view of New Zealand was almost the only one available to German readers (apart from Ngaio *Marsh's few local books). Since 1975, New Zealand literature has been taught in several German universities, including Cologne, Frankfurt, Giessen, Mannheim and Trier; and German language and literature have long had an established place in New Zealand universities.   JBd/NW

GIFKINS, Michael (1945–), is a writer of short fiction, anthologist, editor and literary consultant and agent. He came to prominence with *After the Revolution and Other Stories* (1982) and was established as a leading exponent of innovative short fiction by *Summer is the Côte d'Azur* (1987) and *The Amphibians* (1989). He won the Lilian Ida Smith prize for fiction in 1989, was Auckland University writing fellow in 1983 and Katherine *Mansfield Memorial Fellow at Menton in 1985, and is included in most recent short fiction *anthologies, usually represented by his droll story of encounter across socio-economic groups, 'After the Revolution'. A skilled practitioner of literary gossip, he contributed the 'Bookmarks' column to *NZ Listener* 1984–90.

His entrepreneurial career as anthologist, which began with *The Gramophone Room* (with C.K. *Stead,

1983) and *Listener Short Stories 3* (1984), has recently taken priority. Six volumes since 1988 have collected childhood recollections by prominent people, Katherine *Mansfield's New Zealand stories (illustrated), work by holders of the Mansfield Memorial Fellowship, and stories by Australian and New Zealand writers on the themes of travel, food and lust. It is tempting to characterise Gifkins's own fiction in terms of these three subjects, which are all prominent in his sketches of leisured New Zealanders at home and abroad; but the stories go well beyond such a hedonist account in the intelligence of their enquiry into the apparent meaninglessness of contemporary lives and the challenging conjunctions of modern mobility. Agile, unpredictable, perplexing, yet always lucid, they leave the reader, like one character, 'thrilled to the expected sense of dislocation' ('Metamorphosis'). They consist of entrances and exits, new arrivals who disrupt and reconstruct the dynamic of groups, incongruous flirtations and impulsive couplings, foreign customs observed with 'merciless antipodean curiosity' ('Summer is the Côte d'Azur' is a classic in that New Zealander Overseas genre), or puzzling and stimulating encounters across divides ('After the Revolution', 'Natural Histories'), always seeking pattern in perverseness, as the central character of 'Metamorphosis' struggles to comprehend the chequerboard of New Orleans.

Though often classified as *postmodern, Gifkins resists analysis in terms of 'experimentalism' or 'high fictionality', partly by his tolerant amusement at human idiosyncracy, partly his delicate precision of language.

His off-stage contributions to literature have been considerable. As a freelance editor for *Penguin Books, he has worked with texts by many major writers, while as a successful literary agent he has achieved international exposure for Ming *Cher, Debra *Daley, Lloyd *Jones, Peter *Wells and others.   RR

GILBERT, G.R. (Gavin Robert) (1917–94), born in Greymouth, worked in broadcasting, served in the RNZAF both during and again after World War 2, and was for a time assistant keeper at Tiritiri lighthouse. He published a collection of short stories, *Free to Laugh and Dance*, in 1942, mostly in the first-person vernacular mode in the manner of Frank *Sargeson and William Saroyan, set in the Great *Depression and World War 2. At the time he was considered to be one of the more promising writers of the 'Sargeson school', and Sargeson himself had high hopes for him, encouraged him in correspondence, and attempted to help him find publication. He published further stories, poems and sketches and an excerpt from a novel in periodicals and in Sargeson's anthology, *Speaking for Ourselves* (1945), in the later

1940s and early 1950s, but the only further book of fiction to appear was *Glass Sharp and Poisonous* (1952), an allegorical satire. A humorous book based on his lighthouse experiences, *Love in a Lighthouse*, appeared in 1956. Gilbert continued to write, published an excerpt from a futuristic novel, 'Energy Island', in 1985, and was working on an autobiographical novel at his death.   LJ

GILBERT, Ruth (1917–), published poetry for over fifty years. She was born at Featherston, grew up in Invercargill and Hamilton, and wrote poetry from childhood. Publishing from 1941, her first volume was *Lazarus and Other Poems* (1949), with nine further volumes in her long career. She uses conventional, usually rhymed forms confidently and often elegantly, with an essentially lyrical talent. Some notable poems on her war experience, when she practised as a physiotherapist in the Wellington region, are included in *Complete Early Poems 1938–44* (1944). Her work also includes autobiographical sequences (*The Sunlit Hour*, 1955; *The Luthier*, 1966) and travel sequences ('Tusitala's Island' in *Collected Poems*, 1984). Her references are often biblical, as in the anthologised 'Leah', or classical, as in the extensive set of short poems on Sappho themes written after she learned Greek at the age of 75 (*Breathings*, 1992). Three times winner of the Jessie Mackay Prize and a past president of *PEN (NZ Centre), she was a respected member of the Wellington literary scene until the mid-1980s.   NWr

GILDERDALE, Betty, has been the ground-breaking scholar of New Zealand children's literature. Her pioneering study, *A Sea Change: 145 Years of New Zealand Junior Fiction* (1982), won the *PEN Award for best first book of prose, and her chapter in the *OHNZLE is the authoritative survey. She has also written extensively on New Zealand children's authors for such major international reference sources as the *Routledge Encyclopaedia of Post-Colonial Literatures* (1994), the St James' Press *Twentieth Century Children's Writers* (1995), and *OUP's *Children's Literature: An Illustrated History* (1995). Author of many research papers and a regular reviewer of children's books and columnist for the *New Zealand Herald* since 1973, she has also written introductions to children's texts and authors for children (including the award-winning *Introducing Margaret *Mahy*, 1987) and, with Alan Gilderdale, *The Little Yellow Digger* (1992); she compiled *Under the Rainbow: A Treasury of New Zealand Stories* (1990); and translated and wrote an opera libretto, *Sir Gawayn and the Green Knight*, for composer John Rimmer. Her major biography, *The Seven Lives of Lady*Barker*, was published 1996. Gilderdale is a past president and life member of the *Children's Literature

Association of New Zealand, and is founder and president of the Children's Media Watch group.

Born in London, she graduated BA Hons (1949) in English at University of London. She moved to New Zealand in 1967, lecturing at North Shore Teachers' College, Auckland College of Education and in Continuing Education at University of Auckland.   RR

GILLESPIE, O.N. (Oliver Noel) (1883–1957) was a poet, essayist and editor of the first short fiction *anthology, *New Zealand Short Stories* (1930). While this was later attacked for its supposed conformity, Gillespie's Preface and other critical writings celebrate 'the extraordinary variety of subjects' and the range of emergent literary talent. He wrote in 1938 'We are on the eve of a Golden Age in New Zealand literature', citing *Mander, *Lee, *Hyde, *Rawlinson, *Marsh and others (*New Zealand Railways Magazine XIII*); and he frequently sought to make the public more proud of their writers (in the *Short Stories* Preface, or in *Tomorrow*, 30 Oct. 1935, for instance). He was thus not a bad choice as one of the founder members of the *Literary Fund Advisory Committee in 1947, though being on the Prime Minister's information staff was naturally held against him. In fact, that was only a wartime appointment, from 1940, and a major part of his duties had been chairing the NZ Army Brains Trust and lecturing to the troops on cultural topics and on the breeding of sheep and racehorses, on which he was an authority.

Born in Waikari and educated at Christchurch BHS and Canterbury and Victoria University Colleges (LLB), and not to be confused with O.A.(Oliver Arthur) Gillespie, the military historian, he practised law briefly but fell under the spell of the new moving pictures, worked variously in the cinema business, became vice-president of the Theatre-Owners Association and imported 'British talking pictures'. He was also active in broadcasting, repertory theatre, *PEN and the New Zealand Fellowship of Writers.

He had started as a poet, with poems in the *Bulletin, two volumes—*The Road to Muritai* (1919) and *Night and Morning* (1927)—and seven poems included in *Kowhai Gold* (1930). His transformation from poet into generalist man of letters was a wise one. His poems are not mere 'straining for the picturesque', as they have been presented; characteristically they try for an ironic counterpoint between the romantic-picturesque and a deprecatory and bleak realism, often as a wry bathos: 'No rose of gold or red or white / Can flower within the awesome night / That broods in the discreet small hell / Men call a prison cell.' Unfortunately, he lacks the agility of tone to make the device anything more than sardonic chic.   RR

GILLIES, John (1920–), published *Voyagers in Aspic* (1954), a set of four wittily satiric connected stories about New Zealanders in (and on the voyage to) London. The writing quite deftly sustains an English tone of urbane mockery reminiscent of Saki or Waugh, with characters with names like Mrs Wimbledon Willoughby and comic similes reminiscent of P.G. Wodehouse. Mixed with this is a characteristically New Zealand self-deprecation, especially in the posture of wry embarrassment at New Zealand's unsophisticated provincialism. The book is thus entertaining evidence of a transitional post-war phase of *O.E. and attitudes to England, which was coveted yet increasingly seen as alien. Some amusing literary satire also recurs, as in the proposed high-culture study of 'Soccer with the Sitwells' or the hopeful expatriate writer who aspires in imagination to be described as 'Another Katherine Mansfield'.

RR

GINN, Noel (1916–), is known to those familiar with the poems of James K. *Baxter as the addressee of the poems 'Letter to Noel Ginn' and 'Letter to Noel Ginn II'. The titles' suggestion of a correspondence is deliberate. Ginn, a university student, pacifist and occasional poet, was detained in 1942 as a military defaulter. In detention he befriended Baxter's older brother, Terence. Baxter, upon learning of Ginn's interest in poetry, sent him some verse and they began corresponding regularly, discussing literature and criticising each other's work. Baxter was enthusiastic about Ginn's poetry but Ginn, presented with many hundreds of Baxter's poems over the five years of their correspondence, became dissatisfied with his own verse and destroyed much of it. He shared Baxter's triumph when *Beyond the Palisade was published, and was the first in the country to review it (see *Art in New Zealand, Vol. 17, No. 5, Sep.–Oct. 1945, pp. 17–19). Following the war he and Baxter drifted apart: Baxter was caught up in the Wellington scene of the 1950s while Ginn, feeling a need to distance himself from his wartime experiences, returned to his home town of Wanganui, became a horticulturalist and, with the exception of a few poems published in *Landfall and *Mate, largely ceased writing. In 1966 Baxter, who was working as an editor at *School Publications, contracted Ginn to write a journal for schools called *The Market Garden*. Although they resumed a brief correspondence their letters were relatively businesslike with little of the warmth and intimacy of their wartime exchanges. PM

GLEN, Esther (1881–1940), was an outstanding children's author and editor of highly popular children's pages. Born in Christchurch, second in a family of twelve, she learnt early how to amuse children with stories and plays. After office work and freelance journalism in Christchurch and Australia, she was the Christchurch *Sun *children's page editor 1925–35, then moving to the *Press. She wrote plays and pantomimes with huge casts for public performances, as well as pioneering radio broadcasts for children. Her first book, *Six Little New Zealanders* (1917), unlike Ethel Turner's city-based *Seven Little Australians* (1894), is about a city family transplanted to a farm while their sick mother is taken to England. The story romps along with enough highly comic and nearly tragic incidents to bewilder the bachelor uncles; two children narrowly escape drowning, the oldest boy leaves with a friend and returns months later very ill, and the eldest daughter becomes engaged, despite her bad cooking. Glen's feel for humour and character continue in the sequel, *Uncles Three at Kamahi* (1926), with the children returning for the summer. This time a shed explodes, two girls nearly die in the mountains, and a mock Māori tattoo applied with hat dye proves impossible to clean off, causing all to stay an extra month and miss school until it fades. *Robin of Maoriland* (1929) is based more closely on Glen's family life in Christchurch. She also wrote a booklet of fairy stories, *Twinkles on the Mountain* (1919). In recognition of her achievement, the New Zealand Library Association's Esther Glen Award (now Medal) for excellence in children's literature was established in 1945 (see Appendix). JMcC

Glide Time was Roger *Hall's first full-length play, written shortly after he attended the Eugene O'Neill Workshop in Connecticut in 1975. It was first produced at Circa Theatre, Wellington, in 1976 and published in 1977. Its title alludes to the system of flexible working hours, in this case to a total of 'seventy-five hours fifty minutes' per fortnight. The business of signing in each morning is one of a series of running gags used to stitch together a virtually plotless play about one month in the life of the stores branch of a government department. While a story-line of sorts is provided by the Boss's impending resignation and the competition to succeed him, which results in a surprise victory for an off-stage and 'notoriously lazy' character, the play is essentially a deftly woven tapestry of comic routines that reflect Hall's apprenticeship in revue. The target of most of these episodes is the sheer inertia of life in the public service, which Hall had experienced at first hand as an employee of the Department of Education 1972–75. Observations like 'the Public Service Corridor Walk—The secret is, always have a piece of paper in your hand. And look worried' encapsulate an era and at the same time place the play in the tradition of the comedy of manners. For three of the characters—Hugh, an immigrant from

Wales whose off-stage wife is 'going out of her mind with homesickness', Beryl, a woman of early middle age 'living at home with a mother with cataracts and who half the time doesn't know if it's winter or summer', and Jim, whose brash enthusiasm for the three national icons (rugby, racing and beer) masks his failure as a father and husband—the inertia serves as an objective correlative for private despair, so that the play achieves that blend of pathos and humour that is characteristic of Hall's work. The remaining characters show fewer signs of alienation; both the officious Wally and the tight-fisted Boss are unthinking slaves to the system, while John, the play's principal mouthpiece for Hall's famous one-liners, defies its tedium with a stream of quips and practical jokes, until he is finally outquipped by Michael (the office junior), who matures visibly in the course of the play. *Glide Time* has been highly successful both in New Zealand (where it has spawned spin-off series for both radio and television entitled *Gliding On* and a recent stage sequel, *Market Forces*) and abroad (where its name has usually had to be changed to reflect local idiom: to 'Flexi-Time' in Australia and 'Roll on Friday' in the UK).   RCo

Glorious Morning, Comrade, A (1975), is a collection of short stories by Maurice *Gee, later expanded into *Collected Stories* (1986). In the title story, a former war hero and eminent citizen, now geriatric but independent in spirit, 'escapes' from his protective daughters for 'an hour and thirty-one minutes'. One of the best of Gee's several narratives of elderly men, it is a classic of New Zealand short fiction and is included in many anthologies. It was first published in the *NZ Listener, 22 Dec. 1973. David Norton in 'Life on the Edge of Death' (*Climate 29, 1979) calls the old man's escapade 'a little triumph of the human spirit', and shows how 'an unusually strong character for a short story' emerges from the interaction of comedy and the sense of imminent mortality (partly suggested by his name, Pitt-Rimmer). RR

GLOVER, Denis (1912–80), poet, printer, publisher, satirist, sailor and boxer, was born in Dunedin. Following his parents' divorce, he and his mother moved to New Plymouth where Glover spent the 'bow and arrow stage of existence'. At New Plymouth BHS he encountered military-style discipline, as boy scout and school cadet. As a scout Glover made his first foray into publishing, when he wrote, illustrated and printed a magazine called *Signal Fire*, which he sold to troop members for one penny. In New Plymouth too he affirmed the love of mountain-climbing established in Otago, and first experienced boats, paddling unstable corrugated-iron canoes on Lake Pukekura. He moved to

Auckland GS where he met Bob *Lowry; together they produced an unofficial class journal. In 1929 Glover transferred to the sixth form at Christ's College, Christchurch, where he excelled academically and wrote what he later called 'a vast quantity of very bad verse' but won approval from his peers for his swimming, boxing and cross-country running.

In 1931 Glover enrolled at Canterbury University College, completing a BA in English and Greek in 1934. He won a New Zealand University Blue for boxing, and climbed with the Canterbury Mountaineering Club. Student expeditions in Arthur's Pass National Park provided raw material for some of Glover's finest work, including the *'Arawata Bill' sequence, and some of the *'Sings Harry' poems. His love of writing led him towards journalism, editing the student magazine *Canta* (for which he interviewed Bernard *Shaw), the annual university *Review* and the capping *Revue,* and serving as campus reporter on the *Press. Printing, however, was the most significant activity. In 1932, at an Easter Sports Tournament in Auckland, he again met Lowry, who had set up a press for Auckland University College Students' Association: one of its achievements was *Phoenix. Encouraged by Lowry's success Glover bought a hand-operated press and some type.

After a battle with conservative university authorities he was permitted to set up in a campus basement and established the Caxton Club to use and administer the press. Although the ostensible aim was the study of printing and typography, Glover later commented that 'any young man with the means of disseminating opinion would be unworthy of his salt if he didn't try to print something that would practically transform the world overnight' (*Hot Water Sailor*).

The result was *Oriflamme and the furore over 'Sex and the Undergraduate'. The board of governors revoked the Caxton Club's right to use College premises, and Glover, though not editor of *Oriflamme*, lost his job at the *Press; in 1935, two years later, his reputation as a firebrand cost him his job on the Wellington *Dominion*. Undaunted, Glover continued to develop the Caxton Club (see *Caxton Press). He found a venue for his disputatious nature in the independent left-wing *Tomorrow. Throughout its seven years of publication, 1934–40, Glover contributed notes, poems, short stories and satirical verses under a variety of pseudonyms—'Peter Kettle' was a favourite—as well as his own name. An assistant lectureship in English at Canterbury University College helped subsidise this largely unpaid involvement with *Tomorrow* and the Caxton Club.

Twice stymied at journalism, Glover turned his attention more fully to printing. In 1935 he and his partner John Drew bought a power-driven press, setting it up in a disused stable. The following year saw the first publications under the imprint of the Caxton Press, which aimed to publish whatever literature of merit they could afford, and devote to its production what typographic and technical skills they could command. At Caxton, Curnow wrote, Glover 'created ... a centre which, under his care, did more than any other to help good writing in New Zealand and to raise publishing and book production standards'.

At the time, the main venue for locally written poetry was the annual *New Zealand Best Poems*, edited by C.A. *Marris. Glover passionately hated the pallid and sentimental verse Marris appeared to encourage, aiming instead at Caxton to promote socially responsible poetry. Heated mutual criticism culminated in Glover's 'The Arraignment of Paris' (1937), in which he lampooned what he saw as Marris's stranglehold on literary taste. In retrospect, the satire also reveals a vein of sexism endemic in much writing of the time. Glover's work at Caxton was interrupted by war. One of his last typographical works before leaving on secondment to the Royal Navy was *Recent Poems* (1941), with poems by Curnow, *Fairburn, *Mason and Glover, 'The *Magpies' making its first appearance. In London Glover met publisher John Lehmann and in Oxford John Johnson, Printer to the University. Johnson taught Glover 'more about printing than I had ever learned'. In London, Glover often stayed with Charles *Brasch, discussing the possibility of establishing a literary magazine. *Landfall* appeared in March 1947, published by Caxton.

As a serviceman, Glover distinguished himself in the Arctic convoys, and later as a commander during the D-Day invasion. Promoted to the rank of lieutenant commander, his bravery earned him a DSC and a Soviet War Veteran's Medal. He returned to Christchurch late in 1944 and began an extensive programme of publishing. *The Wind and the Sand: Poems 1934–44*, his first volume of mature verse, appeared in 1945. Although he was always emotionally guarded in his verse, perhaps suspicious that writing poetry was not a particularly manly occupation, the war poems in *The Wind and the Sand* contrast sharply with the nonchalant understatements of his autobiography *Hot Water Sailor* (1962), which chronicles his early life and war experiences. *The Wind and the Sand* also contains some early 'Sings Harry' poems. Published complete in 1951, the 'Sings Harry' sequence discovered a new tone of nostalgia and introspection, albeit mediated by a strongly masculine persona.

In 1936 Glover had married Mary Granville, and their only child was born in July 1945. After the marriage ended in 1950, he moved into a relationship with Khura Skelton, which lasted until her death in 1969.

In the early 1950s he worked with sailing companion Albion Wright at Wright's newly established *Pegasus Press, and left Caxton in 1953. In 1954 he and Khura moved to Wellington where he worked for a while as an advertising copywriter. He worked for some time as production manager and typographer at the Wingfield Press and later tutored typography at the Technical Correspondence Institute. In the early 1960s Glover served as president of *PEN and of the Friends of the *Alexander Turnbull Library, which now holds his papers and manuscripts.

Throughout his life Glover was drawn to the sea. Navy service followed years of sailing with Albion Wright and the Banks Peninsula Cruising Club, and he spent several post-war years training volunteers for the Royal New Zealand Navy. All the major works reflect this love. Even 'mountain' poems such as 'Arawata Bill' and 'Sings Harry' conclude with images of the sea, which suggest the inevitability of change, and the spaces separating individuals. The year 1948 saw a verse commentary for Cecil Holmes's documentary *The Coaster*, made for the National Film Unit, a collaboration influenced by John Grierson's work with W.H. Auden on the film *Night Mail* (1936). In 1955 'Towards Banks Peninsula—Mick Stimson' appeared in *Landfall*. Another *'Man Alone' figure, Stimpson (Glover later found this to be the correct spelling) deserted from Queen Victoria's navy and spent his last years quietly fishing and growing fruit at Port Levy near Lyttelton Harbour, where Glover came to know the old sailor. In his long poem Glover put much of his characteristic reticence behind him and paid homage to the 'old wrinkled warrior' he perhaps regarded as a kindred spirit. Glover's last-published collection, *Towards Banks Peninsula*—a long-contemplated series of poems about a much-loved area—appeared in 1979. Short poems capturing the changing moods of Wellington Harbour were among the best work of his final years.

Despite his interest in 'men alone', Glover was not himself a loner. From one relationship after Khura's death came the love-lyrics *To a Particular Woman* (1970) and *Diary to a Woman* (1971). In 1971 Glover married Gladys Evelyn Cameron ('Lyn'). In 1975 they visited Russia at the invitation of the Soviet Writers' Union; the same year Victoria University of Wellington conferred an honorary DLitt. The old warrior never mellowed, however. His fearless opinions and rasping voice enlivened meetings of the Friends of the Turnbull and the *New Zealand Poetry Society and his stage-whisper interjections were notorious, including a memorable comment on the modernised liturgy during the funeral of James K. *Baxter.

A second volume of autobiography, *Landlubber Ho!* and a *Selected Poems*, introduced by Curnow, appeared in

1981. A further *Selected Poems* (1996) was compiled by Bill *Manhire. Commentary includes J.E.P. Thomson's *Denis Glover* (1977) and Gordon Ogilvie's *Introducing Denis Glover* (1983). Three short films exist: *'The Magpies'* (with interview with Glover, 1974), *'Mick Stimson'* (a reading by Glover, 1974) and *The Coaster* (with Glover's verse commentary, 'The Breeze', 1948). Roger *Hall's play 'Mr Punch' (1989) deals with Glover's life.   SS

GLOVER, Marewa (1961–), Ngā Puhi, lives in Te Awamutu. Her first volume of poetry was *Mooncall* (1990) and she has published in several magazines. In *Te *Ao Mārama*, Witi *Ihimaera has written of her 'strong, unflinching voice, one of the finest new voices in the 1990s'.   NW

God Boy, The (1957), a short novel by Ian *Cross, is a small masterpiece of narratorial craft which deserves its classic status and popularity as a student text. It is told wholly in the voice of Jimmy Sullivan at the age of 13, then a homeless adolescent in care of a Catholic school and manifestly disturbed for all his brash indifference and pose of resilience. The action he narrates focuses on three climactic days in the misery of his parents' marriage two years before, so that the text is an interplay of threefold observation and interpretation, between Jimmy childishly impulsive yet anxiously observant at 11, Jimmy more aware yet now defensive and troubled at 13, and the more knowing reader, adroitly enabled to infer much more than Jimmy ever comprehends. So the adult tragedy of resentment, drunkenness, womanising, vituperation, illicit abortion and finally murder is projected through the child's uncomprehending consciousness. The rituals and mantras which he calls his 'protection tricks', and the outbursts of destructive behaviour which he can describe but not explain, reveal only too clearly the psychological damage being inflicted. The novel's power comes not only from witnessing the dark clenching of a bright and open young mind, but from the conviction of inhabiting a consciousness even as it becomes crippled.

Cross's trained journalist's eye for detail, transmuted into the child's fresh particularity of observation, gives vividness to the context in the wholly credible small township of Raggleton, with its dusty streets, sand-dunes and scruffy port. The tone is relieved with plenty of childish high spirits and some memorable comedy, as when the 11-year-old pesters the grossly overweight abortionist or duels with a rival on bicycles. Jimmy's growing sexuality, boyish friendships and complex relations with his older sister are also treated with wit and insight.

A spiritual dimension is also available within the psychological. The title comes from Jimmy's conscientious struggle to comprehend his situation in the religious terms he has been taught, to ask in his schoolboy idiom some fundamental metaphysical questions: 'if [God] is such a hot scone why doesn't he do more day-to-day stuff?' The expression may be naive as Jimmy moves from affirming that he is 'right there on God's side' to being 'annoyed at God for putting one across on me the way he did.... Me so little and he God', but the sense of betrayal and loss of faith, in a Catholic context, is profoundly tragic. Well-handled scenes of dream, delirium and breakdown further raise the narrative above the merely realistic.

Like *Catcher in the Rye* (with which it is often compared) and *What Maisie Knew*, *The God Boy* succeeds in making an immature central figure tragically significant without ever being patronising or sentimental. It is often cited as an example of New Zealand fiction's particular skill with child observers or narrators, as in *Prelude* or *The *Scarecrow*, though the tradition of dramatising limited or partially aware narration extends to other major works such as *A *Soldier's Tale*, *Plumb* or the early stories of *Sargeson. *The God Boy* was published in New York in 1957, by Penguin UK in 1962, by Whitcoulls in New Zealand in 1972 and by *Penguin NZ in 1989, with a still useful reprinted introduction by Joan *Stevens. A film version was directed by Murray Reece, and a stage adaptation was written by Cross in 1997.
                                                               RR

'God Defend New Zealand' was written in 1876 by Thomas *Bracken as a five-stanza poem which he called 'New Zealand Hymn'. It was published in the *New Zealand Saturday Advertiser* on 1 July 1876. A competition for a musical setting was won by John Joseph Woods of Lawrence in Central Otago and the work was first performed in Dunedin in December 1876. The next year Woods purchased the copyright and began actively promoting the publication and popularisation of the song, while George *Grey arranged for translation into Māori by T.H. Smith, a former judge of the Maori Land Court. Seddon presented a copy to Queen Victoria at her Diamond Jubilee. Copyright passed to Charles Begg & Co. at the beginning of World War 1 and was purchased by the government when the work was accorded the status of 'national hymn' in the *Centennial year 1940. It was made the second New Zealand national anthem with the Queen's consent in 1977, to be of equal status with 'God Save the Queen'. A separate edition of the full poem and music, intended for children, was published in 1997, with historical notes by Tim Plant and illustrations by Keith (Nobby) Clark.   WB

GODFREY, Margery, *South for Gold* (1964), see Gold.

GODLEY, Charlotte (1821–1907) was a letter-writer of acumen and vivid observation whose accounts of life in Canterbury and Wellington in the 1850s are of great interest. Born in Denbighshire, Wales, she married John Robert Godley and so came to New Zealand as wife of one of the founding fathers of Canterbury Settlement. Her letters to her mother acquire special value from her unique position in society, but stand on their own merits for their detailed and telling accounts of town and country, living conditions, clothing, wages and prices, the Māori, etc., as well as engaging gossip about church and political leaders and other local personalities. They were printed privately in 1936 and published, as *Letters from Early New Zealand*, in 1951.   EM

'God's Own Country' is the title poem in a volume by Thomas *Bracken, *Lays and Lyrics: God's Own Country and Other Poems* (1893). The poem is said to have been written while Bracken was touring Australia promoting his *Musings in Maoriland* (1890), and it was first published in the *New Zealand Herald* in 1890. It offers a rousing vision of New Zealand as 'God's own country! framed by Nature in her grandest, noblest mold; / Land of peace and land of plenty, land of wool and corn and gold.' The phrase has become associated with the myths of New Zealand as Pastoral Paradise, England's South Pacific farm and New World egalitarian *Utopia. The phrase was originally US, as 'God's country', 1865, and was thence popularised in New Zealand during the political times of Richard John Seddon, Premier 1893–1906. It is frequently shortened to 'God's Own', humorously spelled 'Godzone' and 'Gordzone', often ironically indicating an earthly paradise manqué. 'Taxing Chows as they enter Gordzone Country is a profitable bit of business,' said *Truth* 13 April 1907.

The paradisal myth has indeed most often referred to the goals towards which the society was seen as progressing rather than to an achieved state. New Zealand writers have responded to and engaged in this national mythmaking in several distinct phases. The pioneer writers (*c.*1840–90) consistently projected the dream of 'solitary wastes' being 'converted into smiling pastures', as John *Featon ('Comus') put it in his novel, *The Last of the Waikatos* (1873). Likewise, they projected the dream of the Just City, to be brought about when 'wealth and labour hand in hand / Work out our glorious plan', as John *Barr of Craigielee put it in his poem, 'There's Nae Place Like Otago Yet' (1861). They assumed with poet William *Golder in his *The New Zealand Survey*

(1877) that 'the time appointed' for the fruition of the dream would arrive in a 'long progressive stage'. Such hopeful projections, based on a view of progress and Anglo-Saxon superiority that was given 'scientific' support by social Darwinism, appeared in the next generations of colonial writers (*c.*1890–1935), from Bracken's work and William Pember *Reeves's poems of the 1890s right down to Alan *Mulgan's *Spur of Morning* (1934) or Nelle *Scanlan's series of *Pencarrow* novels (1932–39). However, the *Phoenix and *Caxton writers of the 1930s began to question the idea of progress and debunk the national myths. Partly in response to the sobering implications of the Great *Depression, these writers constructed, as Allen *Curnow said, 'an anti-myth about New Zealand'. D'Arcy *Cresswell, Curnow, Roderick *Finlayson, A.R.D. *Fairburn and Denis *Glover deconstructed the Pastoral Paradise, seeing God's Own Country's farmed by 'miners, not husbandmen' (Curnow, 'The Unhistoric Story', 1941); as subject to the pressures of the mortgage corporations (in Glover's 'The *Magpies', 1936); and as 'an annex of the neo-Christian deity himself … like "The Queen's Own Rifles"' (Cresswell, *Present Without Leave*, 1939).

Similarly, Fairburn, John A. *Lee, Frank *Sargeson, John *Mulgan, Robin *Hyde and others projected pictures of New Zealand as an unhappy and unjust society. James K. *Baxter, a young poet speaking before an audience that included his elders of the 1930s generation, spoke for both generations of writers at the 1951 *Writers' Conference when he stated that 'the pioneering dream … of a Just City' had not been realised and that writers had to 'state the truth (that we now live in an Unjust City)' and thus 'purge' themselves 'of a lie commonly held to be truth and begin to speak meaningfully' ('Recent Trends in New Zealand Poetry'). After the fierce anti-myth activity of the generations of Baxter and Curnow, later writers have accepted their debunking of the myths of 'God's Own Country' and have traced the process of the failure to actualise those myths, the most notable examples being Ian *Cross's *After Anzac Day* (1961) and Maurice *Shadbolt's *Strangers and Journeys* (1972). 'God's Own Country', a phrase which Bracken could take both seriously and enthusiastically, has become 'Godzone', used only humorously and ironically.   LJ/HO

Godwits Fly, The (1938), was begun by Robin *Hyde in 1935 in the Auckland Mental Hospital. Disappointed with this first draft, she reworked the novel at intervals, completing it in 1937. This story of a young New Zealand woman and her working-class family was a major achievement in the development of the New Zealand novel and the portrayal of women in fiction. In its haunting portrayal of female isolation and alienation it has earned a place beside John *Mulgan's *Man Alone* as a seminal work.

The story of Eliza Hannay's childhood, adolescence and passionate first love is closely based on Hyde's own complex experiences. She commented that it was not a novel 'but I had to say it was—the only lies of major importance are camouflage for other people'. While it invokes the power of the imagination as a source of strength and creativity, it is firmly located in the drab square houses of Wellington's Newtown and Berhampore. Underlying the detailed description of these dreary suburbs and the beauty of the surrounding hills and bays, there is a strong sense of tension as Hyde explores her generation's dichotomy of being 'English and not English', caught by the imperialist traditions and cultural heritage of *'Home' while sensing something uniquely New Zealand, 'delicate, wild'. Similarly, Eliza is caught between her father's inchoate but passionate socialism and her mother's social aspirations. Like her creator she becomes a journalist who desires to be a poet—so adding a further resonance. As in her journalism, Hyde is concerned for those on the margins of society, isolated and exploited because of class, race or gender. To be free of the stifling sham of convention Eliza must seek to cross genders ('I'm not a woman; not for ordinary purposes,' she says) and find further freedom by crossing genres, into poetry and the imagination which produces it, 'in the house of her mind'.

Seeking to push stylistic convention and find new images, Hyde's writing at times becomes contrived and mannered. Other passages achieve lyricism, immediacy and a sense of colour, light and shade. Although she recognised its uneven quality, the novel has remarkable power and veracity, particularly in its portrayal of the defiant turbulence of adolescence, the dreary wasteland of the Hannays' marriage and the pain of loss and failed dreams.   GB

Going West (1992), a novel by Maurice *Gee, contrasts Jack Skeat, a librarian and scholar, and his friend Rex Petley, a poet, who share a fascination with literature. Skeat (ironically an anagram of Keats), though more serious about it, is unable to be creative, while Petley, a womaniser, motorcyclist and outdoor man, careless of his relationships with others, is a highly successful poet. Jack narrates most of the novel, so that the more straightforward and reliable person grows familiar to us while his colourful, various, sometimes vicious counterpart remains mysterious—we are even unsure whether Petley commits a murder, though circumstantial evidence suggests that he does. The temptation to make the creative mind more attractive than the archival

one is avoided partly by this dark side to Rex but also by Jack's warmth, especially in his marriage to Harry (Harriet). Their affection makes a central image that leaves Rex sometimes literally out in the rain. In these complementary characters it is not hard to find something of the author, who has been both a librarian and a freelance writer. As in *Sole Survivor*, they are virtually two sides of one person. The other major 'characters' are the cities of Wellington and Auckland, also complementary, contrasted in myriad ways and so intensely experienced that they are more than a 'background'. This awareness of cityscape is a new development in Gee, previously a writer of small towns, but it grows organically from his original sense of place.   NW

Gold. The gold rushes in New Zealand were geographically limited, comparatively short-lasting, and have faded into a sentimentalised past, yet they brought about demographic, political and social developments which affect perceptions of the country to the present day. Materialistic and exploitative attitudes to the land and the widespread get-rich-quick mentality, as well as more positive attitudes such as egalitarianism, can all be traced in part to this historical phase.

Several writers had their beginnings as journalists or entertainers on or near the goldfields. Julius *Vogel followed the rush first to Victoria and then Dunedin, where he founded the *Otago Daily Times*, one of the oldest surviving newspapers in New Zealand. He also tried his hand as a dramatist for Dunedin's gold-stimulated theatres, as did George Darrell, who followed this apprenticeship with stalwart work in Australia, and B.L. *Farjeon, an obsessive writer and a partner of Vogel, who wrote at least three plays for Dunedin theatres, apparently with comic reference to local events and personalities. Farjeon's *Grif* is set on the Victorian goldfields but was published as a novel in Dunedin in 1866 and performed in a dramatised version throughout New Zealand. Theatre and related entertainments were not confined to Dunedin but were taken out to the goldfields towns, such as Queenstown. In nearby Arrowtown the Provincial Hotel offered musical and music-hall entertainment and when their leading lady was seduced by Bully Hayes and began to appear in the United States Hotel, the Provincial responded by putting on a play mocking Hayes. Despite high charges for entrance the play was a huge success. The most famous goldfields entertainer was Charles *Thatcher, who sang satirical ballads on local themes, voicing the democratic concerns of the miners and mocking the more elitist 'Old Identity'. He travelled from goldfield to goldfield and later throughout the country.

These dramatists and balladeers were immediately

involved with the miners as subject matter and audience. Vincent *Pyke was the first to begin looking back in the more leisurely genre of the novel. In *Wild Will Enderby* and *The Adventures of George Washington Pratt* he adapts the *American frontier tradition to local conditions, enthusing whenever possible on the Otago scenery, and creates adventure stories which are still entertaining.

Henry *Lapham was meanwhile publishing sentimental tales of mining life, and Lady *Barker puts some nostalgic references to mining into the mouths of men who have turned to sheep farming. The contrast between the goldfields adventure and the pastoral world, with the moral advantage given to the latter, was to become typical of literature after Barker. Robert Carrick revives the adventure-story mode in *A Romance of Lake Wakatipu* (1892), though even for him the rushes are a thing of the past, as suggested by the ghostly figure who betrays where he hid his gold. The temporal foreground is occupied by an American millionaire rather than a struggling miner.

By the 1890s, the goldfields were tending to provide a field for moral speculation, whether of Carrick's naive kind or that of the more solemn 'Alien' (Louise Alice *Baker), whose novel *In Golden Shackles* (1896), though burdened by its own earnestness, is a competent piece of authorial craftsmanship. It relates the search for gold to the traditional quest topos of classical literature and contrasts the materialism of the gold-seeker with the values of love and stability.

Alexander *Bathgate frames the goldfields action of *Sodger Sandy's Bairn* (1913) with a pastoral existence. The contrast between these ways of life—adventure as against stability and 'constructiveness'—becomes a common theme. In *Young Pioneers* (1934), a children's book by Edith *Howes, the pastoral theme acquires the intensity of fantasy as the settler family comes to live in a house constructed of growing trees bound together. When the *pater familias* is stricken with gold fever and abandons his family, he is brought back to the pastoral idyll by his own children.

The contrast is even more striking in Georgina *McDonald's *Grand Hills for Sheep* (1949). This is really a pastoral novel, with gold seekers introduced as a contrast to the main theme, showing how the virtuous can be tempted astray, like the sheep they tend. Will *Lawson focuses more exclusively on the goldfields in his two relevant novels, although he, too, shows how the search for gold can lead into error and vice. *Forbidden Gold* (1945) is set in Wellington, where gold is found in an old Māori cemetery, setting up a conflict between the two cultures. The Māori prophecy of doom to those who dig is fulfilled, the mine-owner losing his fortune in an explosion and his wife to another man. *Gold in their Hearts* (1950) contrasts the transitory nature of the gold rush with the main character's urge to achieve stability. He is so deeply identified with the town of Charleston that he almost goes under when it does, but escapes to his love, who is more readily able to accept the transitory life.

The Thames goldfields emerge in novels of the 1950s–60s, in E.H. *Audley's *Islands Float at Eleven* (1952) and *Frenchman's Gold* by 'Catherine *Hay' (1955). *Gipsy Michael* (1954) by Ronald *Syme covers the major historical events of the 1860s, the main characters going through conventional goldfields adventures such as claim-jumping, making and breaking fortunes and pursuit by villains. Eileen *Soper's *Young Jane* (1955) is similarly intended for young readers, but here children play at gold-seeking with some success, part of their general encounter with pioneer life.

The best-known fictional account of the goldfields is Ruth *Park's *One-a-Pecker, Two-a-Pecker* (1957) which verges on sensationalism, but touches seriously on serious themes, such as the conflicts between Europeans and Chinese. In Henrietta *Mason's *Fool's Gold* (1960) a young woman goes to the goldfields disguised as a man. Though this sounds emancipatory, she succeeds in her adventure mainly because a 'great man' is watching over her in the background. They marry and disappear in the direction of parliament.

More original is Elizabeth *Messenger's *Golden Dawns the Sun* (1962), which reverses some conventional values, with its portrait of the bushranger William Garret as gentle and generous, a good lover who comforts the heroine after she loses her husband in one of the many flash floods that rush through these novels. Three substantial children's goldfield books were published in the 1960s: in Margery Godfrey's *South for Gold* (1964) two boys search for their father on the goldfields, to settle down in an idyllic southern landscape remote in every way from the dry Northland district they had left; the heroic mother of Elsie *Locke's *The Runaway Settlers* (1965) leads her children to financial success not by prospecting but by selling cattle to those who do; and children in Anne *de Roo's *The Gold Dog* (1966) learn from a character like *Glover's *Arawata Bill that the searching is more important than the finding.

Perhaps James *Sander's *High Hills of Gold* (1973), a conflict-ridden tale of Thames, was intended for adults, but the stream of children's novels continued with three in 1976 for young readers. *No Trains at the Bay* by Anne *Holden is a kind of boys' Robinsonade; *Hunter's Gold* by Roger Simpson betrays its origins as an episodic television series; and in *Green Gold* by Eve *Sutton seeds imported from England to anglify the country are found to be more precious than gold. This recaptures the old antithesis of stable pastoralism and to nomadic gold-prospecting, evident again in Ruth *Dallas's *Shining Rivers* (1979), to the miner's disadvantage.

T.E. Wilson wrote two novels on a young immigrant to the goldfields, *The Newcomers* (1977), where he shows his lack of practical skill in commercial life, and the sequel *Yellow Fever* (1979), where he survives adventures with goldfields villains, and acquires their gold (after another flash flood) and the barmaid (a little reluctant to end her career for marriage).

The most recent goldfields novel is *Guests of the New Gold Hill* (1985) by Jye Kang, where the story of the Chinese is told from their own point of view, an instructive contrast with their appearance in many of the books named, especially *One-a-Pecker, Two-a-Pecker*. The sufferings from racist attacks are borne stoically, but separation from families in *China is a less tolerable evil.

Outside the novel there is little goldfields literature. After the ballads which originated on the fields themselves, poetry remains silent on the theme until a handful of lyrics by James K. *Baxter and Denis Glover, and Glover's major sequence *Arawata Bill* (1953). Here the quest topos is explored more fully than in any novel, Bill reliving the experience of others long after the rush is over, searching for that as much as for gold itself. The search is important, discovery unlikely. The historical original is the subject of Ian Dougherty's *Arawata Bill* (1996), perhaps the first significant goldfields biography. In the only recent goldfields play, Baxter's *Jack Winter's Dream* (1957), as in Glover's poems, the goldfields have grown remote in time, the clairvoyant dream of a dying man who never knew them in his waking life. A significant early example of local academic history is *The West Coast Gold Rushes* (1962) by Philip Ross May.   NW

GOLDER, William (1810–76), wrote 'the first book of verse published in New Zealand', *New Zealand Minstrelsy* (1852). Its aim was to express 'some of the sweets which lie hid among the asperities of colonial life'. MacDonald P. Jackson in the *OHNZLE calls him a 'pragmatist' whose 'conventional appreciations of the country's "lofty ridges covered with evergreen forests"' was always mixed with acknowledgments of the hard labour required to 'subdue' such awesome terrain: 'How hard, in the outset, to clear off a forest,/ With back often aching, and sweat bedewed brow'. He arrived from Scotland on the *Bengal Merchant* in 1840, and was a Hutt schoolteacher. His verse ranged from celebrations of 'Britannia's enterprising sons' who 'Come to the bush, my boys' to 'follow fame and glory', to satirical political ballads, the topographical *The New Zealand Survey: A Poem in Five Cantoes* (1868) and *The Philosophy of Love* (1871). Eric *McCormick wrote that

Golder's most famous topical ballad, *The Pigeon's Parliament* (1854), 'gives a pungent record of colonial life as it appeared to a labouring immigrant with that itch for self-improvement not uncommon in his class and time'.   HMcQ/RR

Good Keen Man, A (1960), the first of many books written by Barry *Crump, was also his most popular, selling 42 000 copies in its first two years and 275 000 copies by 1992. Narrated by Crump himself in the first person, the book's episodes are based on incidents in the author's life when as a youth of 17 in 1952 he began several years as a professional deer-culler for the Wildlife Branch of the Department of Internal Affairs, hunting in the mountainous bush-clad country of the central North Island and the Ureweras. Crump's title popularised a New Zealand catchphrase, characterising 'one who goes at a job, problem, or situation vigorously and often thoughtlessly' (Elizabeth and Harry *Orsman, *The New Zealand Dictionary*, 1994). Each episode describes simply and with deadpan humour and occasional pathos the range of idiosyncratic, would-be 'good keen men'— eccentrics, rugged loners, deadbeats, incompetent *new chums, idlers and schemers—who drift into and out of his life during his seasonal expeditions: 'A few were good, some were hopeless, and most were bloody awful. A week on the block usually separated the men from the boys.' A vivid image of the isolation and rigours of *bush life also emerges, and a sense of the values shaped in the confrontation with nature: physical endurance, knowledge learned through hard experience rather than from books, independence and the capacity to enjoy simple pleasures. Using recognisable male New Zealand idioms unselfconsciously and inventively, *A Good Keen Man* was essentially a recycling of the earlier pioneering myth of the *Man Alone, who discovers himself in a frontier confrontation with primitive Nature. Crump's version of the myth offered a fantasy of escape for a post-war (especially male) readership increasingly locked into New Zealand's burgeoning cities and suburbs. In his later books Crump invoked this social context—of conformism, materialism and domesticity—even more explicitly.   TS

GOODALL, Maarire (1935–), the director of the National Cancer Research Laboratory, is internationally known for his publications in cancer biology, biomathematics, biochemistry and endocrinology. He is also an essayist of note on Māori issues and is editor of Aoraki Press, a Māori publishing house, where he edits the theatre series. He also also writes *waiata and composes piano music. Maarire Goodall's tribal affiliations are Kāti Māmoe, Kāi Tahu, Takatapora.   NW

GORDON, Gaelyn (1939–97), established herself from 1987 as a significant writer of fiction for adults and children. Born in Hawera and educated at New Plymouth GHS, University of Canterbury and Christchurch Teachers' College, she taught secondary English and drama and worked in theatre as actor and director, until the onset of Ménière's disease in 1987 forced her to leave teaching when head of English at Hamilton GHS. Living in Auckland, she immediately began to produce energetic, dramatic, mostly comic work for adults and children, the first children's story collection, *Tales from Another Now*, appearing in 1989.

A trilogy for teenagers, *Stonelight* (1988), *Mind Fire* (1991) and *Riversong* (1995), is enlarged by the weaving of Māori myth through contemporary concerns for relationships and the environment. As science fiction, *Several Things are Alive and Well and Living in Alfred Brown's Head* (1990) and *Take Me to Your Leaders* (1993) impudently challenge contemporary life through the observations of an alien inhabiting a human head. *Prudence M. Muggeridge, Damp Rat* (1991) is futuristic speculation, and *Tripswitch* (1992) mixes power games and contemporary antics with sinister folk-tale elements. Gordon also wrote for the Tui Turbo emerging readers' series, while *Duckat* (1991) and *The Fortunate Flats* (1995) are tongue-in-cheek picture books exploring identity crises and old age. *The Other Worlds of Andrew Griffin* (1995) is a thought-provoking study of the reality of the imagination.

Gordon's adult novels are satiric black comedies with a cunningly sharp edge. *Above Suspicion* (1990) is a murder story ingeniously narrated by the victim, who describes his own violent death on the first page. A campy gay, his ghostly commentaries on the subsequent enquiry make often hilarious reading, without detracting from the serious undertone to the action. *Strained Relations* (1991) is memorable for its disturbingly authentic schoolgirls (over-assertive, self-righteous and sex-crazed) and for its deftly satiric treatment of such normally proscribed subjects as feminism and sex. Both novels feature Sergeant Rangi, New Zealand's first idiosyncratic sleuth, a comic mixture of Hercule Poirot, Don Juan and Billy T. James. The tone is set by a disclaimer stating that 'Any similarity between police in this book and those in the real world is purely fortuitous. It would also be quite alarming.' In the third Rangi book, *Deadlines* (1996), that least intellectual of sleuth-cops encounters the literary and academic worlds. Other titles are *Last Summer* (1993) and *Fortune's Fool* (1994), a black farce directed largely against modern malehood, with tragic undertones (the original title was 'Pity and Terror'). All show skills acquired in drama, and contribute to the New Zealand tradition of darkly comic

gothic represented principally by Ronald Hugh *Morrieson. Gordon also contributed *Marj's Story* (1996) to a set of four titles derived from characters in TV's 'Shortland Steet', and perhaps New Zealand's first examples of fiction as spin-off merchandise.

Gordon won the Choysa Award for children's writers, the Sargeson Fellowship and the Scholarship in Letters.   DH/RR

GORDON, I.A. (Ian) (1908–), a long-serving and distinguished academic, has made contributions to New Zealand literature as administrator, editor, biographer and lexicographer. Born and educated at Edinburgh, Scotland (University of Edinburgh PhD 1936), he was appointed professor and head of the English department at Victoria University College in 1936, arriving 1937. He served as vice-chancellor of the then University of New Zealand 1947–52 and as chairman of the New Zealand *Literary Fund Advisory Committee 1951–73. In World War 2 he was major in the Army Education Service. He initiated and edited *New Zealand New Writing* 1942–45, in emulation of *Penguin New Writing* in Britain. Though an odd partner for the *Progressive Publishing Society, Gordon's academic status and freedom from local literary or political partisanship enabled him to attract a broad range of contributors and achieve remarkable sales and a significant place in New Zealand's wartime culture. His own verse and essays were included, such as his first article on Katherine *Mansfield. In his long post-war career, as well as discovering and editing a significant eighteenth-century manuscript (the Shenstone Miscellany) in the *Alexander Turnbull Library, he promoted the Turnbull's research strengths, including New Zealand literature. He worked valuably on Mansfield, publishing a monograph in the British Council series in 1954, collecting her New Zealand stories as *Undiscovered Country* (arranged to approximate to a continuous narrative) in 1974 and editing part of her unpublished early journals as *The Urewera Notebook* in 1978. Various later essays sought especially to revise views of the supposed parsimony of Mansfield's father. Gordon's work on the development of English prose and the Scottish novelist John Galt is also well regarded.

After retirement in 1974 he held visiting positions at the universities of Edinburgh, Leeds and Waikato, and found new outlets as a popular columnist for the *NZ Listener* on matters of language use (1975–78, collected as *A Word in Your Ear*, 1980) and in the production of the *Collins New Zealand Dictionary*, 1985. He is CBE and has been awarded honorary doctorates by the universities of Bristol, New Zealand and Stirling. At 89, still a regular columnist for the *New Scientist* (UK), he published *Take My Word for It: The Riddles of English Usage* (1997). RR

GORMACK, R.S. (Bob) (1918–   ), established the Nag's Head Press in 1948 as a vehicle for his literary endeavours, which took the form of ★*Bookie*, a good-natured satire on the cultural hegemony of the ★Caxton Press. There were three issues, concluding with a narrative poem in ten-line rhyming stanzas entitled *Swagger Jack*. Denis ★Glover's enthusiasm for his efforts was such that he dubbed Gormack the 'Byron of Burnside'. The Nag's Head Press went into abeyance while Gormack worked for ★Pegasus Press and then ★Whitcombe and Tombs from 1960. In 1964 it was revived, and over the next thirty years over one hundred books were printed on a single treadle press. These included Gormack's own *Centennial History of Barnego Flat* (ten parts to date spread across thirty years), a discursive fictional narrative in the style of Rabelais that satirised pioneer worship. This appeared alongside a number of reprints of historical documents. Other authors published include Glover, Allen ★Curnow, A.R.D. ★Fairburn, R.A.K. ★Mason, Basil ★Dowling, Helen ★Shaw and Dora Somerville. More recently, with the help of his son Nick, Bob Gormack has published poetry by Kathleen Gallagher, Bill Direen and Julia Allen. Since his retirement from Whitcoulls in 1980, he has averaged four mostly hand-set and hand-printed publications per year.   NWt

Gorse Blooms Pale, The (1947), is Dan ★Davin's first collection of short stories. Twenty-six stories written between 1939 and 1946, mostly in Cairo and Sarafand 1942–43, they seek to recapture the experience of childhood in Southland, of student life at Otago and Oxford, and of war service around the Mediterranean. The collection established Davin's reputation as a short story writer, with a skill not only for the form, but also for capturing the idiom and syntax of the ★Irish community in Southland, and the vernacular of the New Zealand private soldier in World War 2. As the title suggests, the tone throughout is one of melancholy and loss, but the eight stories from childhood, and two about wartime, 'In Transit' and 'The General and the Nightingale', are among the best of mid-twentieth-century New Zealand short stories.   KO

GORST, John Eldon (1835–1916), author of *The Maori King*, was born in Preston, England, a graduate of Cambridge and fellow of St John's College there, and arrived in New Zealand in 1860, apparently in search of novelty. Acquaintance in Auckland with Bishop Selwyn, another fellow of St John's, led to his working in the ★Waikato as teacher, inspector, resident magistrate and finally as civil commissioner implementing government policy. Obliged in this role to counter anti-Pākehā Māori policies on self-government and land ownership in spite of his sympathy with them, he was expelled from the Waikato by Rewi Maniapoto and the Kingites in April 1863. Returning to England and entering an illustrious career in the Conservative party, he published *The Maori King* (1864) while the Land ★Wars were still being fought. In this best contemporary analysis of the inter-racial political stresses underlying the wars, which were not simply Pākehā versus Māori, Gorst identifies the conflicting factions in both camps in a work of complex drama, in an antithetical style recalling Gibbon and imbued with the principles of Mill. In essence he saw the King Movement as a Māori response to Pākehā failure to govern them. His view that the colonists were cynically exploiting imperial power in their own greed for Māori land led to deep colonial resentment at the way he represented them to the British public. Later, knighted and much honoured, he returned to New Zealand in 1906 as Special Commissioner for Britain at an International Exhibition in Christchurch. *New Zealand Revisited* (1908), a less passionate work than *The Maori King*, has the simple structure of recounting his 1906 journey through New Zealand and at each place visited recalling the people and events of the 1860s, some of them still alive to welcome him back. It is a lively and engaging work of real literary value, by one of the most gifted Victorian sensibilities associated with New Zealand.
KA

GOUDGE, Elizabeth (1900–84), was a popular English writer of historical fiction, mainly set at sea, in Devon and on the island of Guernsey. One of the most popular of all her books however, *Green Dolphin Country* (1944; US title: *Green Dolphin Street*) was set in nineteenth-century Guernsey and New Zealand. It went into numerous large editions and was translated into all the major European languages, again reaching large editions, so that for a generation of readers, even New Zealand ones, it presented almost the only literary image of New Zealand in popular currency. Its extensive presence on bookshelves in private homes and in multiple copies in secondhand shops today still gives some echo of its popularity.

In fact, never having visited the country, Goudge constrained herself to a very generalised picture, mainly of the Wellington region, the main interest being centred in William, the pioneer hero who brings the 'wrong' sister as his wife from Guernsey and in that sister herself, Marianne. Their marriage 'shakes down' over a long period of years and pages—while the 'right' sister thrives as a nun on Guernsey. The New Zealand highlights are natural disasters and conflicts with Māori. Goudge has it both ways by combining the two most conventional romance-novelists' images of the Māori: big grateful children, and murderous, cannibalistic savages. It is all in one sentence (which saves reading 500 closely printed pages): as Māori attack a stockaded farmhouse, 'the horror burst like a thunderstorm or earthquake, like any of the upheavals that were forever devastating this appalling country….'

In 1947 *Green Dolphin Country* became a very popular film.   NW

GRACE, A.A. (Alfred Augustus) (1867–1942), was the youngest son of T.S. Grace, a well-known and respected missionary among Tūwharetoa, in the Taupo region. Soon after Alfred's birth the New Zealand *Wars forced the family to leave. Nonetheless he came to know and admire the Māori people, their language and culture, even though by later standards the attitudes expressed in his fiction have to be viewed as patronising.

Grace was educated in England, but apparently he had returned by 1890. In a letter from England he tells of a visit from two Māori travellers and of the scandal among the neighbours: this event was the basis of a short story, 'The King's Ngarere', published in his second book, *Tales of a Dying Race* (1901). The book title reveals Grace's acceptance of the theory that the Māori were not likely to survive the 'fatal impact' of European settlement. The stories are coloured by a nostalgic view of an attractive but doomed people, whose loss to the world would be sad but not tragic, since they would merely be yielding to the 'inevitable advance of civilization'. The book was published in London and achieved some success.

The Auckland *Free Lance* considered that 'His stories possess that warmth of colour and feeling which is sometimes considered to be too strong for the constitution of young persons of our nationality', and attributed this characteristic to the Huguenot ancestry of the Grace family.

By 'warmth' the *Free Lance* presumably meant the relative sexual frankness of some of his characters—only, however, Māori ones. The first story ('The Chief's Daughter') in his first book, *Maoriland Stories* (Nelson, 1895), illustrates the point. An Englishman pursued by a Māori girl remains impassive in the face of her passion, until 'he buries his face in his hands and a great sob breaks from him. He is beaten: the girl has won.'

In 1910 Grace published the *Hone Tiki Dialogues* in New Zealand and Australia. In a crude representation of Māori English, which makes Hone seem ridiculous to the reader, and his criticisms of Pākehā relatively harmless, he nonetheless hooks some quite sharp barbs into Pākehā ways. The overall effect is curiously ambivalent. The moral victory is usually on Hone's side, despite the ridiculous language, but it is hard to ascertain Grace's own attitude.

This ambivalence is also found in the confrontation of wily, cunning *tohunga with shallow, opportunist missionaries, the theme of a number of stories. In such encounters neither character comes off particularly well, and yet the defeat of Māori gods by the Christian one is viewed as no less inevitable than the decline of the Māori in general. What is perhaps surprising is that both Māori and Christian spirituality are criticised. The healthy cheerfulness of Māori is contrasted with the *puritan humourlessness of the settlers. In other stories, the cheerful Māori gives way to a blood-thirsty warrior. Grace's attitudes to the Māori seem self-contradictory —but his view of Pākehā life is no less so.

The relative popularity of Grace's stories—many were published in New Zealand and Australian journals before being collected into volumes—suggests that this view of things found quite ready acceptance in colonial minds. In his last novel, *The Tale of a Timber Town* (1914), he tries his hand at something else: a melodramatic tale based on the Maungatapu murders.

After this, Grace appears to have worked as a journalist, but published no more fiction. He died in Nelson.

NW

GRACE, Patricia (1937–), novelist, short story writer and children's writer, is of Ngāti Toa, Ngāti Raukawa and Te Āti Awa descent, and is affiliated to Ngāti Porou by marriage. She has gained wide recognition as a key figure in the emergence of Māori fiction in English since the 1970s (see also Heretaunga Pat *Baker, Keri *Hulme, Witi *Ihimaera, Bruce *Stewart, June *Mitchell). Her work, expressive of Māori consciousness and values, is distinguished also for the variety of Māori people and ways of life it portrays and for its resourceful versatility of style and narrative and descriptive technique.

Born in Wellington, Grace was educated at St Anne's School, St Mary's College and Wellington Teachers' Training College, later gaining Victoria University's Diploma in the Teaching of English as a Second Language. At Teachers' College, she began to seek out books by New Zealand authors, including Frank *Sargeson, Janet *Frame and Amelia *Batistich: 'when I first read some of her stories it came home to me [that] writing was a question of voice and truth, and of a writer finding his/her own way of telling. Amelia was a New Zealander with a different voice' (interview with Jane McRae in *In the Same Room*, ed. Elizabeth *Alley and Mark *Williams, 1992). She began writing at about 25 while teaching in North Auckland, being published in *Te *Ao Hou* and the *NZ Listener*, and continued to write while teaching, raising her family of seven children and moving to Plimmerton, near Wellington, where she still lives. Her first book, *Waiariki* (1975), the first short story collection by a Māori woman writer, won the PEN/Hubert Church Award for Best First Book of Fiction.

The collection is shaped so as to find for Māori, in the words of the first story's title, 'A Way of Talking', and to 'show ... who we are'. This is the task given by an elder to the narrator of the final story, 'Parade', and stands almost as an artistic credo. The collection may be read as a progress from the almost autistic inarticulateness of the schoolgirl Hera in 'A Way of Talking' to the confident choric harmony of the canoe chant in Māori with which 'Parade' ends. The opening and closing of the volume thus establish a meticulous though unobtrusive patterning: this careful craft remains characteristic. The ten stories between elaborate the affirmation of a people's right to speak, each with a narrative voice that is distinctively different, yet distinctively Māori, whether formally oratorical or racily colloquial. Though Grace's style has often been described merely as 'simple' or 'lyrical', she has successfully shown that 'a Maori world is not limited and Maori people are as diverse as any other people'. While not the only writer to make narrative use of the Māori oral tradition, Grace's sheer range is instantly impressive.

She has continued to extend it. Her first novel, *Mutuwhenua: The Moon Sleeps* (1978), tells the story of the love and marriage of a young Māori woman and Pākehā man, the first time this had been done from the Māori perspective and by a Māori writer. It is focused on the effort of Ripeka/Linda to find identity as well as love, as increasingly she commits herself to her Māori being, family and name. The novel ends with her passing the couple's baby to her mother to be brought up in the extended family, so that the effort of what Grace has called the 'very, very large leap' of cross-cultural adjustment is asked of the husband, whereas 'Most often it's the Māori people who have to go across the gap' (McRae interview). His love and moral quality are tested and judged in those terms: 'I went to him confidently. He had not once failed to love.' While committedly Māori, *Mutuwhenua* is pointedly positive and non-polemical, emphasising 'the common ground that all forms of life have in this country', with 'stereotypes ... skilfully flicked aside' (Patrick ★Evans, ★*Landfall* 128, 1978). Its writing also demonstrates a remarkably sensitive ear, with phrases often cadenced and paragraphs almost scored musically, for instance in the rhythmic Eliot-like prose-poems which describe the city, or the several evocations of the sea shore. (Every Grace book has included variations on this aural depiction of the sea meeting the land.)

Grace is acutely conscious of sound, subtle in onomatopoeia, and imbues even visual description with a strong aural quality. The stories in *The Dream Sleepers and Other Stories* (1980), her second collection, extend the diversity of Māori voices and aspects of Māori life, including some robustly sketched children and two memorable mothers—the comic-maverick car-toting mother of 'It Used to be Green Once' and the elemental, mythic yet very human mother of ★'Between Earth and Sky', a three-page monologue which has rapidly become an iconic New Zealand text.

Always writing well of children, Grace in the early 1980s wrote increasingly for them, seeking to add to the 'few stories that Māori children see themselves in and that reflect their lives'. *The Kuia and the Spider / Te Kuia me te Pungawerewere* (1981), illustrated by Robyn ★Kahukiwa, which tells of a spinning contest between the elderly Māori woman and the spider of the title, won the Children's Picture Book of the Year Award. *Watercress Tuna and the Children of Champion Street / Te Tuna Watakirihi me Nga Tamariki o te Tiriti o Toa*, also illustrated by Kahukiwa, emphasises society's multiculturalism, and was also published in Samoan. Grace has also published a third children's book, *The Trolley* (1993) and several Māori language readers.

The collaboration with Robyn Kahukiwa then produced *Wahine Toa* (1984), Grace's text complementing the book-form reproductions of Kahukiwa's striking paintings of the women of Māori mythology. 'We decided to personalise the stories ... realising more and more that the stories are both contemporary and ancient.'

In 1985 Grace held the Victoria University writing fellowship, gave up teaching and completed her third and most successful novel, ★*Potiki* (1986), which won the New Zealand Book Award for Fiction and was third in the Wattie Book of the Year Award. It many ways it is a synthesis of the skills developed in the earlier work (including the children's writing), with carefully crafted cadences and aural effects unifying the prose, and evoking not only the people's diverse individual voices and the sounds of their environment but their harmony with it and each other. The more aggressive political stance struck many reviewers, John Beston commenting that Pākehā readers find themselves charged 'not with past and irremediable injustices, but with continuing injustices' (*Landfall* 160, 1986). Their embarrassment (in Hera's word from 'A Way of Talking') extends to the inclusion of much untranslated Māori, especially the ending, and the absence of a glossary. In *Potiki* as earlier in 'Parade' Grace disempowers the reader who can read no Māori at crucial points within the cultural form of fiction in English. *Potiki* makes more evident how subtly subversive a writer she habitually is.

Her third collection, *Electric City and Other Stories* (1987), adds to the group of stories in *The Dream Sleepers* centred on the girl Mereana, which Grace originally thought 'would add up to a novel, but they didn't'. The volume's more successful stories are the darker adult ones, such as 'Hospital', with its harsh, hallucinatory version of childbirth and surgery, and its close on a despondent and aimless journey ('... not to know what's round this bend, the next, the next one after that'), thus ending where *Cousins begins.

Grace's third novel, Cousins (1992), followed a Selected Stories (1991). In what may now be seen as a characteristic shaping principle, it moves from that initial wandering journey, silent, blind and objectless, to the vocal, visionary, firmly rooted communal harmony of the ending, with its sense of membership and continuity even in the face of death.

The Sky People (1994), her fourth story collection, is more explicitly and consistently concerned with the disoriented, dispossessed and despondent—'The Haurangi, the Wairangi, the Porangi—those crazy from the wind or what they breathe, those crazy from water or what they drink, those crazy from darkness or depression' (prefatory epigraph from 'conversation with Keri Kaa'). From sisters damaged by childhood abuse by their famous and respected father to a teenage boy tipped into suicide by sexual jealousy and its consequences, these stories refute any suggestion that Grace sentimentalises relationships among Māori. Some are political, like the zestful Swiftian satire 'Ngati Kangaru' (in which Māori from Australia reverse colonisation by appropriating a luxury weekend residential development), some are half-jocularly mythical, like the racy retelling of Māori creation myth in 'Sun's Marbles', and some are realistic and sympathetic sketches of people on the margins of society. The writing is versatile and self-assured, and the stories stronger and more often surprising than before; several ('Flower Girls', 'The Day of the Egg', 'My Leanne') end with a dramatic twist or punch. The title story, about a group of people who live by re-making rejected clothes in a Wellington attic, shows a developed skill in combining entertaining storytelling with a telling underlying significance. It also (with others in this collection and earlier) illustrates a paradox that frequently sustains Grace's art—stories of loss, isolation and sadness which yet are bright with colour, stories where the details of life's sights and sounds tumble out in vivid lists, and where a childlike innocence and insight intersect with the most knowing adult awareness.

Patricia Grace has won enthusiastic recognition among non-Māori readers, was awarded the Queen's Service Order in 1988 and an honorary DLitt of Victoria University in 1989. She makes a significant early statement of her artistic aims in Tihe Maori Ora, ed. Michael *King (1978). Significant critical discussion includes Rachel Nunns, *Islands 26 (1979), John Beston, Ariel 15 (1984), W.H. New, Dreams of Speech and Violence (1987), Mark *Williams, *Journal of New Zealand Literature 5 (1987), the *OHNZLE, ed. Terry *Sturm (1991), and Roger Robinson in The Commonwealth Novel in English Since 1965, ed. Bruce King (1991), and the Centre for Research into New Literatures in English Reviews Journal (New Zealand issue, 1993), which also reprints the interview with Jane McRae.   RR

GRANT, A.K. (Alan Keith) (1941–), is a satirist, parodist, columnist, lyricist and scriptwriter. Born in Wanganui, he was educated mainly in Christchurch, at Linwood HS and University of Canterbury (LLB 1964). After legal work in New Zealand and London, he practised as a barrister in Christchurch 1976–80 and then became a full-time writer and (1980–87) TV script editor. His satiric history of New Zealand is a comic classic. First published as Land Uprooted High (1971), it was rewritten and enlarged as The Paua and the Glory (1982), and the sequel dealing with recent events, Corridors of Paua, was added in 1996. It includes memorable passages of absurdist literary history. His literary parodies are also notable, such as his anthologised 'An Inquiry into the Construction and Classification of the New Zealand Short Story' (in I Rode with the Epigrams, 1979), his VCR update of Katherine Mansfield's 'The *Doll's House' ('I seen "The Attack of the Killer Tomatoes"') and his version of Denis Glover's 'The *Magpies', which after six quardle oodle ardling stanzas ends: 'Tom said, "I know I'm finished, / But I couldn't give a hang. / I'll take that bloody magpie / With me!"—Bang!'

Other publications include The Bedside Grant (1985), The Dictionary of Wimps (1989) and I'm glad I asked you that: Exclusive interviews with charismatic Kiwis (1989), in which 'The Feminist Actress' and 'The Writer' have significant literary content. These volumes mostly collect columns and occasional pieces from NZ Listener and elsewhere. He wrote TV scripts for A Week of It, 1977–79, McPhail and Gadsby, 1980–87, the Billy T. James Show and Letter to Blanchy (1996–). He has also written lyrics for musicals, notably 'Footrot Flats' (1983, book by Roger *Hall). Together with Hall and Tom *Scott, who is frequently his collaborator, Grant is a key figure in the renaissance of satiric comedy since about 1975, his downbeat absurdist wit being among the best of the deadpan self-deprecation which characterises much New Zealand humour.   RR

GRANT, Alison (1901–), published poems in various periodicals in Australia and New Zealand, especially in the Christchurch Sun, New Zealand Free Lance and, in 1925, The Spinner (Australia). A good selection is found in the anthology *Kowhai Gold* (1930). She wrote as 'Fairiel' for the *NZ Times* and the *Evening Post* children's pages 1925–28, earning praise from Robin *Hyde for being 'perhaps the most popular personage with the small fry that any New Zealand journal has known, for she has a habit of treating her youngest readers as if they were very wise in a magic sort of way'. After a few years in Sydney in the 1920s, Grant went to London, where she was a successful freelance for British papers, and during several returns to New Zealand she wrote for the *Mirror*, *NZ Listener, Sydney Morning Herald* and *Truth. In 1937 she had a broadcasting job in Wellington. In London she lived in bohemian circles and was for some forty years the clandestine partner of the Chinese translator and scholar Arthur Waley. She married Hugh Ferguson Robinson in 1930 and finally married Waley one month before his death in 1966. Her secret relationship to him is wittily and romantically described in the autobiographical *A Half of Two Lives* (1982) using the author's name Alison Waley. At an advanced age, she continued to live in London surrounded by Waley's books and manuscripts. Her poems are delicately phrased and their thoughts are hinted rather than stated, with a liberal use of three dots to suggest the inexpressible. Although at their worst they tend to be effete, at their best they have the strength of a genuinely musical use of vowels and rhythms.   NW

GRANT, J.G.S. (James Gordon Stuart) (1838–1902), one of the liveliest polemicists New Zealand has ever seen and heard, was born in Banffshire, Scotland, and educated in Aberdeen and Edinburgh. He was awarded first prize in moral philosophy and political economy at St Andrews, and at the age of 17 he emigrated to Melbourne, where he was recruited by Otago immigration agents, apparently believing that he was to be the rector of the new high school. His ship's captain (on the *Gil Blas*, 1855) took eleven days searching for the entrance to Dunedin Harbour.

On landing he immediately took to lecturing his fellow citizens on weekdays and preaching on Sundays, in both English and Gaelic. When he failed to get the appointment of rector, he founded his own school, the Dunedin Academy. In his hugely prolific writing, he refers to this 'betrayal' again and again, with bitter irony. When the high school opened, he had almost no pupils and set off on a tour of the country 'to inspire life into the other languid provinces'.

Returning to Dunedin he made a failed attempt to start a newspaper and then reopened the Dunedin Academy. Intrigue and persecution (real or imagined?) were his reward. When *gold brought a huge rise in the population, some paused to listen to Grant, who found a new audience for his lectures.

His dazzling rhetoric related poverty in Otago to the gods of Greece and the Dunedin city council to the dictators of Rome. His flourishes included anti-Semitic attacks on Julius *Vogel (although in other places he praises Hebrew culture), whose newspaper, the *Otago Daily Times*, he consistently referred to as the Jew's Harp. Vogel took a libel action. Grant spent two months in prison before the trial but apparently dazzled the jury with his passionate defence, so that he was found not guilty.

At the beginning of 1864 he started a large weekly newspaper, *The Saturday Review*, which he wrote by his own hand. Apart from the help of a printing company, the entire staff of this fascinating enterprise was Grant himself—the sole means of distribution was that he sold it in the street. In his first number Grant explains the reasons for his publication: 'The Colonial Press comes in very conveniently for rolling up parcels, igniting fires, or perhaps, for more equivocal purposes; but it never draws a tear from the eye, or swells the bosom with emotion, or lightens the darkness of the mental horizon....'

Grant wrote both bitterly and wittily of the unemployment problem in the rapidly expanding colony. He called a meeting of the unemployed which passed two resolutions: '1. That in the opinion of this assembly it is the bounden duty of the Government to dispense with the services of all government officials. 2. That this great body of men shall escort and protect Mr Grant to the Government House to demand satisfaction from the Government in reference to this urgent business.' The Superintendent told the men that he could do nothing, and they dispersed. A few weeks later another assembly disturbed a sitting of the council. Grant was arrested and fined £1 before being sent home. It seems that others took him less seriously than he did himself. Nonetheless his account of the incident in *The Saturday Review* is long and dramatic, comparing himself to Cromwell and his unemployed followers to the Light Dragoons.

After several libel and assault actions, the *Review* started to fade—it was closed for its debts in 1871—and Grant turned to politics. He stood candidate to join his enemies on the council, using the slogan 'Don't pay the members and they will the sooner get through their work'. He found himself elected. His passionate attack on attempts to eradicate thistles, the emblem of Grant's home country and 'a stalwart strong emblem compared to the pigmy rose', was greeted with mockery and his political speeches were never taken seriously again. In 1867 he made an attempt to stand for the Superintendency. The result was Macandrew 2259 votes, Dick

1392 and Grant 2 (one of which was presumably his own). This silenced accusations that he had tried to split Macandrew's vote. Later, for many years he offered himself for parliament and consistently received very few votes.

Irrepressibly he started another review: *The Delphic Oracle* (1866–70). Since no one could, it seems, be bothered taking a libel action against him, he filled many of its pages with bitter diatribes against notables of the city. But not all pages: he read recent philosophical, religious and historical publications assiduously and wrote lively, witty and perceptive, if prejudiced, reviews of them. In praising Scott above Dickens, probably for nationalistic reasons, he made some acute as well as wrong-headed judgments. At this distance in time one cannot help but admire his rhetorical skills, his striking imagery, his ability to vary his polemics so that they never become repetitive or dull, and his diligence, energy and wit, which make some compensation for his jaundiced view of his contemporaries.

Eventually even Grant's spark died and for many years he lived in great poverty, selling pamphlets on the street for various organisations as well as those he wrote himself. There were about sixty of the latter including *Classical Education, Philosophical Thoughts on Evolution* and a variety of libellous effusions. He left behind him a niggardly reputation and some of the most entertaining prose ever written in this country. In quantity it is matched only by that of the most prolific romance novelists.   NW

GRAY, Alison (1943–), has combined social research, oral history and prose fiction, always with a focus on narrative as a means to understanding personal lives, relationships and their social contexts. As well as extensive social research reports, mainly on issues of health and disability, she has published eleven books. *The Smith Women* (with Rosemary Barrington, 1981) perfectly caught the rising tide of feminist awareness with revealing interviews that cut across age and socio-economic barriers, and was highly successful. It was followed by other contemporary oral history such as *The Jones Men* (1983), *Expressions of Sexuality* (1985) and *Mothers and Daughters* (1993). Gray had already published well-received fiction, *The Marriage Maze* (1979), and went on to *Stepping Out* (1987), both of which deal vigorously with the issues of women's self-perception and expectations which her research explores. She has also written children's books. There is an interview in Neville Glasgow, *Directions* (1995).

Born in Lower Hutt, she returned to Wellington in 1973 after eight years in Auckland. She was research assistant and lecturer in sociology and social work at Victoria University 1978–86 and is director of 'Gray Matter Research', in Wellington. She has received a *PEN Fellowship for fiction (1996), ICI Writers' Bursary (1984) and a New Zealand Commemorative Medal (1990).   RR

GRAY, Zane, see **Sport**.

Great Depression, The, see **Depression, The**.

Greenstone Door, The (1914), is the fourth, last and best known of William *Satchell's novels. For many readers it offers an image of the relationship between Māori and Pākehā which is not idealised yet almost ideal: tolerant, warm and humane on both sides.

Told in the first person, it traces the experiences and mental development of a boy into manhood, and gains much from the perspective of the mature Cedric Tregarthen on his immature but growing self. Cedric's father is killed by Māori and he is raised by the trader, Purcell, who occupies a balanced position between the two races until war breaks out, when his sympathies are for the Māori, so that he is treated by the settlers as a traitor. Cedric is adopted by Purcell's friend Te Waharoa as the chief's 'Little Finger'. In this way he grows up with his foster sister Puhi-Huia and his close friend Rangiora. At the end of their childhood, Cedric and Rangiora take the oath of the Tatau Pounamu, the Greenstone Door, which is to be closed on enmity between peoples. In his teens, Cedric lives in Auckland, acquiring as much learning in European culture as he has already acquired in Māori ways. He is set up to be a meeting-point and an intermediary between cultures. As events unfold he meets Sir George *Grey and falls in love with Helenora. Cedric's equilibrium is tested when war breaks out between the peoples to whom he owes equal loyalty. Like one of Walter Scott's historical heroes, he stands between the warring parties, not so much split between them as unifying both in himself. He accompanies General Cameron to the famous siege of Orakau, where the defiant words known to all New Zealanders were spoken by the besieged: 'E hoa, ka whawhai tonu ahau ki a koe, ake, ake!' ('Friend, I shall fight against you for ever, for ever!') In the novel they are spoken by Cedric's friend Rangiora. (One can be reminded of Wilfred Owen's line 'I am the enemy you killed, my friend.') In the battle Puhi-Huia, Cedric's loved sister, is killed. With his friends on both sides dead, Cedric falls ill and is nursed to health in Auckland by Helenora. Satchell does not have the strength to avoid Victorian sentimentalism at this point, a fault which detracts from but does not destroy a very moving plot idea. E.H. *McCormick sees the same flaw throughout—'the plot is more improbable and melodramatic than ever'—but generations of readers have not let this disturb their affection for a powerful, if flawed, masterpiece, a New Zealand *Nathan der Weise*. More than any other novel of its time, except perhaps The**Story of a New Zealand River*, *The Greenstone Door*, sometimes categorised as a young persons' book, has been reprinted and reread, again and again.   NW

GREENWOOD, Lisa (1955–), novelist, was born in Westmere and returned to Auckland after a period in various itinerant jobs and the birth of a daughter in 1977. Her first novel, *The Roundness of Eggs* (1986), is the story of a 52-year-old woman who undergoes psychological crisis and dreams of an autonomous life as a painter. The novel's humour comes from her family's expectation that she will continue as the self-effacing, nurturing wife, mother and cook, completely failing to comprehend her increasing alienation from their values. The basic realist mode changes unexpectedly to a symbolic ending, which Greenwood describes as 'a metaphor for a shift within the protagonist'. The novel was well reviewed, as was its very different successor, *Daylight Burning* (1990), a powerful and darkly bizarre account of an Auckland businessman whose yuppie life is transformed by an apparently prophetic vision of Auckland destroyed by nuclear holocaust. Unable to reconcile his foreknowledge with daily life he flees, and ends in a mid-island timber-milling town. Amidst the mud and violence of the settlement he is protected by a wise, 40-year-old Māori cook who also has visions of impending catastrophe, under which she too gradually breaks down. The book's unrelenting pace makes it almost obsessively gripping to read. Greenwood was the 1990 Katherine *Mansfield Memorial Fellow, working on a novel set in fourteenth-century England.   AMcL

GREIG, Rhondda (1940–), poet, children's author and artist, lives and works in the Wairarapa. As well as painting, Greig designs and makes banners, and she has employed the techniques of both skills to illustrate her children's book, *Matarawa Cats* (1984), in which watercolour paintings have been cut and pasted to create images. Her second book for children, *Matarawa House* (1990), describes the pandemonium that results when children explore the ceiling of the house and disturb the animals living there. In sharp contrast, *Eavesdropping with Angels* (1994), her first collection of poetry, is an intensely personal record of a seven-year grieving process for her husband, the acclaimed potter Jim Greig, who died suddenly while in Japan. But Greig's statements of grief, in their lucidity and precision, negotiate the potential pitfalls of such a focus by ensuring, in the words of Margaret *Mahy (*Landfall 188, 1994), that 'sentimentality is held at bay by a style intense but plain.

Emotion, reflected in something other than tranquillity (although tranquillity becomes part of it), floods between reader and page'.   PM

GREY, Sir George Edward (1812–98), was the most commanding figure, and perhaps the most controversial one, in New Zealand public affairs in the nineteenth century. He was Governor from 1845–53, ruling autocratically under the remote British Colonial Office, again from 1861–68, when New Zealand had some degree of independence, and Premier from 1877–79.

Grey was born in Lisbon and educated at Sandhurst Military Academy. He served four years in Ireland (where the economic extremes gave him a permanent distaste for large estates), spent the period December 1837 to April 1840 in Australia, partly on official exploration in Western Australia, before becoming Governor of South Australia, which he led from bankruptcy to relative affluence, while studying and expressing sympathy for Aborigine cultures. Within three years of arriving in New Zealand in 1845 he had quietened the rebellion in the north, acquired a fluent command of Māori and established great *mana with the Māori leaders. He encouraged settlement in the Wellington area and the South Island but dealt firmly with the questionable pre-1840 land purchases in the North. After leaving in 1853 he was Governor in Cape Colony, where he was less successful and found disfavour in London for his self-assured way of ignoring commands from there. His second term in New Zealand, marked as it was by the Taranaki wars, ended with dismissal when he kept the British forces in New Zealand despite the contrary orders from London. After a period in London seeking a seat in parliament he returned to Kawau Island, near Auckland—there is a good description of his home and extensive collections there in Anthony *Trollope's account of New Zealand. He returned to politics, becoming an MP for twenty years, and was briefly Premier, but was generally disliked for his egotism and arrogance. He was highly talented in many ways nonetheless and New Zealand literature owes him a debt for his investigations and preservation of Māori traditions—even though there is some controversy over them as well.

Enjoying great mana among *ariki and rangatira, Grey travelled the country with many of them accompanying him, and from them he learned the language. He copied down their stories and *whakapapa, or, more frequently, persuaded them to write or dictate to an amanuensis. His main informant was *Te Rangikāheke. However, when he came to publish the results of such work he ignored the informants and used only his own name—this was just one example of his arrogant approach to affairs. It should also be borne in mind that his interest in these matters, though remarkable, was always tempered by his assimilation policies and insistence on the use of English in schools.

Grey's contributions to literature included founding important libraries in Cape Town and Auckland by gifting his own collections, which extended to manuscripts, incunabula and other rare books. His botanical collections were of considerable scientific value. He wrote books on Australian Aboriginal languages and on his explorations of Western Australia. His books in Māori were *Ko nga *mahinga a nga tupuna Maori* (the deeds of the Māori ancestors, London 1854; translated as *Polynesian Mythology*, 1855), *Ko nga *moteatea, me nga hakirara o nga Maori* (the songs, chants and poetry of the Māori, Wellington 1853), *Ko ngā waiata Maori* (Māori songs; according to the *New Zealand National Bibliography* this was printed in 1857 but not published until 1950, after copies were found in the tower of the Auckland Public Library) and *Ko nga whakapepeha me nga whakaahuareka a nga tipuna o Aotea-roa* (proverbs and sayings of the ancestors of *Aotearoa, Cape Town and London 1857).

There are various literary portraits of Grey but the most notable is in William *Satchell's *The *Greenstone Door,* where he is contrasted with Cedric's stepfather, Purcell, Grey representing English civilisation and Purcell the 'noble savage' quality of an Englishman who has gone native. In 1980 Keith Aberdein published a fictionalised biography of Grey, *The Governor,* based on a TV series of the same name.   NW

GRIEVE, Hamilton (pseudonym for Beatrice Scott Grieve, born Lake, 1902–90), was an author of stories and *romances with New Zealand settings aimed mainly at an English readership. Her first marriage to the principal of a country school in Northland provided the material for *Sketches from Maoriland* (1939, 1961), scenes and anecdotes of school and social life among a Māori community, engagingly humorous and affectionate, if of its time in being lightly patronising. *Spring Manoeuvres* (1944) is a romance mostly set in a replica Scots castle overlooking Cook Strait near Wellington, escapist material for wartime Britain. *Something in the Country Air* (1947) uses a Hawkes Bay setting for a romance plot lifted above the norm by a wry, almost flippant humour. *It's Nothing Serious* (1950) was the last of these light and amusing love stories that Joan *Stevens describes as 'gay trifles with merit in their kind' (*The New Zealand Novel 1860–1960*, 1961).   PN/RR

Griffin Press, The, was established in its first form in 1934 by Ronald Holloway (born 1909). Holloway's mentor in printing was Robert *Lowry whom he met at Auckland University College in 1932, assisting him

with printing *Phoenix and Allen *Curnow's *Valley of Decision* (1933) for the Auckland University College Students' Association Press. When the press ceased operations in 1934, its equipment was used to establish the Griffin Press at 34 Kitchener Street, Auckland, the first publication being *Modern Poetry and the Ideal* (1934), a radio talk by D'Arcy *Cresswell. The premises were occupied jointly with Lowry's Unicorn Press in which (after R.A.K. *Mason pulled out) Holloway became a partner from 1934 to 1938. In 1937 Holloway married Kay Harvey, who became his partner in Griffin. When the Unicorn Press was dissolved, the Holloways took over its equipment and continued printing and publishing as the Griffin Press in the same premises, beginning with Roderick *Finlayson's stories, *Brown Man's Burden* (1938), originally intended for Unicorn. ('Unicorn Press' is on the title page, 'Griffin Press' on the dustjacket.) Griffin subsequently published four other Finlayson titles. Other authors published by Griffin over a fifty-year period (together with much jobbing printing, such as work for the Catholic Church) included A.R.D. *Fairburn, Ian Hamilton, J.C. *Reid, Arthur Sewell, Helen *Shaw and Riemke *Ensing. In 1945 the Press was moved to the Holloways' property in Panmure. Much lively and opinionated detail about the activities of the Griffin Press and the people associated with it is contained in Kay Holloway's three volumes of memoirs, *Beta Plus* (1992), *Meet Me at the Press* (1994) and *A Sort of Sabbatical* (1996). Ron Holloway's memories of his partnership with Lowry are recorded in 'Remembering Bob Lowry', *Landfall 69 (1964). In 1993 the Holloways donated much of the library, archive and equipment of the Griffin Press to the University of Auckland, leading to the establishment of the *Holloway Press at the university's Tamaki Campus with Alan *Loney as printer-manager.   PS

GRIFFITHS, David (1950–), composer, singer and university teacher, born in Auckland, has carried his long professional experience as choral singer and soloist into his compositions for the 'richness, colour and intensity of voices'. Although most of his vocal music is based on religious texts, he has set Charles *Brasch, A.R.D. *Fairburn, James K. *Baxter, Bill *Manhire, Kevin *Ireland, Albert *Wendt, Sam *Hunt, Ruth *Dallas, Hone *Tuwhare and M.K. *Joseph, in evocative and atmospheric music of wide-ranging moods.   JMT

GROSSMAN, Edith Searle (1863–1931), a novelist, whose first novel was published under her unmarried name, Edith Howitt Searle, was born in Australia, the daughter of a newspaper editor, and arrived in New Zealand with her parents in 1878. She attended Invercargill

Grammar School, Christchurch GHS and Canterbury College of the University of New Zealand (MA with first class honours in Latin and English 1885). Professor John Macmillan *Brown called her 'an indefatigable worker ... (whose) talents placed her amongst the foremost'. From graduation to 1890 she was a mistress at Wellington GHS, when she married a master at Wellington BHS. The marriage was not happy. Her husband pursued a university career in Christchurch and Auckland but was twice in difficulties for financial dishonesty, blaming his problems on his wife, though no evidence supports the claim.

For many years she lived apart from him, in London and Europe for eleven years and in separate houses in Auckland for many more, following a career as a writer. Her journalism appeared in New Zealand and British papers. She was also active in the *women's suffrage movement, holding very progressive views, which are reflected in her novels. She was interested in more than the vote, advocating total equality of opportunity in the workplace and economy, and social recognition for women. She lectured on the Married Women's Property Act of 1884, believing in complete economic equality in marriage. Despite her own unhappiness, she advocated marriage as 'the source of the new race' and wanted women to be a positive force at home as well as outside the home. Sadly, in her brief 'Life of Helen Macmillan Brown' (1905), she concluded that this almost ideal woman was crushed by 'home duties'.

Her first novel, *Angela, a Messenger* (1890), set in the Wairarapa, is dismissed by her critics as a 'narrow crusading affair' (Joan *Stevens), but undoubtedly her work grows in strength from book to book. In this first book, a young woman, finding herself wrongfully ostracised for sins she had never committed, joins the Salvation Army and serves the poor in both Wellington and Sydney. *In Revolt* (1893) and its sequel *A Knight of the Holy Ghost* (1907)—both set in Australia—explore with greater subtlety the fictional possibilities in the very real problems of a feminist idealist shackled to a heartless husband. Hermione must first face the prejudice that study and intellectual activity are not 'feminine' activities. Her farmer husband, Bradley, thinks nothing of such a life, for man or woman, preferring to curse his servants and animals in a state of drunkenness. When she gives evidence against another brutal husband in a murder trial, Bradley turns violent and beats her. He also causes the death of their infant son. At the end of *In Revolt* Hermione escapes across the mountains, while Bradley goes 'mad with delirium tremens' before sinking into 'lethargy': 'He kept on drinking hard, but only seemed to have drunk himself stupid.'

The book contains some powerful scenes, as does its sequel, although the latter is marred by its sensationalist elements and its melodramatic ending. Fourteen years after leaving her husband, Hermione conducts a crusade for women's rights on behalf of the Holy Ghost. Bradley, however, with the full support of 'society', takes her through the humiliation of the divorce courts, after which there is nothing for her to do but die. This surprisingly defeatist ending to a vigorous attack on a wide range of injustices is disappointing, but passages in the book can still inspire a sense of heroic anger.

Grossmann's finest book, indeed one of the two or three best New Zealand novels of the first two decades of the twentieth century, is *The *Heart of the Bush* (1910) which contains its advocacy of feminism in a less vengeful tone and more skilful structure, while broadening its themes to face the major literary question of its time: how is a colonial culture to be defined, and must it 'cringe' before the metropolitan tradition? With its fascinating use of *bush and mountains for meaningful symbolism, the book merits republication.

In her journalism Grossmann covered more themes than her fiction might suggest: educational topics, in particular Māori education; the significance of old buildings in a young country and the need for their conservation; the need for parks in cities; criticism of fiction and theatre. Like others of her generation, such as William *Satchell, she seems to have found the rewards of writing fiction too slight for the effort involved, so that after 1910 she wrote no more novels, although she lived a full and active life for two more decades. She died in Auckland.   NW

GUNN, Kirsty (1960–), is a short story writer and novelist. She attended Queen Margaret College in Wellington and graduated BA (Hons) in English from Victoria University of Wellington in 1982. She tried to get her stories published in New Zealand, but found editors were 'only interested in *New Zealand* stories'; hers lacked this exclusive focus. She left soon after graduation and two years later completed an MPhil at Oxford. Gunn then moved to London, where she now lives. Here she continued to write fiction while holding a string of temporary jobs: writing feature articles, fashion columns, film reviews and agony aunt columns for magazines such as *Vogue*, *Brides* and *Setting Up Home*, writing advertising copy and direct mail leaflets; and for some time she was the London correspondent for *More* magazine (NZ).

Overseas editors were more willing to recognise her talent. Her stories were published in various *Serpent's Tail* anthologies and three stories were published in *First Fictions 11* (Faber and Faber, 1992): 'The Swimming

Pool', 'The Hook' and 'Grass, Leaves'. Gunn's first novel, *Rain* (Faber, 1994), was extremely well received here and abroad. New Zealand readers clearly recognise the Lake Taupo setting. Narrated in the first person by a girl on the cusp of adolescence, it is a story about familial breakdown, parental betrayal and the death of a much-loved younger brother. The writing is elegant and understated, characterised, as in her other fictions, by evocative and densely imagistic prose. The award of a London Arts Board Literature Award in 1995 enabled Gunn to write full-time. Her second novel, *The Keepsake* (Granta, 1997) is again written in first-person, spare and imagistic prose. It records the fragmented memories of its female narrator, again figuring memory as a creative and redemptive act. Remembering allows the narrator to rewrite the painful stories of her past, a past which is closely linked to—but finally separable from—that of her abusive mother. *The Keepsake* has also been well received in the USA.   KWo

Gus Tomlins, in the *Me and Gus* stories, see **Anthony, Frank**.

GUTHRIE, John, was the pseudonym adopted by John Brodie (1905–55) for his seven novels and the much admired portrait of his father, *The Man in Our Lives* (1946). The best-known of his novels is *The Seekers* (1952), which portrays the early impact of European settlers on the Māori and became a controversial film, but some of his admirers tend to prefer *Paradise Bay* (1952), described by the English critic Marghanita Laski as 'an excellent book and a potential New Zealand classic if ever there was one'. His first book *The Little Country* (1935), like many novels of the 1920s–30s, was an attempt to portray New Zealand life through a representative small community, in this case, a Taranaki town in pioneer times.

Guthrie was born and educated in New Plymouth, where he became a journalist with the *Taranaki Daily News*. He completed a Diploma in Journalism at Canterbury University College, which he represented in rugby. A leg was amputated after an accident on the rugby field. After a period as editor of the *Radio Record*, he went to London in 1938 and joined the RAF as an intelligence officer. He did not return to New Zealand but edited the London journal *Books of Today* and was later assistant editor of *World's Press News*.   NW

GUTHRIE-SMITH, W.H. (William Herbert) (1861–1940), was born in Scotland, and spent his early childhood in Hamilton, Lanark. At Rugby School he fostered his writing and bird-watching skills but was not a notable scholar, so that he forged a plan with a fellow pupil, Arthur Cunningham, to go off to New Zealand, earn a fortune and return to Scotland for a life of ease. In 1880 they set off to stay with Guthrie-Smith's uncle in Canterbury. After an apprenticeship in sheep farming there they bought a rugged property at Tutira in Hawkes Bay. Wealth did not fall into their hands, but Guthrie-Smith learned to love and closely observe every detail of the land he was on and its animal inhabitants. He noted how introduced species thrived, or failed to, and how the native species reacted to these rivals, and he observed how the movements of water and air changed the shape of the land itself. Cunningham returned to Britain in 1887 but Guthrie-Smith went on observing and noting for fifty years.

In the evenings he wrote up his observations and also wrote poetry and a play, *Crispus* (published in Edinburgh in 1891), using Gibbon's account of the son of the Emperor Constantine. Criticism protested that it 'nowhere reached the height of sublimity demanded by tragedy', but its polished verse style was acknowledged. Disappointed, he turned to prose and published several short stories in the British paper *Good Words*. His notes on his observations became essays, published by the Selborne Society (which commemorates the English natural history writer Gilbert White) in their magazine. In 1895 he published 'Bird Life on a Run' in *Transactions of the New Zealand Institute*, and in 1910 his first major work on natural history, *Birds of the Water, Wood and Waste*, which included his own photographs of birds in Tutira. It was received enthusiastically in New Zealand and England. His next book, *Mutton Birds and Other Birds* (1914) extended his range, after notable journeys through the South and Stewart Islands. His other books include *Bird Life on Island and Shore* (1925) and *Sorrows and Joys of a New Zealand Naturalist* (1936). However, he is best remembered for ★*Tutira: The Story of a New Zealand Sheep Station* (1921), which he began by organising his extensive notes while living in Britain and working for the war effort 1914–19. On his return to New Zealand he undertook extensive research and completed the book.

There is a biography by A.E. Woodhouse, *Guthrie-Smith of Tutira* (1959), and an excellent MA thesis on *Tutira* by C.P.K. Wells (Waikato, 1979).   NW

H

HAAST, Julius von (1822–87), was one of the founders of science in New Zealand. He studied at Cologne and Bonn, travelled extensively in Europe, worked in the book trade in Frankfurt and travelled to New Zealand in 1858, where he met Ferdinand von *Hochstetter, the beginning of a lifelong friendship.

After exploring with Hochstetter, Haast stayed on to study the geology of Canterbury and Westland for the provincial government. His reports were famous for their meticulous maps, illustrations and detailed accounts, and his book *Geology of the Provinces of Canterbury and Westland, New Zealand* (1879) summarised his work to that time. He was one of the founders of Canterbury University College, its first professor of geology and a member of the senate of the University of New Zealand. He received many honours from European governments and universities, and was known in New Zealand as a singer, a violinist and a lively character. John Macmillan *Brown called him 'a boy at heart until the day he died'. His descendent H.F. von Haast brought out a large collection of his extremely articulate scientific and personal papers in 1948: *The Life and Times of Sir Julius von Haast*. NW

HABIB, Rowley, see **HAPIPI, Rore**.

Hairy Maclary, see **Dodd, Lynley**.

Haka is a dance-chant, a series of postures accompanied by rhythmic shouting, a major genre in Māori oral literature as well as in popular New Zealand culture generally; but it is not exclusively a war dance as is popularly thought. In fact there were several kinds of haka, some performed by men, some by women and some by children. Several early sources describe it as a social enter-

tainment, often carried out in the evenings, but used at any time of the day and in many different circumstances. Haka evenings are compared by Mervyn McLean in *Maori Music* (1996) to 'the later European small-town social dance or "hop" and had similar associations in terms of courtship behaviour'. He quotes J.C. *Andersen to the effect that people often fell in love after admiring each other's haka performance. Its use as a form of welcome on the *marae has a long tradition.

Its importance is emphasised by Alan Armstrong in his book *Māori Games and Haka* (1964): 'The haka is a composition played by many instruments. Hands, feet, legs, body, voice, tongue and eyes all play their part in blending together to convey in their fullness the challenge, welcome, exultation, defiance or contempt of the words.'

The form of haka used strictly as a war dance is called *peruperu*, which was performed immediately before battle and at intervals in the fighting, and again after a successful battle. Elsdon *Best calls it 'a dance, and song of defiance, and also an expression of the joy of the victors'. McLean quotes from Arapeta *Awatere, 'a renowned exponent of haka', as describing how the physically and mentally conditioned warriors aim to demoralise the enemy, 'to roll the fiery eye, ... to spew the defiant tongue, ... to stamp furiously, ... to carry the anger, the peru, of Tūmatauenga, the ugly-faced war god, throughout the heat of battle. Peruperu is the intensive form of peru, "anger", and this is how the war-dance got its name'.

McLean's book gives much detail of traditional haka, based on a close study of more than fifty early accounts, while Tīmoti S. *Kāretu has written an account including popular uses of the form in his book *Haka! Te Tohu* o *Te Whenua Rangatira: The Dance of a Noble People* (1993). The numerous examples he quotes make it plain that the basically unchanged form is used today to speak of modern concerns, such as the dangers of smoking, the risks of drinking and driving or the wish of young Māori to have their voices heeded by the elders. A startling example is a haka performed before the Prime Minister, Sir James Carroll, in 1911, when he—a member of the rival Ngāti Kahungunu—visited the Tūhoe to discuss a land issue. Kāretu's translation begins: 'Smoke rises above Wellington / Beneath it is the Governor / Bedmate of James Carroll / Whose penis is wrapped with hundreds of notes / And studded with many pieces of silver / So that my land can be consumed with ease / Ā! Hā! Hā!'

The *Aotearoa Māori Performing Arts Festival, inaugurated 1972, has been significant in encouraging new and innovative haka to be created, and something of a revival of the traditional form. That it is essentially a literary form has been emphasised by Kāretu: 'The word is far more important than its manifestation in action and movement. Without the word there is no haka.' In the current efforts to increase the effectiveness of the Māori language, haka and other literary forms have a vital role to play.   NW

HALE, Keron, a pseudonym used by Edith *Lyttleton, who also wrote as 'G.B. Lancaster'.

HALEY, Russell (1934–), poet, short story writer and novelist, was born in Dewhurst, near Leeds in Yorkshire. He spent two years of National Service in the RAF and was stationed for a period in Iraq. He began writing while attending Teachers' Training College in Buckinghamshire. He emigrated to Australia in 1961 and then to New Zealand in 1966, attending the University of Auckland (MA 1970). He was closely associated there with the student group which founded *Freed (1969–72), editing the final issue, *Freed at Last*, himself. Haley initially concentrated on poetry. His first book, *The Walled Garden* (1972), was notable for the surrealistic and psychedelic character of its imagery, while his second, *On the Fault Line* (1977), explored the dislocations and changes associated with a return visit to his birthplace in Yorkshire. During the 1970s Haley turned to prose fiction, publishing his first collection, *The Sauna Bath Mysteries and Other Stories*, in 1978. *Real Illusions* (1984), published both in New Zealand and the United States, carries the subtitle *A selection of family lies and biographical fictions in which the ancestral dead also play their part*. In an Afterword, 'Here and There', Haley quotes a passage from Salman Rushdie's *Shame* relevant to his own practice: 'As for me: I, too, like all migrants, am a fantastist. [*sic*] I build imaginary countries and try to

impose on them the ones that exist....' *The Transfer Station* (1989), a series of closely linked stories which fuse French and New Zealand elements in a futuristic scenario, was written during his tenure of the Katherine *Mansfield Memorial Fellowship in 1987.

Haley was a leader in the movement away from critical realism in New Zealand fiction; his work featured prominently in *The New Fiction*, ed. Michael *Morrissey (1985), an anthology devoted to charting this development. Haley edited (with Susan Davis) *The Penguin Book of Contemporary New Zealand Short Stories* (1989), including many texts 'which disrupt readers' expectations as to how prose stories function'. The introduction also questioned the established perception 'that the powerful influences of *Sargeson and *Mansfield have created a kind of bi-polar literary force-field in which the whole of present day short fiction is still magnetically articulated' and noted a movement away from 'the search for a New Zealand identity'. In the 1980s Haley began writing longer fictions, publishing two novels, *The Settlement* (1986) and *Beside Myself* (1990), which elaborated some of the techniques and devices of his short fiction. He also wrote *Hanly: A New Zealand Artist* (1989), a biographical study of the painter Patrick Hanly. Haley has written scripts for several radio dramas broadcast in New Zealand and Australia, and has received several awards and fellowships, including the Auckland University writing fellowship in 1985. He has also worked as tutor in English at the university. In 1994 he moved to a smallholding near Puhoi, north of Auckland.

PS

Halfmen of O, The (1982), is the first novel in a trilogy for children by Maurice *Gee. Two children travel to the planet of O, where people are either 'good' or 'evil', and there they are able to carry out the mystic activity which unites these two halves in people again, to the benefit of society. In *The Priests of Ferris* (1984) they return to the planet of O, where evil is ruling again in the form of the priests. Again the earthling children restore the natural order. Yet another variant of the good–evil mix restored is told in *Motherstone* (1985).   NW

HALL, Bernadette (1945–), poet and playwright, was born in Central Otago, has an MA in Classics from University of Otago and teaches at Villa Maria College, Christchurch. She was the 1996 *Burns Fellow at Otago University. Like a number of New Zealand women writers, she did not begin to publish until her 40s. Her first collection of poems, *Heartwood* (1989), was described by Ken *Arvidson as 'the work of a poet of very individual sensibility'. Three subsequent collections, *Of Elephants etc* (1990), *The Persistent Levitator* (1994) and

Still Talking (1997), have cemented her reputation as one of the more distinctive poetic voices to have emerged since the late 1980s. Friendship, love (religious and secular) and the process of writing are recurrent preoccupations in her work, which is characterised by a crisp, often cryptic, lyricism, combined with a visionary intensity. *The Persistent Levitator* was shortlisted for the Poetry Section of the New Zealand Book Awards in 1995. She has also written two plays, *The Clothesline* (1991) and *Glad and the Angels* (1994), and a musical, *Questing* (1995). HRi

HALL, Margaret (1925–), children's novelist, was born and educated in Christchurch, and worked as a librarian there and for the Girls' Nautical Training Corps in England, a unit of which she established in Christchurch. For her work with youth, she was awarded the BEM in 1973. She later moved to Westland and worked for the National Park Board, her interest in the region leading her to write *Black Sands and Golden Years* (1979). Her first children's novel, *After the Earthquake* (1989), is a dramatic, contemporary, family Robinsonade on the West Coast. Her second, *Swag and Tucker* (1993), is a lively historical novel, set in the *gold-rush days of the same area. DH

HALL, Roger (1939–), the most successful playwright of his generation, was born in Essex. The most authoritative account of his life is his own, given in the Radio New Zealand series 'Hallmarks' (1995). He was educated at University College School, Hampstead (1952–55), before following his father into insurance. A desire to write and to act was kindled by his father's talent as an impersonator, frequent family visits to the theatre, especially revues, and by his love of post-war British radio comedies such as 'ITMA' (see Ted *Kavanagh) and 'Hancock's Half Hour'. But the opportunity to do both came only after Hall moved to New Zealand in 1958. He appeared in amateur productions while working (still in insurance) in Wellington in the late 1950s. After a brief return visit to England (via Australia and India) in 1960–62, Hall attended Wellington Teachers' College and then Victoria University, where he completed a BA. At the same time he participated as an actor and scriptwriter in various revues, both on campus and downtown.

He began teaching, at Berhampore School, Wellington, in 1966, and the short stories and plays he wrote for use in the classroom were the beginnings of a prolific output of children's writing which has continued ever since, most of it published either in the *School Journal or by educational specialists Shortland Publications. He returned to Victoria University in 1967 to complete an MA, then resumed teaching at Berhampore, all the while

maintaining his involvement in local theatre, especially revue. His debut as a scriptwriter for television came in 1969, when he collaborated with Joseph *Musaphia on New Zealand's first television comedy series, 'In View of the Circumstances'. Resigning from teaching to become a freelance writer in 1970, he achieved some stage successes as well as television credits in both New Zealand and Australia, but by 1972—now married with one child—he resumed the security of life with a salary in the education sector, this time as editor of *Education* in *School Publications, a job he held until 1975.

He continued his writing for children and for television, including the 'Spotlight' and 'Buck House' series (both 1974). By 1975 he had produced sufficient work to qualify for an *Arts Council travel grant, which took him to England and America. The Eugene O'Neill Drama Workshop in Connecticut proved to be a decisive influence. On his return to New Zealand he wrote *Glide Time*, and saw it progress triumphantly after its Circa (Wellington) première on 11 August 1976. It became the first publication in the Price Milburn–*Victoria University Press series of New Zealand Playscripts.

Glide Time set the pattern for most of Hall's work, a series of gently satirical sketches linked by running gags and the gradual revelation of the characters' generally dismal predicaments. The blend of comedy and pathos probably owes much to Tony Hancock, though Alan Ayckbourn is often cited, as is Chekhov, to whom Hall paid tribute in *A Dream of Sussex Downs* (1986).

In 1977 Hall moved to Dunedin as *Burns Fellow (1977–78), then stayed on as a half-time teaching fellow in the university's English department. He relinquished this position in 1994, publishing his tribute to the university (*Otago, the University*, with photographs by Bill Nichol, 1994), and moving to Auckland early in 1995. Also in 1977 came *Middle Age Spread*, his best-known play, thanks to the film version and a successful West End production. He found it particularly difficult to write. Running a writing workshop at Otago University in 1977 helped him to turn these difficulties to account in *State of the Play*—a play about playwriting. Hall's own favourite, though by no means his most successful play commercially, it premièred at Wellington's Downstage Theatre in 1978.

In 1978–79, reverting to his apprenticeship in revue, he devised two pantomimes, 'Cinderella' and 'Robin Hood', both with music by John *Drummond, in place of Otago's traditional student capping revues, which were subsequently revived under his guidance in 1983. Also revue-like is *Prisoners of Mother England*, a play in fifty-nine short scenes about English immigrants to New Zealand. The title uses the phrase which may be the source for *'pommie' (if the word does indeed come from an acronym POME). Though written as a straight play, since Tony Taylor's inaugural production at Downstage in 1979 *Prisoners of Mother England* has generally been performed with musical interludes. *Fifty-Fifty*, the most dismal of his straight plays and the only one set in England, in a vain attempt to woo English entrepreneurs, followed in 1981, and *Hot Water*, his only true farce, in 1982. Other work at this time included the 'Gliding On' scripts for radio and television and three other radio plays, 'The Quiz', 'Last Summer' and 'Hark Hark the Harp'.

From the time of his arrival in Dunedin, Hall was also very active in community affairs, serving on the New Zealand *Literary Fund and the board of the Fortune Theatre, founding Monitor (an organisation that had considerable influence as a television watchdog, especially in relation to children's programmes), and laying the foundations for what eventually became (in 1989) Dunedin's annual New Zealand Writers' Week. For the inaugural week Hall devised 'Mr Punch', a portrait of Denis *Glover. A certain amount of experimentation is evident in Hall's work of the mid-1980s. In 1983 he collaborated with Philip *Norman (music) and A.K. *Grant (lyrics) as author of the book for *Footrot Flats*, based on Murray Ball's syndicated cartoon strip. The same team produced the equally successful *Love Off the Shelf* (a satire on popular romantic fiction) in 1986. Norman was again Hall's musical partner in the country-and-western spoof *Making It Big* (1991), while *Where Would A Songwriter Be Without Love?* (1995) is a tribute to Norman's music, devised by Hall. For another musical, *The Hansard Show* (1986)—an anthology of New Zealand parliamentary speeches—John *Drummond and Nigel Eastlake provided the music.

A more radical departure from his usual bitter-sweet sitcom formula was the flawed expressionistic one-acter *The Rose* (1981), a thinly veiled attack on New Zealand's Prime Minister of the time, Robert *Muldoon. It was followed by a full-length problem play about home education, *Multiple Choice*, completed at New Mexico State University, Las Cruces, where Hall held a writing fellowship in 1983. After a controversial production in 1984, from which Hall dissociated himself, at Auckland's Mercury Theatre, *Multiple Choice* has been neglected by the professional theatres, and it was no surprise to find Hall subsequently resuming his old style, first with his underrated adaptation of Chekhov's *Three Sisters*, *A Dream of Sussex Downs* (1986), then with a pair of plays written on either side of the 1987 sharemarket crash—*The Share Club* (1987) and *After the Crash* (1988). The characters of these plays were exploited further in the television series, 'Neighbourhood Watch' (1990). A more melancholy stage sitcom, *Conjugal Rites* (1990), spawned two television series, this time for Britain's

Granada television, after a pilot failed to impress TVNZ. In the lighter *Market Forces* (1995) Hall tests the old maxim that 'the more things change, the more they stay the same', depicting the characters of *Glide Time* and 'Gliding On' in the environment of the restructured public service.

While Hall's play's are funny, their comedy is that of sorrowful resilience, like Chekhov's, and of serious social criticism, for all their unfashionable willingness to treat the middle classes with some sympathy. His one-liners can show truth about human manners as well as wit. His characters have sometimes been dismissed as stereotypes, and his female characters have provoked particular criticism. As if to justify himself, he has written two plays for all-female casts: *Social Climbers* (1995), a comedy about a group of women teachers forced to spend three days and nights together in a tramping hut, and *By Degrees*, a more serious study of four women's experience of tertiary education, written for radio in 1992 and adapted for the stage in 1993. He achieved another popular success with *C'mon Black!* (1996), a solo play about a devoted rugby supporter on tour in South Africa, where actor Grant Tilly brilliantly caught the characteristic Hall mix of uproarious comedy, understated pathos and perceptive political and social comment. The play toured successfully, including performance in the Southwark New Zealand Arts Festival, London, and the Edinburgh Festival in 1997. Hall received an Honorary DLitt of Victoria University in 1996 and the Katherine *Mansfield Memorial Fellowship at Menton for 1997. A musical comedy, *Dirty Weekends*, with music by Philip Norman, was performed in 1998.   RCo

HALL, Winifred, see **MALLORY, Clare**; **Oxford University Press**.

HAMILTON, David (1955–), composer, has a large output of vocal and choral works. Though his musical settings are mainly of traditional and European texts, he has turned to New Zealand writers such as James K. *Baxter, Katherine *Mansfield, Denis *Glover and John Charles, as in *These Islands* (1992), four New Zealand songs for unison voices and piano. He has been influenced by American composers such as George Crumb and the minimalists Philip Glass and Steve Reich. He was born in Napier.   JMT

HANFLING, Brian (1939–), is known for his remarkable junior novel, *The Mind Musicians* (1988). Its witty, succinct dialogue and complex layering of realism, mystery, classical and pop music, fantasy other dimensions, explore (for 11 to 13-year-old readers) the balance required in music between interpretation and technique, emotion and intellect, change and preservation. Born in Te Puke and educated at Seddon Memorial TC, Hanfling began a career in banking and after a period overseas now works as a clerk and writer.   DH

HAPIPI, Rore (also published as Rowley Habib, 1935–), of Ngāti Tūwharetoa, born in Oruanui, played a pioneering role in the development of a Māori literature in English. Initially writing short fiction and poetry, his growing interest in drama led on to work for theatre, film and radio. He began writing while training at Ardmore Teachers' College, and his first success was with the short story 'Death in the Mill', which appeared in Te *Ao Hou—for a long time the single significant outlet for his poetry and fiction—in 1956. Over time he has also had sporadic publication in small magazines, some international anthologies, *Landfall and the *NZ Listener; however none of this substantial body of work has been collected. Patrick *Evans argues that Hapipi's early short stories, which reflect a tradition of realist fiction epitomised in the 1950s by *Duggan and *Gee, are the work of a writer 'feeling [his] way towards a tradition of [Pākehā] male realism that inherently excludes [him]'. His later fiction and poetry is more distinctive: 'Fletcher's Mill, Early Mornin' Blues' for example—'Sneakin' on home at 4 in the mornin' / I'm feelin' tired and my mouth is yawnin''—testifies to the suitability of forms of Negro Spiritual to express the experience of urban Māori.

Always in the forefront of Māori struggles towards self-determination, in particular the land protests of the 1970s, Hapipi worked in theatre to promote Māori control of their own affairs by supporting young Māori writers and performers and helping found Te Ika a Maui Players in 1977. Outside readers of Te Ao Hou, Hapipi was known (as Rowley Habib) as author of politically radical dramatic works adapted from earlier works of poetry and prose that reflected his political preoccupations. 'Death of the Land', for example—which was written in 1975 and anthologised in He Reo Hou, 1991—shows affinities with American protest literature of the 1970s as it rehearses debates over the sale of Māori land to Pākehā. Although documenting avarice on both sides the play essentially questions the convolutions of the coloniser's judicial process and endorses the traditional notion that land should be held in trust for future generations. Hapipi was the 1984 holder of the Katherine *Mansfield Memorial Fellowship in Menton.   PM

Happy Colony, The, a novel by Robert *Pemberton dedicated to 'the Workmen of Great Britain' and published in 1854, is constructed as a dialogue between a 'Philosopher' and his 'Learned Friend' followed by an 'Address' by the philosopher to the workmen of Britain; then comes a dialogue between them and him and finally a discourse on education. The argument is that all the countries of Europe and most of their colonies are corrupted by the pursuit of wealth and that only New Zealand (seen as a kind of 'Terra Nullius') offers the opportunity for creating a happy society based on 'labour and perfect education'. The only disadvantage of New Zealand is its proximity to Australia, 'that fatal spot of attraction and confusion, where all the energies of manual labour are exerted to augment the slavery of mankind', the error underlying this slavery being the 'grand philosophical hypothesis' that gold and labour are equivalents. The philosopher proposes to purchase huge areas of land, 'somewhere in the neighbourhood of Taraniki (sic) now called New Plymouth' and to establish a Happy Colony where there is to be no private property and where the equality of people is to be assured by building towns laid out in perfect circles, avoiding 'all crooked lanes, angles, narrow streets, filthy alleys and nasty courts and *impasses*'. No mention is made of the Māori or any claims they might have to land in Taranaki. 'As the object of this philosophy is the perfection of man and all his works, and the development of all his capabilities and divine endowments, the colleges must be placed in the centre of the intended town.' Part Three of the book is a discourse in which the fictional stance is virtually abandoned and in which the 'perfect education' to be pursued in 'the Elysian Academy or Natural University for the Happy Colony to be founded by the workmen of Great Britain in the Island of New Zealand situated in the Pacific Ocean' is described. In fact it emerges that New Zealand is not totally necessary to the enterprise since any place which offers no resistance to circular towns and geometrical colonies would do as well. The academic idealism of the work was the half-ironic starting point of Roger Robinson's essay on New Zealand literature and the universities, 'Colleges for the Happy Colony' in *Landfall 125, 1976.   NW

Hapū is often translated as 'sub-tribe' and is a subdivision of an *iwi. Its size can vary from a few dozen to a few hundred people, all of them claiming descent from a common ancestor, who in turn was descended from the original figure in the iwi. Traditionally, large-scale projects such as building an assembly house (whare rūnanga) or a canoe (*waka) and often the conduct of war were carried out by the hapū. Normally a part of the iwi's territory was recognised as that of the hapū so that they had special hunting, fishing and agricultural rights within it. The leader of the hapū is the rangatira.   NW

HARDING, Ray (1949–), as scriptwriter of several globally distributed television series, is one of the most successful of all New Zealand writers in terms of mass reception of his work (Neil *Finn probably his only rival). Based with Sydney's Channel 7, he has written many instalments of *A Country Practice* (1985–93) and *Neighbours* (1985–89), and about 200 episodes of *Home and Away*, currently watched by an international audience of 68 million for every instalment. He has also written for children's television, including *Mirror, Mirror* and *The New Adventures of Skippy*. By November 1996 he had written a total of 540 episodes of serial and series television, winning one award and three nominations for Australian Writers Guild awards, three Australian Film Institute nominations and one international 'Emmy' nomination (1989). Two television films, *Sisterly Love* (1987) and *I Can't Get Started* (1985), have been screened in the USA and UK as well as Australia and New Zealand. He is also a playwright, two plays having been produced professionally, 'The Weekenders' (1985), performed in Adelaide and at the Shaftesbury Theatre in London's West End, and 'The Importance of Being Jewish' (1986), performed by the Sydney Theatre Company. He won the Theatre Critics' Circle award for best playwright of 1985.

Born in Christchurch, where his father was a publican, and educated at Cashmere HS and University of Canterbury (BA English 1970), Harding spent periods in secondary teaching (at Kaikoura), teaching English as a second language (in South Vietnam, Sydney and elsewhere) and as a commissioned officer in the British army, before writing full-time from 1985, usually on a freelance basis. RR

HARLOW, Michael (1937–), born in the USA of a Greek father and American-Ukrainian mother, travelled extensively in Europe before arriving in New Zealand in 1968. Known primarily for his poetry, which appears in several New Zealand anthologies, he was also in the 1980s an editor of the *Caxton Press poetry series and poetry editor of *Landfall. Harlow first published in New York (*Poems*, 1965), in Greece (*Events, Greece, 1967–1974*, 1974) and in England (*The Book of Quiet*, 1974). Subsequent titles reveal his Eurocentrism: *Nothing But Switzerland and Lemonade* (1980), the first book of prose poems in New Zealand, *Today Is the Piano's Birthday* (1981), *Vlaminck's Tie* (1985) and *Giotto's Elephant* (1991), shortlisted in the 1992 Book Awards. Harlow's sensibility is also identified by a whimsical, questioning persona, and a persistent engagement with the workings of the unconscious. Operating through strategies of defamiliarisation, and predisposed to emotional ambiguity, his voice often appears enigmatic. But seemingly idiosyncratic elements in his verse—play with poetic conceits, fantasy and dream elements, sexual innuendo—may be underpinned by psychological insight and a sense of the unconscious point of view. His poems have been called 'personally colourful if rarely confessional'. Consistently independent of local literary models, Harlow 'found' materials, and he works in other genres such as the prose poem, performance piece, dream poem and musical performance. His collaboration as librettist with the New Zealand composer Kit *Powell, now living in Switzerland, is extensive: Powell's scores appear in *Vlaminck's Tie*; their pieces include *Texts for Composition*, performed in Christchurch and Switzerland (in German) in 1981; *Nelson Songs* in Laufen and Zürich in 1986; *Les Episodes, Conversation with Questions*, commissioned by the New Zealand Symphony Orchestra to celebrate its fortieth anniversary, in Wellington in 1987, and *The Tower of Babel*, commissioned for performance at the Kykart II Festival, St Petersburg in 1995. He also wrote the script for the short film *Heavy Traffic in the Dark* (1991) (in collaboration with Stephanie McDonald) and edited *Christchurch Teachers College Centennial 1977* (1977). Harlow has been awarded *Literary Fund Bursaries (1977, 1990) and the Katherine *Mansfield Memorial Fellowship (1986). He lives in Christchurch where he practises as a Jungian psychotherapist, and is completing a book, 'Cucumbers and Mad Apples'. JW

HARPER, Theodore Acland and **Winifred**, both New Zealanders, wrote children's fiction in the 1920s–30s from their later home in Portland, Oregon. Theodore spent much of his young life on horseback in the Canterbury sheep ranges when there was 'scarcely a fence on the land'. Graduating as a mining engineer, he followed that profession in Arizona, Alaska, Siberia and Central America, marrying Winifred Hunter-Brown in about 1905. Some editions of their books identify Theodore as author 'in collaboration with Winifred Harper', but joint authorship is probably the accurate description (and is so accepted by Betty *Gilderdale in *A Sea Change*). Their titles, usually published in the USA, include *The Mushroom Boy* (1924), *Siberian Gold* (1927), *The Janitor's Cat* (Sydney, 1928), *Kubrick the Outlaw* (1928) and *Forgotten Gods* (1935). The two set in New Zealand are *Windy Island* (1934) and *Seventeen Chimneys* (1938, by Theodore Harper). Both deal with some sympathy with Bob Cornish, growing up on the opposite side of the world from his cultural heritage and eventually coming to terms with his colonial identity. The Harpers' writing has the strength of deep knowledge of places and situations, and of imaginative sympathy with situations like Bob's, though it tends also to didacticism and to rely on stock characters and formula adventures. PN

HARRIS, Dick (1887–1926), was a poet of lyric melancholy and considerable technical accomplishment. Mostly publishing in newspapers and weekly journals, he produced one volume, *Monodies* (1910), and after his suicide Pat ★Lawlor 'gathered together' his poems in *The Poetry of Dick Harris* (Sydney, 1927). An introduction by Mona ★Tracy pays tribute to his 'wistful harmonies' and descriptive 'word-painting', while Lawlor's personal note recalls Harris's 'subtle wit', 'tempestuous laughter' and 'immense' talent as a storyteller among his friends in Wellington. The poems include skilful use of forms like pantoum, triolet and villanelle, and of demanding metre: 'There's a noise of fretful voices where the troubled stream is calling, / In a turbulence unwonted through its stony bed impelled….' The neo-Tennysonian plangency of lines like 'There, scarves of silver fringe the purple deep' or 'Nothing is stable, nothing stays—/ As listless leaves are we, / Adrift upon Time's windy ways / Across Eternity', admired by Tracy and Lawlor, has since been mocked by commentators from ★Fairburn to Patrick ★Evans. But tastes change, and Frank ★Morton could with some justice describe Harris as the finest lyrist New Zealand had then produced. He is represented in ★*Kowhai Gold* (1930) and also has a story in O.N. ★Gillespie's *New Zealand Short Stories* (1930).

RR

HARRIS, Norman (1940–), wrote in the 1960s some of New Zealand's best sports books, notably the biography of Jack ★Lovelock, still unmatched for its drama and insight into that enigmatic near-mythic figure. Born in Te Kowhai and educated at Hamilton BHS, where he was a versatile sportsman, Harris worked in teaching and broadcasting before becoming a sports reporter with the *New Zealand Herald*, 1960–65. Reporting on the golden years of athletics, he won the Baird Award for sports writing in 1964 and produced such successful book-form records as *Silver Fern at Perth* (1962) and *Silver Fern at Tokyo* (1964). His most significant work is in historical and biographical narrative, in *Lap of Honour* (1963), *The Legend of Lovelock* (1964) and *The Lonely Breed* (1967), all of which combine acute psychological perception with vivid reportage, and so communicate the inner as well as the outward drama of sport with rare power. They led the *Times Literary Supplement* to describe him as the outstanding writer on athletics in the English language.

Harris moved to London as an aspiring writer in 1965. His autobiographical *Champion of Nothing* (1965) was well ahead of its time in dramatising the personal significance and rewards of participation in sport among those not gifted for success, and in getting convincingly into the mind and emotions of the competitor. A virtually stream-of-consciousness narrative, it is a kind of 'Rosencrantz and Guildenstern Are Dead' of sports history, with legendary figures like Snell and Lydiard glimpsed shadowily in the background. From 1969 Harris wrote on sports for the London *Sunday Times*, also initiating and organising that paper's hugely successful National Fun Run, 1978–93. A well-received book on English soccer, *The Charlton Brothers* (1972), and an athletics anthology, *Running: The Power and Glory* (1986), have been his major British publications in book form. He now lives at Barnes near London and writes primarily for the *Observer*, mainly on cricket, receiving accolades for his writing from the doyen of English cricket writers, E.W. Swanton, among others. RR

HARRIS, Ross (1945–), composer, was born in Amberley, North Canterbury. He has devoted a large part of his creative energies to the writing of opera. His setting of a libretto by Witi ★Ihimaera in the opera *Waituhi* (1985) aroused national interest following its première in the State Opera House, Wellington, amidst impressive Māori ritual. Based on incidents from Ihimaera's novel ★*Whanau*, *Waituhi* deals with contemporary Māori issues such as land disputes, the drift of the young to the city, the loss of traditional values, combined with a central love theme involving rivalries and jealousies. Harris used the traditional operatic framework of arias, duets, ensemble pieces and choruses, interspersing them with ★haka, ★poi, action song and ★waiata. He merged aspects of traditional Māori chant with contemporary Māori and European harmonic idioms, both tonal and electro-acoustic. Most of his singers were untrained Māori. Harris's earlier works based on Māori culture have included *Kia Mau te Rongo* (1983), a setting of a well-known passage from Corinthians, in Māori, for synthesiser, drone and voices. New Zealand poets he has set to music have included Denis ★Glover and Alistair ★Campbell. In 1989 Harris completed Tanz der Schwäne ('Dance of the Swans'), again to a libretto by Ihimaera, which recounts the dramas and rejection suffered by a young German nurse in a provincial New Zealand town after World War 2. Its première took place in Wellington in 1993. His latest project is an opera on *King Lear*. JMT

HARRISON, Craig (1942–), was born in Leeds, Yorkshire, and emigrated in 1966 to a position at Massey University, where he is now senior lecturer in English, specialising in fine arts, film and media scriptwriting. He has exploited the tension between his Yorkshire roots and his adopted country in several works, including a comic novel *Ground Level* (written in 1972, but not published until 1981), a play (quarried from the novel manuscript and bearing the same name) which won the J.C. Reid Award in 1974, a second play as yet unperformed ('Home Truths') and a spin-off television series, *Joe and Koro* (1976–77).

In all these works the principal New Zealand character (Koro) is Māori. In another suite of works written over the same period Harrison took a more serious look at Māori issues, anticipating the activism which swept New Zealand from the late 1970s. Again these works all stem from a novel, *Broken October*, which was published in 1976 but written some five years earlier. From this Harrison developed a short story, 'The Whites of Their Eyes' (1971), a play of the same name which won the Theatre Federation Prize in 1974 and was performed at Unity Theatre (Wellington) in the same year, and another play *Tomorrow Will Be a Lovely Day*. This won the Elmwood Players' Jubilee Prize in 1974, was published in 1975 and had its sole professional production at Mercury Theatre in 1978. Other plays from the 1970s which explore ethnic issues are 'Perfect Strangers' (performed at Downstage Theatre in 1976, and reworked and published as *White Lies* in 1994), 'Treed' (a one-acter performed by the Elmwood Players in 1976) and 'Western Powers' (as yet unperformed).

Although plays constituted his most conspicuous early successes, Harrison has always regarded himself first and foremost as a writer of fiction, and, with a few exceptions (such as 'Hearts of Gold', a play based on Somerset Maugham's story 'Rain', performed at Bats Theatre in 1983, and a one-acter, 'Amateurs and Professionals', which won the Western Players Award in 1981), he has largely eschewed the stage in recent years. His most celebrated novel is a work of *science fiction, *The Quiet Earth* (1982), better known to many in Geoff Murphy's film adaptation (1985). The title comes from Yorkshire (the last paragraph of *Wuthering Heights*), but the setting is New Zealand, and the plot takes to an extreme the motif of *'Man Alone'. The central character appears to be the sole survivor of some cosmic catastrophe, although a second man (a Māori) makes an appearance in due course, and a Samoan woman (mute, as a result of a serious injury) joins them near the end. The novel's surprise ending suggests that—like William Golding's *Pincher Martin*—the whole story is an hallucination in the mind of a dying (or dead) scientist, who is evidently doomed to relive a series of variations on the self-absorption which characterised his life. His dead son's autism reflects this self-absorption, while the more passionate temperaments of his Polynesian companions provide a foil to it.

Days of Starlight (1988) is another science fiction novel, less complex than *The Quiet Earth* in design, but equally well crafted. Again the clash between human complexity and scientific autism is examined (with the help of allusions to T.S. Eliot's 'Love Song of J. Alfred Prufrock'), and again Harrison invests the struggle with racial overtones, a black American serving as a foil to the Prufrockian white scientist. The satiric novel *Grievous Bodily* (1991) also features a mysterious black (African) in a minor role, but the character has no obvious thematic or symbolic function. Indeed the book as a whole is innocent of any deep thematic significance; it is a brilliant farce, somewhat similar to *Ground Level* in tone, but markedly more sophisticated in execution. It is New Zealand's funniest university novel and full of zanily astute observations of small-town life. Harrison has published more than a dozen short stories, many of them prizewinners in national competitions, and—in addition to 'Joe and Koro'—has had several radio and television plays broadcast.   RCo

HART-SMITH, William (1911–90), was the first poet to be published by Denis *Glover at the *Caxton Press and an equally active writer in *Australia, where he was even one of the nationalistic group called Jindyworobaks. In interviews he tended to avoid the inevitable question of whether he was a New Zealand or an Australian writer, saying, for example, that he remained 'the English boy who arrived with his parents in Auckland in 1924'. The interviewer (and friend) of the poet commented that 'In later life Bill Hart Smith was to become a gonad nomad, pulled back and forth across the Tasman by the wonders of the next woman.'

His response to the Australian desert environment was sensuous and intense. The many poems he set there have a slightly surprised air, as if he is astonished at liking something so exotic. Nonetheless after serving in the Australian forces in World War 2, Hart-Smith returned to New Zealand, in the company of a famous woman pianist. Their dramatic separation occurred in Christchurch, and there he stayed for some twenty years in the advertising business and as a teacher. During those years he wrote vigorous landscape poems set mainly in the Southern Alps. Many were collected in *On the Level* (1950). That first Caxton Press book was *Christopher Columbus* (1948), of which E.H. *McCormick has said: 'So successfully has he avoided the trap of romantic inflation that he has almost reduced the epic to nullity.' Viewed as a poet of dramatic landscapes rather than as an epic one, Hart-Smith can still impress.

In 1962 he moved to Australia and in 1978 back to Auckland. His own comment on these changes of residence and partner was, 'The poetry, that's all that matters. The rest is just messing around.' NW

Hawaiki is the ancestral home of the Māori people, not geographically definable, indeed largely mythological and spiritual, yet with a strong sense of reality to people who speak of it. The first visitor to New Zealand from Hawaiki was *Kupe. Later, it became overpopulated, war broke out and people remembered Kupe's voyage. They came, according to legend, in a fleet of 'canoes' (see *Waka).

Early interpretations tried to see the Hawaiki stories as in some sense historical, but in the Macmillan Brown Lectures at the University of Canterbury in 1983, published in 1985 as *Hawaiki: A New Approach to Māori Tradition*, Margaret *Orbell argued that it is much more fruitful to approach them as religious literary texts, since although Māori 'formerly believed Hawaiki to be a real place, we must now regard it as a paradisial land similar to other such lands spoken of in religious traditions: similar, for example, to the Garden of Eden in the Christian tradition.' She explores narratives from many tribal areas, pointing out similarities and differences, and constantly making the point that earlier interpretations limited the force of the stories by seeking the element of historical 'truth' they might 'conceal', whereas if they are seen as expositions of religious 'truth' their value is much greater as 'powerful religious narratives which shaped human lives and made the world meaningful'. Orbell's book is an important step in making us aware of Māori traditions as religious and literary texts—as imaginative interpretations of the world. NW

HAWES, Peter (1947–), is a playwright, scriptwriter and novelist. He was born in Westport and educated at University of Canterbury (BA 1969), then working as a television reporter and travelling to Spain. He lived there for four years and wrote—in Spanish (with the help of a translator who won a literary award for the project)—a best-selling novel about the Spanish Inquisition: *La Hoguera (The Bonfire)*, published in 1974.

Returning to New Zealand in 1975, he resumed work for television, as a researcher and journalist, and as a scriptwriter for various series, including 'A Week of It', 'Fraggle Rock', 'Yours for the Asking' and 'Against the Law'. In the early 1980s he began to write for the stage, quickly producing a string of absurdist plays: 'Alf's General Theory of Relativity' (first professional performance at the Court Theatre, 1981), 'Ptolemy's Dip' (Court, 1982) and 'Armageddon Revisited' (Mercury, 1983). Closer to realism (but still full of surprises) are 'Goldie: A Good Joke', a portrait of the early New Zealand painter (Downstage, 1987), '1946 The Boat Train',

which examines the effect of the World War 2 on the lives of four women (Christchurch Arts Network, 1991) and 'Aunt Daisy' (Downstage, 1989), a portrait of the New Zealand radio personality of the 1950s, with music by 6 Volts. 'The 1944 Olympic Games' (one-act) remains unperformed, as do two full-length plays, 'A Higher Form of Killing' (about Ernest Rutherford) and 'The Inquisition Dies' (developed from material in *La Hoguera*).

In 1995 Hawes published his first novel in English, *Tasman's Lay*, an inventive and irreverent account of Abel *Tasman's discovery of New Zealand. This was quickly followed by *Leapfrog with Unicorns* (1996), a satirical work based on material gathered in the mid-1980s, when he was the associate director for a Barry Barclay film (*The Neglected Miracle*), about the ways in which multinational corporations control the world's food resources, to the detriment of many third-world economies.

On the evidence of his novels and plays, Hawes emerges as perhaps New Zealand's foremost current exponent of the comedy of ideas. But, always willing to diversify, he has also turned his hand from time to time to children's books and to acting (in both his own and others' plays). RCo

Hawk Press (1975–83) was a private press established by the poet and printer Alan *Loney and operated by him in a variety of locations in or near Christchurch and Wellington. Initially the press was located at Taylors Mistake (1975–76), then in Sumner (1977), Paraparaumu (1977–78), Day's Bay (1978) and Eastbourne (1978–83). In a 1976 checklist Hawk Press was described as 'a private printer of poetry in limited editions, where all books are designed, handset, printed & handsewn by Alan Loney. The aim is simply to produce books appropriate to content.' A later checklist (December 1990) noted under the heading 'Hawk Press Poetry 1975–1983': 'These books were printed on an Arab treadle platen, with machine made papers. The handset types were Perpetua & Centaur, and the pages were sewn into card with a printed wrap-around cover. Some twenty titles were made in this way.' Normally 200 to 300 copies of each book were printed, an exception being *Hello: Poems* by the American poet Robert *Creeley, which came out of his New Zealand tour in 1976; 750 copies of this were printed, plus fifty signed and numbered by the poet. Other poets included in the series were (in chronological sequence) Ian *Wedde, Stephen *Oliver, Loney, Alan *Brunton, Graham *Lindsay, Rhys Pasley, Russell *Haley, David Miller, Anne Donovan, Murray *Edmond, Joanna Margaret *Paul, Martin Harrison, Bill *Manhire, Bob *Orr, Michael *Harlow, Elizabeth *Smither, Ted Jenner, Pascal Burton and Roger Horrocks. Hawk Press also printed occasional books on commission. From 1979 the press diverged into more elaborate productions and into material other than contemporary poetry. *Dawn/Water* (1979) was a collaboration between Loney as printer and designer, Manhire as poet and Andrew Drummond as artist. In the same year Loney printed J.C. ★Beaglehole's essay *The Death of Captain Cook* for the ★Alexander Turnbull Library to mark the bicentenary of ★Cook's death, and in 1982 Beaglehole's *The New Zealand Scholar*, both these were printed on damped hand-made paper on a handpress, as was *11.2.80 On Creation* by Edgar Mansfield (1981), consisting of texts and drawings by a famous bookbinder. Fittingly, the last Hawk Press title was *Breaking the Bones* (1983), which combined a verse text by Loney with typographic multi-coloured prints, and came closest to fulfilling his William Blake–like conception of 'making a whole thing, from writing to book, as a single creative procedure'. See also ★Black Light Press and ★Holloway Press.   PS

HAWKEN, Dinah (1943–), is a poet who combines powerful inwardness with international awareness. She was born in Hawera, trained as a physiotherapist, psychotherapist and social worker in New Zealand and the United States and is currently a student counsellor at Victoria University. Most of the poems in her first collection, *It Has No Sound and Is Blue* (1987), were written during a three-year period in New York in the mid-1980s while she was studying for a Master of Fine Arts in Creative Writing at Brooklyn College and working with the homeless and mentally ill. The volume's centrepiece, 'Writing Home', is a sequence of sixteen unrhymed sonnets, formally modelled on James K. ★Baxter's ★*Jerusalem Sonnets*, but focusing on women's issues, specifically the need to achieve a state of inner balance in a world under threat. Other notable literary influences include Wallace Stevens, John Ashbery and Adrienne Rich. The collection won the Best First Time Published Poet section of the Commonwealth Poetry Prize for 1987 and at once established Hawken locally as one of the most distinctive new voices of her generation. *Small Stories of Devotion* (1991, UK edn 1995), described by Hawken as 'the diary of a woman it takes time to love', was equally well received. Closer to prose poetry, this second collection fuses dream, myth and the everyday into a series of meditations about female spirituality. *Water, Leaves, Stones* (1995), with its wary celebration of the natural world, further develops Hawken's central concerns.   HRi

HAWKESWORTH, John (1715?–73), was a man of letters selected by the Admiralty to write up British voyages to the 'South Seas'. The result was work of vigorous, hypnotically readable prose superbly bound into three massive volumes: *An Account of the Voyages undertaken by the Order of His Present Majesty for making Discoveries in the Southern Hemisphere, and successively performed by Commodore Byron, Captain Wallis, Captain Carteret and Captain Cook … (1773)*. These masterpieces of the printer's and binder's craft have come in for much criticism from historians for their 'elaboration' of the seamen's journals.

The journals of all four seamen and of Joseph ★Banks were available to Hawkesworth, who turned them into the prose one might expect of a friend of Dr Johnson. He did not hesitate to add philosophical commentary and use classical references and vivid imagery in place of the original 'plain prose'. He wrote in the first person, so that the words seem to be by ★Cook and the others, and differences between four 'voices' are subsumed in Hawkesworth's own style.

The work was immediately controversial. Alexander Dalrymple pointed out that the seamen were maintaining 'silence' rather than 'acquiescence' about its inaccuracies. The accounts of Polynesian mores led to attacks on the book's morality, Joseph Cockfield writing in 1773 that 'our Women may find in Dr. Hawkesworth's Book stronger Incitements to vicious Indulgences than the most intriguing French Novel could present to their Imaginations'.

Hawkesworth's version of Cook's first voyage was the standard one, until J.C. ★Beaglehole's meticulous editions (1955–). Most historians share the view of Geoffrey Moorehead (1966) that now 'few people will bother to read Hawkesworth's volumes. The rough sailor's account is incomparably the better of the two.' But the history of ideas has much to learn from Hawkesworth: he placed the voyages in the philosophical context of the day more clearly than Cook could. His book can even be read as a first-person novel, the first in a long tradition of tales of the magnanimous seaman encountering 'natives', and, for good or ill, it was an early example of the theory of the power of 'Pax Britannica', which underlay the colonisation of much of the world, including New Zealand.   NW

HAY, Catherine (1910–), is the pseudonym of Ivy Rose Hughes, who was born in Te Kuiti and grew up in the King Country, but later lived in Auckland. Her first story was published in the *Daily Mirror* when she was 14 and she published many more in such magazines as *Home Journal, Life Digest, Auckland Weekly News* as well as on radio. She said that she drew on the poverty of the ★Depression years to create the atmosphere of pioneer days in her historical novels. The first of these was *Julia Deverell* (1962). *Halo Round the Moon* (1964) is a Gothic tale centred on a teenage girl set in the 1870s. *A Falcon*

Rising (1960) is set at the time of the New Zealand ★Wars and *The Barrier* (1968) is set on Great Barrier Island. She also wrote *The Singing Waters* (1963) and *The House at Stormy Waters* (1970).   NW

Hazard Press was begun in 1986 in Christchurch by Quentin Wilson to help singer/song-writer Andrew Fagan, of the Mockers, publish his first book of poems, *Salt Rhythms*. With the book's success, a press was launched that now publishes over fifteen titles a year. Wilson's major literary accomplishment is the Hazard Poets series, edited by Rob ★Jackaman and ★Australian poet and academic Philip Mead, which has published established and new poets of both countries to critical acclaim, in beautifully designed volumes featuring original artworks and four-colour covers. For logistical reasons, publications are heavily weighted in New Zealand's favour, though the four Australian titles by Jill Jones, Peter Hay, Louise Crisp and David ★Herkt have been highly praised. Among the New Zealand titles are collections by Rob ★Allan, Alistair Te Ariki ★Campbell, Riemke ★Ensing, Rhondda ★Greig, Jackaman, Helen ★Jacobs, Graham ★Lindsay, Alan ★Loney, Mike ★Minehan, James ★Norcliffe and Stephen ★Oliver. Hazard has also published Alistair Campbell's *Pocket Collected Poems*, which was shortlisted for the 1997 Montana New Zealand Book Awards. Wilson has also instituted a short fiction series under the editorship of David Ling and Patrick ★Evans.   PM

Heart of the Bush, The (1910), a novel by Edith Searle ★Grossmann, tells, in its first part, of the dilemma of Adelaide Borlase, who has to choose between a rather effete Englishman, with the prospect of a prosperous and cultured life in London, and a sun-tanned New Zealand farmer. It is a variant of the town-and-country theme familiar from centuries of English literature, and is representative of a strong thread running through New Zealand literature, especially of the period 1890–1914. Adelaide decides in favour of Dennis, the warm-hearted farmer.

The qualities of Horace and Dennis are almost schematically contrasted with each other: reserved–spontaneous, civilised–barbarous, cultured–philistine, intellectual–emotional, spiritual–materialistic, artistic–natural, effeminate–masculine, aristocratic–working-class, polite–blunt, leisured–industrious, fashionable– timeless, believing in 'honour'—believing in 'honesty'. Although Horace is effeminate and Dennis masculine, it is Dennis who treats women as his equals, and this turns Adelaide's heart, in exchanges such as: '"You do not really want to take lessons from a girl, Mr. McDiarmid?" "Why not? ... don't you bother about my dignity if I don't."'

Interestingly, New Zealand critics have focused almost entirely on this first part of the book. In Part 2 England is almost forgotten and the image of New Zealand is extended beyond the social to the natural: the bush, into the heart of which the newly-weds travel. The journey is presented as a sexual and spiritual journey of discovery for both. But the highest peaks of the Southern Alps—the peaks of married bliss—are reserved for the ★'Man Alone'. While Dennis climbs them, Adelaide falls into 'a hollow gap of stones'. The chapter is entitled ★'Hine-Nui-te-Po', but, with a restraint that marks this book off from her others, Grossmann leaves the reader to find out the sexual-spiritual-mortal symbolism of the title—this part of the book is dense with sexual symbolism, but only for the attentive reader.

Part 3 returns to the social dimension. Having been united in the natural world, the lovers are now torn apart by colonial materialism, which Dennis of necessity embraces, while Adelaide starts hankering for England again: 'the frozen meat trade was quite beyond her.' There is a transition phase in which Dennis is aroused by Adelaide to value England and 'art', while she turns more to New Zealand values. Given at last the opportunity to travel she says, 'Do you think I would go away to Europe and leave my lover working here?' The book ends with reconciliation and contentment.   NW

Hemlock was the irregular publication of the Canterbury University Socratic Society, published 1957–70. It featured articles on philosophical, political, theological and literary subjects by contributors such as J.G.A. Pocock and Elsie ★Locke.   SH

HENDERSON, Kennaway (1879–1960), was the founder and editor of ★*Tomorrow* in 1935. A gifted cartoonist and caricaturist, he worked for newpapers in New Zealand and Australia. His earlier paintings and drawings were delicate, fanciful and of a wry humour; but from the time of his imprisonment as a conscientious objector in World War 1 his satire became more severe and even savage, both in his drawings and in his commentaries. In personal terms Denis ★Glover described him as 'the nicest, quietest kindliest man in the country'. Co-founders of *Tomorrow* were Frederick ★Sinclaire and H. Winston ★Rhodes, both holding pacifist and left-wing socialist convictions similar to Henderson's own. He contributed scores of squibs, lampoons and short articles, most of them illustrated. The journal was closed in May 1940, following the outbreak of World War 2. Various collections of his work were published: *Fun* (1903), *New Zealand Illustrated Annual* (1907–17), *Quips and Caricatures* (1915), *Cartoons from 'Tomorrow'* (1942) and *Fools' Carnival* (1949). Rhodes wrote about

Henderson in two articles, 'The Beginning of Tomorrow', in *New Zealand Monthly Review, August–September 1979, and a full-length study, Kennaway Henderson (1988).   RCp

HENDERSON, Michael (1942–), wrote one of the key books of the *Vietnam War era and of the 'new fiction' of the 1970s, the novella The Log of a Superfluous Son (1975). Described by Vincent *O'Sullivan as 'our one fine political fable', its complex experimental verbal textures convey the memories and emotions of a young man's passage to independence while working on a cattle-boat from New Zealand to Korea. At the time of Vietnam and the height of influence of Catch-22, the voyage is pointedly allegorical of New Zealand's record of herding its young men off to foreign wars for basically commercial motives. The most powerful episode is a scene of Guadalcanal surrealistically littered with the debris of wars, visited on the day of the Massacre of the Innocents. The other emphasis, a youthful critique of the establishment values of social conformity, marriage, material comfort and obeisance to Britain, depends heavily on satiric caricature, especially of Nelson College. The linguistic virtuosity offers an alternative energy but the story's assertion of freedom is weakened by the ending, its central character disoriented, whisky-sodden and still obsessing about Nelson College.

Born and educated in Nelson, Henderson graduated in law at Canterbury University (also excoriated in Log) and was a career diplomat before subscribing to the other conformity of the 1970s as an experimental writer. He lived in USA 1974–80, including a period at the Iowa Writers' Workshop, and then in Australia, returning to New Zealand in 1982. His other book is The Lie of the Land (1991), a collection of short fictions, some of which had appeared in *Islands, *NZ Listener and journals in USA and Canada. Like the novella, they consist largely of dialogue and are thin on narrative, winning high praise from reviewers for 'the power and possibility of words' (Andrew Mason) and 'masterly control of language' (Chris *Else). Variants of colloquial idiom are painstakingly reproduced, with malapropisms often prominent in a way that seems literary by comparison with the vernacular of, say, Gordon *Slatter or Alan *Duff. The most apparently innovatory of the sixteen stories, 'Freedom's Ramparts', is a reprinted extract from Log, though this is not acknowledged. Henderson lives as 'part-time writer' at Motueka.   RR

HENDERSON, Paul, pseudonym for Ruth *France.

Henry Ancrum: A Tale of the Last War in New Zealand (1872), novel, see **War literature: New Zealand Wars**.

HENTY, G.A., see **War literature: New Zealand Wars**.

'Her First Ball', a short story by Katherine *Mansfield, was written in July 1921 as one of six stories commissioned by the Sphere, in which it was published in November of that year. It was subsequently included in Mansfield's third collection, The Garden Party and Other Stories (1922). The whereabouts of the MS is unknown. The experience of a naive 18-year-old country girl, Leila, at her first dance is characteristically presented in interior monologue interspersed with the direct speech of secondary characters. The epiphanic excitement of the first part of the story ('she thought breathlessly, "How heavenly; how simply heavenly!"') changes to distress and fear after she has danced with 'the fat man' who has been going to dances for over thirty years and who prophesies 'you can't hope to last anything like as long as that'. Leila leaves the dance temporarily but forgets her distress when dancing with her next partner. The ball as rite of passage from Edenic childhood into an adulthood fraught with the responsibility of knowledge and experience makes this a popular introductory piece at school level. The rite-of-passage theme links the story with 'The *Garden Party'. According to *Alpers, Mansfield was not entirely happy with it, writing in the margin of the now lost manuscript 'All that I write … is on the border of the sea.… I want to put all my force behind it, but somehow, I cannot.' He characterises the six Sphere stories, written to help pay medical bills, as 'harming [Mansfield's] critical reputation'. However (unlike 'Sixpence', 'Mr and Mrs Dove', 'An Ideal Family' or 'Marriage à la Mode') 'Her First Ball' and 'The *Voyage' remain popular and have thematic and technical qualities in common with some of Mansfield's finest work.   SSa

Here & Now was 'an Independent Monthly Review' issued from Auckland 1949–57 by an editorial panel that (at least at first) included A.R.D. *Fairburn, M.K. *Joseph and Bob *Lowry. Mostly political or economic commentary, largely with a left-wing emphasis, it had considerable overseas content, partly through contributions by writers such as Rewi *Alley, John Kennedy and Greville *Texidor then living abroad. Striking now, for such a journal in 1951, is the almost total absence of discussion of the *Waterfront Strike: 'Owing to the very wide powers taken by the Government … we are unable to comment on what appears to be the most important issue of the day', said Number 6 (March 1951). Occasional literary content included poems by Keith *Sinclair, Kendrick *Smithyman and Anton *Vogt, fiction by David *Ballantyne and O.E. *Middleton, and irreverent commentaries by Fairburn on subjects from the state health service to the New Zealand Sunday. Some of the best work was the film reviewing in early issues by M.K. Joseph and later Isobel *Andrews. Book reviews were sparse, but Dan *Davin on *I Saw in My Dream and Allen *Curnow on the first two issues of *New Zealand Poetry Yearbook were memorable, the latter for his adroitness in painting Louis *Johnson's new direction as merely 'not so remote … from the spirit of *Kowhai Gold'. RR

HERKT, David (1955–) is a New Zealand–born poet who lives in Melbourne, where he works as an HIV/ AIDS educator. Herkt's poetry was widely praised when it first appeared in periodicals and small press publications, and his poem sequences 'Satires' and 'Neolithic', along with the unusual prose poetry of 'Hooded in Darkness: The Letters of Robert Schwartzhelm to Wolfgang von Tiefurt 1802–1808' were awarded Australia's Wesley Michel Wright poetry prize in 1989. Rob O'Neill (*Quote Unquote, June 1995) described 'Satires' as 'shocking and exhilarating and driven by one of the most sexually forceful and amoral narrative voices I've encountered anywhere'. These three sequences join 'Notes from a Plague Year' and 'The Last Delirium of Arthur Rimbaud' to make up the five parts of Herkt's first major collection, The Body of Man (1994). Herkt's poetry reveals a range of literary influences—from early-nineteenth-century *German literature to *Australia's renowned hoax poet Ern Malley—but its problematising of masculinity and heterosexuality allows it a degree of thematic uniqueness. 'By refusing any complacent phallocentric assumptions of universality,' argues Kathleen Mary Fallon, 'Herkt has effected a strategic expulsion allowing different processes, questions, reading positions to take centre stage' (1995). PM

HERVEY, J.R. (1889–1958), born in Invercargill and educated in Christchurch, was an Anglican clergyman during the period 1915–38, retiring through ill health. He served as vicar at Sheffield, Temuka and Shirley. His 'Salute to Youth' and 'War Refugee' won first and first-equal prizes in the long and short poems sections of the New Zealand *Centennial Literary Competition of 1940. Published in a wide range of New Zealand and Australian journals, and in Poetry Quarterly (London), his verse was collected in four *Caxton Press books: Selected Poems (1940), New Poems (1942), Man on a Raft: More Poems (1949), and She Was My Spring (1954). In a memorial tribute to Hervey, published in the eighth *New Zealand Poetry Yearbook (1959), Louis *Johnson judged him the best New Zealand poet of his generation. The verdict is not unreasonable. Hervey's style

owed something to the mature Yeats and something to Auden and other British poets of the 1930s, while also harking back to Donne, Herbert and the seventeenth-century metaphysicals. It is cerebral and contemplative, but carries the true voice of feeling when the abstractions mingle with clearly visualised images or boldly dramatised situations.

Hervey's poetic manner remains fairly consistent from volume to volume: there is little technical development. He deals mainly in traditional metres and in rhymed stanzas, though often the latter are makeshift concoctions of longer and shorter lines. She Was My Spring contains several Italian sonnets. But he can also make effective use of a fluid free verse haunted by the ghost of iambics. A trademark is the unexpected polysyllabic (and often Latinate) epithet or noun, linked to something more familiar: 'immaculate arch', 'curtains of hebetude', 'the … simpering plain', 'death's habiliment', 'runnels of renovation', 'caught in cascading trivialities'. He also packs meaning into compound adjectives, such as 'pomp-pauperised', 'heavy-lidded' (applied to the 'year'), 'history-ridden'. Three lines from 'Variations on a Theme of John Donne' will illustrate his peculiar dense rhetoric. The poem has an epigraph from Donne's 'An Anatomy of the World': 'only death adds to our length, nor are we grown / In stature to be men till we are none'. Hervey meditates on the nature of man with this text as his theme, arriving at the thought: 'Migratory, he shall seek and find pastures / Pretending wealth, / But through the wound of death shall he emerge / On the lush levels.' The biblical echoes are strong, and there are hints of the liturgical in the rhythms and in the third line's inversion of natural word order. But the imagery might also appeal to a Canterbury hill-country sheep-farmer. 'Migratory' gives the notion of the spiritual wanderer a special New Zealand slant. 'Pretending' carries its full weight of 'laying a false claim'. The alliterating 'lush levels' is a mint-new formulation, at once surprising and exact.

Legends, anecdotes, literature, historical snippets, news items, and major contemporary events may provoke Hervey's poetic ruminations, but he also celebrates the domestic and pastoral routine. She Was My Spring, dedicated 'to the dear memory of Ethel, my wife', contains moving tributes. 'I have made friends with time although I have seen / His fingers close on many a meek treasure', he wrote in Man on a Raft. That is a difficult 'friendship' to sustain: Hervey's poetry records the struggle. A fine pencil portrait of Hervey by Leo *Bensemann was included as frontispiece to New Poems and is reproduced in *Landfall 44 (1957). MPJ

Hilda books (school stories), see **GARRARD, Phillis**.

HILL, Alfred (1870–1960), composer, conductor, violinist, violist and teacher, was born in Melbourne. Trained in Leipzig from 1887 to 1891, he played a leading role in late-nineteenth-century New Zealand and Australian musical life, setting many of the works of his contemporaries when he sought literary texts. The cantata *Hinemoa* (1896), for instance, was written by the young poet and journalist Arthur *Adams. Hill collaborated with Adams again in his romantic opera *Tapu* (1902–03) and utilised some of the fruits of his own collection of Māori themes in such internationally successful songs as 'Waiata Poi' and 'Waiata Maori' in the early years of the century. Alfred *Domett provided the source of the Māori cantata for soloists, chorus and orchestra, *Tawhaki* (1895), and John Youlin Burch, an Auckland journalist, wrote the libretto for the comic opera in two acts, *A Moorish Maid* (1905). Johannes C. *Andersen's *Exhibition Ode*, a lyrical rodomontade written for the International Exhibition held in Christchurch from 1906 to 1907, stimulated Hill to provide an ambitious work for soloists, chorus and orchestra. Hill's vast output of songs, many of these settings of Australian and New Zealand writers, has still to be catalogued.

Alfred Hill became friendly with many of the leading literary and cultural figures of his day in both Australia and New Zealand. In 1916 he finally settled in Sydney, following his appointment as professor of composition by Henri Verbrugghen, first director of the New South Wales State Conservatorium of Music. He was a lifelong advocate for the Australian and New Zealand artist and a strong believer in the integrity of Māori, Aboriginal and other indigenous cultures.   JMT

HILL, David (1942–), is a versatile journalist, reviewer, fiction writer, playwright and children's writer. Born and educated in Napier, a graduate of Victoria University (MA Hons, 1964), he spent fourteen years secondary school teaching before writing full-time. He has contributed stories, articles, reviews and plays to newspapers, radio and most New Zealand journals, including *Landfall*, *NZ Listener* and *School Journal*, as well as overseas. His books include *The Seventies Connection* (1970), on New Zealand literature, and *Taranaki* (1987), both in collaboration with Elizabeth *Smither; *Introducing Maurice Gee* (1981); and *On Poetry: Twelve Studies of Work by New Zealand Poets* (1984). *Moaville Magic* (1985), illustrated by Eric Heath, was the first of three collections of comic and gently satirical pieces on an archetypical small New Zealand town, first broadcast on radio and published in the *Dominion* and elsewhere. *The Boy* (1988), illustrated by Chris Slane, amusingly explores a father's perspective on his teenage son. *The Games of Nanny Miro* (1990) is a bilingual story, illustrated by June Grant, translated by Irene Curnow. Plays for teenagers include *Ours But to Do* (1986), *A Time to Laugh* (1990) and *A Day at a Time* (1994).

Hill's first teenage novel, *See Ya, Simon* (1992), is an absorbing story of friendship with a boy dying, at 14, of muscular dystrophy, whose gritty humour and determination expunge sentimentality. Shortlisted in New Zealand and runner-up for two awards in the UK, it won the 1994 *Times Educational Supplement* Award for Special Needs. His next three novels in 1995 perceptively explore relationships and problems among teenagers involved in activities such as Tae Kwon Do in *Kick Back*, a disastrous tramping expedition in *Take It Easy*, and a drama production in *Curtain Up*. Also in 1995, *The Winning Touch* features an intermediate class's efforts to win at New Image Rugby. A more satiric touch is evident in *Second Best* (1996), about cricket. Hill was awarded an ICI Bursary in 1980 and is an occasional performer for *'Metaphor'.   DH

HILLIARD, Noel (1929–97), was a major novelist of the 1960s, now fallen somewhat into neglect. He was born in Napier, the son of a railway construction worker and a waitress, and lived through the *Depression in Hawkes Bay. His father, now on the dole, became bitter and angry. Hilliard became a journalist for *Southern Cross* and attended Victoria University College part-time 1946–50. There he was active in the Socialist Club. He and another journalist, Alexander Fry, became tubercular while sharing an unheated flat. While recovering from lung surgery in Pukeora Sanitorium, 1950–52, Hilliard joined the Communist Party only to leave it again after the Hungarian crisis of 1956. After a variety of jobs he trained as a teacher, married Kiriwai Mete (Ngāti Kahu–Ngā Puhi (to whom he was introduced by Hone *Tuwhare) and taught in a Khandallah (Wellington) school. Although disillusioned with the Party, he remained active in left-wing politics, and this strongly coloured his first published novel, the 'social-realist' *Maori Girl* (1960). After further years as a teacher, in Mangakino, he joined the staff of *NZ Listener* (1965–70), then a major reviewing journal. After a year on the *Burns Fellowship (1971) he returned to the Wellington region. He worked as a sub-editor for three large series of informative journals, *New Zealand Heritage*, *New Zealand Today* and *New Zealand Nature Heritage*, and as proofreader—later sub-editor—of the *Evening Post*. He had no illusions about such work, pointing out that the sub-editor 'is not, as you may think—and as many sub-editors would like you to think—the person next in charge after the editor'. This is in the introduction to a collection of sub-editors' work in the form of headlines, *Nude Chooks Stun Farmer* (1992), which includes such gems as 'Married Students Get More' and 'Wild Oats a Worry in Wairarapa'.

In the Hawkes Bay workmen's camps of Hilliard's childhood racism was not an issue, but when he arrived in Wellington he was shocked to see the phrase 'No Maori' appended to advertisements for work and accommodation. In his fiction this became a major pre-occupation, and *Maori Girl* was in large part a response to it, but in his journalism other left-wing issues, such as opposition to peace-time conscription and the 'American Big Brother influence' played a larger role. However, in reviewing Allen *Curnow's *A *Book of New Zealand Verse 1923–45* under the heading 'New Zealand's Jim Crow Verse Book' (in *Here & Now*) he expressed annoyance at 'the fatuous assumption in Curnow's introduction that poetry in New Zealand began only when the white man arrived'. Curnow's next anthology (1960) did in fact include a little Māori poetry.

Maori Girl was followed by *A Piece of Land: Stories and Sketches* (1963), dealing mainly with the impact of capitalism and urbanisation on New Zealand. The title story gives a vivid account of Māori attitudes to land and how they are damaged by the different, personal-ownership culture of the Pākehā. The entertaining stories in the second part deal with two Māori children, Bubby and Paikea, in a rural setting. In *Monthly Review*, Winston H. *Rhodes wrote, 'because the best stories deal with social attitudes and problems as well as with the details, the small disturbances and joys and dis-appointments of daily living, they more broadly con-tribute to our slender stock of human understanding and sympathy.'

Hilliard went on to turn *Maori Girl* into a tetralogy with the sequels *Power of Joy* (1965), *Maori Woman* (1974) and *The Glory and the Dream* (1978). (See *Maori Girl*.)

Meanwhile Hilliard wrote another novel and another volume of short stories. *A Night at Green River* (1969) tells of a farmer, Clyde Hastings, who offers to pay his Māori neighbours to help harvest his hay, not realising that such payment breaches the custom of mutual help in the community. The Māori fail to come but celebrate the end of Tiwha's harvest, leaving Clyde's hay to be ruined by rain. In the course of a tense night Clyde and his wife discover that there are other ways to think of money and of human labour. The values of capitalism encounter those of Māori communalism. Both Māori and Pākehā learn that cultural differences require non-judgmental tolerance from all participants in social trans-actions. This short novel has something of the character of a parable. It was warmly greeted by critics, who admired its conciseness and the subtle differentiation of character as well as the balance maintained between Māori and Pākehā views, which all make the book less moralistic than a summary might suggest. *Send Somebody Nice* (1976) is a collection of twenty-five stories covering a wide and typical range of political and social themes.

Hilliard's non-fiction arises from his journalism but always has a touch of the unconventional because of his determination to be unclouded in his view of society. *Wellington: City Alive* (1976) has the appearance, superficially, of a conventional picture book; but the photographs by Ans Westra reveal much more of unro-manticised human life than might be expected and Hilliard's text is not afraid to mix the negative with the positive: 'On a fine, calm day Wellington is among the most beautiful cities on earth. But like cities everywhere it can be ugly deep down....' The result is an honest but not harsh account, good for those who know the city and for those who do not. Hilliard also worked with Westra on a story of two Māori children illustrated with photographs: *We Live by a Lake* (1972), set at Mangakino. His last book, published in Moscow, was a personal view of travelling through the Soviet Union shortly before its dissolution: *Mahitahi: Work Together: Impressions of the USSR* (1989). He and his wife had been appointed 'cultural ambassadors' by the New Zealand government in 1988.

Maori Girl and most of Hilliard's short stories have been translated into Russian. In New Zealand terms his books were a considerable commercial success and *Noel Hilliard: a preliminary bibliography* by Jeffrey Downs (1976) shows that by that time the work had been very widely discussed. Probably the findings would be much thinner for the period since then. There is a Canterbury University thesis by T.J. Mullinder (1974) and an exten-sive study in Italian of the Netta Samuel books by Tiziana Nisini (1983). NW

Hilltop was published in three issues in 1949 by the Literary Society of Victoria University College. Successor to the Society's *Broadsheet,* it was itself suc-ceeded in 1950 by *Arachne*. Edited first by J.M. *Thomson and then W.H *Oliver, *Hilltop* featured poetry and fiction by Oliver, David *Ballantyne, James K. *Baxter, Alistair *Campbell, Louis *Johnson, Kendrick *Smithyman and Pat *Wilson. SH

Hinemoa and Tūtānekai are the lovers in one of the most popular of Māori stories. Hinemoa lived on the shores of Lake Rotorua, Tūtānekai on the island of Mokoia. When her disapproving family hid canoes, Hinemoa swam the long journey guided by Tūtānekai's flute.

The story caught the Pākehā imagination in *Grey's

Polynesian Mythology. There were many retellings in pamphlets or collections of *Māori myths and legends.

The tale is told in verse by Edmund Lee (1898), Rathmell Wilson (1905), Mrs. A. Perry (1910), C.O. Palmer (1918), James Izett (1925) and Mrs Adele Schafer (1959). Visitors such as *Froude and *Trollope could never resist retelling it when they wrote of Rotorua, and many novelists use it for a romantic thrill. In *War to the Knife* Rolf *Boldrewood calls it '… a tale of woman's love and man's fidelity. They had better fortune in those old days.' Reminiscent of the ancient story of Hero and Leander, it is enough that it is a touching story of faithful love with a happy ending (the lovers had many descendants).

Anna Flaxman's *Hinemoa* (1941) is the story of a New Zealand girl, set in Europe and Puerto Rico. *Hinemoa* is also a popular name for ships and boats.   NW

Hine-nui-te-pō (Great Woman of the Night) brought death into the world. She dwelt in the underworld, waiting for her children to come to her. The story of *Maui entering her vagina to destroy death but being crushed by her thighs when the fantail woke her with its twittering laughter is one of the best-known of Māori legends and is used in fiction, for example, by Witi *Ihimaera and Albert *Wendt. Hirini *Mead explains: 'The way to secure immortality was to reverse the process of birth, grasp the spark of life and remove it from the goddess.… Thus life can be viewed as an active pursuit of the spark of life. To give up the struggle is to succumb to the goddess of death.'   NW

Hine-te-iwaiwa, an ancestral and legendary woman, is, according to Margaret *Orbell, 'the exemplary figure of a wife and mother, the woman who provided the pattern that women now follow. All girls, therefore, were dedicated to Hine-te-iwaiwa at birth'. One of her achievements was to create pounamu (greenstone) by turning her two jealous co-wives into this substance.

A *karakia associated with Hine-te-iwaiwa aids women in childbirth. Another gives a girl strength when her lips are being painfully tattooed. Others use her name to remove *tapu from objects, another important female function.

Consequently, her name was present in poetry in women's work and social functions in traditional society and recurs frequently in the writing of contemporary Māori women.   NW

HINEWIRANGI (1947–), Ngāti Kahungunu, Ngāti Ranginui, whose full name is Hinewirangi Rosemary Kohu-Morgan, was born in Gisborne and raised in Nuhaka, Opoutama, and Mahia on the East Coast. She is known as a community activist, trainer, counsellor, poet and writer, artist and social entrepreneur. A traditional education, largely instilled by her kuia, was supplemented by schooling at Bethlehem Native School, where Sylvia *Ashton-Warner was her teacher, at Church College of New Zealand, Hamilton, and through adult education at Tauranga Girls College, Fraser High School and at Waikato University. Her teachings and writings, grounded in her Māori heritage, enable her to bring Māori issues to the global arena in support of indigenous peoples working for political, social and economic justice. Hinewirangi has been particularly active on behalf of Māori women and their families as director and international representative for the Māori Women's Centre in Hamilton since its inception in 1984, founding member of the National Women's group Te Kakano o te Whanau (1984), and in involvement in health centres and husing resource management. A tutor in creative arts, Hinewirangi also tutors and lectures at Waikato Technical Institute, Waikato Foster Care, Waikato Hospital and Waikato University. She has also served as a board member on several bodies such as the International Indian Treaty Council (1986) and Nuclear and Independent Pacific (1987).

Hinewirangi's creative writing, the powerful evocation of the pain of cultural loss and celebration of its recovery, includes books of poetry: *Broken Chant* (1983), *The Turning Face* (1984), *Screaming Moko* (1986) and *Kanohi ki te Kanohi* (1990). She has scripted many plans for young Māori, videos for children in the area of sexual abuse and a short story, *Kahurangi the Raindrop*. Currently she is working on two short story collections, 'Te Wa Moemoea' and 'Whakaaro', a novel 'Ko au', and a poem 'Aroha ki te tangata o te ao'. She is represented in *Te *Ao Mārama* (1993), *Daughters of the Pacific* (ed. Zohl De Ishtar, 1994), *Toi Wāhine* (ed. Irwin and Ramsden, 1995), *He Wai* (ed. T. *Menzies, 1996), and contributes poems to the *International Treaty Council Newsletter* (San Francisco), the *Pacific News Bulletin* (Australia) and *Tok Blok* (Canada). Her writing evinces the status inherent in the moko she received with distinction, which empowers her to say 'I wear my people', a whole nation of Māori people.   JBa

HOAR, Stuart (1957–), is a playwright and screenwriter, born in New Plymouth. He began by writing a number of radio plays before coming to the attention of the theatre, which he did spectacularly when he submitted a huge script to the 1986 New Zealand Playwrights' Workshop. Much pared down, the final workshop production of *Squatter* was enthralling. The play is set in 1894 at Carnegie, a Canterbury estate. In 1890, the newly emergent middle class had elected a Liberal government on its promise to break up the extensive *squatters' estates to create smallholdings for the flood of potential farmers coming into the country. Now the inhabitants of Carnegie—its owners, the Bilstrode family, and their workers—must face up to the consequences of this policy. Its first production was directed by Sarah Peirse at Mercury Theatre, Auckland, in 1987, followed in 1988 by a production at Circa, Wellington, directed by Mervyn *Thompson (the director of the original Playwrights' Workshop presentation). Subsequent plays have been 'The Three Musketeers', commissioned and produced by Mercury in 1988, 'Scott of the Antarctic' (Allen Hall, Dunedin, 1989), 'Exile in Stonehurst' (Allen Hall, 1990, later retitled 'Exile'), 'A Long Walk off a Tall Rock' (commissioned for Te Kura Toi Whakaari/The New Zealand Drama School, 1991), 'The Horse and the Lolly Machine' (Young Stagers, 1989, for children), 'The Boat' (Maidment Theatre, Auckland, 1992, directed by Simon Marler), 'Yo Banfa' (Maidment Theatre, 1993, directed by Murray *Edmond), 'Cool Gangs'/'Alice in Cyberspace' (two plays for adolescents), 'Not so Poor' (commissioned by Allen Hall Theatre, Dunedin) and 'Folie à Deux' (co-written with Stephanie *Johnson and presented at the Watershed, 1996). He wrote the libretto for 'Bitter Calm', an opera composed by Christopher *Blake, and the screenplays for two short films: *Lovelock, which won the Writers' Guild Award for best screenplay, and I'm So Lonesome, I Could Cry, an official selection at Cannes, 1994. His radio plays have included 'Terror and Virtue' (commissioned by Radio New Zealand to commemorate the French Revolution) and 'The Voyage'. Hoar's best work is witty, satirical and overtly political. Using challenging non-naturalistic approaches, he questions contemporary political developments (Squatter, 'The Boat') and revisits some of the emblematic figures of the country's cultural history (the literary lions of the 1940s–50s in 'Exile'; Rewi *Alley in 'Yo Banfa'; Lovelock, Scott). In 1988, he was playwright-in-residence at Mercury Theatre and was awarded the Bruce Mason Playwrights' Award in the same year. In 1990, he was Literary Fellow at the University of Auckland and in 1993 *Burns Fellow at Otago.   SG

HOCHSTETTER, (Christian Gottlieb) Ferdinand von (1829–84), studied theology and natural science in Tübingen and worked as a geologist in Bohemia and a university lecturer in Vienna before joining the Austrian scientific expedition around the globe in the Novara. The expedition reached Auckland on 22 December 1858. There Hochstetter met Julius *Haast, who accompanied him on his explorations. The New Zealand authorities persuaded him to stay for further geological expeditions

when the Novara returned. He travelled extensively on both islands, and spent ten years writing up the results of his research. His magnificently produced volume Neu-Seeland, now a collector's piece among early accounts of New Zealand, appeared in 1863 and its English translation in 1867. In this and twenty-one further papers on New Zealand topics, he was the first to describe the country's geology in detail. His subsequent career in Europe was very distinguished: for example, he was president of the Geographical Society of Vienna 1866–82.   NW

Hocken Library, The, the second largest historical research collection relating to New Zealand, is separately housed within the University of Otago library system. It has substantial collections of printed books with supporting collections of periodicals, newspapers (very strong for Otago and Southland), music, sound, maps, paintings, drawings, prints, photographs, and archives and manuscripts (again, strong for Otago and Southland, but with significant national holdings). It has particular strengths in New Zealand literature, both printed and manuscript materials. Writers' papers include those of James K. *Baxter, Charles *Brasch, James *Courage, Ruth *Dallas, Roderick *Finlayson, Janet *Frame, Ruth *France, Roger *Hall, Noel *Hilliard, Peter *Hooper, Robert *Lord, Cilla *McQueen, R.A.K. *Mason, O.E. *Middleton, Elizabeth *Smither and Philip *Temple, and are supplemented by recorded interviews. Archives include those of local publishers, literary magazines, theatres and other cultural institutions (see Friends of the Hocken Collections Bulletin, No. 4, March 1993). Manuscript and archive holdings were reported to the Union Catalogue of New Zealand and Pacific Manuscripts, Part 1, 1968, and to the National Register of Archives and Manuscripts, 1979–94, but are not fully reported. Current acquisitions are listed in Archifacts and the Library's Annual Report.   JT

HOCKEN, T.M. (Thomas Morland) (1836–1910), was an eminent bibliographer and collector, who donated his great collection of books and documents as a 'library or Museum of Information and reference by the general public'. The *Hocken Library at University of Otago was opened in 1910, a few weeks before the benefactor's death. By profession Hocken was a leading physician. Born in Rutland, England, he went to school in Leeds, received medical training in St Helen's, Newcastle on Tyne and Dublin, and reached Dunedin in 1862 after service as a ship's surgeon. He quickly developed interests in ethnology and New Zealand history, collecting New Zealand, Australian Aboriginal and Pacific artefacts which later became the basis of the Otago University

Museum's ethnology holdings; and giving the well-regarded lectures which were developed into his *Contributions to the Early History of New Zealand [Settlement of Otago]* (1898). He published the text of Abel ★Tasman's journal, translated by his wife Bessie Hocken, in *Transactions and Proceedings of the New Zealand Institute*. His magnum opus, however, was his *A Bibliography of the Literature Relating to New Zealand* (1909), which remained a standard reference source through most of the twentieth century. The same interests in New Zealand and its Pacific context directed his lifetime of collecting books, manuscripts, maps and other documents, with special collections in literature relating to exploratory voyages, the missionaries and the early history of Otago. S.R. Strachan in the ★*Dictionary of New Zealand Biography* affirms that Hocken was 'unrivalled' as a bibliographer of the documents of New Zealand history, and that 'as a collector of them and public benefactor he stands with George ★Grey and Alexander ★Turnbull as one of the pre-eminent New Zealand trinity'.   PN/RR

HODGE, Merton (Horace Emerton) (1904–58), achieved the greatest West End success of any New Zealand playwright with *The Wind and the Rain* (1933; publ. 1934), which had a three-year run of over a thousand performances at the St Martin's, Queen's and Savoy Theatres, London. Born at Gisborne, educated at King's College, Auckland, and Auckland and Otago university colleges, he had written and acted in 'extravaganzas' while studying medicine. After graduating MB, ChB 1928 and practising briefly in New Zealand, he travelled to Edinburgh, where he wrote his famous play, with its influence of Noel Coward, in 1931. He continued to practise as an anaesthetist, in London and Cork, until travelling to New York for the play's production there in 1935. He published a version in novel form in 1936 and was acting in a wartime London revival which was interrupted by air raids. No other work matched its success, nor recaptured its gently nostalgic atmosphere which so well caught the current taste for slightly melancholy and rather mannered romance. He tried, in further plays, such as *Grief Goes Over* (1935) and *The Island* (1937), which won him praise as 'the English Chekhov' but not commercial success. He wrote a dramatisation of *The Story of an African Farm* (1938, pub. 1939), and after the war 'All of Whom We Know' and others, and also worked for film and radio. He returned to New Zealand near the end of his life.   RR

HODGKINS, Frances (1869–1947), is New Zealand's best-known expatriate artist, who is acknowledged as an important painter in the British modern movement. She was born in Dunedin, the elder daughter of the leading amateur artist, William Mathew Hodgkins. After studying there and establishing herself as an artist and teacher, she left New Zealand, first on extended sojourns to England, Europe and North Africa (1901–03 and 1906–12), before settling permanently in England in 1913. Here she struggled with poverty and personal setbacks to paint full-time, assimilating the lessons she learnt in Paris, London and the artists' colonies of Cornwall and the South of France, to paint semi-abstract landscapes, still-lifes and portraits which gradually gained her a noted place among Cedric Morris, Paul Nash, John and Myfanwy Piper, Christopher Wood and others. Her literary contributions are twofold. Her letters (ed. Gill, 1993), written to friends and family in New Zealand, offer a vivid picture of her life and attitudes as a painter, and insight into the private thoughts of a New Zealand–born artist. Secondly, her life and work have been the subject of E.H. ★McCormick's skilled work as biographer and historian. In particular, *The Expatriate: A Study of Frances Hodgkins* (1954), *Portrait of Frances Hodgkins* (1981) and *Late Attachment: Frances Hodgkins and Maurice Garnier* (1988) are rare examples of monographic literature on New Zealand artists.   CB

HOGGARD, Noel Farr (1913–75), was a journalist who enjoyed editing small literary magazines as a hobby. He founded ★*Spilt Ink* (later *The New Triad*) in 1933 and ★*Arena* in 1943. He also founded the *Upper Hutt Advocate* and ran a monthly newspaper in Pukerua Bay. His magazines were hand-set, as were a number of books, at the Handcraft Press. These included various of his own poems, an autobiographical essay and *Centennial Miscellany: An Anthology of Short Stories and Verse* (1939), which Hoggard edited.   NW

HOLCROFT, Anthony (1932–), writer of children's fiction, was born in Christchurch, son of M.H. ★Holcroft, and educated at Southland BHS and Canterbury University. He taught at rural schools, worked on farms and now, while also writing, runs an orchard near Rangiora. His masterly short stories take their structure from traditional folklore and reflect his fascination with energies or spirits in the landscape, often of New Zealand. In practical yet poetic and mystical ways they embody three recurring themes: the need for conservation, the destructive nature of greed and the redeeming power of love. Picture books include *The Old Man and the Cat* (1984) and *The Oldest Garden in China* (1985), both illustrated by Fifi Colston, *Rosie Moonshine* (1989) and *Chen-Li and the River Spirit* (1990), both illustrated by Lyn Kriegler (1990). *Chen-Li and the River Spirit* first appeared in *Cricket*, an American children's magazine, where it won the International Reading

Association Paul A. Witty Award in 1991. Holcroft also won the Choysa Bursary for 1986. Collections of his stories, many originally published in international magazines, anthologies and on radio, are: *Tales of the Mist* (1987), illustrated by Elspeth Williamson; *The Boy at the Door and Other Stories of the Supernatural* (1991), illustrated by Julian Holcroft; *The White Bird* (1995); and *The Night Bees* (1995), illustrated by Timothy Ide.   DH

HOLCROFT, M.H. (Monte) (1902–94), was a writer, journalist, editor, critic and essayist. Born in Rangiora and educated in Christchurch, he spent five years in Australia from 1921, working mainly as a freelance writer. Returning to Christchurch, he was sub-editor of the *Weekly News* until it ceased in 1928, whereupon he went to Europe. During this time he was also writing fiction: the first of his novels to be published was *Beyond the Breakers* (1928), followed by *The Flameless Fire* (1929) and *Brazilian Daughter* (1931). Finding it impossible to support himself as a writer in London, he returned to Christchurch in 1930 where he continued to write fiction and literary essays (the *Press published many of them; a selection, *Timeless World*, appeared in 1945). In 1937 he joined the *Southland Times* as leader-writer, becoming acting editor in 1942 and editor in 1945.

A long essay, *The Deepening Stream*, on the problems of cultural and geographical isolation for a writer in New Zealand, won first prize in the 1940 *Centennial Literary Competition's essay section. This theme of the place of the writer in society was developed in two further essays, *The Waiting Hills* (1943) and *Encircling Seas* (1946)—all three being collected as *Discovered Isles* (1950), regarded as still the most considerable work of cultural criticism of its kind written here—and distilled in the monograph *Creative Problems in New Zealand* (1948). Two later works of literary criticism were *Islands of Innocence* (1964), exploring the unusual emphasis on childhood in New Zealand literature, and the account of an earlier Christchurch friend, poet Mary Ursula *Bethell, the first in the Oxford University Press *'New Zealand Writers and Their Work' series (1975).

In 1949 Holcroft was appointed editor of the *NZ Listener*. His twenty-year editorship was noted for its purposeful coverage of literary and artistic activities and its wide-ranging analysis of New Zealand society and values, particularly in his editorials, which broke new ground by discussing contentious or uncomfortable issues with clarity, good sense and humanity. Two collections were published, *The Eye of the Lizard* (1960) and *Graceless Islanders* (1970), later republished together as *A Voice in the Village* (1989). Holcroft's account of the people, events and controversies of his term, *Reluctant Editor*, appeared in 1969.

His descriptive essay accompanying the photographic study *New Zealand* (1963) was so well received that it was reissued separately. After his first retirement from the *Listener* in 1967 (he returned in 1973–74), Holcroft took on several similar assignments, including contributions to *New Zealand's Heritage* and an associated illustrated book, *The Shaping of New Zealand* (1974). Two regional works followed, *Old Invercargill* (1976) and *The Line of the Road*, a centennial history of Manawatu County (1977), as well as the aptly titled essay *Carapace* (1979), detailing the undesirable physical and social effects of the motor car. A final rather pessimistic essay on the wider processes of social change in New Zealand through the twentieth century, *The Village Transformed*, appeared in 1990.

An earlier essay, *Dance of the Seasons* (1952), had traced the youthful Holcroft's expanding thought while working as a farm labourer in Canterbury. Personal experience, particularly as it shapes the writer, is a thread throughout his work. The rounded, detailed and remarkably frank portrait in the two late volumes of autobiography, *The Way of a Writer* (1984) and *A Sea of Words* (1986), draws the various personal, public and philosophical strands of his life together in prose that remains characteristically uncluttered, supple and precise. Holcroft's most personal book, however, was *The Grieving Time* (1989), a meditation prompted by the death of his third wife, Lorna, the great love of his life.
                                                              AM

HOLDEN, Anne (1928–   ), novelist, was born in Whakatane, educated at Hamilton HS and graduated MA (Hons) from Auckland University (1950), and later in law from Victoria University (1989). She has lived in London, Washington DC, taught at a number of schools and in the 1990s served on the Indecent Publications Tribunal. Her first novel *Rata* (1965) is the story of Rata Lovell, the 12-year-old orphan child of a Pākehā father and a Māori mother. In depicting her escape from the dull, inhibiting life of her foster home with Miss Carter, and the contrasting vibrancy of the Māori whānau at the Hikapu pā, Holden was in many ways ahead of her time in portraying the challenges for many who straddle those two worlds. *The Empty Hills* (1967) describes the struggles of a family of women to find some happiness in their monotonous existence or escape the conventions that stifle them. The book is memorable for the vividness of its depiction of small-town New Zealand life in the 1960s: a world of six o'clock closing, cardigans and gloves, Saturday night dances, lengthy engagements and glory boxes or the shame of a sudden marriage, all linked by the inexhaustible voice of small-town gossip. In *Death after School* (1968) a young New Zealand teacher becomes involved in a series of mysterious events at a

London school. With *The Witnesses* (1971), a cleverly plotted psychological thriller, Holden became one of New Zealand's most translated and best-selling authors through the novel's sales in a number of languages including Dutch, German, French and Scandinavian languages. Sales in East Germany alone have been close to 250 000. It was successfully adapted for the American film, *The Bedroom Window* (1987), set in Baltimore. *The Girl on the Beach* (1973) provides a further example of the way in which ordinary lives can be suddenly transformed by violent events. Although the novel is set in Wellington, the American edition required numerous changes, including transposition to California. Her most recent book was *No Trains at the Bay* (1976), a children's nineteenth-century adventure story. She has continued to write non-fiction and has maintained her involvement in women's issues, particularly in relation to education and pay equity, as a recent past president of the New Zealand Federation of University Women, and a member of the Council for Equal Pay and Opportunity.　　　GB

Hole in the Zero, The (1967), marks M.K. *Joseph's debut in *science fiction. The novel begins in what seems to be a comfortable old-fashioned English country house complete with hollyhocks, aged butler and rheumy-eyed basset hound. We soon discover that this idealised place is actually a space station at the boundary of the known universe. Its artifice creates a feeling of secure normalcy in opposition to the numbing chaos beyond the boundary, where 'anything is probable, anything is possible'.

Living at the space station is a 'Limitary Warden' called Paradine, whose name, echoing 'paradigm', indicates his later function as a human exemplar. Three people arrive intending to pass through the 'hole in the zero' into the realm of 'unlaw, untime, unspace and unpossibility'. Their names are again almost allegorically significant: Kraag, a self-made materialist with no time for things imaginative; his beautiful daughter, Helena; and an exquisitely dressed albino male, Kraag's official heir-executive and Helena's contracted fiancé, Hyperion Merganser—Hyperion the sun god and merganser a species of hook-beaked fish-eating duck suggesting the selfishness and appetite that are central to his character.

These four characters journey beyond the known universe, and by an act of Merganser's become stranded in the realm of shifting realities. At this point the novel transforms from linear narrative into a series of brilliantly realised episodes, which range from vignettes of warfare (always a strong point in Joseph's writing) to explorations of those moments in a lifetime at which alternative possibilities arise. The contrasting narratives have the overall coherence of a kaleidoscope, though gradually

one becomes aware that certain themes are recurring. Thus Kraag, the materialist, eventually disappears, perhaps because materialism lacks intrinsic variety. Merganser and Paradine are revealed as anti-types, locked in opposition, but Merganser the self-centred hedonist is finally defeated. Helena undergoes various refining incarnations until finally she is as simple and quintessential as Eve. Paradine experiences a range of lives, from hero to fool, from fanatic to saviour, finally appearing as a man reborn, an Adam. He and Helena seem to presage a new and stable creation.

The Hole in the Zero is remarkable not only for the intensity of its narrative, the variety of its episodes and the dexterity of its prose but for its informing moral vision, which seems to focus on the question of the nature of goodness in a universe without absolute values.　　PMn

HOLLAND, Harry (Henry Edmund) (1868–1933), led the Parliamentary Labour Opposition 1919–33 and was unusual among politicians in also being a competent poet. (See also Alfred *Domett, William Pember *Reeves, Peter *Simpson.) He arrived in New Zealand in 1912 with a reputation as a radical journalist and militant socialist from his native Australia, where he had been gaoled for political agitation. For five years he edited the *Maoriland Worker* and was also a prolific pamphleteer. His career in poetry had begun during a period of illness in 1911, when he left hospital lame and impatient at his slow recovery, pouring out his yearnings, beliefs and protestations in verse. This writing seems to have ceased on his attaining political success. He did, however, publish a selection, *Red Roses on the Highways* (1924). Many poems are in rousing socialist vein, a revivalist mix of sentimentalism and belligerence: 'O the war-drums of Labour are throbbing / Their call from the depths of the years, / And they'll end the young children's wild sobbing / And sorrow of sad mothers' tears' ('They Shall Take and Hold'). Setting the tone for 'The Friendly Road' radio station of Reverend C.G. Scrimgeour ('Uncle Scrim'; see Mervyn *Thompson) during the *Depression, this visionary belief in a *Utopian future, moulded by the people themselves, runs through Holland's writings, as it did through his public life: 'The Sun shall rise Tomorrow / And flood the World with Light.' He is the only New Zealand poet to be commemorated by a nude stone statue, which stands at the top of Wellington's Bolton Street cemetery.
　　HMcQ/RR

Holloway Press, The, was established in 1994 at the Tamaki Campus of the University of Auckland, after the gifting to the university of printing equipment, books and archival material by Ronald and Kay Holloway of the *Griffin Press, Panmure, Auckland. Alan *Loney, formerly of *Hawk and *Black Light Presses, was appointed printer-manager, with Peter *Simpson, associate professor of English, as co-director. All Holloway Press books are designed and printed by Loney. The publication policy of the press is to publish a range of texts appropriate to the technology of hand-printing which have unusual literary, scholarly or historical interest, and which are unsuitable for commercial publication. The press has a particular interest in the history of typography and small press printing in New Zealand. The first publication of the press was Allen *Curnow's *Looking West, Late Afternoon, Low Water* (1994), followed by *The Victory Hymn, 1935–1995* by Robin *Hyde with an essay by Michele *Leggott (1995), and *Tomarata* by Kendrick *Smithyman, with an afterword by Simpson (1996). Other Holloway Press authors and artists are Helen *Shaw, Wystan *Curnow, Leo *Bensemann, the Greek poet Ibykos (translated by Ted Jenner, illustrated John Reynolds) and Robert *Creeley (with drawings by Max Gimblett). PS

HOLLOWAY, Ronald (1909–), typographer, see **Griffin Press**, **Holloway Press**.

Home is where the heart is, and for many British immigrants to New Zealand that meant the land they had come from; to such a degree that it was taken over by their children. For more than a century (*c.*1815 to World War 2) 'home' (often with a capital) was understood to mean (at first) England or (later) the British Isles, alternating with 'the Old Country' and less often 'the Old Dart'. In *Life's Vagaries* (1970) Marguerite Johnson tells how a school principal 'a stickler for British teachers, asked her where she was educated and she replied quite honestly "at home". He understood her to mean England, so she was given the position'. Similarly, 'to go home' meant to visit (in the nineteenth century often 'return to') Britain. Thus, in 1927 the *New Zealand Tablet* reported that 'Miss Nelle *Scanlan, a vivid reporter and journalist ... is going home to widen her sphere of work'. A character in Jean *Devanny's *River* (1927) says, 'I want to go Home, Mother. To London. To Paris. I *must* go Home, Mother.' It is frequently to be found as an adjective and in compounds, especially 'home boat', a former name for a ship plying between Britain and New Zealand. In 1907 William *Satchell used such a ship as the setting for a novel, *The Elixir of Life*. It is worth noting the reversal of the word's use in his phrase 'colonists returning home from the long-anticipated European tour.'

In early writing, unsurprisingly, 'Home' meaning 'England' is more frequently found in settler than adven-

ture literature; one of the earliest novels is entitled *Distant Homes* (Mrs J.E. *Aylmer, 1862). The response there when a character hears the name Canterbury is 'Ah, that will sound almost like home', while Lyttelton Harbour has 'such a busy home look about it'. Mrs. C. *Evans's *Over the Hills, and Far Away* (1874) also implies melancholy distance in its title, Evans writing in the preface of 'the mighty waste of waters which separates me from the home-country'. Much of the conversation in such novels is about 'friends at home' and the women often exchange 'home journals', such as *Cornhill*. The *locus classicus* of the expression is Alan *Mulgan's book *Home* (1927), where the first chapter explains the effect of growing up in the antipodes but reading English books: 'The trend of all this literature ... was to fix my thoughts ever on England. Nor do I suggest for a moment that my experience was unique or even exceptional.' By about the 1950s a generation was becoming irritated by their parents' use of 'Home' for a place so unknown. Denis *Glover anticipated that reaction in 'Home Thoughts' (*Tomorrow*, 1935): 'I do not dream of Sussex downs / Or quaint old England's quaint old towns: / I think of what will yet be seen / In Johnsonville and Geraldine.' HO/NW

HONA, Te Rangianiwaniwa (1938–97), Ngā Puhi, Ngāti Ruamohoe, Ngāti Kahu, Te Aupōuri, Te Rarawa, who also published as Te Aniwa Bosch, was born in her 'grandmother's washhouse' at Mahinepua and raised near Whangaroa Harbour. Her base *marae was Ngātiruamahue, though she became connected to many in the north through lineage and her personal status. Her father, 'the local native policeman', was active in the eradication of home brew and alcohol abuse generally, concerns that enter Hona's writing. Ani, or Te Aniwa as she was known, attended school at Wainui (a 17-km horseback journey) and later Northland College. After training and working as a psychiatric nurse, she studied at Wellington Teachers' College and taught extensively, returning to Whangaroa College in her home area.

Publication of her stories and poems began in the 1960s in *Te *Ao Hou, Te Maori, *Pacific Moana Quarterly, Ocarina* (India) and *Into the World of Light* as Te Aniwa Bosch. She also commenced a biography of Sir James Henare and two novels. A prolific writer for *Te Kohanga Reo*, she was a contributor also to the children's readers *Te Wharekura* (*Learning Media) and *Nga Pukapuka Iti* (*Price Milburn) and she also wrote personalised stories for her children and grandchildren. A regular participant at Maori Writers' and Artists' Conferences, her involvement in performance art was exceeded only by her activities on behalf of northern *iwi. She also worked as a translator for the Maori Land Courts and *Alexander

Turnbull Library, from whom she received a grant for her writing. She was head of Maori Studies at Whangaroa College 1980–82. She worked as an intermediary between the *tangata whenua and the Department of Conservation: at whale strandings, for example, she encouraged a recognition of their value as a resource to the tangata whenua, the whale as tupuna (ancestor), their song as *tangi and the need to honour them with *karakia. Her recognition as Te Aniwaniwa o te Rangi Hona, the rainbow of heaven, was appropriately marked at her tangi by the symbol for which she was named.   JBa

HOOPER, Peter (Hedley Codwill) (1919–), is best known for his 'Forest' trilogy of philosophical futuristic novels, 1979–86. In all his fiction and poetry he is a committed 'forest and bird' writer, working more within the older tradition of nature writing than contemporary ecological or cultural concerns. His poem 'Distance Pacing With 3G', for instance, is like a reworking of Wordsworth's 'One impulse from a vernal wood', with the teacher rejecting classroom literature ('chopping Chaucer / into digestible gobbets') in order to 'learn again from leaves / the wholeness of man outside walls' and 'startle to delight / in the throat of a blackbird'. Hooper's vision is consistently of a holistic and pantheistic world—the god Pan even makes an appearance in his story 'The End of the Road', thinly disguised as a *swaggie with hooves. He writes intimately of plant, animal and bird life, the elements and *backblocks work and survival skills. The poem 'Homage to Thoreau' is characteristic, and 'Thoughts of Westland from London' is like a yearning for a distant lover.

Born in England, he came early to New Zealand and grew up on the West Coast, school teaching mainly there, becoming deputy principal of Westland HS at Hokitika before retiring to a Walden-like retreat near Greymouth in 1977 to write full-time. Poems had appeared in *NZ Listener, *Mate and several English journals, and *Pegasus Press published A Map of Morning and Other Poems in 1964. Through poems set in Italy, England and elsewhere the imaginative effort is always to capture the rhythmic continuity of nature, the way 'earth's inmost sense burns with a greener fire', and to aspire to join it: 'A good poem stands like a daffodil / brave to the chill of spring, attains the strength of an oak / and possesses the secret of the returning seasons.' A pamphlet, 'Profiles in Monochrome' (1974?), sketches a less affectionate view of suburbia. He edited a verse collection, A Pleasure of Friends, in 1970. His Selected Poems appeared in 1977, and The Goat Paddock in 1981, short stories which bring an insistent moral awareness to scenes of rural life.

The moral and philosophical element became more prominent with The Song of the Forest (1979). Set in a post-cataclysmic future, the fiction painstakingly constructs a small community in the West Coast forest, struggling for survival, understanding and social codes. The main narrative is a journey across the Southern Alps by two boys, one destined to become a priest and the trilogy's central character. Scenes of devastated civilisation evoke familiar Christchurch locations while being also reminiscent of John Wyndham's The Chrysalids (1955). The base of realism from which the fantasy is sprung is the intimate and informative presentation of the terrain and skills of bushcraft. The religious dimension, with a self-sacrificial stag that merges Pan with Christ, is less successful. The sequel, People of the Long Water (1985), won the New Zealand Book Award for Fiction. It puts the 'Stag People' in contact with the more pacific 'Shepherd People' and again takes its climax in a symbolic journey, this time to the 'Country of the Newly Dead'. Time and the Forest (1986) completes the trilogy by bringing Tama the priest through old age to death, with the emphasis moving further towards the mystical and the imagining of a more harmonious relationship between human society and the natural rhythms of time, into which even love is finally subsumed.

These preoccupations place Hooper partly within the 'peace and love' context of the 1960s–70s, evident also in the title of his illustrated conservationist essay, Our Forests, Ourselves (1981). But he is more than a city-shunning mystic, and constantly evokes the land and the skills it demands with both expert knowledge and sustained passion.   RR

HORNE, R.H. (Richard Henry) (1803–84), wrote probably the first New Zealand ghost story by a European author, the curious tale of 'The New Zealand Zauberflote', published in Household Words, under the editorship of Charles *Dickens, 19 Oct. 1850. It tells of a Māori chief, Taonui, King of Mokau, who makes 'a native flute' from the legbone of a defeated rival, Te Pomar. It is unclear whether Horne, who had never been to New Zealand, understood that the Māori nose flute is a quite different instrument from the one featured in Mozart's opera, as Taonui has his carved with representations of his victories. But 'The sound of the instrument was truly strange and doleful', so he may have heard one. It is still inhabited by the spirit of his enemy, however, and at critical moments 'vibrated with electrical force' and highly coloured atmospheric effects. The story is embellished with such authentic-sounding detail as the construction of a 'pah', *tapu conventions and the dangers of the mere pounamu, and Horne knows enough to explain that the kangaroos which feature in a crucial hunt scene are, in fact, not native. They nevertheless become spectacularly galvanised by demonic spirits after death. Other details are less convincing, like the explanation that the call 'cooey' is derived from the Māori 'koo-i' ('where are you?'). All ends in harmony, with a romantic marriage and Taonui seeing 'the benign Phantom of Te Pomar slowly rise towards him'. The basic premise seems to be in the statement that 'The interior of New Zealand contains so many natural wonders, that it need not require any great stretch of imagination among the natives to pass over to the supernatural.'

Horne was a colourful character who served in the Mexican navy among other youthful adventures, then wrote the successful epic poem *Orion* (1843) (publishing it for a farthing in protest against 'public contempt' of epic poetry), wrote tragedies and ballad romances, was a friend and literary collaborator of Elizabeth Barrett Browning, went to Australia in 1852, where he commanded the gold escort from Ballarat to Melbourne and wrote his *Australian Facts and Prospects* (1859), returned to England, now calling himself 'Hengist', published Barrett Browning's letters to him, and finally attained a civil list pension in 1874. In this context, the ghoulish eccentricities of 'The New Zealand Zauberflote' appear quite bland.   RR

HORSMAN, E.A. (Ernest Alan) (1918–), retired Otago University professor, contributed to New Zealand literary studies as scholar, reviewer and administrator. Born in Yorkshire, he arrived in New Zealand as an infant and was educated at Northcote College, Auckland University College (MA 1942) and, after war service, Oxford (MA 1952). After lectureships at Auckland and Durham universities he held Otago's Donald Collie Chair of English from 1957 to 1983. Unusually for that time, he began his scholarly career with 'colonial' texts, editing Alfred *Domett's *Diary 1872–1885* (1953) and *Canadian Journal* (1955). He edited Jonson, Shakespeare, Dickens and the 1956–57 Supplement to the *Oxford English Dictionary* and wrote books on Disraeli and, in the Clarendon History of English Literature, *The Victorian Novel* (1990). A friend of Charles *Brasch, Horsman lent his scholarly weight to the early *Landfall* with reviews in issues 8–18, and was the university administrator most responsible for the establishment of the pioneering *Burns Fellowship in 1959. His 'Words at the Funeral of Charles Brasch' was published in *Islands* 5 and the citations for honorary graduands which he wrote and delivered as Otago University's public orator make an eloquent contribution to biographical writing. He lives in Dunedin.   RR

HOTERE, Ralph (1931–), of Te Aupōuri, is an artist whose paintings and three-dimensional works are highly regarded for their formal rigour and evocative messages. Often these are conveyed by abstract symbols, words and texts, on surfaces which are painted and constructed with the most minimal means, including monochromatic colour, spare line, gestural brushwork and use of raw materials like corrugated iron. Hotere was born at Mitimiti in Northland. He studied at the King Edward Technical College, where he trained in art education, before working as an art adviser to schools in Northland and Auckland. He was New Zealand Art Societies Fellow in 1961, at the Central School of Art in London, and spent four years working in England and France, where his (then) minimalist paintings were seen in group and solo exhibitions. Returning to New Zealand in 1965, Hotere was awarded the Frances Hodgkins Fellowship (1969), which resulted in his permanent move to Dunedin and Carey's Bay.

Hotere's work is now regularly included in major exhibitions throughout New Zealand and internationally. He has remained committed to a severe modernist abstraction, complicated by varied usage of words and texts: Māori names, *Māori sayings and traditional laments; references to specific places and historical events; extracts from the Bible; and the poetry of a number of New Zealand writers. This has enriched his work, allowing the artist to engage larger themes and articulate his political stance concerning human rights and environmental issues. Though their message is universal, Hotere is deeply committed to the evocation of the particularities of place. He draws both on his Māori heritage of traditional songs and poetry conveyed particularly by his father, Tangirau Hotere, a noted transcriber of tribal narratives, and on the precedent of Colin *McCahon's use of words in painting. Hotere's sensitivity to the meaning and shape of language has drawn him to the poetry of Bill *Manhire, Hone *Tuwhare, Cilla *McQueen and Ian *Wedde, all of whom deal with the vernacular, but who are also strongly visual in their imagery and word constructions. Hotere's collaborations with these writers, both illustrating their work and using their words in his paintings, have been profiled in Gregory *O'Brien's exhibition for the City Gallery in Wellington: *Hotere: out the black window* (1997).   CB

Houses by the Sea and the *Later Poems of Robin Hyde* (1952) was a posthumous selection from some 300 unpublished poems written between 1935 and August 1939, edited and introduced by Gloria *Rawlinson and published by Denis *Glover. Negotiations over publication were protracted, partly because of Glover's dislike of Rawlinson's introduction and the extracts from Hyde's letters included in it. The earlier poetry is often affected by the predominant influence of the ★Georgian and Romantic poets, resulting in some overuse of elaborate imagery, archaisms and sentimentality. But the collection also contains some of Hyde's finest, many written or reworked in ★China and England. Some of the later New Zealand poems, including the title sequence, evoke a sharp sense of place and the nostalgia of loss. Poems such as 'Sweeping the Gutter Clean' and 'Written at Hsuchowfu', set in China, are imbued with a sense of otherness. In one of the most powerful, 'What Is It Makes the Stranger', she writes with sensuousness and spare strength creating an encompassing vision of reconciliation which embraces her own breadth of experience and the disparate worlds of China and New Zealand. This collection is characterised by a sense of immediacy and actuality, places and people in sharp focus, powerful feelings forcefully conveyed.   GB

HOWES, Edith (1874?–1954), earned the MBE (1935) and King George VI's Coronation Medal (1937) for her children's writing. Born in England, she was educated in New Zealand and drew on her own classroom experiences as pupil and teacher, particularly teaching infants at Gore School 1899–1917. With a special empathy with young people, she wrote many children's stories for newspapers under the pseudonym 'Aunty Jack'. Because of a dearth of child-centred New Zealand school reading matter, she wrote her own booklets (published by Whitcombe & Tombs), using story and song to teach such subjects as nature study, in which she was expert, being made a life member of the Otago Institute in 1911. The most famous of her thirty children's books are *Fairy Rings* (1911) and *The Cradle Ship* (1916). A landmark attempt to provide children with sex education, this ran to eighteen reprints, with translations into French, Italian and Danish, and publication in USA, with four reprints.

Provoked by classroom overcrowding, rote learning and heavy discipline, Howes wrote articles later published as *Tales Out of School* (1919) to set out an educational philosophy which still seems enlightened. In retirement in Dunedin, she drew about her a literary circle. Her three-act play, 'Rose Lane' (1936), won a British Drama League prize and was performed during ★Authors' Week. As first Dunedin president of the ★League of New Zealand Penwomen, she arranged an exhibition of the work of sixty-four women writers, herself having twenty titles on display. At the 1951 ★Writers' Conference in Christchurch, she struck Frank ★Sargeson as both 'incredibly old' and 'incurably famous'.

While much of her work centres on a mythical fairy world which now seems naïve, the best shows a fine eye for natural detail. Howes wrote guide books to Stewart Island (1913) and the Marlborough Sounds (1919), and newspaper articles on women's education and political responsibilities.   HM

Howrah Bridge and Other Poems, James K. ★Baxter's fifth collection, the last poem of which dates from 1959, was published by ★Oxford University Press in 1961. It evinces the tremendous changes, personal and poetic, Baxter went through in the late 1950s—changes that were brought into focus by the months he spent in Asia in 1958–59. Of its forty-three poems, two sections of eighteen flank a smaller section of seven based on Baxter's Indian experiences (the 'Howrah' in Calcutta is the massive iron bridge spanning the Ganges River). The first part, wrote Baxter, 'was written some time ago by a man who thought he was a New Zealander; the second part, lately, in the past two or three years by a man who had become almost unawares, a member of a bigger, rougher family. The poems in India mark this change.' Stylistically, the Indian poems reflect the strong influence of Lawrence Durrell.   PM

Hui is the Māori term for a meeting and is sometimes used in ★New Zealand English for a meeting of any kind. Most commonly, however, it refers to a formal meeting on a ★marae. Māori organisations of many kinds hold hui regularly or exceptionally, and the ★tangata whenua will use their marae for important birthdays, funerals (★tangi), weddings, memorials for ancestors and tribal gatherings. Often hundreds or even thousands of people are accommodated on the marae. As the guests arrive they are greeted with ★karanga, ★pōwhiri, ★waiata and ★whaikōrero, so that the hui provides an occasion for the contemporary development of the oral tradition.   NW

Huia was an annual published in Auckland in 1903 and included work by Edith ★Lyttleton ('G.B. Lancaster'), Jessie ★Mackay, Alan ★Mulgan, Will ★Lawson, Alice ★Kenny and Johannes C. ★Andersen.   SH

Huia Publishers was established in 1991 with the primary aim of publishing and promoting writing by Māori and on subjects of interest to Māori, in Māori and in English, including children's and adult literature. Major publications in Māori include the *Mātāwai* series, three ★Māori newspaper anthologies, and *Kati Au i Konei*, a collection of fifteen Ngāti Toarangatira and Ngāti Raukawa ★waiata. Publications in English include two novels: *He Tangi Aroha* (1993) by Apirana ★Taylor and *The Claim* (1994) by Sally Marshall. In 1995 two collections of short stories, in separate Māori and English books, were produced as a result of the inaugural Huia Publishers short story competition: *Nga Pakiwaitara Huia* and *Huia Short Stories*. Writers published in Māori include Hepora Young, Charles Royal and Esther Tamehana. RRB

HULME, Keri (1947–), novelist, short story writer and poet, gained international recognition with her award-winning *the *bone people*. Within New Zealand she has held writing fellowships at a several universities, served on the *Literary Fund Advisory Committee (1985–89) and the Indecent Publications Tribunal (1985–90), and in 1986–88 was appointed 'cultural ambassador' while travelling in connection with *the bone people*.

Born and raised in Otautahi, Christchurch, Hulme is the eldest of six children. Her father, a carpenter and first-generation New Zealander whose parents came from Lancashire, died when Hulme was 11. Her mother came from Oamaru, of Orkney Scots and Māori descent (Kāi Tahu, Kāti Māmoe). Hulme was schooled at North New Brighton Primary School and Aranui HS (Christchurch). Her holidays were spent with her mother's extended family at Moeraki, on the Otago East Coast, a landscape filled with the residue of its Māori past, which remains important for linking Hulme with her Māori ancestors: 'I love it better than any place on Earth. It is my turangawaewae-ngakau, the standing-place of my heart….' Partial accounts of her childhood are in 'Okatiro and Moeraki' in *Te Whenua, Te Iwi/The Land and The People* (ed. Jock Philips, 1987) and *Homeplaces: Three Coasts of the South Island of New Zealand* (words by Hulme, photographs by Robin Morrison, 1989). Hulme has remembered that as a child she was possessed of 'a relish for telling stories and an obsessive desire to communicate'. After her father's death the sun-porch of the family home was turned into a study for the young writer; she recalls rewriting Enid Blyton stories the way she thought they should have been written, writing poetry from the age of 12, and composing short stories, a few of which were published in school magazines.

After leaving school, Hulme shunned university and worked instead as a tobacco picker in Motueka. It was here, aged 18, that she had the first of many dreams about a mute, long-haired, grinning child with strange, green eyes, from whom the name Simon Peter 'seemed to resonate'. She began to write about him in a short story, 'Simon Peter's Shell'. In the course of the next seven years, the child continued to appear in Hulme's dreams; notes, drawings and stories about him, and other allied characters, accumulated. These fragments eventually formed the basis of her novel *the bone people*, which was published in 1983, more than seventeen years after the first dream-appearance of Simon Peter. In 1967 Hulme began an honours law degree at Canterbury University, but left after four terms, returning to tobacco picking. By 1972, at 25, she was obsessively reworking her dream material and associated drawings and stories: 'I had a kind of theatre going on in my head each night and it was getting out of control.' She decided to turn her hand to writing full-time in order to make sense of the mass of material she had accumulated but despite family support survived only nine months before poverty again forced her to undertake an 'endless stream of menial jobs', in Woolworths, as fish-and-chips cook, woollen-mill winder, postie, journalist and television production trainee. Hulme continued to write and publish poems and stories in journals, magazines and anthologies. Some of her earliest work appeared in *Lost Voices* (1979) under the pseudonymn of Kai Tainui, who also made a brief appearance in *Landfall 138* (1981) with the story 'A Nightsong for the Shining Cuckoo'. 'Nightsong' subsequently appeared in Hulme's collection of short stories, *Te *Kaihau/The Windeater*. Despite a fairly small output Hulme won several awards for her writing, including the *Katherine Mansfield Memorial Award for her short story 'Hooks and Feelers' (1975), the Maori Trust Fund Prize (for writing in English; 1977), the ICI Writing Bursary (1982) and the New Zealand Writing Bursary (1983). In her first collection of poetry, *The Silences Between (Moeraki Conversations)* (Auckland University Press, 1982), six 'conversations' are separated (or linked) by pieces called 'silences'. Together, these comprise a kind of poetical dream diary, recording the thoughts, memories and actions of a central persona, which it seems natural (if mistaken) to assume is Hulme herself.

Throughout these years, Hulme continued to work on the material which had its origins in the dreams, gradually shaping it into a novel. Linked to the figure of the child, other characters appeared in her dreams and writing, notably Kerewin Holmes and Joe Gillayley, who, together with Simon form the triad at the centre of *the bone people*. Hulme has said of Kerewin that although she 'has always been a bit of an off-shoot of me—a sort of wish-fulfilment character for what she owned, … a shallow alter ego', nonetheless 'she escaped out of my control and developed a life of her own'. Eventually a first draft of the novel was completed and submitted. The first publisher's response was to prove characteristic, suggesting that the manuscript be trimmed by about half. Hulme's mother helped edit out unnecessary material from the first three chapters and Hulme continued to rework the manuscript, offering it to a variety of publishers and eventually rewriting it seven times. (Some of this manuscript material has been deposited at the Hight Library, University of Canterbury; two further draft manuscripts are in the possession of Hulme's mother and another three have been kept by the writer.) Four publishers refused the novel in its submitted form, apparently for different reasons. It was not only the intrinsic Māori elements of the novel and its stylistic experimentation that were a problem. Several more publishers recommended severe editing but Hulme adamantly refused to allow anyone to 'go through [her] work with shears' or be 'a silent partner' in her work. The novel was finally accepted by the Spiral Collective and published with the assistance of two Literary Fund grants. Typeset by members of the Victoria University Students' Association, and proofread and pasted up by members of the collective, the first edition of the novel is striking for, if flawed by, a remarkable lack of editorial intrusion and the idiosyncrasies of its many typographic errors. It was launched with a *hui at Wellington Teachers' Training College in February 1984. Extremely well reviewed, copies of the small first print run, and the second, sold out very quickly. The novel was awarded the Mobil Pegasus Award, allocated that year to Māori fiction (1984) and the New Zealand Book Award for Fiction (1984). A new edition, jointly published by Spiral and Hodder and Stoughton, appeared in 1985 and went through several print runs; Louisiana State University Press published the first American edition. That year *the bone people* was awarded the prestigious international Booker Prize.

Hulme acknowledges the need to respect all facets of her ancestry. Māori, Celtic and Norse mythology, in homage to her mixed heritage, is threaded through all of her writing, as are fragments of Māori language, and allusions to European (notably English and Irish Modernist) writing and a variety of inherited narrative conventions. However, she has on numerous occasions declared herself to be wholly Māori by spirit and inclination: 'I think of myself as a Maori writer rather than Pakeha … that's the strong and the vivid and the embracing, the good side of things. That's where I draw my strength from.' She has time and again defended her right to identify and write as Māori, despite criticism which undermines the 'authenticity' of this identification. Most notorious is C.K. *Stead's *Ariel* article (1985) in which, while praising the 'imaginative strength' of *the bone people*, he criticises Hulme's receipt of the Pegasus Award for Māori writers. Stead suggests that the Māori elements of the novel are 'willed, self-conscious, not inevitable, not entirely authentic', arguing that as Hulme is only one-eighth Māori, her upbringing was substantially European and she was raised speaking English, she

has no right to write as and for Māori. Hulme has never made any public response to Stead's criticism.

the bone people was followed by a collection of poems, *Lost Possessions* (Victoria University Press, 1985) and a collection of short stories *Te Kaihau: The Windeater* (Victoria University Press, 1986). Both have received very little critical attention. In 1987, Hulme was awarded the Chianti Ruffino Regional Award and in 1989 published *Homeplaces*, her homage to Okarito, Moeraki and Stewart Island. A further collection of poems, *Strands*, was published in 1992 (Auckland University Press). Many critics have commented on the deeply negative nature of Hulme's writing, despite her wry humour and the celebration in her work of what she calls the 'good things' in life: fishing, cooking, eating, drinking, playing the guitar and painting. Arguably, it is this which accounts for the popular and critical success of *the bone people* and the somewhat ambivalent and muted response to the other writing. The novel manages to contain its negativity, at least for the imaginative duration of the fiction, concluding with an optimistic reconciliation of the (cultural, ethnic, interpersonal and narrative) tensions played out in the fiction. In the short stories and poetry, however, these tensions are laid bare for the reader; redemptive resolution is rarely, if ever, achieved. Critics have tended to read many of the characteristic aspects of Hulme's writing in terms of her situation as a postcolonial writer. Her negativity is often read as reflective of her ambivalent and pessimistic appraisal of New Zealand's 'postcolonial crisis' in which Pākehā and Māori struggle to negotiate differences in the attempt to forge a new bicultural identity. Hulme's postcoloniality, it is argued, accounts for her persistent use and subversion of binary categories (whether Māori/Pākehā, male/female, realism/fantasy or life/death) and her celebration of multiplicity. Similarly explained is the cultural eclecticism of her writing, its multiple literary, linguistic and religious/mythic sources; and her linguistic experimentation is interpreted as attempts to merge and meld both English and Māori into a new language capable of expressing (postcolonial) experience. Other critics have read Hulme's work in terms of its feminism, although Hulme is typically ambiguous in her response to such readings: 'I'm a feminist because I was born female but I've never belonged to a feminist group in my life.'

A self-styled neuter, like her character Kerewin, Hulme lives alone in the octagonal house she built in Okarito, on the West Coast of the South Island, where she engages her creativity (writing, painting and drawing) for nine months of the year; the other three months are spent entertaining family. She writes from the main room of her home which overlooks the

Tasman Sea—the importance of this coast, too, to Hulme has been reaffirmed in numerous interviews and throughout her writing. Her twinned novels *Bait* and *On the Shadow Side*, on which she has been working for a number of years, are awaited.   KWo

HUME, Fergus (1859–1932), novelist, arrived in New Zealand from England as a small child and left for Australia in 1885 shortly after completing a law degree at Otago University. In Dunedin his father was the founding director of Ashburn Hall, the only private mental hospital in the country at that time. In Melbourne in 1886 Hume published *The Mystery of a Hansom Cab*, which has sometimes been described as the first mystery novel in English (anticipating Conan Doyle by one year), and which became an enormous success, with many subsequent reprintings and translations (see Detective Thrillers). Hume did not profit from this, having sold the copyright for £50 to the 'Hansom Cab Publishing Company', but he wrote tirelessly for the next thirty years, producing no less than 137 novels at an average length of 300–400 pages. Most of these are set in England, where he lived from 1888, but a handful are set in Australia. References to New Zealand are few. In the short story 'The Greenstone God and the Stockbroker' in *The Dwarf's Chamber and Other Stories* (1896) the criminal gives himself away by leaving a greenstone 'idol' at the scene of the crime and it is traced back to his visit to the New Zealand ship, the *Kaitangata*. However, any other distinctive object would have served the purpose as well. More interesting is the story 'A Colonial Banshee' in *The Dancer in Red and Other Stories* (1906), which is set in Queenstown and contains some amusing comments on the tourist resort: 'When not climbing I wandered about Queenstown, and employed my spare time in dodging the goats.... When I was there, the principal amusements were riding, driving, climbing, and visiting the cemetery.' The story is of a lonely Banshee called Bridget, who has become a colonist by pursuing an Irish couple to New Zealand and yearns for the old ruined tower in County Mayo where she used to howl so happily.

This may seem a meagre harvest of New Zealand references, and yet Hume and his contemporary readers united in perceiving him as a New Zealand writer. In the 1911 preface to a revised 'Hansom Cab' he wrote 'I may state ... that I belong to New Zealand, and not to Australia', and bibliographies listed him as a New Zealander. This seems to have distressed the more earnest propounders of a national literature, one of whom, William Freeman, wrote a very scathing review of *The Picadilly Puzzle* in **Zealandia* (1889): 'The most remarkable feature about the characters is that very nearly all of them (the hero included) scatter about a reckless profusion of lies, introduced not at all because they are necessary but solely to mystify the reader. The author leads the way himself in this deception.... I take this opportunity of expressing our regret that one who in the eyes of the world is representing us in the Old Country should not take up his stand on the side of that which is clean, wholesome and pure-minded.'   NW

HUNT, Sam (1946–), poet and performer, was born at Castor Bay in Auckland. His distinctive appearance —tall and rangy, usually wearing drainpipe trousers ('Foxton Straights' he calls them) and open-chested shirts, with long hair curling wildly above a weathered face—is complemented by the familiar gravelly drawl that has made him one of New Zealand's most recognisable figures. Virtually single-handedly, Hunt has created a broad general audience for poetry; and if it was up to the crowds who flock to hear him on stage and the school pupils he has galvanised into enjoying verse, he would be the country's poet laureate. The value of Hunt's approach, suggests Alan *Riach, is that 'If poetry is performance then it's also education. If you're reaching people who have never been touched like that before, you're in the business of teaching.'

Part of Hunt's appeal is also his unabashed romanticism: 'Romantics, so they say, / don't ever die!' (Second 'Song'). He is, to quote one reviewer, a 'freewheeling ordinary bloke, a kind of Kiwi Jack Kerouac, laconic— somewhat gauche—whose poems or "roadsongs" are direct and simple, surprised by their own powerful emotion.'

Hunt's commitment to writing poetry probably came from his mother. His father, a barrister, was 'sixty when I was born, / twice my mother's age ... when I wanted him most ... He was somewhere else' ('My Father Scything'). Yet Hunt also reveals a love for this unconventional parent, and early poems featuring his father remain among his best. He attended St Peter's College, Auckland, from 1958 to 1963; a period during which his individualism came into conflict with the Christian Brothers' authoritarianism. (He has said that he was strapped at the age of 14 for reciting a poem by James K. *Baxter, which had sexual imagery, in the classroom.) Life was not made easier by a bad stutter, and poems working through the tensions and fantasies of adolescence became a form of release. Despite school's problems, Hunt, who was a good sprinter and diver, did not leave until asked to. He benefited, in his final year, from having poet Ken *Arvidson as his English master, and he obtained University Entrance.

Leaving school and home coincided. After the briefest stop at the grave of his mentor A.R.D.

*Fairburn, Hunt hitch-hiked 400 miles south, appearing uninvited at the home of another poet he greatly admired, Alistair *Campbell, whose family took him under their wing. The years 1964–67 were a period of oscillation between Wellington and Auckland: Hunt attended university in both cities; was taught by Kendrick *Smithyman; got to know Denis *Glover; and became lifelong friends with his fellow exuberant, Gary *McCormick. Along with brief periods truck-driving and panel-beating, Hunt graduated from teachers' college and taught briefly before deciding, in late 1960, that poetry was his vocation. At about the same time another friend and mentor, James K. *Baxter (whose 'Letter to Sam Hunt' exhorted him to retain his individuality) was deciding that poverty was his vocation.

From then until 1997 Hunt lived in a number of creatively named homes around the Pauatahanui estuary, north of Wellington. The events each dwelling represents are inscribed in his verse. For example, it was at his Bottle Creek boatshed that he was joined by renowned black and white sheepdog Minstrel (survivor of a fall from the back of a truck and dedicatee of his own series of 'Bow-Wow' poems); while at Battle Hill Hunt's son was born. From there Hunt moved to Death's Corner (formerly the farmhouse of a Mr Death), then back to a boatshed in Paremata, before heading, in 1997, for Auckland's Waiheke Island.

Through the seventies and eighties, Hunt's increasing popularity was not enough to offset serious problems caused by alcohol. However, from a low point in 1983 when he tried to take his own life, he turned things around, although it took Minstrel's death (see 'Minstrel Makes Trip Alone', *Dominion*, 21 Dec. 1988) to make him stop drinking. These days there is about him less of the 'solitary, doomed, restless, ever-on-the-move figure' that Campbell once identified as part of Hunt's personal myth-making.

Hunt's book sales far exceed most New Zealand poets. He has published *From Bottle Creek: Selected Poems 1967–69* (1969), *Bracken Country* (1971), *From Bottle Creek* (1972), *South Into Winter: Poems and Roadsongs* (1973), *Time To Ride* (1975), *Drunkard's Garden* (1977), *Collected Poems 1963–1980* (1980), *Running Scared* (1982), *Approaches To Paremata* (1985), *Selected Poems* (1987), *Making Tracks* (1991), *Naming the Gods* (1992), *Down the Backbone* (1995), and, with Gary McCormick, *Roaring Forties* (1997). Reviewers have discovered the need to be sure of their ground before taking a critical knife to these collections. Patrick *Evans, for example, earned for his negative review of *Collected Poems*—in which he called Hunt the 'Pam Ayres of New Zealand poetry'—a considerable correspondence from Hunt's many admirers.

It is a fact that Hunt's strongly autobiographical verse sometimes seems heavy and lifeless, excessively sentimental (or even banal) on the page. But as McCormick argues, the 'literary critic cannot hope to understand a Sam Hunt by merely studying his work and ignoring the man'. Everything Hunt writes is geared for personal performance: his lyrics are deliberately uncomplicated and colloquial; their traditional forms and regular rhythms allow 'the stories and myths [to be] fleshed out and invested with energy and power'. Yet Hunt is also widely read and, as Anne *French notes, such New Zealand literary influences as Baxter, Fleur *Adcock (in 'Ice on the Jetty') and even Katherine *Mansfield (in 'Just Like That') are discernible.

In 1975 Hunt was *Burns Fellow at the University of Otago. But his popularity has brought greater rewards than academic fellowships can provide. Once describing himself as the 'megabuck bard', Hunt has (among his many engagements) read in the New Zealand legislative chamber; performed in Australia, New York and Washington DC; fronted an America's Cup yachting promotion; featured with the New Zealand Symphony Orchestra and members of the group *Split Enz; and made regular television appearances. He was awarded a QSM in 1986 for his contribution to New Zealand poetry.

Angel Gear: On the Road with Sam Hunt (1989), with Colin Hogg, is biographical; as is Peter Smart's *Introducing Sam Hunt* (1981), which also includes a certain amount of critical material aimed at students. Hunt has been interviewed in *Landfall* 107 (1973) and *JAAM* 5 (1996/97).   PM

HUNTER, (Maurice) Reginald or **Rex** (1888– 1960), was a journalist, playwright, poet and fiction writer who spent most of his career in America. His poem-sequence *The Saga of Sinclair* (USA 1927) is an impressionistic autobiographical travel-journal, from his boyhood memories of school and a Māori friend, through the 'Wanderlust, a witch with sea-green eyes' that took him to Australia, Fiji, Honolulu and on across America to 'the beat and drive' of New York, and London, where the poem is composed. With moments of descriptive vividness and confessional force when it is not too mannered, the sequence is refreshingly unlike anything written in New Zealand at that date. The emphasis is on the persona of Sinclair as detached outsider.

Hunter was born in Southbrook, North Canterbury, studied at Canterbury and Victoria university colleges, worked on newspapers in Wellington and Sydney, began his travels in 1914 and held posts on the *Rocky Mountain News* (Denver), Kansas City *Star* and Chicago *Daily*

News, where in 1920 he became a friend of its labour editor, Carl Sandburg, and another journalist, Ben Hecht. He published a volume of four one-act plays and sketches, *Stuff o' Dreams* (Chicago, 1919), which had been produced in Chicago and, like the later poem, romanticise the figure of the wanderer. He moved to the New York *Sun*, living in the literary quarter of Greenwich Village, where Welsh novelist John Cowper Powys became a friend. After a period from 1923 in London and Paris, Hunter freelanced in New York until returning to New Zealand in 1949, spending his last decade in Dunedin, contributing to the *Timaru Herald* and giving radio talks on topics such as 'Literary America' and 'The Lure of the South Seas in Literature'. A brief obituary appeared in *Arena 53 (1960).

Hunter's American journalism includes frequent articles on the *Pacific, Australia and New Zealand (e.g. 'Wild Rhythms of the South Seas', *Dance Magazine*, New York 1927). As Rex Hunter he published numerous poems in newspapers and journals such as *Poetry World* (e.g. Aug., Sept. 1937), and two collections: *And Tomorrow Comes* (USA, 1923) and *Call Out of Darkness* (USA, 1946). His most successful book was the novel *Porlock, A Portrait* (USA, 1940, as Reginald Hunter), which includes a laudatory introduction by Powys. It is about a timid Englishman of cluttered erudition struggling with the go-getting hubbub of Greenwich Village in the Prohibition era. Reviews nationally praised it highly: 'An American classic', 'genuinely funny', 'accurate picture of … the hilarious twenties'. Two Hunter volumes were republished by the English poet and critic Kenneth Hopkins on his Warren House Press in Norfolk, *The Saga of Sinclair* (1981) and *And Tomorrow Comes* (1982). A manuscript collection is in the *Alexander Turnbull Library. No copy of the plays or of *Porlock* is known in New Zealand.   HMcQ/RR

HYDE, Robin (1906–39), who at first published under her actual name as Iris (Guiver) Wilkinson (and later various other pseudonyms), was one of New Zealand's most significant writers in poetry, fiction and journalism.

Born in Cape Town, she was brought to Wellington as a baby. Her early years when the family lived on the edge of poverty, her parents' quarrels, their conflicting social attitudes, her schooling and early career as a journalist and aspiring poet are depicted in the autobiographical novel *The *Godwits Fly* (1938). Her father's ardent socialism was a lasting influence.

Although she wrote dismissively of her secondary schooling at Wellington GC, she was introduced there to the work of poets who profoundly influenced her. Over twenty of her poems and short stories were published in the school magazine and she was second in a Royal

Colonial Institute Essay competition for 'The Lives of Drake and Raleigh … as Empire Builders'.

Gaining a Senior National Scholarship, Hyde briefly studied at Victoria University College, then took up a position as 'Aunt Mary' on the children's page of the *Farmers' Advocate*. Joining the *Dominion*, she began her 'Peeps at Parliament' under the name of 'Novitia', in mid-1925. Reflecting the newspaper's view of what women wanted to read, the style was only slightly modified from 'Aunt Mary'. Nevertheless she succeeded in broadening the range of subjects.

She had been hospitalised for a knee operation in 1924; lameness and pain haunted her for the rest of her life, later entering her fiction and journalism. Likewise her discovery that the young man with whom she had fallen in love, Harry Sweetman, had left for England, and the news of his death soon after, became part of Eliza Hannay's story in *The Godwits Fly*.

Pregnant after a brief love affair, she resigned from the *Dominion* in April 1926. A bleak period in Sydney culminated in the death of her newborn son, Robin. The emotional and psychological turmoil led to hospitalisation at Queen Mary Hospital in Hanmer Springs. Recovering, she began to write again, now adopting the pen-name Robin Hyde. By September 1927 her poetry had been published in the Christchurch *Sun, Auckland Star and New Zealand Times. Engaged by the *Mirror to write a regular 'Breezes from the Capital' column, she intended to return to full-time journalism.

At Hanmer she had begun a correspondence with John *Schroder of the *Sun*. Their correspondence (now in the *Alexander Turnbull Library) illustrates his role as Hyde's mentor, and her gradual growth to independence.

A period with the Publicity Bureau followed, while she continued to write for the *Mirror* and *Sun*, buying a typewriter from her prize-winning South African story 'One Soldier'. Editorial expectations continued to be a frustration—the *Mirror* desired a purely social column, while the *Otago Witness* and Christchurch *Press required, she believed, 'a mat and a mere apiece' to satisfy the demand for New Zealand content in short stories.

She met C.A. *Marris, who published her work in *New Zealand Best Poems*. When Denis *Glover lampooned Marris, Schroder, Alan *Mulgan and women writers in 'The Arraignment of Paris', he exempted Hyde as 'one who's fairly good' from his denunciation of Gloria *Rawlinson, Eve *Langley and Eileen *Duggan. Privately, he was later to dismiss her as one of 'our lady writers. A bunch of bores in stuffy drawers.'

After a period of unemployment punctuated with freelance journalism Hyde began writing 'women's stuff' for ★*Truth* in September 1928. A complex private life and the relentless pressure of journalism left little time for poetry. In December, dismissed without notice, she moved to Christchurch where she shared 'Penelope's Column' in the *Sun* with Esther ★*Glen*. She spent time with Schroder, and met the controversial Jean ★*Devanny* and Jessie ★*Mackay*, the respected poet who later commented, 'Eileen Duggan and Robin Hyde may between them lay the foundation of a New Zealand literature.'

Moving as Lady Editor to the *Wanganui Chronicle*, she further challenged the boundaries of women's journalism. Her first volume of poetry, *The Desolate Star and Other Poems* (1929), was dedicated to Schroder and positively reviewed by Jessie Mackay and Alan Mulgan.

Halfway through 1930 Hyde suddenly moved back to the South Island and in October gave birth to her son. Unemployed again, forced to hide his existence from her family and influential figures such as Schroder, she spent a despairing few months in Wellington before moving to Auckland as Lady Editor on the *New Zealand Observer*.

Though described by Allen ★*Curnow* as 'a shabby little weekly', the *Observer*'s stance as 'Smart but not vulgar, fearless but not offensive, independent but not neutral' enabled Hyde to produce an extraordinary range of contributions. Cynical, provocative or arch, the style and perspective varied as she tackled political and social issues, book and film reviews. Frequently she wrote of the poor and marginalised, their injustices and loss of dignity. Yet often she was forced to suppress this anger, to write instead of balls, cocktail parties and fashion. She still worked on the poetry that was her first love. By mid-1933 the demands of work, combined with financial and emotional stress, led to a suicide attempt. She was hospitalised and charged in court.

She admitted herself to the Grey Lodge, in Auckland Mental Hospital. After some empty months she resumed writing, and flourished in the new freedom from the demands of daily journalism. *Journalese* (1934), a quickly written commentary on life and literature, was praised by the popular novelist Vicki Baum but largely ignored. In Hyde's view 'much of the really unfair criticism … is based on sexual grounds'. By the beginning of 1935 she had finished the first version of her historical novel ★*Check to Your King* (1936), which returned to the theme of her most powerful *Observer* articles, the role of colonisation in creating the contemporary plight of Māori. Her 'Lonely Street' was the winning story in *Art in New Zealand* in March 1935. She continued to write for the *Mirror* and *Observer*, developing her articles on '"Starkie", Outlaw of the NZEF', into the remarkable war novel ★*Passport to Hell* (1936). Much of Hyde's prodigious output early in 1935 remains unpublished but included a draft of *The Godwits Fly*. By September 1935

she was also working on ★*Wednesday's Children* (1937), an extraordinary 'dream novel' which defiantly rewrites women's experience.

During her Auckland years Hyde got to know journalists and writers such as Gloria Rawlinson, a young poet whose Princes Street apartment became a popular meeting place, Ron ★*Holloway*, Eve ★*Langley*, contributors to Auckland University's ★*Phoenix*, Dorothea and John ★*Mulgan*, Frank ★*Sargeson*, Jane ★*Mander*, D'Arcy ★*Cresswell* and the young Warwick ★*Lawrence*. Her introduction to Lawrence's *Vulcan Lane and Other Verses* stated her preference for 'small, simple and restrained' poems rather than Ezra Pound's 'miles of paper and rivers of ink'. Her second collection, *The Conquerors and Other Poems* (1935) was the first by a New Zealander to be included in Macmillans' Contemporary Poets series. It included some of her most haunting poems such as 'Babel Tower' and one of her own favourites, 'Nirvana'.

She returned to Grey Lodge in January 1936. In its own way it provided protection from her vulnerability, financially, physically and professionally. Later in 1936 she travelled to Dunedin hoping to write a historical novel based on the ★Hocken Library papers of Edward Markham, a nineteenth-century Englishman who had lived with the Māori of the Hokianga. When the library trustees withdrew permission she abandoned the project, although her research provided the basis for her hauntingly beautiful poem *Arangi-Ma*.

She completed the final draft of *The Godwits Fly* at Whangaroa Harbour and early in 1937 wrote *A Home in This World* (1984), a painfully honest account of the previous ten years. By September she finished another 'Starkie' book, the novel ★*Nor the Years Condemn*, a powerful commentary on New Zealand between the wars, distinguished, like her travel articles for the ★*New Zealand Railways Magazine* and her best poetry, by a remarkable sense of place. Unlike some contemporaries, Hyde recognised that 'One cannot make a poem or a story, "New Zealand" by sticking a spray of kowhai in the corner like the brand on the side of frozen mutton.'

Around this time she worked on the horrifying fragment *A Night of Hell*, later published by her son as the epilogue to *A Home in This World*. With *Persephone in Winter:Poems* (1937), Hyde's poetry moved away from the English and European influence, especially the ★Georgians and Romantics, that had restricted her earlier work: 'it's just dawned on me that I am a New Zealander, and surely, surely, the legends of the mountains, rivers, and people we see should mean more to us than the legends of any other country'.

Nevertheless, she accepted a Coronation medal and decided to visit England. New Zealanders were, after all, 'English and not English'; her mother had raised her on images of *'Home', bluebells and robins in the snow. On 18 January 1938 Hyde sailed on the SS *Changte*, recording the voyage in articles for *Woman To-day* and in poems. Arriving in Hong Kong she made the momentous decision to travel to *China, then at war with *Japan.

In Shanghai she met Rewi *Alley, already committed to his lifelong work for the Chinese people, and in Hong Kong James *Bertram, who was to have a significant part in the remainder of her life. She travelled to the war front, the first woman journalist to do so, witnessing the barbaric realities which she had only imagined in *Passport to Hell*. Her carefully documented articles for *Woman To-day*, the *Mirror* and *Radio Record* became the basis for *Dragon Rampant* (1939).

Family and friends were alarmed when she disappeared for a month, but despite a vicious assault by Japanese soldiers she succeeded in reaching Tsingtao and then Hong Kong. She finally arrived in England in September, ill and penniless. There she became involved with the China Campaign Committee, the Left Book Club and the Suffragette Fellowship. She was now convinced that New Zealand's future lay in the *Pacific, not with England and Europe.

Living in a caravan in Kent, then in London boarding houses, she continued to work on poetry and *Dragon Rampant*, with support from Bertram. *The Godwits Fly* was published in November and there were negotiations for a dramatisation of *Wednesday's Children*. Hospitalised twice, she convalesced at Charles *Brasch's home outside London. Neither the sales nor reviews of *The Godwits Fly* were as good as she had hoped, but *Dragon Rampant*

received positive reviews. She continued to write the poems which were posthumously published as *Houses by the Sea* (1952). She was ill, financially desperate, anxious to return home, and troubled by the increasing prospect of war. Her old friend John A. *Lee negotiated for government assistance to bring her home but on 23 August Hyde took her own life by benzedrin poisoning.

Schroder's obituary spoke of her 'perpetual struggle against odds', Terry *McLean wrote of her as 'a fighter of rare courage. Her writing was the best of present-day New Zealanders. Her sympathies were always with the under-dog.' Her reputation was enhanced by *Houses by the Sea*, with its vivid poems of New Zealand and China, but her originality in prose and poetry is only slowly being recognised. *A Home in This World*, a *Selected Poems* (ed. Lydia Wevers, 1984), recent reprints of her prose works and *Disputed Ground: Robin Hyde Journalist* (ed. Boddy and Matthews, 1991) have all contributed. Successfully crossing genres, she was a hard-working journalist who published ten books of prose and poetry in ten years. Given such output and diversity, it is not surprising that the writing is uneven. The consistent themes are compassion for those on society's margins, a passionate desire to find 'community' in a hostile world, a search for balance in her own emotions, and assertion of the full equality of women.

Her expression of these ideas became tauter, more precise and more immediate. The context of an external world is always clear, but her poetry, especially, reveals a contradictory and movingly perplexed inner life, for which her unpublished poems and journals provide further intimate record. GB

I

I Saw in My Dream (1949) was Frank *Sargeson's first published novel, and the second of his books to be published in England by John Lehmann. Its first part, a story of childhood and adolescence of Henry Griffiths, was published by *Caxton Press in 1945 as a novella entitled *When the Wind Blows*. A section had previously been published in *New Zealand New Writing* (3 June 1994), and the novella was reprinted in two successive issues of *Penguin New Writing* in 1946.

The novel tells of a young New Zealander's growing to maturity, reflecting Sargeson's own experience and view of the world, though it cannot be simply called autobiographical. In retrospect its closest literary companion-piece is the memoir first published as 'Up onto the Roof and Down Again'. In its first part particularly it owes much to Joyce's *A Portrait of the Artist as a Young Man*, though the culmination here involves recognition of sexual rather than artistic destiny, and a sense of the need to break from the religious and spiritual confines of a family rather than those of a nation. The child paralysed by religious precepts and a sense of sinfulness is a theme that several earlier stories had touched on. In the novel it leads eventually to the reviving confidence of the central figure when he breaks with the ethical and economic constrictions of his supposed destiny and establishes himself as a reconstructed figure, with a new name and new personality. The title's allusion ironically points to the narrative as a pilgrimage away from *puritanism. (It is the narrative refrain of Bunyan's *Pilgrim's Progress*.)

The novel's second part, set on a *backblocks farm, shows the principal character now independent and renamed Dave Spencer. The description of the farm and the circumstances of the character's renaming seem to reflect the influence of the writer's uncle, Oakley Sargeson, the farmer whose name Frank Sargeson adopted when he rejected his given name of Norris Davey in the 1920s. Sargeson's skill in this second part is less in plotting than in the evocative descriptions. These are both negative and affirmative, the one illustrated by the shrewish farmer's wife, who appears little different from the embittered Aunt Clara of the first part, the other by the poor *bush farms, created with great labour in a harsh but beautiful environment. In the ironically named 'Waiamihea' the story depicts a world where the struggle to develop the farms is countered by the eroding land taking destructive revenge.

Sargeson's characters inhabit a world where even the sympathetic characters such as the farmer Anderson are ultimately flawed by the puritan work ethic. That ethic leads to a Pākehā view of Māori which is essentially self-righteous, while ensuring that the sexual awakening which had troubled the character of Griffiths-Spencer in the novel's first part is sustained and further complicated. It is finally a grim and uncompromising view of the New Zealand rural identity, from which the protagonist must escape to return, apparently temporarily, to his point of origin and departure, where he is now in a position to replace negation with affirmation. Sargeson was to pursue his quarry of puritanism throughout his literary career. His first novel marks an important imaginative stage in this pursuit.   WB

IHIMAERA, Witi (Witi Tame Ihimaera-Smiler) (1944–   ), novelist, short story writer, anthologist and librettist, was born in Gisborne. He has the distinction of being the first Māori writer to publish both a book of short stories and a novel. He is of Te Aitanga-a-Māhaki descent, with close affiliations to Tūhoe, Te Whānau-a-

Apanui, Ngāti Kahungunu, and Ngāi Tāmanuhiri, and links to Rongowhakaata, Ngāti Porou, and Te Whakatōhea. His family *marae is the family house of the Pere family, Rongopai, in Waituhi, near Gisborne. The extraordinary paintings, rather than carvings, decorating the meeting house's interior, have been described in rich detail in his writing.

Much of Ihimaera's fiction is based on fact, but his work is never simply autobiographical. Waituhi, for example, the village setting for many of his narratives, is an imaginative recreation of the actual place. The fictional Waituhi's 'physical cohesion [providing] an "objective correlative" to the ethos that binds the *tangata whenua together'.

Ihimaera spent three years at Te Karaka DHS and a year at the Mormon Church College at Tuhikaramea, Hamilton. He completed his University Entrance at Gisborne BHS and then attended Auckland University from 1963 to 1966. Having acquired six units he returned to Gisborne without completing his degree, and began working as a cadet journalist with the Gisborne Herald before becoming a postman. In 1968 he moved to the Post Office, Wellington, and, in 1969, enrolled part-time at Victoria University, completing his BA in 1971. His first book, published in 1972, was read by then Prime Minister Norman Kirk, who decided that Ihimaera would be valuable in the Ministry of Foreign Affairs. He began there in 1973 as a writer, producing the booklet Maori in 1975 and a film script: although the film, Maori (1981), is a promotional exercise with little resemblance to his original intentions. He remained with the ministry until 1989, apart from leave in 1975 to take up a *Burns Fellowship at the University of Otago and, in 1982, the writing fellowship at Victoria University. During his time with Foreign Affairs he worked for the New Zealand High Commission in Canberra and spent four years in New York and Washington, two of them as New Zealand consul. Since 1990 he has lectured in the English department of Auckland University. In 1991 he was awarded a Scholarship in Letters and, in 1993, he travelled to France as the Katherine *Mansfield Memorial Fellow.

Ihimaera was interested in writing from an early age, and recalls scrawling stories across the whole wall of his room at the family farm at Whakarau. In 1969 he began writing seriously. His first story, 'The Liar', was accepted by the *NZ Listener in May of the following year. From the start, he saw writing as a valuable opportunity to express in print his experience of being a Māori.

Ihimaera's publications are often the products of intensive periods of writing. In London, in 1970, the short story collection *Pounamu Pounamu (1972; awarded third prize in the Wattie Book of the Year Awards) and the two novels *Tangi (1973; first prize in the Wattie Award) and *Whanau (1974) were completed within a six-month period. The politics in these first books is implicit, and they primarily represent his horizontal view of the culture and history of his fictional Waituhi.

A second intensive period of writing took place when Ihimaera was Burns Fellow in 1975, and he wrote the more overtly political stories of The New Net Goes Fishing (1977) and began editing the anthology *Into the World of Light (1982), the precursor to the extensive, five-volume, Te *Ao Mārama series. In December of that year, concerned that his work might be considered the 'definitive portrayal of the world of the Maori' when in his opinion it was 'tragically out of date', he determined to stop writing for a time. His fiction's initial purpose, 'to establish and describe the emotional landscape of the Maori people', suddenly seemed to him less important than describing the political and social reality.

At Victoria University, with his politics now explicit and his ten-year embargo on his own writing ended, Ihimaera plunged 'vertically' into Waituhi's culture and history, with the 'past placed firmly in front' of him, to write The *Matriarch (1986)—which again received the Wattie Book of the Year Award. He also produced the libretto for an opera by Ross *Harris based on Whanau.

The Whale Rider (1987) was written in New York and Cape Cod in the space of three weeks. A magical, mythical work about a young girl whose relationship with a whale ensures the salvation of her village, it is, says Ihimaera, the work of his 'that the Maori community accepts best'. He followed this in 1989 with Dear Miss Mansfield, a response to the Katherine *Mansfield centenary celebrations which rewrites her stories from a Māori perspective. Interestingly, this collection of experimental fiction was slated by New Zealand critics (who seemed to feel he had in some way molested a literary icon) but received excellent reviews internationally.

Another novel set in Waituhi, Bulibasha: King of the Gypsies (1994), was awarded the 1995 Montana Book Award. Described by Ihimaera as an attempt to write a Māori western, this 'exuberant novel ... with a New Zealand brand of magical realism' recounts the rivalry between two great Māori families of shearers and sportsmen and women spanning the period from World War 1 to the 1990s. The conflict between the patriarch, Bulibasha—whose 'marriage' to grandmother Ramona conceals a terrible secret—and Himiona, the rebellious youngest male in the extended family, generates the most tension.

In 1996 Ihimaera's writing moved in a significant new direction when he decided to foreground his sexuality and write a gay novel, Nights in the Gardens of Spain. To come out so explicitly was not an easy decision, but

Ihimaera describes it as keeping faith with his gay audience as, in similar fashion, he attempts to keep faith with his Māori audience. *Nights* is, writes Roger Robinson, 'a good story of conflict, growth and reconciliation, with subplots heroic, political and tragic. It wears its throbbing heart on its shoulder (for in many scenes no one's wearing much else you could put it on)' (*★NZ Books*, Mar. 1995).

There is a substantial body of critical, biographical and bibliographical work about Ihimaera. Among his autobiographical articles, the ones in *WLWE*, Vol. 14, 1975; *Tihe Mauri Ora* (1978); *New Zealand Through the Arts: Past and Present* (1982); and *Through the Looking Glass* (1988) are useful. Two extremely good interviews are by J.B. Beston in *WLWE*, Vol. 16, 1977, and Mark ★Williams in *In the Same Room* (1992). Book-length studies include Richard Corballis and Simon Garrett's *Introducing Witi Ihimaera* (1984) and Umelo Ojinmah's *Witi Ihimaera: A Changing Vision* (1993), which includes a useful bibliography.

Central to Ihimaera's fiction is the fact that the kaupapa he writes to has as its central goal the interpretation and reinterpretation of the concerns of the ★iwi from the viewpoint of the past. He sees himself as a Māori in the world, and thinks of 'the world I'm in as being Māori, not European'. Just as he grew up in a society transforming from rural to urban, so his writing developed during another period of change when, in 'the 1970s and '80s … [Māori] began to demand … sovereignty'. The legacy of this period, Ihimaera suggests, is a 'new strength of which Alan ★Duff is a beneficiary'. PM

Image was published in Auckland 1958–61, edited by Robert Thompson. Initially produced as a quarterly, it was largely sustained through the support of a private sponsor, with ★Literary Fund grants being received in 1959 and 1961. It published work by, among others, James K. ★Baxter, Louis ★Johnson, Kendrick ★Smithyman, Barry ★Mitcalfe, Mary ★Stanley, Helen ★Shaw, Maurice ★Duggan, Charles ★Doyle and Australian poet Bruce Beaver. SH

'In a German Pension', the first collection of short stories by Katherine ★Mansfield, was published in 1911 and comprises 'Germans at Meat', 'The Baron', 'The Sister of the Baroness', 'Frau Fischer', 'Frau Brechenmacher Attends a Wedding', 'The Modern Soul', 'At Lehmann's', 'The Luft Bad', 'A Birthday', 'The Child-Who-Was-Tired', 'The Advanced Lady', 'The Swing of the Pendulum' and 'A Blaze'. Aspects of the stories have a well-documented autobiographical source in Mansfield's seven-month sojourn in Bad Wörishofen, where she was taken by her mother in 1909 after her disastrous one-day marriage to George Bowden, and where she miscarried the child she had conceived with Garnet Trowell. All but three of the stories had been previously published in *The New Age*, a controversial English weekly edited by A.R. Orage, to whom Mansfield wrote in 1921 'you taught me to write…'. As the title implies, they are mostly set in lodgings in a German spa town for visitors 'taking the cure'. They are of two broad types. Typically in the first a cynical English female 'I' narrator notes and recoils from the coarse habits and intellectual arrogance of Germans. Many of the others (written in a mixture of omniscient narration and interior monologue) describe the physical exploitation and repression of women by men. 'The Child-Who-Was-Tired' has been controversial since 1935, when Elisabeth Schneider suggested that Mansfield's 'unconscious memory' drew on Chekhov's 'Spat'khochetsia' when writing it. Whilst many claim plagiarism, ★Alpers contends in the *Life* that '"The Child-Who-Was-Tired", while proving that its author had now made contact with her supposed "master", at the same time proved her imaginative freedom from his influence'. In 1920, Mansfield refused permission for another edition to be printed on the grounds that they were juvenilia and that they might contribute to post-war jingoism. Further editions were however published posthumously, in 1926 and 1964. SSa

In Fires of No Return (1958), James K. ★Baxter's fourth major volume of poetry, was published in England by ★Oxford University Press. Despite this international recognition and the book's selection as the Poetry Book Society's choice, the collection, which is divided into three sections, was not judged successful by critics. Section one with some stronger early poems, and section two, a number of previously uncollected pieces, received little criticism. However Baxter's more recent work in section three was censured for its many poems that contain superb lines or phrases yet fail to achieve wholeness. PM

In My Father's Den (1972), the third novel by Maurice ★Gee, opens with a picture of the wages of violence, the first of many such scenes in the author's books. The use of a newspaper 'quotation' gives it an objectivity which is only apparent: a 17-year-old schoolgirl has been strangled. Wadesville (like Gee's boyhood home, Henderson), a once quiet rural valley, has been turned into an Auckland industrial wasteland, and for Paul Prior this transformation seems paralleled by the gruesome murder. Paul has grown up in a family torn by tension between his devout mother ('the demon of godliness would not let her rest') and his intelligent, free-thinking father: 'She withdrew from the edge of his discovered countries as though from a red light district.' While his brother is a believer, Paul spends time in his father's den—significantly, once a poisons shed—reading his books. Years later, he is suspected of the murder of his brilliant pupil, Celia Inverarity, and although innocent he senses a connection between her death and his encouragement of her reading in a resentfully anti-intellectual community. The attitudes that have killed her are then turned against Paul, as first his books are attacked and then himself, narrowly escaping with his life.   NW

Incense to Idols (1960), a novel by Sylvia *Ashton-Warner.

Incorrigible Music, An, is a sequence of poems by Allen *Curnow, published by *Auckland University Press in 1979. One of Curnow's most powerful collections, this densely reticulated sequence juxtaposes poems (several in multiple sections) with New Zealand settings ('Canst Thou Draw Out Leviathan with an Hook?') with poems set in *Italy both historical ('In the Duomo') and contemporary ('Moro Assassinato'), all linked by a pervasive concern with violence and murder and reflecting a perception that 'All the seas are one sea, / the blood one blood / and the hands one hand' ('Moro Assassinato': I, 'The Traveller').   PS

Indecent Publications Tribunal, see **Censorship**.

'Indiscreet Journey, An', a short story by Katherine *Mansfield, was published posthumously in *Something Childish and Other Stories* (1924), though probably written in 1915. No MS is known. It presents the journey of a naive and self-congratulatory young woman from England into the war zone of France early in World War 1 for an illicit assignation with a lover in the French army. The eager frivolousness of the first part of the story ('What beautiful cemeteries we are passing!') gives way to a much more sombre tone in the second part, when the narrator visits cafés in the unnamed town with her lover and other soldiers. The darkening of tone and images of disorientation, disgust and dissension make this one of the most subtle renderings of the sorrow of war. A description of a soldier suffering the effects of chlorine gas must follow closely, *Alpers suggests, on the Germans' first use of gas in April 1915. The story is based closely on Mansfield's own rendezvous with Francis *Carco at Gray in February 1915, though it omits the sexual encounter detailed in the *Journal*, and comparison with the journal and letters shows how carefully crafted is the shift in tone that is the story's fictional essence. Not one of her most popular works, its reputation is rising as Mansfield's significance as a commentator on the war is appreciated, and it is one of the two Mansfield texts in the *Oxford Book of New Zealand Short Stories*, ed. Vincent *O'Sullivan (1994).   RR

INGLEWOOD, Kathleen, pseudonym, see **ISITT, Kate**.

Intensive Care, the eighth novel by Janet *Frame (New York, Toronto, 1970; Wellington, London, 1971) was awarded the Hubert Church Prose Award and the Buckland Literary Award (1972); no MS is known. This is one of several novels by Frame that overtly critique the inanity of war and the evil of the human desire to classify the 'sane' and the 'normal'. The narrative structure of the three-part novel is typically complex. The two initial parts, a loose family saga, are narrated in the third person, but are interspersed with poetry and prose in the first person, spoken or written by a variety of characters. The first part deals with Tom Livingstone, his brutalising experiences during World War 1 in which he is injured and nursed back to health by Ciss Everest, 'alias the War' (with whom he falls in love); his return to his wife in Waipori City, New Zealand, and their raising of two daughters, Pearl and Naomi; and his journey, at 65, back to England to try to find Ciss (he does, she is decrepit and dying, he murders her in rage). The second part focuses on Tom's brother Leonard, Tom's daughter Pearl, and his grandson Colin Torrence who leaves his wife and three children after falling in love with Lorna Kimberly (he eventually murders her, along with her parents, before killing himself). Intrinsic human brutality, fostered by and engendering a cyclic pattern of violence and war, culminates in the anti-*Utopian third part of the novel, a pessimistic vision of post-nuclear-war technocratic perfectionism. Set in a futuristic Waipori City, it is narrated by three interchanging first-person narrators: Colin Monk's retrospective narrative forms a frame for the large central section, which ostensibly comprises the diary of an autistic child-woman, Milly Galbraith. Sandy Monk, a figment of her imagination, also 'speaks' in this section. Judgment day draws near—the 'Human Delineation Act' is soon to be experimentally enforced in New Zealand. Colin Monk is the 'Guardian of the Great Computer' that will assess, on the basis of 'physical data, I.Q. results' those 'who are more clearly animal than human'. All who do not comply with the requirements of the latter category, 'those who are deformed, diseased, handicapped in any way', will be terminated in '*a Clean Sweep*'. Among those deemed unfit to live are the 'dull-normal' Milly and the surgically reconstructed Sandy. After a period in which the Human Delineation Act is brutally enforced by sanitised mass-murders and brainwashing the novel ends with the triumph of the underdog, as the ill and maimed gain ascendancy. But Frame's vision is far from optimistic: in the new economy of power the formerly oppressed turn on their oppressors, utilising precisely the same strategies of violence. As the ironic pun of the novel's title suggests, the condition of a brutalised and brutalising human race that lacks care is indeed one that needs 'intensive care'.   KWo

Into the World of Light: An Anthology of Maori Writing (1982), edited by Witi *Ihimaera and D.S. *Long, represents the period of 'stunning achievements' taking place in Māori literature during the 1970s by collecting the work of thirty-nine prose writers, poets and dramatists. Whereas Margaret *Orbell's anthology *Contemporary Maori Writing* (1970) selected its authors on the basis of a 'shared experience and similarity of approach', *Into the World of Light* is more overtly political. Its editors expand the definition of Māori writing to recognise its diversity and argue that the apparently recent phenomenon of Māori literature must be appreciated in the context of a long oral tradition. Similarly, the apparent dearth of Māori writing in the preceding decades—although partially attributable to social policies responsible for alienation, loss of identity, geographical dislocation and language decline—is, they suggest, due less to a lack of quality than publishers' refusals to produce books by Māori writers because their target readership, other Māori, 'don't read books'. This argument is given substance by the uniformly high standard of the material collected. Graham Wiremu argues that behind this 'prodigious and powerful' anthology lies an indication of the real scope of the Māori literary movement (*NZ Listener*, 22 May 1982). Ihimaera's five volume *Te *Ao Mārama* series, of which *Into the World of Light* is the forerunner, provides an even greater sense of the extent of this movement.   PM

Ireland had an early impact on New Zealand and its literature thanks to the significant percentage of Irish among the early settlers. Irish New Zealanders (some 17 per cent of the total population) have always been outnumbered by the English and Welsh (50 per cent) and the Scots (22 per cent), but until recently they retained a strong sense of identity. Religion was the basis of this; the Irish constituted the only substantial congregation of Catholics. About a quarter were Protestant Ulstermen, but this group merged easily with the prevailing Anglo-Scots culture. Alan *Mulgan, perhaps the best-known writer from the Orange fraction of New Zealand Irish, remarked that 'Ulster was a shadowy place. England and English things were always before my eyes…'.

Nineteenth-century journals such as *The Freeman's Journal*, *The Tablet* and *The Irish Catholic* were based—in name, policy and format—on Irish models. Visiting fund-raisers for the Irish nationalist cause (the Redmond brothers in 1883, John Dillon in 1889, Michael Davitt in 1895) met with a generous response. Irish plays (e.g. by Boucicault) were often performed. And the literature of the New Zealand Irish was modelled on forms which had been popular back home—witness the ballads of David McKee *Wright and Thomas *Bracken.

The New Zealand Irish were thus able to use the Irish Literary Renaissance as a model for New Zealand's nascent nationhood. In 1923 the Irish Society of Wellington produced a journal boldly entitled *Roisin Dubh*. The greater part of it was devoted to a defence of Bishop James Liston, who had been arrested in 1922 for giving a speech in favour of Irish—and therefore by implication New Zealand—independence. *Roisin Dubh* also contained poems and articles by two of New Zealand's most prominent authors: Jessie *Mackay and Eileen *Duggan. To these two really belongs the credit for initiating the dialogue with Ireland which contributed crucially to the shape of New Zealand literature 1920–70.

Mackay seems to have been the driving force behind *Roisin Dubh*. Although her parents were Scottish, they were highland Gaelic-speakers, with a natural affinity for the Irish. She was an obvious choice to represent New Zealand at the Gael Race Conference in Paris in 1921, and on her way back she visited Dublin and attended a soirée at the house of 'Æ' which she describes in loving detail in an article in *Roisin Dubh*. Several of Mackay's poems (which began to appear in 1889) examine the case of Ireland. Others relate Māori myths, which suggests that she saw more clearly than her immediate successors the form that New Zealand's self-image must inevitably take. These successors (beginning with Duggan) took up the Irish analogy, but failed to identify the Māori as the counterpart to the autochthonous peasants celebrated by Yeats, Æ and Synge; their New Zealand is an empty landscape.

Duggan was the daughter of immigrants from County Kerry. In her first collection, *Poems* (1922), she wrote exclusively about Ireland, in a symbolist mode reminiscent of Æ and the early Yeats. Not surprisingly, Æ contributed a warm—if somewhat patronising—review to *The Irish Homestead* in 1923. Following Æ's advice, Duggan turned her attention to New Zealand in her next volume, *New Zealand Bird Songs* (1929). As the title suggests, however, she could find only fauna to celebrate. Although in her later poems (especially 'Centenary Ode') there are some self-conscious gestures to Māori history and legend, she increasingly eschewed all sense of place to explore the mysteries of the Catholic faith.

Allen *Curnow seems to have seen himself in part as

the New Zealand Yeats, fond of quoting Yeats's 'One can only reach out to the universe with a gloved hand—that glove is one's nation, the only thing one knows even a little of'. Curnow's New Zealand, however, lacked Yeats's autochthonous population fully at home in a richly mythic landscape.

Curnow also looked to Northern Ireland's Louis MacNiece as model. Others such as Frank *Sargeson took Joyce, for a 'scrupulous meanness' of style derived from *Dubliners* to suggest the limited quality of life during the *Depression, for the alienated artist Henry in *When the Wind Blows* (1945) resembling Stephen Dedalus, and for the continuation of Henry's story in *I Saw in My Dream* (1949), an anti-*Ulysses* with no Bloom to turn to.

As late as 1965 the Irish-born poet Charles (Mike) *Doyle in 'For Yeats's Centenary' found New Zealand lacking in resonance by comparison with Ireland. Elsewhere there were signs that something like Yeats's 'legendary heroes' had been glimpsed. Dan *Davin, the most self-consciously Irish of New Zealand's writers, wrote about an enclave of expatriate Irish in Southland, which he liked to think of as a 'transplanted Galway'. At the centre of many of these is a hero with the initials M.C. (usually Mick Collins or Martin Cody), a tribute to the Irish patriot, Michael Collins. Typically Davin's fiction depicts the passing of an old order, instinctively Catholic and respectful of Irish custom, but occasionally there are intimations of an older culture which imbues the landscape with dimly perceived significance. In 'Bluff Retrospect', when a family violates a Māori burial ground, 'It seemed worse that it should have been … Irish people who were in this country because life in their own had been made impossible … another conquered race.'

The stories of Roderick *Finlayson, who had an Irish grandmother and a Gaelic-speaking Scots father, also stressed 'the annihilation of [Māori] culture', with the occasional warm-hearted Irish policeman (Constable O'Brien in 'New Year' and Sergeant O'Connor in 'The Totara Tree') who bridges the gap, sympathising with Māori even as he enforces Pākehā justice. Irish and Māori characters also rub shoulders (and more) in the work of Maurice *Duggan, whose parents were of Irish origin, whose earliest stories were published there, and whose diffuse style is comparable to Joyce's and Beckett's. But it was left to James K. *Baxter to effect a fusion between Irish and Māori, and so open the way to a Māori Literary Renaissance which would provide a sense of cultural identity equivalent to that achieved by the Irish Literary Renaissance. Baxter came from a highland, Gaelic-speaking background. His father, Archibald *Baxter, admired James Connolly (leader of the Irish Citizen Army in 1916), and named his elder son Terence McSwiney Baxter after the 1920 hunger-strike martyr.

Yeatsian elements were always evident in Baxter's poetry, but his conversion to Catholicism in 1958 gave rise to works ('Lament for Barney Flanagan', *The Devil and Mr Mulcahy, O'Dwyer's Dancing Party*) with Irish titles and themes. The plays were written for Dunedin's Globe Theatre, owned and administered by an Irishman, Patric Carey. The spirit of Synge and O'Casey seems to underlie their unremitting focus on social outcasts.

Baxter remarked that 'the Irishman … has seemed at times to be a Maori in disguise', and even as he recreated himself as Māori at Jerusalem his Irish affiliations were not forgotten; the title of *Autumn Testament* alludes to Louis MacNiece's record of earlier hard times, *Autumn Journal*.

Baxter's conversion from Irishman to Māori opened the way for writers like Witi *Ihimaera, Patricia *Grace and Keri *Hulme to supply local equivalents to the myth-crammed peasants and sages of Yeats and Synge. Hone *Tuwhare perhaps intimates this connection when he has his old man in the story 'Don't Go Past Me with Your Nose in the Air' exclaim 'kia ora begorrah! Amen.'

In the greatest work of the Māori Literary Renaissance, Hulme's the *bone people*, the Irish scaffold is explicitly pushed away. All three principal characters have Irish affiliations, while Kerewin Holmes inhabits a tower with obvious Yeatsian associations. By the end she has renounced her Irish background in favour of Māoritanga, and rebuilt the tower as a ground-level dwelling on the Māori model. Joe Gillayley also eschews Irishness and assumes (by means which ironically bring to mind the Irish penchant for the fantastic) a wholly Māori identity. But most interesting is Simon P. Gillayley, who turns out to be the illegitimate child of the dissolute heir to an Irish title. His salvation, too, lies in entrusting himself to his Māori mentors.

By *the bone people*, homogeneous national identities were already outdated. Increasingly New Zealanders have recognised and expressed cultural diversity. Writing with an Irish flavour or content still appears (e.g. in stories by John Bentley, plays by Dean *Parker, poems by Bernadette *Hall or the work of Vincent *O'Sullivan), but presented simply as another cultural variant, not as blueprint for a national literature.   RCo

IRELAND, Kevin (1933–), poet, short story writer, novelist and librettist, was born Kevin Jowsey in Auckland. In his 20s he lived for a time in the army hut of his mentor Frank *Sargeson, that Janet *Frame once occupied. Co-founder of *Mate*, Ireland headed for England in 1959, remaining there for twenty-five years (with the exception of a short interval in Bulgaria, translating Bulgarian poetry into English). For two decades he was employed by *The Times*.

Reviews of Ireland's verse tend to mention his spare and witty style, his resolute minimalism, his regular use of imagery and extended metaphors, his carefully patterned forms and recurring themes of love. In interviews he characterises himself as a fossil; a lyricist of 'the ★Glover, ★Fairburn, ★Mason tradition ... that he feels is now decidedly old hat'; part of a generation with an 'anxiety about identity' obsessed 'with what it meant to be New Zealanders'. Even in self-imposed exile, Ireland considered himself a New Zealand poet and published all of his work here. But distance exacted a cost, and much of the poetry written outside New Zealand attempts to anchor identity by focusing on detail; as if to recapture the people and the country through a collage of remembered impressions.

In *Face to Face: Twenty-Four Poems* (1963) and *Educating the Body* (1967) there is the growing impression of identity coming adrift. Familiar places and people become necessary touchstones around which a nagging current of placelessness flows. By the third collection, *A Letter from Amsterdam* (1972), a pervasive sense of isolation is evident: the title city has little apparent significance, the poet's lover is distant and anonymous, and the sense of loss is crushing. In *Orchids, Hummingbirds and Other Poems* (1974) the craving for direct contact with New Zealand contemporaries is made poignantly obvious by 'A Way of Sorrow', dedicated to James K. ★Baxter. With no one who knew Baxter to grieve with, the shock and grief are necessarily private: 'I did not weep / or talk at length or write / but read the poem you sent'.

Ireland has published nine further volumes of poetry. *A Grammar of Dreams* (1975) was followed by *Literary Cartoons* (1977)—winner of the New Zealand Book Award for Poetry—a witty donning of a poetic mask through which the author drolly examines the ironic correspondences between loving and writing. Next came *The Dangers of Art: Poems 1975–80* (1980), *Practice Night in the Drill Hall: Poems* (1984) and *The Year of the Comet: Twenty-Six 1986 Sonnets* (1986), an exploration of the poet's past through a humorous evocation of the cinema heroes of his childhood. Ireland's return to New Zealand was marked by ★Oxford University Press's publication of his *Selected Poems* (1987), and then a volume of finely crafted political satire: *Tiberius at the Beehive* (1990). *Skinning a Fish* (1994) is arguably Ireland's first substantial collection of poems written, as well as published, in New Zealand, to represent the full range of his verse. In comparison with the poetry written in 'exile', *Skinning a Fish* evokes a society, and a poet immersed within it. *Anzac Day: Selected Poems* (1997) is Ireland's selection from earlier volumes, with a few recent poems—for example, a series to 'mother' and one called 'Mururoa: The Name of the Place'.

Ireland has begun publishing prose. *Sleeping With the Angels* (1995), a collection of short stories, is reminiscent of his lighter, wryly ironic, verse. These dozen fables are written by a raconteur who delights in placing his characters in idiosyncratic situations. Similarly, Ireland's first novel, *Blowing My Top* (1996), is comic fiction—a satirical look at events surrounding Auckland's 1951 ★Waterfront lockout through the eyes of testosterone-afflicted student Darby Fulljames. Neither the bolshie Waterside Workers' Union, nor the Holland government, escape Ireland's look at one of the defining moments in New Zealand labour relations.

Ireland has edited *The New Zealand Collection: A Celebration of the New Zealand Novel* (1990) and published two autobiographical essays, one in ★*Islands* 28 (1980) and the other in *One of the Boys?* (1988). He received a New Zealand 1990 Medal and an OBE for services to literature. He was writer-in-residence at Canterbury University in 1986, the Sargeson Fellow in 1987, the University of Auckland's writing fellow in 1989, assistant editor of ★*Quote Unquote*, and, in 1990–91, president of ★PEN.　　　　　　　　　　　　　　　　　PM

ISITT, Kate Evelyn (1876–*c*.1955), a journalist, wrote a significant political novel under the name 'Kathleen Inglewood'. She was born in New Plymouth into a family of Prohibition supporters; her father Rev. Francis W. Isitt and uncle Leonard M. Isitt were leaders of the movement. As private secretary to her uncle in Wellington in the early 1900s, Evelyn would have gained further inside knowledge of Prohibition, the subject of her novel *Patmos* (1905). Set in Christchurch where the movement was strongest, *Patmos* covers the period 1895 to the year the Prohibition cause gained its greatest parliamentary triumph, 1902. Leonard Isitt was among the successful candidates. *Patmos* deals mainly with the male leaders, and is the only Prohibition novel concerned with the political aspects. From 1907 to 1910 Evelyn Isitt was a reporter and first women's page editor on the newly founded *Dominion* newspaper, where she became known for her interest in women's rights, and as founder of the Wellington Pioneer Club for women. In 1910 she went to Britain, where she attended Suffrage League meetings and wrote about the women's movement for New Zealand newspapers. She became a London correspondent for the then *Manchester Guardian*, a position she held until after World War 2.　　　　　　　　JMcC

Island & Time, poems by Allen ★Curnow, was published by ★Caxton Press in 1941. Among the twenty-five poems are several of his best known, including 'The Unhistoric Story', 'House and Land' and 'Wild Iron' —the earliest of his poems which Curnow has regularly preserved in later collections. A note on the dust-jacket (probably written by the poet) states: 'These are frankly the poems of a New Zealander native & untravelled, convinced now that the need is for legend rather than for "realism".... His time-images provide him with a dynamic of his own, & though they represent no metaphysical system they give a humanity & a tragic sense wanting in the earlier work. There has been an increase in his technical range; and he has sought a variety of forms and images to sustain the imagination in its thrust across the Pacific and through Time.'   PS

Islands, a predominantly literary quarterly, appeared 1972–81 and as 'New Series' 1984–87. All issues were edited and published by Robin *Dudding. Previously editor (in succession to Charles *Brasch) of *Landfall, Dudding's choice of a thematically related name and similar physical appearance and contents made clear his intention was to supplant Landfall as New Zealand's flag-ship journal of 'Arts and Letters'. The debut issue in Spring 1972, with Brasch's *mana behind it, featured the major coup of a substantial selection from Allen *Curnow's forthcoming *Trees, Effigies, Moving Objects, the first poems published under his own name since 1962. There were also key Landfall contributors such as James K. *Baxter, C.K. *Stead, James *Bertram and Brasch himself, as well as Vincent *O'Sullivan, Ian *Wedde and Bill *Manhire among younger writers.

The first series continued Landfall's mix of poetry and short fiction, non-specialist literary criticism (usually writers assessing their peers or predecessors), illustrated essays on contemporary art and architecture, occasional social and political comment, and reviews of contemporary New Zealand publications. With rare exceptions, contributors and subject matter were New Zealand–based. After Sleeping Dogs in 1977, increasing attention was paid to New Zealand film. A regular autobiographical section featured accounts by New Zealand writers of their literary 'Beginnings', continuing the Landfall series collected by Dudding in Beginnings: New Zealand Writers Tell How They Began Writing (1980). Dudding showed willingness to depart from the standard template, however. Special anthology editions of contemporary short fiction (Vol. 3, No. 1 and Vol. 4, No. 2) and contemporary poetry (Vol. 3, No. 2) allowed him to offer useful snapshots of the literary scene, while a special double issue (Vol. 8, No. 4; Vol. 9, No. 1) was devoted largely to critical writing. Wedde's novel, Dick Seddon's Great Dive, occupied the entirety of Vol. 5, No. 2; and Vol. 6, No. 3 is a tribute to Frank *Sargeson, with extracts from his writing, and 'Tributes, Memoirs & Commentaries' from others. Regular contributors included Wedde, Manhire, Stead, Kevin *Ireland, Bob

*Orr, Peter *Bland, Murray *Edmond, Lauris *Edmond, Jan *Kemp, Rachel *McAlpine and Elizabeth *Smither among the poets, and Michael *Henderson, Wedde, Michael *Gifkins, Yvonne *du Fresne, Patricia *Grace, Owen *Leeming, Helen *Shaw, Michael *Morrissey and Russell *Haley among the writers of prose fiction.

Islands was never financially secure, depending on grants from the New Zealand *Literary Fund and sometimes soliciting donations. In the late 1970s its appearance was increasingly erratic, and in 1981 it ceased. The 'New Series' (beginning with Vol. 1, No. 1 in July 1984) ran, also erratically, until Vol. 3, No. 2 in December 1987. The 'New Series' was more single-mindedly literary than the original's generalist mix. Newer voices included Elizabeth *Nannestad, Jenny *Bornholdt, Greg *O'Brien, Dinah *Hawken, Anne *Kennedy, Jennifer *Compton and Owen *Marshall.

Islands contained virtually no editorial content. The first issue concludes its short 'Tailfeather' with the only statement of mission: 'the banner "Arts and Letters" means ISLANDS must concern itself with almost every aspect of life in New Zealand, without ignoring life beyond these three islands.' This is recognisably the same impulse that led Brasch to form Landfall. Inevitably, it is the more radical journals of the period that now seem representative: *Freed, *Climate, *Frontiers, *AND, *Parallax, *Splash and *Untold, all more clearly partisan with particular movements. Islands by comparison seemed uncomfortably institutional in an anti-institutional age. Nonetheless, Islands is second in importance only to Landfall among New Zealand literary journals for its encouragement of local writers and the quality of its contents.   HRo

Issue was a broadsheet published in two issues in Christchurch in 1952. Illustrated by Colin *McCahon, it showcased the poetry of John *Caselberg and J.M. *Thomson.   SH

Italy and New Zealand literature have been related in various ways since the time of Katherine *Mansfield. Their most intense and protracted contact occurred in the years 1943–45. The New Zealand division landed at Taranto, moved up to the Sangro River, crossed to Cassino, and fought the whole Italian campaign, being the first Allied troops to arrive in Trieste. The history of the division was written in two volumes of the Official History of New Zealand in the Second World War 1939–45 and in The Road to Trieste (1947) by Geoffrey *Cox. This experience also found expression in literary works, represented most notably by some short stories by Dan *Davin, centring particularly on Cassino,

Guthrie *Wilson's novel *Brave Company* (1950) and the novel *A Gun in My Hand* (1959) by Gordon *Slatter, which recalls the latter part of the campaign, from Forlì northwards across the tributaries of the Po. Slatter's later memoir *One More River* (1995) is a vivid non-fictional account of the 'Silver Fern Trail' up Italy. More trenchantly than anyone, John *Mulgan, in *Report on Experience* (1947), expressed scorn for Italians as soldiers. This is balanced by the New Zealand soldier's admiration of the Italian peasantry, seen in another memoir, Malcolm Mason's *The Way Out* (1946), which narrates his escape as a prisoner of war; he followed this up with *The Water Flows Uphill* (1964), recounting his return to the courageous people who sheltered him. The poems and songs of the Kiwi soldier have been edited and discussed by Les Cleveland in *The Iron Hand* (1979) and *Dark Laughter* (1994). See also *War literature: World War 2.

The war in Italy has continued as a theme of fiction, for instance in Maurice *Shadbolt's *An Ear of the Dragon* (1971), based on the life and stories of Renato *Amato, in Natasha *Templeton's *Firebird* (1994) and in James *McNeish's *My Name is Paradiso* (1995). Having written a biography of the social reformer Danilo Dolci, *Fire under the Ashes* (1965), McNeish used the search for a New Zealand father lost in action in Sicily, apparently operating with the Americans, as a structuring idea for a New Zealand novel which demonstrates a remarkable feel for southern Italy. Another writer whose work shows a deep acquaintance with Italy is the New Zealand–born John *Sligo, whose complex novel *The Faces of Sappho* (1990) includes material on and around the war, from the point of view of collusion and resistance rather than soldiering.

Although the New Zealand experience of war outweighs the kind of English response to Italy typified by *A Room with a View,* a visit to Italy via England was a part of the *overseas experience for many New Zealand writers maturing before or after that war. Probably the earliest such influence is in the work of Samuel *Butler, who drew the landscape of *Erewhon (once over the mountains) explicitly from Lombardy, and frequently used references to Italy and Italian art in evoking his pioneer's view of Canterbury. (In the text which gives the title to the collection *How to be Nowhere* (1995), Ian *Wedde, mindful of the Italian connection, translates 'Erewhon' backwards into Italian as 'Ogoul Nussen'.) Butler wrote three subsequent books about his visits to Italy and the artistic and literary theories he formulated there. More recently, Frank *Sargeson in his first volume of autobiography mentions a visit in the course of a walking tour, Maurice *Duggan writes well of Italy in 'Voyage' (in *Immanuel's Land*, 1956), and Charles *Brasch

includes a record of his passionate response to Italy in his memoir *Indirections* (1980): 'Italy made all of us more alive, keener to do and see.'

By far the best known New Zealand resident in Italy, however, was Katherine Mansfield, who spent a period of black depression at Ospedaletti, on the Italian riviera, between October 1919 and January 1920. Having escaped 'that hell of loneliness', as she called it, she was roundly abused by D.H. *Lawrence for her minimal contact with Italians. Lawrence's translations of the Sicilian peasant stories of Giovanni Verga were also to influence New Zealand, especially the realism of Roderick *Finlayson in *Brown Man's Burden*.

For the winter of 1920–21 Mansfield transferred to Menton, just across the border into *France. Of subsequent visitors to Menton as holders of the Katherine *Mansfield Memorial Fellowship, it has been Michael *Gifkins in particular who, in *The Amphibians* (1989), made literary sallies into Italy. In *Beside Myself* (1990) by Russell *Haley, a later Fellow, Italy tends to function as a stick with which to beat France. Works by a number of other writers record the pleasures and stresses of visiting Italy, often as part of a European tour. Short stories by Vincent *O'Sullivan and Jan *Kemp have as theme the seductive effect of Italian art on New Zealand women. Barbara *Anderson includes a visit to Italy as a key episode in *Portrait of the Artist's Wife* (1992) and, more extensively, in *Proud Garments* (1996). In Anderson's fiction and in a number of the other texts associated with tourism, a visit to Italy inevitably spells trouble for married couples. In C.K. *Stead's *Villa Vittoria* (1997) the emphasis is more on Italian politics. With a much earlier setting, the medieval *Kaspar's Journey* by M.K. *Joseph (1988) still reads allegorically rather like a Eurail trip round Europe, including Italy, by innocent youngsters bearing a charmed life. Joseph's fascination with Italy's past is also shown in his sequence of poems 'The Lovers and the City', which evokes Renaissance Verona. The city of Venice, figuring as prison and labyrinth in *Kaspar's Journey* and in the short story 'Afraid' by Elizabeth *Knox, appears most notably as a kind of mirror city in *The *Matriarch* (1986) by Witi *Ihimaera. In this epic novel, Italian opera is important as providing a parallel mythology, while the sea serves both to divide and connect New Zealand and Italy.

The sea 'which is one sea' is also the image which binds together there and here, then and now, in Allen *Curnow's *An Incorrigible Music* (1979), the most significant volume of New Zealand poetry to come from an extended stay in Italy. This work contains sequences of poems devoted to the assassination attempt on the lives of Giuliano and Lorenzo de' Medici in Florence

Cathedral in 1478, and the kidnapping and assassination of the leading Christian Democratic politician Aldo Moro 500 years later.

The chief representative of Italian culture in New Zealand has traditionally been opera. Plays by Goldoni, Pirandello and Fo have at various time made an impact on the New Zealand stage, but not noticeably affected dramatic writing. Mervyn *Thompson introduced into his *First Return* (1974) Dante's 'In the middle of the journey of my life …' as a song to be sung by 'some sort of grotesque pop group'. As regards subject matter with a local Italianate interest, however, the play *Eugenia* by Lorae *Parry (1996) appears unique. Here a dramatic voice is given to members of Wellington's community of migrants from Massalubrense. Recorded testimonies of families' experiences of immigration and settlement are contained in the oral history archives of the National Library, but there are no notable literary works produced by writers of Italian origin writing in English, with the striking exception of Renato *Amato. After traumatic experiences with both fascists and anti-fascist partisans as a teenager, Amato emigrated to New Zealand and wrote short stories which were collected under the title *The Full Circle of the Travelling Cuckoo* (1967). Like a number of the other writings drawn from connection between Italy and New Zealand, Amato's stories gain their power and tension in large measure from the extreme difference between the two, and are haunted by the shadow of war.

DG

Iwi, commonly translated as 'tribe', was the largest socio-political organisation among Māori, and is now increasingly the basis of many political activities and decisions. Sometimes, at a more spiritual level, several iwi feel related as descendents of the same *waka. The iwi itself is usually divided into smaller units, *hapū and *whānau, which take over much of the organisation of everyday life, while the iwi administer larger matters. Traditionally warfare was managed at iwi level. The leader of the iwi was the ariki ('chief'). NW

J

Jack Winter's Dream (1958), a play by James K. *Baxter.

JACKAMAN, Rob (1940–), a poet and critic who emigrated from England in 1968, lives in Christchurch where he lectures in English literature at the University of Canterbury. His critical works include *Creative Writing/Creative Reading* (1977), *The Course of English Surrealist Poetry Since the 1930s* (1989) and *Poets and Publishers: A Study of Cultural Centres and Margins in British Poetry Since 1950* (1995). He co-edits, with Australian poet Philip Mead, the Hazard Australasian Poets Series published in Christchurch by the *Hazard Press. He has also translated, with Dennis Logan and Tsutomu Shioda, the *Hiroshima Poems of Sankichi Tōgé* (1977).

Jackaman's own poetry is typically written in extended poem sequences with a typography involving stepped lines and significant spaces. Jackaman denies that such layouts are wilfully idiosyncratic because to him the text is 'akin to a musical score, with the timings and rhythm (particularly the ambiguous pause)—crucial to the overall effect'. Alistair *Paterson, writing of the long poem *Fate of Franklin* (1980), makes an observation that applies to much of Jackaman's work when he notes that the 'textual qualities are strengthened and enhanced by its being offered in a form intended for the page rather than for spoken presentation or performance' (*15 Contemporary New Zealand Poets*, 1980). Jackaman's poetry is collected in ten volumes: *Arthur the King* (1975), *Hemispheres* (1976), *Lee: A Science Fiction Poem* (1976), *The Suffolk Miracle* (1978), *Shaman and Charlatan* (1981), *Solo Lovers* (1981), *Triptych* (1988), *Palimpsest* (1988), *Distances* (1992) and *Buried Ships* (1996). Paterson has written a feature article, 'Rob Jackaman:

An Introduction to the Poetry and the Poet' for the *Journal of New Zealand Literature* (No. 10, 1992).   PM

JACKSON, Michael (1940–), has parallel careers—as an anthropologist and academic, and as a poet and fiction writer. Born in Nelson, he studied at Victoria, Auckland and Cambridge universities, before lecturing in anthropology at Massey University. Extended periods of fieldwork—living with the Kuranko people in Sierra Leone through the 1970s and in 1985, with the Warlpiri of Australia's Northern Territory 1989–91, and with the Kuku Yalangi of Cape York, Queensland, 1993–94—have been interspersed with academic terms at the Australian National University in the mid-1980s and at Indiana University, USA, 1989–96. Academic and ethnographical awards are balanced with literary distinctions including the 1981 New Zealand Book Award for Poetry, the 1983 Katherine *Mansfield Memorial Fellowship and third placing in the 1995 Montana Book Awards.

Jackson's publications include articles on a wide diversity of issues, such as the impacts of literacy on early-nineteenth-century Māori society, or divination, shape-shifting and myth in Kuranko society. Anthropological books include *Allegories of the Wilderness: Ethics and Ambiguity in Kuranko Narratives* (1982), *Barawa, and the Ways Birds Fly in the Sky* (1986), *Paths Toward a Clearing: Radical Empiricism and Ethnographic Inquiry* (1989) and *At Home in the World* (1995). His poetry has all been published in New Zealand—*Latitudes of Exile* (1976), *Wall* (1980), *Going On* (1985), *Duty Free: Selected Poems 1965–1988* (1989) and *Antipodes* (1996). Two publications of prose fiction are *Rainshadow* (1988) and *Pieces of Music* (1994).

Jackson's poetry is characteristically low-key and unpretentious—lean, tightly crafted lyrics or longer sequences. He works often with suggestion or implication, in sharply empathetic observations of Kuranko communities and traditions, in landscape pieces such as 'Australia' or 'Macrocarpas' from *Wall*, and in powerful personal poems of love, loss and family. Reviewer John *Newton noted a consistency of approach through Jackson's poetry over the years, a freedom from the theoretical fashions of the 1980s and 90s, and a general concern with alienness, 'the opposite, the other ... division or separation'.

Jackson's prose is equally lyrical, blurring the distinctions between formal academic study and more creative and philosophical writing. *Barawa* explores the history of North-Western Africa, focusing on particular families or dynasties, and drily assessing the expectations and exploits of earlier European 'discoverers', before relating his own experience as an anthropologist, the slow processes of building trust and understanding, the recognition that some things are beyond his comprehension. In *At Home in the World* Jackson addresses questions of belonging and being 'at home', both in a landscape—the Tanami Desert of the Australian outback—and in a community. Tracing the significance of place, his ethnographical research follows back into the sacred Dreamings, the stories of archetypal ancestors that define both the natural landscape and the contemporary relations among the Warlpiri community. This work leads increasingly to considerations of the practice and purposes of anthropological study, and to personal issues of knowledge and identity.

The prose sequence *Pieces of Music* is similarly contemplative and difficult to categorise—a mix of fiction, anecdote, history and notebook references, a glorious assemblage of interlinking details and fragments. Restlessly international, it skips from Africa to Singapore, Cairo, France, Taranaki and a farmhouse on the Whangaparaoa. Jackson's concerns include 'the interplay between real and invented lives'—the ways in which story can take on an irresistible momentum of its own, quite regardless of the ostensible facts—and the eccentric connections and echoes between fundamentally disparate experiences. Jackson's achievement is to challenge our assumptions about knowledge itself, with warmth, intelligence and compassion.   RCr

JACOBS, Helen (1929–), a retired mayor and a keen gardener, has published three volumes of poetry: *This Cording, This Artery* (1984), *Wind Quick* (1994) and *Pools Over Stone* (1997). While elements of her first volume endure in her two later collections—for example the clever use of an idiosyncratic vocabulary and a tendency to work personal symbolism into landscape references—the later volumes also show a clear development. This development may, in part, represent Jacobs's response to initial criticisms that her technique of layering words was not always successful and she overused landscape. Alan *Riach rightly praises her later work for being 'closely crafted, good humoured and keenly observant of the value of single words'. These poems are equally notable for drawing more widely, and with greater effect, from the world Jacobs inhabits. She succeeds in braiding its everyday occurrences—those domestic incidents, mundane defeats and tiny victories—into the universal cord of human experience. The smaller the moment in a Jacobs poem, the greater its significance.   PM

JACOBS, Henry (1824–1901), was the genial archdeacon of Christchurch and an early poet of Canterbury. Born on the Isle of Wight and educated classically at Charterhouse and Oxford, he took orders and in 1850 was appointed foundation classics professor of the proposed Christ's College. He was one of the original 'Canterbury Pilgrims', conducted the first church service at Lyttelton and opened the College in 1852. He edited the *New Zealand Church News*, wrote the volume on New Zealand in the *Colonial Church Histories* series (1889) and produced two volumes of poetry, *Shadows of the Old Church* (1870) and *A Lay of the Southern Cross* (1893). The poems are metrically well-turned and pleasing in a rather formal 'isle-embroidered sea' manner. They mostly celebrate English traditions and institutions, anticipating the coming time for the Province when 'A little while shall see thy wastes grow lovely' and 'Heaven-pointing spires shall beautify thy plain' ('The River Avon'). 'Patriotism' interestingly precedes Rupert Brooke in its claim that, however distant, ''Tis England, where an English spirit dwells'. For all his conventional diction Jacobs catches well a tension between the sense of loss suffered by the early settlers and their determined cultural and spiritual creativity.

HMcQ/RR

JAGOSE, Annamarie (1965–), academic and fiction writer, was born in Ashburton, studied at Victoria University of Wellington (PhD 1992) and then moved to a lectureship in English at Melbourne University. Her published books began with *Lesbian Utopics* (1994), theoretical academic essays on the 'cultural space' of the lesbian, and a well-received novel, *In Translation* (1994). Numerous short stories have appeared in journals and in collections such as *New Women's Fiction 3* (1989), Cathie *Dunsford's *The Exploding Frangipani: Lesbian Writing from Australia and New Zealand* (1990) and *Speaking with the

Sun: New Stories by Australian and New Zealand Writers (1991). The stories and the novel work with the fragility of relationships, the ambivalence and imperfection of our efforts at communication. 'Lulu's Fourth Birthday' and 'Charades' deal with a linguistic researcher, experimentally training a chimpanzee in sign language. Dialogue with the humans in her life—friends, colleagues and a grimly sulky lover—is more complicated and less successful. The multi-layered *In Translation* centres on the actual work of translating a manuscript from one language into another, a metamorphosis that eventually takes on a momentum of its own. Continually shifting and changing, moving from a Kelburn garden to a courtyard in an Indian city, Jagose's novel addresses issues of identity and creativity, sensual attraction and cool indifference, emotional need and independence. Her second academic book is on 'Queer Theory', and a second novel, *Lulu: A Romance*, was published in 1998.   RCr

Japan and New Zealand are still in the early stages of literary awareness of each other, the exchange being so far much less active than in such fields as business, tourism, sport and the visual arts. There artists such as Leo ★Bensemann, Len Castle, Reiko Elliott and Jim Greig have been part of a significant reciprocation, especially in pottery and print-making, that has been charted in Peter and Dianne Beatson's *The Crane and the Kotuku* (1994).

In literature, unless Katherine ★Mansfield's silky *japonaiserie* phase is counted, the first interaction came probably in the experiments with haiku by Ruth ★Dallas from 1937, prompted by Ezra Pound's engagement with oriental forms. Events leading to World ★War 2 brought a different awareness, best reported in the eye-witness dispatches by Robin ★Hyde from Japanese-occupied ★China. 'I Travel Alone' (*Mirror*, Oct. 1938) and 'Paradox at Hsuchow' (*Woman To-day*, July 1939) are reprinted in *Disputed Ground: Robin Hyde, Journalist*, ed. Gillian Boddy and Jacqueline Matthews, 1991. Another skilled reporter of wartime was James ★Bertram, who provided several accounts of the conquest of Hong Kong and his internment as prisoner of war near Tokyo. In poems and the retrospective *Capes of China Slide Away* (1993) he writes with remarkable lack of rancour, even praising the 'stoical endurance', the 'courage and devotion' of the Tokyo people under Allied firebombing. Bertram also wrote well on Japanese (and Chinese) art in ★*Landfall* 1 (1947).

Bill ★Pearson wrote more obliquely of his time in Japan with the 'J Force', transposing to Italy the incident that gave rise to the story 'Purge' (*Six Stories*, 1991; originally 'Social Catharsis', *Landfall*, 1947). That story, and 'Indemnity', which is set in Japan (*Six Stories*, originally

'Aint Gonna Grieve My Lord No More', *Canterbury Lambs*, 1947), and the beginning of ★*Coal Flat*, were all written in occupied Japan ('Beginnings and Endings', ★*Sport* 5, 1990).

Fewer writers than might be expected have sought to give literary expression to the Pacific War and its apocalyptic ending. James K. ★Baxter, visiting Japan for a conference on school textbooks in 1958, imagined, in 'For a Child at Nagasaki', the lasting trauma of 'Having seen an ocean of fire and then / An ocean of ashes', and perceptively saw the Japanese people post-war as 'like people in a bamboo boat on a rough sea' (taking the image from Hokusai's print 'The Wave'). His visit, recounted in Frank ★McKay's *Life of James K. Baxter* (1990), also produced 'Eioko', a poem of sympathy for a nightclub woman's 'deadlier martyrdom, / At drunken midnight tables', and 'Tokyo 1958', which was translated into Japanese and distributed to conference delegates. A collaboration in the other direction was that between poet Rob ★Jackaman and translators Dennis Logan and Tsutomu Shioda in English versions of the *Hiroshima Poems of Sankichi Tōgé* (1977).

Errol ★Brathwaite in *Fear in the Night* (1959) and *An Affair of Men* (1961) gave two related narratives of the pursuit of crashed allied airmen by Japanese patrols on Bougainville, rising well above the basic genre of war action fiction with the inwardness of his presentations of the military mentality on both sides, and the interest of the cultural clash between Japanese warrior values and those of a Christian native village. 'His ability to misread the evidence letter by letter … makes [Captain] Itoh's mind fascinating', wrote R.A. ★Copland (*Landfall* 61, 1962). Cultural incomprehension is also the theme of Vincent ★O'Sullivan's play ★*Shuriken* (1985). A Japanese account of the same 1943 incident at Featherston prisoner-of-war camp is available in *The Path from Guadalcanal* by Michiharu Shinya, a naval lieutenant who was converted to Christianity during his internment (translated by Eric H. Thompson, 1979). The performance history of *Shuriken* in New Zealand and Japan is a study in cultural attitudes in its own right. The Japanese translation (1995) is by Ezawa Sokushin.

There have been scattered attempts to write of Japanese culture or employ Japanese literary forms. They include Gary Langford's poetic sequence 'The Samurai, 1387–1422' in his *Bushido: The Warrior in History* (1987); C.K. ★Stead's 'Uta: 50 free translations from Japanese classical collection' in *Poems of a Decade* (1983); and the ★New Zealand Poetry Society's *New Zealand Haiku Anthology*, ed. Cyril Childs, 1993. Lack of knowledge of the language remains a problem in all these. K.O. ★Arvidson and Albert ★Wendt have both written poems for Nobel Laureate Kenzaburo Oe, Arvidson catching the same disorientation as Baxter, seeing Oe as expressing 'the strange songs pulsing in their minds since Hiroshima'. Other poems on Japanese subjects include Lauris *Edmond's 'The Noh Plays', Allen *Curnow's 'Narita', O'Sullivan's 'Hiroshima', Stead's 'Girl under the Plane Tree', Bill *Manhire's 'Hirohito' and Rachel *McAlpine's collection *Tourist in Kyoto* (1993). Treatments in fiction include a section in Wendt's *Ola* primarily concerned with criticism of the gender attitudes of Japanese culture.

The most sustained writing about Japan to date is Ian *Middleton's trilogy of novels, *Faces of Hachiko* (1984), *Sunflower* (1986) and *Reiko* (1990). Informed by extensive experience of living there, they seek to explore Japanese character, thought and attitudes to foreigners, as well as the externals of social organisation. Above all, they adopt the Japanese viewpoint; *Sunflower*, for instance, neatly inverts Western cultural expectations by giving that name, reminiscent of *Madama Butterfly*, to a beautiful Swedish-American visitor. The comic-strip tendency of Middleton's sex-and-splatter scenes may also be derived from Japanese magazine conventions.

Non-fictional writing is also sparse, though travel writing may be found in sports literature, such as Norman *Harris's *Silver Fern in Tokyo* (1964) or Roger Robinson's 'Thirty-six Views of Mount Fuji' in *Heroes and Sparrows* (1986), translated into Japanese by Mifuyu Komatsu. Travel in the other direction has, of course, become a visible part of New Zealand life. Japanese honeymooners provide the subject of one of the best recent fictions, Peter *Wells's 'Of Memory and Desire', in *Dangerous Desires* (1991), and also feature in Middleton's *Reiko*.

Japanese attention to New Zealand literature has been assiduous by a small group of specialist translators, critics and biographers. These notably include Rikutaro Fukuda, Ginsaku Ohsawa (translator of Mansfield and of Gillian Boddy's studies of her), Ezawa Sokushin (translator-annotator of *New Zealand Short Stories and Poems*), Mieko Tamai and Keiko Mizuta, both specialists in Katherine Mansfield, and the translators of *An Anthology of New Zealand Short Stories* (1981: editor Yuroko Momo and Atsuko Onogi, Akiko Sukigara, Akiko Tanaka). The Japan/Australia/New Zealand Teachers Association and New Zealand Literature Society of Japan arrange lectures and readings.

The recurrent theme of New Zealand's literature of Japan remains perplexity—in Brathwaite, *Shuriken*, 'Of Memory and Desire', even parts of Middleton. This is deepened by the seeming impenetrability of the language. One of Wendt's 'Three Poems for Kenzaburo Oe' plays with the joke that 'In Samoan your name means "You"', but there is no closer engagement; in Vivienne

*Plumb's title story 'The Wife Who Spoke Japanese in Her Sleep' (1993) Japanese language and culture symbolise total alienation, in this case between husband and wife.

A new generation of New Zealanders with experience in Japan and knowledge of the language is beginning to write with more understanding. Recent publications include Peter Dowling's essay on contemporary Japanese fiction in translation, in *Landfall* 192 (1996), an issue which also included a story by Ryu Murakami; and Ingrid Horrocks's poetry and prose in *Landfall* and *Sport*, and especially her volume of poems, *Natsukashii* (1998). RR

'Je ne parle pas français', a short story by Katherine *Mansfield, was written 1918, privately published under Mansfield and *Murry's imprint the Heron Press (Jan 1920), and included in *Bliss and Other Stories* (Dec. 1920). The MS is at the Newberry Library, Chicago. In letters to John Middleton Murry from France, Mansfield wrote that her 'kick off' for the story was 'a cry against corruption' (3 Feb. 1918) and that it was 'a tribute to Love and the very best I can do right now' (10 and 11 Feb. 1918). The story is that of Raoul Duquette, a young Parisian writer and critic, 'author of False Coins, Wrong Doors, Left Umbrellas and two in preparation'. An ironic and grubby-minded version of Francis *Carco, Duquette obsesses about his 'submerged life' on the margins of respectable society. His encounter with Dick Harmon (presented as his English counterpart) and in particular Dick's abandonment of his lover 'Mouse', whom Duquette also betrays, form the nexus of his reminiscences, prompted by sighting the only words that Mouse spoke in French, 'je ne parle pas français'. *Bliss and Other Stories* contains a bowdlerised version of the story, reluctantly agreed to by Mansfield under pressure from the publisher, Michael Sadleir. *Alpers's *Stories* present it as intended, the most significant change being the restoration of these lines to the conclusion: 'I'd rather like to dine with her. Even to sleep with her afterwards. Would she be pale like that all over? But no. She'd have large moles. They go with that kind of skin. And I can't bear them. They remind me somehow, disgustingly, of mushrooms.'

With the use of an unreliable (adult) narrator and the uncompromising treatment of sex, love and betrayal, the story marks new developments which foreshadow the later, uncompleted work 'A *Married Man's Story'. SSa

JEFFERY, Margaret (1910–92), novelist, born in Havelock North as Gretchen Constance Weyergang, spent her childhood in the orcharding area of Mapua, near Nelson. She trained and worked as a kindergarten teacher, and married in 1938. The family lived first in Auckland and then moved to Wellington, where she taught creative writing. Widowed, she worked as matron of a boarding school for girls in Masterton, later retiring to the small settlement of Raumati on the Kapiti coast. Six novels, all with local settings, were published in New Zealand and the UK. *The Forsaken Orchard* (1955), *Too Many Roses* (1956), *Tree Without Shade* (1958) and *Mairangi* (1964) are conventional romantic fiction with an element of domestic realism. *Cabin At Your Gate* (1973) indicates a shift away from the more traditional style and themes of the earlier novels, placing a stronger emphasis on the development of characterisation, and addressing the subject of pederasty. *The Black Shore* (1980) is a historical romance set against the arrival at New Plymouth in 1841 of the sailing barque *William Bryan*, and the resultant period of conflict between the new settlers and Taranaki Māori in the 1860s Land *Wars. Jeffery also wrote children's fiction.   SW

JEPSEN, Vivienne (1950–), won the 1992 Reed Fiction Award (for new writers) with *The House of Olaf Krull* (1994). This recounts the return of Olivia Krull in early middle age from a somnolent marriage in New York to visit family in New Zealand, but as reviewer Ronda Cooper commented, 'what's meant to be a nostalgic reconciliation turns into a kind of jihad'. Olivia rampages and ravishes her way through family, farm and then the even more peccant fields of Wellington and its university's English department. A boisterous, braggadocious, ranting, randy, maverick mélange of confessional fiction, *roman à clef*, literary allusion and savage satire, it won praise from reviewers who confessed to shell-shock. David *Eggleton called it 'rambling, manic and aggressive' but praised 'its fine sense of social hierarchies' and 'fearless deconstruction of Wellington party-life' and Cooper recognised that though 'driven by the need to unload' its 'sheer emotional weight has its own momentum'. Jepsen was born in Otaki, has lived in Rerewhakaaitu, Hamilton, Auckland, Christchurch, London, New York and Wellington and is enrolled as a doctoral student at Victoria University.   RR

JEPSON, Margaret (1907–), novelist, co-wrote her first book, *Miss Amogee in Africa* (London, 1932), with her father, the prolific British novelist and editor Edgar Jepson (1863–1938). Soon after this she accompanied her husband, Dr Frank Birkinshaw, to New Zealand, where they lived in Amberley. Their daughter, the successful British novelist, Fay *Weldon, who was born in Worcester, spent the next twelve years of her life in New Zealand. She later remarked of her parents 'I learned from them both what it was to have something

to say, and how to say it.' Jepson's novel *Via Panama* (London and New York, 1934), the story of the voyage of the *Taipo* from England to New Zealand, was reviewed by Robin *Hyde for the *New Zealand Observer*. Describing it as entertaining and 'a sort of maritime "Grand Hotel"', Hyde expressed particular ironic interest in some of Jepson's statements, such as 'Fewer exceptional people go to New Zealand than to any other country in the world, and no exceptional person ever stays there if they can help it', and 'They've got the village mind in New Zealand—if you can imagine a village run on strictly democratic lines.' Jepson's husband Birkinshaw, too, was productive, writing articles, publishing several magazines and beginning one of the first radio stations in Christchurch.   GB

Jerusalem Daybook, James K. *Baxter's ninth collection, was published by *Price Milburn in 1971. It is the first of Baxter's volumes to combine verse with prose, although the two forms do not meld as smoothly in it as in his next collection, **Autumn Testament*. The rather didactic tone of many of the pieces, as well as a more ostentatious rhetoric in some of its verses, seems at odds with the deceptive simplicity of the **Jerusalem Sonnets* and *Autumn Testament* sonnet sequences that flank this collection. Baxter's personal perspective on the practice and philosophy of communalism as it relates to the initial phase of his Jerusalem commune does, however, give the book greater value as an autobiographical work.   PM

Jerusalem Sonnets: Poems for Colin Durning (1970), James K. *Baxter's eighth collection, was published by the University of Otago's Bibliography Room (rpt. *Price Milburn, 1974). The thirty-nine sonnets—which may as readily be understood as a long poem in thirty-nine stanzas—were sent, during the first phase of the Jerusalem commune, with letters written to Baxter's friend Colin Durning. Appropriately, they form an extended verse epistle, their loose, unrhymed couplets (reflecting Lawrence Durrell's influence) expressing friendship, discussing everyday life and meditating on God. There are hints of a restless quest for meaning in references to journeys, but Baxter also reflects on the ubiquitous 'gap': that place of stillness, where the mind is silenced and God is experienced. Behind their deceptive simplicity the poems display a remarkable unity of voice, theme and setting. With humour and piety, in tones both personal and universal, Baxter's sonnets create that 'tension of belief' that, he once stated, 'gives the poem its edge'.   PM

JNZL, see ***Journal of New Zealand Literature***.

John McIndoe Ltd was established as a printery in Dunedin in 1892. In 1949 the founder's grandson and namesake joined the firm. With a particular interest in the arts, in 1968 he set up a publishing department, with Peter Stewart as editor, concentrating on titles with a local flavour. In 1975, poet Brian *Turner moved from an editorial post at *Oxford University Press. Together, they increased the annual output from around six to twelve publications, many of which were poetry and fiction. With the assistance of NZ *Literary Fund grants, these usually paid their way, but were ultimately an act of patronage by the owner. Although their general list was broad, taking in history, biography, sport, politics, art and architecture, the literary list was slightly more circumscribed. There were books of fiction by Michael *Henderson, Peter *Hooper and O.E. *Middleton, poetry by Denis *Glover, Hooper and Elizabeth *Smither, as well as volumes four, five and six of *Poetry New Zealand. Five authors were particularly well represented: Michael *Jackson, Owen *Marshall, Cilla *McQueen, Vincent *O'Sullivan and Turner. In 1985 John McIndoe retired and Turner left to concentrate on his writing, succeeded by Barbara Larson. They continued to work in conjunction with the University of Otago Press, and, with the editorial assistance of Paula *Boock, broadened into young adult fiction. Ownership changed to Alliance Textiles in the 1980s, followed by a name change to McIndoe Publishers in 1992. By 1995 the company had ceased to publish.   NWt

JOHNS, Atihana Moana (1937–), Ngāti Kahu, Te Whānau Moana, Ngāti Ruaiti, Ngati Whakaeke, was born in Kaitaia and grew up on a small rural *marae where much of his early life was influenced by the uncompromising Māoritanga of his mother's distinguished *hapū. Educated at Rangiawhia Maori School (the location of later writing), Te Aute College and Auckland Teachers' College, he graduated in 1958 and taught in rural and then urban primary schools. After part-time studies, he graduated BA at Victoria University (1972) and MEd at Waikato University (1985). His literary experience widened from the English classics to American, New Zealand and other writers of English. He also developed interest in Māori oral narrative and *mōteatea. Much of his writing has been occupational, given his long experience as teacher and in teacher education, and involvement in teacher unions and in the promotion of the Māori language in New Zealand education. Occasional work has included being shark-fisherman, mail-carrier, freezing-worker and barman. Initially published in Te *Ao Hou and Te Maori, Johns's short stories have been described as 'brilliant', and are anthologised in Short Stories by New Zealanders One

(ed. P. Meikle, 1972), *Into the World of Light (1982) and elsewhere. His short-fiction collection, Just Wondering (1986), reveals his belief in the importance of personal experience and skilled use of binary form, making sensitive and ironic contrasts of rural/urban, youth/age, past/present to examine the subterfuge and honesty in human relationships. Recently he has worked in scriptwriting with a first novel 'still in his head and heart'.

JBa

JOHNSON, Louis (1924–88), Wellington poet ('a doll-sized city … how many capitals are so human?'), had many volumes of verse published over a period of forty-five years. His first work appeared in 1945 and his posthumous last poems in 1990. His constant themes include suburbia, domestic life, childhood, love (with its attendant lust) and the folly of the contemporary world. His early poems, while energetic, had a tendency to vagueness and a lack of centrality, but his later much more controlled poems have been considerably underestimated. Throughout his life he spent considerable time fostering young or neglected poets; indeed, his own poetry probably suffered from his generous spirit and support for other writers.

His poetry books include Stanza and Scene (1945), The Sun Among the Ruins (1951), Roughshod Among the Lilies (1951), The Dark Glass (1955), Poems Unpleasant (with James K. *Baxter and Anton *Vogt) (1955), Two Poems (1956), New Worlds for Old (1957), The Night Shift: Poems on Aspects of Love (with Baxter, Charles *Doyle and Kendrick *Smithyman) (1957), Bread and a Pension: Selected Poems (1964), Land Like a Lizard: New Guinea Poems (1970), Onion (1972), Selected Poems (1972), Fires and Patterns (1975), Coming & Going (1982), Winter Apples (1984), True Confessions of the Last Cannibal (1986) and Last Poems (1990).

In his youth Johnson was at the centre of the 'Wellington group'—so-called because the group defined itself in reaction to their perception of Auckland-based Allen *Curnow. Accordingly its interests were claimed to be what his were not—less concern about physical landscape and the New Zealand identity, more about universal issues which transcend borders. As a group they—and particularly Johnson—wrote about actual life, society and the city suburbs with their state houses and backyard vegetable gardens. In retrospect the dispute was personal, regional and intergenerational rather than ideological. Later, Johnson himself wrote about early European exploration, envisaging Young Nick reminiscing about 'the lost / islands of Tasman uplifted high into further murdering'.

In 1951 Johnson established the *New Zealand Poetry Yearbook. He edited it annually until 1964, when

*Literary Fund support was withheld—with a resultant furore—on the grounds that six of the poems he had chosen were obscene. It was his policy to encourage unknown writers as well as including established poets. This catholic policy led to criticism about standards, a charge led by Curnow. Johnson, allied with Baxter, thus challenged the supremacy of the old master on two fronts. The dispute turned nasty, Curnow's caustic comments (especially in *Here & Now) leading to Johnson's bitter irreverent replies. Nevertheless, a considerable number of budding writers were published, and many continued writing. Johnson deserves full credit for encouraging others as well as for his own accomplishment in poetry. Throughout these years he continued to write prolifically, which he combined with editing the quarterly *Numbers, running the Capricorn Press, and frequent reviewing and broadcasting.

In 1968 he moved to Papua New Guinea, and a year later to Melbourne, where he worked as a journalist. In 1971 he took a tertiary teaching position at Bathhurst, returning to New Zealand in 1980 as the second Victoria University writing fellow. Settling on the Kapiti coast, he became active again in literary politics, becoming president of *PEN, as well as starting his own press, Antipodes. Through this he published *Antipodes: New Writing* (1987), like the old *Yearbook* a generous and practical shopfront for rising writers. This time, however, he included prose. His introduction says 'literary journals and miscellanies … take the pulse of the literary life as it develops and endures around us. They are closer to gossip than history and therefore more interesting. History may awe and shape us, but it's the gossip and the daily tucker that enable us to endure it.' He died in 1988 in England having just completed a year as Katherine *Mansfield Memorial Fellow at Menton. His wife Cecilia established the Louis Johnson New Writers Award to continue his encouragement of developing talent.

Johnson's poems are often a tentative reverie, speculations about the nature of reality. Common images are windows and mirrors, openings onto and reflections on experience and being. 'Words are bricks you throw into every discussion / hoping to break a window, make a mark / in the nervous system of identity.' He was a strongly moral man, angry at injustice, critical of the smug and self-satisfied, but with a well-cultivated sense of humour. His poems reflect his consciousness of the absurdity of human behaviour, while the romantic in him saw the transitory nature of existence, as well as the futility of action. 'Let me not think of these / cruel facts of life in this valley of green trees.' And near the end, 'A point of view; a domestic art—meals / on the table and a warm bed. We do not need large events; / a sense of history clamping its jaws.'

As his style is discursive, a raconteur's approach, the reader is rarely conscious of poetic form. The argument is usually all. In his early poems this was advanced by affirmation and anger; later there was a more perceptive acceptance and wry humour. In this period, his poems grounded in his new family are as good as any New Zealand poetry on this theme: his children's pets, his son awe-struck before an elephant, his daughter learning to read, welcoming him home, delivering make-believe letters. 'All / of it is there, all of it with you, shimmering: / a music: memory: the woman / the soft curled limbs of the children.' 'The Last Cannibal', a poetic persona created by Johnson in a memorable sequence, presents a forceful later public face: 'Memory is as rich as gravy.' This authoritative assurance is illustrated even more clearly by the domestic poems in which Johnson re-explores early themes. 'I tell myself / that love is quite as extreme as any entrance or exit, and does not come too late'. In these and similar poems he traverses and dissects with confidence and skill the issues of being human in the modern world. 'Change has indeed come. / They console themselves, between one suburb / of the global village and others. / The road-houses serve blander plastic steaks: their sons / commute to bread in the dying days of Ford.'   HMcQ

JOHNSON, Mike (1947–), novelist and poet, was born in Christchurch, lived in Europe, Asia and Africa 1972–80, and settled on Waiheke Island in 1982. A graduate of the University of Canterbury, he was a teacher of English as a foreign language, secondary teacher, bookshop owner, then in 1986 became a creative writing tutor at the University of Auckland's Department of Continuing Education. His first book publication was as co-author (with A.T. Johnson) of *Dialogue, A Text for Senior English* (1973). In the 1980s he began an impressive output of fiction and poetry. His prose can be described in terms of magic realism, though with a distinctive *science fiction component, influenced by such US writers as Philip K. Dick and Barry M. Maltzberg, and with idiosyncratic Gothic elements. His novels are *Lear—The Shakespeare Company Plays Lear at Babylon* (1986), *Anti Body Positive* (1987), *Foreigners: Three Novellas* (1991), *Lethal Dose* (1991) and *Dumb Show* (1996). By contrast, his poetry is minimalist with flashes of lyricism, formerly in the style of Robert *Creeley and translations of Chinese poets, though increasingly in the elusive manner of Pablo Neruda. His collections are *The Palanquin Ropes* (1983), *From a Woman in Mount Eden Prison* and *Drawing Lessons* (1984), *Standing Wave* (1985) and *Treasure Hunt* (1996). He was writer-in-residence at the University of Canterbury in 1987.   KI

JOHNSON, Stephanie (1961–), is a versatile writer, moving from poetry to prose to plays for radio and the stage. Born in Auckland, she has lived in that city and in Sydney 1985–90. After university studies in the early 1980s, she began her diverse output with *The Bleeding Ballerina* (1987), a powerful first collection of poems. This was followed by two collections of short stories, *The Glass Whittler* (1989) and *All the Tenderness Left in the World* (1993), and two novels, *Crimes of Neglect* (1992) and *The Heart's Wild Surf* (1996). Her dramatic writing includes two stage plays, *Accidental Phantasies* (1985) and *Folie à Deux* (1995, with Stuart *Hoar), and the radio dramas *Castle In the Harbour* (1987), *Hard Hitting Documentary* (1995), *Sparrow's Pearls* (1996) and *Trout* (1996). She won the Bruce Mason Playwrights' Award in 1986.

Johnson's work is marked by a dry irony, a sharp-edged humour that focuses unerringly on the frailties and foolishness of her characters. Pomposity and self-delusion are favourite targets—the creative writing tutor in 'A One-Page Statement', the eager New Age clients in 'The Deep Resounding', the arrogant Werner in 'Menschenfresser', or the vicar's wife in *The Heart's Wild Surf*. There is compassion, though, and sensitivity in the development of complex situations. *The Heart's Wild Surf*, set in Fiji in 1918, is a subtle, delicately drawn, yet passionately intense portrayal of a family under immense strain. Johnson explores the McNabs' personal and social crises within the wider contexts of late colonialism and the beginnings of new freedoms for women. A purposeful sense of such larger concerns balances Johnson's precision with the small details of situation, character and voice that give veracity and colour.   RCr

JOHNSTON, Andrew (1963–), poet and editor, won the New Zealand Book Award for Poetry with his first volume, *How to Talk* (1993). Born in Upper Hutt, he was editor of the books page of the *Evening Post* 1991–96. His poems have been published in *Meanjin* and *Scripsi* in Australia, *London Magazine* and *Verse* in UK and *Sport* and elsewhere in New Zealand. He received the Louis Johnson New Writers Bursary in 1991. Associated with the Wellington school of *Manhire and *Bornholdt, Johnston writes with a finely judged sense of poetic presence and occasion, and in the first volume projects the image of the wryly detached conversationalist for whom poetry is essentially an art of communication. Emotion is manœuvred into formal strategies designed for the poet–reader encounter: engaging, sustaining, then signing off, often with a punning touch—'when I leave /I leave a lot to be desired'. Titles like 'Haiku Beach' and 'The Poetry Inspector' suggest the formal qualities of Johnston's aesthetic: a willingness

to let grammar provide guiding constraints; a fascination with the sound of the lyrical voice, a recognition of the artefact's capacity to manipulate reality.

His second volume, *The Sounds* (1996), demonstrates the familiar linguistic poise, but is further distinguished by mastery of the elaborate sestina form, with its repeated line-endings and formally varied order. Johnston establishes a thematic dialogue with *How to Talk*, reviving his fascination with grammatical concepts in 'Syntax', playfully alluding to language's apparent conquest of distance in 'How to Walk', 'Wire', and ringing the changes on seasons, spaces and communicative modes in several travel poems. Throughout, he speculates on the ambiguous nature of silence and sound: 'What does sunlight sound like? / A white flower in darkness knows…'. Johnston received a Writers Bursary in 1994, and attended the International Writing Program at the University of Iowa as New Zealand representative in 1995. He is living as a journalist in London.   JW

JOHNSTON, Christine (1950–), adult and children's novelist, was born and raised in Dunedin, studied at the University of Otago, trained as a teacher, and travelled widely in Europe. For a time, she worked as a teacher of German and of English as a second language. After numerous short stories were broadcast and published, in *Landfall* and elsewhere, her first novel, *Blessed Art Thou Among Women* (1991) won the Reed New Fiction Award. It explores the lives of three generations of Dunedin women in what Angela Carter calls 'a cameo history', and has been praised for its 'intelligent and crafty narrating' and 'richness of psychological and social texture'. Johnston held the 1994 *Burns Fellowship. Her love of old houses and of Dunedin and the surrounding Otago landscape led her to make haunted houses and the solving of historical and family mysteries central to her children's novels, *Goodbye, Mollie McGuire* (1994) and *The Haunting of Lara Lawson* (1995).   DH

JOHNSTON, Phyllis (1935–), children's writer, was born in Morrinsville, educated at Rotorua and Thames High Schools, and trained in nursing at Waikato Hospital. She taught singing and piano 1970–82, and tutored in creative writing. Apart from the imaginative exploration of collecting treasures in *My Things and the Hidden Light* (1984), her inspiration for writing comes from family stories—'the great saga of genealogy'. In *No One Went to Town* (1980), *Black Boots and Buttonhooks* (1984), *A Comet in the Sky* (1985), *… Then There Were Nine* (1989) and *No Lily-livered Girl* (1992), she tells in fictional form her mother's family stories at the turn of the twentieth century, recording the lives of isolated, hard-working pioneer families in forest-clearing farm days in Taranaki and the King Country.   DH

JONES, Lawrence or **L.O.** (1934–), is a leading historian of New Zealand fiction as well an editor, reviewer and promoter of New Zealand writing. Born and educated in California, he moved in 1964 to a lectureship in English at the University of Otago, where he is now professor. He initiated the first undergraduate paper in New Zealand literature there, became editor of the *Journal of New Zealand Literature in 1990 and played a major role in establishing the *Association of New Zealand Literature and its regular conferences. He served on the NZ *Literary Fund and Literature Panel of the Arts Council 1991–94.

His critical-historical *Barbed Wire & Mirrors: Essays on New Zealand Prose* (1987, rev. edn 1990) and his historical essay on 'The Novel' in the *OHNZLE* (1991, 1998) have become essential reference. He has also written significantly on *Shadbolt, *Baxter and the 'Search for Identity' and has edited Dan *Davin's *Roads from Home* (1976) and (with Heather Murray) *From the Mainland: An Anthology of South Island Writing* (1995).
                                                              RR

JONES, Lloyd (1955–), is a fiction writer drawn to a sympathetic portrayal of ordinary middle-class life, a suburban realist who simultaneously challenges realism, subverts fictional norms, defies categories and writes narratives which are challenging, original and in some cases controversial. He was born in Lower Hutt, which has remained a frequent setting and subject, and graduated from Victoria University, then working as a journalist and consultant, but always as a committed writer. He has continued to live in the Hutt Valley or Eastbourne, apart from several periods in USA and in 1988 as the Katherine *Mansfield Memorial Fellow at Menton. He has also held the Scholarship in Letters and other awards.

Gilmore's Dairy (1985) is a first novel about a young man's growing up in a small New Zealand community, distinguishing itself from that well-worn tradition by its skilful reportage and fast-paced narrative, and also by teetering unpredictably on the edge of bizarre fantasy, black comedy and parodic satire, as the dairy of the title goes through a series of eccentric transformations. *Splinter* (1988) is that rare creation, an interesting novel about Lower Hutt, that 'town of modest achievement'. Its two primary narratives are the letters and reminiscences of Aurielle Moran, an early immigrant who survives desertion, solo motherhood and persistent floods, and the perplexed personal history of Nick Freear, editor of *Tomorrow's Bride*, an ironic occupation for a man who

lives in the past while his marriage breaks up. The feigned blindness of Aurielle in old age, the supposedly deaf-mute marriage counsellor who obliges Nick and his wife Donna to document all their shifting perceptions, the memorable passages of Nick's schoolteacher father reconstructing the 'Battle of Boulcott Farm' and post-colonially reversing its outcome, even the huge splinter which skewers Nick's ring finger from the the first chapter to the last page, all indicate that this is much more than a realist narrative. Yet it also manages to record historical and contemporary Lower Hutt with conviction and colour, from scenes of sickening nineteenth-century racism against *Chinese to inter-club softball at Naenae Park and small business deviousness in the 1980s.

Jones's short fiction collection, *Swimming to Australia* (1991) was shortlisted for the New Zealand Book Award in Fiction, and his stories have been anthologised in *Vital Writing*, the *Oxford Book of New Zealand Short Stories* and elsewhere. Again, the mixture of realism with the uncommon, absurd or fantastic is striking, especially in the bizarre triptych 'Baggage', which opens with the young narrator collecting a mountain of cans tossed from passing cars on a motorway, and ends with him and a Vietnamese refugee living rough in the backyards of Grey Lynn, 'trying to create new lives for ourselves in the heart of the old one'—a tension which recurs in Jones's fiction. The everyday is always liable to carry perplexing significance, whether in 'Broken Machinery', an extension from *Splinter*, or a family reconstituted after divorce adjusting to new relationships and locations in the title story, or a middle-aged couple rediscovering physical affection in a Russian bus ('The Simpsons in Russia'), or a couple confronting the complexities of their relationship in the black depths of a railway tunnel ('The Waiting Room'). Departure, distance and readjustment of vision are images that recur in the collection's imaginative response to New Zealand in a time of flux. Little is tidily or reliably resolved, yet the significance of individual life is affirmed with a sometimes numinous affection and detail (perhaps best in 'Who's That Dancing with My Mother?').

Two projects have reinforced this concern. In *Into the Field of Play: New Zealand Writers on the Theme of Sport* (1992) Jones compiled a collection of fifteen pieces of *sports writing by such prominent literary and sporting authors as Owen *Marshall, Brian *Turner and Warwick *Roger, almost unique in demonstrating the 'wider culture' of New Zealand sport as well as in the literary quality of the work it includes. And in 1994 he curated (with photographer Bruce Foster) an exhibition at the National Library that illustrated the phenomenon of the New Zealand Saturday. With historical photographs and contemporary ones by Foster, and an essay by Jones, this was published as *Last Saturday* (1994), again unusual in its examination of genuinely popular culture.

These preoccupations with the inner significance of the ordinary and with the nature of reality provide a helpful context for the controversial success of *Biografi* (1993), essentially the extraordinary quest of one ordinary man in search of another. As a drab and officious surface concealing tragic absurdities and uncertainties, Jones's Albania has much in common with his Lower Hutt, as the narrative itself more than once implies.

A collection of three novellas, *This House Has Three Walls*, was published in 1997.   RR

JONES, Pei Te Hurinui (1898–1976), was born in Kennedys Bay (Coromandel Peninsula), the son of Daniel Lewis, a storekeeper, and Pare Te Kōrae of Ngāti Maniapoto. He later took the name of his stepfather, David Jones of Ngā Puhi descent, although some of his work is published under the name Pei Te Hurinui. He was raised bilingually and schooled in a Māori traditional manner by his uncle, Te Hurinui Te Wano. From an early age he was intensely curious to study the traditions of his ancestors. In a memoir written in 1975 for Witi *Ihimaera's anthology *Into the World of Light* (1982) he recorded that 'my granduncle often would recall me from my youthful games and set me to work on his manuscript books. These books contained genealogical tables, tribal traditions, ancient songs, and ritual.' At an early age he began to collect stories and songs of the Tainui people and to record them in Māori, an activity that went on throughout his life.

His professional career began as an interpreter to the Native Land Court in Wanganui. In 1928 he was appointed officer for consolidating land titles in the King Country and he was in charge of the Te Kuiti office of the Native Department, responsible for land development and housing. He resigned from this position in 1940 to work as a licensed interpreter in Hawera. From 1938 to 1943 he was the Labour MP for Western Maori. In 1962 he was awarded the OBE for services to Māori and in 1968 an honorary doctorate from Waikato University. His many public offices included founding president of the New Zealand Maori Council, first secretary of the Tainui Maori Trust Board, chairman of the Maori Dictionary Revision Committee (which revised H.W. *Williams's *dictionary) and member of the New Zealand Geographic Board. He was a close adviser to King Koroki and Princess *Te Puea Herangi and later to Koroki's daughter and successor, the present Māori Queen, Te Arikinui Dame Te Atairangikaahu.

Pei Te Hurinui's skills in the Māori language were greatly admired, and he translated two plays of Shakespeare (*The Merchant of Venice* and *Julius Caesar*), Fitzgerald's *Rubaiyat of Omar Khayyam* and Thomas *Bracken's *'Not Understood' into Māori. His book *King Potatau: An Account of the Life of Potatau Te Wherowhero, the First Maori King* (1959) is an elegantly written biography incorporating a generous selection of *waiata, *haka and other literary material, including an extensive genealogy (*whakapapa) of Te Wherowhero. Another biography from his hand is *Puhiwahine: Maori Poetess* (1961). Jones contributed much of the original material and all of the translations to the four-volume collection Nga *Moteatea, which he edited with Sir Apirana *Ngata.

In 1995 his definitive collection of Tainui historical and literary lore was at last published—supplemented, translated and annotated for this bilingual edition by Bruce *Biggs under the title, *Nga Iwi o Tainui: The traditional history of the Tainui people; nga koorero tuku iho a nga tupuna*. The bibliography in that volume lists a further twenty-six works by Pei Te Hurinui Jones.   NW

JONES, Stella (1904–91), wrote the successful play, *The *Tree* (1957). She was already known for her short stories and articles published in *Landfall* and elsewhere. Later she wrote mainly radio plays, the best-known of which was 'Between Seasons' (1965), discussed, with *The Tree*, in Howard McNaughton's *New Zealand Drama* (1981).   RR

JORDAN, Sherryl (1949–), children's fantasy writer, won the national competition in 1980 for illustrations to Joy *Cowley's *The Silent One*, but soon abandoned illustrating for writing. In five years, she produced twenty-seven picture books (three published) and four novels (none published). Finally, with her fifth novel, she gained the 1988 Choysa Bursary Award, and the futuristic *Rocco* (1990) won the 1991 AIM Book of the Year. Through time-slips to the future, Rocco learns basic survival skills in a mountain environment, reverence for non-violent, spiritual living, and the urgency of anti-nuclear strivings.

Afflicted with Occupational Overuse Syndrome in 1989, Jordan recovered enough to continue writing novels for teenagers and junior readers. All up to 1995 have been shortlisted for awards. *The Juniper Game* (1991) provides her only hint at Southern Hemisphere origins, but like *The Wednesday Wizard* (1991) and *Denzil's Dilemma* (1992) features time-slips to medieval England, where her picture book, *The Other Side of Midnight* (1994), is also set. *Winter of Fire* (1993) and *Tanith* (1994) feature teenage girl protagonists in love and seeking power against oppression in exotic worlds of the distant future or past. Jordan's 1995 novel, *Sign of the Lion*, again features a girl's struggle for power. Though at times she stretches credibility, Jordan writes with passion and dramatic imagery. She was born in Hawera. In 1993 she was granted a Fellowship to the University of Iowa's International Writing Program. DH

JOSEPH, George (Israel) (1912–89), was a prodigiously prolific writer, a flourishing but flawed lawyer and a colourful character still remembered in Wellington for his energy and pugnacity. He claimed that his first publication was at the age of 12 and that he had subsequently had more than a thousand short stories published in such magazines as *John Bull*, *Esquire* and *Argosy*. This may be a New Zealand record. Many of his novels were published in America or UK and widely translated. His life provided ample material. Born in Glasgow, he came to New Zealand at the age of 4 and was educated at St John's, Wanganui, Wellington College, Victoria University College and, as a New Zealand senior scholar in law, Oxford University. There (according to his *Who's Who* entry) he gained blues in two sports, represented England as a boxer, edited *Isis*, the prestigious student newspaper, and published two novels (*Destiny Road*, 1934, and *Time Will Tell*, 1935); he then worked on Fleet Street for the *Daily Mirror* 1936–37, fought as a pilot for the International Brigade in the Spanish Civil War and was twice wounded.

Returning to New Zealand, he practised as a defence barrister, was a member of the Victoria University College Council 1943–48 and continued to publish fiction, such as *The Horse with the Delicate Air* (1945), a collection of neatly turned stories with an international variety of settings. In the 1950s he wrote racy thrillers for the American Bloodhound series: e.g. *The Case of the Tattooed Torso* (1950), *Three Strangers* (1956) and *Venom in the Cup* (1958). With *Lie Fallow My Acre* (1957) he took up New Zealand themes and settings, in a somewhat unpleasant story of a colour-prejudiced American (later himself revealed as one-quarter black) whose scorn for 'coloured' people provokes the community of Hawkes Bay sheep *station owners into warm if paternalistic support of their Māori neighbours. Happily the unpopular American dies in a stable fire which the novel scarcely troubles to explain. Among his many later books, those with New Zealand settings include *When the Rainbow is Pale* (1962), based on the true story of an early-nineteenth-century English sailor enslaved by Māori (and ultimately elevated to chiefdom); and *Take Any City* (1970), a hastily written tale of 1960s sleaze in a sketchy version of Wellington, where a hard-drinking English writer is set up for an under-age sex sting. He also continued to publish bulk short stories modelled on O. Henry, many in the Wellington *Sports Post*.

In his later years Joseph was active as a Zionist, raising funds for Israel during the 1976 Seven Day War; and was struck off as a lawyer after forging some divorce documents which he had been dilatory in obtaining. Perhaps that is why he turned to courtroom thrillers, such as *Trial and Error* (1978), which Terry *Sturm in *OHNZLE* describes as showing 'urbanity and professional skill'; and to books of legal and criminal anecdote, such as *Wigs and Weepers* (1980), which has a foreword by Sir David Beattie, and *By a Person or Persons Unknown: Unsolved Murders in New Zealand* (1982). See also *Detective fiction. PN/RR

JOSEPH, M.K. (Michael Kennedy) (1914–81), was a poet and novelist of the 1950s–70s, one of the most important writers of that period, best known subsequently for his *science fiction and the novel *A *Soldier's Tale* (1976). Diverse in subject and genre, his work combines intellectual with populist elements, international with local interests, and experimentalism of form with a more traditional moral and metaphysical enquiry.

He was born at Chingford, Essex, near London, a month before the outbreak of World War 1, and retained 'sharp but disconnected memories' of wartime London, including an incinerating zeppelin, according to an unpublished memoir of his early life which is the source for some of the following information. His 'highly retentive visual memory' would later give his writing a vividness that interacts with his intellectual inclination. His early life was secure but itinerant. Both parents were well-educated Catholics from families recently risen to middle-class, his mother a successful teacher and his father a talented polyglot and businessman. They lived in various places in post-war Belgium and France 1920–23, Joseph learning French and English simultaneously. A period of schooling in Rouen is affectionately remembered in the poem 'Fragment of an Autobiography' and in *School Journal* (July 1953), and also left its mark on *A Soldier's Tale* (see also *France). Returning to England in 1923, Joseph attended St Aloysius's College, Highgate Hill, and would make use of the recollection for the filmic climax of *The *Time of Achamoth*, set in Highgate Cemetery.

The family emigrated in 1924, settling at Bethlehem, near Tauranga, where Joseph's father became a founder of the fruit industry and made close friendships with the Māori community through his fluency in the language. Joseph attended Tauranga District High School (travelling five miles by horse), then Te Puke HS and, as a junior scholarship holder, Sacred Heart College, Auckland, where J.C. *Reid and Dan *Davin were among his lasting friends. A voracious reader, he had already discovered Jules *Verne, H.G. Wells, Hugo Gernback's *Amazing Stories* magazine and the other originators of modern science fiction.

At Auckland University College from 1931, he studied law for two years before transfering to a BA and MA in English (first class honours 1934). Also in his student years he served as special constable during the 1932 Queen Street Riots (with James *Bertram and John *Mulgan), attended meetings of the Friends of the Soviet Union (with Robert *Lowry and R.A.K. *Mason) and was, in his own words, the 'simple-minded' and 'completely inexperienced' secretary of *Phoenix when it went through its fatal 'shift in emphasis' from literary journal to instrument of 'Party strategy'. After two years as a junior lecturer under Arthur Sewell at Auckland, he entered Merton College, Oxford, in 1936, financed by a grandmother and grand-uncle now also in New Zealand.

His Oxford graduation coincided with the outbreak of World War 2, and he joined the Royal Field Artillery and later an Air Observation unit, serving in England, France, Belgium, Holland and Germany, and reputedly declining promotion above bombadier. This experience recurs in his poetry and fiction and is briefly recounted in his contribution to the 'Beginnings' series (*Islands 27, 1979), source for direct quotations below.

Joseph returned to Auckland as a lecturer in English in 1946, carrying 'absurd burdens of lecturing and marking', and therefore able to write only as he had done during the war, 'in random scraps of time'. He also found time for scholarly work, especially Byron the Poet (1964) and his *Oxford University Press edition of Mary Shelley's Frankenstein (1969), and was promoted to professor in 1970. Professionally he was remembered as a lucid and popular teacher of wide literary sympathies and as an urbane, peacemaking colleague (Forrest Scott's obituary in Zealandia, 22 Nov. 1981). His novel A *Pound of Saffron (1962) gives a less gentle though still charitable view of Auckland's academic life.

He began publishing poetry in the 1940s in *Landfall, *NZ Listener and *Yearbook of the Arts. His collections are Imaginary Islands: Poems (1950), The Living Countries: Poems (1959), A Selection of Poetry (Poetry Magazine supplement, with notes by the author, 1965) and Inscription on a Paper Dart: Selected Poems 1945–72 (1974), which contained significant new work. He has usually been described as a poet of scholarly elegance and erudition, a 'university wit' (W.H. *Oliver), and is indeed skilled in wordplay, satire, literary pastiche and learned meditation. Yet words like 'academic' do not recognise what K.O. *Arvidson called 'a certain richness in the poems', or what MacD.P. Jackson meant when he asked 'what other New Zealand poet could conduct a philosophical argument in relaxed blank verse to the point where the bland voice of the logician rises to something akin to passion?' While Joseph eschewed intensely subjective verse, his best work often obliquely frames personal feeling, as when the perfect metaphysical pastiche 'Meditation on a Time-Piece' emerges as a deeply felt affirmation of marital love; or when the apparently light impressionism of 'Girl, Boy, Flower, Bicycle' takes on intimations of eternity. (For many years this poem was widely anthologised in overseas collections and textbooks.) He brings learning and a highly resourceful diction to confront the moral complexities of cruelty and mercy, apocalypse and hope, art and philistinism, but is capable also of creating a visual, even filmic sense of cosmic scale, as in the awesome Wellsian montage of past and future disguised under the innocent title of 'Epitaph to a Poetry Reading'.

His meditative and metaphysical inclination works in fruitful tension with the belief stated in Byron the Poet that 'art ... is about itself'. Images of mirrors, 'shadows dancing' and reflexivity thus recur, two decades before *postmodernism took hold in New Zealand; so do variations on popular culture ('Murder Story', 'Cinema', 'Funfair'); so do complex games of what later became called intertextuality. The opening page of I'll Soldier No More alludes to Joyce's 'The Dead' ('The rain was falling softly, all over Germany'), the opening of The *Hole in the Zero to Yeats ('nine bean rows') and in The Time of Achamoth one time-travel stopover is in the mind of the unnamed H.G. Wells as he conceives the word 'Morlocks'. All significantly enrich the immediate text.

Though habitually and expertly literary, Joseph is likely to link radio's space-adventurer Jet Morgan with Botticelli ('Mars Ascending'), TV's 'Gunlaw' Matt Dillon with Samuel Johnson ('The Rosy Cats of Doctor Paracelsus'), Plato's Republic with the movie matinee ('Cinema'). He can be a poet of collages and connections and evasions ('Unoriginal Poem') as readily as of the pathos of war ('Elegy for the Unburied Dead') or of paternal love ('For My Children', adapted from the earlier 'For My Son').

His imagination mostly worked beyond the local; a poem for Allen *Curnow and Kendrick *Smithyman is an updated version of the legend of Icarus. But his contributions to specifically New Zealand poetry are considerable, including the satiric 'Secular Litany', one of the best-known 1950s poems for its attack on the Kiwi philistinism of 'Saint Allblack / Saint Monday Raceday' (see also *Sport); grey city sketches like 'Elegy in a City Railyard' and 'The Drunkard and the Crane'; and meditations on the history and geography of New Zealand like 'Mercury Bay Eclogue' and 'Distilled Water'. Joseph was co-winner, with Keith *Sinclair, of the 1953 Landfall Poetry Award for the sequence 'The Lovers and the City'. He is well represented in all anthologies, most substantially the Oxford Book of New

Zealand Writing Since 1945, ed. MacD.P. Jackson and Vincent *O'Sullivan (1983).

About 1951 Joseph began 'writing a series of sketches ... recording impressions of ordinary life in wartime Britain, France and Germany'. These became 'a kind of low-key semi-documentary novel', *I'll Soldier No More* (1958), published by *Paul's Book Arcade and by Gollancz in England, where it was well received by reviewers such as Nancy Spain for its authenticity and balanced human insight. The novel provides a history of the European war from 1940 to 1946 through three conscripted artillerymen, one a New Zealander, Harry Gillies, who reappears briefly in *A Pound of Saffron*. It is a war novel with almost no close-up violent action, where a death is cause for prolonged grief and recrimination, and where the men's internal lives are dominated by personal preoccupations—a wife's infidelity, a mother's death, a lover's rejection, a sustaining Catholic faith, greed, fear, sleeplessness, toothache. Yet their essential heroism is all the more credibly established. The impressionistic sketches of war's impact on the people of England, France, Belgium and Germany are extraordinarily sensitive, and as convincing as the novel's minor cast of utterly unstereotyped soldiers. Lifting the book above realism and routine are eloquent passages that bring a cosmic dimension, especially a visionary overview of the world at war on Christmas Day 1943, which acts as a centrepiece of the narrative.

Joseph's university novel, *A Pound of Saffron*, was conceived as 'a tight plot with simplified "humours" characters, like a Ben Jonson comedy', but 'everyone insisted on reading it as some kind of *roman à clef*', and 'perhaps that has helped to give me a preference for science-fiction, historical romance and other forms of obvious fantasy'. His subsequent novels are the science fiction *The Hole in the Zero* (1967), a return to the moral issues of the European war in *A Soldier's Tale* (1976), a time-travel exploration of evil and 'the mysterious alternatives of history' in *The Time of Achamoth* (1977), and the posthumously published historical novel of the medieval debacle of the Children's Crusade, *Kaspar's Journey* (1988). Two further novels remain unpublished, one an adventure fantasy set in a Europe controlled by victorious Nazis.

Joseph wrote quite often on New Zealand topics; for example, in a discerning study of the artist John Weeks in *Landfall* 34 (1955) or in his conservative but perceptive review of Janet *Frame's *The *Adaptable Man* in *Landfall* 77 (1966). His professional views tended to be conservative, resisting the teaching of creative writing or contemporary literature, dismissing the concept of *nationalism in literature, but these are not wholly consistent with his practice as an innovative teacher as well

as practitioner of science fiction or his expert commentaries on film as a serious art form as early as 1949 for *Here & Now*. Nor was his urbane, Edwardian image wholly consistent with the adventurousness and idiosyncrasy of his writing. The narrator of *Kaspar's Journey* has 'a power of remaining apart', casting a cool 'spectator's eye' on the often lurid adventures that embroil him. Joseph sought the same detachment, writing of the great themes of European history in the idiom of a participant who yet remains at heart outside it all. The strategy of *A Soldier's Tale* and *The Time of Achamoth* as well as *Kaspar's Journey*, this can be read as an imaginative rendering of some of the formative experiences of modern New Zealand history. It produces moments of rare fictional power—the final pitying vision in *Kaspar's Journey* of army after army struggling across Europe towards carnage, or the perplexed contemplation of brutal compassion that ends *A Soldier's Tale*.

His ultimate importance may lie in such searching meditations on aggression and violence. Allen Curnow's attack on Joseph's moral integrity in the poem 'Dichtung und Wahrheit' may have been prompted by the recognition of the threat to his own status as the poet of violence. The craft and compassion of *A Soldier's Tale* survived the assault. The novel stands as a statement of the duality with which 'Cruelty and mercy share the same human heart', just as *I'll Soldier No More* ends with 'the rude soldiery' who are also 'men walking like gods' and the unspeakable final violence of *The Time of Achamoth* ends with a 'terrible radiance on the face of the Holy One'.

Joseph has received little sustained critical attention. E.H. *McCormick, Joan *Stevens and J.C. Reid all wrote sympathetically on *I'll Soldier No More*; W.H. *Pearson considered the treatment of Māori characters in *Essays on New Zealand Literature*, ed. Wystan *Curnow (1973); K.K. Ruthven's structuralist analysis of *A Soldier's Tale* (*Islands* 27, 1979) is of its time, highlighting the narratorial craft; and Roger Robinson placed Joseph as one of four significant recent novelists in *The Commonwealth Novel Since 1960*, ed. Bruce King (1991). An obituary by Dennis *McEldowney (*NZ Listener*, 14 Nov. 1981) gives the most judicious overview, and is especially good on the care with which Joseph 'achieved perfection time after time' in such a variety of forms that 'many future tracers of trends and categories will have to start at or near M.K. Joseph'.   RR

Journal of New Zealand Literature, The, was initiated by Roger Robinson as the first scholarly forum for the discussion of New Zealand literature, and was endorsed by a meeting of the six university departments of English in 1981. The first issue appeared in 1983

under the editorship of Frank *McKay, who also edited No. 3. Other editors have been John Thomson, William Broughton, J.C. Ross and Lawrence *Jones, since No. 10 conjointly with Heather Murray. Editorial, production and distribution responsibilities at first rotated among the English departments, Victoria (Nos 1–3) and Massey (4–6), and have remained at Otago since No. 7. As well as critical, historical and bibliographical contributions, *JNZL* originally, now occasionally, includes surveys of genres of New Zealand writing on a year-by-year basis, intended in part to provide information for overseas readers and institutions. Recent editorial policy has devoted some issues to particular topics or authors, e.g. immigrant and emigrant writers (No. 10, 1992), Janet *Frame (No. 11, 1993) and James K. *Baxter (No. 13, 1996).   RR

Journal of the Polynesian Society *(JPS)*, which first appeared in 1892, is published quarterly. At its inception it contained the transactions and proceedings of the society, whose aim was to promote the study of the Polynesian peoples. S. Percy *Smith, the founder of the Polynesian Society, its president from 1904–22 and sole editor from 1905 to 1922, believed that there was no time to be lost in recording oral traditions, as the people who knew the ancient lore were passing away. According to Smith it was a question of now or never. For over 100 years the *JPS* has been stimulating research and debate on the history, ethnology, anthropology, sociology, archaeology and linguistics of the New Zealand Māori and other Pacific peoples, and it continues to do so.

As one of the prime purposes of the society was to preserve Polynesian oral traditions, the *JPS* began by recording Māori oral literature, including incantations, songs, genealogies and stories. Many of the contributions were published in Māori with English translations. For example, in No. 2, 1893, the first five of thirteen incantations provided by a society member, Tuta Tamati, were published in Māori with English translations. In No. 4, 1893, the story of 'How Ngarara-Huarau was killed', by Te Whetu, was published in Māori with a translation by T.G. Poutawera. In the same issue, 'The Coming of Te Arawa and Tainui Canoes from Hawaiki to New Zealand' (including *whakapapa) was recounted in Māori by Takaanui Tarakawa and translated into English by S. Percy Smith. In this early period there were several enthusiastic contributors and editors of note, including Elsdon *Best and Johannes *Andersen.

By the 1950s, fewer contributions were coming from the amateur scholars recording oral traditions and more from professional anthropologists, archaeologists and others. When the Auckland University anthropology department took over the journal, the editors aimed to maintain a level of interest for both amateurs and professionals, though it has gradually become a publication by and for academics. In 1992 M.P.K. Sorrenson published a history of the Polynesian Society, *Manifest Duty*, which contains much information on the *JPS*.   CL

Joy of the Worm (1969), see **SARGESON, Frank**.

K

Ka mate, ka mate, a traditional Māori *haka, is one of New Zealand's best known and most distinctive compositions, familiar as a *sports challenge before football matches and frequently performed at Māori gatherings. It has been one of our national songs for over a century.

There are two main versions of 'Ka mate'—the Māori traditional version and the sports version; it is a bicultural composition. The story of its origin is well known: it is generally attributed to the warrior Te Rauparaha, who conceived of it while hiding from his pursuers. Most frequently a small portion of Te Rauparaha's haka is performed in both Māori and sports contexts. For Māori it mainly functions as a ngeri—a short, energetic burst of haka performed impromptu. Because it is so well known, this ngeri is likely to be supported by many at a gathering as they salute a particular decision or test the mettle of a speaker or visiting party. The ngeri can act as encouragement or warning.

In the sports context 'Ka mate' is equally well established: the haka was first used by the Natives team on their 1888 tour of Britain. With a few exceptions it has been used ever since in international rugby matches. It has also been used by other representative sports teams (hockey, polo, etc.) and by women as well as men. But its predominant use has been by the All Blacks, and this has encouraged a range of other Pacific dances: the sipi tau from the Tongan rugby team, the manu samoa from the Samoan and others from the Cook Islands. The Fijian sports challenge dance, cibi, appears to have been used as long as the football haka.

The haka as performed by the All Blacks has the same text, delivered with the same shouted voice style and aggressive dance actions as the Māori ngeri. The differences in performance are, however, significant: in the Māori style the leader patrols through the ranks of dancers, exhorting the group to greater efforts, whereas in the rugby version the leader performs at the front; the sports version ends with a leap, which is not appropriate to this style of haka in the Māori tradition.

Sports performances, which may initially have been something of a gimmick, are treated seriously, scrutinised by Māori and sports commentators alike and closely filmed by television. Many teams and institutions have haka modelled on 'Ka mate'.

The controversies which frequently erupt around this haka indicate that 'Ka mate' is a composition of competing claims and a highly volatile national symbol. In sports this haka is a very specific indicator of rugby football; the use of it by other codes (and the use of haka by female as well as male sportspersons) can create some controversy. In Māori society there is a tug between specific tribal ownership and the use of this haka by all of Māoridom. In the wider society there is apprehension at the violence that is apparently sanctioned by the haka's use as a national symbol.   AT

KACEM, Alie, wrote *For Father's Sake, or, A Tale of New Zealand Life* in 1897, published (unusually for the time, when much New Zealand writing was published in England), by Brown, Thomson and Co. of Wellington. The story is of the saint-like Nellie Main who after her father's ruin lives an independent life and longs 'to know of something brighter than paint or canvas'. Kacem writes of drink, racing, slums, marriage and matters of race and class: 'Poor Maoris we rob you of your land …'; '… when the Governor visited … only *one* man had the courtesy and grace to raise his hat in dutiful obeisance.…These are the kind of people we want in New

Zealand...' She says her 'predominating motive' is to 'show the close connection there is between Heaven and Earth' and ends the book with a plea 'For Both Father's Sakes' as Nellie ascends to Heaven. Kacem may have included autobiographical material as some names could be disguised anagrams—I wand Enswav, and the Rettos, Remay, Uregn, Alan and Sebof families. 'Alie Kacem' itself may be a pseudonym: no record has been found of her birth, marriage or death.   ALa

KAHUKIWA, Robyn (1940–), was born in Australia to New Zealand parents, and moved to New Zealand as a young woman. Trained initially as a commercial artist, she is a painter with an international reputation. Her distinctive idiom blends Māori and Pākehā influences, and she is noted especially for arresting images of Māori women.

Kahukiwa is also a prolific illustrator and a more occasional writer of picture books for children, some of which have been issued in Māori or bilingual editions. She has worked in close collaboration with Patricia *Grace. Especially popular are *The Kuia and the Spider* (1981) and *Watercress Tuna and the Children of Champion Street* (1984), which celebrate Māori and multicultural values.

Her own books, such as *Taniwha* (1986) and *Te Koroua and the Mauri Stone* (1985), incorporate elements of Māori myth and tradition into narratives with modern settings; the combination is paralleled in the illustrations by traditional motifs and patterns in the representations of mythical entities, conventional realism in the handling of the characters and settings. They celebrate traditional lore, and assert its continuing validity for the Māori child of the sceptical present.   JH

Kaihau, Te / The Windeater, a collection of stories by Keri *Hulme, was published in 1986 (*Victoria University Press). The collection sold poorly despite the fact that a number of the stories were written contemporaneously with Hulme's best-selling novel, *the *bone people*. The two works have many stylistic and thematic affinities, and even share characters in common: Simon's parentage is further elucidated in 'A Drift in Dream' and the narrator in 'Te Kaihau / The Windeater' is remarkably like Kerewin Holmes. Other similarities can be noted: supernatural and mythic elements are frequently integrated into realistic representations of everyday life; gender roles are consistently subverted; language and character are creolised (Māori–Pākehā being the most common variation, a feature signalled by the collection's bilingual title and underscored by the frequent use of Māori mythology and fragments of Māori language in the English text). There is a recurrent concern with the failings and dangers of language and, linked to this, much linguistic and syntactic experimentation and literary allusion. In typically Modernist fashion, language constantly threatens to fail the writer: 'Have I told you anything? / Has it meant anything to you? / Or is it all just writing? / All just words?' ('Kiteflying Party at Doctors' Point'). Most familiar of all is the recurring figure of the lonely, isolated outcast, the alienated wanderer (pertinently, 'kaihau' means both wanderer and loafer). Where the collection deviates from the novel, as several critics have noted, is in the unrelentingly bleak vision of the short fiction, despite moments of what Ian *Wedde, in his *NZ Listener* review, calls Hulme's 'garrulous humour'. While in *the bone people* alienated individualism is reconciled with community, racial tensions are averted in the reconciliation of Māori and Pākehā, and love triumphs over death and violence (all via the medium of the supernatural), *Te Kaihau*'s stories do not offer such happy endings. The supernatural is not redemptive; creolised pairings or trinities do not engender new beginnings; violence, unrecuperated, is simply destructive; characters remain alienated and are not reintegrated into healing communities; death and violence prevail.

The collection begins with a prefatory diptych ('Tara Diptych'), the first part or 'wing' in prose, the second in poetry; and concludes with a poetic afternote which, while concluding this collection, is apparently the headnote to another ('Headnote to a Maui Tale'). The eighteen stories thus framed by the paired foreword and afternote (binary structuring occurs throughout) are striking for the variety of different narrative styles and voices used by Hulme. This composite aspect of the collection has appeared to some critics to invite *postmodernist frames of interpretation, despite the perceived antagonisms of such critical approaches to Hulme's ostensible postcolonialism and her persistent modernist themes and concerns. Other critics suggest that the poems should be read from the perspective of Māori oral poetry, for although none of the stories can be said to be a traditional *waiata, they may be seen to echo and transform traditional narrative patterns.   KWo

Kaioraora, see **Pātere**.

KALMAN, Yvonne (1940–), author of the blockbuster trilogy *The Greenstone Land*, was born in Hawera and taught for fifteen years before becoming a full-time writer in the later 1970s. Her first book was a children's animal story, *Sparkles* (1979), followed by *Summer Rain* (1980) and *Midas* (1983), torrid *romances released only on the American mass market. She achieved international recognition when she broke into the American blockbuster market with *The Greenstone Land* (1981), the first of a trilogy of three historical romances set in colonial Auckland. The other two volumes in the saga were *Juliette's Daughter* (1982) and *Riversong* (1985). *Bridge to Nowhere* appeared in 1986, and then two further historical romances set in colonial Canterbury: *Mists of Heaven* (1987) and *After the Rainbow* (1989).

Kalman was the first New Zealand popular novelist to revive the historical romance in a major way after Edith *Lyttleton ('G.B. Lancaster') in the 1930s, although Georgina *McDonald, in *Grand Hills for Sheep* (1949) and *Stimson's Bush* (1954) had written about colonial Otago and Southland, and in the 1960s–70s Frank *Bruno, James Tullett and James *Sanders wrote on historical subjects in the male genre of action and adventure. Kalman's romances are colourful evocations of colonial life, laced with often lurid scenes of sex and violence, and written from the point of view of rebellious heroines struggling against the self-seeking and often brutal behaviour of the rich and powerful with whom their destinies are enmeshed. In the *Greenstone Land* trilogy, power is vested in the expanding Auckland business interests of a family dynasty, engaged in ruthless internecine feuds; in *Mists of Heaven* and its successor, in the power politics of Canterbury's ruling colonial elites. Despite their sensationalism the novels offer a richly detailed account of nineteenth-century social customs—hair and dress styles, cuisine and fashions in decor—and *Juliette's Daughter* in particular addresses nineteenth-century race relations with considerable sensitivity.   TS

Kapiti: Selected Poems 1947–71 (1972) by Alistair *Campbell presents his work in a more coherent way after *Mine Eyes Dazzle* (1950) and *Wild Honey* (1964). It takes over most of *Wild Honey*, and *Blue Rain* (1967), though here the poems are rearranged and three excluded, and adds new poems. The poems of his first volume, constantly changed and reordered through new editions and selections, undergo similar transformations. 'The Waterfall' vanishes completely, while others undergo sometimes very slight changes (such as the removal of the indefinite article from the line 'To the glitter of a printed leaf on (a) stone' in 'Bones'). With familiar poems placed in new contexts, the effect is less that of a 'Selected Poems' than a new view of the oeuvre.

The new material includes two poems previously printed as sturdy broadsheets. 'Drinking Horn' is a melancholic drinking song, intensely erotic but painfully aware of the distance between the middle-aged speaker and the youthful girls he admires (a theme treated more

gently in 'To a Young Girl'). 'Walk the Black Path', with its mosaic of violent, slightly crazed images, is reminiscent of German Expressionism. There is also an address to the poet's grandfather ('I would like to think / that he was fierce and proud.... He was probably gentle'), significant for the poet's increasing concern for his ancestors and Polynesian origins. Within a few years he would find that this grandfather had, in fact, deeply loved his grandchild.   NW

Karakia, or 'spells', were used by Māori to increase achievement and performance in all parts of life: children used them with their toys, adults with their various activities or to cure illnesses, and priests used esoteric ones for supernatural purposes. *Williams (see *Dictionaries) lists more than 130 kinds. They were not so much sung as chanted on a monotone, very rapidly, gliding down at the end of a phrase. Raymond Firth pointed out that they were spoken extremely fast and that the flow of sound should be unbroken, so that long ones were spoken alternately by two performers. If they were not word-perfect they would be ineffective and possibly harmful. 'Magic was a double-edged tool, dangerous to the wielder if not properly handled' (Firth, *Economics of the New Zealand Maori*, 1959). Their effectiveness also partly depended on the *mana of the person reciting them. In post-Christian times 'karakia' is also used as a translation of the English 'church service' and the church itself is the 'whare karakia'.
                                                                NW

Karanga are calls performed on the *marae by women to welcome or farewell guests. Greeting calls are called karanga *pōwhiri and farewell calls poroporoaki. They are often extemporised but use conventional phrases. The occasion will determine the nature of the karanga. In *Te Marae: A Guide to Customs and Protocol* (1987), Hiwi and Pat Tauroa write: '... there are basic calls and responses, but ... the feelings expressed are a major ingredient. There will be feelings for the marae, for the *tangata whenua, for the manuhiri (guests), and for the tipuna (ancestors), as well as the personal feelings of the kai karanga (caller) herself.' The most expert calls draw on mythological language, ancestral names and the names of local natural features, in words adapted to the particular occasion. The invocation of the dead links the living to the dead and through them to *Hawaiki and the original Pō (Underworld). Anne Salmond, in *Hui: A Study of Maori Ceremonial Gatherings*, writes: 'The words of the karanga have a great deal in common with the language of Maori oratory, and people say in fact that karanga is the women's equivalent of speechmaking.' (See *Whaikōrero.)   NW

KĀRETU, Tīmoti Sam (1937–), of the Tūhoe, is an acknowledged authority on the Māori language, author of an innovative language text, *Te Reo Rangatira* (1974; using the Tūhoe dialect), *Concise Māori Dictionary* (1984), *He Hingātore* (1987), *Ngā Waiata me ngā Haka a Tāua e te Māori* (1978), *Ngā Waiata me ngā Haka a te Kapa Haka o te Māori* (1978), *Ngā Waiata me ngā Haka a te Kapa Haka o te Whare Wānanga o Waikato* (1987), *He Pitopito Kōrero nā Ngā Iwi o te Motu* (1976) and of a major study of a Māori literary form: *Haka! Te Tohu o te Whenua Rangatira: The Dance of a Noble People* (1993).

Educated at Victoria University of Wellington (Te Whare Wānanga o Te Upoko o Te Ika a Maui), and formerly a schoolteacher in Taumaranui, Waikato, and in Waimārama, Hawkes Bay, he had a period as information officer at the New Zealand High Commission in London and was then professor of Māori Studies at Waikato University (Te Whare Wānanga o Waikato). He is now head of the *Māori Language Commission (Te Taura Whiri i te Reo Māori), a member of the Te Kōhanga Reo board of trustees (responsible for 'language nests', or Māori-language kindergartens) and chairman of the *Aotearoa Māori Performing Arts Festival Committee.

Tīmoti Kāretu is widely admired for his compositions of *haka and *waiata. Four of his poems are included in Volume 5 of *Te *Ao Mārama. In one of them he laments the loss of his language; in another he defends Māori universty students against the charge that they should learn more of Māoritanga on the *marae rather than in a 'Pākehā' university; in a third he insists that Māori must take responsibility for their own destiny; and in the fourth, 'Te Kuika Māori', he sings: 'Reach for the handle of the paddle, keep the canoe head to the wind, for then we might reach the land of prosperity, a land free from strife, which is the desire and wish of the Māori world.' (Translation by Witi *Ihimaera.)   NW

KAVAN, Anna (1901–68), the English novelist and *science fiction writer, spent nearly two years in New Zealand 1941–42, publishing some short fiction. Her name is best known through Bill *Pearson's essay *'Fretful Sleepers', which refers four times to her retrospective article 'New Zealand—Answer to an Inquiry' (1943). This was her first contribution on arrival in London to Cyril Connolly's prestigious *Horizon*. She had come to New Zealand to live with the playwright and pacifist Ian Hamilton, who is 'the Australian' in her *My Soul in China* (1975). A *Tomorrow and later *Here & Now contributor, Hamilton (described in Michael *King's *Frank Sargeson*, 1995, as 'a wealthy and debonair socialist') introduced her at their Torbay home to a literary circle that included *Sargeson, who, King says,

recommended her to Ian *Gordon's *New Zealand New Writing*. Her story 'Ice-Storm' in Number 1 (1942) has a narrator struggling with a decision to leave America during a New York blizzard, which fills the story with images of extreme cold. These recur in her writing, explained by her biographer David Callard as a symptom of heroin addiction, manifested in New Zealand by her preoccupation with the Antarctic. In 'Ice-Storm' the 'ice-coffined' world becomes an image of 'Negation of everything', and she carried something of that impression away from New Zealand: 'it's null, it's dull, it's tepid, it's mediocre; the downunder of the spirit'.

Pearson quotes from this *Horizon* essay her conviction that New Zealanders had not yet cut free of Britain and cites her views on the exclusiveness of New Zealand intellectuals. Other works written in New Zealand or with a connection include 'The Red Dogs', which appeared in *Penguin New Writing*, the stories 'Banjo' and 'The Gannets' in *I Am Lazarus* (1945) and the unpublished 'The Cactus Sign', which Denis *Glover referred to when he wrote that *Caxton 'will probably be publishing a curious travel book shortly for her'.

Born Helen Woods in Cannes, France, and first publishing under her married name of Helen Ferguson, she adopted the name Anna Kavan in 1940 from the autobiographical character in her early novels *Let Me Alone* (1930) and *A Stranger Still* (1935). *Sleep Has His House* (UK 1948, USA 1980) is an intense, imagistic childhood autobiography. The 'slight hysteria' noted by Pearson was characteristic of her feverishly impressionistic prose. She found her métier late in fantasy and science fiction, with *Eagle's Nest* (1958) and *Ice* (1967). With praise (from Brian Aldiss) as one of the great science fiction writers, her reputation is rising, with recent American editions and Callard's 1992 biography.   RR

KAVANAGH, Ted (Henry Edward) (1892–1958), was the main scriptwriter of the famous BBC radio comedy programme, 'ITMA', a key source of Britain's resilient morale during World War 2 and a major influence on later radio and television comedy. He was born and educated in Auckland, and was long remembered for his part in the 1912 Auckland University capping revue. Travelling to England in 1914 to study medicine, he turned instead to writing journalism, humorous monologues and revues, forming a partnership in the 1920s with the quick-fire Liverpool-born comedian Tommy Handley. In July 1939, with war imminent, the pair found their moment with the satiric, irreverent, roguish, absurdist 'ITMA'. The title itself parodied wartime acronyms, code for 'It's That Man Again', the mocking headline coined by the *Daily Express* for Adolf Hitler. Kavanagh was a master of comedy by catchphrase, many of his eccentric characters and their identifying phrases entering British cultural consciousness for at least half a century. The morose Mona Lott ('It's bein' so cheerful as keeps me going'); the bibulous Colonel Chinstrap ('I don't mind if I do'); the loquaciously servile Mrs Mopp ('Can I do yer now, sir?' and 'Ta-ta fer now', coded as 'TTFN')—all can still sometimes be heard in England. Kavanagh's ability to capture recognisable British types perhaps came, as with that other wartime observer, David *Low, from his semi-detached position as a New Zealander. His Dickensian fertility with character and phrase was perfectly articulated by Tommy Handley's crisply mischievous delivery and acute timing, and by a strong cast of English character actors.

Kavanagh's 310 weekly (every Thursday) episodes pioneered many aspects of British radio comedy, and he helped train other major writers for radio and later TV, including Frank Muir, Denis Norden and Roy Plomley. He thus stands at the head of a tradition which inspired Roger *Hall and John *Clarke, among many more. The show's popularity can scarcely be exaggerated. Modern films about wartime Britain, which show every house engrossed in 'ITMA' as the Blitz rains destruction among them, tell no more than the truth. It held its place beyond the war, too, until Handley's sudden death in January 1949. Kavanagh then wrote the biography, *Tommy Handley* (1950).

A dedicated Roman Catholic, Kavanagh was awarded a knighthood of St Gregory by Pope Pius XII. His son P.J. Kavanagh wrote a family history that deals with their New Zealand origins, *Finding Connections* (1990). RR

KAYE, Bannerman (1854–1923), novelist and journalist, was born Eliza Bannerman Maclaren in Lossiemouth, North Scotland, her father a Presbyterian minister. The family emigrated to Port Adelaide, Australia, and after marriage she moved in 1883 to Christchurch. There she was active in the YWCA, becoming president from 1901 to 1920. She was also editor, and a leading contributor, for the Presbyterian Women's Missionary Union paper, *The Harvest Field*, for many years. As Bannerman Kaye, she wrote a novel, *Haromi: A New Zealand Story* (London, 1900), a challenging treatment of sexual and race issues. Haromi, a young part-Māori woman, is seduced, made pregnant and abandoned by English visitor and artist Robert Agnew who has fallen in love with her European half-sister Milly, who in turn loves Presbyterian minister Dugald. When Robert learns that Haromi has his baby he reluctantly decides to marry her, regarding this as a social disgrace that will ruin him. He is saved from this fate when Haromi accidentally drowns. He repents,

and returns to England with his daughter, whom he names Haromi for her mother. Milly also travels to England where some time later she marries Dugald. Themes include racial and sexual double standards, sin, chastity and fears of Māori 'reversion' to savagery. Bannerman Kaye died at Island Bay, Wellington, and her tombstone at Karori Cemetery is inscribed 'They rest from their labours and their works do follow them.' ALa

KEANE, M.C. or **Mick** (Michael Cormack) (1888–1929), was described by Alan *Mulgan as 'the most brilliant journalist of his day'. Born in Hokitika, he was educated at Christchurch BHS, where his teachers included Ernest Rutherford, and Canterbury University College, where he emulated Rutherford by taking first class honours in mathematics and physics and was regarded as an outstanding science scholar. He chose journalism, working for the *Lyttelton Times, *Truth, for the Wellington *Evening Post* as parliamentary reporter and for the *New Zealand Times* and *Dominion* as assistant editor, before joining the *Press as assistant editor in 1913. In 1919 he became the *Press's* first editor to be New Zealand born and educated, and quickly recruited writers who similarly represented the first full generation of outstanding local talent. His own Saturday column, 'Obiter Dicta' (as 'K.'), was nationally popular, and the *Press's* literary page through the 1920s was a major outlet for New Zealand's emergent literature. Ngaio *Marsh, M.H. *Holcroft, Ursula *Bethell, D'Arcy *Cresswell and others all gained from Keane's rigorous and professional expectations. He published his own poetry regularly in the Sydney *Bulletin. Alan Mulgan said 'As a writer of light topical verse he was unequalled, but some of his serious verse was admirable.' Two of the more serious poems were included in Alexander and *Currie's *New Zealand Verse* and were recently revived in Harvey *McQueen's *The New Place* (1993). 'The Blind, Obedient Dead' is a *Kipling-like memorial to the many horses killed in the *Boer War, which succeeds in being compassionate without being sentimental: 'Knowing nothing of the combat, recking nothing if they won / When the echoes of the last shot died away; / They are dreaming of the far-off bush and creeks, and shade and sun, / And gallops at the breaking of the day.' 'Two Voices' (in the 1926 *A Treasury of New Zealand Verse*) shows the same adroit craft with longer lines and difficult metre in evoking the colours and sounds of the New Zealand landscape: 'The threads of fire on mountain-sides in purple of the night—/ The dusted gold of tussocks and the music of the fords...' Keane held the editorship of the *Press* until his death. HMcQ/RR

KEINZLEY or **KEINZLY, Frances** (1922–), pseudonym for Mrs Frances Hunt, born Keinzly, is best known for the novel *Tangahano* (1960). Born in Ireland, she was raised in New Zealand in a large and poor family, leaving school at 13. During the war she served as a WAAC in a New Zealand military hospital in the Pacific. *Tangahano*, published as by Frances Keinzly, is in the tradition of Jane *Mander and Jean *Devanny. Although it shows signs of inexperience and is sometimes melodramatic, it survives as a vivid social document of a 1950s construction town. It also describes with some insight a marriage stressed by that raw environment. In 1961 it won the *Literary Fund Award for Achievement. The thriller *A Time to Prey* (1969) (with the pen-name now spelled Keinzley) is more professional but lacks the immediacy, passion and documentary clarity of *Tangahano*. It is a story of flawed people cooped in a mountain lodge by a blackmailer. The contrived plot rarely transcends its Agatha Christie origins. *Illusion* (1970) is also a thriller, this time with a Jekyll and Hyde plot, and is set in England and on an ocean voyage. It was well received by British reviewers. Keinzley seems not to have applied her developed writing skills to themes of the sort that had stimulated her imagination in *Tangahano*, to the detriment of the New Zealand realist novel.   RG

KEITH, Sheridan, was born in Wellington and studied at Victoria University, combining zoology and English literature. She lived in London for ten years and now lives in Auckland. Her work has included broadcasting, reviewing, journalism, selling advertising space on London buses, teaching creative writing, and running her own Northcote Point antique shop. Her stories have been published in *London Magazine* and *Landfall*, and her articles in *Art New Zealand* and *NZ Listener*, and elsewhere. Her first collection of short stories, *Shallow Are the Smiles at the Supermarket* (1991), was shortlisted in the Best First Book category of the Commonwealth Writers Prize. The second story collection was *Animal Passions* (1992). Then came the successful novel, *Zoology* (1995), winner of the 1996 Montana Book Award for Fiction.

Keith's fiction focuses on personal, intimate situations, analysing relationships and emotions, families and marriages. She has identified a concern in her work with intensity and sensuality, 'that intersection between animal and civilised behaviour'. The stories are economical vignettes—a woman gains the courage to ditch a married lover, a suburban mother defies her husband and digs a swimming-pool, a girl left to stay with her grandmother falls in love with a boy at her new school. *Zoology* is a retrospective of its hero's relationships

with women—wives, lover, daughters—each hopelessly unequal yet building a cumulative understanding. The action illustrates the paradox of free will: 'We seem to be programmed to believe in free will, and yet if that's a programme, how can it be free?' she remarked in an interview. The novel also explores the belief that 'men and women are geared for different sorts of biological situations'. Though the issues are serious, Keith relieves a bleak recognition of failure, inadequacy and loss with gentle humour and a tart sense of the eccentric.   RCr

KELLY, John Liddell (1850–1925), has been called 'the epitome of local Victorianism in verse' (by MacD. P. Jackson). Born near Airdrie, Scotland, he emigrated in 1881 and worked as a journalist. His paper *The Making of a Journalist* was published in 1900. An exploration in 1885 of trade possibilities in the Pacific inspired his poem *Tahiti: The Land of Love and Beauty* (1885) and the libretto of a comic opera, *Pomare*. *Tarawera or the Curse of Tuhoto* (1887) followed, and then the patriotic *Zealandia's Jubilee: An Ode* (1890), with its apostrophe to 'Auckland! Queen City of the Austral Seas, / Seated majestic on thy hundred hills'. Sounding even more uncomfortable was the poem *All Balls*, separately published *c*.1910. His main collection was *Heather and Fern: Songs of Scotland and Maoriland* (1902), which Jackson discusses quite fully, with its sections titled 'The Poet's Creed', 'The Voice of Nature', etc., and its poems on subjects from 'The Phantom Canoe' and 'The Taniwha' to 'The Coronation of Edward VII' and 'The Bonnie Braes o' Blamire'. Kelly was included in the first national anthology, *New Zealand Verse* (Alexander and *Currie, 1906).   HMcQ/RR

KEMP, Henry Tacy (1821–1901), was born in Kerikeri, where his father James was blacksmith for Samuel *Marsden's mission. Subsequently James became the proprietor of the famous stone store at Kerikeri. Henry Tacy Kemp was not for shopkeeping. In 1834 he was sent to the Pottersgate Academy in Norwich, England. His earliest surviving writing dates from this period: letters home and a journal of the voyage. Both survive in the Kemp family papers in Auckland's War Memorial Museum. He spoke both English and Māori from an early age, and on returning to New Zealand became an interpreter. His main activity, until 1862, was the purchase of Māori land on behalf of the Crown. Most notoriously he purchased the bulk of the South Island—some 20 million acres—from the Ngāi Tahu—for £2000. The Ngāi Tahu deed of sale still bears his name. With Governor *Grey's approval he published government-sponsored translations into Māori of Defoe's *Robinson Crusoe*

(1852) a 'Work', Kemp thought, 'likely to be interesting to the Natives', and Bunyan's *Pilgrim's Progress* (1854). A thousand copies of the Kemp *Crusoe* were printed. Those few still known to exist are in Pākehā hands, so the project may have missed its target market. The few Māori reactions to the translations suggest they thought of them as factual rather than fictional documents. In his last months Kemp was preparing a new edition of both translations, but died before completing the project. His revised texts, with corrections in his own hand, are now in the Grey Collection of the Auckland Public Library. Kemp's English–Māori phrase book *First Step to Maori Conversation* (1848) went through four editions. His *Revised Narrative of Incidents & Events in the Early Colonizing History of New Zealand* (1901) holds some interest for its feisty reflections on the early settler period.   MH

KEMP, Jan (1949–), is a poet, short story writer and accomplished public performer of her work, whose career has been mostly expatriate. Born in Hamilton and graduating in English from the University of Auckland in 1974, she has since lived in Canada, the Pacific region, Hong Kong, Singapore and Germany, writing and publishing poetry and teaching English as a second language. She now lives in Frankfurt, and returns regularly to New Zealand. She was first published by Arthur Baysting in *The *Young New Zealand Poets* (1973), and was the only woman among nineteen poets from the *Freed* group. In the late 1970s she toured New Zealand, once more as the only woman, with the 'Gang of Four', the others being Sam *Hunt, Alistair *Campbell and Hone *Tuwhare. She became known as a warm and lively public reader of her verse. Yet despite her public prominence at a time when this was still relatively rare for women poets, she has never been an overtly feminist writer. With their unmistakably feminine voice, many poems are confessional and concerned with discovery of self and the world through engagement in *les affaires de cœur*. By making herself vulnerable to love's dangers, she projects a personal drama of sexual desire and disappointment. But the ultimate message of her verse is optimistic—less about the failure of love than about the illuminations that the challenge to discover intimacy can bring. Her public poetry is often flamboyantly exuberant; showing an ear for mimicry and an ability to incorporate into a distinctive rhythm fragments of other languages, street cries, animal noises, the diverse sounds of exotic environments. Her volumes are *Against the Softness of Woman* (1976), *Diamonds and Gravel* (1979), *The Other Hemisphere* (1991) and two pamphlets, *Ice-breaker Poems* (1980) and *Five Poems* (1988). Known

more recently for her prose readings, she has published a number of short stories in journals and anthologies. She was awarded a PEN-Stout Fellowship at Victoria University in 1991.   JW

KENNEDY, Anne (1959–), is a writer of fiction and filmscripts, one of the most successful of the innovative younger *postmodernists. Born and educated in Wellington, she has been a piano teacher and music librarian and since 1986 a freelance scriptwriter and editor, co-writing with Peter *Wells and others. Her short fiction has been chosen for most recent anthologies, but has not yet been collected. *100 Traditional Smiles* (1988) is 'a brief work of fiction in many small sections'. Her novella, *Musica Ficta* (1993), plays ingeniously between *music and language, between the medieval and the modern, and between New York, Auckland and wartime Nottingham. It, too, is constructed of short, apparently discontinuous fragments, using multiple points of view, some in verse, some with the lyric intensity of haiku, often dependent on wordplay ('During a London peasouper a woman disappeared into thin air'). Places, possessions and colours feature strongly as people try to make sense of memory and create connectedness. Kennedy's essay in *The Source of the Song* (ed. Mark *Williams, 1995) comments on her Catholicism, including reference to *Musica Ficta*. The influence of film and television is evident throughout her work, as well as a rich weaving of musical elements and allusions, including in *Musica Ficta* parodic entries for the *Oxford Companion to Music*.   RR

KENNY, Alice Annie (1875–1960), was a prolific writer whose poetry caught the attention of Ezra Pound. Born in Ngaruawahia, she worked as librarian in Paeroa and contributed verse, short stories and children's stories to New Zealand and Australian magazines. Selections of her lyrical poetry appear in anthologies including *A Treasury of New Zealand Verse* (1926) and *Kowhai Gold* (1930). Despite her conventional *Georgian style and anti-modernist sentiments, Kenny's verse in the magazine *Triad* led Pound to invite her in 1912 to submit work to the new international experimentalist journal, *Poetry*. Although this did not eventuate, the contact precipitated an extended ideological literary dispute sustained by the editor of the culturally reactionary *Triad* against the high modernism propounded in the American journal. Kenny wrote a number of adventure novels, volumes of poetry, and Christian biographies for children, as well as adventure novels for adult readers under the pseudonym 'Alan Armitage', including a western, *Wild Horse Gulch* (1947).   SW

KER, Dorothy (1965–), composer, was born in Carterton, graduated MMus (Hons) from the University of Auckland in 1987 and has subsequently been awarded several prizes and scholarships and taken part in composers' workshops. She has set texts by Denys *Trussell, Ruth *Dallas and Hone *Tuwhare (*And the Rain ...*, 1991). Her expressive and lucid style shows a preference for rich instrumental combinations.   JMT

KERR, Bob (1951–), writes and illustrates children's books. Born in Wellington (where he now lives), he grew up there and in Tokoroa, graduated DipFA(Hons) from Auckland University and worked as a union organiser and freelance illustrator. He illustrated two picture books, *Lucy's Big Plan* (1977) and *Lucy Loops the Loop* (1979), before collaborating with Stephen Ballantyne in the successful adventures of Terry Teo: *Terry and the Gunrunners* (1982), later televised; *Terry and the Yodelling Bull* (1986); and *Terry and the Last Moa* (1990). These are satirically humorous variants on the models of Tintin or Astérix. Kerr's own junior novel, *The Optimist* (1992), about sailing misadventures, won the 1993 Best First Children's Book Award. *The Paper War* (1994) examines political issues concerning those working a paper-run. He also edited, with Linda Mitchell, *For a Living* (1991).
DH

KIDMAN, Fiona (1940–), is a versatile writer and one of the most popularly successful of contemporary serious novelists. Born in Hawera, she has worked as a librarian, writer, producer and critic. Her first novel, *A *Breed of Women* (1979), is the story of an unconventional young woman's confrontations with a narrow-minded small town society characterised by the grim judgment, 'There's no way outa Ohaka, 'cept by flying young, or dying here'. *Mandarin Summer* (1981) has a more exotic setting—the subtropical north of the North Island—and a more exotic cast—the 'China Set', colonial expatriates, whose Gothic family relationships are seen through the eyes of a young girl, Emily, whose parents work for the family as housekeeper and handyman. *Paddy's Puzzle* (1983, issued in USA under the title *In a Clear Light*, 1985), is set in Hamilton during the *Depression and Auckland during World War 2. It tells the story of Clara, her childhood and adolescence, and her attempt to escape from the confinement of her upbringing. *The *Book of Secrets* (1987) is based on a historical account of Norman McLeod, a Scottish preacher who led a band of immigrants to Nova Scotia and subsequently Waipu in the Bay of Islands. It focuses on three generations of women, and deals with issues of transgression and nonconformity within a moralistic culture. *True Stars* (1990) is unusual in Kidman's oeuvre

in its specifically political slant, being an uncompromising critique of new right economics and the changes that New Zealand society underwent in the 1980s. *Ricochet Baby* (1996) is an examination of the effects of post-natal depression on an individual and a family.

Kidman has published three short story collections: *The Foreign Woman* (1993); *Mrs Dixon and Friends* (1982); and *Unsuitable Friends* (1988); and four collections of poetry: *Honey and Bitters* (1975); *On the Tightrope* (1978); *Going to the Chathams: Poems 1977–84* (1985); and *Wakeful Nights: Poems Selected and New* (1991).

Her writing is concerned with the effects of suburban and provincial lower middle-class life, its morals and its hypocrisies. Her style is realist, often filtered through the consciousness of the main (usually female) character. Many of her novels and short stories involve outsiders in a narrowly conformist society. This outsider status is often dramatised by sexual transgression and punishment. Kidman writes, 'As a writer I don't believe I am wholly responsible for the choices my characters make; they are lodged somewhere in my psyche, in my personal histories.' Her poetry tends to be descriptive, autobiographical and confessional, with a strong undercurrent of feminist self-discovery and fulfilment.

Kidman's non-fiction works include *Gone North* (with photographer Jane Ussher, 1984), and *Wellington* (with Grant Sheehan, 1989). *Palm Prints* (1994) represents a range of her non-fiction—autobiographical pieces, speeches, literary journalism dating from 1969. She has written a radio play, *Search for Sister Blue* (published 1975), and a semi-documentary radio series, 'Fire of the North' (1972).

Kidman is a powerful advocate for writers and literature. She has been active in several national organisations concerning literature. She was the national president of *PEN from 1981 to 1983. She has been involved in the *New Zealand Book Council since its inception in 1972, being its first secretary, and president from 1992 to 1995. She writes of the council as 'a concept which held such a profound vision for books in our lives'. She has played an active part in book festivals such as the Women's Book Week, and the *Writers and Readers Week of the New Zealand International Festival of the Arts. She was involved in the United Women's Conventions in the 1970s, and was particularly influenced by 1975 International Women's Year. She writes, 'No story of the last two decades of women's writing in this country is complete without recounting the events of that year.'

She has won a number of awards and scholarships: the Ngaio Marsh Award for Television Writing (1971), the 1988 New Zealand Book Award for Fiction for *The Book of Secrets*, the Literary Fund Award for

Achievement. She has been awarded the Scholarship in Letters on a number of occasions. In 1988 she was the Victoria University writing fellow and was awarded the OBE, and in 1998 was made a Dame of the Order of New Zealand for services to literature.   JS

KILLEEN, Richard (1946–), painter, was born in Auckland and graduated from Elam School of Fine Arts in 1966. He is known for his 'cut-outs', in which images drawn from a wide variety of sources are painted on individual pieces of aluminium. These may be hung in any combination so that any internal compositional structure or linear, narrative relationship of parts is eschewed. This practice, motivated by his critique of traditional representational systems, extends to his production (since 1989) of small-scale, self-published artist books, where Killeen combines text and image, or reproduces elements drawn from his compendium of visual resources. He perceives these as 'interventions' into the arena of book production and alternatives to the immediacy of his wall-based practices. Such works include: *The Politics of Geometry* (1991), *How May We Learn* (1992), *Handbook* (1993), and *Objects and Images from the Cult of the Hook* (1996). Killeen has also undertaken a number of collaborative works in this published form with Francis Pound (*Two Sign Writers Two Fathers*, 1991), Alan ★Brunton (*Ephphatha*, 1994) and Margaret ★Orbell (*The Presence of Dew*, 1996).   CB

KING, Michael (1945–), writer, historian and biographer, recounts his early childhood in his 'selective and ethnic autobiography' *Being Pakeha: An Encounter with New Zealand and the Maori Renaissance* (1985); and the development of his professional life in the sequel *Hidden Places: A Memoir in Journalism* (1992). Together these display the twin threads of King's writing life: his commitment to being a professional writer, scholarly yet accessible to a wide public; and his desire to account for the difference ethnicity has made in his own life, as well as to the history of New Zealand, which has driven his many efforts 'to make Maori preoccupations more intelligible to some non-Maori New Zealanders'. During the late 1970s–early 1980s Pākehā scholars of Māori issues were frequently viewed with deep suspicion. The self-justifying rhetoric of *Being Pakeha* thus at times sounds like special pleading; King's contributions to social history, 'Māori' history and to biography have nonetheless been substantial.

King was born in Wellington. His family was Irish and Scottish: his elders nurtured their ethnicity through Catholic ritual, and longing for their 'old countries', with their ancient pasts and their mournful songs. From an early age, King set himself a different task, encountering

the New Zealand histories which lay all around him, in the archaeology and terrain of Paremata. His interest in the local was fostered by immersion in classics of New Zealand writing such as James ★Cowan's *The New Zealand Wars*, with its skirmish-by-skirmish account. He studied history at Victoria University (BA 1967) and the University of Waikato (MA 1968); and then joined the staff of the *Waikato Times*, where he was assigned to cover Māori issues. This brought him into close contact with the Tainui tribes and their power base at Turangawaewae ★marae in Ngaruawahia. King's knowledge of Māori protocol and access to a wide range of Māori informants were crucial to his writings throughout the 1970s and early 1980s. These included *Moko: Maori Tattooing in the 20th Century* (1972), with Marti Friedlander's elegiac photographs of surviving kuia with moko, and *Maori: A Photographic and Social History* (1983). King's strongest work in this 'Māori' period was in the two biographies *Te Puea* (1977) and *Whina* (1983), the lives of two charismatic Māori leaders. He draws admiring but not uncritical portraits of both women, deftly weaving oral testimony with documentary archive material, thereby revealing as much of the times in which ★Te Puea Herangi and Whina Cooper lived (and which they sought so much to influence) as of themselves. King's later biography *Frank Sargeson* (1995) deploys the same skill for lively narrative, coupled with access to the ★Sargeson archives and correspondence, as well as to numerous friends and enemies whose recollections flesh out the heroic narrative of the birth of Pākehā literature in New Zealand, in which Sargeson was as significant to his culture as Te Puea and Whina were to theirs.

The Sargeson biography, together with the eagerly awaited edition of Sargeson's salty correspondence which is to follow it, climaxed King's work of the 1980s and 1990s, when he shed the mantle of being champion and chronicler of exclusively Māori figures and culture. Those decades saw him account for his own ethnicity in *Being Pakeha* and tackle the wider question of the nature of Pākehā New Zealand cultures. As with his Māori writings, King answered these questions by studying representative figures: Sargeson; E.H. ★McCormick; Andreas Reischek, the Austrian naturalist of King's *The Collector* (1981); and King himself. His interest in the lively yet typical life made him an ideal contributor to the ★*Dictionary of New Zealand Biography*, for which he wrote the life (among others) of Tommy Solomon, the so-called 'last of the Morioris'. This led further to the revisionist history *Moriori: A People Rediscovered* (1989) and the photojournalist essay (in collaboration with the photographer Robin Morrison) *A Land Apart: The Chatham Islands of New Zealand* (1990). King has published also a wide range of populist histories and touristic picture books, tribute to his passion for his country, as well as indicating the projects still necessary for New Zealand professional writers to secure even an adequate income. He held the Katherine *Mansfield Memorial Fellowship in 1976 (see Patrick *White), writing fellowships at Victoria University in 1983 and at Waikato in 1994, the Sargeson Fellowship in 1995 and the *Burns Fellowship in 1998. He is writing a life of Janet *Frame.   MH

KINGSTON, W.H.G. (1814–1880), a prolific English novelist, mainly of boy's adventure stories, wrote occasionally of New Zealand, which he apparently never visited. *Holmwood: or, the New Zealand Settler* (1868) is part of a series edited, and probably entirely written, by Kingston for 'the cottagers and humbler classes of England, whose knowledge of reading and whose vocabularies are limited'. Its didactic and patronising tone towards the 'cottage' reader is echoed in the childlike-primitive image of the Māori. A fatherly settler who for sheer poverty could bring only three servants to New Zealand, treats them and the Māori as children. Though he pacifies some aggressive Māori with a Christian speech, the Major's daughter and maidservant are captured, to be saved when a Māori princess pleads that women among the English 'are their equals and friends, and never their slaves, as are most of the Maori women....' The story ends suddenly with a reference to Major Parry's success in the wars against the Māori. In *Waihoura; or, the New Zealand Girl* (1872?), the 'very good' Lucy saves Waihoura, the 'New Zealand Girl' of the title, both medically and spiritually, affirming that 'In spite of their badness, God loves the Maori people as much as he does us'. She continues to preach to Waihoura, and to the reader, continuing this career after capture in the course of war. Waihoura is responsible for Lucy's escape. *The Three Admirals* (1878) is one of a series dealing with the advance of three friends through the ranks of the navy, in this case detailed to New Zealand to fight the 'savage' but 'gallant' Māori. One of many adventurous settings all over the Pacific, New Zealand is a strange and violent place which provides the protagonists with opportunities for heroism and promotion.   NW

KIPLING, Rudyard (1865–1936), the major English short story writer, novelist and poet, visited New Zealand in October–November 1891. His visit, vividly recalled in his posthumously published autobiography, *Something of Myself* (1937), resulted in two stories, 'One Lady at Wairakei' and 'Mrs Bathurst', and the well-known quatrain on Auckland, beginning 'Last, loneliest, loveliest, exquisite, apart' ('The Song of the English',

1893). 'One Lady at Wairakei', first published in the *New Zealand Herald* on 30 January 1892, anticipates the major role played by women writers in the development of New Zealand literature and astutely observes that cultural independence relies on economic independence. Uncollected, the story was republished in an edition by Harry *Ricketts (1983) and subsequently included in Vincent *O'Sullivan's *Oxford Book of New Zealand Short Stories* (1992). According to *Something of Myself*, 'Mrs Bathurst' (*Traffics and Discoveries*, 1904) was triggered off by overhearing a New Zealand woman described as someone who 'never scrupled to help a lame duck or put her foot on a scorpion'. Now considered among the earliest examples of modernist fiction, the story, told by a series of narrators, offers a tantalisingly fragmentary account of the adulterous relationship between a naval warrant-officer, Vickery, and Mrs Bathurst, the former owner of a small hotel at Hauraki.   HRi

KITCHEN, William Freeman (b. 1873), wrote under the pseudonym 'William Freeman'. He was most notably the editor of *Zealandia* but was also the author of a melodramatic novel set in Italy but published in Dunedin: *He Who Digged a Pit* (1889). He modelled his work and ideals on Charles *Dickens and also had high praise for that other Dickensian, the Australian Marcus Clarke. He hailed Clarke's *His Natural Life* as 'the one star in our Southern firmament, and what a star!' He also enthused over Edward *Bellamy's *Looking Backward, 1000–1877*, a book which was very influential among New Zealand liberals and which he called 'one of the few modern works that it is a positive moral duty for all who profess to be thinking beings, or to have the slightest regard for their fellow creatures, to read'. After the collapse of *Zealandia* Kitchen edited a union daily, *Globe*, during the maritime strike of 1890. In 1891 he left for Australia.   NW

Kiwi, the magazine of the Auckland University Students' Association, was published 1905–80. Issues published prior to *Kiwi* becoming an annual in 1928 were dominated by light verse, reports on student activities and lists of graduands. Individuals involved in the publication of *Phoenix* were also connected with *Kiwi* during the same period, including R.A.K. *Mason, Allen *Curnow, A.R.D. *Fairburn and Robert *Lowry. In the late 1940s Denis *Glover, Kendrick *Smithyman, James K. *Baxter, Mary *Stanley, Keith *Sinclair, Maurice *Duggan, Robert *Chapman, David *Ballantyne, John Reece *Cole and G.R. *Gilbert contributed to its pages with Frank *Sargeson, C.K. *Stead, Maurice *Gee and Vincent *O'Sullivan joining their ranks during the 1950s. During its final two decades *Kiwi* appeared less frequently and included contributions by Albert ★Wendt, Wystan ★Curnow, K.O. ★Arvidson, Ian ★Wedde, Michael ★Morrissey, Michele ★Leggott, Riemke ★Ensing and Peter ★Wells. Other literary periodicals to emanate from Auckland University include ★*Conspectus*, ★*Nucleus*, ★*Crucible*, Te ★*Maarama*, ★*Freed* and ★*Tango*.   SH

KNOX, Charles Henry (d. 1855), an English writer, translated Goethe's *Faust*, collected German legends and was the author of several novels, one of which, *Harry Mowbray* (1843), contains extensive reference to New Zealand. Mainly this involves a sub-plot in which mysterious Englishmen are living at 'Wairangoa' (i.e. Whangaroa). It is told with an irony suggesting that though Māori are violent savages, the white men are no better. Even Māori tattoos are compared with the excessive use of cosmetics by 'our great-grandmothers', and the two Englishmen are as much at war with each other as with the Māori around them, 'in a country in which there was neither conscience, law, justice or mercy'. One Englishman kills the other, and sails home with shrunken heads for a willing European market, a voyage marred by the discovery of his former partner's putrefying head among the cargo, and by food poisoning which kills the whole crew, except the lonely murderer. All this melodrama is subordinated to the picaresque main plot, and summary does little justice to the novel's ironic and entertaining style. The descriptions of New Zealand scenery seem authentic, but the social image is of lawlessness and brutality.   NW

KNOX, Elizabeth (1959–), is a full-time fiction writer who defines her bearings in time and space as 'conviction and glee'. Her style is poetic and intense. The title of her first novel, *After Z-Hour* (1987), stands for 'zero hour' (usually the scheduled time for the start of a military operation), a moment of intense significance for all characters involved. Because of a storm, six characters, of whom three are also narrators, spend time together in an old house. A seventh character is the ghost of Mark Thornton, a young New Zealander who fought in France during World War 1 and who died shortly after returning to New Zealand. The plot strands of her second novel, *Treasure* (1992; shortlisted for the 1993 New Zealand Book Award for Fiction), are set in Wellington and in the Christian settlement of White Steppes, North Carolina, and involve the doings of charismatic Christians, faith healing, museum management and a love story between a postgraduate student in English and her supervisor, which lends it also an element of the campus novel. A third novel, *Glamour and the Sea* (1996), gradually unveils a mystery set in and

around Wellington during the 1940s. It focuses on the lives of New Zealand women in their involvement with American men. All novels are characterised by an absence of a linear plot and a variety of time-frames, settings and narrative voices. Plot as such, or even the depiction of character development, is of minor importance in Knox's novels; the emphasis lies on intensely rendered detail, on capturing a succession of highly charged moments. In addition to these three novels, Knox has published a trilogy of novellas which offer finely observed moments of a girl's childhood and emergent adolescence. *Paremata* (1989) and *Pomare* (1994) are partly based on autobiographical experiences of a childhood near Wellington, in 1969 and 1966 respectively. Both concentrate on two sisters, Jo and Lex Keene, and their family, friends and neighbours. The trilogy was completed by *Tawa* (1998).

Knox has been co-editor of and a frequent contributor to ★*Sport*. Born in Wellington and a graduate in English of Victoria University, she has won several awards and fellowships, including the ICI Young Writers Bursary, a Scholarship in Letters (1993) and the Victoria University writing fellowship (1997). A further novel, *The Vintner's Luck*, was accepted in 1998 for American and international publication.   HT

Ko nga Mahinga ..., see *Mahinga ..., Ko nga*.

Ko nga Moteatea ..., see *Moteatea ..., Ko nga*.

KOEA, Shonagh, fiction writer, was born in Taranaki and grew up in Hawkes Bay. An assiduous writer as a child, at the age of 8 she won two guineas in a *Woman's Weekly* competition. She became a journalist, and in her late teens married a fellow journalist, later editor of the *Taranaki Herald*. He died suddenly in 1987 and three years later Koea left New Plymouth and moved to Kingsland, Auckland, pursuing her interest in antiques and paintings, which had already resulted in a number of articles.

Koea's fiction was first published when she was in her early 30s. In 1981 she won the Air New Zealand Short Story Competition and since then stories have appeared regularly, several being anthologised. Now a full-time writer still living in Auckland, she has published two collections of short stories and three novels, and has won three major literary grants. In 1993 she was writing fellow at Auckland University, completing the short story collection *Fifteen Rubies by Candlelight* (1993) and her third novel, *Sing To Me, Dreamer* (1994). A fourth novel, *The Wedding at Bueno-Vista*, was published in 1996.

A contrast between domestic misery and various forms of withdrawal or escape recurs in Koea's fiction.

Several stories in her first collection, *The Woman Who Never Went Home and Other Stories* (1987), describe the lives of women who escape spiteful families and sanctimonious friends by fleeing to romantic locations. *Fifteen Rubies by Candlelight*, her second collection, contains comedies of manners and tales of everyday cruelty alongside stories of great poignance; 'Good Order and Naval Discipline' and 'The Magic Way' evoke Katherine *Mansfield and Frank *Sargeson, filtering familiar characters, situations and language through a late-twentieth-century sensibility.

Koea's first novel, *The Grandiflora Tree* (1989), describes the protagonist coming to terms with the death of her husband. Hindered by his self-absorbed friends, her sense of emptiness is worsened by the discovery of his youthful diaries, which cause her to revaluate her understanding of their life together. Fending off unwanted attention of all sorts, she finally withdraws to anonymous isolation.

The title of *Staying Home and Being Rotten* (1992), Koea's second novel, refers to the efforts of the protagonist to escape her past following the death of her husband. After being lured to London by a cruel and incorrigible seducer, she returns dispirited and impoverished to New Zealand to her tiny city cottage and her cat. Coming to an arrangement with a wealthy businessman, she finds the promise of real autonomy through her knowledge of paintings and work as an art dealer; her stock initially comes from her own crowded walls.

In Koea's fiction, male characters are sometimes oppressive, and the women correspondingly humiliated and helpless; her female characters often go to great lengths to maintain their composure in the face of intolerable bullying. After a period of helplessness, however, they ultimately take charge of their own lives. Koea's third novel, *Sing to Me, Dreamer*, revisits the territory of the apparently defenceless woman alone. After years living in India as a Maharaja's consort, the unworldly Margaret Harris returns to the composite city of Hillingdon to sort out her mother's rambling estate. Installing an elephant in her back garden, she holds out against plundering neighbours and a rapacious lawyer, finally triumphing through calculated resistance.   SS

Kōrero frequently means 'talk' or 'tell' but is also the name of a literary genre: the story or tale. Stories of alliances and battles between tribes have often become legendary and are an important part of the sense of identity of tribes or *iwi (see *Māori tribal histories). Myths might also be called 'kōrero', but the term is more aptly applied to popular or 'folk' tales. During the nineteenth century many of them were written down, and it is not always easy to distinguish between traditional tales

and those composed at the time of writing. More precisely, as is typical in the oral tradition, very ancient stories were often told in new and distinctive ways.

The stories often tell of people's usually endangered relationship to the supernatural, such as pale-skinned fairies or monsters like the ngārara (giant lizards), *taniwha (water dragons) and man-eating birds. Such beings are usually defeated by the superior intelligence of their human adversaries. Margaret *Orbell has pointed out that 'instead of the struggle between good and evil, virtue and vice, to be found in many European and Asian narratives, there is a struggle between the natural, proper order—that is, human society—and inhuman forces that threaten it'. There are also tales of struggles between family members. Another theme is the visit to or from the underworld, and *Hawaiki, the ancient home of the Māori, is a major source of stories. Themes common to folk stories all over the world—incest, patricide, adultery, jealousy, the search for one's right place in society or other quests, dangerous journeys, the consequences of doing the forbidden (breaking *tapu) —can also be found in Māori tales.

Stories of this kind were often collected in written versions by settlers and missionaries, including Governor *Grey whose papers contain a rich store of them. He had many informants, of whom the most prolific was *Te Rangikāheke. However, the first Māori king, Potatau (1800?–60), at that time still known as Te Wherowhero (see Pei Te Hurunui *Jones), was another of his informants. Only in a few cases are the names of storytellers known but a Waikato woman named Hariata told some to missionaries (including Richard *Taylor); another Waikato writer was the *rangatira Wiremu Te Wheoro of Ngāti Mahuta (a major informant for John *White), while Mohi Ruatapu and Mohi *Turei, both of Ngāti Porou, were recognised as master storytellers. Other known writers or tellers of tales are Wiremu Hoeta from Toihau, near Kāwhia, Wiremu Kauika of Ngā Rauru, Hōri Patara of Ngāti Toa (who used an unknown rangatira informant) and Timi Wāta Rimini from Maraenui. Valuable bilingual collections of kōrero, with detailed annotations and bibliographies, are those complied and translated by Margaret *Orbell: *Māori Folktales in Māori and English* (1968) and *Traditional Māori Stories: He Kōrero Māori* (1992).

Joan Metge distinguishes between kōrero pūrākau (stories, myths and legends) and kōrero pakiwaitara (light-hearted story). The earliest collection of the former was Sir George *Grey's *Ko nga *mahina a nga tupuna Maori he mea kohikohi mai* (London: Willis, 1854) and its translation: *Polynesian Mythology and ancient traditional history of the New Zealand Race* (London: Murray, 1855), which has been in print almost ever since.   NW

KOUKA, Hone (1966–), Ngāti Porou, Ngāti Raukawa, Ngāti Kahungunu, achieved early recognition with his plays on Māori themes, the youngest playwright to win the Bruce Mason Award (for *Hide 'n' Seek*, with Hori Ahipene, 1992). He is also a short fiction writer, poet, children's writer and actor, and has worked as a theatre artistic director and in journalism, sawmilling and forestry. He graduated in English from University of Otago 1988 and from Toi Whakaari / New Zealand Drama School 1990. After *Mauri Tū*, performed and published 1992, *Hide 'n' Seek* and *Five Angels*, he collaborated with director Colin McColl in the popularly successful *Ngā Tāngata Toa*, a version of Ibsen's revenge play *The Vikings*, performed in Wellington and Auckland 1995. Set on the East Coast in 1916, it deals with family conflicts (a recurrent Kouka theme) on the return to the *marae of a war hero, and the dramatic dominance of the woman warrior Rongomai.

Waiora Te U Kai Po (The Homeland) was commissioned for the 1996 New Zealand International Festival of the Arts, revised for a national and international tour in 1997, and published (*Huia, 1997) with an introduction by Roma *Potiki and afterword by Judith Dale. It includes *waiata and *haka by Hone Hurihanganui, performed by spirit characters who observe the action in a manner reminiscent of a Greek chorus, but eventually go beyond that to conflict and interact with the living. The play again presents a tempestuous gathering, a birthday party in a sawmill worker's family who have left their North Island homeland in search of material improvement near Christchurch. It draws irony from the 'immigrant' status of the Māori family. The 1965 setting enables social and racist attitudes to be simplified, while the play also shows the complex pressures of social aspiration and of increasingly global culture. Its centre, however, is the plangent sense of disruption and loss of home.   RR

Kōwhai (pronounced 'koe-fie' or 'koe-why') is the name for trees of the Sophora genus, distinguished in spring by masses of golden-yellow flowers like hanging bells. The original Māori 'kōwhai' or 'kōhai' derives from a conjectural Proto-Polynesian 'kofai', 'tree species'. In early South Island settler texts it is often spelt and pronounced with an initial 'g' as 'gowhai', 'gowai', 'goi', etc. *Butler writes in 1863, 'I remember nothing but a rather curiously shaped gowai-tree' (*A First Year in Canterbury Settlement*, 1863). Later, with its distinctive colour and springtime association, kōwhai became a popular romantic emblem: 'There was a riotous spring colour in the forest, voluptuous gold and red in the clumps of yellow Kowhai and crimson Rata' (Jane *Mander, The *Story of a New Zealand River*, 1920). In literary use the word is enshrined in the title of the 1930 national verse anthology, *Kowhai Gold*, which since Allen *Curnow's condemnation has been associated with a shallowly romantic 'school of versifiers'.   HO

Kowhai Gold: An Anthology of Contemporary New Zealand Verse (1930), chosen and edited by Quentin Pope, was published in London by J.M. Dent and Sons. In his brief introduction, Pope characterises New Zealand—'the youngest Dominion, last, loneliest, most self-satisfied'—as 'living in a state committed to paternalism and agriculture'. However, he argues that increased opportunity for publication 'has acted as a stimulus, writers have sprung up in scores … the foundations of a New Zealand literature are being laid'.

Pope undoubtedly imagined that his anthology of fifty-six poets—thirty of whom do not feature in either of William Alexander and Ernest *Currie's *anthologies—would be the foundation of a new tradition in New Zealand verse. He can hardly have anticipated that it would become a negative standard against which the succeeding generation of poets would define itself and that posterity would remember him as the infamous editor of this country's most vilified poetry anthology.

The criticism of *Kowhai Gold* began mildly enough. On the second page of his introduction to *A *Book of New Zealand Verse: 1923–45*, Allen *Curnow argues gently that there was little justification for publishing so much that is 'trivial if sincere' because the 'body of New Zealand verse is not to be enlarged by seeking numbers of additional names'. With significantly greater force he wrote in the 1960 *Penguin Book of New Zealand Verse* that *Kowhai Gold* is a 'lamentable anthology', its editor's selections 'could only corrupt the better, as it encouraged the worse'. Pope's little ship, and many versifiers who sailed in it, was scuppered. It came to represent 'A sickly second-growth of verse, in which imported insipidities were mixed with puerilities of local origin.'

Numerous critics have since endorsed Curnow's assessment, seeing the anthology as covering 'the poorest years for New Zealand verse', a time dominated by an 'unreal because unexperienced, conception of the "Home Country"', which 'rendered sentimental their view of their own land and people'.

Trixie Te Arama *Menzies is a lone voice in defence of Pope. In 'Kowhai Gold—Skeleton or Scapegoat' (*Landfall* 165, 1988), she argues that it is 'time to lay the ghost' of the '"lamentable anthology"'. *Kowhai Gold* is, she suggests, 'an earlier and obviously more *Georgian version' of later New Zealand anthologies, and 'a valuable link in the continuum of anthologies' stretching back to 1906. She concludes that Curnow, rather than breaking new critical ground was, in 1945, 'continuing and shaping a considerable poetic tradition already in existence'. Almost a third of *Kowhai Gold*, Menzies calculates, is allotted to poems by 'the following "respectable" names, who in some cases are represented quite generously: *Adams, *Baughan, *Beaglehole, Eileen *Duggan, *Fairburn, *Hyde, *Mansfield, *Mason, and *Wall.'

Despite this revisionist view, Pope's anthology, which in his opinion contained 'some poems which no future anthologist of Modern English verse can afford to ignore', is likely to remain, as Menzies describes it, 'a perpetual whipping person for whatever anyone doesn't agree with or like'.   PM

KUIPER, Koenraad (1944–   ), poet and linguist, born in Germany, emigrated from the Netherlands in 1951. He studied at Victoria University and did his PhD in linguistics at Simon Fraser University, Canada. After briefly teaching at secondary level in Christchurch, he has been a lecturer in linguistics at Canterbury University since 1975. His poetry has appeared in journals in New Zealand and Canada. *Signs of Life*, which first appeared in a separate volume published by *Waite-ata Press in 1981, was reproduced, less one stanza, in *Mikrokosmos* (1990), which also included illustrations by Chris Moisa. The poems are primarily glimpses, the evocative small world of the revised title. Despite their brevity, there is often a mischievous wit in the observation. Kuiper has also written *Smooth Talking: The Linguistic Performance of Auctioneers and Sportscasters* (1996) and he co-wrote the text *An Introduction to English Language: Sound, Word and Sentence* (1996).   NWt

Kupe, the legendary explorer, is said, in Māori tribal histories, to be the first to have left ancestral *Hawaiki, in central Polynesia, and travelled to the south in search of a southern land. Guided by stars, currents and weather patterns, Kupe arrived at what his wife, Kuramārotini, called *'Ao-tea-roa', popularly translated as 'Land of the Long White Cloud'. Journeying on a *waka called Mātā-hourua (a double-hulled waka, or sailing vessel),

they left Hawaiki, ostensibly to pursue an octopus owned by Muturangi.

Variations occur in Kupe traditions, but most say that he caught the octopus at Rangiwhakaoma on the south Wairarapa coast. Afterwards he named a number of localities in the area and then travelled to Raukawa Moana (Cook Strait), where a large number of Kupe names can be found.

Generally the greatest number of placenames associated with Kupe can be found at Te Ūpoko-o-te-Ika (Greater Wellington), Te Tauihu-o-te-waka-a-Māui (northern reaches of the South Island) and in Hokianga. However, they are also found in other areas. The general pathway of Kupe's voyage can be discovered by viewing the pattern of place names associated with him.

When Kupe left the southern reaches of the North Island, he journeyed to a harbour that eventually became known as Te Hokianganui-a-Kupe or 'The Returning of Kupe'. It is said that it was from this place that he left to return to Hawaiki and vowed never to return.

Kupe remains a towering figure in the canon of Māori history. His epic journey is recounted time and again and, indeed, his instructions subsequently given to the navigators of the various waka were to have influence in Māori tribal society for a thousand years. Hence, Kupe's voyage established the precedent that the many Māori ancestors who came from Hawaiki were to follow as they settled Aotearoa.

Kupe also retains a mystical presence in tribal psyche as he has now come to represent the prerequisite figure in subsequent tribal movements and endeavours. It is as if his presence remains immovable. For example, many tribes have lived in Te Ūpoko-o-te-Ika but the Kupe traditions remain strong and live as a part of the histories and traditions of all subsequent tribes. The tremendous esteem in which Kupe has been held by subsequent Māori leaders is exemplified in praise by the Ngāti Toa chief Te Rauparaha, to whom he was 'Te tangata nāna i topetope te whenua' (the man who traversed the land).

CR

L

LABAN-ALAMA, Ester Temukisa (1949–), writes innovative adaptations of Samoan legends and stories for children living in New Zealand. Born and educated in Western Samoa, she worked as a teacher there before moving to Lower Hutt in 1976. After primary teaching, she won a scholarship to take Victoria University's Diploma in Teaching English as a Second Language (ESOL) and is now an ESOL tutor at Whitireia Community Polytechnic, living in Wainuiomata. Her stories, songs and plays interpret traditional Samoan narratives gathered from her own research, accounting for regional variations and incorporating the experiences and perspectives of Samoans living in New Zealand. Several have been published by *Learning Media and translated into English, Māori, Nuiean, Rarotongan and Tokelauan, and are used in Western Samoan schools as well as New Zealand schools and ESOL programmes. Her principal publications are *O le ofu o Ane, Su'i se ùla mo Tina* and the play *Sina ma lana Tuna* (1995). She produces them as 'an investment towards keeping Samoan alive as a living New Zealand language'.   RR

LANCASTER, G.B., pseudonym for Edith *Lyttleton.

Land of the Lost, The (1902), was the first novel of William *Satchell, remarkable for its lively and atmospheric evocation of the gumlands—the region north of Auckland where 'gum' (fossilised resin) from ancient kauri trees could be dug up for use in varnishes and other products. The overall picture of a very masculine society and the set scenes, such as the rough-and-tumble of the gumlands pub or the day at the races, with its groups of Māori gamblers, are more successful than the plot itself, which reverberates with coincidences, such as

sudden salvation through inheritance. The minor characters—drunken *remittance men, tough ruffians and the weaklings they dominate, the forlorn, the homesick, and people living from hope, very like those who searched for *gold—justify the title and suggest a kind of hellish emptiness concealed behind feverish activity. This atmosphere is close to that created by other contributors to the Sydney *Bulletin* (Satchell was one of them). It might be compared, too, with frontier fiction in other colonies. However, it concludes with a prophecy of the eccentric, Jess Olive—a character whose visions bridge the majestic past of the kauri forest and the radiant future while he lives in the wretched present: 'There is a better day coming.... The men we know—the reckless, the hopeless, the unhappy—are gone to their appointed places. I hear the voices of children at play among the thick-leafed trees. I hear the mothers singing at their work. Over all the land rests the peace of God.'

Like other books of Satchell, *The Land of the Lost* was largely ignored after its first publication until the 1930s. In 1938 there was a 'second edition' with an introduction by the former Governor-General, Lord Bledisloe, who seemed to think (despite the *Depression) that he was living in Jess Olive's vision and looking back on the bad old days: '"*God's Own Country" … its salubrious climate, its fertile soil and its lovable people of both races. But on its gumfield of 60 years ago … men of gentle birth and breeding and adventurers of degraded and unknown antecedents intermingled in their search for a valuable subterranean deposit.' Such distaste for social intermingling is not to be found in the introduction by Kendrick *Smithyman to the reissue of 1971, which makes much more of the problematic relationship of fiction to fact. The melodrama, so obviously based on

Sensationalist conventions, nonetheless has a basis in the violent facts of gumland life, while the 'realistic' set pieces are indeed that—'set' in a certain artificiality. Most important for Smithyman, though, is that '*The Land of the Lost* is still a readable book.... That it does not totally succeed hardly matters. What matters is that it does not fail.' NW

Land of the Moa, The, brought the Tarawera eruption to the stages of Wellington, Dunedin, Christchurch and Auckland in 1895, featuring 'a rain of fire of red hot stones ... hurled from the crater ... the summit of Tarawera vomiting fire.... Streams of red hot lava run down the mountain.' This spectacle, together with an exploding bridge, gunfights, throttlings, steaming hot-pools, waterspouts and waterfalls, an abducted heroine ('She is in my power!'), a villainous American known as Black Angel, utu, operatic Māori song, dance and a full *tangi, a chief's daughter who tells how 'with the flocks of little birds I welcomed the rising sun' but is then blinded by the explosion, and dialogue like 'You lie, you canting hound!' was the creation of English actor and theatrical entrepreneur George Leitch (1842–1907, born George Goodyear). But despite all this, and Leitch himself hamming up as an old sea pilot who gets comically scorched in the hot pools, an 'animated' rendering of 'Rule Britannia' to bring down the curtain and the presence on the first night on 29 July 1895 of the Governor and Premier Richard Seddon, the tour of New Zealand and Australian cities produced less than red hot receipts. The first publication was in John Thomson's *Victoria University Press New Zealand Playscripts series in 1990, edited from the manuscript in the Mitchell Library, Sydney, and informatively introduced by Adrian Kiernander. He indicates ways in which it differs from the model of English melodrama of the time, especially in the female and Māori characters. The play is more briefly discussed by Howard McNaughton in the *OHNZLE (1991, 1998). The last performance so far was in Melbourne on 16 March 1896. RR

Land Wars, The, see **War literature: New Zealand Wars**.

Landfall, which celebrated its half-century in 1997, is the most important and long-lasting journal in New Zealand's literature. Several periods can be discerned in its distinguished history. First was 1947–66 (Nos. 1–80) under Charles *Brasch, the founder and longest-lasting editor, the era of *Landfall*'s almost unchallenged pre-eminence in literary and artistic life. Then for two decades of fluctuating fortunes (1967–86) *Landfall* had four different editors, each in charge for three to six years:

Robin *Dudding 1967–71 (Nos. 81–101), Leo *Bensemann, 1971–75 (Nos. 102–115), Peter *Smart, 1975–81 (Nos. 116–140) and David *Dowling, 1982–86 (Nos. 140–159). From 1986 to 1992 (Nos. 160–174), the journal was edited by successive boards, usually three or four people, including (for two years or more) Dowling, Hugh *Lauder, Mark *Williams, Iain *Sharp, Anna Smith and Michele *Leggott. Through all the changes of editorial personnel from 1976 to 1992 in-house continuity at the *Caxton Press, which published *Landfall*, was provided by Judith Baker, first as assistant editor, later as editorial manager. A fourth phase began in 1993 when ownership passed to *Oxford University Press, with Chris Price (after a transitional issue) as sole editor, and then, from No. 189 in 1995, to the University of Otago Press, still edited by Price. The journal switched from quarterly to twice-yearly publication with No. 185. In 1996 *Landfall* completed fifty years of unbroken publication.

The magazine originated in conversations in London between Denis *Glover of the Caxton Press and the poet Charles Brasch, with whom Glover stayed while on leave from the navy during World War 2. They agreed on the need for a new, professionally produced literary journal in New Zealand when the war ended. According to Brasch in *Indirections*, 'Denis had looked on all the small periodicals he had run or supported, *Tomorrow*, *Book*, and the rest, as keeping the pot boiling for something more substantial, a mature professional *Phoenix*'. Brasch studied current British, European and American journals such as John Middleton *Murry's *Adelphi*, T.S. Eliot's *Criterion* and Christopher Dawson's *The Dublin Review* as exemplary models of journals in which literature was considered within a wider cultural context, though he also believed the new journal must 'show that the country could stand on its own feet, and ... build up a body of New Zealand work'.

Back in New Zealand, Brasch and Glover canvassed options for a title; some favoured *Tuatara*, Brasch apparently wanted *Antipodes* or *South*. *Landfall* was arrived at by a process of elimination, its immediate source presumably Allen *Curnow's *'Landfall in Unknown Seas'. The title linked the journal to the geography and history of New Zealand, and hence to a perspective that was implicitly national (as distinct from nationalistic), focused (in Curnow's relevant phrase) on 'the condition of being a New Zealander'. *Landfall*'s preoccupation with the New Zealand condition was dominant during Brasch's editorship but less so under later editors.

Initially, *Landfall* was an octavo-sized quarterly of seventy-six pages with a brown paper cover elegantly and chastely laid out and plainly printed in two colours. The basic size and format was retained for forty-six years (174 issues), apart from variations in typographical design and the number of pages. Changes to the cover design were introduced every year or two until 1964. From 1965 each issue had a new cover, with a change from two-colour to four-colour printing in 1979. Eight hundred copies of the first issue (March 1947) were printed, a figure that rose to around twice that number at the height of *Landfall*'s popularity in the early 1960s. *Landfall* paid for contributions and after five years received a grant for each issue from the New Zealand *Literary Fund.

Except for the absence of fiction, the contents of the first issue established a format which was retained with minor variations for fifty years. In the Brasch era each issue began with several pages of editorial Notes followed by a judicious arrangement of poems, stories, essays, illustrations (usually a four-page insert of black-and-white photographs), commentaries (on art, music, theatre, film, architecture, etc.) and book reviews. With few exceptions contributors were New Zealanders. Later editors made the editorials and cultural commentaries occasional.

Brasch's high-minded and carefully considered Notes in the first issue established themes which dominated his editorship: '*Landfall* is a literary review. Its chief concern is with the arts, of which literature is one. But the arts do not exist in a void.... Any serious consideration of them is bound to involve an inquiry into their place in society and the social functions which they fulfil—what part they play in life, what use they are.' Another theme addressed in this inaugural editorial was New Zealand's relationship to Europe. While Brasch's perspective was provincial and Eurocentred, he also commissioned newsletters from *Australia, *Canada, India and South Africa and encouraged occasional attention to Asia and the *Pacific.

A convenient survey of *Landfall*'s contents and main contributors during the first fifteen years is provided by the anthology *Landfall Country: Work from Landfall, 1947–61* (Caxton, 1962), chosen by Brasch. In its 459 pages the book included stories by twelve writers: E.S. Grenfell, Maurice *Gee, Frank *Sargeson, C.K. *Stead, David *Ballantyne, Maurice *Duggan, Roderick *Finlayson, Maurice *Shadbolt, James *Courage, A.P. *Gaskell, John *Caselberg and O.E. *Middleton. There were poems by seventeen poets including Glover, Alistair *Campbell, Ruth *Dallas, Curnow, Basil *Dowling, Stead, James K. *Baxter, Kendrick *Smithyman, M.K. *Joseph, Fleur *Adcock, Charles *Spear, Hubert *Witheford and W.H. *Oliver. In a section called 'Explorations' Brasch included prose by T.H. Scott, Bill *Pearson, Dan *Davin, Sargeson and H. Winston *Rhodes. There were reproductions of paintings by Evelyn Page, W.A. Sutton, Leo *Bensemann, Colin

*McCahon, Louise Henderson and M.T. *Woollaston among others, sculptures by Molly MacAlister and Russell *Clark, and photographs by Hester Carsten and John *Pascoe. Brasch also included thirty pages of selections from his editorial Notes. Important aspects of *Landfall* that the anthology did not represent were the topical cultural commentaries and the indispensable reviews of current books, which included almost all New Zealand publications of interest.

In 'Twenty Years Hard', an essay written during his last year as editor, Brasch isolated three ideal editorial qualities: 'literary flair', to 'seize on the quality of any new work'; 'intellectual grasp', the ability to locate strengths and weaknesses; and 'a sense of the relevance of work on many disparate subjects to the central continuing concerns of literature and the arts' (*The Universal Dance*). For the most part Brasch lived up to these lofty ideals, though his sense of cultural mission gave a rather unremitting solemnity to *Landfall*, which later editors could not or did not want to sustain. He was meticulous without losing sight of the broader picture. Occasionally a narrowness of sympathy limited his success with regard to his first criterion, and some writers of a younger generation such as Baxter, Smithyman, Shadbolt and Louis *Johnson (all nevertheless published in *Landfall*) chafed under what they considered his conservatism. Journals such as *Numbers* and *Mate* emerged in the 1950s to provide an alternative voice.

Landfall never again achieved the stability and cultural ascendancy it possessed while Brasch was editor. Robin Dudding, formerly editor of *Mate* and Brasch's chosen successor, made *Landfall* more purely literary. This was due partly to editorial preference and partly to the increased number of active writers from the late 1960s. The new generation Dudding brought in included Ian *Wedde, Bill *Manhire, Michael *Henderson, Sam *Hunt, Russell *Haley, Murray *Edmond, Fiona *Kidman and Albert *Wendt, while many older writers continued to appear regularly, especially Duggan, Stead, Sargeson, Baxter, Gee, Brasch, Smithyman, Dallas, Johnson, Keith *Sinclair, Davin, Owen *Leeming, Kevin *Ireland, Peter *Bland, Vincent *O'Sullivan, Michael *Jackson and Dennis *McEldowney.

A Dudding innovation in 1968 was commissioning artists to illustrate short stories, including Garth Tapper, Olivia Spencer Bower, Philip Trusttum, Anthony Stones, Colin and Anne McCahon, Jeffrey Harris, Michael Illingworth, Barry Cleavin, Murray Grimsdale and Ralph *Hotere. Noteworthy among Dudding's twenty-one issues was an enlarged No, 100, which included a lengthy interview with Brasch and contributions from several who went back to *Landfall*'s beginnings, including Sargeson, Bensemann and E.H.

*McCormick. One issue later, in 1972, Dudding was dismissed, reputedly for failing to deliver an issue on time. He immediately set up a new journal called *Islands, supported by several of *Landfall's* key contributors. Among those who transferred allegiance (though some also contributed to *Landfall* later) were Brasch, Curnow, Glover, Duggan, Stead and Wedde.

Bensemann, who had been intimately involved on the production side from the beginning, filled the vacuum. Assisted by Philip *Temple as associate editor, Bensemann edited fourteen issues. Outwardly the journal did not change much but the defection of key contributors left Bensemann struggling to maintain high standards. Not surprisingly the visual element flourished during his term, the illustrations insert often being increased from four pages to eight. Among artists treated to an eight-page spread were Tony Fomison, Don Peebles, Patrick Hayman, G.T. Moffit and Patrick Hanly.

Next to Brasch, Peter Smart was *Landfall's* longest-serving editor, operating for six years with Michael *Harlow and David Dowling as associate editors until his sudden death in December 1981. A talented English teacher and compiler of school texts, Smart was energetically eclectic. His first editorial expressed determination to give more space to beginning writers, 'to publish some stories and poems which I feel are only partly successful … to encourage those on the way' (*Landfall* 116). Some indifferent work dismayed many readers and contributors. More effective was Smart's plan to 'vary the programme', using guest editors and theme issues. For example, Howard McNaughton edited an issue on drama in New Zealand (116), while *Landfall* 130 (June 1979) focused on women writers. Other guest editors were Dowling, Harlow, Lauris *Edmond and Rob *Jackaman.

Dowling succeeded Smart in 1982, with Harlow as associate. Aided by the gradual faltering of *Islands*, they recovered *Landfall's* status as the leading literary journal. A significant development was the 'craft interviews' initiated in No. 143 (September 1982) with Hubert Witheford and Fleur Adcock. Subsequent subjects were Edmond, Rachel *McAlpine, Michael *Morrissey, Stead, Owen *Marshall, Elizabeth *Smither, Harlow, Wedde, Leigh *Davis and the international visitors Robin Morgan and Alain Robbe-Grillet. With No. 152 Hugh Lauder began a long association as poetry editor; through 1985 he deputised while Dowling was overseas (as W.H. Oliver had for Brasch in 1957), editing one issue himself while others were guest-edited by Fiona *Farrell and academics Mark Williams and Linda Hardy. As Dowling noted on his return, these 'brought a new range of perspectives' to 'arouse and inform future debate' (*Landfall* 157).

Landfall in the 1980s was clearly responding to the literary climate created by innovative journals such as *Parallax, *AND, *Antic and *Untold, which reflected international movements such as *postmodernism, feminism, post-structuralism and postcolonialism. One visible change was the adoption of an editorial board from December 1986, explained in terms of the breakup of 'the myth … that New Zealand was culturally homogeneous' (*Landfall* 160). Also announced was the intention to devote 'special numbers to other cultures', a tendency already begun with a Canadian issue (No. 159), followed by Australian, British, African and Caribbean issues. Special issues were also devoted to Katherine *Mansfield, Kendrick Smithyman and to Hamilton writers. Further *Landfall* interviews included Margaret *Mahy, Hone *Tuwhare, Smithyman, Epeli Hau'ofa, Anne *French, Curnow, Janet *Frame and Witi *Ihimaera.

Changes in the editorial board led to a more experimental profile, poetry editor Michele Leggott proving influential, especially in Nos. 177 (which reproduced material from the *Now See Hear!* exhibition at Wellington City Gallery, 1990) and 182, a radically unconventional issue devoted to 'page works' by about forty-five invited artists. This lively experimentalism brought *Landfall* new respect from advanced practitioners, while alienating some more conservative readers and contributors.

The sale of Caxton Press in 1992 brought *Landfall* to a crisis. The new owners did not want the journal. After negotiation, *Oxford University Press bought it and took over from No. 185, a special issue on the 1950s, prepared by the old editorial board and guest-edited by Francis Pound. On the Contents page it was listed as New Series, Volume One, Number One. The next issue, with Chris Price as sole editor, established a new format of larger (approximately 180 pages) twice-yearly issues. The new editor wrote: 'It is our intention that *Landfall* feature a variety of perspectives … opening up discussion rather than pursuing any single line of opinion. The balance of contents will vary from issue to issue' (*Landfall* 186).

In 1995 *Landfall* was bought by Otago University Press, with Chris Price retained as editor. The return to Dunedin, where Brasch had edited the first issues, completed something of a circle for this venerable literary institution. PS

'Landfall in Unknown Seas' by Allen *Curnow, which has become one of the best-known of all New Zealand poems, was originally commissioned by J.C. *Beaglehole (on behalf of the New Zealand government) for a publication commemorating the tercentenary of ★Tasman's visit to New Zealand in 1642. The poem was included with an essay by Beaglehole and a new translation of Tasman's journal in *Abel Janszoon Tasman and the Discovery of New Zealand* (Department of Internal Affairs, 1942), and later appeared in Curnow's ★*Sailing or Drowning* (1943); it has been very frequently anthologised. Soon after composition the poem was set to music by the composer Douglas ★Lilburn as a suite for string orchestra in three movements, in which each movement is followed by a reading of one of the three parts of the poem. The first of many performances (with the poet as reader) was given in Wellington in December 1942. There are two sound recordings of the piece, one with Curnow as reader, the other with Sir Edmund Hillary. Partly as a consequence of this setting, the poem's title, its opening, 'Simply by sailing in a new direction / You could enlarge the world', and lines like 'Always to islanders danger / Is what comes over the sea' and 'The stain of blood that writes an island story' have gained common currency.   PS

Landscape and the natural environment have always had a particular significance for New Zealand writers. As Janet ★Frame observed, 'Nature is never out of fashion' (in ★*Living in the Maniototo*). The importance of landscape in New Zealand literature reflects its importance in the wider culture—in painting, photography, film, advertising, tourism and more recently the campaigns of the conservation movement. A diverse yet consistent tradition continues to evolve, following New Zealanders' changing attitudes towards the landscape, and their expectations of the influence of place both for individuals and the wider society. Anthologies such as *Countless Signs*, a collection of landscape writing (1986) and *The New Place: The Poetry of Settlement in New Zealand* (1993) recognise and perpetuate this preoccupation.

Not surprisingly the concern with landscape begins in New Zealand's colonial experience—a determined engagement with the original ecology and landforms, an impossible conflict between eighteenth-century aesthetic conventions and the muddy realities of the new land. Contemporary colonists' accounts, represented in Paul Shepard's *English Reaction to the New Zealand Landscape before 1850* (1969), and most subsequent treatments of the colonial era, share an overwhelming sense of alienation from the indigenous landscape. Despite the glowing publicity encouraging emigration, despite occasional vague resemblances to the landscapes of ★'Home', nature in New Zealand was wild, primeval and unnervingly evergreen, 'dreary and desolate', 'gloomy forest and repulsive rugged waste'.

The most useful of the conventional European concepts of nature was the Sublime, defined by philosopher Edmund Burke as a blend of terror and exhilaration when confronted with intimidatingly powerful, extreme landscapes. From the opening sections of Samuel ★Butler's ★*Erewhon* (1872), New Zealand writers relied on the Sublime as a way of accommodating and managing the magnitude, the sheer drama of the scenery—especially the Southern mountains and the dense ★bush. Human frailty and insignificance are invariably emphasised. William ★Satchell's *The Toll of the Bush* (1905) and Maurice ★Shadbolt's *The ★Lovelock Version* (1980) similarly demonstrate the puny inadequacy of human endeavours against overwhelming forest landscapes. A Wordsworthian response to Nature as awesomely inspirational is evident in the novels of George ★Chamier or Edith Searle ★Grossman. Katherine ★Mansfield reacts ecstatically to the Urewera wilderness in terms of the grandeur of Wagner's operas, while the lowering sunset across the harbour in ★'At the Bay' (1921) is an ominous reminder of human smallness. Brian ★Turner's 'Crossing the Canterbury Plains' (1989) celebrates a 'haughty' landscape of autumn austerity, 'where a leaf might be blown a hundred miles / and end up somewhere much the same'. James K. ★Baxter's 'Poem in the Matukituki Valley' (1949) and Owen ★Marshall's story 'Coming Home in the Dark' (1995) deal with alpine landscapes as places of incomprehensible forces and random violence.

Such huge and difficult Sublime environments, however, offer great opportunities for drama and heroism. New Zealand's wild country became the essential setting for the epic journeys of numerous ★'Man Alone' heroes, rugged figures proving their own sublimity in relation to hostile landscapes. The pattern for Women Alone in such alien scenery tends to be less heroic. Jane ★Mander's heroines in *The ★Story of a New Zealand River* (1920) and ★*Allen Adair* (1925), Lauris ★Edmond in *High Country Weather* (1984), and Mansfield's 'The ★Woman at the Store' (1911) become victims of the landscape and its alienness, destroyed by isolation and hardship and the 'savage spirit of the country (that) sneers at what it sees'.

The principal colonial enterprise of taming the recalcitrant landscape soon became a powerful literary theme. The metamorphosis of landscape into countryside allows writers both to celebrate the settlers' noble enterprise and to employ the more optimistic literary conventions of the Pastoral and the Picturesque. Characters such as ★Guthrie-Smith of ★*Tutira* (1921), Amos Polson in James ★McNeish's *Mackenzie* (1970), Ned Livingstone in Shadbolt's ★*Strangers and Journeys* (1972), Guthrie ★Wilson's high-country pastoralist *Julien Ware* (1952), and Tom Roland, the timber tycoon in Mander's *Story of a New Zealand River* are essentially defined by the landscapes they engage with, and their determined pursuit of the colonial dream. Even the little boy in the newly cleared valley in Blanche *Baughan's 'A Bush Section' (1898) is an adversarial figure, asserting an authority over nature: 'Daytime and Night spring in turn to thy battle, / Time and Decay run in yoke to thy plough'. Metaphors of battle, defeat and victory are common—for example, Ursula *Bethell's 'By Burke's Pass' (1936) describes the farmer's 'assault' on antagonistic Nature, with his 'trophies' his corn-stacks and English trees. Such tough farmer-heroes soon establish themselves in the literature as a quintessential Kiwi archetype, laconic, stoical, struggling for a living and for a sense of identity on the land.

The rural heartland offers writers a distinctively New Zealand Arcadia, rich with inherent tensions and ambivalence. The lush dairy country of Jean *Devanny's The *Butcher Shop (1926), the Taranaki *backblocks in R.H. *Morrieson's novels, the farmhouse 'shaded with macrocarpas' in Baxter's *Pig Island Letters (1966) or the gorse-choked Waikato farmscapes of Vincent *O'Sullivan's Let the River Stand (1993)—these classic rural landscapes are marked by disturbing undercurrents of desperation and violence. Then there are the Hohepa farm in Maurice *Duggan's *'Along Rideout Road that Summer' (1965), the dusty East Coast sheep stations in Witi *Ihimaera's The *Matriarch (1986) and Bulibasha (1994), the rich green of Northland farms rolling away to the blue hills in C.K. *Stead's The *Singing Whakapapa (1994), or the ultimate rural icon, Denis *Glover's 'The Magpies' marking the passage of time (1945)—New Zealand's literary countrysides are rarely without their qualifications, their underlying sadnesses, loss and compromise.

Through the years there have been deliberate attempts to to establish a sense of *nationalism and identity in the mythologised version of New Zealand's settler history. The noble rhetoric of William Pember *Reeves and Alfred *Domett, or the sentimentality of the *Kowhai Gold anthology (1930), reflect the sensibilities of their eras. In the 1930s–40s Allen *Curnow, Charles *Brasch, John *Mulgan, Roderick *Finlayson, Bill *Pearson and Frank *Sargeson—and more recently Shadbolt, O'Sullivan and Stead—focus on the processes of exploring, taming and settling the land as a means of representing the New Zealand character. Conscious of the uneasiness of many Pākehā in their environments, and the traditionally based identification of Māori with the land, these writers strive to develop a sense of belonging, of being at home in the landscape. Brasch argues that such comfortable integration with place can only evolve through the generations: 'Man must lie with the gaunt hills like a lover / Earning their intimacy in the calm sigh / Of a century of quiet and assiduity' ('The Silent Land', 1945).

As the country became more comprehensively settled, and more New Zealanders came to live in cities and towns, which became increasingly violent, polluted and unhappy places, the relative ideals and priorities undergo a not unexpected shift. Many writers develop an explicit contrast between the values and virtues of the country—especially the wilder unspoiled parts of it—and crowded, hectic, artificial urban environments. Wilderness has a renaissance. No longer seen as alien and hostile, natural landscapes are valued as inspirational, reminders of freedoms and instinctual energies lost in the bustle of modern life. Stead's *Smith's Dream (1971) takes its hero off to a remote Coromandel island in retreat from personal and political mayhem; Frame's heroine in A *State of Siege (1966) seeks creativity and inspiration in retirement; Peter *Hooper's primitive forest people of the future in A Song in the Forest (1979) and its sequels are rebuilding human lifestyles in close relationship to the natural rhythms and spiritual qualities of their patch of the West Coast; and in Marshall's 'Cass Robbins' (1995) the refuge is an isolated cottage on the Moeraki coast.

This preference for the perceived simplicity and tranquillity of natural landscapes is, like the concepts of the Sublime and the Picturesque, a tradition going back into the Western cultural inheritance, through Wordsworth, Rousseau, *Shakespeare and Virgil. From the 1960s New Zealand writers were also exposed to a new ethic of environmental conservation, with strong *American influences contributing to the local understanding of landscapes and an appropriate human presence in them. Hone *Tuwhare's 'No Ordinary Sun' (1964) and Ian *Wedde's 'Aluminium Smelter' (1980) are examples of environmental protest.

Wild landscapes have always, however, been a means for New Zealand writers to connect with the eternal and the elemental, with fundamental universal forces. Bethell's poems celebrate the great cold starry night skies over Canterbury, and the ancient geological processes that shaped the Southern Alps and the plains. Geology is also central to Stead's gritty sequence on Auckland's volcanoes, 'Scoria' (1982), and Kendrick Smithyman's 'Where Waikawau Stream Comes Out' (1974), an assessment of human insignificance in the landscape: 'The black terraces by middens streaked / are only streaked / at that one evident layer. We have scarcely scratched / Waikawau.' Tuwhare's poetry addresses the basic elements of the natural world—rain, rivers, sea, snow, sun and storms: 'rain / that demure leveller / ocean-blessed / cloud-sent / maker of plains' ('Reign Rain', 1978). Marshall's A Many-Coated Man (1995) features regular vignettes of place—humble familiar landscapes and little details of nature, each a small but perfectly complete archetype of the New Zealand environment—establishing a context for the more Sublime settings crucial to his hero's development, the sweeping Wairau plains and the lunar salt-flats of Lake Grassmere.

For many writers landscape can be a means of access to larger personal and spiritual dimensions, the forces of history and ancestry. In Māori traditional oral literature, and in the work of contemporary Māori writers, the natural landscape is inextricable from questions of spirituality and identity. Māori relationships with the land are addressed by Pākehā writers also—Finlayson, Barry *Mitcalfe, Shadbolt in the novels and 'The People Before' (1963), or Yvonne *du Fresne in the 'Astrid Westergaard' series, finding parallels with the traditional culture of a Danish immigrant community on the Manawatu plains.

The bonds between Māori and the land are visceral, inescapable, central to the *whakapapa (genealogy) of each individual and the *iwi (tribe), essential for maintaining mauri (the spiritual energies) of each person and thing. Keri *Hulme's the *bone people (1983) focuses on these indigenous forces in the land, powers inherent in the stone, protected by their own kaumātua (wise elder), providing the healing necessary for the resolution of her characters' shattered lives. Hulme's poetry and *Home Places: Three Coasts of the South Island of New Zealand* (1989) return to ancestral landscapes: 'I have, one way or another, been here all my life. I am not often here, in the physical sense … but I never leave it.' Ihimaera, Apirana *Taylor and Bruce *Stewart each emphasise the necessity of links with the land to identity. In *Potiki (1986) and *Cousins (1992) Patricia *Grace explores the strength of family connections with place through the generations, and the community's responsibilities to protect and respect the land; however, in her 'House of the Fish' (1994) the spiritual forces in the natural environment are less warmly sustaining. Alistair Te Ariki *Campbell also works with the darker energies in the landscape, in particular the arrogant spirit of the early-nineteenth-century warrior chief Te Rauparaha, an ominous, ruthless presence imbuing Kapiti Island with violence and dread: 'This island is alive with ghosts. / Tonight every leaf is an ear / attuned to your heartbeat, / every stick a spear …' (*'Sanctuary of Spirits', 1972). Tuwhare's poetry continually turns to strong landscapes, from the jittery 'Walker' (1974) to the sensual *'Papa-tu-a-nuku (Earth Mother)' of the 1975 Land March, the defiance of 'A talk with my cousin, alone' (1982), or the powerful elegy 'A fall of rain at Mitimiti, Hokianga' (1974): 'Mountain, why do you loom over us like / that, hands on massive hips? Simply / by hooking your finger to the sea, / rain-squalls swoop like a hawk, suddenly.'

The immediacy of landscape, vivid and intense, drives many New Zealand writers at the most direct level of response to the environment, the celebratory and lyrical. Tuwhare's 'Snowfall' (1982) or Sam *Hunt's poems of the Paremata harbour, John *Newton's *Tales from the Angler's Eldorado* (1985) or Brian Turner's delicate, precisely drawn high-country poems—these landscapes are fresh, visual, up-close, tactile, places of beauty and joy. Cilla *McQueen's Otago harbour poems and Carey's Bay vegetable-garden sequences (1982) focus crisply on the finer detail of the natural world. David *Eggleton's poetry takes in the full range of constituent parts within the landscape, using unexpected frameworks: 'the capital is a cakescape on a glittering silver salver.… Sunlight white as vanilla icecream / slides along the clean curved tongue of the coast' ('I Imagine Wellington as a Delicatessen', 1995).

This ongoing preoccupation with landscape in New Zealand writing, and the diversity of treatments of landscape and nature, reflect both broader social and historical contexts and the personal priorities and experience of particular writers. Some writers have returned repeatedly to special places and environments, defining them as their own, giving them a distinctive signature—Ihimaera's Waituhi, McQueen's Aramoana or Curnow's Karekare, the wide open spaces of Central Otago in Marshall's stories, rural Northland in Fiona *Kidman's *Mandarin Summer* (1981) and *The *Book of Secrets* (1987), or Maurice *Gee's portraits of the orchards and estuaries of Nelson and Henderson. Such well-loved, characteristic landscapes, and the prolific ongoing tradition from which they evolve, are perhaps some indication that New Zealand writing is at last coming to be 'at home'.

RCr

LANGFORD, Gary (1947–), was one of the most productive of the young poets who emerged in the heady radical days around 1970, and has gone on to success as a playwright, TV scriptwriter and novelist, based since 1974 mainly in *Australia. Always a committed professional writer ('I sold my first story when I was 17 and have gone on selling them'), he has also worked as an actor (1970–76) and since 1977 as a creative writing lecturer, currently at the University of Western Sydney. A native of Christchurch, he returned as writer-in-residence at University of Canterbury in 1989.

He is prolific in many forms, including film (*The Bushranger*, 1975), musical theatre ('Flappers', 1982; 'Playing Molière', 1985), radio drama ('Quartet', NZBC 1972) and multi-media ('Don't Jump Out That Window, You're Feeling Fine', 1981); and has edited fifteen anthologies. There have been more than 250 productions of his plays, revues, musicals and scripts, and he has written under four other names.

Influenced early by radical American writers, especially Gary Snyder and the Beat poets, Langford's work has remained irreverent of conformist values and outspoken on issues such as drugs and sex. In tension with this runs a conservative impulse, driving him recurrently to make sagas, based on locality, domesticity, New Zealand history and most of all family. These extend from his first volume of poems, *The Family* (1973), to his novel *Newlands* (1990), both telling a New Zealand family history over several generations. Characters who veer between establishment and subversive roles also recur, as in the businessman–revolutionary of the poetry cycle *Strange City* (1988) or the centenarian capitalist–poet who narrates *Newlands*. This establishment–radical tension is evident in such titles as *A Classical Pianist in a Rock 'n' Roll Band* (novel, 1989), *The Pest Exterminator's Shakespeare* (poems, 1984) or *Jesus the Galilee Hitchhiker* (performance poetry, 1991), and in poems such as 'Five Minute Romeo and Juliet'; as if Langford (to take two episodes from his own *Newlands*) needs an officer to shoot, a family to shock.

He has won several awards in Australia, and is included in numerous anthologies, including in New Zealand *The *Young New Zealand Poets* (1973) and *The New Fiction* (1986). His many other publications include *Death of the Early Morning Hero* (novel, 1976), *Getting On* (plays, 1977, 1986), *The Death of James Dean* (short fiction, 1978, 1979), *Vanities* (novel, 1984, 1987), *A Library is a Place of Love* (short fiction, 1989, 1991), *Love at the Traffic Lights* (poetry, 1990) and *The Politics of Dancing* (novel, 1994, 1995).   RR

LANGLEY, **Eve** (1904–74), a versatile writer, especially novelist, was born at Forbes, New South Wales. Her father, an itinerant rural labourer, died when she was a child, leaving her mother to support the family in impoverished circumstances. Langley received little formal education. During the 1920s, she and her younger sister June dressed as males, adopted the names Steve and Blue and worked as seasonal labourers in Gippsland, Victoria. In 1929 she undertook a lone crossing of the Australian Alps on horseback. Following her mother and sister to New Zealand in 1932, she at first supported her writing with a variety of mainly domestic work. An extensive body of short stories, poetry, plays and articles was published in literary journals and newspapers in both Australia and New Zealand. A daughter born in 1935 died in early infancy. Langley became involved in the Auckland literary scene, associating with local writers including Henry Brennan, Robin *Hyde, Ruth *Park and Gloria *Rawlinson. In 1937, Langley married Auckland artist Hilary Clark. The experiences of 'Steve' and 'Blue' in Gippsland form the basis of

Langley's two published novels, both written in a distinctive prose-poetry style. *The Pea-Pickers* (1942), joint winner of the S.H. Prior Memorial Prize, was received at the time with substantial acclaim, which included that of influential critics Norman Lindsay, Hal Porter and Douglas *Stewart. *White Topee* (1954), also published by Angus & Robertson, received a more muted reception, in part due to its introduction of an idiosyncratic 'Oscar Wilde reincarnation' theme, which was continued in subsequent unpublished novels.

Despite literary success, difficult economic and domestic circumstances led to Langley's mental collapse, and she was committed to Auckland Mental Hospital in 1942. The family was broken up, and she was divorced in 1951. After her final release from hospital in 1950, she obtained work in the bindery of Auckland Public Library, and resumed a period of prolific writing. She changed her name by deed poll to 'Oscar Wilde' in 1954. Returning to settle in Australia in 1960, she continued to write obsessively, but without success. A trip to Greece in 1965 was cut short because of ill health, and Langley lived as a recluse in a hut in Katoomba in the Blue Mountains until her death in 1974. The Mitchell Library, Sydney, holds an extensive collection of material, including the MSS of ten unpublished autobiographical novels, which together form a detailed account of her early life in Australia and New Zealand. All were rejected for publication, despite the writer's acknowledged originality and 'genius for poetry and fantasy', for reasons including their failure to conform to traditional novelistic expectations of plot and characterisation, their highly introspective nature, and their unconventional attitudes towards personal issues of gender and sexuality. A major biography by Joy Thwaite, published in 1989, has contributed to a renewed interest in Langley's writing.   SW

Language in literature, see **New Zealand English**.

LAPHAM, **Henry** (1852?–87), was a popular essayist for the *Otago Witness*, which published a touching obituary on his early death, referring to him as a schoolteacher and a 'voluminous writer'. *We Four and the Stories We Told* (1880) is a small volume of short stories associated with the *goldfields. It includes a frame in which four men, tiring of playing cards, decide to tell stories on the subject of 'frights'. The fictional status of these yarns is doubtful. Rather than the miners themselves, Lapham's implicit sympathy is with the women and children who suffer loneliness and worse while their husbands are away. He also contributed New Zealand stories to a volume in which his sister Mrs Nugent (i.e. Susan Wood) wrote of her experiences in Australia: *Waiting for the Mail and Other*

Sketches and Poems (1875). These short stories, essays in conversational style, ballads and sentimental iambic poems were mainly reprinted from *Australian Journal, Otago Witness* and other periodicals.   NW

LASENBY, Jack (1931–), writer of children's fiction, was born in Waharoa. He attended the University of Auckland from 1950 to 1952 but left in dissatisfaction and spent ten years deer-culling in the Urewera. Returning to Auckland in 1962, he began teaching and, from 1969, editing school journals. A lecturer at Wellington Teachers' College from 1975, he resigned in 1987 to write full-time. He often writes of heartland New Zealand: small towns, farms, and the *bush frame narratives that are 'observant, erudite, witty, often caustic, scathingly anti-bullshit, [and] alert to fit the fable to the moral (and vice versa)'. His writing is predicated on a belief that although modern entertainment sates children's hunger for stories, it fails to provide sustenance. His early publications include *Lost and Found* (1970) and *The Chatham Islands* (1973), and two picture books from 1976: *Charlie the Cheeky Kea* and *Rewi the Red Deer*. However, it is his novels that inspired Judith Holloway to rank him with Margaret *Mahy and Maurice *Gee as children's writers 'whose themes, originality, and sheer literariness make them almost as important and entertaining to adults' (*New Zealand Books, Dec. 1994).

Lasenby's first novel is characteristic of much of his writing: childhood is not idealised (pain is real and lessons are hard) but adventure abounds and the end is self-sufficiency and individual empowerment. Thus *The Lake* (1987) tells of a girl learning to survive in the bush and, in the process, finding the strength to handle her stepfather's sexual advances. Similarly, in *The Mangrove Summer* (1989), children staying in the Coromandel in the 1940s to escape a possible Japanese invasion fend for themselves, although with certain tragic consequences. The popular 'Seddon Street Gang' trilogy—*Dead Man's Head* (1994), *The Waterfall* (1995) and *The Battle of Pook Island* (1996)—despite being set during the 1930s *Depression, are in a lighter vein. The gang inhabit childhood's mildly anarchic world (adults hover peripherally) yet their experiences teach belief in oneself and the value of friendship. Two darker novels of a post-apocalyptic future convey Lasenby's dislike of inequity and strong views on social justice. In *The Conjurer* (1992) a teenage couple attempt to escape a cruel, hierarchical society stratified according to eye colour, while in *Because We Were Travellers* (1997) an outcast boy and old woman struggle to survive in the land of Whykatto, near the ruined city of Orklun. As a short story writer, Lasenby is unfailingly entertaining: *Harry Wakatipu* (1993), the world's most recalcitrant pack-horse, stacks

up well alongside Uncle Trev's hilarious yarns about travelling asparagus beds, fast grass, and giant kauris with a view of the South Pole, from *Uncle Trev* (1991), *Uncle Trev and the Great South Island Plan* (1991) and *Uncle Trev and the Treaty of Waitangi* (1992). Lasenby has received numerous honours for his writing, including the 1991 Sargeson Fellowship, 1993 Victoria University of Wellington writing fellowship, and 1995 Dunedin College of Education writing fellowship.   PM

LAUDER, Hugh (1948–), poet, editor and education writer, lived in New Zealand 1977–95. Born in occupied Germany of Australian parents, he was educated in England, graduating BSc, MA London while also pursuing literary interests as co-editor of *Omphalos* and secretary of England's Poets' Workshop. As lecturer in education at the University of Canterbury, where he took his PhD, he again published poetry and in 1984 became poetry editor of *Landfall, from No. 152. He was acting editor of Nos. 153–156, and remained poetry editor or on the editorial board to 1990, always committed to avoiding 'narrow sectarianism'. He then moved to Victoria University as professor of education. His poems and prose-poems have been anthologised in the Penguin Books of *Contemporary New Zealand Verse* and *Contemporary New Zealand Short Stories* and the *Caxton Press Anthology* (1987). In this last anthology Mark *Williams discussed Lauder's work up to *Over the White Wall* (1985) wholly as 'political'. This simplifies the ingenious and sometimes passionate intercuttings between the domestic and local (especially New Zealand), and a strong moral concern with international history and its most potent recent images—the *Depression, Dresden, the war in Italy, terrorism. Iain *Sharp brought out the 'subtle and incisive' complexities of the collection, the 'hallucinatory, neurasthenic quality', the interrogation of 'the value of art' and the essential 'compassion', in a key review article in *Landfall* 157 (1986). The human, personal commitment became more apparent in *Knowledge of the Left Hand* (1990), where several poems, like the title prose-poem, are concerned with revisiting *Germany and the various dislocations of the poet's migratory experience. Mobile and international, juxtaposing Van der Velden's paintings with modern advertisements, Māori with Teutonic myth, they explore the interactions of language, history and the individual. Lauder departed 'temporarily' in 1995 to become professor at the University of Bath, England.
          RR

Laura's Poems was a publishing phenomenon of 1995, a best-selling collection by Laura Ranger 'written between the ages of six and nine'. Their colourful and often witty imagery and wordplay ('Some tulips / have red lips / and dark black eyes. / They bow and curtsy / in the wind') and unthreatening treatment of childhood experiences and concerns ('My Zoo', 'God', 'My Dog') made the poems attractive to an unusually wide readership. Their language is accessible and poised, resourceful phrases like 'One wuthering wet day in May' or 'the rosellas / are a crimson streak of light' suggesting remarkable reading or receptiveness of ear. Her first published poem was in the American children's magazine *Stone Soap* in 1991, her second shared a competition first prize with Lauris *Edmond, and her 'Two Word Poem' became what Bill *Manhire called 'the hit poem' of his popular *100 New Zealand Poems* (1993). Manhire's preface to *Laura's Poems*, appropriately ingenuous in tone ('She's a real poet, and plenty of people think so'), credits Ranger's parents with encouraging her writing by 'permission to stay up for an extra hour or so'. No comment is made on the editorial and other processes by which the poems reached America, were entered in competitions or were collected.   RR

LAWLOR, Pat or **P.A.** (Patrick Anthony) (1893–1979) was a journalist, novelist, poet, pamphleteer and Catholic publicist. He was born in Wellington, joined the *Evening Post* in 1911 and transferred to *The Dominion* two years later. In 1914 he freelanced in Sydney and visited Melbourne, whose bohemian tradition he unsuccessfully tried to establish in Wellington on his return. In 1916 he became chief reporter for the *Hawke's Bay Herald,* but returned to Wellington the following year to join the Press Gallery and work with the *New Zealand Times.* He became chief subeditor of *New Zealand Truth* in 1920, also editing *Aussie*, an Australasian soldiers' magazine, and founding the *New Zealand Artists' Annual* in 1926 and the Ex Libris Society in 1930. With the poet Dick *Harris he produced his first collection, *Maori Tales* (1926), over one hundred stories he had gathered and 'rewritten'. The following year, after Harris's suicide, he edited *The Poetry of Dick Harris,* and in 1930 produced *Still More Maori Tales.*

The 1930s saw his most serious attempts to achieve literary recognition, with his two 'Templemore' novels, *The House of Templemore* (1938) and *Daniel Mahoney's Secret: being a new chapter in the House of Templemore* (1939). More successful was his *Confessions of a Journalist* (1935), an important source of literary gossip and historical detail from the period, to which *Books and Bookmen, New Zealand and Overseas* (1954), is something of a sequel. His only other novel, *The Mystery of Maata* (1946), is based on the early life of Katherine *Mansfield. During World War 2, Lawlor invented a second pseudonym (after the better-known 'Shibli Bagarag'), 'Christopher Penn', for *What's Wrong With the*

War? (1942), *War Songs* (1943), *Church Etiquette: Six Lay Sermons* (1945) and *The Last First Friday* (1945); *St. Joseph and Pope John* (1964), *The Demanding God* (1972) and *Prayers for Everyone* (1975) all appeared under his own name.

In 1934 Lawlor was the driving force behind the foundation of *PEN in New Zealand, becoming its president in 1948–49. He was also advocate on PEN's behalf for the foundation of what became the New Zealand *Literary Fund, and served as the Advisory Committee's first secretary, 1947–55. At the *New Zealand Writers' Conference 1951, he led a vituperative rearguard action against the generation of new young writers until being converted by the young James K. *Baxter's address on their behalf. His *The Two Baxters: Diary Notes* (1979) is a record of his friendship with Baxter. In the 1950s Lawlor began to write popular local histories, beginning with *Wellington in Verse and Picture* (1955) and *Old Wellington Days* (1959), which took the form of a diary preceding an account of the ships of Wellington and the Wellington of Katherine Mansfield, and continuing with another diary-history, *More Wellington Days* (1962), and *Pat Lawlor's Wellington* (1976), *Old Wellingon Hotels* (1974) and *Memories of Wellington Trams* (1969). He was awarded an OBE in 1976 and has a street on Mount Victoria named after him.   PE

LAWRENCE, D.H. (1885–1930), sent a postcard to Katherine *Mansfield from Wellington when his ship berthed there for a few hours on 14 August 1922. He wrote the single Italian word 'Ricordi', meaning 'memories'. It succinctly acknowledged both the importance of her early New Zealand experiences to her writing and the value of the past friendship between the two authors, who had recently quarrelled. Lawrence had included a version of Mansfield as Gudrun in *Women in Love* (1920). 'Ricordi' was taken as the title for a play-opera based on *Prelude and *'At the Bay' by Peter *Wells, first performed in 1996. Patrick Waddington has shown that some discarded passages from *Kangaroo* refer irritably to the treatment Lawrence and Frieda received from a Wellington customs officer during their 'cold and stormy' hours in Wellington.   RR

LAWRENCE, Warwick (1915–   ), journalist and poet, wrote *Three Mile Bush* (1934), an illustrated history of the Wairarapa and Carterton, at the age of 18. *Vulcan Lane and Other Verses* (1935) was written during his time in Auckland as a journalist and assistant to the editor of the *Mirror. Among his friends were Eve *Langley, Robin *Hyde and other writers whose meeting places included Blake's Inn in Vulcan Lane. The brief introduction to this slim volume of short lyrics was written by Hyde. He edited *Yours and Mine* (1936), a collection of fairy-tales to which Hyde, Langley, Gloria *Rawlinson, Ngaio *Marsh and Lawrence himself contributed. His unpublished manuscript 'Huzza for New Zealand', on the life and work of Captain William Mein Smith, first surveyor-general of the New Zealand Company, was second in the Rothman's Book of the Year Award in 1969.   GB

LAWSON, Henry (1867–1922), Australian short story writer, journalist and poet, spent two significant periods in New Zealand. The first—lasting seven months—was during the 1893 depression when, penniless, he travelled to Wellington on the slim possibility of editing a newspaper. Unsuccessful, he joined a gang laying telegraph cable between Picton and Dunedin. This experience inspired the early 'Maoriland' stories; 'Stiffner and Jim', 'His Country After All' and the Steelman series. A travelling companion was the original for the 'sharper' Steelman: whose easy abuse of a mate's hospitality was marginally more excusable because he 'was big and good-looking, and good-natured in his way', than it was in his cringing offsider Smith. In their spare prose, laconic tone and unsentimental portrayal of mateship, these narratives are characteristic of his best early writing.

In 1897, recently married, Lawson returned to teach at a Māori school at Mangamaunu, near Kaikoura. Initially, isolation seemed to suit his writing and he commenced a book, *Native School*. But loneliness, difficulties with his pregnant wife, and conflict with Māori created problems. The racist story, 'A Daughter of Maoriland', in which 'Maori' is an adjective of contempt, is indicative of the attitude he had developed. W.H. *Pearson documents the episode in *Henry Lawson Among Maoris* (1968), and argues that, unsympathetic to Māori cultural values, Lawson experienced an artistic crisis and withdrew to 'a recognition of the limitations in time and place in which his talents could operate'. After seven months the couple returned to Wellington, where their son was born. Then it was back to Australia—never again to undergo 'exile in Toadyland—New Zealand'. Had either period led to permanent employment, one of Australia's great writers might instead be celebrated among the founders of the New Zealand literary tradition.   PM

LAWSON, Will (1876–1957), was born in Low Fell, Co. Durham, but moved to New Zealand with his family in 1880 and completed his education in Brisbane when his father was transferred there in 1884. He returned to New Zealand in 1892 as a clerk in the Union Steam Ship Company and later in the AMP in Wellington.

He began writing ballads, notably on railway themes, publishing some in the Sydney *Bulletin* (e.g. 'Stokin'' in 1900), before moving to Sydney to join the *Evening News* in 1912. During World War 1 he was again in New Zealand, as a journalist, returning to Sydney in 1923. For another ten years he continued to alternate between New Zealand and Australia, also travelling widely in the United States and Asia.

His first book, *The Laughing Buccaneer* (1935) is an account of the American adventurer Bully Hayes, partly set in Queenstown during gold-rush days. His second, a novel set in Australia, is often considered his best: *When Cobb & Co. Was King* (1936). From 1938 he lived on an Australian Commonwealth literary pension. He published sixteen novels, seven volumes of verse, four books of non-fiction, and many uncollected poems, short stories and articles. He remained something of a specialist in 'railways literature' (it has even been argued that one can identify different kinds of locomotives in the differing rhythms of his ballads), but his novels cover a wide range of historical themes. He was an alcoholic and when his wife left him in 1942 he was befriended by Bertha, the widow of Henry *Lawson (no relation), who 'saved me from the grog', and with whom he wrote *My Henry Lawson*.

His novel *Forbidden Gold* (1945) is set on the coast near Wellington. It involves the discovery of gold in a Māori burial ground (see *Gold), and consequent prophecy, blackmail, travel, revelation of the secret of the gold's location, duplicity and the continued enactment of the Māori prophecy by explosion and violent death.

Gold in their Hearts (1950), which is called *Mary Smith's Hotel* in later editions, is set in the gold-mining town of Charleston on the West Coast, with an interesting evocation of the transitory world of the miners. The central character almost tragically identifies himself with the shortlived town, while his romantic love is the contrasting prototype of the transient being, fascinating in the liveliness that results from her constant movement. They end the narrative together in Waihi, another gold town doomed to fade in its turn.   NW

LAY, Graeme (1933–), fiction writer and editor, was born in Foxton, spent the formative years of his childhood in Taranaki, graduated from Victoria University of Wellington, became a secondary-school teacher and then settled on Auckland's North Shore in 1970. A prolific writer of stories and magazine articles, television plays and fiction and non-fiction books, he became books editor of *North and South* magazine in 1992. He has published two novels, *The Mentor* (1978) and *The Fools on the Hill* (1988), two collections of short stories, *Dear Mr Cairney* (1985) and *Motu Tapu* (1990), and edited two short story *anthologies, *Metro Fiction* (1987) and the popularly successful *100 New Zealand Short Short Stories* (1997). He has moved the focus of recent work to non-fiction, with *Passages: Journeys in Polynesia* (1993), *Pacific New Zealand* (1996) and, in the planned 'Pacific Pride' series, his working titles are *The Cook Islands*, *Samoa*, *Tonga* and *Fiji*. These books and his many magazine features (often accompanied by his own colour photographs) on the islands of the South *Pacific aim to modernise perceptions of an area that has often been projected as distant and exotic, and to place New Zealand intimately within a South Pacific context.   KI

Learning Media is a Crown-owned company that was set up in 1989 to replace the old *School Publications Branch of the Department of Education, together with what had been the Audio and Visual Productions Unit. Learning Media Limited now publishes on contract to the Ministry of Education and other clients who wish to supply schools with educational materials. It continues the School Publications tradition of seeking out and developing literary and artistic talent, and is marketing many of its productions overseas. Most of the former School Publications publishing programme, including the *School Journal*, *Ready to Read*, *Te Wharekura* and the *Tupu* series, has been continued. The programme of Māori publications now makes up one-fifth of its total output, and Learning Media also plays an important role in the production of texts in Pacific languages (see *Pacific writing for children). A major project, the *Ngata dictionary, was runner-up in the 1994 Montana Book Awards.   BS/RR

LEE, John A. (1891–1982), was born in Dunedin to Scots Romany parents. His father Gipsy Alfredo Lee deserted the family before Lee knew him, becoming a vagrant acrobat and entertainer. The extreme poverty of the family's life is the context of Lee's novel *Children of the Poor* (1934) and of his mother Mary Lee's proud autobiography *The Not So Poor* (1992). Poverty breeding crime, Lee became an habitual thief and was sentenced to Burnham Industrial School in April 1906, effectively being made a ward of the state until 21. He broke away time and again, labouring and living on the *swag until finally gaoled in Mt Eden. He was freed at last in March 1913. Although no criminal in any real sense, he had lived at odds with the law for seven years. In World War 1 he lost his left forearm and was awarded the DCM for gallantry at Messines Ridge. On the day he landed back in New Zealand he joined the Labour Party. He became MP for Auckland East 1922–28, and for Grey Lynn 1931–43. From 1936 to 1939 he was Under-Secretary to the Minister of Finance and responsible for the

introduction of state housing. The 1930s also saw him achieve fame as a novelist and writer on socialism. In 1940 he was expelled from the Labour Party for attacking the Prime Minister Michael Savage in the pamphlet 'The Psychopathology of Politics'. Ill with cancer, Savage died just three days later. Lee's political career was destroyed. He founded the Democratic Labour Party but was never re-elected. He continued to disseminate left-wing socialist views, however, through *John A. Lee's Weekly* (1940–48) and other journals well into the 1950s. From 1950 he was a successful Auckland bookseller and writer, adding to his fiction of the 1930s and publishing a number of political memoirs and analyses. As his formal education had stopped at Standard Four he was an exemplary self-educated, self-made man. And although he miscalculated politically in 1940, he never lost the legendary status he had achieved by that time, a status owed in large part to his writings and gift of oratory.

With the exception of the Shiner stories, most of Lee's best-known works of fiction are autobiographical in origin. Although not published until 1976, his first novel, *Soldier*, was written in 1918 in England as he recovered from his arm injury in a German grenade attack, and is about that and other personal war experiences. In a later war novel, *Civilian into Soldier* (1937), Lee writes of the war of 'John Guy': Guy was his wife's maiden name. These are melodramatic novels, stylistically heavy-handed in their attempts to mime war's assault on the senses, and bold in their sexuality. Written between them, Lee's first published novel *Children of the Poor* (1934) and its sequel *The Hunted* (1936) are very much finer. Dealing with Lee's life to his imprisonment at the age of 14 and his vain attempts subsequently to escape from Borstal, they are his richest treatment of a theme that pervades his work, man's inhumanity to man. Both books are marred, the former especially so, by Lee's inability to achieve aesthetic distance, his constant intrusions in the manner of tracts on economics, criminology, the legal system, sociology, and so on. The wonder is that they survive as 'novels' at all, and there is of course a measure of cultural collusion in this. Lee has real talents for creating characters, dialogue, action, incident and place, and writes with such energy and pace that negative critical judgments come to seem inappropriate. The reader is held by a quality of the writer's personality. The first edition of *Children of the Poor* was published anonymously. When George Bernard *Shaw read it on his way back to Britain in April 1934 he wrote to Lee, 'Do not remain anonymous longer than you can help. It takes a long time for a name to become known in the world of literature; and you cannot afford to lose a minute of it.' In the non-autobiographical, amusing anecdotes and yarns of *Shining with the Shiner* (1944), written almost flauntingly in the year he entered the political wilderness, and in the related volume *Shiner Slattery* (1964), Lee turns the Otago regional folk hero Ned Slattery (1840–1927) into a national icon, the spirit of beating the Protestant work ethic and surviving by one's wits. Completely inferior fictions are the potboilers he wrote originally as serials to boost the circulation of his *Weekly*, *The Yanks are Coming* (1943) and *Mussolini's Millions* (1970). A posthumous novel *The Politician* (1987) was written fifty years earlier as *The Politician and the Fairy.*

Lee's chief political books include *Socialism in New Zealand* (1938), to which the British Labour Party leader Clement Attlee wrote an introduction, and more importantly his political autobiography *Simple on a Soap-Box* (1963). Commentators who have difficulty reconciling Lee's socialism with his exaltation of individual freedom can find assurances in this latter book, such as that 'Socialism without democracy is merely mechanical regulation of life.' *Rhetoric at the Red Dawn* (1965), *Political Notebooks* (1973) and *The John A. Lee Diaries 1936–1940* (1981) shed light on the fortunes of the Labour Party since World War 1. *For Mine is the Kingdom* (1975) is a scurrilously borderline biography of the 'Booze Baron' Sir Ernest Davis. Next to *Simple on a Soap-Box* the most important of all these works of non-fiction is the openly autobiographical *Delinquent Days* (1967), which carries on where the novel *The Hunted* leaves off and ends with Lee's release from Mt Eden gaol in 1913. More effectively in this book than any other Lee describes the foundations of his humanistic political socialism while on the run from Borstal, in the companionship of labourers and swaggers, and in the left-wing writings of Jack London and Upton Sinclair that he came upon in labourers' huts. It was that philosophy that sustained him to the end, and informed everything he wrote, that and his ability to respond lyrically to the natural world, seen nowhere more movingly than in *Delinquent Days*. There are excellent studies of John A. Lee by Erik Olssen and Dennis *McEldowney. KA

LEE-JOHNSON, Eric (1908–94), was a painter, illustrator and photographer. After Elam School of Fine Arts 1924–26, he worked as illustrator, designer and typographer in Auckland, London (1930–38) and Wellington. From the 1940s, Lee-Johnson applied his expertise in pen-and-ink drawing and watercolour to drawings and paintings of the landscapes of Northland, Auckland, Coromandel and the Bay of Plenty, focusing on iconic motifs like burnt tree-stumps, historic buildings and the ramshackle architecture of small-town New Zealand. These were exhibited and published, for instance in *Landfall and the collection of his drawings of Northland, *As I see it* (1969). Acclaimed in the

1940s–50s as uniquely emblematic of New Zealand, his works found special favour with literary associates like Charles *Brasch and A.R.D. *Fairburn. Given his more critical subsequent re-evaluation, it may surprise that E.H. *McCormick chose Lee-Johnson for the first monograph on a contemporary New Zealand artist (1956). Lee-Johnson was also an editor and author, editing *Arts Yearbook* 1950–51, publishing essays in *Landfall* and *New Zealand Studio* and, most recently, his autobiography: *No Road to Follow: Autobiography of a New Zealand Artist* (1994). CB

LEEMING, Owen (1930–), was born in Christchurch, studied French and music at Canterbury University College, and set out to study composition in France, only to abandon music for poetry. There followed a career in broadcasting in London, New Zealand and Australia; he has lived in Paris for more than twenty years. Leeming wrote a number of plays, some for stage but most for radio, where he drew upon his production experience to make adventurous use of the medium. He spent a period at Menton as Katherine *Mansfield Memorial Fellow.

Leeming published poems in various periodicals and in the *New Zealand Poetry Yearbook*, and a single collection, *Venus Is Setting* (1972). Having 'evolved' from Catholic to atheist, by his own account he set about 'exploring a secular metaphysic' through poetry, influenced in particular by contemporary French verse. His contemplative, rather academic poems are characterised by jagged prosody and an idiosyncratic syntax, and intermittent lyricism. Best known is his long poem 'The Priests of Serrabonne'. For subjects he ranges widely across his experience and reading—religion, travel, earthquakes, a headcold. While they can be intellectually dry and harsh on the ear, at their best the poems suggest a mind passionately at work, interrogating the processes of perception and interpretation. JH

Left Book Club, The, Victor Gollancz's London-based club, was quickly established in New Zealand, with the first books arriving only three months after it was initiated in England. The principal agent was *Blackwood Paul, who secured New Zealand distribution rights. Twenty-six groups were formed 1937–40, with around 1000 members nationally. A national association was formed in 1939 with H. Winston *Rhodes as president. Like *Tomorrow*, it sought to provide a forum for public debate, with an increasing emphasis on civil liberties. Its aim of political education was encapsulated in the motto, 'Knowledge, Unity, Responsibility', and its lending libraries were an important focal point. Although it did not enjoy widespread popular support, it did succeed in making progressive literature available outside the main centres. The club's social and cultural activities, which included drama productions and film screenings, became a focus for an intellectual avant-garde, but as wartime censorship grew stricter the organisation increasingly focused on issues of freedom of speech. The outbreak of war and the resultant undermining of the Popular Front line meant that much of the momentum for the club was lost. After 1941, it had virtually ceased to operate as a political organisation in New Zealand, although there was a short-lived attempt to reconstitute the remaining New Zealand membership in 1948, when the parent body finally collapsed. Rachel Barrowman devotes a chapter of *A Popular Vision* (1994) to the club. NWt

LEGGOTT, Michele (1956–), poet, critic and editor, was born in Stratford, Taranaki, and educated at New Plymouth GHS and University of Canterbury (MA in English 1979 for a thesis on the poetry of Ian *Wedde). She spent 1980–85 in *Canada completing a PhD at University of British Columbia. Her dissertation on the American poet Louis Zukofsky was published in America as *Reading Zukovsky's '80 Flowers'* (1989). Her academic work on the experimental tradition in American and New Zealand poetry directly influenced her own poetic practice. Her poems began appearing in periodicals from about 1980. A small selection, *Sound Pitch Considered Forms* (1984), was published (with two Canadian poets) in Vancouver. She returned in 1985 to a lectureship at the University of Auckland. Her first book of poems, *Like This?* (1988) was selected (as a cover note says) 'almost chronologically, from ten years' writing and the shifts made in that time from Christchurch to Auckland to Vancouver, Canada, and back to Auckland'. It won the *PEN First Book of Poetry award. The poems range from brief, short-lined lyrics such as '*on white*', reflecting the influence of Zukofsky in their elaborate wordplay and musical effects, to expansive long-lined poems such as the richly evocative 'An Island', which despite its length (seven pages) has been twice anthologised. *Swimmers, Dancers* (1991) is dominated by poems with a domestic focus sometimes directed towards childhood and memories of her parents, and sometimes towards her own children. The effect of a kind of verbal family photograph album is enhanced by the inclusion of actual snapshots. Leggott's third book *DIA* (1994) won the New Zealand Book Award for Poetry. It includes, together with several pieces which experiment radically with layout, the long poem 'Blue Irises', a set of thirty 'sonnets' (in the sense that each one is fourteen lines long). Among other things this sequence is a homage to the tradition of women poets, especially the New Zealand poets Robin *Hyde, Ursula *Bethell and Eileen *Duggan, whom she believed to have suffered undeserved neglect. This theme is also explored in various critical essays, for example, 'Opening the Archive: Robin Hyde, Eileen Duggan and the Persistence of Record' in *Opening the Book: New Essays on New Zealand Writing* (1995), which Leggott edited with Mark *Williams, and in a series of radio talks, '"Don't forget the girl is a genius": Re-reading New Zealand Women Poets' (1993). Leggott was poetry editor of *Landfall* 1991–93 (Nos. 177–85), and guest editor (with Jenny Penberthy) of *West Coast Line* (No. 11, 1993). She wrote the introduction to Robin Hyde, *The Victory Hymn, 1935–1995* (1995). PS

LEITCH, George, see *Land of the Moa, The*.

Letters, see *Arena*.

'Life of Ma Parker', a short story by Katherine *Mansfield, first published in the *Nation and Athenaeum* (1921) and included in *The Garden Party and Other Stories* (1922), was the last story written at the Villa Isola Bella, Menton, France, early in 1921. No MS is known. The story presents an elderly 'charwoman' whose grandson, Lennie, has just died (apparently of TB), her encounter with the 'literary gentleman' whose flat she cleans, her reflections on a life marred by poverty and loss and her inability to weep about this. It is almost a dramatic monologue in form, and the ironic oppositions set up between Ma Parker's voice and the direct speech of the 'literary gentleman' make the story an exposé of bohemianism (like *'Bliss') as well as a commentary on social class (like 'The *Garden Party' and 'The *Doll's House'): '… because these people set such store by funerals he said kindly, "I hope the funeral went off all right." "Beg parding, sir?" said old Ma Parker huskily.' The pathos of her self-thwarted desire to cry her grief out is one of the ways in which the story is a commentary on the effects of illness and death on the living. In this respect, it has a connection with 'Six Years After', 'The *Stranger', 'The *Daughters of the Late Colonel' and 'The Man Without a Temperament'. In *The Lonely Voice* (1964), Frank O'Connor asserts that the story is imitative of Chekhov's *Misery*, a charge which *Alpers does not repudiate. SSa

LILBURN, Douglas (1915–), composer, was born in Wanganui, endowed with considerable literary as well as musical gifts. These are evident not only in his well-known settings, but in his talk 'A Search for Tradition', given at the First Cambridge Summer School of Music in January 1946, and in its successor 'A Search for a Language', delivered at the University of Otago on 12 March 1969. His long friendships with Allen *Curnow, Denis *Glover and poets of a younger generation, such as Alistair Te Ariki *Campbell, betoken a highly sympathetic response to words which carries over into a number of notable settings. While a student at the Royal College of Music at London he became friendly with expatriate writers such as Robin *Hyde, D'Arcy *Cresswell and James *Courage.

His first and almost only major vocal work, *Prodigal Country* (1939), for baritone, chorus and orchestra, won first prize in the choral class of the 1940 Centennial Music Competitions, the judges describing it as showing 'fine work and judgment with never a stodgy line'. The text was drawn from Hyde's poem 'Journey from New Zealand', Curnow's 'New Zealand City' and Walt Whitman's 'Song of Myself'. Apart from a perfunctory broadcast in 1940 this moving and powerful work lay unperformed until Sir Charles Groves recorded it for Radio New Zealand in 1987. To commemorate the tercentenary of *Tasman's arrival in New Zealand in 1642, Curnow sought Lilburn's collaboration to provide the musical framework to his poem for narrator and strings *'Landfall in Unknown Seas' (1942), an arrangement described by the poet as 'one of those rare and happy circumstances'. This work has fully established itself in the repertoire.

Lilburn's *Elegy in Memory of Noel Newson* (1945) for soprano, alto and strings drew on English poets Herrick, Blake, Herbert and *Shakespeare, whereas his *Elegy* (1951), a song cycle for baritone and piano, sets Alistair Campbell's memorable sequence of poems with powerful intensity. In an altogether different vein is Lilburn's cycle of songs for baritone and piano or guitar, *Sings Harry* (1953), Denis Glover's evocation of an archetypal back-country character. This aroused a deep response, sections of it often being quoted by the composer in other contexts, especially the lines 'Sing all things sweet or harsh upon / These islands in the Pacific sun, / The mountains whitened endlessly / And the white horses of the winter sea, / Sings Harry.' Both Glover and Curnow have celebrated Lilburn's birthdays with poems, and Campbell delineates the essential personality in his poem 'Wild Honey'. Lilburn set Campbell again in his electro-acoustic work for tape *The Return* (1965), based on the poem of the same name. Other poets who have attracted him include James K. *Baxter, Ursula *Bethell and R.A.K. *Mason (*Three Songs for Baritone and Viola*, 1958), Ruth *Dallas and Basil *Dowling. Lilburn's close association with leading poets and sensitivity to the nuances of words has resulted in the creation of a highly expressive body of work.   JMT

LINDSAY, Graham (1952–), published his first book of poetry, *Thousand-Eyed Eel* (1976), with Alan *Loney's *Hawk Press, and has retained the scrupulous care that implies for the *typographic as well as aural structures of his verse. His subsequent volumes are *Public* (1980), *Big Boy* (1986), *Return to Earth* (1991) and *The Subject* (1994); their poems range from the meticulously controlled forms of *Public* to the expansive, conversational, longer lines of *Big Boy*. Though usually seen as avant-garde, Lindsay has been published in journals or anthologies ranging from the esoteric (*Parallax*; *Edge*, Tokyo) to the populist (*Metro*; *100 New Zealand Poems*), including mainstream recognition in *Landfall and *NZ Listener. He edited *Morepork 1979–80. Reviewers have concurred on the 'meditative', 'probing' nature of his thought, the flexibility of his voice and his commitment to the endlessly renewable resources of language. 'He knows how to put a spin on a phrase ... searches for the magic in the mundane' (David *Eggleton). Lindsay's essential and most frequent subject is thus poetry itself, from an early narrative of James K. *Baxter ('The Embrace') to many meditations on language, such as 'Life in the Queen's English': '... The way words / like images lift / pull back peel / from their referents, leave us / longing for the intimacy / that preceded their birth.'

Though born in Wellington and brought up in Porirua and Havelock North, Lindsay has spent his adult life in Dunedin and, since 1988, Christchurch, both cities featuring in his verse; *Big Boy*, especially, is a strongly Dunedin book. He is thus included in the South Island collection *From the Mainland as well as several anthologies of contemporary verse.   RR

Lion in the Meadow, A, by Margaret *Mahy was first published in 1965 as the title story in an issue of the *School Journal devoted to Mahy's stories and poems. The story was illustrated with an effective line-drawing by Jill McDonald. Included in an exhibition of New Zealand printing sent to New York in 1968, the issue was noticed by an American editor, Sarah Chockla Gross, who drew Mahy's work to the attention of the publishing firm Franklin Watts. Released in 1969 as a 24-page picture-book by Watts in the US and by J.M. Dent in the UK, *A Lion* was Mahy's first work to achieve commercial publication. It was an enormous success throughout and beyond the English-speaking world; in New Zealand it received the Esther Glen Award in 1970. The story contains echoes of Mahy's earliest memory—of her father telling her a story 'about a great big black-maned Abyssinian lion'. When a little boy insists on the presence of a lion in the adjacent meadow, his mother, having first dismissed his story, offers him a matchbox containing, she says, a baby dragon which will grow and frighten the lion away. The dragon materialises, and the lion takes refuge in the little boy's house, becoming his playmate. The story's conclusion ('The mother never ever made up a story again') sounds like the ending of a straightforward cautionary tale, but with the humour telling against the adult instead of the child.

A Lion makes a distinction between two kinds of fiction—that which carries conviction, and mere calculated falsehood. Mahy has continued to explore this distinction; in the 1985 adolescent novel *The Catalogue of the Universe*, for instance, solo mother Dido tells her daughter Angela a romantic 'white lie' about her father; Angela is dangerously shocked when she discovers the truth.

In a revised version of *A Lion* published in 1986, new illustrations (again by Jenny Williams) show the mother preoccupied with a new baby; these pictures imply that the little boy's claims are pleas for attention. The text, which remains unaltered until the final page, makes no reference to the baby. But a new conclusion—replacing 'The mother never ever made up a story again' with an account of the lion's full incorporation into the household's comforting bedtime ritual of 'apples, stories and a goodnight hug'—does complement the new illustrations by inviting a reading of the lion as a projection of the boy's temporary sense of displacement and alienation; both the lion and the boy gain security in the end. Mahy created this new ending at the suggestion of her then editor Vanessa Hamilton; many readers had been dismayed by the original conclusion, which they interpreted as a dispiriting attack on 'stories'. Mahy now looks back on her decision with some ambivalence.

A Lion reads like a traditional tale, thanks in part to its formulaic and subtly formal prose. Its protagonists, being unnamed, are types rather than individuals, and archetypal material is subtly evoked; in their final harmonious relationship the lion and the boy are reminiscent of Isaiah's vision of paradise as a holy mountain, where the lion and lamb lie down together, and 'a little child shall lead them' (Isa. 11:6).   KWa

Literary Fund. The New Zealand Literary Fund, often known as the State Literary Fund, was established by the Labour government in 1947, within the Department of Internal Affairs. An approach by ★PEN in about 1937 was renewed with some lobbying 1944–46. By that time, some patronage of literature was being distributed by the Secretary for Internal Affairs, Joe Heenan, who was persuaded to support the proposal and secured an initial grant of £2000. A Literary Fund Advisory Committee was appointed and drew up its terms of reference, and a public announcement was made in August 1947.

The founding members were three PEN nominees, Sir James Elliott, a surgeon and author who was PEN's president and the committee's first chairman, Professor Ian ★Gordon and G.H. Scholefield; and six government appointees, O.N. ★Gillespie, Pei Te Hurinui ★Jones, Mary Mackenzie, Ngaio ★Marsh, J.H.E. ★Schroder and Ormond Wilson MP. Honorary secretary was Pat ★Lawlor, secretary of PEN.

PEN's proposal for a public fund had not received unqualified support from the literary community, with A.R.D. ★Fairburn and E.H. ★McCormick prominent critics, but there was little comment on the announcement of the Fund. Early grants were mostly made to publishers, for instance ★Caxton Press for M.H. ★Holcroft's *Discovered Isles*; early individual grants included two that aroused some criticism, to Antony ★Alpers to research his biography of Katherine ★Mansfield in London, and to Allen ★Curnow, also for overseas travel. The terms of reference covered support to publishers and authors of 'such works as historical works, contemporary creative literature, reprints of New Zealand classics, and Maori literature'. The inevitable dilemma of arts patronage, granting public money to works of which the public was presumed to disapprove, soon surfaced with David ★Ballantyne's *The ★Cunninghams*, at first deemed too offensive but eventually given a grant. In the *New York Times* in 1949 Ballantyne castigated the Fund for preferring 'new editions of out-of-print books'.

Scholefield became chairman in 1948. The next notable event was the ★New Zealand Writers' Conference in Christchurch in 1951, which the committee sponsored, but where it was attacked for being 'conservative and inaccessible'. Scholefield resigned and was succeeded by Gordon, who held the chair for twenty-two years. With an Internal Affairs official, Andrew Sharp, as secretary from 1955, an era of stability ensued. Support was extended to ★*Landfall* in 1950, and soon after to other journals; the Hubert Church and Jessie Mackay awards were established in 1952 to encourage new writing; the Scholarship in Letters was created in 1956 and the Award for Achievement in 1957.

There was occasional philistine protest, as when the *Evening Post* criticised the support for a 'salacious' issue of ★*Numbers* in 1959; and criticism from the other extreme, as when Charles ★Brasch wrote in *Landfall* in 1962 about the committee's policy of the 'deadly safe'. A more serious controversy arose in 1964, when the committee tried (on a split vote) to make Louis ★Johnson remove some offensive poems by James K. ★Baxter and others from the ★*New Zealand Poetry Yearbook*. Margaret Dalziel of Otago University resigned from the committee in protest and the debate raged in the ★*NZ Listener* and elsewhere, Holcroft defending the committee's intervention.

Another kind of intervention saw the Fund's income severely cut by incoming Finance Minister Robert *Muldoon in 1967 and 1969. With the election of a Labour government, C.K. *Stead became chairman in 1973, funding was increased, the New Zealand *Book Awards introduced in 1976 and the separate Authors' Fund (providing writers with some modest return for books in public libraries) in 1973.

Increasing pressure on funding led to the commissioning in 1977 of a report, 'Patronage and New Zealand Literature, an Investigation of the New Zealand Literary Fund', by Department official Owen St J. Vennell. This highlighted the need to diversify sources of funding. At the time only the *Burns Fellowship and Wattie Award supported literature from private sources. The Vennell Report, seconded by a NZ Listener editorial, led directly to the establishment of the country's second writing fellowship, at Victoria University in 1979, funded jointly by the university and the Literary Fund. This pattern was followed later by the other universities. A range of new travel and exchange fellowships, children's literature awards and other forms of joint funding also ensued.

Direct government funding was also increasingly supplemented by money from the Lottery Grants Board, so that overall support for literature through the Fund continued to increase. By now the emphasis had shifted from supporting publishers' projects to direct assistance to writers. R.A. *Copland and (from 1982) Terry *Sturm chaired the Advisory Committee through the relatively calm and prosperous times.

In 1988, however, after a period of discussion about its relation to the Queen Elizabeth II Arts Council, the Literary Fund was reconstituted as the Arts Council's Literature Programme. By 1994 legislation, the Council was itself replaced by the Arts Council of New Zealand Toi Aotearoa, known in its funding capacity as Creative New Zealand. In 1995 this new organisation disbanded all the old Arts Council's panels and committees, including the one that had succeeded the Literary Fund Advisory Committee. These changes and the negotiations that preceded them aroused a major controversy, especially about the termination of the separate Literary Fund and the loss of representation of active writers (nominated by PEN) on the body responsible for distributing their funding. PEN (in 1994 renamed New Zealand Society of Authors/PEN) and other literary interests remain strenuously opposed to this exclusion from a system which they helped to create and had conscientiously supported. NZSA's policy priority in 1996 became 'to regain influence in the distribution of grants.'

An anniversary history of the first twenty-five years, The New Zealand Literary Fund 1946–1970 by Andrew Sharp, was issued by the Department of Internal Affairs in 1971. The fullest account of the history of the Literary Fund is by Dennis *McEldowney in the *OHNZLE (1991, 1998). McEldowney's summary sees the Fund's considerable influence on literature during its forty-eight years as having been largely benign, and argues that early fears of intolerance, bias and bureaucratic intervention were not in that period fulfilled. He overlooks only the credit due to the many active writers and academics who generously gave their time and expertise to serve on the committee, in the onerous and largely thankless task of reading and assessing manuscripts and proposals. For almost fifty years, these judgments were made almost without exception with care and integrity. The full effect of the Fund on this formative period of New Zealand literature remains to be documented and assessed.   RR

Living in the Maniototo, the tenth novel by Janet *Frame (New York, 1979, Auckland, London, 1981), won the Buckland Literary Award (1980) and the New Zealand Book Award for Fiction (1980); no MS is known. It is an intricate, five-part novel of deceptive narrative surfaces, mirrorings and duplications that contemplates the imitative but also creative nature of language and art (and life), offering an exalted vision of the artist as able to construct imaginative truths in a world of imitations. In the first part the narrator— Mavis Furness Barwell Halleton (who has 'buried two husbands' and written two novels), or 'Alice Thumb' (the artist able to plumb the 'manifold' of the unconscious) or 'Violet Pansey Proudlock, ventriloquist'—offers a long disquisition on the deceptive nature of language. Mavis begins by offering autobiographical information, telling of the death of her husbands and of her life in the 'suburb-city' of Blenheim, felt by its inhabitants to be a poor imitation of other 'real' cities (in USA)— but Frame shows those cities to be equally imitative; imitation is the condition of contemporary life. These details provide a frame for the rest of the novel in which Mavis recounts events during her recent visit to *America. In the course of her narrative Mavis systematically overturns everything she has learned at writing classes about 'proper' novelistic procedure. In the second section Mavis tells of her journey to Baltimore, the twin city of Blenheim (they mirror each other in various ways), to stay at the house of a friend, Brian; of the visit of his nephew and the life (and death) of his cleaning lady. In one disturbing scene, recounted dispassionately, Mavis tells how Brian's friend Tommy disappeared in a puff of cleaning fluid. The setting for the third and fourth sections is a Berkeley 'house of replicas' belonging to the Garretts, wealthy art patrons travelling in Italy. Mavis minds their home while working on her next novel. A few weeks after the departure of the Garretts, Mavis receives news that they have died in an earthquake and that she is named in their will as the sole inheritor of their estate. Two couples arrive soon after, apparently invited to stay by the Garretts: Theo and Zita, Roger and Doris. Mavis abandons her current writing project to record the life-story told by each guest; her prose is realistic, believable. In the fifth section, the guests leave reluctantly (each believes thay have a stronger claim on the house than Mavis). As Mavis herself leaves the house, the Garretts return from their holiday: they didn't die, the will never existed. Nor, it transpires, did the guests. Disconcertingly we discover that the 'real' guests were in fact Mavis's fictional inventions, 'killed off' by authorial fiat as easily as Tommy had been wiped off the page earlier: the people she has been living with are her own novelistic creations—and she herself may be the creation of someone else. Frame has thus deliberately tricked the reader into believing that the embedded narrative, realistically dealing with the guests, is the primary narrative. Mavis returns to Baltimore and discovers that Brian has died. She travels back to Stratford, Taranaki, where she ostensibly begins to write the novel we are reading.

KWo

LOCKE, Elsie (1912–), has made a remarkable contribution to New Zealand society as a writer, historian and leader in peace movements and women's affairs, for which she received an honorary DLitt from the University of Canterbury in 1987. Born in Hamilton, she has described the hardships and delights of her early life in Waiuku and at Auckland University, where she was known by her surname as 'little Farrelly' and where she graduated in 1933, in *Student at the Gates* (1981). This autobiography details life in the 1920s–30s, illuminating both some dominant political and literary personalities of the time and also the influences which shaped her idealistic socialist philosophies. In the 1930s she edited the early feminist journal *Woman Today*. In 1941 she married Jack Locke, both having been members of the New Zealand Communist Party. They moved from Wellington to Christchurch, where they raised four children. Elsie Locke served on the national executive of the Campaign for Nuclear Disarmament (1957–70). She also continued writing for adults: *The Shepherd and the Scullery Maid* (1950), *The Human Conveyer Belt* (1968), *The Gaoler* (1978) on early Otago, and two privately printed family histories. She edited *Gordon Watson, New Zealander, 1912–1945* (1949). In 1959, she received the Katherine *Mansfield Award for Non-Fiction for her essay in *Landfall* 48, and in 1992 published her major study, *Peace People: Peace Activities in New Zealand*.

However, she is probably more widely known as a writer for children. Drawing her topics and themes from her interests and commitments, she carries out diligent research, often historical or relating to outdoor exercise. Her preparation has included learning Māori to understand the Māori point of view, which she expresses with sympathy and insight in novels that in this respect were in advance of general perceptions and political correctness. Inevitably, her first novel is based on a true story. *The Runaway Settlers* (1965), illustrated by Anthony Maitland, and reissued with illustrations by Gary Hebley (1993), portrays a remarkable historical-fiction mother in the character of Mrs Small, who changes her family's name to Phipps and flees with her children from her violent husband in Sydney to a hard but successful family life in Governor's Bay. Her experiences include driving a herd of cattle over the Southern Alps and down the Teremakau River (Taramakau or 'Terrible Cow') to the West Coast. This novel has been in continuous print for longer than any other New Zealand children's book.

Other historical novels include *The End of the Harbour* (1969), illustrated by Katarina *Mataira, a compassionate exploration of land issues from Māori and Pākehā perspectives; *Journey under Warning* (1983) illustrated by Margaret Chapman, an exploration of political posturing in the Wairau Affray through the historical character of Locke's own ancestor; and *A Canoe in the Mist* (1984), illustrated by John Shelley, a dramatic portrayal of the famous Tarawera eruption of 1886. *Explorer Zach* (1978), illustrated by David Waddington, is about Canterbury farming life in the 1920s for younger readers, while *The Boy with the Snowgrass Hair* (1976), with co-author Ken Dawson, illustrated by Jean Oates, extols mountaineering in a contemporary boy's search for self-confidence. Other contemporary stories show Locke's concern for wildlife: *Moko's Hideout* (1976), a collection of four good stories, illustrated by Beatrice Foster-Barnham and Elizabeth Plumridge, but poorly produced; and *Look Under the Leaves* (1975), illustrated by David Waddington and Trevor Lithgow, in verse and prose to extend ecological awareness.

In the field of children's non-fiction, Locke has made many contributions to the Department of Education historical bulletins and to the *School Journal. She also published *Maori King and British Queen* (1974); *The Kauri and the Willow* (1984), containing various contemporary extracts to illuminate historical circumstances; and *Two Peoples, One Land: A History of Aotearoa* (1988).

Locke's long and varied career in children's literature was honoured by the Margaret Mahy Lecture Award in March 1995, and extended by *Joe's Ruby* (1995), illustrated by Gary Hebley, the remarkable story of a man who raised an intelligent pet rook from an egg. DH

Log of a Superfluous Son, The (1975), a novel by Michael *Henderson.

LONEY, Alan (1940–), poet and printer, was born in Lower Hutt and attended Hutt Valley HS. He has since lived in Dunedin, Christchurch, Wellington and Auckland. He began publishing poetry in the late 1960s and has described his discovery of Charles Olson's *Maximus Poems* as decisive: 'Everything I have written since then has been informed by the lessons learnt in that, for me, extraordinary and illuminating encounter' ('The Influence of American Poetry on Contemporary Poetic Practice in New Zealand', *Journal of New Zealand Literature* 10, 1992). His first book *The Bare Remembrance* (1971) juxtaposed personal and local elements with references to early European contact with Māori. He printed it himself and in 1975 set up *Hawk Press, originally at Taylors Mistake, near Christchurch, to print his own and others' poetry. His *dear Mondrian* (Hawk, 1976), which won a New Zealand Book Award, is a sequence in which personal elegies alternate with reflections on the Dutch painter. In the preface to *Shorter Poems 1963–77* (1979) Loney wrote: 'Nothing is so sacred or so despicable that it cannot, at some time, by a voice that on occasion is equal to it, be uttered as poetry.' In 1982–83 he edited the three issues of *Parallax, a journal of *postmodern literature and art reflecting the influence of American poetics and theory. The last of some thirty Hawk Press publications was *Squeezing the Bones* (1983), a spare text about the death of his father treated with simultaneous multi-colour printing on a handpress. From 1987 to 1991 he operated *Black Light Press, to further develop the art of fine printing. Among its products were two which used his own writing: *Swell* (1987), poems and prints utilising wood and metal types and printer's blocks in several colours, and an essay *& the Ampersand* (1990). In 1988–90 he edited *New Zealand Crafts* magazine, and in 1989 founded the Book Arts Society. In 1992 he was writing fellow and in 1993 became a tutor in English at the University of Auckland. His *Missing Parts, Poems 1977–90* (*Hazard Press, 1992) contains nine sequences, including 'Squeezing the Bones' and 'Swell'. He described *The erasure tapes* (1994) as 'an autobiography in which I refuse to tell the story of my life'. In 1994 he became printer and co-director of the *Holloway Press at the Tamaki Campus of the University of Auckland.   PS

LONG, D.S. (Donald Stuart) or **Don** (1950–), is a poet, editor and, as Don Long, children's author. Born in Walla Walla, USA, he was a leading figure in the 1970s avant-garde movement of young poets (Gary *Langford, Alan *Loney, Ian *Wedde, et al.) to make New Zealand

poetry more international, eclectic and adventurous. His own volumes were *Borrow Pit* (1971), *Storing Stones for Winter* (1974), *In Search of a Poem* (1976) and *Poems from the Fifth Season* (1977). He was also the innovative editor of *Edge, 1971–77.

Moving in 1979 from Taylors Mistake, Christchurch, to Days Bay, Wellington, he began a collaboration with Witi *Ihimaera, again with a mission to break down old assumptions and encourage diversity and innovation, but this time by fostering Māori writing. Their co-edited anthology, *Into the World of Light: An Anthology of Maori Writing* (1982), was a crucial vehicle for the then nascent Māori voice in written literature. It has been followed by their five volumes (to date) of *Te *Ao Mārama* (1992–96).

Working for *School Publications and its successor, Learning Media, Long began in 1988 to edit children's books by contemporary *Pacific nations writers. He has published over seventy, some in up to five separate language editions. He edited *Matariki* (1990–94), *Te Ata Hāpara* (1990–91) and the *Tupu* series (1988–), all for Learning Media. By fostering publication of New Zealand writers working in Cook Islands Māori, Niuean, Samoan, Tokelauan and Tongan, Long contributes to what he calls 'the breakdown of the idea that New Zealand literature is essentially a Pakeha/Maori art form'.

He summarises his career as 'contributing to three sea-changes to the face of New Zealand literature'. Each is in retrospect consistent with the multicultural character of his own work, both in his earlier poetry and recent children's writing, where the affirmation of multiple ancestries and rejection of restrictive categorising can be seen as the core of work that retains its freshness and conviction.   RR

LONIE, Iain (1932–88), a poet of both classicism and passion, was born in Cambridgeshire, England, and arrived in New Zealand when his Scottish father was appointed medical officer of health in Palmerston North. According to Don McKenzie (see *Wai-te-ata Press), a lifelong friend from their years at Palmerston North BHS, Lonie showed an excellence in English and precocious interest in philosophy, fostered through adult education classes. He completed a BA at Otago, where he married the poet Jean *Lonie, and went on to read Classics at King's College, Cambridge, specialising in ancient philosophy and the history of medicine. He taught at the universities of New England and Sydney, before returning in 1965 to the University of Otago, where he taught until 1974. Although highly regarded as both scholar and teacher, he was often anxious about his ability to convey what he felt about the materials he taught, and resigned to take a job as a deckhand on the

Otago Harbour Board dredge. By this time, he had published two slim volumes of poetry: *Recreations* (Wai-te-ata, 1967, 1970) and *Letters from Ephesus* (The Bibliography Room, University of Otago, 1970).

He returned to London with his second wife, Judith ★Lonie, whom he had met at Sydney, to take up a position as research fellow at the Wellcome Institute, continuing research on the history of medicine. The fellowship was renewed, but did not lead to the expected academic post. Soon after this, in 1982, Judith Lonie died with tragic suddenness, and a little later he returned to Otago. *Courting Death* (Wai-te-ata, 1984) records the intense grief he felt at her death, and the difficulties of coming to terms with the loss and absence and the curiously continued presence of a loved one. That grief still informs the two later volumes, *The Entrance to Purgatory* (McIndoe, 1986) and the posthumous *Winter Walk at Morning* (Victoria University Press, 1991). Iain Lonie took his own life.

Lack of recognition, even at times rejection within New Zealand literary circles, deeply distressed him, for in spite of his impeccable scholarship and erudition, it was as a poet that he sought to be acknowledged and remembered. His classicism is apparent in much of his poetry, not only in his reworkings of familiar legends, but also in his deep interest in mythology and its links with the imagination. Firmly located within particular places, and enriched by traditional cultural echoes, his poetry reveals a strong lyric voice and intense feeling, always tempered by controlled handling of verse forms and by very discriminating choice of language.   PW

LONIE, Jean (1930–), is the author of three volumes of poetry: *Towards the League of Strong Women* (1987), *Angle of Repose* (1991) and *Working within Restraints* (1996). Born in Wanganui, she studied in Dunedin, where she met and married Iain ★Lonie, with whom she subsequently lived in Cambridge (UK) and Australia. They returned to New Zealand in the mid-1960s, but later parted; she settled in Wellington, working at the ★Alexander Turnbull Library and the Correspondence School, and raising her four children. Much of her poetry is very personal and intimate; it attends with care (and with increasing control and sureness) to the task of recording the troublesome business of daily living, in which individual relationships often occasion difficulties, but equally often provide great richness.   PW

LONIE, Judith (1935–82), Australian born, arrived in New Zealand in the mid-1960s, where she subsequently married Iain ★Lonie, whom she had met when he taught at Sydney University. Her first, slim volume of poetry, *Earth into Moon*, was published in 1971. Subsequently

they went to England for further study and research, Judith studying linguistics at Newcastle upon Tyne. She graduated in 1982, but died suddenly that December. Her second volume, *The Remembering of the Elements* (★Wai-te-ata Press, 1984), incorporates most of the earlier collection. Her unstructured verse has an often impersonal tone, contrasting with its personal subject matter. She looks at strangers, at intimates and at self with a slightly curious, and sometimes judgmental detachment. Not always assured with lineation, the poetry relies for much of its effect on precision of imagery, while many of the poems have as their subject aspects of perspective and of illusion.   PW

Look Back Harder is a collection of Allen ★Curnow's critical writings, 1935–84, edited by Peter ★Simpson and published by ★Auckland University Press, 1987. Beginning with the early manifesto *Poetry and Language* (1935), the collection includes the introductions to Curnow's two poetry anthologies *A ★Book of New Zealand Verse 1923–45* (1945) and *The Penguin Book of New Zealand Verse* (1960), plus a miscellany of reviews, articles, lectures, prefaces, book introductions, letters to the editor and interviews.   PS

Loop in Lone Kauri Road, The, is a collection by Allen ★Curnow, subtitled 'Poems 1983–85', published by ★Auckland University Press in 1986. Poems of childhood memory ('A Raised Voice', 'A Sight for Sore Eyes') are mixed with poems deriving from travel in Europe ('Gare SCNF Garavan') and others evoking urban and marine landscapes in contemporary Auckland ('Canto of Signs Without Wonders', 'The Loop in Lone Kauri Road').   PS

LORD, Robert (1945–91), was an internationally known playwright of the 1970s–80s. Born in Rotorua, he was an Arts undergraduate at Otago and Victoria universities. In 1969, he won the Katherine Mansfield Young Writers' Award and, in 1974, was writer-in-residence at Mercury Theatre in Auckland. In the same year, an Arts Council travel bursary enabled him to travel to New York, where he remained until returning in 1987 to take up the ★Burns Fellowship. In 1990 he was writer-in-residence at the Fortune Theatre in Dunedin. He also formed a fruitful relationship with Circa Theatre in Wellington, which resulted in fully-fledged and well-received productions of his mature work: 'China Wars' (Circa, 1987), 'Glorious Ruins' (Circa, 1991) and, most notably, *Joyful and Triumphant* (Circa, 1992). This play, which has also toured to Australia, tells the story of the Bishop family in a series of scenes set on Christmas Day over a period of forty years. While on one level it is a witty situation comedy, on another it unfolds in loving detail a history of fundamental cultural change from the 1950s to 1980s.

Lord was New Zealand's first professional playwright, and the first since Merton *Hodge in the 1930s to have his plays produced abroad; Roger *Hall followed in his footsteps soon afterwards. Lord's work is essentially intimate theatre concerned with the success—or lack of it—of relationships between people. His dialogue is witty and precise, and he uses puns and double meanings to create a sense of the brittleness of social intercourse. His first full-length play, 'It Isn't Cricket', premièred at Wellington's Downstage in 1971. The best-known and most controversial of his early plays was Well Hung (Downstage, 1974), an extensive revision of an earlier play, 'The Body in the Park', in which the central action was drawn from the Crewe murder case. This play was directed by Anthony Taylor, who had already directed 'Meeting Place' (Downstage, 1972) and was to be a future artistic director at Downstage, and it established an ongoing partnership between playwright and director. Other plays that have been produced or published (or both) in New Zealand, Australia and the United States include 'Heroes and Butterflies' (Mercury, 1974), Glitter and Spit (1975), 'High as a Kite' (Downstage, 1978), Balance of Payments (1978), 'Unfamiliar Steps', later retitled Bert and Maisy (Court, 1983), Country Cops, a revision of Well Hung (Circa, 1985) and 'The Affair' (The Globe, 1987). In 1988, he successfully adapted his play Bert and Maisy for television. He wrote a number of one-act plays and radio plays as well as screenplays for Tony Williams's short film, The Day We Landed on the Most Perfect Planet in the Universe, and for the feature film, Pictures.   SG

LOVELOCK, Jack (1910–49), the great one-mile runner of the 1930s, has become one of New Zealand's few near-mythic figures. The innovations of live radio and film newsreel made his achievements public on a previously unknown scale, while his bashful manner and intensely private personality have kept him a perplexing hero. The highly-charged background enhances the story. He was a Rhodes Scholar in 1930s Oxford, competed frequently in America at that nation's most noisily emergent phase and won his greatest victory at the 1936 Olympic Games in Hitler's Berlin. Recent New Zealand writers have placed emphasis, as with Katherine *Mansfield, on the ambivalence of the expatriate colonial, absorbed back into British society yet always a New Zealander, very publicly so in Lovelock's case.

Early New Zealand literary reception can be represented by the Otago University poet who heralded his entry for the 1932 Olympics, 'And not an athlete there

will see the way our Lovelock goes', through to the 'Flight of falcon, bound of deer' of the New Zealand Herald's obituary. Elsewhere, Lovelock was the subject of some excellent writing, especially in British newspapers in that golden age of sports journalism, and his Berlin race is a key sequence in Riefenstahl's film, Olympia; but the first significant New Zealand account was Norman *Harris's biography, The Legend of Lovelock (1964). Vividly written and with a strong sense of the special drama of competitive running, this is still the best interpretation of Lovelock's reticent personality. Christopher Tobin's meticulous Lovelock: New Zealand's Olympic Gold Miler (1984) made extensive use of Lovelock's excellent diaries.

The mythic potential was then perceived by James *McNeish, whose Lovelock (1986) is a skilled biofiction. It mixes detailed research, some original, with invented material, cunningly blurring the distinction, especially in the treatment of Lovelock's sudden death, killed by a fall under a New York subway train while suffering from dizziness and influenza. Speculation about suicide is added to the already colourful historical material.

McNeish's novel has gone through three editions and caught the imagination of younger writers, inspiring a TV docudrama with an award-winning script by Stuart *Hoar and a successful stage play by David *Geary, Lovelock's Dream Run (1993). Particularly strong in its comic writing, this relates the international material such as English class attitudes and German fascism to local issues presented through the boarding-school setting, such as conformity, *puritanism and New Zealand's ambivalent treatment of its heroes. These versions of Lovelock's story all make somewhat self-congratulatory use of his insightful and often droll diaries, which are preserved at Timaru Boys' High School. Apparently so revealing, but still so elusive, these may yet have the last word.   RR

Lovelock Version, The, a novel by Maurice *Shadbolt, was published in 1980. It is in many ways his finest, certainly his most exuberant novel to date, and the first in which he explores the rich vein of New Zealand's nineteenth-century colonial history. It picks up some of the themes from earlier stories such as 'Ben's Land', the opening story of Summer Fires and Winter Country (1963), his second collection of short fiction, and introduces others that he would later return to in his play, *Once on Chunuk Bair (1982), in the second novel of his *New Zealand Wars trilogy, Monday's Warriors (1990), and also in his autobiographical One of Ben's (1993). These connections highlight both the considerable unity present in Shadbolt's large body of work and the central position this novel occupies. Using the realist form of the

Victorian family saga spiced with the magic realism which has become the stock-in-trade of so much Spanish-American fiction, and introducing metafictional techniques before they became fashionable, *The Lovelock Version* presents New Zealand's post-colonisation history through the stories of the three Lovelock brothers—Herman, Richard and James—and their families. Intersecting with these three central strands, each of which represents an aspect of the Pākehā dream of New Zealand, are many digressions which weave into the fictional world of the Lovelocks a web of historical figures (including Bully Hayes, Tītokowaru, Kimball Bent, even Shadbolt himself), locations, and events (the Hokitika *gold rush, the battle of Chunuk Bair).   RC

LOW, David (1891–1963), is secure 'as one of the master cartoonists of the twentieth century' (Colin Seymour-Ure) and author of an excellent autobiography. Born in Dunedin and brought up in Christchurch, he drew cartoons from a very early age and worked from the age of 15 in New Zealand for *New Zealand *Truth*, *Canterbury Times* and others, before moving to the Sydney *Bulletin* in 1911 and gaining notoriety for caricatures of the Australian Prime Minister, Billy Hughes. In 1919 Low was appointed to the London *Star*, also drawing for *Punch* before joining Beaverbrook's *Evening Standard*, having stipulated total political freedom. There his witty derision of European fascism (the 'Nasties') and England's blundering myopic 'Colonel Blimps' gained him world syndication, except for being blacklisted in Germany and Italy. Before and during World War 2 his cartoons gave vivid expression to the dark tragedy of those times and dramatised British defiance with succinct force, like a populist focusing of Churchill's patrician eloquence. 'We shall fight (just in case there's any mistake)', 'Very well, alone' and 'Bombs on Germany' fused verbal phrase with visual image with an intensity that made the message seem an absolute. It is little exaggeration to say that Low's strutting Hitler, pompous Colonel Blimp and, after the war, lumbering cart-horse Trade Union created images that still shape responses to those eras.

In 1949 Low moved to the Labour *Daily Herald*, and in 1952 to the Liberal *Manchester Guardian*. He received honorary doctorates from the universities of New Brunswick and Leicester and accepted a knighthood in 1962.

His verbal gifts made him a good broadcaster, on the BBC's Pacific Service, 1941–44, and an outstanding autobiographer, with *Low's Autobiography*, 1956. There his irreverent and colourful narrative is further enlivened by a habit of memorable simile. Richard Seddon 'always acted heartily, as though he had just dug up a large nugget', Sir Joseph Ward 'always dressed as though he had a lunch engagement at Downing Street', phrases as reminiscent of the skills of P.G. Wodehouse as of Low's own caricaturist's art. In such interaction between visual and verbal, Low's best successor in New Zealand is probably Tom *Scott.

Low's Autobiography gives full credit to his New Zealand upbringing, in 'the middle of a twenty year period of bold radicalism', for shaping his fearless socialism and independence of mind. Low is subject of a book by Colin Seymour-Ure and Jim Schroff (1985) and was celebrated in an exhibition, 'Kiwi cartoonist on Hitler's blacklist', that toured New Zealand 1995–96, with an valuable catalogue by Susan E. Foster, Colin Seymour-Ure and John Roberts. The David Low Fellowships annually enable outstanding New Zealand journalists to study at Oxford University and participate in a Reuter Foundation programme.   RR

LOWRY, Robert W. (Bob) (1912–63), *typographer, printer and publisher, was born in Thames. He began printing at Auckland GS, where he became friends with Denis *Glover (whose development as a typographer he influenced strongly). He enrolled at Auckland University College in 1931 and printed all four issues of *Phoenix* (1932–33), introducing to New Zealand modern printing practices derived from English typographers such as Stanley Morison and Eric Gill. Lowry also printed a notable edition of *Kiwi* (1932) and Allen *Curnow's first book, *Valley of Decision* (1933), for the Auckland University College Students' Association Press. Due to business mismanagement and political radicalism, however, he was proscribed by the university and moved briefly to Christchurch where he assisted Glover with the fledgling *Caxton Club Press. Back in Auckland he established the Unicorn Press in partnership with R.A.K. *Mason. But after the publication (by Spearhead Publishers) of Mason's *No New Thing: Poems 1924–29* (1934)—a superbly designed book, probably Lowry's masterpiece—he fell out with Mason and went into partnership with Ronald Holloway (see *Griffin Press). Among Unicorn's publications were T.I.S. [B.E. *Baughan], *People in Prison*; D'Arcy *Cresswell, *Lyttelton Harbour*; Arthur Sewell, *Katherine Mansfield*; and Frank *Sargeson, *Conversation with My Uncle* (all 1936). When this partnership in turn broke up, Lowry briefly established the Phillips Press in Devonport which printed A.R.D. *Fairburn's parody of Michael Joseph Savage, *The Sky is a Limpet* (1939). In 1940–41 Lowry attended Auckland Teachers' College, where he printed a noteworthy issue of *Manuka*, the college magazine, including the first published poems of Keith *Sinclair and Kendrick *Smithyman.

During a stint in the army 1942–44 Lowry produced a divisional magazine, *Kiwi*, under the aegis of the Army

Educational Welfare Service for the 2nd NZEF in New Caledonia. After the war he worked briefly as a teacher before establishing the Pelorus Press (1945–53) whose publications included Fairburn's *How to Ride a Bicycle in Seventeen Lovely Colours* (1947), described by Glover as 'hot-house tropical typography, where a flamboyant lunacy burgeons on every page' (*Book* 8, 1946). Pelorus also published first collections of poems by Smithyman (*Seven Sonnets*, 1946), and Hubert *Witheford (*Shadow of the Flame*, 1950), printed the magazine *Here & Now* (1949–57), and several books for Caxton, including *Speaking for Ourselves*, ed. Sargeson (1945), and Greville *Texidor's *These Dark Glasses* (1949). Financial problems forced Lowry to leave Pelorus and set up the Pilgrim Press (1954–61) where he published Maurice *Duggan's *Immanuel's Land* (1956), the Fairburn and Glover collaboration *Poetry Harbinger* (1958), O.E. *Middleton's *The Stone and Other Stories* (1959), and printed the literary magazine *Mate* and several satirical pamphlets by Curnow. Hurricane House and Wakefield Press were other establishments with which Lowry was briefly associated as printer. At the time of his death he was preparing for publication Hone *Tuwhare's first collection *No Ordinary Sun* (1964). Glover wrote in 1946: 'If typography is a word that some of us now understand, the credit is Bob Lowry's. That we have not only a more general interest in the appearance of printed matter, not only a few critics of typography but several zealous practitioners, is almost entirely due to the impetus provided by Lowry in the early thirties'. Peter Hughes in a 1995 conference paper summed up Lowry's career thus: 'He founded, partnered, or was associated with no fewer than fourteen presses in his 35-year career as printer, publisher, and typographer.... Typographically his "excesses"—such as the works produced for Fairburn—have been singled out for comment to the exclusion of others, but his classicly inspired design is equally assured'. (See also Peter Hughes, '"Sneers, Jeers ... and Red Rantings", Bob Lowry's Early Printing at Auckland University College', *Turnbull Library Record*, Vol. 22, No. 1, May 1989.) Lowry was known for his many friendships and almost legendary hospitality among New Zealand writers. PS

LYE, Len (1901–80), was a visual artist and prose-poet who earned an international reputation in the 1930s–50s for his kinetic sculptures and experimental film making. He pioneered 'direct film'—that is, manipulation of film to create images without photography. His kinetic sculptures were articulated so that they moved in any breeze, or sometimes under their own power. In both forms he was preoccupied with the abstract beauty of motion, which he called 'kinaesthesia'.

Born in Christchurch, Lye was educated at Wellington Technical College and briefly at Christchurch College of Art, where he was influenced by Māori forms. He experimented with kinetic sculpture in the early 1920s, while living in Auckland, Australia and Samoa. He moved to London in 1926, becoming involved with the Surrealist movement and with writers such as Robert Graves, and took part in the 1936 Surrealist Exhibition. His first book was published in England in 1930. In 1944 he settled in New York, working in conventional documentary film making for some years before returning to experimental film and sculpture in the 1950s, when he exhibited in Europe and USA. He remained in New York, with occasional visits to New Zealand.

Some of his theoretical and creative writing is collected in *Figures of Motion: Selected Writings*, ed. Wystan *Curnow and Roger Horrocks (1984). The prose-poems are almost frenetically allusive in colloquial phrases, in a way that now recalls Joyce and Beckett. Some are included in *An Anthology of New Zealand Poetry in English* (1997), Lye's first such recognition. JH

LYTTLETON, Edith ('G.B. Lancaster') (1873–1945), was one of New Zealand's most widely read popular novelists overseas from the 1900s to the 1940s. Born near Epping in Tasmania, she grew up after 1879 on her parents' sheep station, 'Rokeby', at Rakaia near Ashburton, and in the early 1900s began to contribute short stories regularly to the *New Zealand Illustrated Magazine*, the Sydney *Bulletin* and the Melbourne-based *Australasian*. The need for economic independence, after the death of her father in 1897 and the decline of 'Rokeby', was a major influence on her determination to become a professional writer. However, because of her mother's disapproval she was forced to write under a pseudonym—at first, Keron Hale, then (after the revelation of her identity in the *Illustrated Magazine* in 1901) G.B. Lancaster—and until the 1930s she refused all requests for interviews, photographs or biographical information.

Partly in reaction to her restricted Victorian upbringing, which confined her reading to improving literature for young women, she was passionately drawn to male writers who took Empire as their theme: *Kipling, Stevenson, and later Jack London and Conrad. Kipling's early India-based *Plain Tales from the Hills*, in particular, were a powerful influence on her early stories, which explored the often violent lives and codes of conduct of back-country sheep and cattle *station workers in Otago and Southland, against a harsh environment which she saw as formative of the distinctive colonial qualities of self-reliance, courage and physical vigour. Her first book, *Sons o' Men* (1904), was a collection of such tales. Although few copies reached New Zealand, it was widely read and praised in England and (especially) in the United States, where reviewers (although puzzled by the New Zealand vernacular on which she drew) were quick to make comparisons with American frontier fiction. Her next two novels—*A Spur to Smite* (1905), set in in New Zealand, *Australia and Samoa, and *The Tracks We Tread* (1907), which returned to the remote South Island setting of *Sons o' Men*—were similarly well received overseas, although local reaction, emphasising the 'virility' of their characterisation and style, was mixed.

In 1909 'Rokeby' was sold, and Lyttleton accompanied her mother and sister to London, where she was based until 1925. She had completed two further novels before leaving New Zealand—*The Altar Stairs* (1908), set in the Solomon Islands, and an Australian 'frontier' novel, *Jim of the Ranges* (1910)—and shortly after her arrival in England published *The Honourable Peggy* (1911), an English touring romance exploring the difference between British and *Canadian character. Two years later she published her first really substantial novel, an epic of law and order on the Canadian north-west frontier, entitled *The Law-Bringers* (1913), based on a visit to the region prompted by her American publishers. In the wake of its success, all of her earlier books were reprinted, and she was able to break into the then flourishing English and American magazine markets. During World War 1 she became actively involved in soldier support organisations, visited Belgium and France, and wrote journalism. Two further novels appeared later in the decade—*Fool Divine* (1917), a Cuban-based political romance, and *The Savignys* (1918), an English political romance—but between 1915 and 1925 she mainly wrote short stories and serials, almost all of them set in Canada, Australia and New Zealand, for which she could now command good prices. In the early 1920s she also began to break into the Hollywood film market, and three of her novels—*The Altar Stairs*, *Jim of the Ranges* and *The Law-Bringers*—were made into silent films.

However, in 1924 Lyttleton's writing career went into an abrupt decline after the deaths, within six months, of her sister and mother. For the rest of her life she lived an unsettled, wandering existence, travelling alone between New Zealand, Australia, North America, England and Europe. In 1926 she returned to New Zealand for four years, and in the late 1920s after a visit to Australia began to write the first of four substantial historical romances published between 1933 and 1943. *Pageant*, set in nineteenth-century Tasmania where she was born, was eventually published in 1933, fifteen years after her previous novel and ten years after her name had ceased to appear regularly in short story magazines, and it effectively inaugurated a second writing career. A bestseller in mid-Depression United States and winner of the Australian Literature Society's Gold Medal for the best Australian novel of its year, it was followed by a historical romance set in late nineteenth-century Yukon, *The World Is Yours* (1934). At the end of 1933, with the idea of a 'dominion-historical' series of novels now firmly in mind, Lyttleton returned to New Zealand again to research and write what was to become her best-known New Zealand book, *Promenade* (1938), a vivid three-generational historical romance of nineteenth-century settlement in New Zealand, set in Kororareka, Auckland and Canterbury.

Much of *Promenade* was written during a two-year period spent in Australia, and in 1938 Lyttleton left New Zealand for the last time, travelling to England via Nova Scotia, where she assembled materials for her last novel, *Grand Parade* (1943), a 'dominion-historical' romance of the British settlement of Halifax in the eighteenth and nineteenth centuries. However by the end of the 1930s Lyttleton's health was in decline, and during World War 2 she found herself trapped in England, not strong enough to travel back to New Zealand, although she struggled to assist in the war effort as she had during World War 1. Shortly after completing her last novel on a remote farm in the north of England she suffered a serious relapse from which she never fully recovered, and she died in London shortly before the end of the war.

Throughout her career Lyttleton saw herself as trapped between the popular novelist she had to be in order to survive by her writing and the serious novelist she always aspired to be. Her central subject was Empire: in particular, the kinds of society and the kinds of moral character and national identity taking shape during the process of colonial settlement. Her earlier male-centred fiction tends to idealise the process. However her later books—whose titles suggest Thackeray's *Vanity Fair* and whose power-seeking male egoists evoke another of her favourite authors, George Meredith—register an increasingly ironic, feminist perspective on the triumphalism of Empire, articulated through a succession of deeply intelligent central female characters, at once its bruised survivors and its dispassionate observers.   TS

M

Maarama, Te, appeared in place of the University of Auckland Students' Association annual *Kiwi in 1975 and featured poetry, short fiction, photographs and illustrations by students.   SH

McALPINE, Rachel (1940–), poet, novelist and playwright, was born in Fairlie, where her father was a vicar. Educated at Christchurch GHS, Canterbury University College and Victoria University, she holds a BA (Hons) and Diploma in Education. From 1994 to 1995 she lectured at Kyoto's Doshisha Women's University .

McAlpine began writing poetry in 1974. Elizabeth Caffin, in *OHNZLE, groups her debut collection, *Lament for Ariadne* (1975), alongside Lauris *Edmond's and Elizabeth *Smither's first books, as markers of an important new era for women's poetry. By 1988 McAlpine had published six further collections: *Stay at the Dinner Party* (1977), *Fancy Dress* (1978), *House Poems* (1980), *Recording Angel* (1983), *Thirteen Waves* (1986) and *Selected Poems* (1988). Her lyrical, apparently effortless, verse, makes the personal and local engaging: 'Some days Wellington behaves—/ the air is sedimentary, / and workmen smoke on girders / and forget to demolish Lambton Quay' ('Energy Crisis'). Its unpretentious chattiness is complemented by witty and imaginative wordplay, although some critics have commented on a tone of excitability in her assertion of herself as a woman. *Tourist in Kyoto* (1993), which is suffused with *Japanese iconography, pays particular attention to the haiku.

McAlpine's first play, *The Stationary Sixth Form Poetry Trip* (1980), explored New Zealand adolescence through the medium of a sixth form class's reinterpretation of Coleridge's 'Ancient Mariner'. Another large-cast play for young actors, *Driftwood* (1985), incorporating surfers and break-dancers, followed, and then *Peace Offering* (1988) and *Power Play* (1990). McAlpine's facility with dialogue works well on radio: the powerful drama *The Life Fantastic*, documenting a young girl's shift from fantasy to violence, was followed by *Cats Don't Marry, Quite Nice Really* and *The Op Shop Quartet*.

Three novels, *The Limits of Green* (1986), *Running Away from Home* (1987) and *Farewell Speech* (1990), have polarised critics. In the futuristic *Limits*, a pair of greenies defeat the evil industrialists and destroy their lethal enterprises. Fay *Weldon was moved to praise McAlpine as the only New Zealand writer taking risks and letting herself go, but Mark *Williams commented that *Limits'* 'magic realism without the realism merely makes one nostalgic for the tradition derived from Sargeson such writing is supposedly replacing' (*JNZL 5, 1987). *Running*, which reuses *Limits'* setting, was judged more successful, with Anne *French praising its 'pace, narrative drive, crackling, energetic prose, and … satisfactory resolution' by comparison with its overloaded and 'weakly mythic' predecessor (*Landfall 163, 1987). *Farewell Speech* steps back into the past to fictionalise the lives of three historical characters, the passionate suffragists Kate Sheppard and Ada Wells, and Ada's eccentric daughter Bim. McAlpine felt *Farewell* 'got nearer to the truth than … a biography', but critics decried its inaccuracy and its major slurs against the women. McAlpine remained unbowed, calling her detractors 'modern puritans … trying to freeze-frame [Sheppard] in one position, in an act of prayer' (*NZ Listener, 18 Sep. 1993). She has also published one volume of short stories for children, *Maria and Mrs Kominski* (1990).   PM

McCAHON, Colin (1919–87), is undoubtedly New Zealand's most important modern artist, for his treatment of the local landscape, idiosyncratic adaptations from the history of art, integration of words and texts into painting, and interest in and use of Māori culture. His example is acknowledged as definitive of the situation of the artist in New Zealand.

Born in Timaru and educated in Dunedin, McCahon received only minimal art training under the guidance of Russell *Clark and Robert Nettleton Field, before embarking on his career as a painter, supporting himself with odd jobs which found him moving between Nelson, Dunedin and Wellington. It is in these years that he met and spent time with Toss *Woollaston, Doris Lusk, Rodney Kennedy and his future wife, Anne Hamblett. McCahon was first noticed for his starkly elemental landscapes of the Otago Peninsula and his crudely painted biblical scenes, whose participants were relocated into the bare hills of the South Island. When these were exhibited by local art societies and by The Group in Christchurch, a pattern was quickly set whereby an emerging cultural intelligentsia championed the artist in the face of incomprehension from the general public and the conservative establishment. In 1953 McCahon took up a position at Auckland City Art Gallery. He became a leading figure in the Auckland art scene as an artist, curator and teacher, through his time at the gallery (1953–64), at Elam School of Fine Arts (1964–70) and as a full-time artist from 1970.

From 1953 until he stopped painting in the early 1980s, McCahon's works engage with the language of modernism—in particular the example of cubism, de Stijl and American abstract expressionism—but also register his refusal of formalist abstraction, in preference for painting which conveys meaning, via the incorporation of language, to address central metaphysical and political issues. Over time his works grew in scale, thus emphasising the public nature of his address, but increasingly he preferred a restricted palette of black and white and made greater use of texts borrowed from the Bible, from poetry and popular song, and from traditional Māori sources.

Although he does not use his own words in his painting, McCahon was a powerful writer, in insightful commentaries on his work published in exhibition catalogues and journals (*Auckland City Art Gallery Quarterly* and *Landfall*). He has enjoyed the critical attention and support of key literary figures, including Charles *Brasch, James K. *Baxter, John *Caselberg (whose poetry he has used in major works like *The Wake*, 1959) and Wystan *Curnow, whose exhibition of McCahon's word and number paintings, *I Will Need Words*, travelled to Australia and Edinburgh in 1984. McCahon has drawn extensively on the oral traditions and history of Māori, notably in his adaptation of narratives and songs included in Matire Kereama's *The Tail of the Fish*, a collection of texts relating to the Aupōuri of Northland, which serves as the basis for works like *The Lark's Song* (1969).   CB

McCARTEN, Anthony (1961–), is a commercially successful playwright, also writing poetry and fiction. He was born in New Plymouth. His first play was 'Invitation to a Second Class Carriage' (Depot Theatre, Wellington, 1984). His next, 'Yellow Canary Mazurka', was selected for the 1986 New Zealand Playwrights' Workshop and premièred the following year at Circa in Wellington. At the workshop McCarten met Stephen *Sinclair and, in six weeks in 1987, they wrote 'Ladies' Night', a play about male strippers, which opened at Mercury in December of that year and went on to become the most commercially successful play in New Zealand's theatre history. It has been translated into six languages and was the most successful touring production in Britain between 1990 and 1994. Subsequent plays have been 'Pigeon English' (Playwrights' Workshop, 1988; Depot, 1989), 'Weed' (Circa, 1990), 'Via Satellite' (Circa, 1991, and the winner of the *NZ Listener* Best Play and Wellington Theatre Critics' Best Production awards for 1991), 'Hang on a Minute, Mate', an adaptation from a series of novels by Barry *Crump (Downstage, 1992), 'Let's Spend the Night Together' (Bats, 1994, and afterwards toured nationally), 'FILTH (Failed in London, Try Hong Kong)' (Circa, 1995) and 'Four Cities' (Los Angeles, 1996). As well as 'Ladies' Night', McCarten has co-written with Stephen Sinclair 'Ladies' Night 2' (which relates the fortunes of the characters five years on) and 'Legless'. He has directed two short films: *Nocturne in a Room* (1992) and *Fluff* (1995) and has published a short story collection, *A Modest Apocalypse* (1991), and a number of poems.   SG

MACAULAY, Thomas Babington (1800–59), poet, politician and great British historian, seems now in some danger of being remembered principally for 'Macaulay's New Zealander', his famous vision of the future ruins of British civilisation under the gaze of 'some traveller from New Zealand'. In fact, he intended the image as a tribute to the 'long dominion' of the Church of Rome, in a review of Leopold Ranke's *History of the Popes of Rome* in the *Edinburgh Review*, October 1840: 'She was great and respected before the Saxon had set foot in Britain.... And she may still exist in undiminished vigour when some traveller from New Zealand shall, in the midst of a vast solitude, take his stand on a broken arch of London Bridge to sketch the ruins of St. Paul's.' Macaulay may have had in mind a returned colonist, since emigration was a topical subject in 1840; or it is equally likely that he meant a Māori (then the dominant sense, for instance, of '*New Zealander'). He was liberal-minded enough for such an idea. Later in the review he denies that the Catholic Church has any special claims in theological matters by the argument that in spiritual questions 'we do not see that a highly educated European … is more likely to be in the right than a Blackfoot Indian'.   RR

McCAULEY, Sue (1941–), fiction writer, scriptwriter and journalist, was born in Dannevirke, grew up on a farm in rural southern Hawkes Bay and was a boarder at Nelson GC. She worked as a copywriter and journalist in Napier, Wellington, New Plymouth and Christchurch, beginning her writing career with radio and TV plays and short stories in the 1970s. Her first novel *Other Halves* (1982) won both the Wattie Book of the Year Award and the New Zealand Book Award for Fiction. An autobiographically based account of a relationship between a separated Pākehā mother and a much younger Māori man, it explored ethnic, gender, age and class differences. It has been frequently reprinted, selling more than 20 000 copies, and was made into a feature *film. Her second novel, *Then Again* (1986), is set on an offshore subtropical island and deals with the increasingly intertwined lives of several residents. *Bad Music* (1990) focuses on the relationships between an ageing rock musician, a young woman half his age and the girl's mother. *A Fancy Man* (1996) also involves an apparent mismatch between an older man and a much younger woman. McCauley's novels are characterised by a mix of humour, realism and compassion, with strong sympathy for the underdog. She has also written many scripts for film, television and radio and has published numerous short stories. She has worked as a teacher of scriptwriting and fiction and as a judge of story competitions. She edited (with Richard McLachlan) *Erotic Writing* (1992), and wrote the text of *Escape from Bosnia: Aza's Story* (1996), the narrative being worked up from recorded interviews. She was writer-in-residence at the universities of Auckland (1986) and Canterbury (1993). After living in various parts of the North Island 1970s–80s she moved with her husband to Christchurch in 1991.   PS

McCORMICK, E.H. (Eric Hall) (1906–95), born in Taihape, became New Zealand's pre-eminent literary and cultural scholar, rivalled in the depth of his historical comprehension only by J.C. *Beaglehole, and without peer in his grasp of the nation's cultural evolution. He signalled his abiding commitment to the study of New Zealand culture early, in his 1929 MA thesis at Victoria University College, 'Literature in New

Zealand'. His insights were subsequently amplified at Cambridge with guidance from F.R. and Q.D. Leavis and the historian of ideas Basil Willey, in the MLitt thesis 'Literature in New Zealand: an essay in cultural criticism'. The thesis methodically explores New Zealand literature through the idea that literature is a function of cultural identity and integrity, themselves the products of complex historical, intellectual and social pressures. *Hocken Librarian and later in the 1930s assistant to the Dominion Archivist, McCormick was made editor of *Centennial Publications in 1939–40, and in the Centennial series published a revision of his earlier thesis as *Letters and Art in New Zealand* (1940), his chief aim being 'to bring out their relation to social changes in the years since European discovery'. Alert to whatever is distinctively New Zealand in the works considered, this watershed in criticism marks the end of belletrism and the start of profounder *nationalistic cultural preoccupations. Its status as a classic text is unlikely to be challenged.

Having spent the war in the infantry, the medical corps and army archives, becoming finally Chief War Archivist (1945–47), McCormick was briefly senior lecturer in English at Auckland University College (1947–50), resigning when he realised that the constraints of teaching imperilled his freedoms as a researcher. In a later context he told Michael *King of his independence, '… I refuse to be a specialist … I decide what I want to do and then I find a means of doing it.' In a number of later academic roles he was senior research fellow in the University of New Zealand (1951–52), editor of publications and senior research fellow in the University of Auckland (1963–64) and honorary research fellow in history at Auckland (1965–85). He was also involved in researching and curating some major art exhibitions, *Frances Hodgkins and Her Circle* (1954; with the monograph and catalogue *Works of Frances Hodgkins in New Zealand*), *The Land and The People* that toured Russia in 1958, *Frances Hodgkins, Paintings and Drawings* (1959), and *The Two Worlds of Omai* (1977). His major achievements, however, were in his books.

A 'NZ nationalist whose great theme has been exile, in either direction or both', as Dennis *McEldowney has deftly put it, McCormick dealt in all his major works with the relation of New Zealand and South Pacific cultures to the source-cultures of Britain and Europe. Ahead of his time he exemplifies the postcolonial theorist, in jargon-free writing of a stylistic purity and narrative richness rare in contemporary English-language prose. The southern cultures are related to the northern cultures dialectically; the exile is not in isolation but in interaction. In *New Zealand Literature: A Survey* (1959), an updating of *Letters and Art,* McCormick reminds us that 'the literary antiquarian' will reflect that the Pacific journals of ★Cook's voyaging companions 'numbered Samuel Johnson among their original public, that they stood in the libraries of Jane Austen's country houses, that they fed the mind and imagination of the youthful Coleridge'.

So it is that in *The Expatriate: A Study of Frances Hodgkins* (1954) McCormick studies 'the relations between Frances ★Hodgkins and New Zealand' from her departure to Europe in 1901 to her death in 1947, expecting the book to 'throw some light on a phase of New Zealand history that may not yet have passed'. His later *Portrait of Frances Hodgkins* (1981) and *Late Attachment: Frances Hodgkins and Maurice Garnier* (1988), while centrally concerned with the European cultural context of the artistic imagination in the early twentieth century, are aimed at antipodean readers. It is sometimes observed that McCormick is not primarily an art critic in these works. It needs only to be said that few art critics are capable of recreating the conditions of the artistic life as he has done, paving the way for alternative aesthetic approaches. *Eric ★Lee-Johnson* (1956) focuses on the simple rural and natural symbolism in the work of a painter who like McCormick had spent time in England and returned, seeing New Zealand with eyes that had learned to see elsewhere. The same process is at the heart of *The Inland Eye: A Sketch in Visual Autobiography* (1959), recounting how McCormick's own eyes that had learned to see in Taihape were later informed by the art galleries and architectures of New Zealand and Europe as steps in his vision of his own country.

So it is again that McCormick makes subjects of ★Grey, ★Hocken and ★Turnbull, three antiquarians and book collectors whose libraries became so important to him in his research and the development of his historical imagination. *The Fascinating Folly: Dr Hocken and his Fellow Collectors* (1961) recounts the achievements of all three in establishing their cultural repositories. Turnbull, whose phrase for book-collecting 'the fascinating folly' gave McCormick his title, and who especially among the three built up the New Zealand component of his collection, is the subject of the later monumental *Alexander Turnbull: His Life, His Circle, His Collections* (1974). McCormick has described this book as 'the most arduous job I've ever undertaken. I used to think it was a fight to the death between Alexander Turnbull and myself …', presumably because of the threat posed to McCormick's meticulousness of method by the plethora of documentation in the Turnbull family archives. The book is remarkable for the power of its discipline and the recurrence of certain motifs central to McCormick's intercultural vision like the family's endless journeys between New Zealand and England. It is one of the four

finest things he wrote (the others being *Letters and Art, Omai* and *The Friend of Keats*).

Travellers' accounts of cultural encounters have an obvious place in the framework of McCormick's interests, and he edited two such works, Edward Markham's *New Zealand or Recollections of It* (1963), and closer to his enthusiasms the records of a painter, Augustus ★Earle's *Narrative of a Residence in New Zealand; Journal of a Residence in Tristan da Cunha* (1966). More important is *Omai, Pacific Envoy* (1977). Omai, taken from Raiatea in 1774 by Cook's second expedition to the Pacific, spent three years in England before being returned to Huahine on Cook's next expedition. His reception and experiences in England, conditioned by the same mindset that commissioned the voyages of discovery, enables McCormick to present him 'as a kind of catalyst, provoking discussion of many issues—moral, philosophical, religious —concerning eighteenth-century society. In his person, moreover, he dramatized dilemmas which still confront Europeans in their dealings with Pacific peoples.' Here and in *The Friend of Keats: A Life of Charles Armitage Brown* (1989), McCormick's historical and cultural understanding is at its most lucidly profound. His interest in Brown began in 1923 while he was still a student at Wellington College, his interest in Omai in 1935 while Hocken Librarian. Both works had long, patient gestations. It was while living with Brown in Hampstead that Keats wrote his major Odes, among other things, and their friendship was a long and close one. Brown's understanding of Keats underlies Milnes's great *Life* of the poet. Years after Keats's death Brown migrated in 1841 to a raw New Plymouth as a founding settler and within a year died there deeply disillusioned, believing himself to have been deceived by the Plymouth Company with false expectations. Through Brown, McCormick writes Keats into the cultural history of New Zealand, and the chapters on the two friends and on Keats's death in Rome are among the finest things available on the poet. It is an extraordinary culmination to a career spent clarifying what exile means, and making it something worth having.

Excellent recent studies of McCormick are the essays of *Writing a New Country* edited by James Ross, Linda Gill and Stuart McRae. *An Absurd Ambition: Autobiographical Writings: E.H. McCormick* has been edited by Dennis McEldowney, the title McCormick's own ironic recollection of his youthful ambition to be a writer.

KA

McCORMICK, Gary (1951–), is a poet, entertainer and television performer whose street readings and collaborations with Sam ★Hunt have done much to popularise poetry in performance and give poetry life outside the classroom. Born in Upper Hutt and educated at Titahi Bay, Mana College and (briefly) Victoria University, he began writing poetry in 1968. His published volumes are *Gypsies* (with Jon Benson, 1974), *Naked and Nameless* (1976), *Poems for the Red Engine* (1978), *Poems by Request* (1979), *Scarlet Letters* (1980), *Zephyr* (1982) and *Lost at Sea* (1995). He also wrote *Performance—A Guide to the Performing Arts in New Zealand* for the Department of Internal Affairs (1979) and the satiric 'secret diary of Jacques Chirac', *Honey, I blew up the atoll* (with Scott Wilson, 1995).

McCormick's poems reveal more emotional anxiety than the irreverent and compulsively ludic public persona. Brian *Turner called those in his latest volume 'fraught, distraught, tender, now and then a bit sentimental'. A deft sense of locality and ordinary New Zealand life is characteristic, with particular empathy with the sea, its shores and weather, which the poet attributes to his experience as a surfer. The poems' lyricism and confessional drama complemented Sam Hunt's incantatory balladic resonance in their many pub readings together in the 1970s, a partnership which they renewed, with the greater promotional savvy of middle age, in their successful 'Roaring Forties' tour of 1995. This attracted sell-out audiences and produced spin-offs of a glossy illustrated souvenir book, a TV documentary and new volumes of poetry by both.

McCormick's roguish satiric patter at readings led to work as MC with rock bands and festivals, developing through public debating (with Tom *Scott and others), solo comedy and after-dinner speaking to national fame as television frontman, personality and performer in commercials.   RR

MACDONALD, Caroline (1948–97), children's novelist and playwright, was born and educated in Taranaki, and lived in South Australia where she worked as an editor of teaching material. Having grown up by far the youngest in a family of four, she had a particular interest in isolated characters. Her work also explores concepts of time and issues such as environmental pollution. She won the 1984 Esther Glen Medal for her first novel, *Elephant Rock* (1983), in which the permanence of the rock is contrasted to the passing of life, as a 12-year-old, through time-slips and identity changes, comes to understand her dying mother's preference for the quality of life rather than its length. Winning the 1983 Choysa Bursary helped Macdonald write *Visitors* (1984), the 1985 Children's Book of the Year. Here, a withdrawn boy and a physically disabled but outgoing girl join in communicating with aliens who need help to escape from our world. Even more successful is the futuristic *The Lake at the End of the World* (1988), shortlisted three

times for awards in New Zealand and overseas and winning the 1989 Alan Marshall Prize for Children's Literature in Australia. Technically interesting through the dual narration of isolated teenagers, the novel explores the political nature of people faced with post-cataclysmic problems.

Other novels include *Yellow Boarding House* (1985), which realistically treats the drug world; *Speaking to Miranda* (1990), a search for racial origins in Australia and New Zealand; and *The Eye Witness* (1991), another futuristic novel exploring a dystopian society. *Joseph's Boat* (1988) is a long short story illustrated by Chris Gaskin (who won the 1989 Russell Clark Medal), portraying a lonely boy's attempt to row to the mainland. Other successful titles include *Earthgames* (1988) and *The Seventh Head* (1988). *Hostilities* (1991) is a book of short stories ranging from the realistic to the futuristic. Macdonald wrote six one-act plays, *Act It Out* (1988).

                                                    DH

McDONALD, Georgina (1904–59), a Southland historical novelist, was born (Blaikie) into a Scots farming family at Waitahuna. She took an MA at Otago University, taught at secondary schools, and after marriage in 1934 to a Presbyterian minister was involved in church work and became president of the Southland Presbyterial Association. Her historical novel *Grand Hills for Sheep* (1949) won the *Otago Daily Times* competition marking the Otago Centennial. It is an account of Scottish Presbyterian pioneers in Southland, the Gaelic-speaking McCallum family leaving Scotland to seek 'grand hills for sheep' in New Zealand. McDonald's theme is hard work and Calvinist moral rigour, with a particular focus on the life of heroine Shona. The book was a New Zealand best-seller, reprinted several times to sell 15 000 copies. Her second novel, *Stinson's Bush* (1954), was not so well received. This is an account of a Protestant Irish family in Southland, again with the emphasis on hard work, focused especially on the lives of the women, who bear children and labour ceaselessly to ensure the family's success in their new environment. McDonald also wrote non-fiction, notably *The Flame Unquenched* (1956), a history of the Presbyterian Church in Southland 1856–1956. She wrote for *The Outlook*, the official journal of the Presbyterian Church.   ALa

McELDOWNEY, Dennis (1926–), writer and publisher, was born in Wanganui and grew up in Christchurch. A congenital heart condition (he was a 'blue baby') kept him an invalid until the age of 24. An account of his medical adventures formed the subject of his first and probably best-known book, *The World Regained* (1957, 1976), which won the 1958 Hubert

Church Memorial Prize for prose. Educated by the Correspondence School, McEldowney was a freelance writer until he took a clerical job at the School of Physical Education in Dunedin, 1963–66. A diary of these Dunedin years was published as *Full of the Warm South* (1983). In 1966 he entered publishing as the first editor of *Auckland University Press, becoming managing editor from 1972 until his retirement in 1986, when he was awarded an honorary doctorate by the university. *Then and There: a 1970s diary* (1995) focused primarily on his activities as a publisher and on the Auckland scene. Most of his other books are either biographical or autobiographical in impulse. They include *Donald Anderson, A Memoir* (1966), about the brilliant but severely disabled young scholar; *Arguing with my Grandmother* (1973); and *Frank *Sargeson in His Time*, a short illustrated account (1976). *Shaking the Bee Tree* (1992) is his life with his wife Zoë Greenhough, also a 'blue baby', who died in 1990. He also edited *Presbyterians in Aotearoa: 1840–1990* (1990) and *An Absurd Ambition: Autobiographical Writings: E.H. *McCormick* (1996). McEldowney contributed the chapter on publishing, patronage and literary magazines in the *OHNZLE (1991, 1998) and has written reviews, commentaries and criticism for radio and many periodicals.   AM/PS

McGEE, Greg (1950–), theatre, television and film writer, was born in Oamaru and educated at Waitaki BHS and the University of Otago (LLB 1972). During his university years he also played rugby to the highest level, playing for his university, the province of Otago, the South Island, New Zealand Universities and the Junior All Blacks. He was twice an All Black trialist. Rugby provided both the setting for his spectacularly successful first play, *Foreskin's Lament, and the metaphor for a society in which old codes and hypocrisies were anatomised. Professional performances of *Foreskin's Lament* around the country in 1980 and 1981 happened to coincide with the political and civil upheaval leading up to the 1981 Springbok rugby tour of New Zealand, and McGee's humour, savagery and lament for lost innocence made the play provocative and influential far beyond the usual realms of theatre audiences. His second play, *Tooth and Claw* (first performed 1983; published 1984) drew on his legal qualifications and background to use a law office as a metaphor for society. He implies that lawyers and others, like rugby players, can ignore the unfortunate and bend the rules when it suits them. *Out in the Cold* (first performed 1983; published 1984) was based on his short story published in *Islands 27 (1979). A solo mother disguises herself as a man in order to get a job in the freezing works, where she becomes an effective mouthpiece for social and feminist critiques of the male working world. Unlike the earlier plays, 'Whitemen' (performed 1988) was a box office failure. In satirical farce, using revue-style caricature and energetic bad taste, Rugby Union administrators were lambasted for their decision to proceed with the 1985 All Black rugby tour of apartheid South Africa. (McGee wrote no further stage plays for a decade after 'Whitemen', although a new play called 'This Train I'm On' was workshopped in 1997, and is scheduled for production in 1999.) All McGee's stage plays are centrally concerned with the loss of collective values and individual altruism in an increasingly materialist and selfish society. Their dramaturgical power relies on vigorous comedy to relax an audience into familiar territory; then bitter paradoxes and social pain emerge to leave the audience uneasy about the society it shares with the characters of the plays. McGee's liberal protagonists face the same anguished dilemma, since affection for such established structures as the world of rugby, or the law, confounds the social critique. These overtly socio-political concerns have led McGee to television and film writing, intending thereby to reach a wider popular audience. His television writing has won several awards, including Best Drama Writer for his two most significant political documentary dramas: 'Erebus: The Aftermath' (1987), which examined the judicial inquiry into the Mt Erebus air crash, and 'Fallout' (1994), a dramatisation (with Tom *Scott) of the ANZUS anti-nuclear row with the US and its political implications for the Labour government of David Lange. 'Free Enterprise' (1982) was a drama; and McGee has written for a number of series, including *Roche, Marlin Bay*, and *Cover Story*. He also writes for film, notably the award-winning *Old Scores* (1991), co-scripted with Dean *Parker.   DC

McINDOE, John, see **John McIndoe Ltd**.

McKAY, Frank (Francis M.) (1920–91), critic, editor, poet and priest, is best known for *The Life of James K. *Baxter* (1990), which won the New Zealand Book Award for Non-Fiction in 1991. Judiciously evaluating Baxter's literary achievement and personal life, eschewing both sensationalism and hagiography, the biography showed the benefits of McKay's friendship with the poet, the access he was given to private materials, and his own astute critical judgment and spiritual insight.

Born in Dunedin, McKay was educated at the Catholic St Thomas's Academy and St Kevin's College, both in Oamaru, and at Canterbury University College (1940), before ordination in the Society of Mary in 1948. Teaching at St Patrick's, Wellington, he also studied and tutored at Victoria University College, then gaining his PhD at Cambridge University (1962–65) for work on seventeenth-century religious poetry. Returning to lecture at Victoria, he published and taught increasingly in New Zealand literature, retiring as associate professor in 1985. He edited the first five volumes of *Poetry New Zealand* (1972–82) when it replaced *★New Zealand Poetry Yearbook*, and issues 1 and 3 of the *★Journal of New Zealand Literature* (1983, 1985). Writing perceptively of poets such as Alistair Te Ariki ★Campbell and Eileen ★Duggan, he focused mainly on Baxter, in, for instance, *James K. Baxter as Critic* (1978) or an essay in *★Landfall 137* (1981) on the Jerusalem poems.

McKay's generosity in friendship and his deep but non-judgmental spiritual commitment made him the confidant of many writers, the dedicatee of poems by, among others, Baxter ('Letters to Frank McKay') and Elizabeth ★Smither ('Listening to Gregorian chant in bed: for Frank McKay'), and the subject of poems and prose by, for instance, Lauris ★Edmond, celebrating his hospitable role in Wellington's unusually amiable literary world of the 1970s–80s: 'so we no longer lean our elbows / at Frank's narrow table, his trout mornay / steaming under the lifted spoon …'. His own verse was published in *Landfall* and elsewhere, and a small collection published as *Once* (★Wai-te-ata, 1985). He wrote eloquent poems on faith and literature ('St Jerome, Patron of Literary Men'), on friends ('Piha, for Maurice ★Shadbolt') and on the natural world ('Weasel', or his heartfelt fisherman's prayer for 'just one fish, Lord, / and not too small'). His last years were divided between work in Rome on the reform of the international Marist Order, and in Wellington on the Baxter biography. His extensive collection of Baxter materials and other private literary papers, including his own unpublished fiction and poetry, was left to Victoria University Library. RR

MACKAY, Jessie (1864–1938), was born in the Rakaia Gorge of Scottish parentage and educated in Christchurch. She has been described (by MacD.P. Jackson in *★OHNZLE*) as 'the first poet of any importance to be born in New Zealand'. In the introduction to her first collection, *The Spirit of the Rangatira and Other Ballads* (1889) she expressed the hope that at least a few of the poems 'might have a flavour of the colonial soil' from which they had sprung. The title poem of *The Sitter on the Rail and Other Poems* (1891) is a Kiplingesque satire on those who decline to involve themselves in the political concerns of the day and reflects Mackay's life-long commitment to prohibition, universal suffrage, Irish and Scottish Home Rule and liberal causes generally. She wrote on these as 'Lady Editor' of the *Canterbury Times* and was an active member of the Women's Christian Temperance Union and the National Council of Women. Her subsequent collections are *From the Maori*

Sea (1908), *Land of the Morning* (1909), *The Bride of the Rivers and Other Verses* (1926) and *Vigil* (1935), the title poem, 'Vigil: The Eve of April 10, 1919' referring to the first Prohibition Poll. Despite her reliance on reworkings of Longfellow, Tennyson, Swinburne and the Burnsian tradition of Scottish dialect ballad and song, Mackay achieved what Jackson calls 'greater metrical and verbal facility than any of her [New Zealand] predecessors' and a verse that at times 'taps unconscious yearnings that a Freudian analysis might explore'. She can also be seen as in some senses a nationalist poet, especially in her use of Māori mythology and subject matter and her treatment of contemporary social issues. 'We plowed a lonely furrow,' she wrote of the early New Zealand poets. Her puzzled reaction to *★Kowhai Gold* in 1930, 'No New Zealand', shows an awareness of what a national literature might consist of. Allen ★Curnow recognised this in his approving reference to her in his *★Book of New Zealand Verse* (1945), while Eileen ★Duggan wrote 'You have united an old tradition with a new loyalty, and blended without loss the heritage of one land with the ideals and aspirations of another.' This is a more balanced judgment than some recent ones.

A Voice on the Wind: The Story of Jessie Mackay by Nellie F.H. Macleod (1955) provides a selection of poems, as more briefly does *The New Place*, ed. Harvey ★McQueen (1993). JS

McLEAN, Denis (1930–), is a senior diplomat and author of a notable travel memoir, *The Long Pathway: Te Ara Roa* (1986). The account of a family walk along the eastern coastline from East Cape to Wellington, it is one of the best later expressions of New Zealand's tradition of environmental-philosophical journey narratives, sensitive in describing the land and in meditating on its significance. It is informative and eloquent on geology, personalities past and present, history, and especially on the earliest Māori–Pākehā encounters, narrated from a viewpoint—looking from the shore out to sea—that interestingly reverses the one familiar since ★Cook. Born in Napier, McLean was educated at Nelson College, Victoria University College (MSc 1954) and as a Rhodes Scholar at Oxford, then rising as public servant to be Secretary of Defence 1979–88 and Ambassador to Washington 1991–94. Besides numerous policy and strategic papers, he also published an essay in *What I Believe*, ed. Allan Thomson (1993), again based on the metaphor of the journey, this time as pilgrimage. RR

McLEAN, T.P. or **Terry** (Sir Terence Power) (1913–), has been New Zealand's most popular *★sports* writer for almost half a century, and received a knighthood in recognition of this service in 1997. Born at

Wanganui, educated at New Plymouth BHS, he entered journalism as a teenager in 1930, and after war service was sports editor, columnist, feature writer and senior rugby correspondent for the *New Zealand Herald* from 1946 to 1983. Reporting on more than fifty international rugby tours, he worked very successfully in the genre of the Tour Memoir, from *Bob Stuart's All Blacks* (1954) through classics like *Red Dragons of Rugby* (1969). Among nearly thirty popular books, the more reflective such as *New Zealand Rugby Legends* (1987) or *Silver Fern* (1990) show skills beyond the topical, while his biographical craft is probably best seen in *I, George Nepia* (with George Nepia, 1963). Clear narrative, an intimate though forthright tone, strong historical sense, expert knowledge and deft colouring with digressive anecdote and literary quotation constitute a satisfying commentary unmarred by sensationalism or cliché. Profiles of such controversial figures as Arthur Lydiard or Ces Blazey (in *The Best of McLean*, 1984) show a judiciousness and percipience that belie accusations of hagiography; and in a piece such as that on Jimmy Hunter (in *NZ Rugby Legends*) he puts sport into its full historical context of poverty, polio epidemic, the *Depression and the war. McLean is still, in his eighties, a vigorous and entertaining columnist.   RR

McLEOD, Jenny (1941–), composer and lyricist, was born in Wellington. Her first ambitious music-theatre work for children, *Earth and Sky* (1968), drew on a variety of indigenous and contemporary idioms to bring to life the Māori genesis myth (see *Rangi and Papa) from texts retranslated by the composer; it also utilised McLeod's immense organisational abilities, galvanising into action the town of Masterton. Its successor *Under the Sun* (1971), written partly in rock style for children and amateurs in Palmerston North to her own script, contemplated the history of the universe. In *Childhood* (1981) she used her own poems in ten short songs, as she did with *Dirge for Doomsday* (1984) for unaccompanied choir, and *Hymn for the Lady* (1986) for large and chamber choirs, flute, piano and percussion. William Blake provided the text for her major song-cycle *Through the World* (1982) for mezzo-soprano and piano. She has also set e.e. cummings and Edward Lear and texts by the Palmerston North scholar-poet W.S. Broughton, in an early song cycle *Epithalamia* (1964). Her incidental music ranges from radio plays by C.K. *Stead, *Dialogue on a Northern Shore* (1963), and James K. *Baxter, *Mr Brandywine Chooses a Gravestone* (1967), to plays by Shakespeare and Chekhov. Other music composed in association with well-known New Zealand writers includes the feature film score to *The Silent One* (1984), screenplay by Ian Mune based on the children's book by

Joy *Cowley, music for the TV series *Cuckooland* (1984), including some thirty satirical songs, each in a different popular style, with lyrics and screenplay by Margaret *Mahy, and the TV film score *The Haunting of Barney Palmer*, screenplay by Mahy, based on her award-winning book *The Haunting*. More recently McLeod has turned to Māori texts. *He Iwi Kotahi Tatou* (1993), for instance, is a dialogue between Māori and European New Zealanders for both large and chamber choirs, Māori singers and two pianos, settings of six poems in Māori which she wrote herself, including a *haka. The music as a whole is based on a traditional Māori tribal song 'Kati Ano Au', from Ngāti Rangi, which appears complete, set to a 'birdsong' and choral accompaniment, in the middle of the piece.   JMT

MACMILLAN BROWN, John, see **BROWN, John Macmillan**.

McNEISH, James (1931–), born in Auckland, is a novelist, playwright, journalist, broadcaster and biographer. He has travelled widely and his work reflects his knowledge of many lands. In 1958 he went to the UK as a deckhand on a Norwegian freighter. Travelling around Europe, he recorded folk music in twenty-one countries. He worked with Joan Littlewood in the Theatre Royal in the East End of London, and her spirit of socially committed drama left an impression not only on his plays but also on his novels. As a freelance journalist he also worked for the BBC, the *Guardian* and the *Observer*. In New Zealand, too, he has been a prolific writer for radio and newspapers.

For four years he lived and worked with Danilo Dolci, a courageous non-violent opponent of the Mafia, sometimes called 'the Gandhi of Sicily'. Out of this experience came *Fire under the Ashes* (1965), McNeish's clear, remarkably objective biographical account of Dolci.

His first book, *Tavern in the Town* (1957), is an almost formless series of anecdotes about New Zealand pubs, extensively researched and often of some historical interest, but with no acknowledgment of sources so that verification is difficult and reliability uncertain. *Mackenzie* (1970) is an ambitious novel based on the life of a legendary sheep-stealer who discovered a huge rich pasture in central Otago. Its strength lies less in the heroic portrayal of the protagonist, however, than in its study of the tensions and ambitions in small-town and rural settler communities. There is a suggestion of a symbolic or mystical perception, somewhat obscured by an imprecision of style. The novel was followed by a non-fiction book on the same subject, *The Mackenzie Affair* (1972), which retells the novel's tale twice more. The first part professes to be a historical account of Mackenzie, but is full of unauthenticated dialogue, so that it reads like fiction. The second part is a commentary on the legend, trying to separate fact from myth.

Much more successful was *The Glass Zoo* (1976), where McNeish revealed that he had remarkable narrative powers, carefully constructing a suspenseful tale which is part mystery story but also the account of a highly gifted child in an educational system which demands conformity—namely the British comprehensive school. The New Zealand teacher who narrates the story is also an outsider to the system, and the failure of both teacher and pupil to accept or to cope with the egalitarian ethos—well-meaning, but oppressive to unusual individuals—is sensitively narrated. McNeish showed strength and commitment in writing of such social issues. He combined his skill in analysing small communities with a touch of fantasy in the novel *Joy* (1982). It has many felicities in characterisation and humour, though some found its ultimate point unclear. Is it a study of small-town morality? A satire? An idyll? A Kafkaesque fantasy? The plot centres around an epidemic, which might or might not be real, and a doctor who initially seems threatening and dictatorial but later turns out to be an ideal of selflessness.

The next novel, *Lovelock* (1986), is another documentary fiction, telling the story of another legendary figure, the famous athlete who won a major event at the 1936 Berlin Olympics. The effort to make fiction of this rather than write a biography is not totally successful. Lovelock tells his tale in the first person, but his enigmatic character stands in the way of inner conviction and the strain on credibility is intolerable when he has to narrate his own death. Here again the inner perspective is comparatively unsuccessful, though the novel has gone through three editions and has influenced other versions of the story of Jack *Lovelock. (See also *Sport.)

All of McNeish's special sympathies and skills are, however, combined in *Penelope's Island* (1990), a novel set in New Caledonia at the time of political upheavals in the 1970s–80s. As in *The Glass Zoo*, the key to success lies in the perfect choice of narrative voice: Penelope is a foreigner, but married to a Caldoche, a native New Caledonian of French ancestry. This places her well within the political tensions, but with the perceptions of an outsider, and by following her responses the reader is drawn into the political events just as she is. The use of the setting with its tropical vegetation and enervating climate finally succeeds on both naturalistic and symbolic levels. After three decades of imaginative industry, McNeish achieved an inspired work of fiction.

McNeish's non-fiction includes *As for the Godwits ...* (1977), describing life in the remote and tiny community of Te Kuaka on a promontory overlooking the Tasman Sea. Tales of birds and fishermen are accompanied by very evocative photographs (by James and Heather McNeish) of treeless landscapes, weatherbeaten faces and shy Māori children. In 1980 James and Heather combined their efforts again to produce *Belonging*, oral history in which the interviewer's voice has been deleted so that a virtual monologue results. The interviewees were immigrants to Israel from all parts of the world. A similar technique had been used by McNeish to produce the texts which accompany Brian Brake's photographs in *Art of the Pacific* (1979)—some of the material from this book has been incorporated into *Penelope's Island*. McNeish also wrote the texts to Marti Friedlander's photographs in *Larks in Paradise* (1974), a vision of a 'dull' New Zealand with portraits of people standing unsmiling in urban or rural settings.

As a playwright McNeish is best known for *The Rocking Cave*, first produced at the Mercury Theatre, Auckland, in 1973 and published in 1981. Here he again exercises his talent for portraying a small community, this time a rigidly puritanical Presbyterian town in the 1860s, where an unmarried mother must suffer harsh treatment. Echoes of the hard-headed small town in *Mackenzie* are noticeable, and it is in creating a vision of such communities that McNeish has had his greatest successes. A study of a controversial murder case and trial, *The Mask of Sanity: The Bain Murders*, was published in 1997.

NW

McPHERSON, Heather

McPHERSON, Heather (1942–), poet, was born in Tauranga, trained as a primary teacher (1961), graduated BA at University of Canterbury (1971) and, as a solo mother, worked at various 'survival' jobs as well as writing and publishing. She has published occasionally in literary journals, including *Landfall, since the late 1960s, though from the 1970s she mostly preferred to publish in feminist magazines. She was involved in the Wellington Women's Gallery and was a founding member of the Spiral Collective, before settling for several years in a remote area of the Bay of Plenty. Her two collections are *A Figurehead, A Face* (Spiral, 1982) and *The Third Myth* (1986). They received little recognition, though she is included in the 1985 Penguin anthology. Living in Hamilton in the 1990s, she began publishing again, with work in *Hecate* 20, and is writing a lesbian detective novel. Her poems are strongly feminist, combining myth with the implications of being a woman and a lesbian in New Zealand. They have a distinctive witty intelligence together with a sensitive and lyrical voice. Her 'To the poet who called himself a fox among the hens', addressed to Sam *Hunt (*Landfall* 156, 1985), is a New Zealand feminist classic: 'Remember Maui. He thought / to snatch immortality /

till a fantail laughed / and Hine closed her thighs ...' (see *Maui, *Hine-nui-te-pō).   AMcL

MACPHERSON, Margaret (1895–1974), was a journalist and travel writer. She was born in Leeds, educated at a Quaker school and St Andrew's University, Scotland, and had early work published in Yorkshire and London papers, writing as a suffragette, Marxist and anti-war campaigner. She emigrated to New Zealand in 1916 with her husband, living first at Kaitangata. She had poems and articles published in various New Zealand journals, wrote as 'Wahine' for the women's page of the *Maoriland Worker* 1916–22 and edited the *Northlander*, a new progressive paper in Kaitaia, 1923–28. She later broadcast talks and travelled the world sending travel articles to the *New Zealand Woman's Weekly* etc. She remarried, to an Australian, and lived in Australia, Britain and mainly USA before returning to New Zealand in the 1960s. Her books include collections of travel articles: *Antipodean Journey* (1937), followed by *I Heard the Anzacs Singing* (1942) which contains much of the same material, and two for a young people's travel series, *Australia Calling* (1951) and *New Zealand Beckons* (1952), featuring an American family. She also wrote *A Symposium Against War* (1934) and a novella, *The Love Horse* (1954). She died in Kaitaia.   JMcC

McQUEEN, Cilla (1949–), poet, born in Birmingham, England, arrived in New Zealand in 1953. She was educated at Dunedin's Columba College and University of Otago (MA Hons 1970). She has taught French and English, and currently teaches part-time. She is accomplished and popular as a performer of her poetry.

Writing poetry developed out of McQueen's habit of keeping a diary, which explains its approach to life as a rich mixture of days, moments, casual acquaintances, intimate confessions and occasional shopping lists: 'One Marmite one coffee one flour.... One / fine day with or without frost' ('The Shopping'). Despite its eclecticism, certain characteristics recur. She writes of the Otago region with an intensity reminiscent of Ruth *Dallas or James K. *Baxter, yet with a unique personal perspective on these landscapes 'that we trample / or stroke with our toes or eat or lick / tenderly or pull apart' ('Living Here').

McQueen has published five volumes: *Homing In* (1982)—which was awarded the New Zealand Book Award for Poetry and the Jessie MacKay Award 1983; *Anti Gravity* (1984); *Wild Sweets* (1986); *Benzina* (1988)—New Zealand Book Award for Poetry, 1989; *Berlin Diary* (1990)—New Zealand Book Award for Poetry 1991; and *Crik'ey: New and Selected Poems* (1993).

These collections confirm the consistency of McQueen's talent. Never one for rigid forms, her work has a linguistic exuberance and inventiveness. She is capable of using the present tense dramatically and employing a direct syntax that creates pace or immediacy: 'I look up from walking at / a shy grey heron on / the point of flight' ('Low Tide, Aramoana'). The same devices generate intimacy in poems that may deal with domestic life, fantasy, memory or history.

Nor does McQueen's poetry want for humour. 'The Dream of Jenny Shipley' satirises the politics of the then Minister of Health: 'And Jenny squeals with delight / As the small green roll-on roll-off ferry / jumps right out onto the road, sturdy little thing, / Like a man with no legs jumping out of a wheelchair.'

Other poems draw distinctively on modern science, generating tension when science's analytical perspective meets the poet's idiosyncratic view, the finite mind's attempt to impose order on the infinite universe. 'Quark Dance', for example, suggests the absurdity of scientific investigation, and delights in the world of subatomic particles: 'here come the colours / to settle on our lips and eyes / and rainbow lighting all the edges'. One symbol that she has made her own is the 'meniscus': 'See, Ben, the water / has a strong soft skin, / and all the insects dance / and jump about on it' ('To Ben, At the Lake'). The proposition behind her 'meniscus' poetry is that if this barrier (at times permeable and at others impenetrable) fails to hold, chaos results.

McQueen's recent poetry has an experimental edge, and *Berlin Diary* represents a major departure. Based on diary entries from 1988, the lengthy work combines sequences of poetry and prose, further developing the idea of the meniscus, the barrier that then separated Berlin's opposing worlds (see *Germany).

Crik'ey: New and Selected Poems contains sixty-one poems from four previous books, selections from *Berlin Diary*, seventeen new poems and two new passages of prose, clearly demonstrating the development of McQueen's writing since *Homing In*'s spectacular debut.

McQueen has held the University of Otago's *Burns Fellowship, 1985–86; a Fulbright Visiting Writers' Fellowship 1985 and the Scholarship in Letters, 1991.   PM

McQUEEN, Harvey (1934–), is an anthologist, poet, memoirist and educational writer. Born in Little River, Banks Peninsula, and educated at Canterbury University College and Christchurch Teachers' College, he was a secondary-school teacher and inspector, then curriculum officer and manager in the Department of Education, resigning in 1986 to freelance as a writer and educational consultant. He was appointed personal educational adviser to David Lange, then Minister of Education as well as Prime Minister, during the crucial reforms of 'Tomorrow's Schools'. McQueen's memoir of that time, *The Ninth Floor* (1991), provides an informed commentary on the educational and political history, while his sympathetic treatment of Lange gives a narrative undertow close to tragedy.

He has shown a flair for *anthologies that are both innovative and judicious. *Ten Modern New Zealand Poets* (ed. with Lois Cox, 1974), modestly aimed at schools, gave a central place (only a year after The *Young New Zealand Poets*) to the generation of Sam *Hunt, Bill *Manhire and Hone *Tuwhare, and the *Penguin Book of New Zealand Verse* (ed. with Ian *Wedde, 1985) was the first to juxtapose the poetic traditions of the Māori and English languages. McQueen's eclectic taste was further evidenced by the *Penguin Book of Contemporary New Zealand Poetry* (ed. with Ian Wedde and Miriama Evans, 1989) and *The New Place: The Poetry of Settlement in New Zealand 1852–1914* (1993). This treated New Zealand's Victorian poets with discriminating seriousness for the first time for more than half a century.

McQueen's own poetry is mostly meditative or conversational, giving engaging expression to the mental life of a contemporary educated New Zealand male. Poems range over relationships, family, love, work, politics, office life, domestic concerns like gardening or cats, music and reading, with a sensitivity that is never merely fashionable and a commitment to the significance of private thought that is never pretentious. The wry humour, observation of small-scale detail and natural recurrence of reference to New Zealand's fauna and flora are all pleasures. His volumes are *Against the Maelstrom* (1981), *Stoat Spring* (1983), *Oasis Motel* (1986) and the exquisitely produced *Room* (Black Robin, 1988).

McQueen was president of *PEN (NZ) in 1987, guiding the momentous shift of headquarters from Wellington to Auckland. Until 1997 executive director of the New Zealand Council for Teacher Education, he edited the provocatively titled *Education is Change: 20 Viewpoints* (1994).   RR

MACTIER, Susie (1854–1936), sometimes called 'The Takapuna Lake Poet', published one volume of poetry and three novels. Born Susan Seaman, she arrived in New Zealand at 11 and eventually become a schoolteacher, being headmistress of Takapuna Primary School 1877–80, running a Sunday school and founding Takapuna Public Library.

Thoughts by the Way (1884), by 'Susie Seaman', is a collection of poems, some religious but others using the local environment to some effect.

The title of *The Far Countrie: A True Story of Domestic Life at Home and in the Bush* (1901) suggests that the author identified with British readers rather than the local scene. Central is the danger of becoming 'godless' when far from home. Once the protagonist discovers the truth of Christianity—'and the angels of God rejoiced that night over another soul gathered home'—and is visited by Bishop Selwyn, we are suddenly told 'We need not follow Nigel McLean's fortunes further.'

In *The Hills of Hauraki, or, The Unequal Yoke: A Story of New Zealand Life* (1908) Christina is lost to good society when she marries a man 'who was not a child of God'. She moves through the *goldfields, a sawmilling community and life as a female publican to a wretched death.

In Mactier's most substantial novel, *Miranda Stanhope* (1911), three sisters emigrate to seek independence. Miranda discovers that her husband has been sent to the colonies because of his alcoholism, but her greatest problem is coping with the environment without his support: 'What scope was there in that isolated place for her dainty accomplishments?' When her husband dies in the Tarawera eruption 'her heart [finds] a refuge' with her son.

Although she is sometimes thought of as a 'Temperance novelist', in fact her heroines face loneliness, conflict with Māori, struggles with poor land, distance from family and friends in addition to their husbands' alcoholism.   NW

Magazine appeared irregularly 1942–45, edited and mostly written by the teenage (and precocious) Dennis *McEldowney. It featured poetry and fiction, often experimental or satiric in form, and articles on New Zealand literature, including informed discussion of the schism between the *Art in New Zealand and *Caxton Press 'schools'.   SH

'Magpies, The', Denis *Glover's best-known poem, first appeared in *Recent Poems* (1941). Anthologised in Allen *Curnow's A *Book of New Zealand Verse* (1945), it quickly entered the canon of New Zealand poetry, and the anecdote of its writing is part of literary folklore. Curnow remembered how Glover, driving up to join him at a holiday *bach at Leithfield, north of Christchurch, 'got out of his little tiny baby Austin in the middle of a wild nor'wester to have a pee by the roadside. There were magpies squawking everywhere. And when Denis arrived and came to the door of the bach he didn't say anything at all except "quardle oodle ardle wardle doodle"—just like that' (*New Zealand Herald*, 29 July 1987). Glover added that in the same storm, both poets sat down to write, Glover cursing the 'blasted magpies'. 'When we'd finished, Curnow read his "Wild Iron" to me, and I said "My God, Allen, I'm wasting my time, trying to scribble verse. This is a brilliant, curious piece of Gothic verse." And then I said "I'll read you mine." I read that, and he said "What? I wish I could have written that."' Its ingenuous tone, simple rhyme-scheme and chortling 'quardle oodle ardle wardle doodle' refrain make 'The Magpies' popular in collections for children. Only superficially naive, however, this 'cross between a ballad and a grim nursery rhyme' (MacD.P. Jackson) laments the fate of the small farmer in harsh times, victim of an anonymous system. It is a tale of frustration, waste and loss, perhaps specifically a response to the *Depression, but also recalling the 1880s and 1920s, years when oppressive financial conditions also made it difficult for farmers to stay on their land. Glover maintained that although his farming couple were 'generalised', they represented all the small farmers whose suffering he witnessed in Canterbury during the 1930s. (At that time, magpies were almost unknown outside Canterbury.)

A narrator tells Tom and Elizabeth's story. In the first three stanzas they start work on a farm under rough conditions. Despite their work, lending institutions have first claim on the farm's produce, and ultimately the farm itself. As time takes its toll, Elizabeth dies and Tom becomes senile. Each verse closes with the magpies' persistent, indifferent chorus, highlighting the futility of human endeavour, a local version of 'Fine flowers in the valley' and other dispassionate, ironic refrains in the English and Scottish ballad tradition. The narrator comments colloquially that in the end the farm couldn't even be given away. The final refrain brings the poem into the present: 'And *Quardle oodle ardle wardle doodle* / The magpies say.' Having witnessed all, the birds are now sole guardians of the abandoned farm (again like the 'twa corbies' of the old ballad).

Denis Glover reads 'The Magpies' on *New Zealand Poets Read Their Work for Children* (Waiata, 1974) and a short film, *'The Magpies'*, directed by Alistair Taylor (1974) includes two treatments of the poem and an interview with Glover. His poem has inspired parodies by A.K. *Grant and others, and more serious derivations such as the play *Skin Tight* by Gary Henderson, first produced 1994.   SS

Mahinga a nga Tupuna Maori ha mea kohikohi mai, Ko nga (1854), was—according to himself—the fruit of eight years' labour on the part of the Governor of New Zealand, George *Grey, who also carried out the translation, *Polynesian Mythology and ancient traditional history of the New Zealand race*. This English version was published in 1855 and has been constantly reprinted—with some variations in the subtitle—ever since. Grey gave the original manuscripts to

the South African Public Library at Cape Town, but after long and difficult negotiations they were returned to New Zealand in 1922–23 and deposited in the Auckland Public Library.

Although Grey's preface implies that he transcribed the texts from oral informants, in fact many of the manuscripts are in Māori handwriting, and it was his practice to give the informants exercise books to fill. The most distinguished of the informants was Wiremu Maihi *Te Rangikāheke of Ngāti Rangiwewehi, who provided hundreds of pages and therefore deserves acknowledgment as a writer working close to the oral tradition. In other cases a Māori scribe wrote at the dictation of an informant (for example, Mātene Te Whiwhi of Ngāti Toa took down legends from the great *ariki Te Rangihaeata). Other writers included Wī Tako Ngātata of Te Āti Awa and Te Pirikawau of Taranaki. The authors of some writings cannot be identified. Although Grey also acted as scribe, the overall ascription of the work to himself seems less than just. Bruce *Biggs notes various ways in which the texts were altered during translation, sometimes obscuring rather than clarifying the meaning. It is also true, however, that without Grey's efforts these texts might not have been written or might not have survived.

The most extensive commentary on the manuscripts in relation to Grey's book was provided by *Biggs in the *Journal of the Polynesian Society* in 1952. Biggs judged that Grey was inaccurate in claiming that his translation was 'close and faithful' and suggested that true scholarship of the texts must be based on the originals rather than on *Polynesian Mythology*. On most occasions Grey had to make major editorial decisions in order to convert manuscripts into a publishable form. For example, most of the writings in these manuscripts follow the conventions of oral literature, such as the use of *whakapapa to connect stories together and to illuminate the identities of certain characters. The manuscripts dictated to Te Whiwhi by Te Rangihaeata use whakapapa in this way, and as the storyteller comes to a certain name, the background story concerning that character is told. However, there is no single whakapapa that can link all thirty-seven sections, because they are drawn from a variety of tribal areas and sources. Consequently Grey thought it advisable to remove the genealogical links entirely.

The thirty-seven sections include some of the great classics of Māori oral literature, such as genesis narratives, the stories of *Māui, the journeys of various *waka from *Hawaiki to *Aotearoa, the love stories of Te Kahureremoa and Te Huhuti and the tragic tale of Te Aohuruhuru of Wairarapa, who committed suicide in the face of her husband's indiscretions. There are many more.

In 1928 a superior version of the Māori texts, revised from the manuscripts by H.W. *Williams, was published and this version is now most commonly used.

CR/NW

MAHY, Margaret (1936–), the most acclaimed of New Zealand's children's writers, was born and raised in Whakatane, eldest of five children. Her father, a bridge builder, told stories and read to his children; his taste for adventure was to influence Mahy's writing. Her mother had been a teacher. With many relatives living in the same town, Mahy had a largely happy childhood, excelling at high school as a swimmer. Though regarded at primary school as academically 'slow', her first publications were at the age of 7, in the *children's page of the *Bay of Plenty Beacon*; she also entered *Junior Digest* competitions. Mahy worked as a nurse's aide for six months before going to Auckland University College 1952–54 and Canterbury University College 1955, graduating BA. In 1956 she entered the New Zealand Library School in Wellington, and with her Diploma (1958) went on to embrace librarianship with enthusiasm, taking a position at Petone Public Library. For personal reasons she moved to Ohariu, near Wellington, and then to Governor's Bay, Lyttelton Harbour, in 1965. In 1967 she began working for the School Library Service in Christchurch, and in 1976 was appointed Children's Librarian at the Canterbury Public Library, a position she held until she resigned in 1980 to become a full-time writer. She lives in Governor's Bay.

Working as a librarian and bringing up two daughters, Mahy continued to write stories and poems. Her work was rejected by commercial publishers in New Zealand (who were concentrating on explicitly New Zealand books for the local market), but many pieces were accepted by the *School Journal. The Little Witch* was the first to be accepted, and *The Procession* the first to be published (in 1961). In 1968 an American editor, Sarah Chockla Gross, discovered A *Lion in the Meadow and in 1969 Franklin Watts in America published five Mahy stories as picture books, launching her international career. 'It was one of those romantic things that happen,' Mahy has said, although she in fact received another independent enquiry from America a few months later. Watts went on to publish more stories, including many which had originally appeared in the *School Journal*, now adapted to their new picture book format. By the mid-1970s Mahy had added junior fiction to her repertoire; by the early 1980s she was writing adolescent novels— at least one of which (*Memory*, 1987) could have been marketed for adults. She has published about 120 titles (including school readers), and has written and adapted for television. Her work has been translated into fifteen languages. Awards include the New Zealand Library Association's Esther Glen Medal (*A Lion in the Meadow*, 1969; *The First Margaret Mahy Story Book*, 1972; *The Haunting*, 1982; *The Changeover*, 1984; *Underrunners*, 1992); the Goodman Fielder Wattie Award for Junior Fiction (*Underrunners*); the British Library Association's Carnegie Medal (*The Haunting; The Changeover*); the Young Observer Fiction Prize (*The Tricksters*, 1986); the Italian Premier Grafico Award (*The Wind Between the Stars*, 1976) and the Dutch Silver Pencil Award (*The Boy Who Was Followed Home*, 1977). In the United States her works have been included in prestige listings made by journal editors, librarians and educationalists; *Memory*, *The Tricksters* and *Dangerous Spaces* (1991) have all appeared on the Horn Book Fanfare list. She has held writing fellowships in New Zealand and Australia, and in 1993 was awarded the Order of New Zealand and an honorary doctorate of the University of Canterbury. In the many accounts of her life written for children (the most substantial of which is Betty *Gilderdale's *Introducing Margaret Mahy*, 1987), the no doubt complicated contours of Mahy's past and present existence have been simplified into the archetypal narrative of the hero who is despised at first, but who—thanks to persistence and good fortune—wins through. Mahy does in fact live (with her pets, and visited by her grandchildren) in an Edenic garden by the sea. She is a remarkably generous person, replying to all of the many letters she receives, and frequently visiting schools and libraries (sometimes in fancy dress). One of the more substantial of many published interviews is Sue Kedgley's (*Our Own Country*, 1989).

Mahy's work until 1996 has been judiciously described by Gilderdale in *A Sea Change* (1982) and in *OHNZLE (1991, 1998). Most of the picture books and junior novels are humorous. Mahy describes impossible scenarios in a matter-of-fact tone, she parodies literary conventions, she satirises human foibles, and her virtuosity with language is such that the English poet James Fenton, advocate of 'the new recklessness' in poetry, rose to applaud her poem 'Bubble Trouble' (1991) when she recited it during *Writers and Readers Week in Wellington in 1990. Humour may however be laid aside—as in the mystical picture books *The Wind Between the Stars* and *Leaf Magic* (1976). Mahy's modes are primarily fantasy and adventure, but her witches, dragons, pirates and millionaires do engage with the ordinary world—indeed, she focuses on this engagement. Her fabulous characters embody the liberating power of the imagination; 'perhaps,' Mahy has said, 'when I write about witches, the person I am really writing about is ... myself.' But the stories nevertheless deal with more universal fears and longings. By the mid-1970s Mahy had begun to write about what she has called 'the sort of experience that really could happen'. In the picture book *Stepmother* (1974), for example, the folk-tale archetype of the wicked stepmother exists merely as a figment of a resentful stepdaughter's imagination; it is countered by a real—thoroughly kind—stepmother. The junior novel *The Pirate Uncle* (1977), despite its 'adventure story' title, is also notably realistic. Similarly, some of the adolescent novels (including *The Catalogue of the Universe*, 1985, *Memory* and *The Other Side of Silence*, 1996) are based in what Mahy has called 'consensus reality', where nothing technically impossible happens. But even the realistic novels have fairy-tale analogues (which Mahy emphasises through allusion and metaphor): Tycho, the awkward young hero of *Catalogue*, is a frog prince figure; the elective mute who is the narrator-protagonist of *The Other Side of Silence* resembles the archetypal sulky princess; and the old woman with Alzheimer's disease who befriends and is befriended by the young hero in *Memory* is as weird as any good fairy (even though Mahy apparently based her on an aunt). Furthermore, Mahy has continued to write in an overtly supernatural tradition—with novels like *Aliens in the Family* and *The Tricksters* (both 1986), *The Changeover: A Supernatural Romance* and *Dangerous Spaces* (1991). *The Changeover*, one of Mahy's personal favourites, features a female hero (Laura) who becomes a witch in order to save her younger brother from annihilation by a demon. Laura's powers suggest the creative imagination, while those of the demon seem to project her fears, her insecurity which springs from the separation of her parents and her mother's preoccupation with a new partner. Mahy's novels often develop in a sunny atmosphere, but her recurrent themes include marital infidelity, parental abandonment, jealousy, self-deception, lies, mental illness and brain damage, and death (the latter often tragically accidental). The novels have happy endings, however, and inspire faith in the capacity of the young to overcome quite serious difficulties.

Mahy is an astute commentator on her own work. Characteristic lectures include 'On Building Houses that Face Towards the Sun', published in *A Track to Unknown Water* (1987), and the Arbuthnot lecture for 1989, published by the American Library Association in 1990. She is preoccupied with two topics—the relationship between the 'truth' of the imagination and factual truth; and her failure to depict New Zealand in her earlier work. The themes are connected, since—as Mahy has explained—both her predilection for fantasy and her typically European settings derive from the fact that the books available to her as a child were set elsewhere (chiefly in England). Mahy did include some New Zealand details in her first *Journal* publications, and the

tension between the New Zealand setting and European traditions is both pivotal and explicit in her 1968 poem 'Christmas in New Zealand'. But it was not until *The Changeover* that Mahy began to incorporate New Zealand in her commercial fiction. The New Zealand setting has become increasingly strong in the novels, and a pohutakawa tree adorns even the largely incredible landscape of *Telephone, Tuckletubs and Tingleberries* (1995). Mahy is interested in science; her belief that science and the imagination ultimately validate each other is evident in *The Catalogue of the Universe*. Some commentators have found Mahy's fiction feminist. It has been noted of the picture book *Jam, A True Story* (1985) that it is the father and not the mother who sets about jam-making in response to an oversupply of plums. Mahy herself (although she has described her younger self as a 'tomboy') rejects such readings; the subject of *Jam*, she has said, is the 'prodigality of nature'. Claudia Marquis takes a sophisticated feminist approach to *The Haunting* in ★*Landfall* 162 (1987).

Mahy has been published by Franklin Watts (until 1979), Dent (until 1988) and Hamish Hamilton. Titles not listed in the 1998 *OHNZLE* (excluding those mentioned above) include: (picture books) *Making Friends*, *The Pumpkin Man and the Crafty Creeper*, *The Seven Chinese Brothers* (1990), *The Dentist's Promise*, *Keeping House*, *The Queen's Goat* (1991), *The Horrendous Hullabaloo* (1992), *The Three-Legged Cat*, *A Busy Day for a Good Grandmother* (1993), *The Christmas Tree Tangle* (1994) and *The Big Black Bulging Bump* (1995); (collections) *A Tall Story and Other Tales*, *Bubble Trouble and Other Poems and Stories* (1991) and *Tick Tock Tales* (1993); (junior novels) *Cousins Quartet* (1993). KWa

'Mainland, The', has come since World War 2 to be a term for the South Island; originally used semi-ironically by South Islanders, it is now in widespread, mostly jocular use. It reflects the rueful sense that the South Island, the largest and once the wealthiest and most populous New Zealand land mass, is being progressively marginalised as population, wealth and power come to be concentrated in the northern half of the North Island. The literary centre of gravity has likewise moved northwards as Auckland and Wellington have become the primary literary centres, both in the number of writers resident and in publishing. However, that literary shift northwards lagged significantly behind the shifts in population and wealth.

The South Island in the nineteenth and early twentieth centuries had its share of recognisably southern writers, such as John ★Barr of Craigielee, Thomas ★Bracken, Vincent ★Pyke and Jessie ★Mackay, with Lady ★Barker and Samuel ★Butler among the visitors, and

George *Chamier, William Pember *Reeves, David McKee *Wright and Arthur *Adams among the expatriates. In the 1930s–40s, with the arrival of a new generation of literary nationalists, the South Island seemed actually dominant in literature, despite its political and economic decline. Although a significant Auckland group gathered around *Phoenix, the major means of literary publication were concentrated in the south, with *Tomorrow (1934–40) and the *Caxton Press located in Christchurch, and *Landfall (1947–) edited in Dunedin by Charles *Brasch and printed in Christchurch by Caxton. The key figures, Brasch, Denis *Glover and Allen *Curnow, editor of the canon-setting A *Book of New Zealand Verse 1923–1945, were all South Islanders. Other recognisably South Island writers included Dan *Davin, James *Courage and Basil *Dowling among the expatriates, and James K. *Baxter, Janet *Frame and Ruth *Dallas among the younger writers. By the early 1950s, however, with Baxter and Glover now in Wellington and Curnow in Auckland, and with important groups of new writers in both cities, the centre of gravity was obviously shifting, and the major literary geographical competition in the 1950s–60s was between Auckland and Wellington, with Baxter and Louis *Johnson leading the Wellington group and Curnow the Auckland one. Johnson and others inveighed against what they claimed was a 'South Island myth' in Curnow's earlier poetry and criticism and in Brasch's work; they complained about the hegemony of Landfall and set up rival journals. They viewed both the 'myth' and Landfall as anachronisms, out of place in an urban, internationalised society. The period of South Island dominance was clearly over.

The shift in gravity continued, with the establishment of *Islands as an Auckland-based competitor to Landfall in 1972, and the move to the North Island of such previously strongly southern writers as Janet Frame and Mervyn *Thompson. Since the 1980s, however, there has been a resurgence of South Island writing, but more as regionalist rather than as the 'national' literature that Curnow had announced. Between 1984 and 1988 the Christchurch periodical *Untold, a journal of South Island writing, provided one focus, while the literary programme of the Dunedin publishing firm *John McIndoe provided another. Peter *Hooper was an early South Island regionalist in the 1970s, and was joined by a host of such writers in the 1980s, including Keri *Hulme, Michael *Henderson, Graham *Billing, Brian *Turner, Cilla *McQueen, Owen *Marshall, Rob *Jackaman and Philip *Temple, with John *Newton, Rob *Allan, Kate *Flannery and Christine *Johnston among more recent names. It is now with these

regionalist writers that the 'Mainland' tag has come to be associated. A compilation of such writing is provided in From the Mainland: An Anthology of South Island Writing, ed. Lawrence Jones and Heather Murray (1995).   LJ

Mākereti (Margaret Thom, 1872–1930) was also known as Maggie Papakura. It is said that her name was shortened to Maggie for tourists and that when one of them asked if she had a second name, rather than use her English one she responded spontaneously with the name of the geyser she was standing beside: Papakura. For years she was a popular guide in the thermal region near Rotorua, and she wrote a Guide to the Hot Lakes District and Some Maori Legends in 1905. Its cover title is Maggie's Guide to the Hot Lakes. The appended legends were of the kind tourists asked to hear—tales of *Māui, the story of *Hinemoa (with her *whakapapa) and stories of witches and *taniwha in the thermal region —but they gained in authenticity from Mākereti's education in two cultures.

Her most significant book is The Old-Time Maori, published in London in 1938, with a biographical introduction by her Oxford professor of anthropology T.K. Penniman, and republished in the 'New Women's Classics' series in Auckland in 1986, with an introduction by Ngahuia *Te Awekotuku. It is a scholarly but by no means dull book, enlivened with personal notes and anecdotes by the author, who is always ready to leave the general and tell us of incidents which in sum amount to an autobiography. These are seamlessly connected with stories of her ancestors. The chapter titles are 'Social Organization and Relationship Terms', 'Marriage', 'Children', 'Food', 'Fire', 'Houses' and 'Weapons'.

The personal quality of her style might be illustrated from the chapter on marriage, where there is a detailed and sensitive account of interracial marriages. In fact, while her mother (Pia Ngarotu Te Rihi) was a Te Arawa 'chieftainess' or member of the rangatira class, her father was an Englishman (William Arthur Thom). She was raised by a couple of her mother's family in a relatively remote area, where she grew familiar with many ancient customs and was given an extensive education in whakapapa and other traditional knowledge. As a teenager she attended Hukarere, the famous Anglican school in Napier, where she acquired a Western education. As a bilingual, bicultural, attractive young woman she became a popular guide in her native area, the climax coming with a royal visit in 1901 (described in her guidebook), when the press made her an international celebrity.

She travelled frequently to Australia and led a Māori cultural group on a tour to Britain in 1910. Te Awekotuku writes: 'The group's reception by the British press and public was little short of triumphant, and the many artefacts they took with them, including a house and a pataka, excited great wonder among all who saw them.' A year in Britain and another at home preceded her return to Britain in 1912 to marry Richard Staples-Browne, an Oxford landowner. By the time her marriage dissolved in 1924 she had become a part of the new discipline of anthropology at Oxford University. She submitted *The Old-Time Maori* as a thesis, but one day later she died of a heart attack. After its publication it was soon forgotten, although Arawa people kept copies as a 'taonga' (heirloom), and a more recent paperback publication has drawn it to the attention of scholars and general readers alike.   NW

MALE, John (1913–), a little-known but interesting war poet, was born in Auckland and attended Auckland University College. Prior to his war service he was a *NZ Listener feature writer. He had his first poems published in *New Zealand New Writing and the *Yearbook of the Arts. He served in *Italy and North Africa during World War 2 and then, after a year as national organiser for CORSO NZ, worked for the United Nations for eighteen years. He served on the committees of several organisations and was co-founder in 1974 of the New Zealand Foundation for Peace Studies. His only publication, *Poems from a War* (1989), had a long and colourful publishing history. With the previously unpublished drawings of Russell *Clark, it was initially to have been printed by Male's friend Bob *Lowry, but this never eventuated. Much later Male took it to Alan *Loney, who finally printed it under his *Black Light imprint in a limited edition of thirty-three copies. The poetry and short prose pieces (which appeared with a foreword by Sir Guy Powles) provide a subtle portrayal of a soldier's war. The poems utilise Mason's hanging indent and are written in an abstemious but particularly evocative style, uncharacteristic of the period.   NWt

MALLORY, Clare (pseudonym for Winifred Hall, born McQuilkan, 1913–91), wrote a series of popular girls' school stories, 1947–51, largely but not entirely on the English model. Betty *Gilderdale in *A Sea Change* (1982) says 'They not only have the expected ingredients, but go further to explore the nature of authority and its place in the school system'. The books advocate excellence equally in academic, sporting and cultural fields, especially literary, one gauche non-sporting heroine finding fulfilment by winning a debating contest for a speech on Jane Austen. *Merry Begins* (1947), *Merry Again* (1947) and *Merry Marches On* (1947) are set at 'the Mary Tremayne Ladies' College' in Dunedin, though no world outside school is apparent; *Tony Against the Prefects* (1949) at 'a great English school'; *The New House at*

Winwood (1949) and *The League of the Smallest* (1951) again at private girls' boarding schools in New Zealand, centered mainly on games; and *Leith and Friends* (1950) and *The Pen and Pencil Girls* (1950) are set at more credible day schools, the latter a co-educational Southland school where an interest in writing acts as an incentive and bond among girls of disparate home backgrounds. The 'Merry' books, published by *Oxford University Press, sold more than 23 000 copies in Australia and New Zealand in little more than a year.

Winifred Hall went to Southland GHS and Otago University College, where she was on the council of *Critic* with Dan *Davin, and wrote a gossip column as 'Susan Schnozzletippet', as feared in her day as Felicity Ferret of *Metro. She then went to Oxford, returning to teach and becoming headmistress of Colomba College, Dunedin. She served on the executive of the *New Zealand Women Writers' Society 1954–56 and in her later years was tutor in English at Victoria University of Wellington.   PN/RR

Man Alone, the novel by John *Mulgan, was published in 1939 by Selwyn and Blount, and in a new edition in 1949 by Paul's Book Arcade (*Blackwood and Janet Paul), which has been many times reprinted.

'Man Alone' appears frequently as a topos in New Zealand literature, as in the literatures of most New World societies in which frontier experience has made people aware of solitariness. It takes its name here from John *Mulgan's *Man Alone of 1939 (and Mulgan in turn was alluding to Hemingway), but the topos existed long before it was given a name, and has been a constant element in New Zealand literature from its beginnings. The interpretation given it, however, has changed through different periods of social and literary history. In writings before 1930 the unattached male was often seen as heroic, acting out the society's pioneer values. Sometimes he appears as that stock figure of Victorian melodrama, the wronged man who redeems his reputation, as with Will Enderby in Vincent *Pyke's *Wild Will Enderby* (1873) or William *Satchell's Hugh Clifford of *The *Land of the Lost* (1902) or Jane *Mander's Dick Rossiter in *Allen Adair* (1925). Sometimes he is a bushman or miner pitting himself against the forces of nature, as with Eileen *Duggan's unnamed hero in 'The Bushfeller' (*c.*1930), married but struggling alone clearing the *bush, or Pyke's eponymous hero on the Otago *goldfields in *The Adventures of George Washington Pratt* (1874), or Samuel *Butler's sheepman-explorer in *Erewhon* (1872), or Edith *Lyttleton's South Island high-country sheepmen tested by the rigours of a difficult environment in *Sons o' Men* (1904). A few of these earlier Men Alone are used to question rather than to support their society's values: George ★Chamier's Richard Raleigh in ★*Philosopher Dick* (1891) and *A ★South-Sea Siren* (1895), who learns to question both his view of himself as self-sufficient and his view of New Zealand society as untainted and progressive; Satchell's Byronic Purcell of *The ★Greenstone Door*, who becomes the victim of his society's land–greed and mistreatment of the Māori. A special case is the Christ of R.A.K. ★Mason's poems of the 1920s–30s such as 'Nails and a Cross' or 'Ecce Homunculus', a stoic hero who is victim both of his society and of an uncaring God.

After about 1930 the Man Alone figures tend to be rebels against their society's values or victims of their society. Some of these characters are pioneer types now marginalised, like Denis ★Glover's Arawata Bill from ★*Arawata Bill: A Sequence of Poems* (1953), or Roderick ★Finlayson's Uncle Ted from *Tidal Flat* (1948), or Frank ★Sargeson's maternal uncle in his autobiography, *Sargeson* (1981). Others are characters who have the daring and independence to be successful on the frontier (or in war) but who have become rejects and outlaws in their more staid societies, such as John A. ★Lee's Albany Porcello in *The Hunted* (1936) or Robin ★Hyde's Douglas Stark in ★*Passport to Hell* (1935) and ★*Nor the Years Condemn* (1938). Some of the outlaws are based on the historical character of Stanley Graham, who killed in response to what he felt was social persecution and was then hunted down; Owen Marley in Randal Burdon's *Outlaw's Progress* (1943) and Gerald Milsom in Erik ★de Mauny's *The Huntsman in His Career* (1949) are such figures. The manhunt is also a feature of *Man Alone* itself, but Mulgan's Johnson is not an outlaw so much as an independent man who values his freedom and does not live by the ownership ethic of his society. Such drifting, independent characters who might or might not run afoul of the law include Bill in Sargeson's ★*That Summer* (1943–44), the narrators of such Sargeson stories as 'An Affair of the Heart' (1936) and 'The Making of a New Zealander' (1939) or of G.R. ★Gilbert's 'A Girl with Ambition' (1942), or the speakers in A.R.D. ★Fairburn's poems 'Walking on my Feet' (1946) and 'Down on my Luck' (1952). Drifters who are persecuted for what society perceives as their threatening sexuality include Sargeson's Bandy in 'Old Man's Story' (1940) and Finlayson's Frankie in 'Frankie & Lena' (1976). Other types of Man Alone as victim include Phillip ★Wilson's Jim Hotene in *The Outcasts* (1965) and O.E. ★Middleton's Sonny King in 'Not for a Seagull' (1964), both as Māori victims of racism; or Toby Withers, an epileptic, in Janet ★Frame's ★*Owls Do Cry* (1957) and *The ★Edge of the Alphabet* (1962); and Peter, an introverted closet homosexual in Middleton's 'Confessions of

an Ocelot', both rejected for their difference.

After World War 2, although some Men Alone continue to appear as victims, there is a shift in emphasis in that many are held at least partly responsible for their lives, often viewed from an ★existentialist perspective. This existentialist approach was evident in the treatment of Peter Villiers in de Mauny's *The Huntsman in His Career* and of the ambitious and less sympathetic Mark Burke in Dan ★Davin's ★*Cliffs of Fall* (1945), and became more pronounced in such later novels as Guthrie ★Wilson's *Strip Jack Naked* (1957), Gordon ★Slatter's *A Gun in My Hand* (1959), Redmond Wallis's *Point of Origin* (1962), Graham ★Billing's *Forbush and the Penguins* (1965) and Maurice ★Shadbolt's *A ★Touch of Clay* (1974). A similar tendency to see the Man Alone figure as at least to some extent reponsible for his solitariness is evident in such stories of Maurice ★Duggan's as 'Chapter' (1950), 'Riley's Handbook' (1961), ★'Along Rideout Road that Summer' (1963) and ★'O'Leary's Orchard' (1970), and Maurice ★Gee's ★*In My Father's Den* (1972). The extended range of interpretation of the topos is evident in such diverse works as James ★McNeish's *Mackenzie* (1970), with Man Alone as mythic hero; C.K. ★Stead's 'A Fitting Tribute' (1965), which parodies the topos; Sargeson's 'Man of England Now' (1972), with a traditional view of Man Alone as social victim; Sargeson's *The Memoirs of a Peon* (1965), with Man Alone as comic picaresque rogue; Gee's 'A ★Glorious Morning, Comrade' (1975), with Man Alone as a humorously sympathetic geriatric runaway; and Russell ★Haley's *Beside Myself* (1990), with Man Alone as self-conscious unemployed middle-aged intellectual. Albert ★Wendt provides a Polynesian postcolonial rebel variant in *Black Rainbow* (1992), recurring to the manhunt thriller mode, and Laura ★Solomon, recalling in despair exam questions on the figure, called her novel *Black Light* (1996) a 'discussion of the man alone in New Zealand literature' (in this case an egregious would-be novelist).

Man Alone in New Zealand writing, then, has evolved in about a hundred and thirty years from frontier hero through social victim or rebel to existential agent and currently to a protean figure capable of multiple incarnations.

LJ

Mana is a word taken into English by anthropology and there applied to a variety of cultures. It is not easily defined in English terms, which is why it has been 'borrowed' in this way but also why its use is often questionable. It can be translated as 'pride', and yet it involves a necessary degree of humility: 'self-esteem' may come a little closer. It is in fact accorded by others, in a way neither of these English terms implies, so that 'status', 'prestige' and 'honour' are also elements of it. In *The*

Marae: A Guide to Customs and Protocol (1986), Hiwi and Pat Tauroa write, 'An individual cannot demand that mana be bestowed upon him or her. Others recognising and wishing to acknowledge that individual's continued service to other people may in their own way show a respectful deference to him or her.'

Mana might arise from a person's family status: being the eldest brother, or the senior family person. But behaviour can increase or diminish mana, so that the mana of the person who is senior in years may have declined in comparison with some younger person's achievement or talents. Certain skills, especially those associated with traditional arts, crafts and activities, can result in high mana. Achievement in the Pākehā world can also lead to mana in the Māori world, but this is not always the case. Hiwi and Pat Tauroa write, 'A principal of a school has status in the Pakeha community. However, that same principal may not be accorded any degree of mana.'   NW

MANDER, Jane (1877–1949), novelist, was born in Ramarama, a small settler community near Auckland. Her father forwent the limited opportunities of settler farming soon after his marriage in 1876, choosing the life of a pioneer lumberman and sawmiller in the great kauri forests north of Auckland. In 1881 he bought a *bush mill at Awhitu, the first of many endeavours which caused the family to move (Mander estimated) twenty-nine times during her upbringing, often living in hardship. One such home was Pukekaroro, a tiny settlement near Kaiwaka on the Otamatea river which subsequently provided the details of the setting for her first novel, The *Story of a New Zealand River*. The conditions of Mander's nomadic childhood find expression in her fiction: settler characters and concerns remain largely peripheral to her four novels set in New Zealand, all of which deal with pioneering life. Unlike her mother, who succumbed to invalidism in the face of years of isolation and discomfort, Mander viewed change as opportunity; this is evident in the note of change, weighted with expectation and promise, on which many of her novels end. Her sporadic education at schools often great distances away was supplemented by her mother's tuition, and she reached standard six in 1892. As there was no high school nearby (the family was now living in Port Alfred), she became a teacher-pupil at the local primary school, teaching in a variety of schools in the ensuing years. She matriculated through extramural study in 1897. When the family moved to Whangarei in 1900 Mander gave up teaching, temporarily capitulating to expectations that she conform to the model of passive Victorian daughter. Two years later her father Frank ran for parliament on the side of Massey's Reform Party and,

aided in his campaign by his eldest daughter, narrowly ousted the sitting member for Marsden. He spent twenty years as a member of parliament and a further seven as a member of the legislative council. That same year his purchase of the main newspaper of the north, the *Northern Advocate*, provided Mander with the opportunity to try her hand at journalism; she worked as sub-editor and reporter, and eventually ran the editorial department single-handed.

After a brief trip to Sydney in 1907, Mander took over the editorship of the Dargaville *North Auckland Times*. She returned to Sydney in 1910 and was befriended by W.A. Holman, who became the Labour Party premier of New South Wales. Here Mander occupied herself writing freelance journalism (she submitted articles to the *Maoriland Worker* under the pseudonym of 'Manda Lloyd') and studying languages. Determined to win her father's favour (and financial support) to study journalism at Columbia University in New York, she again returned to New Zealand in 1912. In June that year, aged 35, she sailed for New York, travelling via London, carrying with her the script of a novel which she offered to four publishers, all of whom declined it.

At Columbia Mander excelled, achieving the highest grades in examinations at the end of her first and second years, a remarkable feat given that she also held numerous part-time jobs—lecturing, coaching younger students, writing for magazines—to supplement her meagre income. During this time she continued to rework her novel but, after another rejection, finally abandoned it. While she may have inherited tenacity, courage and energy from her father, Mander did not inherit his good health. Financial pressure and overwork exacerbated her poor health, and she was forced to abandon her studies in her third year. Known for her liberal feminism, she joined the suffrage movement in 1915 and campaigned for the New York State referendum on women's franchise. In the course of the next two years she ran a hostel for girls, pursued research at Sing Sing prison and worked for various war effort organisations, taking an administrative post in the Red Cross when the United States entered World War 1. During this time she worked on a new novel, which was accepted by John Lane in 1917 and published in 1920: *The Story of a New Zealand River*.

Despite being well received in England and the USA, *The Story of a New Zealand River* was poorly reviewed in New Zealand. Lacking precedents for a local literature, critics reproved the novel's failure to conform to the familiar conventions of the nineteenth-century regional British novel in theme and content. Reviewers expected documentary literalism in a novel so liberally sprinkled with real place names and details of actual events; many were critical of the creative fiat with which the novelist altered geography and population to suit her artistic vision. Furthermore, colonial readers found the novel too outspoken on matters of sex and religion. The *New Zealand Herald*, in 1920, proclaimed *The River*'s liberal ending 'too early for good public morality'; it was set aside in the 'Reserve' section of libraries to be borrowed by approved adults only on special request to the librarian.

Mander's next three novels were all set in New Zealand, drawing directly on her childhood experiences of pioneering life in the north. *The Passionate Puritan* (1921) is a rather cheerful account of kauri milling, apparently written with an eye on the cinema ('a mistake', Mander claimed, she 'ever afterwards regretted'). Two long documentary sections—the tripping of the dam and the bush fire—are woven into the light-hearted romance theme, which centres around the liberation of the central character, Sidney Carey, from the shackles of *puritanism. *The Strange Attraction* (1922), the weakest of Mander's New Zealand novels, focuses on the concerns of a thriving second-generation community in Dargaville on the Wairoa river: the rivalry of two newspapers and a contested parliamentary election. Her political concerns and vivid portrayal of an emergent community sit uncomfortably alongside the somewhat indulgent melodramatic romance plot detailing Valerie Carr's love for Dane Barrington, and her release from their disintegrating secret marriage when Dane heroically departs on learning he has terminal cancer. Despite their moderate success abroad, the New Zealand response to these novels was again almost wholly negative. Critical attention focused on Mander's purported failure to portray convincingly 'representative' members of the communities she chose to sketch, on her putative moral deviance, and her continued obsession with what was labelled 'the sex problem'. Mander responded from London to her critics in a letter to the *Auckland Star* in 1924: 'a writer who is trying to be an artist, as I sincerely am, has nothing whatsoever to do with being a tourist agent, or a photographer, or a historian, or a compiler of community statistics.... I am simply trying to be honest and loyal to my own experience'; and 'as a matter of fact I'm not half sexy enough for thousands of readers here'.

In 1923 Mander had left New York for London, where she worked as a publisher's reader and then as the English editor for the Harrison Press of Paris. During this time she wrote some sketches, short stories and essays and acted as the London correspondent for various New Zealand newspapers. As almost all of Mander's private correspondence has been destroyed, one cannot be sure of the novelist's response to negative reviews of her books as they trickled in from her own country. It is

worth noting, however, that *Allen Adair* (1925) was her last novel with a New Zealand setting, as if she wilfully turned her back on the unreceptive readers of her home country and directed her writing towards those more willing to appreciate its strengths and tolerate its weaknesses: *The Besieging City* (1926) is set in New York; and *Pins and Pinnacles* (1928) is set in London and Paris.

Mander completed another novel in 1931, but destroyed it after its rejection by one publisher. The death of her mother imminent, and her own health failing, she returned to New Zealand in 1932. Having championed the advances of New Zealand abroad for two decades, Mander was now bitterly disappointed in her country, which to her mind had failed to fulfil its potential and had become 'one of the backward people of the earth'. The puritanical malaise, so often attacked in her New Zealand novels, was a condition she now found rampant, threatening to dissipate the energies and promise of the pioneers. It is deeply ironical that it is precisely this puritanical, imitative colonialism which marked the response of her original New Zealand readers to her novels. Illness, years of pedestrian literary work, and an intolerant local audience combined to wither her creativity. Her energy drained in the care of her father, Mander's attempts at writing her commissioned seventh novel and reminiscences all ended in illness, and she wrote nothing more than a few articles, reviews and radio scripts until her death in Whangarei, at the age of 72.

By no means New Zealand's most accomplished novelist, Mander remains one of its most important, for in a relatively early period she was willing to make a creative commitment to life in New Zealand. She writes with an intimate sense of belonging to this country and a fervent love of it; her work is undistorted by either exaggerated enthusiasm or the colonial cultural cringe. In this she resembles Olive Schreiner, whose novel *The Story of an African Farm* greatly influenced Mander's first novel (as the title suggests); she hoped to write of New Zealand as Schreiner had done of Southern Africa, evoking a genuine and vivid sense of local flavour. Technically, Mander's novels evidence ample flaws for the critical reader. Her conventional style is mannered and derivative, strongly influenced by nineteenth-century English novels, although her fine management of terse and controlled dialogue stands in contrast to the overblown wordiness of her descriptive prose: spoken language in the novels is rich in variety and aural nuance and provides a good index to character. But Mander's greatest strength is in the rendering of the internal conflicts, feelings and attitudes of her characters so that despite their stylistic clumsiness, the novels have enduring emotional intensity and appeal.

Typescripts of the last four novels are held in the Auckland Public Library, along with Mander's own collection of her journalistic and other prose writing. Copies of this material are held by the *Alexander Turnbull Library in Wellington. The standard critical biography is Dorothea Turner's *Jane Mander* (1972).

KWo

MANHIRE, Bill (1946–), was born in Invercargill. He graduated from the universities of Otago and London, and has since 1973 lectured in the English department of Victoria University of Wellington, where he is now a professor. The winner of many literary prizes, including New Zealand Book Awards in 1977, 1984, 1992 and 1996, he is recognised as among the two or three finest New Zealand poets of his generation. Published in many international, as well as local, journals, his verse has been collected in the following volumes: *Malady* (1970), *The Elaboration* (1972), *Song Cycle* (1975), *How to Take Off Your Clothes at the Picnic* (1977), *Dawn/Water* (1979), *Good Looks* (1982), *Locating the Beloved and Other Stories* (1983), *Zoetropes: Poems 1972–82* (1984), *The Old Man's Example* (1990), *Milky Way Bar* (1991), *Sheet Music: Poems 1967–1982* (1996) and *My Sunshine* (1996). There is considerable overlap between books, *Sheet Music* incorporating five earlier ones, with *My Sunshine* offering new work.

Manhire was represented in the important anthology, *The *Young New Zealand Poets* (1973), where he explained: 'The chief joy of the shorter lyric I take to be its ability to carry the reader out of the sequential, linear world into its own moment: as it were, Snap.' His poems refuse to tread a straight path, but get from starting to finishing point with the aid of gracefully executed sidesteps of register, image or narrative. They depend on a kind of wit, linguistic playfulness, quirks of fancy, mild shocks of surprise, readjustments of focus, a touch of whimsy. For the reader, crossing a line-break can be an adventure. The poems are elliptical, and often enigmatic. Among Manhire's earliest pieces were adaptations of Anglo-Saxon riddles and spells and the cryptic 'Wulf and Eadwacer', and his later style retains something of that fragmentary dramatic lament's elusiveness, allusiveness and ability to stir the imagination.

Manhire has a postmodern, or perhaps simply an alert poet's, consciousness of the strangeness of language, the apparent arbitrariness with which meanings accrue to signs. In 'Jalopy: The End of Love', for instance, the word 'jalopy' conjures up not only a special kind of 'old car' but bygone youthful days: Manhire contrives a delicate mix of nostalgia, ruefulness, amusement and acceptance. In savouring the disused term, he savours much more, and 'Whatever it is, it's finished'. 'Magasin'

dramatises the poet's early fascination with his medium. As a high-school boy he brings his hospitalised father magazines to read, and remarks on the similarity of 'the word for shop / in French', because 'I am learning a language'. But he is also sharpening the poet's eye for resemblances, as the shape of his father's liver traced on his skin 'for the third-year students' reminds the son of 'the map of Africa'. And English has its own oddities: the one-legged man in the next bed comments, as everyone in the ward listens to the races, on 'the second leg at Trentham'! In 'Out West' the cowboy world of a youth's imagination is as much a linguistic as a cinematic construct—of 'varmints' who say 'doggone' and 'ornery critters' who 'mosey along'.

Manhire's manipulation of the clichés of popular culture allows him to move in and out of the fictional and real worlds, blurring the boundaries between life and art, as in 'Princess: The Treatment'. Idiom creates a whole order of experience: 'Wh-wh-what'll we do if we're captured?' Even a poem more securely grounded in location, such as 'Wellington', is almost a collage of those banalities from the media and suburban chit-chat that mediate our perception of reality: Manhire uses them knowingly, as though they were within speech marks. He is often at least half way towards parody, pastiche or burlesque. His methods may also collapse distinctions between the literal and the figurative. A reader encountering the opening couplet of the fine 'A Death in the Family', for example —'His face is gone golden with the dusk / You would think he burned, he burned'—with which the poem also ends, is uncertain about the status of the 'he', so that sunset and a man's death become inextricably linked, while the lyrical 'golden' and the ardent 'burned' romanticise and mythologise the subject. In 'Wingatui' (a South Island racecourse), the reader as disappointed punter, contemplating what 'might have been', is invited to 'Sit in the car with the headlights off' (like so many movie heroes who have, in one way or another, 'blown it'), and 'Look out there now / where the yellow moon floats silks across the birdcage'. The 'birdcage' is the enclosure where horses are paraded and saddled up, and the jockey's 'silks' are his cap and blouse, and the line evokes movements of light and shadow, as if they were the phantoms of the mounted jockeys in their colours; 'silks' is used figuratively, but 'birdcage' might be taken either as the actual racetrack birdcage or as the paddock of the sky, which in the poem's last line becomes an 'azure violin'. In 'The Swallow' John Keats is not counting 'on his fingers', but 'on the morning', but the fingers soon reappear. By taking the idea of 'following' other poets literally, 'On Originality' creates scenes from a spy drama.

Manhire's manner is tentative. He mistrusts the words he relishes, hedges with 'almost', 'I suppose', 'sometimes', 'apparently', 'perhaps', 'as it happens', and the like. Yet these hesitancies are subsumed within an elegant music, marked by artfully sliding cadences. Traditional romantic images—moon, water, snow, clouds, stones, wind, birds, trees—are worked into his own idiosyncratic, thoroughly modern utterance. Many poems handle standard poetic themes, glancing obliquely at their predecessors. Manhire has the lyricist's sense of our subjection to Time, the transience of joy, the fragility of love. He writes about domestic events, personal relationships, families. He is a master of tender, close-up observation, as in his well-known reference (in 'Song') to 'watching the small explosions / under your wrists'. He ranges through a semi-fabulous Brazil, Japan, Europe, Antarctica. Abroad or (in 'Breakfast') flying home, he is consciously a New Zealander. Not only do such pieces as 'Poem for Vanessa', 'Zoetropes' and 'Milky Way Bar' speak to our condition, but through using snippets of the vernacular Manhire weaves his nationality into the fabric of his verse. His styles are various, encompassing incantation both magical ('A Song About the Moon') and jocular ('Declining the Naked Horse'). Over the last decade or so, especially, he has attempted longer poems. Several are built up of fragments that echo one another and are joined by a thin narrative thread. 'An Amazing Week in New Zealand', the penultimate poem in *My Sunshine*, is the most complex and impressive of these. Memories of the Billy Graham crusade in 1959 raise questions of 'faith': Manhire, opting for 'small signs' in a physical 'world of loss', ends with the sceptic's 'Lord, I am / not going forward', which is not without its ambiguities.

Manhire's more expansive recent poems may have been influenced by his turning to short fiction in the late 1980s. In his prose, as in his verse, he is apt to move forward by making 'a jinking little run' ('Ventriloquial'). *The Brain of Katherine Mansfield* (1988) and the stories in *The New Land: A Picture Book* (1990) are reprinted, with additions, in *South Pacific* (1994) and *Songs of My Life* (1996)—the same collection under different titles. The 'Katherine Mansfield' booklet is an open-ended choose-your-own adventure story: the reader picks his or her way through up to fifty chunks of narrative that, while packed with the local and the special, burlesque several literary and sub-literary genres. 'Cannibals' is propelled by the conventions and phraseology of South Seas exploration novels and *Boy's Own* tales of derring-do, zestfully mocked. 'Some Questions I am Frequently Asked' is a spoof interview. 'Wings of Gold: A Week Among Poets' reports drily on the World Poetry Reading in Kuala Lumpur in 1990. Manhire himself has spoken of 'the sort of disenchanted-cum-whimsical-cum-satirical tone' of these stories, which 'try to come

at New Zealand in a variety of … ways', from the surreal to reportage. But ingenious, self-referential and subversive game-playing prevails.

Manhire is author of the critical study, *Maurice Gee* (1986), and editor of two volumes of *NZ Listener Short Stories* (1977–78), *Some Other Country: New Zealand's Best Short Stories* (with Marion McLeod, 1984, revised 1992 and 1994), *Six by Six: Short Stories by New Zealand's Best Writers* (1989), *100 New Zealand Poems* (1993), and *Denis Glover: Selected Poems* (1995). His creative writing course at Victoria, which he began teaching in 1975, has had a major influence on New Zealand literature. *Mutes & Earthquakes* (1997), an anthology of work by former class-members, many now very well known, serves as a showcase. Manhire's introduction begins with two pieces of advice: '1. Write what you know, and / 2. Write what you don't know'. His own verse and prose, where the words are 'instruments of exploration' in a 'process of discovery', achieve this difficult balancing act. MPJ

MANING, F.E. (Frederick Edward) (1811/12?–83), trader, writer and Land Court Judge, was born in Dublin to a Protestant family. He arrived in New Zealand in 1832 after nine years in Tasmania. His arrival is described in detail, with many Shandean digressions, in his entertaining, purportedly autobiographical book *Old New Zealand: A Tale of the Good Old Times* (1863), which has occupied a proud place on many a colonial bookshelf and has rarely been out of print through more than 130 years. When his ship anchored he paid a 'native' to carry him ashore; the man slipped and both fell into the sea; a wrestling match ensued in which Maning defeated his Māori opponent, who congratulated him warmly, as did the assembled people of both races. Maning's acceptance was assured.

Most readers hesitate to believe everything in *Old New Zealand* (published under the pseudonym 'A Pakeha Maori'), but the story of his arrival was confirmed by witnesses and supported by the fact that he was a powerful and fearless man. It is hard, then, to be sure where the facts cease and Maning's love of extravagance begins. It is clear, however, that the book was skilfully and indeed wittily constructed by a master of sinewy prose, so that it can be read as a novel or as autobiography with equal pleasure. It is equally certain that he was as much a master of the Māori language as of English and greatly respected by the people among whom he (at first) kept a store.

Maning's *History of the War in the North of New Zealand against the Chief Heke* (1862) is remarkable for being written from the point of view of a fictitious Māori supporter of Hone Heke, again blurring the border between fact and fiction and suggesting that the façade of down-to-earth natural vigour concealed a sophisticated literary mind.

The 1876 edition of *Old New Zealand* (published by Bentley of London) has an introduction by the Earl of Pembroke. Apparently the Duke of Manchester offered to edit another book, should there be one. Maning wrote to a friend, 'Just think—one editor an earl—and a Duke volunteering! If I was not a philosopher I should be writing away like a 'phool' to please others and not myself. The maggot *does* bite sometimes and I have all the material in the shape of notes, but—the internal music has been extinguished.' In fact he became a misanthrope, wrote of his detestation of all things Māori, and burned not only every copy of *Old New Zealand* he could find but also manuscripts for *Young New Zealand, The Land of Many Conquests* and a history of the Ngā Puhi.

After a series of comments that place him clearly among the enemies of a liberal approach to Māori, Pembroke gives us an interesting personal picture of Maning: 'He was, I believe, sixty years old when I first saw him, but, in spite of his age, looked the finest man for strength, activity, and grace I had ever seen. Six feet three in height and big in proportion, with a symmetry of shape that almost disguised his immense size, I felt I could well understand the stories I had heard of his popularity and his feats amongst the Maories, especially when I watched the keen, bright expression of his humorous Irish face.... With a real love, and a considerable knowledge of literature, a keen appreciation of all intellectual excellence, and a most delightful humour, I think I never came across so charming a talker as [this] man.'

Later editions had a biographical introduction by T.M. ★Hocken. There is an interesting thesis by W.F. Wietmeyer (University of New Zealand, 1935) and a full account of Maning in R.M. ★Burdon's *New Zealand Notables* (Series 3, 1950).

In 1865 Maning was appointed Judge of the Native Land Court, largely because of his familiarity with Māori customary law as well as British law, and some of his judgments are still quoted as a skilful balance between the two systems. Like many other Pākehā, he was fascinated by the story of ★Hinemoa and Tūtānekai and published *Hine-moa: A Maori Love Story* in 1881. In 1885 he published *Maori Traditions*. His reputation depends, however, on *Old New Zealand* and *A History of the War in the North*, both now recognised as classics of New Zealand literature. NW

MANN, Phillip (1942–), is a leading theatrical director and ★science fiction writer. He was born in Yorkshire and graduated in English and drama at Manchester University and in theatre at Humbolt State College, California. He arrived in 1969, initially working as director for Downstage Theatre and actor with the New Zealand Opera Company, and was involved in the formation of what became Toi Whakaari o Aotearoa: New Zealand Drama School. In 1970 he was appointed lecturer in drama at Victoria University, the first position of its kind in the country, became professor in 1997 and took retirement in 1998. He has retained his involvement in professional theatre, directing memorable first productions of Alistair ★Campbell's *When the Bough Breaks* (1970), Vincent ★O'Sullivan's ★*Shuriken* (1993), Greg ★McGee's ★*Tooth and Claw* (1983) and ★Renée's *Pass It On* (1986).

He has written extensively for theatre and radio. In 1978–80 he spent two years in Beijing, studying oriental theatre and working at the New China News Agency, and there wrote his first science fiction novel, *The Eye of the Queen* (1982). Inspired in part, he says, by the experience of living in an alien culture, it documents the traumatic contact between Earth and an advanced alien civilisation. The book was well reviewed in UK ('rarely have I been made aware so credibly of creatures so utterly unlike us,' said *The Times*). The next two works, *Master of Paxwax* (1986) and *The Fall of the Families* (1987), form the 'gardener' sequence, recounting the saga of Pawl Paxwax and his struggle against the Eleven Families which control the explored universe. The style is more uninhibited than the classically SF *Eye*, and was described as 'superior space opera'. *Pioneers* (1988) confirmed that Mann writes in the intellectual and moral tradition of M.K. ★Joseph, as well as being the first of his novels to have a New Zealand setting. Its story is of a cloned creature and his attempts to understand the limits and demands of human nature. *Wulfsyarn* (1991) develops the concern with individual morality, especially in regard to masculinity and the human capacity for violence and self-delusion. Images of St Francis, Dionysus and Achilles symbolise the choices confronting the distraught hero Wilberfoss as he captains a doomed hospital ship.

Mann then produced the major quartet, *A Land Fit for Heroes*, set in an alternative universe in which the Roman Empire was never defeated and Christianity did not become a dominant religion. A rationalist, urban but militaristic Roman aristocracy is contrasted (in a city–pastoral antithesis that goes back in science fiction to Wells) with the intuitive native British community who inhabit the forests. The four individual titles are *Escape from the Wild Wood* (1991), *Stand Alone Stan* (1993), *The Dragon Wakes* (1995) and *The Burning Forest* (1996).

A versatile craftsman in various SF modes, Mann persists in his concerns with complex technologies, alien life forms, and variants on zoological and botanical variety—the giant Hammer in *Paxwax*, for instance, has its origins in the New Zealand weta. Most characteristically, he explores ethical, political and social themes, always with awareness of the mystical dimension and a distrust of the wholly rational. Published and known in the UK, his work has received little attention in New Zealand, a review article by David Groves in *New Zealand Books* being the most sustained commentary to date. JS

MANSFIELD, Katherine (1) (1888–1923), was born in Wellington as Kathleen Mansfield Beauchamp, into a family with vigorous social ambitions. Her mother was the delicate and aloof Annie Dyer; her father, Harold Beauchamp, a canny and successful businessman. A first cousin in Sydney became the best-selling novelist, and Mansfield's first role model, Elizabeth von Arnim.

Mansfield's early school years were spent in Karori, a village in the hills a few miles from Wellington, until the Beauchamps returned to Wellington, to an impressive merchant's mansion and a more select social programme, when she was 11. At first she attended Wellington GC, then Miss Swainson's private school. In 1903 Beauchamp, now director of the Bank of New Zealand, chose Queen's College, Harley Street, London, an institution founded by Charles Kingsley for the liberal education of women, to add metropolitan polish to his clever and handsome daughter. She immersed herself in French, German and music, and began writing sketches and prose poems. In the *Queen's College Magazine* she published 'About Pat', her first re-creation of childhood in Karori, written in direct and simple prose, as well as 'Die Einsame', redolent with *fin-de-siècle* motifs and *symboliste* elaboration of mood. The New Zealander and the European had begun their never quite resolved engagement.

Kathleen Beauchamp returned to Wellington, rebellious and unsettled, in late 1906. Although her life was comfortable and socially expansive, for the next twenty months she warred against parental vigilance, and found Wellington understandably provincial. She filled what she later called 'great complaining notebooks', published her first work under noms de plume in *The Lone Hand* and *The Native Companion* in Australia, and moved through a number of furtive infatuations with men and women. She also made an extended caravan journey into remote Urewera country in the middle of the North Island, her one experience of 'roughing it', returning home with a liking for Māori and English tourists, 'but nothing in between'. Her father accepted her plea for musical training in England and she arrived again in London in August 1908, 'Katherine Mansfield' already decided on as her pen-name.

Within weeks life was, as she had hoped, complex and sophisticated. She was in love with Garnet Trowell, a young violinist whose father had taught her the cello in Wellington. When the affair collapsed some months later, she impulsively married G.C. Bowden, a singing teacher whose name she officially bore for the next nine years, but whom she left the day after the marriage. She returned to Garnet, travelled with his opera company, became pregnant, and again separated. During those months she depended, as she was to do for the rest of her life, on her close but exasperating friendship with Ida Baker, her Rhodesian school chum from Queen's College. Usually referred to as L.M. ('Leslie Moore') or Jones, she was also variously nicknamed over the years as the Albatross, the Cornish Pasty, the Faithful One. A coldly efficient Annie Beauchamp, wrongly suspecting an 'unhealthy' friendship with Ida, arrived from New Zealand to install her daughter at Wörishofen, Bavaria, hoping that the famous water cure might restore normality.

After the birth of a stillborn child, Mansfield stayed on in *Germany until the next January. She formed a liaison of sorts with the Polish translator, journalist and con-man, Floryan Wyspiansky. Later he would attempt to blackmail her with letters she wrote at this time, but he encouraged her to read Russian writers, especially Chekhov, and was indirectly responsible for her finest poem, 'To Stanislaw Wyspiansky'. Ostensibly a tribute to a Polish patriot and poet, it prompted her to consider her own country, 'Making its own history, slowly and clumsily / Piecing together this and that, finding the pattern, solving the problem, / Like a child with a box of bricks' and remarking of herself, with a Whitmanesque bravura, 'I, a woman, with the taint of the pioneer in my blood'.

The months in Bavaria also provided the occasion for the satirical stories she began contributing to A.R. Orage's journal, the *New Age*, once she was back in England. The stories spared neither Germans nor family life, and presented sex, pregnancy and social divisions with almost ferocious candour. These *New Age* stories, and a number of others, were collected in 1911 as *In a German Pension. As well as presenting her as a fresh and incisive voice, Mansfield's association with the respected Fabian weekly led to a close and ultimately bitter friendship with Orage's eccentric South African mistress, Beatrice Hastings. Still dependent on Ida Baker's homely loyalty, but drawn to the modish insouciance of her new literary circle, Mansfield took her most decisive turn when, at the end of 1911, she met the precociously gifted, lower-middle-class Oxford undergraduate, John Middleton *Murry. He was already the founding editor of *Rhythm*, a quarterly self-consciously dedicated to the spirit of Modernism, to Mahler in music, Post-Impressionism in art, and Bergson in philosophy, yet calling also for 'guts and bloodiness', an escape from both Englishness and aestheticism. It was a call that brought from Mansfield the small group of New Zealand stories that depicted the emotional and physical violence of raw colonial life. In 'The ★Woman at the Store', 'Millie' and 'Ole Underwood', she moved the popular colonial low-brow yarn towards a fresh psychological depth and an awareness of impressionist technique. Although Dan ★Davin excluded them from his *Selected Stories* (Oxford University Press, 1953) as dealing 'with scenes she had glimpsed only superficially', they are an essential part of her oeuvre, the first New Zealand stories to thread human behaviour with the brooding grimness of landscape. In a much-quoted sentence from 'The Woman at the Store', which Allen ★Curnow took up as epigraph to his *Penguin Book of New Zealand Verse* (1960), she noted 'There is no twilight in our New Zealand days, but a curious half-hour when everything appears grotesque—it frightens—as though the savage spirit of the country walked abroad and sneered at what it saw.'

Within weeks of meeting, Mansfield and Murry had set up house together, assuming the literary role of 'the two tigers', and begun their habit of addressing each other as Tig and Wig. Her new allegiances drew a series of savage satirical attacks in Orage's portrait of her as 'Mrs Foisacre' in the *New Age*. When *Rhythm* folded in mid-1913, she and Murry jointly edited the three issues of its successor, the *Blue Review*. Soon after they began an intense and troubled friendship with D.H. ★Lawrence and Frieda Weekley, at whose marriage they featured as official witnesses.

At the end of the same year, their attempt to set up as writers in Paris was cut short by Murry's bankruptcy in the wake of his collapsed journals. Mansfield had written only ★'Something Childish but Very Natural', and life back in England meant frequently changed addresses and meagre funds. Soon after the outbreak of World War 1, they moved to Great Missenden, with the Lawrences not far off, and Mansfield began her deep and lasting friendship with the Ukrainian Jew, S.S. Koteliansky. When her relationship with Murry seemed close to falling apart, she set out for Paris in early 1915, to the borrowed apartment of the French novelist, journalist and committed bohemian Francis ★Carco. But first she visited Carco at Gray, in the Zone des Armées where he was posted. The brief affair contributed to her war story, 'An ★Indiscreet Journey', as did Carco himself to the cynical roué, Raoul Duquette, three years later in her 'cry against corruption', ★'Je ne parle pas français'.

Before her return to Murry, Mansfield began in *The ★Aloe* what she hoped would be a novel based on her own family, and the move when she was a child from Tinakori Road to Karori. Memories were further revived when she met up with her beloved younger brother Leslie, who had joined a British regiment. For the Autumn issue of the *Signature*, a short-lived periodical put together by Murry and Lawrence, she wrote 'The ★Wind Blows', an exquisitely controlled re-creation of adolescence and the Wellington of her girlhood. But the enduring motive for a return to New Zealand settings, and her intense focusing on both memory and a new narrative technique, was the death of her brother in Belgium in October 1915. As she wrote soon after, 'the form that I would choose has changed utterly. I feel no longer concerned with the same appearance of things.' Two years later, when Virginia Woolf asked for a story for her Hogarth Press, Mansfield reshaped *The Aloe* into ★*Prelude* (1918). Now a shorter fiction in twelve discrete sections that cut and overlap in a method she derived from cinema, it ran together symbolism and realism with a vivid emotional resonance, achieving 'that special prose' she equated with both elegy and celebration. 'And won't the "Intellectuals" just hate it', she said. 'They'll think it's a New Primer for Infant Readers. Let 'em.' She continued to mine her early memories, while also writing clever, more brittle stories, such as ★'Bliss' and 'Psychology', that drew on her friendship with the Garsington and Bloomsbury 'sets', and allowed her the satirical stance that was also a self-protective play.

Mansfield's friendship with the Lawrences had reached crisis point in Cornwall in mid-1916. Although she felt Lawrence's dark spasms of rage were so close to her own temper, the 'dear man', as she wrote to a mutual friend, had become lost in 'the immense german Christmas pudding which is Frieda. And with all the appetite in the world one cannot eat one's way through Frieda to find him.' She grew closer to Lady Ottoline Morrell and, more cautiously, to Virginia Woolf. For a time Maynard Keynes was her landlord, Lytton Strachey was attracted to her because she was like a Japanese doll, Bertrand Russell admired her mind and attempted an affair, while T.S. Eliot warned Ezra Pound she was 'a dangerous woman'. But Mansfield's wary colonial elusiveness allowed more relaxed friendships with artists and the mildly eccentric—for a time, with the East End painter Mark Gertler, and the androgynous Carrington; more enduringly, from 1912 onwards with the Scottish painter J.D. Fergusson, and the American Anne Estelle Rice, whose portrait of her is in the National Museum in Wellington; and increasingly with the deaf aristocrat, Dorothy Brett, who also painted. But it was illness, rather than choice, that led to her gradual separation from most of her friends in England.

From early 1918, when her tuberculosis became a matter of serious concern, Mansfield moved constantly between London and the Riviera. Even after her marriage to Murry in mid-year, she remained dependent on Ida Baker as companion and quasi-nurse, while Murry was committed to his war work in MI5, then later to his journalism. With various winterings-over in Bandol, Ospedaletti, San Remo and Menton, and summers back in Hampstead, Mansfield accumulated enough stories to put together *Bliss and Other Stories* (1920). In early 1919 Murry had taken over editorship of the *Athenaeum* and separation, reuniting, and again separation established itself as the rhythm of their lives, while there flowed between them a highly charged correspondence. Mansfield's letters were always an amalgam of wit, *joie de vivre*, and direct emotional exchange. Those written to Murry took on the added poignancy of a constant but frequently tested love, with the sharp tracing of her illness in the recurring sequence of elation as she first moved, regret and confusion while they were apart, then restored delight. Her vivacity and frankness as a correspondent increasingly prompts critics to value her letters as highly as her fiction. Taken with her numerous notebooks, they offer a richly detailed account of a modern woman's engagement with love, art, solitude, impending death and war. 'The war is in all of us,' she wrote, even after hostilities were over, as she increasingly drew an analogy between the corruptions of civilisation and her own physical decay.

The most fruitful period in Mansfield's creative life began when she rented the Villa Isola Bella in Menton in September 1920. In the previous eighteen months, much of her energy had gone into almost weekly reviews for the *Athenaeum*, and translations of Chekhov's letters, in collaboration with her friend Koteliansky. Although diverting and astute, she seldom had the chance in her reviews to discuss any but inferior fiction. She was now determined to concentrate on her own work—'they are already chopping down the cherry trees', as she wrote in her awareness of limited time. At Menton she wrote the bitter and posthumously published 'Poison', touching again on the tensions of her marriage, but also the compassionate *'Miss Brill' and 'The *Stranger', and 'The *Daughters of the Late Colonel', which attracted critical acclaim and the admiration of Thomas Hardy, when published in the *London Mercury* in May 1921. That same month Mansfield left for Switzerland, where she and Murry, who had resigned from the *Athenaeum*, took a chalet at Montana-sur-Sierre. She worked diligently to produce made-to-measure stories for the high fees paid by the *Sphere*, but also some of her strongest New Zealand stories—'I long, above everything else, to write about *family love*.'

Returning to the characters of *Prelude*, and her own projection as the child Kezia, she wrote *'At the Bay', as well as *'Her First Ball', 'The *Garden Party', 'The *Doll's House', and in a very different key, the enigmatic and unfinished 'A *Married Man's Story'.

Disillusioned with current medical practice, Mansfield decided on an expensive and useless X-ray treatment. The move to Paris early in 1922 brought her into the circle of Russian emigré intellectuals, while her own reading of Ouspensky, her conviction that she must now 'risk anything', and the renewed influence of her early mentor Orage, led her to seek a cure that was spiritual as much as physical. She wrote little in Paris, but early in the year produced 'The *Fly', her classic final statement on war, futility and courage, and the last of her many attempts to depict her father. In her final story 'The *Canary', the image of the singing and ailing bird is to some extent a representation of herself and the limitations of her own writing, a low-key elegy in which grief becomes acceptance and, ultimately, mystery.

After a brief return to Sierre, and two months in London, in October Mansfield entered the Gurdjieff Institute for Harmonious Development at Fontainebleau. Commentators and biographers remain troubled by her decision to place herself under the direction of a guru who is often presented unsympathetically, and to live in a commune of Russians and truth-seekers—'my people at last', as she called them. Although Gurdjieff treated her kindly, she was by no means a disciple. Her quest was very much along personal lines, a movement against what she regarded as the crippling intellectualism of post-war European life. In almost her last letter, she declared her goal to be total honesty. 'If I were allowed one single cry to God, that cry would be: *I want to be REAL.*' She died at Fontainebleau on 9 January 1923, a few weeks before the publication of *The Garden Party and Other Stories*, which confirmed her place among the Modernists of her generation.

Murry was criticised by his contemporaries, and savagely satirised in Aldous Huxley's *Point Counter Point* (1928), for his enthusiasm in publishing his wife's literary remains, and by later critics for his reverential management of her reputation. But our debt to him is considerable. From her uncollected and unpublished stories he produced *The Doves' Nest and Other Stories* (1923) and *Something Childish and Other Stories* (1924). He followed these with *Poems* (1924), *The Journal of Katherine Mansfield* (1927), the two-volume *The Letters of Katherine Mansfield* (1928), *The Aloe* (1930), *Novels and Novelists* (1930), *The Scrapbook of Katherine Mansfield* (1937), *Katherine Mansfield's Letters to John Middleton Murry, 1913–1922* (1951) and a misnamed 'Definitive Edition' of the *Journal of Katherine Mansfield* (1954).

There have been numerous editions and collections of Mansfield's stories in over twenty languages, although Antony *Alpers's *The Stories of Katherine Mansfield* (1984) was the first scholarly edition, establishing definitive texts. A comparative text of 'The Aloe' with 'Prelude' (1982), an enlarged edition of *Poems* (1988) and *The New Zealand Stories of Katherine Mansfield* (1997) were edited by Vincent O'Sullivan. Four of the five volumes of *The Collected Letters of Katherine Mansfield*, edited by O'Sullivan and Margaret Scott, have appeared between 1982 and 1996. The *Journals*, edited by Margaret Scott, were published in two volumes in 1997. Alpers's *The Life of Katherine Mansfield* (1982), successor to his ground-breaking *Katherine Mansfield, A Biography* (1953), remains the fullest and essential account of her life. Other biographical studies include Ruth Elvish Mantz and J.M. Murry, *The Life of Katherine Mansfield* (1933), Jeffrey Meyers, *Katherine Mansfield* (1978) and Claire Tomalin, *Katherine Mansfield: A Secret Life* (1987). VO

MANSFIELD, Katherine (2), is at best a qualified national icon in New Zealand. As an expatriate writing in the London literary world and reflecting European movements of thought she had little connection with early New Zealand writing, which accorded her little recognition. In Europe Francis *Carco, John Middleton *Murry and Aldous Huxley put versions of her into novels, and other accounts were published by A.R. Orage, Olgivanna, Beatrice Hastings and others. Robin *Hyde caught the ambivalence of the local response in her article 'The Great New Zealand Novel' (1929): we 'murmur sympathetically if vaguely "Katherine the Great".... But she went far from us ... most of her tales were written in a subtle foreign language which is not yet fully understood out here ... the language of twentieth century art'. O.N. *Gillespie included her in *New Zealand Short Stories* (1930) but observed that 'the average New Zealander is prouder of Sir Ernest Rutherford than of Katherine Mansfield'. There was little published response, imaginative or scholarly, apart from her father Harold Beauchamp's *Recollections and Reminiscences* (1937), until Pat *Lawlor's *The Mystery of Maata: A Katherine Mansfield Novel* (1946). D.M. *Davin's *Selected Stories* for Oxford University Press (1953), Antony *Alpers's first version of the life, *Katherine Mansfield, a Biography* (USA, 1953; UK 1954) and Joan *Stevens's discussion in *New Zealand Short Stories* (1968) were similarly early as treatments by New Zealand scholars.

The establishment of the Katherine *Mansfield Memorial Awards in 1959 indicated growing recognition, as did the *Mansfield Memorial Fellowship in 1970. Only then, fifty years after her death, did New Zealand imaginative writing begin to engage with this complex presence in the country's cultural history (Lawlor's book excepted). Brian *McNeill's successful play *The Two Tigers* (1973, publ. 1977), about the Mansfield–Murry relationship, began this process, though Pat Evison's readings, 'An Evening with Katherine Mansfield' (1971, recorded 1972) were a precursor. In scholarship, Ian *Gordon's editions of the New Zealand stories, *Undiscovered Country* (1974) and the *The Urewera Notebook* (1978), were followed by editorial and critical work, by (among others) Vincent *O'Sullivan, Helen McNeish, C.K. *Stead, Cherry Hankin, Margaret Scott, Gillian Boddy, Lawrence *Jones and Andrew Gurr, with Alpers's revised *Life* (1980) and edition of the *Stories* (1984) the seminal books in establishing the significance and nature of Mansfield's New Zealand identity. Michael *Gifkins edited *The Garden Party: Katherine Mansfield's New Zealand Stories* (1987) and Vincent O'Sullivan *The New Zealand Stories of Katherine Mansfield* (1997).

Cathy *Downes's solo *The Case of Katherine Mansfield* (1978, publ. 1995), compiled entirely from Mansfield's words, has now been performed more than 500 times. Mansfield stories have also been adapted in New Zealand for film (*The Doll's House*, dir. Rudall Hayward, 1975), television ('The Woman at the Store', 1974), workshop theatre (Craig Thaine, *Today's Bay*, 1982, publ. 1983), ballet ('Bliss', Royal New Zealand Ballet, 1986), opera-drama (Peter *Wells, 'Ricordi!', 1996), chamber-opera (Dorothy *Buchanan, 'The Woman at the Store', libretto by Jeremy Commons, 1998) and frequently for radio, the earliest probably 'Daughters of the Late Colonel' in 1947 and the most important the 1988 Centennial Year series produced by Elizabeth *Alley. Mansfield's life has produced two films involving New Zealand artists, *Leave All Fair*, directed by John Reid (1984) and *A Portrait of Katherine Mansfield: The Woman and the Writer*, script by Gillian Boddy, directed by Julienne Stretton (1987).

New Zealand's attitude to its national icons being what it is, most literary energy has gone into challenging, subverting or displacing her status. Examples of canonising, sanitising or elevating her into a literary progenitor are hard to find. Her stories and life are often now used as the starting point of updated or 'reinscribed' variations. Janet *Frame alludes somewhat ironically to Menton and Mansfield (as 'Margaret Rose Hurndell ... our famous writer') in *Living in the Maniototo* (1979). Rachel *McAlpine provides new angles and narrators for five stories in poems in *Fancy Dress* (1979). Patricia *Grace indicates the cultural distance between a teacher's adulation for 'Kay Em' and a Māori schoolboy's priorities in 'Letters from Whetu' (*The Dream Sleepers*, 1980). Ian *Wedde in *Symmes Hole* (1986) presents Mansfield largely as a figure of death and of distraction from an essentially *Pacific culture. Mansfield's illness and death are again the dominant allusions in poems by Fleur *Adcock and Marilyn *Duckworth (see *Landfall 172, 1989, a special Mansfield issue), and her exile, 'an old / woman / living in Menton', in Bob *Orr's 'K.M.' (in Breeze, 1991). O'Sullivan's dark mock music-hall frolic, Jones and Jones (1988, publ. 1989), irreverently explores the Mansfield–Ida Baker relationship. Alma *de Groen's feminist play on power, The Rivers of China (1988), focuses on Mansfield's elusive or fragmentary identity ('You have dozens of selves, all calling themselves "Katherine Mansfield"'). Bill *Manhire's jocund title The Brain of Katherine Mansfield (1988) has more to do with the Centennial year than the book's contents, Mansfield appearing only as another icon to mock, along with Samuel *Marsden and Colin Meads. Witi *Ihimaera's Dear Miss Mansfield (1989) provides a 'Māori response' and equally challenging cinéma noir versions. A poem by Anne *French and short story by Lloyd *Jones deal less than predictably with the Menton connection. Stead in The End of the Century at the End of the World (1992) has his 'Katya' faking her 1923 death and returning to New Zealand, dying in the 1950s. Chris *Orsman's poem 'Another Country' (Ornamental Gorse, 1994) has the Mansfield said to be 'imaginative to the point of untruth'.

And so on. No other New Zealand figure has troubled or challenged so many writers to irreverent, defiant or merely exploitative responses. Perhaps the most curious aspect is the underlying assumption that she ever has been an establishment icon. As Hyde said in 1929, 'we've never exactly hung her portrait on the drawing-room wall'. Corporate sponsorship of the Award and Fellowship, and the carefully restored Birthplace (a winner of the New Zealand Tourism Award) are the only signs of this. The resistance in 1988 even to the idea of a *Mansfield Centennial is discussed in a commentary in Landfall 171 (1989). Scholars are taunted about the 'Mansfield industry', yet major work remains to be done. Publication of the letters is still approaching completion, the notebooks remained one of the crucial unpublished texts in modern world literature until Margaret Scott's 1997 edition, the stories are still lacking a truly complete edition, and critical understanding is far from adequate to the work. If an icon at all, Mansfield stands for elusiveness, instability, fragmentation, incompleteness and absence. RR

Mansfield Awards, The, known fully as the Katherine Mansfield Memorial Awards, were founded in 1959 by the *New Zealand Women Writers' Society, originally with categories for the short story and the essay. Now only for the short story, the award is biennial, though exception was made by the present sponsors, the Bank of New Zealand, in recognition of the centenary year of 1988. Entries are submitted anonymously. The award has continued to be administered by past members of the Women Writers' Society, currently by a small ad hoc committee. Past winners are: 1959 Maurice *Duggan (story), Elsie *Locke (essay); 1961 C.K. *Stead (story and essay); 1963 Maurice *Shadbolt (essay discontinued); 1965 Frank *Sargeson; 1967 Maurice Shadbolt; 1969 Alice *Glenday; 1971 Wystan *Curnow; 1973 Margaret *Sutherland; 1975 Keri *Hulme; 1977 Jennifer *Compton; 1979 Vincent *O'Sullivan; 1981 Daphne de Jong (see Daphne *Clair); 1983 Anne *Kennedy; 1985 Susan *Reidy; 1987 Wendy Pond; 1988 Judith *White; 1989 Gary File; 1991 Kate *Flannery; 1993 Alistair *Paterson; 1995 Maurice Shadbolt; 1997 Rowan Metcalfe. RR

Mansfield Centennial, The, in 1988, marking the centenary of Katherine *Mansfield's birth in Wellington, was the first such celebration in New Zealand's literary history. Events were held in Wellington, at the Newberry Library, Chicago (which holds a major collection of her manuscripts), at the University of Liège in Belgium and the University of Nice in France, at Fontainebleau and Avon near Paris and Bad Wörishofen, Germany. New Zealand's Ministry of Foreign Affairs supported several of these, and commissioned a photographic exhibition compiled by Gillian Boddy that toured internationally.

In Wellington a conference at Victoria University was the largest event, attracting nearly one hundred contributing scholars, writers and performers and large audiences over five days. Mansfield's Birthplace at 25 Tinakori Road was officially opened on the birthday itself (14 October), after several years' research and restoration. There was an exhibition at the National Library, productions of two new Mansfield plays (by Alma *de Groen and Vincent *O'Sullivan), a ballet, performances of music and Mansfield's own dramatic pieces, the announcements of the Katherine *Mansfield Memorial Fellow and the Bank of New Zealand Katherine *Mansfield Short Story Award, vice-regal and mayoral receptions, tours, an extensive Radio New Zealand series of talks, interviews, dramatisations, readings and music (produced by Elizabeth *Alley) and a television documentary. The Department of Internal Affairs provided support for the co-ordination and promotion of this programme.

The conference featured New Zealand writing equally with international academic commentary, with readings by almost all former holders of the Memorial

Fellowship and many other writers, including new work relating to Mansfield by, for instance, Riemke *Ensing, A.K. *Grant, Michael *Harlow and Witi *Ihimaera. *Katherine Mansfield: In from the Margin*, a selection of papers from the Wellington and Chicago conferences, edited by their convener, Roger Robinson, was published in USA in 1994.   RR

Mansfield Fellowship, The, known fully as the Katherine Mansfield Memorial Fellowship, annually enables a New Zealand writer to live and work for most of a year in Menton, *France. This prestigious award began as an idea of Cecil and Cecilia *Manson on a visit to Menton, where *Mansfield had written so creatively in 1920–21. The stories she wrote at the Villa Isola Bella include 'The *Daughters of the Late Colonel', 'The *Stranger' and 'The *Life of Ma Parker'; but the room on the lower level of the Villa where she worked was derelict when the Mansons called in 1967. Back home in Wellington, they formed a committee to raise funds for an overseas literary bursary, receiving support from such benefactors as Donald Prater of the *Times Literary Supplement*, Sheila Winn of Wellington (also the main benefactor of Downstage Theatre), the *Queen Elizabeth II Arts Council and the Department of Internal Affairs. The 'Winn-Manson Menton Trust' was formed and the Fellowship established. Over the years the government has increased its contributions, support has also come from the French government and the City of Menton, and the Fellowship is sponsored on a generous scale by ECNZ. The Katherine Mansfield Room at the Villa Isola Bella has been furnished for the Fellows' use by the City of Menton.

The vision of Cecil and Cecilia Manson was 'to give a selected New Zealand writer a period of leisure to write or study … [in] a different and more ancient culture, and thereby to see [their] own remote country in a better perspective'. Many considerable works have emerged. Fellows have been: 1970 Owen *Leeming, 1971 Margaret Scott, 1972 C.K. *Stead, 1973 James *McNeish, 1974 Janet *Frame, 1975 David *Mitchell, 1976 Michael *King, 1977 Barry *Mitcalfe, 1978 Spiro Zavos, 1979 Philip *Temple, 1980 Marilyn *Duckworth, 1981 Lauris *Edmond, 1982 Michael *Jackson, 1983 Allen *Curnow, 1984 Rore *Hapipi, 1985 Michael *Gifkins, 1986 Michael *Harlow, 1987 Russell *Haley, 1988 Louis *Johnson, 1989 Lloyd *Jones, 1990 Lisa *Greenwood, 1991 Nigel *Cox, 1992 Maurice *Gee, 1993 Witi *Ihimaera, 1994 Vincent *O'Sullivan, 1995 Fiona *Farrell, 1996 Owen *Marshall, 1997 Roger *Hall, 1998 Maurice *Shadbolt.
                                         CM/RR

MANSON, Cecil (1896–1987) and **Cecilia** (1908–87) conjointly wrote lively books, some for children, on New Zealand biography and history, and initiated the Katherine *Mansfield Memorial Fellowship. Their titles include *Tides of Hokianga* (1956), *Doctor Agnes Bennett* (1960), *Curtain-raiser to a Colony* (1962) and *Pioneer Parade* (1966). Some of these developed from radio scripts, as they worked extensively as freelance journalists and broadcasters. Their children's books include *The Lonely One* (1963) and *The Adventures of Johnny van Bart* (1965), both centred on friendships across ethnic boundaries. Cecil's memoir of his early life is *A World Away* (1981). They are remembered and honoured primarily for the imaginative idea of the Mansfield Fellowship for New Zealand writers in Menton, and their practical energy in raising the funds for it 1967–69. Their own experience linked New Zealand with Europe. Cecil was born in England and attended Repton School before active service in World War 1, followed by work in journalism and insurance before his move to New Zealand, where he became a portrait photographer and artist. Cecilia was born in Carterton and educated at Wairarapa College and Victoria University College. They married in 1939, before Cecil's second period of war service.
                                         RR

Manuka has been the magazine of the Auckland Teachers' College since 1909. Issues for 1932 and 1941 were printed by Robert *Lowry, with the latter number featuring work by students Kendrick *Smithyman and Keith *Sinclair. The 1960 issue included 'Only Connect (a presumptuous note on the teaching of English Literature)', a significant essay by Maurice *Duggan, which led to his story *'Along Rideout Road that Summer'.   SH

Manuscript collections containing manuscripts and archives of value for research into New Zealand literature are nearly all held in public institutions or private hands in New Zealand. Some small and incomplete collections are held in public institutions in Australia and the United States, notably at the Mitchell Library in Sydney (a few nineteenth and early twentieth-century writers), and the University of Texas at Austin and Boston University (a few mid to late twentieth-century writers). Katherine *Mansfield MSS are in Austin, the Newberry Library, Chicago, and Queen's University, Toronto (see *Alpers), as well as the large collection in the *Alexander Turnbull Library. The British Library holds manuscripts of major British–New Zealand works such as *Erewhon*.

The earliest systematic collecting was by government officials, settlers and missionaries of Māori-language versions of myths, legends and traditional history, which included song-poetry. Most were commissioned from Māori scribes, but some were written by Europeans from oral accounts. Notable collections were made by Sir George *Grey (now in the Auckland Public Library), Edward *Shortland (*Hocken Library), John *White, S. Percy *Smith, Elsdon *Best (all Alexander Turnbull Library) and George Graham (Auckland Institute and Museum and Auckland Public Library). The major collection of song-poetry was undertaken by Sir Apirana *Ngata, beginning in the 1920s and published as *Nga Moteatea* in 4 volumes, 1929–90, many of the manuscripts for which are in the Alexander Turnbull Library. The oral tradition has also been preserved as sound recordings. The major collection is the Archive of Maori and Pacific Island Music at the University of Auckland. From the 1850s personal manuscripts books were created by Māori scribes to record family and tribal histories. Some of these have gone to public institutions, but many thousands of notebooks, often written in school exercise books, are still held privately by individuals and tribes. See also *Maori manuscript collections.

From 1840 an increasing number of archival and manuscript records were created in New Zealand but collection and preservation was haphazard in the nineteenth and early twentieth centuries. Records accumulated by government agencies were not well cared for until the National Archives were created by the Archives Act of 1957, so that some major gaps exist in the official record before that date. None of the major libraries, governmental, university or public, showed an interest in collecting manuscripts until well into the twentieth century. Such deliberate collection and preservation as there was remained the province of the private collectors, and both Dr T.M. *Hocken and Alexander *Turnbull built substantial collections of manuscripts and archives to supplement their collections of printed materials, all of which are now in the public institutions named after them.

Sustained and directed collecting of manuscripts and archives by public institutions began only in the late 1940s, with the Auckland Institute and Museum Library, the Alexander Turnbull Library, the Canterbury Museum Library and the Hocken Library leading the way, and provincial museums, such as those in Gisborne, Taranaki and Hawkes Bay, playing minor roles. University collecting (apart from the Hocken at Otago) dates from the late 1960s, and small but significant collections have been developed at Auckland, Waikato, Massey, Victoria and Canterbury. Public art galleries have also begun collecting manuscripts and archives relating to New Zealand art. In recent years local public libraries, historical societies and museums have become active collectors of local and regional manuscripts and archives. Today there are several hundred repositories which are actively collecting and preserving manuscripts and archives.

In recent years manuscripts and archives relating to New Zealand held in repositories in the United Kingdom, France, Germany, the Vatican, the United States, Australia and the Pacific nations have been copied, mostly on microfilm, for a small group of New Zealand libraries. The Alexander Turnbull Library has the largest collection of such copies but there are significant holdings in the National Archives and the Hocken Library. A summary of the Turnbull's holdings is given in the *Turnbull Library Record*, Vol. 24, No. 1 (May 1991), 19–30.

Most institutions in New Zealand have broad collecting policies and do not draw a clear distinction between manuscripts (letters, diaries and other texts created by individuals, either handwritten or typescript) and archives (the records created by organisations, including files of correspondence, minutes of meetings, financial records, etc.)

The major directories of archives and manuscripts repositories are Frank Rogers's *Archives New Zealand 4: Directory of Archives and Manuscripts Repositories in New Zealand, the Cook Islands, Fiji, Tokelau, Tonga and Western Samoa* (1992) and his *Archives New Zealand 3: Medicine and Public Health* (1990) and the more specialised *Te Hīkoi Mārama: A Directory of Māori Information Resources* (1993). The major finding aids for non-governmental archives and manuscripts are the *Union Catalogue of New Zealand and Pacific Manuscripts in New Zealand Libraries*, published in 2 volumes 1968–69, and its successor, the loose-leaf *National Register of Archives and Manuscripts in New Zealand, 1979–1994*, both compiled and edited at the Alexander Turnbull Library. They include entries for material copied from overseas repositories. Neither the *Union Catalogue* nor the *National Register* are comprehensive records, and they should be used with care. Major acquisitions of manuscripts and archives for a wide range of institutions are listed regularly in *Archifacts*, and the *Turnbull Library Record* and the *Annual Report of the Hocken Library* provide more comprehensive listings for these two institutions. A few inventories and calendars of collections have been published, notably by the Alexander Turnbull Library and the Auckland University Library. Most institutions have in-house inventories or series lists for their archives and manuscript collections.

The Alexander Turnbull Library with some 6000 metres has the major collection of non-governmental manuscripts and archives in New Zealand. Under the National Library Act 1965 it is responsible for maintaining a national collection of library materials, including manuscripts and non-governmental archives, relating to

New Zealand. It is strong in Māori language manuscripts, including the Polynesian Society and Maori Purposes Fund Board Archives and papers of John White, Sir Donald McLean, W.B.D. Mantell, S. Percy Smith, Elsdon Best, James *Cowan, and Pei Te Hurinui *Jones. It has extensive collections of papers of New Zealand writers and archives of several publishing firms and literary journals. It also has fragmentary holdings of manuscripts of overseas authors, mainly Australian, and an important collection of papers of James Hogg, the Scottish writer. Other strengths are political papers, labour and business archives, the archives of women's organisations, scientific papers, and the archives of churches and community organisations, especially for the greater Wellington area.

The Hocken Library in Dunedin is particularly strong in archives and manuscripts relating to the Otago-Southland area, especially community organisations, churches, business firms, local authorities and trade unions. Its collections of literary papers are of national importance, including papers of James K.*Baxter and Janet *Frame.

The Library of the Auckland Institute and Museum has particular strengths in the Auckland provincial area, notably in the archives of churches, business firms, community, cultural and women's organisations, scientists' papers, war archives, Māori language manuscripts, and material relating to the Pacific nations.

The Canterbury Museum has strong collections relating to the Canterbury area and a major Antarctic collection with both archives and personal papers.

The Auckland Public Library specialises in the Auckland City and Province with good collections on local government and community and cultural organisations. The literary papers include Sir George Grey's Māori manuscripts and letters, and papers of John A. Lee, Jane *Mander and Robin *Hyde.

The *University of Auckland Library's New Zealand and Pacific Collection has over 200 collections of archives and manuscripts, mostly relating to the Auckland area and the University. Strengths are trade union and political archives and papers and the papers of writers associated with the university.

The *Victoria University Library specialises in archives and personal papers relating to the university, trade unions and professional associations, and literary manuscripts.

The University of Canterbury Library's collections are mostly trade union, political and business archives and papers relating to the Canterbury area. Literary papers include those of Ursula *Bethell and J.E. *Weir.

Levels of care and conservation are uneven. The first full-time professional conservator of library and archival materials in New Zealand was appointed to the Alexander Turnbull Library in the early 1970s. There is widespread concern for the preservation of archival and manuscript records, but the resources available are inadequate. Demand is high from users of Māori manuscript and archival materials, especially those relating to land ownership, and from family history researchers.   JT

Maori Girl (1960), a novel by Noel *Hilliard, first of the 'Maori Girl tetralogy', caused great public excitement when it appeared but is rarely mentioned in current debates. It is the story of Netta Samuel's migration from a rural background in Taranaki, described lovingly in the first quarter of the book, to the city of Wellington. There she is exploited sexually and in the workplace by the negative forces of capitalism. She seeks security and love, but in the end is left by her lover, Arthur, when he finds that the child she is bearing is not his. *Maori Girl* was awarded the Hubert Church Memorial Award of *PEN.

On the whole, Māori readers and those who sympathised with their lot were more enthusiastic than others. Melvin Taylor in Te *Ao Hou (March 1961) said that 'it is a story that has been lived many times though no other writer has seen it so clearly or painted it so vividly as Mr. Hilliard.... For those who have waited years for this theme to be dramatised, and there are many, I would say that this is it—the New Zealand novel of our time, in that it deals successfully with perhaps the major social problem of our time.' By contrast, Paul Day in *Landfall summarised his negative view with the words: 'Hilliard has fallen between the two stools of reporting and imaginative creation.'

Ironically, the former group of readers have led to the decline of respect for Hilliard's novel, on the grounds that a book written by a Pākehā cannot give an adequate account of Māori life. On the other hand, the book has never really lost favour with general readers, has never been out of print since 1960 and was reprinted in 1997 with, at the author's suggestion, a picture of his wife on the cover. (He always denied that Kiriwai and Netta were identical but admitted that racism experienced by his wife and himself went into the book.)

Over almost two decades, Hilliard worked on three sequels to *Maori Girl*. The first was *Power of Joy* (1965), the story of Paul Bennett's childhood and adolescence. The authoritarian attitudes prevailing in his family in a railway works settlement are matched by those of the boarding school he is sent to, and it is mainly in the beauty of Taranaki landscapes that he finds relief. He finds life in Wellington no easier as he struggles to make a living. From a distance he admires a woman, Netta Samuel, the 'Maori Girl' of the earlier book; but this novel is the story of Paul and his struggle with the economic forces of the *Depression. On the whole, critics did not enthuse, finding its realism dreary, although Joan *Stevens in *NZ Listener made the same point more positively: 'no aery-faery stuff, but rooted in specific and salty actualities'.

In *Maori Woman* (1974) Paul and Netta are drawn into a closer relationship. Netta, depressed after the loss of a child and working in a clothing factory, seeks consolation from a Māori friend, Jason Pine. Paul brings her out of her depression and both return to Taranaki before marrying. Paul's parents are hostile to the idea of a Māori daughter-in-law. Their intolerance is mirrored by Jason Pine's dislike of Pākehā, and the novel ends with Netta in hospital after a violent confrontation between Jason and Paul. The narrative point of view moves between the characters to reveal the range of attitudes towards race. In the *Public Service Journal* Conrad Bollinger noted, 'it succeeds in presenting a compositive vision of contemporary New Zealand life which will strike at the emotional solar plexus of all of us'.

The final volume of the tetralogy, *The Glory and the Dream* (1978), finds Netta and Paul married and soon with a baby daughter. To the surprise of both parties, the cultural difficulties that emerge as they live together are deeper than their tolerance led them to expect. This mature novel of married life is more subtle than its predecessors and less open to the charge of unsuccessfully blending fiction and documentary.   NW

Māori Language Commission, Te Taura Whiri i te Reo Māori, was established by the Maori Language Act 1987, which also declared Māori to be an 'official' language of New Zealand. In the Act the Commission's functions are described as: 'to promote the Maori language amongst New Zealanders in general, but more particularly in those communities where its use is strongest; to encourage and assist government departments and other public institutions in the development of Māori language services; and to liaise with existing Māori language organisations with a view to coordinated action.' The commission consists of a full-time commissioner, four other members and a permanent secretariat.

One of the tasks of the commission has been to conduct research in order to produce a database of new Māori terminology. This project includes finding and coining new words for objects, concepts and activities not available to traditional Māori situations (just as English vocabulary is continuously and rapidly evolving). Such terms have been published in the commission's two-way Māori–English *dictionary, Te Matatiki, which was first published in 1992 and in a revised edition in 1996.

A major part of the commission's work is encouraging the use of Māori in all public institutions and other sections of the community such as television and radio broadcasting. This recognises the fact that among the many minority groups in New Zealand, Māori have a special status as the *tangata whenua. There is a daily television news programme in Māori (*Te Karere*) as well as two current affairs and cultural events programmes (*Waka Huia* and *Marae*). The maintenance of very high standards in these programmes, despite limited resources, has been a remarkable achievement. The development of local Māori radio stations has also been remarkable for strong initiatives in the face of material difficulties.

The fact that the Māori language is a national treasure (taonga—one of those guaranteed by the Treaty of Waitangi), because it is unique to New Zealand, is widely recognised. The provisional results of the recent National Māori Language Survey have shown that there are about 10 000 high to very high fluency speakers of Māori remaining and perhaps ten times as many of 16 and older who speak or understand some Māori. More significant than such statistics is the long historical and powerful cultural heritage associated with it. The Māori Language Commission is the main government institution charged with preserving and actively developing that heritage.   NW

Māori literature is a term that makes sense only in terms of Western literature and raises many difficulties. Publications such as New Zealand poetry collections have wrestled with the place of Māori poetical forms, both traditional and temporary. Clearly Māori did and do create poetical compositions which might be described as literature, particularly oral literature; yet the term fails to capture the entirety of the tradition. For example, most writers in the West have since the Renaissance intended their works to be represented on the written page. *Moteatea composers on the other hand conceive their work essentially for performance, while the 'literary' quality of the texts cannot be denied.

'Māori literature' as a term has other difficulties. Much so-called 'Māori literature', the material found in *Grey's *Ko nga *mahinga a nga Tupuna Maori*, was not composed within an ethnic grouping known as Māori. Traditions related in that publication are written representations of oral traditions handed down since pre-contact times, when the term Māori, as we know it today, was not employed and where identity in the pre-Māori world was delineated by tribe and sub-tribe. There was no such thing as a 'Māori' person prior to the arrival of Europeans. The implied homogeneity of 'Māori' literature is a misrepresentation. Nor can the term reflect the world-view from which, say, the *Māui round of stories was created. It suffers from the same problem as the terms 'myth' and 'legend'. It is undeniable that the stories relating to *Hawaiki, for example, do exhibit some of the elements customarily associated with myth and legend in the West, but the terms cannot bring us closer to how those who created these traditions and stories viewed them. What purpose did they serve?

Finally, the difference between pre-contact and post-contact forms requires a series of terms rather than the broad categorisation of 'literature'. We need to identify the forms that arose from a philosophical paradigm that can be confidently described as unaffected by European influence.

The traditional Māori world-view is related in the concept entitled 'Te Ao Mārama', literally 'the world of light'. Pre-contact Māori viewed the world in these terms and everything that subsequently arose in Māori society is drawn from and reflective of this world-view. Hence, one can argue for a Te Ao Mārama literature. Clearly, this world-view changed rapidly with exposure to European culture. Māori noted this change and came up with terms to symbolise the new world they inhabited. One such is 'Te Ao Hurihuri', a term that recognises that although Māori views on existence, the Māori world-view, had not entirely disappeared, it was now sharing the stage with Western culture. 'Te Ao Hurihuri' literature may include compositional forms from pre-contact times, but also adopts non-Māori forms to meet a Māori goal. This adoption is evident in the novel, in the use by Māori of a Western model of theatre, and in Māori poetry in English. It is time to develop a terminology that goes beyond the ethnicity-centred hold-all of 'Māori literature', one that reflects the complex paradigm in which that literature is now created.   CR

Māori manuscript collections (see also *Manuscript collections) are a very valuable part of the corpus of Māori literature. Many manuscripts remain unpublished, and many of those used in nineteenth-century publications might be re-evaluated in the light of twentieth-century attitudes and scholarship. Much is known about Māori society because of this literary inheritance, and much remains to be learnt from it, particularly about ancient times. The earliest material (1840s–50s) offers remarkable evidence of the transition to literacy of a once oral people, and of classical Māori language. Moreover for Māori who as a result of colonisation and the dominance of English language suffered a drastic decline in their language and cultural life (and disruption to the oral communication of knowledge), these writings are direct and tangible evidence of their ancestors' world. Some are the only source of past knowledge.

This literature is extensive. There are numbers of letters which represent political, social and personal events and experiences. There are diaries and domestic papers which recreate the ordinary course of an individual's life. There is documentation, in letters, petitions, minutes of meetings, and submissions, of interaction with government, and of the development and doctrines of nineteenth-century political and prophetic movements. But the singular material is that which records tribal history, custom and knowledge in compositions which exemplify the genres favoured in the oral tradition and the arts of language use.

These intimate, often poetic, texts are to be found in great quantity. There are chronicles of noteworthy events and prominent people, as well as informative and entertaining stories of, for example, humans' encounters with the gods and supernatural creatures. Accounts of customary practices reveal the rituals and texts of incantations associated with them. Genealogies (*whakapapa) explain kinship relationships or the origins of mankind and the natural world. A great range of *Maori sayings encapsulate proverbial wisdom, preserve quotations from narratives, define and characterise individuals and tribes. And an extraordinary number of songs (*waiata and *moteatea) and chants (*karakia) demonstrate the common use of music and poetry for all manner of occasions. A great many of these texts remain to be published.

Most of that kind of writing is a legacy of the nineteenth century, but those traditions continue to be preserved in handwritten papers in the twentieth century and brought into the public domain. Main city libraries keep the largest manuscript collections: the Auckland City Library and Auckland Museum Library, *Alexander Turnbull Library in Wellington, and *Hocken Library in Dunedin. University, provincial and tribal libraries and archives are also repositories of these important sources of information, and photocopying and microfilming have led to the availability of significant collections in several centres.

In-house catalogues provide the best information about Māori manuscripts, but the scope of them can be read from a few publications. Specific holdings are documented at a general level in *A Guide to Māori Sources at National Archives* (1995) and in detail in Jenifer Curnow's catalogue of Māori manuscripts in the Auckland Museum Library, *Ngā Pou ārahi* (1995). *Nga Iwi o te Tai Tokerau: ngā kōrero nōnamata me nāianei hoki* (1981) locates material in Māori relating to one region. A diverse range of repositories is listed in *Te Hīkoi Mārama* (1993), and an extensive survey of them in the *National Register of Archives and Manuscripts in New Zealand* (1979–1993). Computerised databases promise better access in future. At the *University of Auckland Library, for instance, database indexes are being compiled for the Maori Land

Court minute-books which, since the Court's establishment in 1865, have kept record (largely, but not only in English) of accounts of tribal life given in support of claims to ownership and administration of land.

There are considerable private holdings of manuscripts but these are often restricted to use by family members or carefully chosen researchers. Because of a close connection between knowledge and religious beliefs some Māori are opposed to public access to these valued possessions; others are cautious about giving them over to a public which has long been unappreciative, even disdainful, of Māori culture. Nevertheless personal papers have been deposited in public archives, and some contain invaluable material which is distinctive because it portrays a close, integrated view of tribal tradition and identity as it is expressed through the diverse genres of song, saying, narrative and genealogy. Pei Te Hurinui ★Jones's manuscripts, published with Bruce ★Biggs's translation in *Nga Iwi o Tainui* (1995), provide such an example.

The best-known collections of Māori manuscripts are those that were accumulated by renowned writers about Māori society such as Sir George ★Grey, John ★White, S. Percy ★Smith, Elsdon ★Best, George Graham. Papers catalogued under their names contain within them writings by many Māori. Twentieth-century scholars have brought some of these writers into prominence, for instance, in the translations and commentaries by Jenifer Curnow (★*Journal of the Polynesian Society*, 1985, 1990) and Agathe Thornton (1992) of Wiremu Maihi ★Te Rangikāheke's writing for Sir George Grey. David Simmons's analysis of Grey's editing of material for *Ko nga ★Mahinga a nga Tupuna Maori* (1854), and Michael Reilly's history of John White's collecting (*New Zealand Journal of History* 1989, 1990) have traced the origins of their manuscripts and acknowledged many Māori writers of last century.

Private and government bodies have also given rise to manuscripts of traditional knowledge. At the Alexander Turnbull Library, for instance, the papers of the Polynesian Society contain writing by Māori, not all of which has been published in the *Journal*, and the Maori Purposes Fund Board (established in 1924 with a particular objective of publishing manuscripts on Māori subjects) has deposited a similar store of papers. Mention has been made of the Maori Land Court minute-books. Other government bodies occupied with questions of land forced the oral repetition and written recording of tribal histories as minutes, submissions and reports. The subsequent value of these is exemplified in *Karanga Hokianga* (1986), which is one tribal community's publication of their history based on the minutes of turn-of-the-century land committees. The Waitangi Tribunal,

established in 1975 to hear claims against the Crown for breaches of the Treaty of Waitangi, continues this literary production, with microfiche and on-line access to submissions available in major libraries.

Māori manuscript collections have long been used by individuals in search of their family history and by scholars of Māori studies. Over the last forty years works of literary history by scholars such as Apirana ★Ngata, Pei Te Hurinui Jones, Bruce Biggs, and Margaret ★Orbell have made evident that the manuscripts are a treasure-house of the literary arts. At the end of the twentieth century, a new emphasis in the future publication of this literature might be suggested by the books which members of the Ngāti Porou people have produced in the last five years. The 1870s manuscripts by Mohi ★Ruatapu in *Ngā Kōrero a Mohi Ruatapu* (1993), and the compilations of manuscript and published writings by Reweti ★Kohere (1994), Apirana Ngata (1996), and Mohi ★Turei (1996), all acknowledge that the unpublished writings of these elders are pertinent to the future of their people as well as to a public readership.

JMcR

Māori myths and legends retold in English

make up a diverse but little developed literature. There are books for scholars and general readers, and especially for the young. There is also a journal literature, of scholarly translations and popular writing, primarily in the ★*Journal of the Polynesian Society* and Te ★*Ao Hou*. Legends associated with certain places have been reproduced in local history journals and regional magazines. The books have been abundantly illustrated, in an effort to depict a world which has seemed ancient, foreign and wonderful. Much of the literature is out of print. It attracted most interest from the late nineteenth century to the 1970s, but since then has been available only in a few works and children's books.

The myths and legends are universal in their appeal. They celebrate remarkable accomplishments of famed ancestors, report on the origins and mysteries of life and comment on fundamental aspects of human behaviour and morality. Most are anchored by names: people, creatures, canoes, places. There are a great number of such narratives in the repertoire of Māori oral tradition, because of the anecdotal style and of versions particular to the time, teller and occasion. Writers of English versions have necessarily been selective and have sought order by chronology or story type—the gods and ancestors in ★Hawaiki, voyages of migration, tribal life in ★Aotearoa, encounters with the supernatural, and so on. A distinction has sometimes been attempted between fiction and history but with little success in a tradition which combines the imaginary, the real and the religious.

Certain preferences are notable in the transfer to English. Of the cosmogonic accounts, it is common to tell of the separation of the primal parents, ★Ranginui (Sky Father) and Papatuanuku (Earth Mother), and their children's divine guardianship of different realms provides the subject of other narratives. The antics of demigods or culture heroes are favoured, especially the tricky deeds of ★Māui or ★Tāwhaki's escapades. Also recurrent are the voyages of Te Arawa, Tainui and other canoes (★waka) from the mythical homeland of Hawaiki. From ★Māori tribal histories, the rewriters have taken the romantic or the valiant—★Hinemoa's long swim across Lake Rotorua to meet her beloved Tūtānekai has captured writers' imaginations again and again. Visits to the gods and spirit world also recur, such as Hutu's poignant journey to the underworld to bring back Pare. And there has always been fascination in marvellous meetings between humans and supernatural creatures—Hatupatu's contest with the giant bird-woman Kurangaituku, or Kahukura's discovery of the craft of netting from the fairy people.

The English versions have so far been generally conservative, repeating the same stories, taking little licence with style, and generalising to Māori rather than specifying tribal individuality. Prose narration has usually weakened the poetic and dramatic power of the traditional accounts. There have been occasional recastings in verse, such as J.E. Ollivant's *Hine Moa, the Maori Maiden* (1879) or J.C. ★Andersen's *Tura and the Fairies, and The Overworlds of Tu* (1936), but poets and dramatists have preferred to use allusive reference rather than retell complete narratives.

The retelling of age-old stories is, of course, essential to the oral tradition of Māori, and familiar also to literate English-speakers from Biblical, classical, dramatic and poetic literature. Variation is of the essence. Māori myths and legends are not retold verbatim. But a greater variation is introduced into English retellings, by the cultural origins of Pākehā writers, and the huge shift across languages and cultures. Two other factors are significant. Firstly, bringing stories from oral to print form has almost always lost the cryptic, rhetorical and audience-centred oral mode of composition. Some writers have tried to compensate for this loss by using a narrator (an old chief or priest), or by generous use of dialogue; and perhaps the common use of illustrations was designed to rescue some sense of the dramatic. Secondly, retellings inevitably reflect their age. Nineteenth-century versions evince the colonial sensibility seeking to understand a strange, uncivilised, indigenous culture. Late twentieth-century writing reflects the Māori renaissance and respect for the cultural value of the texts.

The publication of rewritings in English has been extraordinarily influential. It began with Sir George ★Grey's *Polynesian Mythology* (1854), a representative selection from the Hawaiki, voyage, tribal and supernatural classes of stories, and a model for all that followed. Grey retold from the writings and talk of Māori acquaintances. His Māori version, an earlier publication, was a retelling; his translation to English yet another. John ★White created history and fiction from the integrated whole of the tradition when he edited Māori manuscripts for his six-volume, bilingual *Ancient History of the Maori* (1887–90) (a thorough review of all kinds of narratives), and composed a romantic novel, *Revenge: A Love Tale of the Mount Eden Tribe* (published posthumously by A.W. ★Reed in 1940).

The mythological and legendary lore as reworked by Grey and White has become established in popular thinking, not least because they have been so often reproduced. Translation is a valuable part of this literature of retelling. It is to be remarked in the ancient accounts, most concerning the canoe voyages and incidents of tribal life, which were contributed to the *Journal of the Polynesian Society* from 1892. The earlier texts show greater licence than the later, and all have tribal designations. Translation in the later twentieth century has been the preserve of scholars. Nineteenth-century manuscripts are the main source of Margaret ★Orbell's *Traditional Māori Stories* (1992), tales about human encounters with the supernatural or extraordinary feats, and of the extensive summaries in her book *The Illustrated Encyclopedia of Māori Myth and Legend* (1995). Bruce ★Biggs turned tribal history into English in *Nga Iwi o Tainui* (1995). And the extent of Grey's adaptations has been demonstrated by Agathe Thornton's *The Story of Māui by Te Rangikāheke* (1992), a close translation of a manuscript written in the 1850s by Grey's primary informant. Hirini ★Mead has translated his own modern Māori version of Tāwhaki in *Tāwhaki: The Deeds of a Demigod* (1996). By meticulous attention to the Māori, these translators have intervened as little as possible in the retelling and, by commentary and annotations, have clarified the densely allusive language.

Much rewriting of myths and legends has been as authority for description of Māori society. The exploitation of this inherited knowledge for information as well as entertainment, and so the creation of versions for specific audiences, was the habit of Māori oral narrators. Late-nineteenth-century and early-twentieth-century Pākehā writers often combined the tasks of storytelling with ethnographic reporting, sometimes awkwardly. It was common for these writers to cite their sources, give introductions, explanatory notes and glossaries, set the scene of narration—in a meeting house or as an old man talking—and, except for those whose purpose was new fiction, to disclaim embellishment. Their work suggests readers who were curious about Māori culture but more familiar with Greek and other European myths.

Examples are Edward ★Tregear's succinct refashioning, *Fairy Tales and Folk-lore of New Zealand and the South Seas* (1891), and Andersen's *Māori Fairy Tales* (1908) and *Maori Tales* (1924), which informed his fictionalised portrait of traditional Māori society: *Māori Life in Ao-tea* (1907) and *Myths & Legends of the Polynesians* (1928). James Izett also drew on the work of Grey, White and Tregear for the many tales in *Maori Lore* (1904). A.A. ★Grace wrote inventive short stories from local history in *Folk Tales of the Māori* (1907), and W. Dittmer supplemented his brief revisions of the stock stories with lavish illustrations in *Te Tohunga: The Ancient Legends and Traditions of the Māoris* (1907). Arawa tribal life and traditions were recreated in Frank ★Acheson's fiction *Plume of the Arawas* (1930), and Charles A. Wilson revisited the popular stories and told new ones in *Legends and Mysteries of the Māori* (1932). A large assortment was brought together by Sir Maui Pomare and James ★Cowan in the two-volume *Legends of the Māori* (1930–34). As his *Fairy Folk Tales of the Māori* (1925) shows, Cowan enjoyed the roles of raconteur and reporter of stories told to him by elders. Some books of this era were intended for the young—Kate McCosh Clark's informative *Maori Tales & Legends* (1896) and Edith ★Howes' fanciful *Maoriland Fairy Tales* (1913). None could replicate the ways in which accounts were handed down in Māori tradition, by speech and often with ritual in the intimacy of family or tribe, as information about life, religious beliefs or the past. But they are evidence of interest in the myths and legends and a desire to disseminate them.

Other writers, including Richard ★Taylor, Edward ★Shortland, Elsdon ★Best, S. Percy ★Smith and Herries Beattie, made less of storytelling but used summaries or informants' renditions as witness for their ethnographies of Māori society. Another kind of rewriting occurred in the new genre of tribal histories, spanning from J.H. Mitchell's *Takitimu* (1944) to Jock McEwen's *Rangitane* (1986). These arranged the episodes of the oral narratives into the chronologic coherence which readers of English histories might expect. Regional versions of myths and legends, localised stories of the fabulous, and picturesque events of tribal history can also be found in collections of the kind of *O te raki* (1963) in which Florence Keene revisits excerpts of northern Māori history.

The work of A.W. Reed is a singular and substantial part of the literature of retelling. Literary, didactic, informative and almost always amply illustrated, it was aimed at all readers but often at the young. Over some forty years he published an extraordinary number of books,

under titles like *Myths and Legends of Maoriland* (1946) and *Favourite Māori Legends* (1965); his comprehensive compilation being *Treasury of Maori Folklore* (1963). A few books he classified by subject, such as *Maori Myth: The Supernatural World of the Maori* (1978) and *Treasury of Maori Exploration* (1977), experiences of canoe voyages and settlement.

Respectful of the myths and legends and genuine in his desire to portray a Māori response to life, Reed knew the repertoire and drew widely from it. He accepted the religious and imaginary aspects without trying to separate fact from fiction; the spirited performance and transmission of the oral texts were important. He strove to retain the integrity of the old stories, but at the same time explained them through introductions, footnotes and glossaries. He frequently expressed the hope that this literature would come to be valued as part of the national heritage. The sparseness of such work since his time suggests that his wish has yet to be fulfilled.

A serious and literary recrafting is found in Antony ★Alpers's *Maori Myths and Tribal Legends* (1964), narratives of Hawaiki and the canoe traditions which incorporate the values and associations of the world described. Alpers writes as storyteller, but includes a preface and appendix setting out his intentions and sources. He treats much the same material as Grey, but represents the quite different attitudes of his time.

In modern rewritings there is some experimentation, and a move away from the ethnographic to subjective transformations which credit the stories with relevance to the present. Jean Irvine adds spiritual and psychological insights into ★Kupe and Ngahue's journey to Aotearoa in *To the Land of Light* (1995). Witi ★Ihimaera makes the story of Kahutia-te-rangi's journey by whale from Hawaiki the basis for a contemporary novel in *The Whale Rider* (1987). And as short stories, Ngahuia ★Te Awekotuku writes of Hatupatu and Kurangaituku (1993), and Patricia ★Grace alludes to Rangi and Papa in ★'Between Earth and Sky' and gives a delightful contemporary slant to a story about Māui in *The Sky People* (1994). Another striking innovation is Robert ★Sullivan and Chris Slane's cartoon or graphic novel, *Māui: Legends of the Outcast* (1996).

The children's literature of myths and legends since the 1970s has been more sustained, most books richly illustrated, often with Māori motifs and decorative patterns. Notable are Peter Gossage's recreation of the Māui myths, Ron ★Bacon's series *Māori Legends* (1984) and local tribal traditions in Katerina ★Mataira's *Warrior Mountains* (1982) and Mere Whaanga-Schollum's *The Legend of the Seven Whales of Ngai Tahu* (1988). Passing this literature on to the next generation is the prime motivation for these books; but they also epitomise the essential task of the myths and legends, composed as they were to convey colourfully and memorably the important cultural knowledge passed down from the ancestors.

JMcR

Māori newspapers have been a major place of publication for writing in both classical and modern Māori. The *Alexander Turnbull Library catalogue of serials partly or wholly in the Māori language numbers seventy-five titles, and other holdings are in the following libraries: Auckland Public Library, *University of Auckland Library, Auckland Institute and Museum, Waikato University, the Parliamentary Library, and the *Hocken Library. The earliest was *Te Karere o Niu Tireni* (Auckland, 1842–46), which first appeared at the command of the Governor. The first fully Māori newspaper was *Te Hokioi o Niu Tireni* (Ngāruawāhia 1862–63) after two Waikato chiefs, Wiremu Toetoe Tumohe and Te Hemara Rerehau Paraone, had been taken by Ferdinand von *Hochstetter to Vienna, Austria, where they were taught printing skills in the State Printing Works and were given a press, which they brought back to New Zealand with them. During the Land *Wars the Māori King movement published its views in *Te Hokioi* (which is the name of a legendary bird of ill omen), and they were countered by another paper edited by John *Gorst, *Te Pihoihoi Mokemoke*, which caused so much offence to the King Movement that some of its adherents destroyed Gorst's press. The Waikato-based King Movement continued a strong involvement in the publishing of newspapers with another, *Te Paki o Matariki*, which appeared in 1892. In 1897 *Te Puke ki Hikurangi*, which was widely viewed as the newspaper of Te Kotahitanga, the Māori parliament, appeared in the Wairarapa. The Rātana movement began publishing a newspaper in Māori in 1924: *Te Whetu Marama*. There were many others.

Māori newspapers included material that can be classified as literary, including *waiata, hymns, stories of deeds and battles of earlier times, canoe traditions, *whakatauāki and *Maori tribal histories and legends, while some of them, especially those after the turn of the century, included extensive series of articles by such writers as Reweti *Kohere, Paratene and Apirana *Ngata, Tutere Wi Repa, Paraire Tomoana and many others who are less well known. All of them contain examples of classic writing in valedictory letters and mihi, *whakapapa, prose forms and so on. Te *Ao Hou, even though produced so recently (from the 1950s to the early 1970s), emanating from official sources and usually edited by Europeans, included some classic Māori writing by Pei Te Hurinui *Jones, Pine Taiapa, Takurua Tamarau and others. Other recent Māori magazines are

Te Kaea (Wellington, 1979–81), *Te Maori* (Wellington 1970–74; 1979–81), *Tu Tangata* (Wellington 1981–?), *Te Karanga* (Christchurch, 1985–?) and *Mana* (Auckland, 1993–), which is the only one in circulation at present. The newspapers were often the only outlet for Māori writers, since until recently publishers were not interested in producing in Māori.

These newspapers, which are most easily accessed in the National Newspaper Collection of the Alexander Turnbull Library, are one of the few available written sources of exemplary nineteenth-century Māori language and are widely read by students of the language today.

AB/RRB/NW

Māori sayings constitute a highly significant genre in the oral literature. They are revered by Māori as wisdom inherited from the gods and ancestors, and as a means of preserving and passing on traditional knowledge. Sayings are heard in speeches, songs and incantations at tribal meetings, and in the oral teaching of tradition by elders. Carvings and artwork contain representations of them, and a small diverse literature gives insight into their nature, scope and use.

Two words are generally used to distinguish sayings: 'whakataukī' (in some areas, 'whakatauāki') and 'pepeha' which, in modern times, has come to be used for tribal sayings. Words which refer to any speech ('kupu', 'kī', 'kōrero') may also denote proverbial wisdom, and a text labelled a saying in one context may be termed differently in another.

As is common to oral traditions, Māori sayings are numerous and of many kinds. There are epithets, proverbial phrases and complete statements which arise out of casual observation or comments. There are intentionally composed texts and quotations from tribal histories, for instance, exchanges between opposing chiefs during battle, challenges, prophecies, or farewells. There are also formulaic expressions which are conventional to narrative and abundant in song—as is apparent in the texts and annotations to songs in Apirana *Ngata and Pei Te *Hurinui's *Nga *Moteatea* (1959, 1961, 1970).

A representative sample of Māori sayings can be found in the first publication of them, Sir George *Grey's *Ko nga Whakapepeha me nga whakaahuareka a nga Tipuna o Aotea-roa* (1857). Although long out of print, with its wide range and translation and interpretation of examples, it remains important as a record of the currency of this genre some thirty years after the settlement of Europeans and the acquisition of literacy had had an impact on Māori oral tradition.

Saying texts, if not always short, are remarkable for their expressive concision. They may be simply stated with clear messages. But they are more often opaque, even cryptic, because of symbolic associations created by complex metaphors and imagery which depend for meaning on knowledge of Māori history and custom and the natural environment. The artifices of poetry are especially notable: rhythm, symmetry of idea and form, onomatopoeia, alliteration, personification and allusion all contribute to texts which claim attention and are memorable.

The very large number (over 3000) of entries in *Nga Pepeha a Nga Tūpuna* (1981, 1989, 1991, 1994) testifies to the scope of form, content and poetry in this genre. In the latest volumes Neil Grove and Hirini Moko *Mead provide translation and some explanation of selected texts from the first edition. That edition lists only the Māori text and its published source, but demonstrates another characteristic feature of Māori sayings, the variant forms in which they occur.

Changes to wording have resulted from either deliberate alteration or simply the passage of time. Some retain the same or similar meaning despite many changes, others are significantly altered, yet others become the subject of debate as to the correct version. Something of the art of sayings can be read from published lists, but saying meaning is often dependent on contextual use. It is skill in quotation of them, especially in the oratory of ceremonial occasions, that is highly regarded. Examples of this art in speeches can be read in *Whaikoorero: Ceremonial Farewells to the Dead* (1981).

Saying subject matter is wide-ranging, but two broad categories, neither exclusive of the other, might be proposed as a way of summarising content. In the first category there are sayings which encapsulate widely held precepts and customary lore. These may refer to the evolution of the universe and gods or to life in and migration from the Polynesian homeland of *Hawaiki, or be suggestive of social etiquette or comment on human behaviour. Though widely used, individual claims may be made as to the origin of such sayings, and some, although deriving from the circumstances of a local event, come to have a general representation.

Popular collections, as A.E. Brougham and A.W. *Reed's long-running *Maori Proverbs* (1963) or lists supplied to journals (*Te *Ao Hou*, for instance), favour this class, arranging them in the classical style of proverb collection, by topic ('Love', 'Anger', etc.), although this limits appreciation of the potential for meaning in them. Publications about Māori society have long drawn on this body of the oral literature as a source of cultural knowledge. Raymond Firth's investigation of proverbial opinion relating to economic life (published in the journal *Folklore*, 1926) and John Patterson's *Exploring Maori Values* (1992) result from intensive analysis of saying meaning.

Of sayings shared across Māori society there is a distinct group which arose from nineteenth-century prophetic and political movements in conflict with European government. Tāwhiao, the Waikato chief who became the second Maori King, is known for his wise words, as is *Te Kooti, the prophet leader and founder of the Ringatu faith, whose legacy of sayings is well documented in Judith Binney's history of his life, *Redemption Songs* (1995).

In the second category of sayings, and of great value and interest, are those particular to tribal life. Some show similarity of purpose, style and wording across tribes, although versions of them are jealously guarded. Others are entirely original to the tribe. There are terse, highly pragmatic records of territorial boundaries and rights, and of intertribal relationships and obligations. There is witness to the attributes of chiefs, commemoration of historical incidents, and characterisation of individual or group behaviour. The collection *He Pepeha, He Whakatauki no Taitokerau* (1987) typifies some of those preserved among a group of closely related tribes in one region. Such sayings are highly functional. They serve to define and publish tribal identity and, more significantly, they work as mnemonics to tribal history. They appear as descriptors in the recitation of genealogies. And numbers of them are incorporated, sometimes in a progressive series, in historical narratives. No reading of *Māori tribal histories such as J.H. Mitchell's *Takitimu* (1944) or Pei Te Hurinui *Jones and Bruce *Biggs's *Nga Iwi o Tainui* (1995) would leave any doubt that retention of historical matter relies to a large extent on information that has been captured in the many and diverse forms of these lively, picturesque and highly allusive sayings.

JMcR

Māori theatre is rooted in the very structure of the culture itself, with its emphasis on the dramatic formality of *marae protocol when welcoming, debating with, and farewelling visitors. In the context of the theatre as such, a Māori tradition can be most clearly traced to the founding of the Maori Theatre Trust in 1966, though this was the culmination of years of activity by actors and administrators. Early New Zealand stage dramas, such as *The *Land of the Moa* or *Marama* often incorporated or exploited the dramatic potential of Māori forms such as the *haka. Individuals and groups, in both professional and amateur capacities, produced forms of theatre in concert parties and in educational institutions, and such events as the Maori Musical Society's 1941 production of 'Hinemoa' in Rotorua. The Maori Theatre Trust began as a consequence of the New Zealand Opera Company's production of *Porgy and Bess*, starring Inia Te Wiata, which in turn prompted the New Zealand Broadcasting

Corporation to commission Bruce *Mason to write a play using Te Wiata; the result was *Awatea*, a production which had to be postponed until a collaboration in 1968 with Wellington's Downstage Theatre made it possible. Meanwhile, the Trust (in effect, made up of the Māori cast of *Porgy and Bess*) undertook productions of 'He Mana Toa' (by James Ritchie, music by Douglas *Lilburn, choreography by Leigh Brewer, and directed by Richard Campion), *The Golden Lover* (by Douglas *Stewart, directed by Richard Campion), and were involved, with the New Zealand Ballet, the National Band and Kiri Te Kanawa in the production spectacular, 'Green are the Islands', for Expo 70 at Osaka.

The 1970s were a period of consolidation for Māori theatre, and the 1980s of building on those foundations. In 1972, Harry *Dansey became the first published Māori playwright with *Te Raukura: The Feathers of the Albatross* (1974), presented at Mercury in Auckland by Central Theatre with George Henare playing the Māori prophet, Te Whiti. In 1977, Jim Moriarty founded Te Ika a Maui Players specifically to produce Rore *Hapipi's 'Death of the Land'. Hapipi went on to write three further plays: 'Nga Morehu', 'Tupuna' (both Depot Theatre, 1987, in a double bill) and 'Fragments of a Childhood' (Depot, 1988). In 1978, in Dunedin, Rawiri *Paratene began writing plays: 'Gepetto and his Magic Fiddle' (Four Seasons, Wanganui, 1978), 'Saturday Morning' (Newtown Community Centre, Wellington, 1980), 'Directions' (Fortune Theatre, Dunedin, 1981) and 'Nga Korero Paku' (Theatrerevue Electra, Hamilton, 1991). Maranga Mai, a home-grown agitprop theatre, was founded in 1979. In 1982, *Renée began her playwriting career, and Rangimoana Taylor directed Selwyn Muru's 'Get the Hell Home Boy' for the Māori Writers' and Artists' Association. Taylor founded Te Ohu Whakaari, which went on to produce plays by his brother Apirana *Taylor ('Kohanga', 'Te Whanau a Tuanui Jones'), Riwia *Brown ('Roimata', 'Te Hokinga', 'Nga Wahine'), and Haina Stewart ('Iwitaia'). For Wellington's International Festival of the Arts in the sesquicentennial year of 1990, Te Ika a Maui combined with Te Ohu Whakaari and, as Te Rakau Hua O Te Wao Tapu, produced a programme at the Depot which included Bruce *Stewart's *Broken Arse* and John *Broughton's *Nga Puke (The Hills)*. In the early 1990s, Broughton made a substantial career as a playwright with plays like *Te Hokinga Mai / The Return Home* (first produced in front of the meeting house, Mataatua, in the Otago Museum), *Michael James Manaia* (seen at the 1991 Edinburgh Festival in Downstage's production, with Jim Moriarty playing the solo role) and 'Marae', which was commissioned for the 1992 Festival of the Arts. Also in 1990, Roma *Potiki, formerly with Maranga Mai,

formed the group He Ara Hou which collaborated on the production of their play 'Whatungarongaro', which, after touring the country, travelled to Adelaide for the 1992 Festival. Rena Owen, whose first play, 'Te Awa i Tahuti' had opened in London in 1987 (and was reviewed in *The Times*), wrote 'Daddy's Girl' for Taki Rua/ The Depot in 1991, featuring Wi Kuki Kaa. For the 1986 International Festival of the Arts, Circa presented 'Waitangi', directed by Richard Campion and Don Selwyn and designed by Selwyn Muru.

Meanwhile, in Auckland, Don Selwyn directed the first production of Hone *Tuwhare's 'In the Wilderness Without a Hat' (1985), and has continued to produce plays at Waiatarua, his Freeman's Bay base, including Pei Te Hurinui *Jones's Māori translation of *The Merchant of Venice* (1990). A collection of five of these scripts of the 1970s–80s, edited by Simon Garrett, was published as *He Reo Hou* (1991; plays by Hapipi, Tuwhare, Owen, Riwia *Brown and Broughton).

Māori have been engaged in many aspects of theatre, such as Ralph *Hotere's designs for the Dunedin plays of James K. *Baxter and Para Matchitt's for Witi *Ihimaera's opera, *Waituhi*, and in the 1990s became prominent in writing, acting, directing and production. The 1990s also saw the development of a more specific definition of Māori theatre: marae theatre. This involves treating the theatre space as a marae and following the protocol of greeting, speaking and farewelling that would be expected there. The audience is called into the theatre space, greeted with *waiata, encouraged to support the actors during the performance, expected to reply at its conclusion and, in general, to treat the theatre as a marae for the duration of the performance.

Taki Rua in Wellington established itself as the base for the continued development of Māori theatre, as well as for bicultural theatre, its kaupapa (philosophy) based on the principle of partnership inherent in Te Tiriti o Waitangi. This was expressed in productions of plays by playwrights such as Riwia Brown, Renée, Hone *Kouka, Apirana Taylor and Willi Davis. The theatre mounted two significant annual seasons: the Te Roopu season and the Te Reo Māori season of plays fully or largely in Māori. The first two years of Te Roopu were notable for interpretations of Ibsen's *The Vikings of Helgeland* (as Kouka's *Nga Tangata Toa*) and Brecht's *Mother Courage* (as Taylor's 'Whaea Kairau'), both directed by Colin McColl. Newer writers were introduced, particularly Briar Grace-Smith, whose first play, 'Nga Pou Wahine', won the Peter Harcourt Memorial Award for Best Short New Zealand Play in 1995, the same year in which she won the Sunday Star Times Bruce Mason Playwrights' Award. Two more of her plays were produced in 1996: 'Flat Out Brown' (Te

Roopu Whakaari season, Taki Rua) and 'Don't Call Me Bro' (Young and Hungry season, Bats).

The first Te Reo Māori season was in 1995, when four short plays were commissioned and presented: Hinemoana Baker's 'Maua Taua', Esther Tamehana's 'Korowai', Karlite Rangihau's 'Taku Rakau E' and Godfrey and Toroa Pohatu's 'Kapa Haka Blues'. In 1996, the season consisted of Tamehana's 'Hawaikinui' (with additional material by Wi Kuki Kaa), Muru's 'Te Ohaki a Nihe' and Grace-Smith's 'Waitapu', which had earlier that year toured to Canada with the theatre group, He Ara Hou. Taki Rua theatre closed in 1997.

Besides text-based theatre, there has been Māori input into performance-based groups, such as Tama Huata's Hastings group, Kahurangi. It is difficult, too, to draw a line around 'Māori theatre': many Māori practitioners, including playwrights like Broughton and Renée, have played important roles in 'mainstream' theatre. Commercial theatre is increasingly taking account of the totality of New Zealand culture. Nevertheless, it is clear that the ultimate definition of 'Māori theatre' is 'by Māori, for Māori, preferably in Māori'.   SG

Māori tribal histories and traditions in written representations are subject to a fickle relationship with Māori people. On the one hand many Māori lament or even resent the fact that they often turn to publications for sources of tribal historical information, as reading a book is a tacit acceptance that the continuum of oral instruction in Māori culture is under threat. On the other hand, much contemporary Māori development could not take place without the vast array of written sources, a huge 'canon' of written material, which began accumulating as soon as literacy arrived. The following paragraphs can only introduce the huge range of written material concerning tribal histories and traditions.

Almost immediately on the arrival of literacy, stories from tribal history and tradition were rendered into written form. At first they appeared as journal entries, in diaries, in letters and so on, as Pākehā recorded what they heard and encountered. As Māori became literate, they began to write down tribal histories and traditions, and some of the most important *Māori manuscripts in popular use today arose in the early to middle nineteenth century. They ranged from manuscripts dictated by Te Rangihaeata of Ngāti Toa and written by his nephew Mātene Te Whiwhi to the many and varied manuscripts by such writers as *Te Rangikāheke of Te Arawa, Hāmiora Pio of Ngāti Awa, Mohi Ruatapu of Ngāti Porou and many more.

Contiguous to the writings of these was the growth of the substantial records of the Native Land Court and, later, the Maori Land Court. Tribes and sub-tribes who contested land titles brought their evidence, primarily oral, before the court, where the proceedings were recorded in longhand. These records grew extensively from the 1860s to the 1920s and today, despite their many flaws, are considered a very important source of information on tribal histories and traditions.

Probably the first major publication of tribal histories and traditions was *Ko nga *mahinga a nga tupuna Māori* by Sir George *Grey, published in London in 1855. This book is a compilation of writings extracted from manuscripts Grey had collected from many Māori throughout the country. The final publication was by no means a faithful representation of what can be found in the original manuscripts, as Grey extracted pieces and connected them together in odd ways, leaving out crucial materials and reinterpreting others. Despite the questionable integrity of such methods, Grey seems to have set a trend which continued into the twentieth century, as he was followed by another intrepid collector of tribal histories and traditions, John *White.

Like Grey, White was less than neutral in editing Māori stories. His most famous publication is *Ancient History of the Māori* (1887–90), a seven-volume attempt to create a national, orthodox account of the origins and history of the Māori people. White shamelessly interwove stories from diverse tribal backgrounds, and where consensus could not be found, many points were ruthlessly edited out.

While not working with exactly the same material, S. Percy *Smith covered much of the same territory in his work *The Lore of the Whare-Wananga* (1913–15). This book is again a compilation of other people's work; the title-page states: 'Written down by H.T. Whatahoro from the teachings of Te Matorohanga and Nepia Pohuhu ... Translated by S. Percy Smith'. *The Lore of the Whare-Wananga* is drawn entirely from the dictation of the two named *tohunga and others of the Wairarapa schools of higher learning (see *whare wānanga). *The Lore of the Whare-Wananga* includes a very interesting account of Te Mātorohanga's struggle with recording sacred oral knowledge in written form.

Elsdon *Best rightly deserves his reputation as the greatest Pākehā collector of tribal histories and traditions. His mammoth *Tuhoe: The Children of the Mist* (1925, rpt. 1996) is a classic of its kind. A brilliantly flawed tome containing a vast array of information on the Tūhoe people, *Children of the Mist* draws on the extraordinary memories and thinking of several Tūhoe elders.

Best published many other books, primarily through the National Museum, where he worked as an ethnologist. His many publications touch upon almost every aspect of Māori culture, tangible and intangible, esoteric and temporal, real and imagined. Unfortunately, Best could not entirely escape the racism of his times, and maybe that of his own spirit, as his writing leaves one in no doubt that, despite his personal investment in his work, he still considers Māori a barbaric and backward people. Best lived during the ascendency of perhaps the most famous modern Māori collector of tribal histories and traditions, Sir Apirana *Ngata. Sadly even Ngata could not change Best's mind as to the fundamental nature of the Māori world.

Ngata's most famous contribution to published tribal histories and traditions is Nga *Moteatea (1928, 1961, 1970 and 1990), a monumental four-volume collection of songs published by the Polynesian Society over six decades. Written in Māori and English, it set the standard for Māori scholarship and today retains a great deal of prestige, although it, too, is not without its faults.

In completing Nga Moteatea Ngata was joined by a talented Tainui scholar, Pei Te Hurinui *Jones. He too published a number of important, but small, books containing valuable information on tribal histories and traditions. It was not, however, until 1995, nineteen years after his death, that his potential was fully realised in Nga Iwi o Tainui (1995). It comprises a compilation of historical stories drawn from a variety of manuscripts, of both the nineteenth and twentieth centuries, brought together expertly by a tribal historian who was trained in the traditional manner.

Don Stafford is a Pākehā writer who has lived all his life in Rotorua. In his youth he took a keen interest in the stories of the Te Arawa people of the Rotorua lakes district and began to write these stories down. Slowly he filled many notebooks with stories and traditions heard at first hand from elders, which formed the basis of Te Arawa (1967).

Another Māori writer and publisher of tribal histories and traditions is Sir John Te Herekiekie Grace, whose Tuwharetoa was published in 1959. This book is now the standard work on the history of the Ngāti Tūwharetoa people of the Taupō area. It is interesting for the parochialism of the writer, and this parochialism, which relates to the status of his own family within Ngāti Tūwharetoa, makes its way onto the written page.

J. Herries Beattie was another Pākehā collector of South Island tribal histories and traditions. In 1920 he visited many of the pā and kāinga (villages) from Bluff to Canterbury, recording and collecting information about the history, traditions and culture of those people. This material was subsequently published as Traditional Lifeways of the Southern Māori (1994, edited by Athol Anderson). Beattie's manuscript contains a phenomenal array of information about all aspects of their culture, but it has one important fault. Beattie failed to record comprehensively the names of his informants. Consequently, their identities are silenced in the text. (Anderson as editor attempts to identify these in his introduction.)

The entire canon of written material containing Māori tribal histories and traditions is vast and complex, testimony to the extent of the centuries-old literature. Even those recorded since the nineteenth century are far more numerous than has been discussed here. The written tradition, as it can now be called, is, however, fraught with difficulties, especially the essential issue of an oral society transmitting and maintaining its knowledge bases in written form.   CR

Maoriland originally denoted the country as the land of the Māori before the coming of Pākehā: 'It was … from the deck of a small trading schooner … that I first cast eyes on Maori land. It *was* Maori land then; but, alas! what is it now ?' wrote *Maning in Old New Zealand, 1863. It could also refer to continuing Māori society or culture: 'nowhere in Maoriland are there such varieties of legends [as among the Tuhoe]' (T. Lambert, Pioneering Reminiscences of Old Wairoa, 1936). Most commonly, however, it was used as a romantic name for the country as a whole, originally a journalistic or popular literary term recorded in Australia from 1859, in New Zealand from 1865 and popularised from the 1880s especially after adoption by the Sydney *Bulletin and its associated writers and by Thomas *Bracken. Bracken's *Musings in Maoriland established the term, already used as a title in J. Kerry-Nicholls, Maoriland: An Illustrated Handbook to New Zealand (1884). The RSA magazine Quick March indicated the literary flavour of the word: 'As New Zealand the world knows us, for better or worse, and the title will stick…. As for Zealandia, Maoriland, and the like, we may safely leave them to the poets' (1922). For a while a 'Maorilander' was, at least in Australia, a non-Māori New Zealander: 'A recent arrival from New Zealand walking along Collins St, Melbourne, a short time since encountered another Maorilander.' (Bracken, Lays & Lyrics) See also *Aotearoa, *New Zealand, *Niu Tirani, *Zealandia.   HO

Maorilander was the earliest of the periodicals edited, printed and published by Noel Farr *Hoggard. A monthly directed towards an adolescent readership, it grew from a circulation of two handwritten copies in the late 1920s to a duplicated run of one hundred by mid-1932. Hoggard's ability to solicit material from both new and established writers was to be an ongoing feature of his periodicals. Later issues carried work by Dulce *Carman and Enid Saunders.   SH

Marae is the central area of a Māori community, a place where the local people (*tangata whenua) can meet to conduct many of their familiar and sacred events and the place to which they return when they seek spiritual refreshment and contact with the Māori way of life. Although there are no precise statistics, it is assumed that there are about 1000 marae in New Zealand. Anne Salmond reports 'Maori people themselves see the marae as a last outpost of their culture. "Without it," said one old man, "we are nothing"' (*Hui*, 1975). In *Te Marae: A Guide to Customs and Protocol* (1986), Hiwi and Pat Tauroa write: 'The marae is the wāhi rangatira mana (place of greatest *mana), wāhi rangatira wairua (place of greatest spirituality), wāhi rangatira *iwi (place that heightens people's dignity), and wāhi rangatira tikanga (place in which Māori customs are given ultimate expression).... This spiritual aspect of the marae is its most important facet.'

Originally the word marae referred to the open area in front of the main building of the village, but today it often refers to the entire village or complex of buildings and seems to have replaced the words 'pā' and 'kāinga' to a large extent for this purpose. In order to make the distinction, the open area is now sometimes referred to as marae-ātea. It is the place where guests are welcomed and speeches exchanged when a hui takes place. Such welcoming ceremonies involving *whaikōrero and *waiata are one of the most distinctive functions of the marae.

Physically, marae vary greatly both in size and layout, but common features include a distinction between the *tapu areas, such as the wharenui (largest building, often a carved 'meeting house') and the marae-ātea on the one hand and 'noa', or non-tapu areas, such as the cooking and eating buildings, on the other. No food should be consumed in tapu areas. Many marae have their burial ground, the most tapu area of all, nearby. See also 'marae theatre' in *Maori theatre.   NW

Marama, or, The Mere and the Maori Maid

(1920) by Syd Ribbands, with music by Archie Don, is a musical comedy, described by its author as 'a New Zealand opera, the first of its kind' (but see also Alfred *Hill). It was a sensational hit on its national tour in 1920–21 and was successfully revived in 1940. Its multicultural story of a Māori princess is framed as a vision from the battlefields of Flanders, where Ribbands himself had fought with the New Zealand army. 'Highlighting a growing sense of national identity after the misery and horror of the trenches' (Chris Fogarty), it opened in Ribbands's home town of Hastings and everywhere won praise like the *Auckland Star*'s 'a production of colonial genius'. The lost script was rediscovered in Hastings by theatre historian Peter Harcourt, who judges that 'For the first time it gave music and words not just to the aspirations but to realities of New Zealand life.' A further revival, directed by Richard Campion and Tama Huata, was produced by the Hastings Operatic Society in 1996.   RR

'Married Man's Story, A',

an unfinished short story by Katherine *Mansfield, was written in August 1921, first published posthumously in the January–June 1923 issue of the *Dial* and subsequently in *The Doves' Nest and Other Stories* (June 1923). The MS is in the Newberry Library, Chicago. It is confessional in tone, the 'I' narrator, Gregory Powder, recounting his innermost thoughts about his destructive, dependent relationship with his wife, whom it appears he is poisoning, as his father (a chemist) supposedly poisoned his mother before him. Poisoning is a unifying metaphor, with 'the broken bust of a man named Hahnemann' invoked ironically as a symbol of the relationship. (Hahnemann was the founder of homeopathy which advocates the prescribing of minute doses of poison to accelerate the body's immune response.) Schadenfreude pervades the description of a suffering, insecure wife 'nobody is going to ... take her in his arms.... Nobody is going to call her.... And she knows it.' Persistent animal imagery contributes to the effect of emotional savagery. The story breaks off at a point of apparent psychological collapse, described however by the narrator as a moment of positive transformation. There are obvious technical and thematic connections to *'Je ne parle pas français': an unsympathetic, unreliable male narrator who recounts his personal history in an attempt to explain himself, with recall, fantasy and conjecture contributing to a fluid sense of time. Both narrators are aspiring writers who critique themselves as they write. Both have had damaging childhood experiences, obsess about sex and revel in making women suffer. Although John Middleton *Murry described 'A Married Man's Story' to Sydney Schiff as 'the longest and last of her stories for her new book', Mansfield did not finish the work. In the *Stories*, Antony *Alpers suggests this may have been in reaction to the excisions forced on 'Je ne parle pas français'. Critical interest in the piece is growing along with recognition that it ranks alongside Mansfield's best work.   SSa

MARRIOTT, Janice (1946–   ), writer of teenage fiction, was born in Coventry, England, arriving in New Zealand aged 11. Educated at Napier and Gisborne GHS and Victoria University, she took a librarianship course in rare books in San Francisco, and worked in radio and TV in California and Vancouver. After temporarily losing her eyesight in England, and now widowed with a son, she graduated from the Wellington College of Education, but in 1983 went from teaching to audio production for *Learning Media. In 1994, she was the inaugural writer-in-residence at the Auckland College of Education. Her realistic, humorous novels feature teenage embarrassment and a desire to change the world. *Letters to Lesley* (in England called *Marrying Off Mum*) (1989), and its sequel, *Brain Drain* (1993), introduced the irrepressible Henry Jollifer; the trilogy was completed by *Kissing Fish* (1997), which updated the joke of the eccentric Henry trying to elude a persistent penfriend, now using a fax machine. Other titles include *I'm Not a Compost Heap* (1995), and *Crossroads* (1995), which deals more seriously with death and grieving, its compelling exploration of two teenagers in crisis deepened by metaphor and literary resonances, especially echoes from *Hamlet*. It won the 1996 Aim Supreme Award and Senior Fiction Award. Marriott's writing for adults has appeared in magazines and on radio.   DH

MARRIS, Charles A. (1874–1947), journalist, edited a number of literary periodicals and *anthologies. Although Allen *Curnow's anthology *A *Book of New Zealand Verse 1923–45* is generally recognised as marking the dawn of a coherent tradition of authentic New Zealand poetry, Marris's claims (a decade before Curnow's book), that he deserves credit for the arrival of a new generation of New Zealand writers, have some modest substance.

Born in Melbourne, Marris was a teacher in Australia and Wellington before joining the *Evening Post* and then the Christchurch *Sun*, where he was associate editor 1914–25. Shortly after World War 1, he championed New Zealand literature by opening his newspaper's columns 'to this country's literary talents' (see *Annals of Literature*, 1936). He was inundated with manuscripts, among them contributions from Eileen *Duggan, Robin *Hyde and A.R.D. *Fairburn. Apparently as a consequence, he became involved in publishing literary periodicals. From 1927 to 1942 he edited the literary pages of the quarterly *Art in New Zealand; from 1931 to 1933 a Christmas yearly with literary content called *Rata; and, most significantly, from 1932 to 1943 *New Zealand Best Poems, an annual anthology combining new and previously published poetry. He also published such now-familiar names as J.C. *Beaglehole, Charles *Brasch, D'Arcy *Cresswell, Denis *Glover, J.R. *Hervey, Monte *Holcroft, John *Mulgan, Gloria *Rawlinson, Mary *Stanley, Douglas *Stewart, Anton *Vogt and Arnold *Wall.

In Marris's mind he, a journalist, was providing a service that scholars had failed to deliver. In *Annals of Literature* he wrote scathingly of the part taken by universities in the postulated revival of New Zealand letters, accusing them of playing 'an insignificant role' because of insensitivity 'to everything but the prosaic necessity of building for themselves, and not for posterity'.

In fact within the academies Auckland's *Phoenix group and Glover's *Caxton Club were the first swellings of a wave that would swamp numerous lesser writers, and change the shape of New Zealand's literary coastline. Glover responded to Marris's criticisms with scathing satire. In *The Arraignment of Paris* (1937) he mocked *Best Poems*, likening its predominantly female contributors to a 'ladies' sewing guild' (plus an incidental male coterie 'who by their faces / should be in shoulder-straps instead of braces') trailing after Marris because they 'are his sheep and he their pastor dear'. Curnow considered this 'not too scornful' as Marris had 'printed much bad work', although he also conceded that he 'made and kept an audience of a sort for a few of the better writers' (*Penguin Book of New Zealand Verse*, 1960). With the publication of one final selection, *Lyric Poems 1928–1942* (1944), Marris set the seal on *Best Poems*. The following year Curnow's anthology would supplant for good the 'Hobbyists and ungifted amateurs [that had] crowded' his pages.

Trixie Te Arama *Menzies, however, puts Marris's anthologies into some perspective by arguing that although, between them, Marris and Quentin Pope, editor of the vilified *Kowhai Gold* anthology, published some lamentable versifiers, they also published eleven of those selected for *A Book of New Zealand Verse*. 'Curnow', she concludes, 'was continuing and shaping a considerable poetic tradition *already in existence*' (*Landfall*, 165, 1988).   PM

MARRYAT, Emilia (1835–75), was the third daughter of Frederick ('Captain') Marryat, one of the most popular English writers of boys' adventure stories in the nineteenth century. All three sisters followed in his footsteps in a modest way. Emilia wrote fiction from an early age, *Temper* (1854) being her first novel. *The Early Start in Life* (1867) is about a boy who goes to the bad in Australia.

Amongst the Maoris: A Book of Adventure (1874) is a lively tale of two youths walking from Wellington to Auckland, one of them, Jack, looking for a certain Maitland, who has deprived him of his inheritance. On the way he is captured by Māori and tortured by *tohunga, but has 'fun' as well. On the whole Jack prefers the Māori and the wild *bush (described in some detail) to the cities. In Wellington's Barrett Hotel, he is astonished at the number of flies. '"Always the way in Wellington, sir," answered the waiter, as if Wellington had reason to be proud of the fact. "… There asin't no swallows in New Zealand." Jack learns much from his travels before he encounters Maitland, finally discovering 'a lesson of God's own teaching … that love is better than revenge'. The book was reprinted as *Jack Stanley, or, The Young Adventurers* in 1883.   NW

MARSDEN, Samuel (1765–1838), the first missionary in New Zealand and a skilled writer, was a major influence on society in the early settlement period both in New Zealand and in New South Wales (where he was active from 1794). In 1814 he established a mission in the Bay of Islands, where he held the country's first Christian service on Christmas Day. From 1815 to his death he alternated between residences in New South Wales and New Zealand. His enormous energy and courage, aided by his unswerving conviction that, apart from a few 'superstitions', Māori minds were totally blank and waiting for him to write his doctrines on them, did much to impress Wesleyan puritanism and British 'civilisation' onto the people he encountered.

That he was one of the most skilful writers of English in nineteenth-century New Zealand was not totally clear before the publication of his *Letters and Journals* in 1932 (edited by J.R. Elder). ★McCormick described his style with both reserve and penetration: 'There is no conscious striving for literary effect—such artifices he would have scorned as instruments of the Prince of Darkness—but the earnest, simple narrative, relieved here and there by a metaphor of scriptural beauty and aptness, is as dramatic and effective as the most skilfully contrived work of literary art.' Indeed it seems to foreshadow the sparse restraint of the school of ★Sargeson, though with more of the 'manliness' of his times and beliefs. His no-nonsense style is a reflection of his attitude, for example, to the Māori, whom he admired for their 'mental endowments and bodily strength', which he hoped to see 'favoured with the ordinary means of instruction in those civil arts by which men are gradually refined and polished'. He believed that Māori would be better pronounced with English vowels and said of the language that 'at present it is very unchaste and offensive'. His confusion must have been great when his fellow-missionary, Thomas Kendall, found himself more attracted to Māori beliefs (and women) than Christian ones, but he managed to conceal confusion behind evangelical rage: 'His mind has been greatly polluted by studying the abominations of the heathens, and his ideas are very heathenish…. He never will recover from his fall, as he is now a man without strength and in the most awful state as it respects his soul.'
          NW

MARSH, Ngaio (1895–1982), was born and educated in Christchurch, where she spent most of her adult life, despite long periods in England and extended trips to other parts of the world. She began writing at an early age, publishing in school magazines and winning prizes for poems and prose. Her interest in theatre also began during her schooldays, when she acted and wrote for several productions. Nonetheless she chose to study painting, entering Canterbury College School of Art in 1913, where she and Evelyn Page (Polson) were the most successful students of their generation. Marsh stayed at the college until 1919 and left determined to be a professional painter. At the same time she was publishing occasional pieces for the Christchurch ★*Sun*. She was distracted, however, by the opportunity to tour the North Island with the Allan Wilkie Shakespeare Company (1919–20) and followed this by touring with the Rosemary Rees Comedy Company. These experiences laid the foundation for her later work in the theatre. During the 1920s Marsh continued to paint, exhibiting with 'The Group', seven Christchurch artists, most of them women, who made a powerful impression. She also continued to write poetry and stories, mainly for the *Sun*. In 1928, aged 33, she travelled to England for the first time, at the invitation of the wealthy Canterbury family of Rhodes, who maintained connections with ★'Home'. Although her first youth was past, Marsh felt that Britain was as much a home to her as New Zealand, perhaps more so. The ambivalence is not, of course, untypical of her generation. She threw herself into the life of the theatre in London and into social life opened to her by the Rhodes family. In 1929 she and a friend set up a small shop in Knightsbridge.

Throughout this period she wrote journalistic accounts of her travels and other experiences, but her attempt to write a novel with a New Zealand setting was a failure because, she said, 'figures' and 'background' refused to combine into a unified picture: 'I turned, more successfully, to crime fiction.' In an essay of 1977 ('Birth of a Sleuth') she describes how she came, in 1931, to invent the figure of Roderick Alleyn, the very English detective-inspector who was to dominate her fiction. This was set mostly in English theatres and country houses, although the European continent is significant (e.g. in *When in Rome*, 1970) and four of her thirty-two novels have New Zealand settings.

In 1932, hearing that her mother was ill, Marsh took ship for New Zealand. During the next five years she wrote four novels set in England and tried to create an English garden around her Christchurch house. Nonetheless these 'English' novels were often inspired by events in Christchurch and she also exhibited some landscapes in oils which reflected the New Zealand environment. At the same time she produced plays for amateur groups.

In 1937 she returned to England and undertook a car trip through France, Germany, Italy, Austria and Luxemburg with some friends. Again she made use of these experiences for excellent travel journalism. During the voyage to England she wrote her sixth novel—*Artists in Crime* (1938)—in which Roderick Alleyn meets Agatha Troy, a painter who can be seen as an alter ego of the novelist herself. Alleyn and Troy marry in *Death in a White Tie* (1938). By this time Marsh could be described (in the *Times Literary Supplement*) as 'in the front rank of crime story writers'. She was at the height of her powers, writing fluently and publishing at least one novel each year. They are all set in England, but in *Surfeit of Lampreys* (1940) a major character is Roberta Grey, a New Zealander, rather over-impressed by English high society life, even though she also believes that as a colonial she has more energy and a more practical approach to things, which, in some circumstances at least, give her the edge over the effete society idols. This ambivalence, according to which the English are admired for their superior command of social skills but held to be inadequate in practical situations, was to characterise Marsh throughout her career. This stay in Britain was a comparatively short one and in April 1938 she returned to New Zealand.

In 1942 she collaborated with R.M. *Burdon on a book about New Zealand, expressing intense wartime patriotism, and her next novel, *Colour Scheme* (1943) was set in Rotorua, making much of the drama of the thermal region. It was during the forties, too, that Marsh began to make her most striking contributions to New Zealand theatre. Her first Shakespeare production was a modern-dress *Hamlet* with the Canterbury University College Drama Society in 1943. This was the beginning of a 'golden age' in which she cooperated with such musicians as Douglas *Lilburn and Frederick Page (husband of Eve) as well as with many young actors who were later to become well-known. Shakespeare was her main love, but she also produced plays by Pirandello, Chekhov and others. New Zealand dramatists formed no part of her repertoire. The climax was a tour of Australia in early 1949.

In the same year Marsh again travelled to England and from this time dates her habit of signing British hotel registers with her New Zealand address and New Zealand ones with her London address. After three theatre seasons and much literary and social activity she returned to Christchurch in 1951, sailing by way of Sydney with a British Commonwealth Theatre Company, which she directed with only moderate success. Despite the destruction of her old Christchurch

theatre, she was much more successful with her production of *Julius Caesar* and she threw herself into theatrical life again. Nonetheless she soon returned to England. Meanwhile her detective fiction had been so prolific and so viable financially that Ngaio Marsh Ltd was formed as an independent company. Paperbacks, hardbacks, dramatisations and radio serials of her work amounted to a small industry. During this extended stay in Britain Marsh also became something of a public personality, taking part in radio games, etc.

The fiction continued to pursue the same formula, but through various settings, most of them English. These variations extend the application of the formula, for example by describing the survival of pagan rites in an English village in *Off with His Head* (1956), but the formula itself remains unchanged. Marsh also liked to use the theatre as a setting in her novels, and the theatrical element extends into plotting and characterisation. Perhaps this, more than anything else, distinguishes her work from that of her main rivals in the genre.

She returned to New Zealand in 1956 and began work on her next Shakespearean production, *King Lear*. She spent some three months each year on theatrical work, and nine months on writing. On her next trip to Britain, in 1960, she toured several countries in the Far East as well as the United States. Again she tasted theatrical life in London but returned to Christchurch in 1961. She was awarded an honorary doctorate by the University of Canterbury in 1962 and presented the Macmillan Brown Lectures there, speaking of 'Shakespeare in the Theatre'. At this time she also entered into a fruitful cooperation with the composer David *Farquhar on the opera 'A Unicorn for Christmas'.

In 1965 she was again in Britain and was awarded the DBE, New Zealand literature's first such award. Other honours included the Mystery Writers of America Grand Master Award.

In 1966 she published her autobiography *Black Beach and Honeydew*, which disappointed many readers with its reticence on matters of public interest, and it was in response to some of this disappointment that she added chapters on the background to her fiction in the revised edition of 1981. Now a very public figure, Marsh continued to do the things she did best, writing a continuous stream of detective fiction and devoting much of her energy to the theatre. She was tireless in her support of young actors and directors. Her writing had made her an international figure, as the tributes after her death made plain, but in New Zealand she was remembered equally for the contribution she had made to developing local theatrical talent. (One tribute is in Mervyn *Thompson's *Passing Through*. See also *Shakespeare in New Zealand.)

In 1967 the University of Canterbury named its new theatre after her, and she came from semi-retirement to direct the gala opening production at the new Christchurch Town Hall in 1972. She chose *Henry V*, and this was her last production.

In her fiction, Ngaio Marsh shares many of the snobberies and other conventions of the detective novel of the 1930s, where the Depression has little impact, where working-class people do not exist except as humble and loyal servants in large houses, where the solving of a crime confirms the basic reliability of the 'system' and suggests a security comfortably surrounding whatever violence occurs, and where the conventional structure of the narrative adds to the reader's security, without the threats to established thought arising from experimental literature. Some of her critics have suggested that the rigid form and the stylisation of detective fiction provided a shelter for her reticent personality. The English country settings similarly provided an escape from the more demanding task of establishing a New Zealand novel tradition.

The four novels with New Zealand settings are *Vintage Murder* (1937), *Colour Scheme* (1943), *Died in the Wool* (1945) and *Photo-Finish* (1980). The first of these is based on the author's experiences with travelling theatre companies. The theatrical detail is spiced with Māori 'superstitions' surrounding a tiki, and Alleyn inquires almost as much into Māori culture—using Dr Te Pokiha as his informant—as into the crime. For all this 'exoticism' the novel has the conventional structure of a crime committed by someone in a limited and closed group of people. There are moments, which must embarrass some readers, when the colonials submit obsequiously to the great detective from the metropolis, but also some obvious attempts to show sympathy for the Māori predicament—from the outside.

Colour Scheme has aroused more interest than any other of her novels. The use of death by boiling in a mud pool could be seen as an attempt to locate the novel in the country, but equally as a sensational appeal to the exotic for international readers. It is only the rather startling setting which makes the plot differ from the conventional style. The English country village has been replaced by a Māori one and the quiet countryside by boiling mud and geysers. There is some treatment of the loss of cultural artefacts to unscrupulous dealers. Nonetheless the view is still external and though Marsh treats her Māori characters with respect, she seems remote from their concerns. As in the case of the tiki, the artefacts are surrounded by superstition.

Died in the Wool, completed between productions of *Hamlet* and *Othello*, is set on a mountain sheep *station in the South Island. It calls on *landscapes which can also be seen in Marsh's paintings. They are lovingly described, and yet the basic tale is another country-house murder, transported to the antipodes. An extra touch of the exotic is added by Alleyn's search for Nazi sympathisers.

South Island landscapes also play a prominent role in *Photo-Finish*, where Alleyn's wife Troy accompanies him and observes the scene with a painter's eye. She believes that this land belongs to birds rather than humans. In this novel, again, Māori *tapu is used to add an exotic touch to the action. The restriction of characters to a closed group is achieved this time by placing them on an island in the middle of a lake, and the murder victim is a famous opera singer. Despite the exotic setting the conventions of the genre are never really challenged, here or elsewhere in Marsh's work; rather they are exploited with consummate skill.

A complete list of Marsh's fiction is appended to Margaret Lewis's *Ngaio Marsh: A Life* (1991). NW

MARSHALL, Heather (1927–), writes novels and young adults' fiction, mostly about the lives of girls and women set against historical events of New Zealand in her lifetime. Thus *Second-Hand Children* (1984) describes growing up during the *Depression, *A Nest of Cuckoos* (1985) narrates a widow's struggle for independent identity, *Secret Diary of a Telephonist* (1985) is a satire on business derived from experience in personnel management (1974–84) and *Anneliese* (1988), probably the most substantial, tells the tragic story of an anorexic girl living through World War 2 in New Zealand, her problems linked with newsreels of Jewish sufferings, the commonplace news of death of men overseas and the complications of American servicemen at home. The novels are all easy reading and have been readily adapted for radio. Her young adult books include *Gemma, Brooke and Madeleine* (1988), *Marie on Her Own* (1990) and *Picking Up the Pieces* (1993), a finalist in the Esther Glen Awards. Born in Otautau, Southland, Marshall has lived since 1932 in Lower Hutt, where she brought up her family and now lives with cats who have more than once (like the ill-fated Wilfred in *Anneliese*) appeared in her fiction. RR

MARSHALL, Owen (Owen Marshall Jones) (1941–), short story writer and novelist, was born in the North Island town of Te Kuiti, where his Welsh grandfather farmed. The third son of a Methodist minister, he grew up in an environment in which his father read aloud to his family, scholarship was revered, and the value of books unquestioned. His mother—whose maiden name was Marshall—died when he was 18 months old. His father remarried when Marshall was 5, and there were six more children. His childhood, a happy time lived mainly in provincial South Island towns, would provide background for a number of stories. After a boyhood spent in Blenheim—'Seven years of summer days, tar bubbling on the streets'—the family moved, when he was 12, southwards to the town of Timaru, on South Canterbury's east coast. In this region of South Canterbury and North Otago Marshall has spent his adult years, and the affinity he feels with its people and landscapes is evident in much of his writing.

From five years as a student at Timaru BHS, Marshall went on to study for four years at the University of Canterbury—a period punctuated by two intervals of National Service in the military—before graduating MA (Hons) in 1964. He received his Diploma in Teaching in 1965 and went into employment, firstly at a school in Timaru, but shortly after at Oamaru's renowned Waitaki Boys' High School where he rose to deputy rector before resigning, after some twenty-five years as a teacher, to write full-time.

Marshall, a voracious reader as a student, admired writers as diverse as Austen, Faulkner, Hemingway, Huxley, Chekhov and A.E. Coppard. To this list he later added great short story practitioners like Joyce, Babel, Pritchett and Sherwood Anderson. However, he consistently rated two lesser-known writers, H.E. Bates and Theodore Powys, among his most important influences: 'Their writing', he stated, 'shares two elements that particularly attracted me: firstly a marked felicity of language, secondly a persistent affection for the countryside and rural people.'

As a young teacher in his mid-twenties Marshall directed his powerful urge to write into two novels, neither of which found a publisher, but one of which he later 'cannibalised—[with] a certain perverse satisfaction' to fill in the background of many stories. Still unpublished in his early thirties Marshall decided to concentrate on short fiction, a form that interested him as a reader and continued to interest him as a writer because of its 'constraints—possibilities [and] challenges'. Changing genres did not lead to immediate publication, but Marshall looked back on the period as a necessary apprenticeship.

Success came in 1977 when the *NZ Listener* published 'Descent from the Flugelhorn'—a story set in rural Otago about a rugby player's encounter with a dying old man. It was against Marshall's nature to announce himself as an author—'I have always valued the fulfilment of being a writer, rather than that of being seen a writer'—so using his Christian names as a pseudonym ensured some anonymity. More periodical publications followed, but there seemed little prospect of a book. Finally Marshall gambled on the quality of his writing and paid to publish his first collection, *Supper Waltz Wilson and Other New Zealand Stories* (1979). The return was handsome: New Zealand's master of the short story, Frank *Sargeson, in his last review, confessed himself unprepared for the book's powerful impact and passed his mantle to Marshall with the assessment that it was 'As fine a book of stories as this country is likely to see.... And because of [its] density, one that will stand close re-reading for many years to come' (*Islands* 30, 1980).

Marshall admired Sargeson, and once said of *'Conversation with My Uncle' that 'I have read whole novels that have less to say, and say it less well' (*NZ Listener*, 17 Sep. 1988), but it is also clear that Sargeson exerted no stylistic influence on the younger man. Lawrence *Jones, in his essay 'Owen Marshall and the Sargeson Tradition' from *Barbed Wire and Mirrors,* argues that the similarities in their fiction come, in practice, 'from the experience of a common New Zealand provincial environment'.

Following his debut, collections of Marshall's stories appeared regularly, but now reviewers were almost universally enthusiastic, and he never paid for another publication. *The Master of Big Jingles and Other Stories* (1982) was followed by *The Day Hemingway Died and Other Stories* (1984); *The Lynx Hunter and Other Stories* (1987); *The Divided World: Selected Stories* (1989)—a mix of new and previously published material; *Tomorrow We Save the Orphans* (1992); *The Ace of Diamonds Gang and Other Stories* (1993); *Coming Home in the Dark* (1995); and, most recently, *The Best of Owen Marshall's Short Stories* (1997), which collects sixty-seven stories from some one hundred and fifty published.

Marshall is too versatile, too adept at adjusting his narrative technique, ever to be described as a formulaic writer, but the body of his work does reveal certain themes, characters and settings recurring. For example, the unlovely Ransumeen family, and the fictional town of Te Tarehi—the focal point of a predominantly Pākehā rural community—weave threads of consistency through segments of his work. Marriages, families and small-town life are often the focus, as is the relationship between the individual and those exclusive male preserves—societies of schoolboys, rugby players, farmers or war veterans—that dominate and confer identity in provincial New Zealand. And at the centre of many of these stories is a solid moral core of esteem for individual integrity.

Against this backdrop Marshall frequently fastens on the outsiders—the loners and misfits, underdogs and losers—who fail to conform. Some characters make grand gestures they alone understand, others live 'lives of quiet desperation', still others—the unlikeable and unredeemable—are caricatures, products of the writer's 'corrosive eye'. It may be, as Marshall says, that 'you can get a lot of emotional mileage' from such characters, yet the way he uses them is often so idiosyncratic that what he illuminates confounds both expectation and pre-conception. It is Marshall exposing what he calls 'the fallibility of the real', revealing the 'things of great horror and ineffable joy' that shimmer beneath the objective world.

Marshall's empathic identification with small-town New Zealand is tempered by a penetrating realism. Lydia Wevers describes the story 'Mumsie and Zip' as 'the blackest and most brilliantly sinister portrait of the sub-urban marriage in New Zealand fiction' (*New Zealand Books*, Dec. 1995). And Vincent *O'Sullivan notes how 'A Southland Girl' only succeeds when a missing context —'one defining word [that] has been held over'—is supplied ('The Naming of Parts: Owen Marshall and the Short Story', *Sport* 3, 1989). When the girl's lover is abruptly revealed as Māori, the narrative reassessment demanded exposes her protective parents as racists.

Marshall is acutely aware that his early stories have a male emphasis that tends to portray women as aggressive, self-righteous and hypocritical. It has, he explains, much to do with his experience as a heterosexual New Zealand male who was a pupil, and later teacher, at a single-sex boys' school; who spent time in the army—where 'I was confronted with the antithesis of individual integrity and the values of group loyalty and support'; and who played 'a good deal of sport largely with young men of my own age'. Time, marriage and the birth of two daughters have tempered this, and recent depictions of women elicit a broader spectrum of responses and evidence a wider range of narratorial sympathies.

Often labelled a realist writer, Marshall prefers to think of himself as an impressionist, and experimentation with narrative technique is a hallmark of his writing. In 'Choctaw Princess' his stated intention is to use the 'rhythm, cadence and hypnotic quality of words' to produce a 'language mosaic creating pattern and mood'. In contrast, the narrator of 'The Lynx Hunter', who is walking to work, sets up in free indirect discourse a series of surreal self-representations, projecting himself onto his external environment, then interrogating and evaluating the self he sees reflected back.

Many critics rank Marshall among the finest, if not the finest, of New Zealand's short story writers. O'Sullivan defines the terms of reference by which such an assessment is possible when he argues that Marshall 'constantly tests and breaks expectation [and] drives the form and its possibilities further perhaps than any other New Zealander apart from the three it is necessary to think of if one wants to place him correctly. With Sargeson, *Duggan, *Frame.'

Marshall's stories have been anthologised inter-nationally and he has received numerous honours, including the Canterbury University writing fellowship, 1981; the PEN Lillian Ida Smith Award for fiction, 1986 and 1988; the *Evening Standard* short story prize, 1987; the American Express short story award, 1987; two second places for the Katherine *Mansfield BNZ Short Story Award; the 1988 Scholarship in Letters, as well as an achievement award in 1990; the 1992 Otago University *Burns Fellowship; and the 1996 Katherine *Mansfield Memorial Fellowship in Menton, France.

The award of the Burns Fellowship enabled Marshall to write his first published novel, *A Many Coated Man* (1995), which was shortlisted for the 1995 Montana Book Awards. The novel, set in twenty-first century New Zealand, begins with Christchurch dentist Aldous Slaven—out house-painting precariously close to live power lines—narrowly escaping electrocution. While recuperating from burns Slaven discovers that his near-death experience has gifted him with powers of oratory so compelling that he can spellbind crowds for hours, although afterwards he has no recollection of what he has said. In the dry world of New Zealand politics such ability to pull crowds and sway the masses by articulating simple truths is threatening, and his enemies attempt to silence him by incarcerating him in a 'hospital'. Slaven escapes, however, re-establishes himself as the head of his Coalition for Citizen Power, and resumes his mission to put a sense of moral community back into politics.

A Many Coated Man is not realist fiction; rather, a subtle current of magic realism charges the narrative: characters die only to reappear later; a short doctor becomes tall and elegant; an enigmatic bald-headed man frequently appears, helping but never speaking; and of course there is Slaven's own startling transformation. But Marshall's underlying moral is a realist one of world-weary cynicism. The insidious political process triumphs as Slaven begins making the kinds of compromises all too familiar in recent New Zealand politics—negotiating potential coalitions with mainstream parties in return for concessions on his ideals.

Andrew Mason summed up the critical response to *A Many Coated Man* when he observed that most 'reviewers, while admiring the lyrical character of the writing, have found the book flawed in technique and puzzling, even obscure, in its direction. Measured against Marshall's short stories ... the novel was judged a disap-pointment—interesting, yes, but a failure' (*Landfall* 190, 1995). Given such responses, it seems unlikely that novels will supplant short stories as Marshall's most acclaimed genre. As Mason concludes, 'with Marshall less is more.'

Since leaving teaching to pursue his writing, Marshall

has run a fiction writing course at Timaru's Aoraki Polytechnic and edited three books: *Burning Boats: Seventeen New Zealand Short Stories* (1994), *Letter From Heaven: Sixteen New Zealand Poets* (1995), and *Beethoven's Ears: Eighteen New Zealand Short Stories* (1996). He collaborated with poet Brian ★Turner and painter Grahame Sydney on *Timeless Land* (1995), a volume reflecting the three men's passion for the Central Otago region, and he has written a radio play commissioned by Radio New Zealand. Marshall has been interviewed twice: by Lawrence Jones for *Landfall* (150, 1984) and by Patrick ★Evans for *In The Same Room: Conversations with New Zealand Writers* (1992). A brief autobiographical essay, 'Tunes For Bears To Dance To', in *Sport* 3 (1989), recalls his beginnings as a writer.   PM

Martin Tobin, a novel by Lady Campbell, was published in three volumes in London in 1864. It has not been possible to find any details of its author, but the novel is of considerable interest for its image of New Zealand some quarter of a century earlier. It can be viewed as representative of an early ★'romance' tradition in New Zealand fiction. Martin decides to become a colonist when he hears of the 'mismanagement' of New Zealand, to be put right by ★Wakefield's New Zealand Company. As in many similar novels, he leaves behind the weeping Miny. At the first sight of the ★bush, England 'became a sweet but dreamy memory', and this power of the ★landscape over the colonists' minds pervades the novel. Equally impressive is the noble savage type of Māori Martin encounters: 'erect as an arrow, every muscle developed, and every limb moulded by exercise and action, difficult indeed would it have been to find his compeer, impossible to surpass him in natural beauty.' The first of many violent adventures occurs when the lover of Te Rauparaha's daughter is shot in Martin's presence. The action moves to a whaling station where the historical character Dicky Barrett is introduced, while several of the vividly described characters can be taken equally for Pākehā or Māori. A journey north leads to Martin being shot by a villain called Black, the pursuit of Black, a delirium, romantic scenes and an episode where Martin lives with the Māori. When war breaks out between the tribes of 'Wirimu Kingki' (Kingi) and Te Heu Heu (both historical characters) Martin and Black's former lover Clari are taken to Lake Taupo, where she dreams accurately of the marriage of his old love Miny in England while he lyricises on the central North Island landscape. While Te Heu Heu is distracted by another war, Martin and Clari escape to the mission station at Tauranga where, in one of several 'typical' descriptions, the missionary couple have tried to recreate England. As the adventurers travel on via Coromandel to 'Korrorariki', Clari wears trousers to avoid the dangers awaiting women in that 'sink of iniquity and all uncleanliness'. After complications involving letters misappropriated by Black, older family feuds and a revenge shooting, Martin reaches Wellington, where he finds the Company's settlement in disgraceful disarray. This leads him to moralise on the qualities needed in a colonist. Nonetheless, he sees the colony progress to 'even a few shops', while a newcomer waxes lyrical about the 'lovely bay, with white cottages all about the shores…'. News comes of Miny's 'seduction' by Martin's old family enemy, whereupon Martin feels all bonds with England broken, and falls into a fever. Then he renews his travels and finds a new love, Lucy, by saving her from drowning in Lake Taupo. They marry, and in Wellington enjoy the first ball, which 'excited no small amount of envy in Auckland', and a horticultural exhibition with 'old country fruits and flowers'. When Miny turns up at the wharf, Martin needs a stiff brandy. The two women become 'sisters', although both suffer. Martin is carried off by Māori to the north but is again rescued, again by Clari. Lucy loses her trust in her husband and dies on the grave of her baby. War breaks out and Martin, in the force that advances on Te Rauparaha's pā, engages in hand-to-hand conflict with Black, disguised under heavy tattoos. The story is wrapped up with a series of deaths, and Martin returns to England; which does not prevent the author adding a postscript recommending New Zealand to readers who find life hard in Britain.   NW

MASON, Bruce (1921–82), playwright, critic, fiction writer, was born in Wellington, moving at age 5 to Takapuna, where his experiences formed the basis of his most famous work, *The ★End of the Golden Weather*. He graduated (BA 1945) from Victoria University College, where he was active in drama and in the literary magazine ★*Hilltop*. After service with the New Zealand Army 1941–43, and the Naval Volunteer Reserve 1943–45, he married Diana Shaw, a Wellington obstetrician, who continues to promote his work. From 1951 to 1957 Mason was senior public relations officer for the New Zealand Forest Service. From 1960 to 1961 he was editor of the Māori news magazine *Te ★Ao Hou*, where he challenged his readers to ask, 'since I am a Maori, what part do I want it to play in my life?' A leading force in founding New Zealand's first professional theatre, Downstage, in Wellington in 1964, he was also music critic with a weekly column 'Music on the Air' for ★*NZ Listener* 1964–69, theatre critic for the Wellington newspapers, the *Dominion* 1958–60 and 1973–80, and *Evening Post* 1980–82), and editor of *Act* magazine 1967–70. He was awarded an honorary degree by Victoria University in 1977 and a CBE in 1980, and in 1996 the Bruce Mason Theatre was opened on the North Shore.

In his first major success, *The *Pohutukawa Tree* (1960, revised 1963, first performed by the New Zealand Players Theatre Workshop in Wellington in 1957, and produced on BBC TV in 1959), Mason critiqued both Pākehā and Māori societies. In the following decade he created what for a time he called 'Te Hoe Pakaru / The Broken Gourd', but later published as *The Healing Arch* (1987). This is a cycle of five plays which focus on Māori culture since European contact: *Hongi* (1968, published 1974) (the clash of religions); *The Pohutukawa Tree* (the Māori in exile); *The Hand on the Rail* (1967) (the Māori in the city); *Swan Song* (1967) (the Māori returning to his roots); *Awatea* (1969) (creating a modern Māori myth). These go beyond a social history of Māoridom where individuals are alienated from their culture; in the lineaments of Greek tragedy, they show the universal pain of children alienated from parents and vice versa. *Awatea*, the last play in the sequence, was Mason's 'greatest single success'. Recorded for radio in 1965 by Inia Te Wiata and the cast of *Porgy and Bess* (the New Zealand Opera Company), it is a simple story of unmasking youthful deception, but shows how (in the stage direction) 'everywhere in their lives, Maori and European rituals are mixed without incongruity'. When the Māori hero Matt resolves to become a writer at the end of the play, Mason (as he put it) 'symbolically retired from the field', having encouraged Māori culture tirelessly at a time when it was unfashionable to do so. A powerful revival directed by Mervyn *Thompson was the highlight of cultural events organised in conjunction with the 1974 Commonwealth Games in Christchurch.

Māori culture also gave Mason a perspective from which to scrutinise his own. His critique of Pākehā society asks, 'What kind of a society can develop under corrugated iron?' It began with *The Evening Paper* (1953), one of a domestic quartet of plays. The others were *The Bonds of Love* (1953), *The Verdict* (1955) and *The Light Enlarging* (1963). In 1965 *The Evening Paper* was the NZ Broadcasting Corporation's first TV play. Mason described it as 'a sour little piece' about a New Zealander returning from overseas to a stifling suburban life. While *Birds in the Wilderness* (1957) shows how New Zealand society crushes a different immigrant culture, and *We Don't Want Your Sort Here* (1963) is a revue which satirises New Zealand's jingoism, *Zero Inn* (1970) is more hopeful in the way that at least the female parental figure is converted by a dropped-out, dope-smoking youth.

Mason's works of solo theatre were collected as *Bruce Mason Solo* (1981), comprising 'The End of the Golden Weather' (first performed in 1959), 'Not Christmas, but Guy Fawkes' (1976), 'To Russia, with Love' (1965)—the first half of *The Counsels of the Wood*—and 'Courting Blackbird' (1976). To read them together is to appreciate how Mason longed for a larger life than he saw possible in his society, or in the equally repressed and repressive Russian society in which he took an informed interest, with its 'Petrouchkas. Stuffed men. Straw.' (He gave a memorable valedictory lecture at Victoria University on the death of Vladimir Nabokov in 1977.) In his thirty-fourth and last play, *Blood of the Lamb* (1981), he skilfully combines Māori and Pākehā cultural traditions in a story which reverses Mason's typical protagonists to make the parental generation the self-made rebels, and the child (Victoria) the force of conservatism. This 'three-part invention in homage to W.A. Mozart and G.B. Shaw', proudly insisting on its New Zealand setting, focuses on a lesbian couple whose feminism cuts across all macho cultures, both European (aggressive, 'a bloody charnel-house' where the male secretly desires the male) and Māori ('the Maori world is a male chauvinist pigsty').

In *Theatre in Danger*, an exchange of letters with John Pocock (1957), Mason discussed the art of the theatre. He always had a strong musical sense of overarching structure, 'the totality' of a play's theme, and spent his life searching for workable dramatic shapes 'in a country which will admit only games as viable rituals'. All his works, including his fiction, draw on such literary models as Sophocles' Greece, O'Casey's Ireland, Faulkner's South, or Chekhov's and Nabokov's Russia, to articulate and mythologise a dull, parochial landscape. He deliberately places his local and often Māori themes in the aesthetic conventions of European theatre, so that (as he puts it) 'they become bi-cultural exercises'. Like Bernard *Shaw, Mason mingled sophisticated artistic intertextuality with political activism, because he always believed in the galvanising social function of theatre, especially amateur theatre. In *New Zealand Drama: A Parade of Forms and a History* (1973) he argued from the point of view of McLuhan and cultural studies that in the amateur theatre 'the information chaos of the media ... can be transcended and made sense of'. His own oeuvre covers the genres of fiction, poetry, theatre, radio, television and journalism. Only opera is missing, although many of his plays (*Awatea*, *Swan Song*, *Blood of the Lamb*) are highly operatic. Mason's analysis of Māori culture in *Hongi* and elsewhere is informed by ideas of media—the Europeans asked the Māori 'totally to restructure their sensory lives, from the modes of aural resonance, to the abstractly visual'—and this leaves the new generations without even an access to a sustaining mythology.

His best-known works are decidedly undramatic, involving long sections of storytelling, although these are punctuated by set pieces of grand ritual such as a wedding or homecoming. His solo works are predominantly narrative, too. The challenge is, for the imagined listener on stage—old or young—and always for the audience, to reject or embrace the 'myth' that is being created before them. The plays exhort us consciously and energetically to choose a culture and live in it; the last words of his book on New Zealand drama are 'What exactly is Maoritanga?' He translated Chekhov's *The Cherry Orchard* for radio in 1960 (it was later staged in 1981) because it focuses on a group of people who don't have the courage to make this choice. To read just some of his journalism, collected in *Every Kind of Weather* (1986), is to see how Mason tried to make his concerns a matter of public debate, working tirelessly in all the media to reach all New Zealanders. In many ways, he was himself a 'made man', who created, among his many other myths, the myth of himself. Mervyn Thompson called him 'a Don Quixote tilting away at a landscape that doesn't quite live up to his heroic aspirations'. Highly cultured and literate, he nevertheless longed to make contact with the 'average New Zealander', and did so in the inexhaustible performances of *The End of the Golden Weather*. As he puts it, recalling his Takapuna childhood in his monologue *Not Christmas, but Guy Fawkes*, 'I in my flaxbush and the people on the lawn, form a context: if I could not communicate with them, it was because they refused communication with me, or the likes of me. And the reasons for this refusal have become the mainspring of my work.'

Mason was therefore fascinated by 'mid-racial' people who fit in neither culture. In *Swan Song* the hero is a Māori opera lover now learning Māoritanga, and in *The Pohutukawa Tree* Johnny is possessed by the myth of Robin Hood. This interest extends to his work with European settings, such as the German officer in *The Waters of Silence* (1965), or Dmitri in its companion piece *To Russia With Love*. His works often focus on sensitive individuals trying to create personae to satisfy a culture's or elder's demands, but being either unmasked or proved unequal to the role. The sympathy at that point is usually with the individual and against the crucifying society, whether Māori or Pākehā, capitalist or communist. In his life and art, Mason never lost an optimism that one day people would sort out their allegiances. *Blood of the Lamb* is therefore the fitting climax to his career: its exuberant heroines are citizens of the world yet thoroughly embedded in and committed to their local culture. When the daughter Victoria awkwardly accepts their unorthodox behaviour and roles in her life, Eliza observes, 'Well, I guess that's the most we can expect from this time and clime.' While Aroha dies at the end of *The Pohutukawa Tree*, and Matt only sketchily promises to become a Māori writer at the end of *Awatea* (Mason attempted to fill in this sketchiness in 1978 when he published some letters purportedly written by Matt), Eliza's understatement is the first firm stone laid by Mason in building his longed-for healing arch.   DD

MASON, Henrietta or **Etta** (1889–1989), wrote a trilogy of New Zealand historical novels, a family saga mainly of high-country farmers and their women. *Fool's Gold* (New York 1953, London and Christchurch 1960) takes 17-year-old Bridget from England to 1860s New Zealand where, disguised as boy, she goes ashore in Hokitika with a *gold prospecting party and has melodramatic adventures. *Our Hills Cry Woe!* (1963) takes her and her descendants through World War 1 and the *Depression, the farmer-hero becoming a member of parliament and champion of high-country interests; and *High Acres* (1966) brings the sheep *station of that name close to the present. All show skill with women characters. Mason must have sustained a passion for the South Island high country from a distance, since she left New Zealand about 1920, after teachers' college and university, to serve first in the Melanesian Mission and then to study creative writing in America. Her first book was *On Our Island* (1926), published in London as by Etta Mason. She spent twenty-five years as executive secretary of the Department of English at Columbia University in New York City. The novel, *White Orchid* (1953), was published at that time in the USA and UK and serialised in translation in Europe. Its New Zealand heroine works in the New Hebrides in a French-Polynesian family. Mason returned to New Zealand about 1960. PN/RR

MASON, R.A.K. (1905–71), was New Zealand's 'first wholly original, unmistakably gifted poet' (Allen *Curnow). He was born in Penrose, Auckland, the son of New Zealand–born parents and, on his mother's Irish Kells side, the grandson of 1840s colonists. After his father's unexplained death about early 1912, he and his brother were sent to stay with a schoolteacher aunt at Lichfield in the southern Waikato. She taught the boys until the end of 1915, when Mason returned to Auckland for a year's primary schooling at Panmure. In 1917 he was enrolled at Auckland GS, where he formed a close association, lasting more than a decade, with the future poet A.R.D. *Fairburn, and distinguished himself in English and Latin (his well-known translation of Horace's ode 'O Fons Bandusiae' was apparently done as a class homework exercise). In 1923, because of his poor record in mathematics, Mason was unable to go on to Auckland University College, where he had hoped to continue his classical studies, and instead became a tutor at the private University Coaching College. In his spare time he was pursuing his boyhood interest in writing verse, and in 1923 he produced his first 'book' (handwritten, handbound, three copies) of four poems (including three 'Sonnets of the Ocean's Base'), titled *In the Manner of Men*.

His first true publication, however, was *The Beggar*, printed by ★Whitcombe & Tombs in an edition of 1000 copies and published by Mason privately in 1924. Although a number of these twenty-two poems have since been anthologised many times (Harold Monro of the Poetry Bookshop in London published two, 'Latterday Geography Lesson' and 'Body of John', in No. 39 of his miscellany *The Chapbook* in 1924, and two others, the sonnets 'The Spark's Farewell [to its Clay]' and 'Miracle of Life [I]' in *Twentieth Century Poetry* in 1929); and although some (those mentioned plus 'Old Memories of Earth' and 'Sonnet of Brotherhood') have now entered the New Zealand literary canon, the booklet did not sell; so disappointed by the lack of interest locally was the young poet that he is supposed later to have dumped a bundle of 200 copies in the Waitemata Harbour. Despite this failure, in 1925 he had five new poems (including 'Song of Allegiance') printed on a folded sheet of card, under the title *Penny Broadsheet* and dedicated: 'To (?) the Unknown Hero who sent me £3 in appreciation of "The Beggar" ... as a Token of Gratitude to himself (and a Hortatory Example to Other People!).' On the back it announced: 'If you are anxious to help the cause of young New Zealand Literature, buy / "THE BEGGAR" / A rather remarkable / LITTLE BOOK / Price One Shilling / POST FREE—from the Author'.

In 1926 Mason began part-time studies towards a BA in Latin at Auckland University College. For the next three years he wrote little poetry, possibly because of the poor reception of his earlier work combined with his growing interest in radical and student politics. Some poems appeared in the Auckland ★*Sun*, which also published a sympathetic evaluation of his work by Ian Donnelly at the end of 1928. By then Mason had determined to adopt a more public position ('I do want to brighten life and make this world a better place for my being in it'); he wrote later (in *Making a Poem*, 1959) of his developing feeling that 'poetry should and could be as it was so long in Scotland and Ireland, a thing of the people but at the same time profound. So the poem has a simple surface appearance but with deeper layers of significance beneath.' At the same time, 'I felt strongly the need for poetry and drama to move more closely together ... with drama benefiting by the bite and precision of poetry, while poetry should learn again the simple and open texture of drama'. One result was the verse play *Squire Speaks* (published as a play for radio by the ★Caxton Press in 1938, ten years later), generously

described by J.E. ★Weir in his critical monograph on Mason as 'a fashionable example of the Marxist popular drama of the period ... primarily a political, not a literary exercise'.

By 1929 he was writing poetry again and already planning his next collection. Late that year he lost his tutoring job and spent the summer back in the Waikato, working as a farm labourer. An extended diary-letter to his friend Geoffrey ★de Montalk (by then in London), written during January 1930, was published in 1986 by the Nag's Head Press, Christchurch, as *R.A.K. Mason at Twenty-Five*; this offers considerable insight into his creative thinking (he transcribes the original version of what, with little alteration, has become possibly his best-known poem, 'On the Swag') at the start of the year that is generally regarded as the most intensive of his writing life. Besides completing a good number of poems, in 1930 he began a 'partly autobiographical' novel and wrote uncompromisingly radical articles for the *New Zealand Worker* and articles condemning New Zealand's administration of Western Samoa. Between 1931 and 1934 poems from his unpublished manuscripts appeared in the Auckland University annual ★*Kiwi* and in the new university-based literary quarterly ★*Phoenix*. Mason was asked to take over the editorship of *Phoenix* from its third issue (March 1933), transforming it in its last issues into 'an aggressive and polemical instrument' (Weir), writing out of 'passionate indignation against social wrong and inequality, and scorn of public stupidities ... with a vehemence and directness rare in New Zealand during those years of economic crisis and depression' (Curnow).

Mason's next collection of poems, *No New Thing*, was meanwhile being rejected by publishers in Boston and London. Its troubled history was by no means over even after Bob ★Lowry agreed to design and hand-set the work at his Unicorn Press in Auckland in 1934. The project was ambitious, with a simple, elegant design and hand-woven binding cloth; but because of a dispute with the binders the 100 signed copies intended for public sale were never issued (though some copies were later released privately under the imprint Spearhead Publishers). As Weir comments: 'The collection was of such excellence—one of the best single collections by a New Zealand poet—that it deserved a kinder fate.' That kinder fate did await Mason's work after Denis ★Glover established the Caxton Press in Christchurch in 1936, for Caxton published nearly all of his poetic output from about 1936 onwards. Their first volume was *End of Day* (1936): only five poems, including 'Prelude' and the call to revolution 'Youth at the Dance'. To *Recent Poems*, the 1941 collection of new work also by Curnow, Fairburn and Glover, Mason contributed a group of five love poems, including the lyrical 'Flow at Full Moon'.

The same year also saw the publication of *This Dark Will Lighten: Selected Poems 1923–41*. This was the first proper selection of Mason's poetry and made the best of his early work widely available for the first time. It included three poems from *In the Manner of Men* and eleven from *The Beggar* (revised to remove archaisms); the format of all these, and the three from the *Penny Broadsheet*, was altered to conform with the 'hanging indent' style he used for his poems from about 1930. Also included were fifteen of the twenty-five poems in *No New Thing*, four from *End of Day* and 'Flow at Full Moon', as well as one new poem, another 'Prelude', beginning 'Here are the children / of the best part of a lifetime'. There were to be few more such 'children': only one, the denunciatory 'Sonnet to MacArthur's Eyes' of 1950, was subsequently published in the *Collected Poems* assembled for Glover and the ★Pegasus Press in 1962 (second edition 1963; new edition 1971; reprinted by ★Victoria University Press 1990). This gathered together nearly all of Mason's published poems, including some hitherto uncollected pieces, and a selection of unpublished poems from 1924 to 1930; it had an unabashedly evangelical yet critically acute introduction by Allen Curnow (from which the quotations in this article are taken).

His poetic activity may have virtually ceased by 1941, but Mason had a busy thirty years of life left. He continued to work for left-wing theatre groups in Auckland and to write didactic plays for stage and radio (the dance-drama, *China*, was published in 1943, and republished as *China Dances* with other verses in 1962); he became a strong advocate for a national theatre after the war. From 1941 to 1943 he edited a communist newspaper, and from then until 1954 was assistant secretary of the Auckland Builders' and General Labourers' Union, for whom he also edited the journal *Challenge* and under whose auspices he published *Frontier Forsaken: An Outline History of the Cook Islands* in 1947. Suffering ill health, he then worked as a landscape gardener, but was able to visit ★China as first president of the New Zealand–China Society in 1957. In 1962 he received the ★Burns Fellowship at Otago University, where he wrote some new poems (three were published in the Students' Association *Review*) and a verse-play, *Strait is the Gate* (broadcast by the NZBC in 1969). Also in 1962 he married his longtime companion, Dorothea Beyta, and in 1965 they returned to Auckland, where Mason died at Takapuna.

Most critics share Curnow's view and regard R.A.K. Mason as New Zealand's first authentic poet, who could unselfconsciously populate the Waikato, the Waitemata, Otahuhu and Papatoetoe with figures from European myth and history such as Chatterton, Gaius Marius, Diana, Herostratus and Aeneas ('Wayfarers'). Yet his poetic vision was only incidentally local. The earlier poems are preoccupied mainly with the temporariness and yet connection of all human lives, with the 'individual soul standing grimly' between past and future and the wider human brotherhood that our predicament must engender. Later poems often dramatise the suffering, as in 'Judas Iscariot' or 'Footnote to John ii 4' ('Each one of us must do his work of doom'), making its individuality unique yet universal. These philosophic themes are treated in a distinctive and highly personal way: a combination of defiant desperation, dour stoicism, classical pessimism, dismayed emotion and shocked religious faith, tempered with a rather macabre humour and occasional tenderness.

If philosophically Mason places himself in the grand English tradition of 'Shakespeare Milton Keats' and Shelley—'They are gone and I am here / stoutly bringing up the rear' ('Song of Allegiance')—stylistically he belongs in the line of English poets from Dowson, Hardy and Housman to the ★Georgians (with echoes of Catullus and Horace). His poetic voice is equally distinctive: despite the archaisms, the forced rhymes, the sometimes overblown or stilted language, there is also an energy, a dramatic urgency expressed with colloquial spareness, a supple 'muscularity', which achieves a 'ruggedly individual voice that, as it puzzles over what to say, transforms even gaucheness into a kind of authenticity' (MacD.P. Jackson). This 'peculiar intensity' is in part a consequence of his extraordinary youth: Mason was only nineteen when he published *The Beggar*, which so struck Curnow, and over four-fifths of the *Collected Poems* were written before he turned 25. In one of his journals Mason noted: 'I do not invent the words; I do not even repeat them from memory. I say them at the bidding of some invisible prompter far back in the dark stage of my mind.' This confirms the impression defined by C.K. ★Stead (*In the Glass Case*) that Mason's best poems were 'spontaneous expressions of feelings not always perfectly understood by the mind as it brought them forth', and that he was 'a poetic medium rather than a maker of poems'. The 'increased self-awareness' evident in *No New Thing*, even though it contains his finest work, suggests that 'the qualities distinguishing the earlier work could not be maintained', and Mason's poetic silence after about 1940 is compellingly attributed to 'the failure of a gift for which the will could provide no substitute'.

AM

MATAIRA, Katerina (Te Heikoko) (1932–), is a children's writer, artist, illustrator, linguist and Māori-language programme developer. In the early 1970s she was a pioneer in writing texts which presented Māori heritage and language from an inward perspective. As a teacher at Kaikohe in 1959, she was 'the first person to teach Maori in a New Zealand state secondary school, creating many of her own resources, writing Maori poetry, short stories and material for school publications' (*New Zealand Times*, 23 June 1985). She was first published as an illustrator, of Elsie *Locke's young adults' historical novel *The End of the Harbour* (1968). In the 1970s she wrote many Māori-language readers for *School Publications, probably the most enduring being *Te motopaika* (the motorbike), with photographs by Ans *Westra (1971). In English she wrote and illustrated *Maui and the Big Fish* (Christchurch and Sydney, 1972) and wrote *Maori Legends for Young New Zealanders*, illustrated by Clare Bowes (1975), *The Warrior Mountains* (1982) and *The River Which Ran Away* (1983). She also continued to produce books in Māori for School Publications, several being more significant than merely educational readers. *Maori Poetry* (1975) is original writing by Mataira at an early date for such a publication, *Te Ata* (Space) (1975) demonstrates vividly that the Māori language can be adapted to science and technology, and *Junior Primary Maori Language Readers and Teachers' Materials* (1977) presents from behind its functional title a rich resource of knowledge and insight that shows Mataira's centrality to the renaissance of Māori language and culture associated with the Centre for Maori Studies and Research at the University of Waikato, which published this part of her work.

For adults, Mataira's publications include *Whaiora: The Pursuit of Life* (1985), a photo record of Māori people 1976–88, with Mataira's text in Māori and English; and *Taura Tangata* (the joining of people), with her sister Keita Ngata and Denis Mahuika (1988), a limited edition *whakapapa of the people of Ohinewaiapu.

Mataira was born in Ruatoria and educated at St Joseph's Maori GC, Napier, and Ardmore Teachers' College, specialising in arts and crafts. After teaching at Kaikohe she moved with her husband to Wellington, working with the Māori Educational Foundation and studying at Victoria University; and then to Hamilton and Fiji. There she worked with the University of the South Pacific, travelling extensively, and was a contributor to the Peacesat radio conferencing network. Returning to a fellowship at University of Waikato to research Māori language teaching, she developed Te Ataarangi, also known as the rakau method, a total immersion language-learning method which she had observed among Peace Corps volunteers in the South Pacific. In 1987 Mataira was appointed a foundation member of the *Māori Language Commission.

PN/RR

Mate: A Literary Periodical made a momentous debut with a first issue (1957) described by Denis *Glover as 'never to be seen again'. Edited in Auckland by Kevin *Ireland as a 'platform for young writers', it started by recruiting the elite: *Baxter's 'In Fires of No Return', *Sargeson's 'A Sketch', R.A.K. *Mason's 'Sonnet to McArthur's Eyes', Janet *Frame's 'Face Downwards on the Grass' and work by *Fairburn, Charles *Doyle and Ireland himself, disguised as Kevin Jowsey; it was designed and printed by Bob *Lowry. No. 2 (1958), under David Walsh and Robin *Dudding, was almost as memorable, with Maurice *Gee, Doyle, Ireland and Sargeson again, Gordon *Challis and Barry *Crump as 'A *Good Keen Man'. No. 3 (1959) became Dudding's first solo flight, and *Mate* then developed his hallmarks—quality contents, a balance of established and new, elegant appearance and mysteriously dysrhythmic publication. Sargeson and Ireland (now overseas) continued to be featured, Louis *Johnson and Maurice *Duggan (as poet) published there quite often, and by the time he handed over to Tom McWilliams with No. 15 (1967), Dudding's list included *Amato, *Bland, *Brasch, *Duckworth, *Pearson, *Smithyman, *Tuwhare, *Weir and *Wendt.

In the transition to Bert Hingley's brief editorship (Nos. 21–22, 1972–73, after No. 20 jointly with McWilliams), *Mate* had taken on an avant-garde, *postmodern, especially new fiction emphasis, with writers like *Brunton, Wystan *Curnow, Murray *Edmond, *Else, *Fraser, *Haley, *Kemp, *Langford, *Morrissey, *Paterson, *Southam and *Wedde now prominent. Alistair Paterson became editor with No. 23 (1974), when the bigger names, both old guard and avant-garde, were moving elsewhere. His catholic editorial taste gave opportunities to the emerging women writers (*Compton, Lauris *Edmond, *Ensing, *McAlpine, *Smither) and others not associated with any movement or faction. The emphasis shifted towards poetry, and Robert *Creeley's visit was marked in No. 25 (1976).

No. 27 (1977) announced a new direction as 'a magazine of Australasian writing', though this proved as hard to implement as to sell to readers, even with the change of name to *Climate* with No. 28 (1978). Number 30 managed to get the Australian representation up to seven among twenty New Zealanders. Interesting new (not necessarily young) writers were still finding a place—Rangi *Faith, Graeme *Lay, Harvey *McQueen, Gregory *O'Brien—and Sam *Hunt and Elizabeth Smither were featured. But *Climate* had lost *Mate's* pivotal just-off-centre position, and No. 32 (1981) announced union with Dunedin's *Pilgrims*. The demise of both ensued.

RR

Matriarch, The, Witi ★Ihimaera's third novel, was published in 1986, twelve years after his second, ★*Whanau*, with a notable difference in emphasis. Where *Whanau's* pastoral narrative makes the politics of Māori alienation subordinate to its focus on unity and community, *The Matriarch* is overtly political, its protagonist, Tamatea, a tool being sharpened by the matriarch to bring about the Pākehā's destruction. To this end, Ihimaera fragments his narrative and uses abrupt changes in voice and tone (ranging from polemical and didactic to domestic) to make the novel's politics explicit.

Although beginning in 1974, and remaining rooted there, the novel also spans five generations of Tamatea's family. Ihimaera's matriarch, Artemis, becomes the focus of Tamatea's investigation into her history and background. Because he and Artemis are linked by identical circumstances of birth, their destinies are intertwined. His intention is to understand her, but he comes instead to a new self-knowledge, while she remains an enigmatic figure. In her ambitions for herself and her people, Artemis casts Tamatea in a central role. But her demands on him as a child make her seem frightening, and her contest with his mother, Tiana, over him, supplies one of the novel's key tensions.

Tamatea's investigations take him back to other ancestors: to ★Te Kooti, and to the matriarch's great-uncle Wi Pere Halbert, the forgotten parliamentarian. As part of this telling, Ihimaera recounts the history of Pākehā settlement from a Māori perspective—making explicit the rapacity with which they acquired land, abetted by laws to ensure Māori disadvantage; and tracing these patterns of dispossession to the present day.

The Matriarch is an involved and complex work. Among the devices Ihimaera employs to organise it are arias from Verdi (*Aida*, for example, links Artemis to Te Kooti through their refusal to be enslaved by Pākehā and their lament for lost land), which have proved surprisingly contentious.

Given *The Matriarch's* range of reference—to Māori cosmology and mythology, the biblical Exodus, colonial New Zealand history, the Italian Risorgimento, and the Parliamentary Hansard—it is perhaps not surprising that it has met a mixed critical response: C.K. ★Stead called it 'a gross piece of personal mythologising' (*London Review of Books*, 18 Dec. 1996) and Atareta Poananga took issue with its promotion of 'colonial myths on the sexist nature of Maori society' (★*Broadsheet,* Jan./Feb. 1987). At the other end of the scale, Alex Calder praised it as an 'epic which is concerned not with restoring the past but with piecing together a future out of the hopes of the past' (★*Landfall* 161, 1987).　　　　PM

Māui is both a hero and a trickster-figure in Māori mythology, with a status between divine and human. In *Ngā Pepa a Ranginui: The Walker Papers* (1996), Ranginui ★Walker explains that Māui-tikitiki-a-Taranga is a demigod, one of the heroes whose role is to mediate between gods and humans, 'to fetch knowledge from their ancestors above them in the ★whakapapa, and transmit it to human descendents who come after them'. As a hero, he is a model for young people and Walker lists his admired characteristics as 'intelligence, cunning, initiative, boldness and determination'. On the other hand, notoriously, he gets away with breaking ★tapu and, unlike other heroes, he 'performs no feats of arms, concerns himself often with practical, domestic matters, and tends to do things the "wrong", non-prestigious way' (Margaret ★Orbell, *The Illustrated Encyclopedia of Māori Myth and Legend*, 1996). ★Mead points out further that he 'provided the model of death. He was the first to die and, since he died, we must all follow him.'

The stories concerning Māui are simultaneously heroic and comic. His actions—such as slowing the sun to lengthen the days, bringing fire from the gods to mankind and fishing up the North Island while using the South Island as his vessel (★waka), thus creating New Zealand—are comparable to those of heroes in other cultures, but the manner in which he achieves them is comic, and tellers of the tales make the most of their entertainment value. Typically, his death—which brings death as such into the world—is the comic result of a failed heroic action: when he tried to achieve immortality for mankind by entering the vagina of the goddess of night, ★Hine-nui-te-pō, the watching fantails found the sight so hilarious that they giggled and awakened the goddess, who crossed her thighs and crushed Māui. Mead comments: 'How he died provides one cultural model of behaviour for the modern-day Maori. He attempted to expand the fronters of immortality by challenging the goddess of death.'　　　　NW

MAXWELL, Vicky, see **EYRE, Annette**

Me and Gus stories, see **ANTHONY, Frank.**

MEAD, Hirini (Sydney) Moko (1927–), of Ngāti Awa, is a senior academic anthropologist and scholar of arts and culture, who in retirement writes increasingly on Māori language, culture and political aspirations. Born at Wairoa, he was educated at St Stephen's and Te Aute Colleges and Auckland Teachers' College 1944–45. After teaching Māori arts and crafts and appointments as principal in primary schools 1957–63, he graduated MA in anthropology at Auckland University 1965 and PhD at University of Southern

California 1968. After lectureships at Auckland and McMaster (Canada) Universities and a Commonwealth Fellowship at University of British Columbia, he became foundation professor of Māori Studies at Victoria University of Wellington (Te Whare Wānanga o te Upoko o te Ika a Māui), 1977–91. His many appointments include the management committee of the Te Māori Exhibition which famously toured the USA in 1986, and the selection committee for the Mobil Corporation's Pegasus Prize in 1986 (won by *the *bone people*). He was the second Māori scholar to be admitted to the Royal Society of New Zealand. His early publications include *Taniko Weaving* (1952), *The Art of Māori Carving* (1961) and *Traditional Māori Clothing* (1969), and a number of Māori language learners. His major publications on Māori art include *Art and Artists of Oceania* (with Bernie Kernot, 1983), *Te Toi Whakairo; The Art of Māori Carving* (1986) and *Magnificent Te Māori—Te Māori Whakahirahira* (1986). Recent work on political and cultural themes includes the research report *Te Murunga Hura—The Pardon* (1989), *Tawhaki: The Deeds of a Demigod* (1996) and the collection of essays, *Landmarks, Bridges and Visions: Aspects of Māori Culture* (1997). RR/NW

Meanjin, the leading literary journal of *Australia, founded 1940, has shown interest from time to time in fostering understanding of New Zealand literature. Allen *Curnow contributed 'Aspects of New Zealand Poetry' to Volume 2 (1942) and Nettie Palmer a wartime overview to Volume 3, in which she suggested that '*Meanjin* could begin to put these two experimental democracies in literary touch again'. However, while the journal has always been perfectly hospitable to good New Zealand writing, James K. *Baxter could still ask there in 1956 'What can a New Zealander say to an Australian?—except, "we've met before"' ('A Note on Henry Lawson'). *Meanjin* in its first quarter-century published (among others) poems by Baxter, Curnow, *Dallas, *Smithyman, *Stead and *Wolfskehl, fiction by Baxter and essays by Rewi *Alley, *Milner and Helen *Shaw (on *Mansfield). More recently Greg *O'Brien, Andrew *Johnston and Elizabeth *Smither have published there quite often, and several others on one or two occasions. Probably the only writers of New Zealand affiliation to publish significant quantities of new work there have been those born or based in Australia, such as Douglas *Stewart and Louis *Johnson. Lynne Strahan's *Just City and the Mirrors: 'Meanjin Quarterly' and the Intellectual Front, 1940–1965* (1984) confirms this by omission, mentioning only Curnow, Smithyman and Wolfskehl.

The September 1985 issue focused on New Zealand literature, however, with creative or critical work by Patrick *Evans, *Manhire, Smither, *Wedde and others, and the 1994 'Oceania' issue featured *Hawken, *Sullivan, *Were and others. Occasionally major New Zealand topics have been discussed, notably in recent times *Once Were Warriors* ('The Book, the Film, the Interview', 1995). There has been a marked increase in New Zealand content since 1994 under editor Christina Thompson, with Jamie *Belich, Annamarie *Jagose, Vivienne *Plumb, John *Pule, Peter *Wells and Mark *Williams (and others) placing work. Now based in Melbourne, the journal started life in Brisbane as *Meanjin Papers* (1940–47) and was *Meanjin Quarterly* 1961–76. Its name is the Aboriginal word for Brisbane, meaning a spike of land. RR

Meg, the second novel in a trilogy by Maurice *Gee, see **Plumb**.

MELBOURNE, Hirini (Sydney) Raureka (1949–), of Tūhoe, is a leading composer of *waiata, a musician, translator, editor, children's writer and historian. Born in Ruatoki near Whakatane, he was editor of Māori publications for *School Publications 1975–78, editing *Te Wharekura* and *Te Tautoko* and initiating the series *He Purapura*. With an MA for a thesis on Māori land confiscation, he is senior lecturer in Māori at the University of Waikato and serves as head of department. His diverse literary research and creative work includes composition of waiata and lyrics, published for instance in *Toiapipi: he huinga o nga kura puoro a te Maui* (1993; book and sound cassette) and the sound cassette *Te ku te whe* (1994). These give creative expression to the research Melbourne has carried out with musicologist and performer Richard Nunns, in words by Melbourne and music composed and performed on traditional instruments by Melbourne and Nunns.

Melbourne's translations are mainly of children's texts such as *Te kuia me te pūngāwerewere* (1981, with Keri Kaa), a translation of Patricia *Grace's *The Kuia and the Spider*, and the parallel Māori text, *Te poti mau pōtae* (1983), for Dr Seuss's *The Cat in the Hat*. He is also co-author of *People, Land and Forests* (1986, with Evelyn Stokes and J. Wharehuia Milroy), a social and economic report on land use strategies in Te Urewera. 'Waka huia', a television documentary on Melbourne's career and music, with performances, was broadcast in 1989. PN/RR

MELVILLE, Herman (1819–91), the US novelist and poet, first presents Queequeg in *Moby-Dick* (1851) when the harpooner from the South Pacific is engaged in selling ''balmed New Zealand heads'. Queequeg has sold a string of embalmed heads, the landlord of the

Spouter-Inn reports, and only one head remains. It has been suggested that Queequeg was based on the description and illustration of Ko Toatoa of Kororarika in Charles Wilkes's *Narrative of the United States Exploring Expedition, 1838–42*, which Melville owned and quoted. More significantly, Melville thus registers the demand for New Zealand—and specifically Māori—'curios' in New Bedford, Massachusetts. He also conveys the cultural and economic exchanges that were occurring apace within and beyond the Pacific. But perhaps most telling is the process by which these heads become separated from the physical and cultural bodies that define them.

Melville's sea-novels repeatedly associate New Zealand with far-off wilds, romance, and the extremes of geography and human experience. The young protagonist in *Redburn* (1849) imagines journeying to 'the coast of Africa or New Zealand' to fulfil his desire for 'remote and barbarous countries'. Melville creates a Pacific spectrum, from 'the Feejee islands, cannibalism, saltpetre, and the devil', in *White-Jacket* (1850), to the declaration in *Clarel* (1876) that Christ should have been born in Tahiti. He both exploits and questions typical presentations of New Zealand: a doctor pretends to eat a piece of cancerous human flesh in *White-Jacket*, explaining, 'I was in New Zealand last cruise, Cuticle, and got into sad dissipation there among the cannibals.'

Perhaps the fullest portrait of New Zealand emerges in *Omoo* (1847) in the presentation of Bembo, 'a wild New Zealander, or "Mowree"'. Jay Leyda's *The Melville Log* (1951) establishes that the character was based upon the harpooner Benbo Byrne. Melville presents this Māori character as 'a dark, moody savage', 'a man, or devil'. Bembo slips out of the narrative, and his fate remains indefinite even in Ian *Wedde's bravura reconsideration of Byrne in *Symmes Hole* (1986).   JE

MENZIES, Trixie Te Arama

MENZIES, Trixie Te Arama (1936–), born in Wellington of Scottish and Tainui descent, has published three collections of verse through Waiata Koa, an Auckland-based collective of Māori women and artists formed during the 'Karanga Karanga' exhibition in 1986. Many poems were originally performed in Auckland at the Gluepot, the Globe, the Albion, the annual hui of Ngā Puna Waihanga (the New Zealand Maori Artists and Writers Society Ltd) and the Mount Eden festival. All volumes are illustrated by Toi te Rito Mihi and include forewords by Ramai Hayward. *Uenuku* (1986) won the *PEN Best First Book Award. Aiming to continue traditions crucial to Māoritanga, Menzies celebrates collective activities like mussel and pupu picking and symbolically acclaims flax-making and weaving as 'Our work (which) will fashion the nets

to catch the star'. *Uenuku*, like *Papakainga* (1988) and *Rerenga* (1992), includes poems by Dorothy Calvert, Menzies' mother; *Rerenga* also has a poem by her daughter, Georgina Stewart. Menzies's skill is in reconciling European and Māori perspectives and traditions. Linking the earth with its offerings of pūhā and watercress to ancestral time, she is equally likely to view the ancient world of the gods within a contemporary context. *Rerenga* dwells on an overseas trip, an open-hearted encounter with the British and French. Particularly striking is her eulogy to Stephen Hawking, seen as a modern day *Māui, 'keyboard happy / Plucking the fiery fingernails of Time…'. Menzies has also edited *He Wai: A Song: First Nations Women's Writing* (1996), a Waiata Koa anthology of prose, verse and photographs which comprises work from twenty-one ethnic writers, including Hawaiian, Tongan, Canadian Indian and Māori. She has also published critical articles in *Landfall* (reprinted in *Te *Ao Mārama* II), the *Journal of New Zealand Literature* and *Printout*, and wrote on Māori women songwriters for *Standing in the Sunshine* (ed. Sandra Coney, 1993).   JW

MERRETT, Joseph Jenner (1816–54), poet and artist, settled as a young man north of Auckland, and married Maria Rangitetaea Koa of Ngāti Kura. A trader who acted as interpreter during the Northern War, Merrett also made historically important sketches of Hone Heke, Kawiti, and scenes of settlement and Māori life. His poetry was published in Australia, where in the 1840s he antagonised the foremost Australian poet, Charles Harpur, by publishing poems on New Zealand in the *Maitland Mercury*. Harpur, who enjoyed a virtual monopoly on verse in the *Mercury*, counter-attacked by mockery, choosing particularly the phrase 'azure wing' in Merrett's poem 'Scraps of a Wanderer' (1844). In a note to his own long verse satire, *The Temple of Infamy* (1846), Harpur observes 'Perhaps this tendency to *blueness* in Mr Merrett's mental vision is mainly attributable to his having rubbed noses with the *tattooed* Genius of New Zealand. 'Tis a pity his rage for notoreity does not confine itself to portrait painting.'   VO

MERYON, Charles (1821–68), French artist, projected an exotic image of New Zealand into the European visual consciousness, and inscribed the Māori place name 'Akaroa' across the top of a key etching, 'Voyage à Nouvelle-Zélande' (1866). A sub-lieutenant on *Le Rhin*, he was stationed at Akaroa 1843–46, voyaging extensively through the *Pacific islands and producing historically important sculptures and drawings. His famous 'Death of Marion du Fresne', the French navigator killed in the Bay of Islands in 1772, in crayon, pencil and chalk, is in the *Alexander Turnbull Library. His later artistic work in Paris, praised by Baudelaire, alternated between gloomy cityscapes and idyllic images from the Pacific, especially Akaroa. In his last years in the St Maurice mental asylum the two worlds became mixed, Polynesian canoes, birds, whales and fish appearing against harsh Parisian stone, and the Māori language, 'Akaroa', positioned as a symbol of affirmation, an image as potent as *Macaulay's New Zealander sketching the ruins of St Paul's. CM

MESSENGER, Elizabeth, see **Detective fiction**; **Gold**.

Metaphor is a group of writers and performers for children established in 1992. Founding members were Martin *Baynton, Tessa *Duder, Gaelyn *Gordon and William *Taylor. David *Hill and others have also been co-opted as writers. Performances have been given in Australian schools as well as widely in New Zealand. Scripts include *Foreign Rites* (1992), in which Baynton and Duder present New Zealand books in an international publishing context; *Ghost Writers*, a next-world post-mortem on the writers' own work; *Eyeopeners and Gobstoppers, A Tribute to A.A. Milne*; for adults *Love, Lust and Lewd Libidos*; and Duder and Baynton's *Joan* (1995), a reassessment of Joan of Arc in a futuristic setting. DH

Metro, the monthly Auckland magazine, has been one of the most significant literary outlets since its first publication in May 1981. Founder-editor Warwick *Roger, as well as setting unprecedented standards for New Zealand in feature journalism, included short fiction on a regular basis. An anthology, *Metro Fiction* (1987), edited by Graeme *Lay, included Marilyn *Duckworth, Lauris *Edmond, Lloyd *Jones, Michael *Morrissey and Vincent *O'Sullivan. The commitment to fiction increased as responsibility passed to Stephen *Stratford 1987–93, Nicola Legat 1993–96 and Nigel *Cox in 1996, short stories now appearing monthly and the 'Summer Fiction Six-pack' an annual feature since January 1988. Stratford also initiated the publication of a short poem each month. *Metro*'s catholic taste and confidence that its sophisticated readership can cope with the shock of the new have given a wider public and the country's best financial returns to established writers such as Kevin *Ireland, Elizabeth *Smither and C.K. *Stead and to emerging ones such as John *Cranna, Elizabeth *Knox and Damien *Wilkins. The magazine is also notable for the consistent excellence of its literary reviews, especially by Ronda Cooper and Michael *King. RR

Middle Age Spread was Roger *Hall's second full-length play, first produced at Circa Theatre in 1977 and published in 1978. Thanks to a film adaptation, directed by John Reid in 1978, and a production in London's West End which won the *Evening Standard* 'Comedy of the Year' award for 1979, it is probably Hall's best-known work. The story-line is stronger than in his other plays. The main centre of interest is an extra-marital affair between Colin, who has just been appointed a school principal, and Judy, a younger teacher. The affair is pieced together retrospectively in flashbacks which punctuate a celebratory dinner-party hosted by Colin and his wife Elizabeth, with four guests: Judy, her husband Robert, Reg (a Teachers' College lecturer) and his wife Isobel. Scenes one, four, seven and ten depict the dinner party; scenes two, three, five, eight and nine show the progress of the affair, reluctantly ended by Judy in scene nine so that she can return to Robert and their children. Reg blunders in on the lovers in scene nine, and then reveals the affair to the respective spouses in scene ten. Isobel has already revealed (in scene four) that Reg himself has been having an affair with a 'little nineteen-year-old', who has 'just thrown him over'. Thus none of the characters is untouched by suffering, and the title invites us to conclude that they are all in the throes of a mid-life crisis—a syndrome to which Hall has returned again and again, most obviously in *State of the Play*, *Fifty-Fifty* and *Conjugal Rites*. For good measure *Middle Age Spread* also features an adolescent crisis in an off-stage subplot; in scene seven Elizabeth discovers that Colin and Elizabeth's daughter Jane, who has been crying off-stage throughout the dinner party scenes, is pregnant to Stephen, Reg and Isobel's son. For all this unhappiness, however, the tone of this play (and of Hall's others) is not uniformly bleak; the pathos is continually leavened by humour, much of it in the form of the polished one-liners for which Hall is famous. These are generally contributed by a quipster character—in this case Reg ('Here's old Colin, putting it on round the middle, his opinions hardening almost as fast as his arteries …'; 'Now she's into leather—though not in a way I might appreciate. Little clicks and snips—Christ, I'm expecting a bunch of elves to appear any moment.') Like Hall's other quipsters (e.g. John in *Glide Time), Reg is not altogether likable, and his favourite target, Robert (an accountant), gets in one particularly effective retort. But Reg's observations are always funny and often poke effective satire at aspects of New Zealand society. RCo

MIDDLETON, Ian (1928–), is a novelist who has made a particular mark with fiction about post-war *Japan. Brother of O.E. *Middleton, born in New Plymouth and brought up in Taranaki, Te Kuiti and wartime Auckland, his work experience included periods as a merchant seaman and as an English teacher in Japan, 1974–82. He now lives in Auckland and has been a full-time writer since 1982. His first novel, *Pet Shop* (1979, rpt. 1990), dealt with a small-town New Zealand childhood, Auckland wartime adolescence and experience on board a Norwegian tanker, and with a fervid sexuality rendered in lavishly metaphoric and descriptive prose. Kevin *Ireland praised it on republication as 'an absorbing picture of the ... repressions that passed for a moral code'. The fourth, *Mr Ponsonby* (1989), vividly recreates the atmosphere and characters of an Auckland suburb threatened by reconstruction. In the 'Japanese trilogy', comprising *Faces of Hachiko* (1984), *Sunflower* (1986) and *Reiko* (1990), a personal dimension focuses the convincingly complex portrayals of the society and psychology of modern Japan and its conflicts of understanding with foreigners. The sense of inwardness with Japanese culture and thought is a rare attribute in Western writing. The strong metaphoric colour, sensual—often erotic—quality and lush verbal richness of his writing have been attributed to Middleton's blindness, which he himself describes as giving a special perspective but 'without limitation'.   RR

MIDDLETON, O.E. (Osman Edward) (1925–   ), Christchurch-born fiction writer, worked at a variety of jobs, including farm worker, clerk, seaman, construction worker, adult education tutor, telephonist and landscape gardener, gaining the experience of New Zealand working life that is evident in his stories. He served in the New Zealand air force and army in 1944–45, and after the war journeyed to the United States in an unsuccessful attempt to get special medical treatment for his deteriorating eyesight. He has also travelled extensively in Europe. He began publishing stories in 1949, brought out a pamphlet, *Six Poems*, in 1951, and then published five overlapping collections of short stories in twenty years, each volume after the first containing a selection of earlier work combined with more recent previously uncollected stories: *Short Stories* (1954), *The Stone and Other Stories* (1959), *A Walk on the Beach* (1964), *The Loners* (1972) and *Selected Stories* (1975). In 1979 he published a volume of two short novels, '*Confessions of an Ocelot*' and '*Not for a Seagull*'. He has also several unpublished novels and other stories, and a book for children, *From the River to the Tide* (1964).

Middleton's work clearly belongs to the vernacular critical realist tradition of Frank *Sargeson, but he has made his own place within that tradition. Typically his stories, like Sargeson's, are from a first-person or limited third-person point of view, with a vernacular style in keeping with it, and with a structure working through indirection or accretion rather than through tight plotting. Again, like Sargeson's, most of his narrators and central characters are working-class males or children, outside the centres of power in society, and his underlying attitude of egalitarian humanism is roughly similar to Sargeson's. However, within this broad framework of similarity he has defined his own special qualities. His fictional world is richer in sensuous detail than Sargeson's, especially in tactile and aural detail, as in the intense evocation of the hawk in 'Killers' or of the fishing experience in 'Drift'. His range of setting and character is much wider, reflecting his diverse experience. Thus 'The Collector' takes place in a prison in the United States, from his experience as an illegal immigrant there, while 'The Doss-House and the Duchess' is set in an itinerant seaman's world in England, and 'The Crows' and 'For Once in Your Life' are set in Europe. His character range extends from Māori in 'Drift' and 'Not for a Seagull', and Pacific nations immigrants in 'The Loners', to a German immigrant in 'The Man Who Flew Models', a Spanish artist in 'Crows' and a female German student in 'For Once in Your Life'.

In his attitude to his characters, Middleton, like Sargeson, tends to sympathise with the outcasts, the loners, the victims, and to judge adversely the comfortable and the exploiters, the 'arrogant rich'. He tends, too, to stand beside his working-class characters rather than reaching down to them with a sympathetic irony as Sargeson does. At his best he maintains an implicit double perspective in which the reader both shares the character's experience yet sees more than the character can see. In 'The Married Man', for instance, the reader fully shares Tony's grief over the death of his baby daughter and his deeply felt need to take care of her burial himself, but at the same time comes to see that Tony's unquestioned New Zealand male working-class culture does not give him opportunity to express fully what he feels. At the end, when a workmate sincerely offers him the only consolation that he knows, drink and a bar-room pickup, the reader does not judge the characters but realises, as Tony cannot, that his finer feelings have no scope or cultural framework for expression. There is a similar handling of the Islander immigrant Luke in the often-anthologised 'The Loners', and of the naive and sensitive Peter in the novella, 'Confessions of an Ocelot', as he discovers what the reader has already sensed, that he is unconsciously homosexual and that he finds it difficult to face the extent of hidden human suffering and evil. In his weaker stories, Middleton fails to hold such a subtle tone, tending to identify too completely with his social outsiders and score points too easily off his bourgeois characters, as in his implicit excoriation of the American tourist girl in Spain in 'The Crows'. In such stories he crosses over from social commitment to an oversimplified didacticism. At his best, however, he is a subtle artist who can extend the sympathetic imagination of his readers, increase their awareness of basic human worth and show the evils of racial and economic injustice, without didactic manipulation. Such work shows how a literary tradition can be used and modified to express an individual vision.   LJ

MIKAERE, Buddy (1951–   ), of Ngāti Pūkenga, Ngāti Ranginui, Te Arawa, Tūhoe, is Director of the Waitangi Tribunal and a distinguished historian, author of many articles and of two books: *Te Maiharoa and the Promised Land* (1988) and *Ka Kaute Ahau! He Pukapuka Mahi mō te Tamariki* (1986).   NW

Mills & Boon, the most successful British publishers specialising in light *romance, has since the 1950s featured at least a dozen professional New Zealand women authors. These are New Zealand's most widely read novelists, whose readership locally and overseas runs into many millions. Mills & Boon was founded in 1908, but it was not until the 1930s, when it developed a profitable base in commercial lending libraries and pioneered marketing by brand name and format rather than by author, that it began to dominate the light romance market. Until the 1950s New Zealand romance novelists were mainly published by Mills & Boon's competitors, firms such as Ward, Locke (Isabel Maud *Peacocke and Dorothy Quentin), Wright & Brown (Rosemary *Rees, Dulce *Carman and Mavis Winder) and Robert Hale (Nelle *Scanlan, Grace Phipps and later Ivy *Preston). In the late 1950s two of New Zealand's most prolific romance authors, Essie *Summers and Nora *Sanderson (the latter specialising in doctor–nurse romances) began publishing with Mills & Boon.

Summers, in particular, influenced numerous other writers into the Mills & Boon stable. From the mid-1960s she and Sanderson were joined by Mary Moore, Karin Mutch, Gloria Bevan, Miriam McGregor (who previously wrote romantic mysteries in the mode of Dorothy *Eden) and Helen Bianchin (who later moved to Australia). By the mid-1980s, as Mills & Boon romance formulas underwent substantial change and the firm became closely tied to the North American Harlequin Books, yet another generation had emerged, writing in significantly different ways. These included Rosalie Heneghan, Daphne *Clair, Robyn *Donald and Susan *Napier.

Summers, the best-known New Zealand Mills & Boon author, published more than fifty novels 1957–85, and wrote in the older 'wholesome' mode which Mills & Boon had popularised in the 1930s. Although her novels are generally set in highly scenic, mainly South Island sheep *station locations suggesting property and wealth, their actions pivot on relatively commonplace events in the lives of her initially rootless or disillusioned heroines, many of whom are English or have English connections, as in older colonial romances. A great deal of propriety is observed in the handling of sexual encounters ('as far as the bedroom door and no further'), and the patterning of her novels emphasises the importance of family networks and values.

Her autobiography, *The Essie Summers Story* (1974) is a lively source of information about her writing and about her relations with her publisher and mentor Alan Boon and other Mills & Boon writers. New Zealand contemporaries like Moore, Mutch and Bevan (initially) wrote in the same 'wholesome' mode, though with a noticeable narrowing of focus onto the relationship of the hero and heroine, often in isolation from any family or social context. This tendency is pronounced in Gloria Bevan's later novels, after the mid 1970s, where the concern is almost exclusively with the drama of the couple, locked in a battle of wills which is often explicitly sexual in character. Such novels reflected a new international trend in the Mills & Boon romance.

Bevan's novels, with their North Island, Auckland and Pacific settings, also reflected a shift in geographical locations, away from the leisured rural gentility of the South Island. With the exception of Rosalie Heneghan, the new generation of writers (Clair, Donald and Napier) focused on the new, frenetically acquired wealth of Auckland's expanding business and professional elites, drawing their heroes from upmarket legal firms, property speculators, advertising agencies and jet-setting executives in multinational corporations who live in luxurious penthouses. Although the romance conventions remain the same, requiring marriage or the promise of it at the end, their heroines are more independent and assertive, claiming the right to careers and to sexual equality, and much of the writing contains graphically coded or explicit sexual reference. Despite the formulaic requirements of the genre—virginal heroines, macho 'alphamale' heroes who have to learn sensitivity in order to win the heroine, an exclusive focus on heterosexual relationships—the writers differ in their emphases. Clair's novels are informed by an explicit feminist consciousness, Donald's by an interest in female sexual fantasies and Gothic conventions, and Napier's (often) by a lightly humorous playing with the conventions themselves.

Clair and Donald were two of nineteen best-selling international romance novelists who contributed to *Dangerous Men and Adventurous Women* (ed. Jayne Anne Krentz, 1992), a book designed to 'explode the myths and biases that haunt both the writers and readers of romances'. Nevertheless, attitudes to contemporary Mills & Boon romances—whether they are simply escapist fare reinforcing gender stereotypes or whether they reflect new kinds of feminist awareness—remain deeply divided. In 1993 Luigi Bononi, a senior Mills & Boon editor, also sought to explain why New Zealand had produced so many successful authors. Compared with their American counterparts, he commented, they are distinguished by 'a balanced, sensible approach': 'There is a relaxed, leisurely style to the writing and a psychological underlay which appeals.' TS

MILNER, Ian (1911–91), journalist, critic and translator, was one of New Zealand's most committed socialists. As a student he formed close friendships with James *Bertram and Charles *Brasch. Later, at Canterbury University College, he helped Denis *Glover found the Caxton Club—forerunner of the *Caxton Press—and was instrumental in its first publication, the controversial *Oriflamme. From 1934 to 1937 he studied politics at Oxford University, flatting, in 1937, with John *Mulgan. Between 1935 and 1939 he contributed fifty-five articles to *Tomorrow, which provide 'perhaps the most sustained and intelligent assessment of world politics written by any New Zealander in the thirties' (Vincent *O'Sullivan, introduction, Intersecting Lines: The Memoirs of Ian Milner, 1993). He was a civil servant with Australian Foreign Affairs and the United Nations 1944–46 and, from the 1950s, professor of English at Charles University, Prague, where he translated a considerable amount of Czech poetry. His years in Australia produced unexpected repercussions when he was named, in 1955, as a KGB agent by the Royal Commission on 'the Petrov Affair'. He maintained his innocence, but thirteen years later the universities of Canterbury and Auckland, which had invited him to lecture while on leave from Charles University in 1968, withdrew their invitation under pressure that he was 'a Red menace' and a 'spy' (see *Truth).

Milner remained in Prague. His later publications included The Structure of Values in George Eliot (1969, reviewed in *Landfall 94, 1970) and a life of his father, Milner of Waitaki: Portrait of the Man, with a foreword by James *Bertram (1983, reviewed in Landfall 149, 1984). Translations of Czech poetry into English became his main later literary activity, as in 'Four Czech Poets' (translated with Jarmila Milner), Landfall 150 (1984). The poet Miroslav Holub paid tribute to Milner's skills when he visited *Writers and Readers Week in 1998. PM

MILROY, Te Wharehuia, see **Whaikōrero**.

MINCHER, Philip (1930–), was born and lives in Auckland, where he worked as an administrator in light engineering until retirement. He is a prolific and widely published writer of short stories, many of which have been included in anthologies. He has published two collections, The Ride Home (1977) and All the Wild Summer (1985), and a volume of poems, Heroes and Clerks (1959). He was a regular contributor to *New Zealand Poetry Yearbook. The two story collections were adapted as radio series, and he has also written drama expressly for radio.

Mincher writes observantly about youth and adolescence in an elegant but direct and accessible prose, his stories often reflecting a delight in outdoor life and the natural world. Many New Zealand writers have explored such territory; Mincher stands a little apart in his emphasis on pace and action. He also relies less than most on reconstructing youthful thinking and speech, more on an explicitly adult hindsight. This affords scope for reflection and eloquence, and imparts a nostalgic coloration to the stories.

The poems deal with mainly personal material in an oracular, richly figurative manner; one critic speaks of his 'superb, ferocious gift of metaphor'. Their mixed reception reflected divisions of critical opinion at the time, especially over the value and place of rhetoric in poetry. JH

Mine Eyes Dazzle (1950) was Alistair *Campbell's first volume of verse and the first book published by the *Pegasus Press. A collector's item, this edition of 300 copies was exquisitely printed on hand-made paper. From the first, most reviewers and critics agreed that the printing did no less than justice to the exquisite quality of the writing. In 1951 it was reprinted in a plainer format, with an introduction by James K. *Baxter, as No. 1 in a series called 'Pegasus New Zealand Poets', and it appeared again, in a 'new revised edition', in 1956. In fact there are significant differences between the 1950 and 1951 editions as well, and the later volume *Wild Honey (1964) is in part yet a fourth reworking of the same material. Often seen as a 'romantic' poet, Campbell is clearly a painstaking craftsman.

In the first edition there were three named parts: 'Elegy', 'Love Poems' and 'The Cromwell Gorge'. The 'Love Poems' used Campbell's uniquely mellifluous language to evoke sensuous images of women, but rising beyond the sensuous with the symbolist, suggestive quality of their gestures: 'Dressed in green she came, and like / A tulip leaned her head against / The door, and looked at me. Her hand / Lay cool as a stone against her dress…' (From 1964 on this poem has been printed unchanged in words but with different lineation.) In

'The Cromwell Gorge' the same atmosphere of loving connection flowing through the senses was evoked with reference to the landscape, while in 'Elegy', which many readers think is Campbell's finest achievement, the human and the natural worlds were blended and the same love embraced them both. In this sense the entire book is a collection of love poems. Its title combines the themes of sudden death and intense, tragic love, since it is from the words of John Webster's play *The Duchess of Malfi*: 'Cover her face; mine eyes dazzle; she died young.'

'Elegy', a sequence of eight poems, carries the dedication 'In Memoriam Roy M. Dickson, killed in the Alps 1 January 1947, aged 20'. The title and dedication lead us to expect poems of grief, but the first is an evocation of the Hollyford Valley. Nonetheless the valley itself seems to be grieving ('... waterfalls, like tears / From some deep-bowed head / Whose colossal grief is stone'), and this has led some commentators (including Baxter in his *Recent Trends in New Zealand Poetry*, 1951) to speak of Campbell's 'animism'. One can also see the technique as a form of Symbolism, suggesting rather than directly expressing the emotion by attributing it to the natural world. It characterises all eight poems. Symbolist, too, is the proximity of the poetry to the nature of music, manifest in its suggestiveness and in the seemingly effortless (but probably hard-won) way the sounds of the words blend into each other, making such terms as assonance or rhyme too mechanical to describe the effect. These musical sounds can range from the slow and funereal ('... the pale moon's steaming disk ...') through the sharp and brittle ('In a sun-rinsed rock-pool, / An intensity of weathered wood / Caught and dazzled my eyes') and the harsh ('Dear head, struck down') to the thunderously forceful ('Everywhere the hidden sound / Of water, like hives of bees / Up-tilted deep underground'). Douglas *Lilburn's setting of 'Elegy' is justly admired, but the poems already carry much music in them. What James *Bertram said of Lilburn's song-cycle could also be said of its text: '[It was] something of a post-war landmark: it seemed that colour, passion, the true voice of feeling, had returned to these islands again.'

Frequently reprinted, 'Elegy' has never been altered, but Campbell has felt the need to rework other parts of *Mine Eyes Dazzle*. Although it is called a 'reprint', the 1951 edition reorders the sequence of the 'Love Poems', omits one of them and inserts two new ones. The poem omitted, 'O Catch Miss Daisy Pinks', returns in the 1956 edition and the problem is clear enough. Of its own kind it is superb, but its kind is different to that of the others: ironic and witty rather than Symbolist, yet blending its wit with tenderness. It reveals a perkier side to the poet's personality than the sombre lyrics around it. Some compensation for its absence is provided, in 1951, by the insertion of 'Meeting my childhood love one day' (called 'August' in 1956), which fits more easily, despite its lightness, but is unfortunately a less successful poem. The other addition in 1951 is 'I never knew the spring was there'. The 1956 edition is radically different: in two parts rather than three. 'Elegy' remains untouched, but the 'Love Poems' and 'The Cromwell Gorge' have become a loose collection of poems, rather than two sequences. They are reduced in number from seventeen to fifteen, some of which are new while others have been radically shortened or re-worded.

Welcoming the first edition in a newspaper review, Louis *Johnson said: 'At a time when poetry neither pays the writer nor profits the publisher, the appearance of this book is more than a brave publishing venture. It is something of a minor miracle.' It remains a major event in the history of New Zealand poetry. Each edition is an attractive book, but only the careful reader of all three can perceive the meticulous and sensitive poet at work, reconsidering his visions and ideas.   NW

MINEHAN, Mike (Judith M. Blumsky) (1947–), poet and broadcaster, was born in Waiuku. She lived in Auckland until 1969, when she met James K. *Baxter and joined his commune in Jerusalem. The two became partners, with Baxter accepting paternity for her son, who was born in 1971. Minehan recalls this period in some detail in 'The Man Who Shot Angels' (*More*, May 1990). In 1972 she moved to Christchurch where, in 1989, she published *No Returns*, winner of the 1990 *New Zealand Poetry Society's international competition. Minehan sees silences—'the way we do not say'—as a central concern of her 'confessional ... part biographical' poetry. Riemke *Ensing in a review of *Embracing the Dark* (1991) calls many of its poems 'unrelentingly tough and harrowing' in their exploration of 'a number of archetypes', in particular the companion and the 'daddy's girl' who lives in danger of being caught in the thrall of men and becoming the 'eternal daughter' (*NZ Listener*, 23 Sep. 1991). Minehan's third collection, *Suicide Season*, was published in 1997.   PM

Mirror, originally titled the *Ladies Mirror*, was a monthly women's magazine published in Auckland 1922–63. It published most of the successful writers of popular fiction of its period, including Alice *Kenny, Edith *Lyttleton (G.B. Lancaster), Isabel Maude *Peacocke, Grace Phipps, Ruth *Dallas, Dorothy *Eden, Essie *Summers and Jillian Squire. While few of the canonical names in New Zealand literature appeared, contributions by Jane *Mander, A.R.D. *Fairburn, G.R. *Gilbert, M.H. *Holcroft and Robin *Hyde were published. (*Mirror Magazine* appeared in a single issue in Christchurch in 1910 with a cover by David *Low.)

SH

'Miss Brill', a short story by Katherine *Mansfield, was first published in the *Athenaeum* (1920) and subsequently in Mansfield's third collection *The Garden Party and Other Stories* (1922). No MS is known. The story presents an excursion to 'les jardins publiques' by Miss Brill, a lonely, ageing English spinster living and working in France. In an indirect interior monologue, she anthromorphises her fur toque, habitually dramatises her own and others' situations and eavesdrops on others' conversations: 'She had become really quite an expert, she thought, at listening as though she didn't listen, at sitting in other people's lives for just a minute…'. The denouement resembles that of *'Bliss', for it is at the point when she imagines herself to have a special empathy with those around her in the park that she overhears a young couple describe her as a 'stupid old thing' and liken her beloved fur to a 'fried whiting'. In *A Literature of Their Own*, Elaine Showalter cites Margaret Drabble's reaction to the 'cruelty' of the denouement: '"I think it changed something in me forever … one would not like to have written it oneself, however fine the achievement."' The story is an excellent example of the way perfection of 'voice' was important to Mansfield's technique—she wrote in a 1921 letter 'I read it aloud—numbers of times—just as one would *play over* a musical composition, trying to get it nearer and nearer to the expression of Miss Brill—until it fitted her.' The theme of the 'femme seule', betrayed, rejected or unwanted, links the story to 'Psychology', *'Je ne parle pas français', 'The Little Governess', 'The *Daughters of the Late Colonel' and 'The *Canary' .

SSa

Missionary Register was an annual publication containing, as stated on the title page, the proceedings of the principal missionary and Bible societies throughout the world. It was published in London from 1813. While containing news from all the major British missionary societies, it focuses on the Church Missionary Society. Each volume contains monthly reports on the activities of missions and missionaries at home and abroad and was sent to interested associations throughout the Empire to communicate the news to all missions.

New Zealand first appears in Volume II, 1814, under the heading 'South Seas'. This reference is in the form of a letter written by Rev. Samuel *Marsden to Governor Macquarie on November 1 1813 on the subject of the criminal conduct of many masters of vessels toward the 'New Zealanders' (Māori). The letters, journal entries and narratives that appear in the succeeding volumes provide a step-by-step account from initial contact to the establishment of the first missionary settlement. The *Missionary Register* of 1816 reports that Marsden made his first trip to New Zealand on the brig *Active*, and that he was accompanying Thomas Kendall and other missionaries who were going to settle there. His visit lasted from November 1814 to March 1815, and during this time the first missionary settlement was formed at the Bay of Islands. This volume contains Marsden's account of obtaining the grant of land for missionary settlers. The 1817 volume contains extracts from Kendall's journal from March 1815 to January 1816.

However, it is the 1822 volume which contains most information about New Zealand, as it prints extensive extracts from Marsden's journals of his second and third visits. He wrote of the Māori people he met and recorded his conversations on a wide range of topics with chiefs and others. He wrote, for example, of his visit to meet the chief Murupaenga. 'When I arrived at Moodeepanga's, he was ready to receive me. His Children were all dressed and their heads ornamented with feathers; and his Head Wife had got her dog-skin garment on. Moodeepanga had placed the stump of a tree where he intended me to sit; and had made a cushion of bulrushes, which was put on it…. We then entered into conversation…'.

Marsden also described in detail things such as the tattooing process: 'In walking through the village of Rangheehoo, one morning, I observed Towhee tattooing the son of the late Tippahee. The operation was very painful. It was performed with a small chisel made of the wing-bone of a pigeon or wild fowl … like a little pick, with one end. With this chisel he cut all the straight and spiral lines, by striking the head with a stick about one foot long…'.

CL

MITCALFE, Barry (1930–86), was a versatile writer notable especially for his work in Māori poetry. A teacher, journalist, linguist, social and political activist, he once described himself as 'a hedonist, living and loving life'. Born in Wellington, his childhood spent at Whangaroa, Northland, and later New Plymouth formed his early interest in the country's natural and social history. From an early career as reporter for the *Dominion* in Wellington, he later turned to schoolteaching. He graduated BA(Hons) in history from Victoria University of Wellington in 1965, and joined the staff of Wellington Teachers' Training College as a lecturer in social studies, where he developed courses in Polynesian studies. A political activist concerned with anti-war, anti-nuclear and environmental issues, he was instrumental in establishing the Committee on Vietnam and the journalists' organisation Peace Media. He later led opposition to the expansion of gold-mining activities in the Coromandel district, where he had made his home. *Boy Roel: Voyage to Nowhere* (1972) is an account of the experience of sailing to Mururoa atoll in protest against French nuclear testing in the South *Pacific. A prolific writer of poetry and short stories, he contributed to a wide range of New Zealand and overseas journals and anthologies, was a member of the executive of *PEN, and founded the small cooperative Coromandel Press. In 1977 he was awarded the Katherine *Mansfield Memorial Fellowship in Menton. His extensive body of writing and publishing covers his wide interests in education, politics, history, environmental issues and anthropology, with a particular concern for Māori and Polynesian society, art and culture, which he actively promoted to a wider readership. He wrote poetry in the Māori language, in which he was fluent, published translations of Māori literature, and compiled school texts on Māori culture and history. His collections of translated Māori verse and music include *Poetry of the Māori* (1961) and *Māori Poetry: The Singing Word* (1974). *Sun, Moon and Stars* (1982) is an illustrated version of Māori legends for children. His many fictional works for children include *The Long Holiday* (1964), *I Say, Wait for Me* (1976), *The Square Gang* (1981), *Up Down and Around with Mr Obolong* (1984), and *Hey, Hey, Hey* (1985). *Look to the Land* (1986), a collection of poetry published at the time of his death, is based on the history of the Taranaki region.   SW

MITCHELL, David (1940–   ), poet, was born in Wellington and first published in student publications in the late 1950s. He spent 1960–65 in Europe (see the pamphlet *The Orange Grove: Valencia, 1962*, published 1969, and 'The Singing Bread' in the third issue of *Freed*, 1970, for poems based on experiences in Spain and France). Back in New Zealand he became a familiar figure at poetry readings—which enjoyed a great revival in the late 1960s—reading from an unpublished manuscript entitled 'Davy Mitchell's Trip Book'. The publication of *Pipe Dreams in Ponsonby* (1972, 1975)—thirty-eight poems from the period 1968–71—elevated him to something of guru status among the emergent poets of the 1970s. Reviewing *Pipe Dreams*, C.K. *Stead wrote: 'He is probably very much the man of the moment, or the man of the mode, among the young who are interested in poetry in Auckland' and noted how his poems were permeated by 'the personality of the poet and the music of the poetry, and the two were not really distinct' (*Islands* 1, 1972), while Ian *Wedde said: 'At their simplest level these poems are scores, unambiguous and perfectly timed in the way in which they suggest a realization, a voice' (*Cave* 2, 1972). *Pipe*

Dreams contains a note: 'All the poems in this book have been read aloud in public.' Mitchell remained chary of publication; only occasional poems appeared in periodicals after 1972 and there is a small selection of previously unpublished work in *15 Contemporary New Zealand Poets*, ed. Alistair *Paterson (1980). In 1980 Mitchell initiated a popular series of poetry readings in Auckland's Globe Tavern under the title *Poetry Live. He also worked as a primary school teacher, and was Katherine *Mansfield Memorial Fellow at Menton in 1976.   PS

MITCHELL, June (1918–   ), wrote *Amokura* (1978) to recapture imaginatively her ancestor, Te Akau Meretini Cook (Horohau), 1826–97, and in doing so created a significant and precursive rendering of the Māori woman's point of view in a historical novel. Originally from Taupo, Meretini was brought up by a wife of Te Rauparaha on Kapiti Island, married an Englishman and raised their large family in the Manawatu River area. The first-person narrative of her life blends, largely successfully, documentary materials such as newspaper reports, letters and court transcripts with Māori stories, songs, prayers and chants and imaginatively inward fiction. The metaphor of tāniko-weaving is used appropriately for this process. Mostly constructed of separate scenes which each originate from a documentary source, the narrative nevertheless fulfils the author's intention 'to let [Meretini] speak with her own accent and use her own rhythms of discovery, her own imagery, her own beliefs'. Domestic and personal matters—love, motherhood, the deaths of children, the ageing of her husband, intimacy with the land, friendship with Hurihuri the cat—are the foreground of historical events—the later years of Te Rauparaha, erosion, flood, earthquake, the Tarawera eruption. Dominant is the unceasing effort at every level of life for understanding and respect between two races whose destinies, through lives like Meretini's, became inextricable. Herself of Ngāti Raukawa, Te Arawa, English and Irish descent, Mitchell was born in Wellington, and was educated and lived at Wanganui.   RR

Monday's Warriors (1990), a novel by Maurice *Shadbolt, see **New Zealand Wars trilogy**.

Monocle was a glossy monthly set up in opposition to the *Mirror. Published in Wellington 1937–39 it was edited by former *Mirror* editor O.N. *Gillespie. Jane *Mander contributed a book review column almost identical in format to that which she had previously contributed to the *Mirror*. While the *Monocle* solicited local literary contributions, most fiction published was syndicated from overseas sources. Among New Zealand writers to appear in its pages were Hector ★Bolitho, Eve ★Langley, Quentin ★Pope and George ★Joseph.   SH

MONTGOMERY, Eleanor (active 1885–96), one of the earliest published women writers in New Zealand, was a poet and dramatist. Little is known about her life. Her family farmed near Wanganui and she appears on electoral roles 1899–1907. She was a quite productive late-Victorian poet in an antipodean-Tennysonian, 'songs of a Southern Isle' mode, including ecstatic if conventional love poetry: 'Each twinkling star on Heaven's blue breast, / Smiled on my Allan's love confest!' ('The River Song'.) Her five volumes were all published in Wanganui: *Songs of the Singing Shepherd* (1885), *Hinemoa* (1887), *Land of the Moa* (1890), a tribute to Tennyson, *The Pilgrim of Eternity* (1892) and *The Tohunga and Incidents of Maori Life* (1896). Fiona ★Farrell describes 'Retrospect' as her most interesting poem, a long dramatic verse tale set on a Wanganui farm, mingling ★station life with romance and the return to England of the disappointed suitor. The dramatic gift showed also in her published one-act play, *Madame Béranger* (1887), which Howard McNaughton calls 'rich in passionate bombast' but with 'some awareness of stagecraft'. A three-act manuscript, 'At Bay', also remains from her drama scripts.   HMcQ/RR

Monthly Review (1) was a journal edited by J.R. ★Blair from November 1888 to October 1890. From June to September 1888 Blair had issued *Hestia*, subtitled 'A Magazine Devoted to the Teachings of the Ancient Sages and the Study of Philosophy and Science' and containing pseudonymous articles on 'The Egyptian Priesthood', etc. According to the opening number of *The Monthly Review*, *Hestia* 'had proven too esoteric to be popular'. The new journal published poems by Edith Howitt Searle (later ★Grossman), Edward ★Tregear, G.B. ★Davy and others. There were short stories by Edwin Wooton and Thomas McDonnell, who also contributed first-person accounts of the New Zealand ★Wars. Tregear contributed articles on Polynesian poetry, the need for a national archive and the *Kalevala*, Searle on 'The Divorce of Religion and Morality' and the survival of 'philosophy' in an age of science. Oscar ★Alpers wrote on Ibsen, and there was a long series of articles on 'Nga Tangata Maori' by W.E. Gudgeon, in which he asserted the virtues of the 'old' Māori over his modern, allegedly degenerate counterpart. There was also an account of Darwinism by Earnest Beaglehole. After two years the journal followed its predecessor into oblivion.   NW

Monthly Review (2), see **New Zealand Monthly Review**.

MOORHEAD, Diana (1940–   ), began writing fantasies for children at a time when there was little support for such work. Born in England and educated at Waihi College and Auckland University, she became Community Librarian at Glenfield. Her first children's book, *In Search of Magic* (1971), follows the adventures of an English fairy family who travel north from Wellington, seeking the indigenous fairy folk, the Tūrehu. Her next two novels, *The Green and the White* (1974), and *Gull Man's Glory* (1976), illustrated by Sam Thompson, are each set in a fictional, Europeanised fantasy world where the protagonists must challenge corrupt absolute power that threatens to destroy the land. The second of these is strikingly original in its setting after a future nuclear disaster has produced strange forms of life, particularly gull people with wings. Since 1976, Moorhead has forsaken fiction to concentrate on library work.   DH

Morepork was a literary magazine, edited by Graham ★Lindsay and published by Ridge-Pole, Dunedin. For No. 3, Alan ★Loney joined as editor of reviews and criticism. It ran for three issues, the first in 1979, the others undated but appearing in the early 1980s. Coming ten years after ★*Freed*, it shared many of that magazine's interests and authors, but with a more catholic range of writing that never lost its sense of contemporaneity. Its covers carried artwork by Derek Cowie, Andrew Drummond and Jeffrey Harris, and its sole critical review was on the artist and writer Joanna ★Paul in the final issue. On the title page of No. 1, the words 'Find out what's useful in New Zealand writing' signalled a divergence from the concerns of mainstream magazines, and many different compositional tactics are evident in its pages. The risks for such magazines are high in terms of readership and economics, yet *Morepork*'s list of contributors is justification. They include Paul, Loney, Wystan ★Curnow, Bill ★Manhire, Cilla ★McQueen, Ian ★Wedde, Mike ★Johnson, David ★Eggleton, Peter ★Olds, Elizabeth ★Smither, Michael ★Harlow and Michael ★Morrissey; but not editor Graham Lindsay himself.   AL

MORGAN, Teupoko Ina Utanga, or **Poko** (1934–), is a writer-translator of Cook Islands oral narrative and author of a pioneering series of early readers and song books to introduce children and families of Cook Islands origin to their mother tongue. Her *Te Ma'ara'anga—Te 'Imene e te Pe'e* (1986) is a collection of orally preserved stories from her native Rarotongan village of Ruatonga, which incorporate, she says, 'the cultural elements which enhance the lives of folk heroes'. Accompanied by specially composed melodies, they can be read as poetry. She has lived in Rarotonga, Fiji and since 1973 in New Zealand. She is director of the Anau Ako Pasifika project in Tokoroa, creating resources for learning Pacific languages. She was awarded the QSM in 1986 and a Fulbright study grant in 1990 for her work in early childhood education.   RR

MORICE, Stella, see *Wiremu*.

MORRIESON, Ronald Hugh (1922–72), novelist and short story writer, was born, lived, wrote and died in Hawera, South Taranaki. He was domiciled entirely in the home of his mother, with very occasional breaks of a few days in Auckland in his early twenties and later in New Plymouth and, towards the end of his life, at a writer's conference in Palmerston North. Until the age of 37 he worked as a casual dance-band player in the Hawera area, but then became a private music-teacher in order to free his evenings for the career in writing which he had always intended. His first novel *The *Scarecrow*, a tragicomic story of a sex killer in a small town not unlike Morrieson's own, was published in Sydney by Angus & Robertson in 1963. It was well received by reviewers as a Gothic melodrama with a strong popular-culture component. His second, **Came a Hot Friday* (1964), is a tragicomic morality tale about gambling in and about another small Taranaki town. The less favourable reviews began a decline in critical reception which, together with his continuing alcoholism and the death of his mother in 1968, was to darken his last decade. Conservative critics had difficulty with the violence and sexuality of his writing and its failure to conform to the high culture models that dominated the literary values of the period, an attitude summed up in one protestation that the New Zealand in *Came a Hot Friday* was 'certainly not the New Zealand that I know'.

Morrieson's fear, expressed to Maurice *Shadbolt, that he might be 'another of those poor buggers who gets discovered when they're dead', was to be cruelly prophetic. Despite support after 1965 from Shadbolt, Frank *Sargeson and the historian Dick Scott, all his subsequent writing was to be published posthumously. In 1974 *Landfall* published two short stories, in March 'Cross My Heart and Cut My Throat' and in December 'The Chimney'. The first is a comic account of a crapulous male guitar-teacher's attraction to a 13-year-old female pupil. This leads to the loss of his girlfriend but concludes comically, with his mother's naive assurance that he has 'had [his] first little pupil today' and with the appearance of the pupil's father, who seems bent on vengeance but in fact has merely turned up to retrieve his daughter's guitar. 'The Chimney' is far more sober and one of Morrieson's subtler achievements as a work

of art, a sensitive evocation of a boy's first apprehension of mortality and sexual desire that stands as one of the finest of the tradition's many accounts of the onset of adolescence. Both stories indicate something of the writer's excessive intimacy with his mother.

His third novel, *Predicament* (1975), a powerful and disturbing account of the psychological fantasy world of adolescence with the familiar small-town setting, was declined by Angus & Robertson and went through numerous drafts, many abandoned, before being published by John *Dunmore's Dunmore Press in Palmerston North in 1975. *Pallet on the Floor* (1976), a brief and black story, is set in the shadow of a freezing works and features rape, murder and suicide. Again published by Dunmore, it reads more perfunctorily than the earlier works, as if in draft form. A New Zealand edition of *The Scarecrow* (Heinemann) appeared in 1976, and of *Came a Hot Friday* (Penguin) in 1981, and both novels were made into feature *films. Apart from reviews of the first two novels and the odd negative observation, critical commentary on Morrieson was largely posthumous, as indicated in the bibliography to the standard critical work, Peter *Simpson's *Ronald Hugh Morrieson* (1982). Julia Millen's *Ronald Hugh Morrieson: A Biography* (1996) emphasises the strange creativity that arose from the contradictions between his matriarchal home life and his rebelliously dissolute night-time activities. His reputation now stands high, as in Lawrence *Jones's comment that 'it is doubtful whether the anti-puritan underside of New Zealand small-town life … has ever been so vigorously caught'.   PE

MORRIS, Ted (1913–), is a literary curiosity for the numerous honours he has accumulated by association with various overseas organisations, including over a dozen diplomas and medals, the 'International Poet Laureateship' for New Zealand conferred by the United Poets Laureate International (Manila) and 'Diploma Laureateship' of the World Academy of Arts and Culture (Taiwan). His many volumes, mainly self-financed, include a *Collected Poems 1953–88* (1988) and verse autobiography, *A Contradiction in Terms* (1988–95). Born in Granity, he served in Egypt and Italy 1940–45, lived in Wellington and Te Puke and settled in Tauranga in 1968.   KI

MORRISSEY, Michael (1942–), is a versatile and often innovative poet and fiction writer. He was born in Auckland in 1942 and, apart from short periods in Sydney and Christchurch, has lived there for most of his life. He attended Auckland University, received the Writer's Bursary for 1977, and published his first book of poetry, *Make Love in All the Rooms*, the following year.

He was writer-in-residence at the University of Canterbury in 1979, and in 1981 gained a Fulbright travel grant to visit America. In this same year he also published a further three volumes of poetry under his own Sword Press imprint: *Closer to the Bone*, *She's Not the Child of Sylvia Plath* and *Dreams*. The poems range across free verse and metrical forms and tend to focus primarily on sexual relationships. Observation gives way to a more uninhibited surrealism in *Voices*, which is something of a transitional work. In 1981 he also published his first collection of short fiction, *The Fat Lady & the Astronomer*, which won the 1982 *PEN Award for Best First Book of Fiction. This was an avowedly *postmodernist and experimental collection but, as in his poetry, the stories range agilely across a variety of styles and forms. The use of 'factions'—stories where historical figures interact with an obviously fictional world, thereby undercutting realist expectations—is prominent, as is the influence of Donald Barthelme. In 1985 he edited and provided a 30 000-word introduction to *The New Fiction*, a collection of postmodern New Zealand fiction. Like many of his own poems, the stories (by writers including Jennifer *Compton, Chris *Else, Russell *Haley and Keri *Hulme) explore the disjunction between language and reality while challenging realist assumptions about writing. Morrissey also co-edited *The Globe Tapes* (1985), which combined recordings of live poetry performance with an accompanying printed version. *Taking In the View* (1986), his fifth volume of poetry, appeared on his return from a period at the University of Iowa International Writing Programme. Accompanied by Gregory *O'Brien's illustrations, this was a more assured collection that assimilated his experiences in America. Poems such as 'Comic Book Heroes' anticipate his later volume, *The American Hero Loosens His Tie* (1989), which was dedicated to Charles Bukowski. In this period he published a further three volumes of poetry. *New Zealand—What Went Wrong?* (1988) is a quick-fire interrogation of the title country; *Dr Strangelove's Prescription* (1988) is an elegiac treatment of nuclear extinction; and *A Case of Briefs* (1989) is a more playful collection that takes pleasure in the brevity of poetry. Similarly, his collection of stories, *Octavio's Last Invention* (1991), is less sardonic and more playfully fantastical. Stage, radio and film are among his other writing credits, and he teaches a number of creative writing classes in Auckland and publishes frequently as a reviewer and essayist. He compiled *New Zealand's Top 10* (1993), a book of lists. Morrissey has retained a place as a talented innovator, alert to developments overseas, especially in America. He is frequently anthologised, for instance in the *Oxford Book of New Zealand Short Stories* (1992). Two novellas under the title *Paradise to Come* were published in 1997. NWt

MORTON, Elsie K. (1885–1968), pioneering journalist, born Katherine Elizabeth Morton in Auckland, is best known for *The Crusoes of Sunday Island* (1957), the story of the Bell family who settled on Raoul Island 1878–1904. Beginning as a freelance writer, Morton became a general reporter on the *New Zealand Herald* from World War 1, and in the 1920s was the first woman to achieve senior reporter status on a major daily. In 1927 she represented the *Herald* during the royal tour of the Duke and Duchess of York. As editor of the *children's pages, 1927–36, she encouraged such writers as M.H. *Holcroft, Gloria *Rawlinson and Ruth *Park, who 'worshipped that lady; she was the literary light of my life' (*A Fence Around the Cuckoo*). Morton continued to write her own popular feature articles and columns for the *Herald Saturday Supplement*. A collection of these, *Along the Road* (1928), ran to five impressions with 3000 sold in two years, at that time a New Zealand publishing record. Her next, *Joy of the Road* (1929), sold over 2000. A keen tramper and photographer, Morton wrote and illustrated several books and booklets about Westland and Fiordland. Two collections of her 'Friendly Road' radio talks were published, *Gardening's Such Fun* (1944) and *Sunrise at Midnight* (1948), which covers her 1937–38 travels in Europe, the Middle East and North America. JMcC

MORTON, Frank (1869–1923), was a versatile and prolific writer, best known as editor and main author of the *Triad*. Born in Stoke-on-Trent, he was an excellent student in classical and French literature. After emigrating to Australia with his parents he worked as a journalist in Singapore, Calcutta and Hong Kong, then travelled widely in Australia and New Zealand, settling in Wellington in 1908. For the *Triad* he wrote much of the copy on almost every conceivable topic under a series of pseudonyms, as well as editing its monthly sixty pages. He enjoyed what he called 'baiting prudes' and Dennis *McEldowney in the *OHNZLE gives examples of his scourging reviews and 'talent for invective'. The dedication and some of the poems in his volume *Laughter and Tears* (1908) equally vigorously castigate the political and literary establishments: 'Smug city-men exchange their dingy thoughts / And snigger anecdotage, mostly lies…' His best poems have an idiomatic vigour unusual at that date, and unusual frankness on sexual matters (e.g. 'The Dancer'). They draw a scene well, a talent he carried into fiction, publishing a volume of two novellas, *The Angel of the Earthquake* (1909), and a novel, *The Yacht of Dreams* (1911). He returned to Australia around 1914, settling in Sydney and publishing an interesting mix of light love poems, children's verse and erotic verse, and editing a new series of the *Triad*. HMcQ/RR

Mōteatea and *waiata both refer to Māori 'song', or poetic composition with music, many of them chanted rather than sung. In notes to a lecture series at Victoria University of Wellington (Te Whare Wānanga o te Upoko o te Ika a Maui) Joan Metge explains: 'Moteatea is a generic term for poetic compositions, whereas the word "waiata" refers more specifically to songs with a melodic line.' Some scholars prefer to reserve the term 'moteatea' for traditional chants, uninfluenced by European musical traditions. Although they are still performed, 'the chant repertoire seems to be shrinking' (McLean and Orbell, *Traditional Songs of the Māori*, 1975—a valuable published source for texts and music). However, cultural and educational institutions are doing much to preserve the tradition.   NW

Moteatea, Ko nga, me nga hakirara o nga Maori. *He mea kohikohi mai na Sir George Grey ... i tera kaumatua, i tera kuia; na ona haerenga, e maha, ki nga pito katoa, o enei motu* (i.e. 'The laments and chants of the Māori. A thing collected together by Sir George *Grey ... from this old man and that old woman, in his many journeys to all parts of these islands') is a collection of 533 songs and is generally recognised to be a primary source of information on early Māori literature. There are no translations provided and only occasional footnotes, leaving a challenge that later scholars such as Sir Apirana *Ngata have been glad to take up. The collection was published by Stokes in Wellington in 1853. Forty-eight supplementary songs were printed in Cape Town in 1857 but not published until 1950. A related volume, the principal published source of traditional *Māori sayings, is Grey's *Ko nga whakapepeha me nga whakaahuareka a nga tipuna o Aotea-Roa* (i.e. Proverbial and popular sayings of the ancestors of the New Zealand race; Cape Town, 1857).   NW

Mōteatea, Ngā: he maramara rere no ngā waka mahaa (i.e. The Songs: scattered pieces from many canoe areas) is the most important modern collection of Māori song-literature. Originally Sir Apirana *Ngata planned an eight-volume work covering all of Māori literature and history, and he worked towards that end for thirty years. Pei Te Hurinui (*Jones) assiduously continued Ngata's unfinished work and by early 1998 four volumes had been published. Part I (1959) contains ninety songs, some collected from the Ngāti Porou by Ngata, others taken from manuscripts collected by various scholars. Ngata's preface discusses the nature of Māori poetry and provides notes on *oriori, *waiata *tangi, *pātere and waiata *aroha. Introductions and extensive explanatory notes are provided for each text. Part II (1960) is a continuation of the work by Pei Te

Hurinui with 110 songs, including some song types not previously included. The introduction adds more information on such matters as the great significance of woman composers (eleven names are listed for Ngāti Porou alone) and the men's responsibility for 'priestly' songs, which reflect the language of the *whare wānanga. There is also a discussion of how the songs were obtained and selected. As in Part I the texts are present on parallel pages in Māori and English and there are extensive notes. Part III (1970), also edited by Pei Te Hurinui, adds a further ninety songs. It includes a succinct essay on 'The Music of Maori Chant' by Mervyn McLean. Part IV, with an introduction to the series by Ngata, adds ninety-one songs, bringing the overall total to 393.

The total number of songs is only a small proportion of what is available (see *waiata and *Ko nga *Moteatea*) but the introductions and annotations provide the best overview of the topic ever published.

Great care has been taken with the English versions, which are sometimes felicitous and poetic, but the editors conceive them mainly as aids to understanding the Māori texts. In Part I Ngata says of himself, 'the compiler, as a Maori himself, is happier and freer in his own language ... the language of ... that noble generation of singers ... who depicted ... the elations and the disappointments, that men of every race enjoy or suffer, but find the most satisfying expression in the languages they inherit.'   NW

Motherstone (1985), the third in a fantasy trilogy of novels for children by Maurice *Gee, see **Halfmen of O, The**.

MOUNTAIN, Julian (pseudonym of Donald Cowie, *c.*1909–), wrote two novels set in Canterbury, both self-published at Tantivy Press, Malvern, England, which despite post-war restrictions gave quite elegant production to books that it described as 'works of modern literature that may have permanent value'; namely by 'Julian Mountain' and Donald Cowie (the 'important ... young poet' and 'important new satirist'). *The Pioneers: A Romance* (1946) is a settler-family history over three generations, 1850–90. The Christchurch ('Bishopstoke') detail is authentic, but the miseries of the voyage out, contests over land and dingy discomforts of the raw little town are rendered through a mannered and elevated style which now reads strangely as a product of the age of *Sargeson. According to promotional material in Mountain's next novel, *Love is Vanity* (1947), Frank O'Connor thought the book 'superb ... a star' and the *Melbourne Herald* considered it New Zealand's best novel.

Love is Vanity autobiographically follows Matthew

Dittany from his last days at (Canterbury) University College about 1930 through work as a cadet journalist on the 'Godsholme News', involvement in political writing and activism, romantic entanglements and philanthropic work during the *Depression to his almost supernatural escape when an English beauty abducts him by early-model helicopter from a religious meeting on the Summit Road. This gives rise to a new religion in the naive province, an idea taken from *Erewhon Revisited which also anticipates *Stead's 'A Fitting Tribute'.

Poetry volumes by both 'Mountain' and Cowie are advertised by the same publisher, for instance *Representative Lyrics* ('Shelley might have written it') and *Prose and Verse* (*c.*1946). Cowie is remembered as a pipe-smoking Canterbury student who then worked on the *Press, was 'let go' during the Depression, and was assistant in the public library before leaving for England. After 'struggles … to make a literary living in hardest London', recorded in *Diary of a Young Married Man* (*c.*1948), he put out a successful yearbook for antique dealers and collectors, before vanishing from the New Zealand literary horizon as mysteriously as his levitated hero.   RR/RCp

MUIR, Robin (1918–), was a partner and editor in *Pegasus Press, and drawing partly on that experience wrote the novel *Word for Word* (1960) about the world of New Zealand book publishing. The book reads engagingly if self-consciously. It has the interest (post–*bone people*) of envisaging an unknown part-Māori female writer submitting a novel in which violence and the oppressed situation of Māori are aggressively prominent. It is also quite adroit in tracking the overlap between that novel, 'Wahine', and the experiences of its life-scarred young author. It is best, however, as a flippant satire on commercial publishing and especially book promotion. For all its strengths, 'Wahine' is made into a sales success only when a promotional gimmick convinces the public that it contains accurate coded prophecies of racing results. There is satire against the literary-moral establishment, too, as when one steamy sex passage elicits the comment 'that'd make the Lit. Fund boys come out in spots'. From a Gisborne newspaper family, Muir was educated at King's College, Auckland, and Canterbury University College, served as a pilot in World War 2 and founded Pegasus in Christchurch with Albion Wright in 1947.   PN/RR

MULDOON, Robert (1921–92), Prime Minister 1975–84, was the first politician to publish autobiography successfully while still fully active in politics, beginning with *The Rise and Fall of a Young Turk* (1975), and ending four books later with *Number 29* (1986). John A.

*Lee's fictional *Children of the Poor* (1934) has autobiographical aspects, but does not address his political career. Politicians who have since contributed to this genre include Michael Bassett, Roger Douglas, David Lange, Ross Meurant, Mike Moore and Richard Prebble, with more promised. Muldoon is also the most studied recent politician, with full biographies by Spiro Zavos, Robert Jones and Barry Gustafson.

Political satire flourished in the Muldoon era, most notably in the writing and cartoons of Tom *Scott, but Muldoon's role as a subject, icon or target in imaginative literature is unparalleled. There is a long tradition of political satire in New Zealand poetry (see *Canterbury Rhymes), but nothing to match Muldoon's appearance in poems by James K. *Baxter, David *Eggleton, Sam *Hunt, Louis *Johnson, Bill *Manhire, Vincent *O'Sullivan and Ian *Wedde, with his most notable poetic appearance probably in Kevin *Ireland's *Tiberius at the Beehive* (1990). Ireland's introduction comments '[t]he 1980s saw two intuitively gifted, gloriously larger-than-life New Zealanders go into political exile…'.

In fiction and drama, Muldoon's figure is even more dominant. A few earlier appearances by Sydney Holland, Keith Holyoake, Norman Kirk and others are overshadowed by Muldoon's cameo and star appearances in at least twelve novels and four plays. During his political rise and ascendancy these include C.K. *Stead's *Smith's Dream* (1971), with its prophetic Muldoon-like dictator Volkner, Bill Maughan's *Good and Faithful Servants* (1974), with its hero Sir Harry Drinkwater, 'the youngest and fattest Turk of them all', and Jason *Calder's thriller *The Man Who Shot Rob Muldoon* (1976), where the Prime Minister is more target than character.

One curious appearance at this time is as a dog called Muldoon in Maurice *Gee's *Games of Choice* (1976), a 'malevolent' creature owned by Gunter whose father was a Nazi, which draws blood with its bite, although its teeth are less than sharp. Muldoon also appears in person in Gee's *Sole Survivor* (1983) (see *Plumb), perhaps because Gee did not want Duggy Plumb equated too closely with Muldoon despite some common characteristics. The political content of *Sole Survivor* has been undervalued, as it becomes a prophetic parable of the fourth Labour government reflecting in its generational pattern (the sins of the father visited on later generations) the relationship to the first Labour government, and contrasting the ultimately ineffective Raymond Sole with the effective but unprincipled and ambitious Duggy Plumb. Published in 1983, it places Gee in the pantheon of literary prophets.

Other Muldoon manifestations include the kea boss, Highfeather, in Philip *Temple's *Beak of the Moon*; 'the

Prime Minister' in Bob Jones's *The Permit*; Kevin Grogan in Keith ★Ovenden's *Ratatui* (1984); and in drama the ruthless Clean in Greg ★McGee's *Foreskin's Lament* (1980). Roger ★Hall's *The Rose* specifically cautions that 'Leader' is not to be played as Muldoon, seeking to portray the universal rather than the particular (an indication of the compulsive power of his image). Muldoon appears briefly in Mervyn ★Thompson's *The Great New Zealand Truth Show* (1981), based on material from ★*Truth*; and a corrupt local councillor named Muldoon featured in the Australian television drama, *A Country Practice*, while the serial's main scriptwriter was New Zealander Ray ★Harding. (Other topical in-jokes included a low-life babysitter named 'Betty Windsor'.) Even after he left the political scene, Muldoon continued to appear in fiction. He is almost undisguisedly the power-corrupted Howie in Natasha ★Templeton's *The Firebird* (1995), and the Prime Minister/Boss in James ★McNeish's *Mr Halliday and the Circus Master* (1996). The charismatic leader, Aldous Slaven, in Owen ★Marshall's *A Many Coated Man* (1995), is not Muldoon in any significant way, but the public response to Slaven is recognisably that of Rob's Mob, the followers of Muldoon.

It is perhaps indicative of the impact of Muldoon's colourful personality that writers seem to have found it harder to write about the post-1984 political scene. No longer able to simplify the political process as embodied in a tyrannical prime minister, the two most obviously political novels, Stead's *The End of the Century at the End of the World* (1992) and Fiona ★Kidman's *True Stars* (1990) look respectively at a politician and politician's wife in the context of decaying ideals in a disintegrating government.

Perhaps Muldoon would have had to be invented if he had not existed. In a way Stead did invent him, though Muldoon was being widely perceived, especially in Auckland, as a dangerous rising opportunist when *Smith's Dream* was published. If there was any other New Zealand politician in mind—and Stead probably had some foreign dictators too—it was Holland. Volkner was readily transformed into a Muldoon in the later film of the book, *Sleeping Dogs*. Baxter, too, has some claim to prophetic status for his *a death song to mr mouldybroke* (1968). An even earlier prophet was Bill ★Pearson, who may have met Muldoon as an army corporal in Italy in the 1940s. Mr Tribe in Pearson's ★*Coal Flat* (1963), the victualler's representative from Wellington, reads now as a Muldoon figure even though the man himself was not on the national scene when the novel was written. Responding to the original 'Mr Tribe' and others like him was a stimulus of Pearson's classic 1951 essay, ★'Fretful Sleepers'. Perhaps it does not matter whether Pearson really met the original or another corporal with similar

characteristics. Muldoon in literature has long ceased to represent the actual man. Increasingly he, and his followers, have become a grotesque mythical symbol of the anti-intellectuals the literary community fears.　BE

MULGAN, Alan (1881–1962), born in Katikati, became one of the leading men of letters of his generation, and, to the young ★*Phoenix* generation, a symbol of an entrenched literary establishment. He began as a journalist with the Auckland *Star* (1900–04), transferred to the Christchurch ★*Press* (1904–16), and then returned to the *Star* (1916–35), where he became literary editor and leader-writer as well as lecturer in journalism at Auckland University College (1924–35). From 1935 until his retirement in 1946 he was supervisor of talks for the New Zealand Broadcasting Service in Wellington. Through much of his working life and in his retirement he wrote a prodigious diversity of books. His plays included *Three Plays of New Zealand* (1922); his poetry *The English of the Line and Other Verses* (1925), *Golden Wedding* (1932), *Aldebaran and Other Verses* (1937) and *Golden Wedding and Other Poems* (1964); and his fiction *Spur of Morning* (1934) and many uncollected short stories. He wrote an autobiography, *The Making of a New Zealander* (1958), and literary criticism and history such as *Literature and Authorship in New Zealand* (1943) and *Great Days in New Zealand Writing* (1962), and compiled anthologies such as *A Book of Australian and New Zealand Verse* (with Walter Murdoch, 1950). He produced travel books such as *Home: A New Zealander's Adventure* (1927), *A Pilgrim's Way in New Zealand* (1935) and *Pastoral New Zealand: Its Riches and Its People* (1946), essays collected as *First with the Sun* (1939), civics and political history—*The New Zealand Citizen* (with E.K. Mulgan, 1919), *Maori and Pakeha: A History of New Zealand* (with A.W. Shrimpton, 1922), *From Track to Highway: A Short History of New Zealand* (1944); and local history—*The City of the Strait: Wellington and Its Province: A Centennial History* (1939).

Although he did not distinguish himself greatly in any of these genres and probably wrote too much too rapidly, Mulgan did produce some important work. His plays dealt with questions of a national culture and for many years were produced by amateur theatrical groups; the best of them, 'The Daughter', still reads as a strong one-act play. A few of his poems, such as 'Dead Timber', 'Soldier Settlement' and 'Success', have lasting value, and both 'Golden Wedding' and *Spur of Morning* deal with his generation's major theme, 'nation building', in significant ways: 'Further the plough's quest, fresh fields breaking; / New life, new hope, new nation in the making.' However, both are seriously flawed, the first by sentimentality and tepid imitations of Goldsmith and

Crabbe, the second by the conventional plot resolution and the tendency to journalistic cliché that Frank *Sargeson so mocked in his parody of the novel in *Tomorrow in 1937.

Mulgan's power as literary editor and later as supervisor of talks, and his many publications, led to his being cast by Denis *Glover as one of the establishment triumvirate, 'Mulgan, Marris, Schroder', who stood in the way of the new generation of writers associated with *Phoenix* and with the *Caxton Press. He was one of the 'literary pre-Adamites', in Robert *Chapman's phrase. Many of his values and loyalties made it possible to cast him in that role: late-Victorian moral conservatism, Empire loyalty and a sense of England as *'Home', the *Georgian cast of his poetry and the conformity to a genteel tradition in his fiction. As late as 1953 he was complaining in *Landfall that the critical realists of the 1940s and 50s had 'a strong bias towards deliberate sociological probing and exposure as the main business of the novelist', and he was insisting that the novelist should try to portray not 'what is *wrong* with society' but 'what is *right* with it'. It was clear that he had not accepted the kind of literary and social attitudes represented by his son John *Mulgan's *Man Alone* (1939); his son's work has, in fact, been interpreted as a reaction against his own. However, a reading of *Spur of Morning*, his best poems and *The Making of a New Zealander* reveals that his attitudes were more complex than he was given credit for. For example, the two heroes of *Spur of Morning*, Mark Bryan and Philip Armitage, represent different values important to Mulgan—one the extroverted, egalitarian New Zealand nationalist and man of action, the other the introverted, literary Anglophile; and neither is favoured. Similarly, 'Dead Trees' holds in tension the frustrated desire for European high culture and the New Zealander's pride in practical pioneer accomplishment, and in much of his work his faith in progress, typical of his generation, is tempered by his awareness of the obstacles to it and the tragic side of history. Mulgan's aim was to synthesise these opposites. Thus in *Spur of Morning* 'The thoughts of Mark and Philip converged into one channel—nation building'. Similarly, in *The Making of a New Zealander* Mulgan's Anglophile traditionalism and his New Zealand nationalism converge in his hopes for New Zealand literature: 'New Zealanders must use, cherish, and pass on the magnificent body of English prose and verse, ancient, modern, and ever-growing, that is their joint possession, but it will not entirely suffice for their needs. In the imported soil of language and tradition, but in new sunshine, wind, and rain, we must grow our own prose and poetry.'

In 'Golden Wedding' this cultural synthesis is presented symbolically: 'The jasmine flower is English rhyme, / The rose an English tale / But censered from the open hills / The native tang comes drifting in, / Prayer of two worlds my garden fills, / Born of two worlds I watch a third begin.'

More than a negative cultural symbol, Mulgan remains an interesting figure in his own right, one attempting to synthesise some of the most significant opposing forces felt by his generation.   LJ

MULGAN, John (1911–45), was born in Christchurch, where his father, the poet, critic and essayist Alan *Mulgan worked on the *Press,* and his mother Marguerite (Pickmere), one of the first women graduates of Auckland University College, was active in intellectual and musical life. Most of Mulgan's boyhood and adolescence was spent in Auckland, apart from one year in 1926 as a boarder at Wellington College, when his parents visited Britain, and Alan wrote *Home,* a celebration of the heart of Empire.

Mulgan was good at sport as well as academic work, and from Auckland GS he went on to Auckland University College, where his main subjects were English and Greek. Active in student journalism, he ran foul of the college authorities in a freedom of speech controversy, and his views moved decidedly to the Left after the Auckland riots—facts which undoubtedly contributed to his not being nominated for a Rhodes Scholarship in 1932. As a student too he first revealed what would become an increasing reservation about academics and intellectuals, refusing to contribute to the self-consciously progressive *Phoenix,* edited by his friend James *Bertram, and submitting his rather Dowsonian and vaguely melancholy poems to the less elitist *Kiwi. But his preference already was for a straightforward, functional prose.

Towards the end of 1933, on money borrowed by his father and that John paid back over several years, he entered Merton College, Oxford, and two years later took a first class degree in English. At the invitation of Kenneth Sisam, himself an Auckland graduate, and now an eminent scholar and secretary to *Oxford University Press, Mulgan joined the Clarendon Press, and quickly learned the skills and routines of publishing. In 1936, with his close friend Geoffrey *Cox, he began a fortnightly newspaper column, 'Behind the Cables', which was run in the *Auckland Star,* and provided an alert, informed commentary on current European politics. That same year he shared a house with two other New Zealand friends, the medievalist Jack Bennett, and Ian *Milner, an ardent Soviet supporter. Although repelled by right-wing European politics and British foreign and social policies, Mulgan's leftist views remained elusive of party and doctrine. His emphasis on the individual, on modern alienation rather than political panacea, is at the core of the novel he began soon after his marriage in 1937 to a young Oxford woman, Gabrielle Wanklyn.

Mulgan took the title of *Man Alone* from a remark in Ernest Hemingway's *To Have and Have Not*, 'a man alone ain't got no bloody fucking chance'. This is the story of Johnson, an English survivor of the World War 1 trenches, who comes to Auckland during the *Depression, is caught up in rioting, farms first in the grim northern *Waikato and then in the centre of the North Island. After an affair with his boss's Māori wife, and the accidental killing of the boss, he survives an epic crossing of the Kaimanawa Ranges, to leave the country and set out for the Spanish war.

Man Alone has become a classic of New Zealand fiction. It is a set text in most New Zealand courses in universities, and is often grossly misrepresented as a kind of celebration of the Kiwi bloke going it alone, getting offside with the law and women, and making a fist of it on his own terms. It also has been glibly accused of misogyny and racism. For all its local emphases and colour, the novel must be read in the context of post-war Europe, as it takes a hard look at the reality of 'ordinary' life, without the self-congratulatory assurances common to both British and New Zealand conservatism. The starkness of the novel is also a philosophical one. Such values as emerge are what the individual manages to put together as the historical moment allows—fiction as *existentialism, before such a term became modish. At the same time as he was working on the novel, Mulgan edited for Victor Gollancz *Poems of Freedom*, an anthology of poets who 'were unafraid', and whom W.H. Auden, in his Introduction, valued not for their wisdom, but for raising their voices against oppression.

Mulgan remained at Oxford University Press, gradually extending his competence in economics and political thought, until September 1939, when he joined the 5th Battalion of the Oxford and Bucks. Much of the next two years he spent on officer training manœuvres in Northern Ireland, at times close to where his great-grandfather had lived as a Church of Ireland cleric before emigrating to the Ulster settlement in Katikati sixty years before. During brief visits to London, Mulgan recorded a number of radio broadcasts, 'Calling New Zealand', which revealed a flair for radio journalism. Then in 1942 he was posted to the Middle East.

As second-in-command of an infantry regiment, Mulgan fought in the front line at Alamein. It was here, after nine years away from his country, he again met up with large numbers of New Zealanders. He was emotionally stirred by the meeting. 'It was like coming home…. They were mature men, these New Zealanders of the desert, quiet and shrewd and sceptical. They had none of the tired patience of the Englishman, nor that automatic discipline that never questions orders to see if they make sense…. Everything that was good from that small, remote country had gone into them, sunshine and strength, good sense, patience, the versatility of practical men. And they marched into history.'

After the desert engagement, Mulgan risked severe consequences when he challenged the competence of his commanding officer. He transferred to another British battalion, served in Iraq, then in May 1943 he joined the Special Operations Executive with Force 133. A few months later he was parachuted into Northern Greece. For the next year he worked in guerrilla actions against the occupying German forces, and in the increasingly complex slide towards Greek civil war. He was the only SOE officer to directly command Greek *andartes*, and was awarded the Military Cross for his strikes against German communications. Ill and exhausted, Mulgan was flown to Cairo in October 1944, and soon after began work on *Report on Experience*, his account of his war years and his current thinking. He completed this during his months in Athens early in the new year, where he directed the British payment of compensation to Greek families who had assisted the Allies. Although he touches only lightly on his own extraordinary exploits of the previous twelve months, the essay is a brilliant, thoughtful exposition of what war means to a local people, and what peace might offer a post-war world. Since his meeting with New Zealanders in the North African campaign, Mulgan had thought much about his country, its singular merits and aspirations, and its possible future. Although his leisure reading while with the guerrillas had been Boswell and Gibbon, Mulgan came to reject purely intellectual values. He was now drawn to a more direct life of physical openness, classless social exchange and simple domestic satisfaction. He returned from Athens to Cairo in mid-April, where he wound up a number of obligations, including a report to the New Zealand Department of Foreign Affairs on the suitability of Greeks as immigrants, and made arrangements to transfer to the New Zealand Division. The day before that planned homecoming, as it were, on Anzac Day 1945, Mulgan took an overdose of morphia from his medical kit. The reasons for his suicide remain unexplained.

Mulgan has suffered in recent years from his reputation as 'the golden boy', the handsome and personable athlete and scholar, who seemed to succeed at whatever he turned his mind to. The praise of his contemporaries, his choosing to enter the English academic establishment, his impressive military career, and the instant 'classic' status of his work, inevitably have provoked the desire to question that reputation, and to deconstruct the race and gender issues of his novel. But his centrality to

New Zealand literature and self-fashioning seems in little danger of being challenged. Although his reputation is based on only two texts, each is ground-breaking within local traditions. His novel's direct narrative and spare diction cut through a prevalent sentimentality about both this country and Britain, and his style anticipated the tenor of much subsequent New Zealand fiction; while in his final ruminative essay, Mulgan engaged with aspects of New Zealand life and character more imaginatively than any writer since *Mansfield.

Mulgan's publications were *Poems of Freedom*, 1938, *The Emigrants: Early Travellers in the Antipodes*, with Hector *Bolitho, 1939; *Man Alone*, 1939; *Report on Experience*, 1947. He also edited the *Concise Oxford Dictionary of English Literature*, 1939, and a work completed by D.M. *Davin, *Introduction to English Literature*, 1947. Two essential biographical and critical studies have been written by Paul W. Day: *John Mulgan*, New York, 1968, and the shorter *John Mulgan* in the OUP *'New Zealand Writers and their Work' series, 1974.   VO

MURRY, John Middleton (1889–1957), English critic and editor, never visited New Zealand but has a place in its literature through his association with Katherine *Mansfield and his inspiration of the *Phoenix* group. He lived with Mansfield from 1912, was married to her in 1918 and was present at her death in France in 1923. As her editor, adviser and executor his influence on her work and reputation was considerable and mostly positive, despite some questionable dealings with her personal image and manuscripts after her death. New Zealand's view of him has generally been somewhat resentful, echoing Aldous Huxley's satire of the calculatingly grief-stricken Burlap in *Point Counter Point* (1928). Antony *Alpers, however, perceived that Murry, a London scholarship boy, was as much an outsider as Mansfield to the British literary and social establishments, and Vincent *O'Sullivan and Cherry Hankin have given full recognition to the importance to Mansfield of a relationship that was in many ways fulfilling, however uneven. If nothing else, Murry was the recipient and inspiration of Mansfield's love letters, some of the most remarkable in English. Himself influenced by Mansfield and his friend D.H. *Lawrence, Murry had ample literary achievements in his own right, as editor (*The Adelphi* and *New Adelphi*, 1923–30), critic (*The Problem of Style,* 1922; *Keats and Shakespeare,* 1925) and religious-philosophical writer (*God,* 1929). As editor of a literary quarterly, his vision of a serious and progressive new literature, presented with impressive elegance of form, was the model for *Phoenix*, which adopted its name from the signet ring presented to Murry by Lawrence when the *New Adelphi* rose from the ashes of

the *Adelphi* in 1927. Murry's later use of Mansfield's manuscripts as a source of income also benefited New Zealand, by enabling the *Alexander Turnbull Library to acquire at what now seem modest prices a literary collection of the highest importance. This has now been supplemented by a substantial acquisition of Murry's own personal papers.   RR

MUSAPHIA, Joseph (1935–), playwright, was born in London, but emigrated as a child to Melbourne, where he received his primary schooling, and then (in 1946) to Christchurch, where he attended Christchurch BHS. He worked as a commercial artist and cartoonist in both New Zealand and the UK before establishing himself as a writer, and to a lesser extent as an actor and director, in New Zealand. In 1961 his first play, *Free*—inspired by John Osborne's *Look Back in Anger*—was performed at Victoria University by the New Zealand Theatre Workshop, an offshoot of the New Zealand Theatre Company. *Free* was broadcast on radio in 1962, and a revised version was published in *Landfall* 68 in 1963. The dearth of professional theatre in New Zealand forced Musaphia to concentrate on radio in the 1960s, and he has produced more than 120 radio scripts. He also wrote the screenplay and lyrics for Pacific Films' musical comedy *Don't Let It Get To You* (1966), and was active in the early days of New Zealand television, hosting his own children's show (*Joe's World*) and contributing, often with Roger *Hall, to popular series such as *Buck House*, *In View of the Circumstances* and (in Australia) *Australia A–Z*.

An early radio play, *Virginia Was a Dog* (1963), was staged in Wellington in 1968, and, further encouraged by the advent of New Zealand's professional community theatres and by the theatrical renaissance in Australia at that time, Musaphia went on to produce a string of mostly full-length stage plays in the 1970s and early 1980s: *The Guerrilla* (one-act, first produced at the Ensemble Theatre, Sydney, in 1971); *Victims* (Downstage, 1973); *Obstacles* (Downstage, 1974); *Mothers and Fathers* (Fortune, 1975); *Hunting* (Circa, 1979); *Shotgun Wedding* (Circa, 1980); *The Hangman* (Depot, 1983); *Mates* (Circa, 1986); and *The New Zealander* (Fortune, 1988). His success, especially with *Mothers and Fathers*, helped pave the way for the more extended career of his erstwhile television collaborator Roger Hall. Though the comedies of both men are superficially similar, Musaphia's are distinguished by a stronger visual sense, and by his unsettling ability to conjure troubling issues (often on gender-related topics, with a bias towards the male side) out of farcical situations.

Musaphia supplemented his earnings from the stage with newspaper columns for the *Dominion, Sunday Times* and *NZ Listener in the 1970s and 1980s. In 1979 he was the first holder of the Victoria University writing fellowship, producing four plays that were subsequently performed professionally. The waning of his output in the 1980s coincided with a return to full-time employment at the Consumers' Institute (1980–91). He is currently a consultant, newspaper columnist and TV commentator on consumer matters, his forthright irreverence as evident there as in his plays. Several of his more recent scripts—'The Plague' (1983), 'A Fair Go for Charlie Wellman' (1986, based on an earlier radio play), 'Heart of Hearts' (1993) and 'Snakes and Ladders' (1993)—remain unperformed.   RCo

Music and New Zealand literature have enjoyed some close associations, contributing distinctively to an age-old tradition which in English alone includes such major texts as *Beowulf*, Shakespeare's plays and the entire genres of ode and sonnet. This emerges first in the pre-European culture of the Māori, whose music is based on the spoken, sung and chanted word, through the multifarious forms of the *waiata (song), including lullabies, laments, love lyrics or justifications: 'one created songs for a social or religious reason', writes Te Puoho Katene. These have not only given continuity and inspiration to their own people but have also permeated European music written in New Zealand from the early nineteenth century onwards, notably in the works of Alfred *Hill.

On the other hand European folksongs and operatic melodies attracted many Māori. This cross-fertilisation is well illustrated in the journals of Sarah Harriet Selwyn (*c.*1846), wife of the venerable bishop, who on one occasion played her piano to an old chief who had never heard of such an instrument: 'he wondered and wondered, and listened, and put his ear to it, and at last said, "Is there a man inside?"' Lady Martin, wife of the first Chief Justice of New Zealand, in her *Our Maori* (published in the year of her death in 1884) describes Māori boys and girls singing English catches and glees 'with great spirits' at a Māori wedding held at St John's in Auckland. She heard Māori girls give fine performances of Mendelssohn chorales and a young woman who could sing 'Ah! che la morte', from *Il Trovatore*, and 'He shall feed his flock', from Handel's *Messiah*, with 'great pathos and sweetness'.

Missionaries translated favourite hymns into Māori with rewarding ecumenical effect: on many a notable occasion today such as the Queen's 1990 visit to Waitangi they are sung fervently in a slow tempo. The pioneer collection *Traditional Songs of the Maori* (1975) by Margaret *Orbell and Mervyn McLean shows how the waiata has continued to evolve through the nineteenth century to depict the perfidies of the Land Courts, the entrenched attitudes of Wellington bureaucrats and so on. *Te Kooti's many waiata composed in defence of the values and the integrity of his own people are detailed in Judith Binney's monumental *Redemption Songs: A Life of Te Kooti Arikirangi Te Turuki* (1995): 'wherever Te Kooti went—wherever he step foot from one area to another—he's singing,' said the Whakatōhea elder Jack Kurei.

Victorian ballads, an epitome of British social and domestic life, easily transplanted themselves to New Zealand, producing a rich colonial crop, some published locally, others bearing the imprint of a famed Leipzig house. These range from the poignant 'Night-Watch Song of the "Charlotte Jane"' (words by J.E. *FitzGerald, music by a former wine merchant J. Townsend) (*c.*1851), to the bizarre 'The Maniac Maiden, a Dream Song' by Gordon Stables (*c.*1905), to E.W. Secker's famed football ballad 'On the Ball' (Charles Begg, Dunedin), salutations for royal visits, outbursts of patriotism as in Bessie Ferguson Hume's 'Pass Friend, the Jack's A-flying', dedicated to the army and navy of the Empire, and the opening of exhibitions and town halls. The apotheosis of the period is undoubtedly found in John J. Woods' setting of Thomas *Bracken's oleaginous words in *'God Defend New Zealand' (1878).

The high Victorian musical culture of the latter part of the century coincided with a fervent sense of *nationalism and the innovative legislation of the Liberal regime. Writers, poets and musicians worked together to produce works that, however dated and perhaps naive many of them may seem today, yet were the first crystallisation of an incipient search for identity, not to be repeated until the more realistic and critical declarations of the artists of the 1930s.

After the traumas of World War 1, the devastating flu epidemic and the *Depression, a vigorous revival of the arts emerged in Christchurch in the 1930s including the poets Allen *Curnow and Denis *Glover, the artists Rita Angus and Leo *Bensemann and the composer Douglas *Lilburn. A similarly gifted circle arose in Auckland with R.A.K. *Mason, Blackwood *Paul, Hector Monro, Bob *Lowry and others who launched the polemical literary magazine *Phoenix* (1932). Lilburn's literary gifts equalled his musical ones and have so far found permanent expression in the publication, many years after their delivery, of two seminal talks 'A search for tradition' (1946) and 'A search for a language' (1969). The first has the spontaneity and conviction of youth, the second a measured reaction to intervening experience. John Amis and Michael Rose included a telling extract from the latter in their Faber anthology *Words About Music* (1989).

Words and music are closely associated in opera and theatre. A history of opera libretti in New Zealand would reveal struggles similar to those undergone elsewhere, from Beethoven to Chabrier and Britten. Many New Zealand writers lacked experience in combining dramatic craft with the needs of music. Ngaio *Marsh, an accomplished professional, adapted her own play for David *Farquhar's *A Unicorn for Christmas* (1962). Jenny *McLeod's literary skills underpinned her theatre piece *Under the Sun* (1971) and so infused the work that it enjoyed spectacular success. Operas in many different genres continue to be written despite the difficulties of achieving performance. Katherine *Mansfield's stories have received musical treatment, most recently in Peter *Wells's *Ricordi!* and collaborations between Dorothy *Buchanan and librettist Jeremy Commons.

Music for theatre found its apogee in the substantial body of work Douglas Lilburn wrote for Ngaio Marsh's renowned *Shakespeare productions in Christchurch, from *Hamlet* (1943) to *Othello* (1944), *King Henry V* (1945), *A Midsummer Night's Dream* (1945) and *Macbeth* (1946). A selection from his scores for these productions has now been published. Lilburn continued such activities in Wellington with Richard Campion, founder of the New Zealand Players, as in *Dandy Dick* (1953) and *St Joan* (1955). For the New Zealand Broadcasting Corporation he prepared music for *The Pitcher and the Well* (1964), an early use of electro-acoustic sound. Ashley Heenan's orchestral score for James K. *Baxter's *Jack Winter's Dream* (1958), another NZBC commission, is now an integral part of that play. During this heyday of radio drama the NZBC proved a leading and imaginative patron. A distinctive theatrical form was created by Mervyn *Thompson in song-plays like *O, Temperance!*, *Songs for the Judges* and *Passing Through*, influencing several current dramatists.

Music has been part of the creative imagination of many writers in New Zealand, as elsewhere. It flows through Katherine Mansfield's stories as it did in her life. She fell in love with the cellist Arnold Trowell, then with his violinist brother, Garnet, learned the piano from the doyen of Wellington's music, Robert Parker (1847–1937), and formed intense friendships with visiting artists such as the Venezuelan pianist Teresa Carreño. In 'The *Wind Blows' Mr Bullen is a gentle evocation of Robert Parker, a dignified Victorian gentleman. 'Let's have a little of the old master,' he says as he opens a Beethoven sonata. 'But why does he speak so kindly—so awfully kindly—and as though they had known each other for years and knew everything about each other,' thinks his young pupil. Miss Bray, in the unfinished story 'Second Violin', 'darts along to orchestra practice' where 'two Violas sat on a bench, bent over a music book, and the Harp, a small grey little person, who only came occasionally, leaned against a bench and looked for her pocket in her underskirt...'. In the posthumous fragment 'Weak

Heart', Edie Bengel, who plays the piano, receives from her father for her fourteenth birthday 'a silver brooch with a bar of music, two crotchets, two quavers and a minim headed by a very twisted treble clef'. Mansfield gives an intriguing title for a story she never wrote, 'Aunt Anne: Her Life with the *Tannhäuser* Overture'. The barrel-organ in 'The *Daughters of the Late Colonel' ('A perfect fountain of bubbling notes ... round, bright notes, carelessly scattered'), the band in *'Miss Brill' ('Now there came a little "flutey" bit—very pretty—a little chain of bright drops'), the piano ('more desperate than ever') and the band in 'The *Garden Party' all provide a kind of musical accompaniment which is a common element of Mansfield's stories. She may not have been exaggerating when she wrote in her journal entry of 22 March 1914: 'I'd rather be with musical people than any others...'.

Sylvia *Ashton-Warner's *Spinster* (1958) revolves around Anna Vorontosov, 'gifted in art and in music, as in human relationships, but a little barmy', as Joan *Stevens puts it. Germaine de Beauvais, a notable pianist, in *Incense to Idols* (1960), has rather curiously left Paris to come to a small New Zealand city in search of her old French maestro. Ashton-Warner's autobiography *I Passed This Way* (1979) contains a hilarious account of two brusque educational inspectors who arraign her for taking French leave and coming to Wellington to hear the Hungarian pianist Lili Kraus. Janet *Frame, in *An *Angel at My Table* (1984) describes how she began to listen to classical music in the gramophone room of the Dunedin school where she was briefly a teacher, and later her 'rash move into the world of time payment when I bought a radiogram and one record, Beethoven's Seventh Symphony.... The Dance. For me it *was* the dance, filled with a special joy and freedom.'

Music teachers, prominent in small-town life before the advent of modern entertainments, appear frequently in fiction. Lyttelton, in Frederick Page's childhood, boasted six in a population of some four thousand. 'Miss Henderson was a red-fed, took the *Lyttelton Times* rather than the *Press*, voted Labour, was against the Monarchy and let you know she was one "with the people ..."', he wrote in his autobiography *A Musician's Journal* (1986). Ronald Hugh *Morrieson's mother taught the piano and he not only played in dance bands around South Taranaki halls but became a teacher of guitar. 'I have these majestic themes in my mind', he said to Maurice *Shadbolt, 'you see, big things, shapes like music, but the trouble is getting the characters to fit.' The central figure of Maurice *Gee's *Plumb* (1978) makes his first contact with the girl he intends to marry by pretending he wishes to have piano lessons from her. Edie Hamer, younger daughter and assistant to her mother, soon catches on. 'I don't think you've come here to play the piano, Mr Plumb,' she asks.

Close connections between writers and music continue to be too numerous to list. Anne *Kennedy, for instance, weaves words and music inextricably in *Musica Ficta* (1993) and elsewhere, Brian *Hanfling has explored music in his remarkable children's novel, *The Mind Musicians* (1988), and the creative response to Māori song and music continues in writers like Trixie Te Arama *Menzies. Composers such as Dorothy Buchanan and Gillian *Whitehead are drawn to texts by Janet Frame, Fleur *Adcock, Cilla *McQueen or others, while the resonant themes of Charles *Brasch ('In these islands', for instance) and the lyricism of Alistair Te Ariki *Campbell continue to attract composers from different generations. The many lively choral and vocal ensembles are increasingly seeking New Zealand texts. This collaboration between music and literature can only continue to develop and find new forms.   JMT

Musings in Maoriland (1890) was Thomas *Bracken's most ornate and ambitious publication, the fourth book of verse that he published in New Zealand. Like other books of that time, it expressed the hope that an indigenous literature of some value might be emerging as the colony celebrated fifty years of European settlement. In retrospect the poems show little of enduring worth, chiefly interesting as indicators of the taste of the period, when Bracken was both prolific and immensely popular as a writer and reader-performer of verse.

The poems reveal a strong sense of nationalism, enthusiastically celebrating the natural beauties and modest human achievements of the new land. They are for the most part conventional in metre, prosody and stanza form, sentimental in their appeal, and suited to a robust recitation rather than to any closer scrutiny.

The book itself was elaborately bound and printed in Leipzig. Dedicated to Alfred, Lord Tennyson, it was prefaced by a long essay, 'The rise and progress of New Zealand' by Robert Stout, and a shorter introduction to the poems themselves by Sir George *Grey, both of whom Bracken had associated with as a member of parliament. Sales were below expectations, in spite of Bracken's reputation and energetic promotion. An attempt by the author to market a deluxe edition on a sales trip to the Australian colonies only intensified the financial difficulties of his last years.   WB

N

Nag's Head Press, see **GORMACK, R.S.**

NANNESTAD, Elizabeth (1956–), poet, was born in Auckland, trained as a medical doctor, practised as a psychiatrist and is currently a full-time writer. She has been widely anthologised and has been a regular contributor to *Landfall*, *Islands*, *Poetry New Zealand*, *Sport* and *Quote Unquote*. With 'Queen of the River' she was the youngest poet represented in the *Penguin Book of New Zealand Verse* (1985) and is also in the 1997 Oxford *Anthology of New Zealand Poetry*. Her first collection, *Jump*, which brought together poems of the previous ten years, was published in 1986; and in 1987 *Jump* shared the New Zealand Book Award for Poetry with Allen *Curnow's *The Loop in the Lone Kauri Road*. *Jump* consists of six sections and a separate final poem, 'Jump'. A main preoccupation of the poems is how experiences and memories substantiate the speaker's identity at the moment of writing: 'my eye / bends what I see with distance and time.' In her more recent poems Nannestad continues to question domestic detail with calm and sometimes ironic insistence. With a couple of exceptions, the lines are short, the diction plain, the tone relaxed. In a review in *Islands* Michele *Leggott calls her a 'portraitist', and this indicates well Nannestad's subject matter of family, self, friends and lovers. The poems in *Jump* which deal with faraway settings dwell more on the uneasy experience of the traveller than on the exotic locale itself. In addition to the continued discovery of the familiar, Nannestad often contemplates writing itself, because, as she points out: 'The empty page, it's hell / to live with. / And to live without.'

HT

NAPIER, Susan (pseudonym of Susan Potter, 1954–), is one of *Mills & Boon/ Harlequin's most widely read and translated *romance novelists. Since her first novels in the mid-1980s, she has published more than twenty-five novels in many editions. She was previously a journalist on the Auckland *Star*. Napier's novels, often set in the sophisticated high-rise office blocks of downtown Auckland and in trendy inner-city apartments and penthouses, are written, she says, about 'mature, sophisticated heroines for an over-25 readership'. Uninhibited in their treatment of sex and sexual fantasy, her novels are pure entertainments, distinguished from other New Zealand Mills & Boon novels by their lightness of touch, humour and, increasingly, their playfulness with the romance conventions. For Napier, 'You never let reality get in the way of a good story'. Although she acknowledges that 'conventional morality' underpins the formula, and that 'the most important ingredients in a romance are feelings, emotions and passions', the humorous self-reflexiveness with which she treats the genre invites readers to distinguish between reality and the fantasies the novels embody.

TS

Nationalism has been a recurrent and often dominant theme in New Zealand literature. The idea that literature should lead the way in forging a national identity became explicit in such magazines of the 1890s as the *New Zealand Illustrated Magazine* or *Zealandia*, which declared itself 'a distinctively national literary magazine' (July 1889). This proved premature in an era of continuing antipodean fealty. Even Arthur *Adams—'Poet of a newer land, / Confident, aggressive, lonely, / Product of the present only, / Thinking nothing of the past' ('Myself—My Song', 1899)—or William Pember

*Reeves—'Who serve an art more great / Than we, rough architects of State / With the old earth at strife?' ('A Colonist in His Garden', 1904)—seem more interested in New Zealand's potential for national identity than in its content.

While the Boer *War and the Gallipoli campaign of World *War 1 did much to forge popular nationalist sentiment, the New Zealand intelligentsia remained mainly Eurocentric. Alan *Mulgan's Home: A New Zealander's Adventure (1927), recounting his profound satisfaction with England and things English, typifies this displaced colonial identity.

In the late 1920s–30s, writers, mostly poets, began directly addressing a postcolonial identity: R.A.K. *Mason, Ursula *Bethell, A.R.D. *Fairburn, Robin *Hyde, Frank *Sargeson, Allen *Curnow and Charles *Brasch. Many were associated with *Phoenix (1932–33) which, in an influential conjunction of preoccupations, fused a socialist critique of *Depression-era New Zealand with an attempt to wrest the country's intellectual orientation from its British focus.

These writers were never a 'school' or coherent movement. Bethell and Brasch, apparently expecting something much like England only with an antipodean flavour, seemed more sanguine than Mason and Curnow, who aspired to 'Something different, something / Nobody counted on' (Curnow, 'The Unhistoric Story', 1941). What they had in common was belief that New Zealand literature must satisfy our hunger 'for the words that shall show us these islands and ourselves: that shall give us a home in thought' (Phoenix, 1).

The most sustained and influential poetic attempt to satisfy this hunger was the work of Curnow. Poems such as 'House and Land' (1941), 'The Unhistoric Story', 'Sailing or Drowning' (1943), 'The Skeleton of the Great Moa in the Canterbury Museum, Christchurch' (1943) and *'Landfall in Unknown Seas' (1943) analyse colonial guilt and the burdens and opportunities of nation-building with an unsettling mixture of ironic detachment and unrepentant oratory: 'Not I, some child, born in a marvellous year, / Will learn the trick of standing upright here' ('The Skeleton of the Great Moa'). In prose, Frank Sargeson in the late 1930s invented a New Zealand idiom in a sequence of short sketches published in the radical weekly *Tomorrow. Sargeson's New Zealand male—inarticulate, laconic, stoic and loyal to his mates—gave fiction a distinctive New Zealander and a dialect for him to speak.

The *Centennial of 1940 focused attention on questions of nationhood. State sponsorship of the occasion gave birth to two influential essays: E.H. *McCormick's Letters and Art in New Zealand and M.H. *Holcroft's The Deepening Stream. McCormick's perceptive and intelligent account let New Zealanders know that they did in fact have a literary and artistic history. Holcroft's inquiry into the 'deeper impulse[s] within the nation's life' concluded optimistically that New Zealanders 'are still strangers in the land' but increasingly finding themselves at home.

The Deepening Stream was an early success of *Caxton Press, which played an important role in the nationalist movement of the 1930s–40s. By providing a local outlet for the best New Zealand writing, previously often published in London, it allowed not only the possibility of *'speaking for ourselves' (in the significant title of Sargeson's 1945 anthology), but speaking to ourselves as well. It was Caxton which, from March 1947, published *Landfall, its title taken from Curnow and promising arrival after a long voyage. As Brasch wrote in the first issue, 'the first condition of good work here is that for the artist the tradition must be localized'.

In the 1950s this nationalist imperative began to be questioned. Louis *Johnson's *New Zealand Poetry Yearbook contained, in its first issue in 1951, a 'Commentary' by Erik Schwimmer attacking the 'Curnow– Holcroft myth' and arguing that the 'consciousness of the internationalisation of culture is too vivid in New Zealanders' for the myth to survive. This led to a schism between the 'internationalist' Wellington school and the 'nationalist' Auckland school, fought out largely in the Yearbook (1951–64), while articles by Curnow argued that for writers 'to write poems that transcend time and place, they must achieve a correct vision of their own time and place'. Through the 1950s–60s the imperative of a 'home in thought' became the driving force behind literature. There were exceptions; Bill *Pearson's *Coal Flat was hailed as The Great New Zealand Novel in 1963, but in retrospect it is not surprising that its genesis lay over a decade earlier. An emergent professional theatre and Bruce *Mason's indefatigable touring of The *End of the Golden Weather allowed many people to see New Zealand–based drama for the first time. Similarly, the nascent *film industry of the late 1970s was preoccupied with reflecting New Zealand realities in what had been an overseas-oriented medium. In poetry and prose, however, increasing interest in American literature among the *Freed generation of the 1970s made anxiety over identity or allegiance to Britain seem thoroughly outmoded—what Ian *Wedde in a 1977 interview called 'kicking this dried goose turd around the back yard'.

In the 1980s–90s, as allegiances have increasingly splintered, writers show more interest in exploring specific community identities (gay, lesbian, female, elderly, Māori, Islander) than in defining 'national' identity. Concerns about 'speaking for ourselves' have shifted towards the amount of New Zealand content in television programming. Nationalist myths like Sargeson's Kiwi bloke and Kiwi dialect remain available but their invocation is usually either ironic and playful (as in Jane *Campion's film *The *Piano*, 1993) or nostalgic (as in much television advertising). HRo

NATUSCH, Sheila (1926–), has published more than twenty books, mostly on natural history and early New Zealand historical subjects, reaching considerable popular audiences by the vigorous clarity with which she communicates detailed research information. This is often enhanced by her illustrative skills. Her early books include *Native Rock* (1967) and *New Zealand Mosses* (1969), but she turned increasingly to historical topics, her biography of her ancestor, the Ruapuke pioneer *Brother Wohlers* (1969) winning the Hubert Church award, followed by *On the Edge of the Bush: Women in Early Southland* (1976). Probably her best-known book is *Hell and High Water* (1977, 1992), the story of the German mission established in the Chatham Islands in 1843, full of unexpected human detail and pithy narratorial comment (as when she points to the irony of writing in 1975, the International Year of the Woman, about marriages where women were beaten and imprisoned). Equally strong in narrative and research documentation is *The Cruise of the 'Acheron'* (1978), about the British survey vessel in New Zealand waters 1848–51. Her more recent books include characterful biographies such as *William Swainson ... The Anatomy of a Nineteenth-Century Naturalist* (with Geoffrey Swainson, 1987) and *Roy Traill of Stewart Island* (1991). A Stewart Islander of German missionary ancestry, Natusch graduated MA at Otago University and now lives in Wellington, still a full-time writer and illustrator. RR

NELISI, Lino (1952–), is a pioneering writer for Pacific nations children, her stories being published in Cook Islands Māori, English, Māori, Samoan, Tokelauan, Tongan and her native Nuiean. Born in Nuie, she taught there for seven years, moved to Auckland in 1977 and has worked as a primary teacher since 1984. In 1995 she was made an adviser on Pacific Islands education at Auckland College of Education. She began to publish reading texts that 'my hundred Pacific Islands children at school can relate to' after encouragement from Don *Long of *Learning Media. Some draw on the myths and legends of Niue she heard in childhood, others deal with contemporary experiences of Nuieans in Auckland, job-hunting, sharing their pay-packets or being robbed in Grey Lynn. 'Ko e Ama Uga' tells of a girl travelling to Nuie and learning ways of hunting the giant coconut crab, while the best-known, *Sione's Talo* (1992) reminded the *NZ Listener*'s reviewer

of the Russian folktale, 'The Enormous Turnip'. It is now in use in American as well as New Zealand schools, and was an AIM award finalist, as was *Fishing with Spider Webs* (1994). Lino Nelisi also publishes translations for children of other Pacific nations' stories. RR

Netherlands, The, had their first contact with New Zealand when the Dutch explorer Abel *Tasman visited in 1642. In the period of European settlement, the Dutch are the largest immigrant group after the British. From 1950 to 1953 more than 10 000 Dutch people left their country, devastated by war and floods, to settle in New Zealand. A preferential immigration policy was in effect for potential Dutch immigrants until the end of 1992. Because of aggressive promotion of assimilation, most Dutch immigrants tried to fit in as New Zealanders as soon as possible, even though this included relinquishing their language and culture. As a result remarkably few explicitly Dutch elements are discernable in New Zealand literature. The only writer to make her Dutch origins significant to her work is Riemke *Ensing, who, like Tasman, was born in Groningen. Poet Koenraad *Kuiper and photographer Ans *Westra also emigrated from Holland. During the Abel Tasman Year of 1992 a chair of Dutch studies was endowed at the University of Auckland, and the popularity of Dutch studies, particularly in a context of postcolonial criticism, may point to an increased interest in Dutch–New Zealand literary relations. HT

New chum was originally Australian for a newly arrived convict (1812), thence there and in New Zealand a newly arrived immigrant, and later a novice or one new to a job: 'some take delight in ... frightening "new chums", as they term them, with all kinds of disheartening accounts of the colony' (C.W. Adams, *A Spring Time in the Canterbury Settlement*, 1853). 'There's an Auckland proverb, that a new-chum never does any good until his nose has grown' (W.D. Hay, *Brighter Britain*, 1882). Canterbury satirist G.W. *Williams called his last volume of poems *A New Chum's Letter Home* (1904) and in *The New Chum and Other Stories* (1909) Arthur *Adams comically contrasts the 'English' views of a new immigrant with the 'colonial' ones of those who arrived earlier. HO

New Digest, see ***New Horizon***.

New Horizon was a monthly *Readers' Digest* style magazine published in Auckland May–December 1940. Retitled *New Digest* from June 1941 it continued under that name until 1954. As a digest it reprinted articles and other items, initially from local periodicals and newspapers such as *Tomorrow*, *Kiwi*, *Truth* and the *Dominion*, but later from international sources. John Gifford *Male, editor of the first eight numbers, stressed its independence from political, financial or religious affiliations and published work by R.A.K. *Mason, Allen *Curnow, J.R. *Hervey, Anton *Vogt, G. R. *Gilbert, James *Bertram and Helen *Shaw. As *New Digest* the local content gradually disappeared as it became more of a men's magazine featuring sensational articles about war, syndicated stories, and female pin-ups.   SH

New Nation was a monthly published in Wellington 1924–25, when it was absorbed into *New Zealand Life* (see *New Zealand Magazine*). With a policy of promoting local literary endeavour, it published stories and poetry by Eileen *Duggan, Alan *Mulgan, J.C. *Beaglehole and Mona *Tracy.   SH

New Triad, published monthly in Wellington 1937–42, was the second of the series of periodicals edited by Noel *Hoggard which culminated in the long-running *Arena. Although an improvement on its predecessor *Spilt Ink, New Triad* failed to emulate the original *Triad of Charles Baeyertz. However, Hoggard's earnest attempt to promote local writing through his periodicals cannot be dismissed as a total failure. Numerous writers gained encouragement from publication by him and many prominent contributors continued to support him long after their need for such support had passed. C.R. *Allen, David *Ballantyne, G.R. *Gilbert, J.R. *Hervey, Alice A. *Kenny, and Keith *Sinclair all contributed work to *New Triad*.   SH

New World: An Organ of Reconstruction was published in Christchurch 1921–22. Preceded by the *Breeze and edited by Maurice Hurst, it sought to assist in the creation of the 'One Big Class of the future'. It featured poems by Will *Lawson and Margaret *Macpherson and articles by B.E. *Baughan and Elsdon *Best.   SH

New Zealand, derived from a translation either of Dutch *Nieuw Zeeland* or modern Latin *Zelandia Nova*, appears on Frederick de Wit's world map of 1660 first printed in Hendrick Dronker's atlas, and later in de Wit's atlas of 1671, for those parts of New Zealand discovered by *Tasman. Zeeland is a Dutch maritime province. Early forms include 'New-Zealand', 'New Zeeland', 'New Zeland' and occasionally 'Newzealand'; and more recent jocular pronunciation includes 'New Zillun(d)', 'Noo Zilland' and 'NyaZilnd'. Synonyms of various registers include *'Aotearoa', 'Aotearoa–New Zealand', 'Enzed', *'Maoriland' and *'Niu Tirani': '... the land dis-

cover'd by Tasman and now called New Zeland' (James *Cook, *Journal*, 1768); 'The Dutch named it "New Zealand".... English writers ... protest strongly.... Taylor proposes names such as "Austral Britain" or "Austral Albion"' (F. von *Hochstetter, *New Zealand*, 1867); 'Tasman did not call the country New Zealand but Staten Land, on the supposition that it was ... a westward extension of the Staten Land off Tierra del Fuego ... who it was conferred the name New Zealand, within the next few years, we do not know. The reason for it may have been analogy with New Holland' (J.C. *Beaglehole in Cook, *Journals*, 1961).

'New Zealand' as an adjective in its biogeographical use refers generally to the country: 'The Natives are very fond of New-Zealand green stone' (J. *Forster, *Resolution Journal*, 17 Aug. 1774). In its early socio-cultural use, until about 1850, it carries various senses of 'Māori', including that of 'indigenous' or 'native' applied to plants and animals, such as 'New Zealand clematis' or 'New Zealand rat'. After the arrival of the main body of European settlers about 1840–50, predominant usage progressively includes reference to non-Māori society and culture. 'We had not yet sufficient experience of New Zealand troops to trust them too far' (Monkhouse, in Cook, *Journal*, 10 Oct. 1769); 'It is easy to make a serious mistake in the New Zealand tongue, or *reo maori*' (James *Buller, *Forty Years in NZ*, 1878); 'The energising force in New Zealand life up to now has been this myth of the pioneer, the frontier' (Phillip *Wilson, *Pacific Star*, 1976).   HO

New Zealand Artists' Annual was published in Wellington by Pat *Lawlor 1926–32. Similar in content to Lawlor's New Zealand edition of *Aussie, it featured little of lasting literary interest. A.R.D. *Fairburn's tribute to R.A.K. *Mason, published in the issue for August 1929, rails against the very attitudes the *Artists' Annual* seems determined to cultivate. A number of poems and stories by Robin *Hyde, Eileen *Duggan and Jessie *Mackay raise the general standard of material published.   SH

New Zealand Best Poems, see **MARRIS, Charles A.**

New Zealand Book Awards, see Appendix.

New Zealand Book Council, The, was founded in 1972 to increase community interest in books, to improve access to them, to provide a forum for interested individuals and institutions, to publish information about books and to lobby government. Funded by Creative New Zealand, publishers and a number of sponsors, it fosters encounters of writers and readers with its Meet the Author Programmes, Writers in Schools Scheme (which introduces writers to 45 000 students each year), tours by overseas writers and other activities. With its quarterly *Booknotes* it provides information about book-related events and organisations. NW

New Zealand Books was founded in Wellington in April 1991 to provide for the first time a journal of serious and substantial reviewing. The first editorial of J.M. ★Thomson argued that 'Books are one of our chief cultural assets however undervalued they may be by economic policy makers' and aimed 'to provide a forum for the finest available writing and criticism of books'. The increasing numbers, range and renown of New Zealand books have been the journal's justification and greatest problem, as it retains a generally more wide-ranging policy than either of its main models, the *New York Review of Books* and *London Review of Books*. Lauris ★Edmond was, with Thomson, a prime mover, and has continued as the most long-lasting literary figure on the managing board of Peppercorn Press; others have included Phillip ★Mann, Harry ★Ricketts and Bill ★Sewell. After Thomson stepped aside, a series of guest editors—Nelson Wattie, Jane Stafford and Paula Wagemaker—sustained standards until the appointment of political journalist Colin James as editor, 1994–97. He balanced his political interests with literary content, so that by 1996 *New Zealand Books* could win the Reviews Pages section of the Montana Book Awards. In 1997 Ricketts and Sewell became joint editors. A selection of outstanding reviews edited by Edmond, Ricketts and Sewell was published as *Under Review* (1997). RR

New Zealand Bookworld was founded in June 1973 incorporating *The New Zealand Bookseller and Publisher*, and soon established itself as a highly informative source for everything connected with the writing, publishing and selling of books in New Zealand. Its editors included William Riley, John Ewan and Elizabeth Parker. Profiles of authors, articles by writers on the creation of their books, a good coverage of children's books and schools' reading activities, advance information on coming publications, information from libraries, bookselling statistics, short but informative reviews and a variety of lists—local publishers, best-sellers, award-winners (from Britain and America as well as from New Zealand), decisions of the Indecent Publications Tribunal, recommended reading lists for various age-groups, publishers' series and, above all, updates of the *New Zealand National Bibliography*—made the journal an uncontroversial, perhaps unexciting, but also invaluable monthly. The reviews were not confined to New Zealand publications but included many major books that had come on to the market from overseas. *New Zealand Bookworld* expired with its sixty-fourth issue in May 1981. NW

New Zealand Children's Book Foundation, Te Maataa Pukapuka Tamariki o Aotearoa, was established in 1990 as a division of the ★New Zealand Book Council to promote children's books and reading. It liaises with groups and agencies in the field, organises new groups, runs a lecture series, grants the Margaret Mahy Lecture Award to a person 'who has made an especially distinguished and significant contribution to children's literature, publishing or literacy', liaises with overseas groups and organises visits from overseas authors and illustrators. Its objectives include cultivating scholarship and research, encouraging the development of grants and other funding and furthering international understanding among children by the two-way flow of books. NW

New Zealand Children's Literature Association (NZCLA), The, was formed by a group of enthusiasts in Auckland in 1969. Auckland remains the centre of its activities, although branches exist elsewhere. From 1972 to 1988 it published the *CLA Yearbook*, replaced by the thrice-yearly *CLA Voice*. Reaching out to parents and children, it sees itself as grass-roots-based, in contrast to the ★New Zealand Children's Book Foundation, whose activities are aimed at book professionals. NW

New Zealand English (NZE) in the broad sense is the entire range of English used by New Zealanders, including the very large body of written expression belonging to all geographical varieties of the language. It is not difficult to find New Zealand literary works which either in their entirety (especially shorter poems) or for many pages at a stretch are written solely in the common core of international English, with nothing identifiably or uniquely New Zealand in their language. Frequently, however, the writing is clearly recognisable as New Zealand in origin, through linguistic features of NZE in a narrower (and more usual) sense, that is those by which New Zealanders' use of English is distinguished (sometimes along with Australian English) from other regional dialects of the language. These features may be highly conspicuous (as in representations of colloquial New Zealand speech or in works by or about Māori), or at the other extreme present only sparingly in local usages (for example in Katherine ★Mansfield's ★'Her First Ball', where only the reference to Leila's 'sitting on the veranda … listening to the baby owls crying "More pork" in the moonlight' indicates a New Zealand rather than European setting).

An antipodean setting can be established by means other than the use of peculiarly New Zealand words or place names, as Maurice *Duggan shows at the beginning of 'O'Leary's Orchard', with its description of 'a wind of incredible bitterness ... blowing from the south west, carrying from grinding ice floes ... a few penguin feathers'. Some New Zealand writers in the past appear to have deliberately eschewed a strong local flavour in their language, often to avoid alienating the wider readership implied by overseas publication. The monologue and dialogue of Ian *Cross's The *God Boy (1958), for example, are natural enough, but contain virtually no distinctive New Zealand idiom; the contrast with a slightly later novel narrated by a young adolescent, Ronald Hugh *Morrieson's The *Scarecrow (1963), which is rich in Kiwi colloquialism, is striking.

Linguists commonly refer to three levels of language structure for analytic purposes: pronunciation, grammar and vocabulary. Of these, pronunciation and vocabulary are the most important in differentiating among the regional dialects of English, but only the distinctive vocabulary and idiom of these varieties are able to be fully and freely incorporated in literary discourse, if authors so wish. This is because characters' accents are notoriously difficult to render using the normal resources of English spelling, especially for serious purposes. Established and 'respectable' British accents such as Scots and Irish have often been portrayed in literature through selective respelling, even if this makes for heavy going for the reader. Most regional forms of English speech, however, including New Zealand's, have traditionally been stigmatised as degenerate and uncouth, and attempts to suggest pronunciation usually have only comic and satiric effect, as with Constable Ramsbottom in The Scarecrow, whose broad Kiwi 'Oi', 'moi', 'toipewriting', etc., sabotage his attempts at polite discourse.

In fact, many of the key features of the New Zealand accent (which is itself variable) cannot be conveyed at all by this kind of respelling (the fronted long vowel of farm and last, for example), and most writers wisely make no attempt to represent local pronunciation. Occasional instances can be found, as when Sergeant Robbie refers to 'those jokers down at Wullington' in Bruce Mason's The *End of the Golden Weather, or in the common rendering of a Māori-accented pronunciation of 'fellow' as 'fulla(h)' or 'fullar'. Some writers have tried to reproduce other (real or supposed) characteristics of Māori English pronunciation: '"I don' t'ink you like t'at pakeha fullar no more, eh? ... I t'ink you like this fullar best, eh?"' (Maurice *Shadbolt, 'The Woman's Story'); or 'Hey! You fullas' little brother, he done a mimi. Na!' (Patricia *Grace, 'Valley').

New Zealand writers, especially from Frank *Sargeson's time on, have frequently been praised for their skill in imparting to their characters an authentically and recognisably Kiwi speaking voice. The praise is well merited, but critics sometimes mistakenly imply that the accent itself is explicitly reflected in the writing. One asserts of Ma Poindexter in The Scarecrow that her 'accent is broad Kiwi', whereas only universal features of English colloquial and non-standard pronunciation are written into her speech (elisions, unstressed forms like 'yuh', etc.). Given her social class and the novel's setting, a broad New Zealand accent can be projected appropriately on to the character's written speech, but it is not overtly marked in the text itself. There have been similar misinterpretations of the non-standard syntax commonly found in representations of demotic and juvenile New Zealand speech (such as Else's 'I seen the little lamp' at the end of Mansfield's 'The *Doll's House'). The traditional disparagement of NZE as non-standard has sometimes led to any non-standard construction of the language being read as indicative of New Zealand origin. Features such as double negation, 'ungrammatical' verb and pronoun forms, adjectives used adverbially, etc., function in characterisation as indicators of class and education, and lend verisimilitude to the dialogue, but they are not exclusive to New Zealand use, merely part of the international component of NZE referred to earlier.

Since its accent cannot satisfactorily be rendered in writing, and its grammar is rarely divergent, it follows that it is the distinctive lexical items and idiom of NZE that most clearly and most often reflect a New Zealand identity in and authorship of literary works. One part of the singularity of the New Zealand vocabulary consists in terms without equivalents in other varieties of English, deriving from the uniqueness of New Zealand as a place, the interaction of its two principal cultures, and the development of its own social institutions and customs. Another part is made up of words and expressions, particularly in informal use, which are merely local variants for universal sentiments and experiences.

Mistaken views of New Zealand usage as largely a collection of slang items have often obscured the full range of its distinctive items. The range is such that New Zealandisms will be found in all literary styles and modes, sometimes without readers (and perhaps even authors) being aware that expressions peculiar to New Zealand are being used.

Many changes can be observed throughout the development of New Zealand literature in the kinds of New Zealand words that are found and the manner of their use. The self-conscious, sometimes clumsy highlighting of New Zealand landscape terms in what Eileen *Duggan called the 'physiographical rhapsodies' of colonial and early twentieth-century writers has often been noted. So too has the achievement of Katherine Mansfield in providing a model for a more natural amalgamation of local expressions with the rest of the English text, as argued by Ian ★Gordon in the *New Collins Concise* dictionary (New Zealand edition 1982). A reluctance to give New Zealandisms unqualified admittance to the literary language remained for some, however, as seen in Jean ★Devanny's *The ★Butcher Shop* (1926), with its frequent use of inverted commas for farming and colloquial terms ('lambing', 'sheepo', 'cobber'). In the 1930s and 40s the growth of a more realistic, down-to-earth fiction embodying the voice of the 'ordinary', often down-at-heel New Zealander brought much more of the characteristic Kiwi vocabulary into natural literary use than previously, with Sargeson's short stories setting a most influential example. Sargeson's colloquialism was still quite decorous, though, and it was not until the more liberated 1960s and 70s that the writer who wished could mine the more indelicate layers of New Zealand slang and vulgarism, now collected in David McGill's *Dictionary of Kiwi Slang* and *Dinkum Kiwi Dictionary*).

Poets as well as fiction-writers in recent decades have exploited the whole range of New Zealand expression. Perhaps the most spectacular example of this was James K. ★Baxter, whose increasingly uninhibited use of language often encompassed New Zealand terms, from the botanical to the colloquial and the indigenous. Baxter's broad Kiwi style is seen in lines such as 'dark as a dunny the under-runner' ('Never no more') and 'drunk / In Devonport on Dally plonk' ('Letter to Sam Hunt'), and in references to various ★'Pig Island' institutions ('The Plunket nurse ran in / to scissor off my valued foreskin', in 'Letter to Robert Burns'). In short, New Zealandisms of all kinds, including place and other proper names, are now part of a reader's normal expectations of New Zealand writing, though the words used are rarely more than a tiny percentage of the writer's total vocabulary.

The most recognisably NZE words are those drawn from Māori, and this is the grouping whose representation in literature has undergone the greatest changes in recent times. For the greater part of the twentieth century Māori words were used almost exclusively by Pākehā writers and rarely ranged beyond well-established names of indigenous flora and fauna and familiar cultural terms. (William ★Satchell's *The ★Greenstone Door* is one exception.) Words were commonly treated as unassimilated and 'foreign', with italicisation or footnoting employed and end-of-text glossaries provided. These practices were no doubt often editorial rather than authorial in origin, especially with overseas publication. From the 1970s onward, however, the growth of literary writing by Māori, as one manifestation of the Māori cultural renaissance, has brought both significantly more native vocabulary into literary use and greater acceptance of Māori as an integral part of the language of New Zealand literature. Since Māori characters and settings are central rather than peripheral in this writing, a greater range of native words has been required in order to convey with sufficient authenticity in English texts the cultural situation, the thoughts and the speech of Māori. Normal processes of lexical borrowing have given way to virtually limitless possibilities for transferring Māori into English, not only in single word items but also in the form of phrases, sentences and even substantial passages as the occasion demands, reflecting the code-switching habits of bilingual authors and their characters.

At the same time italicisation and footnoting of Māori words have largely disappeared, though in some cases glossaries are still provided as a concession to Pākehā readers where extensive Māori is used (in Keri ★Hulme's *the ★bone people*, for example). Some writers have been more inclined to ease the difficulty of Māori lexis for Pākehā readers than others. Witi ★Ihimaera often integrates explanation and 'translation' into his narration and dialogue: 'his tokotoko, his walking stick'; 'it was the manawa, the heart of the whanau, the heart of the family' ('Fire on Greenstone'). Patricia Grace on the other hand in her recent books leaves her Māori largely unglossed, as a challenge to and learning experience for the monolingual reader (see for example ★*Potiki*). The use of English–Māori code-switching to include some New Zealand readers and exclude others may be seen as a marker of the more politicised nature of recent Māori writing.

NZE like New Zealand literature now has a history, and like the English vocabulary as a whole the body of distinctive New Zealand expressions has been subject to both obsolescence and growth in response to social change. Thus New Zealand words may be a significant part of a text's period flavour, as in Gordon ★Slatter's novels or Sargeson's stories, which record a variety of now dated slang and other terms ('benzine', 'bosker', 'deener', 'a skinner', 'counter-lunch', 'Art Union'). Moreover words associated with earlier periods constitute one of the means available to a writer wishing to recreate an earlier New Zealand era for fictional purposes, as in Maurice ★Gee's ★*Plumb*, for example, or the historical novels of Shadbolt. In this connection we may observe a symbiotic relationship between New Zealand literature and the New Zealand ★dictionaries, especially Harry ★Orsman's historical *Dictionary of New Zealand English* and those leading to its publication. Literary works provide the lexicographer with a wealth of citable evidence for the currency and meanings of local expressions in all fields and styles. (Sargeson and Slatter are much mined.) Dictionaries for their part offer valuable elucidation of literary usages which may be difficult for the ordinary reader by reason of obsolescence, novelty or general unfamiliarity. TD

New Zealand Forest and River Magazine was published by the New Zealand Forestry League 1922–23. Edited by Will *Lawson, it featured articles on forestry, acclimatisation, and conservation, and a small amount of verse by Lawson and O.N. *Gillespie. It was incorporated, with many of its concerns intact, into *New Zealand Life* which in turn became *New Zealand Magazine*. SH

New Zealand Fortnightly Review was published in Auckland by its editor W.R. Kingsford-Smith June–September 1933. In addition to articles on the political and economic situation, it published short stories, poetry and reviews by contributors such as A.R.D. *Fairburn and C.R. *Allen. SH

New Zealand Home Journal was a monthly magazine published in Christchurch 1934–74. It featured short fiction by Dorothy *Eden, Grace Phipps, Jillian Squire and Jean Boswell. A magazine with the same title appeared in Auckland 1907–11. SH

N.Z. Home Life: *New Zealand's Family Paper* was a short lived women's magazine published in Wellington during the summer of 1927–28. Its slight literary content included a story by Joyce *West and an article by Will *Lawson. SH

New Zealand Illustrated Annual was published in Christchurch for only two volumes, 1880–81. The contents include poems by Thomas *Bracken, one of them a long narrative called 'Waipounamutu'. There are short stories by C.L. Innes, Marsden Mott, Vincent *Pyke, H. B. Marriott *Watson and others, almost all of them conforming to a curiously uniform plot-line: a rich father refuses to let his son marry a poor girl and in most cases disinherits him, whereupon the girl either scorns or pities the now poor lover until some kind of happy end eventuates. An exception is an anonymous story of a child lost in the Australian bush. NW

New Zealand Illustrated Magazine, a monthly published in Auckland 1899–1905, featured New Zealand poetry, stories, articles and illustrations, including half-tone photo-engravings of work by several nineteenth-century New Zealand landscape painters. A commitment by the founding editor, F.E. *Baume, to producing a magazine with 'a distinctly New Zealand colouring' (see *Nationalism) led to contributions by Jessie *Mackay, B.E. *Baughan, Jane *Mander, Edith Searle *Grossman, Alan *Mulgan, Edith *Lyttleton ('G.B. Lancaster'), Will *Lawson, Alice *Kenny, Isabel Cluett, Dora *Wilcox, Clara *Cheeseman, Charles Owen, A. E. *Currie, James *Cowan, Elsdon *Best, Apirana *Ngata, Johannes C. *Andersen, A. H. Messenger, plus work by the artist Frances *Hodgkins and the cartoonist Kennaway *Henderson. An index was compiled by G.C. Heron in 1943. SH

New Zealand Life, see **New Zealand Magazine**.

New Zealand Listener, The, has made a unique contribution to literary life since its first issue on 30 June 1939. It need not have been thus. Established as a weekly magazine by the then National Broadcasting Service under James Shelley, its brief was restrictive: 'The journal is a broadcasting publication and everything in it (apart from advertisements) should have a fairly direct connection with broadcasting.' The first editor, Oliver *Duff, interpreted broadcasting in its widest sense, however, as having to do with all human affairs but especially the arts; he knew, too, that offering readers good writing of all kinds would give the magazine character and distinction (and support to struggling writers). Accordingly, the first issues included reviews of books ranging from New Zealand mountaineering and education to international affairs, English poetry and Russian fiction. The early short stories, as a kind of conquest by stealth, were mainly light-hearted pieces about the disruptive effects of radio on domestic life; the first, by G.M. Glanville, came in August 1939, the second, by Isobel *Andrews (who was to contribute many fine stories and poems over the years), a month later. The same issue carried the first adult poem, a piece of whimsy called 'The Stein Song' by 'Magnus'. Shortages caused by war soon imposed constraints, but the pattern had been established: reviews of fiction, poetry and non-fiction across a broad range were acceptable, as were occasional short stories and poems.

Even at the height of the paper shortage in 1942–43, when book reviews had to be limited to every few issues, the focus remained on New Zealand titles, especially imaginative writing and social and cultural issues addressed in *Centennial publications, while reviewers still received enough space to develop their ideas. Short fiction continued, much of it of the 'magazine' kind: entertaining and easy to read, but unmemorable. Work by writers of more enduring reputation also appeared, however: stories by Frank *Sargeson and A.P. *Gaskell as early as 1940, by Roderick *Finlayson in 1944 and

Janet *Frame in 1946. The poetry was equally various, from R.A.K. *Mason's 'On the Swag' (1941) and Ruth *Dallas's 'Milking Before Dawn' (1947) to the satiric topical verse of *'Whim-Wham' (Allen *Curnow), taking in A.R.D. *Fairburn and Denis *Glover, J.R. *Hervey and Ruth *Gilbert on the way.

An early (June 1941) sign of reader response was the publication of several poems under a rubric noting 'the great increase in the number of people offering us verses … because they express emotions that most people at present share, it is sometimes a public service to print things that, on their technical merits alone, would not be worth space …', thus establishing a *Listener* tradition of presenting 'popular' poetry—and fiction—which arises out of and captures aspects of the public mood. For many, the magazine provided their only regular exposure to contemporary New Zealand writing; their reactions to some of it periodically erupted in letters to the editor complaining about the lack of rhythm and rhyme and the 'cult of obscurity' in verse (Anton *Vogt's work attracted this charge as early as 1941), and the 'extreme introspection … long screeds of highly private musing, soul-searching and applied psychology' of the fiction (1946). For one 1944 correspondent, 'the short story in our country is in the hands of a coterie of snobs who believe that the sham artistry of a conscious literary style is the sole stock-in-trade of a storyteller'. The debates that ensued, which attracted contributions also from well-known writers and critics, have been a continuing feature of the correspondence columns.

By the time Duff retired in 1949, the *Listener's* literary tradition was firmly established among readers (though not always appreciated in broadcasting). It was the twenty-year editorship of his successor, Monte *Holcroft, which cemented that tradition in place. Holcroft believed that 'the official journal of the NZ Broadcasting Service had a duty to foster imaginative writing', not only to help the NZBS play its part as New Zealand's largest patron of the arts but also to form a pool of talent on which it could draw; the magazine in turn would provide an outlet and source of income for writers, and a forum for discussion of New Zealand's emerging cultural identity. Short stories were soon appearing almost every week: some by well-known writers, others by newcomers getting established (O.E. *Middleton, Amelia *Batistich, Maurice *Duggan, Maurice *Shadbolt, Alice Glenday, Helen *Shaw, Phillip *Wilson, Noel *Hilliard, Albert *Wendt, Joy *Cowley); some were excellent magazine stories (by Marie Bullock, Thomas Hindmarsh, 'Augustus' (R.A. *Copland), Philip *Mincher), others had a promising vitality. Poems too were appearing in all sorts of corners throughout the magazine, with poets as various as Curnow, Glover,

Vogt, James K. *Baxter, Alistair *Campbell, Basil *Dowling, Gloria *Rawlinson, Ruth *France, M.K. *Joseph, Keith *Sinclair, Kendrick *Smithyman, Marilyn *Duckworth, Barry *Mitcalfe, C.K. *Stead, Louis *Johnson, Peter *Bland (whose poem written out as prose by one correspondent sparked a memorable debate on the nature of poetry), Kevin *Ireland, W.H. *Oliver, Hone *Tuwhare, Fleur *Adcock, J.E. *Weir and Peggy *Dunstan appearing regularly.

Book review space was generous and given first to New Zealand books of all kinds, but especially to fiction and poetry. A Holcroft editorial in November 1961 noted with pride that the *Listener* had been able to devote its books pages entirely to New Zealand work in the previous four weeks (reviewing thirty books in total, compared with fifty-seven, including nine novels, throughout 1960) and observed that, whereas New Zealand books had earlier received 'isolated and indulgent treatment', there was now 'a growing company of writers who expect and deserve to be taken seriously'. Regular reviewers included Alan *Mulgan, Baxter, John *Pascoe, David Hall, J.C. *Reid, James *Bertram, J.C. *Beaglehole, F.L.W. Wood, Randal *Burdon, Joan *Stevens, Barry *Mitcalfe, Margaret *Orbell, Christine Cole (later *Catley, on children's books), W.B. Sutch, Owen Jensen, Dennis *McEldowney, Stuart Perry and George Dallard. Using respected regular reviewers helped to cultivate a consistent critical standard, but by the mid-1960s a certain sameness was evident and some reviewers were being regularly attacked by correspondents.

At Holcroft's retirement in 1967 (and despite periodic assaults by the broadcasting bureaucracy, aggrieved literary coteries and perplexed readers), the *Listener* had long occupied a central place in the publication and evaluation of New Zealand writing. Subsequent editors have been made acutely aware of that position, which has been maintained, more or less, ever since. It did waver under Holcroft's erratic successor, Alexander McLeod (1967–72), when publication and reviewing of poetry became sporadic while short stories and letters on literary matters virtually disappeared. These traditions were restored by Ian *Cross (editor 1973–77), who also developed McLeod's use of review articles and literary features, including profiles of New Zealand writers; he introduced a weekly 'Bookmarks' column (initially by Michael *King and subsequently by Bert Hingley, Fiona *Kidman, Michael *Gifkins, Robin *Dudding and Graham Adams until it was stopped in 1994) serving as a kind of national literary noticeboard and forum for discussion of current issues; also brief 'New Zealand notes' reviews (by Ian Mackay from 1977, and Dale Williams from 1982) to keep up with burgeoning local publishing. The greater complexity of the *Listener* as its circulation and size grew meant that Cross's successor, Tony Reid (1977–80), passed the selection of imaginative writing and commissioning of book reviews over to a separate literary editor, Vincent *O'Sullivan (1979–80). Writers whose work began appearing regularly during the 1970s included Bill *Manhire, Margaret *Sutherland, Witi *Ihimaera, Sam *Hunt, Ian *Wedde, Brian *Turner, Patricia *Grace, Jack *Lasenby, Elizabeth *Smither, O'Sullivan, Kidman, Tony *Beyer, Lauris *Edmond, Rachel *McAlpine, Gary *Langford, David *Hill, Norman *Bilbrough, Anne *French and Owen *Marshall. Two collections of *Listener* short stories, chosen by Manhire, were published (1977 and 1978); the first included A.K. *Grant's unrivalled 'An Inquiry into the Construction and Classification of the New Zealand Short Story' (1973).   Regular reviewers depended on editorial preference, but at different times included Peter Cape, Janet Maconie, P.J. Downey, Marilyn *Duckworth, Les Cleveland, Roger *Hall, Pamela Cunninghame, Hill, Stephen O'Regan, Tony Simpson, David McGill, King, Philip *Temple, Elizabeth Caffin, Alan Roddick, Keith *Ovenden, Ray Knox, Bruce *Mason, Sheila Natusch, Natasha *Templeton, Hirini *Mead, Sue *McCauley and Lydia Wevers. A special feature of this era was the guest editorial, as Reid commissioned a number of established writers (such as Lauris Edmond) to write on topics of their choice. The results were often influential or controversial, as well as eloquent. Reid and O'Sullivan introduced a weekly poem 'slot', a six-weekly digest review of children's books (by Vivienne Joseph), and multiple reviewers, whether joint or independent, of significant New Zealand books. These were continued by O'Sullivan's replacement, Andrew Mason, whose ten-year term (1981–91) provided continuity amid editorial change. The *Listener's* huge readership (over one million) and size (regularly 160 pages) in the early 1980s imposed an obligation to make literary coverage as inclusive as possible; both review articles and grouped brief notices were extended and, in a controversial move reflecting the growing diversity of New Zealand publishing, the range of reviewers was widened to allow more representation of specific gender and ethnic approaches. Comprehensive treatment of children's books was provided by, in turn, Dorothy Neal *White, Diane Hebley, Ruth Halliday, Celia Dunlop and Kathryn du Fresne. Favourable reader response enabled the inclusion of more writer profiles, notably by Marion McLeod. Poetry maintained its traditional place, but a series of harried features editors determined that space available for fiction was limited. Newer writers who began to appear during the 1980s included Shonagh *Koea, Lloyd *Jones, Gifkins (who

edited *Listener Short Stories 3*, 1984), John *Cranna, Anne *Kennedy, Fiona *Farrell, Mike *Johnson, Sue *Reidy, Chris *Else, Michael *Henderson, Kate *Flannery, Damien *Wilkins, Ian *Richards, Cilla *McQueen, Gregory *O'Brien, Dinah *Hawken, Anthony *McCarten, Bernadette *Hall, Robert *Sullivan and Bub *Bridger. As circulation began to fall from the mid-1980s and other periodicals started to compete in literary treatment, so the *Listener's* wider role as patron came to be emphasised: in sponsoring events, notably the annual Women's Book Festival, and devoting space and time to literary awards.

After the magazine was sold to Auckland's Wilson & Horton in 1990, perceived commercial considerations and a smaller format severely constrained literary coverage. Poetry and fiction became very occasional. Under arts editor Vanya Shaw (1991–93), what books space remained was given over to short articles and visual display as much as to reviews. The New Zealand focus was maintained under arts editor Chris Bourke after 1993, but space constraints limited breadth and depth.

The *NZ Listener* 'set out to give strength and character to New Zealand literature' (Holcroft, 1992) and achieved that when no other institution could. Its decline in more fragmented times has enabled various small literary or review magazines to spring up. But these are of low circulation and limited resources; what has been lost is the incalculable benefit of regular exposure to imaginative writing and literary discussion for a mass readership.

The Listener Bedside Book (ed. Mary Crockett, Paul Little and Terry Snow, 1997) is 'a subjective collection of pieces that were felt worthy to be included in the first anthology of *Listener* journalism'.   AM

New Zealand Literary Fund, see **Literary Fund**.

New Zealand Literature: A Survey (1959), was E.H. *McCormick's revision and expansion of his earlier volume *Letters and Art in New Zealand*, which in turn had been his contribution to the *Centennial surveys of New Zealand life published in 1940. Although not large, these two volumes, one after the other, were the standard reference works on the subject for some forty years. Today they can still be looked at for their 'survey' quality and especially for the acute, concise critical judgments they contain. Bibliographical, historical and critical resources have grown enormously since their publication, yet they hold their own as historical documents.

McCormick's generous inclusion of ethnological writing—*Grey, *Dieffenbach, *Shortland and others—as 'literature' in his early chapters has since remained an important aspect of the general image of 'New Zealand literature'. In the earlier decades there is no absolute distinction between fact and fiction. Whether a 'narrative' is autobiographical or fiction is not always easy to determine (e.g. *Maning), and most of the early novelists included a 'Preface' assuring their readers that everything in their (often bizarrely imaginative) books is simple fact.

It is also refreshing that McCormick simply ignores the vociferous claims of some New Zealand writers to have their own work seen as the 'first' New Zealand literature, by giving pre-1920s literature all the attention it deserves (but no more). In the 1940 book he does single out the fiction of the 1930s as more interesting than its predecessors but in 1959 he finds that many of the relevant writers had not fulfilled their promise (there were worthy exceptions: *Davin, *Courage and *Ballantyne), but he tried to whip up his own enthusiasm by finding yet another new beginning taking place at the end of the 1950s.

There are gaps in McCormick's vision. In particular he virtually ignores drama and theatre. He has also been accused of emphasising the masculine at the expense of the feminine, but an examination of the index to his *Survey* hardly seems to justify that claim. It is true, however, that the proportions in Joan *Stevens's history of the novel are significantly different and that McCormick is more likely to include a tale of wild adventure than a temperance novel.

Whatever the reservations, McCormick provided the first overview of the topic, one that is still useful, and in a style so lively that the reader might well be tempted to search more widely and deeply in the original materials —the best compliment one can make to a book of this kind. NW

New Zealand Magazine, The, (1) was a quarterly published in Wellington in 1850 for only two issues, It was the country's first literary and 'scientific' journal. It contains articles on geology by Richard *Taylor and Walter Mantell and, most remarkably, a densely argued attack on E.G. *Wakefield's system of colonisation written by William Swainson. Literary content is limited to a few poems, some translations from the Māori and two 'French Tales' whose author and translator remain anonymous. NW

New Zealand Magazine (2) was published in Wellington under various titles 1921–52, edited by Maurice Hurst. Begun as *New Zealand Life*, from early 1923 it was titled the *New Zealand Life and Forest Magazine* (or similar) after absorbing the *New Zealand Forest and River Magazine*. After also incorporating *New Nation* into its pages in 1925, from 1926 the magazine

reverted to its original title, *New Zealand Life*. Finally, in early 1930 it adopted its longest-held title, *New Zealand Magazine*. Contributors to early issues include Blanche *Baughan, Johannes C. *Andersen, Alan *Mulgan and A.H. Messenger. As *New Zealand Magazine* it added A.R.D. *Fairburn, Dulce *Carman, C.R. *Allen, Pat *Lawlor, Hector *Bolitho, James *Cowan and David *Ballantyne. SH

New Zealand Mercury was a monthly published in Wellington by its editor Helen Longford 1933–36. Initially cyclostyled but later printed, the *Mercury* was always open to experiments in Modernist verse but tended to be dominated by a conservative *Georgian poetic, exemplified in its pages by the work of Arnold Cork and C.R. *Allen. Longford's desire to provide an outlet for budding talent bore fruit with the publication of work by poets who were later to gain prominence, including Denis *Glover, Ian *Milner and Douglas *Stewart. SH

New Zealand Monthly Review, a leftist-Marxist journal of comment founded 1960, published or influenced many writers in its first two decades under the editorship of H. Winston *Rhodes. James K. *Baxter, Janet *Frame and Louis *Johnson were among the poets, as well as Riemke *Ensing, Bernard *Gadd, John *Summers and many more, and Baxter's 'Ballad of the Junkies and the Fuzz' and 'Ballad of Stonegut Sugar Works' were published there in Nov.–Dec. 1969. There were articles by Rewi *Alley, Charles *Brasch, Sarah *Campion, Lauris *Edmond, John A. *Lee, Elsie *Locke, Ian *Milner (struggling to accept the Warsaw Pact destruction of the Prague Spring's liberalism in 1968), and others. In the 1970s–early 80s it published David *Eggleton, Michael *Harlow, Gary *Langford, Barry *Southam and others, but it lost its centrality to the major intellectual issues of the day and became more predictable, and in literary terms lightweight. RR

New Zealand National Review was a politically independent monthly published 1917–51. Early issues featured syndicated stories by authors such as W. Somerset Maugham, but with the appointment of Noel Holmes as editor in 1949 work by G.R. *Gilbert, Rewi *Alley and Louis *Johnson began to appear. SH

New Zealand New Writing appeared in four issues in Wellington 1942–45. Published by the *Progressive Publishing Society and edited by Ian *Gordon in emulation of John Lehmann's *Penguin New Writing* (a British publication which had included work by Frank *Sargeson, Allen *Curnow, Roderick *Finlayson, Denis

*Glover and other New Zealand writers), it was an important outlet for local writing during World War 2. Featuring poetry, fiction and criticism by a host of new and established writers, it developed into a very profitable venture for its publishers, thus ensuring it survived their initial intention that it be primarily an outlet for social-realist poetry and writing. Unlike the publishers (and unlike the parallel publication *Australian New Writing*), Gordon pursued a non-political policy, although he preferred a colloquial realism in style. It included work by Sargeson, Curnow, A.R.D. *Fairburn, Kendrick *Smithyman, Keith *Sinclair, Hubert *Witheford, David *Ballantyne, Helen *Shaw, Bill *Pearson, Isobel *Andrews, A.P. *Gaskell, J.R. *Hervey, G.R. *Gilbert, Anna *Kavan, Anton *Vogt, M.H. *Holcroft and Greville *Texidor. Many of these writers were in the armed forces, but the collection anticipated post-war, locally coloured realism.   SH

New Zealand Poetry Society was founded as the Wellington Poetry Society in May 1973 largely on the initiative of Irene Adcock, a published writer and mother of Fleur *Adcock and Marilyn *Duckworth. It now has members in other centres, thanks in part to grants from the Arts Council/Creative New Zealand. Presidents have been Irene Adcock, Lauris *Edmond, Joan Reid, Harry *Ricketts, Bill *Sewell, Cyril Childs, Vivienne *Plumb and Nelson Wattie. Patrons are Alistair *Campbell and (from 1996) Lauris Edmond. The society now focuses on New Zealand poetry and provides a platform for newer poets, though previously it also featured readings of such poets as Hardy or *Lawrence, topics such as War poetry or *Pacific poetry and performance-readings by students of the New Zealand Drama School/Toi Whakaari. In the late 1980s the Society organised regional Orbital Workshops and supported the magazine *Spin*. Later it gave endorsement to *Poetry New Zealand*. The monthly reading is usually by an established writer, frequently from outside Wellington, while members of the audience also present work, and occasional programmes such as 'An evening of Russian poetry' still broaden the range. The society organises an annual international poetry competition, publishing the best entries (*The Old Moon and So On*, 1994) and fosters a special interest in haiku, members such as Alan Wells and Barry Morrall being accomplished practitioners. *The New Zealand Haiku Anthology*, ed. Cyril Childs (1993) was well received. Other publications include *Frosted Rails* (1990) and *Black Before the Sun* (1993). A monthly newsletter publishes a small selection of poems. In 1995 the society promoted the 'Poetry in Motion' arrangement with the Stagecoach Company, for its buses to carry posters of short New Zealand poems. Poetry is also promoted in senior citizens' communities and elsewhere.   WS/RR

New Zealand Poetry Yearbook (1951–64) was started by Louis *Johnson to establish a more open and inclusive alternative to Allen *Curnow's rigorously selective *anthologies, especially the revised *Book of New Zealand Verse* (1951), which omitted developing poets like Johnson and Alistair *Campbell. *Landfall* was also seen as too prescriptive and coterie-conscious. About thirty to forty poets each year were included in the *Yearbook*, with a good balance between established and new and various features that added interest. In the early issues, about four poets were more fully represented for a 'closer view'; commentaries on different aspects of New Zealand poetry were written by people like Erik Schwimmer, Hubert *Witheford, Robert *Chapman and Charles *Doyle; there was a questionnaire one year (Vol. 4, 1954) where several of the poets commented on aspects of the national poetry scene; and Johnson provided an annual introduction, more, he said (Vol. 2), at the publisher's wish than his own. The *Yearbook* sought, successfully on the whole, to be 'revelatory rather than definitive', 'to bring the best of the year's work together', but to do so in a way free of orthodoxy or agenda. Volume 2 pointed out that it contained work from poets aged from under 19 to over 70. One introduction (Vol. 2, 1952) argued that 'it is impossible to talk about a direction' in New Zealand poetry, that this was 'a transitional period' with a 'lack of single purpose'; it denied the existence of 'groups' in the different main centres, though a later introduction (Vol. 7, 1957–58) found a particular vitality among new writers in Wellington.

The *Yearbook* provoked the resentments and faint praise of all enterprises which purport to select an elite, however generously. Curnow was predictably its strongest critic, reviewing Volume 1 in *Here & Now* as symptom of 'some stray local infection' from the English *Georgians, and 'not so remote … from the spirit [of *Kowhai Gold] as the accidents of style might suggest'. His review of Volume 2, again in *Here & Now*, was even more critical, in the form of a disparaging open letter to Louis Johnson. Johnson was relatively muted in reply, though Schwimmer's article in Volume 1 had attacked Curnow, and Johnson's introduction to Volume 8 (1958–59) argued forcefully that Curnow was out of touch with reality. Surveying the 1950s, this editorial also complained of the lack of real poetry criticism (as opposed to reviewing), and described with some pride the range of poets who had been represented in the *Yearbook*, including the increased proportion of women (thirty of 104; four more were added in the remaining three issues). We now recognise the inclusion of Alistair *Campbell, J.C. *Sturm, Hone *Tuwhare and the translations from the Māori of Barry *Mitcalfe as adding another significant dimension.

Writers like James K. *Baxter, Ruth *Dallas and M.K. *Joseph appeared often; but Johnson's catholic range can perhaps be illustrated by some of the very diverse new voices: Alistair *Paterson (Vol. 1), Elsie *Locke (Vol. 2), Iain *Lonie, John *Pascoe (Vol. 3), Richard *Packer (Vol. 4), Karl *Wolfskehl (Vol. 5), Peter *Bland, Janet *Frame, Philip *Temple (Vol. 7), Kevin *Ireland (Vol. 8), Frank *McKay, John *Weir (Vol. 9), Jack *Lasenby (Vol. 10), Ken *Arvidson, Sylvia *Ashton-Warner (Vol. 11). Johnson's enthusiasm may have been flagging, but the beginning of the end was the highly controversial withdrawal of the *Literary Fund grant for Volume 11 (1964) after he refused to remove six poems which had given offence to some members of the advisory committee, chaired then by Ian *Gordon. The poems were by Baxter, Packer and Martyn Sanderson, though it is not easy now to pick which ones were so repellent as to justify this *censorship. Margaret Dalziel of Otago University resigned in protest at the decision (which was on a 'divided vote') and M.H. *Holcroft, a member who supported the decision, unwisely attacked Johnson in the *NZ Listener.

Volumes 1–3 were published by *A.H. & A.W. Reed, the remaining eight by *Pegasus Press. When the concept was revived in 1971 it was as Poetry New Zealand, edited roughly biennially by Frank McKay, and published by *John McIndoe. Elizabeth Caffin became editor in 1984 and Alistair Paterson in 1994. All have followed Johnson in providing generously for lesser-known writers, though none has been as successful in gaining the prestige brought by the leading names of the day. Johnson's achievement was not only to broaden the range of poets considered prestigious or representative, but to broaden the base of readers by attracting those who welcome guidance in selecting 'the best of the year's work'. As editorial entrepreneurship in poetry, the Yearbook was not matched until Bill *Manhire's 100 New Zealand Poems (1993). RR

New Zealand Quarterly Review and Magazine of General and Local Literature was published in

Wellington for only three issues (Jan., April, July 1857). Despite its promising title, it contains little of literary interest—at most an article on Tennyson and a scathing review of Pemberton's *Happy Colony. For the rest it consists of general articles, for example on geology, with a strong bias towards the views of the Anglican church. NW

New Zealand Railways Magazine was published

in Wellington by the New Zealand Government Railways Department 1926–40. From an in-house journal it developed under the editorship of G.G. Stewart into one of the most popular monthlies of the 1930s. Pat *Lawlor ('Shibli Bagarag') contributed a regular book column in which he gave support to a limited range of New Zealand writers. James *Cowan's long-running series 'Famous New Zealanders' was an important contribution to New Zealand historical biography. A 'New Zealand Verse' column presented work by several important poets, including Denis *Glover and Robin *Hyde. Other notable contributors included C.R. *Allen, Winifred Tennant, O.N. *Gillespie, Isobel *Andrews, Isabel Cluett, Will *Lawson and Alan *Mulgan. SH

New Zealand Short Stories (1930), edited by

O.N. *Gillespie, was the first such *anthology of fiction. Like the verse collection *Kowhai Gold in the same year, it was published by J.M. Dent in London and aimed primarily at the English market. Though less infamous than Kowhai Gold became at *Curnow's hands, it is likewise now remembered only for the opprobrium heaped on it by the next generation. Robert *Chapman at the 1951 *Writers' Conference attacked its preface as conformist and dismissed Gillespie and Alan *Mulgan as 'literary pre-Adamites'. This is less than fair. The selection is broad and generous rather than conformist and Chapman's censure that it 'conforms to the major pattern and opinions of New Zealand life' is true only in its representation of the then broad tastes of a public much wider than one of chosen initiates into a literary orthodoxy, however supposedly radical. The whole argument of Gillespie's preface is that no single 'national outlook or distinctive atmosphere' can be identified. His second sentence stresses 'the extraordinary variety of subjects', and in 1930 this would indeed have struck English readers unfamiliar with Māori legends, the pragmatic feminism of Esther *Glen or Edith *Lyttleton ('G.B. Lancaster') (the majority of authors are women), *backblocks stories or the tough low-life yarns of Pat *Lawlor, Will *Lawson and 'Maori Mac'. While there are finely crafted fictions by B.E. *Baughan, Robin *Hyde (writing here as Iris Wilkinson) and Katherine *Mansfield ('The *Voyage'), the book generally treats the short story as a brief popular entertainment. Some stories, the preface admits, are included 'for their pictorial value rather than anything else about them'. Almost all had appeared, as most short stories then did, in newspapers, especially the *Bulletin and Christchurch *Sun. The success in 1997 of Graeme *Lay's 100 New Zealand

Short Short Stories suggests that more artistically highbrow views of the genre have not wholly prevailed, while Lawrence *Jones and others have recently celebrated 'the range of accomplishment' in New Zealand fiction in terms remarkably similar to Gillespie's.   RR

New Zealand Society of Authors (PEN NZ Inc), see **PEN (New Zealand Centre)**.

New Zealand Verse (1906), 'collected' by W.F. Alexander and A.E. *Currie is the first national *anthology of poetry and still the most useful starting point for the study of Victorian verse in New Zealand. Its 'Index of authors and bibliographical reference' suggests where the search might continue, and its informal introduction, determined not to exaggerate the importance of its subject matter, is still worth reading.

'... with a total population numbering in 1905 only nine hundred thousand souls ... there has existed right from the very beginning a tradition that it was a good thing to write poetry.... Every year now one or two fresh volumes come to the birth, and promptly die of neglect ... it is the conviction that some of them contain verse which at least comes well up to the level of modern minor poetry that has led to the making of the present collection.... And even the hardest-headed race of farmers and shepherds and workers in wood and metal has its dreamers and its seers of visions (and even sends some of them to Parliament).... [The poets] must in some sense be always among aliens...'

The editors note that certain subjects which might be expected—such as shipwrecks 'that have strewn our coasts since earlier days than the whalers', football and horses—are not represented, because no poet has written well enough of them. What is most typical, they say, is poetry of the *landscape (such as *Domett, *Adams, *Andersen and Hubert *Church) and of the seascape, as well as 'up-country pieces' (David McKee *Wright). They note the large number of verse retellings of Māori 'legends', but find none of them successful ('Domett lost his legend entirely in the intricacies of his poem').

The selection of poems seems as astute as the introductory comments. Although few of these fifty-five poets are read closely today, one of them is: Blanche *Baughan. Others—Alan *Mulgan, Jessie *Mackay, Arthur Adams, Alfred Domett, William Pember *Reeves, William *Satchell, Arnold *Wall, Thomas *Bracken, Edith *Lyttleton ('G.B. Lancaster')—still strike a chord in the literary memory of the country. In 1926 a 'revised and enlarged' edition—without the preface—was published by *Whitcombe & Tombs under the title *A Treasury of New Zealand Verse*.   NW

New Zealand Verse was a monthly published during 1934 by its editor, Mackellar Giles, and initially printed by him at his Handcraft Press in Oamaru. Largely set up as a source of income by the unemployed Giles, much of its contents were by the editor or the popular song writer James J. Stroud.   SH

New Zealand Wars, see **War literature: New Zealand Wars**.

New Zealand Wars trilogy, The, is a loosely linked trilogy of revisonist-historical novels by Maurice *Shadbolt, which comprises *Season of the Jew* (1986), *Monday's Warriors* (1990) and *The House of Strife* (1993), his eighth, ninth and tenth novels. While each is concerned with different characters and events, they share the three decades of conflict between Māori and the European colonisers now referred to as the New Zealand *Wars. At the centre of each is a major Māori historical figure, whose story is revealed through the sympathetic yet counterbalancing device of a Pākehā hero. *Season of the Jew* marks a new stage in Shadbolt's oeuvre, which leaves behind the metafictional exuberance of his treatment of nineteenth-century New Zealand history in his previous novel, *The *Lovelock Version* (1980), and instead treats history in a relatively straightforward fashion. Set in the 1860s, it tells the story of the Māori warrior-prophet *Te Kooti Arikirangi, founder of the Ringatu faith, largely from the perspective of George Fairweather, an erstwhile army regular, a landscape painter, and a liberal-humanist whose sympathies tend towards the Māori rather than the colonists. In *Monday's Warriors*, again set in the 1860s, Shadbolt retells the story of another warrior-prophet, Tītokowaru, in tandem with that of the rebel Pākehā Kimball Bent, a significant historical figure himself, who provides the sympathetic perspective earlier furnished by the composite character of Fairweather. In *The House of Strife*, the final volume of the trilogy, Shadbolt reaches still further into the past, to the 1840s and the early years of the New Zealand Wars, to take up the story of the celebrated axeman Hone Heke. Here Shadbolt's window to the past (and his link with the present) is the wonderfully realised Ferdinand Wildblood/Henry Youngman doppelgänger, who marks a fascinating progression from the narrators of the earlier volumes of the trilogy. Throughout the trilogy Shadbolt's historical detail is always meticulously researched, and incorporated into his story without ever interrupting the gusto of his narrative.   RC

New Zealand Women Writers' Society (originally (originally Writers' and Artists') was founded in Wellingtonin 1932 to encourage creative work in the arts and promote comradeship. Its presidents have included

Nelle *Scanlan, Celia *Manson, Ruth Mackay and Margaret Hayward. It published five issues of The *Quill (1934–38), including an early cyclostyled magazine in 1934, Poems: An Anthology by New Zealand Women Writers (1953), Women Writers of New Zealand, edited by Margaret Hayward and Joy *Cowley (1982) and History of New Zealand Women Writers' Society compiled by Thelma France et al. (cyclostyled). It assisted the *Alexander Turnbull Library to purchase Katherine *Mansfield manuscripts, marked Mansfield's birthplace and organised from 1959 the Katherine *Mansfield Memorial Awards. The prestigious awards have continued as a major function beyond the society's winding up in July 1991, and are now administered by a committee convened by Sonia Kellett.　　　　　　　　　　　　　　HM/RR

New Zealand Writers and Their Work (NZWW) was a series of critical studies of individual authors published by *Oxford University Press 1975–86. It was the first such series to be locally produced and marketed. Previously, from the 1960s, some New Zealand writers had been subjects in the Twayne's World Authors Series, mostly but not always examined by New Zealand critics. Published in New York, these made little impact in New Zealand. NZWW, initially under the general editorship of James *Bertram, comprised monographs of usually 60–75 pages with select bibliographies and a variable mix of critical and biographical material. Terry *Sturm, in the *OHNZLE (1991, 1998), is disapproving of a concept which tended 'to consolidate a smallish canon'. The time, however, was one of vibrant growth in local literature (see *PEN/Victoria University Writers Conference, 1979) without support from adequate criticism, scholarship or educational promotion. By comparison with the situation at that time in Australia or Canada, New Zealand literature was still on the peripheries of both public and academic attention, and serious study by critics of the substance of Bertram, R.A. *Copland, Margaret Dalziel, M.H. *Holcroft, Frank *McKay and Vincent *O'Sullivan did much to claim a more central place and fulfil the promise of 'a fresh assessment of … a rapidly-developing literature'. The titles still reward reading and, despite their brevity, some remain among the best available commentaries, such as Bertram on *Brasch, Copland on *Sargeson, Howard McNaughton on Bruce *Mason, O'Sullivan on *Baxter and Peter *Simpson on *Morrieson.　　RR

New Zealand Writers' Conference, 1951 (8–11 May) was part of Canterbury's centennial in 1950. It was funded by the Centennial Association and the *Literary Fund, and organised by Canterbury University English department members Professor John Garrett and

H. Winston *Rhodes. Among the writers, three distinct groupings soon emerged. An older group of 'Late Colonial' writers, consisting of Alan *Mulgan, Arnold *Wall, G.H. *Scholefield, P.A. *Lawlor, Johannes *Andersen and C.R. *Allen, were felt by younger writers to be a reactionary influence as editors and in positions of power on *PEN and the Literary Fund. A middle-aged group of men connected with *Phoenix, *Landfall and the *Caxton Press, who felt themselves the true initiators of indigenous writing, included Allen *Curnow, Charles *Brasch, Frank *Sargeson, James *Bertram and Denis *Glover. A third, younger group, mostly from Wellington, wanted to displace both sets of elders as arbiters of literary taste. Largely unpublished in book form, these were depicted in the Star Sun as a bunch of unshaven Bohemian arrivistes who wore strange garb. They included Louis *Johnson, James K. *Baxter, Alistair *Campbell, Pat *Wilson, Erik Schwimmer, John Reece *Cole and Anton *Vogt. 'Spike' (in *Gaudeamus May 1951) noted among the older generation a prevailing 'narrowness of outlook and a propensity for long-windedness not tolerated by younger generations'. Many of the 'old' men had not forgiven the 'middle' men for displacing them: Lawlor was contemptuous of Curnow's *Book of New Zealand Verse 1923–45, which severely culled early poetry; the names of Dan *Davin and Sargeson cut little ice with Lawlor. In a snap debate the younger men said that the Literary Fund was conservative and inaccessible, and PEN was old-fashioned.

A conservative Catholic, Lawlor suspected the morals of the younger men as evidenced by their work in Landfall, which he saw as having no regard for spiritual values; furthermore it was elitist and snobbish. He praised the government for closing down *Tomorrow, the radical paper of the middle group, for sedition in 1940, and he inflamed the conference by praising the government for its strong handling of the current *Waterfront dispute, which had almost kept the Wellington men at home. The younger men felt democracy itself to be under threat. The highlight came when the young and cherubic Baxter spoke on poetry and the artist's role in society. He traced an historical line of development from David McKee *Wright and Jessie *Mackay; he nodded reverently at those who had changed its direction through Phoenix and the Caxton Press; and he introduced the young Wellington poets whom he represented and who expected recognition for new themes and styles. He presented them as the first generation to free themselves from the 'schizophrenia' of the past and to have grown up accepting New Zealand as their true home. Baxter united the whole conference into a sense of common purpose. He was a splendid speaker and any doubts about the morals of the young were dispelled when he insisted that the artist must act as a 'cell of good living' in a corrupt society, and speak for the downtrodden.

Writers had a sociological role, a role which was given the status of holy writ by Robert *Chapman's seminal paper arising out of the conference: 'Fiction and the Social Pattern' (*Landfall* 25, 1951) prescribed that literature should hold a mirror up to the corrupt society, its themes must be 'the formative, constricting and distorting effect of the mores and values of New Zealand puritanism on our human scene', and its mode must be that of critical realism. This largely valorised the work of its chief practitioner, Sargeson, and sired a whole generation who wrote as they thought he wrote, and failed to notice that he was publishing nothing between 1951 and 1965, having come to the end of critical realism.

Post-1951 writers were to argue acrimoniously over subject matter, style, and who deserved inclusion in the canon, creating a lasting rift between Auckland (Curnow) and Wellington (Baxter, Johnson). Whatever divided them, however, writers agreed that society was philistine, hostile and miserly towards them, and most agreed that regardless of which men were in or out, nearly all women were out. Between *Authors' Week 1936, which celebrated a mainly female creative literature, and 1951, women's writing had been demoted by the middle generation of male writers as trivial, irrelevant or ill-disciplined. As literary arbiters, editors (Brasch), critics (Bertram, Curnow, Brasch), publishers and printers (Glover and Caxton), and compilers of influential anthologies (Curnow), this generation shaped the course literature was to take until the 1970s. Only then did women's writing begin its hard-fought move back in from the margins.　HM

New Zealand Writers' Week is a biennial festival held in Dunedin since 1989, the second major literary gathering to be held on a regular basis (after *Writers and Readers Week). It was initiated by Roger *Hall while he was at University of Otago, to 'celebrate New Zealand writing', after he had been 'irritated' by the media's preoccupation with overseas stars at the 1988 Writers and Readers Week. Writers, the book trade, local media (especially the *Otago Daily Times*) and audiences all responded positively, school groups travelling from around the country. Hall describes the week's success as making him 'as proud and excited as any play I've ever written'. He was again convener for an equally successful event in 1991, and the week continued from 1993 under Lynley Hood, renamed 'Wordstruck'.　RR

New Zealander originally (eighteenth and early nineteenth centuries) denoted 'a Māori', with contemporary synonyms 'Aborigine', 'Indian', 'Native' and occasionally 'Zealander'. With increasing European settlement after 1840, the term widened in application to include non-Māori immigrants and was replaced in its original reference by 'native' (in official use until 1947) or 'Māori'. From about 1850 and in modern use it is applied to a person born or resident in New Zealand or accepting New Zealand citizenship.　HO

New Zealanders, The (1959), is Maurice *Shadbolt's first collection of short fiction. Subtitled 'A Sequence of Stories', it is divided into three sections, 'Wave Walkers', 'Cloud Riders' and 'In the Blind Canyon', each of which takes its heading from the book's first epigraph, an excerpt from James K. *Baxter's poem *'In Fires of No Return'. Only two stories, 'After the Depression' and 'Play the Fife Lowly', had been published previously (both in *Landfall). Together the eleven stories chronicle a substantial part of New Zealand's twentieth-century social history. The first section focuses on the inter-war period, particularly the 1930s. Notable among the four stories in this section are 'The Woman's Story', which includes what is perhaps still Shadbolt's most convincingly realised female character, and 'After the Depression', which focuses on the social and political concerns of the 1930s. Those concerns would later resurface in the novel *Strangers and Journeys* (1972), where the short story's central character, Bill Morrison, reappears as Bill Freeman. The next two sections treat the post-war period of the late 1940s–50s (the period of Shadbolt's youth and his own expatriate experiences in Europe). Although some of these now seem dated, they clearly signal the direction of much of Shadbolt's subsequent writing. The overall scope of the stories is characteristically grand. From the pioneer farm of 'The Woman's Story' Shadbolt's sequence guides the reader along a carefully mapped journey, in time and space, through New Zealand and eventually back to England and Europe. The range of characters—male and female, Māori and Pākehā—is broad enough to carry this design. Along the way the stories, severally and together, explore the need for and emergence of a New Zealand cultural identity distinct from that of the imperial centre.　RC

NEWTON, John (1959–　), poet and critic, was born in Blenheim, completed an MA on contemporary New Zealand poetry at Canterbury University in 1987 and won the Macmillan Brown Prize for student writing three times. He taught English at the University of Melbourne 1993–94 while writing a PhD thesis on Sylvia Plath, and since 1995 has lectured in English at Canterbury. His poems have appeared in *Landfall, *Islands, *NZ Listener, *Untold, et al., and his collection, *Tales from the Angler's Eldorado* (1985), was also published by *Untold*. The title, taken from Zane Grey's utopian description of New Zealand in 1926 (see *Sport), is in ironic counterpoint to the poetry's unflinchingly realistic world of rural violence. Elizabeth Caffin writes that Newton 'uses the language and imagery of a later age to revisit the rural contexts of mid-century poets'; his explorations of the outdoors, resonantly expressed, emerge through well-worn themes of discovery and action: fishing, hunting, farming. Characteristic is the understated diction associated with regional South Island poetry, the habit of precise observation, the significant gesture. Newton's precise and vivid images evoke nature's unsentimental indifference: 'Twitch, with its vicious forked feet, / crawls between bricks'; they can transform nature into something more exotic : 'it's spring / and my corn shoots are opening like / parachutes, green and gold, four inches tall'; and often show empathy with the most insignificant of creatures: 'onto this lit plane of paper tumbles / a brown beetle, a winged chip of warmth, / of November'. Highlight of the collection is the long poem 'Night Fishing' reprinted in the 1989 Penguin anthology. As critic Newton has published on Bill *Manhire's poetry.   JW

Nga Mahinga ..., see *Mahinga ... , Ko nga*.

Ngā Mōteatea: ..., see *Mōteatea ..., Ngā*.

NGATA, Sir Apirana Turupa (1874–1950), was one of the greatest Māori leaders and scholars of the twentieth century. He was born to the Ngāti Porou in Te Araroa, a Māori community on the East Coast of the North Island, and educated there in both Māori and Pākehā knowledge and skills. After completing his BA at Canterbury University College, the first Māori to graduate from a New Zealand university, he moved to Auckland, where, in 1897, he gained his LLB and was admitted as a barrister and solicitor. In 1895 he married Arihia Kane Tamati, also of the Ngāti Porou and eventually became the father of eleven children (being the eldest of fifteen siblings himself).

His educational background and extraordinary charisma gave him sufficient *mana to challenge his elders on the *marae, although it was almost unprecedented for so young a man to do so, and, rather than pursuing the lucrative legal career that opened up for him, he devoted himself to Māori welfare at a time when his people were said to be a 'dying race'. In 1905 he became a member of parliament and remained one until 1943, being Minister of Māori Affairs (or the equivalent) 1909–12 and 1928–34. He was less concerned with party matters than with Māori ones and used his parliamentary position when it was useful to do so and

worked outside parliament when that seemed more fruitful. He is remembered for a wide range of activities but especially for his actions in relation to developing Māori lands. Under the stewardship of his father and then of himself, the Ngāti Porou lands were among the most productive and best managed in the country. He was also close to *Te Puea in developing Tainui lands. As early as 1900 he helped Sir James Carroll draft the Maori Lands Administration Act and in 1909 he assisted John Salmond in drafting the massive Native Land Act, while his own Maori Land Development Scheme of the 1930s led to areas of Māori land being the only exceptions in New Zealand to the general economic decline in the international *Depression. For him, land development was inseparable from developing Māori cultural activities of all kinds.

Ngata stimulated new interest in the Māori language and studied and publicised the history and traditions of all tribes or *iwi. He was president of the Polynesian Society for nine years and contributed major articles to its *Journal*; he helped found the Board of Maori Ethnological Research and initiated its publications, including the journal *Te Wananga*; he was chairman of the Geographic Board (responsible for New Zealand place names); he was a member of the Board of Trustees of the Dominion Museum; he was on the committee to revise the standard Māori *dictionary of *Williams; he encouraged Māori sports; he engaged in crafts, such as woodcarving, and encouraged schools for these to be developed; he was responsible for a revival in the various skills required to build 'meeting houses' and all other kinds of wharenui; he wrote *waiata and *haka, of which he was a notable performer; he was a major practitioner of *whaikōrero throughout the country; over forty years he collected and recorded hundreds of songs, some of which he published in the first two volumes of *Nga *Moteatea*, which he edited, and others of which were included in the subsequent volumes, edited by his protégé, Pei Te Hurinui *Jones; his translations made many aware of Māori literary traditions who might not otherwise have encountered them; after retirement he studied more closely the traditions of the Ngāti Porou and helped with revising the translation of the Bible; his essay 'Anthropology and Government of Native Races in the Pacific' (1928) is a classic study of the contact between the British government and Pacific peoples, and is only one example of his awareness of the place of Māori culture within the variety of cultures in the South *Pacific region; he was also the author of a well-known book on civic responsibility, focused on the award of the VC to the war hero Lieutenant Ngarimu, *The Price of Citizenship* (1943), and he contributed four chapters to *The Maori People Today*, a survey edited by I.G. Sutherland as part of the *Centennial publications of 1940.

In land development Ngata seemed to be everywhere, overseeing office administration and engaging in hands-on work, concerned with fertilisers, seeds, equipment, vehicles, livestock and labour. The land was cleared, ploughed, fenced and provided with crops and stock. Not all of those who helped were as efficient as he, and anomalies appeared in the books, for which he eventually took responsibility and resigned. His cultural work continued, however, unabated and with enormous energy until his physical condition deteriorated and he died after a short illness. Throughout his life he used his skills and knowledge of Pākehā culture to encourage the development of Māori culture across a very wide front. He was a literary figure of note, but it is impossible to separate his writing, composing, translating, performing and encouragement of others from his many other, interrelated achievements.   NW

NGĀWAI, Tuini, of the Ngāti Porou is a leading composer of songs and poetry in the Māori language. She has written some two hundred songs, sometimes to European music, sometimes to her own compositions. Her concise, forceful style of language is greatly admired. Her first song, 'He nawe kei roto', was written in 1933 and in 1934 'Karangatia Rā' (still popular today) was sung at the opening of Te Hono-ki-Rarotonga, Tokomaru Bay. (This was one of many carved houses built in the 1920s–30s under the inspiration of Apirana *Ngata to encourage Māori arts.) 'Arohaina Mai' was performed to farewell Ngāti Porou soldiers going to war in 1939, and sings of despair being calmed by God.

After the war Ngata, who greatly admired her work, arranged for her to teach action songs (*waiata-ā-ringa) and the language in East Coast schools. Although she knew many *pao and *pātere she did not teach them because of their *tapu nature.

The melodies she sets her words to are usually popular songs of the day—which has sometimes caused the value of the poems to be underestimated. Typically she writes of the traditional themes of love, death, war and peace, but there are also poems of the working and leisure-time life of the sheep-farming community at Tokomaru Bay where she lived. In commenting on the current interest in traditional *waiata Tīmoti *Kāretu (in *New Zealand Studies*, Vol. 5, No. 2, 1995) notes a contrast at Tokomaru Bay, where the people of the *marae 'rarely if ever sing traditional chants after *whaikōrero but rather sing the songs of Tuini Ngāwai and more recently those of her niece Ngoi *Pēwhairangi'.   NW

NICHOLAS, John Liddiard (d. 1868), was one of the earliest to record European impressions of New Zealand. A New South Wales settler and former London ironmonger, he accompanied Samuel *Marsden on his first voyage to New Zealand, December 1814–February 1815, to found the first Christian mission in New Zealand in the Bay of Islands. His *Narrative of a Voyage to New Zealand ...* (1817) recounts that visit with clearly described observations of the resident people he met from North Cape to the Hauraki Gulf. Written in an eighteenth-century style and referring to Rousseau when pondering his impressions of the Māori people, the book is almost as much about Nicholas's own preconceptions as Māori manners, customs, culture and values. Typical of his approach is his inclusion of an account of the massacre of the crew of the *Boyd* in 1809 by the chief perpetrator. Nicholas makes clear his abhorrence of the event, but is also at pains to present the reason the Whangaroa people had for acting as they did. A good travel book, *Narrative of a Voyage to New Zealand* also has ethnological and historical value. Nicholas returned to England in 1815.   RG

'Night Watch Song of the "Charlotte Jane", The' (or **'Night-Song ...'**), see **FITZGERALD, James Edward**; *Canterbury Rhymes*.

Niu Tirani, also variously 'Niu Tireni', 'Niu Tirini', 'Niutereni' or 'Nu Tirani', was the main early Maori name for *New Zealand; compare also *'Aotearoa'. The early variation Niu / Nu may derive from English variant pronunciations of 'New'. 'Ko te tahi wahi o Te Kawenata Hou ... Ka oti nei te wakamaori ki te reo o Nu Tirani ... ' (Title 1833, in Williams, *A Bibliography of Printed Maori*, 1975); 'Ka tiakina e te Kuini o Ingarani nga tangata maori katoa o Nu Tirani' (*Treaty of Waitangi*, 1840, in *Facsimiles Treaty Waitangi*, 1877, 1976); 'Niu Tirini is in a mist for the loss of his medicine' (*Taranaki Punch*, 19 Dec. 1860).   HO

No New Thing: Poems 1924–29, a collection of poems by R.A.K. *Mason, was published in Auckland in 1934. This book is one of New Zealand literature's tragi-comedies of errors. For years Mason tried publishing the collection in Britain and America. Hogarth, Chatto and the Atlantic Monthly Press were among those who rejected the manuscript. The poems were agreed to be bold and powerful but *Depression economics militated against unknown poets from New Zealand. Mason met Robert *Lowry through his printing of *Kiwi and *Phoenix, and so liked Lowry's clean, modern *typography and layout that he went into partnership with him as Spearhead Publishers. Spearhead existed only for

No New Thing, an artistic success but commercial fiasco. One hundred and·twenty copies were printed, of which a hundred were to be bound in a specially woven linen cloth (made by Marion Champ out of fishing twine); but the amount of cloth fell short, the binder's bill could not be paid and very few copies were completed. A few were produced later in different binding. Some confusion exists about how many got completed; perhaps as few as thirty. After the partnership between Mason and Lowry fell away, Lowry continued with Ronald Holloway as the Unicorn Press, which actually printed *No New Thing* (see also *Griffin Press). The best summary of the aesthetics of the book is Denis *Glover's. '… this is a book for the collector to prize for its appearance no less than its contents…. Mason's verse, always hard to set changing as it does from the ultra-short to full-measure lines, is ranged most happily on the vertical axis provided' (*Book* 8, August 1946). The failure of this ambitious publication must have hastened Mason's renunciation of poetry for theatre and political activism. But the intensity and economy of the poems (a carefully planned sequence), and the clean design and layout, set artistic standards for others, notably Glover and Leo *Bensemann of the *Caxton Press.   PS

No Ordinary Sun, poems (1964), see **TUWHARE, Hone**.

NOONAN, Diana (1960–), is a writer of fiction for children of all ages. Born in Dunedin and educated at Otago and Auckland universities and Auckland Teachers' College, she taught on the West Coast and in Balclutha before moving to the Catlins and virtual self-sufficiency in South Otago. She received a 1991 Children's Writing Bursary, and in 1993 was writer-in-residence at Dunedin College of Education.

Noonan's passion for environmental conservation pervades her fiction, from picture books and numerous readers to junior and young adult novels. Picture books include *The Last Steam Train* (1992), illustrated by Brent Putze; *The Fish are Jumping* (1992), illustrated by Tony Hadlow; *The Best-Loved Bear* (1994), illustrated by Elizabeth Fuller, which competitively ranks children's love according to the condition of their toys and won the 1995 Aim Picture Book Award; *Kangaroo Bill and the Forest behind the Bay* (1995), illustrated by Lyn Kriegler; and, for Telecom, *Dazzling Miss Dynamo* (1995), illustrated by Philip Webb.

Her junior novels include *Goodbye Toss* (1993), *The Deer* (1994), *Room 4 at Cattle Creek* (1994), *Danny to the Rescue* and *A Touch of Jungle Fever* (1995), all illustrated by Keith Olsen; and *A Dolphin in the Bay* (1993), a subtle, sensitive portrayal of self-discovery that won the

1994 Aim Junior Fiction Award. For teenagers, *The Silent People* (1990) evokes totara forests, burial grounds and yellow-eyed penguins, with memories also of the moa-hunter culture; *Leaving the Snow Country* (1991) and its sequel, *A Sonnet for the City* (1992), explore conflict in society's values, including political ideology; and *The Whaler's Garden* (1994), with historical reverberations, explores perceptions of identity through the relationship between a confused teenager and her aunt, a likeable, eccentric nun in a run-down religious retreat. Noonan works in Wellington as editor for the *School Journal*.   DH

Nor the Years Condemn (1938) was Robin *Hyde's fourth and last novel. Continuing the story of Starkie from *Passport to Hell* it depicts New Zealand society as derailed by World War 1 and the *Depression which followed the brief, illusory post-war boom. As in her other novels Hyde is arguing for community. Starkie, 'an unsolved problem' like many others who have returned to a country which does not seem to want them, wanders from place to place in search of freedom but his life of spasmodic work, drinking and fighting becomes a lonely one. There are brief moments of connection: with Bede Collins, his nurse; McNamara, the socialist visionary; and a young Māori woman Ritehei. In a series of *Observer* articles Hyde had argued for the return of land to the Māori. Here, again ahead of most contemporaries, she denounces their dispossession, their enforced dilemma in 'Trying to be *pakeha* … trying not to be *pakeha*.' Hyde is able to describe with equal clarity the physical landscape of mountains, tussock and wild open country and the swarming life and poverty of the city slums, pakapoo dens and pubs with their ephemeral promise of hope and community.

Hyde's condemnation of the exploitation of the working class and of women is particularly powerful in her portrayal of the Queen Street riots, so different from John *Mulgan's *Man Alone*, and the desolate description of a young woman who has swallowed lysol to end her life. Generally Hyde employs a laconic, blunt narrative style in keeping with her central character, but this varies in association with other characters. Likewise she combines narrative and reflection. The sweep of the novel, the correspondingly fragmentary structure and the multiplicity of voices and styles reinforce the novel's moving sense of dislocation.   GB

NORCLIFFE, James (1946–), poet and fiction writer, has taught English in Christchurch, China and Brunei. He followed his debut collection of poetry, *The Sportsman and Other Poems* (1986), with the successful *Letters to Dr Dee and Other Poems* (1993), which was shortlisted for the New Zealand Book Awards 1994. Described by David *Eggleton as an 'Absurdist's grab-bag of whatever is bumped up against that can be made to reveal the sheer numinous strangeness of existence, imagist-style', the collection contains traces of *China in 'a distilled Taoist influence' and poems that are 'fine-spun, like silk screens, or else transparent, like rice-paper' (*Quote Unquote, Apr. 1994). China also features in The Chinese Interpreter (1993), short stories based on cultural clashes Norcliffe observed while teaching English at Nankai University. These lucid, keenly observed narratives have proved popular on radio. Equally popular have been four novels for young adults: Under the Rotunda (1991) employs the powerful magic of an old cornet to restore to normal a brass band maliciously reduced to the size of carrots; Penguin Bay (1993) recounts the scary adventures of children holidaying in an old house on Banks Peninsula; The Emerald Encyclopaedia (1994)—honour award recipient at the 1995 Aim Children's Book Awards—a fantasy based in Christchurch that explores the manipulation of peoples' minds by those wanting control of the masses; and The Carousel Experiment (1995) chronicles a boy's search for his mother in the enigmatic Carousel Caravan Park. Norcliffe has won awards including the Lilian Ida Smith Award 1990 and the *NZ Poetry Society's international competition 1992.　　　　　　　　　　　　　PM

NORMAN, Philip (1953–), composer and music commentator, born in Christchurch, began his career in music theatre with a comic operetta, Crime Never Pays, written when he was 15 and left unfinished. He has become a leading writer of the genre with such popular successes as Footrot Flats (1983), book by Roger *Hall, lyrics by A.K. *Grant, based on cartoon characters by Murray Ball, and Love Off the Shelf (1984), again with Hall and Grant. This satirised the life of a writer of the popular *Mills & Boon series of romantic novels. It had its British première in Southampton in 1986. He has worked with Elric Hooper in Dunedin, written a doctoral thesis on the instrumental music of Douglas *Lilburn, been chief music critic for the Christchurch *Press and compiled an invaluable Bibliography of New Zealand Compositions (1991).　　　　　　　　　JMT

Not in Narrow Seas is Allen *Curnow's first book-length sequence, published by *Caxton Press in 1939, with a frontispiece by Leo *Bensemann. The contents had previously appeared piecemeal in *Tomorrow in 1937–38. In the Author's Note to Collected Poems 1933–73 (1974), where the sequence appears in revised form, Curnow wrote: 'I suppose it could be called my contribution to the anti-myth about New Zealand which a few of us poets—and almost nobody else—were so busy making in those years.' The twelve numbered sections (consisting of a passage in prose followed by a verse lyric) are framed by a Statement (in sestina form) and an Epilogue. In its national focus and dystopian flavour it has something in common with *Fairburn's *Dominion (1938).　　　　　　　　　　　　　PS

'Not Understood' (c.1879) is one of Thomas *Bracken's most popular poems, and gave the title to a posthumous selection that sustained his reputation through the first half of the twentieth century. It is a sentimental homiletic lyric of seven stanzas, each of five lines, each opening and closing with the title phrase, 'Not understood'. It meditates on the human propensity for making false or unfounded judgments, and urges instead a charitable and non-judgmental spirit of acceptance, closing on the hymn-like hope that this would bring us all nearer to God, 'And understood.' Though expressed and usually interpreted wholly in terms of human frailty at large, the poem may have had a personal beginning, when Bracken, at the time a Protestant and a freemason, felt himself discriminated against when he unsuccessfully approached Bishop Moran for appointment as editor of the Catholic New Zealand Tablet. The poem is cast in resonant abstractions, mostly in slightly archaic, Tennysonian language ('We move along asunder, / Our paths grow wider as the seasons creep / Along the years … '). A few images are drawn from industrialisation, but the only phrase of any local resonance is 'Poor souls with stunted vision / Oft measure giants by their narrow gauge'. The tone is plangent and the rhythms liturgical, with a skilfully handled falling cadence to end each stanza: 'How many cheerless, lonely hearts are breaking! / How many noble spirits pass away / Not understood!' This oral strength made the poem popular in recitation, with Mel B. Spurr particularly associated with performances in Australia and New Zealand in the years before World War 1. The 1916 Cambridge History of English Literature describes the poem as 'well-known', Bracken and Alfred *Domett being the only New Zealand poets cited.

The collection 'Not Understood' and Other Poems went to eight printings 1905–28, and at least four more 1942–58. It contains forty-two of Bracken's most popular poems, though only 'Not understood' and 'New Zealand Hymn' (*'God Defend New Zealand') now have any currency.　　　　　　　　　WB/RR

Now Is the Hour / Haere Ra attained its status as a nationally known composition during World War 2. Played by a brass band, it was used to farewell troop ships, but its origin is some four decades earlier.

Its provenance is complex, and some of the aspects summarised here are disputed. The melody is from an Australian piano solo by Clement Scott, published in London in 1913 as 'Swiss Cradle Song'. The Māori words added to this melody—'Haere ra, Te manu tangi pai'—are generally thought to be the work of Maewa Kaihau, or Louise Flavell, or members of the Grace family of Gisborne, or the member of parliament for Southern Māori, Henare Uru. These words were translated as 'Now is the hour when we must say goodbye'. Prominent recording artists who internationalised the English-language version of the song were Gracie Fields and Bing Crosby. Copyright battles in the USA and elsewhere have been complicated by the sale of the original publishing rights and the extensive use of several versions of the song.

From its origin, 'Now Is the Hour / Haere Ra' was widely used in New Zealand. Between the wars it was used in the Rātana Church as a familiar ending or closing hymn. Its near obligatory use as a farewell for parting passengers is described in Janet *Frame's autobiographical *An *Angel at My Table*: 'I stood on deck among a crowd of passengers all throwing streamers that were caught by the watchers on the wharf ... I stayed on deck to catch one more glimpse ... [and] went downstairs, just as the band was playing "Now Is the Hour", and the music reached down like a long spoon inside me and stirred and stirred.' A full account of the song's complex history is in the Auckland University PhD thesis 'New Zealand's Cultural and Economic Development Reflected in Song' by Angela R. Annabell.   AT

Nucleus was published in parallel to *Kiwi by the Auckland University Students' Association 1957–61. Edited by Wystan *Curnow, Phil Crookes and Tony Hammond, its four issues featured poetry, fiction and articles by students and others, including Wystan Curnow, Denis *Glover, R.A.K. *Mason and Vincent *O'Sullivan.   SH

Numbers was a quarterly magazine edited by Louis *Johnson, assisted by James K. *Baxter and Charles *Doyle, ten issues appearing 1954–59. It sought work which 'by its experimental nature or forthrightness, may frighten more timid editors', and which would challenge 'the established order of shop-keeper values and suburban living'. In Number 4 Baxter attacked the notion of established 'standards' associated particularly with Allen *Curnow, *Landfall and M.H. *Holcroft's *NZ Listener. Doyle and J.C. *Sturm were relatively unknown writers who found useful opportunity through *Numbers*, though it was a few years early to be truly experimental. It was strongly a Wellington publication, putting out one 'Special Issue of Wellington Writing' (Feb. 1959), with an agenda, too, of defying what Johnson saw as Curnow's Auckland hegemony.   RR

O'BRIEN, Gregory (1961–), is a poet, painter and editor. Born in Matamata, he trained as a journalist in Auckland and worked as a newspaper reporter in Northland before returning to study art history and English at Auckland University (BA 1984). Apart from two years working as arts editor of the TV3 arts programme 'The Edge' (1993–94), he has written and painted full-time since 1984, first in Auckland, then in Wellington, where he still lives. He held the Sargeson Fellowship in 1988 and was writing fellow at Victoria University in 1995.

O'Brien's literary output is prolific. His poems have appeared regularly in most New Zealand literary journals (including *Islands, *Landfall and *Sport) since the mid-1980s, and in Australia (*Meanjin, Scripsi), Canada and Britain. His first major collection of poems and drawings, *Location of the Least Person* (opening with the 'Old Man South Road' sequence), was published in Auckland in 1987, followed by the smaller *Dunes and Barns* (1988). *Man with a Child's Violin* (1990) comprised three earlier verse sequences, 'Flying Wall Cafe' (1982), 'Sydney Calm Joe' (1984) and 'Entitled' (1986). His next major collection of recent poems and drawings was *Great Lake* (Sydney, 1991), followed by *Malachi*, a charming verse novella (Adelaide, 1993). The collection *Days Beside Water*, which includes the historical verse sequences 'Marsden at Matapouri' and 'The Milk Horse' (about Mother Mary Aubert) and the wonderful imagined life of the sixteenth-century Italian composer Claudio Monteverdi, was published in Auckland in 1993, and in Britain by Carcanet in 1994. Two further collections are in preparation. O'Brien has also published short fiction in New Zealand and Australia, and a picaresque novel with illustrations, *Diesel Mystic* (1989), which attempts to overlay various heightened emotional,

spiritual and imaginative landscapes onto an unassuming stretch of countryside between Dargaville and Ruawai in Northland.

O'Brien's writing is about other ways of seeing, and has been variously described as 'surreal' and 'magical realist'. It both explores and embodies the mystery of creation present equally in the physical, animate world and in human artistic invention. It draws heavily on the Western cultural heritage, and in particular on the images and sounds of traditional Catholicism, yet fuses these with identifiable local references—to people, especially earlier writers and artists (James K. *Baxter is a significant influence), places, objects and events. Highly original, O'Brien's language is constantly surprising and often witty or poignant in its leaps of association and mood; not least among its many paradoxes is a lyrical quality grounded in the rhythms and vocabulary of ordinary speech.

O'Brien's unique iconography incorporates elements of personal, public and religious history, graphically portrayed in his paintings and drawings, many of which illuminate his books. As an artist, he has held solo exhibitions and participated in group shows in Auckland and Wellington, and has illustrated the work of other New Zealand writers as well as designing covers.

Among O'Brien's other work is a collection of interviews with twenty-one New Zealand writers, *Moments of Invention* (1988, with photographs by Robert Cross), a monograph on the painter Nigel Brown (1991), and a collection of profiles of New Zealand painters, *Land and Deeds* (1996). He was founder editor of the deliberately short-lived literary quarterly *Rambling Jack* in 1986–87, and editor of *Sport* 15 in 1995; *Sport* 11 included 'After Bathing at Baxter's', an essay/journal describing the influence of Baxter on younger New Zealand poets. With his partner, poet Jenny *Bornholdt, he edited a collection of New Zealand love poems, *My Heart Goes Swimming* (1996), and co-edited, with Bornholdt and Mark *Williams, *An Anthology of New Zealand Poetry in English* (Oxford University Press, 1997).   AM

O'BRIEN, Katherine (d. 1982), children's fiction writer, was born in Australia, brought up on her grandfather's farm in coastal Southland and later moved to Eastbourne. She wrote many short stories, but is remembered now for her two novels. The idyllic *The Year of the Yelvertons* (1981), illustrated by Gavin *Bishop, involves two Southland farm children who help their old neighbour prepare for English visitors. It won the 1982 Esther Glen Award. *The Golden One* (1983) is an enjoyable mystery adventure set in Eastbourne, involving antique smugglers and Colombian gold treasure lost after a landslip.   DH

OLDS, Peter (1944–), a *Freed poet of the 1970s, was born in Christchurch, left school at 16, worked in a variety of jobs, began writing in 1966 and had his first volume of poems, *Lady Moss Revived*, published in 1972 by Caveman Press of Dunedin. A further five books of poetry quickly followed: *V-8 Poems* (1972), *The Snow & the Glass Window* (1973), *Freeway* (1974), *Doctor's Rock* (1976) and *Beethoven's Guitar* (1980). He also published a number of broadsheets, including *Exit: 2 Poems* (1971), *Schizophrenic Highway* (1971), *The Habits You Left Behind: Poem* (1972) and *Schizophrenic Rhino* by 'Toastie Oats' (1972). He was awarded a mini-*Burns Fellowship in 1978 and his last volume, *After Looking for Broadway* (1985), was published in Christchurch. He has also been the subject of a number of poems, most notably James K. *Baxter's 'Letter to Peter Olds' (1972). After Baxter's death Olds replied to his friend's correspondence in kind in 'Doctor's Rock'. His father was a minister and, like Baxter, he had an ambiguous relationship with Christianity. He was, however, considered a central figure by many of the younger poets of the 1970s because of his ability to incorporate rebellious detail of contemporary experience with music, drugs and the concerns and language of the street, as in the Mandrax poems, 'Freeway' and 'You Fit the Description'. Early influences included Jack London, Allen Ginsberg and Jack Kerouac and, as a result, the poems often display an uneasy and sometimes ironic nostalgia for the adopted language of the rock'n'roll of the American 1950s. The poems often detail alienation from a consumerist, technological society, and there is a confessional aspect when he treats his experience in psychiatric institutions. Later poems tend to be a hallucinatory collage, but music remains a strong influence, with references made to Tom Waits and John Lennon.   NWt

O'LEARY, Michael (1950–), publisher, poet, novelist, performer and bookshop proprietor, has made a colourful contribution to the literary scene in three cities. Born in Auckland, he was educated at the universities of Auckland and Otago, and now lives in Wellington. Under his Earl of Seacliff Art Workshop imprint he has published his own prolific output as well as various other writers, both alternative and mainstream. His works include *Surrogate Children* (poems, 1981), *Ten Sonnets* (1985), *Straight* (novel, 1985), *Out of It* (satirical novel, 1987), *Before and After* (1987), *Livin' ina Aucklan'* (1988) and *The Irish Annals of New Zealand* (1991). He has also written commissioned histories of two Auckland cemeteries, and edited *Wrapper* (1992), a collection of poems by both new and established poets. His work has appeared in *Pilgrims, Te *Ao Mārama and elsewhere.

O'Leary's poetry and novels explore his Māori (Te Arawa)–Irish Catholic heritage, the poetry more conventionally, the prose in an alternative vein which owes something to Joyce and Beckett.   JH

O'Leary's Orchard is Maurice *Duggan's third and final collection of short stories, published in 1970 by the *Caxton Press. The book contains three long works which can be said to constitute the pinnacle of Duggan's achievement. All three works exhibit a prose style which is extremely complex and poetic, particularly 'O'Leary's Orchard', a novella describing an affair between a middle-aged man, Gambo O'Leary, and a young woman, Isobel Bernstein. The story also examines the way in which human relationships are conditioned by past circumstances. Isobel Bernstein and a group of players use O'Leary's barn to rehearse their play, and Isobel's presence brings the withdrawn O'Leary out of his shell of social isolation. During the course of their affair the incidents in their pasts which drive their relationship are gradually revealed. The relationship cannot last, but by the end O'Leary has ended his isolation, Isobel has found maturity, and their affair has overcome the psychological forces which seem to determine it. 'An Appetite for Flowers' is a simpler story using the myth of Persephone to counterpoint the relationship between Hilda Preeble, a florist shop worker, and her ex-husband Ben. Hilda's anger over her relationship with Ben takes the form almost of an addiction, and stifles her relationship with others, until the arrival of her estranged son, Adam. The renewal of the mother–son relationship gives Hilda the emotional strength she needs to live a life beyond Ben and her 'rose simplicities'. The final story in the collection, 'Riley's Handbook', is the demented monologue of an artist named Fowler who has escaped his wife and family to become a barman and caretaker in a sprawling rural hotel. Fowler's attempt to revise his identity requires a new name, Riley, but 'disguise and sudden departure have not been enough'. Riley forms a sexual relationship with Myra, another worker in the hotel, and rails bitterly against the absurdity of both his former and adopted lives. Riley, whose chief relationships are all with women, is a misogynist. An inability to deal with the early death of his mother and the withdrawal of her love is gradually revealed as the source of his attitudes. In addition, the discovery that he is suffering from incurable tuberculosis has caused Riley's flight and almost pathological condition. The story closes with his death and an ambiguous, hard-won salvation.   IR

OLIVER, Stephen (1950–), a poet who came from Wellington but now lives in Sydney, has published four small-press editions and three larger collections. He began publishing in the 1970s with *Chance to Laugh* (1972), followed by *Henwise* (1975)—in which he takes the domestic hen as his unlikely subject—*& Interviews* (1978), *Autumn Songs* (1978), *Letter to James K. *Baxter* (1980), *Earthbound Mirrors* (1984) and, most recently, *Guardians, Not Angels* (1993). Critics have praised the positive tone of much of Oliver's poetry and commented on his tendency to record experiences, thoughts and emotions in such a way that its overall effect is of a verse diary of the life of a mind. There has, however, been a less positive response to his attempts to juxtapose the disorder of an individual's life with more formal technical devices. Nor has his penchant for predominantly American slang and invented words always been favourably received.   PM

OLIVER, W.H. (1925–), besides being one of New Zealand's foremost historians, is the author of three books of poetry. He was represented in the Oxford (1956) and Penguin (1960) anthologies of New Zealand verse, and the various updatings continue to include his work. Born in Feilding, he graduated from Victoria (1951) and Oxford (1953) universities, and lectured at Canterbury and Victoria (1954–63) before becoming professor of history at Massey University (1964–83). On his retirement he was appointed general editor of the *Dictionary of New Zealand Biography* till 1990, when the first volume was published. The best-known poem in *Fire Without Phoenix: Poems 1946–54* (1957), which won the Jessie Mackay Poetry Prize, is 'In Fields of My Father's Youth', in which a journey to his ancestors' English home county provokes sustained, elegiac meditation on migrant dreams, his own political attitudes and

New Zealand's future. English locations inspire the other most striking pieces. In particular, 'In Radcliffe Square, Oxford' describes a quarrel, on a 'wet and wintry' evening, between a soldier and his girl, while, as church bells ring out, the ancient monuments to piety and learning observe 'the decline of their love': 'Heaven was everywhere / Present, everywhere mourned their loss.' Incident and setting combine to create resonant ironies. The poem takes a God's-eye view of youth's intensities. *Out of Season* (1980) includes a tribute to Robert Lowell, and in this collection Oliver makes frequent use of Lowell's form of unrhymed sonnet. Diction and rhythms have become somewhat harsher. Fastidious in phrasing, carefully measured, the poems make their firmest claim on the imagination when the abstract and the introspective give way to dramatisation, as in 'Waitomo' or some of the fairy-tale parables in the third section. The title sequence of *Poor Richard* (1982) is about New Zealand's first Labour Prime Minister, 'King Dick' Seddon: lively and detailed, it gives an historian's perspective on this symbolic figure. 'Dear kanga' uses A.A. Milne's creatures for social satire, while in a series of pieces under the heading 'Leave Report' the poet and academic again visits Britain and wryly reflects on places, people and events.

Bodily Presence: Words/Paintings (1993) contains reproductions of paintings by Anne Munz together with seven poems by Oliver in the genre that goes under the technical name of 'ekphrastic': each represents a response to a painting, or (as Oliver says) 'a parallel text'. Oliver's other contributions to New Zealand literature include *The Story of New Zealand* (1960), which traced 'a history of adaptation and improvisation'; *Challenge and Response* (1971), seeing the history of the Gisborne East Coast as furnishing 'a set of variations upon a New Zealand theme'; and *James K. *Baxter: A Portrait* (1983), a fine illustrated biography. He was co-editor of the *Oxford History of New Zealand* (1981), and founding editor of the quarterly review *Comment* (1959–63, 1978–82). He edited *Landfall* (Nos. 42 and 43) for six months in 1957.   MPJ

Once on Chunuk Bair, a play by Maurice *Shadbolt, was first produced in 1982 at Auckland's Mercury Theatre, published the same year, and filmed in 1991. The action takes place during the hours between dawn and dusk on 8 August 1915, the day that New Zealand soldiers took the hill of Chunuk Bair on the Gallipoli peninsula. But the purpose of Shadbolt's play is not to celebrate a moment of imperial history or rake over a shameful moment of a country's colonial past, but rather to present the climax of New Zealand's Gallipoli campaign as the moment when New Zealand realised its identity as a independent, postcolonial nation, distinct from the imperium. Everything in the play is organised to this end. In Shadbolt's version of events it is a carelessly directed ship's salvo from the all-but-absent British, rather than the Turks, which ultimately does for the New Zealanders in the closing moments of the play. Despite its apparently limited subject and its necessarily all-male cast, *Once on Chunuk Bair* manages to engage with a raft of social and economic issues which continue to be of importance in contemporary New Zealand society. It also dramatically relates the vast tragedy of World ★War 1, and New Zealand's small but horrific part in it, to other wars fought on the same ground, stretching back to the siege of Troy.   RC

Once Were Warriors is the first published novel by Alan ★Duff (1990). It tells the story of the Hekes, a Māori family living on Pine Block, a state housing area in Two Lakes (a fictitious town closely resembling Rotorua). The husband, Jake ('The Muss', for 'Muscles'), is unemployed and spends most of his time drinking beer with his Māori mates in McClutchy's booze barn. His wife, Beth, prefers to stay at home, smoking, apathetically watching television soap operas and drinking. Like most in Pine Block, they seem trapped by a sense that they are lesser people, 'nowhere-going nobodies', accepting that Māori have no future and life is just a daily stumble between dole payments. Relief is found in alcohol, and for Jake in violence: he prides himself on his reputation as a fighter, and sometimes beats up his wife as well. The effect on their children has been disastrous: the oldest son, Nig, at 17 is joining the leading local Māori gang, the Brown Fists; Boogie, 14, after trouble at school is made a ward of the state and sent to Riverton Boys' Home; Grace, the elder daughter, at 13 is looking after Boogie and her younger siblings and cleaning up after her parents' nights of partying.

In symbolic opposition are the Tramberts, a wealthy Pākehā farming family living in a big house across the paddocks and surrounded by walls. For Grace their civilised lifestyle comes to represent all that is unattainable in her own; after she has been raped in her own bed (she thinks by her father) during a drunken party, and after a planned family visit to Boogie, which starts out happy but disintegrates in almost animalistic drunkenness, Grace hangs herself from a tree in the Tramberts' garden. This tragedy takes Beth back to her kaumātua and the positive aspects of being Māori; thus galvanised, she rejects Jake and the resentful helplessness of Pine Block and launches a self-help project for local Māori youth. But the reversal comes too late for Nig: desperate to be accepted by the Brown Fists yet fearful of their violence, he is shot in a confrontation with a rival gang. Jake, rejected even by his own mates and reduced to sleeping rough, is by the end a broken man.

Once Were Warriors is a novel of explosive force. It depicts with graphic intensity what happens to a warrior culture, prizing physical prowess and display, when it has to live within a culture of very different values. The message is explicit: the violence of the male warrior code is no longer appropriate or acceptable, and those who live by it are 'losers'. Yet the novel is not without compassion or sensitivity: there is sympathy for the predicaments of its main characters even while their responses are often harshly judged. The reader comes to understand the feelings and motivation of each of these outwardly inarticulate people through their inner voices, in a series of interior monologues told in the language each would normally use. It is a sophisticated and self-aware literary technique. Its power comes from the authenticity of the language used, in both vocabulary and fragmented syntax, coupled with a strong narrative pull achieved by the progressive juxtapositions of different viewpoints. The male world depicted here is made to seem absolutely real, deriving from close firsthand experience.

This authenticity is what gave the novel its mark. *Once Were Warriors* is the first New Zealand novel to deal full on with the actualities of modern urban Māori life. While some literary critics found its techniques flawed and its message intrusive, for most readers it not only revealed but also made sense of a world hitherto glimpsed only in news reports. Since its publication in 1990 by Tandem Press, *Once Were Warriors* has sold more than 80 000 copies and has never been out of print in New Zealand; it has also been published in Australia, the United States and twelve other countries. In 1991 it won second place in the Goodman Fielder Wattie Book Awards, and won PEN's Best First Book of Fiction award, and its author was awarded a joint Sargeson Fellowship. A new edition was issued in 1994 to coincide with the release of the film of the same name, scripted by Riwia ★Brown from an original screenplay by Duff. This powerful screen version achieved international success and made *Once Were Warriors* the most widely recognised New Zealand book title, especially in America, surpassing even ★*Teacher* and the ★*bone people*.   AM

One-A-Pecker, Two-A-Pecker, a novel by Ruth ★Park was published in Sydney in 1957 and is one of the most accomplished historical novels set in the New Zealand ★goldfields. The title plays on the names of two early goldfields, Wangapeka and Tuapeka, and has been taken from a folk song of the same name. The narrator is a young woman who travels to the Otago goldfields in the company of her mother and her uncle—grotesque, disoriented figures whose presence in the gold rush is explained by their radical alienation from more settled society. There is a touch of absurdist fiction in the opening chapters, when these characters cross a desolate landscape with no clear idea of where they are going or what they might hope to achieve. A central character is a girl called Currency, who was abandoned by her mother and adopted for practical rather than sentimental reasons by a brutalised washerwoman called Mother Jerusalem. After the death of her foster-mother Currency continues the journey with another grotesque, Billy Figg, who plans to sell his numerous cats to the rat-plagued miners. Billy's desperately sick wife is the third member of the strange party. The senselessness of their undertaking is matched by its inevitability, as fate and the lack of alternatives draw them on. There are encounters with ★Chinese miners which also verge on the absurd or the surreal in the total misunderstanding between cultures and the false expectations aroused. More sentimental, and consequently something of a flaw in the structure, is the mystery surrounding Shennadore, who turns out to be an unfrocked priest somewhat incredibly holding to his vows, so that his behaviour is barely comprehensible to the others on the goldfields. He and Billy Figg end their lives melodramatically with a plunge into the flooded Shotover River. With this novel Park goes beyond the conventional adventure story of the search for gold and creates a sometimes credible world of comic desperation.   NW

ORBELL, Margaret (1934–   ), is the author of several books on Māori literature, tradition and belief, an editor of collections of songs, poetry and stories, and a leading interpreter of Māori texts to non-Māori audiences, including international ones. Her major collections include *Maori Folktales in Maori and English* (1968); *Traditional Songs of the Maori* (1975, 1990, with Mervyn McLean); *Maori Poetry: An Introductory Anthology* (1978); *Waiata: Maori Songs in History* (1991); and *Traditional Maori Stories* (1992). Her achievement in such books is to preserve fidelity to the Māori texts and their cultural connotations while arranging, introducing and translating them in ways that make them accessible to other cultures. Her *Illustrated Encyclopedia of Māori Myth and Legend* (1995) is a rich source of information on traditional literature, drawing on versions from many tribal areas and informatively illustrated. Also of literary interest are Orbell's editorship of Te ★*Ao Hou* 1961–65; her compilation of the early anthology, *Contemporary Maori Writing* (1970); her *Select Bibliography of the Oral Tradition of Oceania* (UNESCO, Paris, 1978); and her consultant editorial role in the *Penguin Book of New Zealand Verse*

(1985). Her 1970 anthology put several significant writers before a wider public, including Witi ★Ihimaera (with the story that was the first version of ★*Tangi*), Patricia ★Grace, Harry ★Dansey, Hirini ★Mead and others.

Orbell's MA at University of Auckland was in English; later (after teaching at Ruatoria, editing *Te Ao Hou* and studying Māori in Wellington with Wiremu Parker) she took her PhD at Auckland in anthropology with a thesis on ★waiata aroha (love songs). After lecturing in Māori at Auckland 1974–75, she moved to University of Canterbury, retiring as associate professor in 1994 to become a full-time writer in Auckland, where she was born.   PN/RR/NW

Oriflamme (1) was edited and published in a single issue by the Canterbury College Caxton Club Press in April 1933. The idea for a radical literary journal came from a visit by Denis ★Glover to Auckland, where he was impressed by ★*Phoenix* and helped by Bob ★Lowry to acquire a workable hand-press. Club members included Glover, Ian ★Milner, J.P.S. (Patrick) Robertson, Walter Brooks, C.R. Straubel and Eric Cook, nine members each contributing £1 to launch what Glover projected as a 'spasmodical'. It was intended as a vehicle for radical debate, to bring the major ideological issues of the time into a university which Glover described, writing in the conservative *Canterbury College Review*, as 'nothing more than an architectural curiosity in a tired little town'. Milner recalled (in *Intersecting Lines*, 1993) that he chose the journal's name for its echo of Byron's 'Freedom! yet thy banner, torn, but flying / Streams like the thunderstorm against the wind'; and that when its origin was recalled as the 'golden flame' battle banner of St Denis, 'Glover guffawed approval'. Among essays and verse critical of what Milner's introduction called the 'outworn system' of society and politics, the first issue included an article by Patrick Robertson on 'Sex and the Undergraduate', which recommended 'companionate marriage' as an interim arrangement for young adults before legal marriage. This caused the issue, in its blood-red cover, to sell out instantly and provoked public outcry, with enraged headlines in the national as well as local press.

The embarrassed college board of governors ordered Glover not to produce a second issue, citing, not unreasonably, that his permission to use the college law basement had been 'for the purpose of studying printing and typography', not for a 'publication ... of an objectionable nature'. Glover's 'supporters melted away like ice-cream under a censorious sun'. He appealed and apologised, and the board relented, allowing the Caxton Club to resume its various activities, provided only that all members were genuinely students, that the title of any publication 'be not *Oriflamme*', and that it 'not discredit the College in the eyes of the community'. Thus followed, only three months later (July 1933), *Sirocco*. Its name, a hot wind, suggests that Glover and Milner were not unduly penitent.

Glover was dismissed by the *Press and the episode perhaps prevented him from becoming a journalist. It certainly contributed to the foundation of the independent *Caxton Press. It showed yet again that radical thinking about sex is always most liable to *censorship. The full story shows the college authorities to have behaved less repressively than has often been claimed. They at least bore little grudge, offering Glover a position in the English department three years later. Another ten years later, in 1946, he was elected to the College Council, and as usual had the last word: 'Some time in 1933, / The College Council sat on me, / But now (the nearest rhyme is groundsel), / I'm sitting on the College Council.'   SH/RR

Oriflamme (2), subtitled 'A literary journal of youth and the fine arts' was published in Wellington 1939–42. It had no links to the Caxton Club *Oriflamme* of 1933. A cyclostyled quarterly, it emanated from the *Alexander Turnbull Library where editor Tony Murray-Oliver was employed. Contributors included Murray-Oliver, C.R. *Allen, Ronald Meek, Lindsay Constable, Dorian Saker and Ronald Castle.   SH

Oriori are a kind of song addressed to a child, usually of high ancestry. They are formally distinguished from *waiata by the way the melody varies to match the words. Margaret *Orbell writes: 'The flexible lines and stanzas, the fast tempo, the simple melodies and swift, economical diction of the oriori make it a medium well suited to the rapid conveyance of complex ideas, with abrupt transitions and highly cryptic allusions to people, places and events.' The allusions make them difficult to understand or translate but provide a preliminary educational experience for the child they are addressed to—something to remember and refer to as greater understanding evolves. By surveying the history of *iwi and *hapū they can give the child a sense of his (less frequently her) place in the scheme of things. Many of them urge the child to arise, go forth and right some injustice in the world. A common structure for oriori is discussed in detail in the introduction to Part II of *Ngā *Mōteatea*.

Although the word 'lullaby' is often used to translate 'oriori', it is appropriate only for a few of the songs. Commenting on an oriori, Elsdon *Best remarked: 'Here we have a composition that differs widely from what we would deem a suitable song to sing to an infant. We must conclude that this was a method employed in the preservation of tribal lore, also it would familiarise a child with names mentioned in traditions and myths which such a child would be required to learn in later years' (*Games and Pastimes of the Maori*, 1925). On the other hand *Dieffenbach, an early observer, wrote of 'nga-ori-ori-tamaiti' (children's oriori) which were apparently not confined to aristocratic children and were definitely used as lullabies for naked babies sharing the parents' blanket and 'lulled to sleep' by the songs.

In his book *Maori Music* (1996) Mervyn McLean points out that oriori are among the longest of Māori songs and that 'in contrast with the texts, the tunes are usually very simple'.   NW

ORR, Bob (1949–), was one of the poets most centrally associated with *Freed* and The *Young New Zealand Poets* and has continued to produce a small body of carefully crafted verse. He has also published in *Islands and *Landfall and is represented in the Penguin (1985), Caxton (1987) and 1997 OUP anthologies. His first volumes, *Blue Footpaths* (1971) and *Poems for Moira* (*Hawk Press, 1979), showed a precocious talent for tautly controlled imagistic lyrics, some of intense verbal beauty and force of feeling. The love poems draw images from the natural world into an emotive synthesis with the passion of the body: 'Your eyelids / closed estuaries / of dream. / Your hair rained / in the half dark room. / My veins guttered into / blue oceans' ('Signatures'). *Cargo* (1983) continued with the discipline of short vibrant lines, often now distilling beauty from urban or industrial scenes, as in 'The Black Trawler', 'Wellington', or 'Parable' ('A man in a crane gently moved / a cloud / across the sky'). Orr's propensity for effects of colour and light is best seen in the short haiku-like lyrics of *Red Trees* (1985), strikingly incorporated in paintings by Rodney Fumpston. In *Breeze* (1991) the tone is more conversational, anecdotal and sometimes nostalgic, though sometimes, too, incantatory ('Tahiti', 'After Reading Albert Camus'), several poems working with the tension between Auckland's urban and Pacific identities. The poet's intense and lucid observation still produces memorable images: 'Summer girls walked shining from the surf'; 'The tide like / old dark leather scuffed'; 'Monarch butterflies / on fire / danced by the classroom window'. Born in Hamilton, Orr has lived in Wellington and Auckland.   RR

ORSMAN, Chris (1955–), made an impressive debut as a poet with his collection *Ornamental Gorse* (1994). Its poems mostly recreate and reflect on episodes from family and national history, with strong images recurring of ships, houses, people at work and the often tragic hazards of New Zealand's natural environment, especially the sea. Their verbal resourcefulness perhaps reflects the poet's lexicographic parentage (see Harry *Orsman) but is always rigorously controlled to serve a moral and intellectual seriousness. The effect is of intense cerebration, rich in wordplay but never merely playful, which makes Orsman (for New Zealand) an unusually metaphysical poet. John Donne would enjoy the erotic astronomy of 'Orbit'.

Orsman's second book, *South* (1996), is a sequence in different voices recreating Scott's tragic last expedition to the Antarctic: 'each man saw his face imprisoned / by his reflection in the ice.' It was praised by Alan *Riach as the product of 'a careful imagination at work with a genuine humility', its images 'resonating with a sense of the modest human scale against which the vastness, both real and imagined, of Antarctica could be measured'. Autobiographical prose passages frame and give a personal dimension to the imaginative evocation of the expedition, 'stealthily out of its element, / eyeing the near forbidden...'. In 1998 he added *Black South*.

Born in Lower Hutt, educated in Wellington, Orsman studied architecture at Auckland University and practised briefly before working as an ambulance officer, travelling, and taking Victoria University's creative writing course in 1993. He lives in Wellington. His poems have been published in *Sport*, *Landfall* and Bill *Manhire's *100 New Zealand Poems* and included in *An Anthology of New Zealand Poetry in English* (1997). In 1998 he launched Pemmican Press as a publisher of new poetry.   RR

ORSMAN, Harry or **H.W.** (Harold William) (1928–), is the pre-eminent lexicographer of New Zealand English. Prodigious reading in local literature and a lifetime collection of usages made him for many years contributor to major *dictionaries of English such as the *Oxford English Dictionary*. He began to publish under his own name with the *Heinemann New Zealand Dictionary* (ed., 1979, 1989), the *Macquarie Dictionary* (contrib. ed., 1981) and the *Penguin Tasman Dictionary* (consulting ed., 1986). All these are dictionaries of general English with New Zealand (and in some cases Australian) usages specially included. The first fully dedicated to the New Zealand variety of English is *The New Zealand Dictionary* (ed. Elizabeth and Harry Orsman, New House, 1994). The culmination of Orsman's scholarly career is *The Dictionary of New Zealand English* (*Oxford University Press, 1997), a major compilation by a team of researchers establishing exclusively or significantly New Zealand lexical terms on historical principles with full commentaries and citations. He

was also a member of the Komiti Ārohi of the Ngata *English–Maori Dictionary* (1994).

His work in and on behalf of literature goes beyond this lexicographic research. He co-edited the first *Dictionary of New Zealand Quotations* (1988), and the quarterly *Comment* in the late 1960s–70s, when it was host to some significant poetry and review articles. He was a national committee member of *PEN (NZ) in the same period. He has also published small popular books, light-hearted but useful extracts from his scholarly materials, the *New Zealand Slang Dictionary* and *Quotable New Zealanders* (both with Des Hurley, 1992). A roguishly provocative wit tends also to emerge at unexpected moments in his scholarly writing or when his expert comment is being sought by media interviewers.

Orsman was lecturer, then reader in English at Victoria University 1960–93, after a miscellaneous early career. He was born in Havelock and educated there, at St Patrick's College, Silverstream, and at Victoria University. The several sides of his accomplishment were acknowledged in a festschrift for his 65th birthday, *Of Pavlovas, Poetry and Paradigms* (ed. Laurie Bauer and Christine Franzen, 1993), which included original scholarly and literary work from many of his New Zealand and overseas friends.   RR

ORWIN, Joanna (1944–), writes children's fiction with a strong ecological emphasis and sense of landscape. Born in Nelson and educated at Canterbury University, she worked as a plant ecologist and science editor for the Forest Research Institute before travelling to England, where she developed her interest in landscape. Inspired on her return by New Zealand's terrain and traditions, she began writing novels for children, setting them around Nelson, Kaikoura and the area of the Lewis Pass and Murchison. *Ihaka and the Summer Wandering* (1982) and *Ihaka and the Prophecy* (1984), illustrated by Robyn *Kahukiwa, follow Ihaka's journey to manhood in an early Māori tribe. *The Guardian of the Land* (1985), winner of the 1986 Children's Book of the Year Award, sends David and Rua back through time to find the guardian, a whalebone pendant, that will renew friendship between Māori and Pākehā. *Watcher in the Forest* (1987) draws on the power of greenstone to rectify wrongs done in the past.   DH

O'SULLIVAN, Vincent (1937–), born in Auckland, is poet, short story writer, novelist, playwright, critic and editor. A graduate from the universities of Auckland (1959) and Oxford (1962), he lectured in the English departments of Victoria University of Wellington (1963–66) and (after several months in Greece) the University of Waikato (1968–78), before committing himself to full-time writing. He served as literary editor of the *NZ Listener (1979–80), and then (1981–87) won a series of writer's residencies and research fellowships in universities in Australia and New Zealand: Victoria (Wellington), Tasmania, Deakin (Geelong), Flinders (South Australia), Western Australia and Queensland. These were interrupted by a year as resident playwright at Downstage Theatre, Wellington (1983). In 1988 he resumed his academic career as professor of English at Victoria University of Wellington. The winner of many literary prizes, he was the Katherine *Mansfield Memorial Fellow in Menton in 1994. In 1997 he also became director of Victoria's Stout Research Centre.

O'Sullivan's first book of verse, *Our Burning Time* (1965), contained poems that had been published in periodicals in New Zealand, UK and USA. An exceptional facility for image-making was already on display. The first of five 'Poems of Place' begins: 'Skopelos drops its village like a pack of cards / from clumsy-fisted mountain, the white sides over.' The simile may seem contrived, but it catches well the haphazard sprinkling of chalky Mediterranean houses, is picked up in a later 'shuffled', and gestures towards themes of chance, fate, and the quirks of history. Over three decades O'Sullivan's talent has developed in response to deepening and broadening experience. His verse is collected in *Revenants* (1969), *Bearings* (1973), *From the Indian Funeral* (1976), *Butcher & Co.* (1977), *Brother Jonathan, Brother Kafka* (1979), *The Rose Ballroom and Other Poems* (1982), *The *Butcher Papers* (1982), *The Pilate Tapes* (1986) and *Selected Poems* (1992), which draws on all but the first two volumes, and adds new work. Among the strongest of O'Sullivan's earlier poems are those in which contemporary relationships and states of mind are given a basis in Greek mythology. A traveller, who has visited and lived in diverse parts of the world, O'Sullivan quarries his changing locations for specific reference, while remaining conscious of a contrasting homeland. The sequence of poems *From the Indian Funeral*, written in reaction to three months spent in Central America in 1975, ends with the poet's return from the world of the Aztec goddess, with her 'taloned feet' and 'necklace of severed hands', to 'green sward and Anchor butter'. Among O'Sullivan's most original contributions to New Zealand verse is his creation of 'Butcher', affable dealer in flesh and blood and guts, as mouthpiece for a line of racy Kiwi shop-talk that raises perennial poetic concerns. With a cast that includes 'Sheila' and 'Baldy', the 'Butcher' poems exploit a dramatist's ear for chit-chat, while subsuming the hectoring and reminiscing voices within sheer O'Sullivanese. In *Brother Jonathan, Brother Kafka*, the awesome certainties of eighteenth-century theologian Jonathan Edwards and the personal, political

and metaphysical anxieties of twentieth-century fabulist Franz Kafka represent twin poles between which the poet's reflections take place, as a visit to New England focuses his thoughts about love and time. These poems, each of four unrhymed quatrains, include some of O'Sullivan's emotionally most satisfying. *The Pilate Tapes* imports the colloquial idiom, the dramatic dialogue, and the demotic vigour of the 'Butcher' poems into a miniature Passion Play, rendered in a dazzling variety of tones. A far-flung province of the Roman Empire merges into a postcolonial New Zealand peopled with liberal-minded Mr Pilate, Jesus from Hicksville (alias Jix), sly flunky Rat (who 'doesn't like Jix, one bit'), Barabbas & Son ('doing nicely in second-hand / timber'), and that 'not-bad piece' Magdalene. The sequence condenses O'Sullivan's religious and philosophical preoccupations, while being packed with local realities—political, cultural and geographical.

It was only after he had established a solid reputation as a poet that O'Sullivan turned in the 1970s to the writing of short fiction. His stories have been gathered in *The Boy, The Bridge, The River* (1978), *Dandy Edison for Lunch and Other Stories* (1981), *Survivals* (1985), *The Snow in Spain: Short Stories* (1990) and *Palms and Minarets: Selected Stories* (1992). They cover a wide range, but are particularly apt to explore various kinds of deprivation, betrayal, rejection, sadness, deceit, estrangement and loss. Death is a recurring theme. Many central characters are on the fringe of a social group, whether struggling to join in, blithely unaware of their position, preferring to remain outside or simply recognising their difference. In 'The Boy, The Bridge, The River', the Polish immigrant to New Zealand, Latty, carrying with him his memories of the war, is an alien among marching girls and Lions' Day, but builds a friendship with his landlady's ingenuous brother Len. The dwarf narrator of 'The Snow in Spain' finds a niche for himself in the sport of dwarf-tossing. The main character in 'Terminus', who is teetering on paranoia, says, 'Forget that masking is natural and even beautiful and set the way we want things to be against the fact of how they are.' O'Sullivan strips away masks, exposes pretension and self-deception, reveals all sorts of emptiness and loneliness. 'Testing, Testing …' finds the Tarzan and Jane within a pseudo-sophisticated marriage. But O'Sullivan's stories are not reductive: they exhibit a shrewd understanding that pierces to the heart of what it means to be human. O'Sullivan can mock, satirise and laugh, but he also finds dignity in unexpected places. He is interested in the *art* of living, and in the borderland where truth and lies meet, both in life and in fiction itself. He can move from old folk to children, from rural poverty to metropolitan glitz, from Hamilton to New York. Characters range from retired sugar-works clerk, to company manager, to trendy academics. Technically, his short stories are remarkable for their unsettling shifts of narrative point of view. Their modes span realism and metafiction. Everywhere they are marked by the poet's eye for detail.

Miracle (1976) is a witty *jeu d'esprit*, a comic-grotesque satire on national institutions and attitiudes, laced with fable and fantasy. The novel *Let the River Stand* (1993), which won the Montana New Zealand Book Award for 1994, is O'Sullivan's major achievement to date. Centred on a Waikato country settlement and covering the period from the end of one World War to the end of the next, it begins, epic-style, *in medias res*, but only after an italicised page about a woman hospitalised with a head injury, the first of six such passages, one at the conclusion and four serving like *entr'acte* choruses, as the narrative moves backwards and forwards in time and between groups of characters, whose fates are gradually revealed as interwoven. The everyday life of a typically taciturn rural New Zealand community, with its family feuds and follies, forms the stuff of tragedy and myth. Settings extend to working-class Ponsonby, a Tasmanian apple orchard and Spain during the civil war. There are gestures towards Katherine ★Mansfield, John ★Mulgan and other predecessors, with the ★Depression and the rise of socialism looming in the background. Characters run the gamut from hypochondriac widow to balaclava-disguised prizefighter. The novel has cinematic qualities, both in its visual richness and luminous exactness and in its frequent switches from one centre of consciousness to another. O'Sullivan's verbal camera lens zooms in and out, tilts and pans; there are cuts and dissolves as the spool unwinds. One section is told through a woman's diary. A sense of mystery haunts the multifarious elements, until they converge. The climax is an instant, frozen in time. No New Zealand novel has conveyed more completely a sense of history and of those visionary moments that resist its flow.

In the 1980s O'Sullivan the dramatist emerged. He had written radio and television dramas before his first stage play, ★*Shuriken*, was performed at Downstage, Wellington, in July 1983. It examines the bizarre situation that led to the death of fifty Japanese soldiers and one New Zealand guard in a World War 2 prison camp at Featherston in 1943. The title is taken from the Japanese word for a throwing-dagger. Japanese prisoners, theoretically committed to a military code of no surrender, and New Zealand guards lacking both experience in their roles and understanding of their charges, are forced into uneasy association, until cultural difference kindles violence. The presence among the ill-assorted New Zealanders of the Māori corporal Tai, who has as much in common with the proud yet subjugated enemy as with

his Pākehā mates, creates a significant third dimension, allowing the play to serve as implicit comment on our interracial history. Though the Kiwi soldiers speak the local patois, in structure *Shuriken* is stylised and non-naturalistic, exploiting the freedoms of the post-Brechtian theatre. In *Jones & Jones*, about Katherine Mansfield and her close friend Ida Baker, who nicknamed each other 'Jones', O'Sullivan again uses such techniques as direct address to the audience, and, taking a hint from Mansfield's own passion for music hall, punctuates the dialogue with popular songs. The play was commissioned by Downstage for the Katherine Mansfield centenary and first performed in September 1988. It draws on Mansfield's writings to explore, with considerable wit and verve, an unusual bond, and conjure up the Bloomsbury litterati among whom the two women moved. Animated by Mansfield's own personality in all its histrionic complexity, it shows, among other things, the emotional tug of the childhood homeland that she had so eagerly escaped. But the relationship between the Joneses is central. Katherine needs her awkward shadow-self in order to scintillate. She bullies, cajoles and mocks Ida —and is fortified by her unconditional love. Specialising in the art of living, she must also learn the art of dying. 'Jones', she says, 'life is nothing if not performance'. *Billy*, presented at Bats Theatre, Wellington, in August 1989, employs techniques similarly disruptive of naturalism, including tricks with lighting and a litany-like sequence in which characters speak 'from various points on the stage'. But this is also, in part, a drawing-room drama, with some quite Wildean banter about weighty matters. Set in the New South Wales penal colony of the 1820s, *Billy* has seven disparate English men and women fret, joke and gossip about their situation, and use the mute Aboriginal servant of the title as a screen on which to project their anxieties and desires. As director Aarne Neeme averred, 'Boundaries of behaviour are challenged across class distinctions, sexual relations, racial tensions and religious beliefs, as are the notions of authority and civilisation'. Power and its link with violence are among the themes. Here too O'Sullivan returns to his concern with truth and lies. Billy's dreamlike eruption into speech at the close forms a stunning *coup de théâtre*. *Shuriken* (1985), *Jones & Jones* (1989) and *Billy* (1990) have all been published by ★Victoria University Press. Less accessible are 'Ordinary Nights in Ward 10' (New Depot, Wellington, March 1984), a dense mix of the farcical, the allegorical and the fantastic, 'The Lives and Loves of Harry and George' (Downstage, Wellington, 1994) and 'Take the Moon Mr Casement' (Court Theatre, Christchurch, September 1996).

O'Sullivan has, with Margaret Scott, edited five volumes of *The Collected Letters of Katherine Mansfield*

(1984–), as well as Mansfield's 'The Aloe' with 'Prelude' (1982), Poems of Katherine Mansfield (1988), and a Selected Letters (1989). His An Anthology of Twentieth-Century New Zealand Poetry (1970, revised 1976 and 1987) was a standard text for a quarter of a century. He is also editor of (among other volumes) New Zealand Short Stories: Third Series (1975), New Zealand Writing Since 1945 (1983, with MacDonald P. Jackson), Collected Poems: Ursula Bethell (1985), The Oxford Book of New Zealand Short Stories (1992), and Intersecting Lines: The Memoirs of Ian Milner (1993). In his critical study, James K. Baxter (1976), he demonstrates the centrality to Baxter's verse of the seasonal myth at the core of most mythologies. He edited the Wellington current affairs journal *Comment during the period 1963–66.

When in Jones & Jones D.H. *Lawrence asks Mansfield whether she knows when she is telling the truth, she replies, 'But I'm an artist Lawrence like yourself. Our vocation is to tell the truth as only the born liar can.' O'Sullivan's writing in different genres is unified by his awareness of this paradox.   MPJ

Otago University Review, founded in 1888 and still issued as recently as 1993, is the longest-surviving journal with literary content. It appeared on a monthly basis during the university session until 1913, biannually to 1922 and thereafter annually. The early issues contain poems, stories and articles of general interest, beginning in the first with an essay on Thackeray and a sarcastic note on Fergus *Hume's popular novels. Other articles cover British and American literary topics and subjects like the 'national character of New Zealanders', and 'The Possibilities of a Colonial Literature' (by 'Z' in 1894). Among many undistinguished poems there is one by Arthur H. *Adams. From 1894 to 1910 the Review seems to forget its literary ambitions, but then we find a sudden flourishing of poems and stories by C.R. *Allen. From 1915 on the typography and paper are surprisingly elegant and literary items are found again. The concern for recent British poetry (Yeats, Bridges) is noticeable in the subsequent years and various anonymous stories and poems appear. From the mid-1930s the Review became a more exclusively literary annual. Dan *Davin's early, prize-winning story 'Prometheus' appeared in the issue for 1935, the first of several contributions by 'D.M.D.'. James K. *Baxter began a long association with the Review with several poems in the issue for 1944, including the Macmillan Brown Prize poem 'Convoys'. With the establishment of the *Burns Literary Fellowship in 1959 a tradition was initiated of Fellows contributing work to the Review, raising its standard and helping to ensure its continued appearance. Burns Fellow contributors include Baxter, Ian *Cross, Janet *Frame, Hone

*Tuwhare, Witi *Ihimaera, Maurice *Duggan and Brian *Turner. Other significant contributors include Basil *Dowling, Charles *Brasch, Fleur *Adcock, Barry *Crump, Bill *Manhire, Iain *Loney, Graham *Billing and Alan Roddick.   SH/NW

OVENDEN, Keith (1943–), biographer, satiric novelist and political commentator, became best known for his well-received A Fighting Withdrawal: The Life of Dan Davin, Writer, Soldier, Publisher (1996), with its informative treatment of the social scene of Southland in the early twentieth century, and of *Davin's literary, wartime and private lives.

Born in London and educated there and at the Universities of Keele (UK), Michigan (USA) and Oxford (DPhil 1971), Ovenden first visited New Zealand in 1972 as postdoctoral fellow at Victoria University. He was lecturer in politics at University of Essex, moving to a senior lectureship at University of Canterbury (1975–81). There he quickly developed a reputation as an entertaining commentator on political and social topics, equally at ease with print journalism, radio or television. He carried this experience into his first novel, Ratatui (1984), a comic political mystery with some memorable scenes of Wellington society and sharply satiric parodies of the media. Its sequel, O.E. (1986; see next entry), is a darker political thriller, with suicide, assassination, espionage, missile tests and some serious reflection on World War 2, but most notable as an early and well-informed attack on French policy in the *Pacific. As with all Ovenden's work, thoughtful analysis is expressed in urbanely articulate narrative, the insight into French attitudes and some good scenes of Paris sharpened by the five years he lived there from 1981. A full-time writer since 1981, Ovenden has lived since 1989 primarily in Washington DC. He also wrote The Politics of Steel (1978) and (with Tony Cole) Apartheid and International Finance (1989). A third novel in the Ratatui sequence, 'Parallel Bars', is complete. RR

Overseas experience, more usually 'OE' (attested from 1975), is an originally humorous term for a period of work or holiday chiefly in Britain and Europe undertaken by young New Zealanders as part of their informal education, popularly considered as a mandatory pilgrimage. Contrast *'colonial experience'. After World War 2 relatively cheap sea and air travel brought to large numbers the opportunity previously enjoyed by those who won academic places overseas. 'OE … is the abbreviation for overseas experience—and no New Zealander, it is claimed, is complete without it. As well as being vital to emotional and intellectual (and sexual) development, OE very nicely fills that awkward gap between high school and marriage' (*NZ Listener, 1975). Of innumerable literary versions, those by John *Gillies (Voyages in Aspic, 1954) and Mervyn *Thompson (First Return, 1974) might represent the period of transition from earlier attitudes to Europe (especially Britain) as *'home' to an overriding concern with the changes travel brings to perceptions of New Zealand. HO/RR

OWEN, Rena, see **Māori Theatre.**

Owls Do Cry is the first novel of Janet *Frame (*Pegasus Press, 1957; New York, 1960; London, 1961); it won the New Zealand Literary Fund Award for Achievement (1958); no MS is known. The title is taken from Ariel's song in The Tempest: 'in a cowslip's bell I lie; / there I couch when owls do cry'. The novel focuses on the passage of the four Withers children away from the security of childhood (the 'cowslip's bell') to pernicious adult society ('where owls do cry'). Their parents, Bob and Amy, foreshadow their destiny; stultified by social conformity, they are empty, 'withered'.

The first section, 'Talk of Treasure', deals with the children's childhood; the second section, 'Twenty Years After', portrays them as adults. Although materially poor, the imaginative children are able to find 'treasure' among the debris of society at the city dump, their favourite haunt. The oldest, Francie, at 12 on the cusp of adulthood, is forced by her father to leave school and work at the woollen mills. She dies in a fire at the dump soon after, a literal death that perhaps echoes her father's sacrifice of her to the fire of adult materialism. 'Chicks' (Theresa), the youngest, lacks the imagination of the other children, and is always running behind them, trying to 'catch up'. Likewise, as an adult, Theresa embraces social conformity and is forever trying to 'keep up' with her neighbours. Ironically, she marries the son of the man who was tending the fire in which Francie died, and they live in a house built on land reclaimed from the city dump. Toby and Daphne, the middle children, are typical figures in Frame's fictions: caught between the withering demands of adult society and the alternative truths to which they have access—Toby by virtue of his epilepsy (we are told that he has the 'gift of escape' despite his terror and shame when he has fits) and Daphne by virtue of her madness (she is institutionalised soon after Francie's death). Daphne's final integration into 'normal' society is harshly forced—she endures a series of electric shock treatments and is finally given a lobotomy that makes her 'safe', enabling her to work compliantly at the woollen mills.

The common theme of the loss of childhood innocence is uniquely treated. Written in the third person from the shifting viewpoint of one or other of the children the novel is interspersed with italicised first person sections in which Daphne 'sings' from the 'dead room' (literally the room where she recovers after shock treatments, figuratively the imaginative space she occupies) in fluid, poetic, highly metaphorical prose. The typographic and stylistic distinction of these sections is indicative of Daphne's position on the borders of 'normal' social interaction and communication. The novel concludes with a short, ironic, universalising epilogue that treats each of the characters as a figure in an extract from the Saturday paper, read to the indifferent manager of the woollen mills by his gossipy wife. KWo

Oxford History of New Zealand Literature in English, The (OHNZLE), edited by Terry *Sturm (OUP, 1991), was the first book-length, multi-author history. Its main precursors were E.H. *McCormick's *New Zealand Literature: A Survey (1959) and the composite essay on 'Literature' in An Encyclopedia of New Zealand (ed. A.H. McLintock, 1966), by D.O.W. Hall, N.L. Millar, Joan *Stevens, W.J. Gardner and W.H. *Oliver. Patrick *Evans's Penguin History of New Zealand Literature (1990) appeared while OHNZLE was in press. In its comprehensiveness, detail and, almost without exception, the authority and judiciousness of its essays, OHNZLE instantly became an invaluable resource. The present Companion acknowledges a profound indebtedness.

The very sparseness of precedent meant that OHNZLE's essays had to be built wholly on original research. Its greatest achievement was to perform a task of such magnitude so well. The next greatest was to go so innovatively beyond the narrowly canonical constraints of most previous discussion, and teaching, of New Zealand literature.

Its contents are: Jane McRae, 'Māori Literature: A Survey'; Peter Gibbons, 'Non-fiction'; Lawrence *Jones, 'The Novel'; Lydia Wevers, 'The Short Story'; Howard McNaughton, 'Drama'; MacD.P. Jackson and Elizabeth Caffin, 'Poetry'; Betty *Gilderdale, 'Children's Literature'; Terry Sturm, 'Popular Fiction'; Dennis *McEldowney, 'Publishing, Patronage, Literary Magazines'; and John Thomson, 'Bibliography'. A second edition, revised and updated, was published 1998, with one additional chapter, by Mark *Williams, 'Literary Scholarship, Criticism, and Theory'. RR

Oxford University Press began its commitment to New Zealand literature by publishing the early *anthology of poetry, The Oxford Book of Australasian Verse, chosen by Walter Murdoch, in 1918. This joined a distinguished series begun by Arthur Quiller-Couch's Oxford Book of English Verse in 1900. The history of a

Press under direct University of Oxford control goes back to at least 1690, the first 'Printer to the University' having been appointed in 1584. In literature, the 'Oxford Books of Verse' and other anthologies, 'Oxford Standard Authors' and 'World's Classics' series have done much to preserve and develop literary traditions. The pioneering *Oxford Companion to English Literature* (1932) was compiled by Paul Hervey, who happily received a knighthood. It remained the basis for the most recent editions (1985, 1995) edited by Margaret Drabble, and was the prototype for the series.

A New Zealand connection with OUP, especially in the fields of literature and lexicography, goes back to the group of literary and language scholars of New Zealand origin associated with the Press in the mid-twentieth century. Medievalist Kenneth Sisam, as Secretary to the Delegates, was responsible for the appointments of John *Mulgan and Dan *Davin; the latter became a key figure in the Press's post-war publishing of literature and works relating to its study, and was host to an informal New Zealand literary centre in Oxford.

Another connection in the 1940s–50s was OUP's best-selling girls' school stories of Clare *Mallory (New Zealander and Oxford graduate Winifred Hall). Davin was then responsible for OUP's first significant adult publications in New Zealand literature since 1918, his *Katherine Mansfield: Selected Stories* (1953), and *New Zealand Short Stories*, in collaboration with Eric *McCormick and Frank *Sargeson (1953). Both were in the pleasingly pocket-sized 'World's Classics' series, as was *New Zealand Short Stories: Second Series*, chosen by C.K. *Stead (1964).

OUP began to publish occasional books in New Zealand from the 1960s. The separate New Zealand publishing operation began fully in the 1970s, though the management relationship with Australia has varied.

Writers employed by the Press in New Zealand have included Brian *Turner, its founder-editor, and Anne *French. An alliance with *Auckland University Press became the basis of some prestigious publishing of local literature in the 1970s–80s, with Fleur *Adcock, James K. *Baxter, Lauris *Edmond, Maurice *Gee, Vincent *O'Sullivan and many more on OUP's list. Major volumes in that period included the Baxter *Collected Poems* (1980) and *Selected Poems* (1982), both edited by John *Weir, and *The Stories of Katherine Mansfield*, ed. Antony *Alpers (1984). The Oxford tradition in literary anthologies has been sustained, with volumes such as *An Anthology of Twentieth Century New Zealand Poetry* (1970, 1976) and *The Oxford Book of New Zealand Short Stories* (1992), both edited by O'Sullivan, and *An Anthology of New Zealand Poetry in English*, ed. Jenny *Bornholdt, Gregory *O'Brien and Mark *Williams (1997). Criticism and biography have been served by the *'New Zealand Writers and Their Work' series, Frank *McKay's *Life of James K. Baxter* (1990) and others. The 'New Zealand Classic' series reprinted novels by authors such as Gee, Marilyn *Duckworth and Joy *Cowley. OUP's children's list (under Wendy Harrex's editorship) was also significant, including Cowley, Gee, Gavin *Bishop, Tessa *Duder, Jack *Lasenby, Elsie *Locke, Caroline *Macdonald and others.

The parent publisher in Britain continues to publish books of New Zealand importance, such as the *Collected Letters of Katherine Mansfield*, ed. O'Sullivan and Margaret Scott (1982–) and Keith *Ovenden's *A Fighting Withdrawal: The Life of Dan Davin* (1996).

Two books of major importance to New Zealand literature have been published in the 1990s: the *Oxford History of New Zealand Literature*, ed. Terry *Sturm (1991, 1998) and the *Dictionary of New Zealand English*, ed. Harry *Orsman (1997).   RR

P

Pacific and New Zealand literatures were originally inextricable through Polynesian myths of migration, and continued to be so in the era of European arrival. In the writings of ★Cook, ★Dumont d'Urville, ★Melville and others, New Zealand is one Pacific landfall, and English versions of Māori myths and legends, such as ★Grey's, sustained a wider Polynesian context, as did the twentieth-century narratives of Peter ★Buck, Apirana ★Ngata, Antony ★Alpers and others. The preoccupations of settler society and those concerned with New Zealand ★nationalism were less spacious, however. The Pacific islands became generally less visible in New Zealand writing, despite their presence as a tourist venue (the first Union Steam Ship 'Excursion to the South Sea Islands' was in June 1884), their importance in the two world wars and New Zealand's continuing political and economic influence in the region. There were, of course, exceptions, like the interview of Robert Louis Stevenson in Apia for the London *Bookman* in 1893 by W.H. Triggs, later editor of the ★*Press*; or Roderick ★Finlayson's novel of Samoan cultural conflict, *The Schooner Came to Atia* (1952); or Allen ★Curnow's 'Pantoum of War in the Pacific' (1943) and his play *The Axe* (1948, 1961), based on an episode from Peter Buck; or the attack on New Zealand's Pacific role in ★*Phoenix* (1933); or the writings of R.A.K. ★Mason and Dick ★Scott on Pacific topics. Yet Charles ★Brasch could justly remark in the initial ★*Landfall* (March 1947) that 'No Pacific country is even half as real to us, in the sense that we know not only its superficial characteristics but the quality of its people and their civilisation, as the British Isles.' The title of Marjorie ★Staples's memoir, *Forgotten Islands* (1950), was appropriate.

This began to change in the 1960s. (For the political and cultural relationship since that time, see also ★Pacific writing for children, ★Pacific theatre and ★Tokelau.) As the major migration began from the Pacific to New Zealand cities, especially Auckland and Wellington, New Zealand was increasingly becoming a factor in Pacific nations education. A number of those pioneer Pacific writers who published earlier than (say) 1985 had connections with New Zealand through residence or education: Cook Islander Johnny (Florence) Frisbie (Hebenstreit), Tongan Konai Helu Thaman, and Samoans Sano Malifa, Talosago Tolovae and Mamoe Malietoa Von Reiche. Factors in strengthening the literary connection and fostering awareness within New Zealand of the emergent Pacific literary consciousness included the influence of Alistair Te Ariki ★Campbell, Albert ★Wendt and a small group of literary journals, especially *Mana*. Campbell's part-Rarotongan heritage was always an evident strength in his poetry, though not highlighted until the 1980s. It was Wendt who, from the early 1970s, was the great proponent, promoter and maker of a Pacific literature, who on returning to Samoa and Fiji after his school and university education in New Zealand set out to foster other writers and be the spokesman of their significance. His essay 'Towards a New Oceania' was seminal: published in *Mana* (1976), often reprinted, it was rewritten as the introduction to his *Lali: A Pacific Anthology* (1980). It is an early and substantial exercise in postcolonial criticism, discussing 'Oceania' as a fantasy formation, rejecting the anthropologised and romanticised European and American versions, exploring the nature and meaning of traditions, and identifying the central energy of the vulnerable and dynamic culture as anti- and postcolonial.

Sons for the Return Home (1973), the story of a young Samoan male's experience of life and mixed-race love in 1960s New Zealand, was the first 'Pacific' book (other than studies of myths and legends by Ngata, Alpers and others) to make an impact in New Zealand, increased by the film version (1979) directed by Paul Maunder. While Wendt's middle-period is focused on Samoa, he continued to explore the New Zealand connection in a few poems ('He Never Once Lost His Way', 'Where the Mind Is') and returned to New Zealand as setting in parts of *Ola* (1991) and in *Black Rainbow* (1992), after himself moving to Auckland. His present role as professor of New Zealand literature there puts him again in a pivotal position, actively fostering young Auckland writers of all Polynesian origins. Wendt's *Nuanua: Pacific Writing in English Since 1980* (1995) updates *Lali* and is the authoritative collection, its title ('rainbow') emphasising the region's diverse linguistic and cultural heritage, just as *Lali* ('gong') summoned the people to celebrate a new beginning.

Mana, the publication of the South Pacific Creative Arts Society based in Suva, Fiji, has been the most widely circulated literary journal. Initiated in 1972 by Marjorie Crocombe, a Cook Islander resident in Suva, it was at first a section within *Pacific Islands Monthly*, with an influential series of separate volumes, the *Mana Annual of Creative Writing* (1973, 1974, 1977). From 1976 it was published separately (as *Mana Review* in 1976, then *Mana*). Other significant journals established during the 1970s include *Kovave* (Papua New Guinea), *Faikava* (Tonga) and *Sinnet* (Fiji).

The most important Pacific literary scholars and critics have been Wendt, Crocombe and the Fijian Subramani, whose *South Pacific Literature: From Myth to Fabulation* (1985) was the first specialist critical study. In New Zealand, Ken *Arvidson and Bill *Pearson were first in the field. Arvidson's 'The Emergence of a Polynesian Literature' appeared in the first issue of *Mana* along with Wendt's 'New Oceania' and stands with it as progenitive criticism. Pearson drew earlier work on cultural encounter together in the central *Rifled Sanctuaries: Some Views of the Pacific Islands in Western Literature* (1982). Others early to study or promote Pacific literature in New Zealand include Bernard *Gadd, Norman Simms and Roger Robinson. Several New Zealand scholars are included in *Readings in Pacific Literature*, ed. Paul Sharrad (Wollongong, 1993). Controversy was unleashed by C.K. *Stead's *Faber Book of Contemporary South Pacific Stories* (1994), which attempted to mix and foreground New Zealand and Pacific texts in a new way, but won little support from pioneering authorities like Wendt and Arvidson, being perceived as still centred in English language cultural traditions and inadequately

informed about the Pacific. Wendt and leading Māori writers declined inclusion.

Pacific literature is developing quickly, as Wendt's *Nuanua* shows, and independently, though various connections with New Zealand are still pertinent to the understanding of both literatures, perhaps especially the increasingly multi-lingual nature of New Zealand literature. Cook Islander Kauraka Kauraka, for instance, has published poetry in Manihiki and English, and Rarotongan and English, and Māori and English (with a collection, 'My Dawning Star'). Of sixty-four Pacific writers in *Nuanua*, twenty-five have some New Zealand connection, several, like John Puhiatua *Pule (Nuie) and Johnny Frisbie being long-time residents. The closeness of the connection makes the relationship not wholly easy. Wendt's introduction to *Nuanua* points out that Pacific nations 'lose many of our most energetic and adventurous people' and that 'Colonialism, racism, modernisation and their effects on us remain major preoccupations in our literature.' New Zealand bears part of the responsibility for what Wendt calls the 'sense of profound loss' that pervades Pacific writing.

Several recent or current New Zealand writers have Pacific heritage or experience which enables them to begin a different kind of recognition and contact. These include Gloria *Rawlinson (*The Islands Where I Was Born*, 1955), Hone *Tuwhare (*Something Nothing*, 1974), David *Eggleton (*South Pacific Sunrise*, 1986), Rosie *Scott (*Nights with Grace*, 1990), James *McNeish (*Penelope's Island*, 1990), Janette *Sinclair, Graeme *Lay, Denys *Trussell and Cathie *Dunsford, while Campbell has foregrounded his 'Polynesian strain' in his poetry, fiction and autobiography since about 1980. Joy *Cowley's award-winning *The Silent One* (1981), a contemporary rewriting of a Pacific myth and moving story of friendship between a deaf mute boy and a white turtle, is an international classic of young adult literature, and was successfully filmed.

A significant sub-genre is protest writing against French nuclear testing in the Pacific, initially Barry *Mitcalfe's *Boy Roel: Voyage to Nowhere* (1972) and notably Maurice *Shadbolt's *Danger Zone* (1975, 1985). More recent anti-nuclear fiction includes Keith *Ovenden's *O.E.* (1986), Colin *Peel's *Atoll* (1992) and Gary *McCormick's satiric *Honey, I blew up the atoll* (1995), while protest writings, mostly poems, by more than forty New Zealand writers were collected in *Below the Surface: Words and Images in Protest at French Testing on Mururoa*, ed. Ambury Hall, 1995. This includes Curnow's total revision of his earlier 'Pantoum' as 'Pacific 1945–1995: A Pantoum', drawing irony now from the use of the mainly French pantoum verse form (French by adoption, though originally Malaysian).

With new or reprinted work by many other leading authors, this book perhaps more than any other evinces New Zealand's shift to the perception that 'New Zealand is a South Pacific nation' (in the opening phrase of Judith Devaliant's essay there). New Zealander Roger S.Clark contributed to the legal literature with *The Case Against the Bomb* (with Madeleine Sann, 1996).

New Zealand is a quite frequent presence, of course, in the Pacific's own writings, not always appearing to advantage, as when the Tongan Epeli Hau'ofa features a celibate New Zealand bull and lesbian Australian cow in his comic satire on agricultural aid, 'The Big Bullshit' ('New Zealand never sends duds abroad'), in *Tales of the Tikongs* (1983). As Wendt says in *Nuanua*, 'Decolonisation still inspires much of our writing.'

Pacific children's writing and early readers are a significant literary expression of Pacific nations communities resident in New Zealand, for instance in the writing of Ester ★Laban-Alama (Samoa), Poko ★Morgan (Cook Islands), Lino ★Nelisi (Nuie) and Epi ★Swan (Tokelau), who work mostly with ★Learning Media editor Don ★Long. Pacific theatre groups are also very active, especially in Auckland. Clearly these early voices of a Pacific diaspora are only the beginning.   BW/RR

Pacific theatre in New Zealand has advanced to the point where John Kneubuhl's *Think of a Garden*, directed by Nat Lees at Taki Rua, won Wellington's Best Theatre Production Award for 1995. Besides this independent production, Pacific theatre in New Zealand is represented by two theatre companies: Pacific Underground, based in Christchurch, and Pacific Theatre, based in Auckland. Previously the company Tao Tahi was active in the 1980s, producing the first play on Pacific themes by a Pacific writer, *Le Matou* ('The Fishhook', by Samson Samasoni and Stephen ★Sinclair, 1984). Pacific Theatre was formed by Justine Simei-Barton in 1987 to bring the vitality of Pacific performance traditions into a contemporary theatrical context. Besides mounting productions of plays by a range of playwrights, such as John Kolia's 'Feiva/Favour' (Maidment Arts Centre, Auckland, 1988), Edgar White's 'The Nine Night' (Maidment, 1989), Andy Rashleigh's 'Robeson: Song of Freedom' (Maidment, 1990), *Romeo and Juliet* (University of Auckland Summer Shakespeare, 1992) and August Wilson's *Ma Rainey's Black Bottom* (Herald Theatre, Aotea Centre, Auckland, 1995), Pacific Theatre has also developed and produced its own original scripts. These include 'Lupe and Sima: A Love Story with Cannibals' (Maidment, 1991), 'The Contest', by Paul Simei-Barton (Taki Rua, 1993) and 'Tusitala: The House of Spirits', by Paul

Simei-Barton (Taki Rua, 1996). Pacific Underground produced 'Fresh off the Boat', by Simon Small and Oscar Kightley, at the Rolleston Avenue Theatre in the Christchurch Arts Centre in 1993. In 1996 Oscar Kightley and David Fane were commissioned by the International Festival of the Arts to write 'The Frigate Bird Sings' (Downstage).   SG

Pacific writing for children is a significant component of the developing Pacific voice in New Zealand literature. The relationship is closer than is usually recognised. At different times Western Samoa, the Cook Islands, Niue and ★Tokelau have all been under New Zealand administration. Tokelau legally became part of New Zealand in 1946. Tokelauans, Cook Islanders and Niueans are all entitled to New Zealand passports and have unrestricted rights of entry, and more now live in New Zealand than in those countries of origin. Though Western Samoans are no longer generally entitled to New Zealand citizenship (as was so in the past), Samoan remains (with English and Māori) one of the three most widely published and spoken languages in New Zealand. For example, a new book for children in Samoan is published in New Zealand about every eight weeks. Almost a third of New Zealand's school-age population is now Polynesian. Of this third, about a third are of Pacific nations descent. About half of all the Pacific Islanders in New Zealand are Samoan, though the fastest-growing community is Tongan. Aside from Māori and New Zealand Sign Language (and, formerly, Moriori), there are four other languages in the world only spoken by New Zealand citizens: Tokelauan, Niuean, Cook Islands Māori and Pukapukan (a separate language spoken in the northern Cook Islands). Because of its unique history, a somewhat archaic form of English is still spoken on Palmerston atoll in the Cook Islands, and the oral literature of Palmerston is an interesting, if often forgotten, feature of New Zealand and Cook Islands literature in English.

Writing for children by Pacific Islanders in New Zealand really began in the pages of eleven journals published by the New Zealand Department of Education: *Tusitala mo A'oga Samoa* (1947–54), *Tusitala mo Vasega Laiti Samoa* (1955–62), *Tusitala mo Vasega Tetele Samoa* (1955–62), *Tala mo A'oga i Tokelau* (1951–8, published in Samoan until 1953), *Tuhi Tala mo Tamaiti* (1959–64), *Tohi Tala ma e Tau Aoga Niue* (1950–8), *Tohi Tala ma e Fanau Lalahi Niue* (1959–66), *Tohi Tala ma e Fanau Ikiiki Niue* (1959–64), *Te Tuatua Apii o te Kuki Airani* (1950–66), *Au Tua no te Tamariki o te Kuki Airani* (1959–66) and the ★*School Journal* (1907–   ). While the ten journals published in Samoan, Tokelauan, Cook Islands Māori and Niuean were really published for schools in the islands (then under New Zealand administration), copies began finding their way into New Zealand schools as Pacific nations immigration to New Zealand increased through the 1950s and 60s. Earlier issues of these journals at times betray the colonialist attitudes of the period, and often include translations of European folk tales. Later issues contain a much higher percentage of original material by Pacific writers and, increasingly, Pacific writers writing in New Zealand. Writing in English by Pacific writers also began to appear in these years in the *School Journal*. Albert *Wendt, for example, began publishing stories written for children in the *School Journal* in 1961. Comparatively little writing for children in Pacific nations languages was published in New Zealand between 1966 and 1982. In 1983 the New Zealand Department (later Ministry) of Education began publishing books for children in Samoan, Cook Islands Māori, Tongan, Niuean and Tokelauan for New Zealand schools and (from 1988) preschools. By 1995 *Learning Media, for the New Zealand Ministry of Education, was publishing thirty books for children in New Zealand schools and preschools each year in these five languages. Scholastic New Zealand (formerly Ashton Scholastic), Anau Ako Pasifika and the Pasifika Press are among other publishers who are also publishing children's books in Pacific nations community languages, while Longman Paul has also published a number of Pacific children's books in English.

The *School Journal* arguably remains the best source of writing for children in English by Pacific nations writers. Peggy Dunlop, Emma Kruse Va'ai, Lino *Nelisi and Johnny Frisbie are all frequent contributors. Since 1983 publishing for children in New Zealand in Pacific languages has been characterised by multi-lingual editions. Commonly, the same story is published in a number of separate language editions. New Zealand publishers of books for children in Pacific nations community languages publish more translations than any other sector of the book trade (including, somewhat surprisingly, publishers of books in Māori). By 1995 about two children's books a month were being published in New Zealand which were translations *between* Pacific nations community languages. The major shift in the fifty years between 1947 and 1997 in Pacific writing in New Zealand has not been between languages (it has remained fairly steadily multi-lingual) but in the settings. There has been a steady shift from work set in the islands to writing set within the world of the Pacific communities in New Zealand. Among the more productive Pacific children's book authors currently writing and publishing in New Zealand are Frisbie, Nelisi, Ester Temukisa *Laban-Alama, Feaua'i Amosa Burgess, Teupoko Ina *Morgan and Epi *Swan. It is noticeable that all these children's book authors are women, publishing primarily in Pacific nations community languages. By contrast, the best-known Pacific authors writing for a more general audience in New Zealand in the 1990s, such as Wendt, John Puhitautau *Pule and Alistair Te Ariki *Campbell, are so far mainly men, publishing primarily in English.

LI/DL

Pacific Quarterly Moana, see **Cave.**

PACKER, Richard or **Lewis** (1935–89), poet, playwright and journalist, was born in Taumarunui and educated at New Plymouth BHS. He briefly attended Ardmore Training College before transferring to journalism. He worked on newspapers in Wellington and Christchurch before moving to Melbourne in the mid-1960s. In New Zealand he was something of a protégé of Wellington poet Louis *Johnson and was initially published in *Numbers*, *Arena* and *New Zealand Poetry Yearbook* from the mid-1950s. He was one of the three poets whose poems caused the controversy around the 1964 issue of *Poetry Yearbook*. His only New Zealand book was *Prince of the Plague Country* (1964). Describing himself as 'an existentialist with a religious bias', Packer expounded through his poems a broadly absurdist view of life, often through mythological subjects, and showed some influence of esoteric philosophy derived from Gurdjieff and Ouspensky. He was a follower of Subud, the international mystic movement of Indonesia. He settled in Australia, apart from extensive travel in Europe and some visits to New Zealand, working mostly in advertising. He has published three further books: *The Powerhouse* (1972), a verse play; *Being Out of Order: Some Poems and 'The Uncommercial Traveller'* (1972); and (under the name Lewis Packer) *Serpentine Futures* (1986), a collection of poems which includes a sequence 'Passage Through Oswiecim' derived from a visit to Auschwitz.

PS

Paddy Murphy's Budget, subtitled 'A collection of humorous "pomes, tiligrams, an' ipistols"' (1880), and *Paddy Murphy's Annual*, subtitled 'A Record of Political and Social Events in New Zealand' (1886), both published in Dunedin, were collections of doggerel, political satire, etc., written entirely by Thomas *Bracken. Although much has lost its force with the passing of time, the liveliness of the wit can still raise a smile. Usually the fictional element is confined to the personality of Paddy himself, who is made to comment on real events. Typical is 'Paddy Murphy and Tay Whiti', in which much of the comedy lies in the way the prophet Te Whiti is made to speak in an *Irish accent when reported by Paddy. Several of the texts are printed in both volumes.

NW

Pao are an epigrammatic form of *waiata, usually sung for entertainment, expressing love, extended greetings or satirical comments on events, often with an element of gossip (which can be called paopao in Māori). Unlike more serious waiata, pao were and are composed extempore. Often they are used to illustrate points in the course of *whaikōrero.   NW

PAPAKURA, Makereti, see **MĀKERETI**.

Parallax—a journal of postmodern literature and art ran for three issues, 1982–83, when publisher Brick Row Publishing Co Ltd withdrew the project. Designed by editor Alan *Loney to follow on from *Morepork, it had as contributing editors Wystan *Curnow, Tony Green and Roger Horrocks, with covers by Cilla *McQueen, Andrew Drummond and Richard Killeen. *Parallax* proposed to document and critique *postmodern literature and art on the assumption that these were solid, ongoing concerns, even if not necessarily popular ones, in New Zealand culture, rather than mere fringe activities with a limited lifespan. The magazine was intended as a reminder that a body of work was being produced that owed more to the international modernisms of the century at large than to the achievements of New Zealand poets and artists of the 1930s. Artists John Bailey, Killeen, Drummond, and film maker Mike Sukolski were featured, as were critics Curnow, Horrocks and Francis Pound, while poetry and prose appeared by such as Ted Jenner, Len *Lye, Judi Stout, Graham *Lindsay, Green, Joanna *Paul, John Barnett and Leigh *Davis. The untimely demise of *Parallax* served to stimulate the birth of *Splash.   AL

PARATENE, Rawiri (1954–), Te Rarawa, Ngā Puhi, was born in Motukaraka, and grew up in Otara. Educated at Hillary College as David Broughton, the transliterated form of his family name, he later took back his name as a positive identification for Māori in his chosen career. Inspired by a school visit to *Hamlet* at Mercury Theatre, he graduated from the Toi Whakaari New Zealand Drama School (1972), followed by an apprenticeship with Mercury Theatre and then extensive work as actor, writer, director, producer, tutor and administrator in theatre, radio, television and film. In professional theatre he has played Edgar (*King Lear*), Tranio (*Taming of the Shrew*) and Romeo, and on television lead roles in *Joe and Koro* (1976–78), *The Governor* (1979), *Playschool* (1980–82), *Pioneer Women* (1981), *Once upon a Story* (1982), *The Legend of Pikari* (1983) and *Brunner—At the Risk of Our Lives* (1987). In 1989, he wrote and hosted *Variations on a theme*, a half-hour

drama, and appeared in *Laughinz* (contributor also), and *New Zealand 2000* (contributor/reporter). He was the storyteller in seven of twenty-six episodes of 'Maori Myths and Legends' (1990), was a contributor and performer in '1990 the Issues More Issues' (1990–93) which won best comedy (1993). In 1995, he appeared as Hare in *Dead Certs* (director Ian Mune), a one-hour drama he wrote for the Montana Drama Series, which was followed in 1996 by his role as the father in *Waiora*, a play by Hone *Kouka. His work in radio is also extensive, including hundreds of dramas, thousands of schools broadcasts, the hosting of 'Wags' (1978–79) and reading *Once Were Warriors. His filmwork includes roles in *Footrot Flats* (1987), *Arriving Tuesday* (1987), a feature which he co-wrote in 1985 with Richard Riddiford and Bruce Philips that was nominated for Best Screen Play/Best Supporting Actor, and *Rapanui* (1993). He is currently developing two feature screenplays.

His accomplishments as a writer have been recognised in several awards, such as the Maori Writer's Award for 'Saturday Morning', his one-act play set in an inner-city prison courtyard. His adaptations for secondary and primary schools including 'Varnished Faces' (*Merchant of Venice*), 'Lamb's Tales' (from Shakespeare), 'Rockin Back Magic' (a Musical) and 'Figgy Pudding' (for rest homes) were written while he was resident writer in 1978 for Stagestruck, Downstage Theatre in Wellington. 'Directions' (1979, Youth Theatre) and two theatre revues followed—'Decayed Decade' (1979) and 'The Big Black O' (1980). 'Proper Channels', the first radio play written, produced and directed by him (1980), won the Mobil Award for Best Special Programme. 'The Fabulous Adventures of Foxy' (1981), a children's musical, fulfilled an aim to write and produce further material based on the fables. Other work included 'Thrills, Chills and Spills' (1981, an adaptation of Roald Dahl's stories), 'The Big Black No' (1981, a theatre revue for the general election), 'Untitled' (1982, a collection of performance poetry) and 'Playfool' (1982, a solo kids show). 'Sam's Place to Live', broadcast in 1996, was written in 1983 after he was awarded the *Burns Fellowship. *Te Moemoea* (1989), which he directed for television, has subsequently screened in festivals in France, Brussels and Canada. In 1989 also, the Listener Television Award for Best Writer was awarded for *Erua* (filmed 1987), a one-hour drama based on the book of drawings by Sir Toss *Woollaston.

He has contributed scripts to *Country GP* (1984), *Seekers* (1984), *The Adventurer* (1985), *Open House* (1987), *Kiri Te Kanawa—The Return Journey* and he wrote the radio drama 'Save Us a Place to Live' (1994). 'Whiria' (co-written with Pat Hohepa), which he considers to be his major work to date, followed in 1988. An epic series of six one-hour pre-European dramas which follow the adventures of a female tattooist, her carver husband and their family, 'Whiria' appears in extract in *Te *Ao Mārama* 5 (1996). His work in documentary, in which he excels, includes 'Opo' (1990, writer and appearance), 'Nga Uri Whakatupu' which he also produced (1991, co-writer L. Parr), 'Hikoi' as co-producer (1993, co-written with H. *Melbourne and T. Reedy) and, more recently, 'Te Pahu' (writer/producer), which explores the 'fate of the traditional Maori drum' (1996). Poetry has been a constant concern, including an idealistic poem at age 10, '500 poems in the back of his geography book' at secondary school, and the poignant 'I will give you gold apples and grapes made of rubies' written at age 14, when his mother was dying, and remains the expression of 'something deep inside you'. More recently, 'Pakeha' (*Te Ao Mārama* 5) reiterates the political aspect of his time as president of Nga Tamatoa (Wellington, 1972) and as national co-ordinator (1972) of the inaugural Māori Language Day. In recent years, his public profile has involved work as a New Zealand delegate to the International Association of Theatre for Children and Young People (1990–93) and as deputy chairperson of the organising committee of the Asia Pacific Film Festival (1994–95). He regularly commutes from his home and whenua at Opononi in the Hokianga.　　　　　　　　　　　　　　　　　　JBa

PARK, Ruth (1917–), novelist, autobiographer and children's writer, was born and educated in New Zealand but has spent much of her adult life in Australia and has written extensively on both countries. Much of her childhood was spent in a small King Country town, and she has drawn on that experience to write fiction in which Māori–Pākehā relationships in rural communities play an important role. In *The Drums Go Bang!* (1956) she and the Australian writer D'Arcy Niland tell amusingly how they came to meet as young journalists, how Park went to Sydney to marry Niland (in 1942) and how they then travelled adventurously through the Australian 'outback' before settling in Sydney. Their efforts to get established as full-time writers are described vividly and reveal much about the conditions of literary life in both countries during the war years. In Sydney they lived in a slum area called Surry Hills and made strenuous efforts with partial success to get work published in newspapers, journals and through the broadcasting system.

True success, in fact a major *succès de scandale*, was achieved when Ruth won the *Sydney Morning Herald* novel competition in 1946 with *The Harp in the South*, which was serialised in that year and published as a book in 1948. It is set in Surry Hills and tells of the struggles of the Darcy family trying to live worthwhile lives in that

environment, which is described as horrendously disadvantaged. Not only the Darcys but also the colourful range of other characters meet adversity with humour and courage. Reactions to the book, especially in Sydney, ranged from high praise to shocked fury, some of its readers claiming that such social conditions as those described were impossible in Australia. Park followed up her success with a sequel telling the further adventures of the Darcy family under the title *Poor Man's Orange* (1949). By the time Niland published his own best-seller *The Shiralee* in 1955, the couple were known as people who courageously combined parenthood with full-time writing careers. Altogether they have five children, two of whom, Kilmenny and Deborah Niland, have been credited with the illustrations to some of Park's children's books. After the death of Niland in 1967 Park moved to London for some time, but later returned to Sydney and then, in 1973, moved to Norfolk Island, where she has lived ever since.

New Zealand responses to her early books included a review by 'G.W.' in the *Auckland Star*, 11 Jan. 1950, which suggested that she had found more colourful characters in Sydney slums than would be possible in New Zealand and nonetheless challenged her to write equally vividly of the country of her birth. She met this challenge with *The Witch's Thorn* (1951), set in a small King Country town, Te Kano. It is not short of vivid writing, but seems more credible to foreign readers than to local ones. In part it reads as if it were directed at the tourist market, and it has been one of her best-selling books outside New Zealand. After a purple-prose description of the country it opens with Johnny Gow jumping into the local geyser just as it is due to go off. There is little left of him, but the remainder of the book is a flashback covering the four years which led to his death. Mainly the events are seen through the eyes of Bethell, a girl who is abandoned by her teenage mother and brought up by family members who are totally unsympathetic towards her. She finds warmth, love and understanding in a Māori family. She is told by Pearlie Gow that her father, Johnny Gow, is also Bethell's father. Full of excitement she goes to see him, but is thrust angrily away. The family life that Johnny is trying to preserve in this way is anything but happy, however, and in his thoughts there are gloomy regrets for Queenie, Bethell's mother, and angry hatred for his wife. It is this frustration that ultimately drives him to suicide, while Bethell continues to find comfort with her Māori friends.

A Power of Roses (1953) takes up the story of life in Sydney's slums again, but in *Pink Flannel* (1955) Park returns to the small-town setting of Te Kano. As a child the narrator lived there with 'four radiant aunts' and it is the story of their lives that she wishes to tell. They are dominated by their irascible Swedish father, who stands between them and married happiness. For example, when Louise falls in love with the Pig Man, the father is furious and confiscates the phonograph Louise had received from her lover. Parallel to this story of gentle women who lack the strength to defy their patriarchal tyrant are the ventures of the narrator into the warmer world of the Māori, where generational conflicts are at a minimum. There is some sensitive commentary on the 'colour prejudice' of such a community in the 1950s: the Pākehā children like and admire the Māori ones but 'When they left school they discovered they had put on social inequality with the long trousers'. The narrator observes that there can be happiness in the poorest Māori hovel and unhappiness in the well-off but morally restricted house of sisters. Ironically, when her grandfather sees the (constricted) love life of his daughters and 'cuts them off without a penny', they are all delighted. This is their moment of release, and the novel ends with the wedding of Louisa and the Pig Man.

Park's best-known New Zealand novel is *One-a-Pecker, Two-a-Pecker* (1957), a South Island *goldfields novel, reissued in the US as *The Frost and the Fire* (1958). *The Good-Looking Women* (1961) is a study in religious hysteria with a tragic outcome. After a long pause, Park's next adult novel was *Swords and Crowns and Rings* (1977), the story of an Australian country town from 1907 to 1931. At its centre is Jackie Hanna, a dwarf, who suffers all the disadvantages and miseries arising from his deformity but retains a proud human spirit which ultimately triumphs. The background of World War 1 and the *Depression are vividly conveyed and something of the rough city life of Sydney slums is recaptured from earlier novels.

Ruth Park has also had a considerable career as the author of children's books. Her stories about the 'Muddle-Headed Wombat' have been translated into many languages and sold all over the world. *The Ship's Cat* (1961) is a New Zealand tale of a boy and a cat shipwrecked in early days and being taken over by a group of Māori. The boy, Barnaby, is saved from murder by a girl called Te Inu, who also turns out to be a lost white child, once called Margaret. On encountering moa the Māori show fear, but the cat shows that the moa are harmless. Barnaby suggests burning the tussock to drive the moa against the enemy tribe, a ploy which succeeds. Finally Barnaby and Margaret are picked up by a whaler in Dusky Sound. *The Hole in the Hill* is a longer story of an encounter of white children with Māori, set in more recent times. It includes a series of wild adventures and encounters with *tapu in an old cave. *The Shaky Island* is set on an imaginary island near Australia where a huge turtle is persuaded to leave a cave, where

it had caused the island to be constantly shaking. *Uncle Matt's Mountain* (1962) is a tale of the Tarawera eruption. *Nuki and the Sea Serpent* (1969) is set in a Māori community but is concerned with the difference between 'fiction' and 'lying'. *Merchant Campbell* (1976) is an historical novel of early Sydney.

Park's autobiographical *A Fence Around the Cuckoo* (1992) won the Melbourne *Age* Book of the Year Award for non-fiction, and was followed by *Fishing in the Styx* (1993).   NW

PARKER, Dean (1947–), is a writer for screen, radio and stage, born in Napier and educated at Napier Marist and St John's, Hastings. Comic iconoclasm was evident in his early plays for radio, including 'Joe Stalin Knew My Father' (1974) and 'Where Have You Gone, Wilson Whineray, Lake Taupo Turns Its Lonely Eyes to You' (1974). His first stage play, *Smack* (1974), drew critical attention for the power and anger as well as the humour of the writing, and for the casual violence of its attack on establishment hypocrisy. Parker made no secret of his sympathy for class struggle. Professional theatres were unenthusiastic, however, and *Smack*, like *Two Fingers from Frank Zappa* the following year, was lucky to get even a late night slot. Subsequent plays such as *The Irish Argument* (1978), *The Slippery Opera* (1983) and *The Feds*, a Brechtian critique of fifty years of the Federation of Labour (1989), have been similarly politically engaged, and seldom seen in mainstream theatres. Radio has often been more accommodating, particularly for subjects like the political entertainment 'Engels F: A History of the Ould Sod' (1978), and a 1980 series on workers' strikes in New Zealand. Since the mid-1970s Parker has written mainly for television, including *Thirty Minute Theatre* (1976), *Roche* (1985), *A People Apart: The Irish in New Zealand* (1995) and *Share the Dream* (1997). He also writes for film, notably *Came a Hot Friday* (1984, co-written with Ian Mune), and the award-winning *Old Scores* (1989, co-written with Greg *McGee). He has written occasional articles on labour history, and edits the New Zealand Irish magazine *Saoirse*. He lives in Auckland.   DC

PARKINSON, Sydney (*c*.1745–1771), accompanied James *Cook on his first voyage to the South Pacific in 1769. His posthumously published *Journal of a Voyage to the South Seas* (1773, 1784) is the first visual and written account by a professional artist to describe and illustrate New Zealand subjects. Trained as a botanical artist in Edinburgh, Parkinson came to the attention of Sir Joseph *Banks who invited him to join the *Endeavour* to record the plant life encountered. As well as 955 drawings of plants collected by Banks, Parkinson undertook topographical studies of landforms and figure studies, especially after the death of Alexander Buchan, another of Cook's artists, in 1769. The vividness of expression and gesture in this work indicates a close rapport with Pacific people. CB

PARRY, Lorae (1955–), feminist playwright, was born in Sydney and moved to Auckland for her last school year in 1972. After training at the New Zealand Drama School and working at Downstage Theatre, from 1979 she worked in Britain with other New Zealanders in the 'Heartache and Sorrow Company', writing and performing in London and at the Edinburgh Festival. She co-wrote *Strip* with Lynne Brandon and Celia West, and rewrote it on return to New Zealand, playing the lead in its run at Wellington's Circa Theatre (1983), prior to its performance by several New Zealand professional companies. *Frontwomen* (pub. 1993) enjoyed sellout seasons at the Depot, Wellington, in 1988, and Maidment Theatre, Auckland, in 1989. It examines a rare theme in New Zealand drama, 'the love that exists between women … who lead ordinary and sometimes extraordinary lives'.

As playwright, actor and director Parry has been committed to empowering women in theatre and demonstrating through drama the importance of women's lives. *Cracks*, 'a rough edged contemporary fairy tale', published 1994 and performed that year at Taki Rua, Wellington, is set in Sydney and examines the effects on character of class and roots. *Eugenia* (Taki Rua 1996, pub. 1996) explores the nature of sexuality and gender, while challenging the encircling social mores. Contrasting public and private lives, past and present, and drawing richness from comedy and tragedy, it is Parry's most significant achievement.

Since 1988 she has been involved in 'Hen's Teeth', a women's comedy collective, known especially for the satirical 'Digger and Nudger' sketches, and was instrumental in founding the Women's Play Press which has published *Frontwomen*, *Cracks*, *Love Knots* by Vivienne ★Plumb, *Ophelia Thinks Harder* by Jean Betts and *The Case of Katherine Mansfield* by Cathy ★Downes. Parry held the Victoria University writing fellowship in 1998. GB

Parsons' Packet was published and edited by the Wellington bookseller Roy ★Parsons 1947–55. It rapidly became a literary institution, presenting a mix of news, reviews and articles on New Zealand and overseas writing solicited from a wide selection of local writers, including John Reece ★Cole, Dan ★Davin, Basil ★Dowling, J.C. ★Beaglehole, Lauris ★Edmond, A.R.D. ★Fairburn, Alan ★Mulgan, Frank ★Sargeson, Sarah ★Campion and Louis ★Johnson. SH

PARSONS, Roy (1909–91), was an energetic influence in the book trade for many years. Born in England, he arrived in Wellington in 1939 to manage a new bookshop. In 1947 he established his own bookshop, which has traded ever since at or near the original Lambton Quay location, and devoted himself to improving local access to good books—books, as he put it, with 'the stuff of life in them'. His quarterly house journal, *★Parsons' Packet*, had a substantial literary content. Parsons Books and Music is now operated by his son and daughter.

He served on the council of the New Zealand Booksellers' Association from about 1950 to 1980, with two terms as president, and set about professionalising the hitherto informal body. Among his initiatives were the introduction to New Zealand of book tokens; the establishment of the ★New Zealand Book Council; training courses for booksellers; the Book of the Month scheme; and a clearing-house system whereby the association coordinates overseas purchasing for member booksellers.

Parsons helped establish the Indecent Publications Tribunal; recognising that ★censorship was politically inevitable, he sought to remove it from the hands of the Customs Department, and make it open, informed and consistent. He is also remembered for having taken legal action against the 1981 Springbok rugby tour. JH

Parting of the Mist, The (1963), by Lyndon Rose, is significant among children's novels for its early informed insight into Māori life. Betty ★Gilderdale calls it 'fine and sensitive' in its portrayal of 'a people in many ways perplexed, yet clinging to their traditions' (*A Sea Change*, 1982). Set in the 1930s, it is detailed and realistic in its account of rural Māori lifestyle and the tensions between traditional customs and the attractions and risks of moving to urban areas. It tells of the high-born Tama, discontented and rebellious but gifted in carving and with visionary percipience. Illicitly away from school in the bush, he accurately dreams of his grandfather's death, but on returning for the ★tangi he is insensitively arrested for an earlier crime and committed to Borstal. Working on a Pākehā farm he comes to appreciate the settlers' strengths and what Māori could learn from them. After war service, Tama returns home and is elected rangatira, committed to preserving Māori values and custodianship of the land. RR

PASCOE, John (1908–72), was an environmental and mountaineering writer and historian of the European exploration of New Zealand. An outstanding mountaineer, his writing is always informed by intimate knowledge of the back country and its challenges, and by literary and scholarly skills. The combination makes his narratives informative and literate. In several cases, they bring a significant new perspective to major literary and historical figures such as *Butler or Selwyn, and to the early literary and artistic representations of the country. Among more than a dozen books, *Land Uplifted High* (1952) provides valuable summaries of aspects of mountain culture such as the literature of the Southern Alps, and *Great Days in New Zealand Exploration: The Bush and the Rain* (1959) and *Exploration New Zealand* (1971) unpretentiously lucid narratives of a dramatic era. His biography and edition of the diaries and letters of Charles Edward Douglas, *Mr Explorer Douglas* (1957), brought to attention a significant explorer and spirited writer.

Born in Christchurch and educated at Christ's College, Pascoe worked in Wellington as controller of the then Wildlife Branch of Internal Affairs and later as chief archivist of the National Archives, and he was also secretary of the Historic Places Trust. He achieved the first ascent of more than twenty-five Southern Alps peaks as well as pioneering explorations in the Rakaia–Rangitata area. He was illustrations editor for the *Centennial publications in 1940. As a photographer he is known for spectacular high-country pictures and for revealing portraits, his 1951 study of Frank *Sargeson (in *Landfall Country*) being among the best-known New Zealand literary images.　　　　RR

Passport to Hell (1936) is Robin *Hyde's story of James Douglas Stark, born in the South Island of Native American and Spanish descent. Having interviewed him for her 1935 *Observer* article, '"Starkie", Outlaw of the N.Z.E.F.', Hyde returned to his extraordinary story during her stay in the Auckland Mental Hospital's Grey Lodge. Expelled from five schools, court-martialled nine times yet recognised for his exceptional bravery, Starkie is shown to be an outcast because of his race, class and confrontations with the law. A homeless itinerant on the run from the police, the 16-year-old Starkie finds himself in the army and sailing for Egypt. Describing his adventures in the back streets of Cairo, the swollen, blackened corpses of Gallipoli, the horror of the Somme trenches, Hyde succeeds in denouncing the imperialistic arrogance and hypocrisy of the military hierarchy, the futility of war and the depths of man's inhumanity. At times the style is that of documentary, detached and objective, at others horrifying in its detail or moving in its unexpected description of rare moments of peace and silence, 'droning bees, rows of blue flowers … brick buildings faded to the colour of autumn leaves'. Hyde's subject is not the glory of war, nor the romantic heroism of officers and gentlemen, but 'that most unknown of soldiers, the ordinary man'. Characteristically, Hyde shared the

royalties with Stark whose sudden declaration of love was an unexpected complication. While some of Starkie's contemporaries queried the narrative's factual detail, it was justly described by John A. *Lee as 'the most important New Zealand war book yet published'.　　　　GB

Pātere are a form of traditional song composed as satires or insults to attack—and correct—the behaviour of people who step out of line. They are performed by groups of singers who often underline their feeling with gestures and facial expressions called pūkana (also used in *haka). The delivery is fast and continuous and often the words are shared (as in *karakia) so that continuity is unbroken—for as long as half an hour according to Maui Pomare and James *Cowan in *Legends of the Maori* (1930). Bruce *Biggs remarks that they were usually in reply to slanderous gossip, not by denial but by 'recounting the lineal and lateral kinship of the author…. A pātere often takes its audience on a tour … with introductions to the principal chiefs of the time and genealogical excursions into the past…. Interspersed … are interesting remarks on what the singer will do to her detractors when she meets them.' Pei Te Hurinui *Jones reveals that it is considered 'a high compliment to be the subject of chastisement and castigation, especially in song. The poetesses … would not be bothered with ordinary men and women…. many of the old songs of this nature have been rescued from oblivion by the descendents of those people named in the pātere'. However, if such a song is truly offensive it is called a kaioraora, rather than a pātere. Elsdon *Best says the kaioraora 'expresses savage and deadly hatred, a desire to slay, cook and eat enemies against whom it is directed'.　　　　NW

PATERSON, Alistair or **A.I.H.** (1929–), is a poet, editor, anthologist, fiction writer and critic most associated with the development in the 1970s–1980s of New Zealand awareness of recent American poetics, especially aspects of *postmodernism and the concept of 'open form'. He has also combined a productive literary career with unusual skills as an administrator and entrepreneur, a legacy perhaps of his experience in the Royal New Zealand Navy (1954–74, retiring as lieutenant commander) and in public service education (dean of general studies, New Zealand Police 1974–78, continuing education officer, Department of Education 1979–89). Thus he initiated and organised the important tour of Robert *Creeley in 1976, was behind the later visits of Robert Duncan and Galway Kinnell, served on the national executive of *PEN 1982–89, has frequently acted as literary judge and on various selection committees (*Burns Fellowship et al.) and has been a notably reliable and successful editor, of *Mate* and *Climate* 1974–78, and *Poetry New Zealand* since 1994.

Above all Paterson made himself known as an advocate of contemporary *American ideas in poetry and as a tireless critic of what he has always loosely called *'Georgianism'. Influenced mainly by William Carlos Williams, he argued that poetry is 'not a quantity (in either the metrical or the intellectual sense) but a quality of mind', following the 'Black Mountain poets' (Creeley, Duncan, Charles Olson, et al.) in seeking 'open' or 'organic' form, exclusion of any notion of poetic personality or self and thus the discarding of conventions of lineation, margin and metre in favour of spontaneity and a sense of the exploratory and provisional. From this he adapted his own practice of 'double margin field form'.

Paterson's volumes of poetry are: *Caves in the Hill* (1965), *Birds Flying* (1973), *Cities and Strangers* (1976), *The Toledo Room* (1978), *Qu'appelle* (1982), *Odysseus Rex* (1985) and *Incantations for Warriors* (1986). *The Toledo Room* grew from his interest in the possibility of the longer poem, then well out of fashion, and was well received, being performed as a dramatic piece on radio and at Downstage Theatre, both in 1978. Paterson's poetry has been frequently anthologised both in New Zealand and America and he was co-winner of the J.C. Reid Award for longer poems in 1982 for *Qu'appelle*.

His missionary zeal for the new poetics also made him an active promoter and mentor of younger practitioners of them. As editor he encouraged writers such as Jennifer *Compton, Mike *Johnson and David *Mitchell, and he has written enthusiastically on such poets as Riemke *Ensing (*Metro*, July 1986) and Rob *Jackaman (*Journal of New Zealand Literature* 10, 1992). Yet his success as an editor reflects a catholicity of taste rather than a single-minded orthodoxy. Even his anthology *15 Contemporary New Zealand Poets* (NZ 1980, USA 1982), by including Allen *Curnow and Kendrick *Smithyman, showed a responsiveness to varieties of the contemporary outside Black Mountain or 'open form' doctrines. His long and contentious introduction to *15 Contemporary New Zealand Poets*, expanded and published separately as *The New Poetry, Considerations Towards Open Form* (1981), is more prescriptive, doctrinaire and arguably elitist than his actual editorial practice.

He is currently concentrating on fiction, in which his first recognition came when he won the BNZ Katherine *Mansfield Memorial Short Story Award in 1993. His novel *How to Be a Millionaire by Next Wednesday* (1994) led to a 1996 Creative New Zealand award for work on a further novel. He has also taught novel writing for University of Auckland Continuing Education.

Born in Nelson, Paterson has lived in Christchurch, Wellington and since 1979 Auckland, as well as on-board postings with the Navy. He graduated BA at Victoria University and also gained teaching qualifications. Though he has sometimes described himself as insufficiently recognised by the literary establishment, he has in fact almost always held positions of influence which he has used with some generosity, especially now as editor of *Poetry New Zealand*.   RR

Paul, Blackwood and Janet, see **Blackwood and Janet Paul.**

PAUL, Joanna (1945–   ), was born in Hamilton, daughter of *Blackwood and Janet Paul, a literary and artistic upbringing that contributed to her career as a poet and visual artist. She completed a Diploma in Fine Arts at Elam (1969) and has lived in Auckland, Canterbury, Wanganui and Dunedin. She has worked with a variety of media: poetry, oils, watercolour, drawing, photography and film, often blurring the generic boundaries as she seeks to record impressions of her environment and life as a woman, wife and mother. Her first collection, *Imogen* (1977), which won the PEN First Book of Poems Award, is a moving sequence about the short life of a child. It employs compelling imagery in a compressed, elliptical syntax, achieving emotional intensity yet at the same time a sense of serenity. Published by *Hawk Press, its adventurous typography extends and supplements the imagery visually. She has another volume in preparation.

She has also produced a number of artist's books, including *Rilke's Life of Mary* (1970), *Unwrapping the Body* (1978) and *As I sat …* (1985–86), and shown paintings and works on paper regularly in solo and group exhibitions since 1972. Although Paul keeps her painting and writing separate, the activities intersect. *Unwrapping the Body*, for instance, incorporates both text and images to explore the emotional and political resonances of references to parts of the human body. Her poems characteristically articulate sensitively observed visual images, while her paintings and drawings, which she describes as 'visual poems', often integrate verbal with visual elements, the fragmentary and disconnected objects evoking her sequential encounter with everyday life. These resemble notations in a visual diary, an art form which emerged in the 1970s as vehicle for women artistically exploring their lives.   CB/JH

Paul's Book Arcade, see **Blackwood and Janet Paul.**

PEACOCKE, Isabel Maud (1881–1973), who also wrote under her married name Isabel M. Cluett, was a novelist, playwright, journalist, teacher and broadcaster. Born and resident in Auckland, one of six children of

Gerald L. Peacocke, editor of *The NZ Farmer,* she married at the age of 39 an inventor, George Cluett, who predeceased her by thirty-six years. Though childless, she was closely involved with children, opening her own school for girls when only 16, and from 1910 to 1920 teaching at Dilworth School, where she established traditions of storytelling and nature rambling. Peacocke began writing early: at 10 she had to leave a play on Mary Queen of Scots unfinished because she could not bring Mary to her inevitable end. A novel, *When I Was Seven* (1927), contains autobiographical material. A book of verse, *Songs of the Happy Isles* (1910), collected her poetry published here and in Australia. Most poems use the simple vocabulary and rapid pace that characterise 'The Grand Old Gum', expressing an Australian miner's love for gum trees: 'But give to me the tough old gums / That skirt the boundary-railing; / When skies are brass, and earth is dust / And all the creeks are failing.'

She is best known for her novels for children and for sixteen adult light romances. She wrote some fifty novels in forty years, many published in England, where in 1924, a grateful publisher, Ward Lock, gave her a 'swell party' at the Waldorf Hotel. Many novels sold out in England before reaching New Zealand. 'Wherever they sell them it is all right by me,' said Peacocke, whose chronic insomnia may have contributed to her productivity: 'I … sit up in bed to work at any old hour.' She was a vice-president of the *New Zealand Women Writers Society for forty years, as well contributing to writers' and women's service groups in New Zealand and London. In 1915 she dedicated *My Friend Phil* 'To my Comrades all, the Junior Boys of Dilworth Ulster School … this story of a boy is inscribed'. The novel contains many of Peacocke's usual features: it is a lively, non-preaching story of courage, coolness, and common sense. Above all, she liked children to enjoy themselves, free from fear of being deserted by adults, and from poverty. She hardly ever wrote 'young' stories, but put children into a situation where their cleverness showed up some failing in the adult world: cruelty, failure to care, selfishness or snobbery. There are escapades, dangerous situations and puzzling isolation for the child until proper order is restored, with the adult taught a lesson. She appealed to children's love of words, often using long, difficult ones or humorously misusing others ('ammonia' for 'pneumonia'), and had a penchant for puns. Many of her novels were set in the urban environment of Auckland at a time when children's books were most often set in rural England.

Cathleen with a 'C' (1934) subverts many conventions of children's stories. Lively and irreverent in style, with racy dialogue, the novel features an unusual 'herowine', Cathleen, whose face is fleshy and figure pillowy but who is a wry observer of the adult world. There are camping holiday adventures, with, as some commentators noted, a more than passing similarity to *Swallows and Amazons.* However, though girls may be lively for a while, most Peacocke heroines expect eventually to be rescued by boys and to defer to husbands, once they have been brought to their senses. In a critical article on New Zealand writing (*The Mirror,* 1 Nov. 1929), she argued that in fiction 'most of the more virile and convincing pen pictures of this country have been presented by women', while also conceding the tendency for women writers to decamp to England. She liked novelists to be discreet about love and rejected the modern trend to be 'coarse and vulgar'. During Zane Grey's visit to New Zealand, Peacocke is reputed to have pressed on him his first-ever cup of tea, which the great cowboy novelist and fisherman vowed to drink, 'even if it killed him'.

HM

PEARSON, Bill or **W.H.** (William Harrison) (1922–), fiction writer, essayist and critic, was born and grew up in Greymouth, attended Canterbury University College in 1939 and Dunedin Training College and Otago University College 1940–41. He taught briefly at Blackball School in 1942 and then, after intense inner questioning about conscientious objection and military service, served in the Dental Corps in Fiji in 1942–43, in the infantry in Egypt and Italy and in the occupation force in Japan in 1943–46. After completing an MA at Canterbury in 1947–48, he taught at Oxford District High School in 1949 and then went to King's College, University of London (PhD 1952). He remained in England, writing and working as a supply teacher for London Council Schools 1952–53. He returned to lecture at Auckland University College (later University of Auckland) from 1959 until his retirement as associate professor in 1986, apart from periods overseas, such as a term as research fellow at the Australian National University 1967–69.

Throughout this distinguished academic career Pearson wrote fiction, social criticism and literary criticism. His first published writings were short stories about his childhood and military experience, published in periodicals 1947–51 and much later collected in *Six Stories* (1991). These were in many ways apprentice work for his major novel, *Coal Flat.* Though this did not appear until 1963, he had begun planning it as early as 1946 and wrote it in the 1950s. His influential essay of social analysis, *'Fretful Sleepers: A Sketch of New Zealand Behaviour and Its Implications for the Artist',* appeared in *Landfall* in 1952 and outlined many of the themes that were to be imaginatively explored in *Coal Flat.* Although *Coal Flat* was received as the most important New Zealand novel of its time, Pearson published no more fiction, but rather concentrated on literary criticism and scholarship. He edited Frank *Sargeson's *Collected Stories* in 1964, while his *Henry Lawson Among the Maoris*, a study of *Lawson's experience in New Zealand and the fiction that emerged from it, appeared in 1968. His essays and reviews on New Zealand literature and society were collected in *Fretful Sleepers and Other Essays* in 1974. Some of his most important work had been on the depiction of Māori in New Zealand writing, and he followed this line of interest with a study of imaginative writing about *Pacific Islanders, *Rifled Sanctuaries*, in 1984.

In both his fiction and his critical writing, Pearson helped to define the themes and modes of New Zealand critical realism; he was innovative in giving scholarly attention to representations of Māori and Pacific Islanders; and as university lecturer he was among the first to teach a course in New Zealand literature, first offering a series of lectures, with Allen *Curnow, in 1956.   LJ

PEEL, Colin (1936–), is a prolific author of action thrillers published mostly in the UK. They have high-tech or science fiction content, showing influence from his earlier experience as a research engineer in missile development; and from Ian Fleming. Born in England, he worked there and in Canada and USA before arriving in New Zealand in 1969 to work eventually with Fletcher Challenge. He now lives rustically in the South Manukau. He began publishing in the UK in 1973 with *Adapted to Stress* and *Bitter Autumn*, and produced the commercially successful *Flameout* (1976) and others while still in senior executive employment. Writing full-time since 1990, he added *Hell's Angels* (1991) and others, with currently nineteen titles, belatedly achieving Australasian publication with the 1995 reissue of *Atoll* (1992), which topically envisages catastrophic consequences from France's *Pacific nuclear testing. Mostly aimed at young males, the earlier titles are plain tales of violent Cold War action, with complex technology and simple dialogue. The more recent seem aimed at a more mature audience, with some interest in character and location, especially different parts of the Pacific in *Atoll* and *Dark Armada* (1995)   RR

Pegasus Press (1947–86) took its 'first flight in the typographical air' when Albion Wright, whose successful advertising agency had been a substantial client of *Caxton Press since its inception, decided to establish a rival. Wright aimed both to challenge his close friend Denis *Glover and to emulate the Caxton tradition of patronage for the arts coupled with high production

standards. His partner and Pegasus editor was Robin *Muir, who ensured that rigorous editorial standards were maintained. His novel, *Word for Word* (1960), provides a very readable account of the book-publishing process during this period. Peter Low, factory manager and later a director, details the many people involved with Pegasus in his *Printing by the Avon* (1995); among these were Glover himself and Bob *Gormack. Pegasus first signalled its commitment to New Zealand literature with the publication of Alistair *Campbell's first collection, *Mine Eyes Dazzle* (1950), in an elegant octavo edition, and was rewarded when it went to a further two editions. They followed this success with the Pegasus Poets series, which included volumes by Louis *Johnson, Mary *Stanley and Keith *Sinclair and retailed at a very modest price. Johnson, in particular, developed a close relationship with Pegasus, convincing them to publish the *New Zealand Poetry Yearbook* from 1954 until its final controversial 1964 issue. Perhaps their most successful literary association was with Janet *Frame, for whom they published seven novels, a book of short stories and a volume of poetry. Of particular note in relation to Frame was their groundbreaking work in establishing joint publication with foreign publishers and securing translation rights. In the early 1970s, Pegasus again achieved success with poetry from Glover, Campbell, R.A.K. *Mason and the biennial *Poetry New Zealand. As part of the International Year of the Woman in 1975 they also published volumes of poetry by Marilyn *Duckworth, Lauris *Edmond and Fiona *Kidman. The continued success of the Pegasus was based on judicious use of the *Literary Fund for literary publications, underpinned by a successful commercial printing operation which included publication of many district and family histories. However, as with many publishing houses in the 1980s, they were taken over and stripped of their assets. Nevertheless, their legacy of almost 100 volumes of poetry and over twenty works of fiction, as well as numerous works of history and biography, stands as a significant contribution to New Zealand's cultural heritage.   NWt

Pelorus Press, see **LOWRY, Bob**.

PEMBERTON, Robert (1788?–1879), was an Englishman of obscure birth, thought to be one of the illegitimate children of the court of George III. He published nothing until he was 60 and then brought out eleven books in ten years. Only one of these, *The *Happy Colony* is of relevance to New Zealand. The others have such titles as *The Attributes of the Soul from the Cradle* or *The Natural Method of Teaching the Elements of Grammar*.   NW

PEN (New Zealand Centre), now the New Zealand Society of Authors (PEN NZ Inc), was founded in Wellington in 1934 by the self-styled 'bookman' Pat *Lawlor. It is affiliated to PEN International (the International Association of Poets, Playwrights, Editors, Essayists and Novelists), which began in the UK in 1921. The society serves the interests of writers and of literature in various ways, including many functions of a trade union, of a social organisation and of a lobbying group.

The New Zealand branch quickly established itself as a significant force by organising the first formal literary gathering, *Authors' Week 1936. Membership expanded across the country following this and the establishment in 1938 of the newsletter, *PEN Gazette*, now retitled *The New Zealand Author*. The next important initiative was its campaign for formal state funding for literature, which it began in 1937 and resumed vigorously in 1944. After two years' advocacy the State *Literary Fund was established and three PEN representatives included on its advisory committee. This arrangement continued until, following new legislation in 1994, formal representation by writers in the process of distributing public funding for literature was controversially ended in 1995.

Other successful PEN campaigns have included the establishment of the Authors' Fund, by which writers receive some compensation for books held in public and academic libraries, and of Copyright Licensing Limited, which collects and distributes remuneration for multiple photocopying, especially by educational institutions. PEN also appoints or nominates members of the selection committees of many writing fellowships and literary prizes, its members giving significant time to these responsibilities. PEN itself has created awards, including those for Best First Book (of Poetry, Fiction, etc.), and has initiated or supported further significant conferences, including the *New Zealand Writers' Conference 1951, the *PEN/Victoria University Writers' Conference 1979 and seminars on professional aspects of authorship such as 'The Business of Writing' in 1984. The society's active contribution to the development of New Zealand literature has been an important one.

It has generally enjoyed a remarkably wide acceptance among New Zealand writers, many of the most celebrated having accepted one or two years' appointment as 'President of Honour', and many more serving assiduously on its managing committees. There have also been the more controversial passages natural to an association of writers, such as the censure of its 'old-fashioned' management by the 1951 Writers' Conference, or the debates which preceded the move of the national office from Wellington to Auckland in the late 1980s, or

the 1994 change in title and constitution to the 'New Zealand Society of Authors', indicating a more explicitly political and lobbying role. Its exclusion from the funding process by Creative New Zealand, the present administrative body, has sharpened the renamed society's focus. A statement issued to PEN International in 1996, drafted by Kevin *Ireland and Gordon McLauchlan, defined NZSA's present priority as 'campaigning to regain influence on the distribution of grants'.   RR

The PEN/Victoria University conference, 'New Zealand Writing 1959–1979', held at Victoria University 31 August–2 September 1979, acknowledged in its title the two decades that had passed since the last national literary gathering, the 1959 PEN Writers' Conference. This time the programme made a principle of placing the discussion of literature side by side with its performance, and perhaps as a result the mood was confident and celebratory rather than combative or controversial. Lauris *Edmond has described it as 'a weekend full of intellectual and social fizzing, the making or re-making of connections among writers who lived in different parts of the country … like a sporting tournament—literature as display, as jousting, as team game, festival' (*The Quick World*). For the first time the diversity of New Zealand writing was prominent, rather than any single orthodoxy, with unprecedented sessions on Māori and Polynesian writing, drama, and history and biography, as well as an emphasis on vitality through variety in the sessions on fiction and poetry. C.K. *Stead's *postmodernist reading of recent poetic history, 'From Wystan to Carlos', was received as only one response to an excitingly diverse and developing literary landscape, rather than as the seminal revisionism of *Baxter's presentation at the *New Zealand Writers' Conference 1951. The markedly increasing public with an informed commitment to New Zealand literature was also apparent in audiences of several hundreds, making the conference an important precursor of the success of *Writers and Readers Week and other literary festivals of the 1980s and 1990s. It pioneered an international dimension, too, with a session on Australian writing which Frank Moorhouse and David Williamson turned into a virtuoso display of trans-Tasman mockery, a literary equivalent of underarm bowling.

Contributors were: Bub *Bridger, Alistair Te Ariki *Campbell, Jennifer *Compton, Ian *Cross, Allen *Curnow, Wystan *Curnow, John Davidson, Lauris *Edmond, Riemke *Ensing, Ian Fraser, Patricia *Grace, Russell *Haley, Michael *Harlow, Peter *Hooper, Sam *Hunt, Louis *Johnson, Lawrence *Jones, Jan *Kemp, Michael *King, Graham *Lindsay, Bill *Manhire, Gary *McCormick, Frank *McKay, Frank Moorhouse,

Michael ★Morrissey, W.H. ★Oliver, Bill Parker, Roger Robinson, Peter ★Simpson, Elizabeth ★Smither, C.K. Stead, Bruce ★Stewart, Apirana ★Taylor, Mervyn ★Thompson, J.E.P. Thomson, Hone ★Tuwhare, Ian ★Wedde, Alan Wells, Albert ★Wendt, David Williamson.

Poems by Fleur ★Adcock were read by Anne ★French. Janet ★Frame, M.H. ★Holcroft, E.H. ★McCormick and Bruce ★Mason were all present as guests of honour. A souvenir booklet, *Poems for the Eighties* (1980), published the new poems read at the final session, with commentary by Roger Robinson, who was the programme convener, assisted by Anne French.   RR

Pencarrow books, The, a sequence of four novels by Nelle ★Scanlan (*Pencarrow*, 1932; *Tides of Youth*, 1933; *Winds of Heaven*, 1934; and *Kelly Pencarrow*, 1939) were the most widely read New Zealand novels of their time. They trace the Pencarrow family over four generations, from pioneering times to the late 1930s. The books were reprinted on several occasions in the 1930s, and again in the 1950s, and achieved sales of 80 000 copies in New Zealand alone, according to one estimate. In Alan ★Mulgan's view (*Great Days in New Zealand*, 1962), Scanlan was the first to establish a popular readership for fiction with New Zealand settings, characters and themes. With their celebration of family values during a century of pioneering struggle they held immense appeal for middle-class readers in the unsettled 1930s.

Pencarrow's central characters are the original pioneers, Matthew and Bessie Pencarrow, who establish the 'Home Farm' in the Hutt Valley and a sheep station, 'Duffield', in the Wairarapa. The narrative is also concerned with the intersecting and conflicting lives of their children: Michael, who contracts a disastrous marriage and brings up his daughter, alone, at 'Duffield'; Hester, who marries a reliable farmer in Picton; Miles (later Sir Miles) who becomes a prosperous lawyer and property speculator in Wellington; and Kittie, bored by farming life, who marries a weak-willed ★remittance man, but develops unsuspected strengths when he becomes ill. The novel is episodic, focusing on births, deaths, courtships and weddings, married life, conflict between parents and children, family reunions and their underlying tensions. In its later part, with Bessie as a grandmotherly figure of benign authority, the focus shifts to the manipulative Miles, his long-suffering wife, Norah, and the various fortunes of their children.

Tides of Youth takes the narrative to the end of World War 1, the focus now on the second generation, with central roles given to Sir Miles's adult children. The sense emerges of an ongoing cycle of strong and weak character traits passed on over the generations. The novel opens with the pathos of Bessie's death and develops sympathy

for the ageing Sir Miles. Bessie's strength is inherited by her granddaughter Genevieve; much of Miles's stubbornness reappears in his son Kelly; and there is a suggestion that the sensitivity and indecisiveness of Kittie's first husband is passed on to Genevieve's child, Pencarrow.

The third novel, *Winds of Heaven*, intended as the last, brings events to the present, with Kelly and Genevieve again central. The main action concerns Genevieve's struggle to support her ailing husband Robin and efforts to ensure the survival of the family law firm, but there is increasing focus also on Kelly's children. The end brings an almost pastoral sense of family identity, as the country emerges from the ★Depression.

Although there were signs that the original impulse was becoming exhausted in the third volume, Scanlan allowed herself to be persuaded to write a fourth, *Kelly Pencarrow*, published on the eve of World War 2. Despite the title, the presiding consciousness is again Genevieve, now a widow and the inheritor of Bessie's exemplary wisdom. There are two main actions: the renovation of Kittie's failing marriage, and the failure of Kelly's son, Michael, to reform his feckless uncle. This balancing of success and failure, within the overarching family continuity, is typical of the series. The essentially conservative ideology underlying Scanlan's affirmation of hard work, loyalty, and learning through adversity is explicit in the novel's attacks on the Labour government—elected for the first time in 1935—whose well-meant policies are seen as a threat to the values of individual initiative on which the Pencarrow family dynasty was built.   TS

Penguin Books (New Zealand) has been a force since the early 1980s in the publication of New Zealand literature. The establishment of a New Zealand branch in 1973, with a manager sent from England (Patrick Wright, a nephew of David McKee ★Wright), was part of a general pattern of British involvement in the New Zealand industry which began in the 1960s, when local branches were established by such firms as Heinemann and Hodder & Stoughton. Through the 1970s Penguin functioned as a sales and distribution office for overseas Penguin books, in alliance with the New Zealand subsidiary of Longman, which in 1967 had become Longman Paul after purchasing ★Blackwood and Janet Paul. This alliance for sales and distribution was also important in the establishment of Penguin's local publishing activities in the late 1970s, under Graham Beattie, who became managing director in 1978. Beattie and John Barnett (senior editor at Longman Paul) together set up a list which saw the 'transfer' to the Penguin imprint, among others, of Patricia ★Grace and Albert ★Wendt, of ★Mulgan's *Man Alone* and Frank ★Sargeson's stories, along with the purchasing of paperback rights to hardcover books published by other firms. Penguin's was, in a broad sense, a 'literary' list, while Longman Paul specialised in educational books. A major early initiative was the commissioning of the *Penguin Book of New Zealand Verse*, edited by Ian ★Wedde and Harvey ★McQueen (1985), notable and controversial for its inclusion of Māori poems with translations, chosen by Margaret ★Orbell, alongside the poetry written in English.

In 1985 Geoff Walker, who had worked in journalism and television before joining ★A.H. & A.W. Reed in 1976, became editor (later publishing director). The list expanded rapidly. Māori writing continued to be prominent, including Grace's prize-winning ★*Potiki* (1986), Hone ★Tuwhare's collected poems *Mihi* (1987), new Māori authors Apirana ★Taylor and Bruce ★Stewart, and a second anthology, of contemporary poetry, in which Wedde and McQueen were joined by Miriama Evans, again organised on bicultural principles. In the same year (1989) a contemporary short story anthology appeared, edited by Susan Davis and Russell ★Haley. The list also included numerous other new and established fiction writers (including Maurice ★Gee, from Faber), the beginnings of a children's list, and in particular a broadening range of lively 'current affairs' non-fiction very much in the tradition of the parent company: political commentary, general biography, books on Māori politics and culture like those of Ranginui ★Walker, a book on the Rainbow Warrior affair by Michael ★King, and collections of short autobiographical articles like Virginia Myers's *Head and Shoulders* (1986).

In 1988 Beattie left to pursue his interest in children's publishing at Ashton Scholastic, and a significant shift occurred in the wake of the company's purchase of the publishing list of Whitcoulls. Penguin's list became more diverse, topical and popular, expanding into fields such as natural history, gardening, cookery and travel. The parent company had also purchased the American publishing house of Viking, and the Australian branch of Penguin was planning a similar diversification. Initially the Viking imprint was assigned to the broader paperback categories inherited from Whitcoulls, but in the 1990s it began also to be used for major books in hard covers, like Anne Salmond's *Two Worlds* (1991) and *Between Worlds* (1997), King's biography of Sargeson (1995), and James ★Belich's *Making Peoples* (1997).

Expansion and diversification continued. Serious literature (especially fiction, history and biography) remained essential, including Patrick ★Evans's *Penguin History of New Zealand Literature* (1990), prize-winning novels by Vincent ★O'Sullivan (*Let the River Stand*, 1993) and Witi ★Ihimaera (*Bulibasha*, 1994), and a steady stream of new fiction writers. In 1997 Penguin's publishing programme had reached eighty-seven titles (including reprints), and a major expansion of sales and distribution activities had occurred, including distribution of Hodder Moa Beckett books. Although Penguin has not escaped the upheavals that occurred from the 1980s onwards as corporate entrepreneurs entered the market, it has been less affected than many others and its commitment to literature has held firm.   TS

Penwomen's Club (NZ), The, also known as the League of New Zealand Penwomen, was founded in Auckland in 1925 by a Texan, Edna Graham Macky, and affiliated to the Penwomen's Club of America. Its purpose was to help women have interests beyond the home, especially in the arts, with the motto 'Sincerity—in Friendship, Art and Ideals'. By 1926 there were sub-circles for art, drama, music, gardening, journalism and welfare. A Junior Penwomen's Club and branches in Dunedin, Hamilton, Marton, Tauranga and Wellington were established. The league's publications include the journal ★*Flight*, the *Penwomen's Journal* (for journalists), the magazine *Penpoint*, and *Hyacinths & Biscuits: The Diamond Jubilee Book of the Penwomen's Club (NZ) Inc 1925–1985* (1985), which contains a history.   HM

Pepeha, see **Māori sayings.**

PERKINS, Emily (1970–), won attention when Picador (UK) published her first collection of stories, *not her real name and other stories* (1996), while she was living in London. It was shortlisted for the New Zealand Book Award, won the Best First Book (Fiction) Award and subsequently won the Faber Award in the UK. Born in Christchurch, she grew up in Auckland and Wellington, worked as a TV actor, and studied acting at the New Zealand Drama School / Te Kura Toi Whakaari and writing at Victoria University. Both are evident in the deft narration and tellingly authentic dialogue of her stories of contemporary *weltschmerz*. These are mostly sketches in the joyless lives of the young generation of the modern city, conducting relationships with the same sense of anaesthetised necessity with which they work in shops or restaurants. Tama Janowitz's anodyne New York and Martin Amis's pleasureless London are discernible in the droll despondency of tone, as are the mannered ellipticalness and emotive reticence of the ★Manhire, ★*Sport* or Wellington School of the 1980s–90s. Chad ★Taylor and Maria ★Wickens are the most comparable New Zealand contemporaries, though Perkins's dismal tales are edged with an adroit downbeat wit and aptitude for episodes that tilt into black-absurdist comedy.   RR

PERRY, Anne (1938–), is a prolific and popular British-based author of detective mysteries. Born Juliet Hulme in Liverpool, England, and suffering much disruption in childhood from ill health and separation from her parents, she arrived in New Zealand in 1946 and entered Christchurch GHS in 1952. In 1954, at age 15, she and a classmate, Pauline Parker, were found guilty of the brutal murder of Parker's mother, a sensational case that subsequently gave rise to the play, *Daughters of Heaven,* by Michaelanne Forster, Peter Jackson's internationally successful film *Heavenly Creatures* (1994) and various other accounts. After release from prison in 1959, Hulme left New Zealand and now lives in Portmahomack in the Scottish Highlands. Her crime-writing career as Anne Perry was well established before her identity as Juliet Hulme became known in 1994, when interest in *Heavenly Creatures* led to features in the *New York Times* and elsewhere. Julie Glamuzina and Alison Laurie in their 1991 book on the case commendably chose 'not to intrude into the[ir] new identities'. Perry, perhaps coincidentally, is the name her mother took after divorce from Henry Hulme and marriage to co-respondent George Perry.

Her novels are set in mid-late Victorian England, usually London. They feature either Inspector Thomas Pitt (promoted to Superintendant in the most recent) and his resourceful well-bred wife Charlotte, or the broodingly romantic Inspector William Monk (later a 'private investigator'). Their main period colour comes from the depiction of London locations, English class attitudes and accents, and detailed accounts of domestic furnishings and women's fashions. Some deal in part with contemporary politics and there are usually walk-on appearances by such real-life persons as Gilbert and Sullivan. The crime plots are relieved by treatment of the personal and romantic relationships of the main characters.

At least twenty titles, a number that is increasing rapidly, have made Perry one of the best-known names in crime-mystery fiction, including *Resurrection Row* (1981), *Highgate Rise* (1991), *Defend and Betray* (1992), *The Hyde Park Headsman* (1994), *Traitors Gate* (1995), *Weighed in the Balance* (1996) and *Ashdown Hall* (1997). More than three million copies of her titles are currently in print. RR

Peruperu, see **Haka**.

PĒWHAIRANGI, Ngoi (1922–85), of Ngāti Porou, Te Whānau-a-Ruataupare, was an important composer of *waiata, both classical and modern, and the niece of the famous Tuini *Ngāwai, of whom she wrote a biography (*Tuini*, 1985). Tīmoti *Kāretu praises her

'charismatic, warm personality' and refers to her as a great inspiration to himself and other composers and performers, while Witi *Ihimaera remarks that her waiata 'Ka Nohu Au' and 'Whakarongo' are 'classics of the genre'. NW

Philosopher Dick: Adventures and Contemplations of a New Zealand Shepherd, George *Chamier's first novel, was published in two volumes in London in 1891. For the most part it is set on an up-country sheep station in Canterbury. Dick Raleigh, contemplative and well-educated, seems out of place in the rough atmosphere of the men. The manager finds him 'morbid' and an urbane doctor warns him against the melancholy inherent in preference for solitude. Dick points out that educated people who try to integrate themselves into colonial society end in poverty and misery.

When Dick goes alone to a hut in the mountains there are hints of a Robinsonade in his efforts to make a solitary life comfortable. He tries his hand at painting, and his flute-playing brings a touch of pastoral to the narrative.

It emerges that he seeks solitude out of disillusionment with the values of the industrial revolution, the 'progress and utility' in Britain and 'the gleaming *newness* of everything' in the colony. Slipping into apathy, dulled to the beauty of the landscape, he neglects his work and fills a diary with 'contemplations', noting the irony that solitude has been more 'confining' than liberating. The deep look into his soul has resulted in finding nothing there. When the flock he is guarding is driven over a precipice by dogs, Dick contemplates suicide but, after an accident, returns to the indifferent men at the station.

After episodes surrounding the arrival of a maidservant, Dick is offered the position of manager, but turns it down on the grounds that expending too much energy is the bane of the British people. He leaves, and after scenes of hellish desolation and drunken misery at an accommodation house arrives at a town. Here he observes that lawyers are as essential to a British colony as the Holy Inquisition to a Spanish one. Two eligible young women are introduced, Mary and Alice Seymour, and various people persuade him to become 'a respectable member of the community and be no longer PHILOSOPHER DICK'. How Dick responds is the subject of the sequel, *A *South-Sea Siren.*

Though *Philosopher Dick* has been seen as historically important and significantly different from other colonial novels, E.H. *McCormick found its mixture of attitudes 'baffling', while Joan *Stevens was no less puzzled by the confusion of narrative techniques. More recently Patrick *Evans has spoken of Chamier's 'remarkable sophistication', and the wide range of attitudes and techniques may indeed be seen as positives. The novel's unconventional satirical, indeed cynical view of colonial life sets it far from conventional tales of pastoral progress or spirited adventure, replacing courage with contemplation. Chamier would find more congenial spirits in Australian letters, and the emptiness at the heart of things, Dick's ultimate insight, is very like that in some of Henry *Lawson's more sophisticated tales, while the combination of learning and satire and of narration and reflection is reminiscent of Joseph Furphy. The nihilist melancholy also relates Chamier to Ruth *Park, who, like him, ultimately chose to live in Australia.   NW

Phoenix, the journal which gave its name to an innovative generation of writers, was published by the Literary Society of Auckland University College in four issues: March and July 1932, edited by James *Bertram (then aged 21), and March and June 1933, edited by R.A.K. *Mason. Under Bertram the journal's policy was 'literary' and aesthetic, a 'trail-blazer', 'the integration of national consciousness, the focusing of contemporary opinion upon local needs, the creation of cultural antennae ... ', while he also acknowledged the 'grandiloquence' of this programme. Mason's two issues were more political, using more non-student contributors, with radical articles attacking New Zealand's militarism, colonialism in the South *Pacific, anti-Semitism, and other targets. The four issues were handsomely printed by Robert *Lowry, the impressive appearance confessedly modelled on John Middleton *Murry's New Adelphi in England, just as editorially Bertram especially sought to emulate Murry's promotion of a serious and progressive post-*Georgian English literary movement. Hence the Phoenix symbol, associated with Murry, D.H. *Lawrence and artistic renaissance.

Earnest student articles on 'The Functions of Poetry' by C.R. *Allen or 'The Challenge of Russia' by Charles *Brasch are less than compelling today, and the importance of Phoenix lies in what it came to represent rather than its actual literary contents. Patrick *Evans in his Penguin History of New Zealand Literature (1990) gives a telling account of how his own contemporaries in the 1960s were brought up to revere the 'Phoenix generation' as the heroic progenitors of a new literature, how Phoenix had been mythologised into the defining point of New Zealand literary history. Even now, though the attitudes seem Anglophile and exclusivist, the short-lived journal retains its significance as a meeting point for mostly young writers who would retain their individual and collective importance: Bertram, Brasch, D'Arcy *Cresswell, Allen *Curnow, A.R.D. *Fairburn, Elsie *Locke, Mason, Ian *Milner. It was also the beginnings

of the rejection of what was perceived as the second stage of colonial poetry represented by *Kowhai Gold. A fifth issue was compiled by Mason, his third, but Lowry was 'fed up' with the hard labour of handsetting from the very limited stock of type. Thus, appropriately, Phoenix both died and lived on.   SH/RR

Piano, The, the award-winning film (1992) by Jane *Campion, was published in book form by Bloomsbury, UK, 1993. The film won the 1993 Palme d'Or at the Cannes Festival and was nominated in nine categories for Academy 'Oscar' Awards, including Best Original Screenplay. An Australian production with French finance, it is nevertheless an intensely New Zealand work, and unusually literary for an original film. Campion began writing it in 1984, while working in Sydney, as an imaginative revisitation of her relations with her New Zealand origins, with its colonial past, natural terrain, especially the *bush, and with the Māori people. The story centres on a Brontë-like romantic-erotic triangle in a tiny remote community, with the woman dominant, despite her muteness and the restrictions of convention, most evident in her cumbersome dress. Eroticism is the more powerful for being so little comprehended and so incompetently expressed, Victorian constraints on the body being visually contrasted with its celebratory decoration by the Māori characters. Similarly the sparse and repressed spoken English and sign-language are contrasted with the eloquence and frank wit of the Māori script, which includes verses by Selwyn Muru. Campion's published text amplifies the dialogue with extensive directions, which encompass descriptive and narrative writing ('The kerosene lamp burns fitfully, fluttering a light pulse across their faces') and psychological or moral explication ('He pulls her chair back from the piano. This upsets her, as much of her confidence was associated with the instrument. Baines ... is desperate and romantic'). The full text is thus a semi-dramatised fiction, its strong visual element heightened by stills from the film.

There has been considerable critical discussion, but little of the film's literary aspects, apart from some concern over similarity with Jane *Mander's The *Story of a New Zealand River. However, sources could also include Samuel *Butler's accounts of transporting his piano over incongruous ground in A First Year in Canterbury Settlement or John Huston's memorable scene in The Unforgiven of a settler woman playing her piano outdoors in defiance of the hostile terrain and its inhabitants. More significant is the powerful presentation of the New Zealand bush, especially its almost submarine qualities: 'The wetness, closeness and darkness of the bush is such that the air seems green, as at the bottom of a deep sea.' New Zealand's unique relation between earth, sea and sky—especially the two former—has rarely been more vividly imagined.   RR

Pig Island(s) is a familiar name for New Zealand that celebrates the long (since *c.*1769) association of New Zealand with domestic pigs escaped into the wild rather than the rooting nature of its inhabitants. Earliest use was as 'the Pig Islands': 'Your Worship, for forty long years, and the rest, I've battled the Pig Islands doing my best' (*Truth*, 1906); later as 'Pig Island', as a noun from 1917: 'We wish them a safe return and every happiness and prosperity in our dear old "Pig Island"' (*Chronicles of the NZEF*); as an adjective from 1912: 'He had been let in for it by a "Pig Island mug"' (*Free Lance*).

'Pig Islander' for 'New Zealander', probably mainly 'white New Zealander', is recorded from 1909: '… do yer think … that a whole million Pig-Islanders is a goin' to let the Chows snavel Noo Zealand?' (*Quick March*, 1919).

The best-known literary usage is in James K. *Baxter's *Pig Island Letters*: 'Love is not valued much in Pig Island / Though we admire its walking parody'; 'The censor will not let my lines reveal / Pig Island spinning on the potter's wheel.'   HO

Pig Island Letters, James K. *Baxter's sixth collection, was published by *Oxford University Press in 1966. In its title sequence, dedicated to Maurice *Shadbolt, Baxter identifies with his friend's despondency at an apparent loss of creativity, before taking gloomy inventory of his own failed undertakings. Typically, lost youth is mourned and death looms large in the future, yet the poems also achieve a new, less censorious, realism—of which *'Pig Island', Baxter's colloquial, amiably caustic name for New Zealand, is emblematic. The collection fully anticipates the Jerusalem poetry as Baxter further develops his notion of the 'gap'—that paradoxical site of absence within which one discovers one's true self—and prefigures a full adoption of the role of social prophet by diagnosing society's maladies through a rehearsal of the dramas of his own life. C.K. *Stead, who savagely criticised *The Fire and the Anvil*, was won over by this volume, describing its 'total effect [as] richer than anything Baxter had achieved before' (*Islands* 3, 1973).   PM

Pilgrim Press, see **LOWRY, Bob.**

Pilgrims (1977–82) was a journal that caught much of the period's vitality, though it has suffered from being identified as a Dunedin journal (not mentioned, for instance, in the *OHNZLE*). Editor Stephen Higginson, without subscribing to any particular orthodoxy in the

manner of *Freed and others, in fact assembled most of the progressive writers of that time of rapid development—Russell *Haley, Michael *Morrissey, Peter *Olds, Elizabeth *Smither, Mervyn *Thompson, Hone *Tuwhare, Brian *Turner, Ian *Wedde, as well as excellent art work (Tony Fomison, Ralph *Hotere, Alan Pearson, Marilyn Webb) and some unusually substantial criticism, for instance by David Dowling, Lawrence *Jones and Canadian W.H. New. Newer writers were well represented (Yvonne *du Fresne, Rangi *Faith, Rosie *Scott) and there was a fresh international dimension with issues like the 'Israeli and New Zealand Arts and Letters' double issue 5 and 6 (1978). In 1982 the last issue of *Climate* announced a merger with *Pilgrims* under Alistair *Paterson's editorship, though this seems not to have eventuated.   RR

Pioneer was a family magazine published in Timaru, April 1905–March 1907. Until June 1906, 10 000 copies were distributed free to homes in South Canterbury financed by advertising. Among a predominance of articles on farming, current events, sport, local history and stories by popular overseas writers, it published some local fiction and poetry. Contributors included Jessie *Mackay, Johannes C. *Andersen, Frank *Morton, Dulce *Carman, T.M. *Curnow, A.E. *Currie and Dora *Wilcox.   SH

Plainsman, a Christchurch monthly published 1948–51, was directed towards a regional Canterbury readership and featured articles on local history, farming, sport and women's interests, as well as fiction and poetry, mostly by local writers.   SH

Playmarket was established in 1973 as a script assessment service and playwrights' agency by a group of people on the staff of or associated with Wellington's Downstage Theatre: Robert *Lord (playwright, whose play 'It Isn't Cricket', had been workshopped at the Australian Playwrights' Conference in 1973, the same year he attended the Eugene O'Neill Playwrights' Workshop in Connecticut), Nonnita Rees (director and actor), Judy Russell (secretary, New Zealand Theatre Federation) and Ian Fraser (Queen Elizabeth II Arts Council). Judy Russell became the first administrator, followed by Nonnita Rees, Ann Paetz and John McDavitt. In 1986, Lester McGrath became the first staff dramaturg, followed by Simon Garrett in 1987 and Susan Wilson in 1991. In 1975, as part of Downstage's tenth birthday celebrations, Playmarket organised the first of the Playmarket workshops which, by 1980, were to grow into the biennial New Zealand Playwrights' Workshops. In 1976, the organisation took over the publication of Downstage's *Act* magazine and moved from the theatre to premises at Victoria University of Wellington. The organisation also established itself as a publisher (its first title was Roger *Hall's *Glide Time) and agent for overseas publishers, including Australia's Currency Press. Playmarket's focus has remained on the development of local playwriting. In particular, the national workshops became a centre of theatrical activity in New Zealand, as well as acting as midwife for the decade's most interesting new local plays: Greg *McGee's *Foreskin's Lament (1980), Hilary Beaton's *Outside In* and Carolyn *Burns's *Objection Overruled* (both 1982), *Renée's *Wednesday to Come* (1984), Stuart *Hoar's *Squatter* (1986), Ken *Duncum's 'Blue Sky Boys' (1988) and David *Geary's *Lovelock's Dream Run* (Australia and New Zealand Playwrights' Conference, 1992). By 1988, when four scripts subsequently received full productions ('Blue Sky Boys', Raewyn Gwilliam's 'The Island', Jeff Addison's 'Legitimate Strip' and Anthony *McCarten's 'Pigeon English'), the workshops had become an effective way for playwrights to bring their work to the attention of the professional theatres. In 1990, a playwrights' *hui was held in Nelson which gathered together some fifty playwrights, as well as the collaborative groups He Ara Hou (which presented its collaboratively developed play, 'Whatungarongaro'), Pacific Theatre and *Red Mole and in April 1992, New Zealand practitioners took five plays to the Australian and New Zealand Playwrights' Conference in Canberra. The 1994 Oceania Playwrights' Workshop, held at the University of Auckland, however, saw, for the meantime, the end of this developmental cycle; resources are now being directed towards workshops in theatres. Playmarket's other major activity has been as a playwrights' agency and, in this capacity it has overseen the growth of commercial theatre, in which New Zealand scripts have acquired a central importance. Between 1973 and 1994, audiences paid some $30 million to see New Zealand plays; almost $3 million was distributed to playwrights as royalties. 				SG

Plumb (1978), a novel by Maurice *Gee, is considered here with its sequels *Meg* (1981) and *Sole Survivor* (1983). Together they have become known as the 'Plumb Trilogy', recognised as one of the greatest achievements in New Zealand fiction.

Plumb's story (though not the first chapter) opens at the beginning of the century. George Plumb is a stern Presbyterian clergyman, generous, courageous, intellectual, honest, loving, almost saint-like in his integrity. And yet these qualities lead to his own misfortunes and to the misery of those who are dearest to him. It could be said that the unyielding quality of his integrity makes it ill-suited for survival in a flawed and compromising world. But this would be only half the truth, for from another point of view the flaws can be found in his own personality: he is often so intensely absorbed in his study of major questions that he overlooks the needs of those who are close to him; he is willing to make material and social sacrifices for his principles, but, perhaps unwittingly, forces his wife and children into sacrifices whose benefits they cannot share; he cannot integrate the demands of physical and spiritual life; his belief in an ultimate truth never leaves him through all the changes in his faith (he is forced from the church and moves towards a kind of religious rationalism), so that he is unable to understand the sense of relativity with which others live. Does the world or Plumb cause the unhappiness of others? The novel leaves many such judgments open, so that the reader must undertake serious thinking; and yet the moral dilemmas are never permitted to restrain the dramatic movement of the plot as it traces the ups and downs of the family: George, Edie and their twelve children. 'My life and Edie's together was a tree that bore fruit in its season.' (He is shocked at the thought that his children have chemically 'poisoned' theirs by contraception.) In a relatively short compass these fourteen characters and several important peripheral ones come vividly to life, so that one is drawn into caring about the destinies of each. Among its other strengths this novel is exemplary in its concision, the skill with which few words and brief scenes are given density of meaning.

The story is not told in chronological sequence but follows the wandering yet disciplined memories of George Plumb, so that even on the first page mention is made of people and events that will be clearer and more significant much later. The interweaving time sequences encourage comparisons, so that there are networks of meaning which transcend chronological time. The temporal foreground is often occupied by the remembering Plumb himself, going over events in his mind, but still experiencing and still learning.

In this foreground, the old man is cared for by his daughter Meg and surrounded by people whose lives bear on his in a multiplicity of ways. He is undertaking a journey to Wellington, but readers sensitive to symbolism will recognise the journey as a passage towards unattainable understanding and, simultaneously, a passage through all of life towards death. In this way, the journey figures the entire novel.

The caring, loving yet only partly comprehending Meg is at the centre of the second part of the trilogy, which bears her name. Her nature makes her ideal for this narrational function because her caring draws her into the lives of her brothers and sisters and their offspring. With many of them she goes through experiences from which she learns. As the youngest she is not threatening to the others or competing with them. With Alfred, her brother, violently rejected by their father for his homosexuality, she is able to discuss the nature of love. From Esther, her fat materialistic sister, married to the money-worshipping property dealer Fred Meggett, she learns of sensuality. Her mechanically skilled aviator brother, Emerson, gives her, and her alone, an exciting ride on his motor-bike, so that technology is not fearsome to her. Her mystical brother, Robert, gives her a new vision of spirituality, quite different from that of her father. Each of them has left that father's path in a different way, and Meg, loving and caring, learns from each and encompasses a greater range of human possibility than any, despite her relatively limited intellectual range—or perhaps because of it.

On the other hand, being the youngest gives her a sense of inferiority and uncertainty: the others have grown up, when will she? Even married to Fergus Sole, Fred Meggett's subordinated business associate, and as the mother of children, she worries about her maturity. 'Was it true I had grown up?' When her husband loses his job and they must live in depression and poverty, she can say, 'At last I began to feel I was grown up.' *Meg* is an unorthodox kind of *Bildungsroman*. Meg's goal, typical of the genre, is self-knowledge: bringing her inner world into harmony with that around her.

As narrator, she is also using the act of writing the novel as a part of her growth towards self-knowledge. There are frequent references to the way she is shaping her story by leaving out major parts of her life, including much of her relationship to her children (in part this will be filled in, but from a different point of view, in the third novel). Self-knowledge results not only from discovery but from working and re-working what is experienced and learned. For this reason, Bill *Manhire has emphasised that *Meg* is the story of an artist. The self which Meg is to know is, in part, her creation. It is ironic that *Plumb*, the tale of a self-centred man, tells us more of the world he lived in than *Meg*, the story of a loving person whose most difficult task is to see herself as she sees others. Nonetheless, the glimpses of the commercial minds of Fergus Sole and Fred Meggett and the rigidly legalistic mind of Meg's oldest sibling Oliver, now a judge, suggest a change in the climate of the social world from the emphasis on integrity in *Plumb* to worldly success, money and status in his children's generation.

The third generation is presented through Raymond Sole, Meg's and Fergus's son and the eponymous protagonist of *Sole Survivor*, as well as through his associates. He seems very different from the central figures of the first two novels—Plumb striving for understanding, Meg for love—since, with a world-weary air, he seems to find little worth striving for. Plumb and Meg must both, in different ways, ruthlessly cast off their illusions; Raymond seems to have none, but this absence makes him even more ruthless. His life, privately and publicly (he is a journalist), is intertwined with that of his less cynical but even more ruthless cousin Duggie, who opposes political action to Raymond's passivity. Raymond believes it is 'honest' to have no firm political convictions and to support no party; Duggie thrives in the slash-and-grab world of ambitious politicians. Yet Raymond is not without his own destructive view of others: 'I told myself I followed my sense of right. That was how I justified the dislike of everyone that showed in my writing.' An editor calls his work 'biography-cum-hatchet job'. For all his efforts he is unable to make a book-length work in this manner, only fragmentary essays which see facets of truth but not the truth, parts not wholes. Neither can he initiate. Even in his love affairs he takes up Duggie's cast-off girlfriends and even his father's ex-mistress, Beth Neeley.

He is not unaware of his weakness, and he sees one aspect of it even more strongly in Duggie. For all his activity, Duggie lives on the edge of nothingness, too, because his activity is directed towards a world he scarcely seems to see. Other people are there only to be manipulated for his political purposes. Raymond knows this and is aware of his own emptiness, Duggie is not even aware of it. Gee remarked in an interview: '[Duggie Plumb] has no sense of the reality of other people. They are simply beings who move around within his range of vision and can be used.'

Raymond and Duggie are hollow men, resounding with the lives of others. The comparison with Meg, who grows and learns through sympathy with the lives of others, and with Plumb, who imposes his life on others, is revealing. What seems common to all of them is their awareness that if they change these attitudes they will fall into a terrifying abyss of nothingness. Raymond has a 'vision' of Wellington Harbour at night: 'People showing glow-worm lights on the edge of nothing.' What gives life is the awareness of other people, and in this regard Meg, in the central part of the trilogy, is more alive than either Plumb or Raymond.   NW

PLUMB, Vivienne (1955–), is a playwright and fiction writer, who won the 1993 Bruce Mason Playwriting Award for *Love Knots* (performed 1993, pub. 1994) and the Hubert Church Award for a first book of fiction for *The Wife Who Spoke Japanese in her Sleep* (1993). A professional actor of extensive experience in Australia (where she was born) and New Zealand, she was a founder member of the Women's Play Press in 1992. She lives in Wellington, took Victoria University's creative writing course in 1990 and a BA in 1998, and has edited three collections of new poetry and prose. She was 1996 president of the *New Zealand Poetry Society. Her writing takes an engagingly mobile line between realism and a humorous, fairy-tale-like fantasy where women's activities, especially baking, assume magic powers, the inexplicable occurs in commonplace settings (the wife who unaccountably recites *Japanese), people appear and disappear and men are two-dimensionally goofy or ogreish. *Love Knots* was praised for its 'swoops from the mundane to the miraculous' (Susan Budd) and the short stories for 'surrealistic imagery and deliciously ironic humour' (Sandra Arnold). At her best, in 'Coral and Zetta' or 'Mrs Gittoes' Compleat Art of Baking', the surface naivety can encompass both a comic deflation of human passions ('Zetta felt hot and melty all over, like cheese on toast') and a suggestive glimpse of darker experience—fraught friendship or forlorn childlessness. A second play and a first novel are in progress.   RR

Plume of the Arawas, novel, see **ACHESON, Frank.**

Poems 1949–1957, by Allen *Curnow, is a collection of eighteen poems published by the Mermaid Press, Wellington (a Denis *Glover imprint), in 1957. Sophisticated and highly wrought, some of the poems reflect in their imagery Curnow's sojourn in England in 1949 (e.g. 'Elegy to My Father') and his subsequent move from Christchurch to Auckland (e.g. 'Spectacular Blossom' and 'A Small Room with Large Windows'). Also included were memorial poems to two of Curnow's poetic mentors Dylan Thomas ('In Memory of Dylan Thomas') and Wallace Stevens ('Mementoes of an Occasion'). PS

Poetry Live was started by David *Mitchell in 1980. Over the years its venue has changed from one Auckland pub to another, but the basic principle has been the same: on Monday evenings poets can volunteer to read their own work, with live music adding to the entertainment. An invited guest also reads for half an hour. Poets who found an audience with Poetry Live include John *Pule, Iain *Sharp, Mike *Johnson and Alistair *Paterson. NW

Poetry New Zealand, see **New Zealand Poetry Yearbook.**

Pohutukawa Tree, The, was Bruce *Mason's first success. Written in 1955 and first performed by the New Zealand Players Theatre Workshop in Wellington in 1957, it was produced on BBC TV in 1959, and published in 1960 by *Price Milburn (rev. edn 1963). It continues to be the first exposure to theatre for many New Zealand schoolchildren. One of its great values

during the 1960s was that it presented the two main cultures of New Zealand on stage, with their flaws as well as their virtues. Mason continued to relish the play's social, healing role; in 1972 he revelled in the fifty-fifth season of the play in Dannevirke: 'what impressed me most of all was the community feeling it evoked'.

The play had its origins, in Mason's confession, with his childhood glimpse of a naked Māori girl bathing at Rotorua. There is no noble savage in this play, however: not pregnant Queenie, nor even Aroha Mataira, the oppressive and puritanical matriarch. In 1979 Mason said he would 'never make so ludicrous a presumption' as to think he could speak for the Māori people, and this refusal to judge is what makes the play Aroha's tragedy and not a piece of political or racial propaganda. If anything the play is critical of the old ways of Aroha, from her refusal to move down and live with the tribe, to her preachy mothering which results in two highly rebellious and miserable children. Mason complicates the audience's moral choices by having both Aroha and her son Johnny freely choose the worst features of European society: Christianity and the spurious mythology of Robin Hood. Aroha's respect for her ancestral land is touching, but she romanticises her partnership with Atkinson while she denigrates her tribe at Tamatea. Beside her pride, Atkinson's 'Land must be used some time, not just remembered' seems almost reasonable. But on the Pākehā side, there is little to admire, either. The young seducer Roy's attitude is summed up in his observation of Queenie: 'As Maori sheilas go, you're pretty hot stuff.' The minister Sedgwick is atoning for his sins during the war, and wants to reinstate the noble savage, saying of the marae at Tamatea, 'such joy in simple things … real simplicity of spirit…. For a dispossessed race, they're wonderfully cheerful'—this, just after he has arranged there a marriage between Queenie and a Māori man she has never met. Yet, like all the characters, even Sedgwick has his moments of insight, when he comments, 'They [on the marae] want the past … and they want it now.' Even when the Atkinsons' world is exposed in the great wedding scene of Act 1, Scene 2, Mason makes sure that the moral waters are clouded. The Atkinson family have laboured to turn the land into 'rolling English countryside' and because, as Mason observes elsewhere, that is the great cultural achievement of New Zealanders, there is nothing left over to mark life's rituals. The Europeans' excruciating rendition of the national anthem is replaced by Mrs Atkinson's desperate call, 'Where are our Maoris? We want our lovely Maoris!' Aroha enters and sings her *waiata in 'a voice of piercing sweetness'. Atkinson thanks her ('That was lovely') and confirms the paucity of European ritual, but this is undercut by a drunken Johnny singing 'You are my sunshine'; the scene ends with a clear intimation that all is not well with Queenie and Roy, while in contrast the young married couple of Sylvia and George have at least 'done it right'.

The richness of the text comes from its various *coups de théâtre* and juxtapositions. On the wall of Aroha's house are Holman Hunt's 'The Light of the World' and a photograph of Aroha's ancestor Whetumarama; Queenie has no sooner sung 'Moonlight becomes you' than there is heard 'a rhythmic and barbaric Maori chant'. And while the play has autobiographical roots in Mason's years as a horticulturist and his early friendships (Johnny is based on a real Māori, Eru Karani), it is also a patently allusive play. Mason borrows his tree from Forster's wych-elm in *Howards End*, Aroha's majestic folly from *King Lear*, and his anti-hero Johnny from a decade of angry young men. Although set in 1947, then, and retaining a specificity of time, the play achieves a universality and a moral ambiguity which make it convincing and engaging forty years on.   DD

Poi are a very popular form of song-dance performed with poi-balls attached to long or short strings, which make a rustling accompaniment to the music. They are nearly always performed by women, occasionally by young men. Earlier poi were recited rather than sung and show clear signs of derivation from *haka, the foot-stamping of the latter being replaced by the gentle slap of the poi.   NW

'Pokarekare ana' is the best known of all *waiata, its words probably the most familiar complete text in the Māori language to non-Māori, and with the status of a national song, especially when New Zealanders gather overseas. Written by Paraire Henare Tomoana (1868–1946) early in the twentieth century, it 'has been called a waiata whaiaipo, or love song, a term usually applied to older songs' (Margaret *Orbell). It is a yearning song of parted lovers separated by the always stormy (pokarekare ana) waters of Waiapu (wai o Waiapu), and thus an appropriate expression of the nostalgia for distant loves common among New Zealanders away from home.   RR

POLACK, Joel Samuel (1807–82), was an entertaining if rather conventional early-Victorian travel writer. Probably born in London, he arrived as an early Jewish settler at Hokianga in 1831, where he traded for a year before going into business at Kororareka in flax, timber and brewing. He made journeys along the coastal areas of Northland, Bay of Plenty and East Coast. He also wrote, drew, and fought two duels. Returning to Britain in 1837 he advocated British intervention and colonisation for New Zealand. In 1842 he auctioned some of his New Zealand land and migrated again. His Bay of

Islands business suffered with the transfer of the capital to Auckland and from the Northern Wars, when his property and records were burnt. He spent the years 1845–50 running a business in Auckland before permanently departing for California. *New Zealand: Being a Narrative of Travels and Adventures … between … 1831 and 1837* (1838) includes observations of Māori people but says little about his business activities. *Manners and Customs of the New Zealanders … and Remarks to Intending Immigrants …* (1840) enlarges on what he wrote about the Māori in the earlier book. Polack's narratives are readable and his ethnological observations have value, though limited in perception. Each book is illustrated from his drawings.   RG

Polynesian Mythology (Sir George *Grey), see **Mahina a nga tupuna Maori ha mea kohikohi mai, Ko nga.**

Pom, pommy or **pommie** were originally Australian terms, first recorded there 1912, for an immigrant from Britain, especially England. 'Pommy' was first recorded from within New Zealand in the 1920s, 'pom' from 1946. They did not replace the usually non-derogatory New Zealand 'homey' as the common colloquial term for 'Briton' until World War 2. The derogatory 'pongo', originally applied to British soldiers, also came into general use during that war.

The words derive from a wordplay associating 'pomegranate' (also from 1912 in Australia, and pronounced 'pommy' or 'pummy' 'grannit'), a name for a British immigrant, with the Australian rhyming series 'immigrant', 'Jimmygrant' (New Zealand 1845, Australia 1859), 'Pommy Grant' or 'pummy grant' (the last two recorded in Australia from 1912–13 but not in New Zealand); thence to the elliptical or familiar forms 'pom' and 'pommy'. Unlikely derivations (that is, 'not supported by evidence') include: 'Prisoners of Mother England'; 'Permit of Migration Ireland or England'; 'Pompey', naval slang for Portsmouth; rhyming slang for 'Tommy'; and French slang 'paumé', 'lacking in energy'.

Compounds and derivatives include 'whingeing pom' (Australia 1962, New Zealand 1985), for a stereotypically complaining British immigrant, 'Pomland' (1974), 'Pomgolia' (1976), 'Pongolia'(1967), 'pommie-bashing' (1987), 'Pommy bastard' (1940) and 'pommyism' (1920), the assumption of an air of superiority.

Roger *Hall's play *Prisoners of Mother England* (1979) is a recent literary use of the term and treatment of immigration from Britain as a central theme.   HO

Poohua tau, see **tauparapara.**

445

POPE, Quentin, see **Kowhai Gold**.

POPPER, Karl (1902–93), one of the greatest thinkers of the twentieth century, was born and educated in Vienna, the son of a lawyer whose library, stocked with Greek and Latin texts as well as those of the great European philosophers, was the boy's main source of education. His mother encouraged his love of music. He believed that his sharply critical approach to thought was honed by the traumas of World War 1, which led his teenage mind to be critical of accepted opinions, especially political ones. Briefly he was attracted to Communism's promise of a better world, and the search for such a world filled his life, long after he had rejected all forms of dogmatism in favour of critical thought. In 1934 he published *Die Logik der Forschung*, which attracted the attention of the 'Vienna Circle', even though it contested some of their basic concepts. In arguing with Carnap, von Neurath and other members of the circle he was able to develop his belief that scientific progress is not based on induction—as had been believed since Francis Bacon—but on trial and error elimination. He was able to convince even Einstein that the development of scientific theory is not a methodical 'path' but an act of creativity followed by rigorous criticism. Others who acknowledged his influence were Peter Medawar, Ernest Gombrich, Konrad Lorenz and A.F. von Hayek. His discussions with Einstein, Schrödinger, Bohr and Wittgenstein influenced in various ways the progress of scientific and philosophical thought. This revolution in the conception of science was not available to English readers until the translation, *The Logic of Scientific Discovery*, was published in 1956.

Meanwhile, however, many New Zealand students had been profoundly influenced by his thought through his lectures and discussions at the University of Canterbury, where he was the sole teacher of philosophy from 1937 to 1945. With the aid of English friends, Popper and his wife escaped from Austria before the Anschluss and moved to Christchurch. Here he wrote the two books which are most readily associated with his name: *The Open Society and Its Enemies* and *The Poverty of Historicism*. He said that they 'were my war effort', and they applied his insights into scientific discovery to the social sciences. In all thought an imaginative thrust ('TT'—tentative trial) must be followed by rigorous criticism ('EE'—error elimination). In later work he was to show that this is also the basis of evolution, mutation being the trial and subsequent struggle the error elimination. In the social sphere completely frank and rigorous criticism is crucial to this process, and only a political system which permits this (an open society) can achieve progress.

He found that New Zealand was, in some respects, such a society: 'the best-governed country in the world, and the most easily governed … a wonderfully quiet and pleasant atmosphere for work'. On the other hand, the university itself was less 'open': 'I had a desperately heavy teaching load, and the University authorities not only were unhelpful, but tried actively to make difficulties for me. I was told that I should be well advised not to publish anything while in New Zealand, and that any time spent on research was a theft from the working time for which I was paid.'

Nonetheless Popper found time to do some revolutionary work in logic, inventing 'natural deduction', and on the history of science, as well as to inspire many with his numerous and wide-ranging lectures in Christchurch and Dunedin, while writing his two major books. He called some of the people he associated with 'life-long friends', including Sir John Eccles, who was awarded a Nobel Prize for his work in neurophysiology, and who acknowledged the encouragement he gained from Popper's arguments.

Some of his students later gained prominence in New Zealand life: the medieval historian and philosopher of history, Peter Munz; the mathematician and contributor to atomic bomb research, Robin Williams— later vice-chancellor of Otago University and of the Australian National University; the professor of chemistry at the University of Otago, Hugh Parton; the head of mathematics and science at Wellington Polytechnic, H. Offenburger. But also in many less prominent positions, as teachers, administrators, public servants and researchers, his students influenced New Zealand intellectual life for a generation.   NW

Poroporoaki, see **Karanga**.

Postmodernism in its customary connotation of a post-realist writing with such features as discontinuous narrative, deconstruction or subversion of the autonomous and reliable subject, and intertextuality (each text seen as an 'intertext' in a succession of texts) appears locally in varying manifestations about the late 1970s. Some earlier writing anticipates some of its elements. In fiction, for example, Janet *Frame's *Scented Gardens for the Blind* (1963), *The *Adaptable Man* (1965), and *Daughter Buffalo* (1972), along with Ian *Wedde's *Dick Seddon's Great Dive* (1976) and M.K. *Joseph's *A *Soldier's Tale* (1976), are complex and self-referential narratives that show the contingency of the postmodern on the metafictional and the difficulty of making precise definitions in this area. Significant, though, is K.K. Ruthven's analysis of Joseph's novel in *Islands* 27 (1979), in which he admonishes local critics for lacking a methodology adequate to the work, a challenge variously answered during the following decade by *Parallax (1982–83), *AND (1983–85) and *Antic (1986–). *Splash (1984–85), containing material from the aborted Parallax 4, marks the most clearly identifiable local assertion of the mode, with Wystan *Curnow, Roger Horrocks, Ted Jenner, Judi Stout, Leigh *Davis and others writing creative material as if in deliberate illustration of the other journals' poststructuralist theory, and the entire project demonstrating its links with the postmodern art world of North America.

Davis's poetry collection Willy's Gazette (1983), Curnow's Cancer Daybook (1989), Alan *Loney's Missing Parts: Poems 1977–90 (1992) and Wedde's Tendering (1988) are the most tangible products of the journal, although the latter two volumes stand on the modernist cusp of postmodernism. MacDonald P. Jackson has cited Donald Allen's The New American Poetry (1960) as 'some kind of catchment area' in its influence on New Zealand poetry, while in fiction, the influence of the early postmodern American writing of the 1960s is evident in an Auckland group of short story writers, from the publication of Russell *Haley's The Sauna Bath Mysteries (1978), which he followed with Real Illusions (1984) and the novel The Settlement (1986). Michael *Morrissey's The Fat Lady and the Astronomer (1981) marks his advent into the mode, while Michael *Gifkins's After the Revolution (1982) is the first of three such collections, followed by Summer is the Côte d'Azur (1987) and The Amphibians (1989). Chris *Else's Dreams of Pythagoras (1981) collects stories that show a similar influence.

Morrissey's The New Fiction (1985) assembles an eclectic variety of short fiction in an attempt to establish postmodernism as the way of the future: it features a number of the writers named here as well as Michael *Harlow, Malcolm *Fraser, Gary *Langford, Julia Allen, Alexandria Chalmers and Stephanie *Johnson, all of whom can be said to occupy positions on a widely conceived spectrum of postmodernism. As with C.K. *Stead's *All Visitors Ashore (1984) and The *Death of the Body (1986), there is a sense with these writers that postmodernism is a style consciously adopted and, at its best, requiring adaptation to local requirements. In some cases, such as Else and Haley, the mannerism has faded with further publication later in the decade. Long before this, it had begun to leave its trace in more established fiction writers: Janet Frame's *Living in the Maniototo (1979) and The *Carpathians (1988) are consciously postmodernist, with structural sleight-of-hand, shifting subjectivity and partially North American settings, while even established realists like David *Ballantyne in The Penfriend (1980), Maurice *Shadbolt

in The *Lovelock Version (1980), Maurice *Gee in *Going West (1993) and *Crime Story (1994), and Owen *Marshall in stories such as 'The Day Hemingway Died' (1984) can be found flirting with aspects of self-conscious narration.

Wedde's *Symmes Hole (1986) and Patrick *Evans's Making It (1989) are novels more wholly devoted to postmodernist narrative method and structures, the former anticipating something of Graham *Billing's The Chambered Nautilus (1993) in its creation of 'history' as pastiche. A number of recent works are more obviously identifiable as committed to the postmodern mode. Anne *Kennedy's 100 Traditional Smiles (1988) and Musica Ficta (1993) are demanding and fragmented collocations of verbal (and sometimes visual) cultural bric-à-brac, discontinuous in narration and sometimes opaque in subject. Greg *O'Brien's novel Diesel Mystic (1989) is a similar accretion of fragments and pastiches, of prose and verse, but with more visible gestures towards some relation to historical reality, while Damien *Wilkins's novel The Miserables (1993) successfully and consummately localises the mode. Bill *Manhire's The Brain of Katherine Mansfield (1988) is a game-novella which relies on the regionality of New Zealand place names. Like O'Brien's and Kennedy's works, but unlike his short story collection The New Land: A Picture Book (1990), which contains no pictures, his novella is illustrated (by O'Brien), a reminder of the generically democratic nature of postmodern art. This nature is evident in the link between Manhire's poetry and prose, which from the first share a comfortable detachment from the realist tradition. Manhire's poetry takes a postmodernist praxis in New Zealand back to his early volumes, The Elaboration (1972) and How to Take Off Your Clothes at the Picnic (1977). In the subsequent period a number of his contemporaries have also written poetry which implies its subject and relies upon the verbally constructed nature of experience.

Of the material collected by Miriama Evans, Harvey *McQueen and Wedde in their Penguin Book of Contemporary Poetry/Nga Kupu Titohu o Aotearoa (1989), the poetry of Graham *Lindsay, Michele *Leggott, Rob *Allan, David *Eggleton, Anne *French, Bernadette *Hall, Morrissey, O'Brien, Joanna *Paul and Iain *Sharp can all be identified as belonging somewhere on the continuum between Wedde's cautiously modernist posture, evident for example in Lindsay, and Manhire's more committed postmodernist position, which is evident in Leggott and a number of the others.

The numerous examples of postmodernist influences in poetry and fiction contrasts with local drama writing, in which only Patrick Evans's one-act play Stuff: A Play on Words (1994) and a number of Stuart *Hoar's full-length works, starting with *Squatter* (1988), show a conscious attempt to adapt postmodernist methods to the stage.   PE

Potiki (1986), Patricia *Grace's second novel, won the New Zealand Book Award for Fiction, was third in the Wattie Book of the Year Award and remains both a popular success and a reference point for discussion of Māori writing and international postcolonial fiction.

Though nearly 200 pages long, it sustains the unity and intensity of a novella. It is focused on the short life-span of the visionary child Tokowaru-i-te-Marama, and the conflict over family land which he foresees and is eventually martyr to. It also seeks to embody the belief that each such story is 'a story not of a beginning or an end, but marking only a position on the spiral'. It therefore looks back to the long-term 'loss and grief' of the Māori community since the appropriation of their land in World War 1 and devastation of their children in the post-war influenza epidemic; and forward through Toko's prophecy beyond the book's climax to a time of armed Māori insurrection ('taking the white sticks in their hands ... shouldering the sun-bleached wood').

Toko, the Potiki, last-born, is born crippled and hunchbacked in the edge of the sea, his mother Mary a mentally handicapped innocent, and the probable father a derelict called Joseph, their names alluding to the birth and life of Christ. Grace has said that the story also parallels 'the story of the ancient Māori *Potiki*'. Toko is cherished by Mary's family, the Tamihanas, in which the main characters are her brother Hemi and his wife Roimata, Hemi's mother Granny Tamihana, and their three previous children: James, who is to become a master carver, the activist Tangimoana, and the fearful Manu. Their life near the small community of Te Ope is one of kinship with their inherited land and the sea, 'which hems and stitches the scalloped edges of the land'. In one childhood episode, which again echoes the New Testament, Toko predicts catching a big fish, and then himself hooks a giant conger which feeds the whole community, its remains then nurturing a passionfruit vine: 'The seeds are a new beginning, but started from a death', Toko says, in the childlike but resonant prose which characterises much of the narrative.

The image of new seed leads to the next phase, the closing of the freezing works and Hemi's decision to devote himself to working the land: 'Everything we need is here' becomes a refrain, prompting Roimata to educate the younger children at home through the sharing of 'stories'. Toko's visions of conflict presage Parts Two and Three, when the family's self-containment is shattered by construction work on a nearby tourist resort. The agent Mr Dolman, nicknamed Dollarman,

tries to persuade the community to permit an access road which will destroy their urupa (cemetery) and force the whare tipuna (meeting house) to be relocated. The disillusioned owners refuse: 'If we sold to you we would be dust.' Reduced to 'hate and anger' the developers deliberately flood the urupa and then resort to arson—the 'night of colours' long predicted by Toko. With increasing support and resolve, the community begins rebuilding, James now working on the carvings with which the novel opens and ends.

In the final conflict, the 'night of stars', Toko is killed and Tangimoana incites the Māori construction workers to bulldoze the road and development site and dump the expensive machinery in the sea. After this outburst the novel draws to a close in loving communality and spirituality, as Toko is transmuted into James's carving and in spirit speaks the last chapter and closing Māori incantation. 'Potiki's' meanings of 'penis child' and 'life force', frequently implied in the densely allusive text, become explicit.

His final message is not wholly of love. As with the killing of Christ by a colonising power, the novel implies, his martyrdom will provoke unified faith and activism. While some have found this political message weakened by the caricature treatment of the non-Māori figures, Māori values and vitality are strongly affirmed, the view of 'a broken race' refuted by the insistence on the people's 'special knowing' and determined continuity.

Potiki also affirms Māori values through its imagery, drawn from the land, sea, sky, seasons, community and myth, with a directness which sometimes seems childlike yet is capable of rhapsodic intensity; and through its narrative form, in which overlapping accounts are retold through different members of the family (either in their own voices or through a flexible semi-indirect narration). The effect is indicated in the recurrent image of communal weaving: 'as the strands worked to and fro so did our stories'. Art, whether weaving, carving or narrative fiction, is thus the 'history of patterns and the meanings of patterns to life'. In this structured movement from idiosyncrasy of voice to communality, Grace, it has been suggested, 'begins to adapt fiction in English to Māori forms, rather than the other way round'.   RR

POTIKI, Roma (1958–), Te Rarawa, Te Aupōuri, Ngāti Rangitihi, is a poet, playwright and commentator on Māori theatre. She is also a theatre performer and manager, who was Te Toka-a-Toi (Māori arts) coordinator of the 1998 New Zealand International Festival of the Arts; and a visual artist, who illustrated her own first collection of poems and has work in the permanent collection of the Dowse Gallery, Lower Hutt.

Born in Lower Hutt, she was educated at Wainuiomata College, leaving at 15, and lives at Paekakariki. She held a writing residency at a Sydney theatre in 1996.

Potiki's poems are in the Oxford (1997), *Te Ao Mārama* and other anthologies, while the refrain of her poem 'and my heart goes swimming' became the title of the anthology of New Zealand love poems edited by Jenny *Bornholdt and Gregory *O'Brien in 1996. Her collection *Stones in Her Mouth* (1992) articulates intense feeling across a versatile range of forms and tones. At their best, the poems ground personal emotion in a strongly observed natural world, as in love lyrics like 'flood me', poems of feeling like 'change' ('… to earth / to heal / to return'), or nature poems like 'the flax' ('the smell is someone weeping / fresh life. / the coarse roots hold / round earth / intend to stay'). By contrast there are poems which depend essentially on the rhetoric of an ironic, acerbic or dogmatic spoken voice, usually of political anger, especially directed at racist and gender attitudes ('white boys', 'change is necessary'). A set of six broadsheet poems was published by *Wai-te-ata Press, *Roma Potiki* (1996).

Her play *Going Home* was performed in Sydney in 1996. She wrote the introductions to *He Reo Hou: 5 Plays by Māori playwrights* (1991) and *Waiora* by Hone *Kouka (1997).   RR

Pounamu, Pounamu (1972), by Witi *Ihimaera, was the first published volume of stories by a Māori writer, although, as Ihimaera has been at pains to point out, a vigorous tradition of Māori short fiction in English had existed for two decades involving writers like J.C. *Sturm and Arapera *Blank. In *Pounamu, Pounamu*, he focuses on rural Māori; the greenstone of the title symbolising the value of the traditional rural life these stories celebrate. The real wealth of Māori culture, they suggest, is the spirit generated within *whanau, *hapū and *iwi.

These stories address issues of cultural difference, but with less anger than in the later The *New Net Goes Fishing. In 'The Other Side of the Fence', for example, when attitudes and behaviours do conflict, universal human values of fairness and equity optimistically bring about order and resolution.

The collection is deceptive in its lyricism, and the narrative voice—if not a child's then frequently childlike—generates a sense of naivety and sentimentality that has received some criticism. However, Richard Corballis and Simon Garrett recognise a vein of scepticism running beneath the collection's surface; and Lydia Wevers comments that the division in narrative voice between a complex third person representing Pākehā and the spoken first-person idiom of the Māori narrator cleverly introduces racial and cultural contrasts. *Pounamu,*

Pounamu was awarded third prize in the Wattie Book of the Year Awards.   PM

Pound of Saffron, A (1962), is the second novel by M.K. *Joseph and New Zealand's first 'university novel'. It was published by *Paul's and in London by Gollancz. It centres on the coldly exploitative drama professor, Jim Rankin, a modern Machiavelli who lectures on that Renaissance politician in Chapter 1, while the title and epigraph are from Webster's characterisation of the Machiavel in *The White Devil*. Seeking a powerful UNESCO appointment, Rankin pushes through a controversial scheme for an open-air theatre on the slopes of One Tree Hill, and directs *Antony and Cleopatra* there, at great personal cost to those he manipulates in the process (see *Shakespeare in New Zealand). Much more than an academic novel, it is thoughtful and illuminating on issues of power, personal morality, generational conflict, the arts in New Zealand, racism and biculturalism. Basically realist, it has passages of richly virtuoso writing, especially the capping parade, the account of a painting, and the sustained multi-layered narrative of the play's opening night. Particularly striking is the passage where a Māori lecturer among the audience on that historic Māori site inwardly transposes Cleopatra's keening 'crown o'th' earth doth melt' lament into the language and imagery of the *tangi.

Rankin's downfall seems contrived, but the ending is darkened by unexpected violence and complicated further by Joseph's sly use of literary allusion: Harry and Nancy Gillies from his *I'll Soldier No More* appear in middle age; and Rankin's place of exile proves to be an inventively modernised version of Sulaco, the fictitious setting of Joseph Conrad's great political novel, *Nostromo*. Joseph denied that any of the characters derived from his Auckland University colleagues. But the contrast between Rankin's calculatedly destructive gossip and the ex-soldier Gillies' pragmatic charity does make the novel in part an illustration of his later remark that 'Soldiers are kinder and gentler than one or two of the people you meet around universities' (*Islands 27, 1979).   RR

POWELL, Kit (1937–), composer and teacher, was born and grew up in Wellington but has lived in Switzerland since 1984. Since 1961, when his *Ballad of Reading Gaol* (using part of Oscar Wilde's poem) was recorded by Nelson Wattie (baritone) and the National Orchestra, Powell has worked consistently on short theatrical pieces for voice with instruments and/or computer sounds. In Christchurch, where he and the poet Michael *Harlow were both attached to the Teachers' College, they collaborated on a variety of works including *Texts for Composition* (1979), *Devotion to the Small*

(1980), for singer and five percussionists (winner of the Mobil Award for best recorded music in 1981), *Nothing But Switzerland and Lemonade* (1985) and *Vlaminck's Tie* (1985). The collaboration continued with *Nelson Songs* (1986), for voice and computer tape, written for Nelson Wattie, as was *Father's Telescope* (1988) for singer, speaker and tape. Related works include *Chinese Songs* (1988), a setting of sacred texts for soprano and tape, and a full-length opera, *Hauptsache, man geht zusammen hin* (1992), with a libretto by the Swiss writer Jürg Schubiger. More recently, Powell has been working with a Moscow theatrical group.   JMT/NW

POWELL, Lesley Cameron, see *Turi, the Story of a Little Boy*.

Pōwhiri is a welcoming ceremony for guests (manuhiri) to a *marae, although the term is sometimes used in English for any formal welcome on a public occasion. The word can be used for written invitations to a *hui, which can include poetic incantations and invocations, also called pōwhiri.

After the *karanga, as the guests move onto the marae, the pōwhiri is performed by the lines of receiving people, holding fronds which they beat in rhythmic actions. As Anne Salmond has described it, once the rhythm is established, the leader begins the chant: 'These chants are also performed as war dances, but although the words are the same the performance is very different. War dances are performed by men, and the actions are aggressive and masculine. Pōwhiri, on the other hand, are performed by women, with a gentle, rhythmic waving of greenery' (*Hui: A Study of Māori Ceremonial Gatherings*, 1975).   NW

Prelude, short story by Katherine *Mansfield, was shortened and refined from The *Aloe during the first four months of 1917 and published as a short volume in July 1918, the second publication of the Hogarth Press, owned by Leonard and Virginia Woolf. The text was largely hand-set by Virginia Woolf. Mansfield included the story in her second collection, *Bliss and Other Stories* (1920). No MS exists. According to Antony *Alpers the title was thought of by John Middleton *Murry. *Prelude*, like its later companion piece '*At the Bay' (1922), is one of Mansfield's most celebrated New Zealand stories. Based on the Beauchamps' move to Karori, near Wellington, in 1893, it presents the extended Burnell family as they relocate from the city to the country. In the course of its twelve sections, the story shifts between various characters' interior monologue, charting their reactions to the move: Stanley's delight, Linda's ambivalence, Beryl's fear of isolation and the children's excite-

ment. Some of the defining moments include the children's reaction to the beheading of a duck in Chapter IX, Linda's epiphanic encounter with the aloe in Chapter XI and Beryl Fairfield's self-analysis in Chapter XII. The story from which *Prelude* was drawn was written between March 1915 and March 1916, a period marked by the accidental death of Mansfield's brother, Leslie, in October 1915. Several months later she wrote in her *Journal*: '... the form that I want has changed utterly ... now I want to write recollections of my own country ... I want for one moment to make our undiscovered country leap into the eyes of the Old World ... especially I want to write a kind of long elegy to you [Leslie] ... perhaps not in poetry. Nor perhaps in prose. Almost certainly in a kind of *special prose*' (22 January 1916). Comparison with *The Aloe* shows Mansfield achieving this by excising authorial narration and local colour, paring down characters' dialogue and reminiscences and editing out incidental characters and scenes. The tighter and more poetic 'special prose' that emerges establishes Mansfield's mature style and technique. Structured metaphorically rather than in linear fashion, there is almost a complete absence of a discernible narrator, with interior monologue moving from one character to another. The juxtapositions and synchronicities this affords form the story. Symbols and images are used to illuminate characters' perceptions, with any 'meaning' emerging from characters' own evaluation of their inner lives, often charted through variations on the epiphany (or 'glimpse', as Mansfield called these devices). In a letter to her artist friend Dorothy Brett, Mansfield wrote: 'What form is it? you ask.... As far as I know it's more or less my own invention' (11 October 1917). *Prelude* is established as one of Mansfield's greatest achievements; as Vincent *O'Sullivan states in his introduction to '*The Aloe' with 'Prelude'*, the story has had 'influence on an entire tradition'.   SSa

Press, The, the Christchurch daily morning newspaper, has a distinguished record for publishing and fostering New Zealand literature. Its first issue was 25 May 1861, as a six-page, three-column weekly tabloid initiated primarily by James Edward *Fitzgerald in competition with the established *Lyttelton Times. It became a daily in 1863. Even in those early days an urbane wit and articulate liberalism characterised contributions from such highly educated settlers as Joseph Brittan, Fitzgerald and J.V. Colborne-Veel, who was editor for most of the first two decades. The paper's first undeniable claim to a place in literary history came on 20 December 1862, with the first of a series of challenging satiric articles on Darwin by Rangitata runholder Samuel *Butler, which were the origin of *Erewhon. Butler through 1863–64 continued to contribute quite frequently if unpredictably, under various pseudonyms and in items as diverse as a verse account of a cricket match and a hostile anonymous review of his own first book, *A First Year in Canterbury Settlement*.

The *Press* built a tradition of literate journalism; its own history (1963) speaks of its hallmark as 'the arresting phrase in a column of careful prose'. It became conscious of a specifically literary role, however, when W.H. Triggs, editor 1894–1914, introduced a Monday morning literary column, with contributors including T.M. *Hocken, Sir Robert Stout, Henry *Jacobs and Hone Heke, politician grandson of the famous Ngā Puhi chief. In 1899 the column launched the prolific publishing career of Professor Arnold *Wall, whose contributions were to span more than sixty years. Meanwhile the *Weekly Press* was providing readers with new essays and fiction by Conan Doyle, Rudyard *Kipling, Jerome K. Jerome and Bernard *Shaw, as well as pre-publication serialisations of significant English novels. It also published plenty of original local verse and prose, by, for instance, 'M.C.V.' (Mary *Colborne-Veel, daughter of J.V.) and 'Austral' (Anne Glennie *Wilson).

In the early years of the twentieth century, the literary staff included Guy *Scholefield, W.F. *Alexander and M.C. *Keane (all of whom went on to become editors of various dailies); Alan *Mulgan was a subeditor and Mona *Tracy (then McKay) a reporter. By 1914 the daily paper's literary column had expanded to a full Saturday page.

The literary golden age of the *Press* came under the editorship of M.C. Keane, 1919–29. Publication on the Saturday page became a mark of literary success. Keane recruited established and new writers, several gaining their first publication there, or early experience of rigorous editing. These included Ursula *Bethell, D'Arcy *Cresswell, M.H. *Holcroft, Robin *Hyde, Ngaio *Marsh, Alan Mulgan and Frederick *Sinclaire. Original work as important as Bethell's best-known poem, 'The Long Harbour', made the page a significant creative outlet.

Oliver *Duff, editor 1929–32, was as substantial a writer in his own right as Keane, but clashed with his managers over the 1932 tramway strike and his insistence on publishing extracts from Cresswell's *Present Without Leave*. The *Press* also short-sightedly dismissed the young Denis *Glover in 1933 for his part in the controversial *Oriflamme*. While Pierce Freeth's long editorship (1932–57) brought a more pragmatic journalistic emphasis, J.H.E. *Schroder sustained the Saturday page and the paper's continuing literary influence. Allen *Curnow, Jean Stevenson (Bertram), Jane *Mander and Esther *Glen were each on the staff during these years.

The *Press Junior*, an important outlet for children's writing, was started in 1934 (see *Children's pages of newspapers). In 1941 the subversive satiric verse of *'Whim-Wham' (Curnow) began to appear, with the equally fearless cartoons of David *Low.

Curnow returned to the *Press* after the war, honing his skills as a critic; his criticism from these years is represented in *Look Back Harder*, edited by Peter *Simpson (1987). 'Whim-Wham' continued to lay about him until 1988. The staff in the 1950s included Eric *Beardsley and R.T. *Brittenden, who joined in 1938 and after war service had established himself as the country's best cricket writer. Creative literature of other kinds was no longer included, but the weekly books page was unchallenged (other than by the *NZ Listener*) until the upsurge of interest in New Zealand literature in the 1980s raised standards in other cities' newspapers. Lawrence *Baigent, R.A. *Copland, H. Winston *Rhodes, A.W. Stockwell and others upheld the tradition of urbanely expressed rigour of opinion, and through the 1970s–80s, when Peter Simpson was the regular reviewer of poetry and Owen *Marshall of short stories, every book of New Zealand literature received serious expert consideration. Current reviewers sustain this standard, with Margaret Quigley, Glynn Strange and Tom Weston established and consistent. It was appropriate that the *Press*, then under Naylor Hillary, books editor 1978–94, won the inaugural *PEN Best Books Page Award in 1990.

The *Press*, edging towards the highbrow as it always has, still leaves scope for fireworks and fun, as when A.K. *Grant's review of poems by former Governor-General Bernard *Fergusson produced a riotous exchange of Scots dialect verse. Grant, in fact, established himself as a writer with his comic columns in the *Press*, which proved that the days of new creative writing were not quite over, and in their absurdist-satiric way returned the paper's literary tradition to its Butlerian beginnings.

RR

PRESTON, Florence (1905–82), born Florence Margaret Munro at Oporo, attended Southland GHS and the University of Otago. Her first novel, *A Gallows Tree*, was published by Cassell in London in 1956; the 'tree' is a metaphor for the painful experiences of Joanna Denniston, married to a respectable physician, and Preston writes of exploring 'the real content of living happily ever after'. In the next three years Cassell published *Harvest of Daring* (1957), *Great Refusals* (1958) and *The Gay Pretensions* (1959). The themes of Preston's work have been compared with those of Edith *Grossmann, Jean *Devanny and Jane *Mander, and her focus on the pain women experience in relationships can be compared with that of Marilyn *Duckworth and Ruth *Park. Many of her novels have historical settings; her last book, *Who Rides the Tiger* (1980), published when she was 74, is set in early Central Otago. Preston lived in Queenstown for many years, where she was known for her landscaped garden. She wrote two descriptive books about the Wakatipu–Fiordland region. She was a member of the *New Zealand Women Writers' Society.   ALa

PRESTON, Ivy (1914–   ), was a prolific popular *romance writer, mainly for *Mills & Boon. More than thirty novels, widely translated, pursue romance storylines in settings that tend to isolate a small group of eligible characters against a picturesque background: Stewart Island in *Where Ratas Twine* (1960) and *Island of Enchantment* (1963); a hospital in *The Secret Love of Nurse Wilson* (1966); a Wellington flat rented by four young women in *Romance in Glenmore Street* (1974); or a coach tour of Fiordland in *Mountain Magic* (1979). Terry *Sturm discusses Preston's formulae and predilections quite fully in the *OHNZLE* (1991, 1998), particularly the pattern of 'frenzied intensities of feeling aroused in the heroine by the slightest and most innocent of physical gestures from the hero', and the rigorous repression of these intensities into an 'internal drama of the heroine's sensations'.

Preston's own life is at least as interesting, and makes absorbing reading in her autobiography, *The Silver Stream* (1959). Daughter of a Timaru farming family (born Kinross), she grew up during the *Depression and had to leave school early to learn dressmaking, despite her love of writing and of spoken English. After work as a cook, she married a farmer and had four children. Life remained hard on their farm near Timaru. While her husband also worked in the freezing works, Preston earned pin money by writing 'paragraphs' and stories for magazines; with her prize from one competition she bought her first washing copper. When her husband died young in 1956, with the eldest child 16, she began to write seriously and with a professionalism that has to be admired, however simplistic her treatments often are. She still lives in Timaru, visiting the public library regularly.   PN/RR

Price Milburn, the publishing firm, was founded in 1957 by Hugh Price and Jim Milburn. While studying history at Wellington's Victoria University College, Price's friend, J.C. *Beaglehole, interested him in typography and book design, and in 1954 he attended the London School of Printing and Graphic Arts. Back in Wellington, he found that his friend Milburn had a book but no publisher. So they published Milburn's book and a business developed. A number of productive relationships with, for example, the New Zealand University Press, the Sydney University Press and *School Publications saw their list expand dramatically. Their most significant literary collaboration was with Victoria University Press, with whom they produced the extensive VUP 'New Zealand Playscripts' series; publishing, among others, Bruce *Mason and Roger *Hall. Price, who was a friend of James K. *Baxter, also produced four of his collections: *Jerusalem Daybook* (1971), *Autumn Testament* (1972), a reprint of *Jerusalem Sonnets* (1974) and a collection of children's poems, *The Tree House* (1974).   PM

Priests of Ferris, The (1984), is the second novel in the fantasy trilogy for children by Maurice *Gee. See **Halfmen of O, The**.

Printout is an Auckland-based magazine of poetry, short prose fiction, artwork and criticism, which first appeared in 1991. Its initial impulse was to publish brief, readable work, including that of new writers, without propounding any lofty literary vision: hence the slight format (A5; 64 pages) and casual title. The first issue, closely associated with the weekly *'Poetry Live' readings in Auckland, was limited to poetry and artwork, and only Aucklanders contributed. From its second issue, however, *Printout* set up as a national (and international) magazine, and opened its pages to short fiction. With the ninth issue (Autumn 1995) the format expanded to 96 pages; and from issue ten (Summer 1995–96) the criticism section became extensive. *Printout* has remained principally a venue for poetry, however, perhaps because all the editors have been poets: Susan Allpress, Tony *Beyer, Diane Brown, Grant Duncan, John Herbert, Kai Jensen, Joy MacKenzie and Iain *Sharp. The magazine's rotating editorship has led it on a meandering path between more conservative literary models and the fringes of *postmodernism, and its production values have also been somewhat erratic. Yet *Printout* has produced eleven issues in five years, and has printed most of the country's major poets.   KJ

Progressive Books, established in May 1936 by Jack and Doris Basham, was the first co-operative bookshop to be set up in New Zealand. (Rachel Barrowman devotes a chapter of *A Popular Vision* (1994) to the co-operative book movement.) The operation was founded on socialist principles and aimed to provide a wide range of 'radical literature'. It therefore kept its prices low and established a lending library (closed in 1952 because of financial pressures). Affectionately known as 'Basham's Bomb Shop', it also acted as a vibrant cultural centre for a progressive intelligentsia that included writers like Frank *Sargeson and R.A.K. *Mason and architect Vernon Brown. Arthur Jackson-Thomas took over management of the shop from 1941, and he was to run it until 1966. In the 1940s, by providing one of the few outlets for serious, quality literature, it developed a lively reputation in Auckland. From the mid-1970s, increasing rents forced its move away from the city centre and this, coupled with tighter market conditions, led to its demise in 1980.   NWt

Progressive Publishing Society was established in 1941 to publish progressive and New Zealand literature. Among its instigators were W.B. Sutch, Ian *Gordon and F.L. Coombs. It was initially conceived as a joint publishing venture between the Auckland, Wellington and Christchurch co-operative book societies (*Progressive Books) with the financial and technical support of *Caxton Press and *Paul's Book Arcade. However, by 1943 a tension between the political and literary aims of the society had developed to the point that Caxton and Paul's were excluded. Publications were fairly evenly divided between political and social critiques and literary endeavours. The former included A.R.D. *Fairburn's *We New Zealanders*, Frederick *Sinclaire's essays and *The Waiting Hills* and *The Timeless Land* by M.H. *Holcroft, while Allen *Curnow's *Sailing or Drowning* and Frank *Sargeson's *A *Man and His Wife* were among the significant literary contributions. In 1944 the society ran a short story competition, which was won by Anton *Vogt. One of its most successful ventures was *New Zealand New Writing*, edited by Ian *Gordon, which ran to four numbers 1942–45. Along with co-ordinating the work of the bookshops, the society produced a number of topical pamphlets specifically relating to the New Zealand situation as well as a range of children's books. Always undercapitalised, it could not sustain the costly transition from producing pamphlets to substantial hardbacks, and without a compensatory source of income, independent of publishing, it recorded substantial losses. In the middle of 1945, the society went into liquidation with a debt of almost £2500, proving a costly experiment in cultural democracy for the co-operative book societies. However, during its short lifespan it had achieved sixty-five publications, as well as initiating two of Caxton's most significant publications: Curnow's *A *Book of New Zealand Verse* and Sargeson's *Speaking for Ourselves*. Rachel Barrowman devotes a chapter of *A Popular Vision* (1994) to the Progressive Publishing Society.   NWt

Proverbs, Māori, see **Māori sayings**.

Prowlers (1987), a novel by Maurice *Gee, tells the story of Sir Noel Papps and his grand-niece Kate, who is writing the life of his sister, Kitty. The strategy of using one person writing the life of another and the ironies relating to the perception of self and others that this involves were to be repeated in *Going West*. Kate wants to interview Sir Noel for her biography of the political maverick Kitty, while he remembers his sister more for her personal qualities and part in his own life. While Kitty was involved with left-wing politics, he, a scientist, was a pillar of the community; in different ways their lives were affected by the property-dealing, materialistic, womanising Phil Dockery. Though Kate is interested only in Kitty's politics, Noel's account of the past reveals a range of human foibles, inconsistencies and achievements only partly accessible to Kate's limited view. Meanwhile Kate is pursuing a complex love-affair of her own. Gee thus covers a wide period of social history in a short space, beginning with the youth of Noel's generation in World War 1, and including an anti-German riot presented differently in the children's book *The *Fire Raiser*. The differences reveal much about Gee's writing for children or adults. The historical span simultaneously includes the passions of Kate's generation in the 1980s. As in the *Plumb* trilogy, Gee reveals his skill in evoking the detail of the past and relating it to the present.   NW

PUHIWĀHINE (Rihi Puhiwāhine Te Rangihirawea, d. 1906) was a remarkable poet and a colourful personality. Her life and poems were researched by Pei Te Hurinui *Jones, and the present account is heavily indebted to his *Puhiwahine: Maori Poetess*, first published as a series in Te *Ao Hou* and then (1961) by the *Pegasus Press.

Puhiwāhine was born and died in the lands of the Ngāti Tūwharetoa. Her mother, Hinekiore, a famous song leader and composer of satirical songs (*pātere), taught her age-old traditions, including the techniques of *poi and pūkana (posture dances). From an early age she was recognised as having remarkable talents. She travelled widely and was courted by many chiefs. She also encountered a number of Pākehā and acquired a little English. To the distress of linguistic purists, she introduced English words—in Māori adaptation—into her poems.

On her travels she fell in love with Hauauru of the Maniapoto, but her brothers forbade her to become his second wife. When she heard that he had taken another, she fell ill. During her recovery she wrote two songs known as 'Puhiwāhine's Songs for Hauauru': 'For two years you were lost to me, / And it was I, alas, who left you. / Would that I had clung to the rock; / Then naught on earth, nor in the heavens, / Would have moved above, or here below, / With the howling gales or stormy winds.' (This and subsequent translations are by Jones.) She had been told of Hauauru's marriage by Tanirau at Paripari, and as she left she sang an *action-song to Tanirau filled with the names of many prominent men who had courted her: 'Ah me! a persistent one is Nepia, / Who often daydreams about me; / But Ku and Pateriki, / Like my kerchiefs, are always with me…'.

Stories of Puhiwāhine's innumerable wooers preceded her on her further travels and she was the subject of gossip. After a scandalous affair in Kāwhia her Taupō people carried her on to Whatiwhatihoe, at that time a tribal meeting place. Among the hundreds there, Puhiwāhine encountered Te Mahutu Te Toko of the Maniapoto, 'a striking figure of a man with his face only recently tattooed by the leading artist of the Maniapoto…. Te Mahutu was a fine orator, a good singer and a lively conversationalist. When these two ardent souls met it was a case of love at first sight' (Jones). Again her brothers intervened. At Owaikara near Parawera, Puhiwāhine wrote the most popular of her songs, 'He Waiata Aroha Mo Te Mahutu Te Toko' (A Love-Song for Te Mahutu Te Toko): 'It was I who did forsake you, / Slave heart mine not to seek a lingering farewell; / With two nights more in close embrace.' Occasionally, it was sung to tease Mahutu, who composed an answering song of his own, a blend of whimsy, sentiment and satire: 'Come, cut off my head, / Cast it on to the courtyard / As a wash-bowl for the maiden / Whose memory gnaws on within.'

Shortly afterwards Puhiwāhine married someone with echoes of a very different poetic culture: John Gotty was German and, according to some, the illegitimate son, or grandson, of the poet Johann Wolfgang von Goethe. Jones wisely treats this with some scepticism. Recently journalists—in particular the New Zealand/ Viennese writer Tom Appleton—have tried to trace even the day on which Gotty was conceived, at a time when the great poet's movements are a little difficult to trace. Goethe scholars, slightly scandalised (despite Goethe's known promiscuity), have treated the story even more sceptically than Jones.

As Gotty travelled with her from Tūwharetoa lands to Wanganui she was wooed in classical Māori by the chieftains in three villages. 'It was, perhaps, just as well for Gotty's peace of mind that these declarations were made in this manner—the expressions used were well beyond his limited knowledge of the language' (Jones). During the sporadic hostilities, Gotty's Māori wife was treated with suspicion and she found herself isolated from both her people and her husband's for long periods. At this time she wrote a song of war ('He Waiata Mo Te Pakanga'), quite unlike her earlier verse: 'For seven long years / The patu has opposed / The unsheathed sword, / And the loaded gun. / Be prepared. Be prepared! / The worst is yet to come.'

In peacetime Puhiwāhine's 'sparkling wit and charm' (Jones) won her many friends. Although she spoke little English she became 'a lady of fashion' and was also a welcome guest among the tribes, where she was often asked to sing her own compositions. In response to much teasing about her earlier life, she wrote 'He Waiata Ki Ana Whaiaipo' (A Song of a Coquette) in which she gives 'a long catalogue of her love affairs and many flirtations'. Jones prints twelve verses, but often the descendants of one of her lovers remember only the verse that refers to him. Jones remarks, 'It is no exaggeration to say that mention of an ancestor in this song is like a citation for military honours', and Hauauru successfully asserted his claim to a block of land in the Maori Land Court by quoting a verse of it.

As the years advanced, Puhiwāhine's two sons married, and in 1869, when both were about to be fathers, she wrote an *oriori or lullaby. Normally these are written for an infant, but this grandmother was too impatient for that and wrote a prospective oriori, 'Te Oriori A Puhiwahine', for the two children-to-be. In the 1880s she attended meetings of the Maori Land Court, and her last recorded song is 'He Waiata Mo Nga Mahi Whenua' (A Song about Land Affairs), expressing 'sorrow and regret for the manner in which the tribes were dealing with their ancestral lands' (Jones). Despite certain influences from the English language and European narrative styles, the songs of Puhiwāhine are notable compositions in traditional and classical Māori forms.   NW

PULE, John Puhiatau (1962–), was born in Liku, Niue, and arrived in New Zealand in 1964. He began writing in 1980 after reading the work of Hone *Tuwhare, and has published poetry including *Sonnets to Van Gogh and Providence* (1982), *Flowers after the Sun* (1984) and *Bond of Time* (1985). He took up painting in 1987 with the encouragement of artist Tony Fomison, his dual interests coming together in the late 1980s in a series of paintings of texts in Nuiean which confronted his audience with evidence of his cultural difference. Since his first return trip to Niue in 1991, Pule has taken increased interest in the history, mythology and make-up of his country of origin. This is registered in his painting, which now typically takes the form and employs the colour range of Nuiean tapa, and in his novel, *The Shark That Ate the Sun: Ko E Mago Ne Kai E La* (1992), one of the most significant texts of the immigrant *Pacific community.

This combines sequences of historical, mythical, genealogical and autobiographical narrative. The varied languages of these entangled stories are frequently visionary and poetic as they describe the journeying, survival under difficulty, and the *alofa* among a migrant Niuean family. A prologue takes the reader into an ecstatic present, releasing images of loss and rebirth, city and village, and introducing the novel's themes of anti-colonialism, anti-nuclear protest, desire, family ties and violence. The first of the novel's three main sections comprises letters between family members, with prose and poetic pieces that contrast life in Niue and New Zealand. Part Two is a lush, lyrical and erotic thirty-poem sequence set on nineteenth-century Niue. The narrator of the third section describes his home, school, work and prison experiences in various suburbs of Auckland, interspersed with a chapter of legends which emphasises the disjunction between migrant life and the mythical *Pacific and reconnects the characters to that past. A spiritual poem combining Christian and Niuean symbols forms the epilogue.   BW/CB

Puritanism has been a consistent concern of New Zealand writers, especially in the period 1930s–60s. Frank *Sargeson in his radio broadcast on 'Writing a Novel' in 1950 said that 'what is pervadingly characteristic of New Zealand is its own particular variety of puritanism'. Two years later in *'Fretful Sleepers' Bill *Pearson commented that 'the puritanism of Littledene' was still the dominant social pattern in New Zealand, 'one of the cementing elements of our society'. The following year in 'Fiction and the Social Pattern' Robert *Chapman described the 'puritan cultural pattern' as central to the society. All three writers knew what they meant by 'puritanism' and expected their audiences to relate that meaning to the literature of the previous twenty years, which they saw as predominantly a critique of puritanism. Both the term and the phenomenon, of course, went back well before 1930. Mrs Brayton in Jane *Mander's The *Story of a New Zealand River (1920), set in the New Zealand of the late nineteenth century, states 'Puritanism is an awful disease', and Mander went on to entitle one of her novels The Passionate Puritan (1921), while Constance Clyde's novel A Pagan's Love makes a critique of puritanism as early as 1905. However, it was the writers of Sargeson's generation who especially focused on the theme.

By 'puritanism' these writers did not mean the religious movement represented by John Milton, but rather a secularised pattern of feeling and conduct developing from the Victorian lower-middle-class evangelical morality brought with them by settlers in the second half of the nineteenth century. The secularisation involves the shift from what Sargeson in his autobiography calls the 'pure puritan' (represented by his father), the 'genuinely

religious and moral' person who believed 'that all the heavenly absolutes as he conceived them could and should be made to prevail on earth', to the 'impure puritan' (represented by his mother), who 'insisted that you should do the right thing because of what people would say or think if you didn't', and who was 'indeed truly representative of of the prevailing general sentiment about what life in New Zealand should be'. The 'right thing' involved the work ethic: 'Work, deny yourself and you will be prosperous and saved', as Chapman defined it. The negative corollaries of this work ethic included an anti-aesthetic attitude and a distrust of mere pleasure. Also central was the strict code of behaviour: temperance; linguistic propriety (no blasphemy and no explicit sexual language); a residual sabbatarianism; a sexual repressiveness that included conservative dress, a taboo on sexual knowledge for the young, strict restrictions on sexual behaviour, including 'self-abuse', and sharp fear of and disapproval of homosexuality. More generally, the code discouraged public expression of emotion. The work ethic and behavioural code were assumed to be absolutes, the only 'right thing', and thus there was the tendency to make self-righteous moral judgments on non-conformity. This pattern was enforced by the external mechanisms of public shaming and punishment and by the internal mechanism of guilt. The primary moral guardian was Mother, in puritanism's clearly defined gender roles, for, as Toss *Woollaston put it in his autobiographical Sage Tea (1980), woman's mission in life was 'to oppose sin in boys and men—swearing, drunkenness, and other things that could not be mentioned'.

Criticism of the puritan pattern as 'unnatural' and denying human fulfilment was one of the defining characteristics of serious writing in the 1930–60 period (popular literature, on the other hand, tended to enjoin the pattern or to take it for granted). As late as 1967, James K. *Baxter saw 'the endemic problem of our poets' as 'a struggle with the austere anti-aesthetic angel of Puritanism', while Sargeson in a review in 1950 saw the writer as carrying out the role of 'self-liberator (and perhaps liberator of some of those who suffer under little Bethel)', and Chapman concluded that 'the attitide which the New Zealand writer takes to his society, and which informs his work, will continue to be based on the possibility here of a truly human ease and depth of living and on an attack on the distortion produced by an irrelevant puritanism of misplaced demands and guilts'. However, Pearson warned that the belief that 'the worst enemy is puritanism' may have been an oversimplification, for 'when the puritan shell is cast there is nothing to replace it except perhaps a dimly expectant hedonism' or 'conscientious and enlightened self-indulgence'. The critique of puritanism is everywhere in the New Zealand literature of the 1930–60 period and still present but not so dominant in the years that followed, not only in the texts already mentioned, but in such Sargeson stories and novels as 'A Good Boy' (1936), 'Old Man's Story' (1940), ★*I Saw in My Dream* (1949) and *The Hangover* (1967); in Robin ★Hyde's *The* ★*Godwits Fly* (1938) and *A Place in This World* (1937; pub. 1984); in A.R.D. ★Fairburn's satires and commentaries such as *We New Zealanders* (1944) and 'La Belle Dame Sans Merci' (1941); in Ronald Hugh ★Morrieson's black comic novels of small-town life; in Janet ★Frame's ★*Owls Do Cry* (1957) and ★*To the Is-Land* (1982); and the classic retrospective account, Maurice ★Gee's ★*In My Father's Den* (1972).   LJ

PYKE, Vincent (1827–94), is best known for his two lively and popular ★goldfields novels, *The Story of Wild Will Enderby* (1873) and its sequel, *The Adventures of George Washington Pratt* (1874). Born in Somerset, Pyke emigrated to South Australia at the age of 24, and joined the gold rush to Bendigo, Victoria, before turning to the more reliable life of a storekeeper in 1853. His rhetorical skills led to election as a speaker for the miners in their fight against licence fees, and to represent their community in the Victorian Legislative Council. After a visit to England, Pyke was appointed police magistrate on the mine fields in 1858 and commissioner of trade and customs in 1859. In 1862 he took a trip to New Zealand for health reasons, but it is probably no coincidence that this was the time of the gold rush in Otago. He remained as secretary for the goldfields to the provincial government and from 1873–90 was member of the House of Representatives for Whakatipu, as well as first chairman (1877–82) of the Vincent County Council, the county having been named for him. In 1893 he returned to parliament representing Tuapeka. Pyke framed regulations which were the groundwork of mining legislation in New Zealand and in 1866 drafted the Gold-Fields Act, some of whose features are still law. The Victorian Limited Liability Act, which was adopted in New Zealand, was also his work. Perhaps it is salutary for readers of his novels to find C.S. Ross stating in 1887, 'His *magnum opus* ... is the Otago Central Railway.'

Pyke was also active as a journalist, founding the *Southern Mercury* in Dunedin in 1874 and contributing a humorous coloumn, signed 'Timaru'. Two other papers were briefly under his editorship: the *Guardian* and one of the papers called *Dunedin Punch*. In 1884 he wrote a prize dialect story for the Ayreshire Association (*Craigielinn*, set in Scotland immediately before emigration to New Zealand) and in 1886 a series of old identity portraits in the *Tapanui Courier*.

Pyke's goldfields novels are lively, often amusing tales. Despite a certain crudity in the telling, their loosely connected adventures, struggles between heroes and villains, touches of romantic love and colourful scenic descriptions have lasting appeal, as their long publishing histories show. *Wild Will Enderby* has enjoyed several reprintings. Essentially it is a story designed to make heroes and villains among the golddiggers, whose adventures are told in a prose somewhat too grand for the subject. It comes as close as any New Zealand story to the frontier literature of America, the authenticity of the background being emphasised in footnotes. An unlikely friendship between a reserved Englishman and a garrulous American (George Washington Pratt) leads to scenes of defending their gold against villainous thieves, seduction by 'a large ripe, rich beauty', prospecting, pursuits, poker games and accusations of murder. After a closing mass of complications in which a variety of brutal villains are contrasted with the decent hero, all ends in happy marriage, except for the still wandering American.

His story in *George Washington Pratt* opens with even more rapt descriptions of wild mountain scenery than in the first book. Episodic adventures among this romantic landscape involve courageous rescues (of a mother and baby), a lynching party, enemies named Ginger, Slush, Jimmy and Tripes, a mate called Pegleg Dick, compromising situations with distressed women, attacks and counter-attacks in which the region's rivers and rainfall play a part, deaths by quicksands and drowning, beatings and abandonment and characters called Maori Jack (kindly but lazy) and Old Jack (a donkey whose braying is mistaken for the call of a moa). Finally rich, Pratt decides to return to America, since New Zealand 'do seem to be stacked up rather muchly'. After some closing romantic complications he claims his distant love. Though told with panache, the colourful story has never achieved the high popularity of *Wild Will Enderby*.

Contemporary reference suggests that there was another novel, *Eustace Egremont*, which cannot now be traced. Pyke's 'White Hood: A Tale of the Terraces' was published in one volume with Thorpe ★Talbot's 'Blue Cap' in 1881. It is another melodramatic story of romance, illicit love and murder, set this time in gold mines on natural terraces around Lake Whakatipu. Pyke's *History of the Early Gold Discoveries in Otago* (1887) is an amusing, anecdotal but reliable account which was long recognised as the standard work and a classic of New Zealand historiography. Another comment by C.S. Ross is revealing: 'His life was too active, he was too much a man of affairs and too attractively sociable ... to appropriate the contents of books and heap up stores of knowledge.... But no man we have met could, on occasion, express himself so pithily and to the point as he.'   NW

Q

Queen Elizabeth II Arts Council, see **Literary Fund**.

QUENTIN, Dorothy, see **Romance fiction**.

Quesada: Poems 1972–74 (1975) introduced a decade of poetic experimentation for its author, C.K. *Stead. The greater stylistic freedom of Stead's previous collection *Crossing the Bar* (1972) has been noted by critics, while his longer, free-form sequences of the later 1970s would be collected in *Walking Westward* (1979), *Geographies* (1982) and *Poems of a Decade* (1983). *Quesada* occupies a pivotal point between these collections, comprising a range of new poetic possibilities for Stead. The title sequence is relaxed in form, exploring a myth of Don Quixote as vanquished lover, with a number of its passages employing an unusually long line. '15 Letters from the Zebra Motel', in contrast, is epigrammatic in its concision, and this sequence seems to have been composed on a single occasion—Stead's stay in an Australian motel during a literary conference. It foreshadows Stead's later experiments with spontaneous, journal-like composition, such as his sequence 'Yes T.S.'. *Quesada* also contains the beginning of Stead's celebrated sequence of sonnets, in free verse couplets. On the dust-jacket he suggests that writing these sonnets in the manner of *Baxter 'might have been an unconscious wish to exorcise that dour Kiwi ghost', but the exorcism was unsuccessful. The journal composition principle of these sonnets evidently advanced Stead on his path towards a more personal mode of poetry. The sonnet sequence was reprinted and extended in *Walking Westward*.   KJ

Quill was the irregular annual publication of the *New Zealand Women Writers' and Artists' Society. It appeared in five issues 1934–38 and featured work by the society's members, including Isobel *Andrews, Nellie Donovan and Roma Hoggard.   SH

QUINN, Pat (1947–   ), won the 1994 Senior Children's Fiction Award for her first teenage novel, *The Value of X* (1993), which refreshingly weaves the mathematical symbol of the unknown, 'X', into the home, school and social lives of a girl on the threshhold of adulthood. Born and educated in Wellington (BSc, DipCommns, Victoria University), Quinn began writing for New Zealand and Australian *School Journals, winning a 1989 short story award. Her other books are the non-fiction *Sailing with New Zealand Endeavour* (1993) and *Free Fall* (1994), and the teenage fiction *Sounds Crazy* (1995), as well as readers for *Learning Media. A freelance writer, she lives in Wellington, working actively with New Zealand Society of Authors *(PEN).   DH

Quote Unquote was a monthly magazine styling itself 'New Zealand's guide to books and other pleasures', which ran 1993–97. Winner of both the Commonwealth Media Prize for arts, media and literature and the New Zealand Book Page of the Year Award in 1994, it was published by Quote Publishing in Auckland. It offered a lively and eclectic mix of articles, interviews, reviews, opinion pieces and pithy comment on books, writers, writing processes, literary and cultural issues, the publishing and bookselling scene, along with occasional short fiction, poetry and book excerpts. A popular feature was the 'Poetry File', in which Bill *Manhire discussed the poetic process in individual poems. The magazine also covered the arts, albeit in less depth, concentrating on painting and photography but commenting also on film, music, theatre and other performance arts. The range of its contributors was equally wide. The primary focus was on New Zealand but, particularly in the reviews section, a variety of overseas works and events were also considered. In tone, *Quote Unquote* was irreverent, sometimes cheeky or provocative, and determinedly non-intellectual, even while dealing seriously with serious issues, and in presentation it was slick and professional, literature's first such magazine, with an average of forty-eight pages each issue, some in colour.

Quote Unquote was founded in 1992 and published its first issue in June 1993; its founder and editor was Stephen Stratford, and assistant editor Kevin *Ireland. Despite a circulation about three times that of most New Zealand literary journals, *Quote Unquote* failed to survive the perils of specialist magazine publishing in New Zealand.   AM

R

Rainbirds, The, is the seventh novel by Janet *Frame (London, 1968; Christchurch: *Pegasus Press, 1969; published in the USA as *Yellow Flowers in the Antipodean Room*, New York, 1969; five draft manuscripts are held in the *Hocken Library). Frame's consistent critique of middle-class suburban bourgeois New Zealand ('the average New Zealander possesses no staircase to the [emotional and creative] upper floor') is given its fullest treatment in this novel. Godfrey Rainbird, a successfully integrated English immigrant to New Zealand, has managed to 'fit in' admirably in his adopted city of Dunedin where 'people like everything to go the same way'. A model, conformist citizen, Godfrey becomes alienated from society when he 'returns to life' after being 'pronounced dead' following a car accident (he was in fact comatose). His inconvenient resurrection (funeral arrangements have already been made) occurs on the 'third day', one of many parodic parallels between Godfrey and Christ. Godfrey becomes a social pariah, shunned by a society terrified of the mortality he symbolises. He loses his job as a clerk in the Tourist Office; his children, Sonny and Teena, are taken away by Welfare; his wife, Beatrice, starts drinking and dies in mysterious circumstances (suicide or murdered by Godfrey?). Alienated from others, Godfrey finds his brush with death has given him a new 'view' on life; he turns increasingly from society, rejecting the 'neat domestic path leading up to the front door', journeying instead on the 'inward path' to the source of his new vision. In doing so he rejects 'the convention and the wording' of social language, refusing to trust 'so obvious a deceiver as language'. After the accident he finds he is able to 'get inside the lining' of words and resorts to using an 'icy language'—resonant with punning, anagrams and wordplay—which veers increasingly towards incommunicability. In the final ironic section of the novel (similar in tone to the epilogue of *Owls Do Cry*), set in the future, we are told of the successes of the Rainbird children and of Godfrey's attainment of the unsolicited status of visionary after his actual death: his grave becomes a tourist site. *The Rainbirds* is critically regarded as Frame's least successful (if most comic) novel. Commenting on the novel's bizarre plot and lack of credibility, critics have found Frame's sense of the ridiculous to be a liability, her consistent wordplay intrusive, and her focus on social conditions to be achieved at the cost of convincing characterisation.   KWo

RANDELL, Beverley (1931–), is an internationally recognised author of books for children who has been published by sixteen publishers, in several languages, in six countries. Her total sales approach the forty million mark. Educated at Wellington schools, before going on to take a BA in English and history at Victoria University College, she first worked as a primary school teacher. Her marriage, in 1959, to Hugh Price of the publishers *Price Milburn signalled the start of her involvement in book production. From 1962 she put her knowledge gained as a teacher to good use when she wrote and edited scores of books for children in the early stages of reading. She has been praised by Dennis *McEldowney for her 'genius for devising ... infant readers which used minimal vocabularies to tell actual stories'. The origins of Randell's interest in children's books are explained by her daughter, Susan Price, in *Books for Life* (1991). For a full list of publications see *Beverley Randell: A checklist of children's books written by her, 1955–1995* (1996).   PM

Rangatira is the leader of a *hapū.

RANGER, Laura, see *Laura's Poems*.

Rangi and Papa are the central figures of the popular version of the Māori 'genesis myth'. This term is preferable to 'creation myth', since the world, in this version, originated with the separation of the sky (Rangi) and the earth (Papa) rather than with an act of creation. The best-known version is to be found in ★Grey's *Polynesian Mythology*, originally the work of ★Te Rangikāheke, whose manuscript begins: 'My friends listen to me. The Maori people stem from only one source, namely the Great-heaven-which-stands-above and the Earth-which-lies-below. According to Europeans, God made heaven and earth and all things. According to the Maori, Heaven (Rangi) and Earth (Papa) are themselves the source.' The translation is by Bruce ★Biggs, who points out that Grey deleted the reference to the Europeans here and elsewhere, giving the impression that his informant was speaking without knowledge of European traditions and merely telling the myths without comment.

Because Rangi and Papa were in a seemingly eternal embrace, all was darkness, but their children were determined to discover light and for this purpose drove their parents apart. In particular Tāne, god of the forests, persuaded his children, the trees, to bury their heads in Papa and drive Rangi away with their feet, or branches. The resulting entry of light into the world and the world into light (Te ★*Ao Mārama*) was the beginning of all things.

The myth has found entry into modern literature in many forms, such as the references in ★'Between Earth and Sky', a story by Patricia ★Grace, or in Hone ★Tuwhare's poem 'We, Who Live in Darkness': 'It was light, my brothers. Light. / A most beautiful sight infiltered past / the armpit hairs of the father.'   NW

Rata was an annual published in Wellington 1931–33 by Harry ★Tombs, and edited by C.A. ★Marris. It featured photographs and paintings of New Zealand scenery, and articles, poems and stories by Marris, Eileen ★Duggan, Dora Hagemeyer, Johannes C. ★Andersen, J.C. ★Beaglehole and Robin ★Hyde.   SH

Rata Leaves was published by the Rata Club, a women's literary and social club of Christchurch, about 1898–1901.   SH

RAWLINSON, Gloria (1918–95), poet, was born in Tonga and moved with her family to Auckland at the age of 6. A childhood attack of poliomyelitis confined her to a wheelchair for much of her life. *Gloria's Book* (1933), a collection of juvenilia, was published when she was a young teenager, followed by another book of early poetry, *The Perfume Vendor* (1935), and a novel, *Music in the Listening Place* (1938). She was active in the Auckland literary scene, and associated with other prominent local writers and poets, including journalist and writer Robin ★Hyde, with whom she maintained a correspondence after Hyde left New Zealand. Rawlinson became Hyde's literary executor after her suicide in London in 1939, editing ★*Houses by the Sea* (1952), a selection of Hyde's later work. She contributed a large body of poetry and stories, including children's fiction, to newspapers, literary magazines and anthologies in both Australia and New Zealand. The poetic sequence *The Islands Where I Was Born* (1955) was produced in pamphlet form by the Handcraft Press, and has been frequently anthologised. Later poetry was published in the collection *Of Clouds and Pebbles* (1963), and a small volume, *Gloria in Excelsis* (1995), was produced shortly before her death.   SW

Red Funnel was published in Dunedin by the Union Steam Ship Company 1905–09. Less a travel magazine than a literary journal, it was edited by A.A. Brown and directed towards an international readership. Its content consisted largely of material by British, Americanand Australian authors, although it did publish some poetry, stories, and articles by New Zealand contributors, including C.R. ★Allen, Isabel Cluett, H. ★Guthrie-Smith, Alice ★Kenny, James ★Cowan and Dulce ★Carman.   SH

Red Mole (1974–) has been aptly described as 'perhaps the first, last and best of the numerous non-realist theatre groups to have flourished here in this late capitalist era'. The group was founded as a collective in 1974 by Alan ★Brunton and Sally Rodwell after observing folk theatre in Bali and India. They were also influenced by the avant-garde theatrical tradition in Europe and America. Red Mole aspired also to be 'as totally New Zealand as a can of Watties baked beans'. With other 1970s groups, such as Francis Batten's Theatre Action and Paul Maunder's Amamus, Red Mole sought alternatives to prevailing naturalistic styles. A publicity handout in 1978 stated: 'Red Mole moves easily from puppetry to mimicry and dance, from poetry to spectacle, all to comic ends. Red Mole is in the entertainment business but considers the big questions of existence to be the best entertainment of all. The Red Mole universe is one of metamorphosis and transmigration of imaginations.'

The Historical Note in Brunton's *A Red Mole Sketchbook* (1989) lists forty shows performed 1974–89; the period 1989–94 produced at least five more. In the early years Red Mole concentrated on cabaret-based satirical theatre ('Cabaret Paris Spleen', 1975, 'Cabaret

Pekin 1949', 1976). Later shows became more complex, including elements of myth and symbolism ('Pacific Nights', 1977, 'Crazy in the Streets', 1978). In 1978 Red Mole went to the United States, and except for a New Zealand tour in 1980 ('I'll Never Dance Down Bugis Street Again') remained New York–based for a decade ('Numbered Days in Paradise', 1979, 'Childhood of a Saint', 1982, 'Dreamings End', 1984), with shorter residences in New Mexico ('Circu Sfumato', 1985, 'Lost Chants for the Living', 1986), London ('Blood in the Cracks', 'Dead Fingers Walk', 1979) and Amsterdam ('Playtime', 'Hour of Justice', 1987).

Red Mole returned to New Zealand in 1988 ('Gas Attack!', 'New Hope', 1988), based again in Wellington, though new shows were often toured ('Comrade Savage', 1990, 'Just Them Walking', 1992). They performed in Australia in 1990 and 1992, and in 1993 toured 'The Navigators' to the United States and Europe. Many actors and musicians have contributed for various periods, but the common element was always the partnership of Brunton and Rodwell. Of their 1991 show 'The Book of Life', David *Eggleton wrote: 'The conceptual framework … remains politically pertinent and appositely streetwise. They have always been purveyors of a bizarre, eccentrically grandiose theatre of commitment … theirs has always been a theatre of collective bargaining … against the Power, the repressive received systems….'   PS

REED, A.H. (Alfred Hamish) (1875–1975), was founder of the publishing house that became *A.H. and A.W. Reed and in later life a prolific author and assiduous book collector. Born in England, he arrived in New Zealand aged 12, and spent part of his teens as a gumdigger. After various business experience in Dunedin, as bookseller and importer, producer of Sunday school materials, and other activities, he began publishing books in 1932. In 1938 he and his wife established the Alfred & Isabel Reed Trust which donated a significant book collection to Dunedin Public Library. He officially retired in 1940, though retaining considerable influence on publishing policy, and, like his nephew A.W. *Reed, worked energetically as author to fill gaps in the market. He wrote prolifically for children on religious and historical subjects, his best writing reflecting a commitment to New Zealand's land and culture and to an engagingly populist version of its history. His many histories, often aimed at young adult readers, include *The Story of New Zealand* (1945), *The Gumdigger: The Story of Kauri Gum* (1948) and a series of provincial histories such as *The Story of Otago* (1947) and *The Story of Northland* (1956). All have had many editions. He also edited extracts from the journals of Captain *Cook (1951), *With Anthony*

Trollope in New Zealand (1969) and many others. Equally significant now are his contributions to the literature of New Zealand's terrain and *landscape, the local genre of tramping travel-writing, in titles like *Walks in Maoriland Byways* (1958), *From North Cape to Bluff* (1961) and *Marlborough Journey* (1963). He entered folklore himself with his octogenarian tramping achievements, climbing Mounts Taranaki, Ruapehu and (at 85) Ngauruhoe, and walking from North Cape to Bluff at 85. He lived in Dunedin, and, at age 99, received a knighthood, promptly commemorated in *Personal Recollections of Sir Alfred Hamish Reed* (1975).   RR

Reed, A.H. & A.W., see **A.H. & A.W. Reed**.

REED, A.W. (Alexander Wyclif) (1908–79), a less colourful figure than his uncle, A.H. *Reed, was the driving force behind the growth of the New Zealand publishing firm *A.H. and A.W. Reed, and was also a prolific author. Born into a family deeply committed to education and to the Protestant work ethic, he began work in Dunedin in 1925 in the Sunday school and religious supply business owned by his uncle A.H. Reed. In 1932 Clif (as he was known) agreed to his uncle's suggestion that he open a branch in Wellington and that year the firm published its first major title, *The Letters and Journals of Samuel *Marsden*, which was followed by other religious and historical works. Under Clif's enthusiastic guidance the publishing business expanded during the war and by the 1950s flair, energy and a keen eye for the market had created a very successful publishing enterprise.

A.W. Reed's first book as an author was *First New Zealand Christmases* (1933), written with his uncle and the precursor of an extensive output over the next forty years. Increasingly he left the publishing to a skilled staff and devoted himself to research and writing, often tailoring his product to the firm's needs. He published over 200 books, most of which appeared under the Reed imprint. A sustained interest in Māori topics produced his best-known and most substantial works. He was not himself familiar with life on the *marae, nor did he speak Māori, but he diligently mined the secondary sources available to produce dictionaries, encyclopedias and many books on Māori life and customs for a popular readership. It has to be said that his approach lacked subtlety and complexity and his tone owed much to a paternalistic missionary tradition. Claiming little creative ability as a writer, he saw his role as a simplifier and was amused when *Myths and Legends of Maoriland* (1946) won the Esther Glen Medal for best children's book of the year, although written for adults. Among his most successful books, some of which were still in print in the 1990s, were *Reeds Concise Maori Dictionary* (1948), *A Dictionary* of Maori Place Names (1961), *An Illustrated Encyclopedia of Maori Life* (1963) and *Treasury of Maori Folklore* (1963). A number of matching titles on Australian Aboriginal life quickly appeared from his pen after Reeds opened an Australian subsidiary in 1964. Deeply interested in education, he also wrote many books for schools, particularly at primary level and often in series, on religious topics and on Māori and Pacific life. EC

REES, Rosemary (1876–1963), ★romance novelist, was born in Auckland, the daughter of W.L. Rees, a barrister and parliamentarian, and author of a novel, *Sir Gilbert Leigh* (1878). She pursued a stage career overseas until 1924, when the collapse of a comedy company she had set up to tour New Zealand led her to write her first novel, the light romance *April's Sowing*, in order to pay off her debts. She continued to write prolifically over the next twenty years, and had published twenty-six novels altogether, in both England and the United States, by the time of her last, *The Proud Diana*, in 1962.

Rees's years of greatest popularity in New Zealand, alongside Nelle ★Scanlan, were the 1930s–40s. A considerable number of her novels with overseas settings drew on her experience of the world of the theatre, but her New Zealand novels were especially praised for the romantic intensity of her description of New Zealand scenery, reflected in such titles as *Lake of Enchantment* (1925). In 1933 she wrote a government-sponsored travel book, *New Zealand Holiday*, remarkable for its description of mid-★Depression New Zealand as 'a happy, comfortable country … notwithstanding the outcry from the Labour party about the bitterly hard lot of the unemployed'.

Rees initiated the genre of the 'light' romance in New Zealand, a shorter, more simplified form of romance than the complexly plotted Victorian romance novel, focused much more exclusively on the feelings, character and destiny of the heroine. Although the way she developed her recurrent themes—extra-marital infidelity and pre-marital chastity—often seemed to challenge the accepted moral norms of her time, the resolution of conflict in her novels invariably emphasised that the institution of marriage was essential to the well-being of women. In essence her novels provided none-too-subtle warnings to her female readers to preserve their virginity before marriage and avoid the dangers of extra-marital affairs. TS

REEVES, Amber (1887–1981), though generally known only as the brilliant Fabian daughter of William Pember ★Reeves and for her scandalous affair in 1908–09 with H.G. Wells, in fact became a significant feminist novelist and writer on socio-political topics and popular

psychology. Born in Sydenham, Christchurch, she moved to London in 1896 on her father's appointment as Agent-General. Her novels, published in London and the USA 1911–23, are mainly concerned with the restrictive education and opportunities of women. They include *The Reward of Virtue* (1911), *A Lady and Her Husband* (1914) and *Helen in Love* (1916). She also contributed Chapter 11 to Wells's *The Work, Wealth and Happiness of Mankind* (1932), on 'The Role of Women in the World's Work'. Her later writing, such as *The New Propaganda* (1939) and *Worry in Women* (1941), was published under her married name of Amber Blanco White. RR

REEVES, William Pember (1857–1932), like many early New Zealand politicians (see ★Domett, ★Tregear) was also a writer—of history, poetry and books of scenic description. Educated at Christ's College, Christchurch, he studied law but engaged in journalism and was in turn editor of the *Canterbury Times* and the *Lyttelton Times*. He entered parliament with a reputation as a radical and had a brilliant early career, entering the Liberal Cabinet as Minister for Education and Justice at the age of 33. His labour legislation earned him a worldwide reputation, but financial scandals surrounding his father interrupted his rise and, his ambition thwarted by Seddon, he accepted a position as New Zealand's Agent-General in London, arriving there in 1896. He and his wife Maud became leading members of the Fabian Society. He quarrelled with H.G. Wells over the issue of Free Love, his resentment increasing when his daughter Amber ★Reeves became pregnant by Wells, whom Reeves called 'a vile, impudent blackguard'. The scandal had an 'immense' effect on Reeves, according to Keith ★Sinclair's biography (1965), and the Fabian Society never fully recovered, despite efforts at reconciliation led by Bernard ★Shaw.

Except for one short visit, Reeves did not return to New Zealand, though his history of it, *The Long White Cloud: Ao Tea Roa* (1898) established itself as the classic account for a considerable time. The mythological pattern it imposed upon the English-speaking settlement of New Zealand was hardly questioned until the 1950s. Sinclair, praising it as 'a book of great intellectual and imaginative sweep', also describes it 'as a disguised autobiography'. Certainly upon our historical narrative it placed a South Island perspective and enshrined the originality and importance of the Liberal legislation. This latter theme was repeated in *State Experiments in Australia & New Zealand* (1902).

Reeves produced four volumes of poems, two in conjunction with George ★Williams, *Colonial Couplets* and *In Double Harness*, light verse satirically describing early Canterbury. In his own two volumes *New Zealand and Other Poems* (1898) and *The Passing of the Forest and*

Other Verse (1925) Reeves stressed his vision of New Zealand history. In his title poem 'New Zealand', the new nation appears as a worker's free citadel, surrounded by the 'surges and winds of the masterless deep'. It is a fresh place—not jungle, desert or the industrialised old country—with only one foe, 'the stern soil'.

'The Colonist in His Garden', probably his best poem, from his last volume, wrestles with the dilemma of the exile. In response to the claim of 'England, life and art', the poet responds '"No Art?" Who serve an art more great / Than we, rough architects of State / With the old Earth at strife? … Mine is the vista where the blue / And white-capped mountains close the view…. Friend, could I rear in England's air / A sweeter English rose?' It is ironic that for all this commitment, Reeves did not return to live in the country of his birth.

His poetry cannot compare with his history. *The Long White Cloud* remained a basic text for over sixty years. The fact that recently the revisionists have had a field-day paradoxically illustrates its predominance. Part of its appeal was Reeves's crisp, authoritative style. His vision is exemplified by his revised ending in a later edition, which expresses the 'belief that a young democratic country, still free from extremes of wealth and poverty, from class hatreds and fears and the barriers these create, supplies an unequalled field for safe and rational experiment in the hope of preventing and shutting out some of the worst social evils and miseries which afflict great nations alike in the old world and the new'. Not for him ambiguity or doubt.

The Long White Cloud reflects a legal training underpinning a skilled journalist's polemic, combined with the attention-gaining attributes of the politician and an intellectual's breadth of thought. The opening sentences illustrate these varied strengths: 'Though one of the parts of the earth best fitted for man, New Zealand was probably about the last of such lands occupied by the human race. The first European to find it was a Dutch sea-captain who was looking for something else, and thought it was part of South America from which it is sundered by five thousand miles of ocean. It takes its name from a province of Holland to which it does not bear the remotest likeness, and is usually regarded as the antipodes of England, but it is not. Taken possession of by an English navigator, whose action, at first adopted, was afterwards reversed by his country's rulers, it was only annexed at length by the English Government which did not want it, to keep it from the French who did.' The history thus begun is one of the finest, as well as one of the most influential, works of New Zealand prose.

This is especially true of the first scene-setting chapter, where Reeves essentially defines what it was to be a New Zealander. His descriptive listing of the *bush is characteristic of pioneer writing: 'There are the koromiko bush with white and purple blossoms, and the white convolvulus which covers whole thickets with blooms, delicate as carved ivory, whiter than milk. There are the starry clematis, cream-covered or white, and the manuka, with tiny but numberless flowers. The yellow kowhai, seen on the hillsides, shows the russet tint of autumn at the height of spring-time. Yet the king of forest flowers is, perhaps, the crimson, feathery rata. Is it a creeper or a tree? It is both.'

*Wakefield, 'Good' Governor *Grey (who was not good but 'fond of devious ways and unexpected moves'), 'King Dick' Seddon ('of his power to endure pommelling he had need early')—all the mythology of our early history is there in striking and resonant prose, in a story of progress culminating in great reforming legislation. Reeves placed a Canterbury settler's template on the Land *Wars. His description of the Māori race reflected his time. 'Bold as seamen and skilful as fishermen, the Polynesians are, however, primarily cultivators of the soil. They never rose high enough in the scale to be miners or merchants.' The book portrayed the switching political allegiances of the colony's early parliament as a conflict between oligarchy and democracy, evil and good. It fixed the term *Aotearoa within the national consciousness. Reeves's highbrow belief about the 'fetish of commonplace in public life' (this and the following phrases all come from his revised edition), that 'New Zealanders appeared to distrust distinction, dislike brilliancy, and doubt originality', became accepted as gospel. So too did the idea 'that mainstay of his country, the farmer, set small store in those days by sparkle and vivacity: he pinned his faith on butter and borrowing'. It is perhaps not surprising Reeves stayed in England, even though the roses there would be no sweeter.   HMcQ

REID, J.C. (John Cowie) (1916–72), born in Auckland, was a leading Catholic layman and a professor of English at Auckland University, an important scholar of the Victorian period with books on Coventry Patmore, Thomas Hood and Francis Thompson, and editorial work on *Dickens and Newman. A man of extraordinary energies in fostering and promoting literature and the arts, he was among much else founder-chairman of the Auckland Theatre Trust administering the Mercury Theatre. He was also a prime mover in the introduction of New Zealand literature to Auckland University's curriculum in 1956. His numerous studies of New Zealand writing and culture include *Creative Writing in New Zealand: A Brief Critical History* (1946) and *Australia and New Zealand* (1970), co-written with Australian Profesor G.A. Wilkes. The former is a slighter work than the 1940 critical history by E.H.

*McCormick but retains interest for Reid's scepticism concerning contemporary *nationalist preoccupations in literature, and for evaluations of Eileen *Duggan, Robin *Hyde and Allen *Curnow rather different from the orthodoxies at the time. Reid's anthologies *The Kiwi Laughs: An Anthology of New Zealand Prose Humour* (1961) and *A Book of New Zealand* (1964) provide interesting views of the cultural horizons of the period.   KA

REIDY, Sue (1955–), is a fiction writer distinctive for her complex treatment of female identity and spirituality. Born in Invercargill and trained in graphic design at Wellington Polytechnic, she has worked as a practitioner and teacher of design and illustration, providing the illustrations for her own stories. She won the Bank of New Zealand Katherine *Mansfield Award in 1985 for her story 'Alexandra and the Lion'. The short stories in *Modettes* (1988) are set primarily in South-East Asia, defying notions of realism by shifting between reality, dream and fantasy with an often humorous directness of tone. The tensions within feminism and other modern ideals are also challengingly presented, for instance between natural sexual impulse and resentment of gender roles, or between correct received opinions about other cultures and the damage actually inflicted by intruders, however well intentioned. Asian belief systems are portrayed with unusual inwardness. The novel *The Visitation* (1996) is also concerned with spirituality and responsibility, this time in the context of 1960s New Zealand Catholicism. Its two-sisters story sets the traditional mythology of the Virgin Mary against the antipodean context, as modern Catholicism frustrates a message delivered by divine vision. The novel is again at times magic realist, at times humorous, and often enriched by strong visual and musical senses. It is published by the English Black Swan company.   RR

REILLY, Colleen (1949–), born in Lowell, Mass., USA, and brought up mainly in Omaha, arrived in Wellington in 1972 after four years in Ireland. She was a well-regarded lecturer in English at Victoria University 1972–94 and tutor at the New Zealand Drama School 1975–94, and weekly television critic for the *NZ Listener* (1978–83) and *Dominion Sunday Times* (1988–92). *The Deputy Head* (1986) is a narratorial tour de force remarkable for a first novel. Told entirely in the voice of a 53-year-old male teacher, it takes the reader more deeply than the narrator himself is ever aware into his inhibited consciousness as he declines into nervous breakdown. His damaging effect on women, and theirs on him, are revealed with unusually equitable compassion, while the Wellington settings are an active as well as sharply observed element in the book's deft textures.

Christine (1988) also treats the complex tensions between the individual and her family, and between intense inner life and the ordinary realities. The stories in *Jim's Elvis* (1992) confirmed Reilly's skill in a range of narrative voices that deal perceptively and frankly with modern relationships, their matter-of-fact surface containing subtle depths of compassion, irony and the subconscious. Reilly now lives nomadically on USA's freeways as a certificated (1996) commercial driver of a 23-metres-long semi-trailer.   RR

Remittance man (Australia 1878, New Zealand 1888, also used elsewhere) is of significance to New Zealand's colonial past and as a folk or stock character in popular literature—a British immigrant in some way found undesirable by his usually upper-class home family and for that reason supported 'in exile' by remittances from Britain: 'Two of her loves were just sheep-men, but the third was a remittance-man, if you know what that is, and he had been a gentleman in England' (*Kipling, *One Lady at Wairakei*, 1892).   HO

RENÉE (1929–), feminist dramatist and fiction writer, was born in Napier, of Ngāti Kahungunu and Irish-English-Scots ancestry. She was formerly known in the theatre world as Renée Taylor. She left school and started work at the age of 12; has worked in woollen mills, a printing factory, a grocery-dairy, and as a feature writer and reviewer; and completed a BA at the University of Auckland in 1979. Renée has described herself as a 'lesbian feminist with socialist working-class ideals' and most of her writing is a direct expression of that conviction. She has been involved with community theatre, the Broadsheet Collective, *PEN, radio shows, programme organisation for the Globe Theatre in Dunedin, and with script writing for TV. She started writing for the stage at the age of 50. Her work for the stage includes *Setting the Table* (1982), *Secrets* (1982), which addresses sexual abuse within a family, *Breaking Out* (1982), *Dancing* (1983), *The MCP Show* (1983), *Groundwork* (1985), which is set during the Springbok tour of 1981, *Born to Clean* (1987), *Touch of the Sun* (1990), *Missionary Position* (1990), *Form* (pub. 1993; part of *Song of the Shirt: Three One-Act Plays for Young Actors*, by Paula *Boock, Renée, Fiona *Farrell), and feminist revues such as *What Did You Do in the War, Mummy?* (1982) and *Asking for It* (1983).

Renée's most successful work is a trilogy of historical plays about four generations of working-class women: all three plays, set in three distinct New Zealand locations, have strong roles for women who cope in the absence of men, or despite men's obstructive or insipidly passive presence. *Wednesday to Come* (pub. 1985) is set between Palmerston North and Wellington in 1934, during the *Depression and more particularly at the time of the workers' march from Gisborne to Wellington. It exposes the atrocious conditions in the so-called relief camps and the effect on the women who are left to run households by themselves. *Pass it On* (pub. 1986) is set in Auckland in 1951 during the *Waterfront lockout. Jeannie and Cliff, who were the teenage children in *Wednesday to Come*, are now the main characters. *Jeannie Once* (pub. 1991) addresses the shattered illusions of early immigrants to New Zealand. Set in the Dunedin of 1879, it reveals the spunk and determination of a young woman, Granna in *Wednesday to Come*, who confronts the realities of class and religious hostility in the supposedly promised land. This last play also draws attention to the history of theatre and music-hall entertainment.

In addition to a short story collection, *Finding Ruth* (1987), about a young adolescent girl and her widowed mother, Renée has also written three novels which all criticise traditional notions of the family. *Willy Nilly* (1990) questions the idea of the traditional nuclear family by orchestrating various crises surrounding the preparations of a young woman's wedding. *Daisy and Lily* (1993) is framed as the biography of Daisy who is coming out as a feminist lesbian writer. *Does This Make Sense to You?* (1995) centres on Flora's experience in the House of Unwed Mothers in 1961, and her attempt to make sense to the daughter who was adopted out. Most of Renée's writing is characterised by a straightforward, simple realism with an easily discernible agenda of issues. She was the 1989 *Burns Fellow.   HT

Report on Experience, see **MULGAN, John.**

'Reservoir, The', a short story by Janet *Frame, was first published in the *New Yorker* (12 Jan. 1963) and soon after in Frame's second collection of stories, *The Reservoir: Stories and Sketches* (Braziller, 1963). All but two of the stories in this collection, together with a number from *Snowman, Snowman: Fables and Fantasies* (Braziller, 1963) were collected in *The Reservoir and Other Stories* (*Pegasus Press, W.H. Allen, 1966), which won the Buckland Literary Award in 1967.

Typical of Frame's early work, the story is narrated from a child's perspective and is imbued with the frustrations of a child's limited understanding of the (adult) world. Cutting against this is a foreboding sense of the taint of adult knowledge and experience, carefully suggested by the retrospective narratorial commentary. The narrator recalls how, after considerable prevarication through a long, hot summer, she (if the narrator is indeed female) and her siblings defied their parents' warnings and visited the forbidden 'reservoir'. Much of the story develops the sense of menace that issues from the reservoir, labelled dangerous (literally) by the adults. The reservoir symbolises other taboo 'dangers' the adults will not name or label, notably sexuality; the afternoon journey from the familiar territory of the local creek to the unknown landscape of the reservoir which feeds it becomes a symbolic boundary-crossing from childhood innocence to adult experience. The familiar adult/child, innocence/experience dualisms typical of Frame's early work are further underscored by the use of light and dark imagery. Reaching the shaded reservoir, the children are surprised at its benign appearance but become frightened by their own imaginings of a danger beneath the 'wonderful calm and menace' of the water, afraid they may disturb 'something which must never ever be awakened'. They run from the place in terror, back into the sunlight, but by the time they reach home the experience has enabled them to laugh knowingly at their parents' fears: 'How out of date they were! They were actually afraid!' Despite the triumphant assertions of the children at end, a sense of pervading menace remains. This results, in large part, from the (no longer innocent) narrator's descriptions of the changing, threatening landscape through which the children travel. 'The Reservoir' has been anthologised at least six times.   KWo

Review was the publication of the Wellington John O'London's Club, published in two issues in 1939 and 1940 as a contribution to the centennial celebrations. Contributors included Nellie E. Donovan, O.N. *Gillespie, Ian *Gordon, Roma Hoggard, Gloria *Rawlinson and C.R.H. Taylor.   SH

RHODES, H. Winston (1905–87), was professor of English at University of Canterbury and an early teacher and scholar of New Zealand literature. Australian by birth and educated at Melbourne University under Frederick *Sinclaire, he moved to Canterbury in 1933. His critical books include *New Zealand Fiction since 1945* (1968), *Frank Sargeson* (1969), *Frederick Sinclaire: A Memoir* (1984) and *Kennaway Henderson* (1988). With *Henderson and Sinclaire he was deeply involved in *Tomorrow*, as literary editor giving early publishing opportunities to such writers as *Sargeson, *Curnow and *Fairburn. His essay 'The Moral Climate of Sargeson's Stories' was one of the select seven 'Explorations' chosen by Charles *Brasch for *Landfall Country*. He edited four volumes of the work of Rewi *Alley, 1948–55, including two of his poetry. A committed Marxist, he was editor of *NZ Monthly Review* and president of the NZ–USSR Society, and published Soviet-oriented political commentaries such as *War over the Pacific* (1941) and *Russia: The Coming Power in the Pacific* (1944).   RR

RIACH, Alan (1957–), was born in Lanarkshire in *Scotland, and has devoted his writing life to making the literature of his homeland more widely known. He took a BA at Cambridge University and his doctorate in the Department of Scottish Studies of Glasgow University. His dissertation formed the basis for his monograph *Hugh MacDiarmid's Epic Poetry* (1991), which aims to reclaim MacDiarmid as an unjustly neglected poet, especially celebrating his contribution to the renaissance of Scottish literature in the 1920s–30s. Riach is general editor of Carcanet's multi-volume complete MacDiarmid and since 1992 has been at the University of Waikato, teaching Scottish, American and other postcolonial literatures. His critical writings focus on the Scottish element in the literatures of Great Britain's former colonies, especially in the British Guyanese novelist Wilson Harris and in contemporary New Zealand writers. Riach's own poetry reflects these obsessions, drawing on his life both in Scotland and New Zealand, his adopted homeland, as well as his reading of modern English, American and Scottish writers. Deploying a wide range of modern forms, from 'projective verse' to prose memoir, the poems range in tone from lyric sweetness to wry sarcasm. Riach has published four volumes of poetry in New Zealand: *For What It Is* (with Peter McCarey, 1986); *This Folding Map* (1990); *An Open Return* (1991); and *First & Last Songs* (1995). He was considered 'NZ' enough to qualify for Bill *Manhire's *100 New Zealand Poems* (1993).   MH

RICHARDS, Mark (1922–), born in London, a grandson of the novelist, poet and essayist Maurice Hewlett, arrived in New Zealand in 1927 with his parents, who farmed near Tauranga before moving to Auckland's North Shore in 1933. After an apprenticeship, interrupted by five years in the army and airforce, he became a journeyman printer on the *New Zealand Herald*. He attended Auckland Teachers' College 1949–51, graduated from Auckland University in 1954, then taught at Takapuna GS until 1977. A friend of A.R.D. *Fairburn and R.A.K. *Mason, who deeply influenced his writing, he published early poems in *Arena*. In 1960 he won first prize for 'Go Back, Lazarus' in the Cheltenham Festival Poetry Competition, at that time arguably the most prestigious international prize awarded to a New Zealand poet. For the next ten years his poems, plays (mainly in verse) and talks were frequently broadcast. His books of poems are: *Solomon Grundy and Other Poems* (1958), *Go Back, Lazarus* (1962), *The Ballad of Drunken Bay* (1965), *Jericho Road* (1969), *Long Weekend* (1972), *Liberation Ode* (1975), *At the Point* (1979), *Collected Poems 1952–83* (1984), *Satan's Complaint* (1989), *February Journey* (1991) and *Fire at Anchor* (1994). His other publications are *A Burnt Child, Collected Plays 1960–85* (1989) and a satirical history of New Zealand, *1840 and All That* (1991). His serious poetry and plays have a moral and didactic purpose influenced by his rationalist and liberal socialist beliefs, and are generally against war, violence, cruelty and intolerance.   KI

RICHARDSON, Catherine H. (1858–78), wrote the first book of poems by a woman to be printed in New Zealand, *Gabrielle and Other Poems* (1875). As might be expected of a 17-year-old, they are derivative though accomplished. Born in Sussex, she was brought to Dunedin at the age of 6 and died very young. The potency of Otago's Scots culture at that date is shown by her skilfully nostalgic 'The First News Frae Auld Scotland', with its evocation of the losses faced by the 'first to hae trod on these alien shores'; however well 'I hae made me a hame i' the stranger lan'', there are 'nae memories sae leesome' as those of days when 'the blue heather-bells bloom'd bonnilie'.   HMcQ/RR

RICHMOND, Mary E. (1853–1949), was, like Jessie *Mackay, an early example of the woman poet who also won wide respect for community service. While her poetry circulated largely within a private circle, she was an acclaimed preacher and public speaker and was awarded the CBE in 1949 for services to women and children. She founded the Wellington (originally Richmond) Free Kindergarten Association in 1905 and was a founding member of the Wellington Free Unitarian Church in 1904. Unmarried, she remained active in old age, writing her last known poem at 91.

Daughter of C.W. Richmond, Appeal Court judge and at one time acting Premier of New Zealand, she was born in New Plymouth and lived mostly in Wellington, with long periods in Nelson, Auckland and Britain. Her early publications, the privately printed *Roundels, Sonnets and Other Verses* (Edinburgh, 1898) and *Poems* (London, 1903), were positively reviewed by Professor G.W. von Zedlitz, and she was anthologised in *New Zealand Verse* (1906, 1926). Originally using conventional forms, especially rondeau and sonnet, for personal poetry, she had passages of dramatic intensity and rich natural description in her later serious work, *Arisaig Idyll* (1943?) and *Yet We Believe* (1942, 1943). She also had some gift for comic, political and children's verse, with a spirited use of *Australasian idiom (*Betty B.'s Book*, 1907; *Songs for Children*, 1908; *The Bindy Ballads*, 1924). Many poems remain unpublished and much material is in the Richmond–Atkinson archive in the *Alexander Turnbull Library.   NWr

RICKETTS, Harry (1950–), is a literary scholar, poet and reviewer. Born in London, he grew up in England, Malaysia and Hong Kong, experiences still reflected in his poetry, which is often retrospective. A collection of Hong Kong stories, *People Like Us*, was published there in 1977. He studied English at Oxford University (MLitt 1975) and lectured at Hong Kong and Leicester before arriving in 1981 to a post at Victoria University, where he pursues a policy of teaching New Zealand poems and stories alongside British and American. He has also done much to encourage student literary work, editing the annual *Writings* through the 1980s. His first New Zealand publication was an edition that rescued from obscurity *Kipling's New Zealand story *One Lady at Wairakei* (1983). His book of interviews with New Zealand poets, *Talking About Ourselves* (1986), is an essential resource, partly because his subjects' personalities emerge (for better or worse) in ways that verge on the dramatic. His technique there of mixing a non-threatening manner with alert perspicacity also informs his reviewing. His own collections of poems are *Coming Here* (1989), *Coming Under Scrutiny* (1989), a quarter of the four-poet *How Things Are* (1996), *A Brief History of New Zealand Literature* (parodic limericks, 1996) and *13 Ways* (1998). His best are either deftly satiric 'light' verse, exploiting rhyme, wordplay and traditional forms like the clerihew or limerick, in a manner more common now in Britain; or wry personal commentaries on the perplexities of love, marriage or parenthood. He has edited *Worlds of Katherine *Mansfield* (critical essays, 1991) and *Under Review: A Selection from 'New Zealand Books' 1991–1996* (with Lauris *Edmond and Bill *Sewell, 1997) and is preparing a biography of Kipling and an anthology of New Zealand comic verse. RR

RIDDELL, Elizabeth (1907–), poet, was born in Napier. On the basis of poems written during her school years, she was invited to Australia in her teens and worked on the Sydney *Truth*, *Daily Mirror*, the *Australian* and the *Bulletin* before becoming a freelance reviewer and feature writer. She won the prestigious Walkley Award for journalism. She also worked in England and the USA and as a war correspondent in Europe. Today she is recognised as one of *Australia's most distinguished poets, having published six volumes of poetry, including a *Selected Poems* in 1992. She has won numerous literary awards. Although death has been a consistent theme, her poetry is often lyrical and sensuous. For the National Library of Australia she edited and introduced the exquisitely produced volume *With Fond Regards* (1995), a collection of private letters. NW

RITCHIE, Anthony (1960–), composer, grew up in a musical family, his father being professor of music at the University of Canterbury. He has been influenced by the minimalists and Eastern European composers. His settings include texts by Denis *Glover, Alistair Te Ariki *Campbell, James K. *Baxter, Allen *Curnow, Janet *Frame, Sam *Hunt and Cilla *McQueen. JMT

Roads From Home (1949) is widely regarded as Dan *Davin's most successful novel. He draws fully on his Irish Catholic family origins in Invercargill. The central strand of the plot concerns a young railwayman, John Hogan, and the failure of his marriage to a Protestant woman Elsie, who is still infatuated with an earlier lover, taunting John with the possibility that he is not the father of their child. This story is worked out in a way that critics found melodramatic. This does not detract from the steady focus that Davin maintains on a Catholic society in transition, as in the funeral of an itinerant Irish *seanchai* (storyteller), or the loss of faith and nervous collapse of John's brother Ned, who had been studying for the priesthood. The book includes an affectionate portrait of Davin's own mother in the character of Norah Hogan, and the effective treatment of numerous aspects of life in pre-war Southland: horse-racing, pubs and sly-grog shops, fist fights, ferreting and family life. 'Davin has done with an economy and unobtrusive skill [what] a social historian can only envy...,' wrote D.H. Akenson (*Half the World from Home*, 1990). In an introduction to the second edition (1976) Lawrence *Jones wrote, 'As a provincial history it is of lasting value' and 'one of the landmarks in the development of the New Zealand realistic tradition'. KO

ROBERTS, Anna, see **Dalmatians in New Zealand literature**.

ROCHE, Stanley (1923–85), wrote short fiction and two distinctive books of history and biography, each with some feminist emphasis. Her short stories appeared in *Islands* 12 (1975) and elsewhere. She was joint winner of the *Oxford University Press Quincentenary Biography Award with *Foreigner: The Story of Grace Morton as told to Stanley Roche* (1979). It tells of the daughter of missionaries whose life included traumatic periods in the history of *China and then of Czechoslovakia, compiled from tapes of many conversations between the two women. *The Red and the Gold: An Informal Account of the Waihi Strike* (1982) also presents history through the eyes of the people, especially the women. Narrating this first major confrontation between the Federation of Labour and the employers in 1912, Roche relates the strike to major issues such as the changing sense of national identity (from imperial province towards nationhood) and the increasingly central role of women since the franchise. Her sympathies strongly with the workers and the women, she writes with a sometimes enjoyably tart impatience with outmoded attitudes: 'The women according to the *Herald* were without exception hysterical, unsexed, bedraggled, tired, hoarse, screeching and shrill. Well, you could hardly expect them to be looking their sexy best. They were at the mine entrance by 7.30 every morning. Some of them ... had walked miles. A lot had babies that they brought with them....' The writing is also at times eloquent, even poetic.

Born Stanley Anderson in Wanganui into a family of 'dedicated readers', Roche was a lecturer in English at Palmerston North Teachers' College.   PN/RR

Rock Woman, The, published in 1969, is a selection of fifty-three of James K. ★Baxter's poems, largely chosen by his London publisher ★Oxford University Press. Baxter approved the choices, which were intended to provide an overview of his achievements during the preceding two decades, but critics have commented on a certain unevenness in the book. The title poem refers to a rock, found on the coast, that resembles a woman. The drops of sea water that cover her are reminiscent of the rosary beads found on a medieval statue. For Baxter, the Rock Woman also symbolised New Zealand's bare, stony landscapes, which were for him as familiar as a lover—alone with her, he experienced peace.   PM

ROGER, Warwick (1945–   ), has won numerous awards in journalism, including feature writing, sports writing, environmental writing and investigative journalism. He edited ★*Metro* from its inception in 1981 to 1994. His books are *Places in the Heart* (1989), a collection of personal essays and sketches, particularly good on aspects of Auckland; *Old Heroes* (1991), a reconstruction of the 1956 Springbok rugby tour; and *The Other Side* (1996), a collection of journalism. The introduction to this most recent book by Michael ★King comments on the increasing sharpness of Roger's journalism, while *Old Heroes*, in its skilful melding of reportage, autobiography, investigative biography and cultural history, is one of New Zealand's best ★sports books. Roger has published short stories and many features and essays in magazines and books, for instance in Lloyd ★Jones's literary sports selection, *Into the Field of Play* (1992).

Born and educated in Auckland (Auckland GS and Teachers' College), he worked in advertising and teaching before becoming a reporter in 1969. Various positions in reporting and feature writing included *NZ Weekly News*, *Sunday Times*, *Dominion* and *Auckland Star*, with notable freelance work in *New Zealand Runner* and elsewhere. He is now editor at large of *North and South* and a newspaper columnist, winning the 1996 Media Peace Premier Print Award for a *North and South* investigative feature.

Roger is known for his forceful criticism of modern journalism's 'obsession with the trivial', his commitment to a journalism of 'unease' and 'the other side', and for his outspoken independence of mind, refusing to follow any fashion, probing motive and often exposing the self-interest behind morally self-righteous groups and movements. Naturally, this leaves him less than universally admired, the most common counter-charges being egocentricity and (with less justice) right-wing reactionism. Regardless of viewpoint, his writing is never less than lucid and insightful, gaining its colour from the depth of thought and strong personal voice rather than any surface sensationalism, whatever the subject. Whether he writes on feminism, David Lange, ★overseas experience, the newest Auckland restaurant or an ageing sportsman, the enquiry is perceptive, personal, eloquent and strongly structured. His editorial skills are embodied in the remarkable success of *Metro*.   RR

Romance fiction. From the late nineteenth century to the present, New Zealand has produced a continuous mainstream tradition of vigorous popular romance writing, much of it set in New Zealand and almost all of it authored by women. Because of the smallness of the New Zealand market and the absence of a local publishing industry, until the 1940s and 1950s almost all of this fiction had to be aimed at publication overseas, in Great Britain and the United States. In addition, it was subject to the vagaries of international distribution practices, which often meant, especially in the period up to the 1930s, that New Zealand books widely read overseas were available only irregularly, if at all, in local bookshops. After the 1950s the increasing globalisation of the genre fiction industry continued to require that romance writers publish overseas, but improved distribution practices meant that New Zealand ★Mills & Boon authors, and Yvonne ★Kalman's American-published colonial life blockbusters, were readily available locally, even if (with the exception of Essie ★Summers) the authors were never marketed as 'New Zealand' authors.

If New Zealand's fledgling publishing industry was insufficient to sustain a market for popular romance, from the 1880s on the country did begin to develop an established industry of popular journalism—newspaper supplements, weeklies and monthlies—which provided regular outlets for stories and sketches, and these (especially after the rise of women's magazines in both New Zealand and Australia) became effective apprentice-grounds for many of the women who subsequently went on to establish themselves as professional authors. Louisa ★Baker ('Alien') and Edith ★Lyttleton ('G.B. Lancaster') at the turn of the century, Nelle ★Scanlan, Mary ★Scott and Dorothy ★Eden between the 1920s and 1940s, Essie Summers, Grace Phipps and others in the post-war years, all began their careers in local newspapers, weeklies and monthlies, and often retained contact with their New Zealand and Australian readers through them after they had established themselves primarily as professional novelists published overseas.

Nineteenth-century New Zealand colonial romance, like the male genre of colonial adventure and action, was closely modelled on British conventions, and was the occasional product of isolated amateurs like Clara ★Cheeseman and Jessie ★Weston, with the exception of Louisa Baker, the first New Zealander to attempt to establish a professional career as a romance writer. Between 1894 and 1913 Baker published sixteen novels in England and America, many of them with New Zealand settings, although she regularly complained of publishers' resistance to local content. Baker's novels are close to full-blown Victorian domestic romance, with long, intricate plots and sensational melodramatic effects, but she was also influenced by the feminist movement of her time in her portrayal of inequalities in sexual relationships. Her solution envisaged a reform of the institution of marriage, and the actions of her novels regularly involved the heroine in vigorous forms of intellectual rebellion and self-assertion as part of a process of preparation for a marital union based on an equality of emotional and intellectual participation by each partner. In arriving at her happy endings, which often involved a typically colonial integration of New Zealand and English destinies, Baker never flinched from dealing out death, disaster and maimings to characters who failed to measure up.

The literary formation of Isabel Maud ★Peacocke and Edith Lyttleton was also late Victorian, though their most productive years began after Baker had ceased writing and continued over several decades. Peacocke is better known as a prolific children's author who popularised the family story in New Zealand, but she also wrote sixteen adult romances between 1918 and 1955, all of them carrying strong traces of Victorian melodrama, and most of them addressed to young women, warning them of the dangers of pre-marital 'promiscuity' and promoting marriage as an institution designed for the protection of women. Marital breakdown and adultery are regular themes of her later novels, which warn, again, of their effects on children and of the need for women to stay in broken marriages no matter what the personal cost. Peacocke is only marginally less inventive than Baker in the punishments she metes out to errant characters.

Edith Lyttleton was primarily an exponent of the male-focused colonial adventure genre in her earlier work, but she increasingly came to introduce romantic elements into her plots as a means of testing the moral character of her colonial heroes. Women function as small islands of civilisation in her lawless frontier environments—in New Zealand, Australia and north-west Canada—requiring of her heroes something more than brute physical strength or the ruthless application of inflexible codes of honour. For Lyttleton the true test of the colonial enterprise was an internal test of character, and the fact that so many of her romantic actions result in tragedy, self-sacrifice and loss often seems to suggest uncertainty about the value of the enterprise itself. In the second phase of her career, in the 1930s, Lyttleton turned more directly to one of the major forms of romance—the historical romance—organising her epic treatments of colonial history in New Zealand, Australia and Canada around the perspectives of a series of highly intelligent, independent and rebellious female protagonists. The image of Empire which emerges, despite the colouring of romance, is distinctly critical.

In the work of Rosemary ★Rees and Scanlan, popular in the 1930s and 1940s, romance began to take more specialised, recognisably twentieth-century forms. Rees introduced the 'light romance', shorter and less complicated than the Victorian form, and more narrowly focused on the heroine, with lush scenic descriptions; Scanlan's specialty, in the ★Pencarrow novels and elsewhere, was the family chronicle, a form of domestic romance anticipating radio and television soap opera, offering multiple variations of family rivalries and generational rebellions. Both authors—like Peacocke—used the romance to promote traditional moral and social values, appealing to middle-class New Zealand readers during the insecure years of the ★Depression and World War 2.

Dorothy Eden and Mary Scott, who began contributing regularly to local journals and newspapers in the 1930s and 1940s and became established professional novelists from the 1950s to the 1970s, both developed the romance in quite distinctive ways. Eden's specialty was the romantic mystery novel, replete with spine-chilling Gothic effects of horror and suspense, effective at least partly because her treatment of sexual relations lacks the moralising of either Rees or Scanlan. Nevertheless, her novels are premised on a world of polarised gender relations in which her heroines (and readers) typically experience a breakdown of any sense of normality and are thrust into a nightmare world suffused with the threat of male violence and intimidation. After establishing herself in New Zealand, Eden based herself in London after 1954, where her work became increasingly international in its themes and settings. By contrast Scott was the first New Zealand romance writer to set her fiction entirely in New Zealand and direct it to a New Zealand readership, though many of her books were also published overseas, and they were unusually popular in *Germany. The background of all Scott's light romances—from her humorous stories of a farmer's wife, 'Barbara', in the 1930s and 1940s, to the many novels she published between 1953 and 1978—was the experience of women living in New Zealand's small, isolated *backblocks communities in the North Island. As her romance actions unfold, the novels provide an unusually rich social documentation of these communities, as well as constructing a conservative myth of the backblocks as the 'real' New Zealand, fostering the values of independence, hard work and neighbourliness. In her adaptation of the older colonial romance formula, her heroines typically come not from England but from New Zealand's own cities and suburbs, discovering values largely absent in the urban rat race.

Scott's implicit critique of materialism and conformism had parallels in much of the 'serious' fiction written in the 1950s and 1960s. Other romance writers of the 1950s and 1960s were more sanguine. Grace Phipps, for many years editor of the column 'Over the Teacups' in the *New Zealand Woman's Weekly*, wrote domestic romances celebrating family life in the suburbs. Dorothy *Quentin's romances often read like celebrations of the arrival of American consumerism in the 1950s. Dulce *Carman specialised in a form her English publishers called the 'Maori Romance'. Premised on the official government policy of assimilation, and using plots which might have come directly out of the most sensational Victorian melodramas, her novels are remarkable both for the hostility they direct at Māori youth (while co-opting idealised Māori elders into Pākehā schemes for assimilation), and for their unabashed manipulation of *Māori myths and legends to promote the destinies of her Pākehā characters.

Carmen and Scott, in different ways, clearly reflected in their writing a widespread 1950s anxiety that juvenile delinquency was rife and family values in decline. Mavis Winder, who also wrote as 'Mavis Areta', published many romances between the 1950s and the 1970s which dealt explicitly (sometimes graphically) with 'social problems'—broken marriages, delinquency, alcoholism and drugs. Like Louisa Baker at the turn of the century, she envisaged explicitly Christian solutions to such problems. However, the author whose romances offered the most persuasive celebration of marriage and family life was Essie Summers, New Zealand's first internationally successful Mills & Boon writer. From 1957 to 1985 she wrote more than fifty romances which attracted a huge readership in New Zealand and overseas. Her novels were nostalgic throwbacks to colonial New Zealand, often set on spectacularly scenic sheep *stations in the South Island, and often reworking the older colonial pattern in which an orphaned or rootless heroine of English origins or affiliations discovers her true heritage (confirmed by marriage) in New Zealand. Summers emphasised family networks—grandparents, aunts and uncles, children—in the unfolding of her romance actions, and maintained a great deal of reserve in her description of sexual relationships. The distinctive effect of her novels, reinforced by her attention to scenic detail and to a romanticised historical ambience of place, was of a lyric affirmation of family values in a world remote from the kinds of social dislocation explicitly evoked in the work of other romance writers.

Throughout the 1960s–70s there were numerous contemporaries of Summers, writing in similar or related ways, most notably Ivy *Preston (also from the South Island), and Nora *Sanderson and Gloria Bevan, both Mills & Boon writers. By the mid-1970s, in fact, romance fiction in New Zealand had become virtually synonomous with the imprint of Mills & Boon. However, New Zealand romance writing in the 1980s and after shared in the transformations of the genre which occurred internationally. During this decade Yvonne Kalman revisited the genre of the historical romance with a trilogy of nineteenth-century 'settlement' epics, entitled *The Greenstone Land*, set in the Bay of Islands and Auckland, and a further two set in colonial Canterbury—all of which broke into the American blockbuster market. A new generation of Mills & Boon writers also emerged—most notably Daphne *Clair, Robyn *Donald and Susan *Napier—whose work reflected a much more contemporary mode: upmarket professional business settings (often in Auckland), more assertive heroines with careers, much more explicit descriptions of sexual encounters and sexual fantasies, and an almost exclusive focus on a power struggle between heroine and hero. Often, also, there is direct reference to the discourse of feminism in these contemporary Mills & Boon romances, though its role remains highly problematic. No Mills & Boon romance has been able to dispense with marriage, and the promise of children, as the main goal of the heroine.   TS

ROSE, Lyndon, see *Parting of the Mist, The*.

ROSIER-JONES, Joan, see **Dalmatians in New Zealand literature**.

ROSS, D.M. (David Macdonald) (1865–1933), was a poet in the late-Romantic mode of plangent melancholy: 'Is it cold in the grave, dear one, / When gusts of the south wind blow, / When the clouds overshade the sun, / And shed on the earth their snow?' ('Inflorescent'). To these well-worn conventions of language and cadence he gave a local colouring that did not affect their basically Edwardian English character: 'A horseman came a-wooing me, / In days of Life that have grown old, / When ridges blossomed ti-tree snow, / And rivers mirrored kowhai-gold' ('The Horseman'). This may be where Quentin Pope found his title for the anthology *Kowhai Gold*, which includes three of Ross's poems, though not 'The Horseman'. 'The Flight', which Pope did select, has been called Ross's best. He wrote often of the sea, again in the conventional 'foam-flecked' manner: 'The sea, my mother, with billowy swell, / Is telling her tale to the wave-washed shell' ('The Sea to the Shell'). Born in Moeraki, brought up in Palmerston, he was by profession a stock inspector, and was renowned for equestrian interests in hunting, polo and racing. He published five volumes of poetry, variously in London, Melbourne and Auckland: *The Afterglow* (1904), *The Promise of the Star* (1906), *Hearts of the Pure* (1911), *Morning Red* (1916) and *Stars in the Mist* (1928).   HMcQ/RR

ROSS, Forrest (1860–1936), born Forrestina Grant in England, was a teacher until she married Malcolm *Ross in 1890, when she began accompanying him on climbing trips and writing about her experiences. She became the first female member of the New Zealand Alpine Club, whose journal she edited briefly in her husband's absence. Their son Noel (1890–1917), was to follow them into journalism. In 1897 they moved from Dunedin to Wellington, where Forrest became the first Women's page editor of the *Evening Post*, and took up parliamentary reporting for several papers, continuing both until 1915. She contributed articles and stories to journals such as the *New Zealand Illustrated Magazine* and *Wanderlust*, some illustrated with her photographs. In 1910 she travelled alone to Europe, publishing *Around the World with a Fountain Pen* (1913), a collection of articles, including her conservative observations on the suffrage movement in London. As well as assisting Malcolm Ross in compiling *Noel Ross and His Work* (1919), she included her son's work with her own in *Mixed Grill* (1934). Her articles on politics, literature and art earned her a high reputation.   JMcC

ROSS, Malcolm (1862–1930), born in Dunedin, began journalism on the *Otago Daily Times* in 1882. Sent to cover the disappearance of a professor in the relatively unknown Manapouri/Fiordland Sounds area in 1888, he developed a lifelong interest in exploration and climbing, became a Fellow of the Royal Geographic Society, and in 1891 a founding member and vice-president of the New Zealand Alpine Club and editor of its journal 1893–94. He publicised mountaineering through his many articles, collecting them and extracts from those of his wife Forrest *Ross in *A Climber in New Zealand* (1914). An entrepreneur and photographer, he wrote official illustrated booklets for the developing tourist trade, and others on his own account about such public events as the 1901 royal tour. In World War 1 he was the official New Zealand correspondent in Egypt, Gallipoli and France, publishing *Light and Shade in War* (1916), a collection of his own writing and that of his son Noel, a journalist wounded at Gallipoli. After Noel's death, Malcolm and Forrest compiled *Noel Ross and His Work* (1919). Malcolm wrote the New Zealand chapter of *The Empire at War* (1921–26), edited by Sir Charles Lucas, and returned to the parliamentary press gallery until 1926.   JMcC

Rostrum was the annual of the New Zealand University Students' Association, published 1939–46. It featured articles on both student and university affairs and on a wide range of university disciplines as well as poetry, stories, drawings and photographic studies. Contributors included academic staff, members of the Senate, graduates and students of the University of New Zealand. Editorial responsibility rotated between the constituent colleges of the University. Notable contributors include Antony *Alpers, James K. *Baxter, James *Bertram, Denis *Glover, W.H. *Oliver, Winston *Rhodes, Keith *Sinclair, Kendrick *Smithyman and Pat *Wilson.   SH

RUATAPU, Mohi, was apparently the oral storyteller whose work is recorded in two manuscript volumes in the *Alexander Turnbull Library. Margaret *Orbell has investigated his work and reports on it in the notes to *Maori Folktales in Maori and English* (1968). The first page is dated 28 May 1876 and the last page of the second volume has a note translated by Orbell as 'by Mohi Ruatapu of Ouawiwi. H. Potae of Tokomaru wrote it down.' Orbell notes: 'Henare Potae of Tokomaru Bay was an influential and high-ranking chief of Ngati Porou. He is known to have been a pupil of Mohi Ruatapu.... According to W.E. Gudgeon, a contemporary expert on East Coast history, Mohi Ruatapu was "the most learned of all the Ngati Porou tohungas". He was also one of the three main teachers at Te Rawheoro, the last school of learning (*whare wananga) on the East Coast.' The stories from these manuscripts are among the most popular of Māori tales (*kōrero) and include 'The Woman and the Ngarara', 'Ihurangi, who was possessed by a spirit' and 'Houmea the Shag-Woman'.   NW

S

Sailing or Drowning (1943) contains some of Allen ★Curnow's best-known poems. Printed by Leo ★Bensemann at the ★Caxton Press, and published by the ★Progressive Publishing Society, Wellington, it is dedicated to Denis ★Glover, who is also addressed in the verse letter 'Spring 1942' (and who was serving overseas in the Royal Navy at the time). The collection includes a sequence of 'Nine Sonnets', the well-known 'Attitudes for a New Zealand Poet' (also in sonnet form), and ★'Landfall in Unknown Seas'. The poems are suffused with imagery of warfare, reflecting their composition during the darkest period of World War 2. Several were first published in *Poetry* (Chicago).   PS

Sanctuary of Spirits, a sequence of poems by Alistair ★Campbell, was first published by the ★Wai-te-ata Press in 1963 in a hand-set edition of 150 copies on handmade paper. It had already been broadcast by the New Zealand Broadcasting Corporation, who had commissioned a documentary in verse on Kapiti Island. This is, however, not the only reason why, in his first extensive recourse to Polynesian tradition, Campbell chose not to make use of his Cook Islands heritage, but rather to call on the 'spirits' inhabiting the island of Kapiti and the adjacent coast. The house he was living in (and still lives in) looks out dramatically onto that landscape, and Campbell felt that it was inhabited by the spirits of the past. The Ngāti Toa view the region as their home, although they moved into it with their powerful leader Te Rauparaha only in the early nineteenth century. The powerful chief used Kapiti as his refuge and stronghold, but also had a fortified pā on the site now occupied by Campbell's house.

No other extended New Zealand lyric makes such immediate and vital use of history and landscape. Compared with this immediacy, the justly admired historic poems of Allen ★Curnow seem ironically detached from both. Here they are given voice in the imagined speech of participants in historical events. 'Kapiti', a kind of prologue, could be in the voice of a modern narrator until it starts to address the warriors paddling out from the mainland, warning them of the danger that awaits them at Te Rauparaha's hands. It is as if we move into the scene as the poem progresses and, once in it, we stay there, hearing voices speak out of the land. As spirits, they live in the present, so that time sequences are irrelevant to this 'historical' poem. 'Kapiti' recalls the great victory in 1825 that put Te Rauparaha in control of the region. The battle is not described, though the subsequent cannibal feast is, and the focus is less on war than on a spiritual power invading man and nature. Nonetheless the next two voices, those of an old woman and an old man, mourn the fatal effects of war on those who are not warriors and cannot share the spiritual force of the fighters. The fourth poem uses several voices and works on the implications of the name Te Rauparaha, which means 'convolvulus'. 'Tukitukipatuaruhe', made up of two speeches by Te Ruaoneone and Te Rauparaha, uses rhetoric reminiscent of ★whaikōrero, oratory, drawing on another aspect of Māori 'voice'. In 'Nga Roimata' we hear the voice of a young woman killed by her father to save her from slavery to Te Rauparaha, a reminder of his genocidal attacks on the Ngāi Tahu. There is a sudden change of time and mood in 'Tamihana Te Rauparaha', when the chief's son speaks with prim piety in his praise, presenting a point of view markedly different from the terror that has spoken in all voices till now: 'a kind man / who fed his workers first /

and then his visitors'. Revising for *Wild Honey* (1964), Campbell placed this poem before 'Nga Roimata', giving it a more central position in the sequence and making the contrast between the two poems more shocking. It is followed with a return to terror, the voice of someone of the Ngāi Tahu, defeated by Te Rauparaha at Kaiapoi ('Nothing can touch me now—/ My mind is gone') and remembering the evil omens preceding the event. The final poem, a kind of epilogue, returns to a modern voice: 'Against Te Rauparaha'. But it is much more ambivalent than its title suggests, for the old chief still haunts the modern world, sometimes in the form of a noisy train frightening a little girl at night, but sometimes as an intimidating image of terror and atrocity, haunting an adult mind familiar with more recent acts of genocide. 'But why deceive myself? / I know you as the subtlest tormentor, / able to assume at will / the features of the most intimate terrors.' Here the poet's own voice seems to break through the mosaic and chorus of voices of the sequence, especially when we remember that Campbell had moved to the Kapiti Coast from a mental hospital. Writing in the *NZ Listener* in 1965 he said, 'Te Rauparaha came to be not only a presence, but identified with a feeling of unease, a symbol of mental disorder. Both a spirit and a state of mind.'

'Sanctuary of Spirits' presented a new inner vision to the readers of Alistair Campbell's poetry, not all of whom were delighted by it. Rather than working in the 'universal' traditions of Western thought, as he might be said to have done before, Campbell now opened up the possibility of a greater relativity of cultural perspectives. Writing in *New Zealand Heritage* (1972) he later remarked: 'The key to an understanding of Te Rauparaha is that he was essentially a pre-European Maori, educated in a code that appears at times to be the reverse of the Christian code.' NW

SANDERS, James (1911–), wrote vigorous novels of early New Zealand history, as well as popular histories, war histories and other work. After varied back-country jobs starting from his birthplace of Dargaville, he survived the *Depression on a mix of manual and newspaper work, then saw action as a pilot with the RNZAF in World War 2. After newspaper cartooning and commercial art he went into advertising and headed a successful agency. A pacy autobiography, *The Time of My Life* (1967), unleashed a considerable gift for raconteurship and narrative and he published several good historical novels in London. *The Green Paradise* (1971) and *The Shores of Wrath* (1972) take in early Australia as well as New Zealand, the latter anticipating Patrick *White's *A Fringe of Leaves* (1976) in its story of a society

Englishwoman reverting to nature in the Australian bush in company with convicts. *Kindred of the Winds* (1973) is a novel of early whaling off New Zealand, with scenes ashore among Māori. *High Hills of Gold* (1973) deals with Coromandel *goldmining and the best, *Fire in the Forest* (1975), is a vivid story of Von Tempsky's campaign of 1863, anticipating *Shadbolt this time in its story of an American Civil War soldier caught up in a conflict which is strongly portrayed without ever being condoned or glorified. Personal bonds and tragedies cut across enmities and race. Sanders also published histories (*The Colourful Colony*, 1983), a history of the Press Association (*Dateline NZPA*, 1979) and World War 2 histories and biographies (*Venturer Courageous: Group Captain Leonard Trent VC*, 1983, *The Long Patrol*, 1986) that are enlivened by personal experience and his confessed 'love affair' with piloting aircraft. RR

SANDERSON, Nora (1905–75), was author of twenty-one novels, mostly for *Mills & Boon and the English Women's Weekly library, as well as many short stories for magazines and radio. Her first story was published when she was 16, but her first success was her whimsical children's best-seller, *The Puppycat* (1953). Born Nora Brocas in Opotiki, educated in Auckland and trained as a nurse at Rawene Hospital, Northland, she nursed in and around Auckland until her marriage to a Methodist minister, drawing on her nursing experience for several of her romances, such as *Hospital in New Zealand* (1962) and *No Welcome for Nurse Jane* (1968), also set in New Zealand. She turned to other fields as she came to feel out of touch with nursing, such as flying in New Zealand in *Stranger to the Truth* (1969). She was also willing to include in her romances the forthright opinions that made her a familiar name on talkback radio and in letters to the editor, as in the strongly conservationist theme of *The Sun Breaks Through* (1975), where the enlightened heroine has to dissuade the misguided male from his despoliation of the beech forests.

Widely translated (including in Brazil and Denmark), Sanderson was a member of the British Romance Novelists' Association and a founder of its New Zealand equivalent, and an active and honoured (in 1961) member of the *New Zealand Women Writers' Society. With her clergyman husband and family she lived at Granity (West Coast) and Taitapu (near Christchurch), and they retired at Templeton, where, according to the *Press* obituary, she completed an autobiography. PN/RR

SANDYS, Elspeth (1940–), is known in New Zealand as a writer of mainly historical fiction. Her long previous experience in Britain as stage and radio playwright, author of adaptations and series for the BBC, and as an actor in New Zealand and UK, is evident in the crafted dialogue of her fiction.

Born in Timaru, she spent her childhood in Dunedin, adopted into the Alley family (Sandys is a pseudonym), with Rewi *Alley a visitor, and so was exposed early to literature. Her early working life was mainly as an actor, divided between the NZ Broad-casting Service and London. She then lived in England 1969–89, becoming a full-time writer and editor. Her first three novels were published there: *Catch a Falling Star* (1978), based on the life of the poet John Donne; *The Broken Tree* (1981), published in the USA as *The Burning Dawn*; and *Love and War* (1982), republished in New Zealand in 1992.

Her first novel with a New Zealand setting, *Finding Out* (1991), she has called 'a daydream from the Cotswolds about my Otago childhood in the 1950s'. Strongly evocative of the Otago Peninsula, and of the era of near-traumatised returned servicemen and repressive communities, it deals with the sexual awakening of two schoolgirls and the community's thwarting and exclusion of an idealistic young male teacher. Exclusion is also central to *Best Friends* (1993), a collection of loosely linked short stories set mostly in contemporary London, a city shown as callously disregarding towards the book's disoriented expatriate New Zealanders. Sandys has spoken of her own 'geographic schizophrenia'.

River Lines (1995), probably her most substantial achievement, shortlisted for a UK award, interweaves the histories of two contrasting Canterbury families in a dynastic plot rich in strong action and emotion. The hard-won bond of settlers with the land is particularly well established. Well-reviewed, it was called 'an instant modern classic' by *Quote Unquote*. *Riding to Jerusalem* (1996) deals somewhat polemically with the repression of early unionism in the nineteenth-century Cotswolds, the victimised 'white slaves of England' eventually freed to emigrate to New Zealand. Sandys was the 1992 Sargeson Fellow and 1995 *Burns Fellow.   RR

SAPHIRA, Miriam (1941–), poet and lesbian writer, was born at Inglewood, and educated at New Plymouth GHS, Palmerston North Teachers' College, and the University of Auckland, taking a PhD in Psychology. She has also published as Miriam Jackson. Founder in 1981 of Papers Inc., a small lesbian publishing collective, Saphira served on the Broadsheet Collective where she wrote articles on domestic violence and sexual offending. She has published three books of poetry: *I Ask of You* (1978), *Good Morning I'm Fine* (1982) and *My Mother Taught Me* (1992). Other work includes four books on child abuse, the first non-fiction book about lesbians, *Amazon Mothers* (1984), and an autobiography about discovering her

father's gay life, *A Man's Man: A Daughter's Story* (1997). She edited *The Power and the Glory and Other Lesbian Stories* (1987) and *The Lavender Annual* (1989) and has published short stories in the lesbian magazine *LIP*. Saphira has made a significant contribution to New Zealand lesbian writing and publishing.   ALa

SARGESON, Frank (1903–82), was born Norris Frank Davey, the child of a middle-class family in Hamilton. He was educated there and in Auckland until he completed his training as a solicitor in 1926, when he went for two years to Britain and Europe. Returning in 1928, he decided not to pursue a career in law and instead worked at various jobs before settling on family land near Takapuna, where he was to remain for the rest of his life, most of it as a full-time writer.

He had begun writing in the late 1920s, but did not establish a significant reputation until he began to con-tribute short sketches and stories to the radical periodical *Tomorrow* from 1935. First collected as *Conversation with My Uncle, and Other Sketches* (1936), these saw Sar-geson beginning to master the elements that over the next twenty years were to become the distinctive features of his style: an economic delineation of character, mini-malist narration, and an understanding of the tight range of idiomatic vocabulary and syntax appropriate to his characters.

Sargeson published forty stories between 1936 and 1954, all but two completed by 1945. Most were col-lected in *Conversation with My Uncle* or in two later volumes, *A Man and His Wife* (1940), and *That Summer, and Other Stories* (1946). 'The Making of a New Zealander' was adjudged joint winner in the short story section of the 1940 *Centennial Literary Competition. In these years Sargeson dominated New Zealand short fiction. The stories, showing some indebtedness to Sherwood Anderson and Hemingway, are frequently wry sketches or ostensible yarns about apparently undis-tinguished characters and minor occurrences. The back-ground, explicit or implied, is New Zealand in the years between the two World Wars, and particularly the 1930s *Depression, against which the characters are depicted as itinerant labourers or unemployed men, seldom happily married and frequently without any apparent family connection.

The stories drew praise for their social realism and austere economy of language, appropriate to the ap-parently unimaginative principal characters who were often the semi-articulate narrators and chroniclers of the events. The narrators' starkly limited point of view char-acterises a view of the world that dare not admit openly the emptiness and loneliness that is immanent. This was accepted as true of the limited, *puritanical, emotionally sterile world of the New Zealand working-class male, isolated by gender, economic status and emotional incapacity, relying on the unspoken expectations of 'mateship' for some partial fulfilment that more often than not proved elusive. More than any other works before them, Sargeson's stories captured working-class New Zealand vernacular, the society that gave rise to it and much of its inner spirit.

In 1945 Sargeson published the first part of a novel-in-progress under the title *When the Wind Blows*. The complete novel, a study of youth and self-discovery, was *I Saw in My Dream* (1949), published in England by John Lehmann, who had published earlier work by Sargeson in the wartime *Penguin New Writing*, and the *That Summer* collection. But the small collection by New Zealand writers which Sargeson edited as *Speaking for Ourselves* in 1945 pointed towards post-war roles of mentor to younger writers such as Maurice *Duggan, John Reece *Cole and Janet *Frame, confidant of contemporaries such as Roderick *Finlayson and E.H. *McCormick, and collaborator with arbiters of taste, such as Dan *Davin in the influential 1953 World's Classics selection of New Zealand short stories for *Oxford University Press.

As writer, however, the post-war years were less fruitful for Sargeson than he had hoped. Though sixteen New Zealand writers were to hail his fiftieth birthday with a letter of congratulation and appreciation in *Landfall* (March 1953), the decade that followed was not productive. He published one novella (*I For One*), two stories and a short essay in autobiography; a pair of plays were only partially completed, and a novel presented continuing difficulties.

But in his sixties Sargeson enjoyed a remarkable new burst of creative achievement. In 1964 the first complete collection of his stories was published, with a thoughtful introductory essay by Bill *Pearson. In 1965 the two plays, 'A Time for Sowing' and 'The Cradle and the Egg', were published under the collective title of *Wrestling with the Angel*, and in the same year the novel *Memoirs of a Peon* appeared.

This work, together with its two successors and the half-dozen short stories written before 1970, would establish a new narrative technique through which Sargeson explored a different kind of character, in a world of mostly dark comedy. The characters of Sargeson's later fiction are principally middle-class. In place of the old inarticulate minimalism, the narration is frequently ornate, even verbose, and often expansive, reminiscent of eighteenth-century formalism. The narrators themselves, whether authorial or identified with a character, are now more articulate, much more confident with language. Yet for all their fluency, they reveal themselves to be no less isolated, no less puritanically constrained, no less ultimately defeated, than their hesitant predecessors.

Each of the three later novels is close to dark farce or tragicomedy. In each, the protagonist is left at the end surrounded by images of failure rather than success, with his ambitions achieved at a price that is at best pyrrhic and at worst shocking. In *Memoirs of a Peon* the Casanova-character Michael Newhouse pursues his erotic and commercial ambitions through the stifling world of 1920s provincial New Zealand until a predictable miscalculation and retribution leaves him wryly observing a seemingly inevitable fate. *The Hangover* (1967), possibly its author's favourite, describes the dark fall into homicidal frenzy of a young university student, trapped between the puritanical and potentially incestuous ambitions of his overweening widowed mother, and a nether-world of social and sexual grotesques in 1960s 'Bohemian' Auckland.

Joy of the Worm (1969) owes much to Smollett in its style, but also something to *Butler's *The Way of All Flesh* in its subject matter. Its protagonists, the Reverend James Bohun and his son Jeremy, compete intellectually and sexually for the domination of their respective partners, and by extension, of each other, until, having destroyed the women they are supposed to have cherished, they strike a bargain in the nature of a truce and move laconically towards retirement, each in his own eccentric way.

There is much irony but little real laughter in these novels, and the sombre tones are carried into the several novellas that Sargeson wrote in his last years. He had attempted the form in 'That Summer', the centrepiece of the stories written prior to 1945, and developed it in 'I For One'. He reprinted this in 1972 together with two other stories, 'A Game of Hide and Seek' and 'Man of England Now', the latter giving the 1972 volume its title. Here Sargeson offers his reader studies of the grotesques that figure increasingly in his repertoire of characters from *The Hangover* on. The tendency to emphasise not merely the unorthodox but the thoroughly bizarre is present in stories of the 1960s such as 'Charity Begins at Home' and 'An International Occasion'. In the last four or five novellas, it became a staple of the fiction.

In his seventies, however, Sargeson returned to the subjective but essentially naturalistic style of more orthodox narrative as he composed a trilogy of memoirs. Much earlier, he had written an autobiographical essay entitled 'Up onto the Roof and Down Again' for Charles *Brasch who published it in four parts in *Landfall* between December 1950 and December 1951. Expanded to more than twice the original length with the addition of a memoir called 'Third Class Country' recalling the farm of his uncle Oakley Sargeson, the two pieces were published as one volume of autobiography under the title *Once is Enough* in 1973. The two volumes that followed, *More than Enough* (1975) and *Never Enough* (1977), trace Sargeson's life as a writer discursively but more or less sequentially from the 1930s to the 1970s. They are rich in anecdote, reminiscence and insights into both his life and creativity. The trilogy of autobiographies therefore stands as an important document in the history of New Zealand writing. They were published as one volume, *Sargeson*, in 1981.

Sargeson's last published short story was 'Making Father Pay', in the *★NZ Listener*, 7 June 1975. His last two novellas were *Sunset Village* (1976), a comic crime mystery story set in a geriatric community, and *En Route*, the story of a journey of discovery made by two feminists in middle life, published together with a novella by Edith ★Campion in a joint volume entitled *Tandem* (1979). In 1978 his seventy-fifth birthday was commemorated with a 360-page issue of the periodical *★Islands* (issue 21) containing reminiscences by friends, evaluations and commentary, and excerpts reprinted from his earlier work. His own critical writing, reviewing and essays were collected in *Conversation in a Train and Other Critical Writing*, edited by Kevin Cunningham in 1983.

Frank Sargeson was undoubtedly the most important New Zealand writer of short fiction in the years following the death of Katherine ★Mansfield. Like her, his reputation helped promote the recognition of New Zealand writing beyond the country's shores. Unlike her, he wrote his major works during a lifetime's residence in New Zealand. He focused relentlessly on his male characters and their experiences in a spiritually depressed society, exploring subjects and themes which appeared to him to necessitate an austere style that eschewed the apparently imaginative in favour of a harsh and pessimistic social realism. The romantic and homoerotic subtexts which the contemporary reader discerns suggest that Sargeson's narratives are more than just the social realist fictional records of a section of society, as an earlier generation largely saw him. His work has survived his generation, and he remains a major figure for his achievement and influence in New Zealand fiction.

In 1995 Michael ★King published a biography of Sargeson distinguished for its detailed research and for establishing that Sargeson's withdrawal from the public life of a lawyer, and his change of name, were consequential on homosexual activity. The reception of King's book also reaffirmed Sargeson's continuing significance as a reference point in literature. WB

SATCHELL, William (1860–1942), was the author of four remarkable novels, a volume of poems and a large number of stories and magazine articles. He was born in London and grew up in a highly literary environment,

his father being not only a senior civil servant but also a scholar, bibliographer, student of Egyptology and a contributor to Murray's *Oxford English Dictionary*. William was educated at Grove House Academy 'for young gentlemen' and at the University of Heidelberg. His emigration to New Zealand in 1886, after working as a writer (under the anagrammatic pseudonym Saml. Cliall White) and publisher, has been described by Phillip ★Wilson, his biographer, as a reversal of Katherine ★Mansfield's, in Satchell's case from the literate centre of Englishness to the colonial periphery.

By the time he arrived, and even more obviously by the time he was publishing his novels (1902–14), the colonial phase of New Zealand history had given way to a more settled, pastoral period, but it is the colonial era that marks his work, and to this extent he is the author of historical novels. In fact his first experiences were in the far north, Hokianga, where Māori still predominated and almost half the Pākehā men had Māori wives. Satchell's sympathetic interest in these people coloured his novels. He worked there as a storekeeper.

In 1892 he moved to Auckland, by now a married man and a father, and from this time on his literary activity redeveloped. He contributed many stories and poems to the *NZ Graphic*, a weekly subsidiary of the *Auckland Star*, and he also sent poems to the Sydney *★Bulletin*. When the Thames ★gold rush occurred he earned his first large income as a stockbroker, but his literary work continued. A collection, *Patriotic and Other Poems*, was published in 1900. The 'patriotic' verse is centred on the Boer War while the 'other' poems are mainly ballads of pioneer life.

Clearly determined to succeed, in 1901 he founded his own literary paper, *The Maorilander*, to encourage new writers 'of a literature striving to assert itself in a new land'. In fact he wrote most of the material for the seven issues himself (and wrote merciless responses to people who tried to contribute). He also attended to gathering advertisements and to distribution. It is perhaps significant that he went on to publish all of his novels in England.

The first of these was *The ★Land of the Lost*, published in 1902 when its author was 42. Its gumfields setting must have seemed exotic to English readers, yet it was favourably received, the London *Athenaeum* comparing it with Thomas Hardy. This significant moment in New Zealand literary history was, however, scarcely noticed in New Zealand itself. Alan ★Mulgan (quoted by Wilson) suggested that this was because local people 'were not interested; it was too near home. Romance was something that came from the African spaces or the Hudson Bay Territory, not from the other side of one's own hills.'

Now living in Mount Roskill, Auckland, Satchell

went on to write The *Toll of the Bush (1905), which E.H. *McCormick considered 'his best novel'. The *Athenaeum* was again enthusiastic: 'This is a colonial novel of remarkable merit and distinction. It has a rounded completeness, a full and broad humanity, which are by no means characteristic of contemporary fiction.' But again New Zealand reviewers found the local setting a strange one for 'romance'. Today it has fascination for its literary use of the *bush as a strong, claustrophobic, inhuman force constantly threatening those who venture into it. With its near contemporary, Edith Searle *Grossmann's The *Heart of the Bush (1910), it showed that this local environment could be used as a powerful symbolic instrument in fiction.

Satchell's financial dealings were less successful than his literary work and he moved with his family to a cheaper house in Birkenhead. For all that, another novel, *The Elixir of Life* (1907), was published, though not well received. It is set at sea and in a shipwreck, and its focus is medical. Alan Vincent, a brilliant scientist, is accompanied by Philip Westland, a brooding, depressive figure, not unlike Satchell himself. For modern readers its emphasis on a miraculous elixir—a topical theme of the time—makes the book seem faintly ridiculous, despite the skill of its characterisation. (See also *Science fiction.)

For some years, Satchell devoted himself—unsuccessfully—to playwriting and to horticultural interests, before turning to his next and most famous novel: The *Greenstone Door (1914). It was more carefully planned than any other, Satchell visiting Auckland houses and taking bush walks in places which were to be the novel's setting. It was, however, an historical novel, dealing with the 'New Zealand *Wars' between Māori and Pākehā. This was not a fashionable theme, which might explain the relative lack of interest when the novel was published. Wilson suggests that its anti-war theme was disturbing on the eve of war in Europe. Worse perhaps: the younger characters spend time studying German and reading German poetry. The book's tone is conciliatory, compassionate and humane. Of Satchell's nine children, three of his sons were to fight in France.

Satchell lived another thirty years, but published no more novels, disappointed at the relative failure of The *Greenstone Door*. Near the end of his life he remarked, 'Had I been given any encouragement, it would have been my fourth book, not the last.' In 1928 he wrote a children's story, 'The Book of Joso'. Before his death he was comforted by the fact that his fourth novel, one of the most humane in New Zealand, was finding new readers, some of whom wrote warmly to him and strove for its republication. It was in fact republished in 1935 and several times since then.

A bibliography of Satchell's writing, including many uncollected pieces, is to be found in Phillip John Wilson's *William Satchell* (1968).   NW

SAVAGE, John (1770–1838), was the author of the first general survey of New Zealand after *Cook's voyages: *Some Account of New Zealand; particularly the Bay of Islands, and Surrounding Country; with a Description of the Religion and Government, Language, Arts, Manufactures, Manners, and Customs of the Natives* (1807). Savage visited New Zealand as a ship's surgeon in 1805 and returned to England in 1806. Facsimiles of his book were published in 1966 (Hocken Library) and 1975 (Capper Press). There is also an edition of 1939 where the text is interrupted by annotations by A.D. McKinlay, setting Savage's observations into the frame of a more recent perception of ancient Māori life. In fact Savage's view is relatively 'enlightened', on the one hand seeing 'passions' as the governing force of all 'uncivilized' peoples but on the other noting the 'restraint' exercised by the chiefs and by 'a natural proneness to affection'. He admits that cannibalism is practised, but argues that it is not for 'food', but as an act of hostility against enemies, a view that conforms with other early ones such as those of Cook, Crozet and *Nicholas. In contradicting the established British view that the Māori were unrestrained and brutal, Savage says 'The manners of these people are particularly kind and affectionate upon all occasions.' Several Māori asked him to take them to England, and he selected Moyhanger (Moehanga), 'a healthy stout young man of the military class'. After a few weeks in England, Moyhanger returned on another ship. Savage's book contains some details (probably supplied by Moyhanger) which are surprisingly accurate considering the short time of his stay and the lack of general information on the Māori available at the time. It includes a chapter on the language with an interesting vocabulary list. On the other hand, as a source of information it is outdated and as a narrative of early contact it is disappointingly short and sketchy. Its main claim to attention is its primacy as an account of the country.   NW

SCANLAN, Nelle (1882–1968), author of the popular *Pencarrow novels of the 1930s, was born in Picton of Irish Catholic stock, educated in Blenheim, and around 1900 moved with her family to Palmerston North where she worked as a typist before setting up her own secretarial business. After the outbreak of World War 1 she became a reporter (then sub-editor) on the *Manawatu Times*, and at the end of the War decided to pursue a professional career as a freelance journalist. In 1921 she received national (and international) prominence as the only woman journalist at the first Limitation of Arms

Conference held in Washington, and for several years became an unofficial roving ambassador in the United States, speaking on the Women's Club circuit and reporting on major public events and personalities in syndicated articles which were published as a book, *Boudoir Mirrors of Washington*, in 1923.

She then travelled to England, and for the next twenty-five years divided her time regularly between England and New Zealand, continuing her journalistic career as a lively reporter of social news, royalty and the personalities behind political and cultural events overseas, and during World War 2 speaking regularly on radio in New Zealand. She drew heavily on her earlier overseas experiences in a fictionalised romantic travelogue, *Ambition's Harvest*, which she published in 1935, a novel which later provided much of the material for the last book she wrote, the autobiography *Road to Pencarrow* (1963).

Her dual Anglo–New Zealand allegiance is reflected in the pattern of the fiction Scanlan began to write in the early 1930s. Between 1931 and 1952 she published fifteen novels, five of them set in England and ten in New Zealand. The first two, *Primrose Hill* and *The Top Step*, both published in 1931, were set in London, revealing the author's penchant in her English fiction for light social comedy focused on middle-class manners and stereotypes. In the wake of their modest success her editor, Robert Hale, suggested that she turn to New Zealand for her materials, and in the following year she published the first of the quartet of linked novels—the Pencarrow novels—which established her as the most popular novelist of her generation in New Zealand in the 1930s–40s.

The Pencarrow novels—*Pencarrow* (1932), *Tides of Youth* (1933), *Winds of Heaven* (1934) and *Kelly Pencarrow* (1939)—constitute a New Zealand family saga, perhaps influenced in their conception by John Galsworthy (whom the author had met in England), recounting the varying fortunes of the Pencarrow family from their pioneering origins in Wellington in the 1840s through to the 1930s. The first novel traces the dynasty's rise to prosperity, as the founding pioneers in the mid-nineteenth century expand their farming interests in the Hutt Valley and Wairarapa and one of their sons develops urban-based business and legal interests. However, the 'public' dimensions of Scanlan's characters' lives, like historical events themselves, provide a vague, background ambience only. Her primary focus is domestic, her central aim a celebration of the values of the bourgeois family as the stable, central core of New Zealand society. It was almost certainly this conservative impulse which explained the wide popularity of the books among middle-class New Zealand readers when they first appeared in the mid-*Depression years of the 1930s. The central events of the novels, narrated with a mixture of pathos and sentiment, are births, romantic entanglements, marriages, family reunions and deaths, and conflict is provided through endless variations of family quarrels and rivalries, children rebelling against possessive parents, the testing of outsiders as suitable marriage partners, the renovation of wayward family members. Scanlan shows considerable skill in the way she controls the elements which threaten family stability, suggesting an ongoing, cyclic continuity of values through different generations and different forms of rebellion, with a strong emphasis, throughout, on wives and mothers as providing the solid matriarchal core of wisdom and values on which society is built.

The Pencarrow books, with their focus on commonplace events in domestic settings, set a pattern for all Scanlan's New Zealand fiction. *Leisure for Living* (1937) and *A Guest of Life* (1938) dealt with the familiar theme of English characters in New Zealand; *March Moon* (1944), contrasting a youthful romance against a long-standing feud between a brother and sister, drew on childhood memories of the Marlborough landscape; and *The Rusty Road* (1948), with its central character of the mother who learns the art of 'compromise' and becomes 'the focal centre of [the] home; its unifying influence, and its strength under stress', returned to the family chronicle format of the Pencarrow books. Interspersed with these books were two English society novels: *The Marriage of Nicholas Cotter* (1936), in which an older man abandons a long-standing domestic relationship with his sister in order to marry a young woman; and *Kit Carmichael* (1947), a novel of fashionable London society.

Scanlan returned to New Zealand for the last time in 1948, and published two more novels, *Confidence Corner* (1950), and *The Young Summer* (1952), her last, set in Paraparaumu where the author lived in retirement until her death. Noting in his *Great Days in New Zealand Writing* (1962) that by 1960, in New Zealand alone, *Pencarrow* had sold 30 700 copies, and the series more than 80 000 copies, Alan *Mulgan described Scanlan as a writer who was influential in the 1930s–40s in creating a readership for New Zealand fiction, changing negative colonial attitudes towards locally written work. In 1965 she was awarded an MBE, not only for achievements as a writer but for her long-standing professional involvement in writers' organisations in New Zealand.

TS

Scarecrow, The (Sydney 1963, 1967; Auckland 1976, 1981), was Ronald Hugh *Morrieson's first novel. It is set in the imaginary south Taranaki township of Klynham and focuses on the Poindexter family, a junk-dealer, his big-hearted wife and their children, of whom the youngest, the 14-year-old Neddy, narrates the story. Beginning with its famous statement, 'The same week our fowls were stolen, Daphne Moran had her throat cut', the novel yokes two worlds, the innocently pre-sexual everyday and that of post-lapsarian experience, moving from a pre-adolescent world of petty crimes and schemes involving chickens to the adult world of sex, violence, drinking and gambling into which Neddy's older brother Herbert is slowly declining. The latter is represented by Hubert Salter, the Scarecrow of the title, an itinerant serial killer and necrophiliac who enters the town early in the narrative and pursues the voluptuous 16-year-old Prudence Poindexter, herself an object of interest to her narrating younger brother, his friend Les Wilson and a group of young bullies known as the Lynch gang. In keeping with the novel's underlying emphasis on the workings of male adolescence, it progressively dissolves the line between innocence and experience, revealing the latter in the former in a number of sequences. Thus the Lynch gang's desire for Prudence is shown to link them to the Scarecrow, who is also associated with Klynham's undertaker, and more importantly with Athol Cudby, Neddy's dissolute uncle, who brings the Scarecrow into the Poindexter home and the presence of Prudence for the first time. The Scarecrow's pursuit of Prudence, and Neddy's ultimately successful protection of her, provide the novel's main direction and issue in the ultimate extermination of the Scarecrow, which allows a redemptive conclusion and an affirmation of adult life as a potentially positive experience. A feature film version (1982), directed by Sam Pillsbury, was described by Nicholas Reid as 'a unique example of specifically New Zealand Gothic'. PE

Scented Gardens for the Blind, the fourth novel by Janet *Frame (Christchurch: *Pegasus Press; London, 1963; New York, 1964) won the Hubert Church Prose Award in 1964; no MS is known. Written in England at a time of heightened tension in the nuclear arms race, the novel explores the decay of language as an index of Western Civilisation's cultural and spiritual depravity and its deadly 'progress' towards nuclear self-annihilation: 'the flash in the sky, the deep burn of words that destroy all power to create, the time of a first degree language so articulate that ... those who have spoken one word of it are struck dumb and forbidden ever to speak again.' The novel opens with a chapter in the first person voice of Vera Glace, a woman feigning blindness ('Blind I am safe'), fearing the light of visionary truth. Chapter 2 is written in the limited third person with extensive passages of interior monologue, focusing on Vera's mute daughter, Erlene, who stopped talking without apparent

cause. Chapter 3, in traditional omniscient mode, focuses on Vera's genealogist husband, Edward. This narrative pattern—Vera, Erlene, Edward—is repeated five times with recurrent images and motifs uniting the disparate chapters and characters. Vera's anxious narrative is fraught with guilt; she is terrified that she may be the cause of her daughter's 'affliction' and fears that Erlene's first words, should she begin to speak again, will be words of accusation. Erlene, silent and motionless, lies in her small room in the pose of death. Her only companion is Uncle Blackbeetle, a storytelling beetle who lives in her windowsill. He is the imaginative inverse of the psychiatrist, Dr Clapper, who tries to get her to speak. Edward, we learn, left his wife and child eleven years earlier, travelling to England to research the history of the Strang family in order to show its survival through the centuries despite wars, plagues and natural calamities—and thus, he hopes, the capacity of the human race to survive any disaster. He places his faith in language, believing it will offer 'the final answer to the problem ... the hope for humanity, the future'.

In a destabilising conclusion typical of Frame's fictions, it is revealed in the final chapter (16) that all three characters exist only in the imagination of Vera Glace, a 60-year-old, unmarried, childless patient tended by Dr Clapper in a psychiatric institution. The novel ends apocalyptically with the falling of an atom bomb that destroys England. Following this, Vera utters her first sounds in thirty years, the 'new language of humanity', animalistic grunts that arise 'out of ancient rock and marshland; out of ice and stone'. This is not the saving language Edward anticipated, but rather the 'voice of the beast' of which Erlene warned. If this does not suggest the utter failure of language, it suggests the need to return to a primordial past that disavows alienating Western 'progress'. For as Vera says: 'When there are no human beings on earth who will name the ashes? The winds of love blow only in the forests of people; without them there is no more caring.' KWo

SCHOLEFIELD, Guy H. (1877–1963), was a significant, though now partly out-dated, historical writer. In particular, he was a pioneer in the fields of economic history (*New Zealand in Evolution, Industrial, Economic and Political*, 1909; *The Pacific: Its Past and Future and the Policy of the Great Powers from the Eighteenth Century*, 1919) and historical biography (*Notable New Zealand Statesmen: Twelve Prime Ministers*, 1946). For the *Centennial he wrote *A Dictionary of New Zealand Biography* (1940), in two volumes, covering 2600 persons. Although it suffered from his desire to please (or not to displease) it was an astonishing achievement for an individual and it remains an important first source for biographical information. The monumental volumes of *The *Diction-ary of New Zealand Biography* (1990–), edited by W.H. *Oliver and Claudia Orange, are unlikely to dislodge it completely. Scholefield's other contributions to cultural life included his career as a journalist on the *New Zealand Times* and the Christchurch **Press*, as London and war correspondent for the New Zealand Press Association 1908–19 and subsequently as editor of the *Wairarapa Age*. His industry as Parliamentary Librarian is evidenced by his editorial work on the *Parliamentary Record 1840–1949* (1950), by indexes to a wide range of newspapers and manuscript collections and especially by the massive two volumes *The Richmond–Atkinson Papers* (1960), repro-ducing the letters and diaries of two closely interlinked families, still a major source of information on social history in nineteenth-century New Zealand.   NW

School Publications has a modest but secure place in New Zealand's literary history. Formed as the publishing branch of the Department of Education in 1939, and lasting until the Department's replacement by a Ministry in 1989, it produced a steady stream of exemplary pub-lications for schools. (A successor organisation, *Learning Media Limited, carries on substantially the same tradition.)

Its first task was humble enough: to publish a series of textbooks to replace the dull and unimaginative ones currently available. But it was the time of the first Labour government, and there was a stirring of national con-sciousness in the air. The committee which recom-mended the establishment of School Publications was keen to see material that reflected the experience of New Zealand children; and it gave the new organisation an implied mandate to seek this material not only from educationists and subject specialists but from the best available local writers.

This was a new thing in New Zealand educational publishing, and the success with which School Publications drew on, and fostered, local talent eventu-ally gained it worldwide attention. No doubt it helped that several of the Branch's editors—James K. *Baxter, Alistair *Campbell, Jack *Lasenby and Louis *Johnson, to name only a few—were themselves significant writers.

School Publications did have some notable prece-dents. As early as 1895, *The New Zealand Reader*, a Government-funded miscellany of extracts from local authors, had been published at the urging of that remarkable Minister of Education, William Pember *Reeves. Better known, and well remembered by gen-erations of children in this country, was an Education Department periodical, distributed free of charge, which first appeared in 1907 and has been a fixture in New Zealand schools ever since: the *School Journal*.

By the time School Publications was established, however, the *Journal* had lost the national flavour of its earliest issues. Most of its items were reprints from over-seas sources, and nearly all original pieces were unsigned. Handing the publication over to the new School Publications Branch provided an opportunity for a fresh start.

The infant organisation was fortunate in the appoint-ment of Dr C.E. Beeby as Director of Education. Beeby took a close interest in the development of School Publications, seeing it as central to the whole movement of educational reform; and he had a clear idea of what it should be trying to achieve.

'In a school book,' he later wrote, 'a small child from a barren home may make his first contact with literature and the arts, and his first contact, too, with minds that are trying to say something to him with sincerity and skill and with no hint of condescension.'

The results of this approach took some time to estab-lish themselves. The war intervened; there were paper shortages and shortages of money. But by the late 1940s, School Publications was beginning to achieve some notable successes. There was no shortage of confidence among its editors: writers of the calibre of Frank *Sargeson and A.R.D. Fairburn were being invited to contribute material, and although the work that emerged was not always well adapted to its young read-ership, the adventurousness of the invitation itself was a good sign.

Design and typography had improved, too. Even the Branch's more utilitarian publications—syllabuses, hand-books, the monthly *Education* magazine—by now had a graceful look to them.

The *School Bulletins*, which began to appear after the war, provided a new opportunity for writers to develop a theme at length. Among the best examples were explo-rations of New Zealand history, written with skill and authenticity, but in a form that was readily accessible to children. Some took a notably independent line: *Te Tiriti o Waitangi*, by Ruth Ross, challenged the then-received view of the treaty; and Roderick *Finlayson's series of bulletins on Māori history, later reprinted as *The Springing Fern*, was similarly adventurous. In bulletins such as these, School Publications encouraged its writers to get beyond secondary opinions and recorded facts. The aim was to create living impressions of what people did and how they felt.

The *School Journal* too showed the effects of the new approach. Authorship was now routinely acknowledged, and increasingly the text explored a more personal style and subject matter. Some of its new writers, like Ruth *Dallas and Elsie *Locke, had first been commissioned to write bulletins and decided that they enjoyed the

challenge of writing for children. Others—Amelia
*Batistich, Margaret *Mahy, Maurice *Duggan, Ruth
*Park, Barry *Mitcalfe, Witi *Ihimaera, Joy *Cowley—
gravitated to the *Journal* of their own accord. By the
1960s, the *School Journal* had become established as a
quality periodical whose emphasis was entirely local.

New needs brought other publications. The *Ready
to Read* series of early reading books came in 1963. (New
titles in the series, with a new approach, began appearing in 1984.) *Ready to Read* was yet another successful
attempt by School Publications to provide New Zealand
children with something better, more recognisable as
living reality, than commercially produced series such as
Janet and John.

Since 1947, School Publications had been publishing
in Samoan, and it gradually added other *Pacific
nations languages as time went on. (Its 1954 booklet in
*Tokelauan was the first publication in that language.)
Until 1962, these Pacific publications were for schools in
the Islands under New Zealand administration; with
independence, emphasis shifted to publishing for the
Pacific communities in New Zealand schools. The *Tupu*
series of booklets, first appearing in 1988, is now
published in five Pacific nations languages—Samoan,
Cook Islands Māori, Tokelauan, Tongan and Niuean.

Oddly, as it now seems, publishing in Pacific nations
languages preceded a similar programme for the Māori
language. Although very occasional items in Māori had
appeared in the *School Journal*, even as far back as 1907,
for many years the language was largely ignored.

In 1959, it was suggested that School Publications
produce some texts in Māori suitable for pupils studying
the language at secondary schools. A series of these,
Te Wharekura, began appearing in 1960, followed
some years later by *Te Tautoko*. Both publications were
successful, but by 1978 there was a demand for simpler
material that could be read in the primary schools. The
outcome was *He Purapura*—a series of lively picture
books.

The School Publications Branch formally ceased to
exist in 1989, when it joined the Department of
Education's Audio and Visual Production Units to form
a new entity, Learning Media.   BS

SCHRODER, J.H.E. (John Henry Erle) (1895–
1980), was poet, essayist, educator and broadcaster, but best known for encouraging and promoting
other, more talented writers. Born in Hokitika, he
became responsible for the literary page of the
Christchurch *Sun* from 1927 and of the *Press* from
1929, writing his own popular *Sun* column, 'The
Wooden Horse', and publishing early work by Eileen
*Duggan, Robin *Hyde, A.R.D. *Fairburn, R.A.K.

*Mason, M.H. *Holcroft and others. His own verse
was light, colonial *Georgian and often pastiche in
character, the best being the most comic. His most
famous poem, 'The Street', first published in the *Sun* in
1922, was anthologised in *Kowhai Gold* and elsewhere,
and gave its title to his first collection, *The Street and
Other Verses* (1962). Collections of his newspaper essays,
mostly on literary subjects, appeared as *Remembering
Things* (1938) and *Second Appearances* (1959), and his
radio talks on language as *The Ways of Words* (1969). He
was appointed assistant director-general of the then
New Zealand Broadcasting Service in 1949, was on the
selection committee of the State *Literary Fund from
1947 and later the Queen Elizabeth II Arts Council and
the *Indecent Publications Tribunal. This role as arbiter
and patron provoked Denis *Glover's mockery of him,
along with Alan *Mulgan and C.A. *Marris, as 'Three
men who hold within their hand / The literacy of the
land'. Schroder riposted by correcting the punctilious
Glover's grammar in a nicely turned sonnet, 'Glover!
Thou shouldst be cringing at this hour!' After retiring
from broadcasting as director he resumed writing light
verse for the *Press* and *NZ Listener*, publishing a
selection as *Yet Once More* (1969). The correspondence
over seventeen years between Schroder and Robin
Hyde (in the *Alexander Turnbull Library) provides an
intriguing study in the changing relationship between
an increasingly independent writer and a valued but
ultimately restrictive mentor. Schroder was awarded an
honorary DLitt by the University of Canterbury in
1975.   GB/PE/RR

Science fiction is a colourful and quite significant
genre of New Zealand literature, perhaps because of the
coincidence of history which saw the remote land occupied by Europeans at a time when the industrial civilisation of Europe was suffering a major crisis of confidence.
*Aotearoa's confrontations of old and new, the familiar
and the alien, provoked writers to comment on existing
social orders and speculate about new ones. Many of the
early novels in which we might recognise science
fiction's breath (if not its bellow) have a sociological
agenda, and the form is closely related to *Utopian literature. Robert *Pemberton, for example, in his novel
*The *Happy Colony* (1854) suggests that a lust for wealth
having corrupted Europe, only New Zealand now offers
the chance for an ideal society. Henry Crocker Watson
published a utopian novel *Erchomenon or The Republic of
Materialism* (1879) and the provocatively titled *The
Decline and Fall of the British Empire or The Witches Cavern*
(1890). William Delisle Hay in *The Doom of the Great
City* (1880) explores the notion of a great fog which kills
London leaving the antipodes to retain the best of

English life. Most famous is Julius *Vogel's *Anno domini 2000; or Woman's Destiny* (1889), which contemplates how women might achieve political power, and the consequences for society at large. (See *Women's Suffrage.) Also socially speculative is the work of 'Godfrey Sweven' (John Macmillan *Brown), *Riallaro: The Archipelago of Exiles* (1901) and *Limanora: The Island of Progress* (1903, 1931).

Science fiction in the sense of imaginative writing concerned with issues of science began with the dialogues contributed by Samuel *Butler to the *Press* on Darwin's *Origin of Species* (1872). The first futuristic story, also touching the Darwinian controversy, is probably (Rowan Gibbs has suggested) the comical and spirited 'A Night at the Club; or, Christchurch in 1963', by 'Mrs Raven' (probably Sara Raven, 1821–68), published in *Literary Foundlings: Verse and Prose Collected in Canterbury, N.Z.* (1864). Butler's *Erewhon* (1872), which incorporated some of his *Press* pieces, is, of course, the major work of this period to use fantasy narrative to explore avant-garde scientific ideas, including the still-relevant issue of the effect of technology on society.

A more popular science fiction mix of romance and adventure began to appear towards the end of the nineteenth century. *The Great Romance* (1881) by 'The Inhabitant' is perhaps New Zealand's first science fiction story in the modern sense. It follows the trail blazed by Jules *Verne and demonstrates considerable scientific acumen. Set in 1950, seventy years into the future, the novel follows the adventures of J.B. Hope who, having taken a special sleeping draught, sleeps until the year 2143 when he awakes to discover that the 'civilized' world has developed telepathic powers. With two colleagues, Moxton and Weir, he departs in a space ship called the Star Climber to Venus where…. Unfortunately, only Parts One and Two of the novel exist; Part Three was probably never written, although clearly it was envisaged. The story ends therefore with an appalling cliffhanger when Weir tumbles away into space from a low-gravity asteroid.

The Secret of Mount Cook (1894) by 'Azor' (John Petrie) is an extraordinary love story in which aristocratic escapees from the French Revolution are discovered, cryogenically preserved, on Mount Cook, to be defrosted and revived by the hero. Unfortunately, the storytelling is erratic and lacks concern for scientific fact or probability. *Hedged with Divinities* (1895) by Edward *Tregear is a masculinist response to the growing feminist movement. When all men and boy children suddenly die, the world is left in charge of the women. The sole male survivor, Jack Wallace, who had been put to sleep for three years by a mysterious Māori medicine man, becomes King in Auckland. Learning, however,

that a deputation of women is on its way from Wellington to claim their 'rights', he escapes these 'duties' with his true love Nellie. However paternalistic, Tregear's novel is saved from absurdity by its engagement with the 'what-if' of the situation and a certain compassion for the characters; Victorian morality and sentimentality can be seen struggling with a situation which threatens their very existence.

The Elixir of Life (1907) by William *Satchell describes the adventurous voyage of a steamship from England to New Zealand when the ship's doctor discovers a universal panacea for all germ-based diseases. Though it has received a harsh press, this novel engages with many major topics of its day ranging from eugenics to Social Darwinism.

The next noticeable upsurge of interest in science fiction came in the 1960s–70s, led by the distinguished novels of M.K. *Joseph, *The *Hole in the Zero* (1967) and *The *Time of Achamoth* (1977). Their intellectual and moral depth and Joseph's scholarly and literary eminence helped to validate the genre, and other mainstream writers have since found science fiction an appropriate medium. Maurice *Gee created magical worlds for younger readers in works such as *Under the Mountain* (1979), *The World Around the Corner* (1980) and *Motherstone* (1985). Margaret *Mahy reveals in her more adult writing such as *Aliens in the Family* (1986) and *The Tricksters* (1986) a fine ability to explore the frightening borderland where everyday reality encounters supernatural forces. Peter *Hooper and Philip *Temple worked in fantasy forms related to science fiction, as then did Rachel *McAlpine in *The Limits of Green* (1985) and *Running Away from Home* (1987), novels which display exuberant imagination while retaining awareness of how political decisions shape our lives. Mike *Johnson also made a mark with the post-apocalyptic *Lear* (1986), and continues to push beyond realism in novels like the gothic-magical *Dumb Show* (1996). Johnson regards science fiction as 'still the most potent vehicle for social comment available to the writer'.

The form is now established in New Zealand, as elsewhere, and a growing body of committed science fiction writers explore issues relating to ecology, social change and politics. Among the most celebrated is Cherry Wilder (Cherry Barbara Grimm) who after a period in Germany returned to New Zealand in 1997. Her international reputation is based on excellent narrative skills, careful characterisation and graceful prose. Novels such as *The Torin Trilogy* (1977) and *Signs of Life* (1996), and the short story collection *Dealers in Light and Darkness* (1994) display an interest in alien cultures accompanied by a fierce optimism. Wilder has also written fantasy and horror stories, while her frightening story *Anzac Day* (1996) reveals an equal ability in naturalist vein.

Craig ★Harrison's three novels, *Broken October* (1976), *The Quiet Earth* (1981) and *Days of Starlight* (1988), reveal a sharp political awareness of the threats to democracy posed by urban terrorism and the ambitions of superpowers. The first two are set in New Zealand and comment forcefully on the country without falling into the trap of preaching or losing the momentum of the narrative. An emigrant from Yorkshire, Harrison has commented that living in New Zealand is 'like being on another planet. Everything seems transplanted. It is an ideal setting for the kind of science fiction I want to write.'

Phillip ★Mann, a fellow Yorkshireman, has written nine science fiction novels as well as many short stories and plays. Only one, *Pioneers* (1988), is set in New Zealand. The latest, *The Burning Forest* (1996), is Part 4 of a long work entitled *A Land Fit for Heroes*, displaying Mann's strong interest in alternative histories and bizarre life-forms as well as a growing passion for the ecological protection of our planet: 'the only home we have in the universe'.

Hugh Cook's ten-novel sequence *Chronicles of an Age of Darkness* (1986–), while generically closer to fantasy, nevertheless challenges the limitations imposed by our culture, insisting that 'other realities are possible'.

Futuristic and post-apocalyptic fiction has become quite popular, often with an environmental agenda (e.g. Barbara Ker-Man, *Death of a Sparrow*, 1991) or a feminist one (Sandi Hall, *The Godmothers*, 1982; Lora Mountjoy, *Deep Breathing*, 1984); while writers such as Lucy Sussex and Paul Collins, both currently in Australia, are developing reputations as writers and editors of science fiction.

Two recent New Zealand collections of science fiction stories testify to a growing confidence, even though *Rutherford's Dreams* (1995), edited by Warwick Bennett and Patrick Hudson, takes the more negative position that there is 'little room in New Zealand's literary marketplace for writers of science fiction to develop their craft'. *Tales from the Out of Time Café* (1996, ed. Phillip Mann) collects stories mainly by new authors on the theme of a café that can trap the unwary and carry them to different times and different worlds.

The strength of science fiction and fantasy in New Zealand is also a major element in children's writing, including notable work by Ken ★Catran, Barry ★Faville, Maurice ★Gee and Caroline ★Macdonald.

Among New Zealand's science fiction magazines, *Phlogiston*, an independent quarterly of comment, news, reviews and short fiction, is outstanding for the high standard of its critical writing, and has an expanding international readership. Editor Alex Heatley created it in 1984 with a characteristically Kiwi do-it-yourself motive: 'I wanted to read a NZ SF magazine, so I created one.' His Burning Tiger Press has published *Trimmings from the Triffid's Beard* (1994), a collection of the outstanding reviews of science fiction published by 'The Bearded Triffid' (Alan Robson). Robson, whose knowledge of world science fiction is encyclopedic, has observed challengingly, 'NZ science fiction is either stupendously good or embarrassingly bad and there is almost nothing between those two extremes. Consequently it never fails to make an impression on the reader.'
PMn

Scotland was a major component of the literary heritage brought to New Zealand in the nineteenth century and remains an important part of the fabric of contemporary New Zealand culture. In 1840 the ratio of Scottish to total UK population was 1:7. Among New Zealand settlers it was 1:2. Dunedin was founded as an Antipodean Edinburgh by Scots whose minister was a nephew of Robert Burns.

The international influence of Burns and Sir Walter Scott (as well as James Macpherson's 'Ossian', which gave every minor versifier the title of 'Bard') was at its peak in the early nineteenth century. William ★Golder (1810–76), who left Scotland in 1839, followed Scott's *Minstrelsy of the Scottish Borders* (1802–03), by producing *New Zealand Minstrelsy* (1852), allegedly 'the first book of verse published in New Zealand'. John ★Barr of Craigilee, 'Bard of the Otago Province' (1809–89), emigrated in the year Golder's *Minstrelsy* was published. When Barr sings the praises of colonial life in such vernacular Scots poems as 'There's Nae Place Like Otago Yet', he also imitates Burns, decrying the poverty and class exploitation he had left behind: 'beggar weans … auld men shivering … starving …' while the 'upstart, mushroom lord … feast[s] on roast and boil'. Barr's championship of 'wealth and labour hand in hand' suggests the hopeful new beginning colonial life seemed to offer.

Less optimistic, Dugald ★Ferguson (1833–1920) produced a version of the entire Book of Job in heroic couplets, and expressed sentimental nationalism in 'The Flag of Scotland' and 'The Bagpipes': 'When Scotland's pipe sounds in my ears, / My heart with stirring thoughts it cheers.' Ferguson was also the author of a popular historical novel modelled on Scott: *The King's Friend: A Tale of the Scottish Wars of Independence* (1905).

Moral piety typifies the demotic homilies of Hugh Smith, 'Bard of Inangahua' (1851–1944). By the 1930s, his *Poems by an Ayrshire Scot* had sold 2000 copies. 'Hughie' was popular culture among those for whom Scotland was a land of 'romance, legend and song' rather than industrial squalor, cleared wilderness and poverty. Proverbially, 'exile is the mother of nationalism'.

Not only sentimentalism but also active political thought characterised Jessie *Mackay (1864–1938), an early champion of women's rights, prohibition, New Zealand poetry and Scottish and Irish Home Rule. Her curiously artificial vernacular ballads include 'Strathnaver No More'—a passionate, stilted lament for the Highlanders deported from their communities. 'Scotland Unfree' is a call to undo the imperial union of Scotland and England: 'Mother of martyrs, now hear ye the living.'

These and others such as Marie R. Randle also wrote a plethora of love songs in the debased tradition of Burns. Their popularity should be considered in terms of a society reared on religion, song and story-telling. Allen *Curnow comments on Barr, Ferguson and Mackay in his introduction to *The Penguin Book of New Zealand Verse* (1960).

Charles *Brasch admired the work of the major modern Scottish poet Hugh MacDiarmid and met him in Edinburgh. Ian *Milner published an introductory essay, 'The Poetic Vision of Hugh MacDiarmid', in *Landfall* 64 (1962). MacDiarmid's work was also known to James K. *Baxter. Baxter's complex identification with Scotland is evident not only in his acknowledged sympathy with Burns but also in the more subtle sense of his choosing to privilege that side of his own family background, which allowed him to emphasise affinities between the tribal nature and oral culture of the Scottish clans and those of New Zealand Māori society (see also *Ireland).

Many late-twentieth-century New Zealand writers claim some Scots ancestry or interest: Allen Curnow (whose poem 'An Abominable Temper' deals with the subject), Bill *Manhire (see the strong but delicately poised poems 'A Scottish Bride' and 'Ain Folks'), Cilla *McQueen and Keri *Hulme, who claims mixed descent from Māori, English and Orkney forebears and has valorised that quality of mixed ancestry to oppose notions of 'purity of origin' and patriarchal, linear chronologies. Alistair Te Ariki *Campbell is son of a Cook Islands woman by a New Zealand trader called 'Jock' Campbell. John *Summers's mystery novel *Fernie Brae* (1984) is written almost entirely in Scots. Fiona *Kidman's novel, *The *Book of Secrets* (1987), tells the saga of the Scots immigrants who settled in the North Island at Waipu.

The Scottish academic tradition has been strong in New Zealand literary studies, including John Macmillan *Brown and Ian *Gordon. Waikato University Professor Marshall Walker has produced a major study of Scottish literature and Alan *Riach (also Waikato) an edition of MacDiarmid.

This itemised catalogue might be extended but the question of nationality is most pressing when it reflects anxiety about identity. Multicultural nationality is the late-twentieth-century condition, whether in New Zealand or Scotland. Riach's poetry unsentimentally registers both loss and the opportunities afforded by the distance between New Zealand residence and his native Scotland. Perhaps this continuing dialectic signals the impossibility of considering any literature as something that can be defined in national or even geographical terms as purely autonomous.   AR

SCOTT, Dick (Richard George) (1923–), historian and journalist, was born in Palmerston North and completed a Diploma of Agriculture at Massey College in 1943. From 1946 to 1948 he was farming editor for *Southern Cross*, and from 1948 to 1951 a publicity officer for the PSA. He edited the *Transport Worker* 1949–51, and was a union secretary 1953–61. He edited and published the *Wine Review*, 1964–78, was president of the Auckland Branch of *PEN 1977–79, and member of the New Zealand *Literary Fund Advisory Committee 1989–91. His first book *151 Days* (1952) was an account of the *Waterfront dispute of 1951. *The Parihaka Story* (1954) was the first of two books about the Māori pacifist leader Te Whiti, *Ask That Mountain* (1975) being a much fuller account. He wrote several histories of aspects of the Auckland region, including *In Old Mount Albert: Being a History of the District* (1961); *Stock in Trade: Hellaby's First Hundred Years* (1973), the history of a meat company; *Stake in the Country: Assid Abraham Corban* (1977), the biography of a pioneering wine-maker; *Fire on the Clay: The Pakeha Comes to West Auckland* (1979); and *Seven Lives on Salt River* (1979), an account of settlement around the Kaipara Harbour which won the New Zealand Book Award for Non-fiction and the J.M. Sherrard prize for regional history. More general histories were *Inheritors of a Dream: A Pictorial History of New Zealand* (1962) and *Winemakers of New Zealand* (1964). Later Scott turned to Pacific history in *Years of the Pooh Bah: A Cook Islands History* (1991) and *Would a Good Man Die? Niue Island, New Zealand, and the late Mr Larsen* (1993), an account of the murder of a colonial official and its aftermath. Scott's writing combines thorough research with partisan engagement from a humanitarian and multicultural perspective.   PS

SCOTT, Mary (1888–1979), a widely read author of light fiction from the 1940s to the 1970s, was born in Waimate North, descended on her father's side from the Anglican missionary George Clarke and on her mother's side from the Indian missionary Edward Stuart, who became Bishop of Waiapu at Napier, where Scott spent much of her childhood. Educated at Napier HS and

Auckland GS, she won a John Tinline Scholarship and graduated MA (Hons), first class, in English at Auckland University College in 1910. She became a teacher before marrying Walter Scott in 1914 and moving with him to a remote *backblocks farm in the King Country, inland from Kawhia near Mt Pirongia. The story of the many years of pioneering struggle to develop the property and raise a family is movingly told in an autobiography, *Days That Have Been* (1966), and the harsh conditions of backblocks life also inform a grimly realistic novel which Scott wrote in the late 1930s but did not publish until 1957, entitled *The Unwritten Book*. 'The unwritten book' of the title is a novel, 'Toll'—its theme the human costs of physical and social privation—which the protagonist finds herself never able to complete.

Scott's literary career, however, took her in a completely different direction from the realism of *The Unwritten Book*, into the genres of light comedy and *romance. In order to eke out the family income during the *Depression years she began writing humorous sketches about the life of a backblocks farmer's wife, Barbara, publishing them in the *New Zealand Herald* supplement, where they proved so popular that over the next twenty years five collections of them appeared in book form: *Barbara and the New Zealand Back-Blocks* (1936), *Barbara Prospers* (1937), *Life With Barbara* (1944), *Barbara on the Farm* (1953) and *Barbara Sees the Queen* (1954). By the late 1930s she was contributing fourteen articles a month to various newspapers and had begun a long association with the Dunedin *Evening Star* as a weekly columnist; she had also published two early novels in London, *Where the Apple Reddens* (1934) and *And Shadows Flee* (1935), which she later described as 'better buried in oblivion', and contributed stories to the Manchester *Guardian* and other English newspapers. In the 1940s she wrote numerous playlets for amateur performance by Country Women's Institutes, which were published in three collections.

It was not until the early 1950s, partly to fill the gap created by the departure of the last of her four children from the family home, that she began the career as a light romantic novelist by which she came to be best known, not only in New Zealand but in *Germany, where numerous of the novels were translated. In 1953 she published *Breakfast at Six*, the first and most popular of twenty-six light backblocks romances which appeared regularly until 1978, the year before her death. The next two, *Yours to Oblige* (1954) and *Pippa in Paradise* (1955), were also published in London, but in 1956 she began a long association with the publishing firm of *Paul's Book Arcade. A number of her subsequent novels drew on the same fictional community (Te Rimu) and its 'core' characters as her first—including *Tea and Biscuits*

(1961), *Turkey at Twelve* (1968), *Strangers for Tea* (1975), and her last, *Board but No Breakfast* (1978). Another popular series was a trilogy focusing on the grown-up children of a broken marriage, and their rediscovery of family values: *Families Are Fun* (1956), *No Sad Songs* (1960) and *Freddie* (1965). In the 1960s Scott also collaborated with Joyce *West in the writing of five New Zealand thrillers (*Fatal Lady*, *Such Nice People*, *The Mangrove Murder*, *No Red Herrings* and *Who Put It There?*)—written 'for fun', according to the authors, but also in reaction to whodunnits they regarded as farfetched and illogical.

Scott's main local predecessor in the genre of light romance was Rosemary *Rees, but Scott was the first popular novelist to set all her fiction in New Zealand and to think of her readership as primarily a New Zealand one. She also produced a quite original and historically significant variation of the light romance formula. The social context of her fiction was the opening up of the hinterlands of the North Island to small dairy farming in the first three decades of the twentieth century and the growth of a rural culture of scattered backblocks communities serviced by expanding provincial towns. Scott's romances are based wholly in this rural world and celebrate its essentially conservative, character-building virtues, contrasting them with an increasingly negative vision of post-war urban and suburban New Zealand as materialistic, conformist and stifling to individual initiative. Scott's use of the romance formula involved an adaptation of the older colonial polarity between England and New Zealand to this newly perceived internal polarity between town and country, which was also strongly reflected on the national political scene from the 1930s onwards in the opposition between a rural-based National Party and an urban-based Labour Party.

In the older colonial romance, heroines typically were English and the heroes eligible bachelor sheepfarmers on wealthy South Island *stations, in tourist settings of spectacular natural beauty. Scott's settings were altogether more commonplace, premised not on wealth but the struggle to make a farm pay its way, and her 'ordinary' heroines almost invariably came to the country to escape the rat race of life in towns or cities. Marriage to an eligible backblocks bachelor involved a process of self-discovery closely linked to the discovery of the superior community values of rural life. In effect, the backblocks provided a moral testing-ground for characters, outsiders as well as wayward insiders, challenging them to develop qualities of self-reliance and concern for others. Although the overall effect is an idealisation of the backblocks, Scott is also careful to introduce discordant elements into her close-knit communities: gossip, interference in the lives of others, local snobberies and rivalries. Overall, also, the novels provide insight into the daily lives of rural women and a lively record of the social life of backblocks communities: the importance of the party-line telephone and the local general store, and of events like dances, Women's Institute theatricals, Christmas parties, flower shows, dog trials, and race meetings. They also record the gradual transformation of the backblocks: the improvement of roads and properties and amenities, the invasion of tourism. Despite such changes, one of the last novels Scott wrote, *Away from It All* (1977), still celebrated the spirit of 'spontaneous friendliness' which she saw as surviving the breaking down of remoteness.

TS

SCOTT, Rosie (1948–), is a successful writer of fictions about the energy and anguish of contemporary life. Born in Johnsonville, Wellington, she took an MA (Hons) in English at Victoria University and the Diploma in Drama at Auckland. An itinerant period in social work, publishing, journalism, waitressing and acting in far-flung locations from Nouméa to London provided material for her inventively written tales of career girls, drug addicts, family women and queens of love in the shifting cinematic dreamworld of modern society. She started with a volume of poems, *Flesh and Blood* (1984) and a play, 'Say Thank You to the Lady'. Produced in 1985 at Mercury 2, Auckland, this presents a Pākehā social worker who discovers in a lawless Māori girl a model for the strength she herself needs to break free of oppression in marriage and work. The play was popular and Scott won the 1986 Bruce Mason Award. Its short filmic scenes adapted well to the feature film version, *Redheads*, for which she was script editor.

Her first novel, *Glory Days* (1988), was shortlisted for the New Zealand Book Awards and published internationally. *Queen of Love* (1989) is a collection of clear-sighted, hard-nosed stories about women's relationships, competitiveness and sexiness, and *Nights with Grace* (1990) is equally forthright yet lyrical about 'that lovely drenched expectant silence before sex'. Scott can handle abandonment to a passionate affair on a dreamy *Pacific island without ever using a cliché in language or plot. Her later novels deal more with the dehumanising superficiality and angst of the city: *Feral City* (1992), *Lives on Fire* (1993) and *Movie Dreams* (1995). Their writing fortunately is never as dreary or burnt out as the people they describe, having wit, vitality and a good ear for phrase and image: 'We were lying in bed, the old fan lolloping above us like a live thing … mosquitoes whining tinnily in the hills and valleys of the bedclothes….'

All Scott's recent books have been internationally published and translated; she has published in *Rolling Stone*, *Metro* and elsewhere. She works on film scripting, including *Glory Days*. Since the late 1980s she has lived in *Australia (Brisbane, then Sydney) and has received support from the Literature Board of the Australia Council. Like most literary migrants there, she has lamented (in *Hecate*, 1992) the lack of interaction across the Tasman.

RR/DC

SCOTT, Tom (1947–), has made a distinctive dual contribution to the renaissance of New Zealand comic satire (see also A.K. *Grant and Roger *Hall). Born in London, he arrived in 1949 and was educated at Feilding Agricultural HS and Massey University, where he gained a BSc in Physiology and a reputation for hilarious contributions to student 'capping magazines'. After briefly lecturing at Central Institute of Technology (which sounded, he later wrote, 'like one of those asylums the Soviets maintain high in the Arctic Circle exclusively for dissidents'), he was recruited by Ian *Cross in 1973 as part of his revitalisation of the *NZ Listener. Scott's collections have been published as *Tom Scott's Life and Times* (1977), *Snakes and Leaders* (1981), *Ten Years Inside* (1985) and *Private Parts* (1990). He has also published a humorous travel memoir, *Overseizure* (1978), a book on drug abuse, *The Great Brain Robbery* (1996), and several collections of cartoons, including the *Tom Scott Cartoon Annual* (1992, 1993) and illustrations to A.K. Grant's comic history, *The Paua and the Glory* (1982) and its sequel, *Corridors of Paua* (1996). His scripts for television include the major political docudrama about the end of the *Muldoon era and the ANZUS anti-nuclear crisis, *Fallout* (with Greg *McGee, 1994), and for film *Footrot Flats—The Movie* (with Murray Ball).

Scott's writing exudes personal warmth and projects a characteristically Kiwi persona—insignificant, vulnerable, droll, but fearlessly determined to have his say. This makes his satire less than savage and enhances its sense of moral commitment. Bumbling or Lilliputian though he purports to be, Scott has influenced New Zealand thinking and given offence to prime ministers, supporters of foreign governments and both sides in the 1981 Springbok tour dispute (when his professed membership of 'Cowards Against the Tour' endeared him to many who shared an aversion to batons). The personal dimension also enables him to write or draw from the heart when he so feels, for instance on the death of Prime Minister Norman Kirk in 1974. It also makes him an engaging raconteur of private or domestic events (his accounts in *Private Parts* of his encounter with a rural lifestyle are memorable); and gives his political narratives, even when blatantly whimsical and invented, their beguiling air of being informed insider gossip. In the late 1990s Scott is a cartoonist with the Wellington *Evening*

Post and writes on a freelance basis for the *Listener* and other journals.   RR

Season of the Jew (1986), novel, see **SHADBOLT, Maurice; War literature: New Zealand Wars**.

Selected Poems 1940–1989 by Allen ⋆Curnow (UK, 1990) eschews chronological ordering for a three-part thematic arrangement, in which the book begins and ends with recently written poems evoking childhood, while earlier-written poems are mostly grouped in a middle section. In a Preface the poet notes: 'The poems may or may not, as the reader pleases, seem to describe a kind of circle joining age and youth, a loop in the road.' Only one poem, 'An Evening Light' was previously uncollected.   PS

SEWELL, William or **Bill** (1951–), poet, was born in Athens and spent much of his early life in various parts of Southern Europe (Barcelona, Ankara and Beirut). After primary and secondary schooling in England, he finished his education in New Zealand where he studied German at the University of Auckland and completed a doctorate on the poetry and politics of Hans Magnus Enzensberger. He lectured in German at Otago University, worked as an editor for ⋆John McIndoe and the University of Otago Press and, after obtaining a law degree from Victoria University of Wellington, was a legal researcher for the Law Commission and is a freelance writer and editor.

Sewell was ⋆Burns Fellow at Otago University in 1981 and 1982, and president of the ⋆New Zealand Poetry Society in the early 1990s. He has published three collections of poems, *Solo Flight* (1982), *Wheels Within Wheels* (1983), and *Making the Far Land Glow* (1986), and also *A Guide to the Rimutaka Forest Park* (1989). Sewell's work, though usually local in its setting, demonstrates in its practice his engagement with modern European, particularly German, poetry. His articulate, carefully orchestrated poems are notable for their restrained lyricism, political focus and an undertow of laconic humour. 'Solo Flight', a series of meditations about the South Canterbury aviator Richard Pearse, 'Otago Studies' ('evening crinkles the land / into folds of the brain') and the uncollected 'El Sur' ('Silence has a word / for most things; / if not, a grunted / syllable must do') attest to his liking for the poetic sequence and are among his most impressive achievements in this line. He is a frequent reviewer, especially for ⋆*New Zealand Books*, becoming co-editor in 1997. He edited *Sons of the Father: New Zealand Men Write About Their Fathers* (1997) and co-edited *Under Review: A Selection from 'New Zealand Books' 1991–1996* (1997).   HRi

SHACKLETON, Bernice (1901–), born in Waimate, became one of the highest-achieving women in journalism. Educated at Columba College, Dunedin, she gained a Diploma in Journalism at Canterbury University College in 1928, and became a reporter on the *Christchurch Star*, leaving after a judge ordered her out of the courtroom because of an 'unsavoury' case. Articles about her overseas travels earned her another position on the *Star*, as assistant to the editor, 1930–35, then the highest position a woman had attained on a major daily. She was responsible for the leader page, writing editorials, a column, and a special feature 'A Woman's Point of View'. She became a freelance parliamentary reporter in 1936 and 1938, knowing that no newspaper would send her officially. Returning home in 1939 to look after her ageing parents, she later worked for Corso, and was a member of the Waimate Hospital Board. Her book *The Fifth Schedule* (1984) is 'a significant study of the place of the small hospital in the New Zealand health system'. She was awarded the QSM.   JMcC

SHADBOLT, Maurice (1932–), fiction writer and playwright, was born in Auckland and educated at Te Kuiti HS, Avondale College and Auckland University College. He worked as a journalist for various New Zealand newspapers and as a scriptwriter and director of documentary films for the New Zealand National Film Unit until 1957, when he left for Europe. This period of his life is recorded in *One of Ben's: A New Zealand Medley* (1993). Before he returned in 1960 he published his first book, a collection of stories grandly titled *The* ⋆*New Zealanders* (1959). Although the book brought Shadbolt immediate recognition in Britain, where it was highly praised by such influential reviewers as Alan Sillitoe and Muriel Spark, in New Zealand the critical response was predominantly, and probably unfairly, negative. The eleven stories chronicle New Zealand's social history during the first half of the twentieth century, introducing themes which have remained important throughout Shadbolt's oeuvre. In his next collection of stories, *Summer Fires and Winter Country* (1963) Shadbolt continues to chronicle the lives of young New Zealanders of his own generation. The impressive opening story, 'Ben's Land', draws on his own family history, and introduces material which would later be reworked in his first novel, ⋆*Among the Cinders* (1965), expanded in *The* ⋆*Lovelock Version* (1980), and revisited again in his later autobiographical work, *One of Ben's. Among the Cinders*, which began as a satire on contemporary New Zealand literature, is best read as a realist novel which explores New Zealand's history from the pioneering days to the 1950s through the relationship between the adolescent Nick Flinders and his grandfather Hubert. Here

Shadbolt found a pattern for treating past and present that he would reuse and develop in later works. He then published another collection of short fiction, *The Presence of Music* (1967), a triptych of three novellas which deal with the theme of the artist in society, his last collection of new stories for almost thirty years. (*Figures in Light: Selected Stories* was published in 1978.)

Shadbolt's next two novels, *This Summer's Dolphin* (1969) and *An Ear of the Dragon* (1971) have been referred to as distractions from the task of completing *Strangers and Journeys* (1972). *This Summer's Dolphin* is a short novel inspired by the story of Opo the dolphin, whose famous sojourn at the beach of Opononi had been the subject of a film Shadbolt made in 1956. The novel focuses on isolated characters whose separate stories are linked only by their tenuous connection to the mysterious dolphin. As the coherence here is in the story of Opo, so the pattern for *An Ear of the Dragon* is in the life of Renato *Amato, and Shadbolt's blatant reconstruction of Amato's life generated considerable criticism. The use Shadbolt makes of historical flashbacks in the stories of Pietro Fratta (Amato) and Frank Firth (possibly a persona of the author) is particularly skilful. *Strangers and Journeys* then followed, a long, ambitious novel, both accomplished and flawed, which took Shadbolt ten years to complete. It draws together many of the themes and characters of his earlier work, in what is essentially a contrast between the lives of two representative fathers and sons (and it is worth noting here the predominant focus on male characters in Shadbolt's fiction). The earlier sections, which deal with the lives of the fathers as they battle against both the environment and the harsh economic times, are generally recognised as the strongest. As the work moves closer to the present, to the city, and to the lives of the sons it tends to lose its way.

In many respects *Strangers and Journeys* marked the end of a phase. Shadbolt had largely focused on contemporary New Zealand and explored the position of the artist in society. His next two novels, *A *Touch of Clay* (1974) and *Danger Zone* (1975), are two parts of an unfinished trilogy of the 1970s, and mark something of a digression. *A Touch of Clay* focuses on the relationship between an ex-lawyer turned potter and a drug-dependent young woman from a nearby commune. It continues Shadbolt's interest in the relationship between the artist and society, and between individuals and their environment, but lacks the scope of *Strangers and Journeys*. Of particular note is the nineteenth-century strand provided by the potter's grandfather's diaries, which may have prompted Shadbolt to turn more fully to the past, first in *The Lovelock Version* and later in the *New Zealand Wars trilogy, where he undoubtedly found his métier. *Danger Zone* sits somewhat incon-

gruously in his oeuvre. Linked to *A Touch of Clay* only by its focus on the search for inner meaning of its central characters, it focuses on New Zealand's opposition to nuclear testing the the South *Pacific, and is loosely based on Shadbolt's own voyage to Mururoa on board the protest vessel *Tamure* in 1972.

In 1980 Shadbolt published his first historical novel, *The Lovelock Version*, his most exuberant and possibly his finest novel to date, which marked a shift to engagement with nineteenth-century history, the richest seam Shadbolt has thus far explored. In *Among the Cinders*, *A Touch of Clay* and *Strangers and Journeys*, the past, predominantly in the form of family history, has permeated his fiction while nevertheless remaining in the background; here for the first time it is foregrounded in the three pioneering Lovelock brothers and their families, whose stories (and the many digressions those lead into) present the full sweep of early Pākehā history. In this novel Shadbolt skilfully blends the techniques of magic realism and metafiction with the realist mode to present a tragicomic and above all entertaining version of New Zealand history. It confirms that he is first and foremost a magnificent storyteller. The Gallipoli strand in *The Lovelock Version*, and Shadbolt's consuming interest in those events, led to his only published play, *Once on Chunuk Bair* (1982), and later to a work of non-fiction, *Voices of Gallipoli* (1988). The play treats the battle as a moment of historical definition when a colonial country realised its postcolonial identity.

Following this excursion into drama Shadbolt returned to the historical novel with the New Zealand Wars trilogy, a triptych of revisionist-historical novels: *Season of the Jew* (1986), *Monday's Warriors* (1990) and *The House of Strife* (1993). They form perhaps the most important work of historical fiction yet produced by a New Zealand writer. The first focuses on *Te Kooti's Poverty Bay campaigns of the 1860s (and invites comparison with 'The Song of Te Kooti' section in Witi *Ihimaera's *The *Matriarch*, also published in 1986). *Monday's Warriors* moves to Taranaki, also in the 1860s, and the stories of Tītokowaru and the rebel American Kimball Bent. Here Shadbolt is mining ground already cleared in *The Lovelock Version* where Tītokowaru, Kimball Bent and Von Tempsky all appear. *The House of Strife* moves back in time to the 1845–46 rebellion of Hone Heke, who cut down the flagpole above what is now Russell in the Bay of Islands on four occasions. Common to each novel is a central Pākehā figure —George Fairweather, Kimball Bent and the Ferdinand Wildblood/Henry Youngman doppelgänger—whose sympathies lie more with the Māori side than with the colonisers, and who provide Shadbolt with a detached narrative position. Together the three volumes offer a revised version of the New Zealand ★Wars. More importantly, they remind us that history is above all else story, and that there are many versions of it. Shadbolt's work to date now presents a distinctive version of the whole of postcolonisation New Zealand history.

History is also at the heart of his first autobiographical work, *One of Ben's*, a family history of national consequence which skilfully mixes the myths and legends of the Shadbolt tribe with those of postcolonisation Pākehā New Zealand. After a gap of almost thirty years Shadbolt returned to the short story with 'Dove on the Waters', which won the Bank of New Zealand Katherine ★Mansfield Memorial Award in 1995. That and two more novella-length stories were published in 1996.

Maurice Shadbolt is a major New Zealand writer, with an impressive body of work which also includes successful non-fiction work such as the *Shell Guide to New Zealand* (1968). In a writing career which now spans five decades he has won fellowhips and almost every major literary prize, some on more than one occasion: the ★Landfall Prose Award in 1957, the Scholarship in Letters in 1959, 1970 and 1982, the Katherine Mansfield Memorial Award in 1963, 1967 and 1995, the ★Burns Fellowship in 1963, the Katherine ★Mansfield Memorial Fellowship in 1998, the James Wattie Award in 1978, 1981 and 1987, and the New Zealand Book Award in 1981. In 1989 he was made CBE. Above all, however, Shadbolt should be recognised for his storytelling talent. That almost all his books remain in print is testament to his enduring popularity with a wide reading public. RC

Shakespeare in New Zealand. Shakespeare knew of the 'South Sea of discovery' (*As You Like It* 3.2.197), and referred frequently to what the Renaissance imagined the peoples and landscapes of the 'antipodes'—the reverse of Europe—would be like. Yet F.E. ★Maning's claim, in his joco-serious classic *Old New Zealand* (1863), 'I don't believe Shakespeare ever was in New Zealand', is certainly correct. Nevertheless, since 1769, when a copy of Shakespeare's works sailed on the *Endeavour* as part of Sydney ★Parkinson's library, Shakespeare has exercised a lasting influence on Pākehā culture, a legacy New Zealand shares with all of Britain's former colonies. ★Cook's journals never allude to Shakespeare, but later travellers frequently invoked the Shakespearean sublime to record their reactions to new terrains, as in Edward Jerningham ★Wakefield's praise, in his *Adventure in New Zealand* (1845) of 'the abundance of the second crops in the existing native gardens' which reminded him 'touchingly of Shakespeare's sweet picture of the perfection of agriculture'. Maning's *Tale of the Good Old Times* is the most engaging of such accounts. 'Pigs and potatoes have degenerated; and everything

seems "flat, stale, and unprofitable."' He cites Hamlet's melancholy (*Ham.* 1.2.133), but his title page presents his memoir rather as tales of 'Anthropophagi, and men whose heads do grow BETWEEN their shoulders,' revising *Othello* 1.3.144.

In the settler period after 1840, Shakespeare served as secular scripture, as ★Sargeson records in his essay 'Shakespeare and the Kiwi' with many homes possessing a *Collected Works* 'the one volume copy printed in double columns' surpassed in importance only by the 'supremacy of the family Bible'. Sargeson's essay was first published (together with birthday tributes also by James ★Bertram, Ngaio ★Marsh and D.F. McKenzie) in ★*Landfall* 18 (1964) to mark the Shakespeare tercentenary. Sargeson laments that, despite Shakespeare's status as cultural talisman, his works remained unread by the New Zealand public. New Zealand writers in contrast were, as Katherine ★Mansfield puts it, 'steeped in Shakespeare', as in such neo-Shakespearean dramas as W.H. ★Guthrie-Smith's *Crispus* (1895) and R.T. Hammond's *Under the Shadow of Dread* (1908) which 'shakespearises' King Alfred's combat against Danish invaders. Mansfield was herself a vivid Shakespearean critic, especially fond of the sheep-shearing feast in *The Winter's Tale* (4.2); *Twelfth Night* ; and the 'dream islands' of *The Tempest*, in which she imagined herself and Middleton ★Murry as Miranda and Ferdinand. Hotspur's line, 'But I tell you, my lord fool, out of this nettle danger, we pluck this flower, safety', became a motto of her later years, used in the title of 'This Flower', proposed as epigraph to the collection *Bliss and Other Stories*, and inscribed by Murry on her tombstone. The autobiographies of Ngaio ★Marsh and Janet ★Frame record the inception at high school of lifelong obsessions with Shakespeare. Marsh's fiction depicts Shakespearean actors and productions; *Death at the Dolphin* (1967) features a glove Shakespeare may have given to Ann Hathaway. Her last novel *Light Thickens* (1982) summarises Shakespeare's importance to her: murder takes place on stage during a production of *Macbeth*. The novel lovingly evokes the play and mid-twentieth-century patterns of rehearsal and performance.

Shakespeare pervades Frame's fictions more elusively. Ariel's longing for island freedom shapes the title and text of ★*Owls Do Cry* (1957); Istina Mavet's copy of the *Complete Works* in ★*Faces in the Water* (1961) begins 'to read itself' for 'the book understood how things were', transforming Mavet's evocation of madness from the picturesque, 'easy Opheliana recited like the pages of a seed catalog' to invoking the inhabitants of her asylum in 'the desperate season of their lives'. Frame enlists Shakespeare on the side of those in revolt against 1950s conformity; and should be read against M.K.

*Joseph's satire on provincial campus life, A *Pound of Saffron (1962), in which an unscrupulous drama lecturer stages an outdoor production of Anthony and Cleopatra besides One Tree Hill; the follies the production reveals remain the stock of campus life, and Shakespeare outdoors (which Joseph depicts as a stylish provincial novelty) became increasingly common in the 1980s and 1990s. Marsh, Frame and Joseph seek to define forms of Shakespearean nationalism. Later writers draw on Shakespeare less patriotically. Mike *Doyle's Lear: The Shakespeare Company Performs Lear at Babylon (1986) envisions the tragedy as performed in some dystopian yet biblical future. King Lear's characters perform with postmodern self-consciousness their own stories from the play; the text avoids overt questions of nation. Jean Betts's Revenge of the Amazons (1983) is a comic feminist burlesque of A Midsummer Night's Dream, and her Ophelia Thinks Harder (1994) transforms Hamlet into a feminist cartoon, laying waste to the play's sexism, giving Ophelia Hamlet's best lines. Though written for the centenary of *women's suffrage in New Zealand 1993, its appeal too seems more international than local.

New Zealand writers have also been enthusiastic commentators on Shakespeare's works: Marsh herself spoke frequently as a populariser of Shakespeare; the *Alexander Turnbull Library holds transcripts of many of these talks. Percy J. Marks' Australasian Shakespeareana: A Bibliography of Books, Pamphlets, Magazine Articles &c., that have been printed in Australia and New Zealand, dealing with Shakespeare and his works (1915) lists work by Victorian and Edwardian scholars. Commentators ranged from professionals like John Macmillan *Brown, professor of English at Canterbury College, who published studies of Julius Caesar and The Merchant of Venice (1900), to the truly obsessive: J.G.S. *Grant (1838–1902), who published a barrage of pamphlets anthologising highlights from Shakespeare whilst advocating his own salty opinions on a brace of Dunedin topics. Louis Direy published in Gisborne a French version of the sonnets, William Shakespeare, Son Poème, Les Sonnets (1891); sixty years later Pei Te Hurinui *Jones translated The Merchant of Venice into Māori as Te Tangata Whai-rawa o Weniti (1946).

Macmillan Brown anticipated a later age of professional specialisation. The expansion of New Zealand universities after World War 2, in particular, saw the importing or return home of a number of scholars who achieved eminence writing on Shakespeare and his era: Arthur Sewell, Sydney Musgrove, who encouraged at Auckland the study of Shakespearean texts, as in James Walton's The Copy for the Folio Text of Richard III (1955). This work was taken into the age of computer

stylometrics by MacDonald P. Jackson, whose publications on Shakespeare's texts receive worldwide attention; as do D.F. McKenzie's significant contributions to the study of the printing of texts and the history of the book in Shakespeare's era.

The prevalence of Shakespeare in university curricula ensured him a wide currency, influencing especially generations of high school teachers and students. By the 1990s, Shakespeare had become the only pre-modern author all high school students would have read. The grim compulsion of examination syllabi was attended by a fresh wave of enthusiasm for the Bard. The 1990s saw the creation also of several high school student clubs devoted exclusively to the performance of Shakespeare (similar Shakespeare clubs and societies, such as the Hamilton one to which Frank Sargeson belonged as a boy, were popular in the early part of the twentieth century). Membership of these in the 1990s was doubtless boosted by the popular film versions of Hamlet (both Mel Gibson's 1990 and Kenneth Branagh's 1996 performances); Branagh's Henry V (1989) and Much Ado About Nothing (1993); and the Romeo and Juliet (1996) starring the American 'slacker' heart-throb, Leonardo DiCaprio. The Stratford Shakespeare Festival was formed in 1990, featuring a biennial celebration of Shakespeare in Stratford, Taranaki ('where all the streets are named for Shakespeare'), with screenings, full performances, street parades and workshops for teachers. Dawn Sanders' Very Public Hangings: the Story Behind New Zealand's Gift to the Globe Theatre London (1992) records the material legacy of this late-twentieth-century Shakespearean zealotry; the large tapestries stitched by over 500 New Zealand needleworkers hang permanently in the new Wanamaker Globe in London, which opened in 1996. They depict Renaissance subjects: Venus, Adonis, Hercules, Atlas, in vibrant colours and with piquant New Zealand touches: a taniwha here, a spring lamb there. The visits to Wellington's International Arts Festival of the Royal Shakespeare Company in 1994, performing Adrian Noble's novelistic version of The Winter's Tale, and the Royal National Theatre with Othello in 1998, epitomised this pre-millennial fervour.

New Zealanders have long since become accustomed to New Zealand performances of Shakespeare. These visits were a return to the nineteenth and early-twentieth-century pattern of Shakespeare performed by touring English troupes, including New Zealand as part of their Australasian itineraries. Theatres Royal were built throughout the colony; Shakespeare featured amidst more standard nineteenth-century melodrama and farce. The tone of such Shakespeares is richly evoked by H.F. McKillop's account, in his Reminiscences of Twelve Months' Service in New Zealand (1849), of seeing a Macbeth in Port

Nicholson in 1846, during which, to the 'uproarious … laughter' of the crowd, Macbeth enlivened 'some long soliloquy' by singing and dancing the sailor's hornpipe. This is perhaps the first recorded Shakespearean performance in New Zealand. Probably less uproarious was the *Othello* at Auckland's *Theatre Royal* in 1856. In the 1870s *Hamlet* together with *Othello* dominated the Auckland Shakespeare repertoire. Victorian interest in the latter was recreated by *Theatre at Large*'s excoriating *Savage Hearts* (1993), which dramatised interracial passion within a touring company performing *Othello* in the colony. John Thomson (*The New Zealand Stage 1891–1900*, 1993) and Howard McNaughton (*New Zealand Theatre Annals: Christchurch, 1900–1919*, 1983) record several companies performing Shakespeare in this period; these productions have yet to be analysed in detail. Rose Seager acted a 'deeply impressive' Lady Macbeth in 1890 for George Milne. Her daughter Ngaio Marsh toured with the Allan Wilkie company in the early 1920s; relating her experiences in *Black Beech and Honeydew* (1965) and the fictional *Vintage Murder* (1937). Wilkie was the last of the actor-managers to tour Shakespeare: the novelty of cinema saw audiences for live theatre in the 1920s–30s fall away.

Mid-century performances were dominated by amateur repertory groups, most importantly the Shakespeares performed by students at the University of Canterbury and directed by Ngaio Marsh, beginning with *Hamlet* in 1943, and concluding with the community *Henry V* which opened the James Hay Theatre in the new Christchurch Town Hall in 1972, featuring Jonathan Elsom as the Chorus disguised as Shakespeare. The expatriate scholar J.G.A. Pocock acclaimed the first ten years of Marsh's Shakespeares as a 'golden age' of New Zealand theatre. Marsh was strongly influenced by the famous 1940s–50s productions and performances by Tyrone Guthrie, Ralph Richardson and Laurence Olivier, who also performed in New Zealand in 1948 with Vivien Leigh. Marsh insisted that New Zealanders too could perform to high Shakespearean standards, though she demanded they abandon their flat, unmusical accents to do so. In his 1982 elegy for Marsh (in *Landfall* 144) Mervyn *Thompson lamented Marsh's reduction of Shakespeare's texts to thrillers; yet her productions profoundly influenced Thompson's future career as director and playwright. His 1972 *King Lear* for the Court Theatre was one of the most powerful Shakespeare productions of recent decades. Sam Neill and James Laurenson, who achieved later fame as film and TV stars, learned their first Shakespeare from Marsh. Her company toured New Zealand in 1944–45, and was acclaimed in Australia in 1949. The productions were enthusiastically received by a Bard-hungry Christchurch public. One Dunedin fan, who thanked Marsh for her 1958 *Hamlet,* lamented that she would herself have played Ophelia as a girl, had not 'Scarlet fever stepped in & dealt me a very sad blow'. The Marsh archives in the Turnbull Library contain promptbooks for Marsh's productions; their details record vividly the gloss of her production style.

Marsh longed for a national professional theatre, but this was not achieved until repertory companies were established in the 1960s in the four main cities. Her Shakespeares set an important precedent for Mercury and Theatre Corporate (Auckland), Downstage and Circa (Wellington), the Court (Christchurch) and Patric Carey's Globe (Dunedin), as they frequently strove to marry Shakespearean texts with professional New Zealand actors. The results took competent, live productions to more people than at any time since the Wilkie Company stopped touring; though by the early 1990s most professional theatre companies found Shakespeare too expensive to stage regularly. In 1964 students and staff performed Shakespeare in the quad below Auckland University's clock tower; the production is now an annual event. The practice has spread nationwide: Victoria's drama students perform Summer Shakespeare in the Dell of Wellington's Botanical Gardens or the less pastoral Civic Square; Hamilton actors have presented dawn Shakespeares on the banks of the Waikato, and taken the bard to the beaches of the Bay of Plenty.

Production styles have mirrored larger shifts in Pākehā culture. Standards of excellence must have varied: Mrs W.H. Foley's star turns as both Desdemona and Emilia in the 1860s perhaps made up in brio what they may have lacked in nuance. Until Marsh's time, colonial mimicry of English performances and accents seems to have been the order of the day; Shakespeares since have progressively been influenced by nationalist reinventions and exposure to international performances on film and video, which have assisted a shift in acting from the declamatory to the psychological. Settings have become increasingly experimental, from the Globe's 1971 *Hamlet 2000* with its 'amazing Freudian headgear' to Colin McColl and Warwick Broadhead's visionary 1986 *Tempest* at Downstage, which its eclectic barrage of 'Balinese and Japanese influences … flexible drainpipes [and] wheelchair parades'. Broadhead anticipated a 1990s wave of cultural hybridity: *The Winter's Tale* pastoral replaced by Fred Dagg (John *Clarke) songs, *As You Like It* at a Kiwi beach, *Romeo and Juliet* set within two warring Samoan families. By the mid-1990s, then, Shakespeare remained a fixture of high and popular culture in 'the South Sea of discovery', now frequently recast in multiple Pacific forms.   MH

SHARP, Iain (1953–), poet and critic, emigrated from Glasgow to Auckland at the age of 8 and apart from two years at Victoria University of Wellington, has resided there ever since, working first as a librarian and then journalist. While completing an Auckland University PhD on the Jacobean comedy *Wit at Several Weapons*, he participated in pub poetry readings in the early 1980s. One of his performances is captured on *The Globe Tapes* (1985). He continues to be an effective performer, touring in 1995 with Lauris ★Edmond and David ★Eggleton. He has had three books of poetry published, *Why Mammals Shiver* (1981), *She Is Trying to Kidnap the Blind Person* and *The Pierrot Variations* (both 1985), which all share with the subject of his thesis an uncommon wit. The humour is usually self-directed in the manner of the Pierrot figure featured in the title of his third volume. The poems are predominantly short lyrics marked by a gentle pathos. However, just as the Pierrot character has a rich literary history, Sharp often good-naturedly satirises the high seriousness of his own literary heritage, as in the whimsical 'Jiving with Charles ★Brasch'. He was, for a short time, fiction editor of ★*Landfall* and has also edited ★*Printout*. A prolific columnist, reviewer and critic, he edits the book page of the *Sunday Star-Times*. His latest book, *Sail the Spirit* (1994), is a history of the Spirit of Adventure Trust. He also wrote the chapter on New Zealand for the *Oxford Guide to Contemporary Writing* (1996).   NWt

SHARPE, Alfred (1836–1908), is described by his principal biographer, Roger Blackley, as the 'most communicative of all artists working in nineteenth-century New Zealand'. Highly regarded as a colonial period watercolourist, Sharpe has also come to light as a poet, art critic, theorist and polemical essayist writing regularly in newspapers in Auckland (where he lived 1859–87) and Newcastle, New South Wales (where he lived until his death). Profoundly deaf, Sharpe wrote and painted as a means to contribute to cultural life. His deep regard for nature, evident in the highly detailed, large-scale watercolours he produced for exhibition at the Auckland Art Society in the 1870s–80s, is mirrored in his poetry and writings. Blackley has located some sixty poems, published 1878–86, and hundreds of letters, essays and articles published under various pseudonyms, including 'Asmodeus', 'Amicus' and 'Arboricultus'. Lines like '... aneath some sylvan temple / Where man's foot hath seldom trod / Read I, in the tome of Nature / Wondrous things of Nature's God' (*New Zealand Herald*, 1888) are literary corollaries to the visual records he left of the bush and countryside in the Auckland and Coromandel regions. An archive of his writings has been established in the Research Library at Auckland Art Gallery.   CB

SHAW, George Bernard (1859–1950), the Irish playwright, visited New Zealand memorably in 1934 (15 March–14 April), to a very favourable reception which he described as 'a sort of Royal progress'. He formed equally favourable impressions: 'If I were beginning life, I am not sure that I would not start in New Zealand.' His biographer Michael Holroyd suggests New Zealand seemed like an idealised Ireland. Shaw liked its peacefully attained social reforms, its infant care, the ★Alexander Turnbull Library ('a treasure house'), its opportunities for outdoor exercise (he was photographed resplendent in bathing costume and robe at Mount Maunganui) and true Māori music ('practically a Gregorian chant with a touch of the pibroch'). He urged his hosts to develop a more diversified economy, build a local film industry ('or you will lose your souls') and 'chuck the silly Empire'. He carried away a souvenir copy of ★*Children of the Poor* and wrote from the *Rangitane* on the homeward voyage to New Zealand author George Macdonald Henderson (*Collected Letters 4*, ed. Dan H. Laurence). His other main contact with New Zealand literature was an interview in Christchurch by a student journalist called Denis ★Glover, who warned him that 'anything he said would be newsed against him'. According to the headline in *Canta*, the university paper, the encounter was one of 'Mutual Admiration'. Shaw had long been an advocate of Samuel ★Butler, deriving his own 'religion' of Creative Evolution from the ideas Butler had first explored in the ★*Press* and ★*Erewhon* and had developed fully in evolutionary works such as *Luck or Cunning*, which Shaw reviewed in 1887.   RR

SHAW, Helen (1913–85), was a short story writer, poet and editor. She was born in Timaru. When her father was killed on the Somme in 1916, she was raised by her mother in her maternal grandparents' home. She graduated BA in English literature at Canterbury University College, where she met Antony ★Alpers, who became a lifelong friend. Though graduating from Christchurch Teachers' College, she decided against teaching in favour of casual work and writing freelance features and stories. The ★*Press* and the *Press Junior* began publishing her work in 1937 and she flatted with the editor of *Press Junior*, Jean Stevenson (later married to James ★Bertram). In 1941 Shaw married in Auckland, where she was to remain until her death. In 1942 she became a columnist for the *New Zealand Observer* and began writing short stories. The first published was 'The Two Fathers' in ★*New Zealand New Writing*, ed. I.A. ★Gordon (1943), followed by 'Noah' in ★*Speaking For Ourselves*, ed. Frank ★Sargeson (1947), 'After the Dark' in ★*Arachne* (1950), ed. Erik Schwimmer, and 'The Blind' in *Arachne* (1951). The latter two stories establish the main preoccupations and techniques of Shaw's fiction. A Gothic atmosphere is evoked through the use of expository detail, which symbolises the decaying inner lives of the characters and their environment. There is an emphasis on the past and how it impacts on the present, which the English poet Kathleen Raine, in an unpublished letter to Shaw in 1979, interpreted as 'the faint last echoes of the music ... of a civilisation most have never imagined'. Shaw's Symbolist approach and her mannered prose and dialogue differentiated her writing from the prevailing literary realism. In an unpublished journal entry, Shaw wrote: 'The source of derivation is not an outside scene, observed, but an interior scene, raised up, discovered.' (1976) Her work was not appreciated by some influential critics and publishers. In *New Zealand Literature—A Survey* (1959) E.H. *McCormick wrote that in her stories '[the] point is obscured rather than revealed by a decorative symbolism'. Charles *Brasch, editor of *Landfall, only published a handful of her stories. Over twenty years separated publication of her first collection, *The Orange Tree and Other Stories* (1957), from her last, *The Gypsies* (1978).

Through the 1950s and into the 1960s, Shaw continued to write stories; she also began diversifying into criticism, poetry and meditations. Shaw's poetry and meditations, inspired by her interest in the 'interior scene', mark the development of mysticism which was central to her writing. Her first collection of poetry, *Out of the Dark* (1968), was followed by seven further collections between 1970 and 1985, the last of which, *Leda's Daughter*, was published posthumously. Her first criticism, *The Puritan and the Waif: A Symposium of Critical Essays on the Work of Frank Sargeson* (1954) was self-published, under her Mandala Editions imprint. During the 1970s–80s Shaw edited the sonnets and letters of D'Arcy *Cresswell, culminating in publication of *Dear Lady Ginger, An Exchange of Letters between Lady Ottoline Morrell and D'Arcy Cresswell* (1983), which includes Morrell's essay on Katherine *Mansfield. No full life has been published, though the preface to a collection of Shaw's meditations, *I Listen* (1955), ed. D. Knowles, includes biographical details, as does the Shaw entry in *The Book of New Zealand Women* (1991). For a critical overview, see Lawrence *Jones's 'The Inside Story: Helen Shaw, Russell *Haley, & the Other Tradition', *Islands* 31–32 (1981).   DK/SSa

SHAW, Tina (1961–), born in Auckland, spent her early years in Matangi, near Hamilton, and Christchurch, before returning to Auckland. She won the Newcomer's Award in the 1991 Mobil *Dominion Sunday Times* short story competition, and other stories have appeared in magazines and teenage anthologies, and have

been broadcast on radio. Her first novel, *Birdie* (1996), won praise, particularly for its dynamic portrayal of an alienated young woman working in an Auckland strip club. Her second was *Dreams of America* (1997).   KI

Shining with the Shiner (1944) is John A. *Lee's tribute to a real Otago 'character', the Irish swagman Ned Slattery known to all as Shiner Slattery, who rambled the roads from the 1870s until his death in 1927. It is also Lee's tribute to a romantic ideal of individual freedom obscured by capitalist industrialism. Oddly described on the 1944 dust jacket as a novel, *Shining with the Shiner* is a collection of 'episodes' belonging stylistically to the genre of the yarn, laconic vernacular stories owing much to the influence of the Australians Henry *Lawson and Steele Rudd and others of the *Bulletin school. Lee himself met the Shiner while on the run from Borstal in 1907, and believed that the father he never met, the wandering entertainer Gipsy Alfredo Lee, had done much to popularise the legend of the Shiner. The Shiner of the stories is the legendary figure rather than the biographical one. For a second volume of stories, *Shiner Slattery* (1964), Lee solicited material, and received more stories than he could use, attesting to the Shiner's viability as a cultural icon. He added to the type later again in *Roughnecks, Rolling Stones, and Rouseabouts, with an Anthology of Early Swagger Literature* (1977). The Shiner is a benign figure, sometimes a conman (the vernacular origin of the nickname), a trickster, a loafer, the 'Champion of Anti-Sweat' and an 'anti-dynamo', working as little as possible and living by his wits and the gift of the gab. He is the stuff folk heroes are made of, a born survivor. A tendency to moralise in some of the stories on the evils of idleness and the demon drink suggests Lee's feelings about the Shiner's type contained some ambivalence. The Shiner's link with Lee's father and with Lee's own youthful lawlessness give him perhaps a greater psychological complexity in Lee's imagination than meets the eye. Shiner Slattery is at any rate an enduring comic creation of real cultural significance.   KA

SHORTLAND, Edward (1812–93), was an unusually sympathetic early writer on the Māori. He was born in Devon, educated at Exeter GS, Harrow, Cambridge (MA 1839), and admitted Extra-Licentiate of the Royal College of Physicians in 1839, MRCP 1860. The brother of Willoughby Shortland, Colonial Secretary in 1841, Edward arrived in Auckland that year. He soon took up a series of official appointments which involved exploration, tribal and settler–Māori mediation in the Waikato, Bay of Plenty, coastal Otago up to Akaroa, and Wellington. For a brief period he was translating in the

Northern War. From 1846 to 1861 he lived in Europe, practised medicine in Plymouth and married. The years 1861–65 were spent in New Zealand, from 1863 as Native Secretary, and again 1869–73 and 1880–89. Shortland's peregrinations may have resulted from his ambiguous relationship with officialdom. Quickly becoming fluent in Māori and cognizant with Māori lore and custom, efficent, honest, intelligent and charming, Shortland would have been a useful bureaucrat. On the other hand, he was a man who was not interested in securing Māori souls or their land. When it came to the point he could find his views ignored. *The Southern Districts of New Zealand; A Journal with Passing Notices of the Customs of the Aborigines* (1851), *Traditions and Superstitions of the New Zealanders; with Illustrations of their Manners and Customs* (1854) and *Maori Religion and Mythology: Illustrated by Translations of Traditions, Karakia, etc., to which are added Notes on Maori Tenure of Land* (1882) are the fruit of his experiences with Māori communties, his quick inquiring mind and his ability to gain and keep the trust of highly reputable informants. His findings are presented in a clear and felicitous style. The translations of *waiata, for example, are free of nineteenth-century mannerisms. He was valued highly by his contemporaries in ethnology. His books remain valid and a delight to read.   RG

Shuriken (a Japanese throwing-dagger) is the title of Vincent *O'Sullivan's first stage play, performed at Downstage, Wellington, in July 1983, at Theatre Corporate, Auckland, in 1984, and since in Hamilton, Australia, Germany and *Japan. It is an imaginative exploration of the circumstances in which fifty Japanese prisoners and one New Zealander were killed in a POW camp in Featherston in 1943. Though building towards its bloody climax, the play exploits Brechtian and Noh techniques: a narrative prologue accompanied by a wartime newsreel, direct revelation of characters' thoughts in soliloquies and speeches ignored by others on stage, sudden transitions and striking juxtapositions of parallel or antithetical episodes, the use of music, the enacting of rituals, theatrically exciting set pieces. Yet within this deliberately non-naturalistic framework Kiwi vernacular is put to lively effect. In the crudities of their speech the New Zealand soldiers declare more than they consciously intend. The play's dynamics come from the cultural tensions and mutual misunderstandings between the captive Japanese, pledged to a code of 'no surrender', and the motley assortment of inexperienced local guards. Since these include the immigrant Pom and the Māori corporal Tai, there are implications concerning colonial power relations. Tai, though sustained by his own racial heritage, has as much in common with the subdued adversaries, striving to retain their self-esteem, as with his Pākehā mates.

In production, visual effects are important, the two groups being outwardly as alien to each other as they are in their habits of mind. As the play progresses, the gap between the two races widens. The more they learn about the enemy's language and culture, the less they comprehend. Well-intentioned gestures in the name of international brotherhood prove as dangerous as blind prejudice. The play is set on two levels, reflecting the camp hierarchy, with the commandant and adjutant appearing above, and the lower-ranking New Zealanders sharing the main stage with the Japanese. Conflicts among the custodians thus complicate the clash between East and West and give *Shuriken* a satisfying moral complexity.   MPJ

'Silk, The', a short story by Joy *Cowley, was published in the *NZ Listener, 5 March 1965, and has become an almost inevitable anthology choice since the Oxford *New Zealand Short Stories, Third Series* (1975). It was collected in Cowley's *Heart Attack and Other Stories* (1985) and in *Complete Short Stories* (1997). It deals with the way an unpretentious old couple, Herb and Amy Blackie, of modest means and education, cope with the husband's final illness and death. A piece of silk he had bought in Hong Kong as a wedding present fifty years before becomes their means of expressing a sense of beauty, fineness and their own inarticulate affection, as she makes it up into laying-out pyjamas. Written with subtle and sensitive restraint, sometimes in the Blackies' own limited terms ('When Mr Blackie took bad again that autumn …'), the story manages to convey the beauty not only of the silk, 'always unexpected', but equally of the bond that may exist under the surface of ordinary marriage, even beyond death. Cowley's Prologue to *Heart Attack* recounts the 'clairvoyant' parallels between the story and the death twenty years later of her husband Malcolm Mason (see *Italy).   RR

SIMONA, Ropati (1925–95), was a translator who had a significant impact on the entire published literature of a language, Tokelauan. He was born in Boku, in Papua New Guinea, the year before *Tokelau came under New Zealand administration. His parents were Tokelauan missionaries from Fakaofo. He later wrote about his childhood experiences in Papua New Guinea in *Kua Tukua Tautahi* (1995). Simona was educated in Western Samoa, and then became one of the first teachers (and later principals) in the government schools in Tokelau. In 1967 he became a translator and lecturer in Tokelauan at the University of Auckland. In 1975 he was appointed a research associate at that university, where, working as a lexicographer with Maselino Patelesio, Loimata Iupati, Judith Huntsman, Antony and Robin Hooper and others, he published the *Tokelau Dictionary* in 1986. In 1989–90 the Tokelauan Department of Education increased the number of children's books in Tokelauan from the previous five to thirty-five. Working with Sr Tagikakau Tominiko, Faraimo Paulo and Fuimanu Kirifi, Ropati Simona edited all these books. He then became the principal consultant to the New Zealand Ministry of Education for their publishing programme in Tokelauan. By 1995 he was writing, translating, or checking a new book for children in Tokelauan about every two months. His own translations of children's books into Samoan and Tokelauan include *Ua Tuua Toatasi Au* (1995), *Ko na Fakamalu ma na Aitu* (1995) and *E Olo ki Fea na Punua Fonu?* (1995). He translated songs for *Songs and Stories of Tokelau* (1990) and contributed to the development of *Matagi Tokelau* (1991). He was the co-translator and editor of the Tokelau Pacific Islands Church of Christ's hymn book, *Ko na Pehe ma na Vikiga o te Atua* (1990), and he initiated the process of translating the Bible into Tokelauan, preparing the first translation of St Mark's Gospel, before he died in 1995. There is hardly a book in the *Tokelau National Bibliography/Fakamaumauga o na Tuhituhiga o Tokelau* that he did not influence, either directly as an editor and translator, or indirectly, through his dictionary.   LI/DL

SIMONS, Wendy (1939–   ), has published three novels and a number of short stories. Her first novel, *Harper's Mother* (1977), won the Angus & Robertson Writers' Fellowship and was published internationally, including a Pan Books paperback in the UK. *Odd Woman Out* (1980) and *Naomi* (1984) were also published in Australia, the UK, the USA and New Zealand, and her short fiction has appeared in *NZ Listener, New Women's Fiction 1987* and elsewhere. She also writes tramping and bush-walking guidebooks and resource books for adult learners of English.

Simons's fiction mainly explores the tensions created for women by the changing social and sexual mores of the 1970s–80s, such as conflict between opportunities for love and independence. Thus *Odd Woman Out* narrates in a partly stream of consciousness way an affair with a married Auckland University professor, which leads to resentment of exclusion (as the title implies), the suicide of his wife and the narrator's eventual emergence from grief into emotional liberation. As in *romance, the male characters are external and stylised, the female inward and explored in painstaking emotional detail, with an increased emphasis on their relationships with each other. Simons lives in Auckland, having spent periods in Scotland and Western Samoa, and has worked as a teacher, journalist, editor and adult educator.   RR

SIMPSON, Peter (1942–   ), is a scholar, critic, editor and professor of literature who also served a term as Labour member of parliament. His maiden speech in 1987 was probably the only such occasion when a member has quoted from his own poetry: he delivered part of his 'Birthday Ballad for Woolston', a verse history of the Labour Party which he had composed and performed for celebrations of the oldest Party branch. 'Birthday Ballad' was published in David McGee's biography of Elizabeth McCombs, the first woman MP, *My Dear Girl* (1993). As MP for Lyttelton 1987–90, Simpson specialised in environment issues; but a speech to arts administrators, 'Being Pakeha in 1990', was published in *Metro (June 1990). After Labour's loss in 1990, he was a freelance writer, specialising in art and literature, writing regularly for the *Press and compiling material that led, for instance, to the Auckland Art Gallery exhibition and catalogue *Candles in a Dark Room: James K. Baxter and Colin McCahon* (1996). In 1993 he was appointed associate professor at University of Auckland, establishing literature teaching on the Tamaki Campus.

Born at Takaka and educated at Nelson College and the universities of Canterbury (MA 1964) and Toronto (PhD 1976), Simpson taught at Massey, Toronto, Carleton (Ottawa) and Canterbury (1964–68, 1976–87) universities before his foray into politics. Working with H. Winston *Rhodes at Canterbury in the 1960s, he was one of the first to teach New Zealand literature at university level; later he taught the first full paper in Pacific literature (1980) and currently convenes the first Masters programme in New Zealand studies. Simpson is author of *Ronald Hugh *Morrieson* (OUP *New Zealand Writers and Their Work, 1982); editor of *Look Back Harder: Critical Writings 1935–1984* by Allen *Curnow (1987), *Selected Poems* by Kendrick *Smithyman (1989), *Slow Passes* by Alan *Brunton (1991) and others; contributor to the *Oxford History of New Zealand* (second edition, 1992); and as critic and reviewer has published extensively in New Zealand and internationally. He is co-director with Alan *Loney of the *Holloway Press.
                                    RR

SINCLAIR, Janette (1948–   ), is 'one of the most impressive of the new generation of New Zealand short story writers' (Graeme *Lay). Born in Dunedin, she spent part of her childhood in Fiji, experience on which she draws in some of her most successful stories, notably the anthologised 'Outlines of Gondwanaland', co-winner of the John Cowie Reid Award in 1988. Since making her debut in *Landfall in 1987 Sinclair has published more than twenty stories in ★*Metro*, ★*Sport*, ★*Takahe* and elsewhere. Her novella *In Touch* (1995) is a high-energising, wickedly comic feminist fantasy of a flat-chested West Coast nurse who cross-dresses herself into the All Blacks, exploiting pelvic muscles powerful enough to maim the Welsh opponent who tries to check her gender mid-tackle. Child abuse, advertising and psychiatric medicine are among the other targets of a book the reviewers called 'fizzing', 'hilarious' and 'subversive', impressively inventive if somewhat self-conscious in its zestful metaphoric wit. Educated at Christchurch with a Canterbury University MA in sociology, Sinclair has worked as social worker and researcher and is a survey designer in Wellington. RR

SINCLAIR, Keith (1922–93), poet and historian, was born in Auckland, and grew up in Point Chevalier beside the Waitemata Harbour, the oldest son of a rambunctious and impoverished family of ten. Their idyllic harbourside adventures in the 1920s and 1930s are recalled in Sinclair's posthumously published autobiography, *Halfway Round the Harbour* (1993). His many adventures on the Meola reef, which juts into the Waitemata, form the basis for one of his most anthologised poems, 'The Ballad of Meola Creek', and were recreated in fictional form in *Reefs of Fire* (1977), a vivid foray into children's literature. Both texts testify to Sinclair's lifelong passion for Auckland's land and seascapes, as well as to his obsession with recording the material facts which make New Zealand distinctive. His enduring legacy is his commitment to being a historian of New Zealand trained in New Zealand.

After Mount Albert GS, Sinclair studied at Auckland Teachers' College and part-time at Auckland University. He completed his BA overseas on military service at the end of World War 2. After the war, he took his MA and PhD in history at Auckland. He joined the Auckland history department in 1947, became a professor in 1963 and, apart from a brief dab into national politics (in 1969 he was member for Eden for three weeks, but lost the seat by sixty-seven postal votes), taught there until retirement. By then his reputation as a charismatic lecturer and a gifted, prolific and accessible scholar of New Zealand history had spread far beyond New Zealand's universities. His best-selling *History of New Zealand* (1957), which went through several editions and still sells well after forty years, demonstrates his commitment to readable yet responsible history. In a series of witty and jargon-free chapters, Sinclair traces New Zealand's history, from Māui's fishing up the North Island (Te Ika a Māui) to the cold war alliance with the USA, focusing especially on issues of national character: bicultural, collectivist, yet ruggedly individual. Subsequent revisions

lament the long reign of the National Party in the 1960s–70s and the free-market reforms of the post-1984 period. The *History* set the agenda for much research that followed; Sinclair's old-fashioned romance of national destiny moved generations of readers. He saved scholarly treatment of the 'nature' of the 'nation' for his later cultural history, *A Destiny Apart: New Zealand's Search for National Identity* (1986), which traced the scars of myths of war and sport on the New Zealand psyche. His other populist endeavours were celebratory: several widely read school text books; the lavish *Looking Back: A Photographic History of New Zealand* (1978); and *The Story of New Zealand* (1985), co-authored with Judith Bassett and Marcia Stenson.

Sinclair's prodigious thirst for archival research made him the first and leading historian in many genres of New Zealand writing. He helped found the *New Zealand Journal of History* in 1967. The respect granted Māori issues and personalities in his *History of New Zealand* reflected the depth of research for his doctoral dissertation, published as the ground-breaking *Origins of the Maori Wars* (1957), which was not superseded until the late 1980s by James ★Belich's *New Zealand Wars*. Sinclair sustained his interest in the Māori, becoming fluent enough to read the massive archive of nineteenth-century Māori documents, which lay behind his elegiac social and cultural history, *Kinds of Peace; Maori People After the Wars 1870–85* (1991). His success as a Pākehā historian of the Māori paved the way for later historians, especially his students Judith Binney and Claudia Orange. He never published a novel, though *Reefs of Fire* shows a narrative talent. He developed his interest in prose narrative in his two political biographies, *William Pember ★Reeves: New Zealand Fabian* (1965) and *Walter Nash* (1976). He was among the first to treat New Zealand biography as a serious form. He relates with gusto the public lives of both politicians, surrounding glimpses of their private lives with evocations of New Zealand's political landscape at crucial points in its development as a modern state. His example has been followed, in the works of Raewyn Dalziel (his second wife) and his former colleagues, Barry Gustafson and Michael Bassett. His *Open Account: A History of the Bank of New South Wales in New Zealand* (1961), co-authored with W.F. Mandle, showed the possibilities for engaging and non-sycophantic history of private businesses. Sinclair even managed to make the *History of the University of Auckland 1883–1983* (1983) entertaining and opinionated. Sinclair's colleague, R.C.J. Stone, continues to explore the labyrinthine history of Auckland businesses and businessmen.

Sinclair published five books of poetry: *Songs for a Summer* (1952), *Strangers or Beasts* (1954), *A Time to*

Embrace (1963), *The Firewheel Tree* (1974) and *Moontalk* (1993). These were produced perhaps out of his generation's commitment to creating a national poetry, but they have energy, vividness, a witty resourcefulness of language and tone and a metaphysical quality that R.A. *Copland called 'direct sensuous thinking'. His strongest poems rework historical themes: 'Memorial to a Missionary' was highly praised by *Curnow ('Sinclair has matched a historian's understanding with a poet's insight ... no other poem ... contains, in so many glances of a wary imagination, such a span of our history'). It is frequently anthologised. The love poems are often compellingly sensual. The rollicking castaways' 'Ballad of Half-Moon Bay' shows the varied vigour of voice. Despite Sinclair's modest claim in his autobiography that he and Kendrick *Smithyman together formed the 'Mudflat School' of New Zealand poetry, he is a significant poet of the post-war generation. His greatest literary achievement, nevertheless, remains in his many histories, which record his passion for New Zealand in his distinctively terse, blunt yet convincing style.   MH

SINCLAIR, Stephen (1956–), is a popularly successful playwright, and a screenwriter and poet. He was born in Auckland and educated at Westlake BHS and Auckland and Victoria universities (BA in Māori studies 1979). He worked as a researcher for the Māori studies department for two years, and subsequently as a translator of Māori manuscripts for National Archives. His plays are often concerned with the tensions of race and culture, as in *Le Matou* ('The Fishhook'; jointly written with Samson Samasoni, first performed 1984), the first play to dramatise the experience of Samoan immigrants to New Zealand. Sinclair was also active in the establishment of Tao Tahi, the first *Pacific/*Māori theatre company, which performed *Le Matou* and other plays about Polynesian concerns. In *Caramel Cream* (first performed in 1991) he explores the tensions between Māori and Pākehā racism and sexism, especially for the 'caramel cream' who is 'brown on the outside, white in the middle'. Other plays, such as *The Houzie Show*, a community-based political show written with Simon Wilson (first performed 1981), and the musical *Big Bickies* (first performed 1988), are satirical attacks on aggressive capitalism. Many of his plays have been written in collaboration, most notably the huge box office success *Ladies' Night* and its sequel *Ladies' Night 2: Raging On*, both written with Anthony *McCarten. Although *Ladies' Night* starts with the gritty realism of unemployment for a group of hopeless young men, its enormous popularity (which led to several national tours after its first performance in 1987) was largely due to the inspired showmanship of the male strip show which the young

men develop, and which constitutes a big production extravaganza for most of the second half of the play. A similar determination to flout political correctness lay behind *The Sex Fiend* (written with Danny Mulheron, first performed 1989), and the violently bad taste comedy splatter movies 'Meet the Feebles' (1990) and 'Braindead' (1992), both co-written with Fran Walsh and director Peter Jackson. In addition to other plays and film work, Sinclair has published *Twenty Poems* (Cabbage Press, Auckland, 1976), and his poetry has also appeared in *Landfall*, *Climate* and *Zero* [US], and in the *Cabbage Press Anthology* (1978). This also includes poems by his father, Keith *Sinclair. He has written two books for children, *Thief of Colours* (1995) and *Dread* (forthcoming 1998). He lives in Auckland.   DC

SINCLAIRE, Frederick (1881–1954), essayist and social commentator, had a trans-Tasman career. Born near Auckland, he won scholarships to Auckland GS and Auckland University College, graduating MA with first class honours in Latin and French in 1903. A convert to Unitarianism, he abandoned study at Manchester College, Oxford, to become a minister in Melbourne. A disciple of George Bernard *Shaw, Sinclaire became a prominent radical and pacifist, eventually abandoning Unitarianism for his self-created Free Religious Fellowship. He associated with literary nationalists such as Vance and Nettie Palmer, attacking the provincialism of Australian cultural life in *Annotations* (1920). A long-time socialist, he opposed dogmatic Marxism, and his influence in Melbourne eventually waned. After a period in Western Australia, he returned to New Zealand in 1932 as professor of English at Canterbury University College, where his teaching inspired the likes of Denis *Glover and Ian *Milner, the latter describing him as 'a warm-hearted man passionate in his prejudices as in his radical, humanist faith'. With Glover, Kennaway *Henderson and H. Winston *Rhodes (a follower from his Melbourne days), he helped establish the magazine *Tomorrow*, contributing a quasi-editorial column, 'Notes by the Way', for two years, 1934–36. In the first issue he wrote: 'We inhabit a land of dreadful silence. New Zealand is the country in which no-one says anything, in which no-one is expected to say anything.... We appeal to [our readers] to help us in breaking the uncanny and ill-boding silence.' Increasingly out of sympathy with *Tomorrow's* fundamentalist leftism, he turned to the *Press as the main outlet for his eloquent but old-fashioned literary essays, most of which reflected an Edwardian sensibility. The *Caxton Press published two collections, *Lend Me Your Ears: Essays* (1942, 1943), and *A Time to Laugh and Other Essays* (1951).   PS

Singing Whakapapa, The (1994), is C.K. ★Stead's most accomplished novel, and his most sustained fictional exploration of New Zealand history. The book seems to have emerged from Stead's research into that history and the history of his family, which he undertook in preparation for *Voices* (1990), his poetry collection commissioned by the Ministry of Internal Affairs for the sesquicentennial celebrations of the Treaty of Waitangi. Scenes from *Voices* recur in the novel, such as the moment when the lay-missionary John Flatt, Stead's great-great-grandfather, sees a war canoe being rowed past a jetty. Flatt's story is one of the novel's two main strands; the other is that of Hugh Grady, a present-day character based on Stead himself, as he traces Flatt's history through archival sources. Both Flatt's and Hugh's stories end in the revelation of secrets. Hugh and his research assistant Jean-Anne Devantier eventually deduce that Flatt was in a sexual relationship with Tarore, the young Māori convert whose murder ended the South Auckland war of the 1830s—indeed, that Tarore could not escape her killers because she was in Flatt's bed. In the present, Hugh discovers that his assistant Jean-Anne is his natural daughter, result of an extra-marital affair with one of his students in the late 1960s. Other characters from the author's family history crowd the background. The novel is rich with Stead's characteristic prose style: fluent, sensuous, deft in its choice of detail and pace of narration. It crowns his preoccupation throughout his career with the problematics of New Zealand identity. *The Singing Whakapapa* won the New Zealand Book Award for fiction.   KJ

'Sings Harry', Denis ★Glover's fourteen-poem sequence, was first published in *Sings Harry and Other Poems* (★Caxton Press 1951). The poems had been written over the previous ten years; the first appeared in *Recent Poems* (1941) along with poems by Allen ★Curnow, A.R.D. ★Fairburn and R.A.K. ★Mason. Harry, like Glover's equally famous characters ★Arawata Bill and Mick Stimpson, is a ★'Man Alone'. Masculine, rugged loners, all three commune with the sea and the landscape, if not actively in flight from human company, at least content without it. Harry—the only fictional character of the three—is the only one who speaks directly about his flight from home and family. Facing old age, he muses on his past. He sings about the ephemerality of love, ambition and possessions and the abiding certainty of the mountains and the sea.

Harry's first song is about the ephemerality of his own art: 'Not I but another / Will make songs worth the bother.' Although Harry is not Glover—unlike his persona, Glover lived in or near cities all his life—Harry perhaps speaks for his creator; Glover's assessment of his own talent was also tinged with polite self-deprecation: 'Poetry I gave a good deal of time to but I was never as good as my friends. Some of them really were poets' (*Hot Water Sailor*). The Harry persona also conceals Glover's unwillingness to express his emotions in poetry. Even Harry does not 'sing' directly to the reader: an italicised narrator mediates the singer's nostalgia for things past.

Harry sings for Glover in at least one other way. In this first stanza, Harry occupies a pioneering position within an emerging lineage of 'singers'. He sees himself as a kind of forerunner, who must do his job, albeit inadequately, so that others may do their job better. As a writer and publisher, Glover's efforts were similarly pioneering, directed towards the establishment and development of a local English-speaking literary tradition. Poems such as 'Sings Harry', about identifiable New Zealand 'types' and written in uncluttered colloquial language, were one possible contribution to an emerging local literature, one which consciously set itself apart from the language of ★Georgian sentimentality.

Composer Douglas ★Lilburn, Glover's friend, expressed a parallel desire to establish a Pākehā musical tradition, setting many texts by contemporary New Zealand poets. In 1953 Lilburn set six of the 'Sings Harry' poems for male voice and piano. The musical possibilities suggested by Harry's guitar provided an ideal vehicle for the composer's experimentation with a folk-style musical idiom. Lilburn's settings have become as canonic as the poems themselves. Glover reads 'Sings Harry' on *Arawata Bill and Other Verse* (Kiwi Records 1971).   SS

Sirocco was the second publication of the ★Caxton Club Press, successor to the banned ★*Oriflamme*. It had only a single issue, July 1933. Printed by Denis ★Glover, it featured poems and articles by Glover, Allen ★Curnow ('Philo'), A.R.D. ★Fairburn and others.   SH

SLATER REDHEAD, Janet (1940–), children's writer, was born in Masterton, educated at Wairarapa College and Wellington Teachers' College and taught in country schools as well as studying for missionary work with the Methodist Church. Contributions to Radio New Zealand's *Grandpa's Place* led to many children's stories, including readers. Picture books include *The Big Block of Chocolate* (1985), illustrated by Christine Dale; *Mr Magee Came Home for his Tea* (1986), illustrated by Fifi Colston; *The Duck That Couldn't Swim* (1988), illustrated by Graeme Kyle; *Deep in the Jungle* (1992), illustrated by Tim Tripp; and the *Scaredy Cat, Nosey Parker* series, notable for its sympathetic acknowledgment of children's fears. In *Pins and Needles* (1989), illustrated by Lyn Kriegler, a boy's friendship with a hedgehog helps his acceptance of his mother's remarriage. Slater Redhead's most extensive work is *Call of the Kotuku* (1986), an informative, anthropomorphic novel illustrated by Elaine Power, about a young heron's dangerous journey from Northland to Okarito.   DH

SLATTER, Gordon (1922–), is a novelist, sports historian and autobiographer. His first book, the novel *A Gun in My Hand* (1959), went through five impressions within a year in New Zealand and UK. It is a psychological thriller, the stream-of-consciousness one-day odyssey of a disillusioned man revisiting his Christchurch past, vainly bent on resolving the guilt he carries from traumatic war experiences. This present-day action, which builds a Joycean picture of Christchurch and includes pub scenes unmatched in raw realism until Alan *Duff, is intercut with extraordinarily vivid fragments of memory from the New Zealand Division's *Italian campaign of 1945 and from work experience on the wharves, on farms, in the freezing works, and elsewhere. The overall effect is an intensely painful imaginative rendering of the life and consciousness of the generation of New Zealand males that endured World *War 2 and its long aftermath.

The Pagan Game (1968) is similarly much more than a novel about an inter-school rugby match. Its seven chapters, one for each day of the week of the game, are each centred on the consciousness of a different character—teachers, the team captain, a disgruntled parent, the coach. From these diverse subjectivities is compiled a rich collage picture of the Wairarapa town ('Ruamahanga') and its high school, which are thus more than setting. Chronological and geographical reference is also broadened; war memories are again powerful, shifts and tensions in New Zealand society in the 1960s are acutely observed, and the rugby game itself is narrated with insight into the complex drama of team sport. Both novels are memorable for their virtuoso renditions of New Zealand male vernacular, which has made them as valuable as *Sargeson as a source for the language research of Harry *Orsman. Also striking now is the treatment of Māori, informed, sympathetic but never appropriative. *The Pagan Game* comments, five years before *Tangi, that Māori novelists are needed to reveal the Māori consciousness, while the fine war memoir, *One More River* (1995), includes in its closing section a moving tribute to the Māori who died in that European campaign.

Slatter's four books on rugby, including *Great Days at Lancaster Park* (1974), show the same strength as the novels in narrative reportage, and in moving to a significance beyond action, in this case mainly historical. He also wrote *The Story of Rolleston House* (1977). Though Slatter's subject matter is almost wholly male, his treatment of it is informed, wisely contextualised, often crit-

ical and always insightful. If they were still read, the two novels would be problematic to simplistic 'masculinist' histories of the period. He was born in Christchurch and has always lived there, apart from teenage years in Masterton and his young adult years in the army, with active service in Italy in 1945. He was for twenty-five years a highly regarded teacher and head of history at Christchurch BHS, where the 1959 *Te Kura* magazine included the affectionately parodic 'A Gin in My Hand'.   RR

SLIGO, John (1944–), gained some rather controversial attention when *The Cave* won the PEN (NZ) best first novel award for 1978. A short novel that reflects European experience and influence, it is about the imprisonment, torture and escape of an unnamed political assassin in an unnamed European state, and combines an *existentialist turn of mind with an explicitness about violence and sex not then familiar to New Zealand readers. The physical detail is unremitting and ritualistic: 'The blood spurted in great gushes as if his head had been severed. It covered her breasts and from there trickled between her thighs.' This preoccupation is intercut with metaphysical statements such as 'All action must bear the infirm humilities of flesh', or 'mercy wears many different faces'; but the intellectualised fascination with justified revolutionary violence relates it more closely to *Smith's Dream* (1971) than the more complex moral challenges of A *Soldier's Tale* (1976).

Born in Dunedin and educated at the universities of Otago and Cambridge, Sligo was living in Rome when *The Cave* was published. He also published poems about civil strife in Greece ('And hate must run its course') in *Landfall* 134 (1980), and fiction either set in Europe, like the story 'A Roman Farewell' (*Landfall* 129, 1979), or contrasting provincial sterility with the spiritual vitality of life overseas, as in the novellas of *Final Things*, which won a New South Wales fiction prize in 1988. Also published in *Australia was *The Faces of Sappho* (1990), an ambitious and complex counterpointing of ancient and modern European history, through which a New Zealand–born protagonist finds 'the interior paths' rather than the 'series of moral statements' that mars Christianity. It also objures New Zealand for its 'petty bourgeois experiment in democratic fascism ... the negative history; the vacuum cleaning of its suburban rural realist literature ... an unvital earth that would contrast so vividly with its rumbustious and alive neighbour....' As this would suggest, Sligo lives in Australia.   RR

Small Room with Large Windows, A (1962), was the first of several Selected Poems by Allen *Curnow, published in London by Oxford University Press. Omitting entirely poems from Curnow's first four books, the selection focused on work written after 1940. Only two poems were previously uncollected, 'Pacific Theatre 1943, II' (later called 'Pantoum of War in the Pacific'; see ★Pacific) and 'An Oppressive Climate, a Populous Neighbourhood', written in New York in 1961.   PS

SMITH, Miriam (1926–88), wrote children's books with emphasis on family relationships and Māori perspectives. Born of Ngā Puhi descent and educated in Hawkes Bay, she worked as an officer in the early childhood division of the Department of Education, Wellington. Married and living at Pukerua Bay, she valued relationships between young and old, and this is reflected in her three picture books published in English and Māori, the translations into Maori by Sonny Huia Wilson, John Hunia and A.T. Mahuika respectively. *Kimi and the Watermelon* (1983), illustrated by David Armitage, measures the passing of time by the ripening of a watermelon as Kimi waits with her grandmother for her uncle's promised return home. *Roimata and the Forest of Tane* (1986), illustrated by Suzanne Walker, celebrates time through the growing of trees and a child's relationship with her grandmother. *Annie and Moon* (1988), illustrated by Lesley Moyes, winner of the 1990 Picture Book of the Year Award, warmly portrays a child–mother relationship during a search for a new home, along with the complications caused by a valued pet kitten.   DH

SMITH, S. (Stephenson) **Percy** (1840–1922), was a significant if now dated early historian of the Māori. Born in Beccles, Suffolk, he emigrated to New Plymouth with his family when 9, left school at 14, worked on the family farm for a year and then joined the Survey Department. This proved the most important step in his life as the job led to many exploratory trips into the North Island and years of association with Māori people. In 1857 he climbed Mount Taranaki–Egmont and, late that year, made a thousand kilometre journey into the central North Island. Records were kept of this trip, setting a pattern that was followed for the rest of his life and provided the basis for his later ethnological studies. The years 1859–65 were spent surveying for the Native Land Purchase Office in the Auckland District. Other transfers and promotions followed, including surveying confiscated land in Taranaki and working in the Chathams when ★Te Kooti escaped from there. He was appointed Surveyor-General early in 1899, and retired late in 1900.

Early in 1892, however, Smith had been a prime mover in founding the Polynesian Society, becoming secretary, treasurer and most significantly, editor of its ★*Journal*, holding that post for thirty years. Numerous

articles and many books followed, among the most notable *History and Traditions of the Maoris of the West Coast, North Island of New Zealand prior to 1840* (1910) and *Maori Wars of the Nineteenth Century: The Struggle of the Northern against the Southern Maori Tribes prior to the Colonisation of New Zealand in 1840* (1910). The former encompasses information gathered over the years from his boyhood in Taranaki and the latter his North Island research generally. Some of Smith's work has not stood up to modern research, especially where he speculates on Māori origins or attempts to fit his findings into nineteenth-century preconceptions (see ★Whare wānanga). On the other hand his historical works are comprehensive and detailed and the records he left behind contain material that otherwise would have been lost.   RG

SMITHER, Elizabeth (1941–), poet, novelist and short story writer, was born in New Plymouth where she works as a librarian. She has published twelve collections of poems: *Here Come the Clouds* (1975); *You're Very Seductive William Carlos Williams* (1978); *The Sarah Train* (1980); *The Legend of Marcello Mastroianni's wife* (1981); *Casanova's Ankle* (1981); *Shakespeare Virgins* (1983); *Professor Musgrove's Canary* (1986); *Gorilla/Guerilla* (1986); *Animaux* (1988); *A Pattern of Marching* (1989); *A Cortège of Daughters* (1993); *The Tudor Style: Poems New and Selected* (1993). There have also been two novels, *First Blood* (1983) and *Brother-love Sister-love* (1986); two collections of short stories, *Nights at the Embassy* (1990) and *Mr Fish* (1994); a book for children, *Tug Brothers* (1983); an edition of her journals, *The Journal Box* (1996); and co-edited with David ★Hill *The Seventies Connection* (1987). Amongst other awards, she has received the Scholarship in Letters in 1987 and 1992, and *A Pattern of Marching* won the Poetry Section of the 1990 New Zealand Book Awards.

Smither's first collection, *Here Come the Clouds*, published in her mid-30s, at once established her distinctive, even idiosyncratic, poetic manner. The short poem, usually but not always unrhymed, witty, stylish and intellectually curious, has remained her forte, although 'To Hugh a friend flying to London November 30 DC 10', a 600-line poem in *Professor Musgrove's Canary*, successfully transcends the ordinary limits of her miniaturist technique. As the titles of her collections suggest, literary and legendary figures often provide starting points for poems, a number of which are also characterised by a strong interest in Catholicism. In addition to more perennial subjects, her poetry, though never merely self-referential, celebrates the slipperiness and paradoxical nature of language. She has remarked that the poets she most admires are 'tough', citing as examples Emily Dickinson, Wallace Stevens, e. e. cummings, Elizabeth

Bishop, William Empson and John Berryman: 'They don't pull any punches; they're like Humphrey Bogart. You have to use all your senses to crack them open.' The same comment applies to the best of her own work.

Perhaps because she has been so prolific a poet, Smither's fiction has tended to remain underrated. Like her poetry, her short stories often make use of a literary motif as a springboard: a phrase from Auden, a literary quiz, an academic's journal, a replica of Keats's death mask. The subsequent glimpses into the lives of the characters, usually women, are typified by an ironic sympathy with their ability or inability to deal with the vicissitudes of their relationships with men.

While adumbrating more clearly the strand of Catholicism which runs through her poetry, both Smither's novels deal with areas central to Pākehā New Zealand experience: early settler days in *First Blood* and the mixed response of a contemporary New Zealander visiting England in *Brother-love Sister-love*. The former, set in nineteenth-century New Plymouth, explores the human, social and religious interactions which lead to the new settlement's first murder when Cassidy, an Irish ex-militia man and itinerant worker, stabs a young widow, Mary McDavitt. Although deliberately omitting some of the more conventional features of the historical novel (there is, for instance, little attempt to imitate the spoken or written idiom of the time), *First Blood* nonetheless recreates a powerful sense of period and, flickering back and forth between its gallery of characters, builds up an evocative portrait of a small, intricate, vulnerable world. *Brother-love Sister-love* recounts a trip to England by Isobel, a New Zealand poet, to visit her expatriate brother James. The narrative technique is similar to that of *First Blood*; a range of viewpoints are played off against each other with Isobel's as the dominant perspective. The deft satire of Isobel's adventures among the London literati neatly complements the broader farce of her sculptor husband Angus's attempts to *épater* the local bourgeoisie back in New Zealand. The rapid switches from character to character and scene to scene aptly mimic Isobel's intense, somewhat uneasy reactions to the people and situations she encounters.   HRi

Smith's Dream (1971) was C. K. *Stead's first novel. Though lacking the stylistic flair of his later fiction, it achieved considerable prominence. The topicality of *Smith's Dream* assisted its fame: it is a New Zealand allegory of the Vietnam *War, published when the anti-war protests were at their height. It is also remembered for having provided the basis of the feature film *Sleeping Dogs* (1977), in which Sam Neill played the protagonist, Smith, and Ian Mune his rival and comrade, Bullen.

The story is that of a New Zealand Everyman who,

his wife having left him, retreats to a solitary hut in the Coromandel. His attempt at the *'Man Alone' life is ended, however, when he falls foul of the secret police of Volkner, the dictator recently risen to power (see *Muldoon). Smith is suspected of involvement with insurrectionists, tortured, beaten and, after an interview with the dictator, escapes to join the guerrillas in earnest, witnessing their defeat by *American military power, and the ravages of war upon the civilian population. The narrative considers at some length how New Zealanders' political indolence and love of strong leaders could permit such developments.

Smith's Dream owes a clear stylistic and structural debt to John *Mulgan's *Man Alone* (1939), which Stead has identified as a significant early influence on him. Like Mulgan's Johnson, Smith is an Everyman figure who tries to avoid political commitment, but who becomes politicised as he experiences the disastrous results of apathy. The laconic prose resembles Mulgan's, as do the narrator's disquisitions on national character. Like Johnson's, Smith's story reaches its climax when he narrowly evades death in crossing a bush-clad mountain range.   KJ

SMITHYMAN, Kendrick (1922–95), poet and critic, was born in Te Kopuru, near Dargaville, where his parents ran a boarding house. They moved to Auckland during the *Depression and he went to various primary schools including Point Chevalier and to Seddon Memorial Technical College. He attended Auckland Teachers' College 1940–41 and (with Keith *Sinclair, a lifetime friend) published early stories and poems in *Manuka*, the college magazine. From 1944 he began publishing poems regularly in journals such as *New Zealand New Writing*, the *Yearbook of the Arts*, *Kiwi*, *Book*, *Arena*, *Hilltop* and the Australian journals *Angry Penguins* and *Meanjin*. He also published occasionally in the USA and UK. Serving in artillery (1941–42) and then the air force (1942–45), Smithyman spent the war years in New Zealand, apart from a visit to Norfolk Island in 1945, which suggested an important early sequence ('Considerations of Norfolk Island'—the title was later shortened) included in the second edition of Allen *Curnow's *Caxton anthology (1951).

In 1946 Smithyman married Mary *Stanley, also a poet. From 1946 to 1963 he was a primary and intermediate schoolteacher, specialising in children with learning difficulties. His first book was *Seven Sonnets* (Pelorus Press, 1946), followed by *The Blind Mountain and Other Poems* (Caxton, 1950). In his earlier poetry he assimilated a great many Modernist influences, including T.S. Eliot, W.H. Auden, Dylan Thomas and the Americans John Crowe Ransom, Allen Tate, Robert Lowell and Marianne Moore. New Zealand influences were less evident, Smithyman preferring (at least initially) to avoid the 'land and the people' preoccupations of his elders, which he associated with a South Island Romantic mythology (see *Mainland). His poems were often highly allusive, intellectually demanding and syntactically complex. He defended his work against criticisms of obscurity on the grounds that complexity was unavoidable in the modern world: 'A section of the poetry of an advanced and intricated community must inevitably be complex, and because complex, obscure' (*New Zealand Poetry Yearbook, 1954). During the late 1940s–50s he published frequently in journals, including the first (in 1947) of the extraordinary total of sixty-four poems he eventually placed in *Landfall. But apart from a pamphlet, The Gay Trapeze (Handcraft Press, 1955), and The Night Shift (Capricorn Press, 1957)—a joint publication with James K. *Baxter, Louis *Johnson and Charles *Doyle—he did not publish another book until Inheritance (*Paul) in 1962. This collection was a mix of both very early and more recent poems, including (among the latter) some of memorable subtlety and intricacy, such as 'Parable of Two Talents', 'Zoo', 'Climbing in the Himalayas' and 'Snapshots from the Pigbreeder's Gazette'. Few new poems were written in the early 1960s; Flying to Palmerston (1968) consisted mostly of revisions of poems written in the 1950s, though the title poem pointed in promising new directions.

In 1963 Smithyman joined the University of Auckland as a senior tutor in English, a position he retained until his retirement in 1987. He was awarded an honorary DLitt in 1986. He was a visiting fellow in Commonwealth Literature at the University of Leeds in 1969, and wrote many poems stimulated by his travel experiences in the UK and North America, such as 'English Effigies' and 'Reflections from Golden Gate'. These figured prominently in his next three collections, all with *Auckland University Press, Earthquake Weather (1972), The Seal in the Dolphin Pool (1974) and Dwarf with a Billiard Cue (1978). His return to New Zealand stimulated some of the best of his poems which engage with the landscape, history and people of Northland, including the sequences 'An Ordinary Day Beyond Kaitaia', 'Tomarata' and 'Reading the Maps: An Academic Exercise', which are arguably his finest achievements. Stories About Wooden Keyboards (1985), which won the New Zealand Book Award for Poetry, revealed an increasingly anecdotal and narrative tendency, and the corresponding development of a comically loquacious and self-deprecating persona, directions taken still further in Are You Going to the Pictures? (1987) and Auto/Biographies (1992). A Selected Poems (AUP, 1989), edited by Peter *Simpson, included some previously uncollected poems and revisions of many earlier ones. Shortly

before his death at age 73, Smithyman completed *Atua Wera, a lengthy, idiosyncratic poem-book about Papahurihia, the remarkable nineteenth-century Ngā Puhi religious leader who had been Hone Heke's personal *tohunga. The product of some fifteen years' research and writing, Atua Wera is Smithyman's magnum opus.

In addition to being a prolific poet Smithyman wrote criticism intermittently, especially during the period when he was literary editor of *Here & Now (1949–57). In the early 1960s he wrote four articles about post-war New Zealand poetry for *Mate (8–11), which were later revised and expanded to a book-length study, A Way of Saying (1965). This idiosyncratic book shrewdly revealed the Romantic affiliations of earlier New Zealand poets, and pointed to subtle regional differences, especially between Auckland and Wellington poets, in his own generation. His account of the aesthetics and practice of Auckland poets (notably M.K. *Joseph, Keith *Sinclair, Mary Stanley and C.K. *Stead) in the period 1945–60 also provided insights into his own poetic theory and practice. He also produced critical editions of novels by William *Satchell, The *Land of the Lost (1971) and The *Toll of the Bush (1985); and of the stories of Greville *Texidor, In Fifteen Minutes You Can Say a Lot (1987). He remarried in 1981 and was awarded the OBE in 1990. A prolific, demanding and rewarding poet, Smithyman is perhaps most noteworthy as a kind of literary archaeologist whose self-imposed task was to investigate 'What place means' ('Bream Bay') in terms of the northern parts of New Zealand he knew so intimately.   PS

Soldier's Tale, A (1976), is an emotionally powerful and morally complex short novel by M.K. *Joseph. Late in World *War 2, a British corporal, Saul Scourby, tells the story of a weekend he spent, during the Allied advance through Normandy earlier in 1944, with a beautiful young Frenchwoman, Belle Pradier, in her isolated cottage. For three days he protects her from the Resistance, who wait outside to avenge her betrayal of one of their members to her German lover during the Occupation. The sexual payment Scourby exacts for his protection turns in the course of the weekend to a microcosm of a loving marriage, a relationship that fluctuates through moods of routine domesticity and tender intimacy as well as animal possessiveness and loving passion. The complexity of human love is as much the novel's subject as the tragic determinism of war.

Scourby's efforts to find help for Belle from his own superiors and the Catholic Church are unsuccessful. The survival and hunting skills he has learnt in a parentless youth in rural Wessex enable him to act at once tenderly and brutally. His final efficient mercy-killing of Belle, almost unbearable in the reading, leads quickly to the novel's Blakean conclusion: 'Cruelty and mercy share the same human heart.'

That comment is part of a texture of moral reflection woven throughout the action by the immediate narrator, the educated and contemplative bombardier to whom Scourby told the story, the second soldier whose 'tale' it becomes. Possessed by it 'like a tough old ugly cat that won't drown and won't go away', he writes it in his study at night in 1973, troubled constantly by the multiple ambiguities of its possible meanings, including those induced by the changed context thirty years after the event. A few unobtrusive hints can identify this narrator as a New Zealander, and the sense of involved detachment with which the war is regarded subtly encapsulates New Zealand's changing relation with Europe in the later twentieth century, and is one of Joseph's most significant achievements, here and elsewhere.

The sharply observed authenticity of the wartime background is rendered in vivid, sometimes onomatopoeic language ('Splinters buzzed and clipped and whickered through the trees. Then it was all gone'), including the monotonous routines of everyday existence on the edge of war. The text sustains a stimulating counterpoint between Scourby's limited soldier's slang and the narrator's more resourceful, varied, sympathetic, sometimes lyrical cadences, as he works confessedly 'decoding these messages from the past ... recreating, refining, reinforcing, enhancing'.

This multiple narration, many-layered at times, as when Belle recounts to Scourby her earlier life and how she was trapped into the betrayal, has caused the novel to be discussed in terms of structuralism and *postmodernism. It also made it the object of a savagely unsympathetic reading by Allen ★Curnow in the poem 'Dichtung und Wahrheit' shortly before Joseph's death. In essence, however, *A Soldier's Tale* is a classic lucubration, a philosophical meditation on a text, in this case one whose complex spiritual, moral and political implications make tolerable the tragic pain of the story itself. It is an encounter between Joseph's Catholic consciousness and his formative experience of war.

A Soldier's Tale was published by Collins in Great Britain and New Zealand, reissued in Fontana paperback in 1977 and 1986, and by Godwit in 1995. A feature ★film version was released in 1991.   RR

Sole Survivor, the third novel in a trilogy by Maurice ★Gee, see **Plumb**.

SOLOMON, Laura (1974–), novelist, was born in Auckland, but has also resided in Raetihi, Nelson, Tasmania, Christchurch, Dunedin and Wellington, where she worked in the theatre both as a writer and actor. She completed a BA at the University of Otago, where she also began writing seriously, and BA (Hons) in English at Victoria University. At the age of 21 she achieved the remarkable feat of having two novels accepted for publication: *Black Light* (1996), in part a subversion of the ★'Man Alone' myth, and *Nothing Lasting* (1997). Her high-velocity prose style is violent and lurid. In an interview in ★*Quote Unquote* (Sept. 1996) she remarked: 'I don't want to be easily digestible. I want to go down like a cup of cold sick, and I think I'm achieving my aim.' She has been called 'the young New Zealander best known for writing about youth's rage' (Kate Belgrave).   KI

'Something Childish but Very Natural', a short story by Katherine ★Mansfield, was published posthumously in *Something Childish and Other Stories* (1924), though written early in 1914. The whereabouts of the MS is unknown. The story exemplifies the fashionable Edwardian notion of escape into childhood as well as Romantic ideas, taking for its title the Coleridge poem of the same name, which it misquotes. Romantic child love is presented through the meeting of two innocents, Henry (18) and Edna (16), who play-act a relationship, conceived of by Henry in terms of the title poem: 'Had I two wings, / And were a little feathery bird, / To you I'd fly, my dear—'. The story charts Henry's romantic ideal, Edna's shrinking from physical contact, her seeming absorption into Henry's fantasy followed by her final rejection—Henry rents a cottage for them to share, but Edna sends a telegram that dashes his hopes. Sentimental in tone, this essentially realist story is not one of Mansfield's most popular. It is nonetheless significant as her longest work to that date. It also introduces an episodic structure and characters who engage in fantasy, features which recur in later stories.   SSa

SOPER, Eileen (1900–), born Eileen Service in Sydney, was a journalist, children's novelist and autobiographer. Educated at Otago GHS and Otago University (BA 1924), she became the first women's page editor on the *Otago Daily Times*, where she found herself confined to writing social notes. Later she reviewed books and became 'Dot' of the *Otago Witness* children's page, returning to the *Times* when the *Witness* closed in 1932. Women's page editor again, she developed a new column, 'Patchwork Pieces', for stories, articles and interviews. Resigning in 1938 to marry, she wrote *The Otago of Our Mothers* (1946) and two autobiographical books, *The Green Years* (1969) and *The Leaves Turn* (1973), which includes a valuable account of her work as a journalist. Her first book for teenage readers, *Young Jane: A Tale of New Zealand in the Sixties* (1955), a nineteenth-century South Island story, is described by Betty ★Gilderdale as 'the first book to portray a child's-eye view of early-settler life … rendering sensitively the period atmosphere and day-to-day life of a sheep station'. *The Month of the Brittle Star* (1971) is set in Stewart Island, where a near-drowning causes a young girl to develop a sense of responsibility and awareness of differences in personality.   JMcC

SOUTHAM, Barry (1940–), made a mark as one of the voices of New Zealand's equivalent of the Beat Generation, with poems, stories and plays about alternative lifestyles or people outside the norms of society, often drop-outs. Brought up in Christchurch (Christchurch BHS, University of Canterbury), he accumulated wide work experience in jobs from forestry labourer and ship's scullion to television actor, as well as periods in California. He started as a poet, publishing quite frequently in ★*Cave*, ★*Edge* and ★*Mate*, as well as ★*Landfall* and ★*Poetry New Zealand*. His first volume, *Lovers and Other People* (1973), is a series of vignette character or narrative sketches in direct, colloquial diction, their impact coming mainly from their (for the time) radical frankness on such subjects as sex or suicide. In many ways they are close to the suburban realism of Louis ★Johnson. Southam carried the same candid camera into short fiction with *Mixed Singles* (1981). Forthrightly observed but never malicious, the twelve stories were described by Alistair ★Paterson as using an approach 'closer to that of the anthropologist than the traditional story teller's'. They are at their most perceptive on the stressful encounter between conventional and new lifestyles, particularly in three recording a New Zealander's response to California. A vignette of male disconcertment under women's new sexual power is also notable. More poems followed (*The People Dance*, 1982), again dramatic sketches drawn mostly from New Zealand and America; and several plays for stage, radio and television. Southam now works as an addiction counsellor in Auckland, and his novel dealing with the alternate lifestyle generation of the late 1960s, 'Going Down in Grafton', has been accepted for publication.   RR

South-Sea Siren, A: A Novel Descriptive of New Zealand Life in the Early Days by George ★Chamier was published in London in 1895 as a sequel to ★*Philosopher Dick*. It adopts an unorthodox structure in which chapters of philosophical discussion involving the male characters are dispersed between more straightforward narrative. The first chapter, a discussion on the question of eternal damnation and the relativity of truth, sets the tone. During wedding preparations for Dick's friend Mary Seymour, who with her sister Alice appeared in

the first novel, 'the feminine element is in the ascendant'. It brings in a '★puritanical society' prone to moralistic gossip, usually centred on the 'siren' of the title, who is notorious for her striking appearance and vigorously flirtatious 'conquests', though these do not amount to adultery. She is able to enchant even the bailiffs and entice money out of her male visitors, including Dick, who feels self-disgust at the attraction.

Philosophical discussions on the issue of delusion and truth continue to be interspersed with these episodes. Dick tries to live as a recluse but is constantly visited by amorous women, sometimes with heavy-handedly farcical consequences. He joins a surveying party and meets the ideal 'Contented Man', who avoids extremes of all kinds.

When Dick returns, Mrs Wylde the siren continues the theme of lies and truth by scorning his suggestion that she should maintain appearances, despite an episode where she lies ill revealing her 'bosom', and another where he sleeps at her bedside. Dick, fearful the scandal will reach Alice Seymour, accepts a journalist's position in Wellington. Alice appears and says she too is going to Wellington, and the story ends with the suggestion of a new life in the capital.

A reissue in 1970 in the series 'New Zealand Fiction' (★Auckland University Press) has an introduction by Joan ★Stevens, the only extended comment on Chamier's fiction. She sees the novel's primary interest as 'evidence about New Zealand in the 1860s', which is indeed remarkably rich and detailed, but calls it 'very oddly constructed' and 'inartistic'. In fact, the unifying theme of truth and lies, reality and appearances, fact and fiction can be pursued into every facet. It is most acute in the siren herself, whose unashamed flirtatiousness combines startling 'honesty' about sexuality in a hypocritical world with its own limitations to truth in suggesting more than it yields. Celia Wylde is a splendid image of an irreconcilable confusion of truthfulness and imposture.

Stevan ★Eldred-Grigg takes up characters and themes from this book in his novel *The Siren Celia* (1989).
                                     NW

Speaking for Ourselves (1945) was an ★anthology of short stories compiled and edited by Frank ★Sargeson. Originally commissioned by the ★Progressive Publishing Society, when they withdrew it was taken over by Denis ★Glover for ★Caxton Press, and was also published in Melbourne by Reed and Harris. (To secure this Sargeson included a story by the Australian publisher-author Max Harris.) Younger writers, many mentored by Sargeson, are strongly represented—David ★Ballantyne, John Reece ★Cole, Maurice ★Duggan, A.P. ★Gaskell and Greville ★Texidor. Roderick ★Finlayson and Sargeson's own 'The Hole That Jack Dug' were also included. Michael ★King comments that 'the effort that Frank devoted during the years of the war to friendship and to literary midwifery bore fruit in *Speaking for Ourselves*' (*Frank Sargeson*, 1995). Patrick ★Evans gives the different angle that the choice 'seems to shoulder [the 1930s] into the past', but cites Janet ★Frame's memory of how 'The stories overwhelmed me by the fact of their belonging' (*Penguin History of New Zealand Literature*, 1990). King summarises the reviews as 'mutedly favourable', but the book was not commercially successful despite Sargeson's attempts to cater for popular appeal in some of the selections.   RR

SPEAR, Charles (1910–85), poet, was born in Okawa in the Catlins district of South Otago. He went to Otago BHS (1924–27) and to university in Christchurch and Dunedin (BA Otago, 1933). He returned to Canterbury College for his MA in 1945. Among his close friends and contemporaries were Ian ★Milner, Leo ★Bensemann and Lawrence ★Baigent. Milner recalled that 'He was dedicated to the cult of the beautiful as an end in itself.' He contributed poems to student magazines in the early 1930s including *Canta* and the ★*Canterbury University College Review*, usually under a pseudonym or initials. He collaborated with Lawrence Baigent on poems and fiction, a novel *Rearguard Actions* being published by Methuen in 1936 under the name C.L. Spear-Baigent. A second novel, *No Place for a Gentleman* (1939), was completed but never published. Spear worked in journalism and schoolteaching before becoming a lecturer in English at Canterbury from 1949 until his retirement in 1975. He specialised in Middle English literature and was also widely read in European languages, including Latin, Greek, French, Italian, German and Russian (which he taught himself shortly before retirement). He reviewed plays for the ★*Press* in the 1960s.

After his student years Spear did not publish poetry again until 1948–51, when his poems appeared in ★*Landfall*, ★*Yearbook of the Arts*, ★*Arachne*, ★*Gaudeamus* and the ★*New Zealand Poetry Yearbook*. He was one of the new writers added by Allen ★Curnow to the second edition of his ★*Book of New Zealand Verse* (1951), and also in 1951 published his single (and singular) collection, *Twopence Coloured*, the seventh and last volume in the 'Caxton Poets' series. The title comes from the phrase 'one penny plain and twopence coloured', as used by Robert Louis Stevenson in *Travels with a Donkey*, of the 'sheets of characters of my boyhood' (i.e. for toy theatres). The book has an apt epigraph from James Joyce's *Finnegans Wake*: 'This way to the musey room. Mind your hats goan in.' There were fifty-two short poems in

Twopence Coloured, ranging in length from four to seventeen lines, some being revisions of his student verses from the early 1930s. The poems are noteworthy for their concision, their allusiveness, their almost total avoidance of local or regional reference, and (in Thomas Hardy's phrase) for their 'idiosyncratic mode of regard'. Spear told friends that many were composed word-for-word in his sleep. After *Twopence Coloured* he published very little. He said in 1960, 'My ideas about verse and literature seem to be changing, for which reason I have written nothing for some years.' The silence (at least as far as publication is concerned) continued for the rest of his life.

Although he published relatively little Spear's name has been kept alive as a poet by the fondness of critics and anthologists for his work. Curnow commented in 1951: 'Mr Spear's gracefully formed lyrics come direct from a mind withdrawn upon itself, nourished by nothing we would call indigenous; yet they are a distinctive addition by a New Zealand poet.' Curnow included fourteen poems in his Penguin anthology in 1960, while Vincent ★O'Sullivan chose twenty for his Oxford anthology in 1970. MacD.P. Jackson, who included fifteen of Spear's poems in *New Zealand Writing Since 1945* (Oxford, 1983), wrote: '*Twopence Coloured* looks like verbal cameo-work, but Spear's "studiously minor" muse is (as he claims) "attuned to doom". A post-war temper infiltrates the trim stanzas of a Rhymers' Club aesthete, and disturbing, sharply focussed details loom from a phantasmagoria in miniature of historical, literary, and personal anedote.' Spear is still represented in recent anthologies such as the *Penguin* (1985) and Oxford *Anthology* (1996).

After retirement Spear and his wife Margaret went to live in England, where both their daughters had settled. He died in London. His friend and colleague R.A. ★Copland described him in an obituary as 'a rarely gifted man, so European in his intellectual and imaginative range, and yet so essentially Kiwi in his personality, so self-deprecating in his nature.'   PS

Special Flower, A (1965), the second novel of Maurice ★Gee.

Spike was published by the Victoria University College Students' Association 1902–61. Initially a biannual of student affairs with some literary content, following the establishment of the student newspaper *Smad* in 1930, predecessor of *Salient*, *Spike* became an annual of student literary endeavour. Early issues featured verse by Hubert ★Church, F.A. de la Mare, and Seaforth MacKenzie, much of which was collected into the anthology *The Old Clay Patch*, first published in 1920. From the mid-1940s

Spike was supplemented on campus by *Broadsheet* (1947–1948), *Hilltop* (1949), *Arachne* (1950–51), *Experiment* (1956–63), and several literary issues of *Salient*. Notable contributors from 1940 include James K. *Baxter, Peter *Bland, Gordon *Challis, Charles *Doyle, W.H. *Oliver, Maurice *Shadbolt, Pat *Wilson, Hubert *Witheford and Anton *Vogt. During this period both *Caxton Press and Robert *Lowry were employed to print *Spike*. SH

Spilt Ink was the second periodical edited, printed and published by Noel *Hoggard. It appeared in Wellington 1932–37 and was succeeded by *New Triad*. From an initial single cyclostyled leaf it developed into a professionally printed journal incorporating *NZ Amateur Theatre*. *Spilt Ink* reported on local and overseas literary events and published poetry and stories by members of the 'Spilt Ink Clubs', established by Hoggard and others to promote New Zealand writing. Contributors included Denis *Glover, C.R. *Allen, Jean Boswell, S.G. August and Dulce *Carman. SH

Spin was started in 1986 on cyclostyled A4 as 'the Quarterly Magazine of the Poetry Orbital Workshops', which were 'an initiative of the *New Zealand Poetry Society', and were run from Palmerston North. Under editor David Drummond the magazine developed by Number 7 (1988) a quite professional appearance, could attract writers such as Harry *Ricketts, and had two assistant editors, one in *Australia. It now solicited international submissions, describing itself as 'an independent journal produced on behalf of the Poetry Society Inc.' It included poems, reviews and notices. After Drummond's death and a hiatus in publication, the society gave its endorsement to *Poetry New Zealand*. A 'first reissue' of *Spin*, described as a 'new venture', appeared in March 1991 edited in Auckland by P.N.W. Donnelly, who had contributed poems to the early Palmerston North issues. RR

Spinster (1958), a novel by Sylvia *Ashton-Warner, was greeted with surprise and enthusiasm for its portrayal of Māori children. The dialogue ('That's why somebodies they tread my sore leg for notheen. Somebodies.') seemed to capture the language of such children with startling fidelity. The numerous children were strongly differentiated from each other yet all seemed to be 'authentic'.

The main character is a schoolteacher, Miss Vorontosov, and the action takes place almost entirely in the school. She is devoted to the children and to her otherwise quiet life as a spinster. Even the most difficult of the children is allowed to sit on her knee and is encouraged to develop creativity and spontaneous skills. She is disturbed by the relationship of the attractive teacher, Paul, and a beautiful schoolgirl, Wareparita, and yet she remains curiously innocent. She is fearful of the director and of the school inspectors, and they have little respect for her teaching methods, but these are so successful that, for the reader, she, rather than those more powerful figures, is triumphant. Throughout the stresses of such relationships she is sustained by the *aroha of the children, whose robust health invigorates her. She is less impressed by the Pākehā children however, noting of a 5-year-old that he has already 'had a serious nervous illness'. Her love is for the Māori children and the 'life-force' they represent: 'I am as clay in the hands of this force, this something that told my dephiniums when to bud.'

The gift she has for the children in return is the ability to read. Her technique, which occupies much of the book, is unorthodox: she asks the children what they are afraid of or what excites or moves them, and then shows them how to write the words they use. Not 'The cat is on the mat', but 'butcher-knife, gaol, police, sing, cry, kiss, Daddy, Mummy, Rangi, haka, fight. So I make a reading card for him: out of these words, which he reads at first sight, and his face lights up with understanding.' This is Ashton-Warner's theory of the 'key vocabulary' and the way that the children create what they are to learn—a theory which gave the author a career in education but is here integrated into a strong narrative. The plot includes a 'love interest' which turns out unhappily for Miss Vorontosov at the hands of a treacherous male, but its main interest is the vivid characterisation of Māori children. Reviewing it for *Te *Ao Hou* (March 1959), Erik Schwimmer wrote: 'It has been very well received in England: in New Zealand it is undoubtedly one of the best novels so far written. It is explosive, passionate, exciting all the way.' NW

Spiral Collective, see **HULME, Keri.**

Splash was a magazine in four issues, 1984–86, edited by Wystan *Curnow, Tony Green, Roger Horrocks and Judi Stout. Its first editorial stated: 'The fore-runners were: *MOREPORK, and *PARALLAX which is what got us going as editors, and of course *AND as our example of Xerox publication'. This located *Splash* as part of a genealogy of magazines, stemming from *Freed* in New Zealand, but aligning also with a number of overseas, particularly *American, publications. While it is tempting to treat the members of this genealogy as isolated attempts to get something more durable started, it is more accurate to treat the genealogy as a whole, itself the durable documentation of a continuous activity by the artists and writers included in it. A lot of material by overseas artists and writers appeared, establishing a wider and testing context for the local work, but without overwhelming the New Zealand product or competing unduly with it. Overseas writers included Charles Bernstein, Lyn Hejinian, Robert Grenier, Johanna Drucker, with New Zealand artists Stephen Bambury, Julia Morrison, Bruce Barber, Peter Roche and Linda Buis, Philip Dadson; and writers Alan *Loney, Wystan Curnow, Judi Stout, Leigh *Davis, Tony Green, John Geraets, Roger Horrocks, Ted Jenner, Graham *Lindsay, Alex Calder.   AL

Spleen was a radical magazine, 1975–77, produced by *Red Mole Enterprises, initiated by Alan *Brunton and Ian *Wedde, in succession to *Freed (1969–72). It put literary work into a context of the visual and performing arts, its content and layout assertively unconventional, anti-establishment and aimed at the younger generation.   RR

Split Enz, see **FINN, Neil**.

Sport and literature in New Zealand have had an uneasy, even hostile relationship. Serious writers have tended to castigate the public's preoccupation with 'rugby, racing and beer', and popular sports literature, despite a copious print journalism, is of recent growth and modest quality. For a country with such a rich history of sport, there is a striking scarcity of literature that celebrates, narrates or re-imagines it with any inwardness. Only where sport enters the *backblocks or mountains has New Zealand produced a literature in any way distinct, and that is more as part of the larger imaginative response to the *landscape than as sports writing in the accepted sense.

The earliest sports writing of any literary interest is Samuel *Butler's virtuoso account in the *Press of the Canterbury vs All England cricket match in 1864 in parodic Shakespearean blank verse: 'Fortune turned her wheel, / And Grace, disgracéd for the nonce, was bowled / First ball, and all the welkin roared applause!' It was reprinted in the 1914 edition of *A First Year in Canterbury Settlement* and anthologised in Leslie Frewin's *The Poetry of Cricket* (London, 1964). Sports reporting in early newspapers was mostly confined to events of social significance. From as early as 1864, the *New Zealand Herald* fully reported the annual regatta on the Waitemata and the New Year's Day race meeting, but sports such as athletics, rugby or swimming were not covered until the 1880s. At that time in Christchurch the *Weekly Press* embarked on its major commitment to sports journalism, producing the first identifiable writers of repute,

'Sinbad' (Fred Digby) and 'Senex' (E.G. Griffith).

Away from the cities, early explorers such as Butler, Thomas Brunner, J.H. Baker and Charles Douglas wrote well about the rewards as well the rigours of the mountains, but in the sense that enjoyment is the prime purpose, probably the first sports book about New Zealand was by an early angling tourist, William Senior, whose *Travel and Trout in the Antipodes* was published in England in 1880; and the first written and published in New Zealand was W.H. Spackman's *Trout in New Zealand: Where To Go and How To Catch Them* (1892). These are instructional guides, and field sports writing only began to aspire towards something more reflective with George Douglas Hamilton's *Trout-Fishing and Sport in Maoriland* (1904) ('sport' here meaning game-hunting) and A.H. Chaytor's *Letters to a Salmon Fisher's Son* (1910). Mountaineering, too, now began to produce writing with narrative, descriptive and even psychological depth (for the first time since *Erewhon), as in Arthur P. Harper's *Pioneer Work in the Alps of New Zealand* (1896), which John *Pascoe calls 'one of our few classics' in his summary of Alpine literature in *Land Uplifted High* (1952).

What were then called 'games' found their first expression outside the newspapers with Thomas Rangiwahia Ellison's eloquent *The Art of Rugby Football* (1902) and *The Complete Rugby Footballer* by the literate duo of D[avid] Gallaher and W[illiam] J. Stead (1906). Gallaher, New Zealand rugby captain in 1906, was also progenitor of the 'Rugby Tour' genre with *Why the 'All Blacks' Triumphed! … 'Daily Mail' Story of the Tour* (London, 1906).

The oral dimension should be acknowledged, however hard to recall. Wi Pere's welcome to the Anglo-Welsh rugby team at Poverty Bay in 1908 is still quoted; tramping and mountaineering developed a vigorous tradition of songs and verses (e.g. *The Tararua Songbook*, 1971); sports clubs had their own song books; long-established yarns can still be collected (e.g. Graham Hutchins, *New Zealand Rugby Yarns*, 1996); and the ballad impulse began to produce published verses by David McKee *Wright, Thomas *Bracken or George Phipps *Williams on horse-racing ('How Carbine was left at the Post'), 'fisticuffs' or cricket, as well as, of course, the *bush. The *haka challenge, *'ka mate, ka mate', recorded as first used by the New Zealand rugby team of 1888, has become the most familiar item of oral sports culture in New Zealand.

Sports journalism was firmly established in popular culture by the early twentieth century. The *Press* and especially *Weekly Press* justly boasted that its sports coverage was 'the best south of the Line … known to every player in the two islands for its brilliant descriptions of play' and other qualities, not forgetting 'very capable editorship' of the chess and draughts columns. Notable writers included 'The Warrigal', whose work was reprinted in Britain's prestigious *The Field*, and 'Antithenes', in fact Arthur Henry Bristed, *Weekly Press* editor 1886–1925, a talented sportsman, authority on racehorse breeding, and sportswriter in the *Press* tradition of expert lucidity. *The New Zealand Referee*, a sporting paper, was edited from 1925 by C.A. *Marris, the literary anthologist. Robin *Hyde was one journalist who went beneath the surface and wrote of the popular culture of sport (e.g. in 'All Night Queue', *New Zealand Observer*, 1937).Close to journalism at this time was the short story, almost always published in newspapers, with racing the usual sports subject: Pat *Lawlor's 'The Nag Nincompoop' (in *Gillespie's *New Zealand Short Stories*, 1930) is a good sample of this semi-reportage genre.

A book-based literature was still evolving only very slowly. Two angling classics came from the famous American Western novelist, Zane Grey, the enthusiastically impassioned *Tales of the Angler's El Dorado—New Zealand* (1926) and the posthumously compiled *Tales from a Fisherman's Log* (1978). Field-sport writing was enhanced by T.E. Donne, who wrote well on angling and hunting (e.g. *Red Deer Stalking in New Zealand*, 1924). There was little else—mountaineering and tramping continued to produce literate reflection, but nothing to match European work. Even as the newspapers of the first half of the twentieth century responded to the public's enormous appetite for sportswriting, in works that have survived as literature sport remained almost invisible. John *Mulgan commented in *Report on Experience* (1947) on his generation's preoccupation with rugby ('the best of all our pleasures') and the deprecation this provoked 'by a lot of thinkers who feel that an exaggerated attention to games gives the young a wrong sense of values'. His defence of rugby now sounds worse than an attack: 'in wartime … there was considerable virtue in men who had played games like professionals to win.' Sport's values, he concluded, 'were not so much wrong as primitive'.

That disparaging premise seems to underlie much of literature's treatment of sport from 1940 until about 1990. Sport, and especially rugby, became scapegoat and metaphor for militarism (as Mulgan suggested), violence, competitiveness, profaneness and philistinism. Bill *Pearson in *'Fretful Sleepers' took the Rugby Union's concession to South Africa as evidence of the whole nation's impoverished morality. Bruce *Mason blamed the lack of theatre on a society 'which will admit only games as viable rituals'. M.K. *Joseph castigated the worship of 'the liturgical drone / Of the race-commentator' and 'Saint Allblack / Saint Monday Raceday'

('Secular Litany'). A.R.D. *Fairburn lamented to Charles *Brasch that 'our heroes [are] successful Rugby footballers'. Allen *Curnow noticed New Zealand's extraordinary Olympic achievements in 1964 only when some high-spirited athletes bowed to the Japanese Emperor and provoked a *'Whim-Wham' sermon on conduct: 'This wouldn't be the first (or worst) Display / Of the Kiwi's Habits while abroad—and All / Because the World's so big, and he's so small! / The dear wee Pet …'. After the Springbok tour of 1981 the charges got even graver, as in David *Eggleton's 'Execution of a South African Considered as an All Blacks–Springbok Test Match' (in *After Tokyo*, 1987) or Gary *Langford's use of racing as metaphor for all of society's violent repressiveness, in 'Samuel Marsden and the Convict Race' (in *Jesus the Galilee Hitch-Hiker*, 1991).

Even those few imaginative works that write of a sport with any informed inwardness were mostly critical of its values and role in New Zealand society. Rugby in A.P. *Gaskell's novel *The Big Game* (1944), Maurice *Gee's *The Big Season* (1962) and Greg *McGee's more complex version in *Foreskin's Lament* (1981) is a code of narrow-mindedness and brutishness, an ethic of 'Dominate them!', 'Kick shit out of everything above grass height', of stifling conformity that isolates the one individual (in both the Gee and McGee) who tries to enact a morality of social conscience. Albert *Wendt also writes knowledgeably about rugby in *Sons for the Return Home* (1973) and *Black Rainbow* (1992), but concludes that to play it well is to comply with colonialist values; his talented schoolboy footballer in *Sons* 'chose to win the game; play it their way' but thereafter 'refused to play'. Dan *Davin made rugby and racing a natural part of his record of Southland life, for instance in *Roads from Home* (1949), but his lack of rancour was the exception.

Sport's very competitiveness has made it available as a metaphor of failure or decay: 'The young athletes ran / Nowhere at the Games, / No sporting year-book / Lists their names' (Curnow, *Not in Narrow Seas*, 1939); 'Under the framed photograph / Of his All Black team / His hooked hand trembled' (Ruth *Dallas). Sporting defeat leads to suicide in Gaskell's 'All Part of the Game' (1950), mercenary cruelty in Gee's 'The Losers' (1959), 'huge despair' for Bruce Mason's Firpo in The *End of the Golden Weather* (1962) and death disregarded by a shallow spectator society in Maurice *Duggan's 'Race Day' (1952). Gee's flabby ex-boxer in 'The Champion' (1966), 'dreaming of fights', turns to vindictiveness and self-destruction rather than accept his own decrepitude. The death of a courageous Māori player can elicit only the obituary 'a promising rugby player, and a credit to his race' (in Maurice *Shadbolt's *Strangers and Journeys*, 1972; the remaining ten minutes of the game are played).

In James ★Courage's 'An Evening for a Fish' (1955) dishonesty and stealth, not sporting skill, make the boy's rite of passage.

The claim of the moral and cultural high ground for the arts and intelligentsia is most explicitly made in C.K. ★Stead's poem 'Crossing the Bar' (1972), which prefers poetry (which 'represents') to the momentary art of high jumping ('And falls on foam'), and his story 'A Race Apart' (1961), where a great runner like 'something out of a Greek legend' is belittled, exposed as emotionally obtuse and mindlessly obsessed with diet and training, defeated by the intellectual writer in the contest for the sexual prize and finally humiliated, flat on the ground 'like a spider turned on its back'. Such cultural elitism runs from Bob ★Gormack's parodic version of horseracing 'culture' in ★Bookie (1948), the point being the laughable impossibility of such a thing, through J.H.E. ★Schroder's set of poems scoffing at the idiom of sports commentators (Yet Once More, 1969) to Ian Richards mockingly learning that 'the greatest man of all time was ... named Clarke, a fullback' (1991) or John ★Sligo rejecting a society of 'fearful souls who could never face inside and made do with mountains to climb' (Faces of Sappho, 1990) or Bill ★Manhire playing word games with Phar Lap or the amputees who talk about 'the second leg at Trentham' (Milky Way Bar, 1991). The avant-garde literary periodical founded in 1988 calls itself, with ludic irony, ★Sport.

A few works have begun the task of giving imaginative expression to sport's innate drama, psychological interest and what Lloyd ★Jones has called its 'wider cultural context' (introducing his ground-breaking collection of quality sports writing, Into the Field of Play, 1992). Relatively early attempts include Pat ★Booth's Sprint From the Bell (1966), Stead's poem 'Four minute miler', and, more successfully, Gordon ★Slatter's The Pagan Game (1968) and Ruth ★France's The Race (1958). This novel is strong in its well-informed narrative of a stormy inter-island yacht race, and its insights into inner lives, especially of 'the waiting women'; it recognises, too, the bond between a skilled sportsperson and the physical world ('he was part of the surging ocean'), and the confrontation sport can bring with the fundamentals of life ('It takes ... so little of elemental fear to strip the niceties'). Foreskin's Lament and Mervyn ★Thompson's play A Night at the Races (with Yvonne Edwards, 1981), Patricia ★Grace in 'The Dream' (1975) and Selwyn Muru in 'Te Ohaki a Nihe' all treat with some sympathy the place of sport in popular culture. James ★McNeish combined psychology with myth in his biofiction ★Lovelock (1986), followed by David ★Geary and Stuart ★Hoar. Adrienne Simpson's anthology Cricket (1997) includes excellent writing by Spiro Zavos and others. Notable writing since 1950 about mountaineering and tramping includes books by John ★Pascoe, A.H. ★Reed, Philip ★Temple and Denis ★McLean. Good fishing writing has risen to the surface in the work of O.S. Hince, John Parsons, Douglas ★Stewart and especially the prose and poetry of Brian ★Turner. Turner writes on a wide range of sports, in poems ('Jack Trout', 'Training on the Peninsula', 'Running in the Manuherikia Valley'), drama ('Finger's Up?' won the J.C. Reid Award 1985) and prose journalism (such as his account of riding a mountain bike among the Royal procession at Ascot). Roger ★Hall's 'C'Mon Black!' (1996) presents the drama of rugby from the spectator's point of view with unprecedented percipience. Warwick ★Roger (Old Heroes, 1991), Lloyd Jones (ed., Into the Field of Play) and Roger Robinson (Heroes and Sparrows: A Celebration of Running, 1986) have produced sports books aimed at the serious literary reader as well as the enthusiast. It is even becoming possible to treat sport comically, as in Geary's 'Pack of Girls' (1991), Janette ★Sinclair's satiric In Touch (1995) or Hall's 'C'Mon Black!'.

Some of the best imaginative work on sport has come from writers for children, a tradition established by ★School Journal with writers like Henry Brennan and by 'school story' writers like Clare ★Mallory on hockey, and developed, among others, by Elsie ★Locke on mountaineering and tramping, Jack ★Lasenby on bushcraft, Alan ★Bunn on the Coast-to-Coast and triathlon (Driving Force, 1991, Road Warriors, 1993), Paula ★Boock on softball (Home Run, 1995) and, most notably, Tessa ★Duder on swimming and David ★Hill on tae kwon do (Kick Back, 1995), tramping (Take It Easy, 1995) and, with some irony, cricket (Second Best, 1996).

Sport has also begun to appear in imaginative literature more naturally and maturely, no longer just to be turned on its back as the despised epitome of 'primitive values'. Anne ★French writes poems about jogging and sailing, John ★Newton about fishing, Stead about Murray Halberg; and sports take a place in such significant novels as Lloyd Jones's Splinter (softball), Gee's The ★Burning Boy (running and softball), Vincent ★O'Sullivan's Let the River Stand (boxing), Witi ★Ihimaera's Nights in the Gardens of Spain (jogging), and short stories by Owen ★Marshall and Peter ★Wells, who features 'a flock of graceful runners' as object of the homosexual gaze ('Outing').

Sports books themselves have become one of New Zealand publishing's most popular forms—Alex Veysey's Colin Meads—All Black (1974) sold over 60 000 copies, and John Blackwell's Moa Publications produced 230 titles in twenty-five years. Most are ephemeral, but writers who have proved their literary skills elsewhere quite often now write, or ghost-write, sports biographies or histories, including Pat Booth, Gordon Slatter, Douglas Stewart, Paul *Thomas and Brian Turner. These, and R.H. *Brittenden on cricket, Norman *Harris on running and T.P. *McLean on rugby stand out from the hagiographies and potboilers, doing more, as Lloyd Jones put it, than 'insist that I am between twelve and seventeen years of age'. From other individual titles of more than passing value by writers other than those named above, a provisional canon might include Ivan Agnew, *Kiwis Can Fly* (1976), Phil Gifford, *Smokin' Joe* (1990), Peter Heidenstrom, *Athletes of the Century* (1992), Edmund Hillary, *Nothing Venture, Nothing Win* (1975), Noel Holmes, *Trek Out of Trouble* (1960), Naomi James, *At One with the Sea* (1979), Chris McLean, *Tararua: The Story of a Mountain Range* (1994), Robin McConnell, *Iceman* (1994), Brian O'Brien, *Kiwis with Gloves On* (1960), Paul Powell, *Men Aspiring* (1967), Alex Veysey, *Fergie* (1976) and Jim Wilson, *Aorangi: The Story of Mount Cook* (1968). As sports writing has yet to receive the academic attention given to romance, detective fiction or soap opera, such a list is at best tentative.   RR

Sport is a literary magazine which has been published twice yearly since October 1988. It was launched in part to fill the gap left by *Islands, which although not officially folded had not appeared for some time. Lessons were also drawn from the examples of the designedly marginal and short-lived *AND and *Rambling Jack*. From the start it was intended that *Sport* would be a substantial, professionally edited and produced paperback, which would appear regularly, take a visible place in bookshops and find a general readership. According to John Thomson in the *OHNZLE* (1991, 1998), *Sport* 'at once established itself as currently the leading magazine for poetry and fiction'. Publisher and editor Fergus Barrowman founded *Sport* with editorial support from Elizabeth *Knox, Damien *Wilkins and Nigel *Cox. Later issues have been guest- or co-edited by James Brown (13, 14, 16, 18–), Andrew *Johnston (6–9), Gregory *O'Brien (15) and Sara Knox (17). Barrowman is also publisher of *Victoria University Press, and *Sport* has featured many writers from the so-called 'Wellington group' associated with VUP and Bill *Manhire's Victoria University creative writing course. The first issue featured early work by Barbara *Anderson, Jenny *Bornholdt, Anne *Kennedy, Elizabeth Knox, Virginia *Were, Wilkins and Forbes Williams, as well as established writers such as Cox, Keri *Hulme, Manhire and Vincent *O'Sullivan. *Sport* has continued to give a large amount of space to new writers. It was the first publisher of Emily *Perkins and Catherine Chidgey, and an early publisher of Kate *Flannery, Annamarie *Jagose, Chris *Orsman and Peter *Wells. *Sport* has published occasional review

essays, but not reviews, editorials, letters or other features of the traditional literary quarterly. The average size of the issues has been 160 pages, and the paid circulation is maintained between 500 and 600 copies.   FB

Squatter, originally a US term for a settler with no legal title to the land occupied, is applied in various senses in New Zealand: (1) (Australia 1828, NZ 1840), in historical use, one who occupies without, or with doubtful, legal title, Māori land, or such land as has been alienated to the Crown or a land company: '… the cupidity of land jobbers and squatters' (*GBPP House of Commons* 1841); (2) (Australia 1837, NZ 1847), in historical use, one occupying a tract of Māori or Crown land to graze livestock, having title (or putative title) by lease or other arrangement: 'The front ranges stopped the tide of squatters for some little time …' (Samuel *Butler, *Erewhon*, 1872); (3) in common current use (Australia 1841, NZ 1852), a pastoralist or farmer distinguished by class status and/or size of holding without reference to the title by which the land is held, formerly a member of a social and political elite: '… the prince of all the squatters, Largest holder of runholders' ('Song of the Squatters' in *Canterbury Rhymes*, 1866).

Various compounds are also found, often satirical and mainly archaic, such as 'squatterine' (1913), a contemptuous name for a squatter's wife, or 'squattocracy' (Australia 1843, NZ 1864), the wealthy sheep farmers as a political or social force, often applied derogatorily to wealthy sheep farmers collectively. The term was used as the title of a play, *Squatter* (1986) by Stuart *Hoar, set on a Canterbury *station in 1894.   HO

STANLEY, Mary (1919–80), is a poet whose output, though small, is of high quality. Three of her earliest poems won her the Jessie Mackay Memorial Award of 1945, and she went on from there to publish in periodicals like *Kiwi, *Yearbook of the Arts in New Zealand and *Here & Now. By 1951 she had a sufficiently large selection to publish one slim volume, *Starveling Year* (1953). There is little evidence to support the view expressed by some critics that Stanley was silenced by the male literary establishment of the 1950s. Indeed, her second husband, poet Kendrick *Smithyman, notes in his introduction to Stanley's posthumous edition *Starveling Year and Other Poems* (Auckland University Press, 1994), that 'men as different as A.R.D. *Fairburn, M.K. *Joseph, Robert *Lowry, Frank *Sargeson, Maurice *Duggan, James K. *Baxter, Robert *Thompson and especially Louis *Johnson treated her respectfully'. Stanley's poems are carefully crafted, often employing personal and domestic themes as vehicles for subtle comments on universally significant issues like death, grief, materialism and nuclear war. Her best work is characterised by a brilliance of image that merits comparison with work from the same period by Australian poet Judith Wright.   PM

STAPLES, Marjorie (1910–), travel writer, journalist and novelist, used the name 'Rosaline Redwood' for much of her work, and 'Marjory Thomas' or 'M.C. Thomas' during her first marriage. Her first novel was *Mocking Shadows* (1940; as Rosaline Redwood). Born Marjorie Jefcoate in Invercargill, she had short stories and articles in several New Zealand papers from her high school days, expanding later into Australian and American magazines, including articles on the *Pacific in the *National Geographic*, illustrated with her own photographs. She became a regular broadcaster in the 1940s through *Yeomen of the South* (1940; as M.C. Thomas), on Southland pioneers. Later she broadcast for the BBC and in South Africa based on *Forgotten Isles of the South Pacific* (1950), a history of the southern islands, and *On Copra Ships and Coral Isles* (1966), an account of her South Pacific travels which was New Zealand 'Book of the Month'. She wrote three lively later novels, *Forgotten Heritage*, set in Codfish Island (1966), *Isle of the Golden Pearls* (1967) and *Stranger from Shanghai* (1968), the latter reprinted in large type in 1992 with *Copra Ships*. She contributed gardening features to Australian and South African magazines and wrote *My Wilderness Blossomed* (1964). Her spiritual-autobiographical *He Was There Too, Reminiscences of a Christian Journalist* appeared 1995.

JMcC

State Literary Fund, see **Literary Fund.**

State of Siege, A, the sixth novel by Janet *Frame (New York, 1966; Christchurch: *Pegasus Press, London, 1967; typescript held in the *Hocken Library) won the Buckland Literary award (1967). Minimal in plot, the narrative focuses on the single figure of Malfred Signal, over a period of several days, tracing her solipsistic inward journey that ends in death. Much of the novel is written in the third person, with the exception of several chapters narrated in the first person by Malfred; the details given in these chapters differ in important ways from those given by the omniscient narrator. There are three sections, the titles of which invite allegorical reading: 'The Knocking', 'Darkness', 'The Stone'. In the first section Malfred, a retired art teacher, aged 53, leaves her South Island home (and her 'provincial, prejudiced, puritanical background') to live up North, on the 'subtropical' island of Karemoana, where she has bought a cottage and hopes to live 'alone, in charge and at rest'. She has been freed to do so by the death of her mother whom she has been tending for some years with, it transpires,

considerable bitterness. Malfred is seeking 'the New View', wanting to forgo her old way of seeing life; she no longer wishes to produce mimetic art but rather to 'forget the years of rigid shading, obsessional outlining and representation of objects' that she has practised in her painting, and forced on her students. Malfred equates her desired new view, truth and knowledge uncontaminated by human prejudices or social values, with a shadowless state (an idea Frame was to develop in greater depth in *Daughter Buffalo*). In the second section, one stormy night soon after her arrival on the island, Malfred is besieged by an unknown 'element', a prowler who knocks thunderously on her door and switches the lights off at the outdoor meter box. The knocking continues intermittently throughout the night. Physically trapped in the dark house, Malfred finds no retreat in the 'dream-room' situated 'two inches behind the eyes'; her mind, too, is besieged, invaded by memories of people from her past: mother, father, brothers and sisters, friends, pupils, and, most disturbingly, Wilfred, her lover, who was killed in the war. In the final section, a stone is thrown through the bedroom window, smashing it. The stone is wrapped in a piece of newspaper, written in a language she cannot understand (the ironic reader is better placed to decipher the Jabberwockian phrases), on which are scrawled the words, '*Help Help*'. Malfred is found dead, clutching the stone, three days later. Despite the familiar critique of small-town social conformity, Frame seems to suggest that the quest for an unadulterated, essential way of seeing, a wholly subjective 'new view' that wholly excludes others, can only end in the complete rejection of social language (hence the unintelligible newsprint) and the final excommunication, death. *State of Siege* was filmed by Vincent Ward.   KWo

Station (Australia 1820, NZ 1839), a large grazing property with its buildings and stock, was formerly frequently used in popular literature for the estate and home of the *squatter: 'Suppose you were to ask your way from Mr. Phillips's station to mine, I should direct you thus …' (Samuel *Butler, 'Forest Creek MS', 1860); 'F— says that this beautiful place will give me a very erroneous impression of station life' (Lady *Barker, *Station Life in New Zealand*, 1865); 'Barry's mother had been governess to a neighbouring station-owner's children' (Jean *Devanny, The *Butcher Shop*, 1926). *Stations* is a novel of early settlement by Philip *Temple.   HO

Station Amusements in New Zealand (1873) was written by Lady *Barker to follow on the commercial success of *Station Life in New Zealand*. The difference between the two volumes is explained in the preface to *Amusements*: 'Whereas that little book dwelt somewhat upon practical matters, these pages are entirely devoted to reminiscences of the idler hours of a settler's life.' As in *Life* the narrator is to some degree anonymous and only identical with the author by implication. She plays a vigorous role in pursuits which an English lady might well have viewed as masculine, although she also pays due attention to the 'servant problem' and devotes a chapter to 'cooking troubles'. A new perspective is offered on the great snowstorm of 1867, which was presented as a calamity in *Life* but is here seen as the basis of one of the most lively 'amusements', tobogganing. The sheep which provide the family's livelihood have been buried beneath a huge snowfall, but the narrator and her husband respond by rushing down the snow-slopes, presumably over the corpses of the sheep. The writing suggests exhilaration: 'F— is laughing to such a degree at me that he does not put down his brakes soon enough, and loses control of the sledge … yet in the grand and final upset at the bottom of the hill, the sledge is there too, and we find we have never parted company from it.' The narrator shows no less enterprise when she participates in boar hunts, energetic rides over rough terrain or eel-fishing expeditions. These and many other tales are told with an infectious enthusiasm and humour as well as with a linguistic skill which makes Barker one of the finest prose writers of the nineteenth-century colony.   NW

Station Life in New Zealand, a book of reminiscences of Canterbury life in the 1860s by Lady *Barker, was published in London in 1870. It is clearly addressed to English readers by an English writer who hopes that it 'may succeed in giving here in England an adequate impression of the delight and freedom of an existence so far removed from our own highly-wrought civilization'. The patronising tone is maintained throughout, and yet the evocation of 'delight and freedom' has won the book many readers in the country it looks down upon. The narrator's voice has a charm which can hardly be resisted and her attempt to remain 'ladylike' is continually and fortunately undermined by sheer physical exuberance. These qualities added to the obscuring of personal names and the moral and symbolic weight of the narrative give the book a strong touch of the fictional, so that the borderline between autobiography and novel is obscured. Many emigrant novels follow its pattern of describing the journey from England, the process of settling down and the incidents of daily life on a sheep *station, and the tradition has been carried into the twentieth century by such writers as Mary *Scott. *Station Life*, along with *Butler's *First Year in Canterbury Settlement*, despite their non-fictional status, can be seen as the origin of this novel tradition. The narrator organises life in the station homestead, but also takes part in horse-riding and hunting expeditions, boating trips on the lake and similar activities with seemingly inexhaustible energy, despite the fact that she is also bearing children and recording their progress or—in one case—death. The financial and physical burdens of life on the station are evoked. There is much on the servant problem, which troubled Lady Barker partly because her aristocratic pretensions were not unquestioned by the colonial 'lower orders'. Perhaps the egalitarian ethos was particularly irksome because Lady Barker was not really an aristocrat at all, but the daughter of a colonial administrator. Storms and other natural disasters are described, but never in a tone of despair, always with a sense of adventure and even humour. Most vivid is the account of the great snowstorm of 1867, which has entered into several literary accounts of Canterbury and even into legend. The hunger of the people in the snowed-in homestead is accompanied by the death of thousands of sheep out on the fields; yet, even here, Lady Barker leads the reader on to the 'raising of spirits' when the weather changes. This resilience is one of the qualities that have given the book its lasting appeal.   NW

STEAD, C.K. (Christian Karlson) (1932–), is a novelist, literary critic, poet, essayist and emeritus professor of English from the University of Auckland. He has been a figure in New Zealand literature since the 1950s, when, as an aspiring poet, he was a protégé of Frank *Sargeson and Allen *Curnow, and took Curnow's side in his conflict with the Wellington group of poets. Stead is best known these days, however, for his novel of the Vietnam *War period, *Smith's Dream* (1971), filmed under the title *Sleeping Dogs* (1977); for his string of internationally successful novels published in the 1980s and early 1990s, two of which, *All Visitors Ashore* (1984) and The *Singing Whakapapa* (1994), won the fiction section of the New Zealand Book Awards; and for his outspoken criticism of liberal positions in education and literary affairs. This last feature of Stead's career, his critiques of feminism and the Māori rights movement in the 1980s and early 1990s, has aroused such heated feelings in the New Zealand literary and intellectual community that cool appraisal of his work has been lacking.

A useful key to understanding Stead's writing is the tension between his academic and literary roles. His literary production was restricted in the 1950s, 1960s and 1970s by his work towards academic qualifications (MA Auckland 1955; PhD Bristol 1961) and by the demands of teaching (he rose from his initial appointment in 1959 as a lecturer in English at the University of Auckland to a full professorship in only eight years). *The New Poetic* (1964), a study of modernism based on his PhD thesis, which sold more than 100 000 copies, assisted this rapid rise. Stead's academic career yielded a further respectable handful of books: he edited the second series of *New Zealand Short Stories* (1964), *Letters and Journals of Katherine Mansfield: A Selection* (1977), a collection of critical essays on *Measure for Measure* (1977) and the *Collected Stories of Maurice Duggan* (1981). A second study of modernist poetry, *Pound, Yeats, Eliot and the Modernist Movement*, was published in 1986. Throughout his academic career Stead was an active critic of New Zealand literature, and these writings were collected as *In the Glass Case: Essays on New Zealand Literature* (1981). A later collection, *Answering to the Language* (1989), comprised essays on British, American and Australian writers as well as New Zealand writers and issues.

Stead's academic work and his creative writing have stood in a relationship to one another of conflict, but also of mutual enrichment. His literary criticism has been writerly, accessible, little theorised—and has consequently gained a wide readership. It characteristically expresses a practitioner's viewpoint on other practitioners, in prose of ease and clarity. Stead comments in one essay that 'there is no important difference in tone, in vocabulary, or in the demands they make, between my academic papers and my reviews for journals. I am not interested in arcane dialogue. I would like, where possible, to be understood.' He has been content to view literature through the theoretical lens which he ground in the 1950s and early 1960s, though this has let him in for criticism from academics who have kept more up to date with the diversity of critical approaches and discourse in their discipline.

At the same time, Stead's creative writing was both limited and shaped by his academic career. His reputation in the 1950s and 1960s depended on relatively few poems and a handful of short stories, which were, however, widely admired and anthologised. In particular, his sequence 'Pictures in a Gallery Undersea' was a last-minute inclusion in Curnow's 1960 *Penguin Book of New Zealand Verse*, and was voted by ★*Landfall* readers the best poem from the magazine's first fifteen years of publication. His short story 'A Fitting Tribute' (1965) was reprinted and translated in half a dozen countries. Not until 1964 did his first volume of poetry appear, *Whether the Will is Free*, and it was another eight years until his second collection, ★*Crossing the Bar* (1972). That was the year in which Stead's first novel, *Smith's Dream*, was published, elicited by his involvement in the anti–Vietnam War protest movement. The novel brings the injustice of Vietnam home to New Zealanders by imagining how a similar war might arise here.

Aside from *Smith's Dream*, Stead's only books of creative work had been poetry until 1981, when five of his short stories were collected in a single volume, *Five*

for the Symbol. Many reviewers and critics have commented on the eclectic nature of Stead's poetic corpus. In volumes such as ★*Quesada* (1975), *Walking Westward* (1979) and ★*Geographies* (1982) he experimented with open form, free verse, journal composition, extensive quotation and found text, while also professing more traditional modes, such as personal lyric, translation and imitation. The poet's love of jokes and puns is often evident, as in his well-known transformation of a line from *Macbeth* into the opening line of one of his sonnets: 'To Maurice, and to Maurice, and to Maurice'; or his discreet pleasure in the plumbing anagram for T.S. Eliot, in 'Yes T.S.'.

Stead's booklet-length poem *Paris* (1984) and some sequences in *Between* (1988) offer another kind of experiment, whereby the image, line or sentence constitute the maximum unit of coherent narrative, and these varied fragments are woven together into a larger mood. Throughout his extensive sequence of poetic experiments, however, Stead often turned back to coherent personal narrative, as in his lengthy sequence of sonnets reminiscent of ★*Baxter*, his 'Clodian Songbook' (adaptations of Catullus to the writer's own personal situation), and his 1990 volume *Voices*, commissioned for the sesquicentennial celebrations, which depicts scenes from New Zealand history and from Stead's own family history. Altogether, his poetic career displays verbal facility allied with creative discipline, and a lively, ingenious mind always at work—the academic poet continually drawn to new models: yet there is no committed development of an individual poetic, no coherent theme but the writer's own personality. Michael ★*Morrissey* referred to Stead as 'arguably our most successful literary chameleon'. We may detect behind this restless succession of styles the confessional novelist waiting for an opportunity to reveal himself.

Stead furnished this opportunity in 1986, when he took early retirement to devote himself to writing after the considerable success of *All Visitors Ashore* (1984). Since then his production has been mainly prose fiction, and this work has displayed the unity and conviction, the individual stamp, that the poetry lacked. Indeed, Stead's handful of earlier stories already hinted at his gift of exposition, the sheer nerve (verging on egotism) that sustains him in furnishing his narratives so sumptuously. Stead's fiction of the decade 1984–94 has been distinguished by the sensuous lucidity of its prose (Damien ★*Wilkins* complained of Stead's 'surfeit of lucidity'), and by the highly personal nature of its material. *All Visitors Ashore*, *The ★Death of the Body* (1986), *Sister Hollywood* (1989) and *The ★Singing Whakapapa* (1994) have all contained major characters to some extent based on Stead himself, while *The End of the Century at the End of the World* (1992) revisits the late 1960s Vietnam War protest scene which was so important in Stead's life, as well as presenting, in altered form, a contemporary debacle of literary politics in which Stead was closely involved.

Stead has often been described as a 'metafictional' writer, meaning that his novels underline their own fictional status by devices such as movement back and forth between past and present narratives, the inclusion of documents written by characters as part of the narrative, or having narrators discuss the process of composition. These devices should not, however, obscure the fundamentally realist, confessional nature of Stead's fiction —the same confessional voice that is the one persistent strand of his poetry. Stead has repeatedly emphasised the realist basis of his writing in his critical essays. The method of a writer in one of his novels applies exactly to Stead himself: 'so much of Hilda's fiction is based on the facts of her life, and illustrates her maxim that she writes, not to invent what didn't happen but to come to terms with what did'. Stead's early friendship with Frank Sargeson, his academic career, his marriage, an apparent extra-marital affair which recurs in various poems and two novels, and difficulties surrounding women and their claims: all these matters are presented to us under a veil of fiction that is at times alarmingly diaphanous. Stead has displayed some courage in thus publicly digesting his past at a time when his personal reputation, especially among the literary community, is not universally high. At the same time, because the guise of fiction prevents any sure identification of their scenes with events in his life, Stead's novels constitute a prolonged, elaborate teasing of his critics and opponents.

In 1997 Stead published a novel set in *Italy, *Villa Vittoria*, and *Straw Into Gold: Poems New and Selected*, his first poetry collection for seven years. **KJ**

STEVENS, Joan (1908–90), academic, critic and editor, performed in the 1960s–70s useful service to New Zealand literature through her editions and commentaries, making accessible several little-known texts, mainly journals and fiction. Her *The New Zealand Novel, 1860–1960* (1961; several times reprinted; second updated edition 1966) was like a 'companion', an enticing guide to more than two hundred novelists with plot summaries and judicious comment. She did a similar job in *The New Zealand Short Story: A Survey* (1968). She also edited and annotated the journals of Edward Jerningham *Wakefield, the letters of Mary *Taylor, George *Chamier's *A *South-Sea Siren*, J.L. *Campbell's *Poenamo*, and wrote a good introduction to *The *God Boy*. She was one of the authors of the essay on literature in *An Encyclopaedia of New Zealand* (1966). Her sympa-

thy for obscure earlier texts was related to her other speciality and main teaching area, English Victorian fiction. Born in Sussex, she arrived as a child in New Zealand and was educated at Hamilton GHS and Otago and Oxford Universities. After secondary teaching 1932–42 and lecturing at Dunedin Teachers' College, she was appointed lecturer at Victoria University College in 1946, and was elevated to a personal chair in 1971, two years before retirement. **RR**

STEWART, Bruce (1936–), of Ngāti Raukawa, Te Arawa, is a fiction writer and dramatist who has expressed the anger, confused loyalties and spiritual aspiration of late-twentieth-century Māori. He began writing seriously after a Michael *King workshop in 1974, drawing on his varied experience as a bushman, builder, farm worker, prison inmate, singer and father; and made a big impact when he read his hard-hitting prison story, *Broken Arse*, at the *PEN/Victoria University Conference in 1979. It was published in *Into the World of Light* (1982) and he later rewrote it as a playscript, which was performed in Wellington in 1990, televised and published by *Victoria University Press in 1991. In this dramatic form the strong choric element of the rebellious prisoners stomping and chanting in unison became even more powerful as *haka. While race anger is prominent, it is essentially a story of betrayal from within a group of men, of self-serving manipulation of a code of permitted violence, not unlike *Foreskin's Lament* from the same time. A novel, *Disorderly Girl*, was published in 1980 and a collection of short fiction, *Tama and Other Stories* in 1989, when another play, 'Thunderbox', was also televised. An extract from a novel in progress, 'Te Au', was published in Te *Ao Mārama*, Volume 3, 1993, with a substantial representation of Stewart's recent work.

The 'raw power' and 'anger' (Rangi *Faith) of Stewart's presentation of the Māori underclass makes his early work precursive of Alan *Duff's, but there is also a lyrical and spiritual quality, especially in the recurrent treatments of the child's view of life and of interaction with the land. Memorable passages include the child's communion with a fallen rimu in 'Boy', the journey through bush to mountain top in 'Papa' and the felling of a prime totara in 'Te Au'. The writing frequently moves outside conventional narrative prose and is particularly strong in the oral dimension, including authentic idiomatic dialogue, internal monologue and fragments of intense incantatory poetry.

Born in Hamilton, Stewart grew up in the Wairarapa and was educated at Wairarapa College. He has lived mainly in Wellington, where he successfully set up the first work trust and founded Tapu Te Ranga Marae at

Island Bay, creating a centre for debate and education in Māori culture and protocol and for the redevelopment of native bush. He was president of Ngā Puna Waihanga (Māori Writers and Artists Society) in 1982. An interview with Stewart is in Neville Glasgow, *Directions* (1995).   RR

STEWART, Douglas (1913–85) was born in Eltham, Taranaki, where he attended the primary school before moving to New Plymouth BHS in 1926. The words he wrote there for the school song are still sung. The story of his childhood and youth is movingly and entertainingly told in the autobiographical *Springtime in Taranaki* (1983), which is among the best of the many evocations of New Zealand childhood in literature.

In 1930 he took up studies at Victoria University of Wellington and from 1931 to 1938 worked as a journalist for various New Zealand papers, apart from a brief trip to Australia as a freelance writer in 1933. In 1936 he published his first book of verse, *Green Lions*, in Auckland. The landscapes used here are often bleak and cold, with images of frost, ice and snow (anticipating the Antarctic landscapes of the magnificent radio play *The Fire on the Snow*). Frequently, too, the natural world is found to be aggressive, like the 'green lions' of the title poem, which crouch in 'the jagged hollows' of a bay 'gouged by the wind'. The same poem illustrates his equally pugnacious city imagery, where 'men denied the jungle of young years / Grow taut and clench their fists'. The combination of landscape imagery and human contemplation reaches an even greater degree of vigorous intensity in his second book of verse *The White Cry* (1939).

These two volumes represent his purest New Zealand verse, and were followed by two small volumes of wartime poetry on boyhood friends: *Elegy for an Airman* (1940) and *Sonnets to the Unknown Soldier* (1941), but even in later poems written in Australia references to New Zealand and its people recur, and his statements in articles and interviews reveal that his sense of New Zealand identity never diminished. It is, therefore, a curiosity of literary history that this writer, so profoundly respected and admired in Australia, is comparatively little known in his home country.

In 1938 he travelled to England, where a message reached him that he would be welcomed in Sydney as assistant to the literary editor of the ★*Bulletin*. He took over the literary editorship (i.e. of the 'Red Page') in 1940 and for twenty years in that position and ten as publishing editor with Angus & Robertson he encouraged and aided many Australian writers.

His own poetry continued with *The Dosser in Springtime* (1946), in which he expresses his exhilaration

and wonder on encountering the remarkable natural world of ★Australia. Nancy Keesing has pointed out that his first Australian poems lack the 'intricate, experienced detail' of both his earlier New Zealand work and also his later Australian poems, which suggests a transition from one environment to the other. In *Glencoe* (1947) Stewart used the massacre in the Scottish highlands to protest against cruelty and violence in general. *Sun Orchids* (1952) brings him back to his special skill: the detailed and loving observation of nature combined inextricably with philosophical comments on the nature of life which attain profundity without losing wit and joy. His greatest poems of the Australian outback are to be found in *The Birdsville Track* (1955).

His most ambitious poem is the title one of the volume *Rutherford* (1962), where the New Zealand physicist is called 'the great sea-farer of science' and is the centrepiece of a vast historical view of man's need to explore his inner and outer worlds. Keesing says that this poem 'draws together every major theme that Stewart has explored in his writing'.

His poetical style is superficially 'conservative', preserving regular metres and rhymes, but in fact radically experimental in matching sounds, rhythms and images. This might be illustrated by the use of such rhymes as 'Icarus/licorice' or 'sweeten/button' in serious poems, but extends to every level of sound and meaning. There is an element of irony and wit which constantly lightens but never conceals the serious purpose of the poems.

Stewart was also successful as a dramatist. *The Fire on the Snow*, a verse play for radio about Scott's journey through Antarctica, was first produced in Australia in 1944 and has since been broadcast in New Zealand, England, Canada, Japan, South Africa, Norway, Denmark and Iceland. Its contrasting images of the fire of men's passions and the snow of indifferent nature are both poetic and dramatic. The heroic strain was continued in *Ned Kelly* (1943), but in *The Golden Lover* (1944) Stewart uses a more gentle, humorous and ironic tone. It tells the story of a Māori woman torn in her affections between her mortal husband and her fairy lover. The world of tradition and social convention embodied in the husband and his tribal affinities wins out over the world of fantasy and romance represented by the fairy. *The Earthquake Shakes the Land* (1946), written for radio, is based on the first New Zealand war of the 1840s and reflects the attempts of subject people to retain dignity, some of them by resisting, others by acting with the colonisers. It focuses on Māori attitudes towards a Pākehā named McDonald, who has married a Māori but is viewed by many as a representative of the people who have 'stolen' Māori land. In a powerful soliloquy it turns to the anguish of McDonald himself, torn in his loyalties to his Scottish traditions and his half-Māori son. *Shipwreck* (1947) tells the story of a mutiny following the wreck of the *Batavia* on the Australian shore. *Fisher's Ghost* (1960) takes up an Australian legend and treats it with colloquial humour largely in a ballad metre.

Stewart also published two books of critical essays, *The Flesh and the Spirit* (1948) and *The Broad Stream* (1975), which demonstrate a civilised control of deep feeling, as well as a prose account of fishing in New Zealand and Australia, *The Seven Rivers* (1966). He edited several books of Australian ballads and other verse.

He also wrote one book of short stories, all with New Zealand settings: *A Girl with Red Hair* (1944). The title story is a moving account of an adolescent girl and her emotional tensions in a town which might also be called adolescent. 'The Whare' explores the necessity and the difficulty of grasping the attitudes of people living in a different culture. The other stories in the collection explore other aspects of cultural tension in the Taranaki of Stewart's childhood. Of these stories Clement Semmler has said: 'There is throughout them a warm feeling for his New Zealand countryside and its towns; a generous understanding and compassion for the people who live there; a poet's ear for their speech and conversations; and a poet's evocation of their experiences and emotions.'   NW

STONEY, Henry Butler (1816–94), author of *Taranaki, which is sometimes erroneously referred to as the first New Zealand novel, was born in Tipperary and had a career in the British imperial forces in Malta, the West Indies and Canada before returning to Britain and then emigrating to Australia in the late 1850s. In 1860 he came to New Zealand, where he took part in the Land Wars and later retired into civil administration, being a member of the Auckland Provincial Council 1872–73. He died in Kawakawa. Stoney's work hovers in the grey area between fact and fiction. He published two books descriptive of Australia: *Victoria: with a Description of its Principal Cities, Melbourne and Geelong: and Remarks on the Present State of the Colony; including an Account of the Ballaarat Disturbances and the Death of Captain Wise, 40th Regiment* (1854) and *A Residence in Tasmania: with a Descriptive Tour through the Island, from Macquarie Harbour to Circular Head* (1856). These are less objectively descriptive than might at first appear. In the preface to *Tasmania* the author declares his purpose to be 'to draw attention to those daring pioneers in the far South … and to make known the advantages offered by this colony as a field for emigration'. He deliberately set out to 'improve' the image of the former penal colony of van Dieman's Land. This helps us to understand his purpose in *Taranaki*, neither book being entirely fictional or

entirely factual. Stoney wrote only one work which is clearly a novel: *Reginald Mortimer* (1857), but paradoxically the author here sets up a massive barrier of prefaces, explanations etc. (signing them H.B.S.) to make the story seem authentic. Hence it is catalogued as biography in research libraries. Similarly, the fictional status of *Taranaki* is undermined by long excerpts from non-fictional 'despatches'. For these reasons, the claim of Stoney to be the country's first novelist seems flimsy at best. Earlier works which might also claim to be first include those by *Bowman, *Bennett, *Knox and *Dumont d'Urville.   NW

Story of a New Zealand River, The, Jane *Mander's first novel, was written in New York in 1914–16, published there in 1920 and in London a few months later. In the opening scenes English immigrant Alice Roland travels by river with her young children (including 8-year-old daughter Asia) to join her husband, Tom, who has taken up a bush-felling contract at Pukekaroro on the Kaipara river, north of Auckland. The marriage is loveless. Alice, a single mother with a child to support (she claims to be a widow), was propelled into it by economic hardship; Tom desired a wife. After the initial journey from 'civilisation' into the rugged bush, the focus narrows to the tiny Pukekaroro settlement, alternating with some awkwardness between details of the men's struggle to tame the land and the domestic sphere of Alice's simple home. The main body of the text portrays Alice's prolonged and painful cure from the 'awful disease' of *puritanism. She falls in love with her husband's partner and the local doctor, David Bruce, but despite David's reciprocation of her feelings and Tom's endorsement of their liaison (he takes a number of lovers himself) their love remains unconsummated. They remain passionate friends through years of Alice's illnesses and despair until Tom's heroic death which conveniently occurs only when Alice is sufficiently educated in the tenets of liberalism to finally act on her feelings for David. Intelligent and high-spirited, Asia grows up a modern young woman under the tuition of David and the neighbouring Mrs. Brayton. Asia, it transpires, was the fruit of an illegitimate liaison, not a previous marriage as Alice had claimed; this costly mistake is the source of Alice's puritanical repression. When Allen Ross, a married man, arrives in Pukekaroro he and Asia become lovers despite Alice's horror at the 'experiment'. The novel concludes with movement away from the now thriving Pukekaroro settlement: the young couple leave for Australia; David and Alice depart for Auckland to begin their married life.

The 'solid realism' which Frank *Sargeson found to be Mander's 'greatest strength as a writer' is marred by the inclusion of melodramatic romance elements and cumbersome descriptive set pieces. In retrospect, in 1938, Mander herself found the novel to be flawed by her 'unrefined diet of Shaw and Nietzsche' and her rather naive faith in 'social movements—the bogus and fuzzy ones'. Well-received abroad (including a tolerant review by Katherine ★Mansfield in the *Atheneaum*), the novel was poorly received in New Zealand. It remained out of print until 1938, when Mander initiated a New Zealand edition, was published again in 1960 with the assistance of a grant from the ★Literary Fund, and again in 1973 and 1994 to increasing acclaim, particularly for the vividness of Mander's portrayal of pioneer life and her profound psychological acuity and sensitivity in the rendering of character and emotion. KWo

'Stranger, The', a short story by Katherine ★Mansfield, was written in late 1920 and published in the *London Mercury* (1921), using the place names Auckland and Napier. According to ★Alpers, Mansfield altered the names to 'Crawford' and 'Salisbury' for publication in *The Garden Party and Other Stories* (1922) because the story draws on an actual event which involved her parents. The MS is held at the Newberry Library, Chicago. It presents John Hammond awaiting his wife, 'Janey', who has been in Europe for ten months visiting their daughter, at the dockside in Auckland. Back in their hotel room, fearing that she is aloof but with a heightened desire for her, he learns that aboard ship a man died in her arms: '"You're not—sorry I told you, John darling?… It hasn't spoilt our evening—our being alone together?"… Spoilt their evening! Spoilt their being alone together! They would never be alone together again.' The story effectively juxtaposes the interior monologue of Hammond with the direct speech of Janey to render a relationship in which an inequality of affection and dependency is compounded by a life-altering experience. In these ways it is similar to the ending of James Joyce's 'The Dead'. Mansfield's original choice of title for the story was 'The Interloper'. SSa

Strangers and Journeys, published in 1972, is Maurice ★Shadbolt's major early work. It is a long and ambitious and by turns brilliant and flawed novel which took ten years to write. Essentially a work of social realism, it draws on many of the themes and characters that appeared in his earlier works, particularly the novel ★*Among the Cinders*. It contrasts the lives of two fathers, Ned Livingstone and Bill Freeman, and their sons Tim and Ian, and thus gives Shadbolt considerable chronological scope. The earlier and most successful sections of the novel deal with the lives of the fathers and their battles with the harsh environment and the equally harsh economic times. It has convincingly been suggested by a number of critics that the earlier parts of the novel succeed because Shadbolt uses an organising myth, whereas the later parts, which focus on the lives of the sons, fail because they have no such structural pattern. It may also be that as Shadbolt nears the present some of his objective distance is lost. In the later sections, which move to the city, replicating New Zealand's rural to urban drift, the lives of Tim Livingstone, a painter, and Ian Freeman, a writer, continue the exploration of the position of the artist in New Zealand society that was a consistent concern in Shadbolt's early work. RC

STRINGFELLOW, Olga (1921–), was a novelist, a journalist in the UK for *Modern Woman* and *The Sketch*, and a columnist for the Scottish *Daily Express*. The novel *Mary Bravender* (1960) tells of a Scottish girl who emigrates and becomes tangled up in the New Zealand ★Wars. It was an immediate success and sold 10 000 copies in its first week. Compton McKenzie, who had encouraged her to write it, declared it 'as good a piece of sustained narrative as I have read in a long time. What a relief to be caught up again by a moving and exciting story.' *A Gift for the Sultan* (1962) is based on a true story. A Scottish girl, Helen Gloag, was captured by pirates on her way to America and sold into slavery, eventually becoming a gift to the sultan of Morocco, and his favourite wife. Stringfellow makes much of the contrast between puritanical Scotland and opulent Morocco, but does not sensationalise it.

Her own life is almost equally colourful. Her birth (as Olga Elizabeth Brown) was registered in Auckland, though she later claimed to have been born in Dunedin (in an interview in the *Otago Daily Times*). She was educated at Otago GHS and Elam School of Fine Art, at the age of 13 as their youngest pupil ever. She married in 1943 (later dissolved) and moved to the UK in 1949. There, after journalism, she became (by others' reports) an internationally successful healer by touch, with Middle Eastern princes and New York millionaires among her patients. On her 1984 visit to Dunedin she was reported to have healed the rugby-damaged shoulder of the *ODT*'s photographer, who gratefully pictured her resplendent in a caftan and expensive jewellery. She was no longer writing, she said at that time. PN/NW

STURM, J.C. (Jacqueline Cecilia) (1927–), Māori, of Taranaki, born in Opunake, is a writer of short stories and poetry. In the late 1940s her poetry was published in student newspapers and the ★*Review*. She married the poet James K. ★Baxter in 1948, and in 1949 became probably the first Māori women to obtain a university degree when she completed her BA (begun at Otago

517

University and Canterbury) at Victoria University College. The following year she began an MA in Philosophy, writing a dissertation on 'New Zealand National Character as Exemplified in Three New Zealand Novelists', which was commended as being of exceptional merit and awarded first class honours. Early in the 1950s she began writing short fiction: in 1954 her first story 'The Old Coat' appeared in *Numbers 1 and a year later 'For All the Saints' became the first story written in English by a Māori writer to appear in Te *Ao Hou. Throughout the 1950s and early 1960s she featured regularly in Numbers and Te Ao Hou, both writing and reviewing. C.K. *Stead included 'For All the Saints' in New Zealand Short Stories: Second Series (Oxford University Press, 1966), making her the first Māori writer selected for a New Zealand anthology. Sturm's writing, influenced by *Mansfield and by *Sargesonian realism, is finely crafted and has been compared favourably to others writing at that time, such as Noel *Hilliard and Maurice *Gee. The stories are succinct and lucid and on first reading they appear to embrace the era's dominant ethos—that New Zealanders were one nation—by avoiding specific reference to Māori. However, read against the grain of thought that expected, in Sturm's words, all Māori 'to become respectable middle-class citizens, a lighter shade of brown, as it were', it becomes clear that the society she depicts fosters inequality, and her work conveys a strong and poignant sense of alienation. Her female narrators, although rarely defined by their race, are marginalised figures that give a vivid sense of the constriction and restrictions of a young woman's life in Wellington in the 1950s. Lydia Wevers notes that by supplying 'the missing term "Maori" ... Sturm's stories fall horrifyingly into place'. Sturm herself commented that 'whether my work has any [overt] Maori content or not ...we're talking about a way of looking, a way of feeling and a way of being'.

By 1966 Sturm had a collection of stories ready for publication, but no publisher. Soon after she became a solo parent and the pressures of earning a living left her little time for further writing for over a decade. In 1982 'First Native and the Pink Pig' and 'Jerusalem, Jerusalem' were featured in the anthology of Māori writing *Into the World of Light (ed. *Ihimaera and *Long), but it took her first public reading—in 1980 with, among others, Patricia *Grace and Keri *Hulme—to get the entire collection published. The women's publishing collective Spiral printed her stories in 1983 as The House of the Talking Cat. Reviewers, while commenting that stylistically the stories were of an earlier era, praised the collection, with Witi Ihimaera calling her a 'pivotal presence in the Maori literary tradition' and speculating on the course Māori literature might have taken had 'J.C. Sturm

and Cat achieved success and publication in their time, rather than twenty years later' (*NZ Listener, 17 Mar. 1984).

In the decade following the publication of The House of the Talking Cat Sturm returned to writing poetry. Her recent poems are dedicated to family and friends (including Janet *Frame, Jean *Watson and Peter *Alcock) with the poems to her late husband having a particular poignancy: 'None will ever know where / Those years of exploration / And discovery took us / And what we found there' ('P.S. 22/10/91 (for Jim)'). Published as Dedications (1997) her poetry was an immediate success. By commingling experiences of loss and love, youth and age, and Māori and Pākehā, Sturm's verse conveys a sense of tranquillity through acceptance of the dualities inherent in her own eventful life. Her poems have been published in *Landfall 183 (1992), 186 (1993) and 194 (1997); Kapiti Poems 6 (1992) and 7 (1994); and Te *Ao Mārama Vol. 1. In addition there is an interview and series of poems in Hecate (20.2, 1994). Twelve of her poems are collected in How Things Are (1996).   PM/AMcL

STURM, Terry (1941–), is editor of the *OHNZLE (1991, 1998), professor of English at University of Auckland and an authority on New Zealand popular fiction. Born in Auckland, he was educated at Auckland GS and Auckland University (MA 1963) and did postgraduate studies at Cambridge and Leeds universities (PhD Leeds 1967). He lectured at Sydney University 1967–80 before being appointed professor at Auckland in 1980. He was chairman of the *Literary Fund Advisory Committee from 1982 and was involved in negotiating the transfer of its functions to the Queen Elizabeth 2 Arts Council in 1988, becoming chair of that body's Literature Committee until resigning in 1992 in protest at proposals to restructure the committee (which was disbanded in 1995 by Creative New Zealand). Sturm's scholarly publications, mainly as editor, have been in Australian and New Zealand literature, and he has made a significant contribution towards placing New Zealand literature at the centre of the academic curriculum, especially through the establishment at Auckland of the first chair in New Zealand literature, with Albert *Wendt as the foundation professor.   AM/RR

SUISTED, Laura (1840–1903), was a pioneer woman journalist and advocate of New Zealand literature. Born in Yorkshire, she arrived in Dunedin in 1862, marrying in 1864. Settling in Westport in 1869, she began to publish poems, stories, sketches and serials in 1878, in the Otago Witness and in Australian and English magazines. She won prizes in 1895 and 1896 in story competitions run by Sharland's Trade Journal. From 1884 to 1892 she was the first woman to report regularly on the New Zealand parliament, becoming the first female member of the NZ Institute of Journalists in 1891. She also wrote about Antarctic and Arctic exploration, being elected to the Royal Geographic Society in Australia, and about New Zealand literature, notably in an article in *Author* (December 1891), the journal of the British Society of Authors. She argued that 'nothing can better show the growth of a nation than its progress in literature', applauded 'the characteristic nationalism' of local writing, and refuted those British commentators who saw 'too much Maori' in some works. A journey through Britain and Scandinavia in 1893 is recorded in her travel book, *From New Zealand to Norway* (1894). She was known for her encouragement of young writers. JMcC

SULLIVAN, Robert (1967–), Ngā Puhi, emerged as a distinctive Māori poet with his first collection, *Jazz Waiata* (1990). *Piki Ake* appeared in 1993. Sullivan then had a substantial entry in the first volume of *Te *Ao Mārama*, edited by Witi *Ihimaera (1994). He is a graduate of Auckland University, where he took the course in modern American poetry taught by Wystan *Curnow, Michele *Leggott and Roger Horrocks. The largest single influence on Sullivan is the New York poet Frank O'Hara. Like O'Hara, he alternates relaxed, conversational narratives of everyday events, including frequent allusions to the literary scene and to popular culture, with, in other poems, disjointed, free-associative verse, typographical experimentation, and wild bursts of verbal exuberance. His quieter poems about his *whānau in Northland, such as the Tai Tokerau sequence, also display a debt to *Baxter's *Pig Island Letters* and Jerusalem poetry. Sullivan is a qualified librarian, currently working at Auckland University Library. This bibliophile side of his life is explored in the sequence 'The George Grey Room', where he describes the daily routine of a rare books librarian, and praises the former New Zealand governor as a collector and benefactor, gently rebuking Māori activists who decapitated the statue of *Grey in Albert Park. Sullivan's predominantly urban, *postmodern poetic is enriched by his acute awareness, as a Māori, of New Zealand racial and social issues. In works such as 'Not the 1990 Poem', 'Message from Mangere' and 'The Prophet Rua', he furnishes Māori identity with a new voice, sophisticated yet passionate. KJ

Summer in the Gravel Pit is Maurice *Duggan's second collection of short stories, published in 1965 by *Blackwood and Janet Paul and Victor Gollancz of London. Because this book would appear overseas it also included some work from Duggan's first collection, *Immanuel's Land* (1956). The title appealed to Duggan as an image of life. The new stories in the collection move beyond the autobiographical emphasis of that first book, toward literary artefacts which explore the general nature of life through New Zealand particularities. Thus 'The Wits of Willie Graves' blends the evocation of landscape and the reaction of a debt collector to an encounter with a *backblocks farming family into a tale of psychological corruption. 'Blues for Miss Laverty', one of Duggan's most popular stories, is the unsentimental account of the effects of self-imposed isolation on a spinsterish classical music teacher. Mary May Laverty is bedevilled by a nameless man who plays a record of the St Louis Blues over and over again in their boarding house. Eventually, after a failed attempt at an affair with the father of one of her pupils, May Laverty confronts the nameless man briefly and they recognise the impossibility in life of 'a little human warmth'. *'Along Rideout Road that Summer', Duggan's most famous and probably his best story, is the retrospective confession of Buster O'Leary, who as a young man runs away from home and has a relationship with a Māori teenager, Fanny Hohepa, on her father's farm. A turning point is the arrival of his father at the farm, prompting feelings of guilt in Buster and the realisation that his stay can be only temporary. He hitches a ride with a car that drives off 'through the tail-end of summer'. The remaining four stories form a disjointed sequence detailing the life of Harry Lenihan, the son of Irish immigrant parents, followed by the travel diary 'Voyage', as if this were an account of Harry's escape to a far country. The collection sold well both in New Zealand and England, and was reprinted by Longman Paul in paperback in 1971. IR

SUMMERS, Essie (1912–), is the maiden name of New Zealand's first and most prolific author of *Mills & Boon light *romances. She was born in Christchurch a year after her parents emigrated to New Zealand from Newcastle, England, and left school (Christchurch Technical College) at the age of 15. She worked in a Christchurch drapery department store for seven years, then as a costing clerk in the fashion garment industry, before marrying a Presbyterian minister in 1939. She became a regular contributor of poems, columns and stories to New Zealand and Australian newspapers and weeklies for two decades before publishing her first novel, *New Zealand Inheritance*, in 1957. She wrote more than fifty Mills & Boon romances over the next twenty-eight years, with estimated sales by 1981—worldwide and in a dozen languages—of seventeen million copies. In 1974 she wrote a lively autobiography, *The Essie Summers Story*, which provided an insight into the world of Mills & Boon romance writing from the 1950s–70s.

Summers's romances were essentially a nostalgic

re-creation of the earlier colonial romance formula, notable for the reticence with which she handled sexual relationships ('as far as the bedroom door and no further'), and for their spectacular natural settings—often sub-alpine sheep *station settings in the South Island. Usually the heroine is English, or of English origins, and typically conflict centres on her suspicion of the sexual motives of the hero (usually a prospective inheritor of sheep station wealth) and his suspicion of her mercenary motives. Local family networks, often directly connected to English or European ancestral roots, regularly provide the agency by which conflict is resolved, so that marriage (for the heroine and readers) represents the reassertion of a heritage of Englishness in the antipodes. A highly skilled professional writer, Summers used the romance form to celebrate a deeply conservative view of marriage and family values, appealing especially to older readers, during a period (1960s–70s) when the institutions themselves were undergoing radical transformation.   TS

SUMMERS, John (1916–93) was a bookman, poet, fiction writer, memoirist and reviewer, whose Christchurch second-hand bookshop was for a quarter of a century a literary meeting-place. His immersion in literature came initially from friendships, especially with Ursula *Bethell during the war, and over many years with Winston *Rhodes and Monte *Holcroft, who published some early work in the *Southland Times* and poetry in the *NZ Listener*. He often wrote then as 'Westcliff', after the Essex seaside town where he was born. He arrived as a child in Southland, and was educated at Riverton HS. He was active in *PEN and poetry readings, and published in *Arena*, *Edge* and other magazines, though apart from *Poetry New Zealand* he never gained the endorsement of anthologists and published mostly under his own 'Pisces' imprint. He used a variety of forms, somewhat assuming the role of literary dilettante, even writing in Lallans (Lowland Scots dialect). Hugh MacDiarmid remained an influence. His most notable verse collections are *Letters to Joe* (1967), *Prancing Before the Ark* (1982), *Canticles of Capricorn* (1989) and *Capricorn's Farewell* (1996); and of the prose, *Fernie Brae* (novella, 1984), *O Darkly Bright* (novel, 1987) and *Dreamscape 1* and *2* (memoirs, 1991, 1993). His writing is conversational, playfully bookish, often acknowledging better writers (there are poems for Bethell and Helen *Shaw, elegies for *Brasch and *Baxter, and many more), with a frequent 'pixyish' tone (as Rhodes put it) and self-mockery that do not wholly disguise an underlying warmth, most evident in some good late poems of age and memory: 'Each day comes pregnant with its past.'   RR

Sun, The, was a Christchurch and Auckland newspaper, 1914–34, which devoted special attention to literature. Writing in 1935, Pat *Lawlor claimed that 'the pivot of its enterprise, its literary staff, was unequalled in the history of journalism in this country' and that 'the poets, short story writers and essayists the "Sun" has discovered and helped over the last two decades represent nearly every New Zealand writer who has achieved any distinction in his profession during that period.' Robin *Hyde concurred, writing that it was 'the one and only daily to pay any serious attention to literary work … garnered from the stores of New Zealand writers'. The first literary editor was Charles *Marris and his successors included J.H.E. *Schroder. Every Friday, *The Sun* published 'Among the Books' with poems, reviews and rather chatty essays. All papers serialised novels, but *The Sun* boldly serialised New Zealand ones, such as Edith *Howes's *Young Pioneers* (1923–24). In its special Christmas numbers each year there were poems and stories by such distinguished writers as C.R. *Allen, Hector *Bolitho, Eileen *Duggan, A.R.D. *Fairburn, Monte *Holcroft, Robin Hyde, Will *Lawson and Jane *Mander. Interestingly, for example, Fairburn's poem 'Kowhai' (1928) is as sentimentally *Georgian as any of the poems he and his comrades were later to scorn. *The Sun* also distinguished itself by publishing six of Ngaio *Marsh's earliest stories, including 'The Night Train from Grey' (1919), her first published work. The paper's policy was explained in an editorial on 18 December 1923: 'The Sun is doing its utmost to give aspirants to fame in letters the opportunity to make themselves known…. This policy has assisted to give the death-blow to the snow and holly leaf tradition, whose demise will not be regretted.'   NW

'Sun and Moon', a short story by Katherine *Mansfield, was first published in the *Athenaeum*, October 1920, though written in 1918, just hours after completion of *'Je ne parle pas français'. On the day of its composition, Mansfield wrote to John Middleton *Murry 'I *dreamed* a short story last night, even down to its name, which was *Sun & Moon*…. I didn't dream that I read it. No I was in it…' (10 Feb. 1918). The MS is in the Newberry Library, Chicago. The story was included in *Bliss and Other Stories* (Dec. 1920). Its imaginative source, evocative of Coleridge, is appropriate for a story which draws on Romantic as well as Edwardian notions of childhood. It presents brother and sister Sun and Moon, with Sun's perception of a dinner party exposing adults as predatory, destructive and objectifying of children: 'All the people who couldn't get at Moon kissed Sun, and a skinny old lady with teeth that clicked said: "Such a serious little poppet," and rapped him on the head with something hard.' Though the story has received scant critical attention, it has thematic connections with some of Mansfield's best-regarded work, notably 'The *Doll's House' and *Prelude. (Sun's horrified reaction to the destruction of the ice-pudding house at the end of the story is reminiscent of Kezia's reaction to the beheading of a duck in *Prelude*.) Mansfield herself was always ambivalent about the story, attempting to prevent its initial publication in the *Athenaeum*, yet later allowing it to be included in her second collection.   SSa

SUTHERLAND, Margaret (1941–), born and resident in Auckland, is a popular writer of fiction, whose work has been successful in Britain and the USA as well as New Zealand. Her short stories appeared in various periodicals, and have been collected in *Getting Through and Other Stories* (1977), which was published in the USA as *Dark Places, Deep Regions* (1980); a number of them have been broadcast in New Zealand.

Sutherland received the Katherine *Mansfield Memorial Award in 1973, and her first novel *The Fledgling* (1974) won her the Freda Buckley Literary Award in 1975. A tale of a repressed single librarian who 'adopts' a homeless young woman, then her boyfriend and finally and definitively her child, *The Fledgling* displays the features which persist in Sutherland's subsequent fiction: a domestic compass; wryly acute observation of human behaviour; a countervailing compassion; and a spare, eloquent, distinctive style. Her talent lends itself to comedy, which is not central to her work, but almost always attendant upon the action.

Sutherland has been represented, and perhaps marketed, as a writer of domestic novels about and for women, and *The Love Contract* (1976) fits this mould readily. But it is also atypical—less tart, less humorous, more subdued than the other novels and many of the stories. It aligns Sutherland with the exploration of women's roles and female sexuality undertaken by many women writers in the 1970s, and a number of her short stories operate in the same territory. To focus exclusively on this aspect of her work, however, is to underestimate its variety, breadth of vision, substantial male characters, and especially the detachment which qualifies her sympathy with her characters, and imparts a faintly satirical edge.

This is especially apparent in *The Fringe of Heaven* (1984), which explores life on the fringe—of the *bush, of Auckland, of society, and sometimes of sanity. This novel exemplifies the subtlety of Sutherland's touch, and the skill with which she reanimates the commonplaces of urban fiction. It plays with the rural myth (see *Landscape) of the superiority of life close to nature. Titirangi is bushy, semi-rural, the fringe of Heaven; its

very remoteness makes the eccentric lifestyle of the central character marginally sustainable, and the damp bush undermines physical health while it restores emotional well-being. The establishment figures as saviour as well as enemy, the complex traffic between the fringe and the centre working both for better and for worse, and creating a lively interplay of ironies. At her best, with her tartly eloquent style and sharp eye for folly, Sutherland resembles a rather gentler Muriel Spark.   JH

SUTTON, Eve (1906–92), wrote striking historical fiction for children. Born in Preston, England, and educated at the University of London, she arrived in New Zealand in 1949. For ten years she typed Braille transcriptions. She then collaborated with Lynley *Dodd in *My Cat Likes to Hide in Boxes* (1973), which won the 1975 Esther Glen Award and is still in print. Apart from *Skip for the Huntaway* (1983), illustrated by Ernest Papps, Sutton subsequently wrote mainly historical novels, in which characters variously discover their identity and goals in life. *Green Gold* (1976), *Tuppenny Brown* (1977) and *Johnny Sweep* (1977), all illustrated by Paul Wright, bring unprotected nineteenth-century English boys to New Zealand, on account of death, or petty crime (Tuppenny is from Parkhurst Prison, like Margaret *Beames's Charlie), or desertion from the horrors of a whaling-ship. A longer novel, *Moa Hunter* (1978), illustrated by Bernard Brett, is unique in its pre-historical setting, while *Surgeon's Boy* (1983) and *Kidnapped by Blackbirders* (1984), both illustrated by Fiona Kelly, document nineteenth-century voyaging, including the shameful 'slave' trade in the Pacific. Sutton also, like Ruth *Dallas, explores the *gold-rush era, in *Valley of Heavenly Gold* (1987). Illustrated by Doss, this features the role played by Chinese immigrants. Sutton's lively, concise historical novels and overall contribution earned her the inaugural Children's Literature Association Award in 1990.   DH

SUTTON-SMITH, Brian (1924–), children's novelist and educationist, was born and educated in Wellington, and graduated in 1954 the first PhD in Education from Victoria University. He taught in Wellington primary schools, the University of Ohio, and Columbia Teachers' College, New York, before becoming professor of human development and folklore, University of Pennsylvania. He is recognised internationally as an authority on children's games, publishing, for example, *The Games of New Zealand Children* (1959) and *A History of Children's Play: The New Zealand Playground 1840–1950* (1981). In New Zealand, however, he is probably better known for his novels: *Our Street* (1950, 1975), *Smitty Does a Bunk* (1961, 1975), and

The Cobbers (1976). These portray a boy's world as it often was when Sutton-Smith needed stories relevant to his pupils. However, without probing relationships, without internal judgment against ★'existentialist' infringements of law and accepted behaviour, *Our Street*, especially, provoked criticism on first publication. The third novel remains socially relevant in exposing bullying by staff and students at secondary school level.   DH

Swag (Australia 1841, NZ 1853) commonly denotes in early use a blanket-wrapped roll or bundle of possessions and useful articles, carried by a traveller on foot on the back or shoulders, usually held by straps, or laid round the neck like a horse-collar ('a horse-shoe swag'); also a load carried in or as a swag. In later use it denotes a knapsack or 'pikau', often extemporised from a hessian sugarbag. It probably derives from 'swag', 'a thief's plunder or booty'. The phrases to be or to go 'on the swag' and to 'carry one's swag' (live or travel on foot in the style of an itinerant, often in search of work) were once common, as were the verbal uses of 'to swag', to carry on the back or shoulders as, or in, a swag; also 'to swag it', to travel on foot with a swag, or as a swagger.

'Swagger' (Australia 1855, NZ 1867) denotes an itinerant carrying a swag, especially one in search of work, a tramp. Since *c*.1940 it has been only in historical use. Synonyms are 'sundowner', 'swaggie' (1900), 'swagman' (1876) and 'swagsman' (1869). 'Swagger' was the preferred New Zealand form, though ★Mansfield in ★'The ★Woman at the Store' uses 'sundowner'. 'Swagman' is the main Australian term.

The swagger recurs in New Zealand literature, in poetry from McKee ★Wright ('While the billy boils') through R.A.K. ★Mason ('His body doubled / under the pack ... oh curse that old lag– / here again / with his clumsy swag') to ★Baxter in 'Jack the Swagger's Song' and elsewhere ('"Damn this dry shingle country" / Old Jack the Swagger cried'). Images of dryness and prodigious thirst recur. In fiction, John A. ★Lee's 'The Shiner' is probably the classic version of the swagger as 'incorrigible vagabond', his thirst intensified in conditions 'too hot for a man warmly clad to be on the road carrying a swag and a heavy swag'.   HO

SWAN, Epi (1944–), is a pioneer of writing for children in ★Tokelauan, legally a New Zealand language. Born in Tokelau, at Nukunomu, she was a teacher there for eight years, moving to Auckland in 1971. Now a counsellor, health adviser and writer living at Petone, Hutt Valley, she began writing by translating the *Sunday Missal* (1985) into a bilingual English–Tokelauan resource for Catholic children of Tokelauan origin. *Lost* (1992) is a school reading book set in Petone. *Ko te Nonu*

(English title *Nonu*, 1995), about a Tokelauan fishing canoe, won an AIM Children's Book Award and had the unique distinction of being launched in conjunction with an actual canoe, traditionally built of 'thatched' logs and now in regular use on Wellington harbour. The book captures the pride of the author and community at this opportunity to share old fishing skills with a new generation. *Paheka i Nukunomu* (1996) returned to Swan's birthplace for a Tokelauan story retold for children in New Zealand. She has also translated into Tokelauan children's books by Māori, Niuean and Samoan authors, and her own have been translated into Cook Islands Māori, Māori, Niuean and Tongan. All her works are published by ★Learning Media.   RR

SWEVEN, Godfrey, pseudonym for **BROWN, John Macmillan**; see also **Science fiction; Utopian literature**.

SYME, Ronald (1910–), was born in Lancashire and is essentially an English writer of adventure stories for boys with 'exotic' settings including Australia, the South Seas and New Zealand. He received part of his education (1926–29) at the Collegiate School, Wanganui. From 1930 to 1934 he was a seaman and from 1934 to 1939 foreign correspondent for British papers. The years 1940–45 he worked with British army intelligence. Since 1979 he has lived in Rarotonga, working as a PR officer and parliamentary correspondent for the Cook Islands government. Although the primary impulse of his fiction is sheer adventure, he touches on the destructive impact of industrial civilisation on an Arcadian community on the island of 'Aorangi' in *The Amateur Company* (1957) and deals with a similar theme in *They Came to an Island* (1955). He published a popular history for adults, *The Story of New Zealand*, in 1954. His most notable New Zealand book is, however, *Gipsy Michael* (1954), the story of a boy who runs away from an unhappy home at the age of 14 and ends up in New Zealand. The ship is attacked by a Māori war party in Opotiki, where those who escape, including Michael, are aided by the German missionary Volkner. The party is led to the ★goldfields by their captain, who hopes to acquire enough money to buy another ship. They are very successful, but are robbed by claim-jumpers, whom they chase through a series of bush adventures. They return to gold-panning, become involved in the Land Wars, witness the death of Volkner, participate in the battle of Orakau, where they show more sympathy for the Māori than for the settlers, and recover their ship, only to have it commandeered by ★Te Kooti as he escapes from the Chathams. At last they sail away from this violent country into stiller waters. In *The Spaniards Came at Dawn* (1959) Syme writes of a Spanish 'discovery' of New Zealand with dire consequences to the intolerant seamen. *The Great Canoe* (1957) begins in New Zealand but moves quickly to the Pacific.   NW

Symmes Hole (1986), a novel by Ian *Wedde, interfolds narratives of nineteenth-century whaling and present-day historical research in a quest for, and questioning of, historical reality. Exuberantly *postmodern in its game-playing mix of fictional with documentary materials—both genuine and invented—its prose is loosely structured, richly metaphoric and allusive, strongly influenced by post-war *American fiction, especially Thomas Pynchon. Patrick *Evans calls it 'one of the most remarkable fictions ever likely to be produced in the country'.   RR

T

Takahe is a literary magazine produced since 1989 by the Takahe Publishing Collective in Christchurch. It was formerly *Cornucopia*. With a liberal editorial policy, it has developed from modest beginnings to have national lists of subscribers and contributors, especially of emerging writers.   RR

TALBOT, Thorpe (1851–1923), was the pseudonym of Frances Ellen Talbot, later Ward, a writer of fiction, travel writing and poetry who lived in Dunedin. Her best-known work is the short novel *Blue Cap*, which was published in one volume with a story by Vincent *Pyke, as *White Hood and Blue Cap: A Christmas Bough with Two Branches* (1881). The story opens with a dramatic but presumably satirical account of the wreck of the Picton ferry—most of the stranded passengers are more concerned with flirting and with obtaining cups of tea than with any sense of danger. Of these Gower and Marion continue their wooing on a trip to Christchurch, a town they find likeable only for its trees, and to Dunedin, which suits them better. Unfortunately things go less well when they are separated and in Rotorua Marion becomes engaged to Mr. Scariff, who always wears a blue cap. When he removes it, two horns are revealed—the result of his mother being terrified by a bull during pregnancy. There are some torrid scenes in a lonely house, with some echoes of *Wuthering Heights*. Marion's bull-horned husband has a fit of rage when she wears a red ribbon: he strips her and ties her up. Gallant Gower rides through a storm to find her. Flashes of lightning reveal her in her nightgown, 'every outline of her figure distinctly visible', but she disappears into the dark and drowns herself.

Dunedin researcher George Griffiths has established other information. Talbot's novel *Philiberta* (1883) won a *Melbourne Leader* competition, and is set in both Victoria and Dunedin, with one episode describing a musical tour through Canterbury and Otago. A copy is in the *Hocken Library. She also published at least one poem in the *Australasian*, articles about California in Melbourne and in the *Otago Witness* (1887), and a book about the North Island thermal region, *The New Guide to the Lakes and Hot Springs, and A Month in Hot Water* (1882). She was also described in her other works as 'author of … *Guinevere*', but this may have been published only as a newspaper serial and is not known. She was born in Yorkshire and was in Otago (probably by way of Victoria) by the late 1870s. She married Judge Charles Dudley Ward in 1902, after the death of his first wife, having (Griffiths indicates) included commendatory references to him much earlier in her fiction.   PN/NW

Tangata whenua or 'people of the land' are often the people whose ancestry connects them with a particular *marae, so that the term can sometimes be translated as 'hosts', in contrast to the manuhiri or 'guests' who visit a marae. But the term can be used in a broader sense to refer to the original claim of all Māori to the land of New Zealand, or in any sense which relates people closely and spiritually to a piece of land of any size.   NW

Tangi means 'weep' when used as a verb, but is often used as a shorter form of 'tangihanga', meaning funeral. Elaborate rituals over three days (the period the wairua or soul remains with the body) accompany such funerals, and the modern developments from the tradition can be found evoked in Witi *Ihimaera's novel *Tangi. A powerful account of a traditional tangihanga ('Here were seen for the last time on such a scale some thrilling pictures of old Maoridom.') is James *Cowan's description of the funeral (1894) of King Tawhiao in *The Maori: Yesterday and Today* (1930). A more recent event is described in detail by Earnest and Pearl Beaglehole in 'Contemporary Maori Death Customs', *Journal of the Polynesian Society*, Vol. 54, 1945.

The rituals include loud communal weeping and various forms of address to the deceased, which is an important form of Māori oral literature. The skills of oratory (*whaikōrero) are practised and highly valued, with the speeches referring constantly to history and legend, and especially to *Māui, who had tried to overcome death. Mourners also repeat many *Māori sayings, such as one quoted by *Mead: 'rāranga maunga tū te pō te ao: rārangi tangata ka ngaro, ka ngaro, ka ngaro' (a range of mountains remains standing night and day but a group of people is lost, is lost, is lost). Mead comments: 'Although proverbial comments on death might be repeated again and again … people want to know what their ancestors thought about death and what goodness and advice there is for them.' For 'waiata tangi' see *Waiata.   NW

Tangi, Witi *Ihimaera's first novel (1973), is an expanded version of the final story in *Pounamu, Pounamu*. It recounts Tama Mahana's reaction to the death of his father, but in doing so becomes a narrative equally concerned with the situation of young Māori in present-day urban New Zealand. Tama, who has moved from his home *marae at Waituhi, near Gisborne, to work in Wellington, is devastated by the death of his father. Ihimaera defines the place of individuals within the *whānau, and their relationship to the land, by employing a complicated time sequence that mingles Tama's memories of his family with his present situation. His journeys to and from the *tangi become potent symbols of the personal consequences of his father's death: the hasty flight to Gisborne by plane indicating his panic and confusion, and the sedate train journey back to Wellington representing a growing maturity and self-knowledge. Despite the pastoral nature of the novel, it is significant that Tama does not stay in his beloved Waituhi, but returns to a type of exile in the city.

In addition to the focus on his protagonist, Ihimaera develops a coherent sense of the Māori community, and weaves in a mythical dimension by likening the relationship between Tama's parents to the union of *Rangi and Papa, Sky Father and Earth Mother, with Tama representing the child, born in darkness, whose ability to see and grow is dependent on the separation of his parents.

PM

Tango, edited by David *Eggleton, replaced the Auckland University Students' Association annual *Kiwi in 1982 and featured contributions by Eggleton, Riemke *Ensing, David *Mitchell, Michael *Morrissey, Iain *Sharpe, Kendrick *Smithyman and C.K. *Stead.   SH

Taniwha are water monsters, referred to frequently in Māori oral literature (*Māori myths and legends, *Māori tribal histories), in the fiction, especially, of pre-1914 settlers, in novels and stories by Witi *Ihimaera and other modern Māori writers and quite extensively in literature for children in both languages.

Taniwha can live in any mass of water, salt or fresh, and some can move through the earth itself. Every *iwi and many *hapū or even *whānau have their own taniwha, which are intimidating but often protective as well, and sometimes almost seem like pets.

While making allowances for cultural differences, the taniwha often fills the place in Māori stories occupied by dragons in European legends. There are consequently many tales of heroic struggles between taniwha and humans. Often this is to avenge people eaten by the taniwha. In all cases the human is ultimately victorious.

One category of *karakia is the propitiatory chant to a taniwha, asking for safe passage past his home (usually a dark place such as a cave, deep pool or gorge). Often these songs were accompanied by offerings to the taniwha left on a rock. This friendly interaction meant that a taniwha could act as a guardian of its people and several have been said to come to the surface to mourn the death of a great *rangatira. (Sometimes the spiritual power of a rangatira was expressed by speaking of him metaphorically as a taniwha.) Another oral tradition is to ask for the protection of taniwha during a storm on a lake.

In appearance, taniwha often resemble tuatara (the lizard-like survivor of an order of reptiles otherwise extinct for two million years) but are much larger, sometimes as large as a whale. Some have different forms and some can change their forms, like Proteus.   NW

Tapu is the Māori form of a Polynesian concept which has been taken into English and other languages, primarily by Freudians, as 'taboo'. Often translated as 'sacred', it does indeed have a powerful spiritual base, but from another point of view it is a mechanism of social management and control. People, places and things can be 'tapu' and consequently protected from indignities, misappropriation, exploitation, overuse (of resources) and the like.

Early European writers on New Zealand (such as *Maning) made much of the sanctions imposed on those who breach tapu, but often the exuberance of such writers led them into sensationalism. Although a major breach of tapu could lead to death (death from despair more frequently than from execution), in many situations tapu simply regulated the careful use of resources and preserved *mana and social hierarchies.　　NW

Taranaki: *A Tale of the War, with a Description of the Province Previous to and During the War: Also an Account (Chiefly Taken from the Despatches) of the Principal Contests with the Natives during that Eventful Period* (1861), by H.B. *Stoney, is conventionally called the first New Zealand novel, although there is reason to doubt both its priority and its status as a novel. In the opening paragraph the author seems to imply that the story is true and that only the names have been changed, but in other places there are signs that he at least intended it to be a novel. The issue is confused by the obscure style and faulty and ambiguous grammar. Only patches of the prose are narrative, the rest being descriptive and more frequently polemical. The opening chapter is an accusation in the author's (rather than a narrator's) voice that the New Zealand *Wars were caused by the missionaries, who had encouraged the 'Natives' ('little more than savages') to think themselves equal to the British. The church had also slanderously suggested that the government wanted to take land from the Māori—a curious accusation considering that Stoney's preferred policy was to remove Māori from their land with the purpose of 'reclaiming the Natives to civilization'. He clearly hoped for the end of Māori culture, if not of the Māori people. After some facts and figures about Taranaki he returns to polemics, his anger now directed against students of the Māori language, which should, he thinks, die out as soon as possible. Other arguments are 'contrary to the fundamental principles of colonial polity'. Only after all this does the story begin, but is repeatedly interrupted by digressions.

Love between young members of two settler families in the idyllic fields of Taranaki is hindered by slanders and the outbreak of war. Sadly, the personal outcome remains unclear as the narrative is swamped by battle and destruction. Stoney seems to seek sympathy from English readers for colonials' sufferings, but his weak narrative gives way to impassioned, if ungrammatical, persuasion.　　NW

TARGUSE, V. (Violet) (*c.*1883–1937) was a leading playwright in the 1930s, winning many British Drama League prizes and having seven plays published in BDL collections. Forthrightly exploring contemporary social issues in constrained rural settings appropriate to the one-act format, her plays create an intense emotional atmosphere and psychological suspense. Three were published in *Seven One-Act Plays* (1933), a collection introduced by British stage luminary Dame Sybil Thorndike, whose tribute to 'V. Targuse' disarmingly

stumbles over gender: 'a real aptitude for theatre he has—(I've just seen it's a Mrs—I do apologise to her!) I think her works … spring from life'. 'The Touchstone', set in a sheep *station kitchen, evinces a strong and liberal sense of the history of settlement; 'Fear', set at a freezing works, deals with the legacy of domestic violence. The most powerful is 'Rabbits', centred on a woman trapped by the *Depression in a shack on an isolated railway siding on the Canterbury Plains, with her son's caged rabbit symbolising her condition. The writing is often strongly emotive: 'I no longer lived in a shack, I lived in a cage, and when the door of that cage opened, it would open into a cemetery! … I have watched the dead come one by one to keep me company'. The ending achieves a tragic resonance: 'What's the sense in trying to escape when you know Fate's against you? You silly little creature!' Carol Stevenson in her essay 'Staging Women's Talk' describes Targuse's work as 'an important phase in the development of women's roles … and the interaction of New Zealand women on the stage'. Certainly her kitchen settings and hard-working women anticipate *Renée, while the misery of their isolation with inadequate or violent men may also represent an early refutation of the *'Man Alone' myth from the female viewpoint. According to theatre historian Peter Harcourt, Targuse once described herself on a form as a 'menial', probably an ironic description of her role as a rural housewife. Born in Timaru, she was, Carol Stevenson has established, a regular WEA student, played first violin in the Timaru Orchestra and was an ardent reader. She died in Christchurch.　　RR

TASMAN, Abel Janszoon (*c.*1603–*c.*1659), born in Lutjegast, near Groningen in the *Netherlands, was an explorer employed by the Dutch East India Company. Under his command the *Heemskerck* and the *Zeehaen* arrived in New Zealand from Batavia in December 1642 while searching for the Unknown South-Land. The logbook details the arrival and landfall, and the death of four mariners in an encounter with the Māori at sea, and is thus the first European text of New Zealand. Tasman and his crew did not actually set foot on land, however. A number of accounts survive in manuscripts, and in 1671 a version of Tasman's voyage, based on the diary of the ship's surgeon Henrik Haelbos, was published for the first time in Arnoldus Montanus' *De Nieuwe en Onbekende Weereld*. Both the instructions issued by the Dutch East India Company and the log-book of the voyage are valuable for the perception and presentation of New Zealand and its inhabitants 135 years before James *Cook arrived. A translation by J.E. Heeres, *Abel Janszoon Tasman's Journal of his Discovery of Van Diemen's*

Land and New Zealand in 1642, was published in 1898, also detailing Tasman's life and the historical context. Andrew Sharp's translation, *The Voyages of Abel Janszoon Tasman* (1968), is the current modern text. Tasman's precursive status and the name he gave the country were defended as early as the poetry of C.C. *Bowen. Allen *Curnow's *'Landfall in Unknown Seas' articulates Tasman's attempt powerfully and ironically: 'Simply by sailing in a new direction / You could enlarge the world.' For a recent alternative version of Tasman's voyage, see Peter *Hawes's *Tasman's Lay* (1995), which recounts the trip from the perspective of Tasman's Hindi scribe. HT

Tau or **tau marae**, see **tauparapara**.

Tauparapara are short songs performed by a male on the *marae before performing *whaikōrero (making a speech). Many have canoe imagery and the term is sometimes used for an incantation for moving a canoe (*waka). In his 1974 dissertation on whaikōrero, Robert Mahuta points out that there are various kinds of tauparapara depending on the speech which is to follow. In *Maori Music* (1996) Mervyn McLean says that in various tribal areas tauparapara can be called tau marae, poohua tau or simply tau.

(Tīmoti) Sam *Kāretu, indicating that tauparapara may be distinctive to one tribe, or may have become common across the country, describes them as generally beginning 'with the words "tihe mauri ora" which means literally "the sneeze of life". It serves the purpose of announcing "Here I am. Listen to me. I am about to speak." Some speakers also end their tauparapara with the words "tihe mauri ora"' ('Language and Protocol of the Marae' in *Te Ao Hurihuri: The World Moves On* (1977) ed. Michael *King). Anne Salmond writes that their archaic words and obscure historical references give the chants a 'spell' quality. 'The roll of the voice and the mystery of the words lend the tauparapara its dignity, and the recitation conveys *mana and *tapu rather than specific information ... There are hundreds of these chants and they are still being composed, although only by the most expert elders' (*Hui: A Study of Maori Ceremonial Gatherings*, 1975). On pages 160–164, Salmond gives examples of tauparapara appropriate to various occasions. NW

Tāwhaki is a heroic figure whose place on *whakapapa is soon after the birth of the world. Extremely handsome, he is loved by many women. His greatest accomplishment was to climb to the sky, where he restored sight to his grandmother Whaitiri by giving her the eyes of his brother, Karihi. Because of a sexual misdemeanour Tāwhaki was deprived of his wife, who was taken to an even higher sky. His attempt to reach her there was too bold even for a hero; he turned himself into a harrier hawk but his wings were clipped and—somewhat like Icarus—he fell to the ground. This summary is based on the Ngāti Porou version; there are others in Taranaki and on the South Island.

There are other tales of Tāwhaki. Te Rangihaeata of the Ngāti Toa told of Tāwhaki's war with water sprites. In some places he is the predecessor of the great *tohunga. There are even more variants of the tales in other parts of the Pacific, and his myth is thought to have existed for more than two thousand years. In a sense he was the 'original' Polynesian hero, while *Māui was a later, more comic and ironic version. NW

TAYLOR, Apirana (1955–), of Te Whānau-a-Apanui, Ngāti Porou and Taranaki descent, has published three collections of poetry, two collections of short stories and a novel. He also writes for children and for the theatre, acts, teaches drama and is a member of the Māori theatre group Te Ohu Whakaari.

Taylor's first collection of poetry, *Eyes of the Ruru* (1972), established him as a powerful voice among Māori writers. Although the collection is uneven in places, with few of its poems approaching the poignant intensity of Tu—a casualty of colonialism and Māori urban drift—reciting his *whakapapa in 'Sad Joke on a Marae', Peter *Simpson notes that its 'raw, powerful and angry poems' present 'a Maori voice utterly different from the lyricism and gentle ironies of Hone *Tuwhare' (*Evening Post*, 14 Feb. 1997). A collaborative volume, *3 Shades* (1981), followed, and then in 1997 a third volume of poetry, *Soft Leaf Falls of the Moon*. This volume is evidence of Taylor's development as a poet, with most of its verses making less emphatic demands to be performed, and a number experimenting with language and layout.

It was Taylor's prose that firmly established him as a literary presence. His short stories—collected in *He Rau Aroha: A Hundred Years of Love* (1986) and *Ki Te Ao* (1990)—are written in predominantly realist modes that Lawrence *Jones finds 'reminiscent of O.E. *Middleton, especially in the natural, uncondescending adoption of a working-class perspective, in the vivid but understated naturalistic detail, and in the straightforward moralism' (*Evening Post*, 28 Sep. 1990). His novel, *He Tangi Aroha* (1993), is narrated with the world of urban Māori in the 1990s as its backdrop. While the setting is similar to Alan *Duff's *Once Were Warriors*, Taylor explores the issues, where Duff tends to be more descriptive, by using his characters as emblems of the complex groupings within such a society. He also aims for a more balanced perspective on bicultural issues by developing a rather formalised dialogue between Pākehā and Māori. PM

TAYLOR, Chad (1964–), is a writer of uncompromisingly contemporary short fictions of transience and shifting realities in the modern city. Born and educated in Auckland, where his work is largely set, he graduated BFA at Elam and has carried that interest into the strong visual quality of his writing. His stories have been published in *Landfall, *Metro and *Sport and anthologised in Michael *Gifkins's *Lust* and elsewhere. Published volumes are *Heaven* (1994), *Pack of Lies* (1994), both novellas, and *The Man Who Wasn't Feeling Himself*, short stories (1995). The fictions often work on the edge of such conventions as the murder story ('No Sun, No Rain'), futuristic fantasy ('Somewhere in the 21st Century') or romance triangle (*Pack of Lies*, 'Calling Doctor Dollywell'), often through unreliable or unattractive narrators. As these literary norms are subverted, perceptions of reality and identity are challenged. Strong visual representations, especially of sex and clothing, and filmic treatment with fragmentary and mobile scenes and chronology, provide metaphorical access to these internal concerns. Taylor has written for film, including the script 'Funny Little Guy' (1994). A full-time writer, he lives in Auckland.   RR

TAYLOR, Mary (1817–93), born into a Yorkshire mercantile family, met Charlotte Brontë at Miss Wooler's School in 1831 and, with Ellen Nussey, another Roe Head pupil, became a close friend of the Brontës. Charlotte Brontë was introduced to the extensive Taylor family, which she later used as a basis for the Yorkes in *Shirley* (1849), describing them as 'peculiar, racy, vigorous'. In 1841 Taylor travelled to Brussels with Charlotte and Emily, all three attending school there—Taylor the Koekelberg School, Charlotte and Emily the Pensionnat Heger. In 1845 Taylor followed her brother Waring Taylor as an emigrant to New Zealand, settling in Wellington where she built and ran a draper and general goods' shop. Later called James Smith's, this remained a Wellington landmark until the early 1990s. Her letters to Charlotte Brontë and Ellen Nussey, collected by Joan *Stevens in 1972, provide a lively and somewhat critical picture of the settlement, as well as some acute comments on Charlotte's writing. She kept only one of Charlotte's letters—that which describes herself and Anne Brontë revealing their identity to the publisher George Smith. The loss of the bulk of the correspondence is regrettable, as it seems that Charlotte wrote more confidingly to Taylor than to the conventional Nussey, the source of most extant Brontë letters.

Taylor returned to England in 1859, completing her only novel, which she had begun in Wellington, *Miss Miles, or a Tale of Yorkshire Life 60 Years Ago* (1890). Despite its nostalgic setting, this is an explicitly feminist work which argues the necessity of women earning their own living. Taylor was a source for Elizabeth Gaskell's *Life of Charlotte Brontë* (1857), though she disapproved of the mythologising of the Brontës; and is the original for Rose Yorke in *Shirley*: 'a lonely emigrant in some region of the southern hemisphere'.   JS

TAYLOR, Richard (1805–73), was significant in literary history for collecting and preserving tales and poems from Māori informants, especially from Ngāti Hau, Ngāti Ruanui and Ngā Rauru tribes. A graduate of Cambridge, he had clerical positions there and in Ely before being accepted by the Church Missionary Society for work in New Zealand, where he arrived in 1838. Taylor assisted in drawing up the Treaty of Waitangi and engrossed it on parchment the evening before it was signed (February 1840). He was appointed to Wanganui in 1843, in which district he travelled energetically, and it was there that he did much of his literary work, as well as maintaining peace between various Māori tribes. Governor *Grey was much impressed by the school Taylor opened in Wanganui.

In 1855 Taylor travelled to England taking Hoani Wiremu Hipango, a Christian chief, with him. While there he published *Te Ika a Maui*, an important account of Māori life and customs, as well as a study of geology, natural history, productive economy and climate, with 100 illustrations from his own sketches. After 1860 his son took over much of his missionary work while Taylor himself concentrated on scientific studies, publishing *A Leaf from the Natural History of New Zealand* in 1848 and *The Age of New Zealand* in 1866. In 1868, again visiting England, he also published *The Past and Present of New Zealand*, dealing mainly with his own experiences.

It seems that much of the work in John *White's vast collection, *Ancient History of the Maori*, was taken from Taylor's manuscripts without adequate acknowledgment. Margaret *Orbell and Mervyn McLean have studied this debt in some detail.   NW

TAYLOR, William (1938–), has written novels for adults but now regards these as his 'apprenticeship' for his successful fiction for children and teenage readers. Born in Lower Hutt, he worked in banking before attending Christchurch Teachers' College. His teaching career includes a year in London and the years 1979–86 as principal of Ohakune Primary School, a time when he was also a solo parent, part-owner of a restaurant and (1981–88) mayor of Ohakune. His early teaching experiences are recorded in *Burnt Carrots Don't Have Legs* (1976). Winning the 1984 Choysa Bursary for Children's Writers led to full-time writing from 1986. In 1988, he served with the Volunteer Service Abroad in Bhutan until invalided home. In 1992 he was inaugural writer-in-residence at Palmerston North College of Education.

Taylor's early 'apprentice' novels for adults are *Episode* (1970), *The Mask of the Clown* (1970), *The Plekhov Place* (1971), *Pieces in a Jigsaw* (1972), *The Persimmon Tree* (1972) and *The Chrysalis* (1974). *Pack Up, Pick Up and Off* (1981) shows the subsequent hallmarks of his children's fiction: contemporary realism in rural and small-town settings; concern for justice and compassion for victims; compelling narrative; and acuteness in dialogue. Exuberant humour dominates the 'Greenhill Trilogy', beginning with *The Worst Soccer Team Ever* (1987); the Porter brothers series beginning with *The Porter Brothers* (1990); *The Fatz Katz* (1995); and *Annie & Co and Marilyn Monroe* (1995). Gentle satire enhances the comedy of *Agnes the Sheep* (1990), winner of the 1991 Esther Glen Award, and *Knitwits* (1992). Warmly comic yet moving, this traces Chas's preparations for the birth of a sibling to the mocking of the irrepressible Alice Pepper. Its sequel, *Numbskulls* (1995), is comparatively disappointing.

Serious, critical social realism drives *My Summer of the Lions* (1986); *Shooting Through* (1988); *Possum Perkins* (1987, published as *Paradise Lane* in the USA); *The Kidnap of Jessie Parker* (1989), his most astringent novel; *Beth and Bruno* (1992); and *The Blue Lawn* (1994), winner of the 1995 Senior Fiction Award for its sensitive exploration of the relationship between two adolescent boys.

A contributor of plays, short stories and reviews to various magazines and newspapers, Taylor also edited *Zigzag* (1993), a collection of short stories focusing on adolescent boys, and performs as a member of *Metaphor.   DH

Te Ao Hou / The New World, see **Ao Hou, Te / The New World**

Te Ao Mārama, see **Ao Mārama, Te**

TE AWEKOTUKU, Ngāhuia (1949–), short story writer, essayist and spokeswoman on Māori, feminist and lesbian issues, was born in Rotorua of Te Arawa, Waikato and Tūhoe descent. At Auckland University she was active in gay and feminist movements and Ngā Tamatoa, the emergent Māori rights group. She completed an MA in English (1974), with a thesis on Janet *Frame, and PhD on the socio-cultural effects of tourism on the Te Arawa people (1981). She was curator of ethnology at the Waikato Museum, 1985–87, lecturer in art history at Auckland University 1987–96, and is now professor of Māori studies at Victoria University. Her first short story, 'Tahuri: the Runaway', was included in *New Women's Fiction* (1987) and in her own collection, *Tahuri* (1989). Loosely autobiographical

stories of a young Māori girl's growing up and discovery of sexual identity, this collection makes Māori, and especially lesbian, women central and Pākehā peripheral, carrying out what Te Awekotuku has called her 'responsibility ... to the fierce women fighters, shamans and poets of Maori legend and myth ... the resilient courageous women of my own extended family ... to ensure their stories are not lost in a mawkishly romantic muddle of male translated history'. This statement, rejecting 'colonial and contemporary ethnography', is from *Mana Wahine Maori: Selected Writings on Maori Women's Art, Culture and Politics*, a collection of essays from 1971 to 1990 which weave together the strands in her life as Māori, feminist, lesbian and academic. AMcL

TE HURINUI, Pei, see **JONES, Pei Te Hurinui.**

Te Kaihau / The Windeater, see **Kaihau, Te / The Windeater**

TE KOOTI ARIKIRANGI TE TURUKI (1832?–93) is best known as a prophetic leader and guerrilla strategist and fighter, but he was also the composer of an important body of *waiata (songs). He founded the Ringatū faith, and left an extensive collection of written and oral narratives and predictive sayings, which are remembered as a source of inspiration, and repeatedly acted upon. He was born at Te Pa-o-Kahu at Turanganui (Poverty Bay) and belonged to Ngāti Maru, a *hapū of Rongowhakaata. He spent his youth in Poverty Bay, but was involved in coastal trading to Auckland and Napier in Māori-owned vessels. He aspired to be ordained in the Anglican church, but was rejected. In 1866 he was sent as a prisoner to Wharekauri (Chatham Island) with 300 Pai Marire fighters (men and women) taken in the East Coast wars, although he had not been a supporter of this religious movement. His writing survives in several forms. All derive from his experience of exile, escape and dramatic return to New Zealand in 1868, and his subsequent pursuit by colonial and Māori militia forces. Two holograph diaries from this period exist in public collections (*Alexander Turnbull Library and Hawke's Bay Museum, Napier). The first records his visionary experiences during his exile on Wharekauri, and the beginning of the new faith. The second contains references to fighting in Taupo in 1869, early prophetic utterances and a diagram of a visionary dream. Letters to the government and Māori leaders, allies and opponents, also survive from the war period. They set out his cause—the injustice of his exile without trial—and seek support from Māori, particularly those who had recently experienced land confiscation; above all they request the end of his pursuit by the government. In one letter, he refers to the executions he carried out at Matawhero, Poverty Bay, in 1868, where he attacked Māori and Pākehā families. All were involved in the illegal sale of land, in which he had ownership rights.

As a composer of waiata, he invented and adapted songs from various tribal regions for different occasions. As one Māori elder recalled (in 1981): 'Wherever Te Kooti went—wherever he step foot from one area to another—he's singing.' Te Kooti constructed his own life history in song, beginning with predictions of his birth; he left songs as gifts for the *marae and the people whom he visited on journeys around Te Ika-a-Māui (North Island) after he was pardoned in 1883. There are ninety-eight written song texts, as well as others recorded orally, and they are of great literary significance. The bulk of the texts exist in the original manuscript book of Te Kooti's waiata collated by his secretary Hamiora Aparoa (*University of Auckland Library). Many of the songs warn and cajole Māori communities against land loss and political manipulation. Others talk of the government's misuse of the principle of law ('te ture'). All contain complex allusions to Māori ancestral history, reworked for the present time.

Te Kooti's three secretaries wrote down his sayings and predictions. These form the bulk of the surviving written records. At times intentionally opaque, Te Kooti's visionary words ('nga kupu whakaari') can be interpreted as guides to the future. Through these sayings, Te Kooti set a series of tasks to be fulfilled by his successor, the One whom he predicted would come after him to complete his work. The predictive words exist in many manuscript books held within the several branches of the Ringatū faith.

Even before his death, Te Kooti entered the literary imagination of New Zealand. The earliest poem, 'Te Kooti' (1870), is a satire by an Otago settler, Alan Clyde, on the futile boastings of the northern military men, who kept claiming that they had captured the most elusive of Māori fighters. Te Kooti became the source of poetic outpourings from the scurrilous to the supportive when he attempted to return to Poverty Bay in 1889 but was arrested with dubious legality. More recent, measured poems by C.K. *Stead, 'January 24, 1884 The Visit' (1990), and Kendrick *Smithyman, 'Meeting at Matata' (1992), recreate other historical encounters with Te Kooti: the man who was never captured in war fascinated all who met him. Smithyman recalled the occasion when Te Kooti wrapped a cloak around the shoulders of his former adversary, Gilbert Mair, with the words, '"Wear this in memory of me. If it's not / big enough, let me clothe you with my love."' Te Kooti was first fictionalised by Grace Whitelaw in a prize-winning short story, 'Kiore. A Tale of Ngatapa', in the *New Zealand Graphic and Ladies Journal* (24 Dec. 1891). Better novels were to follow: most notably, Witi *Ihimaera's The *Matriarch (1986) and Maurice *Shadbolt's Season of the Jew (1986; see *New Zealand Wars trilogy). In both, Te Kooti is a distant presence, but for Ihimaera his history interweaves with the life of contemporary Māori families. Ihimaera understands orality: the continuing story, through which Māori transmit their history into the present.

For many Māori, Te Kooti stands as the figure of Moses in their own land: leader and prophet at the time of their dispossession, whose successor will restore the people to their autonomy. If he lives in people's minds, he has also been given life in song, in carving, in painting, in film, in theatre, in opera, and in narrative. He will continue to exist in all these ways. JB

Te Kotare Press, see *Dark Lord of Savaiki.*

Te Maarama, see *Maarama, Te.*

TE MATOROHANGA, see **Whare wānanga**.

TE PUEA HĒRANGI (1883–1952) was an important agent for Māori culture, including literature, and a major composer of *waiata.

She was a direct descendent of the Māori kings Potatau and Tawhiao and is popularly known as 'Princess' Te Puea, although, strictly speaking, there are no princesses in the Māori system. Her name is from the phrase 'Puea ahau i te ao'—'I shall rise to the surface of the world'. At first she was educated by her uncle, Mahuta, but when he became king, in 1894, she was sent to Pākehā schools. She was thus educated in both cultures. In 1898 she returned to Mangatawhiri, a small village but an important meeting place for Waikato *iwi. It was not until a decade later that she became active in politics, helping in the election of Maui Pomare to parliament in 1911. From 1914 she began to organise major King Movement (Kingitanga) *hui at Mangatawhiri. In 1916, when the pacifist Waikato Māori were under pressure from the central government to assist in World War 1, the Pai Mārire religion, which had been introduced into the Waikato by Te Puea's grandfather King Tawhiao, was revived, and from that time on Te Puea held prayer sessions every morning and evening. These prayers gave the people strength to resist the government pressure, and on occasions of direct confrontation with police Te Puea spoke on the Māori behalf. The skills of *whaikōrero thus demonstrated added to her courage (it is usually thought to be a masculine artform), and the love she inspired made her the strongest leader of her people in the coming years. Both Māori and Pākehā recognised her leadership.

After the war, the influenza epidemic, which killed people all over the world, decimated the population of Mangatawhiri. Te Puea gathered many orphans around her and cared for them. Later, these people who owed their lives to her were completely devoted to Te Puea, who also raised their children in turn. By the early 1920s she was organising the king's work. Te Rata, the king, was shy and retiring, while she was bold and imposing, but, although her role was more public than his, she always saw herself as his support. It was under her leadership, in 1921, that the people returned to Ngaruawahia, home of the King Movement, which had suffered in the land confiscations after the New Zealand *Wars. This was felt to be a return home in fulfilment of King Tawhiao's *whakataukī to the effect that his people would be reborn.

To finance the development of Tūrangawaewae Pā at Ngāruawāhia, Te Puea organised a concert party—Te Pou o Mangatawhiri or 'TPM'—which was to have a crucial influence on the development of *waiata-ā-ringa. Indeed it is said that she was so impressed by a visiting concert party from the Cook Islands that, together with Sir Apirana *Ngata, she actually invented the form of waiata-ā-ringa. The forty-four members of TPM travelled widely through the North Island, often walking twenty miles from one concert to the next, because the money they earned was to be used at Tūrangawaewae. As they slept out of doors and skipped meals, the buildings rose at their home village. When Sir Apirana Ngata met Te Puea on one of the concert tours he took her to Wellington, introduced her to the prime minister and encouraged the government to help develop the pā at Ngāruawāhia. Under Te Puea's supervision and with Ngata's help as Minister of Native Affairs, many areas of Waikato land were cleared for dairying. During the *Depression, such land development projects were among the most active parts of the economy.

Te Puea could often be seen working on the land herself, but she also found time to encourage the growth of cultural activities. She set up a carving school and organised the building of large *waka to take part in the *Centennial celebrations of 1940, again using the TPM to finance the work. At her *tangi in October 1952 more than 10 000 people, including the prime minister and other Pākehā and Māori leaders, came to express their respect.

At important times of her life, Te Puea composed waiata to express her awareness of the situation and to encourage her people. A famous example is 'The Song of Te Puea'—E huri rā koe—written in 1917 to strengthen the Waikato men who resisted conscription into the New Zealand army.

Te Puea is said to have been a major influence in the creation of the main character in Witi *Ihimaera's novel *The *Matriarch. Much of the above is indebted, as any account of Te Puea must be, to the researches of Michael *King for his biography *Te Puea Herangi* (1977).   NW

TE RANGI HIROA, see **BUCK, Peter**.

TE RANGIKĀHEKE, Wiremu Maihi (*c.*1815–96), a chief of Ngāti Rangiwewehi, Te Arawa, an important tribe living on the northern shores of Lake Rotorua, was the author of the manuscripts which were the source of most of the prose material in the appendices to Sir George *Grey's *Ko nga *Moteatea, me nga Hakirara o nga Maori* (1853), and of much of the material for his *Ko nga *Mahinga a nga Tupuna Maori* (1854) and hence of its translation, *Polynesian Mythology* (1855). Te Rangikaheke became acquainted with Grey in 1846–47 and by 1849 was working with Grey who, as Governor, wished to learn the Māori language and Māori customs. After Grey's departure in 1853 Te Rangikāheke held several official appointments over a period of eighteen years in Maketu and Rotorua as clerk of works to the Native Department and later as clerk of the Circuit Court and land purchase agent and later again as assessor to the Native Land Court. He was the first Māori to stand for election in a European constituency, contesting the East Coast constituency in 1875–76. He was involved as a witness or claimant in numerous cases in the Native Land Court. Te Rangikāheke was regarded as a brilliant orator by Māori and Pākehā.

Between 1849 and 1854 Te Rangikāheke produced most of his large body of writing in Māori, twenty-one manuscripts of which he was the sole author, and seventeen more to which he contributed, in all nearly 800 pages. The manuscripts, written in a legible, neat, consistent hand, encompass most aspects of Māori culture, including language, genealogies, legends, contemporary history, political commentary, customs, commentary on laments and autobiographical material. In addition Te Rangikāheke contributed to Grey's manuscripts of songs and proverbs. Eight manuscripts deal with myths and tribal history and it is these that were the source of most of the prose material in Grey's published works. His writing is clear and lively; there are many beautiful comparisons, as well as analogies, digressions and effective use of dialogue. His grammar and style are generally regarded as 'classical' Māori. Te Rangikāheke's account of history covers all time, from the evolution of the universe, the origin of man with the separation of *Ranginui and Papa-tu-a-nuku, the quarrels of their sons, the deeds of *Māui, the migration of the seven canoes from Hawaiki, and the voyage and arrival of Te Arawa canoe, down to the spread of Te Arawa from

Whangaparaoa to Maketu and the inland lakes. It is a comprehensive and sequential account, connecting the past to the present and claiming *mana and land for his tribe. Genealogical recital and narrative are the techniques used to recount events. Other manuscripts recount the story of *Hinemoa, and the wars of the 1830s–40s in the Rotorua and Bay of Plenty areas. Others tell of Māori–Pākehā relations, marriage customs, leadership qualities, warfare, religious observances and an exposition of Māori knowledge.

Grey named none of his informants and introduced alterations, combinations and omissions, particularly in his latter two works. Little was therefore known of Te Rangikāheke's writing until after the turn of the century, especially when Grey's library was returned from South Africa to the Auckland Public Library in 1922. A number of Te Rangikāheke's manuscripts have been transcribed as he wrote them and translations made by Bruce *Biggs, Margaret *Orbell, Agathe Thornton and Jenifer Curnow.   JC

TE UA HAUMENE (d. 1866), Ngāti Ruanui, was the founder of the religious movement of Hauhauism and a creator of prophetic texts. As a child and youth he came under the influence of Wesleyan missionaries. During an illness he was visited by the Angel Gabriel, who directed him to found a new religion. As the fame of his miracles spread, so did the Hauhau movement. During the New Zealand *Wars he was captured, and later *Grey took him on a tour of the affected areas. To be seen in the company of the Governor destroyed Te Ua's credibility and after his release he faded from historical records.

Te Ua's writings were based on the Old Testament and his vision of Gabriel. The doctrines are the earliest attempt to reconcile Biblical teaching and Polynesian beliefs. The Māori were identified with one of the lost tribes of Israel and New Zealand became 'New Canaan'. Gabriel told Te Ua how the Māori were to be freed from bondage to the Europeans: *karakia were chanted around the 'Niu' pole—a tall wooden pole with a crosstree on which dwelt the gods of war (Riki) and peace (Ruru), Ruru being the greater. The 'karakia' were in 'Hebrew'—in fact a confusion of Māori syllables and English, mainly biblical, words. Hauhauism is best known as a fighting organisation, with the warriors chanting 'Hapa, hapa, paimarire hau' and raising their right hand to ward off bullets. The chant provides the source of the name 'Hauhauism' and also of the official name of the church 'Paimarire' (which has a few hundred adherents today).   NW

TE WHATAHORO, H.T., see **Whare wānanga**.

TEMPLE, Philip (1939–   ), broke new ground in fiction with his environmental novels, has made a distinguished contribution to the literature of mountaineering and exploration, and is a successful children's writer. Born in Yorkshire and educated in London, he moved to New Zealand in 1957, becoming an explorer, mountaineer and outdoor educator. Two expedition narratives were followed by two notable books on New Zealand mountaineers, *The World at Their Feet*, which won the Wattie Book Award for 1970, and *Castles in the Air* (1973). He was features editor of the *NZ Listener* 1968–72, associate editor of *Landfall* 1972–75 and editor of *NZ Alpine Journal* 1968–70, 1973. Becoming a full-time writer in 1970, he has held several awards, including the Katherine *Mansfield Memorial Fellowship (1979), *Burns Fellowship (1980) and a German government arts award (1987).

Temple's first novels were *The Explorer* (1975; UK 1976) and *Stations* (1979), both strong realist chronicles of early settlement. His most significant fictions, however, are his two-part anthropomorphic saga of the mountain kea, *Beak of the Moon* (1981) and *Dark of the Moon* (1993). These cautionary environmental allegories adapt an English sub-genre (from *Wind in the Willows* to *Watership Down*) into a distinctive local version evincing the author's profound knowledge of the New Zealand mountain locale. He added *Sam* in 1984, and two further novels have been completed in draft. He returned in 1985 to creative non-fiction narrative, with *New Zealand Explorers: Great Journeys of Discovery*, a Wattie finalist in 1986. This became the basis of a three-part TV documentary-drama series, 'At Risk of Our Lives', researched and scripted by Temple, first screened in 1992, one of which (on William Colenso) was runner-up as best drama in that year's Film and TV Awards.

Temple's children's picture books, all illustrated by Chris Gaskin and frequently reprinted, include several award winners and again draw on his knowledge of the terrain and its natural history, particularly birds. Notable are *The Legend of the Kea* (1986; UK 1986), *Kakapo, Parrot of the Night* (1988; UK 1988; AIM Award winner 1990) and *Kotuku, Flight of the White Heron* (1994; AIM Honour winner 1995).

Temple has also written several walking track guides and is a leading outdoors photographer, with six full books and many credits. He has written many articles in journals and newspapers in New Zealand and overseas, including recent commentaries on electoral reform. He has lived in Wellington, Anakiwa, Little Akaroa and Dunedin, with regular periods recently in Berlin. He received the 1996 National Library research fellowship to work on a biographical study of the *Wakefields.   RR

TEMPLETON, Natasha (1936–), is author of the novel *Firebird* (1994), unique in its conscious fusion of the tradition of the Russian novel with New Zealand material and themes. Born in Russia, she spent her childhood in Europe, arriving in New Zealand in 1951 and graduating BA at Victoria University College in 1956. She worked and trained as a broadcaster in New Zealand and London before marriage to diplomat and politician Hugh Templeton in 1961. On various postings she worked as broadcaster, writer and lecturer, graduating MA in Russian literature at Columbia University, New York, in 1964. Reviews and short stories in the *NZ Listener preceded the novel. *Firebird* is an ambitious multiple narrative which connects New Zealand history and politics with the revelation of actual atrocities inflicted on the Red Army at the end of World War 2. New Zealander Major-General Sir Stephen Weir is fictionalised as General Mort Stirling, the key narratorial figure, while other historical figures appear under their own names (Freyberg, Montgomery) or in fictionalised form, such as Dan *Davin or Robert *Muldoon, critically presented as Howie 'Piggy' Hall. Reviews concurred in praising the historical grasp, compelling action narrative and humanitarian commitment, some with reservations about the romanticising of the enigmatic and passionate Nadezhda, the 'Firebird', as linking device. It was published in London, 1994, and New Zealand, 1995.   RR

TEXIDOR, Greville (1902–64), fiction writer, was born in Wolverhampton, England. Though she did not arrive in New Zealand until 1940 and left in 1948, most of her writing took place in her New Zealand years. Between 1918 and 1940 she lived a varied life, with three marriages (to an Englishman, a Spaniard and a German), much travel, and several years of residence in Spain. Her experience included some years in the Hampstead art world with her mother and sister, both painters, time as a dancer in chorus lines and variety acts in Europe and North and South America, participation with her third husband on the Republican side in the Spanish Civil War, and work for relief and aid agencies in Spain and England to help Spanish and later German refugees. This cosmopolitan experience served as the subject matter for some of her fiction and was a source of an outside perspective on New Zealand in the remainder of it. In New Zealand she lived with her third husband, Werner Droescher, and her mother and sister in Auckland, North Auckland and on the North Shore, where she became part of a literary group that included Frank *Sargeson (who was her literary mentor), Maurice *Duggan, R.A.K. *Mason, John Reece *Cole (who lived for some time in a caravan on her property), Ian

Hamilton, Anna *Kavan and others. From 1943 to 1948 she published short fiction in New Zealand, Australian and English periodicals, and in Sargeson's anthology, *Speaking for Ourselves* (1945). She also completed in those years a novella, *These Dark Glasses*, which after some delay was printed by Robert *Lowry and published by the *Caxton Press in 1949. She and her family went to Australia in 1948 and returned to Spain in 1954. After the breakup of her third marriage in 1961 she returned to Australia in 1962; she committed suicide there in 1964. In 1987 her published stories together with a selection of previously unpublished work were brought out as a collection, *In Fifteen Minutes You Can Say a Lot: Selected Fiction*, edited by Kendrick *Smithyman.

Some of Texidor's work, such as the story 'An Annual Affair', deals devastatingly and mercilessly with New Zealand provincial society. The unfinished novella 'Goodbye Forever' presents a European refugee's critical view of the North Shore intellectual world. The remainder of her work, written in New Zealand, deals with her European experience, especially the Spanish Civil War and its aftermath as seen by foreign political and social workers and by the refugees themselves. *These Dark Glasses*, her most substantial fiction, impressionistically presents the experience of a disillusioned communist worker and writer in a world of rootless intellectuals in southern France.   LJ

That Summer and Other Stories by Frank *Sargeson was published by John Lehmann in London in 1946. The first publication of a volume of Sargeson's work outside New Zealand, it reflected the respect which had led Lehmann to include four Sargeson stories in wartime issues of *Penguin New Writing*. Sargeson's work had previously been available only in the limited New Zealand editions of *Conversation with My Uncle* (1936) and *A Man and His Wife* (1941, 1944). A representative selection of his short fiction, twenty-one sketches and stories, now became generally available.

'That Summer', the title story, was first published in three parts in *Penguin New Writing* in 1943–44. It is a tender treatment of a relationship of platonic male love, played out against the background of a seedy boarding house in Auckland during the *Depression, and is Sargeson's most ambitious attempt at the presentation of a 'yarn' by a semi-articulate and completely innocent narrator. Bill recounts the story of his association with Terry, a man in every sense his complete opposite, during one golden summer when both are unemployed. The narrator is motivated by the dimly recognised desire to find 'a mate who won't let him down'. It follows the unlikely couple through their economic vicissitudes, through Bill's brush with the law and Terry's failing health, to the story's inevitable conclusion and the narrator's inability to describe his feelings of loss.

In all these stories, Sargeson's mastery of both the sketch and the longer narrative yarn becomes apparent. Lonely figures isolated in an uncaring society, as in 'Miss Briggs' and 'In the Department', are cryptically presented by a sympathetic but detached narrator for whom the central characters are finally figures of amusement. These short pieces are set beside the major stories in the book where that same lonely world becomes the setting for a quest for love or at least companionship, in which the narratives are presented from a variety of positions, both of comprehension and incomprehension on the part of the storyteller. In 'An Affair of the Heart' a fully perceptive narrator can come to realise both the isolation of his own condition and the terrible beauty of the possessive love of the old mother whom he revisits. The narrator of 'A Man and His Wife', a story of marital breakdown and reconciliation, may well be unaware of the ironies of his own part in the story, while in 'The Making of a New Zealander' Sargeson's quintessential yarn-teller speaks of his uncertainty whether his tale has any significance, though the story's conclusion suggests that he is all too aware that it has. Several of the stories hint at the violence that Sargeson perceives as the inevitable result of a puritanical emphasis on the ultimate virtue of work and denial of physical and spiritual self-expression. The stifling of love by a disapproving society may lead to suicide, as in the moving conclusion of 'Old Man's Story', while self-hatred and the sense of lack of worth may lead to the act of violent and macabre self-assertion that is the culmination of 'A Great Day'.

Sargeson's view in this collection of his New Zealand characters, whether rural or suburban, itinerant and solitary or domesticated, is compassionate but essentially pessimistic. It struck a generation of readers as authentic and insightful into the underlying realities of life in New Zealand in a way totally new to fiction.   WB

THATCHER, Charles (1830–78), was well known on the Australian and New Zealand *goldfields as a balladeer and satirist. He was born in Bristol, England, and began his theatrical career there as a flautist. In 1852 he tried his luck on the Victorian goldfields, where he was unsuccessful as a digger, but gained a reputation as an entertainer. At the height of his fame he followed many diggers from Victoria to Otago in 1862 and was at once hired by the theatrical entrepreneur, Shadrach Jones, to entertain audiences in the 'Theatre Royal', Dunedin (formerly the Commercial Hotel). He shared the billings with his wife, the soprano Madame Vitelli. One of his first songs introduced the famous distinction between

the 'Old Identity' and the 'New Iniquity' into Dunedin society—the puritanical early settlers and the brash gold-diggers—Thatcher being emphatically on the side of the latter. His song mocks the 'Old Identity' as petty-minded and opposed to social progress. The song was sung so frequently as to gain the status of a folk song and the phrase 'Old Identity' became a catchword. Thatcher himself was extremely popular, yet also hated by the targets of his satire. One wrote, 'He is a very clever fellow but he wants a thrashing.'

After his Dunedin season he moved on to Christchurch, where he not only repeated his most popular songs but immediately introduced new ones satirising local conditions and personalities. This was to become a pattern in his concerts—the audience enjoyed the old favourites while the tension rose as people wondered what the new 'local' would be. Sometimes the people attacked would issue public responses, which in turn would stimulate new comic rhymes from Thatcher, so that a public dialogue occurred in which the balladist's rhetorical skills usually gave him the advantage. He and Madame Vitelli travelled on to Wellington and to Hawkes Bay, astonishing audiences with his apparent familiarity with each local scene.

His greatest successes were, however, on the expanding goldfields. By 1863 Queenstown had become the raucous centre of entertainment for the diggers, with dancing halls, hotels and full theatres. The colourful scene provided plenty of material for Thatcher's ready pen. He made a further tour of New Zealand and then settled again on goldfields for a season, this time on the West Coast, especially in Hokitika. As the 'rush' faded, almost as quickly as it had sprung up, Thatcher showed his customary awareness of events and left the country in 1867. He returned, however, for another tour of the entire country in 1869–70. In addition to his songs he presented a comic lecture on the Australian goldfields using changing pictures on a painted diorama.

In 1870 he returned to Australia and from there to England, where he had yet another career as a dealer in antique porcelain, travelling extensively and frequently in China and Japan. Thatcher's songs were published as broadsides, a bibliography of which can be found in Robert Hoskins's 'An Annotated Bibliography of Nineteenth-Century New Zealand Song' (Christchurch 1988). Manuscripts of some forty New Zealand ballads by Thatcher are held by the State Library of Victoria.   NW

Theatre and New Zealand literature. The story of European theatre in New Zealand moves from working-class roots to absorption into middle-class culture, and eventually to a multicultural diversity. It is also a story that largely mirrors the history of European theatre itself in its movement from presenting types of morality plays, such as melodrama, farce and political satire, through to the genres of expressionism, naturalism and modernism.

By 1844, the inhabitants of the townships of Auckland and Wellington and the settlement of Nelson were accustomed to the presentation of regular theatrical performances. These towns were populated by settlers whose background was Protestant and puritan: they were indifferent, even antagonistic to the arts. The indigenous Māori population had no theatre form of its own. Mid-nineteenth-century drama was a pastime for an atypical minority, and viewed only by the more adventurous citizens. The bulk of this audience was working-class and illiterate, and the practice of theatre was somewhat feared by a majority bent on turning the Protestant virtues of hard work and piety to the task of breaking in a new country. These early performances consisted of farces, melodramas and variety shows. They happened almost invariably under the patronage of hotel proprietors. Within a decade, pub theatres had been established in almost all of the European settlements, performing pieces inevitably advertised as 'new' and 'original' but rarely matching these expectations. The first recorded performance of a locally written play was on 11 July 1848, when James Henry Marriott wrote, produced and acted a lead part in 'Marcilina and the Yorkshireman; or the Maid of Urnindorpt'. This two-act drama attracted a full house at Wellington's Britannia saloon but was never published, reported on or revived.

In the early colonial period Auckland developed most quickly: it was relatively cosmopolitan and had close links with Australia, in particular with its Irish immigrants. More importantly, visiting British regiments, engaged in the Land Wars of 1854–70, were accustomed to presenting entertainments as well as providing audiences for what theatrical fare was available. With their departure, theatre in the North Island faded quickly. Meanwhile, in 1861, *gold was discovered in Otago. By 1863, the population of Dunedin had increased fivefold, to 60 000, and hotel entertainment was in demand at the goldfields of Central Otago and the West Coast. The huge increase in wealth also led to the building of substantial civic theatres in Dunedin and Christchurch, as well as other cultural developments, such as the establishment of the University of Otago in 1869. The first recognisably New Zealand playwrights would result from the establishment of these cultural institutions, but, for now, many who contributed to these emerging dramatic efforts could hardly be called New Zealanders; they were itinerants who happened to work briefly in New Zealand. George Leitch's The *Land of the Moa (1895)

was the most successful nineteenth-century play on a New Zealand subject. Another play of this period was George Darrell's 'The Pakeha'. However, the earliest extant dramatic work appears to be *Kainga of the Ladye Birds*, produced and published in Wellington in 1879. Melodrama like this, with its stock characters and hackneyed stories, was the characteristic genre of Victorian New Zealand theatre. Barrie Marschel was one celebrated writer of melodramas, including 'The Murder at the Octagon' (1895), 'Humarire Taniwha' (1898), 'Crime at Cathedral Square' (1903) and 'The Kid from Timaru', best known in its film version of 1918. Nevertheless, the colony was not far behind in awareness of European dramatists such as Ibsen, Chekhov and *Shaw. In 1914, Arthur *Adams described his work as 'modern comedy'; however, social realism would not become established in New Zealand as a genre of dramatic literature for another fifty years. Self-conscious writers, working in a small population, preferred to write political satire, a genre that is a continuing thread in the development of an indigenous drama.

In 1920, *Marama: The Mere and the Maori Maid*, a musical play, with music written by church organist Archie Don and described by its writer, Syd Ribbands, as 'a New Zealand opera, the first of its kind', opened in Hastings. Such was its home-town success that a touring company was formed and the production taken around the country, from Dunedin to Auckland. But success on this scale was not the norm. Until 1918, private enterprise had been the main provider of theatre; from this date, however, the potential of the motion picture diverted its attention. Instead of professional theatre, local amateur organisations were established; civic repertory theatres began to appear in 1926; the universities and the Workers' Educational Association (WEA) began to promote playwriting; and, importantly, a branch of the British Drama League was established in 1932. As a result, and as the country came out of the *Depression, one-act playwriting took on an astonishing vitality. The setting for these plays was typically an isolated *back-blocks farmhouse; the problem was to accommodate the format—one act, one set, little budget—to a presentation of the images of an emerging national identity. Two who worked well under these constraints were Violet *Targuse and Isobel *Andrews, both of whom had several plays published and won British Drama League prizes. It was not until Bruce *Mason's early plays of 1952–55, using urban settings, that it became possible to make substantial social comment in the context of the one-act play. Notable plays published during this period were John *Mulgan's *Three Plays of New Zealand* (1922), Ian Hamilton's *Falls the Shadow* (see *Kavan) and R.A.K. *Mason's *China*, a series of poems to accompany a dance drama. R.A.K. Mason is much better known as a poet but, from the mid-1930s, sought to combine his political and literary activities through the theatre. His attraction to drama was that it was public, dynamic and participatory. His energies were directed towards the People's Theatre in Auckland, primarily a working-class theatre 'encouraging', in the words of a programme note, 'the production of plays with a special working class interest, focussing the efforts of dramatic groups in trade unions and other working class organisations, providing a clearing house of information and guidance for such groups, and encouraging the writing of plays' by members of them. Mason's work for the theatre included sketches and longer pieces, such as 'Squire Speaks' (a dramatic monologue), 'International Brigade', 'Skull on Silence', 'This Dark Will Lighten' and, as well as China, 'Refugee', another script for a dance drama. In Hamilton, a People's Theatre was formed in 1939, presenting Odets' Till the Day I Die and O'Casey's The Star Turns Red. But this group soon identified less with an international socialist theatre movement and more with local amateur theatre. In Wellington, a theatre of the left emerged from the city's academic institutions: Victoria University College and Wellington Teachers' Training College. The 'Extrav', the university's annual capping (graduation) show, filled the 1200-seat State Opera House each year. In the early 1940s, Unity Theatre was founded in Wellington as an agitprop, anti-Fascist theatre, although it lacked a local writer of the calibre and commitment of R.A.K. Mason. From 1945, Unity's main focus was on theatre rather than politics and it attracted an audience for good, contemporary, progressive drama. It provided an apprenticeship in theatre skills for many of the generation of New Zealand's foremost actors, playwrights and directors, such as Bruce Mason, Richard and Edith ★Campion, Nola Millar, George Webby, Grant Tilly and Sunny Amey. It produced plays from the whole spectrum of modern drama—Beckett, Pinter, Genet, Osborne—and was the first theatre in New Zealand to present Brecht's The Caucasian Chalk Circle. Among its realist local plays was Kathleen Ross's The Trap (1950, published in London, 1952), a socially radical study of women's repression across three generations.

In contrast to this activity, the plays of Merton ★Hodge, an Otago Medical School graduate who travelled to Britain as a ship's doctor at the age of 28, were attracting interest in London. The Island saw him hailed as the 'English Chekhov'; his greatest success was The Wind and the Rain, which ran for over a thousand performances in 1933.

In 1936, Eric Bradwell wrote 'Clay', in which he applied the techniques of radio drama to the one-act play format while also adopting Strindberg's principles of

Expressionism that he had read in the preface to A Dream Play. The play opened in the Wellington Concert Chamber on 10 April 1936, drawing considerable publicity, including a newspaper editorial. This play, and those of J.A.S. Coppard, represent a significant move towards Expressionism that parallels the work of fiction writers, such as Frank ★Sargeson (★I Saw in My Dream) in the 1930s, while also anticipating major developments in the locally written drama of the 1960s.

During the 1940s, Auckland and Christchurch were the centres of cultural and literary activity. In Christchurch, Ngaio ★Marsh directed a series of celebrated, mostly ★Shakespearean, productions for the Canterbury University Drama Society, while many of the ★Caxton Press poets, such as D'Arcy ★Cresswell, Allen ★Curnow, Charles ★Brasch and James K. ★Baxter, were involved in theatre. Curnow's 'The Axe' was produced in Christchurch and Auckland, as well as being adapted for radio. Later, he wrote another stage play, 'The Overseas Expert', and two more radio plays. Cresswell's comic play, The Forest, was welcome relief from the characteristic seriousness of the plays of the period. However, the most important of these Christchurch poets-turned-playwrights was Baxter: twenty-four playscripts can be counted among his work. The first, Jack Winter's Dream, was produced as a radio play in 1958, a stage play in 1960 and as a film in 1979. It is a 'dream' story, set in the Central Otago goldfields, and framed by the opening scene where an old drunk is drinking by himself and a final one where his body is found by two hitch-hikers. It brings to the melodramatic tradition the subjectivity of Expressionism. His other plays include The Wide Open Cage, 'The Sore-footed Man', 'The Temptations of Oedipus', 'Mr O'Dwyer's Dancing Party' and 'The Devil and Mr Mulcahy'.

Bruce Mason moved to Wellington (from Tauranga, where he had been managing his father-in-law's orchard) in 1952. Unity produced the first of his plays, 'Bonds of Love', as its entry in the British Drama League's one-act play festival in 1953. More plays with a domestic setting followed—'The Evening Paper', 'The Verdict' and 'The Licensed Victualler'—as well as many revue scripts. Unity's commitment to producing the classics of naturalistic drama was limited by its acting resources and Mason's ability to provide locally written naturalistic drama was welcome. Likewise, Mason was at the forefront of the move to lead Unity beyond realism and towards plays which preferred aesthetic values over political ones. In 1951, the Campions returned from England, where they had been working at the Old Vic, and began planning the formation of a touring professional company. In May 1953, the New Zealand Players opened its first season in Wellington. Mason began writing for the new company, attracted by the opportunity to work with professionals. The *Pohutukawa Tree was premièred by the Players in 1957. His interest in things Māori was heightened when he left his job as theatre critic on The Dominion to take up the editorship of Te *Ao Hou. Four further plays resulted, all written in the latter part of the 1960s: Awatea, 'Swan Song', 'The Hand on the Rail' and Hongi. Mason's most famous play, however, remains The *End of the Golden Weather, a one-man play he performed himself well over 850 times throughout New Zealand and abroad, including at the Edinburgh Festival in 1963.

The New Zealand Players collapsed in 1960. However, in 1964, Downstage Theatre Restaurant was founded in Wellington, presenting Edward Albee's Zoo Story as its first production. The existence of this theatre, and soon others like it in other centres, was but one reason for the spectacular increase in playwriting from the mid-1960s. Others were the establishment of the New Zealand Theatre Federation, which prompted the restructuring and co-ordination of amateur theatre, the formation of the Association of Community Theatres from the group of professional theatres established in the main centres, and the development of the Queen Elizabeth II Arts Council's theatre training and subsidy programmes. Among the playwrights who came and went during the 1960s–70s were poet Alistair Te Ariki *Campbell, who wrote six plays, starting with *'Sanctuary of Spirits' and ending with When the Bough Breaks (perhaps the most sophisticated Expressionist work written in New Zealand) and Peter *Bland, whose plays included 'Father's Day' and 'George, the Mad Ad Man', the latter being possibly the closest to an Absurdist drama written here. Downstage's Gulbenkian Series, presented towards the end of 1969 as a result of an unexpected grant, brought togther plays by Campbell ('When the Bough Breaks'), Warren Dibble, Dora Somerville and Max Richards. The importance of this season lay in a workshop production style—simple sets and an easy relationship between actors and audience—which would influence the playwrights, such as Robert *Lord, of the following decade. Perhaps the most interesting of the Gulbenkian plays was Edward Bowman's Salve Regina. It had won the 1968 Observer television playwriting competition, judged by Harold Pinter, Martin Esslin and Kenneth Tynan, and had already been produced for radio and television. It is set in the basement of a department store which has apparently been wrecked in a nuclear war. But much remains uncertain: the identity of the characters, the state of the rest of the world and the time in which the play is set.

Robert Lord is notable as a writer who came directly to writing for the theatre. His work is characteristically for an intimate theatre and is concerned with the success—or lack of it—of relationships between people. His best known and most controversial early work is Well Hung, which premièred at Downstage in January 1974. It is an extensive revision of an earlier play, 'The Body in the Park', and is loosely based on the Crewe murder case. In 1974, Lord moved to New York where he lived until returning to take up the *Burns Fellowship at the University of Otago in 1987. Since then, many of his plays have received productions in New Zealand: It Isn't Cricket, Meeting Place, Heroes and Butterflies, 'The Affair', China Wars, Glorious Ruins and Joyful and Triumphant. Meanwhile, in Christchurch, Mervyn *Thompson was the co-founder and co-director of the Court Theatre; he moved to Downstage in 1975 and was appointed head of drama studies at the University of Auckland in 1977. His first play was First Return; as in the one-man plays of Mason and Baxter, a highly autobiographical authorial ego is at the centre of this play, as it would be in later scripts, such as Coaltown Blues, Lovebirds and Passing Through. Another series of plays, however, moved from the personal to the political, and used documentary techniques, music and sentimental songs to highlight social issues. These plays include O! Temperance!, Songs to Uncle Scrim, A Night at the Races and Songs to the Judges.

The political and social awareness of the 1970s expressed itself also in the development of collective theatres in which groups of actors, directors, designers and writers developed their own scripts in rehearsal and performed them in informal situations. Probably the best known of these was *Red Mole which performed satirical cabaret programmes, often written by poet Alan *Brunton. These groups, which also included, for example, Francis Batten's Theatre Action and the Amamus theatre company, stimulated a re-evaluation of dramatic practice by the established theatre. Theatre Action, made up largely of former students of L'Ecole Lecoq in Paris, was founded in 1971. Its most substantial specific contribution to New Zealand drama was 'The Best of All Possible Worlds' (1973), a search for national identity and a critique of the *God's Own Country myth. Influenced by Jerzy Grotowski, Amamus made a study tour of Poland in 1975. On its return, Unity Theatre's reputation as a platform for socially responsible theatre was revitalised when the group found that it provided a sympathetic base for its major productions. In the later 1970s and early 1980s, these groups were followed by others, such as the Town and Country Players, Heartache and Sorrow and The Theatre of the Eighth Day, a development by Paul Maunder out of Amamus. This last named led, in turn, to the founding of specifically Māori groups, particularly Te Ohu Whakaari and Te Ika a Maui, which performed plays written by Māori playwrights, such as Rore *Hapipi, Rawiri *Paratene,

Neil Gudsell, Bruce *Stewart and Apirana *Taylor. More recently, Riwia *Brown, John *Broughton, Rena Owen, Hone *Kouka, Willi Davis and Briar Grace-Smith have successfully picked up the challenge of constructing a body of *Māori theatre.

The 1970s also produced New Zealand's first commercially successful playwrights since the nineteenth century. Joe *Musaphia began by writing for radio and and Roger *Hall for television; by the 1980s, however, a commercially viable theatre had been established, allowing playwrights and theatre groups working in other areas to define their differences more precisely. This development was supported by the establishment of *Playmarket in 1973 by a group of Wellington academics and theatre practitioners as a playwrights' agency and script development service. In 1978, it held the first of its biennial National Playwrights' Workshops. These were focused on intensive work on selected scripts: results included Greg *McGee's *Foreskin's Lament, Carolyn *Burns's Objection Overruled, Hilary Beaton's Outside In, Stuart *Hoar's Squatter, Anthony *McCarten's Yellow Canary Mazurka and F.I.L.T.H. (Failed in London, Try Hong Kong) and David *Geary's Lovelock's Dream Run. Substantial playwriting activity continued outside the workshop process, too: *Renée's Wednesday to Come, Vincent *O'Sullivan's Shuriken, Maurice *Shadbolt's *Once on Chunuk Bair, Sarah Delahunty's Stretchmarks, Lorae *Parry's Frontwomen and the plays of James Beaumont were just some results of this huge increase in writing plays for the New Zealand stage. They became the platform for the successful development of professional theatre over a period of twenty-five years.

Most of these were naturalistic plays. Some turned to history to find moments that illuminate the present while recounting the past—Shuriken, Once on Chunuk Bair, Wednesday to Come, Squatter or Michaelanne Forster's Daughters of Heaven, on the 1954 Parker–Hulme murder case (see *Perry), first performed by Christchurch's Court Theatre in 1991 and published in 1992. Others addressed contemporary social issues more directly. *Foreskin's Lament is about the centrality of rugby to the national psyche; Outside In uses its setting of a women's prison to excoriate the destructive hierarchies of society; and Objection Overruled, less naturalistically, addresses through its courtroom fantasy the issue of gender construction as well as violence, nurture versus nature and other topics. The lighter situational comedies of Hall (New Zealand's most successful playwright) and McCarten (who, with Stephen *Sinclair, wrote Ladies' Night, New Zealand's most successful play) are also characteristically naturalistic. Hoar's Squatter, however, is a clearly modernist work, and marks an important point in the story of writing for the New Zealand stage.

Moreover, throughout this period, highly inventive and sophisticated alternative performance groups—Dramadillo, Inside Out, Tantrum, The Front Lawn, Hen's Teeth, Theatre at Large and Justine Simei's Pacific Theatre—continued to generate exciting work.

A strong body of feminist theatre has also emerged, not only serious work from regularly published playwrights like Renée or Parry, but across a range of forms, including one-woman plays (Cathy *Downes's The Case of Katherine Mansfield or Leah Poulter's 'A Working Girl'), cabaret shows ('Vital Statistics'), music-drama (Delahunty's 'Stretchmarks') and satiric-parodic retellings (Jean Betts's The Revenge of the Amazons or Ophelia Thinks Harder).

From 1964, with the founding of Downstage theatre in Wellington, theatre companies in the main centres provided the infrastructure that enabled the development and support of the skills of a wide range of the theatre practitioners. But with the collapse of Auckland's Mercury Theatre in 1991, the story of the 1990s was one of difficulty, despite the increasing popularity of New Zealand plays. Theatre companies have all but disappeared; co-operatives, the strength of the alternative theatre, are now being relied on to take centre-stage in the provision of local drama. Finding themselves unable to rely on the accumulated professional skills and experience of directors, actors and designers, fewer playwrights are writing fewer plays, and these are being produced in fewer and smaller venues. Nevertheless, the energy generated during the previous quarter of a century has carried through. Roger Hall continues to write plays, such as 'Market Forces' (Circa, 1996) and 'C'mon Black!' (a one-man play starring Grant Tilly, Circa, 1996), which attract enthusiastic audiences. *Playmarket calculated that in 1996 50 000 people bought tickets to see Roger Hall plays, and an average of 2400 tickets a week to New Zealand plays. Theatre at Large continues to generate productions such as *'Maua Taua/Savage Hearts', Cyrano de Bergerac and King Lear. Theatre for children, and the use of drama in education, have also developed significantly (see Susan *Battye); one of the most frequently performed of all New Zealand plays is the adaptation by Alannah O'Sullivan of Spike Milligan's Bad Jelly the Witch. Perhaps the most interesting advances, however, have been made in Māori, *Pacific and bicultural theatre. For example, Colin McColl, a leading director, has been engaged in a long-term project that has seen him direct a number of modern classics in New Zealand settings; in 1994, he directed Hone Kouka's Nga Tangata Toa, an adaptation of Ibsen's The Vikings of Helgeland, and in 1995, Apirana Taylor's Whaea Kairau, an adaptation of Brecht's Mother Courage. Both these productions premièred at

Wellington's Taki Rua Theatre, which also closed, in 1997. See also articles on individual playwrights and titles. SG

THOMAS, Paul (1951–), became New Zealand's best-selling local thriller-writer with *Old School Tie* (1994). This ingeniously sustains its high-pitched pursuit through a world of bizarre violence and sex with a downbeat black humour and sharp eye for the weirdness and manic self-interest beneath the surface of Auckland's social establishment. Several Auckland personalities and institutions are recognisable in only slightly exaggerated and therefore luridly outrageous versions, while the settings for the various deaths, investigations and misadventures, from the Harbour Bridge to a basement carpark, are wholly credible. Thomas followed this success with *Inside Dope* (1995), about a race for the ill-gotten hoard of the Mr Asia syndicate, again with skilfully created New Zealand settings. It won Australia's Ned Kelly Crime Writing Award in 1996. *Guerrilla Season* (1996) zestfully subjects a number of Auckland media celebrities to political violence by the Aotearoa People's Army, in a complex plot again embellished by gory corpses, gloomy jokes and sexy kinks.

Born in the UK into a clerical family, Thomas moved to New Zealand as an infant in 1954 and grew up in Timaru, Christchurch and Auckland, graduating at Auckland University. He worked as a reporter and from 1980 to 1987 travelled extensively, working in public relations and as a travel writer, returning as features editor of the *Auckland Sun*. Since 1988 he has worked in public relations in Auckland and, currently, Sydney, where he now lives. Before *Old School Tie* he co-authored three sports books, *Christmas in Rarotonga* with John Wright (1990), *Kirwan—Running on Instinct* with John Kirwan (1992) and *Straight from the Hart* with John Hart (1993). RR

THOMPSON, Mervyn (1935–92), was a playwright, director, autobiographer, teacher and actor. Born in Kaitangata, South Otago, he grew up in a working-class family on the West Coast of the South Island, and left school at 15 in order to work, including several years as a coal miner. He entered Canterbury University as an adult student, and was briefly a schoolteacher before returning to Canterbury as a lecturer in the English department. As a student actor he came under the influence of Ngaio *Marsh (who cast him in the minor role of Proculeius in *Antony and Cleopatra*, whence the name 'Proc' by which he was almost universally known). In emulation of her he became a director, and continued her tradition of high-quality productions with largely student casts. His *Cherry Orchard*, *The Birthday Party*, *Marat/Sade*,

Taming of the Shrew and others were powerful and original. But his own first play, *First Return* (written in 1971, though not performed until 1974 at the Court Theatre), already indicates his rebellion from Marsh's anglocentric vision of drama. His play is defiantly working-class and New Zealand in its subject matter, and Expressionist and Brechtian by turns in much of its ironic style. *First Return* is also representative of his entire career in its autobiographical vulnerability as his protagonist wrestles, sometimes literally, with the daemons of his past (a 'menagerie' controlled by a ringmaster).

Thompson was passionately committed to a national drama honestly rooted in the New Zealand experience and in working-class politics of the left. This vision informed his teaching, and many of his most successful productions as a director were with students. He also worked skilfully with students in collaborative theatre projects. *O! Temperance!* (Court Theatre, 1972; pub. 1974; the ironic title is one of Proculeius' few lines in *Antony and Cleopatra*) is a documentary play with music, based on the linked temperance and women's suffrage movements in early-twentieth-century New Zealand. It was created with students at the newly created Court Theatre, of which he became co-director in 1971. His next three 'song-plays' were virtually a genre unto themselves, and enthusiastically presented Thompson's working-class and political themes. *Songs to Uncle Scrim* (Downstage Theatre, 1976, music by Stephen McCurdy; pub. 1983) is more than a musical about the *Depression (Colin Scrimgeour was the outspoken Methodist minister who championed the poor on radio), since the audience to whom the songs were sung were clearly expected to make contemporary political connections as well. In *A Night at the Races* (New Independent Theatre, 1977, co-written with Yvonne Blennerhassett Edwards, music by Andrew Glover and others; pub. 1981) Thompson is in lighter mode, joyously celebrating both horse racing and its attendant gambling as working-class release. And in *Songs to the Judges* (Maidment Theatre, 1980, music by William Dart; pub. 1983) he is at his most trenchantly political, the satiric songs protesting vehemently against a century of injustice towards Māori. In his autobiographical play *Passing Through* (Court Theatre, 1991; pub. 1992), Thompson refers to this period as fighting for 'the people I thought were allies (women, Maoris, working-class people, even those who believe that you can't have a nation if you haven't got a national drama).' His faith in a cultural 'popular front, that community of interest', was the driving force behind his work as a professional director at the Court, and two years as artistic director of Downstage in Wellington. His autobiography *All My Lives* (1980) gives the reader a vivid picture of New Zealand theatre at this time, as well as inducing some discomfort at his confessional vulnerability.

When he moved to Auckland University as senior lecturer in drama in 1977 he was returning to a student environment where he could anticipate kindling a greater commitment than he had among professional actors. He looked back with some self-criticism on this move in the song 'Why are you running away?', one of several moving sequences in *Passing Through* (1991). He succeeded as before in the university context, however, with his combination of passion, intellectualism and rigorous standards. *The Great New Zealand ★Truth Show* in 1982 followed the *O! Temperance!* formula of collaborative script development with Thompson the writer of material researched by students.

In professional theatre his greatest influence was through his close involvement in the early ★Playmarket Playwrights' Workshops. In 1980 he directed the workshop of *Foreskin's Lament* by Greg Mc★Gee, a play he rightly predicted would 'change the face of New Zealand drama'. He also directed and championed the work of emerging women playwrights such as Carolyn ★Burns, ★Renée and others. His generosity of judgment was one of his special qualities.

Thompson's first work for solo performance, *Coaltown Blues* (Maidment Theatre, 1984; pub. 1986), is both celebration and lament for the working-class roots from which he sprang. The same year his life changed irrevocably after unsubstantiated allegations of sexual harassment and rape, and a brief and violent abduction and torture (based on events in a feminist play he had workshopped) by anonymous vigilantes. The fallout from these events is painfully described in articles in ★*NZ Listener*, and his memoir *Singing the Blues* (1991). It is also dramatically evoked in his final one-man show, *Passing Through*. By the time he started its national tour in 1991 he had left Auckland University, returned to Christchurch, spent a year as writer-in-residence at Canterbury University, and was widely known to be dying of cancer. He had adapted John A. ★Lee's ★*Children of the Poor* for the stage (Court Theatre, 1989; published 1990). Two final plays dealt with the trials and ideals of sexual obsession and love: *Lovebirds* (Court Theatre, 1991) and *Jean and Richard* (Court Theatre 1992); both were published in 1992 in *Passing Through and Other Plays*. *Passing Through* chronicles New Zealand theatre for three decades, from the Reefton Drama Club to Ngaio Marsh to Bruce ★Mason to Jerzy Grotowski to Thompson's own fatal instinct for giving his enemies the fight they wanted. Text, performance and audience were inextricably interwoven as a dying writer charted the performance of his life. *Passing Through* stands as a monument to Thompson's passionate crusade for a national drama of which New Zealand could be proud, and to which he contributed without reserve.   DC

THOMSON, John Mansfield (1926–), is the leading writer on the history of New Zealand music and an editor of literary journals. Born in Blenheim and educated at Nelson College, he served in the Fleet Air Arm of RNZN 1944–46, then graduated BA at Victoria University College. He was founder-editor of ★*Hilltop* there in 1949 before leaving for University College, London, and Camberwell School of Arts. He worked in London in publishing and editing, and was founder-editor of *Early Music* 1973–83. In 1984 he returned as the first research fellow at Victoria University's Stout Research Centre, then becoming founder-editor of the *Stout Centre Review* 1990–95 and of ★*New Zealand Books* 1991–92. He has thus successfully pioneered an important New Zealand literary magazine, a scholarly music journal, a New Zealand studies research journal and the first New Zealand literary reviews periodical. He published poems in journals such as ★*Issue*.

His first major book, *A Distant Music: The Life and Times of Alfred ★Hill 1870–1960* (1980), was joint winner of Oxford University Press's international biography competition in 1978. Other major publications as author include the *Biographical Dictionary of New Zealand Composers* (1990) and the *Oxford History of New Zealand Music* (1991), praised as a substantial piece of cultural history and for the elegance and wit of its writing. Thomson has also edited *Frederick Page: A Musician's Journal* (with Janet Paul, 1986) and the *Cambridge Companion to the Recorder* (1995), among others, and has written two significant exhibition catalogues, *Musical Images: A New Zealand Historical Journey 1840–1990* (1990) and *Landmarks in New Zealand Publishing: Blackwood & Janet Paul 1945–1968* (with Janet Paul, 1995). He curated these and several other exhibitions. He has contributed extensively to musical reference books such as the *New Oxford Companion to Music* (1983) and to newspapers and journals internationally, including *Times Literary Supplement*, ★*NZ Listener* and ★*Landfall*; and has given numerous broadcast talks in England and New Zealand. With his dual expertise, international scholarly standing and his own literary skills, Thomson has made distinctive contributions to music and literature, and to links between them. He received the Composers Association of NZ Citation in 1988 and an honorary DMus from Victoria University in 1991.   RR

Tikera, or, Children of the Queen of Oceania
(*Dzieci Krolowe Oceanii*), a novel by Sygurd Wiśniowski (1841–92), was first published in Poland in 1877. It is superior to any English-language novel of that time relating

to New Zealand. The 1956 edition was bought by the National Library and then translated by Jerzy Podstolski, a senior lecturer at the New Zealand Library School. This translation was edited by Dennis *McEldowney and published by *Auckland University Press in 1972.

Wiśniowski visited New Zealand in 1864–65, landing at Auckland and gold-panning in Otago and Marlborough. *Tikera*, however, tells the story of an unnamed narrator and a well-born German scoundrel who journey through the North Island when the country is rent by war. Much of the novel is set in New Plymouth when it is under threat of attack and the centre of shady oil dealings. The men are caught up in these events and also again meet Tikera, a beautiful part-Māori seeking a white husband. Each man uses her: the narrator to secure freedom from a belligerent tribe and the German for sexual favours.

Although Wiśniowski telescopes history and rearranges geography, *Tikera* excels in its ironical and perceptive depiction of colonial society, where 'as soon as the pioneers of civilization step ashore they erect a church and a gaol' and practise a morality in which "… what is legal is moral".' Few are those who do not strive to better themselves materially by wheeling, dealing and marriage. There is an interesting tension within the narrator. As a Pole, whose country is occupied by foreigners, he has political sympathy with the Māori; as a nineteenth-century European, however, he is unable to accept social equality despite his sympathies.   RG

Time of Achamoth, The (1977), the second *science fiction novel of M.K. *Joseph, won the New Zealand Book Award for Fiction. It is a story of time travel told with Joseph's characteristic vividness in action narrative and engagement with moral issues. From a British research station located in New Zealand, a young man, Mark Hollister, undertakes a series of adventurous time journeys, by a technique of tuning into and possessing the minds of earlier beings rather than the Wellsian notion of travel in person. Thus Hollister experiences in turn the hazards and emotions of the World War 1 trenches, the Paris street uprising of 1871, a Victorian mock-medieval pageant and a murderous Regency house party. This allows Joseph to exploit fully his preferred technique in his science fiction of short self-contained scenes of extraordinary intensity. Strange and threatening anomalies in the events gradually make it apparent that even in these historical locations a cold war battle is taking place between rival Russian, Chinese and American time programmes. Even more ominously, an independently powerful agency seems to be at work, bent on wider destruction, which wrecks all the time-travel facilities except the financially under-resourced New Zealand Tau research station. Under this threat the international powers agree to work together. Hollister is sent into the future, leaping from mind to mind to gain advice finally from a being of the far future called the Caretaker. He learns that the Illuminists, a late Gnostic sect established during the eighteenth century, 'were able to conceive the possibility of hastening the destruction of the world. They took the name of Achamoth….' One survivor has been at work through time, manipulating psychotic personalities, prompting destruction: 'Lincoln, dead, Ghandi dead, the Kennedys … the shame of concentration camps'. In a somewhat melodramatic final sequence Hollister finds and destroys this 'dreadful mind … which had sampled all the agony of war' in the setting of Karl Marx's tomb in Highgate Cemetery, 'a funeral landscape of tombs with the colossal stone head of a wild-haired and bearded prophet….' This release from the world's entrapment is of significance to our own grisly century; but the book's strengths mostly lie earlier, in the pace of the narrative and the gripping detail and realism of the scenes of street revolution in the 1870s or the surreal horror of the trenches.   PMn

To the Is-Land: An Autobiography is the first volume of autobiography by Janet *Frame (New York, 1982, London, 1983, Auckland, 1984; published together with Volume 2, An *Angel at My Table and Volume 3, The *Envoy from Mirror City, as *Janet Frame: An Autobiography*, Auckland, 1989). It won the Buckland Literary Award and the Wattie Book of the Year Award (1983). 'From the first place of liquid darkness' (birth, 1924) and speculation on 'The Ancestors', the autobiography details Frame's childhood experiences during the post-war years of the *Depression in the small provincial town of Oamaru, until she left home to attend Teachers' Training College in Dunedin (1943). It offers a remarkable chronicle of the development of the writer in a childhood fraught with material poverty, familial illness and death. Frame recounts how her profound love of language and literature, fostered by her mother and shared with her siblings, was increasingly coupled with a growing awareness, necessary to the artist, of the deceit and ambiguity of words. She recalls her first attempts at poetry writing, her fierce determination to be a poet not a schoolteacher, and her nurturing of the inner world of her imagination as a retreat from an external world that demanded conformity despite her felt sense of difference from others. For readers familiar with the complexity and narratorial trickery of Frame's novels, the autobiography provides a relatively straightforward account of her life which is nonetheless resonant with the lyrical fluidity of her other writings. The short chapters are broken into even smaller sections with the frequent citation of remembered poems and songs. Prior to the publication of the autobiography the details of Frame's life were the subject of much speculation, with critics often extrapolating from the fictions in an attempt to reconstruct the famously private novelist's life. Frame has vehemently refuted such assumptions, saying in interview that '*To the Is-Land* was the first time I'd written the true story'. Frame has claimed the autobiography was 'my story, … I wanted to have my say about my life because I have been rather disconcerted by some details which are incorrect'. Nonetheless, throughout the autobiography Frame meditates on the slippery nature of memory and the fundamentally artistic process of shaping the 'fact and truths and memories of truths' into a coherent interpretation of one's past: '[M]emories do not arrange themselves to be observed and written about … thus denying the existence of a "pure" autobiography'; 'some memories stay forever beneath the surface.'   KWo

TOCKER, Mahinarangi (1955–), Ngāti Raukawa, Ngāti Tūwharatoa, Waikato, is a major composer of modern ★waiata who performs in all parts of New Zealand and has also toured extensively in Europe, North America and Australia. She has written more than three hundred songs and several short stories.   NW

Tohunga, sometimes translated 'priest', was the most powerful and dreaded man in an ★iwi or ★hapū. The role was hereditary and the father would teach the son secret ★karakia and ★waiata as well as more extended ★whakapapa than those known to the rest of the tribe. Some of this information was also taught at ★whare wānanga.

These spiritual leaders called on a vast oral tradition to conduct ceremonies and as a base for foretelling the future. Their knowledge of that literature, passed on only to chosen successors, was essential for many communal activities, from curing the sick to conducting war.

In adventure novels of the nineteenth century the tohunga was often presented as an ugly, threatening and intimidating figure who goaded the tribe on against intruders or captives. Modern tohunga, on the contrary, can strike the observer as gentle, skilful and well educated.

In spite of the Tohunga Suppression Law, passed in 1907 under the sponsorship of Maui Pomare, then Officer for Maori Health, and revoked in 1962, the power of the tohunga is still felt today. ★Mead has reported that physicians in hospitals sometimes call in tohunga to aid in treating certain patients and big companies might use them 'to convince factory workers that the proper rituals for their protection in the workplace were indeed carried out and hence their families were not in danger'. Whether such uses are within the 'literary' quality of texts is a matter of definition.   NW

Tokelau is legally part of New Zealand, and Tokelauan is thus New Zealand's second surviving indigenous language, providing, with Māori, another literature in a Polynesian language. Tokelau consists of three atolls (Atafu, Nukunonu and Fakaofo), with a fourth 'lost' atoll, Olohega, administered by American Samoa. Tokelau came under New Zealand administration in 1926, and legally became part of New Zealand in 1948, through the Tokelau Act. All Tokelauans are New Zealand citizens. Despite this, Tokelauan writing is rarely published in New Zealand literary journals and anthologies (an exception being ★*Poetry New Zealand*) and books published in the language are excluded from some major literary awards. About 1600 Tokelauans currently live on the three atolls, with another 4000 Tokelauans living mainly in the Wellington area, but also in Auckland, Rotorua and Taupo. The language was first published (by the New Zealand Department of Education) in the journal *Tala mo A'oga i Tokelau* in 1954. The New Zealand Ministry of Education now publishes about six books a year for children in Tokelauan. A complete list of published work in Tokelauan, and in other languages by Tokelauan authors, is provided in the *Tokelau National Bibliography / Fakamaumauga o na Tuhituhiga o Tokelau*, published by the National Library of New Zealand. Most Tokelauan writers now live and publish in mainland New Zealand. Well-known authors include Loimata Iupati, Kelihiano Kalolo, Peato Tutu Perez, Farapikiti (Faraimo Paulo) and Epi ★Swan. Tokelauan writing in English is collected in Teresa Pasilio's *Nuanua of Tokelau* (1992). More traditional material is collected in Allan Thomas, Ineleo Tuia and Judith Huntsman's *Songs and Stories of Tokelau* (1990), Farapikiti's *Fatuga Mai na Kakai Tokelau* (1989), Ingjrd Hoēm, Even Hovdhaugen and Arnfinn Muruvik Vonen's *Kupu Mai te Tutolu: Tokelau Oral Literature* (1992), Aleki Silao's *He Kete Kakai* (1991), and in *Matagi Tokelau* (1990). The most authoritative dictionary is the *Tokelau Dictionary* (1986).

Most Māori and Pākehā would either be unaware that New Zealand has another literature in a Polynesian language, quite separate from New Zealand Māori, or would prefer to argue that Tokelauan gives us a ★Pacific nations literature, not another New Zealand one. Tokelauan writers find their relationship with New Zealand literature ambivalent, and see themselves as contributing equally to South Pacific literature. This makes Tokelauan texts one of the stronger literary links between New Zealand and the South Pacific, and perhaps the body of work where the two most clearly overlap. As the literature of one of the poorest community groups in New Zealand (according to the 1991 census), with a history of slavery (many Tokelauans were taken as slaves to Peru, just five generations ago), Tokelauan literature continues to record a great degree of anguish and, in this aspect, compares to Moriori oral literature in its final moments, and Māori literature at its most despairing.   LI/DL

Toll of the Bush, The (1905), was William *Satchell's second novel. It is a story of pioneering times, set in Hokianga, the northern region where its author had first settled. Like many similar books it contrasts a colonial (Robert) with an English immigrant, or *'new chum' (Geoffrey). The main plot is romantic: Robert loves Lena and Geoffrey loves Eve—but because of an accusation of immorality he loses her to Rev. Mr Fletcher (who suppresses the letter that could clear Geoffrey's name). The adventures, not untypical of colonial novels, include a search in the bush for the lost Eve and a fire, which fortunately kills off the troublesome clergyman rival. There is power in the portrayal of Geoffrey's fine father-in-law, Major Millward. There is even more power in the portrayal of the disintegration of a personality in the bush, in this case Robert's father-in-law, Andersen, a Swede. The bush is threatening and dangerous, best coped with by those born to it, like Robert. On Andersen it takes its 'toll'. Having shown us the gumlands as a source of illness to humanity in The *Land of the Lost, Satchell here presents another colonial environment in a similar light. Frequent references to the Boer *War serve as a broader framework for this story—suggesting that it is only part of a greater colonial enterprise.   NW

TOMBS, Harry H. (1874–1966), served his printing apprenticeship, after Christ's College, in his father's company, *Whitcombe & Tombs. He then went abroad to the London Printing School and to study the violin at Leipzig Conservatory, working for a time in South Africa before returning to Whitcombe & Tombs. He set up his own printing and publishing company in Wellington in 1914. During its fifty-two years of existence (at first as Harry H. Tombs, later Wingfield Press), this company made a considerable commitment to the fine arts. In 1929 Tombs established Fine Arts (NZ) Ltd to produce Maui Pomare and James *Cowan's *Legends of the Maori* in a de luxe limited edition of 300 copies. He launched *Art in New Zealand, which carried the motto 'Nothing but the choicest in Art and Letters', in 1928. This quarterly concentrated on the visual arts, extending so far as to include colour reproductions. Artists included Rita Angus, Russell *Clarke, Mervyn Taylor and the architect Vernon Brown. It also featured authors such as C.R. *Allen, Eileen *Duggan, A.R.D. *Fairburn, Robin *Hyde and Charles *Marris. It changed its name in 1946 to The Arts in New Zealand, and ended life, in 1951, as Arts Year Book. Tombs and Marris produced a Christmas annual, *Rata, 1931–33,

and from 1932 to 1943 *New Zealand Best Poems, which carried new poetry as well as anthologising previously published work. To round out his interest in the arts Tombs also printed and published Music in New Zealand for a time. Jim Henderson's Gunner Inglorious (1945), a memoir of the Desert War, ran to 10 000 copies. Denis *Glover also worked for Tombs's Wingfield Press in Wellington for a short time.   NWt

Tomorrow was edited and published in Christchurch by political cartoonist Kennaway *Henderson from July 1934 until its closure under government pressure in May 1940. While primarily a fortnightly journal of radical and left-wing political opinion written by contributors such as Frederick *Sinclaire, Noel Pharazyn, W.B. *Sutch and John A. *Lee, Tomorrow was also an important outlet for those poets and writers who had first found their voice in the student magazines of the early thirties: *Phoenix, *Kiwi, *Spike, *Oriflamme, *Sirocco and the like. Poetry, short fiction and literary criticism all developed through the pages of Tomorrow, largely because of the influence of editorial committee members Winston *Rhodes and Denis *Glover. There were stories by Frank *Sargeson, Roderick *Finlayson and others, poetry by Allen *Curnow, A.R.D. *Fairburn, and Glover himself, and reviews and articles by these and other writers. In Tomorrow, too, Curnow began to develop, under the pseudonyms 'Julian' and then *'Whim-Wham', his alternative and more populist and satirical literary identity. With such a range, Henderson's magazine was one of the most important periodicals of literary interest published prior to the founding of *Landfall in 1947.   SH

TOPEORA is the name under which Rangi Topeora Kuini Wikitoria is best known. She is one of the best remembered Māori women of nineteenth-century New Zealand. A poet, strategist and influential leader, Topeora was born at Kāwhia, the daughter of Te Ra-ka-herea of Ngāti Toa and Waitohi of Ngāti Toa and Ngāti Raukawa. Her family was powerful and included two of the most famous Māori leaders, her mother's brother Te Rauparaha and her own brother Te Rangihaeata.

Topeora first came to prominence as a young woman at Kāwhia, where she urged her Ngāti Toa people to avenge the death of some of their kin, mostly women, who had been killed while travelling to a funeral. She conveyed her message through song, a technique she was to continue throughout her life. Indeed Topeora is now recognised as one of the great composers of the traditional song form called *mōteatea, and many of her compositions still exist.

Topeora was closely involved in the hostilities and other events which led to the migration of Ngāti Toa from Kāwhia to the southern part of the North Island. Upon their journey southward an incident took place which again sealed Topeora's reputation in the history of her people. She and another woman, Nekepapa of Te Āti Awa, desired the same man, Te Ra-tu-tonu of the Ngā Māhanga people of Taranaki. It was decided that the two women should compete for him by running a race to see who would be the first to lay her korowai (cloak) on this man. Topeora succeeded, and Ra-tu-tonu became one of her numerous husbands.

Once Ngāti Toa were settled in the southern reaches of Te Ika ā Māui (North Island), and even on lands secured in the north of Te Wai Pounamu (South Island), Topeora played a prominent role in the councils of her people and, following her mother's example, became one of the key strategists in warfare and in settling land matters.

Later she was baptised with the name Kuini Wikitoria, or Queen Victoria, while her husband was baptised 'Prince Albert', after Victoria's husband. It was not unusual for Māori to use names of influence and importance in European society: no ordinary name would do.

Topeora is known to have had many lovers, including a man named Hukiki Te Ahukaramū, a close kinsman of Ngāti Raukawa. In commemoration of their relationship Topeora composed two songs for Te Ahukaramū, one of which appears in Sir Apirana *Ngata's Nga *Moteatea. In part it runs as follows: Kati au i konei / Hei ekenga ihu waka / Hei tanga waihoe ma Te Ahukaramū / Ka kopa i te rae ki Ōkatia ra (Let me here abide / as a canoe landing place / Or the paddling splashing of Te Ahukaramū, / Who appears over the rise at Ōkatia).

Although Topeora was baptised and had many dealings with Pākehā people, she did not follow European ways and refused, for example, to wear European clothing. She also signed the Treaty of Waitangi, one of only five women to do so, which is testimony of her influence with her people.

Topeora is an example of the classical wahine toa or 'warrior woman'. Born of important heritage in both Ngāti Toa and Ngāti Raukawa, she excelled as a leader and fighter for her people. Her deeds have served to refine our understanding of a traditional woman leader, whose qualities include fiery speech-making, the use of sexual attraction for political ends, high competence in poetical composition and the responsibility to see vendettas (utu) pursued.

CR

Touch of Clay, A, Maurice *Shadbolt's fifth novel, was published in 1974 and revised in 1995. Along with the novel Danger Zone (1975) it forms part of an unfinished trilogy of novels of the 1970s. The setting is a lush West

Auckland suburb overlooking an estuary, where Paul Pike, an ex-lawyer turned potter (one of the many artist figures who inhabit Shadbolt's fiction) is recovering from a nervous breakdown. Shadbolt carefully establishes Pike's idyllic and deliberately isolated world, then, through the pattern of representative characters entering that world—a commune-leader-cum-guru figure, an environmental campaigner, the drug-dependent girl, Irene, with whom he has a disastrous affair—he explores a series of 1970s social issues including religion, drugs and the environment. The narrative shifts between Pike's present-time story and his grandfather's nineteenth-century journals, passages of which are scattered throughout the novel and highlight once more Shadbolt's enduring interest in history. That the stories of Pike and his grandfather begin to merge at the end when Pike takes flight suggests that this novel may be less about New Zealand society per se, and less about the parallels and contrasts between the pioneer past and the present, than about *existential and moral issues relating to personal responsibility.

RC

TRACY, Mona (1892–1959), journalist and children's writer, was born at Mackay, Adelaide, and grew up in Waipu, then among Māori families in Paeroa, near the Waihi gold mines. After her father left them, her mother became a journalist in 1903 on the Auckland Weekly News. Two years later Mona became a cadet, rising to sub-editor on the NZ Herald. In 1917 she became general and women's page reporter on the Christchurch *Press, resigning to marry in 1921. She contributed stories, poems and articles to New Zealand and Australian journals, and wrote several children's books. Piriki's Princess and Other Stories of New Zealand (1925) was a collection from work published in the Christchurch *Sun. Her Waihi experiences and research into early New Zealand history for The Story of the Pacific (1925), written for secondary schools, provided material also for her three lively children's novels: Rifle and Tomahawk (1927) about *Te Kooti; Lawless Days (1928, 1934), a South Seas adventure; and Martin Thorn—Adventurer (1930). These portray some Māori characters sympathetically and feature strong girls as well as boys. Her non-fiction books are Historic Kawau (1927), and West Coast Yesterdays (1960), adapted from articles and radio talks about places visited and old-timers she met in the late 1920s–early 1930s.

JMcC

Trap Press issued catalogues in artistic *typography for Spring 1977 and Summer 1978, advertising books printed on 'our rare Port Chalmers mangle (now dated positively at 1929) and handmade paper produced from rimu saplings grown in favoured hollows of the

Coromandel Peninsula'. Titles listed included 'state ward' Ivan Weedie's *How I Took My Clothes Off At The Picnic and Nobody Noticed*, Lon Dong's *Poems 5639–1103* ('the first joint Hong Kong–New Zealand publication of an expatriate Chilean') and Will Manheim's *The Coruscations and Other Poems* ('etiolation at its finest … won the national Book Award for poetry by academics between the ages of 33 and 34'). With the Joycean motto 'The Trap lies in Belief', the Press thus fulfilled its object 'to produce books of contemporary writing by printing them'. One of New Zealand's few good literary jokes, Trap Press deftly parodied the *Hawk Press catalogues then produced by Alan *Loney, who featured as Arthur Lonely, along with other avant-garde writers of the time, such as Ian *Wedde, Don *Long and Bill *Manhire (as above), Michael *Harlow (Patrick Marlow, 'variously described as Mexican, Swedish, Polish, Albanian and even Greek'), Michael *King (Mitchell Ring, '*Te Puha ha ha*', a biography of a laughing Māori policeman … a Haka of a book'), Russell *Haley ('Rustle Hustle') and C.K. Porterhouse Steak ('order in packs of a dozen patties or more'). Skilled parodies of poems by Wedde and others were also included. The anonymous perpetrators were in fact Brian *Turner and Philip *Temple (despite his appearance as Phillip Forehead, author of *Trains, Signals* and *Junctions*), with contributions from Bill *Sewell. They have never been brought to account.RR

Tree, The, a play by Stella *Jones, attracted considerable attention when it was produced in 1957 in Bristol, England, toured by the New Zealand Players in 1959 and published by *Whitcombe & Tombs with *Literary Fund support in 1960. Originally placed second in the Southland Centennial Playwriting Competition, it was rejected for production until its overseas success. Set on the back porch of a New Zealand home, it is reminiscent of Arthur Miller's *All My Sons* (1947) in its depiction of a family under pressure, its time movement across fifteen years and its economical and realistic dialogue. It was discussed in *Comment* by Robert *Chapman and in *Landfall* by James *Bertram, who compared it with Bruce *Mason's The *Pohutukawa Tree, concluding justly that 'Mrs Jones's text … reads much more smoothly' but that Mason's achieves a 'range of language and of emotional tone' that hers 'nowhere ventures'. The play's central relationship is between the mother, frustrated in her higher aspirations, and the daughter who by travel has achieved greater freedom of choice. Bertram identified the feminist centre of gravity: 'The Tree, in fact, is deeply rooted in the matriarchal folklore of a post-pioneer society, and draws from this much of its power [and] considerable literary quality'. More recently, it has been discussed by Howard McNaughton in *New Zealand Drama* (1981) and the *OHNZLE (1991, 1998).   RR

Trees, Effigies, Moving Objects (1972) initiated a new phase in the poetic career of Allen *Curnow, his first collection of new work since 1957. A sequence of eighteen poems, it was published by the Catspaw Press, Wellington (a Denis *Glover imprint). *Landscape imagery from the bush and beaches of the West Coast near Auckland figured prominently. Some of the poems also reflected Curnow's visits to Washington, DC.   PS

TREGEAR, Edward (1846–1931), was a versatile writer and influential public servant, one of the energetic polymaths the early colony attracted. He was born in Southampton, arrived in 1863, took part in the Land *Wars and entered the public service. As a surveyor he went into uncharted areas and formed a lifelong interest in Māori society and language. Arguing from apparent similarities between Māori and Sanskrit-derived languages, he wrote his controversial *The Aryan Maori* (1885), proposing theories now discredited that gained considerable attention at the time. He compiled one of the significant early lexicographic listings, *The Maori–Polynesian Comparative Dictionary* (with an English key, 1891). He then produced the first book for children to be published in New Zealand, *Fairy Tales and Folklore of New Zealand and the South Seas* (1891), reflecting an informed interest in folklore and myth. At that time he was appointed first Secretary of the New Zealand Labour Department under William Pember *Reeves, working closely with Reeves in the formulation of New Zealand's progressive labour legislation. After Reeves left for England Tregear worked with the early leaders of the Social Democrat movement, becoming president of the party 1912–14. He continued to write, publishing a futuristic dystopia of female dominance, *Hedged with Divinities*, in 1895 (see *Science Fiction, *Utopias); and his influential *The Maori Race* in 1904, 'for twenty years the standard handbook on "the true Maori"' (Peter Gibbons). Though he had written and occasionally published poetry from the early 1870s, his only volume was *Shadows and Other Verses* (1919). *The Verse of Edward Tregear*, ed. K.R.Howe (1989), testifies to continuing interest, and he has been consistently anthologised, in the Penguin (1985) and Oxford (1997) anthologies, for instance. His best-known poem is probably 'Te Whetu Plains', with the lines that have often been taken out of context to illustrate the supposed sense of deprivation of the early settler-poets, ''tis a songless land, / That hears no music of the nightingale'. In fact, they are part of a remarkable evocation of the New Zealand landscape in terms of still-recent ideas of evolution and the earth's pre-history: 'When Earth was tottering in its infancy, /

This rock, a drop of molten stone, was hurled / And tost on waves of flames.' The same interest informs a personal poem like 'The Veils of Phantasy', with its vision of his baby grandchild as part of 'This subtle net of threads which bind the multitudes of earth', carrying him imaginatively back 'Behind the old dead centuries on some primeval shore', where 'Without is forest-darkness, but within the cave-fire gleams'. Tregear's wide reading and formidable intellect make everything he wrote substantial, challenging and often vivid.　　　　HMcQ/RR

TREMAIN, Ronald (1923–), composer, born in Feilding, describes his vocal and choral pieces as probably his 'best and most characteristic music. I have always loved good poetry and I find it a fascinating challenge to discover apt musical imagery for verse, to unite verbal with musical rhythm and at the same time to make a satisfying musical structure.' His *Four Medieval Lyrics* (1965) for mezzo-soprano and string trio he considers his most successful vocal piece. He has set poems by Ursula *Bethell, Allen *Curnow, A.R.D. *Fairburn and M.K. *Joseph, but most of his other works draw on traditional sources or Arthur Waley's translations from the Chinese. In 1970 he was appointed professor of music at Brook University in Ontario, Canada, but maintains links with New Zealand.　　　　JMT

Triad was founded in Dunedin in 1893 by music critic Charles Nalder Baeyertz and rapidly became an important ingredient of New Zealand's developing intellectual and cultural life. With the appointment of Frank *Morton as co-editor in about 1909 the literary component of the magazine increased. As well as many poems, stories and articles by Morton himself, other noteworthy contributors included Alfred *Grace, Arthur *Adams, C.R. *Allen, Johannes C. *Andersen, C.N. Baeyertz, Jean Boswell, Hubert *Church, Dick *Harris, M.H. *Holcroft, Will *Lawson, Quentin *Pope, Dora *Wilcox and David McKee *Wright. In 1912 its best known contributor became Alice *Kenny, when Ezra Pound invited her to send poems to his *Poetry*, and was rebuffed by Kenny and by a series of attacks on Modernism by Morton. The exchange is discussed in an essay by K.K. Ruthven in *Landfall* 89 (1969). With the shift to Sydney in late 1915 *Triad*'s New Zealand literary connection became somewhat tenuous, although familiar New Zealand contributors and a number of new ones did continue to appear.　　　　SH

TROLLOPE, Anthony (1815–82), the most prolific of the great Victorian novelists, described New Zealand on the occasion of a two-month visit in 1872. His comments are vivacious and reveal something of both the observer and the observed. He arrived in Bluff in the first days of August and left from Auckland on 3 October. On the return voyage he wrote the 690 pages of *Australia and New Zealand*, which was published in February 1873, within weeks of his arrival in London. *New Zealand* was republished separately in 1874 and edited by A.H. *Reed in 1969 with annotations and excerpts from local newspapers. References to New Zealand occur also in two of his novels. *The Fixed Period* (1882) is set on a Pacific island which has been inhabited by immigrants from New Zealand, but its central concern is the consequences of a law that all citizens must be killed when they reach the age of 68, while *The New Zealander*, a novel 'putting the world to rights', which was rejected by his publisher in his lifetime and not published until 1979, is not actually about New Zealand but refers to Thomas *Macaulay's famous remark about some future 'traveller from New Zealand' sketching the ruins of St Paul's.

Trollope said that 'it would be impossible to imagine any country more unlike Australia'. On the other hand the manners of the people, the pastoral scenery and even the animal kingdom ('no animal is to be seen in New Zealand different from those which are familiar to us in England') seemed to amount to a caricature of home: 'The New Zealander among John Bulls is the most John-Bullish. He admits the supremacy of England to every place in the world, only he is more English than the Englishman at home.... If he would blow his trumpet somewhat less loudly, the music would gain in its effect upon the world at large.' He admired the Māori ('they are certainly more gifted than other savage nations I have seen') but shared the fashionable view that they were a 'dying race': 'All good things have been given to this happy land and, when the Maori has melted, here will be the navel of the earth.'　　　　NW

Troubadour was an annual magazine of fiction and poetry published by the University of Canterbury Literary Society 1964–65. Printed by the *Caxton Press, it featured contributions by R.A. *Copland, Rupert Glover and John *Weir.　　　　SH

TRUSSELL, Denys (1946–), is a poet, biographer and essayist. Born in Christchurch, he graduated MA in English at Auckland University in 1971, has been a freelance critic of the arts and is a pianist and piano teacher in Auckland. His long poem for choreography *Dance of the Origin* (1980) was performed by Origins Dance Theatre in Auckland, and selections from his second poetry book, *Words for the Rock Antipodes* (1986), were set to music by Dorothy *Ker and performed in 1990. His other verse volumes are *The Man of Paradise* (1991) and the sequence *Archipelago: The Ocean Soliloquies* (1991), a dramatisation and meditation on the history of the *Pacific, from its origins, 'cycles / of the moon dragging / young water through / the formation / of its stone', to the modern city, 'the opaque runes / of its glass, the upthrust / beams of its welding'. *Walking into the Millenium* was published in 1998. Trussell's biography of the poet *Fairburn (1985) won the PEN Best First Book of Prose Award, and he has also published *Alan Pearson: His Life and Art* (1991). Allusive and intellectually challenging, Trussell's poetry reflects interests also explored in his many essays published in New Zealand and overseas, dealing especially with the arts and environmental issues; a collection of these is in preparation. A large selection of his poetry is included in *Sustaining the Earth: An Anthology of Green Poems in English*, ed. Norbert Platz (1998).   RR

Truth, the populist and often sensationalist weekly tabloid newspaper, began as *New Zealand Truth* on 24 June 1905, an offshoot of *Sydney Truth* and part of the small empire of the colourful John Norton. It was controlled from Sydney until a group of New Zealand shareholders acquired it in 1951. An earlier *Truth*, not connected, had been published in Christchurch from 1887, conceding the name in 1909 and retitling itself the *Evening News*.

In its early years the vigorous Wellington-based *Truth* was 'The People's Paper', socialist and pacifist in its leanings and willing to challenge the established order. It was *Truth*, for instance, that published Archibald *Baxter's account of the horrendous 'field punishments' inflicted on conscientious objectors in France during World War 1, in a letter to his parents which Blanche *Baughan forwarded to the editor. Pat *Lawlor called *Truth* 'the worker's Bible' when he worked for it in the 1920s, though his account (in *Confessions of a Journalist*, 1935) is also forthright about the way 'sales were built up almost entirely on the magistrate's court garbage untouched by the daily press'. *Truth* gave early employment to journalists of the quality of David *Low and Robin *Hyde, as well as developing talents now less well-known such as cartoonist and versifier Tom Glover and witty editor Nelson Burns. A good account of Hyde's time at the decrepit Luke's Lane offices, where 'huge rats rustled and peered among old files', is in *Disputed Ground: Robin Hyde, Journalist*, edited by Gillian Boddy and Jacqueline Matthews (1991). Hyde was given some freedom, for instance to pillory a visiting American peddler of quack medicines as vigorously as the paper protested on behalf of the ageing Edward *Tregear against Wellington's first cabaret club, under the headline 'Gay Goings on in Goring Street'.

Its alliterative headlines and billboards could give *Truth* a not altogether frivolous claim to a place in New Zealand literature. From early examples like 'Householders Hot Over Highborn Hullabaloo' and 'Mirth, Motors and Maledictions' to memorable later outbreaks like 'Pinhead and a Virgin—Blossom Bikie Booked' and 'Nipped In Nude—Girl Liked Jap Seamen', *Truth* sustained pre-Puritan English traditions of alliteration, connotation and the ludic pun. In these, as in Tom Glover's ingenious comic jingles and even its zestful scurrility, it stands in contrast to the dour *puritanism of some more intellectual publications.

Truth's relations with literature deteriorated as it moved politically to the right. Norton changed its slogan in 1928 to 'The National Paper', its World War 2 position was hostile to pacifism, it adopted an increasingly reactionary and philistine stance towards literature (attacking James K. *Baxter, for instance) and it provoked the cancellation of Ian *Milner's visiting position at the University of Canterbury: 'NZ Varsity Post for Ex-Spy' (17 Oct. 1967). Two scathing ripostes came from radical writers, both turning *Truth*'s own tactics of abuse against it. Baxter reshaped scurrility into wit: 'I think it's hardly safe / To rub your ink on my bottom, / The poison might creep up and make / My haemorrhoids go rotten'. Mervyn *Thompson compiled his dramatised history of *Truth*'s repressive right-wing attitudes almost entirely from its own pages, turned into narrative and ironic song in *The Great New Zealand Truth Show*, first performed 1982, published in *Passing Through and Other Plays*, 1992.

Truth has occasionally been featured more tolerantly in literature, usually by writers familiar with the world of journalism, as in Robin *Muir's novel *Word for Word* (1960), which quotes 'Teen Sex Probe Shocks' and other headlines. Perhaps it has had an even worse press than it deserves. Lawlor paid tribute to its aptitude for scoops missed by the more conformist daily papers, and to its incorruptibility by bribes or political pressure. It has habitually challenged New Zealand's extremely protective libel laws. Yet it stands curiously isolated in a journalistic scene which has produced no right-wing intellectual equivalents to *Tomorrow, *Here & Now and *New Zealand Monthly Review, and is probably condemned to continued hostility, if only because it has actually had the ear of the people.   RR

TŪREI, Mohi (*c*.1830?–1914), of the Ngāti Porou was born in the Waiapu district on the East Coast and lived in Rangitukia. He was an Anglican deacon and a passive resister to Hauhauism (see *War literature: New Zealand Wars). He was a skilled carver but was even better known for his oratory (*whaikōrero) and his knowledge of traditional history. He was also a poet (some of his *haka have become famous) and a prolific writer of stories (*kōrero), many of which were published in Māori magazines. The journal *Te *Ao Hou* once called him 'one of the very best of all New Zealand writers'. NW

Turi, the Story of a Little Boy (1963) by Lesley Cameron Powell won the 1964 Esther Glen Award for Children's Literature and is described by Betty *Gilderdale as 'undoubtedly one of the classics of New Zealand fiction for the young' (*A Sea Change*, 1982). It was published by Paul's Book Arcade (see *Blackwood and Janet Paul), illustrated by photographs by Pius Blank of an authentic Māori family; and reprinted by Longman Paul in 1969, 1972 and 1977. Unlike the many previous children's stories that deal with Māori–Pākehā friendship, its focus is almost wholly Māori, and it was widely influential in its treatment of the extended family and its detailed accounts of planting kumara, gathering shellfish, and the social rituals, songs, myths and beliefs of Māori culture. It follows Turi from nine months old, when he goes to live with his Granny, to the point where he has started school and has learned to accept her death: 'It was not that he forgot her; she was in fact part of him'. Its direct treatment of old age, death and grieving is described by Gilderdale as having 'set a pattern for what was to become an unusual and distinguishing feature of New Zealand children's literature in the English-speaking world'. RR

TURNBULL, Alexander (1868–1918), bequeathed his great book collection to the nation and thus founded a research library, the *Alexander Turnbull Library, of world as well as national importance. Born in Wellington into a prosperous commercial family, he was taken to London to be educated at Dulwich College, returning in 1885. Wealthy, unmarried and unclubbable, he was free to devote most of his energies to his passion for books, and stands supreme as a collector in New Zealand, and, with Australia's David Scott Mitchell, regionally. He committed himself early to building a comprehensive New Zealand collection, as well as pursuing interests in naval literature, voyages, James *Cook, Scottish history, the art of the book and English literature, particularly Milton. In the 1890s he extended his acquisitions to materials relating to the Pacific, its Polynesian peoples and particularly the Māori. He travelled quite extensively and spent several periods in London. His only publication was a privately printed journal of a yachting cruise, yet his contribution to New Zealand literature was immense. His library's historian, Rachel Barrowman, affirms that while 'there was nothing especially idiosyncratic' at that date about Turnbull's interest

in New Zealand books, yet the scale and discrimination of his collecting created an incalculable resource for the preservation and study of this literature. He is the subject of a biography by E.H. *McCormick, *Alexander Turnbull: His Life, His Circle, His Collections* (1974). RR

Turnbull Library, see **Alexander Turnbull Library**.

TURNER, Brian (1944–), is an unrepentantly regional Otago poet whose work moves constantly beyond the merely local or descriptive. Wider recognition has come with the Commonwealth Poetry Prize for his first collection, *Ladders of Rain* (1978) and the New Zealand Book Award for Poetry for his most recent, *Beyond* (1992). His other collections are *Ancestors* (1981), *Listening to the River* (1983), *Bones* (1985) and *All That Blue Can Be* (1989). He has also written short fiction and plays, his cricket play, 'Finger's Up?' winning the J.C. Reid Memorial Prize 1985. In poetry and prose, Turner is one of New Zealand's most significant writers on *landscape, environmentalism and *sport, through regular journalism for *National Business Review*, the *Independent* and elsewhere, and books including *Images of Coastal Otago* (1982), *New Zealand High Country: Four Seasons* (1983), *The Last River's Song* (1989)—all text accompanying photographs—*The Visitor's Guide to Fiordland, New Zealand* (1983), *Timeless Land* (with Owen *Marshall and Graham Sydney, 1992) and his cricketing brother's biography, *Opening Up* (with Glenn Turner, 1987). His work is represented in all recent major poetry anthologies and in literary sports anthologies such as *Into the Field of Play* (ed. Lloyd *Jones, 1992), the *Picador Book of Golf* (1995) and *New Zealand's Treasury of Trout and Salmon* (ed. Bryce Hammond and John Parsons).

Turner has eschewed poetic cliques and fashions as rigorously as he rejects the archaic conventions of nature poetry: 'dismiss all talk of "rare beauty" / or "lyric fastness" as piffle … There *are* / always the hills' ('Always the hills'). His imaginative effort is always to establish that emphasised '*are*', to cut away all intrusive pretension or platitude and render directly and with respect the independent reality of the things that matter to him: 'Only the mountains know / where they have come from / and where they are going / and what will happen when we are gone'. Very often these are the hills, winds, clouds and rivers of the back-country landscape which he knows more actually and actively than probably any previous New Zealand poet. (Only the high-country writers like John *Pascoe or Philip *Temple can match him.) His 'nature poetry' is thus of that best kind which works as directly as the sun and the rain, and is a fusion of the poet's roots, experience and reading. Or often his subjects are more domestic, though still always vivid with the elemental processes of life. His 'Carrot' is told 'I understand / your angry new-born look / when you are wrenched / from the earth's warm haven'; a slaughtered pig becomes, by its sheer dead weight, an emblem of grief for mortality ('Pig'); and, refreshingly egalitarian, he writes poems for grass, pebbles, potatoes ('scabby testicles'), autumn blackberries, fingerbones, a craven pet dog or a sleeping cat 'digesting the heart of a bird'. And he writes with the same tough honesty about human emotions, relationships and (increasingly) memories, all subject to the same elemental processes of growth and decay as if they were trees or grass, all affirming the vital worth of emotion while almost passionately resisting sentimentalism. So there are many fine love poems, poems of loss or grief, about happiness or the unseen bond with ancestors or the changing relationship with his father, poems where a creature may become the emblem for a complex of human feeling ('To muse is to escape / which a free-ranging chicken / can't do. There's a squawk / and a chaos of feathers / disappears into straw-coloured grasses'—'Bantam', uncollected).

Quite often Turner adopts a droll bloke role, brushing off anything phoney or pretentious with a quirkily derogatory wit, whether about a hawk ('the smarmy Al Capone / of the air'), or a love tryst interrupted by 'a fat frog / croaking and staring pop-eyed / like a lovesick money-lender', or a moment of wickedly deprecating self-consciousness: 'I shrug off my shirt. / Burly men do it better, I'm sure / but shrugging is manly / so I shrug away and cough….'

Beneath the wit, the no-nonsense honesty, the rigorous clarity of sense and the sinewy rhythmic energy of the poems' surfaces runs the craft of a sophisticated, confident and well-read poet—echoes of Berryman, Merwin, Durcan, ★Baxter, complex sound structures and a fine vibrant lyricism, the more singing because anchored so naturally in observed reality and the effort to make real.

Turner has worked, among other things, as customs officer, rabbiter, sawmiller, editor for ★Oxford University Press and managing editor of ★John McIndoe. He has been a national-class hockey player, senior cricketer and mountaineer, and is still a skilled race cyclist, fisherman and yachtsman. He held the ★Burns Fellowship in 1984 and the University of Canterbury writing fellowship in 1997. He was born in Dunedin, educated at Otago BHS and lives at Sawyers Bay.   RR

Tutira (1921), the best-known work of W.H. ★Guthrie-Smith, was described by E.H. ★McCormick as one of the 'finer products' of 'European civilization in New Zealand'. Its author's intention was to describe the natural history of the Tutira run, but to his readers'

delight he decided to add 'chapters on physiography, native life, pioneer work, and surface alterations' so that his book became a microcosmic history of New Zealand itself, benefiting from its concrete detail and intimacy with its subject matter to such a degree that it is a more vivid and effective history than the generalised ones which claim to cover the entire country. It begins when its mountainous subject was still immersed in the ocean and finishes with an account of the changes wrought by British colonisation. Since the author was the principal coloniser of the region it is also an unintentional and movingly modest autobiography.

The opening chapters on the geology, physical geography, climate and general configuration of the run combine scientific exactitude with the controlled vividness of a master of prose. The account of Māori settlement and its impact on the land is both detailed and imaginative and includes close attention to traditions, poems and tales, illustrating both the literary nature of the oral culture and its intimate association with the minute details of the land. The even more radical human impact that followed European colonisation is shown to result from land use as well as from the arrival of the birds, mammals, insects and plants that came with the settlers. Negotiations between the owners of the land and the Māori people, and the commercial and banking communities, have direct and indirect influences on the land, as do, more obviously, its inhabitants' growing knowledge of soil, climate, agricultural potential and value. Much of what Guthrie-Smith writes has the sensitivity of poetry and often it is blended with a novelist's sense of a narrative. Dramatic events, such as a violent earthquake, add to the tension. The literary skills are combined with the close observation and love of detail of the self-trained naturalist, resulting in a book which has been compared with White's *The Natural History of Selborne*, Thoreau's *Walden* and the books of W.H. Hudson, but which goes beyond all of these by combining its tale of natural history with that of human history into a seamless 'story of a New Zealand Sheep station' and of the country itself.   NW

TUWHARE, Hone (1922–), is New Zealand's most distinguished Māori poet writing in English, and also a playwright and author of short fiction. He was born in Kaikohe into the Ngā Puhi tribe (hapū Ngāti Korokoro, Ngāti Tautahi, Te Popoto, Uri-o-hau). When his mother died his father moved to Auckland, where Hone attended primary schools in Avondale, Mangere and Ponsonby. He spoke Māori until he was about 9, and his father, an accomplished orator and storyteller in Māori, encouraged his son's interest in the written and spoken word, especially in the rhythms and imagery of the Old

Testament. During his time in an apprenticeship (1939–44) at the Otahuhu Railway Workshops Tuwhare met the poet R.A.K. *Mason, who encouraged him to write, and like Mason he became politically involved in trades-union organisations. For much of the 1950s he worked on hydroelectric projects on the Waikato, and until the Soviet invasion of Hungary in 1956 was a member of the Communist Party.

In this year Tuwhare began writing seriously. His earliest poems appeared in *Northland Magazine*, the *New Zealand Poetry Yearbooks*, Te *Ao Hou (though the Maori Affairs Department initially banned his work because of his Communist affiliations) and in the *NZ Listener*. His first published collection, *No Ordinary Sun*, appeared in 1964 to widespread acclaim and was reprinted ten times during the next thirty years—one of the most widely read individual collections of poems in New Zealand history. From the late 1960s he began a long association with the Otago region when he was awarded the *Burns Fellowship in 1969—and he held it again in 1974. In Dunedin he met the Māori painter, Ralph *Hotere, who provided illustrations for his next four volumes—*Come Rain Hail* (1970), *Sap-Wood & Milk* (1972), *Something Nothing* (1974) and *Making a Fist of It: Poems and Short Stories* (1978).

In the 1970s Tuwhare became actively involved in Māori cultural and political initiatives. He was an organiser of the first Māori Writers and Artists Conference at Te Kaha in 1973 and participated in the Māori Land March of 1975. There were also invitations to Germany and to China, both of which he revisited in the 1980s. His earlier poems were kept in print (and new ones added) through *Selected Poems* (1980), *Year of the Dog: Poems New and Selected* (1982) and *Mihi: Collected Poems* (1987). In 1983 he worked on the Edward *Shortland papers as *Hocken Library Fellow, and this revitalised and extended his interest in Māori history and language. His full-length play, *In the Wilderness Without a Hat* (perf. 1985), is a highly original, deeply personal, marae-based tribal drama, begun in the wake of his participation in the Land March and published in *He Reo Hou: 5 Plays by Maori Playwrights* (1991). *Short Back and Sideways: Poems & Prose* (1992) was new work prepared during his tenure of the University of Auckland's Literary Fellowship in 1991. A second collection with new poems, *Deep River Talk* (1993) was followed by *Shape-Shifter* (1997), consisting of poems and stories.

When Tuwhare's poems first began to appear in the late 1950s and early 1960s they were recognised as a new departure in New Zealand poetry, cutting across the debates and divisions between the 1930s and post-war generations. Much of their originality came from the Māori perspective. This was not simply a question of the

subject matter of some poems ('Lament', a reworking of an older *waiata tangi, 'Tangi' and 'Mauri'), but of their direct lyrical response to landscape and seascape, their vivid evocation of Māori myths and images ('A burnt offering to your greenstone eyes, Tangaroa'), and their capacity for angry protest at the dispossession of Māori land and culture ('The mana of my house has fled, / the marae is but a paddock of thistle'). The poems were also marked by their tonal variety, the naturalness with which they could move between formal and informal registers, between humour and pathos, intimacy and controlled anger (as in the anti-nuclear theme of the title-poem of the first volume, 'No Ordinary Sun') and, especially, in their assumption of easy vernacular familiarity with New Zealand readers.

In his next three volumes (of the earlier 1970s) Tuwhare added to this repertoire a distinctive longer form of 'conversation' poem, often deploying narrative elements but containing the same variations of tone, feeling and register: playful humour, edged satire and moments of sustained elegiac intensity. Some of these poems were elegies (like those for his mentor Mason, and for James K. *Baxter); others were intimate 'conversation poems', like 'Country Visit' (a visit to his sister's family), 'Sandra' (a birthday poem) and 'A korero on the beach with Phyllis'); yet others ('occasioned by the newness and press of contrasts') were sparked off by places visited overseas: including Western Samoa ('Village on Savaii') and *China ('Kwantung Guest House: Canton'). In one of his best known poems, 'To a Maori figure cast in bronze outside the Chief Post Office, Auckland', the same elements were deployed in a dramatic monologue, remarkably rich in its edged allusions to the political, economic and class contexts of race relations in New Zealand, and in its imaginative play with formal and colloquial English and Māori idioms, and with the cultural meanings carried by particularities of location in urban and suburban Auckland. The assumption of a familiar context shared unselfconsciously with his New Zealand readership is crucial to the effect of this poem (as in all Tuwhare's mature work); because of the density of local allusion and idiom almost every line would require annotation for overseas readers.

Tuwhare's later poetry continued to expand the range and subtlety of his distinctive style. His interest in Māori self-determination was intensified by participation in the Land March, which produced a series of celebratory poems in *Making a Fist of It* (1978), alongside that volume's angry political title-poem, on South African atrocities at Soweto and elsewhere. Yet Tuwhare's work resists identification in terms of any separatist notion of 'Maoriness'. Increasingly, especially at the level of language, his poetry represents (and often playfully invents) moments and scenes of (multi)cultural exchange and interaction, suggesting a local world of shifting, multiple identities and identifications. His affiliations to the language and aspirations of ordinary working-class New Zealanders have remained strong, however, and his major, recurrent concerns—emergent through the extraordinary cultural diversity of the poems' occasions, the richness of their sense of location, and their highly inventive use of New Zealand demotic idioms—have remained those of the age-old lyric tradition: love, friendship, the life of the feelings, the experience of loss and death.   TS

TWAIN, Mark (Samuel Langhorne Clemens) (1835–1910), the *American author, visited New Zealand in 1895 and wrote about it in his last travel book *Following the Equator* (1897). This immediately sold 30 000 copies and helped him pay off his creditors. During his lecture-tour, he recommended the banishment of English poachers to New Zealand to solve the rabbit plague, observed that the Scots settlers in Dunedin must have thought they were in heaven, and was surprised to find a lavatory equipping every railway car. He studied the skeleton of the great moa in the Christchurch museum, and theorised that it would have made terrific speed when ridden by a native mail-carrier, so the railroad must have exterminated the species to get the business. He was given a present of a stuffed platypus; he started a poem on the fauna of Australasia: 'Land of the ornithorhynchus / Land of the kangaroo / Old ties of heredity link us....'

Impressed by Māori tattoos and carvings (particularly one depicting a shrewd Māori robber escaping on stilts), and appreciative of native representation in government and both sexes having the vote, his account of his visit turns memorably chilling when he reports on the 'Maungatapu Murders'—a 'dark episode ... in the history of Nelson'.

Certain aspects of Twain's legacy in New Zealand literature can be specified. Frank *Sargeson entitled his 1920s travel journal *A New Tramp Abroad*, following Twain's *A Tramp Abroad*, and acknowledging the vernacular spirit and language he wished to adopt. He recommended Twain to his protégés. Sargeson's story *'That Summer' (written 1938–41) and Roderick *Finlayson's novel *Tidal Creek* (1948) are both clearly indebted to *Huckleberry Finn*. But it is more than a matter of similar characterisation or reminiscent scenes. In *Art in New Zealand* (1934) and in reviewing Sargeson's *Conversations with my Uncle* (1936), A.R.D. *Fairburn emphasised Sargeson's kinship with the American 'colonial' tradition; just as *Huckleberry Finn* characteristically represents unrefined America, so Sargeson writes of

similarly representative New Zealanders, Fairburn said. 'The easy-going, gum-chewing attitude towards life of the true colonial is something that concerns us very directly.... We understand Huck, the true colonial, where we can only pretend to understand Tom Brown, the English public school-boy.' This is also true of Finlayson.

Answering the question 'What books are the best you have ever read or have influenced you most profoundly?' in *NZ Listener* (1 August 1987), Ian *Cross began with *Huckleberry Finn*, claiming that there Twain 'released writers and readers from the bondage of colonial belief that literature was governed by a special language'. Drawing attention to the variety of dialects that were all valid modes not only of speech but also of writing, Twain, Cross said, 'was making a declaration of independence for New World writing ... we were being told that we could celebrate ... write and read our own voices.'

Twain's sensationally irreverent humour and his respect for the Māori people might also have influenced authors such as Ronald Hugh *Morrieson and Alan *Duff. More generally, his democratic esteem for a diversity of voices, his subversive wit and acid attitude to cant and hypocrisy are inherited in various ways, but always as gain.   AR

TWEEDIE, Merylyn, see **BUDD, Lillian**.

***Typo*, *A Monthly Journal and Literary Review*,** was written, edited, printed and published by Robert Coupland Harding 29 January 1887 to 1897, at his printing office, Hastings Street, Napier. For eleven volumes and seventy-three issues *Typo* was 'Devoted to the advancement of the typographic art and the interests of the printing, publishing, bookselling, stationery and kindred trades'. To Harding's own list can be added advertising and literary matters, and the magazine exhibited therefore an astonishing range of one man's attentions. *Typo* received international acclaim, mainly in Britain and the United States, for its astute and detailed analyses of contemporary type designs and the wealth of printers' flowers, typographical ornaments and technical innovations that poured out of type foundries and printing supplies manufacturers in the latter part of the nineteenth century. The design and layout of the magazine itself exemplified Harding's beliefs and principles of good *typography, and his predilection was for a very much less decorative style than that which was the fashion of his time. This New Zealand–born friend of William Colenso was probably the first self-conscious typographer in New Zealand, and he stands as a major though atypical figure for any student of the black art. There are only a few extant complete sets of *Typo*, one in the ★Alexander Turnbull Library and another in the library of the Auckland Institute and Museum. AL

Typography has often been considered an essential part of the totality of literary effect, especially in relationship to poetry. For the Māori the introduction of printing presses, like that of writing itself, meant even more: it brought about a transformation of their relationship to their own literature and ultimately of the literature itself. The first book printed in New Zealand was in fact in Māori—a translation of the *Catechism* by Rev. W. Yate in 1830. Yate's press does not seem to have been a great success—the surviving prints are smudged and uneven—and when William Colenso landed another in 1835 many important pieces of equipment were missing: there were no leads, brass rule, galleys, inking table, composing stick or even printing paper. Nonetheless, as the official printer of the Church Missionary Society, he relied on improvisation, printing mostly in Māori. By 1837 the complete New Testament (translated directly from Greek by William ★Williams) could be printed and in 1840 *The New Zealand Advertiser and Bay of Islands Gazette* was founded, as was the local version of *The New Zealand Gazette and Wellington Spectator*, the first issues of which had been printed in London in 1839.

The Māori population took with enthusiasm to reading and writing, and to typography as well. From children to very old men, thousands wanted to learn the new skills. There is a story of a Waikato ★tohunga, Wetere Te Puke, being taught to read by his 12-year-old son and becoming so skilled that he was nicknamed Te Putea-kōrero (the bag of eloquence). For other Māori, books were a more important trading item than blankets or tobacco. English tales told orally (by, for example, John ★White) were already very popular, and George ★Grey had *Robinson Crusoe* published in 1852 and *Pilgrim's Progress* in 1854 in translations by Henry Tacy Kemp.

Who read such books? As early as 1844 George F. ★Angas recorded in his diary, 'One of our natives constantly carries a slate, and whenever we halt to rest, he amuses himself by working sums in arithmetic; he is now lying at full length on the fern, busily engaged with a calculation that Forsaith has set him; and my lad, Pera, is reading aloud from a native testament, extremely fast. Not only do the young people, in this way, improve themselves in education, but they are very fond of teaching others; and many individuals in the interior, who had no instruction whatever from the missionaries, have acquired the arts of reading and writing, merely by the aid of these native instructors, who have a pride in communicating their new acquirements.' The history of ★Māori newspapers also reveals much of the printing and

reading climate. In his *Bibliography of Printed Māori to 1900* (1924), H.W. Williams records more than a hundred printers of books.

Newspapers in English also flourished in the nineteenth century and for many years the government relied on newspaper printers to print its legislation. The same newspapers were often in deep conflict with the government.

On the whole, however, printing was merely that, rather than something rising to the level of conscious art, which is 'typography' in the narrower sense. Some books surviving in research libraries, however, demonstrate great care and skill, in particular those printed by the Brett Publishing Company of Auckland. In such a context the work of Robert Coupland Harding of Napier stands out as a remarkable exception. The assiduity with which he acquired rare and attractive typefaces and the skill and care with which he used them set an example which craftsmen of lesser talent were pleased to follow. A useful survey is *A History of Printing in New Zealand 1830–1940* published as a part of the ★Centennial celebrations in 1940 by the Wellington Club of Printing House Craftsmen.

The fresh flourishing of literary arts in the 1920s–30s was closely interrelated with printers and presses. Just as writers of that time believed they were creating the first truly New Zealand literature, the printers believed they were creating original styles of presentation unique to their country. (But as with the poetry, sources in British styles can be traced.) Bob ★Lowry, with *Phoenix* and other publications, Denis ★Glover of the ★Caxton Press, Bob ★Gormack of the Nag's Head Press and Ronald Holloway of the ★Griffin Press created something of a revolution in printing to match the changes in literature.

This fertile interchange is clearest in poetry, partly because that has most often been designed, set, printed and published locally, on a small scale and with craft aspirations, whereas fiction has only quite recently found a viable local market. A novel such as M.K. ★Joseph's ★*I'll Soldier No More* (published in London by Gollancz and in Hamilton by ★Paul's Book Arcade, 1958), like all of Paul's list, makes a statement by its appearance about the significance of the text and the discriminating taste of the envisaged readers, quite different from the airport-book-stall packaging and 1990s disposability of the latest Paul ★Thomas thriller. But prose's rectangular block of type allows only limited variation of statement or inventiveness. The production of poetry tells a more vital story.

Allen ★Curnow, introducing Glover's *Selected Poems* in 1981, wrote of the 1930s as a time 'when we all began reading Pound and Eliot, or shared our modernity with Auden, MacNeice, Day Lewis or Spender'. These were published by Faber & Faber, Oxford University Press,

Michael Joseph, Jonathan Cape, Hogarth Press, Victor Gollancz—all sustaining reputations for typographical as well as literary distinction and contemporaneity.

Parallels between the published intentions of Glover's Caxton Press and Francis Meynell's Nonesuch Press in England, for example, are striking and instructive of local aspirations at that formative time. The functional clarity of typography advocated by Eric Gill was combined in Nonesuch or Bodley Head, and thence in Caxton, with a conscious quest for distinction of appearance, a projection of significance, so that the literary text is offered to a discerning and perhaps select readership, as to members of a club; as Caxton, of course, originally was, albeit a club of students. Commentators such as J.C. *Beaglehole and E.H. *McCormick had a sharp sense of how the emergent canon was associated with standards and practice of book production, and the fact that writers themselves, with their friends and close colleagues, had taken the means of production literally in hand.

The innovation of the 1930s became the standard for three decades. Caxton's *Landfall embodied, four times a year in the supposedly ephemeral form of the journal, the aspiration to a quality, discriminating, permanent culture. In 1969 things began to change. A group of new writers openly challenged that aspiration, embodying their challenge in the irreverent, informal and insistently ephemeral form of periodicals like the Literary Yearbook of the NZ Students Association, *Frontiers and *Freed. Using cheap, transitory reprographic methods like the photocopier, these magazines presented literary texts as immediate rather than canonical, populist rather than elitist, vibrantly international, rather than reverently striving to create a local but still essentially Anglo–derivative tradition of excellence. They were often irregular rather than periodical, and in the case of Freed declaredly short-lived, a frontal challenge to the growing 'collector's set' format of Landfall and *Islands. It's the more ironic that Freed has become legendary and a permanent point of reference in the narrative of New Zealand poetry.

The new generation looked not to Britain but to the United States and Europe for their poetic models, and to Europe—the Surrealists, the Dadaists, the Constructivists, the Bauhaus—for their typographic ones. The new poems needed a new typography, and the pages of Freed (1969–72) and of David *Mitchell's Pipe Dreams in Ponsonby (1972) are probably the best indications of the new mode of literary composition and its embodiment in printed form. Again, the typographic solutions, or questions of what is now known as 'layout', were modelled directly on the poetry that the new poets were reading.

The break from the past was not, of course, complete, even though it crucially shaped the overall picture of New Zealand poetry over at least the next twenty-five years. The 'thirties' and the 'seventies' traditions still both flourish, a little uneasily together, the former still generally taken as the continuing mainstream. Sadly few commentators have been able to account for both without partisan commitment. The typographical picture is also in process of being fundamentally and probably permanently changed by the personal computer. Now, everyone is a typographer. What once were signs of affiliation to a literary-typographical ideology—symmetrical and conservative or asymmetrical and radical—are now simply options available at the click of a button, mere locations on a list of choices. Through technology, conservative literature can receive radical typographical treatment, and radical texts can be disguised as rectangular blocks of type. Even now works are being written—or constructed—which can be made and read only on the computer, which cannot be printed out on a page without loss of their integrity. Future links between literature and typography will almost certainly be dependent on whatever new technology evolves.   AL/NW

U

Unicorn Press, see **Griffin Press**.

United States, see **America**.

University of Auckland Library has a standard printed collection of New Zealand literature to support the University's teaching programmes and a small collection of archives and manuscripts in the New Zealand and Pacific Collection. Writers' papers include those of Rex *Fairburn, Robin *Hyde, Isabel Maud *Peacocke and Greville *Texidor, and ancillary collections those of Bob *Lowry and the *Oxford University Press (NZ).   JT

University literary magazines, published by the various university students' associations, have been an important site of first publication for many of New Zealand's most notable writers and poets. The first to begin publication was the *Otago University Review* in 1888. The *Canterbury University College Review* appeared in 1897, followed in 1898 by the *Collegian*, published at the Auckland University College, predecessor of *Marte Nostro* (1903–04) and the longer running *Kiwi*, first published in 1905. In 1902 the students of Victoria University College of Wellington published the first issue of *Spike*. Some of the more topical functions of the reviews were taken over by the student newspapers which began to appear from the mid-1920s, generally leading to an increase in the proportion of literary material in the magazines. From around mid-century periodicals such as *Canterbury Lambs* (1946–49), *Hilltop* (1949), *Arachne* (1950–51), *Experiment* (1956–69), *Nucleus* (1957–62), *Rostrum* (1939–46) and the *New Zealand Universities Literary Yearbook* (1960–72), began to replace the established annuals, which, with the

exception of the *Otago University Review*, gradually ceased publication.   SH

Untold, a literary magazine, appeared 1984–88, in eight issues plus a final double issue, No. 9/10. Editors were: No. 1, Simon Garrett; No. 2, Simon Garrett and John *Newton; all others, Simon Garrett and Shona Smith. *Untold* was published in Christchurch by Untold Books, except for the last double issue which was published in Wellington. Nos 1 to 5 were designed by Max Hailstone in an A4 format that was retained after moving to computer typesetting for No. 6 onwards. Each cover featured a different artist, and these included Philip Trusttum, Joanna *Paul, Don Peebles, Bill Hammond and Julia Morison. *Untold* occupied a place somewhere between the mainstream of *Landfall* and its more radical contemporaries *Splash* and *AND*. Poetry, short stories, reviews, articles and photographs appeared by new and some soon-to-be established writers and artists, with no other expressed manifesto than the magazine title itself. Lively, generous with white space, and maintaining an up-to-date editorial line, *Untold* had an important role in providing space for an increasing number of very competent authors at an interesting time in this country. It was a time when New Zealand literary magazines were unusually focused on specific literary-political agendas or on regular stables of contributors. Frequently appearing in *Untold* were Murray *Edmond, John *Newton, John *Dickson, Rob *Jackaman, Owen *Marshall, Bernadette *Hall, Patrick *Evans and Rob *Allan; and articles considered the work of Janet *Frame, Keri *Hulme, Leo *Bensemann, Stuart *Hoar, Cilla *McQueen and Allen *Curnow.   AL

Utopian literature has a rich tradition in New Zealand, both in writing by New Zealanders and by others using a New Zealand setting. Each contributes to a genre that stems from the words *utopia* and *eutopia*, coined by Thomas More in 1516 in the work now known as his *Utopia*. The word *utopia* or *outopia* simply means 'no place' or 'not place' ('topos', place; 'u' or 'ou', 'no' or 'not'). More punned on *eutopia* or *good place*, and others have since added *dystopia* or *bad place*.

The first New Zealand utopia, *The Travels of Hildebrand* ★*Bowman* (1788) was published even before New Zealand was generally known to Europeans, and since settlement New Zealand has been the physical setting for several well-known utopias and dystopias. Major nineteenth-century examples include Samuel ★Butler's ★*Erewhon* (1872), small parts of which were originally written in Canterbury and published in the ★*Press*, and ★*Erewhon Revisited* (1901), Robert ★Pemberton's *The* ★*Happy Colony* (1854), and Anthony ★Trollope's *The Fixed Period* (1882). New Zealand also figured in a large number of works that depicted a collapsing Britain, the most famous of these representations being '★Macaulay's New Zealander'.

In the twentieth century, the widespread belief that New Zealand is the most likely developed democracy to survive a nuclear war has produced a substantial number of utopias with at least partial New Zealand settings, or with New Zealand imagined as a society surviving and going on from catastrophic war. Aldous Huxley's *Ape and Essence* (1948) is a major example, New Zealand scientists exploring the devastation of the northern hemisphere. John Wyndham's *The Chrysalids* (1955) ends with escape from a regressive northern world of mutants, savagery and religious cruelty to an idyllic New Zealand of a 'wide blue bay' and a 'city with its white houses embedded among green parks and gardens', where technology is advanced and the people telepathic. In New Zealand, this same survivalist argument was presented in a brief utopia, 'Apocalypse 1989' (1980) by Peter Wilkins, initially published in a collection entitled *Pictures of the Future* and reprinted in a report of the Commission for the Future (1982).

Utopian literature by New Zealanders developed parallel with the process of settlement by Europeans. Most of the early utopias can be seen as a combination of propaganda extolling the virtues of New Zealand to possible settlers and heartfelt thanks for the better life actually found there. Such literature can be found in the letters of emigrants, both real and fictional, books with titles like *Brighter Britain!* (1882), and the colonisation schemes for Canterbury, Otago, Albertland, and various Special Settlements.

Late in the nineteenth century, the Premier Richard John Seddon popularised the expression ★'God's Own Country', a phrase of obviously utopian overtones. The tradition of literally describing New Zealand as a realised utopia was carried on by George ★Bell, *Mr Oseba's Last Discovery* (1904); Kenneth Melvin, *New Zealand: 'The Small Utopia'* (1962); and Seymour Kopf, *All the Curious Traveller Would Want to Know About the Only Remaining Utopia for the Average Man—New Zealand* (1975) among others. This attitude was satirised in Austin Mitchell's *The Half-Gallon Quarter-Acre Pavlova Paradise* (1972).

What is more narrowly thought of as New Zealand utopian literature emerged in the later nineteenth century in poems, stories, pamphlets, and a few novels, generally centred on specific social, economic, or political issues. One of these issues, women's rights, produced the first full-length novel among New Zealand utopias, Julius ★Vogel's *Anno Domini 2000; or, Woman's Destiny* (1889), which makes a case for almost complete equality between women and men. The issue also produced a number of utopias presenting the evils of equality, including ★Bracken's *The Triumph of Woman's Rights* (1892?)

But economic issues predominated, and, following the publication in the United States of Edward Bellamy's *Looking Backward* (1888), which was a best-seller in New Zealand (including a number of pirated editions), the next decades focused on public solutions to poverty and economic inequality. The predominating influence was Henry George, a US reformer who proposed a single tax on land in his *Progress and Poverty* (1879). This idea appeared in works like Frederick M. King's *The Wreck of the 'Erthshire'* (1899), and the nationalisation of land was the basis of utopia in Arthur Sanford's *Looking Upwards* (1892) and others. Lack of access to land was a major issue in New Zealand and, as a result, became the focus of indigenous utopianism.

The best known works of this period were two volumes by John Macmillan ★Brown, *Riallaro* (1901) and *Limanora* (1903). A third volume, 'Beyond', is in the Macmillan Brown papers at the University of Canterbury. *Riallaro* is a typical example of Gulliveriana in which the protagonist travels from island to island encountering people with differing peculiarities. All these peoples have been exiled from Limanora, which, in order to improve its stock, exiled all those who could not be brought up to the Limanoran physical, moral, and intellectual standard. *Limanora* is an extremely detailed utopia written in turgid prose, with no real plot, and about a hundred invented words like 'duomovamolan' that do not precisely trip off the tongue and require a glossary. Macmillan Brown's grandson, James K. ★Baxter, was struck by the resolute optimism. 'Beyond' is an example of Gulliveriana set in space focusing on religion.

With the exception of Robin ★Hyde's ★*Wednesday's*

Children (1937), the period from about 1910 to 1960 produced little of note. The same themes were continued as in the previous decades, but New Zealand's reforming energies were obviously directed elsewhere. In most of the world, the *Depression of the 1930s saw a significant upsurge in the utopias produced; in New Zealand, there was, if anything, a decline. But *Wednesday's Children* stands out as a foretaste of what was to come. A strongly feminist work, and certainly the best-written New Zealand utopia before the 1970s, *Wednesday's Children* is most frequently described as a fantasy. While there are elements of fantasy, stylistically it has much in common with what became known as Magic Realism.

The 1960s–70s saw a dramatic resurgence in utopias, notably Janet *Frame's *Intensive Care* (1970), the earliest and finest modern New Zealand dystopia. It begins with a fairly straightforward family history but shifts gears dramatically to a future post-war society trying to cleanse itself of its 'inferior' members. Vernon Wilkinson's *After the Bomb* (1984) similarly places New Zealand as part of an evolving worldwide eutopia society. In Frame's dystopia the cleansing backfires through the discovery of important skills among the 'unfit'; in Wilkinson's eutopia the isolation of the unfit is an essential basis of the better future world.

Other titles in a rich period have included C.K. *Stead's *Smith's Dream* (1971, rev. 1973), Sandi Hall's *The Godmothers* (1982) and *Wingwomen of Hera* (1987), James *McNeish's *Joy* (1982), Lora Mountjoy's *Deep Breathing* (1984), Rachel *McAlpine's *The Limits of Green* (1985) and *Running Away from Home* (1987), Mike *Johnson's *Lear* (1986), Ian *Wedde's *Symmes Hole* (1986), John *Cranna's *Arena* (1992), Fiona *Farrell's *The Skinny Louie Book* (1992), Rosie *Scott's *Feral City* (1992) and John Elder's *The Hidden Mask* (1995). Many of these works are dystopias or 'bad places'. This negative projection of the present has been the dominant form of the utopia in the twentieth century, but in New Zealand it took hold quite late, just as the eutopia was reviving in the rest of the world. Overwhelmingly New Zealand dystopias depict an authoritarian New Zealand government determined to ignore environmental concerns in the name of profit for large corporations and uninterested in the needs and concerns of the people. Many seek to extrapolate directly from current events and policies, envisaging a near-future authoritarianism that is either related to the support of corporate power or is simply self-serving, retaining power by force or fraud.

The two main streams of eutopian writings also reflect these concerns. One primary theme is the fictional representation of a future New Zealand communalism, such as in Gordon Kerins, *No Lasting City* (1981) and Barry Rosenberg, 'Sweetwaters 1984: The Final Refuge' (*Pathfinder* 1983). The other primary eutopian theme is feminism. But in both cases the government and big business in league are depicted as destroying the actual or potential idealised New Zealand society.

There is a tension between the *'Man Alone' tradition in New Zealand literature, perhaps best represented in recent utopias by Bob Jones's *The Permit* (1984), and the community basis of most utopian literature, particularly feminist, such as Lora Mountjoy's *Deep Breathing* and Sandi Hall's *Wingwomen of Hera*; and tension, too, with the form of communalism that stems from respect for or idealisation of traditional Māori culture. This is best represented in utopian work by a video by Hall, *Just Passing Through* (1985), but is included in many recent utopias, such as David P. O'Neill's *The Book of Rewi* (1975), Peter *Hooper's *A Song in the Forest* (1979) and Ted Sheasby's *The Coming of the Prophet Bird* (1987). In some such as McAlpine's two fantasies, the natural world is presented as joining women and Māori in revolt against environmental degradation, idealistically reclaiming the land from governmental and corporate greed.

New Zealand utopian literature is a living tradition that has now been established for over 150 years. It includes almost 150 adult titles and many more for young adult readers; and is being added to regularly. Currently it is fulfilling the common role of utopias, opposition to the established state of things; but belief in the hopeful possibility of New Zealand as a utopia in the positive sense is far from dead.   LS

Valley of Decision, Allen *Curnow's first book of poems, is a collection of twenty-three short lyrics published in 1933 when he was 22. It was printed by Robert *Lowry and Ronald Holloway, and published by the Auckland University College Students' Association Press as 'Phoenix Miscellany: 1'. In his Author's Note to *Collected Poems 1933–73* (1974)—the only publication in which these poems were subsequently reprinted (with four omitted)—Curnow wrote: 'In *Valley of Decision*, and after it, some crisis or change from faith to scepticism may be read, however perplexed and precarious the faith was, and the scepticism no less so.'   PS

VASIL, Lisa (1973–), was 13 when her first novel was published. *Just an Ordinary Kid* (1987) draws significantly on her own courage and experience of cerebral palsy to convey with disarming humour the need for *disabled people to be treated as 'ordinary'. Her second novel, *Dark Secret* (1989), deals with teenage blindness, secret guilt, values and friendship. With *Escape from the Future* (1991) Vasil moves into time-twist *science fiction to explore the generation gap, and in *The Apprentice Devil* (1993) she uses a fantasy element for comic effect in a contemporary story. Her youthful success was acknowledged by a Young Achiever's Award in 1986, and in 1993 she was writer-in-residence at Palmerston North College of Education. Vasil was born in Taupo and educated through the Correspondence School while living in Taihape.   DH

VERNE, Jules (1828–1905), the innovative French fantasy novelist, mentions New Zealand in a number of his *Extraordinary Journeys to Lands Known and Unknown*, although he never actually visited the Pacific region. His comprehensive *Histoire générale des grands voyages et des grands voyageurs* (1878) contains many references to the exploration of New Zealand in the eighteenth and nineteenth centuries. His interest started early with *Les Enfants du Capitaine Grant*, Part III, (1865–67). Set in the Waikato–Taupo–Thermal areas during the New Zealand *Wars, this novel makes dramatic use of the distinctive features of the land and its inhabitants—the dangerous coastline and wild hinterland, volcanic activity, earthquakes, unusual bird life and fierce Māori. Accurate documentation is derived from Ferdinand von *Hochstetter's 1859 account of his scientific expedition to the inland North Island (published in the travel magazine *Le Tour du monde* in 1865), complemented by *Dumont d'Urville's earlier accounts. Reference to contemporary events, such as the Māori resistance at Orakau against the 40th Regiment, Reverend Volkner's murder at Opotiki in 1865 and Whitcombe and Howitt's South Island expedition, and to personalities such as Generals Carey and Cameron, King Potatau or William Thompson provide a base of realism for the incredible adventures of the heroes. Local information presented by the eccentric character of Paganel, the secretary of the Paris Geography Society, is manipulated for humour and suspense. For all its 'operetta' atmosphere, Verne's novel was responsible for projecting colourfully romantic images of New Zealand throughout the world.

New Zealand's Auckland and Chatham Islands and its own coastline provide a realistic though temporary anchorage for several unlikely Verne adventures, some based on genuine whaling and shipwreck stories, like his famous *utopia, *L'Ile Mystérieuse* (1874). This owes some characters and incidents to François Raynal's *Les Naufragés ou Vingt mois sur un récif des Iles Auckland*, an authentic tale of shipwreck and survival in the Auckland Islands, first published in *Le Tour du Monde* in 1866. In other Verne stories New Zealand is often mentioned as a distant though civilised point of reference, a credible place to start, pursue or end any adventure, as in *Capitaine de 15 ans* (1878), *Robur le Conquérant* (1866), *Deux ans de vacances* (1888), *L'Ile à Hélice* (1895), *Le Sphinx des Glaces* (1895) and *Maître du Monde* (1904).

Partly set in New Zealand in 1863, *Les Histoires de Jean-Marie Cabidoulin* (1901) combines factual information on whaling with age-old fictions about sea-monsters. It reflects observations recorded by Dr Félix Maynard and edited by Alexandre Dumas in *Les Baleiniers* (1858), and in Dr Louis Thiercelin's *Journal d'un baleinier* (1866). Both described bay-whaling around Banks Peninsula in the 1840s. In Verne's novel, Jean-Marie Cabidoulin, the old superstitious cooper who believes in sea-serpents, is opposed to Dr Filhiol, the scientific young ship's doctor. Traditional whaling areas such as Akaroa, Kaikoura, Cook Strait or the Bay of Islands are evoked as the French whaler *St Enoch* sails in local waters between whaling trips to the Northern Hemisphere.

The first five chapters of *Les Frères Kip* (1902) are also set in New Zealand, starting in the Port Chalmers' 'grogshops' during the gold rush, then moving away to Norfolk Island, New Guinea, the Solomons and Tasmania. The geographic novel soon turns into a detective story with a miscarriage of justice. The New Zealand background is a collage of accurate and fabricated details, mostly derived from Dumont d'Urville's now dated account. However, we are presented with a busy and modern settlement developing quickly through international trade. Glowing descriptions of the 'modern' cities of Wellington and Dunedin as real centres of 'Progress' are underlined by photos which now replaced the fine etchings of Verne's earlier New Zealand novels.

Jules Verne's varied picture of New Zealand associates fiction and information in a unique and influential way. By exploiting the romance of 'Old New Zealand' he appealed to his readers' imagination while passing on substantial factual information. Geographical isolation presented obvious advantages for the storyteller while rapid economic development justified his belief in the exploitation of the planet for the betterment of mankind. Verne's versions of New Zealand combined romance with testimony to the nineteenth-century expansion of capitalism.   CM

Victoria University of Wellington Library has a standard printed collection of New Zealand literature to support the University's teaching programmes and a small but growing collection of writers' papers in the special collections in the J.C. Beaglehole Room. Bruce *Mason deposited his papers in the 1980s and the Literary Archive established with INL sponsorship in 1993 has acquired papers from Alistair Te Ariki *Campbell, Patricia *Grace, Witi *Ihimaera and Jenny *Bornholdt, all writers who have a strong association with the university. The audio-visual suite holds the Wellington Theatre Archive of videotapes and the Stout Research Centre Literary Archive, a collection of audio and video tapes of readings, discussions, lectures and interviews commissioned by the Archive or recorded from Radio New Zealand and other sources between 1986 and 1991. A duplicate set of the recordings is held by the *Alexander Turnbull Library.   JT

Victoria University Press is a scholarly publisher also known for its lively literary list. It was initiated primarily by Professor D.F. McKenzie (also creator of *Wai-te-ata Press), in partnership with Hugh Price of *Price Milburn publishers. The first of a number of books to carry the joint imprint was Barry *Mitcalfe's *Maori Poetry* (1973). In 1977 Price Milburn's 'New Zealand University Press' list of New Zealand drama (mainly Bruce *Mason) became the beginnings of VUP's 'New Zealand Playscripts' under the editorship of John Thomson, with *Glide Time* initiating what became a significant series. It remains the only regular publisher of plays, and has made available over forty scripts by playwrights including Greg *McGee, Vincent *O'Sullivan and *Renée. In 1978 an equivalent 'New Zealand Short Story' series was launched, under Bill *Manhire. Publishing of these series and other titles under the VUP's sole imprint began in 1979 with the appointment of Pamela Tomlinson as editor; and after her death in 1985, Fergus Barrowman. The Short Story series saw the début of Yvonne *du Fresne and collections by, among others, Janet *Frame, Keri *Hulme, Helen *Shaw and Ian *Wedde.

Building on this, VUP became a leading publisher of new fiction, introducing many new writers and winning recognition in the form of successes at the New Zealand Book Awards. Writers introduced since 1987 include Barbara *Anderson, Catherine Chidgey, Annamarie *Jagose, Elizabeth *Knox, J.H. Macdonald, Emily *Perkins and Forbes Williams, and VUP has also published Lloyd *Jones and Damien *Wilkins. The poetry list, again with Manhire influential, has introduced Jenny *Bornholdt, James Brown, Rachel Bush, Dinah *Hawken, Andrew *Johnston, Chris *Orsman and Virginia *Were. In 1997 VUP has a staff of two and an average output of eighteen titles a year, most in its New Zealand History and Nature, Environment and Conservation lists.   FB

Vietnam War, see **War literature: Vietnam War**.

VIRTUE, Noel (1947–), novelist, was born into a Plymouth Brethren family and raised in Lower Hutt, Waikato and Auckland. In 1967 he went to Britain, where he became a zookeeper for the London Zoological Society and eventually head keeper of the Welsh Mountain Zoo.

In the late 1970s Virtue left zookeeping to concentrate on writing. His fourth completed novel, *The Redemption of Elsdon Bird*, was published in the UK in 1987 and in the USA and New Zealand in 1988. Relating the anguished experiences of a young boy in a Plymouth Brethren family in Wellington and Waikato in the 1950s, the novel created an immediate sensation and was shortlisted for book awards in Britain and New Zealand. Five more novels followed in rapid succession. The second, *Then upon the Evil Season* (1988 UK, 1989 NZ), is set in Opononi in 1955–56; it has a lighter tone, with elements of the fantastic. The third, the ironically titled *In the Country of Salvation* (1990), describing a seriously dysfunctional Plymouth Brethren family in Auckland around 1960s, is his darkest novel yet. The fourth, *Always the Islands of Memory* (1991), reflects on the effects of the past on the present for two elderly sisters living in 1950s Te Aroha, and encountering most of the calamities of their era, from the Napier earthquake to the Tangiwai railway disaster; it is more like the second in tone. The fifth, *The Eye of the Everlasting Angel* (1992 UK, 1993 NZ), relating the picaresque adventures of a young man in London in the 1960s, is concerned with personal transformation. The most recent, *Sandspit Crossing* (1993 UK, 1994 NZ), is an episodic comedy set in Northland in the mid-twentieth century. Virtue's first published novels were widely praised for their freshness and originality. His subsequent fiction, however, has been criticised for its lack of development; for its obsession with the *puritanism of the post-war New Zealand of his youth; for its invention of period slang; and for its depiction of bizarre characters and unlikely events, as a New Zealand version of small-town American Gothic.

Virtue has also written two books of autobiography: *Among the Animals—A Zookeeper's Story* (1988) and *Once a Brethren Boy* (1995). The latter makes plain how much of his earlier fiction, especially, was derived from his own family experiences; how much homosexuality, a subtext in his fiction, is central to his life; and why, with 'haunted memory', he chose to live for an extended period in London and recreate New Zealand in his writings.   AM

Visual arts and literature, see **Art**.

VOGEL, Sir Julius (1835–99), was born and educated in London and moved to the Victorian goldfields in 1852, where he ran a drugstore and was editor of two papers, the *Inglewood Advertiser* and the *Talbot Leader*. In 1861 he followed the movement of the gold rush from Victoria to Otago, where he and a partner, W.H. Cutten (1822–83), founded the *Otago Daily Times*. With B.L. *Fargeon as manager, the paper was a brilliant success—and is still appearing daily. In 1868 Vogel was dismissed for obstinately insisting that the South Island should be politically separated from the North, so that only the latter need bear the costs of the New Zealand Wars. He founded another paper, *The Sun*, but soon abandoned it for politics.

Vogel is now best remembered for his dramatic borrowing policy, first as a Minister of the Crown, then as Premier (1872–76), under which the then enormous sum of £10 million was raised to build railways, roads and other items of infrastructure for the colonies.

Vogel was immensely energetic and imaginative and these qualities can be found in his visionary novel *Anno Domini 2000, or, Woman's Destiny* (1899). By the year 2000 'it has come to be accepted that the bodily power is greater in man, and the mental power larger in woman'. The British Empire has become 'United Britain'. At a meeting of the Federal Parliament in Melbourne, New Zealand is represented by the brilliant and lovely Hilda Richmond Fitzherbert. There is much love interest as she is first attracted to and then distressed by Lord Reginald Paramatta, while the Emperor is to marry the daughter of the female President of USA. This leads to a debate on gender equality and Vogel's description of the related political tensions is the finest part of the book: he had clearly learned something from *Trollope. A war between America and the Empire is entirely in the latter's favour, but the Emperor cannot bear to destroy the United States. And so all ends well: the United States President marries the captain of the ship *British Empire* and her daughter a British admiral. The people of New York State vote to rejoin the Empire and New York becomes the capital of Canada. In an epilogue the author assures us that all the marriages were happy. See also *Science fiction, *Utopian literature and *Women's suffrage.   NW

VOGT, Anton (1914–84), was a conspicuous figure in the Wellington literary scene of the 1950s. He was born in Oslo, and arrived in New Zealand in his youth. As a lecturer at Wellington Teachers' College (1949–59) he inspired or encouraged many students to write, among them James K. *Baxter, Louis *Johnson and Alistair *Campbell. He wrote a textbook, *English for Schools* (1953), which was widely used for many years.

Vogt wrote prolifically, contributing poems, short

stories and articles to numerous publications. His three verse collections move progressively away from Auden-esque satiric modernism (*Anti All That*, 1940) towards formal strictness and lyricism. *Poems for a War* (1943) has some of the iconoclasm and rhetorical belligerence of its predecessor—'As if it really mattered that we were eloquent and bitter'—but includes also some nostalgic, rather ★Georgian poems. This gentler vein prevails in *Love Poems* (1952), where historical models, especially the metaphysical conceit and the Petrarchan sonnet, are employed with technical virtuosity and eloquence. Reviewers of the time mistrusted these qualities, as inimical to sincerity and 'depth', and undervalued perhaps the poems' grace and vigour.

Vogt's contribution to *Poems Unpleasant* (with Baxter and Johnson, 1962) is boisterous satire in rough verse, mocking literary figures and politics and reflecting his taste for controversy. As a writer he exercised less influence than as a motivator and organiser, particularly of public readings which contributed much to a vigorous local flowering of poetry, and as an educator. He spent his last years in Menton, where he featured formidably in the experiences of several Katherine ★Mansfield Memorial Fellows there. JH

'Voyage, The', a short story by Katherine ★Mansfield, was written in August 1921 as the last of six stories commissioned by *The Sphere*, in which it was first published in December 1921. It was subsequently published in Mansfield's third collection *The Garden Party and Other Stories* (1922). The MS, on which it can be seen that Mansfield's working title was 'Going to Stay with her Granma', is in the Newberry Library, Chicago. The voyage referred to is that of Fenella Crane and her grandmother who travel by ferry from Wellington to Picton after the death of Fenella's mother. The story, largely written in Fenella's interior monologue, balances the wonder of a small girl's first ferry trip with the knowledge of death implied in the mourning dress worn by Fenella and her grandmother, in other adults' behaviour and in their oblique references to loss. The crossing is made at night and the dawn arrival at Picton is fitting for a story in which characters progress towards reconciliation with loss. In a 1922 letter to William Gerhardi, Mansfield made a rare comment on her imaginative method: '... when I wrote that little story I felt that I was on that very boat, going down those stairs, smelling the smell of the saloon.... Why—I don't know. It wasn't the memory of a real experience. It was a kind of *possession*. I might have remained the grandma forever if the wind had changed that moment.' ★Alpers characterises the six *Sphere* stories, written to help pay medical bills, as 'harming [Mansfield's] critical reputation'. However (unlike 'Sixpence', 'Mr and Mrs Dove', 'An Ideal Family' or 'Marriage à la Mode') 'The Voyage' and ★'Her First Ball' have thematic and technical qualities in common with some of Mansfield's best work. SSa

W

Wai-te-ata Press was established at Victoria University of Wellington in 1962 by D.F. McKenzie, professor of English, originally in two old garages in Wai-te-ata Road. Students of literary scholarship, paleography and bibliography were taught through practice aspects of early book production. Wai-te-ata became a small printing and publishing house, promoting university events and producing first edition poetry and prose, some very significant. Its cast-iron Stanhope Press of 1813, on permanent loan from Cambridge University Press, is the oldest printing machine in New Zealand. The collection of equipment also includes lead and wooden type and historic presses rescued from commercial printeries or on loan from individuals.

During the 1960s–70s, Wai-te-ata published volumes from such writers as Alistair *Campbell, James K. *Baxter, Peter *Bland, Sam *Hunt, Iain *Lonie and Bill *Manhire, and four issues of an occasional journal, *Words: Wai-te-ata Studies in Literature*, 1965–74 (mostly not on New Zealand subjects). Work of visual artists such as Robin White and Don Peebles was often featured, and in 1967 Waiteata Music Editions was established on the initiative of Douglas *Lilburn to print scores by New Zealand composers. Now a separate house under Jack Body, Waiteata Press Music remains a seminal force.

Don McKenzie's departure in 1986 caused a scaling down but in 1995 the University re-established Wai-te-ata through the creation of an Arts Faculty research fellowship. Now directed by Sydney J. Shep, it is a centre for information technology and communication theory as well as printing history. The fine printing division produces limited editions, notably to date poems by Alistair Campbell and Roma *Potiki.   SSh

Waiariki (1975), the first short story collection by Patricia *Grace.

Waiata is a word used to cover a wide variety of songs, traditional and modern, which might be used on special occasions but are often a part of everyday life. Margaret *Orbell remarks: 'The word "waiata" cannot be translated. The term is now also used to refer to all melodic songs including contemporary ones influenced by Western music.' For this reason scholars such as Charles Royal prefer the term *'mōteatea' for classical Māori compositions and modern ones in the classical style. In a narrower sense waiata were laments or complaints usually sung before an audience on a *marae. Orbell, writes: 'Their language is often elaborate, with specialised expressions and complex allusions. They were sung very slowly, with melodies in which endlessly inventive use was made of a small range of notes.' Kinds of waiata include waiata *tangi, or songs of grief or mourning, and two kinds of love song, both composed only by women.

The first of these, waiata *aroha, were 'songs of love and longing' (Orbell) and might well be used to influence the composer's family and that of her lover, or to persuade the lover himself. The second kind, waiata whaiāipo, 'sweetheart waiata', are bolder songs, witty and flirtatious, addressed to several men at once and serving for entertainment. Men sometimes adapted these songs to different purposes—one chief negotiating with another might use a waiata aroha to express his political 'affection' for his potential ally.

Waiata tangi were usually laments for the dead, although they could be sung for any great loss, including that of crops, or for serious illness. They were often sung at funerals, but could also be sung in memory of the dead on other occasions. An important function was to provide, on the one hand, a link to the past and, on the other, a bond for the survivors. Frequently they were composed for a particular person, but if that person was famous the song would survive by being performed at the funerals of his or her descendants. Some, such as Te Ika-here-ngutu's lament for his children, travelled far beyond their original regions and were sung by many who found the words appropriate to their own situation—in this case to that of elderly people who had lost younger relatives.

In the introduction to Part II of Ngā *Mōteatea, Pei Te Hurinui *Jones points out that 'laments' are the most numerous form of song, expressions of the pain of sorrow in intensely lamentatory language of longing and anguish, while scourging one's own flesh: 'the gods are called upon, and a farewell tribute is paid to the dead; following this comes the cursing of the men or people who did the killing, and then the cry is made to warrior relatives to go forth and seek revenge'. If the death was from natural causes, the last section could be replaced, as 'the poet describes the character and personality of the dead'. *Biggs points out that death is commonly related to some aspect of nature and 'the grief occasioned by death is likened to rain, to the moaning of the sea, or to biting winds' ('The Oral Literature of the Polynesians', Te *Ao Hou, 1964).

The texts of waiata are often highly allusive, assuming a knowledge of general and local traditions, so that they can be difficult for the unskilled to understand. In Polynesian Literature (1946) Johannes C. *Andersen points out that this is also true of 'many beautiful creations in English literature, such as "Lycidas", "Adonais" and other widely read favourites'. He suggests, too, that a song which may seem to a Pākehā merely a list of names can be very evocative to a Māori to whom 'every name is a fragment of history, or a picture, or both'.

The Māori tradition differs from the English, however, in that poetry and *music are not divorced from each other but constitute one indivisible unity. An interesting illustration of this is a recording of flute music made by Andersen, who discovered only a year later that words had been softly spoken into the flute (koauau) and could be distinguished on the recording. Mervyn McLean's Maori Music (1996) has a chapter on 'Recited Song and Dance Forms', but these are chanted on monotones or intoned in other ways which suggest that music is integral even to them. In the introduction to her 'select bibliography of traditional songs', The Poetic Genius of the Maori (1979), Leonie Sparrow makes this point: 'With the Māori tradition we are dealing with a blend of words and music, and an art form which, in pre-European times, had no valid existence out of its social and historical context.' A unexpected source of information on this latter point is S. Percy *Smith's Wars of the Northern Against the Southern Tribes of New Zealand in the Nineteenth Century (1904), which, says Sparrow, 'discusses all aspects of the oral literature of the Maori as a part of the total fabric of society'.

A different aspect of Māori poetry is discussed by Elsdon *Best in The Mythopoetic Maori: His Genius for Personification as Seen in His Mythological Concepts (New Plymouth, 1922), where personifications, allegorical fancies and metaphysical abstractions are pointed out, and seem to lift the texts beyond the 'social and historical'.

The coming of the European brought changes to waiata, the poets singing of their need to maintain *mana and their traditions, of protest against land-hungry Pākehā and songs by or about the great prophetic leaders, such as *Te Kooti. Often traditional songs were recomposed to suit a new occasion. Women like *Puhiwāhine and *Topeora continued to assert themselves in waiata, as they had always done.

The singing of waiata is a central feature of contemporary efforts to preserve and revive Māori language and customs. Thousands of waiata have survived in *Māori manuscripts and in early books and *Māori newspapers. Most of them have been neither edited nor translated. The leading twentieth-century scholars involved in conservation were Sir Apirana *Ngata and Dr Pei Te Hurinui *Jones. A rich source of printed texts are the volumes of the *Journal of the Polynesian Society. There are said to be innumerable manuscript books in Māori homes throughout New Zealand. Most important, many ancient waiata are still preserved by being sung on the *marae.   NW

Waiata-ā-ringa, or 'action songs', are a distinctly Māori form, even though they are modern rather than traditional and the European influence can be clearly felt. They evolved around the turn of the nineteenth to twentieth centuries from *haka and related dance-songs. The earliest printed record is in the programme of the Young Māori Party conference in 1908 and *Te Puea Herangi organised the first touring concert party. They seem to have become truly popular through the concert tours organised by Sir Apirana *Ngata during World War 1 to raise money for the Maori Soldiers' Fund. Many of the songs relate to the departure and return of soldiers, in both world wars, or to mourning their deaths. An example is 'Hitara Waha Huka', written in response to the death of Te-Moana-nui-a-Kiwa Ngārimu, VC posth., and translated by Barry *Mitcalfe: 'Hitler, frothy-mouth, wooden-head, / He's the man who wanted to fight, / Beaten here, beaten there, all over Russia, / You can wipe him and his deeds.' From such anger through tenderness to lyrical sadness, the emotional range of the songs is wide.

Today waiata-ā-ringa are a part of every popular Māori concert. Some of them have become so popular that they are national rather than purely Māori songs: in *New Zealand Studies*, Vol. 5, No. 2, 1995, Tīmoti *Kāretu remarks that he has heard 'E Pari Ra' played by pipe and brass bands 'on very ceremonial occasions'. However, he also notes that on the *marae even young people prefer to use traditional forms in connection with *whaikōrero.

In their performance guide, *Maori Action Songs* (1960), Alan Armstrong and Reupena Ngata write: 'The action song is ... a harmonious blending of the old and the new, it embodies the music and poetry which is the very soul of the race, and above all, it is a vigorous expression of ... pride and ... aspirations for the future.'
NW

Waikato 'is used indifferently as the name of a river, a confederation of Māori tribes, and the country inhabited by them', as John *Gorst wrote in *The Maori King* (1864). Gorst was the most assured analyst of the complex interracial politics leading up to the Waikato war of 1863–64. The war itself was recorded in a number of accounts, including William Fox's *The War in New Zealand* (1866), J.E. Alexander's *Bush Fighting* (1873), and John Featon's *The Waikato War 1863–4* (1879), and important later studies of the war include those by James *Cowan, *The New Zealand Wars and the Pioneering Period* (1922), and James Belich, *The New Zealand Wars and the Victorian Interpretation of Racial Conflict* (1986).

There are numerous pre-war descriptions of the Waikato region and people, variously emphasising missionary activities and Māori customs and literacy, the fertility of the land and Māori agricultural successes. Particularly clear descriptions may be found in W.R. Wade's *A Journey in the Northern Island of New Zealand* (1842), G.F. *Angas's *Savage Life and Scenes in Australia and New Zealand* (1847), Ernest *Dieffenbach's *Travels in New Zealand* (1843) and William Swainson's *Auckland, the Capital of New Zealand, and the Country Adjacent* (1853). Lady Mary Martin describes her 1846 journey through the region in *Our Maoris* (1884), reflecting presciently that 'Some day, doubtless, stately mansions will be built there, and the park-like ground be stocked with deer.'

The Waikato war and the years following have been popular subjects for fiction. Early novels include J.H. Kirby's *Henry Ancrum: a tale of the last war in New Zealand* (1872), H.B.M. *Watson's *The Web of the Spider* (1891), Rolf *Boldrewood's *War to the Knife, or Tangata Maori* (1899), and, undoubtedly the best of them, William *Satchell's *The *Greenstone Door* (1914), which culminates in the war years. Among several more recent novels, Errol *Brathwaite's *The Needle's Eye* (1965) and Maurice *Shadbolt's *Season of the Jew* (1986) contain excellent episodes from the war. The significant film *Rewi's Last Stand* (1939), written and directed by Rudall Hayward and put into novel form by A.W. *Reed, deals with the exploits of Rewi Maniapoto up to the battle of Orakau pā in April 1864, the climactic event of the war in this as in *The Greenstone Door*. The journalistic anecdotes of William *Baucke's *Where the White Man Treads* (1905), written when it was still believed that the Māori were a dying people, imply that the race reached its apogee in the war years, and proved ill suited to the conditions of peace and civilisation that followed. (See also *War literature: New Zealand Wars.)

A different kind of peace is the subject of Edward *Tregear's well-known poem 'Te Whetu Plains', written in the heart of the southern Waikato about 1870, where (though only 24!) he longs for the calm of 'the Death-Angel's kiss—/ But not, oh God, such peace, such ghastly peace as this.' For better or for worse something of that feeling has coloured much of the region's writing. Although Hamilton, the largest Waikato city, now has a population of 105 000, it had little more than 1000 at the turn of the century, and even thirty years ago was less than half its present size. Waikato literature has scarcely begun to be metropolitan. Johnson in John *Mulgan's *Man Alone* works on a Waikato farm for a while and later, still on the run towards Auckland, has a beer and a meal in Hamilton, a stop of about six hours. Buster O'Leary disports himself with Fanny Hohepa on a farm near Paeroa for a time in Maurice *Duggan's *'Along Rideout Road that Summer', but realises finally it's not the life for him after all. The best poem by World War 2 casualty Donald McDonald from Ngaroma, miles from anywhere in the wild country between Mangakino and Arapuni, is 'Ngaroma'. Frank *Sargeson's rural stories bear many Waikato and King Country landscape impressions, but of all his stories only perhaps 'The Colonel's Daughter' is set in Hamilton. Born in Hamilton in 1903, his complex reasons for leaving the town in 1925 are told in his Waikato-based memoir *Once is Enough* (1973), in which his love for the mountains and bush of the region is overshadowed by the pressures of small-town respectability. Oddly enough in that book, it is not far from Tregear's Te Whetu that Sargeson sees from the Hamilton bus a bleak Mamaku landscape like 'the desolate surface of some other planet' and finds himself contemplating 'the perfect symbol of my own inner desolation'. The popular romance novels of Mary *Scott, the children's fiction of Joyce *West, and Philip *Wilson's race-relations novels *The Outcasts* (1965) and *New Zealand Jack* (1973), like Maurice *Shadbolt's *Among the Cinders* (1965), belong in the lonely farms and marginal lands of the Waikato–King Country region. In the solitude of Waikato's west coast near Kawhia, James *McNeish wrote the anecdotal studies of a small community *As for the Godwits* (1977) and *The Man from Nowhere, and Other Prose* (1991).

From the 1930s until his death in 1965 Blackwood Paul, one of the Auckland University College *Phoenix group, developed the family bookselling business in Hamilton into Paul's Book Arcade, probably the best bookshop in the country. In 1936 he became New Zealand agent for Gollancz's *Left Book Club. He and his wife Janet Wilkinson met as committee members of the *Progressive Publishing Society, a venture intended to publish books on New Zealand matters at affordable prices, and as publishers they pursued that policy themselves from 1945 under the imprint that became *Blackwood and Janet Paul. 'They put Hamilton on the map as a publishing centre', as John Mansfield *Thomson has written, seeing them to have played a role crucial in those decades to the evolution of a New Zealand literature.

Vincent *O'Sullivan's novel, *Let the River Stand* (1993), set in central Waikato farmland, is the most successful Waikato novel in its evocation of life in the region from the Edwardian period to mid-century. It is the one Waikato novel so far genuinely metropolitan in temper, breaking the myth of regional isolation. Many of O'Sullivan's short stories also deal with the Waikato, and so does much of his poetry, making him a major writer of the region where he lived 1969–78. The Aucklander C.K. *Stead's recent novel *The *Singing Whakapapa* (1994) has as one of its strands the CMS mission at Matamata during the pre-European wars between Te Waharoa and the Arawa in the 1830s, with the figure of Stead's forebear John Flatt in that context. A younger Waikato writer of fictions of considerable power is John *Cranna. Other interesting contemporary fiction writers include Gaelyn *Gordon, Beryl *Fletcher, Katerina *Mataira, Fleur *Beale and Joan Druett.

The Auckland poet A.R.D. *Fairburn remarked while travelling through the Waikato that 'the squalid tea of Mercer is not strained'. Some reasons why may be found in the works of Waikato poets, some born there, some choosing to live there, among them Jan *Kemp, Murray *Edmond, K.O. *Arvidson, Hirini *Melbourne, Heather *McPherson, Joanna *Paul and Alan *Riach.

KA

Waka is often translated as 'canoe', but Ranginui *Walker and others have objected to this word, imported from Native American languages, being used for vessels of a very different culture. In particular, the large ocean-going vessels which carried the original Māori from *Hawaiki are diminished by the translation. The Māori sense of identity involves a hierarchy of kin groups, such as *whānau (extended family), *hapū (sub-tribe) and *iwi (tribe). The largest of these is the 'waka', to which a group of tribes belongs, and according to mythology these vessels carried the ancestors to New Zealand. Well-known waka include Aotea, Te Arawa, Horouta, Kura-hau-pō, Mātātua, Tainui, Tākitimu and Tokomaru. The theory that they came in a 'Great Fleet' is now discounted.

NW

WAKEFIELD, Edward Gibbon (1796–1862), published his theories of colonisation—a pastiche of classical economics, utilitarianism and social engineering—in *A Letter from Sydney* (1829). Masquerading as fact, the book's explicit perspective of intimate involvement with Australian settlement should rightfully rank it among the best imaginative fictions about Australasian colonisation. Wakefield, who was yet to travel outside the Northern Hemisphere, had in fact penned it while languishing in Newgate gaol, serving three years for abducting 15-year-old heiress Ellen Turner in 1826. Released in 1830, Wakefield's theories ensured him an influential role in the reformist National Colonisation Society. Although past misdeeds excluded him from active involvement in politics, as a director of the New Zealand Company between 1840 and 1849 he exerted considerable sway behind the scenes. With respect to New Zealand, he was instrumental in formulating policies—for example, on land division and the make-up of the Pākehā majority through stringent selection criteria for immigrants—that proved instrumental in dispossessing and alienating Māori. From 1850 Wakefield worked towards self-government for New Zealand and, in 1852, departed from England to enter the New Zealand parliament. But his ambition led to a grave miscalculation when a political crisis that he engineered backfired, forcing his resignation from office in 1855. Deeply depressed, he died seven years later. See A.J. Harrop's *The Amazing Career of Edward Gibbon Wakefield* (1928); P. Stuart's *Edward Gibbon Wakefield in New Zealand* (1971); *The Collected Works of Edward Gibbon Wakefield*, ed. M.F. Lloyd Prichard (1969); and *Edward Gibbon Wakefield and the Colonial Dream: A Reconsideration* (1997).

PM

WAKEFIELD, Edward Jerningham (1820–79), born in London, was the son of Edward Gibbon *Wakefield, founder of the New Zealand Company and nephew of William Wakefield, the leader of the first Company settlers. In 1839 he accompanied his uncle with the advance party in the search for suitable sites for settlement. He made overland journeys and took part in establishing the Company's presence in Wellington and Wanganui, where he had a reputation for being a wild young man. His Māori nickname, he wrote, was 'Tiraweke, the name of a small bird … known … for its chattering propensities'. He returned to London in 1845, after being publicly rebuked by Governor FitzRoy, and wrote *Adventure in New Zealand* from the diary-letters he had sent home. He returned to New Zealand with the first Canterbury settlers in 1850. A broken political career followed where he generally took a populist stand. In 1863 he married, but his family suffered along with his political and other activities because of his drinking. Eventually he died in the Ashburton Old Man's Home, 'an asylum for the aged and indigent', as the *Ashburton Mail* recorded it. *Adventure in New Zealand* lives up to its title, tells a good story and is written with pace and imagination. The numerous passages attesting to the impeccable intentions of the New Zealand Company are tedious but his pillorying of persons and arguments which do not share his view of the Company invigorates the book. Uncritically read it misleads, but if the blatant bias is allowed for, *Adventure in New Zealand* is the most lively first-hand account of the early years of settlement. His 1845 *London Journal* contains brief diary entries of his life, loves, parties, politics, books and drinking friends, one of whom was apparently the convivial novelist Thackeray. RG

WALKER, Ranginui (1932–), Whakatōhea, associate professor of Māori studies at Auckland University (Te Wānanga o Waipapa), became known to the broader public in the 1980s with his regular columns in *NZ Listener* and *Metro, although he had published many academic papers before that. The wide range of his interests makes his writing an invaluable source of information on Māori literature, as well as many other topics. His book-length publications include *Ngā Tau Tohetohe* (1987), a collection of his finest columns, and *Ka Whawhai tonu Mātou: Struggle without End* (1990), an unusual book of Māori history, as well as more specialised works: *The Political Development of the Māori People in New Zealand* (1984), *The Meaning of Biculturalism* (1986), *History of Māori Activism* (1983), *The Treaty of Waitangi* (1983), *Perceptions and Attitudes of the New Generation of Māoris to Pākehā Domination* (1981), *Liberating Māori from Educational Subjection* (1991) and *Ngā Mamae o te Iwi Māori: Te Ripoata o te Hui i Tūrangawaewae* (1987). NW

WALL, Arnold (1869–1966), professor, poet and prolific journalist, born in Ceylon (Sri Lanka), left Britain in 1899 to take up the chair of English at Canterbury University College, a position he held until his retirement in 1932. A medievalist and philologist, Wall was known as a less than charismatic teacher but a noted if abrasive proponent of university reforms. In a retirement that exceeded his professorial career in length he became nationally prominent as a newspaper columnist; he wrote an influential prescriptive work, *New Zealand English* (1938), which aimed to remedy what he saw as the inaccuracies and slovenliness of New Zealand pronunciation; and he is best remembered for the weekly radio broadcasts on English language and usage which he gave from 1955 to 1961 under the title of 'The Queen's English'. He began a new weekly newspaper column at the age of 91, 'The Jeweller's Window', and this was still running when he died. He had also been a notable amateur botanist, writing numerous scientific papers on New Zealand's alpine and subalpine flora.

Not least Wall was a prolific lifelong poet, from unpublished juvenilia to a poem 'On His 96th Birthday' written shortly before his death. Most of his poems first appeared (usually one at a time) in New Zealand newspapers or the Sydney *Bulletin. Of his ten published collections the most notable are *London Lost* (1922) and *The Pioneers and Other Poems* (1948), the latter containing 361 poems prematurely offered as a 'final' selection of his work. His poetry is mostly traditional rhyming verse, intellectual and reflective rather than passionate in tone, but with a very broad sweep of theme and subject. A lengthy review of *The Pioneers* by Douglas *Stewart in the *Bulletin* in 1949 gave the collection warm praise for its creation of a rich and varied world and its 'reflection of a completely civilised mind'. Wall's work is represented in all the early anthologies of New Zealand verse up to and including Allen *Curnow's 1945 *Book of New Zealand Verse*, the revised edition of 1951 and Curnow's 1960 *Penguin Book of New Zealand Verse*. (Wall was Curnow's uncle by marriage.) Since then his poetry has attracted less attention, although the Oxford *Anthology of New Zealand Poetry in English* (1997) includes two poems. On the publication of Wall's memoir, *Long and Happy*, in 1965, Curnow wrote, 'Conscience must tell any annotator of the New Zealand verse record that there is more art and less pretence in his kind of work than in a good deal that now passes for poet's currency.' TD

WALLIS, Redmond (1933–), novelist, a fourth-generation New Zealander, was born in Christchurch, studied science at high school but graduated BA in modern history at University of Canterbury in 1956, and then worked as a science and political journalist. Unusual because it portrays an explicitly *Existentialist *'Man Alone', Wallis' first novel, *Point of Origin* (1962), earned him a Scholarship in Letters in 1963. The narrative follows the progress of Peter Hennessy, a young man of scientific bent whose father was cheated out of a farm by a dishonest landowner. Hennessy's development from alienated victim into a character who realises his Sartrean freedom is confirmed when he describes himself as a 'point' which would plot its own curve on the graph of Christchurch. In London Wallis was a journalist and editorial director of a publishing house. Later novels are juvenile science fiction written in Spain and London.

DB

WALPOLE, Hugh (1884–1941), best-selling English novelist, was born in Auckland, where his English father was in his second year as vicar of St Mary's, Parnell (later the Cathedral). The family moved on in 1889 to a more challenging clerical post in New York. At the age of 9 Hugh was sent to England for school and later Cambridge. After work as a teacher and reviewer, he wrote *The Wooden Horse* (1910), partly autobiographical and partly set in Auckland. With *Mr. Perrin and Mr. Traill* (1911), a convincing story of staff-room rivalry, Walpole began to win his vast middle-class readership. *The Dark Forest* (1916), *The Cathedral* (1922), the historical-adventure four-volume *Herries Chronicle* (1930–33), and others, made him one of the most financially successful novelists of his time. He also wrote popular literary studies, for instance of Conrad (1916) and Trollope (1928). He was knighted in 1937. His fame was sufficient by 1924 for Hector ★Bolitho to report (in *The Bookman*) that the people of Auckland 'are very proud … that a "great" man was born there'. The sentiment is unlikely to be heard today. The refined, English-born Mrs Parker in Frank ★Sargeson's story 'The Hole That Jack Dug' (1945) has read 'more than ten books by an author called Hugh Walpole', but when the Kiwi narrator tried one, 'I never got past the first chapter'.   RR

War literature: New Zealand Wars. The imaginative literature of the wars between the European colonisers and the Māori colonised began even while they were in progress. The term 'imaginative' can only be relative in the case of Major ★Stoney's ★*Taranaki* (1861), since its subtitle affirms that the 'tale' is combined with 'A Description of the Province' and that the account of the war is 'chiefly taken from despatches'. The fiction is flimsy and the narrative obscure, but there is some (presumably) first-hand information about the tensions in New Plymouth when the settlers in Taranaki had withdrawn from their farms into the city to avoid massacre. One reason for the inconclusiveness of the plot must be that the book was published before the Taranaki conflict itself was at an end. This is no historical novel.

The first campaign in Taranaki occurred in 1860–61 and was followed by another in 1863. It was not until after the action at Moturoa in November 1868 that the Taranaki Māori grew quieter, though still not overcome.

The causes of war were complex, but essentially the desire of the newcomers to occupy land, combined with vastly different concepts of land ownership, inevitably led to conflict. This was exacerbated by other cultural differences, as in all colonial conflicts. For Stoney the advance of 'progress' was being slowed down a little, but his final words suggest that British dreams for New Zealand are bound to succeed: his heroes will 'once more convert the desolated waste to the flowering glade, and the ruined and devastated sites of their former homes to new and still more happy abodes'. In short the tendency of this book is not historical but prophetic—British decency will conquer all.

This is similar to the message of *The Last of the Waikatos: A Sensational Tale of the Province of Auckland* 'dedicated to the volunteers of New Zealand, by Comus' (1873). Again the borderline between fact and fiction seems flimsy, so much so that ★Hocken thought that this was a non-fictional account of the Waikato wars. In fact, its tendency is futuristic. (See also ★Waikato.) The advance of the British general Cameron into the Waikato region in 1863 can only be called an act of aggression. It aimed to thin out the concentration of Māori forces in Taranaki, create a safe zone around Auckland, occupy the rich lands of the Waikato, where the Māori were growing produce to feed Auckland, and extend British authority over people who had not yet accepted it. *The Last of the Waikatos* exults in the destruction of the people, telling of an invasion of the King Country (not under British authority when the book appeared) and, like Stoney's book, ending with a vision of a glorious future: 'There was now a thorough understanding with the natives; the new territory was rapidly peopled with Europeans, roads were cut in all directions, and everyone looked forward with confidence to the future.' 'Comus' was John ★Featon, whose genuinely historical *The Waikato War* (1923) is a lively, readable but biased account.

A different case is that of J.H. Kirby's two-volume *Henry Ancrum, a tale of the last war in New Zealand* (1872), which has as much to do with settler life—musical entertainments, 'soirees dansants', fashionable conversation—as with the wars. It is also a love romance. Henry falls in love with Edith, takes part in a brief skirmish in Taranaki, returns to social life in Auckland and then joins the Waikato campaign. Again many pages are occupied with descriptions and information that have little relevance to the fiction. There is, for example, some account of the ★Māori newspapers issued in the Waikato. And there is much argumentation against the humanists of Exeter Hall. For most of the second volume Henry is captive to Māori and in danger of losing his heart to a woman in their camp, but all ends happily though melodramatically—the war being little more than a romantic background. With *Henry Ancrum* the 'historical' accounts begin, overlapping by a year the 'prophetic account' of *The Last of the Waikatos*.

Joan ★Stevens says of what follows: 'With Fenimore Cooper, G.A. Henty, and later Rider Haggard to copy, who could go wrong? You needed only the hero, preferably of officer caste, a Maori princess or a settler's daughter or both, tribal jealousies, a ★tohunga or two, some military skirmishes, a few blood-curdling yells, and the trick was done. Mix well with muskets and inaccurate Maori, and serve up to a London publisher.' One of the earliest to follow this recipe was Emilia ★Marryat with her *Amongst the Maoris* (1874), again almost more fact than fiction—except that the facts are questionable. Robert P. Whitworth in *Hine-Ra, or, The Maori Scout: A Romance of the New Zealand War* (1887) compares Māori with dogs, chimpanzees, tigers and spiders, yet Frank, the bold hero, befriends the lovely Hine-Ra and the fine and upright Matariki. The segment of war covered includes the final Waikato battle at Orakau, exploiting the myth that surrounds it, but concentrates especially on the Hauhau (a post-Christian religion founded by ★Te Ua Haumene), presumably because this movement seemed convenient to writers who wished to demonise the Māori enemy.

The two novels of A.A. Fraser, *Daddy Crips' Waifs, a tale of Australasian life and adventure* (1886) and *Raromi, or, The Maori Chief's Heir* (1888), were published by The Religious Tract Society of London, intended to blend instruction with entertainment. In both, the wars provide an opportunity for young men (one is actually called Noble) to demonstrate courage. 'A Tale of Adventure' is also the subtitle of H.B. Marriott ★Watson's *The Web of the Spider* (1891), and clearly the thrill of adventure is the motive of most of these novels of late empire. British schoolboys could identify with the successful colonising daredevils. The spider is Te Katipo, a Hauhau chief, not so much a monster as sarcastic villain ('Come, we cannot stand talking here. You are my prisoners; you must yield to the power of the despicable Maori.') The hero is called Palliser and has, as often in such adventures, his share of pretty women to protect.

Even the master of the colonising novel, G.A. Henty, had one attempt at a New Zealand novel. *Maori and Settler: A Story of the New Zealand War* (1890) was only one of some eighty adventure stories he wrote as he sailed the seas in luxury ships (… *A Tale of Hotspur and Glendower*, … *A Tale of Bush Life in Australia*, … *A Tale of the Zulu and Boer Wars* and so on). Like the early tales of future hope, this ends happily: the 1911 reprint assures readers that 'there are many breathless moments in which the odds seem hopelessly against the party; but

they succeed in the end in establishing themselves happily in one of the pleasantest of New Zealand valleys'.

Ngamihi, or, The Maori Chief's Daughter: A Tale of the War in New Zealand (1895) by Robert H. Scott opens with a chapter on the 'General Character and Superstition of the Maoris' and interrupts its story often for such informative tidbits. It has the rescue of a lovely young woman from a Māori, the murder of the missionary Volkner, a couple of earthquakes ('as a rule, however, earthquakes of recent years have not been productive of fatal results'), hot springs, volcanoes, a wild boar hunt, 'A Tale of the West Indies', a comic Irishman, some sea yarns, to say nothing of 'Miss Munroe's Thrilling Experiences', all similar to stage melodramas such as *The ★Land of the Moa*, which toured in the year in which the novel was published. Although the author ungrammatically claims that 'the following narrative of events … are taken directly from my diary written at the second Maori War', it is hard to trace much war in the story, though blood flows copiously at times.

Rolf ★Boldrewood's *War to the Knife, or, Tangata Maori* (1899) also has much to do before the war starts in the middle of the book. At last the aristocratic hero, Massinger, joins the Forest Rangers and goes to war with von Tempsky. This German adventurer and artist and his voluntary guerilla forces captured the New Zealand imagination; he was killed in battle against the Taranaki chief Tītokowaru at his fortress of Te Ngutu-o-te-Manu in 1868. Boldrewood treats him as a romantic hero worthy of German opera. His Māori foes are described as 'gallant' and ironically compared to Britons defending their lands against the invading Romans.

A curiosity is *Liebet Eure Feinde* (1891) by Rev. Jos. Spillmann, S.J., published in Freiburg im Breisgau. An English translation, *Love Your Enemies*, was published by the same publisher (Herder) in 1895. Injured by Māori warriors, Patrick O'Neal says in delirium 'Love your enemies', remembering that a Christian Māori had used those very words, and when he recovers he says 'I consider the war unjust…. The Maoris have been, for the most part, shamefully deceived, and they fight in defence of their home.' When at the end Māori and Pākehā alike are welcomed to the bosom of the Church, 'Such were the rich fruits of the love of enemies.'

By the turn of the century the wars already seemed less relevant to the agricultural peace of the country. Not until 1911, when James ★Cowan published *The Adventures of Kimble Bent: A Story of Wild Life in the New Zealand Bush* did another literary account appear. Its preface begins 'This book is not a work of fiction', but its subtitle suggests that it wants to tap the market for adventure stories and much of its telling is indistinguishable from the novels already discussed, apart from the fact that Cowan writes better. It tells of a British soldier captured by Māori and fighting with them against his comrades—a story later taken up by Maurice *Shadbolt. It is a well-told account of the war of Tītokowaru from the point of view of a participant.

The finest of all fictional treatments of the wars is William *Satchell's The *Greenstone Door, with its neutral figure who internalises the conflict psychologically, demonstrating its divisive nature yet forging its sides into a unity. This is a discourse on the nature of conflict in narrative form more than a mere adventure story.

Mona *Tracy revived the adventure formula in Rifle and Tomahawk: A Stirring Tale of the Te Kooti Rebellion (1927), treating a later phase of the war with the religious leader *Te Kooti, while A.W. *Reed retold the story of Rudall Hayward's film in Rewi's Last Stand (1939). This uses (the word is precise) the battle of Orakau at the end of the Waikato campaign.

Apart from these sporadic revivals of adventure myths, the wars disappeared for some decades as a subject. More than thirty years passed before the next novels, Leo Fowler's Brown Conflict: A Tale of White Man and Maori (1959), and three novels in 1960: Mary Bravender by Olga *Stringfellow, Black Noon at Ngutu by Frank *Bruno and Dorothy *Eden's Sleep in the Woods. Fowler follows Satchell with a narrator who stands between the conflicting parties, but he alters the balance subtly to take up a pro-Māori stance; his unrelenting seriousness and scholarship can lose the reader's concentration. Mary Bravender (published in the USA as The Flesh and the Salt) also has such a mediating figure in Chase Pendennis, the confidant of Māori chiefs and of the government. Mary also has faithful friends among the Māori and eventually overcomes her initial dislike of Pendennis. Unlike similar love stories, this one lets the more serious themes move into the foreground. Frank Bruno was once a boxer and pummels the poor panicking reader with vigorous, venomous, violent alliteration. His story tells of the siege of Tītokowaru's fortress Te Ngutu-o-Manu in Taranaki. Dorothy Eden lets her heroine take in the social life of Wellington before sending her out to face Te Kooti and the Hauhau in the second half of the novel. Briar can wield a handy rifle, but the main theme is the burgeoning of love. Another romance, A Falcon Rising (1960) by Catherine *Hay uses the conflicts as merely exotic background. Serious literary engagement with the wars resumed with a well-researched trilogy: Errol *Brathwaite's The Flying Fish (1964), The Needle's Eye (1965) and The Evil Day (1967). Although readers must put in some work to follow the course of events and the sequence of battles, these books are a skilful and mature account of men (almost without women) at war.

The gaps in the development of fictional accounts of the New Zealand Wars suggest that for more than half of the twentieth century they faded from the imagination of the country. The sudden flourish of good and bad novels in the 1960s then seems to anticipate the concern with the meaning of the Treaty of Waitangi and the history of Māori–Pākehā relations which has been one of the most prominent strands in New Zealand thought and literature during the last quarter of the century.

For James *Sanders in his Fire in the Forest (1975), as for Brathwaite, the colourful figure of von Tempsky and his Forest Rangers served as inspiration. Brathwaite turned the German into a Welsh officer named Williams, but Sanders retains von Tempsky's name and reputation to build up a romantic account of saving a captured European from 'savage' Māori. For younger readers G.K. Saunders in The Forest Rangers offers a 15-year-old hero, but of the many recent children's books of the wars, the most impressive is R.L. *Bacon's Again, the Bugle's Blow (1973). Its success is due to the device of letting a contemporary Māori boy, Rua, slip through a time warp into the wars, so that the relationship betwen past and present is always vivid to the young reader. Rua experiences the legendary battle of Orakau and reflects on its relevance. Other treatments include Keith Aberdein's The Governor (1977), a fictionalised life of George *Grey based on the author's television script, which approaches the wars from a political standpoint; and Ray Grover's Cork of War: Ngati Toa and the British Mission, an historical narrative (1982). This is something of a sport, deeply researched, illustrated with original pioneer paintings and drawings, with detailed footnotes and a long bibliography, but presented as a novel. The narrator, married to a Ngāti Toa, lives uncomfortably but observantly between the contestants. Unfortunately he often sounds like a twentieth-century historian, so that some confusion of genres detracts from a book that is a considerable and humane achievement, notable for its sensitivity to the Māori point of view and for dealing with tensions in the Wellington region, rather than the more familiar Taranaki or Waikato campaigns.

In 1986 three books were published which revealed new attitudes to the New Zealand Wars. James *Belich's historical The New Zealand Wars and the Victorian Interpretation of Racial Conflict radically revised past accounts by pointing out just how often the Māori were successful in battle and how near they came to winning the war. Belich also examines the way such conflicts have been reported, offering a history not only of the wars but of the perception of war. Maurice Shadbolt's Season of the Jew was influenced by conversations with Belich, but takes a more pro-Pākehā stand, and Witi *Ihimaera's The *Matriarch makes the wars central to a wider presentation of crucial New Zealand issues.

Neither Ihimaera nor Shadbolt achieves the moral balance of *The Greenstone Door*, and the difference reveals a growing gulf between views of the wars and of the Māori–Pākehā relationship in general between 1914 and 1986. In Shadbolt's novel Te Kooti learns his warfare and even his pro-Māori attitudes from studying Europeans such as Garibaldi, while in Ihimaera's he draws on Māori traditions. A comparison of the way these novels present the action at Matawhero ('massacre' or 'retaliation'?) is revealing. Ihimaera's narrator identifies with Te Kooti himself, Shadbolt's with the British soldier Fairweather. For Shadbolt the destruction of the home and family of Major Biggs is a dreadful bloodbath; Ihimaera's narrator deliberately avoids the description of blood and chooses to describe the death as a drowning instead. The death itself takes place in a subordinate clause, and seems justified by the sheer injustice of Pākehā occupation of the land.

Shadbolt followed his novel with two more (see ★New Zealand Wars trilogy), but the three books of 1986 are most revealing of the divisions between the viewpoint of a historian, a Pākehā novelist and a Māori novelist. NW

War literature: Boer War (1899–1902).

New Zealand's twentieth century involvement in warfare began with the enthusiastic dispatch of troops to the Boer War. While no writing of any quality emerged, there was prolific journalistic treatment of the campaign, including a prize-winning short story by H. Dobbie in the *New Zealand Graphic* (Christmas Number, 1900). This has its hero awarded the Victoria Cross and returning, wounded, to claim his beautiful bride. But it was not till 1949 that a brief account by D.O.W. Hall of *The New Zealanders in South Africa, 1899–1902* was belatedly published by the War History Branch of the Department of Internal Affairs. More informative is a historical narrative compiled by Richard Stowers, *Kiwi Versus Boer* (1992) and a brief history of the Mounted Rifles entitled *First New Zealanders to the Boer War 1899* (1899). A succinct and highly readable account of the defence policy build-up to New Zealand's involvement in both the Boer War and World War 1 is in Ian McGibbon's *The Path to Gallipoli* (1991).

Among documents closer to the time, Sarah Elizabeth Hawdon's *New Zealanders and the Boer War* (1902?) is interesting for its account of the country's patriotic response to the war, while pamphlets which attacked participation include *Freedom of Thought and Speech in New Zealand, Nos 1 and 2* (1900) by J. Gratton Grey. Grey was expelled from his post as chief reporter of *Hansard* for writing a letter to the *New York Times* which condemned New Zealand's involvement. His second pamphlet contains details about opposition to the war and the conduct of the Boers. Several personal narratives supply details about the campaign. Joseph Linklater in his *On Active Service in South Africa with 'The Silent Sixth'* (1904) writes in diary form about daily soldiering and comments about ridiculous distinctions between officers and men in the British Army; Ted Andrews in *Kiwi Trooper* (1967) tells the story of Queen Alexandra's Own Mounted Rifles with chapters on the regiment's part in the Boer War; James G. Harle Moore's *With the Fourth New Zealand Rough Riders* (1906) gives his impressions of the South African countryside and its natives; and *With the New Zealanders at the Front* (1902) by F. Twistleton supplies details of twelve months' campaigning. H.P. Valintine's *Ten Weeks a Prisoner of War* (1901) is the only personal narrative by a captive of the Boers, giving them credit for the consideration they showed. Trooper Frank Perham's *The Kimberley Flying Column* (1958?) has detail about life in the field, trekking through the countryside, raiding livestock, rounding up women and children and guerilla warfare.   LC

War literature: World War 1 (1914–18).

The First World War, for all its devastating casualties and patriotic fervour, produced little literature of lasting or distinctive quality. John A. ★Lee's *Civilian into Soldier* (1937) is notable as a realistic account of an infantry soldier's combat experiences on the Western Front, and his *Soldier* (1976) deals with the loss of his arm and a brief love affair while convalescing in a military hospital in England. Robin ★Hyde's biographical novel, ★*Passport to Hell* (1936), tells the story of James Douglas Stark, bomber, 5th Regiment NZEF in France, and the sequel, ★*Nor the Years Condemn* (1938) is a brilliant treatment of the post-war years that follows the struggles of 'Starkie' and his mates through the vicissitudes of ★Depression and hardship.

Personal narratives from World War 1 abound, but the best of them is Alexander Aitken's *Gallipoli to the Somme* (1963). A professor of mathematics, Aitken writes with precision about his life as an infantry soldier on the Western Front. Roy F. Ellis in *By Wires to Victory* (1968) describes the work of the NZ Divisional Signals Company. O.E. Burton in *The Silent Division* (1935) recalls his experiences at the front. William Taylor in *The Twilight Hour* (1978) writes about his part in operations on the Somme and at Messines and recounts how on discharge he went back to his old job on Puketiti Station where his employer welcomed him with 'Here you are, all back again.' 'Not all of us, Boss,' replied Taylor thoughtfully.

Much anecdotal information from diaries, letters and interviews about the campaigns is contained in Nicholas Boyack, *Behind the Lines* (1989); J. Phillips, N. Boyack and E.P. Malone, *The Great Adventure* (1988); and N.

Boyack and Jane Tolerton, *In the Shadow of War* (1990). However, the most impressive of the narrative genre is Maurice *Shadbolt's *Voices of Gallipoli* (1988). This is a fictionalised presentation of the matter-of-fact utterances of twelve actual survivors of the great Gallipoli misadventure, reworking some of the material on which he based his play *Once on Chunuk Bair* (1982), one of the best subsequent imaginative recreations of the war. Like the play, *Voices* debunks some of the sentimental platitudes and military clichés that have obscured the Gallipoli experience.

Recent historical writing has also re-explored the meaning of the campaign and its contemporary significance. Christopher Pugsley's *Gallipoli: The New Zealand Story* (1984) discusses the dual meaning of *Anzac Day as both a symbol of willingness to 'share the burdens of Empire' and a source of national identity. In *Scars on the Heart* (1997) and *Anzac: The New Zealanders at Gallipoli* (1995) Pugsley notes that Anzac Day is an occasion of comradeship that has also become an opportunity of discovery for the contemporary generation. Alistair Te Ariki *Campbell's poem, 'Elegy for Anzac Day', carries implications of this, too. However, 'Anzac, Spirit of', a poem in *The Iron Hand* (1979) by Les Cleveland, visualises the Dardanelles landing as a futile thunder rite and draws a comparison between fanatic Turks and the angry peasants of Vietnam. Kevin *Ireland's 'Selected Poems' (1997) bears the title *Anzac Day*. Ironically, the first poem is 'Antic Hay', but 'Anzac Day, Devonport' comments on the meaning of the day for various generations.

First World War poetry is for the most part unmemorable, but the popular ephemera of the day contain a few amusing examples of soldiers' verse. For example, *New Zealand at the Front* (1918), a compilation by members of the Division, as well as some excellent line drawings, has poems about life in the trenches, going on leave, news from home, and other predictable topics. A few prose items and occasional verses by troops are also to be found in *The Kia Ora Coo-ee* (reprinted 1981), a magazine for Anzacs in the Middle East.

Aspects of World War 1 other than the fighting itself have produced some challenging works. Christopher Pugsley's *On the Fringe of Hell* (1991) examines the severities of military discipline. Archibald *Baxter's *We Will Not Cease* (1939) is an account of the oppressive treatment of conscientious objectors, and *Armageddon or Calvary* (1919) by H.E. *Holland protests at the illegal deportation of a group of conscientious objectors to France and their ill-treatment and torture. Sexual problems of the soldiery are examined by Jane Tolerton in *Ettie Rout* (1992), a biography of a woman who ran a pioneering social and sexual welfare service for New Zealand troops.

A four-volume 'Popular History Series' covers the principal campaigns in which New Zealanders served. This treatment is augmented by A.R.D. Carbery's *The New Zealand Medical Service in the Great War 1914–1918* (1924) as well as a number of unit histories. The part played by the Māori contingent and the Pioneer Battalion on Gallipoli and in France and in Flanders is described by James *Cowan in *The Maoris in the Great War* (1926). *Sons of Te Ramaroa* by Joan Leaf (1983) contains interviews and biographical details about the men of South Hokianga in World Wars 1 and 2.   LC

War literature: World War 2 (1939–45). The activities of New Zealand forces are comprehensively covered in the extensive *Official History of New Zealand in the Second World War* published by the War History Branch of the Department of Internal Affairs. This consists of campaign and service volumes, unit histories and a three-volume series, *The New Zealand People at War*.

Another series of thirteen unofficial narratives deals with the history of units of the Third NZ Division in the Pacific theatre from 1940 to 1944, when the force was disbanded. Other historical works that explore significant aspects of the War are W.D. McIntyre's *New Zealand Prepares for War* (1988), which analyses defence policy in the period before hostilities began; Sheryal Kendall and David Corbett's *New Zealand Military Nursing* (1990), a history of the Royal New Zealand Nursing Corps; Colin R. Larsen's *Pacific Commandos* (1946), an account of New Zealanders and Fijians in action; J.E. Sanders's *Desert Patrols* (1976), dealing with the New Zealanders in the Long Range Desert Group; *New Zealand at War* (1946) by K.R. Hancock, and an unofficial account of the war effort both overseas and at home; and *War Memorial* (1989) by Laurie Barber, a particularly useful chronology of New Zealand's war effort.

Most of the official unit histories make specialised and rather pedestrian reading, except for two that are enriched by informal glimpses of ordinary soldiers' lives and feelings. S.P. Llewellyn's *Journey Towards Christmas* (1st Ammunition Company) (1949) has many memorable descriptive passages, including a vivid treatment of Crown and Anchor games in the Naafi at Helwan in Egypt, a dance in Trieste with violins, drums and saxophones, girls laughing and the sounds mixed in the warm air 'with burnt petrol, magnolias, mosquitoes, the soft, rain-remembering dust', and crowds shouting '*Viva I Neo Zelandia! Viva la Liberazione!*'. Similarly, Jim Henderson, in *22 Battalion* (1950), writes sensitively of the feelings of ordinary soldiers. His own experience of being wounded and undergoing amputation while a prisoner of war is graphically related in his *Gunner Inglorious* (1945). His *Soldier Country* (1978) is a miscellany of sketches, yarns and memoirs that explore the experiences of a great many combatants. Other non-fictional prose writing includes history in the form of personal narratives, POW and escape experiences, biography, oral interviews and home front reminiscences. The personal narratives range from numerous accounts of travels and services life to a light-hearted treatment of the Italian campaign by Leslie Hobbs (war correspondent), George F. Kaye (photographer) and Neville Colvin (cartoonist) in *Kiwi Down the Strada* (1963).

Soldiering On (1989) by John Blyth describes 'the day to day business of being a soldier' in North Africa and Italy, while Gordon ★Slatter's *One More River* (1995) is a spirited account of the ordinary infantry soldier's life during the Italian campaign. Geoffrey ★Cox's *Two Battles* (1987) is a personal memoir about Crete and the Western Desert. Cox, the senior intelligence officer on the NZ divisional staff, also wrote *The Road to Trieste* (1947), an account of the Division's final campaign in North Italy, culminating in the occupation of Trieste and a confrontation with the Yugoslav partisan armies commanded by General Tito.

Lawrence Watt's *Mates and Mayhem* (1996) is a compilation of interviews with Second World War veterans. *Dark Laughter* (1994) by Les Cleveland contains many observations about morale and social behaviour in the Division and discusses twentieth century war in terms of popular culture. *Angel in God's Office* (1997) by Neva Clarke McKenna is an account of her experiences in the New Zealand Women's Auxiliary Corps. *WAAC Story* by Iris Latham (1986) deals with the Corps's evolution and its history. Alison Parr's *Silent Casualties* (1995) examines the persistence of stress-related disorders among veterans.

Outstanding among the adventures of New Zealanders behind enemy lines is *Guerilla Surgeon* (1957) by Lindsay Rogers, who joined the Yugoslav partisans, operated under appalling conditions in their field hospitals, met General Tito, and had some complicated dealings with the Communist leadership. Another New Zealand soldier, John Denvir, became a Yugoslav partisan brigade commander. His exploits are described in James Caffin's *Partisan* (1945). Alternatively, William Jordan's *Conquest Without Victory* (1969) deals, from the point of view of a dedicated anti-communist, with the experiences of a New Zealand officer who saw service with the resistance movements in Greece and France. Murray Elliott's *Vasili: The Lion of Crete* (1987) is about the exploits of Dudley Churchill Perkins who was a special agent on Crete. Gabrielle McDonald's *New Zealand's Secret Heroes* (1991) describes the deeds of members of the Special Operations Executive behind the lines in Greece and Crete. John ★Mulgan in his *Report on Experience* (1947) discusses the problems of morale and the nature of underground operations in Greece, where he was a secret agent.

Freyberg's Circus (1981) by Noel Gardiner is a lively chronicle of his experiences in North Africa in 27 Machine Gun Battalion. He is one of the few writers to discuss such issues as sexual problems of the troops, the nature of fear and courage, and the style of discipline in the Division's combat units. However, the qualities of New Zealand soldiers are critically scrutinised in John McLeod's *Myth and Reality* (1986). McLeod questions the assertion that New Zealanders are natural soldiers 'as good as, if not better than, those of any other nationality' and he discusses disciplinary problems as well as the refusal of duty staged by a furlough draft who returned to New Zealand in 1943. A chapter entitled 'Crimes, Follies and Indiscretions' finds drunkenness to be the New Zealanders' greatest single problem.

Two books throw some light on the aggressive performance of the Maori Battalion, who were shock troops with the highest casualty rate in Division. H.G. Dyer's *Ma Te Reinga: The Way of the Maori Soldier* (1953) contains stories and reminiscences about some of the unit's famous warriors. Wira Gardiner's *The Story of the Maori Battalion* (1992) discusses the question of fear and morale, and also mentions the practices of looting, plunder and the capture and appropriation of enemy weapons.

Notable prisoner-of-war escapes and tales of endurance in prison camps include *Farewell Camp 12* (1945), an account of the adventures of Brigadier James Hargest, formerly MP for Awarua, and one of the Division's most experienced soldiers. *Dare to be Free* (1951) by W.B. Thomas describes how he was imprisoned in Salonica, but hid in the monasteries on Mount Athos until he could reach Turkey in a stolen boat. James ★Bertram's *The Shadow of a War* (1947) is an account of his experiences in ★China, the surrender of Hong Kong and his four years in Japanese prison camps. Other escape narratives include C.N. Armstrong's *Life Without Ladies* (1945), Ernest Clark's *Over the Fence is Out* (1965), R.H. Thomson's *Captive Kiwi* (1964), George Clifton's *The Happy Hunted* (1952), Allan Yeoman's *The Long Road to Freedom* (1991), John Borrie's *Despite Captivity* (1975) and Jack Hardie's *From Timaru to Stalag VIIIB* (1991).

Several narratives describe how escaped New Zealand prisoners were helped by partisans and by ★Italian peasantry. *The Way Out* (1946) by Malcolm J. Mason is the story of his survival in winter in the Abruzzi mountains followed by a difficult journey to the Allied lines. For eight months, John E. Broad hid in a grotto in a mountain gorge in the Apennines. In *Poor People—Poor Us* (1946) he writes vividly of the experience of near starvation under huge snow drifts. Arch

Scott in *Dark of the Moon* (1985) recalls his activities in North Italy where, with cool effrontery, he cycled around the countryside organising the movements of other escapees.

The influence of the Italian experience on some survivors is discussed in 'Twenty Years After', an essay by Les Cleveland in *Landfall* (1964). It is also one of the themes in Maurice *Shadbolt's *An Ear of the Dragon* (1971), which is derived from the life and writing of Renato *Amato, whose short stories are collected under the title of *The Full Circle of the Travelling Cuckoo* (1971). Other short stories that draw attention to aspects of war as well as the experience of homecoming including A.P. *Gaskell's 'No Sound of Battle' and 'Fight the Good Fight' in *The Big Game and Other Stories* (1947); John Reece *Cole's 'Free Rides for Soldier's Brides' in *It Was So Late* (1949); and T.E. Dorman's *The Green War* (1997), which has thirteen poems as well as short stories and prose sketches about operations in the Fiji Regiment.

Errol *Brathwaite (ed.) in *Pilot on the Run* (1986) recounts the adventures of Flight Sergeant 'Chalky' White who walked through the French countryside and the Pyrenees only to be locked up by the British consulate in Barcelona as a suspected spy. *The Pitcher and the Well* (1961) by J.D. McDonald (ed.) is an unusual account of the stresses endured by a pilot dying of burns in a German prison hospital. The experience of being a prisoner of the *Japanese is described by Claude Thompson's *Into the Sun* (1996) and James Bertram in *Capes of China Slide Away* (1993) and elsewhere. David McGill's *P.O.W.* (1987) is the best source for details of daily prison existence.

The history of pacifists and conscientious objectors in New Zealand during World War 2 is detailed in *Out of the Cold* (1986) by David Grant. The story of one man's resistance to being called up for military service is told in *AWOL* (1990) by James Edwards. Walter Lawry's *We Said No to War* (1994) is an account of a conscientious objector's existence in military defaulters' camps, while L.A.W. Efford in *Penalties on Conscience* (1945) examines the defaulters' detention system.

Accounts of RNZAF and squadron activities in the air war include Colin Ballantine's *40 Squadron RNZAF: To the Four Winds* (1985); Alex Horn's *Wings Over the Pacific* (1992); Norman Franks's *Forever Strong: The Story of 75 Squadron RNZAF 1916–1990* (1991). Bathia Mackenzie's *The WAAF Book* (1982) is a fascinating scrapbook of wartime memories about service life, customs and social activities; Keith and Nora Morris's *Wartime Memories of the RNZAF* (1993) is the story of an air force friendship that led to romance. Brathwaite's *We'll Be Home for Christmas* (1994) is a treatment of the RNZAF from the viewpoint of ordinary New Zealanders, using informal anecdotes, diaries, cartoons and light verse.

Personal narratives and biographies that detail the lives of air force personalities include *Cobber Kain* (1992) by Michael G. Burns; *Green Kiwi Versus German Eagle* (1991) by J. Norby King; *Typhoon Pilot* (1982) and *One More Hour* (1989) by Desmond Scott; *Spitfire Patrol* (1990) by Colin Gray; *Of Wind and Water* (1989) by James *Sanders; *The Blue Arena* (1986) by Bob Spurdle and *Popeye's War* (1996) by Lorie Lucas. Biographies by Vincent Orange include *Sir Keith Park* (1984), *The Road to Biggin Hill* (a life of Wing Commander Johnny Checketts) (1987), *Coningham* (1990) and *Ensor's Endeavour* (1995).

Books about the naval war include Denis *Glover's *D Day* (1944), a tautly written account of operations in a landing craft; L.J.H. Wackrow's *Kiwi on the Messdeck* (1984), the story from a lower-deck perspective of five New Zealanders serving in HMS *Aurora*; and D. Grant's *A Working Holiday 1940–1945* (1992), which is about thirteen convoy trips to North Russia in destroyers. Grant Howard's *The Navy in New Zealand* (1981) is an illustrated history; Jack S. Harker's *HMNZS Achilles* (1980) is an account of *Achilles'* part in the Battle of the River Plate against the German pocket battleship *Graf Spee*, and his *Almost HMNZS Neptune* (1991) is about the cruiser *Neptune's* career until sunk off Tripoli in 1941; Timothy Gambrill's *New Zealand Cruisers in Combat* (1988) deals with the wartime activities of *Achilles, Neptune, Leader* and *Gambia*.

One of the most intellectually stimulating of the novels about World War 2 is Dan *Davin's *For the Rest of Our Lives* (1947). Davin draws on his intimate knowledge of the New Zealand Division to treat it as a microcosm of the homeland and an integratory force in the lives of its soldiers. His characters include a Marxist whose self-analysis imparts an underlying philosophical tension to the narrative. Davin's wartime short stories are collected in his *Selected Stories* (1981) and *The Salamander and the Fire* (1986). Two novels by M.K. *Joseph deal brilliantly with the life of the ordinary soldier. *I'll Soldier No More* (1958) follows the fortunes of a group of rank and file soldiers, including one New Zealander, in Europe, while *A *Soldier's Tale* (1976) is a love story narrated later by an artillery clerk in an air observation unit in Normandy. The Italian campaign is the setting for Guthrie *Wilson's *Brave Company* (1950) which deals with the struggle for survival of a typical infantry platoon. His *The Feared and the Fearless* (1954) is a thriller that begins with a manhunt at Lake Como in the closing stages of the war. Gordon Slatter's *A Gun in My Hand* (1959) is another account of life in an infantry company interwoven with a disillusioned commentary on the

New Zealand scene, and the traumatic effects of the war on a returned soldier and his generation of New Zealand men.

Two novels about the Pacific war from a partly Japanese point of view are Pat ★Booth's *Sons of the Sword* (1993) and Errol ★Brathwaite's *An Affair of Men* (1961). In *Fear in the Night* (1959) Brathwaite writes about a forced landing by a bomber crew over Japan.

The many biographical studies of New Zealand's wartime military leaders include Paul Freyberg's *Bernard Freyberg V.C.* (1991); Laurie Barber and John Tonkin-Covell's *Freyberg: Churchill's Salamander* (1965); Peter Singleton-Gates' *General Lord Freyberg V.C.* (1963); Major-General Sir Howard Kippenberger's *Infantry Brigadier* (1949); Kenneth Sandford's *Mark of the Lion: The Story of Capt. Charles Upham, V.C. and Bar* (1962).

Events on the home front are dealt with among many others, in *When the Boys Were Away* (1984) by Eve Ebbett; *The Yanks Are Coming* (1989) by Harry Bioletti; *It Wasn't Easy* (1990) by Bracy Gardiner; *War Stories Our Mothers Never Told Us* (1995) ed. Judith Fyfe; and *Women in Wartime* (1986), ed. Lauris ★Edmond. Fiona ★Kidman's *Paddy's Puzzle* (1983) is one recent fictional treatment of this period. Val Wood's *War Brides* (1991) is about women who married New Zealand soldiers in the First and Second Wars and settled in New Zealand.

The lighter side of military life in the Division emerges in two collections of wartime cartoons and prose sketches by E.G. Webber and Neville Colvin entitled *Johnny Enzed in the Middle East* (1945) and *Johnny Enzed in Italy* (1946). The prose pieces were written initially as a regular feature in the *NZEF Times* by Webber, one of its editors. The cartoons are by Neville Colvin, a brilliant caricaturist who was also on the staff of the paper. Some of the soldiers' songs and comic verse circulating in the Division are reproduced in Les Cleveland's *The Songs We Sang* (1959).

Established New Zealand poets of the 1930s–40s had relatively little to say about the actualities of World War 2, though the apprehensions of the left toward its approach are evident in the periodical ★*Tomorrow* with poems like 'On an Old German War Helmet' by B.C.D. and 'O Can Ye Brew Poisons?' by Allen ★Curnow ('One gas will raise blisters, another will destroy sight'). However, contributions to ★*New Zealand Best Poems* of 1942 by Paula Hanger, L.F. Smaill and Arnold ★Wall show an awareness of distant battlefields and epochal events. A few poems and stories in ★*New Zealand New Writing* (1944) also express some of the anxieties of the times. Curnow's 'In Memoriam', for a dead soldier friend, published in *A ★Small Room With Large Windows* (1962), has a mood of sombre reflection ('Weeping for bones in Africa, I turn / Our youth over like a dead bird

in my hand'). Nancy Bruce's *Home is the Warrior* (1964) has several poems that perfectly capture the loneliness and anxiety of those left behind. Her 'Dawn Parade' speaks of 'hearts that kept the vigil all alone' hearing 'the pipes go crying through the town'. In 'Returning' she invokes the disturbing image of wartime troop train: '"I'll be back," you said. And round the bend the train rolled out of sight.' A satire entitled 'Security' by Denis Glover in ★*New Zealand Poetry Yearbook* (1951), edited by Louis ★Johnson, uses the military imagery of occupied, war-torn cities to celebrate 'these far cleaner days' where no armies clash and the loudspeaker 'exhorts for God, for freedom, and the ballot box'.

A great amount of popular verse was written by people in the services in wartime, but most of it is of little account. More impressive is the output from a small number of soldier poets. Several poems by James Bertram in his *Occasional Verses* (1971) express his feelings on the descent of an American bomber on fire over Tokyo Bay, his bitter thoughts as a POW ('Each day / We pass in organised futility, / And peace more hostile than a field of battle'), and his thoughts of the homeland while on a Tokyo working party. His 'Rondeau in Wartime' reflects the disillusionment of a period in the war when Allied cause was in disarray. ('Far-called out navies melt away / While padres lift their hands to pray.')

H.W. Gretton, while a soldier in North Italy, wrote a long poem entitled 'Koru and Acanthus' which reflects on New Zealand history and the possibility of constructing a new Carthage that will realise the potentialities of Maoritanga as well as 'the beautiful hopes of steamer and canoe'. This was published in ★*Spike* in 1947.

The Iron Hand (ed. Les Cleveland, 1979) contains several poems by Charles Smith whose 'Greece a Year Ago' appeared in the *Palestine Post* and was reprinted in various military newspapers including the *NZEF Times*, which had a regular 'Off Parade' page for contributors. Some of the best poems from this feature are reprinted in *The Iron Hand*. Poems by Dan Davin, Erik ★de Mauny, William E. Morris, Charles Smith, Les Cleveland and Gwenyth Hayes are also included in the Oasis selection of *Poems of the Second World War* (1985), *More Poems of the Second World War* (1989), the Schools Oasis *Poems of the Second World War* (1992) and *The Voice of War* (1995). *Landfall* (September 1950) contains short stories by D.W. Cheer and Leo Sinden, who had won a special prize in the *NZEF Times* 1942 Christmas issue with his poem 'December Night—Western Desert Coast'. A cycle of four poems about the Italian Campaign by Cleveland, entitled 'Aspects of War', also appeared in *Landfall* (December 1964).

Some particularly accomplished World War 2 poems came from M.K. Joseph and John ★Male, whose *Poems from a War* (1989) move deftly through a spectrum of experience from the troopship to the returned veteran's studied understatement that 'There was a job to do / and it was done. Not many / will make a song about it.' With a philosophical sensibility, Male observes 'The arrogant well-spoken young bank clerk' who 'is now Captain X'. In 'Four Italian Seasons' he offers ironic advice to 'seize your short summer, count / your days in flowers, / be desperately romantic.' His 'Stricken Peninsula' conjures up a violent past where 'every night at our staging area near Trasimeno / we encountered ghosts, / tired Roman and Carthaginian still / spear-locked in combat, elephants / palely trumpeting.' But 'Portrait of a Young Man Grown Old' speaks in sombre actuality ('You can't go through this sort of thing / indefinitely and not grow old'). In a different and larger context, James K. *Baxter's 'Thoughts on War on a Spring Day' in *Collected Poems* (1980) sums up the century's bitter experience of War, as kids climbing on the cenotaph 'shout and straddle the loud myth / of historical lightning // that strikes the young leaves down each / two decades.' (See also *France, *Germany, *Italy, *Japan and *Low, David.) LC

War literature: Korean War (1950–52). The Korean War had little impact on New Zealand literature, with the 1951 *Waterfront strike appearing largely to obscure it both at the time and in retrospect. R.A.K. *Mason's 'Sonnet to MacArthur's Eyes' (1950) is probably its best-known literary product; James K. *Baxter wrote 'A Takapuna Business Man Considers his Son's Death in Korea'; and there is passing mention of a non-literary sort in the magazine *Here & Now* (3, 5, 6, 9, 10). Ian McGibbon's two-volume history, *New Zealand and the Korean War* (1992–96), is notable not only for its lucid account of the politics and diplomacy (Vol. 1) and combat operations (Vol. 2) but also for its quotations from manuscript sources, especially letters and diaries. PE

War literature: Vietnam War (c.1961–75). The Vietnam War provoked a somewhat more substantial response than the Korean War. The left-wing *New Zealand Monthly Review* recorded opposition to the war as early as July 1963, with occasional editorials appearing from June 1964 as well as regular features by Freda Cook and others, occasional special supplements (Sept. 1964, July, Sept. 1965) and correspondence. Another left-wing journal, *Dispute*, editorialised against the war from February 1965, publishing articles by I.F. Stone, J.R. Flynn, Roger Horrocks and others (March, July August, 1965; April, Nov. 1966; Jan.–Feb., April 1968). From May 1965 M.H. *Holcroft editorialised

occasionally on the war in the *NZ Listener*, whose correspondence columns attracted letters from Maurice *Shadbolt, James K. *Baxter, O.E. *Middleton, Roderick *Finlayson, C.K. *Stead, Barry *Mitcalfe, Ian *Cross and others; many writers signed a petition in the 26 August 1966 number. Vincent *O'Sullivan, H.W. *Orsman, Lawrence *Jones and others wrote consistently against the war in *Comment* (Vol. 7, Nos. 2 & 3; Vol. 8, Nos. 1–4; Vol. 9, No. 1).

Rewi *Alley's collection *The Mistake* (1965), following his diary *Spring in Vietnam* (1956), was probably the most trenchant poetic response the conflict was to draw from a New Zealander. One edition of the Auckland magazine *Fernfire* (September 1966) was devoted to poetry about Vietnam and included Charles *Doyle, Willow Macky, Mitcalfe, Alan Trussell-Cullen and Hone *Tuwhare, as well as Baxter's uncollected 'The Green Beret'. This and two individually published poems of 1965, 'A Bucket of Blood for a Dollar' and 'The Gunner's Lament', were Baxter's most specific responses to the conflict. In the same year Charles *Brasch editorialised (in *Landfall* 75 and 76, which also contained others' contributions on the Vietnam issue) against what he called 'the Spain of the sixties', and wrote two satires, the individually published 'Twice Sixty' and the uncollected 'Hot Lines from the Hellpress'; 'All Our Days' in his collection *Not Far Off* (1969) also referred to the war, as did two poems in Janet *Frame's *The Pocket Mirror* (1967), 'Napalm' and 'Instructions for Bombing with Napalm'. J.W. Winchester's 'Writing on Vietnam' in *Landfall* 81 (1967) was a valuable contemporary survey, which drew the conclusion that 'not very much has been put between covers on Vietnam—508 pages in all'. He discussed among other things the publications of the Wellington-based Committee on Vietnam and the Auckland-based Committee on South-East Asia. The latter published Tuwhare's 'The Holy Cities' (1966), as a pamphlet; his 'Cambodia: S.E. Asia', in *Something Nothing* (1974), is also anti-war. Two poems in David *Mitchell's *Pipe Dreams in Ponsonby* (1972), both entitled 'my lai / remuera / ponsonby', trenchantly protested against American atrocities. The war lay implicitly in the background of some of those poems in Allen *Curnow's *Trees, Effigies, Moving Objects* (1972) that were set in the United States, and became most nearly explicit in 'A Framed Photograph'. As *'Whim-Wham' Curnow was occasionally more explicit still, as in 'Let's All Talk At Once'. Stead's 'A Small Registry of Births and Deaths', which imagined the war from the point of view of Vietnamese civilians being bombed, appeared first in *Landfall* 78 (1966), and a long poem on the war, 'April Notebook', appeared in *Landfall* 85. In *Landfall*

86 he reported at length on the 'Conference of Peace, Power & Politics' held in Wellington in March–April 1968. He referred directly to the ending of the war in Sonnet 16 of 'Autumn 1975' in *Walking Westward* (1979), whose title poem touched on the conflicts in both Korea and Vietnam, and to the latter again in 'The Revolution' in *Voices* (1990); anti-war protests also figured briefly in his novel The *Singing Whakapapa* (1994).

The wider, formal and stylistic, influence of the *American counter-culture of the time was evident in Arthur Baysting (ed.), The *Young New Zealand Poets* (1973). A small group of novels expressed a curious identification of New Zealand and Vietnam. Frame's *Intensive Care* (1970) imagined a New Zealand of the future policed by American troops enforcing a government policy to exterminate abnormality in the population. In Stead's *Smith's Dream* (1971), New Zealand has been taken over by a dictator, Volkner, who uses American troops to control the populace. Michael *Henderson's *Log of a Superfluous Son* (1975) sent its young protagonist on a sea-journey towards South-East Asia and the battlefields of both Vietnam and Korea. Craig *Harrison's novel, *Broken October: New Zealand 1985* (1975), imagined a Māori uprising on the lines of the North Vietnamese, and his *The Quiet Earth* (1981) focused particularly on a Māori veteran of Vietnam. The concluding section of Shadbolt's *Strangers and Journeys* (1972) took place against a background of anti-war protests. 'Comment' in *Mate 13* (1965) recorded Mitcalfe's view of the war, and his poem 'Cambodia' (*Mate* 19, 1971) noted its widening. His story 'Black Cat' in O'Sullivan's 1975 Oxford *New Zealand Short Stories, Third Series,* took the reader into the mind of a soldier in Vietnam. Middleton's short story 'Demonstration' (*Mate* 15, 1967) was about an anti-war protest. Warren Dibble's dialogue-free anti-Vietnam-war television play, 'How with This Rage' was accepted in 1967 but never televised; the script was published in *Landfall 88*. His play 'Operation Pigstick' was performed at Downstage Theatre in November 1966, to some strong reactions. Philip *Mann's 'Nam: A Vietnam Documentary' was performed at Victoria University in 1972, but was not published. Greg *McGee's play about football, *Foreskin's Lament* (1980) opposed the liberal-humanist values of its protagonist and those of a character who brings a doctrine of ruthless self-seeking and brutality from his time in the Vietnam War. John *Broughton's plays *Te Hokinga Mai* (1988) and *Michael James Manaia* (1994) both examined the effect of the Vietnam War on Māori participants in it. Rod Eder's novel *Deep Jay* (1995), an adventure story set in the deep jungle of the title, has been a late contribution to the genre.   PE

WARD, Crosbie (1832–67), born in County Down, was one of the most outstanding of that multi-talented group of *Irish gentry who dominated early Canterbury's politics, journalism and intellectual and literary life. He was classically educated at Trinity College, Dublin, and was exceptionally widely read. He arrived in Canterbury in 1852 to settle the affairs of two drowned brothers but stayed to marry Margaret Townsend from another Irish gentry family. Ward was reputed to be the richest of Canterbury's generally impoverished young gentlemen but was also a dagger-sharp wit and politically ambitious. In 1855 he bought the *Lyttelton Times*, which under his editorship achieved a reputation for excellence equalled only by the *Nelson Examiner* and J.E. *FitzGerald's Christchurch *Press*.

Ward's prose output was mainly superior journalism, marked by vivacity, clarity and wit. He was the dedicated enemy of pomposity and pretension, and as a writer of high-spirited comic verse and sparklingly malicious satirical parody was the best of his time, in an age when this was both an art form and an effective political weapon. He has possibly not been surpassed in a subsequently rather solemn literary history. His most quoted work is 'The Song of the *Squatters', but others deserve notice, including 'The Summer Road', 'Railroadior', 'Ballad of the Ancient Member' and the 'Bucolic Arcades Ambo, after Virgil'. He wrote almost all *Punch in Canterbury* in the 1860s, and a selection of his verse appeared in his *Book of *Canterbury Rhymes* (1866, 1883). At his best he loses little in comparison with his English contemporaries F.C. Burnand and W.S. Gilbert.

As a politician, Ward was ardent for South Island and, especially, Canterbury interests. He was MHR for Lyttelton 1858–67, Post-Master General in the Fox and *Domett Ministries 1861–63, and negotiator of the important Panama Mail service. He died prematurely soon after becoming Canterbury's London Agent.   EB

WARD, Raymond (1925–), rose quickly to some prominence as a poet in the early 1960s. Born in Wembley, London, he arrived in Dunedin in 1959, after war service in the Royal Navy, a BA(Hons) in English at the University of London and various teaching posts. Already a published poet in England, he received great encouragement from Charles *Brasch. His poems in *Landfall* won admirers for their acute observation, adroit control of tone and gift for vibrant and memorable images: 'The urban day has got her straw hat on'; 'Night grows more stealthily than grass'; 'I slump like a ramshackle house / with broken windows'; 'your outline only, drained like a negative, at last remained, / sharp against the window veiled with steam'. A collection was published by *Caxton, *Settler and Stranger* (1965), and six poems were selected by Vincent *O'Sullivan for *An Anthology of Twentieth-Century New Zealand Poetry* (OUP, 1970, 76). This ranked Ward alongside Eileen *Duggan, Robin *Hyde or M.K. *Joseph. He is now remembered largely for his poem 'Watching Snow', which is much used by speech and drama practitioners.

After some years teaching English, Ward became senior tutor in art history at Otago Polytechnic (retiring 1991), art critic for the *Otago Daily Times*, and wrote on art for the *NZ Listener* and *Landfall* (164, 1987). He has continued to write poems, some in formal modes, and publishes them privately. *Settler and Stranger* is now little known. This may be because his versatility of tone and form makes him hard to classify, or because few poems are identifiably local. Yet several of Ward's poems, including 'Watching Snow', 'Settler and Stranger', 'Ode to an Urban Day' and 'Moods of the Night Wind', still deserve attention.   RR/PN

WARDELL, Phyllis (1909–), wrote children's adventure novels well in advance of their time. Born in Christchurch and educated at Avonside and Christchurch GHS, she worked in an advertising agency, married and raised a son and daughter. A university course in journalism led to various articles and stories before she began a children's series based on family stories about early gold-prospecting days. Set mainly in the South Island mountains, forests and sea coast, and full of action and mystery interspersed with humour, her stories concentrate on the need, then a less fashionable cause, to protect the environment and endangered species from greed and profiteering. *Gold at Kapai* (1960), illustrated by Douglas Maxted, was followed by *The Secret of the Lost Tribe* (1961), illustrated by Keith Money and republished in the Kotare Series in 1986; *Passage to Dusky* (1967), illustrated by Garrick Palmer; *Hazard Island* (1967), illustrated by Albert Wagenvoort; *The Nelson Treasure* (1983), illustrated by Alan Gilderdale; and *Beyond the Narrows* (1985), illustrated by Gary Meeson.   DH

Waterfront crisis, The, of 1951, came about when the Waterside Workers Union, engaged in a wage dispute, refused to work overtime hours until the dispute was settled and were consequently refused work by their employers. The union considered that they were victims of a lockout, but the government, in the context of the Korean *War and Cold War tensions, deemed their actions an illegal strike and brought in the Emergency Regulations, disestablishing them as a union and forbidding any material aid to them or publication of their views. The resulting Waterfront crisis lasted 151 days, with much unrest and civil disobedience, and with the government setting up new unions and using the

military to load and unload vessels. The union finally admitted defeat, and the government called a snap election, increasing their narrow margin by four seats. Feelings ran high, and the crisis strongly polarised public opinion. At the time and subsequently the crisis has provoked a variety of literary responses, most of them critical of the government position. The more immediate responses, from 1951 to about 1963, treated the crisis as a dramatic symptom of current social ills, while post-1970 responses tended to distance the crisis and treat it as part of the pattern of New Zealand social history.

Literary responses began with James K. *Baxter's 'Recent Trends in New Zealand Poetry', his talk at the *New Zealand Writers' Conference held in Christchurch in May 1951, during the crisis. Baxter ended with an added section on 'the function of the poet in modern society, and particularly in this country', a 'consideration' he felt to be 'especially relevant at the present time'. In that section he called for the writer to be a responsible social critic, a 'cell of good living in a corrupt society', obviously with the crisis and what it signified in mind. The conference passed a resolution opposing 'war hysteria' and supporting 'the free expression of opinion'. Charles *Brasch picked up these themes in his *Landfall editorial on the conference, calling for writers to be nonconformists and social critics in a society 'stagnating in mediocrity'. The following year Bill *Pearson in his essay *'Fretful Sleepers' took the crisis as confirmation of his view that New Zealand had become a dangerously conformist society and that the writer's task was 'awakening New Zealanders from their fretful sleep'. Robert *Chapman's classic 1953 *Landfall* essay, 'Fiction and the Social Pattern', similarly interpreted the crisis as the expression of a 'conservative and arid social order' that fiction writers were trying to expose and change.

The crisis appeared in fiction about ten years later, most significantly in Noel *Hilliard's short story 'New Unionist' in 1963 and in Ian *Cross's novel *After Anzac Day* in 1961. Hilliard's story is a sharply critical portrait of one of the new unionists used to replace the members of the Waterside Workers Union, while Cross's novel uses the crisis as an image of the nation's social and political divisions. The novel is set in the middle of the crisis, with tensions so high that they lead to the death of one of the characters, while flashbacks through several generations reveal the historical sources of those divisions. The crisis is seen as an expression of the failure of the New Zealand dream of becoming *'God's Own Country', its decline into a postcolonial society economically based on racial discrimination and the expropriation of land, spiritually disciplined by a deadly secularised *puritanism, socially regulated by a welfare state bureaucracy.

When the crisis appeared again in post-1970 writings

it was seen not as an expression of current discontents but as a part of a cyclical historical pattern. In Maurice ★Shadbolt's ★*Strangers and Journeys*, the novel's 'sons' are involved in the crisis as their fathers were in the Queen Street riots in 1932, with those earlier events marking the beginning of the historical phase that would produce Labour's welfare state, and the later ones the end of that phase. In Maurice ★Gee's *Sole Survivor* (1983; see ★*Plumb*), the crisis is a stage in the education into political cynicism of one of the idealist George Plumb's grandchildren, Raymond Sole, and on occasion exploited in the rise to political power by another grandson, Duggie Plumb. Both Shadbolt and Gee present the crisis historically from a middle-class point of view, while ★Renée and Mervyn ★Thompson, in historical dramas of the 1980s, present it from a working-class position. In Renée's trilogy dealing with three generations of working-class women in conflict situations, the crisis serves as the focus for *Pass It On* (1986), the third play in historical sequence, although the second to be written. Renée treats the dispute as one of the occasions, like the ★Depression or late nineteenth-century exploitation of female labour, when working-class women worked and suffered within an unjust capitalist social order; and tried to change or mitigate its effects. Thompson in *Coaltown Blues* (first performed 1984, published 1986) treats the crisis as one of the rare occasions when the people of his often harsh West Coast coal-mining town came together in common cause. His *The Great New Zealand Truth Show* (first performed 1982, published 1992) similarly treats the crisis as symbolic of the biases in ★*Truth*'s treatment of events. The most historically distanced treatments of the crisis are in C.K. ★Stead's postmodern-flavoured novel, ★*All Visitors Ashore* (1984) and Kevin Ireland's ironic fiction *Blowing My Top* (1996). In Stead's book the crisis is the background which affects in various ways the private lives of the characters (loosely based on Frank ★Sargeson, Janet ★Frame, Stead himself, and others). The action is viewed ironically and nostalgically by one of the characters in 1981, so that the critical view held of the crisis at the time is vividly presented, but also seen as historical product. In Ireland's novel the crisis is played as ironic farce, viewed from the 1990s by the narrator-protagonist as a 'lunatic parody' of the cold war confrontations going on elsewhere in the 1950s, a battle between a government led by a 'drongo' and a union led by a 'mung', and witnessed by a public of 'cretins'. While the farcical action confirms his judgments, the structural irony is also turned back on him; his role then as an inept SIS spy prepared him only too well for his current role as fraudulent New Right investment entrepreneur.

Over more than forty years the Waterfront crisis has been an important topos in New Zealand writing, the developing treatment of it revealing shifts in literary stances and attitudes. LJ

WATSON, Henry Brereton Marriott (1863–1921), was born in Caulfield, Melbourne, and arrived in Christchurch at the age of 9, when his father was appointed to a curacy. In 1883 he graduated from the University of New Zealand and in 1885 moved to England, where he lived the rest of his life. He was the author of forty-one undistinguished yet versatile novels. For example, his first, *Marahuna* (1888), is a mysterious tale of a fire-loving Peruvian; *A Poppy Show* (1908) traces the leisured lives of very wealthy young ladies in London; and *Hurricane Island* (1915) is an adventure story at sea. He is best known now for weaving Poe, Haggard and the New Zealand ★Wars into his melodramatic *The Web of the Spider* (1891). The only other work with a New Zealand reference appears to be 'The Hand of God: A Story of the Waitiri Gorge' in the collection *In Australian Wilds, and Other Colonial Tales and Sketches*, ed. Philip Mennell (1889). In 1891 Watson co-authored a play for the West End with J.M. Barrie. NW

WATSON, Jean (1933–), novelist and short story writer, was born and brought up on a farm near Whangarei, left school at 15 and has for many years lived as a freelance writer in Wellington, also completing a Victoria University degree in religious studies. Her first and best-known novel, *Stand in the Rain* (1965), draws on aspects of her marriage to the writer Barry ★Crump. The story, told with deceptive simplicity, portrays the problematic relationship between the narrator, Sarah, a would-be writer, and Abungus, an itinerant bushman, as the couple travel around the North Island, looking for work and a place to live. A 'woman's "on-the-road" novel' as it has been called, *Stand in the Rain* has become a minor classic of its period, being reissued in 1985 and again in 1995. Four subsequent novels—*The Balloon Watchers* (1975), *The World is an Orange and the Sun* (1978), *Flowers for Happyever: A Prose Lyric* (1980), and *Address to a King* (1986)—have been increasingly informed by Watson's enquiries into the Vedanta philosophy and embody an ongoing search for spiritual truth in a world dominated by materialistic values. These later novels have on the whole received little serious attention, but the sequence *Three Sea Stories* (1994), linked narratives set in southern India, was greeted with considerable critical acclaim. With great subtlety and insight, the stories explore cultural difference through the friendship that develops between the narrator Catherine, a 50-year-old New Zealander, and Satya, a young Tamil man. Watson has also published *Karunai*

Illam: The Story of an Orphanage (1992), an autobiographical account of her involvement with the founding of an orphanage in southern India. HRi

WATSON, Joy (1938–), children's writer, was born in Gisborne, educated at St Mary's, Wellington, and trained and worked as a dental nurse. When the youngest of her nine children was at school, she began writing children's stories, poems and a musical play, *The Circus* (1991). She is most successful with her humorous, accumulative picture books, *Grandpa's Slippers* (1989) and *Grandpa's Cardigan* (1993), both illustrated by Wendy Hodder. In *No Porridge, Please* (1994), illustrated by Jill Parry, she entertainingly exposes prejudices in a grandfather–grandson relationship. DH

Wattie Book of the Year Award, see Appendix.

WEBB, Alice (1876–1963), wrote short stories of New Zealand life, especially that of women, during and after World War 1. Published originally in newspapers, especially the *New Zealand Illustrated Magazine*, some were collected as *Miss Peters' Special and Other Stories* (1925). There is a perky resilience about them which suggests a morale-raising intention, as they show women cheerfully getting things done despite difficulty and shortages. The resourceful Miss Peters of the title story, for instance, rides the train to the city in a goods carriage when no passenger space is available. There is also a determination to establish each narrative situation in New Zealand terms, an affirmation of the local almost in defiance of the global pressures on it. Webb's other book is a short life of her clergyman father, *Pilgrimage: A Biography of Anthony Spur Webb, M.A., Camb., Canon of St. John's Cathedral, Napier, and First Vicar of Ormondville* (1949). Despite this heavily ecclesiastical title, the book is lively, dealing with late Victorian England, Scandinavian settlement in Hawkes Bay, the Boer War and family causes and effects. It remains true to the author's prefatory promise 'to strive not to be prosy'. Webb as a writer is characterful and independent; she came from Warwickshire. Born in Stockingford, she was 8 when the family emigrated and settled to parish work in Hawkes Bay. PN/RR

WEDDE, Ian (1946–), poet, fiction writer and critic, was born in Blenheim and lived there until the age of 7 when he travelled overseas for eight years with his parents, living first in East Pakistan (now Bangladesh) then in England, where he attended boarding school. He returned at the age of 15 and went to King's College and the University of Auckland (MA in English 1968). From 1966 his poems began appearing regularly in periodicals, including *Landfall* and *Freed*. He edited the *New Zealand Universities Literary Yearbook* in 1968. After graduating he travelled extensively, living for periods in Jordan and, from 1970, England, where he wrote criticism for *London Magazine* and published a first pamphlet of verse, *Homage to Matisse* (1971). He returned to New Zealand as *Burns Fellow in 1972, living in Port Chalmers until moving to Wellington in 1975. His first substantial volume of verse, *Made Over* (1974), collected poems from the years 1967–72, including those written in the Middle East and England. In a note for *The *Young New Zealand Poets*, ed. Arthur Baysting (1973), Wedde wrote: 'My own instinct is to write longer poems. I tend to quest about like a dog backtracking & crisscrossing a terrain in search of an odour's source. Most of my poems begin as enquiries of a personal nature, attempts to explain myself to myself.... Most of my poems are concerned with how we live, how we should live, & are political in these senses. At the same time I think I seldom tell; I enquire.'

Poems from his Otago sojourn were collected in several books published in quick succession. *Pathway to the Sea* (1975), a long poem dedicated to the *American poet A.R. Ammons and protesting against the planned siting of an aluminium smelter near Aramoana, was included, despite its length (46 nine-line stanzas), in several anthologies. *Earthly: Sonnets for Carlos* (1975) is a sequence of sixty sonnets spanning the first year of life of his first son. Other poems from this period were collected in *Spells for Coming Out* (1977), co-winner of the New Zealand Book Award for Poetry. Like other poets of his generation, Wedde was especially interested in the experimental tradition in American poetry, Ezra Pound, William Carlos Williams, Gary Snyder, A.R. Ammons, Ted Berrigan, Robert *Creeley, Frank O'Hara, Robert Duncan and John Ashbery being some of the many American voices he attended to.

As well as poetry Wedde also regularly published fiction, influenced in part by the Americans William Gaddis and Thomas Pynchon. In 1977 he won the Book Award for Fiction for his first novel, *Dick Seddon's Great Dive*, which strongly evoked the atmosphere of the late 1960s and early 1970s and which shared many locations and concerns with his poems of that period. It was initially published as complete issue of *Islands* (16, 1976) and reprinted in *The Shirt Factory and Other Stories* (1981), which collected stories published through the 1970s. *Castaly: Poems 1973–1977* (1980) incorporated the pamphlets *Pathway to the Sea* and *Don't Listen* (1977) and covered the transitional period between Otago and Wellington, encompassing a noticeable shift in tone towards irony and satire. New poetry volumes appeared regularly though with less frequency after the mid-1980s, namely *Tales of Gotham City* and *Georgicon* (both

1984), *Driving into the Storm: Selected Poems* (1987), *Tendering* (1988) and *The Drummer* (1993). Two further novels appeared in the 1980s, ★*Symmes Hole* (1986) and *Survival Arts* (1988), a shorter comic novel. *Symmes Hole*, one of the most important novels of its decade, is of epic scope, sustaining a prolonged parallel between the nineteenth-century plot which involves the activities of James 'Worser' Heberley, an early whaler, and a contemporary plot-line concerning a researcher who is investigating aspects of nineteenth-century New Zealand settlement with a particular focus on the whaling industry. There are many points of connection between the novel and the poems written during the lengthy period of its composition and revision.

Another major undertaking of the mid-1980s was the *Penguin Book of New Zealand Verse* (co-edited with Harvey ★McQueen) which included substantial quantities of Māori poetry both classical and contemporary, and in both Māori and English translation (see ★Anthologies of poetry). Wedde's introduction argued for language grounded in the realities of location as a key defining characteristic of New Zealand poetry (see ★New Zealand English). A second anthology, *The Penguin Book of Contemporary New Zealand Poetry*, focusing on poetry of the 1980s (for which Miriama Evans joined Wedde and McQueen), followed in 1989. Between 1983 and 1990 Wedde was art critic for the *Evening Post* in Wellington, a position which led to a progressive reorientation of his career towards the visual arts. He curated several exhibitions which were accompanied by book-length catalogues, notably *Now See Here! Art, Language and Translation*, co-edited with Gregory Burke (1990) and *Fomison: What Shall We Tell Them?* (1994), for a touring retrospective of Tony Fomison's work. A large sampling of Wedde's critical writings was published as *How to Be Nowhere: Essays and Texts, 1971–1994* (1995).

In 1994 he became arts projects manager at the Museum of New Zealand Te Papa Tongarewa. His grants since the Burns include the Writers' Bursary 1974, the Scholarship in Letters 1980, 1989, and the Victoria University writing fellowship 1984. He was a member of the ★Literary Fund Advisory Committee 1977–79, and of the Queen Elizabeth II Visual Arts Panel in 1990. Wedde's literary versatility and significance established him as a leader among the generation of writers born in the immediate post-war period.   PS

Wednesday's Children (1937) was described by Robin ★Hyde as 'a dream novel with no morals'. Set in contemporary Auckland it draws on Hyde's own experience, including a wryly derisory picture of male journalists who 'had long ago lost the habit of going to bed, especially if with their wives'. It is also an excitingly innovative work, a fantasy which demonstrates the liberating power of the imagination, of love and of community. Hyde portrays women's lives as circumscribed by convention but 'neither protected inside marriage nor beyond it', and conjures up their rich potential: 'We have to exchange relationships which gall and goad us, for community, which laughs and is free.' Wednesday Gilfillan escapes the stifling respectability of her in-laws in her role as a fortune teller offering illusory hope to the quietly desperate, and in the dream world of her island, shared with the children of her five lovers. Hyde thus depicts the 'surface truths' of everyday physical reality, and the more powerful 'real' truth of fantasy and imagination. Again she expresses her concern for the oppressed and marginalised so that Wednesday's eccentric Uncle Elihu knows that the source of her behaviour is the 'limitations and onesidedness in matrimonial arrangements, the fetish of illegitimacy, the dual standard of morality'. Despite the novel's humour and whimsy it is founded on irony and so Wednesday's suicide provides its final statement on the irreconcilable nature of the two worlds Hyde knew so well.   GB

WEIR, John (1935–), is a poet, scholar and editor of James K. ★Baxter. Born in Nelson, he was educated at St Patrick's, Silverstream, and Mount St Mary's Seminary, Greenmeadows, being ordained a Catholic priest in 1961. He taught at St Bede's, Christchurch, lectured in English at the University of Canterbury 1970–77 and was rector of St Patrick's, Wellington, 1977–82. He won the Macmillan Brown Prize for Poetry in 1962 and his first two volumes, *The Sudden Sun* (1963) and *The Iron Bush* (1970), established him as a distinctive voice in the Baxter manner of eloquent spiritual autobiography. Baxter praised their 'intellectual honesty … clear, hard images' and 'lyric gift'. Their main strength, however, is the poignant expression of a profound melancholy. Their harmoniously sad descriptive cadences ('Cold as ice under the pale grief of stars') were replaced in *a warning against water drinkers* (1974) by haiku-like sparseness and gnomic bitterness: 'the lecture-room is square / unlike the grave which is oblong / sometimes i can think of other differences.' *Treading Water: Poems 1975–82* (1983) is enlivened by some sharply observed travel poems but is also more intensely personal and preoccupied with death and loss: 'living is such a mortal sickness' ('The Hare'). Some poems ('The Difference', 'The Fall') suppress feeling into a terse monotone or ironic wordplay. 'The Excuse' rejects the charge of morbidity and self-pity, affirming 'And the poems are / a kind of quiet knocking / at the door of the self.'

Weir's *The Poetry of James K. Baxter* (1970) was the first critical study and his bibliographic works (with Barbara

Lyon) on Baxter and New Zealand poetry more generally are still essential resources. His scholarly skills and personal knowledge made him an ideal editor of the *Collected Poems of James K. Baxter* (1980), his most significant book. It will remain standard for many years, despite the absence of then-unpublished poems such as those in *Cold Spring. The *Selected Poems of James K. Baxter* (1982) completed this task of custodianship. Several of Baxter's poems are addressed or dedicated to Weir ('Poem for John Weir'), whose friendly guidance was crucial in the older poet's practice of Catholicism and last years. Frank *McKay records that at Baxter's funeral in 1972 'I gave the panegyric after John Weir didn't feel able to give it.' Though he has continued work on Baxter, Weir is not known to have published as a poet since about 1985.   RR

WELDON, Fay (1933–), the prominent British novelist, spent her childhood in New Zealand. She was born Franklin Birkinshaw in Alvechurch, Worcestershire, the family then moving to New Zealand, where her parents divorced in 1937 (see Margaret *Jepson). Her portrait as a child was painted, together with her sister, by Rita Angas. Living with her mother and sister ('It never occurred to me that women were supported by men'), she briefly attended Christchurch GHS until they returned to Britain after the war. She worked as diplomatic writer, journalist and advertising copywriter, before becoming a distinctively tragicomic voice in feminist literature. More than fifteen successful novels include *Down Among the Women* (1971), *Praxis* (1978), *Puffball* (1980), *The Life and Death of a She-Devil* (1983) and *Life Force* (1992); she has written stage plays, short stories, essays and a study of Rebecca West; writes extensively for television; and is an energetic campaigner against censorship.

Her New Zealand experience rarely enters her work directly, though *Growing Rich* (1992) includes an amusing vignette of an omnicompetent Otago farmer's wife who 'can mend a leaking gutter, wire a shearing shed, milk a cow, deliver a baby and a political address, and dress up to be a Top Table Lady'. She has visited New Zealand as a literary competition judge.   RR

WELLS, Peter (1953–), won the New Zealand and Reed awards for fiction with his first short story collection, *Dangerous Desires* (1991). Extraordinary for the lucid and passionate eloquence of the writing as well as their sexual (mostly homosexual) explicitness, the stories combine emotional intensity with psychological insight and a rare wit. 'One of THEM!', concerning two young men coming to terms with their sexuality, was described as 'a small masterpiece' by the Book Award judges, who also commended 'Of Memory and Desire', about a *Japanese

couple honeymooning in New Zealand, as 'original, sensitive and finally deeply moving' in its tragic outcome. Visually vivid, perhaps reflecting his experience as a film writer and director, the stories have a freshness of image and phrase and a sometimes mannered coruscation of language that work to affirm vitality in the face of the often tragically frank presentation of gay life in the age of AIDS. The last story, 'Dark and Light', ends with a movement out of the 'dark zone of passion' to realisation 'that already it was dawn, the night had ended and there was light, trembling like a membrane, all over the world.'

Wells's second collection, *The Duration of a Kiss* (1994), is more darkened by the shadow of AIDS, 'the fateful diaspora', 'the chaotic dark agent of a virus'. The writing is again remarkably eloquent and metaphorically rich, though less consciously lyrical than at times in *Dangerous Desires*. As there, some coherence is provided by two stories continuing the narrative of Eric Westmore, now after the death of his partner Perrin. The success of many stories in both books lies in part, as Wells suggests in a concluding essay, 'Confessions of a Provincial Pouf', in enabling 'readers simply to experience a world in which their concerns are placed to the side, viewed from a different angle', as in several stories of relations with parents, for instance. But Wells's power of sympathetic insight also makes profoundly moving such topics as the seduction of a schoolboy by a middle-aged antique dealer ('His Eternal Boy'), or obsession throughout the gay community with a charismatic visitor ('The Duration of a Kiss'). Though he is committedly and publicly a gay writer, his range of subject, setting and style is greater than any such definition can suggest. Again, some of the best writing deals with non-gay subjects—the tragedy of Bosnia (and the problem of New Zealand's identity) in 'Hills Like Green Velvet', or an international marriage in 'A Colour Known as White'. Both collections have been published internationally and the stories anthologised in the *Oxford Book of New Zealand Short Stories* and elsewhere.

Wells is equally known as a film and television director and scriptwriter, most notably for 'A Death in the Family' (1986), which won a major New York award for its drama about the loss of a friend to AIDS; and for the feature film *Desperate Remedies* (co-written and directed with Stewart Main), selected to screen at the 1993 Cannes Film Festival. Documentary television work includes *The Mighty Civic* and *The Newest City on the Globe!* With director Colin McColl, Wells was responsible for 'Ricordi!' (see D.H. *Lawrence), an operatic and expressionist dramatisation of Katherine *Mansfield's Wellington stories, commissioned for the 1996 New Zealand International Festival of the Arts, where response to its stylised perplexities was mixed.

With Rex Pilgrim, Wells edited *Best Mates: Gay Writing in Aotearoa New Zealand* (1997). His first novel, *Boy Overboard*, was published in 1997.   RR

WENDT, Albert (1939–   ), has been an influential figure in the developments that have shaped New Zealand and *Pacific literature since the 1970s. Born in Apia, Western Samoa, a member of the Aiga Sa-Tuala, he was educated from 1953 at New Plymouth BHS, Ardmore Teachers' College and Victoria University (MA in history). He returned in 1965 to Samoa to teach, became principal of Samoa College and in 1974 moved to Fiji to the University of the South Pacific. After a period at the Apia campus, he became professor of Pacific literature and pro-vice-chancellor. This was a dynamic and productive period in intellectual life in the Pacific; the developing university was a main focus for debates about independence, identity and cultural exchange. In 1988 Wendt became professor of New Zealand literature at Auckland University, where he continues to play a key role in the debate on issues of indigenous culture, and is active in fostering literature among Pacific nations communities, both in New Zealand and their home countries.

Wendt's first novel, *Sons for the Return Home* (1973), draws on his New Zealand experience to describe the life of a young man from a migrant Samoan family and his love affair with a fellow (Pākehā) student. 'He was bored with the lecture', the first sentence reads, and the narrative goes on to explore the energy and angst of New Zealand society as it entered the dynamic 1960s. Hard-hitting in its descriptions of racism, frank in its evocation of youthful sexuality, even-handed but also harsh and tender in its vision of flawed humanity, the novel was immediately recognised as important, not only for its subject material but because of its success in fusing literary styles with colloquial speech and oral narratives. *Māui, the Māori trickster figure, with his ability to supervise supernatural change, though human in his subjection to death, is an important recurring motif.

The critic Subramani considers the evolution of short fiction from oral to written form to be an outstanding feature of Pacific writing in English, and Wendt was among the most notable experimenters in this genre. The linked narratives in his *Flying Fox in a Freedom Tree* (1974) explore the history of Samoa through a wide variety of characters, settings and narrative points of view. Shifting cultural values, the demands of social ideals of masculinity and femininity on the individual, disease and damage as metaphor, the tension between commitment and freedom, life and death—symbolised by the flying fox—are recurrent themes.

Peggy Fairburn-Dunlop's essay 'Samoan Writing: The Search for the Written Fagogo' also emphasises the importance of oral traditions and Wendt's role in the development of a specifically Samoan literature. She discusses his concern with exploring the construction of identity, especially in the poems. Many of the poems in Wendt's first collection, *Inside Us the Dead: Poems 1961 to 1974* (1976), including the title piece which pushes interpretations of the significance of ancestry to the limits of history, achieve a fusion of verbal sensuality and intellectual detachment. The lava fields, which also form a fertile symbolic backdrop in the fiction, appear in the poems as the mark of distinctive but changing geographical boundaries.

Pouliuli (1977; the title can be translated as 'darkness'), is a short novel which examines the ripple effects of political corruption, family loyalties, external and internal, and individual responsibility in the faa-Samoa against an *existentialist vision. The story outlines the tragicomic course of events when 76-year-old Faleasa Osovae awakes one morning and gives in to the madness and yearning for solitude lurking beneath his years of upright behaviour and social commitment.

With the publication of *Leaves of the Banyan Tree* (1979), a family saga that crossed three generations, Wendt sets what has been called 'a capitalist's tragedy' (*Landfall* 135, 1980) in a 'fallen epic world' (Subramani). An ambitious novel written with what Roger Robinson described as 'muscular vigour which evinces a powerful imaginative grasp on the physical world', it explores a tension between the belief in fiction as a testing ground for sociological reform and the pull of psychological drives towards individualism and self-destruction, again with philosophical enquiry a potent element in the thought. One section is transposed from *Flying Fox in a Freedom Tree*. This subversive, sometimes self-destructive impulse, an underlying trickster's rebelliousness, was identified by Robinson as working in Wendt's texts in counterpoint with the 'responsibilities' of his leadership role.

A number of theoretical publications appeared during the 1970s, in which Wendt elaborated on the relationship between artist or writer, society and Pacific cultures. 'Towards a New Oceania', originally published in *Mana*, Vol. 1, No. 1 (1976), summarised the eras of the colonialist past and looked forward to the future of arts and education in the Pacific by questioning notions of tradition and authenticity. It was reprinted in *A Pacific Islands Collection*, ed. Richard Hamasaki (1983). *Mana*, Vol. 3, No. 1 (1978) published 'The Artist and the Reefs Breaking Open', which took the idea of the breaching of a coral reef as a metaphor for the way colonialism both threatened and invigorated Pacific societies, and beyond that, to signify the oppositions (inside/outside, protection/stagnation) that can characterise the relationship between an artist as individual and the social structures engaged with. *Lali* (1980) edited by Wendt, was a ground-breaking anthology that showcased and promoted the new literary writing of the Pacific, prose and poetry.

Poems in *Shaman of Visions* (1984) meditate on the relationship between abstract and physical qualities of language, objects and the human. Many of the poems are set firmly in Samoa, though the ideas of rootedness and transience emerge as ambivalent elements, as do observations on the simultaneous presence of ancient gods and rampant consumerism. In *The Birth and Death of the Miracle Man* (1986), Wendt returned to the forms of short fiction. The characterisations and locations add to the complexity of his representation of Samoa—from Fiasola, a head teacher at Sapepe village whose alienation emerges in his dreams, for example, to Salepa, a family man whose talent for fiction lands him in jail. The village of Saula, caught in the grip of a mysterious stench in 'I Will Be Our Saviour From the Bad Smell' has a chicken-and-egg problem—should the villagers find the cause of the smell or just try and get rid of it? Their search for a solution provides both an entertaining narrative and a discourse on the search for origin.

Wendt's later fiction has continued to be culturally and technically mixed. He has always been a versatile international writer as well as a committedly Pacific one. In *Ola* (1991), set in New Zealand, Israel, *Japan and Samoa, questions about how identity is shaped in a diasporic century are set in the context of religious faith and global mobility. The self-reflexive storytelling techniques Wendt mobilises allow him to play with the possibilities of inter-gender and multicultural communication. Wendt's intellectual and literary enthusiasms are again evident, as in the Borges-like poems he provides as written by his dominant female central character and the impressive lists of her reading. *Black Rainbow* (1992) is a postmodern mix of the genres of dystopian fiction, political thriller and self-conscious intertextuality. Wendt called it an 'allegorical thriller'. The title comes from a series of lithographs by the painter Ralph *Hotere produced to mark nuclear explosions. Thematic variations on how individuals respond to violence, neo-colonialism and state control reverberate throughout the text. *Photographs* (1995) is a varied collection of poems, combining intimate family portraits with experimental form and verbal play. It includes a long extract from a novel in verse, *The Adventures of Vela*, on which Wendt has worked since about 1985. David *Eggleton commented on Wendt's 'restless pursuit of unities', his use of storytelling to turn disorder into 'the woven mat of life', and the 'double consciousness' of his bilingualism.

Nuanua (1995) is Wendt's second anthology of Pacific writing, its introduction again an authoritative statement that celebrates the development, diversity and changing concerns of Pacific literature and comments with insight on the developing work of individual writers. Moving through anti-colonial and postcolonial positions, Wendt argues that Pacific writers have 'indigenised and enriched the language of the colonisers and used it to declare our independence and uniqueness'. To this literature, which he calls 'a fabulous storehouse of anthropology, sociology, art, religion, history, dance and music', Wendt's own work has made a leading and lasting contribution. BW

WERE, Virginia (1960–), poet and prose writer, has published in magazines like *Sport*, *NZ Listener* and *Landfall*. She studied at Elam School of Fine Arts, graduating 1982, was a member of the music group 'Marie and the Atom', and has travelled in the Pacific and India. *Juliet Bravo Juliet* (1989) is a collection of prose and poetry in three sections thematically linked by the idea of tourist travel as a metaphor for life. The book skilfully manœuvres between the different features of these genres, moving towards hybrid forms of verse narrative and prose poetry. Were's writing is precise and lucid: occasionally impressionistic, she always signposts a flight of fancy. Literal images in the short prose pieces of the first section develop a moral perspective, a personal comment, or a future scenario: in 'The Clyde Dam', 'the earth winces as its seams are drawn together by pins'. The poetry in the second section functions like a travelogue, narrating a personal engagement with different people and locations. In the third section four short stories are told by a detached narrator who panoramically surveys the locations described: characters on the road travel to local destinations, registered in titles which are also doubled place names—'Greymouth/Blackball'; 'Timaru /Dunedin'—and visit far-flung cities like Leuka and Delhi. Were now lives in Devonport. JW

WEST, Joyce (1908–85), fiction writer, is best known for her children's novels. Born in Auckland and brought up by teacher parents in remote districts of 'bush roads and river crossings', she began publishing stories and articles as a teenager. She achieved a pioneer family saga, *Sheep Kings* (1936), set beyond Gisborne, and collaborated with Mary *Scott in several murder-mystery romances featuring Inspector Wright. These included *Fatal Lady* (1960), with its horse-racing background, and *Who Put It There?* (1965).

Removed from the grand scale, and with her own illustrations, her children's trilogy successfully uses similar material. *Drovers Road* (1953), *Cape Lost* (1963) and *The Golden Country* (1965) draw convincingly on her knowledge of farming and rural communities, her passion for horses and her taste for the comic, the dramatic, the romantic and for protagonists 'orphaned' through divorce, death or travel. These engaging qualities reach their height in *The Year of the Shining Cuckoo* (1961), illustrated by Dennis Turner. A vivid celebration of almost-bygone Northland isolation, dominated by milking and tidal timetables, its structure rests on Johnny's efforts to raise money to buy the golden filly, 'all fire and silk and beauty'. His crusty grandfather and even crustier Aunt Garance and her entanglements, and various community gatherings, enliven Johnny's progress, culminating in a wedding with hilarious consequences. *The Sea Islanders* (1970), with West's own illustrations, again celebrates isolated Northland in a Robinsonnade featuring three runaway children and a special dolphin. Her final novel, *The River Road* (1980), also set on an isolated farm, is up to date in its confrontation with drug-runners.   DH

WESTON, Jessie (1867–1944), born in Auckland, taught in country schools and began contributing short stories to newspapers at 15. She began her novel *Ko Meri* (1890) at 20, travelling via the United States and Canada to Britain where it was published. The book takes a pessimistic view of the future for Māori, in keeping with the widespread belief at the time that they were a dying race. The main character, a young Māori woman, despite European education, returns after a crisis to her own people to share their fate. A keen imperialist, in London Weston began writing for the *New Review* on imperial matters, adopting the pseudonym 'C. de Thierry', under which a collection of her articles, 'Imperialism' (1898) was published. She contributed leading articles and political or literary reviews to major London papers and wrote for magazines such as the *Globe* and *Cornhill* and for the military magazine, *The Broad Arrow*, for over twenty years. Her topics included politics, colonial defence, naval bases and federation. Though for this work she used her own name, she always worked from outside, so that only her editor knew the articles were by a woman. She married late in life, and died probably in England.   JMcC

WESTRA, Ans (1936–), born in Leiden, Holland, emigrated to New Zealand in 1957 and became a photographic chronicler of the life and times of ordinary New Zealanders. Paying special attention to Māori and Pacific Island subjects, her work has been published in books and journals, in particular Te *Ao Hou*, and for the Department of Education. She has also worked with authors like James Ritchie, on *Māori* (1967); James K. *Baxter (and Tim Shadbolt) on *Notes on the Country I

Live In (1972), and Katerina *Mataira on *Whaiora: The Pursuit of Life* (1985). She is perhaps most known for the controversy surrounding her *Washday at the Pa* (1964), a photo-essay of the life of a Māori family living in an isolated rural community, which was commissioned for a schools publication, but withdrawn due to criticism from the Maori Womens' Welfare League. Westra's book was subsequently published by *Caxton Press (1964), but has continued to be a focus for debate on the politics of the representation of Māori by Pākehā artists.   CB

Whaikōrero is the Māori art of rhetoric, a literary, semi-theatrical skill which is as important to a person's *mana as skill in battle or other valued qualities. Because its deep spiritual significance is inseparable from the language, even today many insist that only Māori be spoken during the welcoming of guests to the *marae. This sometimes leads to misunderstanding on the part of those who speak no Māori, but the forces that bind the marae, the *tangata whenua and the spirits who inhabit the place cannot be separated from the way language is used there.

To be permitted to speak on the marae is a great honour, accorded only to certain people who must earn the right through their actions in all departments of life. An order of precedence is often observed, so that it is rare for a younger person to speak before an older one has done so. In most tribal areas (the exception is Ngāti Porou on the East Coast of the North Island), women are not encouraged to speak on the marae—indeed great offence can be caused in this way. A man may refuse to speak if a woman has done so before him, causing difficulties if the woman holds high office in the Pākehā system, and requiring cultural sensitivity of all parties. This dilemma is explored by Hiwi and Pat Tauroa in *The Marae: A Guide to Customs and Protocol* (1986).

Anne Salmond writes: 'A skilled orator is a master of genealogy, ancient chants, local history and proverbs. Not only is he erudite, but a consummate actor as well. His movements are dramatic and timed to give the best possible effect to the statements he is making.' She describes a clergyman tearing off his collar so that he could 'speak as a man, not as a priest', a gesture still talked of almost two years later. The marae, *Orbell says, is at such moments 'very like the theatre' (*Hui: A Study of Maori Ceremonial Gatherings*, 1975; see also *Māori theatre).

The speech itself is preceded by an introductory *tauparapara, after which the speaker normally pays his respects to the dead of the marae and greets the marae itself and the hosts. Only then will he address the major theme of his speech, and at the conclusion of it he will be supported by the people singing a *waiata. This sequence applies to mihi, the greeting ritual, which is bound by formalities. Later, indoors, whaikōrero is less formal and it is here that the speaker's special oratorical skills can be more clearly perceived. Nonetheless the choice and manipulation of formal elements to suit a specific occasion is a greatly admired skill in the more formal kind of whaikōrero. The forms were studied in detail in a dissertation by Robert Mahuta (1975).

Clearly there is a problem in making this literary activity comprehensible to people whose literature is primarily in writing and in another language. Hirini *Melbourne has addressed this problem, but cannot solve it, citing the celebrated orator Te Wharehuia Milroy, who 'is a reluctant writer. His creativity is so linked to its cultural context that his most commanding works are created on the marae or the wharenui at night.' Any transcription, Melbourne argues, loses the resonances of context; translations of whaikōrero 'have been translated not merely into another language but also into a wholly different conceptual system' ('Whare Whakairo: Māori Literary Traditions', in *Dirty Silence: Aspects of Language and Literature in New Zealand*, ed. Graham McGregor and Mark *Williams, 1991).

Salmond points to the techniques of spontaneity, originality, digression and variations from standard structures, so that 'the best speakers end up discoursing on quite unexpected topics, moving their audience to laughter or tears at will'. The speeches are set in a mythological landscape which, Orbell affirms, 'would be quite unfamiliar to other New Zealanders'. The larger cities are ignored; small villages with a rich mythological and historical background are given prominence. In this way a creative poetic activity is going on all over New Zealand, often unobserved by a majority of the population and sometimes being lost as memories fade. Such loss, however, a feature of all oral literature, is balanced by the preservation of song in constant repetition. NW

Whaka-ara-ara pa is a kind of watch song, sometimes performed in the place of a *tauparapara. Originally it was a call to arms performed by sentries. NW

Whakapapa, genealogies, in Māori traditional literature, record the origins and histories of tribes, families and individuals, giving them an important part of their sense of identity and interrelationship. Whakapapa follow the generations back to legendary and mythical ancestors but are also an essential part of the historical record. They are, however, selective, and therefore flexible. In *Ngā Pepa a Ranginui: The Walker Papers* (1996), Ranginui *Walker writes that the sheer length of history of tribal societies made it impossible for all ancestors' names to be preserved orally. 'Only luminaries who had pivotal roles in the evolution and development of the

Māori world were recorded in the whakapapa.' Genealogies were also often lengthened 'by the insertion of extra divisions in the epochs of creation, or deities in human lines to enhance them'. Their details were not common knowledge but were transmitted to an educational elite in the esoteric lore of the *whare wānanga.

The remoter parts of the whakapapa were an area of poetic creativity. Walker writes of 'the insertion of poetic or compositional layers in the genealogy', with metaphoric names that may be translated as (for example) 'the enchanted wand … the resounding gong … the wailing gong … the panting sob … the dry heavenly breeze of summer'. Their meanings can be complex. In publishing Tainui genealogies in *King Potatau* (1959), Pei Te Hurinui *Jones remarked, 'The translations alone—which do not always conform to the dictionary meaning of the words—will be found to reveal a treasure trove of philosophic thought of a high order.'

Apart from its own literary merits, the whakapapa often serves as an important element in narrative literature (*kōrero), where intricacies of plot can depend on the relationships between characters as illustrated through genealogy. It also plays a major role in oratory (*whaikōrero), where speakers call on various phases of the whakapapa to welcome, gratify or discomfort their hearers. In short, whakapapa is a central component of Māori thought and cultural life.   NW

Whakataukī, see **Māori sayings**.

Whale Rider, The, see **IHIMAERA, Witi**.

Whānau, or extended family, is a subdivision of a *hapū. This is the basic social group among Māori, offering intimacy and mutual support (*aroha). It is also the household unit and can include three or four generations, sometimes numbering more than thirty persons. The leaders of the whānau are the kaumātua.   NW

Whanau (1974), Witi *Ihimaera's second novel, is again concerned with the tightly knit Māori community of the small village of Waituhi. Unlike *Tangi*, which focuses on an individual, the village is as central to the novel as its *whānau. Rather than privilege a single member, Ihimaera brings the community into focus through a multitude of perspectives, thus making the point that the individual is subordinate to the community. Yet *Whanau* also has a number of significant subplots; such as George Karepa's desertion of Mattie, the mother of his child, which symbolises young Māori abandoning traditional responsibilities. Old Nanny Paora symbolises the opposite perspective, his *mana is great because of his lineage and his age, and he is venerated as one of the few full-blooded Māori remaining. In the final chapters, when young Pene helps him escape threats to place him in a nursing home, the novel finally brings the whānau together in an attempt to find the pair. Although the search succeeds, Paora tragically falls into a coma. Yet behind the tragedy, Pene comes to understand the old man's vision of the crucial importance of village *aroha as a way of resisting the disintegration of their culture. Waituhi's *tangata whenua live clustered around its meeting house—the unusually painted Rongopai—which is the heart of the village. Yet Rongopai is, as the novel begins, in a state of decay emblematic of the traditions being lost to the whānau in the modern world. But just as the fugitive pair use Rongopai as a sanctuary, so Ihimaera uses it as a symbol of hope; the whānau's growing pride in it an emblem of Māori culture's essential strength.   PM

Whare wānanga was traditionally a Māori school of learning, where young men of noble birth learned *whakapapa, traditions and, sometimes, secret and esoteric knowledge. Sitting in complete darkness, they learned texts by chanting them. The teachers were *tohunga, sometimes of great fame for their learning. All matters connected with such schools were extremely *tapu.

A famous whare wānanga was Te Rāwheoro at Tologa Bay, founded by a great woodcarver, Hingāngaroa. A school of high reputation, like this one, would attract young men from considerable distances and other *hapū or *iwi. Ngāti Porou history (according to Margaret *Orbell) records that the last session at Te Rāwheoro opened in 1836, when the leading tohunga were 'Rangiuia who recited the genealogies, Tokipuanga who supplemented them, and Mohi *Ruatapu who elaborated upon them.' (Mohi Ruatapu was also one of the experts who dictated traditions to amanuenses, thus recording them for the future.)

The Ngāti Kahungunu tohunga, Te Mātorohanga, spent some time at Te Rāwheoro in 1836. When he and others of his iwi set up their own whare wānanga, for the first time they allowed their 'students' to keep written notes. The notes kept by H.T. Te Whatahoro and Āporo Kumeroa, together with manuscripts collected by Te Whataroa from other sources, formed the basis of S. Percy *Smith's book *The Lore of the Whare Wānanga* (2 vols., 1913, 1915). However, this was very late in the history of the whare wānanga, and Te Mātorohanga was an innovator. What is more, Smith introduced distortions of his own: his description of the god Io as a supreme being and creator was clearly based on Christian thinking and is not even consistent with the (in any case non-traditional) notes of Te Whatahoro and Āporo

Kumeroa. In Māori belief *Rangi and Papa were not created, but always were, and the myth of their separation is therefore a genesis rather than a creation myth. There are other major differences between Smith's account and those of other sources—such as the large number of children of Rangi and Papa—due partly to Te Mātorohanga's innovations, partly to Smith himself. Consequently Smith's account of the literary/religious tradition is dismissed by modern scholars. The notes on which it is based, can, however, be viewed as 'a convincing picture of Ngāti Kahungunu thought at a late stage in its development' (Margaret *Orbell).

There are also mythical whare wānanga to be found at *Hawaiki, and on arrival in *Aotearoa one of the first actions of each *waka was to found one. The first Tainui house of learning, for example, was Te Ahurei. Education was not confined to the whare wānanga. Practical arts and less esoteric knowledge were taught to all young people on the marae. Songs (*waiata), stories (*kōrero) and *sayings all conveyed traditional knowledge in everyday life.

In recent years whare wānanga are places where Māori customs (tikanga), history and traditions are taught. They can be weekend schools for people returning to their *marae, schools for more extended learning and, in one or two cases, places where university degrees can be acquired. New Zealand universities and other institutions of learning include the term in their Māori titles: for example, Victoria University of Wellington is named Te Whare Wānanga o te Upoko o te Ika a Māui (the school of learning at the head of the fish of *Māui).   NW

'WHIM-WHAM' is the pseudonym under which poet Allen *Curnow wrote satirical verses in various New Zealand newspapers. In succession to Curnow's earlier *Tomorrow* pseudonym of 'Julian', Whim-Wham verses appeared in the *Press* in 1939, then in the *NZ Listener* 1942–45, and after 1951 the *New Zealand Herald*, later syndicated. Several compilations were published in book form: *A Present for Hitler* (*Caxton, 1940), *Verses 1941–42* (Caxton, 1942), *Verses, 1943* (*Progressive Publishing Society, 1943), *The Best of Whim-Wham* (*Paul's Book Arcade, 1959) and *Whim-Wham Land* (*Blackwood and Janet Paul, 1967). After nearly fifty years, Whim-Wham made his last appearance on 6 August 1988.   PS

Whitcombe & Tombs was formed in 1882 when a Christchurch bookseller, George Whitcombe, joined with the printer and bookbinder George Tombs. They extended their activities to include publishing and stationery, and then took advantage of the burgeoning demand for locally produced school textbooks. By 1916 they had established offices and printing works in the four main centres, eventually becoming the largest firm of printers and publishers in New Zealand. They also established branches in Melbourne, Sydney, Geelong and Perth, as well as a buying office in London. In 1917 B.E.H. Whitcombe became the managing director upon the death of his father, serving the company for a further forty-five years. School readers formed a major part of their educational list, but perhaps their greatest success was the series of mass-produced children's storybooks, of which some twelve million were produced between 1908 and 1965. Ian McLaren's *Whitcombe's Story Books, A Trans-Tasman Survey* (1984) provides a detailed bibliography of this phenomenon. As well as verse by Blanche *Baughan and Jessie *Mackay and a selection of general books covering biography, natural history, history and Māori subjects, they also published the New Zealand Centennial Survey and a number of legal books. The Whitcombes Library Service, which held the National Library contract, was established in Wellington in the early 1950s. Denis *Glover referred to the company as 'The Octopus', but their Christchurch shop was particularly supportive of *Caxton titles. In 1971 Whitcombe & Tombs merged with the printers Coulls Somerville Wilkie to form the now almost ubiquitous Whitcoulls.   NWt

WHITE, Dorothy Neal (1915–95), was an internationally regarded pioneer in children's library services and writing on children's literature. Born and educated in Christchurch, in 1936–37 she attended the Carnegie Library School in Pittsburgh and in 1937 was appointed children's librarian at Dunedin Public Library, where she introduced a library service to Otago schools. After leaving librarianship to raise a family (her first husband was Dunedin antiquarian bookseller Dick White), she became head of children's services at Dunedin Public Library 1957–74. Her first book, *About Books for Children* (1946, 1958), discussed kinds of writing for children and recommended appropriate reading; her second was the trail-blazing and highly influential *Books Before Five* (1954, 1984), recording her observations of her elder daughter's early reading development. She was resident children's book reviewer for the *NZ Listener* 1982–85 and (as D.N. Ballantyne) general book reviewer for the *Otago Daily Times* from 1981. In 1987 the National Library's historical collection of children's books was named in her honour.   AM

WHITE, John (1826–91), novelist and collector/author of one of the largest works on Māori literary and historical traditions, grew up in Hokianga where he learned the language of his Māori neighbours and acquired a great enthusiasm for their culture and way of life. He was born in County Durham and travelled to New Zealand with his blacksmith father, Francis, and his mother, Jane, in 1834–35.

Hokianga was a fascinating but isolated community —it was easier to travel to Sydney by ship than to Auckland on foot or horseback. The journal White kept from 1846 to 1850, now in the *Alexander Turnbull Library, laments the lack of educational opportunities, but shows that he spent much time reading, writing and, even then, collecting Māori traditions. It seems that he was already working on the latter at the age of 17. In fact he and his siblings attended a mission school.

In exchange for the stories he was told by Māori friends, he would tell them stories culled from Sir Walter Scott or other collections such as *The Arabian Nights*. In an essay on early printing in Māori (1940) Johannes *Andersen recorded that 'it was his skill in story-telling which very largely helped John White to collect the stories in his collection *The Ancient History of the Maori*; it was barter again; a Pakeha story for a Maori story. On 11 June 1846 he told them the story of *Jack and the Beanstalk*. He writes: "they were delighted with it; they listened with all the attention imaginable; they laughed heartily at Jack's stealing of the enchanted wand."' When (on 26 December 1846) he told Scott's 'Lady of the Lake', he comments in his journal, 'it took me from seven till twelve at night to tell it: being in a foreign language I had to explain different parts, which made the tale longer. They all listened with great eagerness to it, and when it was finished they said, "What a pity it is done so soon; it is so pretty."' And elsewhere White wrote of a *tohunga who heard him tell Scott's *St. Clair of the Isles* and went back into the interior to tell his tribe the story. White comments that in return for his tale he got 'a most outaway tale, love, love, a mad love, and death at the end of it. Cupid keep me from such.' To him, at first, the Māori tales seemed largely entertainments—he called them 'anecdotes'—but gradually he developed the plan of organising and publishing such materials. He also enjoyed writing stories and poems of his own and worked assiduously as a translator.

From this often casual yet industrious dabbling arose a collection which has become a standard work, often quoted but not always praised or even acknowledged: *The Ancient History of the Māori* (6 vols., 1887–90). Although each section bears the name of a tribe, and many tales are told in tribal variants, it is not always clear who the informants were in each case. Margaret *Orbell says that much of White's material has been taken from the manuscripts of the missionary Richard *Taylor, and White has been severely criticised by J. Prytz Johansen for his 'untrustworthiness' as an editor, while Kendrick *Smithyman made a minute critical analysis of part of the work, reaching the conclusion that White rewrote most of the Māori while copying from his notebooks. In Orbell's opinion, 'His alterations … do much to damage the stories' swift laconic precision of style.' In the preface to *The Ancient History of the Maori* White gives an explanation of the 'disjointed' nature of the work. He laid the blame on the oral nature of the tradition and its partly esoteric value which led an informant to say 'The parts I have not related are so sacred that I withhold them in dread of sudden death.'

Some question whether all the material was in fact collected or whether some was invention, the result of White's own literary ambitions (this is discussed by Michael Reilly in the *Journal of New Zealand History,* Vol. 23, No. 1, 1989 and in the next issue Reilly traces the complex issue of 'informants'). The mirror image of such doubts is created by his historical novels—are these fact rather than fiction? The subtitle of the first, *Te Rou* (1874), suggests a non-fiction—ethnographic—intention behind this novel: *A Tale, exhibiting the social life, manners, habits, and customs of the Maori race in New Zealand prior to the introduction of civilisation amongst them.* Although it largely imitates the popular English novels of Charles Kingsley, White spoke of this book as an historical account. Another novel, *Revenge: A Love Tale of the Mount Eden Tribe* was published by A.W. *Reed in 1940, but Reilly says that the original typescript was 'much edited' by Reed. There is a third novel in manuscript in the Wellington Public Library ('Tale of Hari').   NW

WHITE, Patrick (1912–89), *Australia's greatest novelist and Nobel Laureate, visited Wellington for three weeks in March 1961, finding it 'so beautiful that it makes Australia seem like a rubbish dump'. He commented less favourably on 'the most astonishing outbreaks of human violence and youthful degeneracy' and on 'the wind. There are grey, tearing days which perhaps explain the high suicide rate and undercurrent of neurosis' (*Letters*, ed. David Marr, 1994). He was visiting a cousin, Peggy Garland, whose lodger, Antony *Alpers, took him to the Katherine *Mansfield collection at the *Alexander Turnbull Library where he 'handled a lot of her original letters and notebooks … tremendously intrigued by the private, sometimes almost automatic outpourings'. Alpers touched White deeply by a present of 'a little greenstone and silver paperknife which had belonged to K.M.'. Also in the house was Peggy Garland's youngest son, Philip, then 14. Brain-damaged in some unknown way at birth, simple, troubled by fits but articulate and sensitive, he and White struck up a friendship, listening to music and visiting the nearby Wellington Zoo. White's biographer, David Marr, shows that images from their walks together, the zoo and

'Philip hanging over the gramophone listening to Schubert' returned to him in writing *The Solid Mandala* (1966), with 'Arthur Brown, the simple man of unexpected gifts … the sort of man his cousin Philip Garland might have been if the boy's "childish wisdom" had matured.' Mark *Williams writes in his study of White's novels (1993) of the 'dualism' of Arthur as the focus of the book's spiritual themes.

The dualities of New Zealand had recurred to White when he was 'bowled right over' by Janet *Frame's *Owls Do Cry* in 1963, writing of the 'despair and confusion under the simple, uncomplicated New Zealand surface…. I shouldn't be surprised if any New Zealander took a gun to his neighbour.' Marr has reported that White enthusiastically wrote to Janet Frame, receiving a reply twenty-two years later.

Marr's biography shows that White was also a lifelong admirer of Mansfield, using her letters and diaries 'as a guide' when he visited the South of France in 1976, and agreeing to join Michael *King, that year's Katherine *Mansfield Memorial Fellow, in urging the Menton authorities to increase their support. White met King again on a brief visit to Auckland in 1984, when he presented awards for the New Zealand Foundation for Peace Studies, endorsed New Zealand's anti-nuclear stand and greeted the plants in the Domain's scented garden 'like old friends.'   RR

WHITEHEAD, Gillian (1941–), composer, was born in Whangarei, where in childhood she absorbed the natural world of the sea, hills and trees and especially their Māori associations. Natural sounds suffuse her music: 'of birds, the sound of wind from nothing, the sound of rain and the great sense of space and the changing light'. One-eighth Māori, she feels strongly she belongs in New Zealand, 'because the Maori part of me goes further back than 1642, the year of Tasman's explorations'.

As a composer, words have meant as much to her as music. While studying for her degree at the University of Auckland from 1959, she sang in the cathedral choir under Peter Godfrey, learning the choral repertoire, especially sixteenth and seventeenth-century English works. This experience bore fruit in her first mature composition, a highly praised *Missa Brevis* (1963). Since then she has written many works for voice including settings of texts by Janet *Frame, Bill *Manhire and Cilla *McQueen. The chamber opera *Tristan and Iseult* (1975), with a libretto by Malcolm Crowthers and Michael Hill, launched her on a career as a successful music theatre composer. Her close collaboration with Fleur *Adcock resulted in a number of works: *The Inner Harbour* (1979), for choir and chamber orchestra, *Hotspur* (1980), a north-England dramatic saga for soprano and chamber ensemble, *Eleanor of Aquitaine* (1982), for mezzo-soprano and orchestra, *The King of the Other Country* (1984), a chamber opera, and *The Virgin and the Nightingale* (1986), five songs from a medieval Latin text translated by Fleur Adcock and others. Anna Maria dell'Oso provided librettos for the operas *The Pirate Moon* (1986) and *Bride of Fortune* (1988). In London she had begun a series of works on Māori themes such as *Whakatau-ki* (1970) for male singer and instrumental ensemble, based on Māori sayings which describe in vivid imagery the seasonal cycle. A number of string and piano compositions which have similar derivations include *Pakuru* (1967), for soprano and instruments, *Te Ahua, Te Atarangi*, a string quartet which won first prize in an NZBC competition and most recently *Awa Herea* (1994) ('Braided Rivers'), a song cycle to texts by the composer and Keri Kaa, which has received much critical acclaim.

After graduating BMus (Hons) in 1964 from Victoria University of Wellington, Whitehead took a Masters in composition at the University of Sydney (1966), and studied with Peter Maxwell Davies in Adelaide and England. She has held appointments as composer-in-residence or as teacher at Newcastle University, UK, and Sydney Conservatorium of Music, among others. JMT

WICKENS, Maria (1966–), won the 1993 Reed New Writers Fiction Award with *Left of Centre* (1994), a fast-paced and realistic sketch of teenage alcoholism and drug addiction. It is a New Zealand small-town ('Mudflats', presumably Masterton) version of what Tom Wolfe has called the American 'anaesthetic novel', as in, for instance, Tama Janowitz, who was a guest of ★Writers and Readers Week in Wellington in 1990. Thus sex, family strife, proffered love, and deaths by suicide and overdose all leave the narrator 'dead inside. Dead numb. Dead dull nothingness.' Any approach to feeling is turned aside by flip quips ('One hot chocolate and I was anybody's') or derivative allusions to ★American electronic culture of film, television and music; while responsibility is passed on by the plot's revelation of sexual abuse by her father and alcoholic evasion by her mother. Its picture of the lost self-respect of a lost generation is depressingly credible, sometimes bleakly funny, with glimpses of what Elizabeth Caffin called an 'anarchic free spirit'. Maria Wickens was born and grew up in Masterton, graduated BA(Hons) in English and BCA at Victoria University in 1989, worked in public relations in Wellington and since 1992 has been in London. RR

WILCOX, Dora (1873–1953), was a popular poet who has a place in the literatures of New Zealand and ★Australia. Born in Christchurch, she taught in Armidale, NSW, and contributed to the ★*Bulletin* before travelling to England for war work during World War 1. The poems from this long absence were published in *Verses from Maoriland* (1905) and *Rata and Mistletoe* (1911), and attracted a wide public by their strong nationalism and fashionable evocation of loss and nostalgia, the note of the 'exile's lyre'. With her second husband, Australian art historian and journalist William Moore, she settled in Sydney, winning a *Sydney Morning Herald* prize in 1927 for an ode commemorating the opening of the Commonwealth Parliament. Two of her plays were published in *Best Australian One-Act Plays* (ed. William Moore and T. Inglis Moore, 1937), and a lecture on *Samuel Butler in Canterbury* for the Sydney Branch of the English Association, of which she was a patron. Her last book of verse, *Seven Poems* (1924) draws largely on her Australian experience. HMcQ/RR

Wild Honey (1964), a book of poems by Alistair ★Campbell, published in Britain, was partly an attempt to re-present his former work in a more perfect form (and for an overseas readership) and partly a publication of new poems. It opens with the sequence ★'Sanctuary of Spirits', minimally revised, and a group of poems not previously published in book form, while the second and third sections are a rearrangement of poems from ★*Mine Eyes Dazzle* with some adjustments and additions. 'Looking at Kapiti' is dated 'December, 1959', revealing that the poet's preoccupation with Te Rauparaha and his island fortress had preceded 'Sanctuary of Spirits' by at least four years. A suggestion of future, autobiographical, tendencies are the four 'Personal Sonnets', which recall members of Campbell's family, notably his Polynesian mother, 'of *ariki* / Descent', who gave him the middle name (Te Ariki) he started to use shortly after this date, and the Scottish–New Zealand father who died of grief after her early death. Ariki are Polynesian nobility. For the first time, too, he directly addresses his troubled mental history, seeking an origin for his illness in the fact that 'Parental love engenders in the soul / Serenity without which we are mad.' In the third section of the book some familiar poems reappear. 'Waterfall' is an interesting case. In the 1951 version of *Mine Eyes Dazzle* it has five stanzas, in the 1956 version only two and in *Wild Honey* three, the third being cleverly constructed to save what was best of the deleted stanzas. In this section old poems are blended harmoniously with new, so that, more than a retrospective, *Wild Honey* suggests a future for the poet secure on the foundations he had laid and (especially in 'The Climber' and 'Forgiveness') a determination to overcome the obstacles his illness had created by stretching the bow between future and past. NW

WILKINS, Damien (1963–), one of the most distinctive fiction writers to emerge in the 1980s, was born in Lower Hutt and educated there and at Victoria University (BA Hons, 1984). After university teaching and travelling overseas, he became assistant editor at ★Victoria University Press in 1988, leaving in 1990 to do an MFA in creative writing at Washington University, St Louis. Since 1992 he has been a full-time writer and occasional writing tutor in Wellington.

Wilkins's short stories first appeared in ★*Sport* and other periodicals in the late 1980s. His accomplished and varied story collection, *The Veteran Perils* (1990), was joint winner of the inaugural Heinemann Reed Fiction Award. He has since published an unexpected book of poems, *The Idles* (1993), and two novels: *The Miserables* (1993), a multi-layered portrait of a young man's developing literary sensibility, which won the 1994 New Zealand Book Award for Fiction; and *Little Masters* (1996), a comedy of manners deriving from intersecting relationships and geographical dislocations. Wilkins is also known for his astute literary reviews and critical essays.

Central to his fiction is the close observation of character, especially the disjunction between the perceptions of self and of others, between desire and outcome, revealed as much in quirky incidents as at times of crisis, and engendering pathos as well as comedy. His writing is exuberant and evocative, subtle and exact, aware of its own artifice yet relishing the idiosyncrasies and possibilities of language; control now seems more sure. Looking to European and American models (his work is published also in the UK and USA), Wilkins is potentially the finest New Zealand fiction writer of his generation.

AM

WILKINSON, Iris, see **HYDE, Robin**.

WILLIAMS, George Phipps (1847–1909), light verse writer, was born in London, went to Harrow and Cambridge, and emigrated to New Zealand in 1869. A civil engineer by profession, he carried out a large number of public works in the North Island and the Canterbury area. At various times he worked for the Rakaia Railway, the Westport–Stockton Company, the Waimakariri–Ashley Water Supply Board and central government and was involved in the construction of the Midland Railway from Canterbury to the West Coast.

Known to his friends as 'Strange Peter', Williams mixed professional with literary and sporting interests. A founder member and long-serving secretary of the Christchurch Savage Club, a columnist for the Christchurch ★*Press* under the pseudonym 'The Bohemian', he was also a lively participant in local amateur dramatics and

a handicapper for the Jockey Club. With W.P. ★Reeves (whom he later described as 'your dine-at-the-Club, like-m'-wine-dry type of socialist'), Williams brought out two highly popular verse collections, *Colonial Couplets: Being Poems in Partnership* (1889) and *In Double Harness: Poems in Partnership* (1891). While Reeves's contributions, both 'grave' and 'gay', have not worn well, Williams's show him to have been a light verse writer of considerable accomplishment. Poems like 'Atra Cura', 'An Old Chum on New Zealand Scenery' and 'A New Chum's Letter Home' with their genial irony, metrical assurance and wry modulations of tone compare favourably with W.S. Gilbert's *Bab Ballads* or ★Kipling's *Departmental Ditties*. The 'Old Chum's' confession strikes a characteristic note: 'The terms I use are such as poets would not love to hear. / What they call a brook or brooklet, or a streamlet, or a rill, / I do only, I confess it, call a *creek*, and always will.' Williams's play, '*A Question of Degree': A Bush Idyll*, was performed by members of the Christchurch Savage Club on Ladies' Night, 16 August 1899, and published the same year; *A New Chum's Letter Home and Divers Verses, Dry and Diverse*, in effect a selected poems, appeared in 1904. HMcQ/HRi

WILLIAMS, Haare (1936–), Te Aitanga-a-Māhaki, Rongowhakaata, Tūhoe, Whakatōhea, is a pioneer of Māori broadcasting, both radio and television. He was manager of Te Reo o Aotearoa and general manager of Aotearoa Radio, but resigned to organise the Māori contributions to the sesquicentennial celebrations in 1990. He is a minister of the Ringatū church, an artist and a writer. His publications include *Karanga* (poems, 1981), *The Raukawa Experience: A Weekend on a Marae* (1980), *Akona te Reo Māori* (1979), *Te Rūnanga o Waitangi—He Kōrero mō Waitangi* (1984) and *He Tohu Aroha ki ngā Tūpuna* (1985). NW

WILLIAMS, Henry, see **WILLIAMS, William**.

WILLIAMS, H.B. (Herbert William), see **WILLIAMS, William**.

WILLIAMS, Mark (1951–), is an academic critic and editor of contemporary New Zealand literature. Born and educated in Auckland, he went from Auckland University to the University of British Columbia for his PhD (1983), returning to lecture at Auckland and Waikato before moving to the University of Canterbury, where he is now senior lecturer. His major publications on New Zealand literature as author are *Leaving the Highway: Six Contemporary New Zealand Novelists* (1990) and his chapter on 'Literary Scholarship, Criticism, and Theory' in the revised *OHNZLE* (1998). As editor he has published *The Caxton Anthology: New Zealand Poetry 1972–1986* (1987), which marked the fiftieth anniversary of *Caxton Press; *Dirty Silence: Aspects of Language and Literature in New Zealand* (ed. with Graham McGregor, 1991); *In the Same Room: Conversations with New Zealand Writers* (ed. with Elizabeth *Alley, 1992); *Opening the Book: New Essays on New Zealand Writing* (ed. with Michele *Leggott, 1995); *The Source of the Song: New Zealand Writers on Catholicism* (1995); and *An Anthology of New Zealand Poetry in English* (ed. with Jenny Bornholdt and Gregory *O'Brien, Oxford University Press, 1997). He is one of the first academics to focus his publications so predominantly on contemporary New Zealand writing. His work also shows some sense of international context, which enables him to argue in *Leaving the Highway* against the 'violent dualities' of New Zealand culture and the 'binary habits of New Zealand criticism' and advocate instead independence, difference, continuities and 'complex wholeness'.   RR

WILLIAMS, Mona (1943–), storyteller and children's writer, was born in British Guiana (now Guyana), won a scholarship to the prestigious Anglican colonial school, Bishops, and went on to Stanford University, USA, as a Fulbright and Ford Foundation scholar. She worked in radio and TV in San Francisco, her storytelling programme, 'Roots and Branches', winning an Emmy in 1971. Known widely for her dynamic storytelling incorporating music and dance, Williams is now a New Zealand citizen and lecturer in English at the Palmerston North College of Education. As an Afro-Caribbean of Jewish faith, she brings perspectives that are unusual in New Zealand. Her stories have appeared in the *NZ Listener, *School Journal and on radio, and she collaborated with Joy *Cowley to produce the story collection, *Two of a Kind* (1984). Her year's fellowship as the 1993 writer-in-residence at the University of Waikato enabled her to concentrate on her vibrant autobiography, *Bishops: My Turbulent Colonial Youth* (1995).   DH

WILLIAMS, William (1800–78), completed an apprenticeship to a Southwell (London) surgeon before going to Oxford, where he graduated BA in classics in 1824, and was ordained soon after. He then followed his brother Henry to New Zealand for the Church Missionary Society, arriving in Paihia in 1826. He spent the next eight years there studying the Māori language, constructing its grammar preparatory to translating the Bible.

His *A Dictionary of the New-Zealand Language, and A Concise Grammar* was published in Paihia in 1844 and, after much revision, it is still in print, the longest surviving book in New Zealand history. After years in missionary work he visited England in 1851–52, where he published his Māori translations of the New Testament and the Prayer Book. In recognition of his services Oxford University conferred on him the degree of DCL (1851). After his return to New Zealand he worked on his book *Christianity among the New Zealanders* (1867). When the bishopric of New Zealand was divided in 1859 he became Bishop of Waiapu, and he ran a large group of schools in Poverty Bay until they were sacked by Hauhau and the library burned in 1865. He died in Napier.

Williams was of a prominent missionary family. His brother Henry, archdeacon of Waimate, translated the Treaty of Waitangi into Māori and personally persuaded many chiefs to sign it. W.L. Williams (1829–1916), the son of William and principal of Te Rau Maori Theological College, was a noted Māori scholar, who revised his father's dictionary for publication in 1871 and wrote *First Lessons in the Maori Language* (1862) and *East Coast (N.Z.) Historical Records* (rpt. from the *Poverty Bay Herald*, 1932).

Work on the *Dictionary* was continued by W.L. Williams's son, H.W. Williams (1860–1937), who was awarded a Doctorate of Literature from the University of New Zealand for his fifth edition of it (1917). He also published a definitive bibliography of printed Māori. Later editions of the *Dictionary* were prepared by committees, prominent members of which were Pei Te Hurinui *Jones and Bruce *Biggs, but they still bear the name of H.W. Williams, the last of a distinguished line of scholars.   NW

WILLIAMS, W.L. (William Leonard), see **WILLIAMS, William**.

WILSON, Anne (Lady) (1848–1930), was a novelist and poet of the late colonial period. Born Anne Adams in Victoria, Australia, she married in 1874 James Glenny Wilson, Rangitikei farmer and for fourteen years member of the New Zealand parliament, becoming Lady Wilson on his knighthood. She was remembered for her culture and intelligence, qualities also evident in her writing, though evinced in strong derivativeness from English models, especially Tennyson and Kipling: 'Hear the distant thunder rolling; surely 'tis the making tide, / Swinging all the blue Pacific on the harbour's iron side.' Patrick *Evans (in the *Penguin History of New Zealand Literature*, 1990) took Wilson's poetry as the period type for what he tartly dismisses as 'a sort of Disneyland of the mind that has no connection with anything in particular'. The pastoralisms in their artifice indeed often evoke the English eighteenth century rather than 1880s Canterbury: 'That idly gads o'er hill and vale'; 'the twinkling windows of the farm'; 'And rosy vapours skirt the pastoral plain' (though Disneyland has never echoed Milton so skilfully). Yet among these gestures of derivation there is effort also to name local habitations, to identify the cause why 'I love this narrow, sandy road'; an effort that names without artifice 'the loud nor'wester', 'shrill cicada' and 'glacier river rattling on'. Wilson is anthologised in Harvey ★McQueen's *The New Place* (1993). As 'Austral', she was a prominent contributor of poetry and prose to the ★*Press*. Her volumes of poetry, all published in London, include *Themes and Variations* (1889) and *A Book of Verses* (1901); her novels (or romances) are *Alice Lauder: A Sketch* (1893) and *Two Summers* (1900).   RR

WILSON, Guthrie (1914–   ), novelist, born in Palmerston North and educated at Victoria University College and Wellington Teachers' College, had a distinguished educational and military career. He taught at Marlborough College in Blenheim, 1937–40, and then joined the New Zealand Territorial Forces in 1941. He served as an officer in the New Zealand Division infantry in the Middle East and ★Italy, 1943–45, was captured just before the end of the war, and received the Military Cross for leadership and gallantry in a battle incident at the Senio River in northern Italy (the incident is the basis for the central episode of ★*Brave Company*). He returned to Marlborough College in 1946 and then served as head of history, geography, and social studies at Palmerston North BHS 1946–55. From 1956–60 he was senior Latin master at Newington College, Sydney, and then senior master in 1961. From 1962 to 1979 he was at Scots College, Sydney, where he was first assistant to the principal, and then, from 1966, principal. In 1977 he received an OBE.

This career in education, with its growing responsibilities, seems to have crowded out Wilson's career as imaginative writer, which had been seen as extremely promising. He published a few poems in ★*Tomorrow* 1936–37, but his career as writer really began with his war novel, *Brave Company*, published in the United States in 1950 and in England and New Zealand in 1951, to much critical acclaim. (See also ★War literature: World War 2.) His later novels divide into two groups: ★'Man Alone' novels of violence, and more social novels of ambition. The 'Man Alone' novels include *The Feared and the Fearless* (1954) and *Strip Jack Naked* (1957). The former deals with a New Zealand soldier who is brain-damaged in combat in Italy, becomes an effective leader of the partisans, and then after the war a violent killer and the object of a manhunt in New Zealand; the latter deals with the destruction of an asocial English seaman in New Zealand after he turns to violence. (See also ★Existentialism.) The novels of ambition include *Julien Ware* (1952), the story of the ruthless struggle of an underprivileged young man to reach wealth and social status, cut off by his death in the war; *Sweet White Wine* (1956), the subject of a libel action by the novelist against a reviewer, which deals with the relationship between a New Zealand writer and his ruthlessly ambitious friend; *Dear Miranda* (1959), a comedy set in Australia focusing on the rise of a good-natured but quite self-concerned young woman; and *The Incorruptibles* (1960), the story of the struggle for the headship of a Sydney public school. There was also a later novel, *The Return of the Snow-White Puritan* (1964), published under the pseudonym of 'John Palotti', as well as several uncollected short stories.

Wilson was seen in the early 1950s as potentially a major novelist, but none of his later works equalled *Brave Company*. All are marred by a tendency to melodramatic devices to move the plot when it threatens to stall, and by the use of stereotyped characters. However, *Brave Company* ranks as one of the best New Zealand novels of World War 2, successfully evoking the community of a platoon caught in extreme circumstances; and *Strip Jack Naked* attains a powerful narrative unity although it threatens, like *The Feared and the Fearless*, to tumble into violent sensationalism. Wilson seems destined to remain one of the might-have-beens of New Zealand fiction.

LJ

WILSON, Pat (or **Patrick** or **P.S.**) (1926–   ), was one of the Victoria University College poets who founded ★*Hilltop* and ★*Arachne* and produced the 1949 *Old Clay Patch* anthology. His collection *The Bright Sea* (1950) was published by ★Pegasus in the same series as ★*Mine Eyes Dazzle*. By understated lyricism and subtly modulated tones, these apparently modest and often melancholy poems achieve more than they pretend—constrained passion in 'Patience', learned wit in lines like 'The trees were taking umbrage once again', and sketches of the ships and seas of Wellington Harbour and Cook Strait that still have clarity. James K. ★Baxter noted Wilson's 'effort to avoid the inflated phrase' and 'romantic imagination governed and reversed by patient intellectual irony' (★*Landfall* 57, 1961), though Allen ★Curnow called him 'renovated ★Georgian' (★*Here & Now*, Dec. 1951).

The poems' light structuring through metre, half-rhyme and flexibility of voice is carried into the intimate and crafted ten-line stanzas of *Staying at Ballisodare*, published in *Landfall* 32, 1954, and in London, 1960, as 'Patrick Wilson'. Dedicated to Alistair ★Campbell, this is a narrative-meditative journal of a visit to Yeats country.

Baxter observed that 'the final tenor of the poem is tragic'. It is valedictory, too, as the restrained, gently mocked eagerness of the literary tourist fades into acceptance that 'Romantic Yeats is dead and gone, / And the great queens, and the god-like men, / All my old ones. Goodbye, / Goodbye, then.'

If this was in part a farewell to New Zealand as well as the poet's youth, it was not quite final. Wilson (born in Tauranga, educated at Nelson College and Victoria University College, PhD 1953) indeed left in 1951 for a London career in music, teaching and lecturing in philosophy and education. He continued to publish poetry in the *Times Literary Supplement* and elsewhere, until a fallow period 1967–79. At this time he wrote academic articles and children's stories, following *Tauranga Adventure* (1963) with stories in the New Zealand *School Journal* in the 1970s under the pseudonym 'John Bates'. Retirement in 1985 brought a return to poetry, with publication in *Outposts, Iron* etc. A selected poems to be published by Nag's Head, Christchurch, will finally enable New Zealand readers to consider the full output.

RR

WILSON, Phillip (John) (1922–), was born in Lower Hutt, served in RNZAF in World War 2, and worked on the staff of the *NZ Listener*. He first became known as a writer of short stories in the late 1940s–50s, and was collected in *Some Are Lucky* (1960). Five novels followed: *Beneath the Thunder* (1963), *Pacific Flight* (1964), *The Outcasts* (1965), *New Zealand Jack* (1973) and *Pacific Star* (1976). Later short stories were collected in *South Pacific Street* (1984), and there were also two critical-biographical studies of William *Satchell, *The Maorilander* (1961) and *William Satchell* (1968). Wilson's fiction is in the line of male critical realism descending from Frank *Sargeson and focuses on one of the central themes of that tradition: the difficulty of human relationships, both sexual relationships and mateship, in an indifferent universe and an imperfect society. The social obstacles to human happiness in his work include racism, a residual *puritanism still strong in the rural society (usually that of the *Waikato) that he depicts, and the continuing harmful effects of World War 2 on the men who took part. The positives that he sets against these difficulties are an *existentialist self-responsibility and self-knowledge and the immediate satisfactions of mateship and outdoor activity. These themes run through all his fiction, with differing emphases. The war and its effects is the dominant theme in *Pacific Flight* and *Pacific Star*, while racism is central to *The Outcasts* and is important in its sequel, *New Zealand Jack*. Wilson has always been a serious writer dealing with significant issues, but his writing has been persistently flawed by an uncertain control of tone, a rhetorical over-explicitness, and a tendency to melodramatic plot resolutions, so that only in some of the individual short stories and in shorter sequences within the novels has he been entirely successful.

LJ

'Wind Blows, The', a short story by Katherine *Mansfield, was originally published as 'Autumns II', under the pseudonym Matilda Berry, in D.H. *Lawrence and John Middleton *Murry's *The Signature* (1915). Renamed 'The Wind Blows', and recast in the third person, it was published in the *Athenaeum* (Aug. 1920) and then included in *Bliss and Other Stories* (Dec. 1920). No MS is known. The story narrates the response of a rebellious and disgruntled young woman, Matilda, to a music lesson on a windy day. Although unnamed, the location is identifiably Wellington. The tone of frustration in the first part of the story: 'How hideous life is—revolting, simply revolting' changes to one of arousal during the music lesson. It concludes with a wish or dream sequence in which the narrator and her brother ('Bogey') look back on themselves from the deck of a boat sailing from the harbour. The story is technically significant. It consolidates Mansfield's use of interior monologue to structure the narrative in episodic bursts from 'inside' the character (thus dispensing with a conventional narrator). It also makes extended use of the dream or day dream, a device increasingly deployed by Mansfield from this point. The wind as a symbol of unsatisfied sexual arousal was also used in *'Bliss'. SSa

WINDER, Mavis, who also wrote as Mavis Areta, see **Romance fiction**.

Wiremu, The Book of, see *Book of Wiremu, The*.

WISNIOWSKI, Sygurd (1841–92), see *Tikera or Children of the Queen of Oceania* (1877).

WITHEFORD, Hubert (1921–), is a member of the post-war generation of poets who has chosen to spend most of his life in England. His first two New Zealand collections, *Shadow of the Flame* (1950) and *The Falcon Mask* (1951) established his distinctive romantic voice and spiritual concerns. James K. *Baxter's famous speech at the *New Zealand Writers' Conference in 1951 identified Witheford with the 'Wellington Group' and its reaction against Allen *Curnow's dominating concept of *nationalism. Witheford also co-edited, with Bill *Oliver and Erik Schwimmer, the journal *Arachne, in which he represented the New Zealand of that period as inimical to the artist, where the individual was isolated, and the community in a state of disintegration.

Graduating in history from Victoria University College, he worked in the Prime Minister's Office during World War 2 and subsequently in the War History Branch, before leaving New Zealand in 1953. The following year he joined the Reference Division of the Central Office of Information in London, whose function was to prepare factual documents for distribution by British diplomats abroad. He retired in 1981 as director and subsequently lived for a few months in Wellington before returning to England.

During his time as a British civil servant Witheford did not become closely involved with literary life. He privately published two major collections in England, *The Lightning Makes a Difference* (1962) and *A Possible Order* (1980), as well as a pamphlet, *How Do Things Happen?* (1972). After retirement he came into contact with a group which included Christopher Reid, the poetry editor at Faber & Faber, who published his most recent collection, *A Blue Monkey for the Tomb* (1994). He has always maintained some literary links with New Zealand, publishing the volume *A Native, Perhaps Beautiful* with ★Caxton in 1967. But although one of his most anthologised pieces is 'Elegy in the Orongorongo Valley' and 'Barbarossa' is a fine poem of the 1931 earthquake, his poetry tends to have little evident connection with his New Zealand origins. Introspective meditation and imagism are more characteristic.

Witheford has been influenced by the teaching of Gurdjieff and by Tibetan Buddhism, and believes that art and religion are closely allied. His preoccupation has been spiritual self-realisation through poetry. This is an elusive goal, however, which may be frustrated by the inadequacy of words: 'I want / A poem, / A true equivalent, / Also / An impossible freedom' ('Compline'). It is part of a larger search for transcendence, which can only be found by first confronting pain and darkness: 'And before it surfaces / Must go deeper / Yet, the wreck of this, our day' ('Si le grain ne meurt'). The result may be 'A native, perhaps beautiful, of the vasty deep' ('Displacement'). Witheford also has a considerable lyrical gift, as in 'Lake Seen Through Pine Branches', and has produced some powerful, if rather acerbic and bleak love poems, such as 'Dying We Love'. His style moved away from the rhetorical and abstract mode, and as early as 1953 he was criticising Baxter for not learning from Ezra Pound. A minimalism with fractured syntax characterises both *A Native, Perhaps Beautiful* and *A Possible Order*. Most recently, however, in *A Blue Monkey for the Tomb*, he has developed a relaxed, gently humorous, conversational tone, which reflects an appreciation of the here and now, and an acceptance of old age and approaching death, examples of which are 'The World in the Evening' and 'Limping'.   WS

WOLFSKEHL, Karl (1869–1948), was born in Darmstadt as the son of a bank manager. His father's wealth was to provide him with a comfortable living for the first fifty years of his life. In fact the family could look back on a line of bankers to the court of the Arch-Duke in Darmstadt, and even further to their origins in the nearby town of Wolfskehlen. According to family legend they had come to this region from Tuscany at the behest of the Emperor Barbarossa in the twelfth century. Wolfskehl therefore felt justified in speaking of 'his' thousand-year residence in the Rhineland and also of his Mediterranean origins. The great cultures north and south of the Alps were as much his 'home' as the Jewish culture which he also inherited and which came to play an important role in his later life. On the basis of this sense of identity he acquired an encyclopaedic knowledge of Germanic and Romance cultures extending back to his great learning in Latin and Greek. The range of his cultural background can be found in the casual references of his essays and also in his translations, which in their time were greatly respected. He translated poetry and prose from older forms of German, from ancient and medieval Latin, French, Italian, English, Flemish, Swedish and Hebrew as well as reworking translations from Arabic and Persian. Notable is his translation of da Ponte's 'Marriage of Figaro'. He also wrote poems in languages other than German, including English. All this meant that his self-image was that of a cosmopolitan European with a solid base in German-language culture.

In 1892, after completing his doctorate in Giessen, Wolfskehl read the poems of the German Symbolist Stefan George, and although he had already written poetry it was from this time that he dated his understanding of 'what a poem is'. George had attended the literary gatherings around Mallarmé in Paris, and one part of his achievement was to introduce Symbolist ideas and practice into Germany. Wolfskehl believed that George had transformed the German language itself into an instrument which could be used to reveal a vast vision of reality and the cosmos which had not been available to earlier writers. He had achieved a revolution in taste, style and perception, and had done this by enormous self-discipline and application. George in fact was an 'Apollonian' personality, a vehicle for the 'principium individuationis', while by contrast Wolfskehl saw himself as a 'Dionysian' personality, bursting through limitations, dissolving hard forms and returning individuated things to their original unity. In his view both kinds of personality have their own significance and his unrestrained admiration of George did not prevent him asserting his own personality. Together with two other members of George's 'Circle', Alfred Schuler and Ludwig Klages, Wolfskehl was a part of the 'Cosmic Circle', which was something between a group of friends and a debating society, where the huge changes in German and European society were discussed against a vision of cosmic proportions.

Ultimately they were to part in acrimony because the others could no longer tolerate Wolfskehl's Jewishness. Absorbed in a German movement which emphasised the Teutonic base of its perceptions, Wolfskehl was forcibly confronted with the fact that he was a Jew. His response was to deny the incompatibility of the two cultures and to the end of his life he believed that the synthesis of German and Jew which he embodied was a greater historical truth than the one-sided German identity that was soon to lead to disaster for Germany and for Wolfskehl himself. George himself believed in the existence of a 'Secret Germany' which was more genuinely heir to Teutonic traditions than the vulgar and brutal forces which had taken over political power. In his later poetry, written in Italian and New Zealand exile, Wolfskehl wrote in an intensely Jewish voice, which was, however, formed by a total mastery of the nuances of the German language. It is impossible to exclude the German or the Jew from this poetry, or to detect any line dividing them, and this synthesis was exactly what he was aiming for. While other Jewish exiles refused even to speak their native German, Wolfskehl prided himself on his Germanness as well as his Jewishness.

After the dissolution of the 'Cosmic Circle' he continued to live mainly in Munich. In 1898 he had married Hanna de Haan and for more than twenty years he and his wife and daughters lived in Schwabing, the artists' quarter of that city. He was at the centre of discussions among artists and thinkers; many of the famous names of the time were on his guest-list; and the anecdotes about this huge, passionate, witty man were a part of the Munich legend. His reputation as a poet was nonetheless limited by his refusal to publish outside the journal of the George circle, *Blätter für die Kunst*, of which he was also one of the editors. He maintained a comfortable and generous lifestyle on a private income, but by 1919 this had begun to dwindle rapidly as a result of post-war inflation. The 50-year-old poet had to change his lifestyle radically. His wife withdrew to a country house and in 1922 he moved to Florence as tutor to an aristocratic family. Altogether he lived in Italy for more than ten years, although he was also active in Munich as literary director of a small publishing house, the Rupprecht Presse. At the same time he worked as a literary journalist with a prolific output of articles on cultural themes, and he distinguished himself, in particular, as an expert on poetry of the German Baroque.

On 27 February 1933, the day of the Reichstag fire, Wolfskehl was celebrating Carnival in Munich, he saw the coming terror and 'still dancing', as he claimed, he boarded a train which carried him out of Germany for ever. At first he stayed in Switzerland, surrounded by friends, but later moved to Italy, where he could still feel at home, even as an exile. He added 'Roman' as a third element to his identity, besides 'German' and 'Jewish'. After some years, in 1937, he noted the sudden appearance of the same anti-Semitic 'poison' in the Italian papers as that which had disfigured Germany. With a sense of disgust that now even this part of his home continent was corrupted, he decided to move as far away as possible, which meant to New Zealand. This sense of distance was his only reason for choosing the country; a negative reason it is true, and yet he was to find a way of life in New Zealand which made it possible for him to create his most masterly poetry.

He arrived in 1938, aged 69, and it would not have been surprising if this had been the end of his creative life; in fact it was the beginning of his greatest period. In Italy he had already begun to write a kind of poetry new to him, and this Jewish-German synthesis was published as *Die Stimme spricht*. Literally the title means 'The Voice Speaks' but an American translation gives the work the title '1933', making its connection to the seizure of power by the Nazis more explicit than Wolfskehl himself did. The 'voice' which speaks through these poems is that of Jahwe, but also of the Hebrew and Jewish tradition in all its complexity, uttering words of comfort and warning to European Jews of the twentieth century. The poet listens humbly to this voice and permits it to speak through him. The poems written in New Zealand extend and transcend this subject matter. The poet identifies himself with that symbol of human suffering, Job, and in the sequence 'Hiob oder Die Vier Spiegel' (Job, or The Four Mirrors) he restructures the myth four times to reveal the constant forces controlling Jewish destiny in all ages of history. The suffering figure at its centre symbolises more than Jewish fate, however; it also expresses the misery of Germany and beyond that the fateful nature of the human condition itself, deprived of salvation in historical time and geographical space and yet permeated with a transcendental quality of salvation.

Wolfskehl's poetry and prose is most readily accessible in the collected edition *Gesammelte Werke*, edited by Margot Ruben and Claus Victor Bock (two vols, 1960), and his fascinating New Zealand correspondence in *Briefwechsel aus Neuseeland, 1938–1948*, edited by Cornelia Blasberg (2 vols., 1988). The first volume of the *Gesammelte Werke* begins with the 'Collected Poems' (*Gesammelte Dichtungen*) which were first published as one volume in 1921, bringing the work of several earlier publications together. These early poems are remarkable for their strictness of form combined with extremely musical vowel and consonant patterns, demonstrating the linguistic skill which was to characterise all his work, but at the same time they can be criticised for their lack of concrete reference, their remoteness from social, political and specific temporal concerns. They approach the status of 'art for art's sake', although their underlying passion pulls them into a less ethereal context. The next section is 'Der Umkreis' (The Surrounds), corresponding to a volume of that title published in 1927. It is followed by 'Die Stimme spricht' (see above) which contains some of the poet's undoubted masterpieces and where the virtues of the earlier work are not diminished although the reference to the poet's own times glows through more clearly.

The final major section of lyric poetry is entitled 'Die drei Welten und das Lebenslied' (The Three Worlds and the Song of Life) and itself contains six major subsections or poem sequences. Whether Wolfskehl succeeded in his plan to combine all of these into a greater unity is a matter for analysis and interpretation. In any case these poems, written or completed in New Zealand, constitute his claim to be considered as a major poet of his time and embody the experience of exile, which he shared with millions of his fellow-creatures. The title refers to 'the three worlds which gave rise to my spiritual being' (Northern European, Mediterranean and Jewish) as well as to his passionate polemic 'To the Germans' (a condemnation of a people's betrayal of its own finest traditions), which together with individual poems of exile constitute his 'Song of Life'. Although most of these poems are too esoteric to become 'popular', they have attained recognition and respect for their blending of intense earthly passion and profound religious vision as well as for the integrity and courage which speak from every line. The extraordinary linguistic skill of the poet attains new heights in this late work. The first volume of the *Gesammelte Werke* closes with more than one hundred pages of dramatic poems, scenes and monologues. The second volume opens with the poetic translation from many languages which are an important part of the poet's achievement, and continues with his prose works, of which the erudite, complex, yet lively essays from the volume 'Bild und Gesetz' (Image and Rule) are the centrepiece. The poems of exile together with the endlessly rich letters from New Zealand to all parts of the world nonetheless remain the works which will continue to draw a small but devoted readership to this remarkable writer. (See also *Germany.) NW

'Woman at the Store, The', a short story by Katherine *Mansfield, was written in 1911 and first published in the avant-garde English quarterly *Rhythm* (Spring 1912). No MS is known. Edited by John Middleton *Murry and Michael Sadleir, *Rhythm's* slogan was 'Before art can be human again it must learn to be brutal.' Mansfield may have taken this as the starting point for this story—the first to be set in New Zealand—which presents *backblocks rural life as brutalising. The story of three travellers (one female and two male) who stop overnight at an isolated store deploys conventions of colonial fiction with 'local colour' provided by close description of the physical environment, attention to characterisation and dramatic dialogue in New Zealand idiom. Out of this, however, loom two unusual figures—the woman of the title, reputed to know 'one hundred and twenty-five different ways of kissing!' and her disturbed young daughter. To the female narrator, the woman appears unhinged: 'Imagine bothering about ironing—*mad*, of course she's mad!', an assessment vindicated when the child reveals, by way of a sketch, that the woman has shot and buried her husband, the child's father. Descriptions of the environment draw on Mansfield's 1907 camping trip through the North Island, jottings from which are published in *The Urewera Notebook*, ed. Ian *Gordon (1978). The story differs markedly in style and subject matter from Mansfield's mature work, and in a letter written to Murry in 1920, she cites it as the type of story she could not have reprinted. It was however republished posthumously in *Something Childish and Other Stories* (1924). A film version with screenplay by Ian Mune and Peter Hansal was made in 1974, and a one-act opera by Dorothy *Buchanan and Jeremy Commons (libretto) had its première in 1998. SSa

Woman Today was a left-wing monthly published in Wellington 1937–39 by an editorial board which included Elsie *Locke. Literary contributions were made by writers such as Isobel *Andrews, Dulce *Carman, Dora Hagemeyer, Elsie *Locke, Jessie *Mackay and Gloria *Rawlinson. SH

Women Writers' Society, see **New Zealand Women Writers' Society**.

Women's suffrage, a major element in New Zealand's self-perception, largely because it was granted at a national level in 1893, before any other nation in the world, prompted surprisingly little imaginative literature at the time. One significant literary response to the movement was Julius *Vogel's vision of a millennial future, *Anno Domini 2000; or, Woman's Destiny* (1889), where a global federation, 'United Britain', is ruled by a woman prime minister, the formidable Mrs Hardinge, partly because 'it has come to be accepted that the bodily power is greater in men, and the mental power larger in women'. Though primarily concerned with the temperance issue, G.M. Reed's *The Angel Isafrel: A Story of Prohibition in New Zealand* (1896) also makes reference to the injustice of drunken men being permitted to vote while women were not, and when the leading character, Isafrel, gives a speech at a women's convention she is challenged as to whether women's interests are not too 'narrow' to let them perceive the public good. She replies that the franchise will change all that.

There was also an early fictional instance of backlash. *Hedged With Divinities* (1895) by Edward *Tregear is a satirical fantasy in which the world is entirely peopled, and mismanaged, by women, men having been wiped out but for a solitary representative who, predictably, saves the day.

Kate Sheppard, a leader in the campaign, has recently entered the popular imagination to the extent of appearing on the ten-dollar note. Yet though William Lovell-Smith, who later became her second husband, wrote *Outlines of the Women's Suffrage Movement in New Zealand* in 1905, the outlines were not filled out until very much later, principally by Pat Grimshaw's *Women's Suffrage in New Zealand* (1972, 1975, 1987), which became a standard source. Kate Sheppard's own story was not told until a century after her campaign's triumph. Judith Devaliant's *Kate Sheppard: A Biography* appeared in 1992, and *Plain Thinking and High Living: The Family Story of Jennie and Will Lovell-Smith*, written by the latter's great-granddaughter Margaret Lovell-Smith, in 1995. She also selected and edited *The Woman Question: Writings by the Women Who Won the Vote* (1992), which documents the suffrage campaign as it was conducted in the press, pamphlets and other ephemeral publications. The following year saw the appearance of Tania Rei's *Maori Women and the Vote*.

Kate Sheppard appears occasionally in fictionalised contexts. The first work to take her and suffrage seriously, and which began the process of mythologising her, was Mervyn *Thompson's song-drama *O! Temperance!* (1974), which focuses on her advocacy of prohibition, and was scrupulously researched. Considerably later a version of her rather unorthodox domestic life features in Rachel *McAlpine's novel *Farewell Speech* (1990), adapted for the stage by Cathy *Downes.

Around the official Suffrage Year in 1993, building on the upsurge of interest in women's issues from the time of the United Women's Conventions of the mid-1970s, there was a flurry of women's histories with wide or popular appeal. Notable are *The Book of New Zealand Women*, a collection of biographical essays edited by Charlotte Macdonald, Merimeri Penfold and Bridget Williams (1991), *Standing in the Sunshine: A History of New Zealand Women Since They Won the Vote* by Sandra Coney, and *Women Together: A History of Women's Organisations in New Zealand* by Anne Else, both of which appeared in 1993, as did the only such book to focus exclusively on the franchise issue—*The Suffragists*, issued by the *Dictionary of New Zealand Biography.

The Suffrage Centennial Trust, administered by the Ministry of Women's Affairs, was established to foster and in some instances help to fund commemorative projects, among them many publications. In their *Celebrating Women: A Suffrage Year Handbook*, the Trust describes these projects and provides a comprehensive bibliography of pertinent publications. Many are specialised histories, covering New Zealand women in a variety of contexts: institutions (government departments, parliament, religious orders, among others); places (Geraldine, Gore, Matamata); occupations, professions and industries (science, health, education, the law, the theatre); and others (art, sexuality, the countryside, feminism, the family). The list also includes a number of biographies of influential women.

As this sampling suggests, the non-fiction coverage of suffrage and related issues has been relatively extensive. In the area of creative writing the pickings continue to be slim: a few stories, songs and poems, a few plays, mostly amateur, some aimed at schoolchildren. That Kate Sheppard has achieved iconic status is beyond dispute, thanks to the banknote and the use of her name on memorials as diverse as a street, a camellia and a bus stop. But apart from Mervyn Thompson, writers have followed rather than created this interest. The minimal imaginative response to suffrage itself is perhaps because interest has been dissipated across a range of current contemporary women's issues, or absorbed into the markedly heightened general awareness of women's writing.   JH

WOOLLASTON, Toss (Sir Mountford Tosswill) (1910–), is an artist known for his powerfully expressive figurative works and landscape paintings of Taranaki, Wellington, the South Island's west coast, and in particular, around Nelson, where he has lived (on and off) since the 1930s. Woollaston studied briefly at Canterbury College School of Art in 1931 and, informally, with Robert Nettleton Field in Dunedin, before staging his first solo exhibition in Dunedin in 1936. Major survey and retrospective exhibitions (1948, 1973, 1991) have established him as a leading figure in New Zealand art history. In the 1930s–40s he associated with literary figures like Charles *Brasch and Ron O'Reilly, and artists like Doris Lusk and Colin *McCahon, becoming a key proponent of modernist ideas and art and participant in debates concerning the role of art and the artist in New Zealand society. Also known as a writer, Woollaston has published a limited edition book of drawings, *Erua* (1966) and his autobiography, *Sage Tea* (1980). His essay, *The Far Away Hills: A Meditation on New Zealand Landscape* (1962) provides insights into Woollaston's response to the New Zealand landscape, which has remained his principal focus through a long career.   CB

WORBOYS, Anne, see **EYRE, Annette.**

Wordstruck!, see **New Zealand Writers' Week.**

WRIGHT, David McKee (1869–1928), one of New Zealand's most popular balladists, is also one of the few turn-of-the-century poets whose work is still valued and anthologised. Born in Ballynaskeagh in Northern *Ireland, he was despatched because of ill health to New Zealand, arriving in 1887. After rural work on Otago *stations, including rabbiting at Puketoi, he entered the Congregational ministry, becoming pastor at Oamaru, Newtown (Wellington) and Nelson. He campaigned actively against the Boer War, against 'sweating' and grasping bosses, but opposed strikes. He left the ministry in 1905 after marital difficulties and differences with the church over temperance (he believed in individual choice). He worked as a freelance journalist in Nelson, then moved to Sydney, where he became editor of the famous literary 'Red Page' of the *Bulletin until ill health forced his retirement in 1926. He also wrote copiously for other papers, often under pseudonyms. His last decade was spent at Glenbrook in the Blue Mountains, with the novelist and poet Zora Cross, who probably contributed to his novel *Luta of Lutetia*, a story of the fourth-century Roman Empire, which was serialised in the *Sydney Morning Herald* in 1930.

It is as a poet that Wright is best remembered in New Zealand. In one decade he published four collections: *Aorangi and Other Verses* (1896), *Station Ballads and Other Verses* (1897), *Wisps of Tussock, New Zealand Rhymes* (1900) and *New Zealand Chimes* (1900). A final volume, *An Irish Heart* (1918), was published in Australia. These accomplished ballads celebrate South Island station life, shearing, rabbiting, gold-mining, mateship, the boiling billy over the crackling speargrass fire, horse-riding, racing, cricket matches won on the last ball, and fisticuffs. Wright's world is masculine, sentimental, democratic, hard-working and unsophisticated. It was also vanishing, so that nostalgia has always been part of the appeal. There is a serious moral dimension, as the earnestness and Christian values of the Congregationalist emerge through the stories. 'The Mother' is compassionate towards the woman who must hang for the murder of her 'fatherless child', evoking the hopeless toil of her life: 'I had worked, when work could be had, in

the close, hot sweater's den, / Sewing for weary hours cheap clothes to be sold to men…'. In poems like 'Our Cities Face the Sea' he dealt, too, with the problems of migration and settlement for those who 'take our homeland with us, however we change our sky', until the time when 'he hailed the windy islands with their flax and fern as his own'. He celebrates the making of a new land by men, 'Bringing up the future with a shout and a song'—Jack from Cornwall, Pat from Donegal, 'Arry from London, Sandy from Aberdeen and Tom who is native-born, 'all mates together in the lands of the morn'.

It proved easier, however, to be a larrikin writer among the quarrelsome literary set of Sydney or the sunlit gum trees of the Blue Mountains than in New Zealand. In his later years Wright turned on the ballad tradition he had used so skilfully, echoing some of the highbrow critics of his own earlier volumes. But his ballads remained popular and admired. In his introduction to *Station Ballads* Rutherford Waddell wrote, 'the sinewy swing of the accomplished balladist is evident in his verse. What I like best is the health and sanity of his song.' The rollicking rhythms made standard by Paterson and *Lawson and the cheerful vigour and resilience of the life they celebrate appealed to settler society, and the appeal has lasted. Wright's poems continue to appear in anthologies such as the most recent Penguin (1985) and Oxford (1997) selections of New Zealand verse. Despite his omission by *Curnow, Wright remains a representative and pleasurable voice of his age.   HMcQ

WRIGHT, Niel (1933–), born in Christchurch, is a prolific poet and literary scholar, with a strongly classical and philosophical inclination. His major work is the continuing epic *The Alexandrians*, currently comprising more than eighty books of 300 lines each, published in more than a hundred instalments and editions. Modelled in part on Dante's *Divine Comedy*, it contains short lyrics, long narratives and philosophical discourses, with consistent consonantal rhyme. This ambitious project has aroused widely conflicting responses, collected by the author in *The Alexandrians: A Critical Scrapbook* (1994). With a PhD in English, Wright has spent his career in the public service.   RR

Writers and Readers Week was New Zealand's first major literary festival held on a regular basis, every two years within the New Zealand International Festival of the Arts in Wellington. The 1979 *PEN/Victoria University Writers' Conference, with its international dimension, was the only precursor, though Adelaide Writers Week, Toronto Harbourfront Festival and others were models. The first, in 1986, established the pattern of mixing both acclaimed and rising overseas writers with a representation of the New Zealand literary community. One distinctive feature has been the emphasis on 'Readers', with participation encouraged from audiences, who have astonished overseas guests by their wide reading and sheer numbers. Sell-out sessions are commonplace, and special venues have accommodated mass audiences for such stars as Alice Walker and Jung Chang. Virtually every New Zealand writer of note has appeared at least once. Book launches, publishers' parties, a gala 'Writers International' and a *marae welcome add other dimensions. For the first five festivals (1986, 1988, 1990, 1992, 1994), publisher Ann Mallinson led the committee, with Elizabeth *Alley also important. The subsequent broadcasting of readings and discussions under Alley's direction until 1996 made the Week's impact national and long-lasting. Highlights (among many) include sessions with (visitors) Angela Carter, James Fenton, Oliver Sachs, Edwin Morgan, Kazuo Ishiguro (before his Booker success), Doris Lessing, and Edmund White, and (home) Keri *Hulme (fresh from Booker triumph), Owen *Marshall, Margaret *Mahy, a charismatic reading from *Intensive Care* by Janet *Frame in 1986, and the emotional celebration of her 70th birthday in 1994. Other literary festivals, including Dunedin's *New Zealand Writers' Week (Wordstruck!) and events in Christchurch and Mount Eden, have followed. A memoir, *Recollections of 5 Festivals* by Ann Mallinson, was published in conjunction with the 1996 Week.   RR

Y

Yearbook of the Arts in New Zealand, The
(1945–51), was edited for four years by Howard
Wadman, briefly by Harry H. *Tombs and then by Eric
*Lee-Johnson. Various associate editors, among them
A.R.D. *Fairburn and Maurice *Duggan, were assigned
to particular arts. Some features were invariable: heavy
coverage of painting and drawing, with numerous reproductions; architecture, with photographs and commentary; theatre reviews from the main centres; and poetry,
selected from submissions. There are essays on particular
artists and events, and other art forms, but with no
attempt at systematic coverage.

The *Yearbook* attracted adverse criticism, some for its
selective, uneven coverage, more for its editorial selection policies. It was damned on the one hand for a modernist bias, on the other for including too much
conventional work of dubious merit. Literature exemplifies the coverage problem, being represented only by
poetry in most issues. Apart from the poems, there are
two general essays on New Zealand poetry; one review
of a play, as distinct from a production; one scene from a
play in progress; a survey of one 'Year's Fiction', and
another 'Year's Work in Writing'. In seven years, that is
all.

The soundness of Fairburn's poetry selection,
however, was cited as a redeeming feature. Unlike the art
editors, he offered small quantities of strong work. Some
names appear year after year: James K. *Baxter, Charles
*Brasch, Allen *Curnow, Ruth *Dallas, Fairburn
himself, Denis *Glover, M.K. *Joseph, Keith *Sinclair,
Kendrick *Smithyman. In that it had such a regular
stable of contributors, the poetry section could not, any
more than the *Yearbook* as a whole, be considered truly
representative of the year's work.   JH

You Will Know When You Get There (1982) is a
collection of poems by Allen *Curnow, subtitled *Poems
1979–81*, published by Auckland University Press /
Oxford University Press. The collection includes short
poems such as the title poem and 'The Parakeets at
Karekare', and two long sequences. 'A Fellow Being' is a
ten-part poem focusing on the career of Dr F.J. Raynor,
a wealthy American businessman prominent in Auckland
in the early twentieth century; and 'Organo Ad Libitum'
is an audacious nine-part fantasia on sex and death which
fuses imagery from (among other things) *Butler's
Erewhon, a Parisian blue movie, and an aircraft crash in
Antarctica.   PS

Young Have Secrets, The (1954), was James
*Courage's fifth novel, the fourth and best of his New
Zealand ones. It focuses on young Walter Blakiston, the
Courage persona who also appears in a group of short
stories in *Such Separate Creatures* (1973). It deals with the
winter and spring of 1914, when Walter is 10 years old
and a boarder at a small preparatory school in Sumner.
He boards with the family of the headmaster, Mr
Garnett, and is caught up there in adult intrigues that he
cannot understand, as the three Garnett daughters,
Muriel, Hilda and Rose, compete for the attention of
Hilda's husband, Geoff Macaulay. The situation is complicated by the class-motivated maliciousness of Mrs
Nelson, the mother of one of Walter's friends, who
extracts from him the secret that Geoff is having an affair
with Rose, and reveals it to Hilda, helping to cause her
death. As in L.P. Hartley's *The Go-Between* (1953), which
probably influenced Courage, the central effect is gained
from the contrast between a young boy's innocence and
the adult sexual tangle in which he is involved, so that

he encounters a 'language of which he did not know the grammar'. However, Courage handles the problems of point of view less adroitly than Hartley, whose first-person narrator looks back on his childish innocence, whereas Courage chooses a third-person limited point of view. All but a few scenes are restricted to what young Walter could see and hear, reported neutrally by a third-person narrator. The result is that Walter has to become the repository of an unlikely number of adult confidences as well as eavesdropping on adult conversations; the contrivance is too evident. Further, Courage resolves his sexual tangle too neatly both for the adults and for the young Walter, in contrast to Hartley, whose young character is marked for life by his experience. Courage's novel establishes quite convincingly multiple conflicts in sexual warfare (against a background of the onset of World War 1)—between the Garnetts and Geoff, between Mrs Nelson and her husband, between Walter's mother and father (a recurrent theme in the short stories), and even in a more benign key between Walter's beloved grandmother and his rather perverse grandfather. However, all this warfare is too easily explained away at the end by Walter's mother, and Walter himself is too easily 'released … from his guilt and pain'. As with the recurrent central symbol of the drowned dog, all is too neatly contrived. Courage does bring in a more sardonic note with Mark, the implicitly homosexual Garnett son, but this is left undeveloped.

The book, though limited by its adherence to the conventions of the English well-made novel, is quite successful in evoking the feelings of the young Walter and the social atmosphere of the school and the Garnett household, with their backward-looking loyalties to England and assumptions about social class and historical stability. These assumptions the forces of history, represented by the War, are about to destroy. LJ

Young New Zealand Poets, The (1973), an *anthology compiled by Arthur Baysting, includes poems by Alan *Brunton, Murray *Edmond, Russell *Haley, Sam *Hunt, Jan *Kemp, Alan *Loney, Bill *Manhire, Bob *Orr, Ian *Wedde and Baysting himself. Most of these were associated with *Freed; none had appeared in Vincent *O'Sullivan's An Anthology of Twentieth-Century New Zealand Poetry (1970). The collection confirmed the entrenchment of Modernism in New Zealand poetry—Kendrick *Smithyman acknowledges in his 'Afterword' to the volume that its poetics are 'recapitulatory more than remarkably novel'. Nevertheless many of the 'young' poets were to enjoy prominence in the 1970s–80s, and a few into the 1990s.

They draw liberally upon *American models and poetics, and Modernist methods such as open form, speech-based rhythms or ordinary language are taken for granted. The collection reflects the Vietnam *War climate of protest and iconoclasm, manifested in two distinct ways: thematically, in irreverent social comment, in gritty explorations of a very male urban counter-culture, and in a taste for macabre images, urban fable and emotional pathology; and formally, in a rejection of the language of high culture and the constraints of discursive logic. The counter-culture strain has come to seem dated, and even at the time of the volume's appearance it could be seen as mannerism, marking the exhaustion of high modernism. But some of the poems clearly anticipated the concerns and methods of the *post-modern era, in which Wedde and Manhire in particular were to be prominent. JH

Z

Zealandia, subtitled 'A Monthly Magazine of New Zealand Literature by New Zealand Authors' was edited in Dunedin by William Freeman, who modelled his editorial principles on those of Charles *Dickens. It lasted for twelve issues (July 1889–June 1890) before it expired as the result of 'insufficient capital, lack of advertising support, the extraordinary amount of credit which the large majority of agents and booksellers seem to consider they have a right to, the inability of the editor to continue to devote his time to the work, insufficient advertising on our part, and the too early increase in the size of our magazine'. Nonetheless *Zealandia's* publishing record was remarkable. The final issue managed to complete the novel *The Mark of Cain* by Grahame Owen, which had been running from the beginning. Other prominent authors of fiction were William Pember *Reeves ('A Helpless Spectator'), Jessie *Mackay, who used the pseudonym 'Jessica', Edwin Wooton, Paul Black, Thomas *Cottle and William Freeman himself. Published poets included Thomas *Bracken, Jessie Mackay, H.L. Twistleton, Mary *Colborne-Veel and Richard Ellis Richmond, who was also the poetry editor. General articles covered a large variety of subjects, some of them literary such as Richmond on 'Verse Making', but more on such topics as 'What is the State?' (Sir Robert Stout) and 'Some Social Responsibilities of a Young Community' (Rev. Rutherford Waddell). There were regular reviews of New Zealand musical compositions by 'Tutanekai' as well as a series on 'The Human Voice: Its Use and Abuse' by 'Anacreon'; and, as in most journals of the time, touristic articles on the country's scenery were frequent.   NW

Zealandia was once a popular romantic name for New Zealand, no doubt intended to match the Britannia of *Home and Pallas Athene of the Hellenic Empire. She can be seen on the nation's Coat of Arms: on the 1911 design with her hair stoically raised in a bun and wearing a chaste, body-concealing, vaguely Greek robe, and on the 1956 revision with a flowing perm and a clinging V-necked robe high enough to reveal two bare feet. In the later design she and the Māori chieftain on the opposite ('sinister') side have turned to face each other, so that Denis *Glover (in *An Encyclopedia of New Zealand*, ed. McLintock, 1966) thought she was 'solicitously chatting him, or chattingly soliciting him, in a sexless sort of way'. At the turn of the century, Glover pointed out, she appeared on music scores and concert programmes where 'she wore her cloche helmet—a sad sort of coal scuttle … the right hand clutching a cornucopia pouring forth apples and pears while from the left there dangled the caduceus. Depending on the skill of the artist, her expression ranged from vacuous insipidity to a crystal-gazing trance.' He also recalled that 'from 1901 to 1909, in a well-washed red, her figure was daily battered by the cancellation mark of every post office in the land'. Her most recent image may be as the face on another postage-stamp in 1995, a globe replacing one eye and a symbol of antinuclear policies gently held between her pouting lips. This design was the subject of scandal, being held by some to be demeaning to womanhood; its role as Zealandia was not fully publicised nor, perhaps, comprehended.

An early appearance of the word was in Charles Hursthouse's *New Zealand* (1861): 'Drowsy matrimonial four-posters give place, in Zealandia, to elastic iron bedsteads and hair mattresses.' Rarely used now, it was formerly a proprietary name for such practical objects as soap, knife-polish, bicycles, and, as Glover said, 'a pub or two'. There was a journal with some literary pretensions called ★ *Zealandia*, and it is still the name of a long-standing Roman Catholic weekly. More to our purpose, again in Glover's words: 'would-be bards, agonising in the Poet's Corner of their local news sheet, ceaselessly extolled her charms—Zealandia of the sea-girt isles!' One such sentimental versifier was Cornelius O'Regan: 'While song-birds greet Zealandia's natal morn, / And seem to say "Rejoice, a Nation great is born"' (*Poems*, 1896). Another was Mary Sinclair, who included 'Excelsior Zealandia' in her book *'Tena Koe'* (1903). Its rousing chorus seems spookily to prefigure a later political party: 'Then boldly raise the toast and sing, / Let this the burden be: / New Zealand first, New Zealand last, / And Auckland still for me.' Wilhelmina Sherriff Elliott published (in London) *From Zealandia* (1925), which included one poem named 'Beautiful Zealandia' and another entitled 'A Patriotic Chant'. This uses the word 'Zealandia' thirty-two times, which is probably a record. It begins: 'Our Britain of Antipodes: / Zealandia! / All hallowed be thy destinies: / Zealandia! / Oh, fair thy forests evergreen: / Zealandia! / Encrowned with Flora's starry sheen: / Zealandia!' HO/NW

New Zealand Literary Awards

Sir James Wattie/Goodman Fielder Wattie Book Award

(This was a 'book' award, recognising the quality of the total publication, not only literary merit. Works placed second or third are also listed below where they are of particular literary interest.)

1968 John Morton and M. Miller, *The New Zealand Sea Shore* (Collins).

1969 A. Murray-Oliver, *Augustus Earle in New Zealand* (Whitcoulls).

1970 John Dunmore, *The Fateful Voyage of the St Jean Baptiste* (Pegasus).

1971 Rosemary Rolleston, *William and Mary Rolleston* (Reed).

1972 Gil Docking, *200 Years of New Zealand Painting* (Reed); 2. J.B. Condliffe, *Te Rangi Hiroa: Sir Peter Buck* (Whitcoulls); 3. C.K. Stead, *Smith's Dream* (Longman Paul).

1973 Maurice Shadbolt, *Strangers and Journeys* (Hodder & Stoughton); 2. Janet Frame, *Daughter Buffalo* (Reed); 3. Witi Ihimaera, *Pounamu, Pounamu* (Heinemann).

1974 Witi Ihimaera, *Tangi* (Heinemann).

1975 Edmund Hillary, *Nothing Venture, Nothing Win* (Hodder & Stoughton); 2. Noel Hilliard, *Maori Woman* (Whitcoulls); 3. Marti Friedlander and James McNeish, *Larks in a Paradise* (Collins).

1976 Harry Morton, *The Wind Commands* (McIndoe); 2. M.K. Joseph, *A Soldier's Tale* (Collins).

1977 James Bertram, *Charles Brasch* (OUP).

1978 J.D. Raeside, *Sovereign Chief: A Biography of Baron de Thierry* (Caxton); 2. Erik Olssen, *John A. Lee* (University of Otago Press); 3. Vincent O'Sullivan, *The Boy, The Bridge, The River* (McIndoe/Reed).

1979 Maurice Gee, *Plumb* (OUP).

1980 Albert Wendt, *Leaves of the Banyan Tree* (Longman Paul); 3. Charles Brasch, *Indirections* (OUP).

1981 Eruera Stirling and Anne Salmond, *Eruera: The Teachings of a Maori Elder* (OUP), and Patricia Burns, *Te Rauparaha* (Reed); 3. Maurice Shadbolt, *The Lovelock Version* (Hodder & Stoughton).

1982 Doreen Blumhardt & Brian Brake, *Craft New Zealand* (Reed), and Sue McCauley, *Other Halves* (Hodder & Stoughton).

1983 Janet Frame, *To the Is-Land* (Hutchinson).

1984 Michael King, *Maori: A Photographic and Social History* (Heinemann); 3. Janet Frame, *An Angel at My Table* (Hutchinson).

1985   Janet Frame, *The Envoy from Mirror City* (Hutchinson).

1986   Witi Ihimaera, *The Matriarch* (Heinemann); 3. Patricia Grace, *Potiki* (Penguin), and Keri Hulme, *Te Kaihau / The Windeater* (VUP).

1987   Maurice Shadbolt, *Season of the Jew* (Hodder & Stoughton); 3. Judith Binney and Gillian Chaplin, *Ngā Mōrehu: The Survivors* (OUP).

1988   Claudia Orange, *The Treaty of Waitangi* (Allen & Unwin/Port Nicholson); 2. Stevan Eldred-Grigg, *Oracles and Miracles* (Penguin).

1989   Lynley Hood, *Sylvia!* (Penguin).

1990   Michael King, *Moriori* (Viking); 2. Russell Haley, *Patrick Hanley* (Hodder).

1991   W.H.Oliver (ed.), *The Dictionary of New Zealand Biography, Volume One, & Ngā Tāngata Taumata Rau: 1769–1869* (Dept of Internal Affairs/Bridget Williams); 2. Alan Duff, *Once Were Warriors* (Tandem); 3. Brian Boyd, *Vladimir Nabokov: The Russian Years* (Chatto & Windus).

1992   Barbara Anderson, *Portrait of the Artist's Wife* (VUP); 2. Brian Boyd, *Vladimir Nabokov: The American Years* (Random House/Chatto & Windus); 3. Anne Salmond, *Two Worlds* (Penguin).

1993   Maurice Gee, *Going West* (Penguin); 2. Witi Ihimaera (ed.), *Te Ao Mārama: Contemporary Māori Writing, Volume 1* (Reed); 3. Martin Edmond, *The Autobiography of My Father* (AUP).

Montana Book Awards (formerly Wattie)

1994   Vincent O'Sullivan, *Let the River Stand* (Penguin); 2. H.M. Ngata, *English–Maori Dictionary* (Learning Media); 3. Bill Manhire (ed.), *100 New Zealand Poems* (Godwit).

1995   Witi Ihimaera, *Bulibasha* (Penguin); 3. Michael Jackson, *Pieces of Music* (Random House).

New Zealand Book Awards

(These awards are for literary merit in each genre. The award for Book Production, introduced 1980, is not listed here.)

1976   **Poetry**: Louis Johnson, *Fires and Patterns* (Jacaranda), and C.K. Stead, *Quesada* (Shed). **Fiction**: Maurice Gee, *A Glorious Morning, Comrade* (AUP), and O.E. Middleton, *Selected Stories* (John McIndoe). **Non-fiction**: Mervyn McLean and Margaret Orbell, *Traditional Songs of the Maori* (Reed).

1977   **Poetry**: Ruth Dallas, *Walking in the Snow* (Caxton), and Alan Loney, *dear Mondrian* (Hawk Press). **Fiction**: Ian Wedde, *Dick Seddon's Great Dive* (Islands). **Non-fiction**: Keith Sinclair, *Walter Nash* (AUP).

1978   **Poetry**: Bill Manhire, *How to Take Off Your Clothes at the Picnic* (Wai-te-ata), and Ian Wedde, *Spells for Coming Out* (AUP). **Fiction**: M.K. Joseph, *The Time of Achamoth* (Collins). **Non-fiction**: Michael King, *Te Puea* (Hodder & Stoughton).

1979   **Poetry**: Kevin Ireland, *Literary Cartoons* (Islands). **Fiction**: Maurice Gee, *Plumb* (Faber). **Non-fiction**: Harvey Franklin, *Trade, Growth and Anxiety in New Zealand: Beyond the Welfare State* (Mallinson Rendel).

1980   **Poetry**: Allen Curnow, *An Incorrigible Music* (AUP). **Fiction**: Janet Frame, *Living in the Maniototo* (Braziller). **Non-fiction**: Sylvia Ashton-Warner, *I Passed This Way* (Reed).

1981   **Poetry**: Michael Jackson, *Wall* (McIndoe). **Fiction**: Maurice Shadbolt, *The Lovelock Version* (Hodder & Stoughton). **Non-fiction**: Antony Alpers, *The Life of Katherine Mansfield* (Cape).

1982   **Poetry**: Alistair Campbell, *Collected Poems* (Alistair Campbell). **Fiction**: Maurice Gee, *Meg* (Faber/Penguin), and Vincent O'Sullivan, *Dandy Edison for Lunch* (McIndoe). **Non-fiction**: Robin Morrison, *The South Island of New Zealand from the Road* (Taylor).

1983 **Poetry**: Allen Curnow, *You Will Know When You Get There* (AUP/OUP), and Cilla McQueen, *Homing In* (McIndoe). **Fiction**: Sue McCauley, *Other Halves* (Hodder & Stoughton). **Non-fiction**: Ray Grover, *Cork of War* (McIndoe).

1984 **Poetry**: Fleur Adcock, *Selected Poems* (OUP). **Fiction**: Keri Hulme, *the bone people* (Spiral). **Non-fiction**: Janet Frame, *An Angel at My Table* (Hutchinson).

1985 **Poetry**: Bill Manhire, *Zoetropes* (Allen & Unwin/Port Nicholson). **Fiction**: Marilyn Duckworth, *Disorderly Conduct* (Hodder & Stoughton), and C.K. Stead, *All Visitors Ashore* (Collins). **Non-fiction**: Peter Mahon, *Verdict on Erebus* (Collins).

1986 **Poetry**: Kendrick Smithyman, *Stories About Wooden Keyboards* (AUP). **Fiction**: Peter Hooper, *People of the Long Water* (McIndoe). **Non-fiction**: Janet Frame, *The Envoy from Mirror City* (Century Hutchinson).

1987 **Poetry**: Allen Curnow, *The Loop in the Lone Kauri Road* (AUP), and Elizabeth Nannestad, *Jump* (AUP). **Fiction**: Patricia Grace, *Potiki* (Penguin). **Non-fiction**: Virginia Myers (ed.), *Head and Shoulders* (Penguin).

1988 **Poetry**: Anne French, *All Cretans Are Liars* (AUP). **Fiction**: Fiona Kidman, *The Book of Secrets* (Heinemann). **Non-fiction**: Dick Scott, *Seven Lives on Salt River* (Hodder & Stoughton).

1989 **Poetry**: Cilla McQueen, *Benzina* (McIndoe). **Fiction**: Janet Frame, *The Carpathians* (Century Hutchinson). **Non-fiction**: Ronald Kean, *Tarawera* (R. Kean).

1990 **Poetry**: Elizabeth Smither, *A Pattern of Marching* (AUP). **Fiction**: John Cranna, *Visitors* (Heinemann Reed). **Non-fiction**: Frances Porter, *Born to New Zealand* (Allen & Unwin).

1991 **Poetry**: Cilla McQueen, *Berlin Diary* (McIndoe). **Fiction**: Maurice Gee, *The Burning Boy* (Penguin). **Non-fiction**: Frank McKay, *The Life of James K. Baxter* (OUP).

1992 **Poetry**: Bill Manhire, *Milky Way Bar* (VUP). **Fiction**: Peter Wells, *Dangerous Desires* (Reed). **Non-fiction**: Anne Salmond, *Two Worlds* (Penguin).

1993 **Poetry**: Brian Turner, *Beyond* (McIndoe). **Fiction**: Fiona Farrell, *The Skinny Louie Book* (Penguin). **Non-fiction**: Jane Tolerton, *Ettie: A Life of Ettie Rout* (Penguin).

1994 **Poetry**: Andrew Johnston, *How to Talk* (VUP). **Fiction**: Damien Wilkins, *The Miserables* (VUP). **Non-fiction**: Harry Evison, *Te Wai Pounamu: The Greenstone Island* (Aoraki).

1995 **Poetry**: Michele Leggott, *Dia* (AUP). **Fiction**: C.K. Stead, *The Singing Whakapapa* (Penguin). **Non-fiction**: Phoebe Meikle, *An Accidental Life* (AUP).

Montana New Zealand Book Awards

(Amalgamation of Montana Award and New Zealand Book Awards; main literary categories only are listed below.)

1996 **Book of the Year/Cultural Heritage**: Judith Binney, *Redemption Songs: A Life of Te Kooti Arikirangi Te Turuki* (AUP/Bridget Williams). **Poetry**: Bill Manhire, *My Sunshine* (VUP). **Fiction**: Sheridan Keith, *Zoology* (Penguin).

1997 **Book of the Year/Cultural Heritage**: Jessie Munro, *The Story of Suzanne Aubert* (AUP/Bridget Williams). **Poetry**: Jenny Bornholdt, Gregory O'Brien and Mark Williams (eds), *An Anthology of New Zealand Poetry in English* (OUP). **Fiction**: Alan Duff, *What Becomes of the Broken Hearted* (Vintage).

1998 **Montana Medal** (non-fiction): Harry Orsman (ed.), *The Dictionary of New Zealand English* (OUP). **Deutz Medal** (fiction): Maurice Gee, *Live Bodies* (Penguin): 2. Catherine Chidgey, *in a fishbone church* (VUP) and Kirsty Gunn, *The Keepsake* (Granta). **Poetry**: Hone Tuwhare, *Shape-Shifter* (Steele Roberts). **A.W. Reed Lifetime Achievement Award** (inaugural): Margaret Mahy.

NEW ZEALAND CHILDREN'S BOOK AWARDS
New Zealand Library & Information Association Awards

Esther Glen Medal/Award
(A selective annual award for the most distinguished contribution to literature.)

1945 Stella Morice, *The Book of Wiremu* (Progressive Publishing).
1947 A.H. Reed, *Myths and Legends of Maoriland* (Reed).
1951 Joan Smith, *The Adventures of Nimble, Rumble and Tumble* (Paul's Book Arcade).
1959 Maurice Duggan, *Falter Tom and the Water Boy* (School Journal, Faber).
1964 Lesley Powell, *Turi, the Story of a Little Boy* (Paul's Book Arcade).
1970 Margaret Mahy, *A Lion in the Meadow* (Dent).
1973 Margaret Mahy, *The First Margaret Mahy Story Book* (Watts/Dent).
1975 Eve Sutton, *My Cat Likes to Hide in Boxes* (Hamish Hamilton).
1978 Ronda Armitage, *The Lighthouse Keeper's Lunch* (Deutsch).
1979 Joan de Hamel, *Take the Long Path* (Lutterworth.)
1982 Katherine O'Brien, *The Year of the Yelvertons* (OUP).
1983 Margaret Mahy, *The Haunting* (Dent).
1984 Caroline Macdonald, *Elephant Rock* (Hodder & Stoughton)
1985 Margaret Mahy, *The Changeover* (Dent).
1986 Maurice Gee, *Motherstone* (OUP).
1988 Tessa Duder, *Alex* (OUP).
1989 Jack Lasenby, *The Mangrove Summer* (OUP).
1990 Tessa Duder, *Alex in Winter* (OUP).
1991 William Taylor, *Agnes the Sheep* (OUP).
1992 Tessa Duder, *Alessandra: Alex in Rome* (OUP).
1993 Margaret Mahy, *Underrunners* (Hamish Hamilton).
1994 Paula Boock, *Sasscat to Win* (McIndoe).
1995 Maurice Gee, *The Fat Man* (Viking).
1996 Janice Marriott, *Crossroads* (Reed).
1997 Kate De Goldi, *Sanctuary* (Penguin).

Russell Clark Medal/Award
(A selective annual award for the most distinguished illustrations.)

1978 Robert Jahnke, *The House of the People* (Waiatarua).
1979 Bruce Treloar, *Kim* (Collins).
1982 Gavin Bishop, *Mrs McGinty and the Bizarre Plant* (OUP).
1984 Gwenda Turner, *The Tree Witches* (Kestrel).
1985 Robyn Belton, *The Duck in the Gun* (Shortland).
1986 Pamela Allen, *A Lion in the Night* (Hodder & Stoughton).
1987 Robyn Kahukiwa, *Taniwha* (Viking Kestrel).
1988 Dick Frizzell, *The Magpies Said* (Century Hutchinson).
1989 Chris Gaskin, *Joseph's Boat* (Hodder & Stoughton).
1990 Chris Gaskin, *A Walk to the Beach* (Heinemann Reed).
1991 David Elliott, *Arthur and the Dragon* (Nelson Price Milburn).
1992 Sandra Morris, *One Lonely Kakapo* (Hodder & Stoughton).
1993 Christine Ross, *Lily and the Present* (Methuen).
1994 Kerry Gemmill, *The Trolley* (Viking).
1995 Chris Gaskin, *Kotuku: The Flight of the White Heron* (Hodder & Stoughton).
1996 Linda McClelland, *The Cheese Trap* (Ashton Scholastic).
1997 Murray Grimsdale, *George's Monster* (Learning Media).

Te Kura Pounamu Award

(The first Te Kura Pounamu Award covered all previous publications in Maori.)

1996 Katerina Mataira, Terewai Kemp, Hone Ngata, *Marama Tangiweto (Cry Baby Moon)* (Mallinson Rendel; Ahura, 1992).

1997 Katerina Mataira, Te Maari Gardiner, *He Tino Kuia Taku Kuia (My Kuia is a Special Kuia)* (Te Pou Taki Korero: Learning Media).

Young People's Non-Fiction Award

1987 Olive and Ngaio Hill, *Gaijin: Foreign Children in Japan* (Longman Paul).

1989 Claire Patterson, Lyndsay Quilter, *It's OK to be You! Feeling Good About Growing Up* (Century Hutchinson).

1990 Deborah Furley, *The Web: The Triumph of a New Zealand Girl over Anorexia* (Collins).

1991 John Reid, *Model Boats That Really Go* (Random Century).

1992 Peter Garland, *The Damselfly* (Nelson Price Milburn).

1993 Kim Westerkov, *Albatross Adventure* (Nelson Price Milburn).

1994 Robyn Kahukiwa, *Paikea* (Viking).

1995 Barbara Cairns and Helen Martin, *Shadows on the Wall: A Study of Seven New Zealand Feature Films* (Longman Paul).

1996 Laura Ranger, *Laura's Poems* (Godwit).

1997 Diana Noonan, Nic Bishop, *I Spy Wildlife: The Field* (Heinemann Educational).

Children's Books of the Year

(These awards began in 1982, funded at first by the Government Printer before being sponsored by AIM and then by New Zealand Post. From 1993 on, the story categories were divided into Junior and Senior Fiction. From 1995 on, an overall best book was named, identified here by ★.)

Children's Book of the Year

1982 Joy Cowley, Sherryl Jordan, *The Silent One* (Whitcoulls).

1983 Maurice Gee, *The Halfmen of O* (OUP).

1984 Anne de Roo, *Jacky Nobody* (Methuen).

1985 Caroline Macdonald, Garry Meeson, *Visitors* (Hodder & Stoughton).

1986 Joanna Orwin, *Guardian of the Land* (OUP).

1987 Barry Faville, *The Keeper* (OUP).

1988 Tessa Duder, *Alex* (OUP).

Picture Book of the Year

1982 Patricia Grace, Robyn Kahukiwa, *The Kuia and the Spider* (Longman Paul/Kidsarus).

1983 Gavin Bishop, *Mister Fox* (OUP).

1984 Lynley Dodd, *Hairy Maclary from Donaldson's Dairy* (Mallinson Rendel).

1985 Ron Bacon, Robert Jahnke, *The Fish of Our Fathers* (Waiatarua).

1986 Lynley Dodd, *Hairy Maclary Scattercat* (Mallinson Rendel).

1987 Robyn Kahukiwa, *Taniwha* (Viking Kestrel).

1988 Lynley Dodd, *Hairy Maclary's Caterwaul Caper* (Mallinson Rendel).

Non-Fiction Award

1986 Judith Bassett, Keith Sinclair, Marcia Stenson, *The Story of New Zealand* (Reed Methuen).

Aim Book of the Year

1990 Tessa Duder, *Alex in Winter* (OUP).
1991 Sherryl Jordan, *Rocco* (Ashton Scholastic).
1992 Joy Cowley, Robyn Belton, *Bow Down Shadrach* (Hodder & Stoughton).

Senior Fiction

1993 Tessa Duder, *Songs for Alex* (OUP).
1994 Pat Quinn, *The Value of X* (Heinemann Educational).
1995 William Taylor, *The Blue Lawn* (Harper Collins).
1996 Janice Marriott, *Crossroads* (Reed).★

Junior Fiction

1993 Margaret Mahy, *Underrunners* (Hamish Hamilton).
1994 Diana Noonan, *A Dolphin in the Bay* (Omnibus).
1995 Maurice Gee, *The Fat Man* (Viking).★
1996 Jack Lasenby, *The Waterfall* (Longacre).

Picture Books

1990 Miriam Smith, Lesley Moyes, *Annie and Moon* (Mallinson Rendel).
1991 Pamela Allen, *My Cat Maisie* (Hodder & Stoughton).
1992 Lynley Dodd, *Hairy Maclary's Showbusiness* (Mallinson Rendel).
1993 Christine Ross, *Lily and the Present* (Methuen).
1994 Gavin Bishop, *Hinepau* (Ashton Scholastic).
1995 Diana Noonan, Elizabeth Fuller, *The Best-Loved Bear* (Ashton Scholastic).
1996 Joy Cowley, Linda McClelland, *The Cheese Trap* (Ashton Scholastic).

Non-Fiction

1993 Chris Gaskin, *Picture Magic: Illustrating a Picture Book* (Ashton Scholastic).
1994 Mary Taylor, *Old Blue: The Rarest Bird in the World* (Ashton Scholastic).
1995 Andrew Crowe, Sandra Parkkali, *Which Native Forest Plant?* (Viking).
1996 Trish Gribben, Jenny Scown, *Aya's Story* (Ashton Scholastic).

New Zealand Post Children's Book Awards

Senior Fiction

1997 Kate De Goldi, *Sanctuary* (Penguin).
1998 Paula Boock, *Dare, Truth or Promise* (Longacre).★

Junior Fiction

1997 Jack Lasenby, *The Battle of Pook Island* (Longacre).
1998 Joy Cowley, *Ticket to the Sky Dance* (Penguin).

Picture Books

1997 Jennifer Beck, Robyn Belton, *The Bantam and the Soldier* (Scholastic).★
1998 Lesley Moyes, *Alphabet Apartments* (Mallinson Rendel).

Non-Fiction

1997 Chris Gaskin, *Picture Book Magic: Illustrating a Picture Book* (Reed).
1998 Diana Noonan, Keith Olsen, *The Know, Sow and Grow Kids' Book of Plants* (Bridge Hill).